To the memory of my mother,
and to my other mother, Frieda.

CONTENTS

PREFACE

The project of writing the first edition of *The SAP R/3 Handbook* started in the first half of 1996, not long after the major release 3.0 of R/3 began to be installed on the first sites. At the time, most SAP customers were still working with releases 2.1 and 2.2 and thinking of migrating to 3.0. The book project spanned about one year, coming to fruition in July of 1997. During that time R/3 Internet release 3.1 came out, meaning that from month to month I had to change contents and features to be as current as possible.

The pace of technology upgrades and technical enhancements is exponentially increasing, and that has been particularly true also for SAP and for R/3. So, two and a half years later, in the middle of the much anticipated EnjoySAP release, there is much change and news around the SAP world. And 1999 saw the announcement and first demonstrations of the major Internet initiative mySAP.com.

We have seen how SAP has changed from being a single-product company (R/3) to a full business solution software company (SAP Industry Solutions, New Dimension Products).

Business Framework, Internet Business Framework, and BAPIs redefined R/3 architecture and connectivity options. A major initiative for a revolutionary user interface came to light with front end enhancements and the EnjoySAP role-based interface. As new releases are coming, there are also new and enhanced installation and upgrade procedures and tools to make these activities easier and less time consuming.

Other enhancements and options that have been added and that you can find in this book are related to subjects such as the following:

- Availability is increased, and there are now further options for distributing the system, along with new powerful platforms.
- There is a new change and transport system, including all the facilities of the Transport Management System (TMS).
- In the ABAP workbench, there are a host of new utilities, a step-forward object-oriented ABAP, the replacement of matchcodes with search helps, and more.
- Windows NT is now a very popular platform with thousands of customers. For this reason, this new edition is operating system independent, dealing with both UNIX and Windows NT where appropriate.

- The authorization system and administrator duties have been facilitated with the profile generator.
- Since release 4.0 there is a new object-based monitoring architecture and alert monitors.
- The well-known OSS has now become SAPnet, with two variants: R/3 front end and Web front end.

In this edition you will find lots of new things to discover and enjoy. I hope you enjoy this book and enjoySAP.

José Antonio Hernández
Madrid, Spain

ACKNOWLEDGMENTS

This second edition was almost harder to review than if a new book would have been written. The fact that it is now in press has to do with the tremendous friendliness and collaboration of a lot of people, to whom I owe much gratitude because without their help I would not have made it.

Many thanks to Enric Roca and José Ramón Sierra, of Compaq Computer, for their contributions in many of the chapters and for coming home from out of town to cheer me up and work with me.

Special thanks go to SAP Spain people who provided me with material and help, specifically Javier Millares, for his contribution of an excellent section in the first chapter, Rafael Cano, José Manuel Nieto, Angel Fernández, Sandra Ordóñez, Mario Dabán, and the friendly specialists at the service support center.

Extraordinary help on R/3 systems, the infoDB, CDs, information, and more was provided by realTech, a specialized technical consulting company that is leading the market in Technical R/3. Thanks to José Pablo de Pedro, longtime SAP consultant and managing director of realTech Spain.

Finally, I want to thank my family and friends for their support and understanding: my father, Manuel, my brother Manuel and sister Maria, my close friend José Muñoz, and my dearest American family, Blanca and her daughter Lucy.

CHAPTER 1

What Is SAP R/3?

After the Internet, SAP R/3 is one of the hottest topics in the computer industry, and the company that developed it, SAP AG, has become one of the most successful in the software market.

The SAP R/3 system is targeted to most industries: manufacturing, retail, oil and gas, electricity, health care, pharmaceutical, banking, insurance, telecommunications, transport, automotive, chemical, and so on. The customer list includes most of the U.S. Fortune 100 companies, 97 percent of the most profitable German companies, and other impressive figures from companies around the world.

All major hardware vendors, without exception, are fully engaged to partner with SAP: in 1999, ACER, Amdahl, Bull, Compaq, Comparex, Data General, Dell, Fujitsu, Hewlett-Packard, Hitachi, IBM, Intergraph, NCR, Sequent, Siemens, SUN, Unisys, and others have supported and certified SAP R/3 platforms.

The biggest international consulting firms, numerous smaller ones, and most of the hardware vendors system integration departments have built an impressive army of experts around SAP-related business: Andersen Consulting, Arthur Andersen, Price Waterhouse Coopers, Ernst & Young, KPMG, Deloitte Consulting, Cap Gemini, Origin, CSC-Ploenzke, EDS, Sema Group, and others. Additionally, SAP has a growing group of first-order technological partners including Microsoft, Informix, Oracle, Apple, Next, Adobe, iXOS, Software AG, and many others that have participated in the Complementary Software Certification program.

With this presentation card, it is well assumed that SAP R/3 is not something that can be learned at home or in universities with the aid of a PC and standard PC software.

SAP AG: The Company Behind R/3

SAP AG was founded in 1972 by four former IBM employees. The company headquarters are based in Walldorf, a small German town close to Heidelberg, where the university is a continuous source of employees at SAP. Many of the gurus behind this phenomenal system known as R/3 come from this university.

Since its foundation, SAP has made significant development and marketing efforts on standard application software, being a global market player with its R/2 system for mainframe applications and its R/3 system for open client/server technologies.

The company name, SAP, stands for *Systems, Applications and Products in Data Processing.* After the introduction of SAP R/3 in 1992, SAP AG has become the world's leading vendor of *standard* application software. One of the reasons for SAP's success is that since it is a standard package, it can be configured in multiple areas and adapted to the specific needs of a company. To support those needs, SAP includes a large number of business functions, leaving room for further functionality and enhancements or adaptability to business practice changes. More and more, corporations are deciding to use standard software systems that are highly flexible and configurable and able to support most of their business practices and information needs. This kind of package leaves the development of custom software only for exceptional cases.

The maturity and solid experience of SAP in solving the information management problems of businesses around the globe have made its R/3 system the clear market leader in the development of standard applications.

Profile and Evolution

In 1995, SAP AG was ranked fifth among independent software vendors and was making gains with annual growth rates of more than 40 percent in sales and profit and approximately 30 percent in headcount. In 1999 SAP AG was already ranked third. The SAP global evolution for a five-year span is shown in Figs. 1-1, 1-2, and 1-3. Figures are approximate due to currency fluctuations.

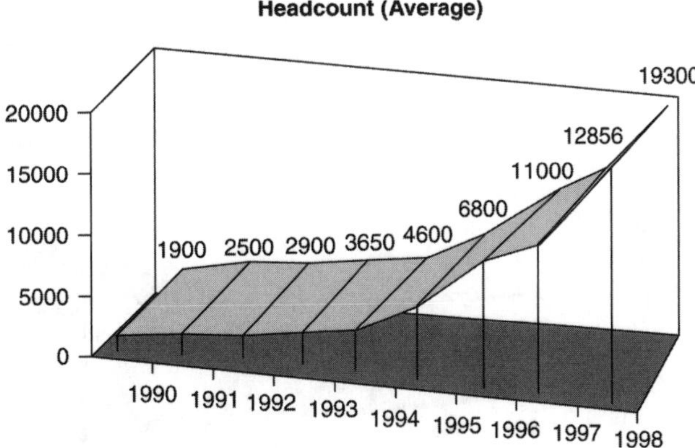

Figure 1-1 SAP headcount evolution.

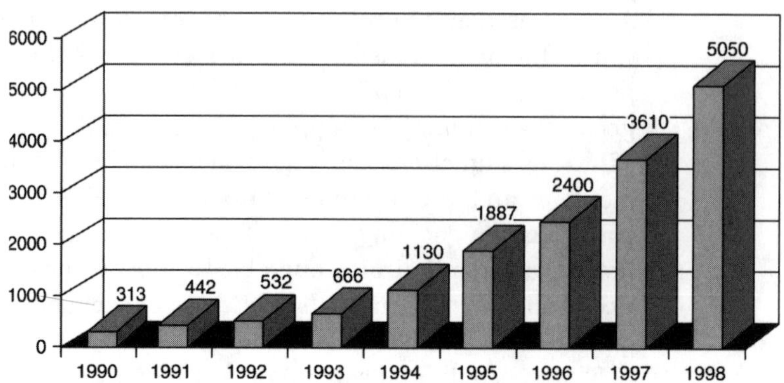

Figure 1-2
SAP revenue.

SAP AG has become the top European software vendor. It has formed a considerable number of subsidiaries in more than 40 countries; SAP America is the largest one, with corporate headquarters in Wayne, Pennsylvania. It has also established a technology development center in Foster City, California, and sales and support offices throughout North America. The company is committed to further expand into new international markets and to gain multinational support. That is one of the reasons SAP has developed a Kanji version of the R/3 system for the Japanese market and a new Mandarin version for the Chinese.

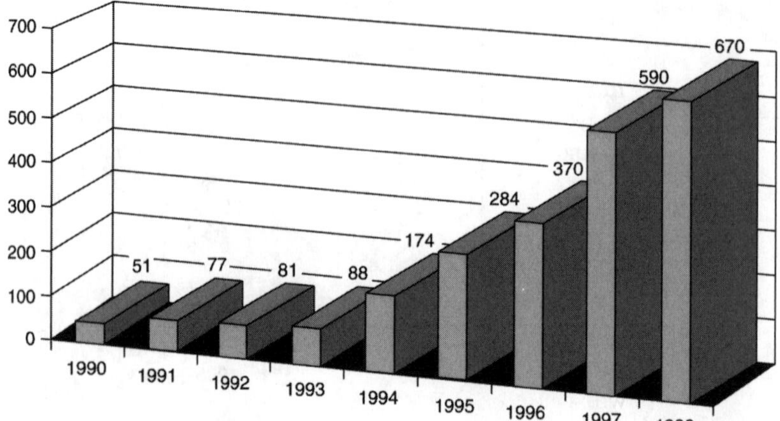

Figure 1-3
SAP net profit.

By the time this book is published, the number of SAP R/3 installations should be more than 20,000, and the number of productive users should easily surpass 1 million. This means that thousands of companies will rely on SAP software for their most critical business needs.

SAP AG values customer feedback very much and tries hard to meet customer requirements by constantly enhancing its products and offering valuable and state-of-the-art services which combine to make probably the best integrated solution for enterprise applications. SAP also offers an extensive range of training courses and consulting services for its customers and partners.

The marketing effort is determined by the SAP presence at the most important trade shows, by participating in numerous user groups around the globe, by organizing infodays, and by helping partners to market new products and solutions for the SAP environment. Special mention is made of its own event, the SAPPHIREs, in which top executives, engineers, partners, and others hold workshops, presentations, exhibits, and conferences, and where main releases and announcements are made.

Strategy and Products

SAP invests approximately 20 percent of its annual sales revenue in research and development in order to remain at the edge of technological innovation. With more than 25 percent of its employees working in the research area, SAP wants to make sure that it can maintain a constant dialogue with customers and users and exchange with them experiences and ideas to enhance its systems and service offerings. This information exchange is vital in order for SAP to maintain a long-term relationship with its customers and to attract new ones to the R/3 wave.

In the mid-1990s SAP had two main products in the business software market: mainframe system R/2 and client/server R/3. Both were targeted to business application solutions and feature a great level of complexity, business and organizational experience, strength, and integration. SAP software systems can be used on different hardware platforms, offering customers flexibility, openness, and independence from specific computer technologies.

SAP has greatly based the functionality of its R/2 and R/3 software systems in the business process concept. For SAP, a *business process* is the complete functional chain involved in business practices, whatever software module has to deal with it. This means that the chain might run across different modules. SAP sometimes refers to this kind of feature as an *internal data highway.* For instance, what travel expenses, sales orders, inventory, materials management, and almost all types of functions have in common is that most of them finally link with the finance modules. R/2 and R/3 are particularly noted for this type of comprehensive business functionality which qualifies the systems as being *highly integrated.* SAP understands that business practices and organizations change often and quickly, so it left the system flexible enough to be able to adapt efficiently.

With release 4.5 and 4.6 of R/3, SAP had already incorporated a library of more than 1000 predefined business processes across all functional modules which customers can freely select and use for their own way of doing business. SAP makes new business functions available regularly.

International applicability is another important part of the strategy to meet today's complex and global business needs. For SAP, this does not only mean having the software available in different languages, but also covering the differentiating aspects of each country: currency, taxes, legal practices concerning human resources, import/export regulations, and so on. Users from a multinational company in different countries can work simultaneously in the same system using their own language, currency, and taxes.

An additional aspect of the software integration capability is *real time.* In fact, the *R* from R/3 originally is meant for *real time.* When new input is made into the system, the logical application links will concurrently update related modules so that the business can react to immediate information and changes. This type of updating reduces the overhead of manual processing and communication and enables companies to react quickly in the nonstop and complex business world, which makes SAP software systems a very valuable tool for executive planning and decision making.

R/2 Mainframe Solution. R/2 is SAP AG mainframe software that runs on IBM, Siemens, Amdahl, and compatible equipment. This type of solution cannot claim to be open, although with the help of Application Link Enabled (ALE) technology, R/2 can be linked to R/3 systems and share online data.

Nevertheless, and despite the emergence of new technologies and the significant decrease of hardware prices, some companies some companies preferred the approach of the mainframe solution. This is mainly targeted at enterprises with data-intensive and centralized industries.

R/2 is the antecedent of the client/server R/3 system and also offers comprehensive, fully functional business applications to satisfy the demands of mainframe users.

SAP will still continue to support R/2 systems till the year 2004, and so it is advising customers to migrate to R/3.

R/3 Client/Server Solution. SAP R/3 technology is the logical evolution of the SAP R/2 system, and it is the product that has really fueled the expansion of SAP since its introduction in 1992, establishing itself as the leader and de facto standard in the industry. This complex client/server system is the core of this book.

SAP consultants divide themselves into functional or technical categories. *Functional* SAP consultants are experienced people in some business areas who have learned how to customize those modules to meet their customers' needs. On the other hand, *technical* consultants get acquainted mainly with the *basis system* of R/3—installation, operating system management, network and database administration, and so on. Administrators clearly fall into this category.

SAP explains the implicit complexity of R/3 systems by reasoning that the business world is complex, and for a standard system to cover it, it had to include a large number of functions. But SAP not only includes business functionality, it also includes efficient implementation tools, a comprehensive development environment, and a full-featured set of tools to efficiently monitor and manage the system.

R/3 has become the system of choice for those companies anchored in character-cell legacy applications wishing to downsize their centralized mainframe class computer system to newer and cheaper client/server technology.

The following paragraphs introduce some of the features of subsequent R/3 releases, showing some of the points where SAP concentrated its strategic efforts and directions.

R/3 Release 3.0

R/3 release 3.0 was a major step forward for SAP, both in starting to build the Business Framework architecture and in making customization tools easier. Some of the most important features introduced in 3.0 were:

- *Application Link Enabled (ALE) technology.* With these interfaces to link different SAP systems and external application systems, SAP overcomes the problem of having a unique centralized database server and allows big companies to further distribute their business processes without losing integration. ALE is now a basic cornerstone of the Business Framework architecture.

- *Integration with standard PC applications, mainly the Microsoft Office suite.* With this version, SAP included standard links to interact with MS-Excel, MS-Word, MS-Access, and others, using OLE technology.
- *Enhanced Graphical User Interface (GUI) with lots of new options, buttons, captions, and images.* There was also a set of utilities for interacting with SAP, such as the SAP Automation, RFC interfaces, and so on, included in standard Desktop SDK.
- *Technological enhancements in the architecture of the system,* such as new memory management features and easier installation and upgrade procedures.
- *New APIs and standard calls for software developers,* further opening the system and broadening the spectrum of functionality, with add-ons like Archiving, EDI, Forms management, external work flow, plant data collection devices, mail and fax solutions, and so on.
- *First steps to a more business-object-oriented system* with an enhanced SAP Business Workflow and the introduction of business objects.
- *The introduction of the Business Framework architecture* with the goal of making it faster and easier for customers to introduce new functionalities into the system, as well as making the system even more flexible and open.

R/3 Release 3.1

By year end 1996, SAP announced availability of release 3.1. This version was known as the Internet release, since the main new features and capabilities related to the possibility of to expanding the capacity of the R/3 systems, using the Internet for doing business while preserving the functionality and support of the core R/3 applications. Users will be able to make transactions with the system directly using their Internet browsers. Release 3.1 allows for efficient communication in the business world between companies, customers, and providers.

SAP R/3 release 3.1 was the first to broaden the typical three-tier client server architecture to a multitier one by introducing a new layer, known as the Internet layer, located between the presentation and application layers. With this approach SAP increased the potential access to the system of thousands of users (better known as *business partners*).

To support this new architecture, SAP introduced several modifications to the application level, based on the *thin client* concept, which is in turn based on making a very reduced data transfer between the presentation and the application levels. This is a very important concept considering the limited bandwidth often found on Internet connections.

R/3 release 3.1 offered the same functionality as the previous 3.0 release but enabled the ability of business processes using both Intranets and the Internet. Some of its features were:

- *Java enabling,* with the possibility of avoiding the code for the presentation server in clients and making presentation software distribution easier.
- *Support for new presentation platforms* such as Network Computers (NCs) and NetPCs.
- *Introduction of Business Application Program Interfaces* (BAPIs), which can be used as a mechanism to communicate R/3 with external applications using Internet. BAPIs are object-oriented definitions of business entities. The concept behind BAPIs is the key in the Business Framework architecture as well as in the overall SAP R/3 Internet and electronic commerce strategy, as the object-oriented interface to integrate external applications. Based on business objects, such as company, vendor, employee, material, and so on, a BAPI defines the methods that can be used to interact and communicate with those objects. Release 3.1 included more than 100 predefined BAPIs ready to integrate R/3 with third-party solutions and applications.
- *Internet Application Components* (*IACs*) were the new components on R/3 application servers that allow the use of software modules to support business transactions through an Internet layer. Initially SAP provided a small number of IACs (around 40), including components for human resources applications.
- *Web Browser* is an Internet browser including Java-enabled components that becomes a new user interface (a new presentation). Most typical browsers, such as Netscape Navigator and Microsoft Internet Explorer, are fully supported.
- *Web Server* is the typical Internet server, which, in the case of R/3 applications, links the Internet or Intranet world with the SAP business processes.

- *Internet Transaction Server* (*ITS*) is the component located at the Internet level in the architecture and connects the Web Server with the SAP Internet Application Components.
- *SAP Automation* is the programming interface that allows Internet components and other applications to interact with R/3.

Besides total support for the Internet layer, within the business engineering tools, release 3.1 incorporated a new process configuration based on models. This feature allowed for a quicker and more dynamic configuration of the business processes, oriented to the processes, and the system included several "industry" models that could be used directly by customers, thus reducing the time needed for configuring and customize the system.

With the introduction of the R/3 solutions for supporting business processes through the Internet, it was possible for companies to widen their businesses by providing a new communication channel between companies and between customers and companies.

Standard with release 3.1 of SAP R/3 was the possibility of using three different types of Internet and Intranet scenarios for supporting electronic commerce:

- Intranet corporate applications
- Intercompany applications, extending the possibilities of the supply management chain
- Applications from consumer to companies, enabling final customers with a simple Internet browser to communicate and trigger transactions with an R/3 system

R/3 Release 4.0

With the introduction of release 4.0 and in the context of the Business Framework, SAP's strategy for enterprise computing was to develop R/3 into a family of integrated components that can be upgraded independently.

Following a well-known study by the Gartner Group, SAP closely watches the strategy depicted for the survival of the Enterprise Software Vendors and put the corresponding actions in place well before 1997. The four actions indicated were:

- *Move toward componentization,* both in products and sales force. This move can be clearly seen with the emergence of R/3 release 4.0.
- *Add consulting content.* This is another step that SAP has added to its overall business, although in a more silent way, in order not to provoke the legion of consulting partners. SAP figures show that 1997 and 1998 have seen a percentage growth both in revenue and people from services and consulting.
- *Develop industry-specific components or templates.* This is not a new strategic direction for SAP, although it is true that for the year there has been more marketing than real products. With release 4.0, some industries such as retail and the public sector can find some additional and specific business processes; however, telecom companies have been waiting since 1995 for their piece of the cake.
- *Focus on fast implementation: methodologies and solutions.* ASAP and TeamSAP are excellent examples of SAP's reaction to the continuous criticism of implementation times and overbudgeted projects.

In addition to the logical evolution of technological aspects besides the increment on functionality on release 4.0, there are two features that should be particularly highlighted: componentization and inclusion of industry solutions. To these features, from a strategic and pragmatic point of view, we should also add the increased accent on the use of solution sets for rapid implementation, such as AcceleratedSAP or ASAP.

Componentization is a practical consequence of possibility enabled by the Business Framework architecture. When SAP introduced release 4.0, it explained that R/3 has evolved into a family of distributed business components.

Among the new components and functional add-ons to the kernel R/3 application modules are:

- *Introduction of new distributed scenarios* using ALE and its integration using BAPIs.
- *Enhancements for the management of the global supply chain* (from the provider of the provider to the customer of the customer) together with the New Dimension products within the Supply Chain Optimization Planning and Execution (SCOPE) and SAP Advanced Planner and Optimizer (APO) initiatives.
- *Introduction of new specific functionality* for particular industry solutions, starting with retail and the public sector.

- *New Business Framework architecture components.* With these new components customers can add new enhancements to the system independently of other R/3 functionalities. For instance, there is a large group of new Internet scenarios that can be used for business processes.
- *Some of the new business components* within New Dimension that were introduced at the time of the release of R/3 4.0, for example Product Data Management (PDM), ATP Server (Available-to-Promise), the Business Information Warehouse or the system of catalog and purchase requisitions using Internet. These products are installed separately and are release independent.

It was SAP's goal to include substantial improvement for implementing R/3 more quickly, making it a business solution that is easy to use and easy to upgrade. With new R/3 Business Engineer components, the system includes an advanced mechanism for model-based configuration (business blueprints) and for continuous change management.

Technologically, the programming language ABAP/4 has also evolved toward a completely object-oriented language based on the so-called ABAP objects, and from release 4.0 on it is called simply ABAP. These new objects allow interoperability with other types of external and standard object architectures.

There are also enhancements in security and data integrity by means of using authentication and electronic signature techniques.

There was also the extension of the SAP Business Workflow via the addition of new wizards for rapid work flow scenario configuration and deployment as well as the possibility of launching Workflows from the Internet using forms with HTML formats.

R/3 Release 4.5

Release 4.5 was announced in 1998; with it SAP continues its process of introducing new functional components for logistics, financial, and human resources modules, many of which are based on a new open standard provided by the Business Framework architecture.

Strategically, release 4.5 is the strongest SAP bet to introduce and enhance industry solutions. In this version solutions for automotive, distribution, and consumer products are especially strong.

Among new and enhanced technological features of this release, special mention must be made of the new extensions for centralized systems management; new GUI components for integration with PC applications, including new ActiveX controls; more BAPIs; more enhancement and ease of use and configuration of the Business Workflow; enhanced features for object-oriented ABAP; and the capability of accessing archived documents from the Internet using an enhanced Web ArchiveLink Interface.

There are also some major changes in the programs and utilities used for systems installations as well as for upgrading.

By using the architecture provided by the Business Framework, release 4.5 introduces new possibilities of extending the system using third-party solutions via BAPIs in many R/3 areas: enhanced system administration and control with CCMS, human resources management, enhanced global supply chain, report generation, and so on.

EnjoySAP: R/3 Release 4.6

EnjoySAP was an initiative announced by SAP at SAPPHIRE'98 in Madrid, targeted to receive as much feedback as possible, mainly on R/3's usability—that is, on enhancing the system from an end user point of view. Customer and user feedback, together with new strategic and marketing campaigns such as the New Dimension Solutions and the Next Generation, have established the cornerstone for release 4.6, known as EnjoySAP.

Previous R/3 releases included hosts of new components, functionalities, add-ons, industry solutions, and technology advances, and also new but not revolutionary user features. EnjoySAP has dramatically changed the user interface, going beyond just designing appealing and colorful features to fundamentally distinguishing between different types of users by delivering a role-based user interface. One of the features included in EnjoySAP more demanded by users is the ability to tailor the interface, so that now users can add their own icons for their most-used functions to the application toolbar.

SAP Transformation: From a Single-Product Company to a Global Business Solutions Company

The evolution of information technology systems from the beginning was quite similar in all industries and activity areas. In the 1960s and 1970s companies chose a hardware provider, and from there and basic software development products (programming languages) they started to develop their business applications. Most companies started with critical areas, like accounting and financial applications, that were somehow easier. Later, these companies advanced and introduced applications in other, more complex areas like distribution, production, and others. In any case, they always made their own development using the previously chosen hardware and software.

Already in the 1970s there were some companies that realized the possibility of developing business software that could be used by different companies, creating the opportunity to develop the applications only once and then sell the software to other companies. Among these companies was SAP AG, created in 1972.

Obviously the development of "standard" software was more viable in those business areas that were more "standard," like the accounting and financials. There were also more "standard" processes common to companies from the same or similar industry sectors (like manufacturing or financial industries).

At the beginning there we many problems with and obstacles to selling these systems in important quantities. One of these problems was the dependency of the hardware and software platforms in which the systems were developed. At the time, it was not possible to use the same software in different hardware platforms. Another problem was that companies did not behave as standardly as initially thought. For instance, payroll calculation was quite different between companies, and even more different between countries, since each country has its own laws and legal rules, agreements, contract types, and so on.

In late 1970s and during the 1980s, these problems led to companies developing standard applications to follow a strategy to enrich their systems toward a standard product that had to be flexible enough to provide functional features to different types of companies and in different countries. During the 1980s, with the emergence of PCs and the massive deployment of computing and computer networks in companies, it was the time to make applications independent of hardware platforms, and also to make those applications portable among platforms. This was the open systems wave, when different hardware vendors were designing computers that could work with (nearly) the same operating systems (UNIX flavors, Windows NT) and with the same database engines (Oracle, Informix, and others). This technological advance also enabled the development of standard applications that could be independent of hardware and software platforms.

At the beginning of the 1990s, SAP AG had a product, SAP R/2, that covered reasonably well the needs of different types of businesses in different countries and in different areas like financials (accounting, accounts payable and receivable, controlling, and so on), logistics (materials management, warehousing, distribution, sales and production), and human resources (payroll, time management, personnel development). This system was installed in approximately 3000 companies around the world.

The logical and natural evolution from R/2 to an open systems environment led to the birth of R/3 in 1992. SAP R/3 was developed through SAP AG's 20 years of accumulated experience in solving the business problems of its customers, along with experience in computing and managing complex networks. The company had experience and enough technological background for R/3 to succeed.

In a few years, the growth in the number of customers of the R/3 system was exponential: 900 installations at the end of 1993, 2,400 in 1994, 5,200 at the end of 1995, and 20,000 by the middle of 1999. In the middle 1990s it was clear that the standard business software (commonly known as ERPs or Enterprise Resource Planner applications) was mature enough that many companies decided for standard software and could abandon the traditional strategy of local and custom development, which was often more costly in the middle term. At the same time, SAP AG started to gain enough critical mass to take a new step in the development of standard software. This was to start developing software for those company areas that were less standard and more dependent on the business or industry area. These were, for instance, the upstream and downstream systems of oil companies, the call center and customer care systems for telecom or utilities companies, the selling of advertisement in the media sector, and so on. It was necessary to make a move from the back office applications (financial, logistics, human resources) to the front office in the different industry areas. It was also necessary to transform a company selling a product (SAP R/3) independently of the target customer to a company offering specific solutions for the needs of its customers.

SAP AG had enough customers in many different industries to think that the development and selling of specific industry solutions could be profitable. Figure 1-4 shows the percentage of R/3 installations according to industry as of December 31, 1998.

SAP Industry Solutions

Until 1996 SAP R/3 was traditionally presented in the classical diamond figure as shown in Fig. 1-5. There was a red area representing financial applications, a green area for logistics, and a yellow one for human resources; the central blue color represented the basis and development system.

In 1996 SAP's industry solutions started to appear. As a base for many of them, SAP used solutions from R/2 or R/3, which had been previously developed by partners or customers in different business areas, like RIVA in the utilities sector for customer billing. The development of these industry solutions is first coordinated through the Industry Centers of Expertise (ICOEs), where SAP's experience in the development of standard software is joined by the business knowledge and requirements of its customers, as well as the experience of big consulting firms for the inclusion of best business practices for each industry sector.

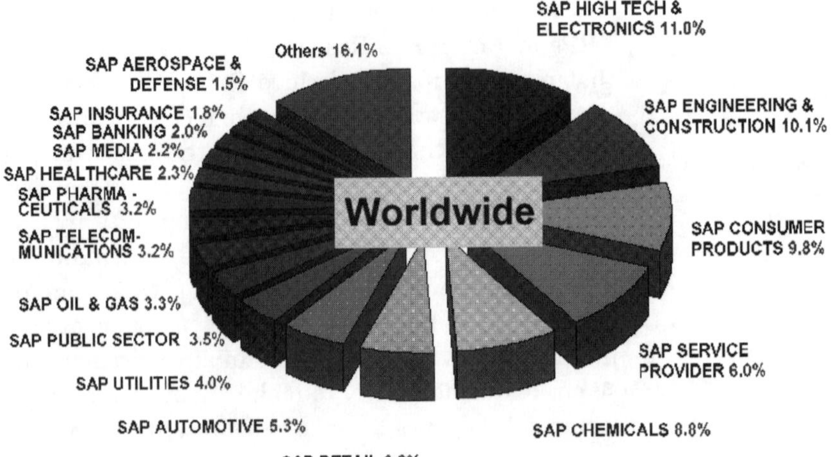

Figure 1-4 SAP R/3 customers' installations by industry. *(Copyright SAP AG.)*

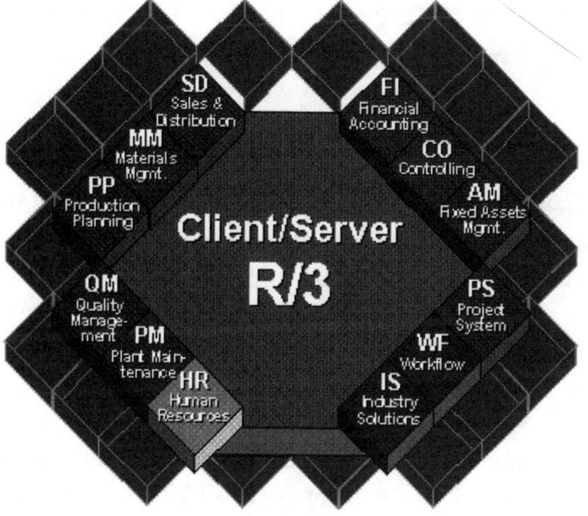

Figure 1-5 Classical representation of SAP R/3. *(Copyright SAP AG.)*

The initial step in developing industry solutions has been steadily consolidated and required SAP to specialize its teams into different industries, called Industry Business Units (IBUs), which included and supplanted the previous ICOEs. These business units are responsible for gathering the market and industry knowledge and developing specific solutions and applications for each of the industry sectors in which SAP is committed to provide. Currently (in mid-1999), there are 18 different industry solutions, as shown in Fig. 1-6.

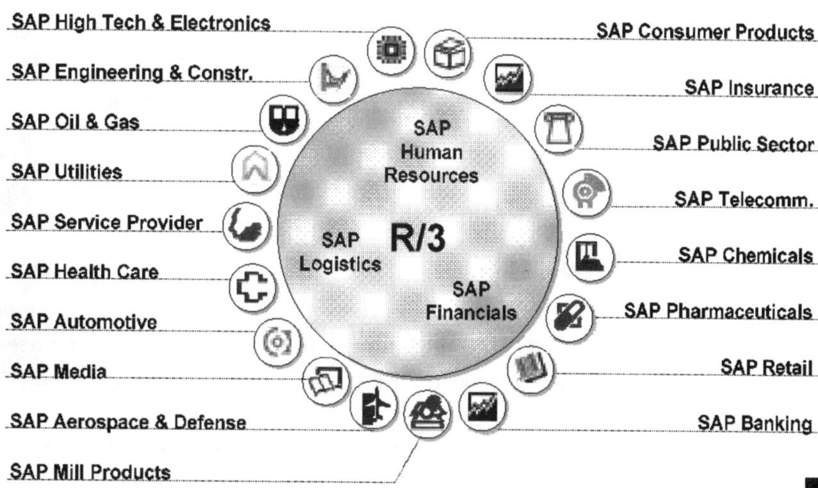

Figure 1-6 SAP's Industry Solutions. *(Copyright SAP AG.)*

The Emergence of the New Dimension Products

Within the last few years, SAP was developing additional modules that initially were included within an IBU; but when looking more closely at these new developments SAP was aware that some of the requested functionalities for these modules were common to different industry sectors. Examples of such common applications are the Customer Interaction Center or Call Center (CIC) or the Sales Force Automation (SFA) that matches those systems that have the objective of automating sales, and that can be deployed in industries as different as consumer products, media, pharmaceuticals, and others.

Since these modules could not be grouped under a specific industry solution, they were positioned by SAP as an equivalent to IBUs called Strategic Business Units (SBUs). Initially SAP created three SBUs:

- SAP Supply Chain Management (SCM), which includes products such as SAP Advanced Planner and Optimizer (APO), SAP Business to Business (B2B), and SAP Product Data Management (PDM)
- SAP Customer Relationship Management (CRM), which includes SAP Sales, SAP Marketing, and SAP Service
- SAP Business Intelligence (BI), which includes the SAP Business Information Warehouse and the SAP Knowledge Warehouse (formerly InfoDB)

Figure 1-7 shows the full picture of SAP New Dimension products.

As can be seen from SAP products and solutions initiatives, from the initial R/3 application modules, SAP has significatively increased the number of solutions that are sold separately from R/3 and that can also be deployed together with non-R/3 applications.

Solution Maps

In 1998 SAP was ready to complete its strategic move from being a single-product (R/3) company to being a company offering complete business solutions to its customers. That was the appropriate launch for the SAP solution maps, for the different industry sectors in which SAP offers these solutions.

The solution maps gather not only the R/3 product vision, but a full and structured view of the customer business as well. This is achieved with a

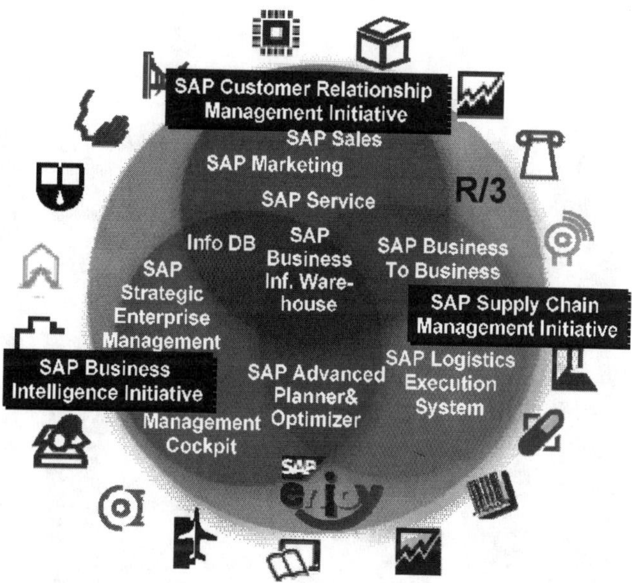

Figure 1-7 SAP New Dimension Initiatives. *(Copyright SAP AG.)*

firm decision to complete the company's catalog of products and services, so that it can offer its customers a complete solution, either directly with SAP products and services or with third-party products developed by complementary software partners.

In the solution maps, the customer business processes are collected in the horizontal colored boxes. Different colors signify different processes within the company.

To build a complete solution for the customer business it will be necessary to deploy different products. As an example, Fig. 1-8 shows the SAP solution map for the media industry.

In this case, the SAP solution for the media industry would include several modules of R/3, such as FI for financial accounting and asset management, CO for the economic and strategic management of business, TR for treasury, MM for procurement, HR for human resources, and so on. It would then include SBU applications like the Business Warehouse, SAP Sales, and SAP Marketing. Finally would come IS-Media with its two modules: Media Advertising Management (MAM) and Media Sales and Distribution (MSD), which include the management of selling advertising for papers, journals, magazines, television, radio, the Internet, and other venues, as well as the management of subscriptions, paper and magazine sales, and distribution.

Additionally, SAP considers it a must to provide its customers with a complete solution by developing required connections with those systems

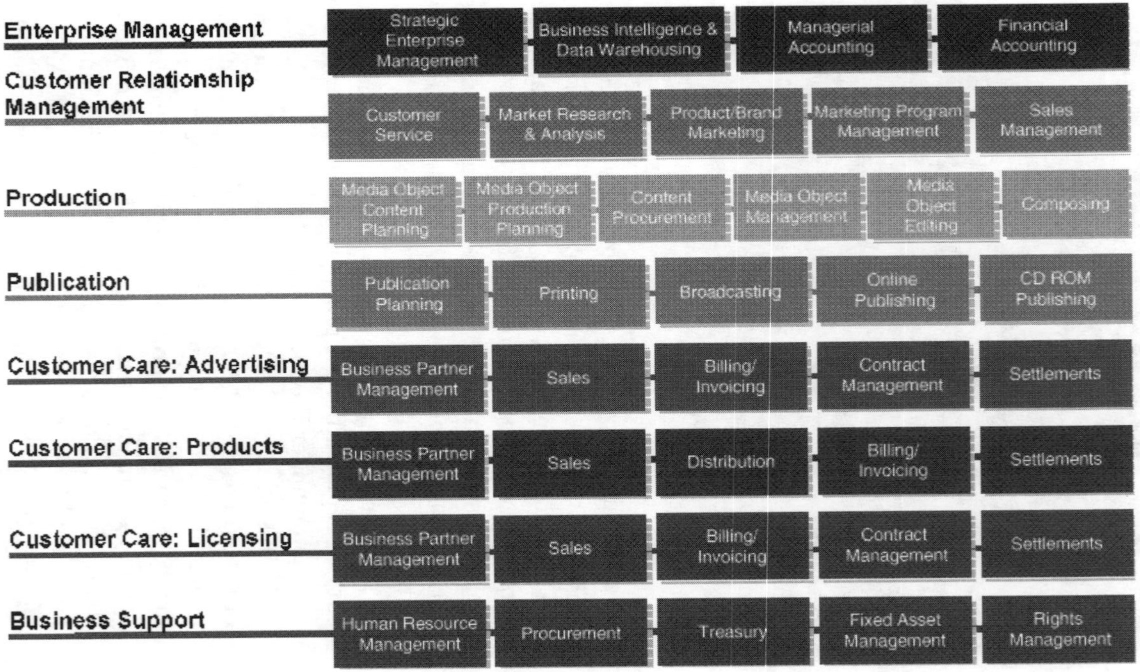

Enterprise Management	Strategic Enterprise Management	Business Intelligence & Data Warehousing	Managerial Accounting	Financial Accounting		
Customer Relationship Management	Customer Service	Market Research & Analysis	Product/Brand Marketing	Marketing Program Management	Sales Management	
Production	Media Object Content Planning	Media Object Production Planning	Content Procurement	Media Object Management	Media Object Editing	Composing
Publication	Publication Planning	Printing	Broadcasting	Online Publishing	CD ROM Publishing	
Customer Care: Advertising	Business Partner Management	Sales	Billing/ Invoicing	Contract Management	Settlements	
Customer Care: Products	Business Partner Management	Sales	Distribution	Billing/ Invoicing	Settlements	
Customer Care: Licensing	Business Partner Management	Sales	Billing/ Invoicing	Contract Management	Settlements	
Business Support	Human Resource Management	Procurement	Treasury	Fixed Asset Management	Rights Management	

Figure 1-8 SAP Solution Map for the media industry, 1999 edition. (Copyright SAP AG.)

that must coexist with SAP. In SAP Media this is the case with production systems that must interface with content servers or with systems for the design and pagination of publications. This is achieved by the Business Framework architecture based on open interfaces that can be used by products of complementary software partners. This structure guarantees SAP customers a complete integration of products, providing a full solution map for the integrated management of their businesses.

SAP Services Overview

SAP has put in place a comprehensive set of quality services to help customers during the process of implementing and supporting the R/3 system. These services include product information, education services installation and upgrade services, consulting, and more. SAP bases its services mainly on remote connections with customers through the international networks.

Administrators, support personnel, and consultants should be particularly familiar with the former SAP *online service system* (OSS), now known as SAPnet-R/3 front end, which is the primary source of service and support. The next section of this chapter includes an introduction to SAPnet-R/3 front end. SAP offers a certification process in the technical, functional, and developing areas of the system and an extensive number of training courses worldwide.

SAP provides several types of services:

- *Consulting services.* This type of individualized consulting can be given on-site or via a remote connection to SAP. With remote consulting, customers receive immediate and updated technical support and answers to their questions. SAP also gives weekend support when upgrades or installations are done outside regular working hours. Customers open the connection so SAP consultants may directly access their systems and evaluate the problems online. Once the consulting session is finished, the customer closes the connection.
- *Maintenance services.* This is the basic and most common type of support for customers in the preproduction and production phases of an R/3 implementation. This service deals with answering questions and helping to resolve the errors or problems with the system. For maintenance, SAP has set up a *helpdesk,* or *hotline,* which monitors the calls and resolves them or directs them to the appropriate

SAP expert, and a *first-level customer service team* that is in charge of resolving the problems, prioritizing the calls, and if needed, referring questions to other experts. Customers obtain this service via phone, fax, or the SAPnet-R/3 front end. It is available 24 hours a day, 7 days a week. For example, if you have a severe problem at 5 A.M., log it in on the SAPnet-R/3 front end, give it a "very high" priority (meaning "my system does not work"), and you might expect a fast call back from Japan, Philadelphia, or Walldorf, Germany.

- *Preventive services.* The primary one is the EarlyWatch service which ensures successful and efficient installation of the R/3 system in all phases. This service makes regular (usually once a month) performance checks and analyzes the system to identify potential problems and help system managers and SAP administrators tune the system and realize its full potential. Soon after an EarlyWatch session, SAP sends the customer a report with the results of the analysis and recommendations for avoiding potential problems, such as database tablespaces becoming full, shortage of system parameters, and buffer tuning.

SAP provides additional services such as the development request service, which submits enhancement requests, and the first customer shipment (FCS), which gives selected customers the opportunity to test new R/3 versions' functionality before the products are officially released.

In the search for total customer services solution, SAP has also designed a comprehensive Service Map that gathers the requirements for a full life cycle of services, including evaluation, implementation, and continuous improvement phases for each of the identified key customer processes:

- Management activities
- Business processes
- Technical management
- Development activities
- Knowledge transfer
- Help and care

For each of these processes and phase, SAP and its partners have an extensive portfolio of services. Updated information and service map can be found at www.sap.com/service.

Online Services. As stated previously, SAP has made online services through remote connections its preferred and most convenient way to support customers. For this reason, obtaining a network connection to SAP can become critical in an R/3 project.

SAP has built a worldwide network of support servers for customers to use to obtain the support they need for successful implementation and operation of their SAP systems. Customers can also download patches and upgrades from those servers via *ftp* (a file transfer protocol very common in TCP/IP networks).

SAP also offers extensive information and correction services for customers and partners through the Internet with SAPnet (sapnet.sap-ag.de or sapnet.sap.com), which gathers most of the facilities previously found on the Online Service Systems (OSS) but with much more content.

However, customers will still need a remote connection to SAP for certain services, like EarlyWatch, Telnet, remote upgrade, and others.

Figure 1-9 includes a very simple scheme of the connection between customer systems and SAP support servers. *SAProuter* is a program provided by SAP which acts like a firewall, giving users control of who accesses their R/3 systems. For more details, refer to Appendix A.

The only thing customers need in order to gain access to these servers is a remote connection to the nearest support server. Currently, SAP has support servers in Walldorf, Foster City, Tokyo, Sydney, and Singapore.

This is the connection that you use for the OSS, EarlyWatch, and remote consulting. It is the only way that you can permit the SAP experts to log on to your system and solve problems online. Imagine the costs saved in travel.

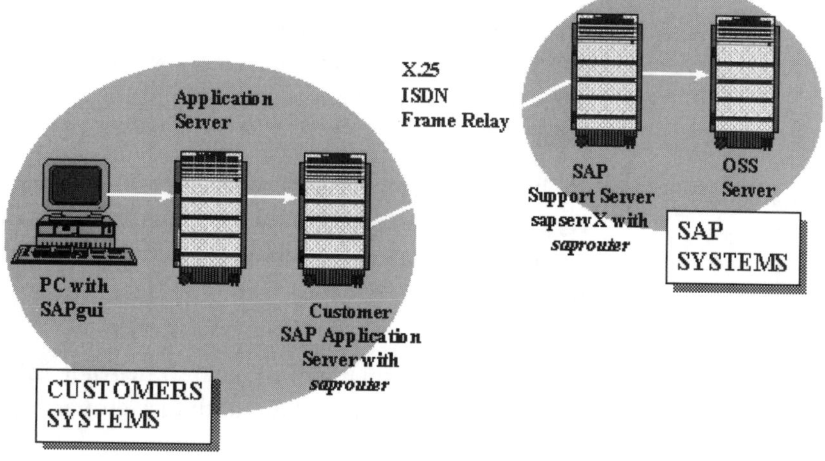

Figure 1-9 Connecting your system to a SAP support server.

In order to use SAP remote services, you must perform the following steps:

1. Select and apply for the most convenient supported type of connection. There are many ways to connect to SAP depending on the geography where you are located: X.25, frame relay, ISDN. To know which one is the most convenient for your organization, contact your nearest SAP subsidiary. You can also find more information in SAP document number 5000 9179, "Remote Connection to the R/3 Online Services," which comes in the SAP software kit.
2. Apply for an official IP network address. Usually your network carrier can help you with this.
3. Select the support server that corresponds to your geography or ask SAP which one is the most convenient.
4. Send SAP your network address specifications so that SAP can add it to its network configuration to be able both to connect to your system and permit your entrance into its support servers.

These steps might concern some information security managers; however, they should not worry too much. In fact, when configuring the remote connection, only outgoing calls from the customer to SAP are permitted. Then, when customers open the connection, they can themselves permit or prohibit the SAP services. For more information, see Appendix A.

SAPnet-R/3 Front End (OSS)

The SAPnet-R/3 front end (formerly known as OSS or Online Service System) is nothing more (and nothing less) than an R/3 system that customers with remote connections to SAP support servers can use free of cost.

This is a brief list of what is available at the SAPnet-R/3 front end system:

- Problem and information database (hint notes), so that users can try to find the solution to their problems before they call SAP or send it a problem report. Looking and reading notes is a great way to learn tidbits about R/3.
- Latest SAP news in the HotNews section.
- Up-to-date release, installation, and upgrade information. To have these very latest notes is a mandatory step in any installation or upgrade procedure of R/3.

- Online problem registry. Problems or questions are treated the same way (and sometimes better) and with the same priority as they are when registered by telephone.
- Training offerings and course descriptions. These have just recently been included.
- Access to the SSCR (SAP Software Change Registration), where customers can register developers and SAP repository objects and get the keys required to continue development.
- Download Support Packages (formerly Hot Packages) for correcting system and program errors.
- Register Knowledge Products CDs.
- Register customer systems and request SAP licenses.
- Define and manage service connections.
- Display EarlyWatch Alert reports.
- Manager user accounts for accessing the system.

SAPnet-R/3 front end is the star service system provided by SAP and the most widely used by SAP customers and partners, especially consultants and administrators. The SAPnet-R/3 front end interface is intuitive and a very easy system to learn and use.

SAP provides initial user accounts for accessing SAPnet. Customers can create and maintain additional user accounts from within the SAPnet-R/3 front end.

EarlyWatch. EarlyWatch is a SAP offering for preventive services, providing proactive diagnosis and analysis online. Through the connection, a SAP expert accesses the customer system and obtains all the information needed for preparing a report that is later sent to the customer.

SAP used to provide a free session before customer systems go into a productive stage. Subsequent sessions must be separately contracted.

The first thing revealed in the EarlyWatch report is a summary diagnosis indicating the problem's level of severity found in the system. This diagnosis might indicate that most parameters are well tuned and that systems are running fine, or it might say that there are some problems, which can be either normal or critical—in which case, customers should solve them as soon as possible.

The checkups done by the EarlyWatch service include detecting potential problems in the SAP R/3 application, as well as in the database and operating system. The service provides information about tablespaces getting full, SAP system log error messages, buffer tuning, and database parameters.

R/3 systems have hundreds of parameters, with many of them directly affecting other values. The EarlyWatch team analyzes the past week's evolution of the system and if it detects bottlenecks or an increase in processing times, it usually recommends new values for the profile parameters.

Partners

SAP standard software and consulting services are complemented by a comprehensive partnership program to help customers fulfill their needs and to help SAP cope with the strong demand for supporting the R/3 system, implementations, additional industry solution developments, new add-on products, training, business process reengineering consulting, outsourcing, and so on.

In 1997 SAP introduced the TeamSAP concept, a significant step in the SAP partner policy and strategy of aiming for efficiency when implementing R/3, with the objective of providing end-to-end service to customers during the full system life cycle. TeamSAP is defined as a symbol of distinction of the best SAP and partner resources, and includes three main areas: persons, processes, and products.

SAP has the following types of TeamSAP partners:

- *Consulting partners.* The world's biggest consulting and multinational system integration organizations provide solid experience in technology, industry solutions, and SAP implementations. Because of their worldwide presence, SAP calls them *global logo partners.* On the national scale, there are many smaller and highly professional consulting firms specializing in SAP projects, customizing, and certain industry areas. These are known as *national logo partners.*
- *Technology partners.* These are leading hardware and software vendors of databases, networking, hardware, operating systems, and add-on products that are tightly integrated in SAP systems.
- *Value-added resellers.* System vendors which provide support to small- and medium-sized companies to implement SAP solutions.
- *Complementary Software Partners.* These include software companies that develop add-on products and solutions certified to work with SAP products.

- *Outsourcing partners.* These are organizations that have the resources and knowledge to run and outsource customers R/3 installations.

R/3 Complementary Software Certification. As previously stated in this chapter, a strategic move by SAP to maintain and further advance its leadership in the client/server market with R/3 is the integration of third-party software that adds value to SAP's solutions.

SAP has established a certification program for the interfacing between SAP applications and third-party software to guarantee ready-to-use solutions for mutual customers. All third-party software must be certified by SAP through this program, which has already certified add-on solutions in the areas of plant data collection devices, process control systems, EDI translators, optical archives, CAD, product management data, laboratory information management systems, mobile data collection systems, and geographical information systems. To date, there are already more than 100 partners with certified solutions.

Description of R/3

From previous sections, it became clear what the use of this software system is and who decides to implement it: SAP R/3 controls business processes and manages essential company information. Enterprises needing those services implement this standard software.

To manage the complex business needs of companies, the R/3 product family offers leading technology solutions:

- Multitier client/server architecture.
- Based on middleware for supporting open systems technology.
- Business Framework architecture, open to total integration with other components and applications, including the Internet world. This is achieved by the use of standard Business Application Program Interfaces (BAPIs).
- Homogeneous user interface among applications.
- Comprehensive development environment.
- Total application integration.
- Solution Sets for configuring the system.

- Wide range of services including hotline support, training, consulting, quality checks, and so on.
- Complete support for solving all the problems arising from the millennium change (Y2K) and the appearance of the new European currency, the euro.

Figure 1-10 shows the R/3 components from a functional point of view. The overall SAP R/3 system is represented by everything included inside the ellipse.

The lower layer is made of the operating system, physical database (whose software is included in the SAP kit), and the network. The *middleware layer,* which is above it, interfaces with the lower one and integrates the SAP R/3 applications on top of it. This middle layer is known as the *basis system,* as the *basis system,* and includes components such as the ABAP development workbench, the system administration tools, batch job handling, authorization and security management, and all *cross-application* modules.

ABAP/4 is a fourth-generation programming language that was used to develop all R/3 application modules. When releases 4.0 and 4.5 were introduced, and SAP's strategy began to focus on object orientation, it was decided to rename the programming language to simply ABAP, abandoning the 4 in reference to fourth generation. Chapter 7, "Introduction to the ABAP Development Workbench," gives an overview of the R/3 development components.

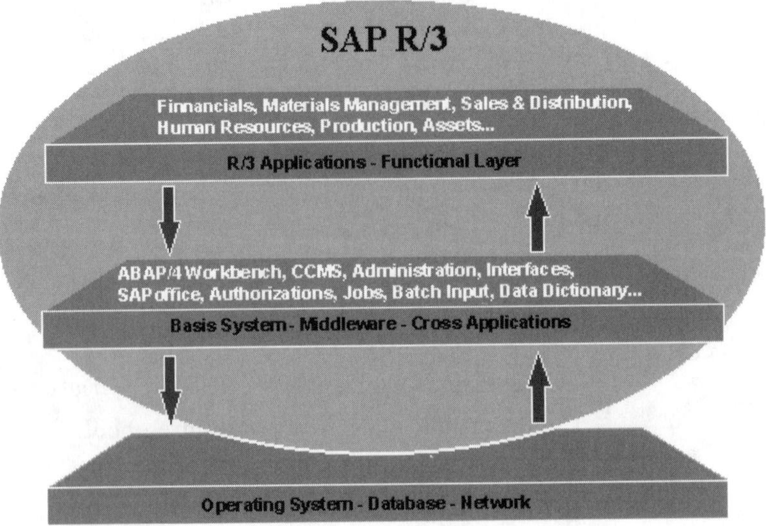

Figure 1-10
SAP R/3 components.

Middleware are the layered software components that facilitate the development of client/server applications that can be deployed in heterogeneous vendor platforms. The basis system, also known as the kernel, is the SAP R/3 middleware.

The upper layer, the *functional layer,* contains the different business applications: financial, human resources, sales and distribution, materials management, and so on. The integration of all applications relies on the basis system.

SAP defines *client/server* also from a business solution point of view: a technology concept that leverages computing power to link core business processes with software, tying together various functions, such as financials, human resources, sales and distribution, logistics, and manufacturing.

A very common way for SAP to illustrate the R/3 system is the one shown earlier in Fig. 1-5, with the R/3 kernel system providing the necessary integration and infrastructure for the R/3 applications.

The R/3 kernel makes use of standard communications and application program interfaces to access the operating system, the database, and the network. This kernel layer is located below the application logic and data layers of the system and operates independently from the applications. This architecture allows users to change system configuration and install new systems without interrupting or altering the applications themselves.

Multitier Client/Server Solutions

In general, *client/server* is a style of computing that distributes the workload of a computer application across several cooperating computer programs. This type of computing separates user-oriented, application, and data management tasks. Client/server is mainly a software concept that includes a set of service providers and service requesters. In client/server computing, individual software components act as service providers, service requesters, or both. These software services communicate with each other via predefined interfaces.

Major advantages of the client/server approach are as follows:

- *Flexible configuration.* With the deployment of standard communication interfaces, there are many possibilities for distributing and planning a client/server installation: from a centralized configuration to a highly distributed system. See Fig. 1-11.

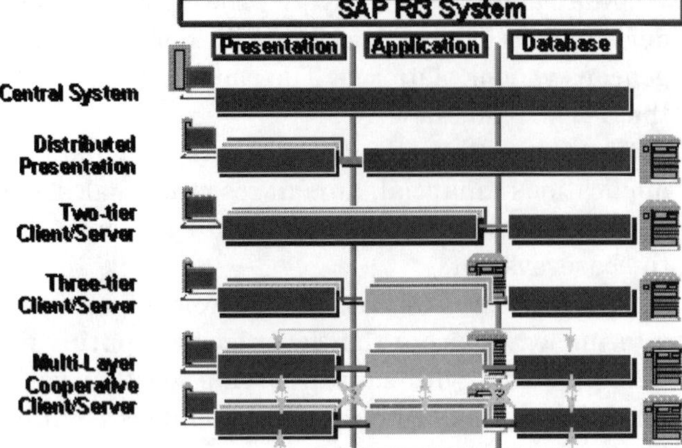

Figure 1-11 SAP R/3 client/server configurations. *(Copyright by SAP AG.)*

- *Workload distribution.* Since application servers work in parallel and communicate with the database, users can be evenly distributed based on their job tasks. Also, there is the possibility of deploying dedicated application servers to specific business areas.
- *High scalability.* Client/server permits users to adapt the capacity of their hardware according to the performance needs of their businesses, such as adding additional application servers when there is an increase in number of users, when additional modules start production, and when the database becomes larger. This enables companies to protect software and hardware investments.

One of the widely used client/server configurations with the R/3 system is the three-tiered architecture (see Fig. 1-12), which separates a system's computers into three function groups: presentation, application, and database. Since client/server is a software concept, it must be clear that an application server includes the software components that make up the provider services for the presentation, acting as a server, but also acting as service requester of the database services.

With the three-tiered architecture, each group is set up to support the demands of its functions. The central server contains the database, widely known as the *database server. Application servers* include the processing logic of the system, including services such as spooling, dispatching user requests, and formatting data. The tasks related to presentation of the data are handled by the *presentation servers,* which typically are personal computers or workstations, enabling easy access to the system.

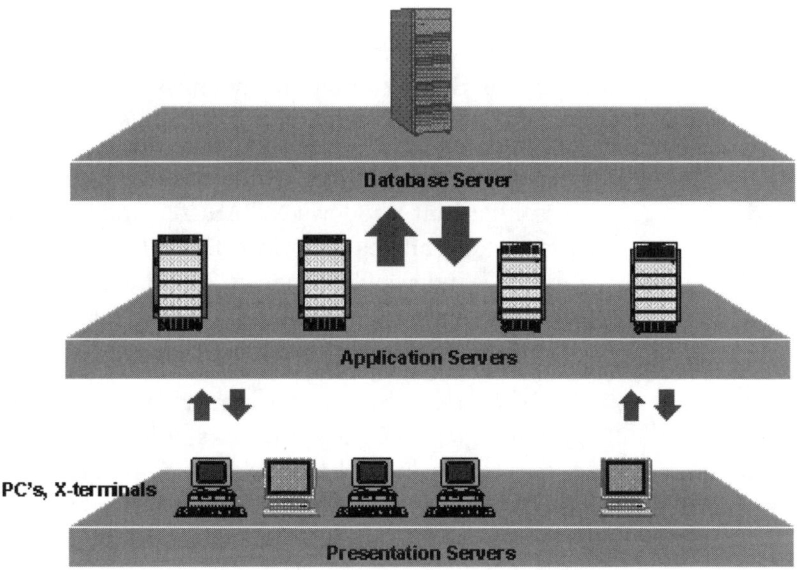

Figure 1-12 R/3 three-tiered client/server architecture.

Communication among the three tiers or server types is accomplished with the use of standard protocol services, such as the ones provided by TCP/IP or CPIC.

CPIC stands for *Common Programming Interface Communication* and includes standard functions and services for program-to-program communication with the ABAP programming language.

The section entitled "R/3 Basis Software" in the next chapter shows in greater detail the services, processes, and components of the client/server architecture of SAP R/3.

Open Technology

The key to SAP R/3 success was the strategy of making *open solutions,* in which the applications can run on multiple operating systems, databases, and communication technologies. This enables customers to remain independent of a single vendor if they wish.

The list of current SAP-supported systems can be found also on the Internet link from the Information Center for Technology Infrastructure at www.sap.com/products/techno/index.htm. Select *Platforms,* then *Hardware.*

What basically makes systems open is the use of standard formats for data exchange, communication interfaces, and program-to-program communication. SAP extends the openness concept in several respects:

- *At the system level.* Support for multiple hardware platforms and operating systems, such as all types of UNIX from main system vendors, Microsoft Windows NT, AS/400, and S/390. Support for a large number of graphical user interfaces (GUIs), such as for all Windows flavors (Windows 95, Windows 98, Windows NT), Macintosh, OS/2, Motif, Internet Browsers, and so on. In 1999 SAP also announced support for the Linux operating system.
- *At the database level.* R/3 supports various relational database systems such as Oracle, Informix, Adabas D, DB2, and SQL-Server. Access to the data managed by R/3 is possible using standard R/3 reports as well as any other SQL standard tool: ODBC, SQL browsers, and so on. SAP has incorporated the standard ANSI-SQL as the database manipulation language, which allows users and programmers to store, view, and retrieve data to and from all different underlying database products.
- *At the application level.* The system is open to be enhanced and extended to meet specific business requirements. The ABAP repository and the R/3 reference model enable users to understand the relationships and inner workings of R/3 applications. The R/3 programming interface lets other R/3 systems and external programs invoke R/3 function modules via RFCs (remote function calls) or RPCs (remote procedure calls), or by using Business Application Program Interfaces (BAPIs). SAP offers the Remote Function Call Software Developer Kit (RFC SDK), a standard interface for customers and complementary software partners to carry out individual extensions to SAP business applications that support the direct communication with the function modules of R/3.

  At the URL www.sap.com/bfw/index.htm (Business Framework Main information center), under *Open BAPI Network,* SAP provides a repository or collection of BAPIs with all the information needed for their use.
- *At the desktop level.* With the deployment of Microsoft OLE (Object Linking and Embedding) technology, R/3 enables desktop users to access SAP data and functions from many OLE client programs. With the introduction of R/3 release 4.0 and especially with 4.5 and

4.6, SAP leveraged the concept of integration with PC programs, mainly with the technology provided by ActiveX and Java.

- *At the communication protocol level.* SAP can use the standard communication protocols TCP/IP, SNA-LU6.2, CPIC, and OSF/DCE/DME for interprogram communications as well as for network communication and data transfer.
- *At the external communication level:*
  - R/3 includes EDI (electronic data interchange) interfaces to automate the exchange of data (invoices, orders, etc.) between R/3 and other applications systems used by business partners.
  - It also uses MAPI (Messaging Application Program Interface) technology, supporting standard X.400 and SMTP protocols. These standards allow R/3 users to communicate with other mail systems and the Internet.
  - Since release 3.1, with the incorporation of the BAPI technology, SAP has actively supported the new *electronic commerce technology* with the deployment of the Internet, which allow business transactions to happen between Internet users and R/3 systems.
  - With the ALE (Application Link Enabled) technology, SAP R/3 allows communication between distributed applications: R/3-R/3 systems, R/3-R/2 systems, R/3-external application systems.
  - Using development environments such as standard ANSI C, C++, Visual Studio, Java, Delphi or Visual Basic, developers can integrate external applications with the R/3 system, exchanging information on the level of business objects.

User Interface

The R/3 user interface is designed for ease of use and friendliness by all levels of staff. The SAP graphical user interface, known as SAPGUI, acts as the presentation server and is available in Windows 95, Windows 98, Windows NT, Motif, OS/2 Presentation Manager, and Macintosh. They all look identical, whatever underlying system they are running on.

The SAPGUI includes all graphical capabilities of modern windows interfaces, with push buttons, menu bars, toolbars, hypertext links, on-focus descriptions, and right-clicking options. The graphical design and functionality is homogeneous across the entire system, which makes training easier and more straightforward for all levels of SAP users.

Depending on which R/3 application or processing tasks are to be run, screens may be very simple or may contain multiple fields and graphical elements. Customers can also customize and create new menus and screens with the help of the development workbench. Chapter 5, "Using SAP," contains all the information needed to learn how to use the system, what the available icons are, how to move around the system, and some very useful hints.

In R/3 releases 4.x, the new GUI was designed to be able to show several types of information at the same time. There is also the possibility of transferring the presentation components on demand from R/3 to the workstations. This is possible because of the enhancements in the architecture introduced using ActiveX under Windows or JavaBeans.

As introduced previously, one of the biggest changes and improvements in the EnjoySAP release is the user interface strategy.

ABAP Development Workbench

ABAP/4 was SAP's own fourth-generation programming language, and that was the name up to release 3.1. When release 4.0 was introduced, the name lost the 4 suffix and the language started to be known simply as ABAP. It is exactly the same language with several new technical improvements, mainly in the field of adding all the features that make a programming language object oriented. The name is taken from ***A**dvanced **B**usiness **A**pplication **P**rogramming **L**anguage* and is the programming language used by SAP for the development of all standard business applications included within the R/3 suite.

On top of ABAP, SAP has designed a full-purpose development environment, known as the ABAP development workbench, which is integrated within the R/3 system and is available for customers to develop their own solutions and enhance or extend the capabilities of the existing applications.

The ABAP development workbench includes all tools necessary to develop and design programs, screens, menus, and so forth. It also contains performance and debugging facilities. Central to the workbench is the ABAP object repository and the data dictionary.

The *object repository* stores all the development objects of the workbench: programs, dictionary data, *dynpros* (dynamic programs), and documentation. The repository is the key to managing and testing ongoing development.

The *data dictionary* contains the descriptions of the data structures used within programs. This is the *metadata* repository that includes table definitions, allowed values, and relationships between tables. Administrators should be very familiar with this SAP component since it is widely and extensively used. The ABAP data dictionary is covered in detail in Chap. 8.

As of version 3.0, the development workbench included the workbench organizer, the evolution of the correction system of previous releases. The organizer handles the transition of new developments and customizations into productive systems. Some of the available features are version management, programs modification control, and team project developments. The transport system handles the movement of development work from one system to another. For instance, migrations to new SAP releases are, in reality, massive objects transported from the systems at SAP to customers' systems. This is a very important tool in the R/3 system and is explained in Chap. 6.

Application Integration

The data from the different SAP functional applications are shared and integrated, building what is often known as an *internal information highway.* This integration can be seen as an implicit applications work flow.

One of the main benefits of the set of R/3 applications is their capacity for creating a perfect integration between the different business processes of companies. It is that integration between applications that ensures that all business and management information is available to all areas of a company.

An accompanying feature that makes application integration stand out is the capacity of doing it in *real time.* This means that information is constantly updated, so when a manager requests a report about the current balance the system provides instant information about the status of the financial statements. This avoids the difficulty of running end-of-period reports and programs from a traditional legacy system, which has to search and incorporate needed data from other applications before the run.

From the point of view of the business processes, the integration of the R/3 application modules is represented using the tools available within the *R/3 Business Engineer.* At the level of data models, this integration can be accessed using the available functions included in the *Data Modeler.*

Customizing Tools

Customizing is the cornerstone of SAP R/3 system implementation. Once you get your kit, you have all the modules with all the business processes. The next step is to *customize* the system to suit your business needs and practices. This is the method of implementing and enhancing the R/3 system, as well as upgrading to new SAP releases.

Some of the customizing tasks are as easy to implement as electronically entering the countries where the company is located. That has an automatic effect on currencies, tax calculations, legal requirements, and so on. Other tasks are very industry-specific and somewhat more complicated.

Customizing the system is a long, time-consuming process because it can only be done by expert company users and with help from consultants that know the real business. Customizing must precisely match business organization, processes, and functions with those of the R/3 system. Figure 1-13 shows an example of one of the multiple screens used by the R/3 system for help in customizing.

SAP includes some standard tools to help customers and consultants with this process and is also planning to provide some templates to be

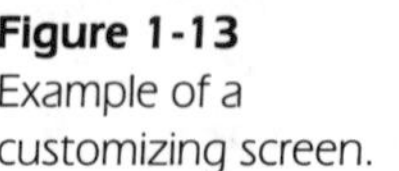

Figure 1-13 Example of a customizing screen.

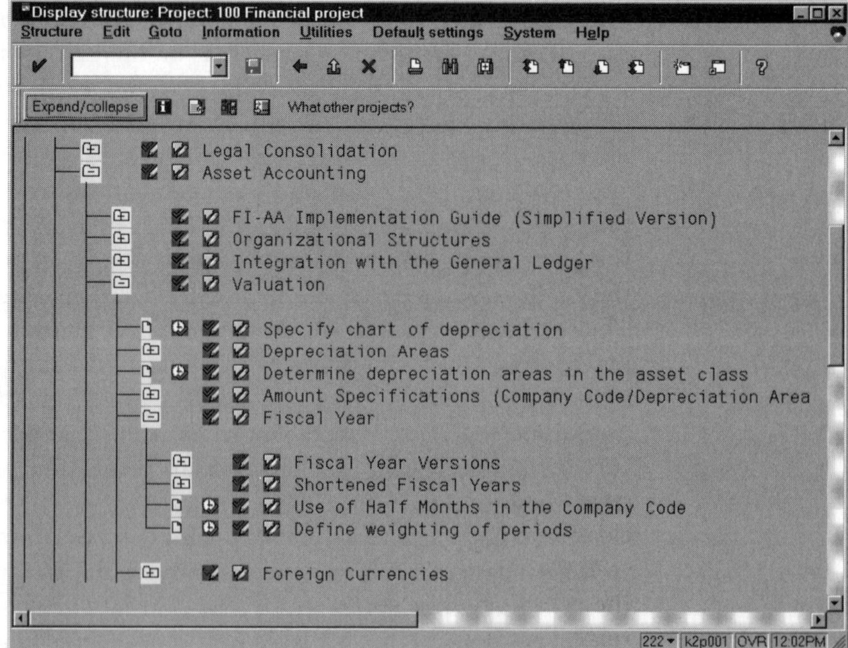

used for adapting the R/3 functions to their corresponding business practices.

Some of the tools and documentation provided are as follows:

- *The procedure model.* A hierarchical project structure designed for helping and guiding customers in their implementation projects. Introduced in release 3.0, this model can be considered the first integrated solution set that SAP included within the R/3 system. The procedure model is integrated into the R/3 system, but it is quickly becoming less used in favor of the ASAP methodology.
- *The IMG (implementation guide).* An interactive model to help users and consultants map company requirements for specific business needs. IMG can handle the automatic creation of recommendations for organizing and implementing the project. It acts like an electronic manual for consultants, linking hypertext documentation with real transactions.
- *The transport system.* Tools for transferring system configuration from test systems to production systems.
- Tools for managing system and release upgrades.

Administrators also have some customization work to do for the basis system, such as setting printers, copying clients, setting up the correction and transport system, and so on.

R/3 Business Engineer

SAP provides the R/3 reference model for helping to depict and describe the business processes, the possibilities offered by the R/3 software, and the relationships between different processes and application modules. This model is very important in the R/3 projects, since it allows customers and consultants to select which processes, alternatives, workarounds, and system components will be necessary to meet the companies' business and organization requirements as well as their technological infrastructure needs. The R/3 Business Engineer is a graphical tool that is used for documenting the business processes included within R/3, providing a clear vision of their integration.

Together with the customizing tools, the R/3 reference model is one of the essential components for implementing SAP. Figure 1-14 shows the relationship and role of the reference model as the intermediate layer

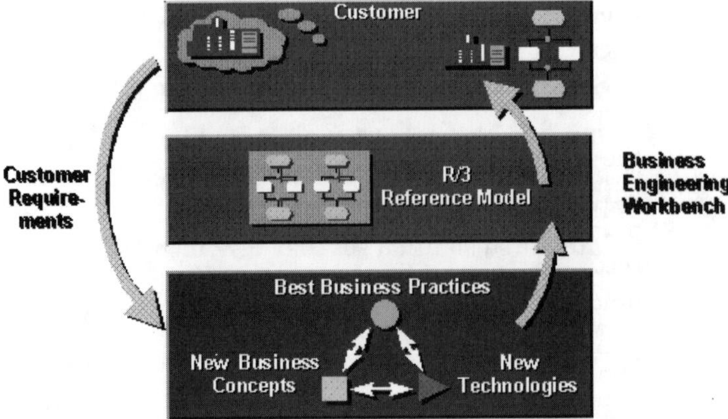

Figure 1-14 R/3 business process integration. *(Copyright by SAP AG.)*

between the business practices and processes included in R/3 and the needs of companies.

The reference model can also be used for other SAP project tasks such as end user training, project scope analysis, integration tests, systems reengineering, gap analysis, and so on.

When there is no SAP R/3 system installed and available yet at the customer site, the reference model is available as independent PC tools, such as the ARIS toolset, LiveModel for SAP R/3, Visio, or Micrografx Enterprise Charter. All these tools can be used for analyzing and modeling the business processes of companies and can be very useful for simulation, prototyping, training, and documentation.

Since release 3.0, the reference model is also integrated intro the R/3 system and is better known as *Business Navigator.*

R/3 Applications Overview

The R/3 applications are usually categorized in three core functional areas: financial, human resources, and logistics. Additionally, SAP actively develops special software packages complementing R/3, targeted to specialized vertical industries. These packages are known as *industry solutions* (ISs). Also, there is a special set of modules, known as the *cross application (CA) modules,* which is positioned between the technical and functional areas of the system, and covers such things as the business workflow, CAD integration, and document system. Since customizing is also a process that must be done for all areas of the system, SAP also refers to it as a CA module.

The core areas include hundreds of business processes to address all the needs of modern business applications. There are many modules within these areas that work equally well when deployed as stand-alone products. For instance, there are companies that might decide to use only certain modules of the R/3 application suite—sales and distribution, manufacturing, and accounting.

The following sections include brief descriptions of the main module groups and listings of the modules for each group. SAP includes new modules as new versions are released, so these listings may not be completely up-to-date.

Financial Applications

SAP financial modules give customers the whole picture of the accounting functions, with extensive report facilities to allow for fast decision-making support. They are also perfectly suited for international corporations with multiple subsidiaries, including support for foreign currencies and multilingual capabilities.

The financial area contains the following module groups:

- *FI.* Financial accounting
- *CO.* Controlling
- *EC.* Enterprise controlling
- *IM.* Capital investment management
- *TR.* Treasury

FI: Financial Accounting. These modules constitute the operational aspects of the general accounting and financial information for the enterprise. They connect and integrate with other financial modules such as treasury and controlling, as well as parts of human resources, such as payroll and travel expenses. Also, the transactions of accounts receivable and accounts payable are directly related to the sales and distribution and purchasing modules. The following list contains the financial accounting modules. Each one includes multiple business processes and capabilities.

FI-AA	Asset accounting
FI-AP	Accounts payable
FI-AR	Accounts receivable
FI-GL	General ledger accounting
FI-LC	Consolidation
FI-SL	Special purpose ledger

An important aspect of the financial accounting system is the real-time generation of the current balance and profit and loss sheets.

CO: Controlling. This module is used to represent the company's cost structures and the factors that influence them. The module includes areas such as cost controlling, product and production cost controlling, and profitability analysis.

The CO module is intended to answer key management questions such as "What does a product or service cost?" To answer that, the CO product costing system uses different valuation strategies and quantity structures, enabling the cost of manufactured goods to be planned as precisely as possible.

With the help of a planned/actual comparison, the CO module enables users to quickly recognize weak points in the production process. The following lists the controlling modules and their descriptions.

CO-ABC	Activity-based costing
CO-OM	Overhead cost control
CO-PA	Sales and profitability analysis
CO-PC	Product cost controlling

EC: Enterprise Controlling. The EC module is another very important decision-making tool which monitors the critical success factors and key figures of the company from a controller's point of view.

The executive information system (EIS) is basically a collection of tools which helps to quickly filter and analyze the enterprise's most important data and get critical and up-to-date business information into graphical form or customized reports.

With the management consolidation (EC-MC) system, subsidiary data, even from different countries and with different legal regulations, passes directly into the central MC system, automatically performing all the required consolidation work.

The EC module allows profit analysis for independent business areas of a company. The system takes care of automatically retrieving and grouping the necessary information for this process. The following list contains the areas included in the enterprise controlling module group.

EC-EIS	Executive information system
EC-MC	Management consolidation
EC-PCA	Profit center accounting

IM: Capital Investment Management. IM is a new SAP release 3.0 module designed to plan and manage capital investment projects and budgets. It is also used for monitoring the bookkeeping functions associated with assets under construction on capital investment projects and orders. It consists of two parts:

IM	Capital investment management (programs)
IM-FA	Tangible fixed assets (measures)

TR: Treasury. The treasury module of SAP R/3 integrates cash management and forecasting with the financial and logistics-related applications. It provides tools to analyze budgeting, process electronic account statements, analyze foreign money markets, and so forth. The following list shows the components of the treasury module.

TR-CM	Cash management
TR-FM	Funds management
TR-TM	Treasury management
TR-MRM	Market Risk Management

Human Resources Applications

The HR module includes all necessary business processes to efficiently manage all the needs of a company's human resource area—from applicant screening to payroll accounting or personnel development. As with the rest of the SAP applications, the aim of the HR module is to enter data just once and make it available to other related applications, such as accounting, plant maintenance, or business workflow.

The HR module includes full support for salary administration and payroll, work schedule models, planning, travel expenses, and so forth.

It must be noted that the HR module and its associated business process are very country-specific, since the software must adhere to specific country laws concerning employment, tax, benefits, and so on. For this reason, SAP includes different procedures and transactions for different countries.

There are two module groups within the human resources applications:

- *PA: Personnel administration,* which includes the following:
  - PA-APP Applicant management
  - PA-BEN Benefits
  - PA-EMP Employee Management
  - PA-INW Incentive wages
  - PA-PAY Payroll
  - PA-TIM Time management
  - PA-TRV Travel expenses
- *PD: Personnel development,* which includes the following:
  - PD-OM Organizational management
  - PD-PD Personnel development
  - PD-RPL Room reservations planning
  - PD-SCM Seminar and convention management
  - PD-WFP Workforce planning

Logistics Applications

Logistics is the most extensive area of the R/3 applications and contains the largest number of modules. The logistics applications manage all processes involved in the supply chain of goods: from raw material procurement to final customer delivery and billing. These applications contain comprehensive business processes for flexible manufacturing systems and lots of tools for decision support. These applications integrate seamlessly with virtually every other R/3 application, from the financial and controlling modules to the human resources processes.

The logistics applications include the following modules:

- *LO.* General logistics
- *MM.* Materials management
- *PM.* Plant maintenance
- *PP.* Production planning

- *PS.* Project system
- *QM.* Quality management
- *SD.* Sales and distribution

LO: General Logistics. These applications contain the intelligence engine of the SAP R/3 logistics system: tools and reports to analyze and manage the status and make forecasts about the supply chain. The following is a list of the general logistics modules.

LO-ECH	Engineering change management
LO-EHS	Environment, health and safety
LO-LIS	Logistics information system
LO-MD	Logistics master data
LO-PR	Forecast
LO-VC	Variant configuration

MM: Materials Management. The materials management module comprises all activities related with material acquisitions (purchasing) and control (inventory, warehouse).

The purchasing module includes a complete range of operations: request for quotations, requisition limits, vendor price comparisons, agreements, order status, and so on.

Inventory management is a great tool for planning and enables users to compare materials ordered with those received. It has direct links with purchasing and quality management. Stock is always controlled since every material movement is immediately recorded.

The warehouse module can manage complex warehouse structures, storage areas, and transportation routes. It links with the sales and distribution modules and capital investment management.

The invoice verification module is the right tool to avoid paying more than necessary. It handles information directly with the accounting and controlling modules and allows users to define tolerance values and analyze the movement of goods.

The MM system is made up of the following components:

MM-CBP	Consumption-based planning
MM-EDI	Electronic data interchanges
MM-IM	Inventory management
MM-IS	Information system

MM-IV	Invoice verification
MM-PUR	Purchasing
MM-WM	Warehouse management

PM: Plant Maintenance. The PM modules take care of the complex maintenance of the plant systems. This include support for having graphical plant representations, connecting to geographical information systems (GISs), and detailed diagrams. The modules support management of operational and maintenance problems, equipment, costs, and purchase requisitions.

The modules' extensive information systems allow users to quickly identify weak points and plan preventive maintenance.

The PM system includes the following modules:

PM-EQM	Equipment and technical objects
PM-IS	Plant maintenance information system
PM-PRM	Preventive maintenance
PM-PRO	Maintenance projects
PM-SMA	Service management
PM-WOC	Maintenance order management

PP: Production Planning. This business area is a very complex and extensive part of the R/3 logistics application system. It contains modules for the different phases, tasks, and methodologies used in the planning of production (product quantities, product types, materials procurement, time, etc.) and the process of production itself.

From version 3.0, the new PP-PI (production planning for process industries) module is included, providing an extensive planning tool for batch-oriented manufacturing. This module also enables the connection with external plant control systems and the management of different plants.

The PP modules are extensively integrated and connected to other R/3 applications, such as sales and distribution and materials management.

The production planning application is made up of the following modules:

PP-ATO	Assembly orders
PP-BD	Basic data
PP-CRP	Capacity requirement planning

PP-IS	Information system
PP-KAB	Kanban/just-in-time
PP-MP	Master planning
PP-MRP	Material requirements planning
PP-PDC	Plant data collection
PP-PI	Production planning for process industries
PP-REM	Repetitive manufacturing
PP-SFC	Production orders
PP-SOP	Sales and operations planning

PS: Project System. The PS application is a complete project system that handles all aspects of activities, resource planning, and budgeting of complex tasks. It includes a complete information system to keep track of current project status. It connects with the accounting and logistics applications and has many graphical capabilities as well as the ability to interface with external applications such as Microsoft Project. The following lists the modules included in the project system application.

PS-APP	Project budgeting
PS-BD	Basic data
PS-EXE	Project execution/integration
PS-IS	Information system
PS-OPS	Operative structures
PS-PLN	Project planning

QM: Quality Management. The SAP R/3 system as a whole, and the R/3 applications independently, take care of quality control of the managed business areas: human resources, financial controlling, and so on. As integral parts of the logistics application, the QM modules handle the tasks involved in quality planning, inspection and control, and complying with internationally defined standards on quality.

The main tasks of the QM modules have to do with the quality control of the sales and distribution processes, the materials management, and all production-related quality issues. The following is a list of the QM modules:

QM-CA	Quality certificates
QM-IM	Inspection processing

QM-PT	Planning tools
QM-QC	Quality control
QM-QN	Quality notifications

SD: Sales and Distribution. The SD modules are the most intensive transactional applications and usually are used as a base for benchmarking different platform architectures since they virtually connect and integrate with every other R/3 application: production, materials, accounting, quality, project, human resources, and so on.

This collection of modules enables the management of all aspects of sales activities: ordering, promotions, competition, sales leads, call tracking, planning, mail campaigns, and so forth. Other useful features include immediate product availability information and the ability to make early quotations. Customers benefit with better and faster service and can receive direct order confirmation by fax or mail.

These modules also allow the definition and control of the pricing structures and, with the connections to accounting and controlling, the receivables and revenues are immediately updated.

The SD system is made up of the following components:

SD-GF	General sales functions
SD-BIL	Billing
SD-CAS	Sales support
SD-EDI	Electronic data interchange
SD-FTT	Foreign trade
SD-SIS	Sales information system
SD-MD	Master data
SD-SHP	Shipping
SD-SLS	Sales
SD-TR	Transportation

Cross Application Modules

The CA (cross application) modules or components include all R/3 functions and tools which are not directly related to a unique part of the system. These are general-purpose applications that can be used independently or in connection with any of the functional application modules. Applications included are as follows:

- *SAP Business Workflow.* A workflow automation system which allows the integration of transactions across different R/3 applications. This is a very powerful tool that SAP is going to promote and enhance further.
- *SAPoffice.* An integrated mail and office system. This allows message exchanges within the SAP system and to and from outside mail systems. The folder system allows the integration of internal SAP and PC documents. The messaging features extend beyond the mail capabilities, allowing integration and processing with other business applications. For instance, a message might have a transaction associated with it, which can be triggered when a user processes a message.
- *SAP ArchiveLink.* This enables the optical and physical archiving of important input or output documents or print lists.

Other CA tools and applications are CAD integration, document management system (DMS), classification guide, characteristics guide, Application Link Enabled (ALE) technology, EDI, and external system communication interfaces.

The implementation tools including SAP customizing, procedure model, and reference model are also considered CA modules, since they are overall activities of SAP R/3 projects.

CHAPTER 2

The Architecture of SAP R/3

Now that you know what SAP R/3 is, what its foundations are, what its main functions are, and what the company profile is, the next step is to get a closer look at the architectural principles of the system: how it works, the main processes involved, how communications are handled, how the system uses the underlying database, and the way it interfaces with the operating system.

Architecture is basically the art of building, and to be able to construct or build something, two elements are needed: a design and the building materials. SAP R/3 includes both: it has a sound design based on a modular multitier software client/server principle and it has architectural components, the processes and software modules which offer the services.

This chapter deals with such issues as defining which elements make up the system and how they join together. Using this approach, we will come upon how SAP defines and implements the client/server architecture of the R/3 system. For simplicity reasons, the figures and examples shown are mainly based in the UNIX and Windows NT operating systems and Oracle database. However, the R/3 software's modular design and its openness make these examples conceptually the same as for other database engines (Informix, Adabas D, SQL-Server) and other operating systems.

R/3 Basis Software

The R/3 *basis software* is the set of programs and tools which interfaces with the computer operating system, the underlying database, the communication protocols, and the presentation interfaces. This software enables the R/3 applications (FI, CO, SD, etc.) to have the same functionality and work exactly the same way no matter what operating system or database the system is installed on. The R/3 basis software is an independent layer that guarantees the integration of all application modules. When referring to the basis software in this sense, it is generally known as the R/3 *common kernel* or R/3 *middleware.* Kernel and middleware have become generic computing terms which are widely used: *kernel* usually refers to the core or nucleus of a system; *middleware* means a set of programs which allows an independent interface between an upper layer and a lower layer (it stands in the *middle*).

NOTE *Although applications functionality is the same on all platforms, there are some differences, for instance in the transactions that deal with the management of the database or the operating system. Additionally, adjustments in the ABAP code must sometimes be made on the AS / 400 platform, since it runs on the EBCDIC character code, instead of ASCII—for example, some SELECT statements might differ from those used in other platforms.*

Often these terms are also referred to as the R/3 *basis system* or simply R/3 *basis,* both of which have a broader meaning. Besides the interfaces with the other system elements such as the operating system, database, network, and user interface, the tools and components of the R/3 basis provide the following:

- The environment for the R/3 applications, built on the ABAP development workbench and the ABAP repository, which includes the ABAP data dictionary (centralized logical repository with all the business and system data). This environment also has the workbench organizer and the transport system to facilitate the modification and enhancement of the system and the integration of new developments across systems.
- System administration and monitoring tools, including a common printing system and a complex and comprehensive set of management transactions within the CCMS (computer center management system), which is used to monitor, tune, and control the R/3 system.
- Architectural software client/server design, which permits system growth and allows the distribution of available resources.
- Authorization and profile management tools, which take care of user management and internal access control to system and business objects.
- Database monitoring and administration utilities.

These R/3 basis topics are covered in greater detail in the following chapters. This chapter discusses the central interfaces and the client/server architecture.

As shown in Fig. 2-1, the R/3 middleware uses common APIs (application program interfaces) and has the function of interfacing with the underlying operating system, the database, the communication protocols, and the GUIs. The features of the R/3 basis system which enable these types of interfaces are as follows:

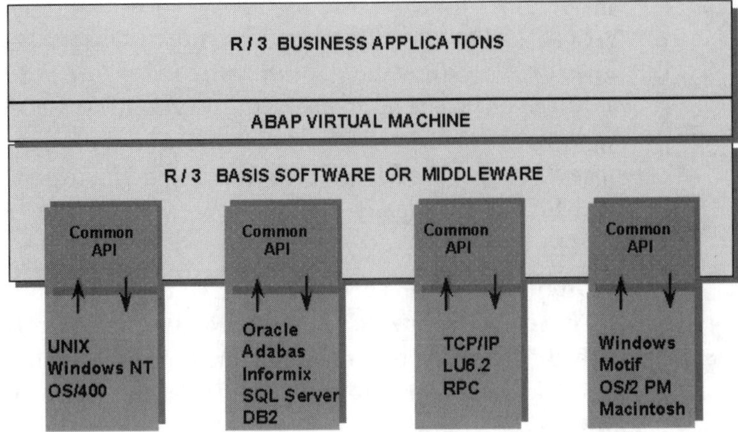

Figure 2-1
SAP R/3 middleware.

- The client/server architecture and configuration
- The use of relational database management systems
- Graphical user interface design for presentation

The R/3 basis system is based on standards: ANSI-C and C++ for the programming of the runtime environment, Open SQL for embedded SQL calls inside ABAP for interfacing with the database, communication standards such as TCP/IP, and standard graphical interfaces such as Microsoft Windows, Motif, or Macintosh.

Basic Architectural Concepts

The R/3 system uses some widely known terms to which SAP gives specific meanings. This section includes some of those terms, needed for a clear understanding of the architecture of SAP R/3.

Transaction

Generally, a *transaction* is an operation that lets a user make changes to a database. The overall R/3 system must be seen as a business transaction processing system. This means that the whole data flow that runs across application modules is executed using transactions.

In the SAP system, a transaction is a sequence of related steps. These logically related steps, known as *dialog steps,* are screens in which data is introduced causing the generation of other events. There is a special transaction monitor, the *SAP dispatcher,* which takes care of handling the sequence of those steps.

The final task of a transaction is to modify the information which ultimately goes into the database. The database is not updated until a transaction has finished. For the sake of consistency, if the transaction has not finished, all changes are still reversible.

The transactions usually contain two phases: an interactive phase and an update phase. The interactive phase may be at least one step, but can have many. This phase is responsible for preparing the database records that can update the database. The update phase may have no steps or many. This phase processes the previously prepared records and updates the database.

Since many users have the ability to access the same information, in order for the transactions to be consistent, there is a lock mechanism engaged during the time it takes to process the transaction.

All the transactions in the R/3 system have an associated *transaction code.* A fast and useful way to move around the R/3 system is by typing the transaction code directly in the command field of an R/3 window. The available transaction codes are held in table TSTC. To see this table, from the main screen menu, select the following options from the menu bar in this sequence: *Tools → ABAP Workbench → Development → Other Tools → Transactions.* Or, type *SE93* in the command field. Then click on the possible list arrow (the down arrow to the right of the field). Chapter 5 deals with the basics of using and moving around the R/3 system both with menus and with transaction codes.

A fast way to specify table entries is by using transaction *SE16* (Data Browser) and entering the table name in the input field.

Dialog Step

A *dialog step* is a SAP R/3 screen, which is represented by a dynpro. A *dynpro,* or *dynamic program,* consists of a screen and all the associated processing logic. It contains field definitions, screen layout, validation and processing logic, and so forth. A dialog step is controlled exactly by a dynpro.

The processing logic means that the dynpro controls what has to be done before the screen is displayed (process before output, or PBO) and what has to be done after the user finishes entering information (process after input, or PAI).

When users are navigating in the SAP R/3 system from screen to screen, they are actually making dialog steps. A set of dialog steps makes up a transaction.

Logical Units of Work (LUWs)

Conceptually, a *logical unit of work* (LUW) is defined as an elementary processing step which works as a locking mechanism to protect the transaction's integrity. A LUW is a set of steps within a transaction, and all of those steps must be correctly completed to go ahead with the transaction logic. If there are errors before the end of the transactions, the current LUW is canceled, but not the previous ones.

Within the SAP system, three conceptually different types of transactions may be distinguished:

- A database transaction, known as LUW or database LUW, is the period of time in which the operations requested must be performed as a unit. This is known in the database world as an *all or nothing* operation. At the end of the LUW, either the database changes are committed (performed) or they are rolled back (thrown away). As you can see in Fig. 2-2, there are four database transactions (database LUWs) corresponding to the period of time from the beginning of a new database operation to the DB-commit operation.
- An update transaction or SAP LUW is the equivalent to the database concept for the SAP systems. It means that as a logical unit, these SAP LUWs are either executed completely or not at all. Generally, a SAP LUW can have several database LUWs. The special ABAP command, COMMIT WORK, marks the end of a SAP LUW and the beginning of a new one.

  In Fig. 2-2, the SAP transaction or SAP LUW comprises all the database operations until the COMMIT WORK statement; in this case, it is made up of four database LUWs.
- A SAP transaction or ABAP transaction is made up of a set of related tasks combined under one transaction code. This concept is related more to the programming environment, in which an ABAP or SAP transaction functions like a complex object containing screens, menus, programming logic, transaction code, and so forth.

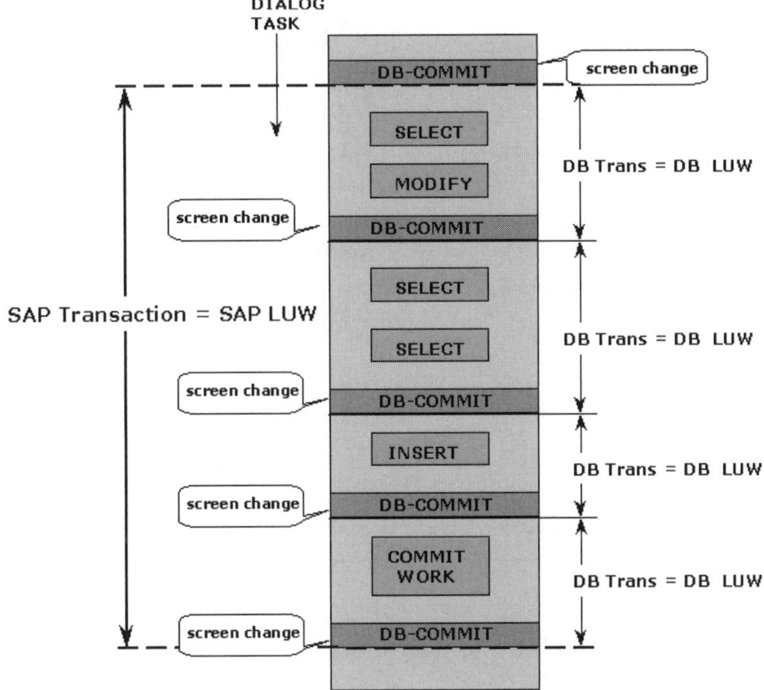

Figure 2-2
Example of SAP LUWs.

Clients

A *client* is defined as a legally and organizationally independent unit within the R/3 system, for example, a company group, a business unit, or a corporation.

At the beginning of the R/3 technical phase of the implementation, right after installation of the software, one of the first things that usually must be done is to copy one of the standard clients included in the package. With the copied clients, customers can make tests, can use them for training, or can start real customization.

SAP comes with three standard clients: 000, 001, and 066. Client 000 contains a simple organizational structure of a test company and includes parameters for all applications, standard settings, configurations for the control of standard transactions and examples to be used in many different profiles of the business applications. For these reasons, 000 is a special client for the R/3 system since it contains the client-independent settings.

Client 001 is a copy of the 000 client, including the test company; if this client is configured or customized, its settings are client-dependent. It does not behave like 000. It is reserved for the activities of preparing a system for the production environment. SAP customers usually use this client as a source for copying other new clients.

Client 066 is reserved for SAP access to its customers' systems to perform the EarlyWatch service.

The R/3 system includes tools for creating, copying, transferring, resetting, deleting, and comparing clients. When the loads of individual clients differ, the buffer manager of the application service is able to respond and allocate resources appropriately. As shown in Fig. 2-3, the client is the first field when logging on to the system.

The System Central Interfaces

In this section the main system interfaces are described in greater detail. The R/3 middleware or common kernel is made up of central interfaces. These are as follows:

- The interface with the operating system.
- The interface with database.

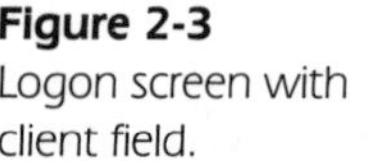

Figure 2-3
Logon screen with client field.

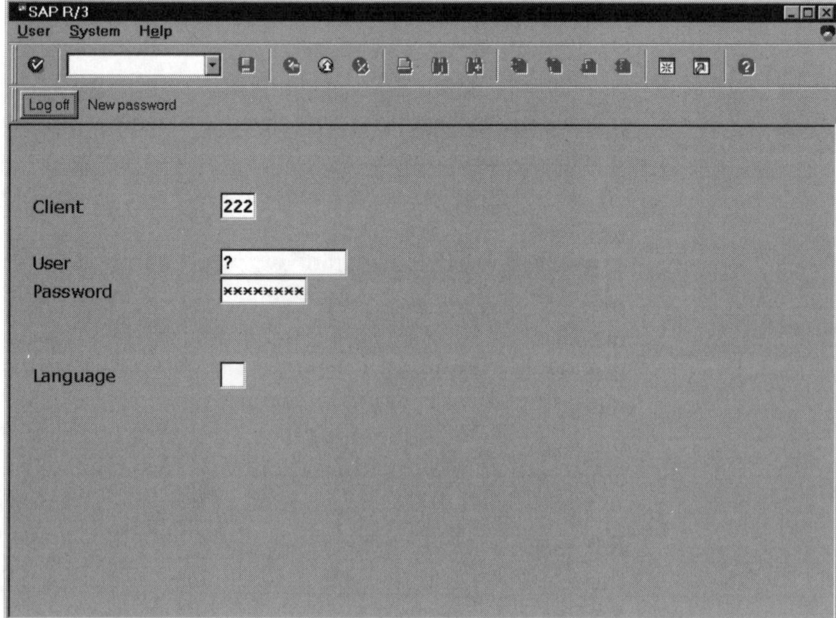

- The interface for presentation.
- The communication interface could be seen as a special type of interface which directly or indirectly is present in the other three types.

For compatibility and portability reasons, all these interfaces are grouped together in the central interface functions of the SAP system kernel. The interfaces in the SAP system are a group of software programs running as *daemon processes* in the UNIX operating system, or as *services* on Windows NT.

Operating System Interface

One of the main tasks of the basis system is to guarantee the portability of the whole system. That is done using an internal SAP portability layer. This layer offers to the applications the nearest services to the system, such as message handling and memory management, independently of the platform and optimized for performance. The inherent openness of R/3 makes it run over different operating systems, which have to be POSIX standard–compliant. For a list of the supported technical and platform environments for SAP R/3, refer to www.sap.com/products/techno/index.htm and then click on *Platforms.*

The mission of the system interfaces is to provide services such as scheduling, memory management, and similar tasks, which could be partially done by the operating system software, but SAP executes them internally for performance and portability reasons.

The R/3 system runtime environment, commonly known as the kernel, is written in ANSI-C or C++, but all application programs inside R/3 are written in the interpreted programming language ABAP developed by SAP.

The components in charge of controlling the user dialogs are the dynpros (dynamic programs). The technology base for the R/3 applications is made up of the interrelation of the dynpro interpreters and the ABAP language. For their tasks, both use the global image of the data environment of R/3, which is held on the ABAP dictionary. The runtime environment of the R/3 applications consists of two processors: one for the dynpros and the other for the ABAP language.

From the point of view of the operating system, the runtime system of R/3 can be seen as a group of parallel processes (work processes). Among these processes there is a special one, the dispatcher, which controls and assigns tasks to the other processes.

The Dispatcher Process

The SAP *dispatcher* is the control program which manages the resources of the R/3 applications. It works like a typical transaction monitor which receives screens and data from the presentation services and passes them to the corresponding work processes. Figure 2-4 illustrates this concept.

The work processes are special programs in charge of some specific tasks. Using client/server terminology, a *work process* is a *service* offered by a *server* and requested by a *client.* The dispatcher manages the information exchange between the SAPGUIs or other type of presentation interface and the work processes, enabling users to share the different work processes available.

The main tasks of the dispatcher are as follows:

- Balanced assignment of the transaction load to the work processes
- Buffer management in main memory
- Connection with the presentation level
- Organization of the communication processes

The logical flow of execution of a user request follows:

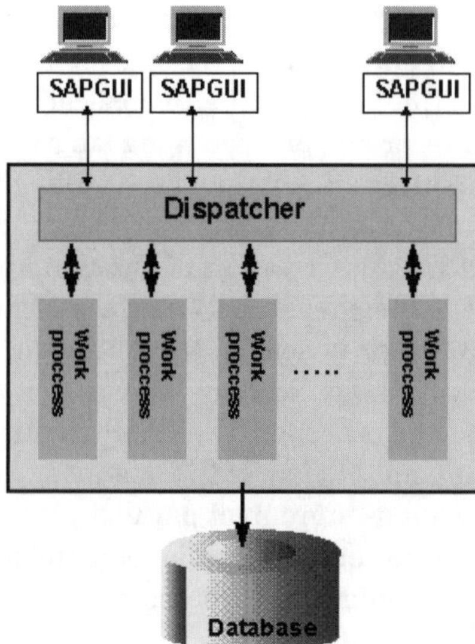

Figure 2-4 SAP dispatcher process.

1. Users enter data in their presentation server; the data is received by the SAPGUI, converted to a SAP format, and sent to the dispatcher using an special optimized protocol called DIAG.
2. Initially, the dispatcher keeps the requests in queues, where the dispatcher later processes them one by one.
3. The dispatcher allocates the user requests using the free work processes. The real execution takes place inside the work processes themselves.
4. At the end of execution, the result of the work process task goes back to the SAPGUI through the dispatcher. SAPGUI interprets the received data and fills up the user screen.

SAP has optimized the data flow between the presentation and the application servers. Typically the quantity of data that goes in the network from the dispatcher to the SAPGUI does not exceed 2K (for dialog processes). This network traffic does not include the print requests that are managed by spool or print managers on users' PCs or workstations. The communication is established via standard TCP/IP sockets.

The dispatcher has a special *advanced program-to-program communication* (APPC) server built into it which communicates and responds to requests submitted by the work processes. On each application server there is one dispatcher but multiple work processes.

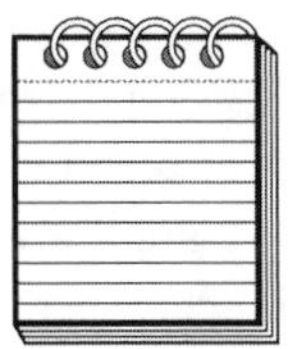

NOTE *If an application server (hardware point of view) is running more than one SAP instance (application server, from a software point of view), there is one dispatcher for every instance.*

Work Process Architecture

A work process is a program in charge of executing the R/3 application tasks. Each work process acts as a specialized system service. From the point of view of the operating system, a group of parallel work processes makes up the R/3 runtime system.

As shown in Fig. 2-5, a work process consists of a task handler, a dialog or dynpro interpreter, an ABAP processor, and a database interface. The work processes execute dialog steps for the end users. These steps generally relate to the processing or display of a single screen, which means that right after one work process finishes the execution of a dialog step for a user session, it is immediately available for use by another user session.

For its processing, each dialog step needs code, dictionary objects, and data. These elements may come from the database server or from the memory buffers which reside on the application server. The dialog processes usually request read-only information from the database and rely on other types of work processes for read-write information. This is explained in the following sections.

The activities within a work process are coordinated by the task handler. It manages the loading and unloading of the user session context at the beginning and end of each dialog step. It also communicates with the dispatcher and activates the dynpro interpreter or the ABAP processor as required to perform its tasks. The ABAP processor is in charge of executing the ABAP programs, while the dialog interpreter (also known as the dynpro processor) is in charge of interpreting and executing the logic of R/3 screens. The database interface allows the work processes to establish direct links with the database.

The work processes might need the same data for more than one dialog step, in which case, the data is held in shared memory areas (buffers) and are available for other work processes. It must be noted that users of the same or similar R/3 business applications, such as FI (financial accounting) and CO (controlling), logging in to the same application servers will benefit from this feature, since they very often access the same tables. If these tables already reside in the buffer areas, the system doesn't have to go to the database to get them, and thus performance will be improved.

Work processes make use of two special areas: paging and roll. The *paging area* holds application program data such as internal tables or report listings. The *roll area* holds the user context data entered in previous dialog steps and other control and user information such as authorizations. Where there is main memory available, these areas are held in the main memory of application servers; otherwise they are *paged out* or *rolled out* to physical disk files. The size of these areas is configurable using SAP system profile parameters. With the release of 3.0, the memory

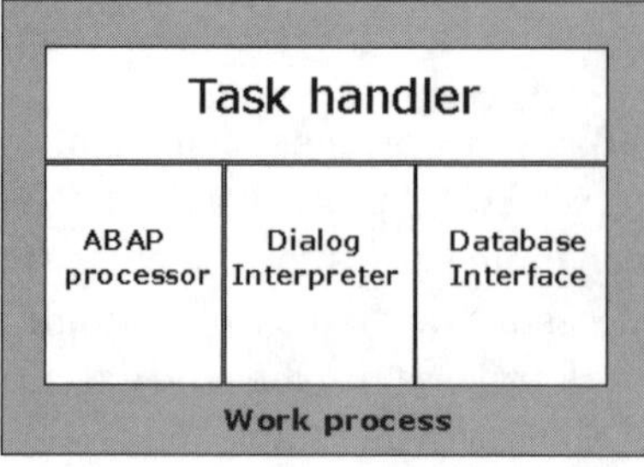

Figure 2-5 Work process architecture.

management of the SAP system changed; for instance, the paging file is no longer used except for special conditions. This new memory management concept and the associated profile parameters are discussed later in this chapter.

The system shared memory areas also contain read-only images of other parts of the R/3 system, such as the program or table buffers. The sizing and configuration of these buffers are very important for overall performance of the system. Refer to Chap. 11. The configuration and refresh rate of these caches are critical to the overall performance of the system.

To make a more efficient use of available resources, work processes are run in parallel, which makes this architecture especially suitable for multiprocessor equipment and able to run the group of work processes distributed among different CPUs.

The number of available work processes per application server is configurable using the appropriate SAP system profile parameters. The following sections include examples of such parameters. For more information about profiles, refer to the section entitled "Instances Profiles" in Chap. 4.

There are several types of work processes: dialog, background, update, enqueue, and spool. Additionally, the R/3 runtime system includes three other special types of services: message service, gateway, and the system log collector.

Since the work processes are in charge of executing the ABAP programs and applications, a group made of a dispatcher and a set of work processes is known as the *application server.*

Services: Work Processes Types

Every work process is specialized in a particular task type: dialog, batch, update, enqueue, spool, message, or gateway. The last two types are somewhat different than the rest. In client/server terms, a work process is a *service,* and the computing system that is running the particular services is known as a *server.* For example, if the system is just providing dialog services, this is a *dialog server,* although commonly called an *application server.*

The dispatcher assigns tasks to the free work processes, making optimal use of system resources and balancing the system load. The dispatcher knows and distributes accordingly the pending tasks according to the processing type of the defined processes. The difference among the various work processes only affects their mission or special services as assigned to the work processes through the dispatching strategy.

Figure 2-6 shows the work processes from within R/3. To get to this screen, select *Tools → Administration → Monitor → System Monitoring → Process Overview,* or type */NSM50* in the command field.

Figure 2-7 shows the same work processes from the perspective of the Windows NT processes. If you look at the PID (process identification) numbers on both screens, you might notice that they are the same.

Dialog Work Processes

The dialog work processes are in charge of the interactive tasks of the R/3 system. A dialog work process performs the dialog steps corresponding to the interactive user sessions.

The jobs held by the dispatcher in the request queues after user input are assigned to the next free work process. The dialog work processes execute just one single dialog step at a time and become immediately free for the next user request (dialog step), which is assigned by the dispatcher. This means that the dialog work processes can be constantly switching between different user sessions. This type of processing allows a great

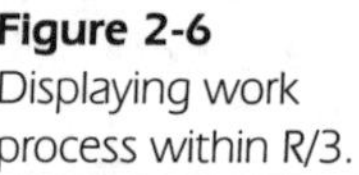

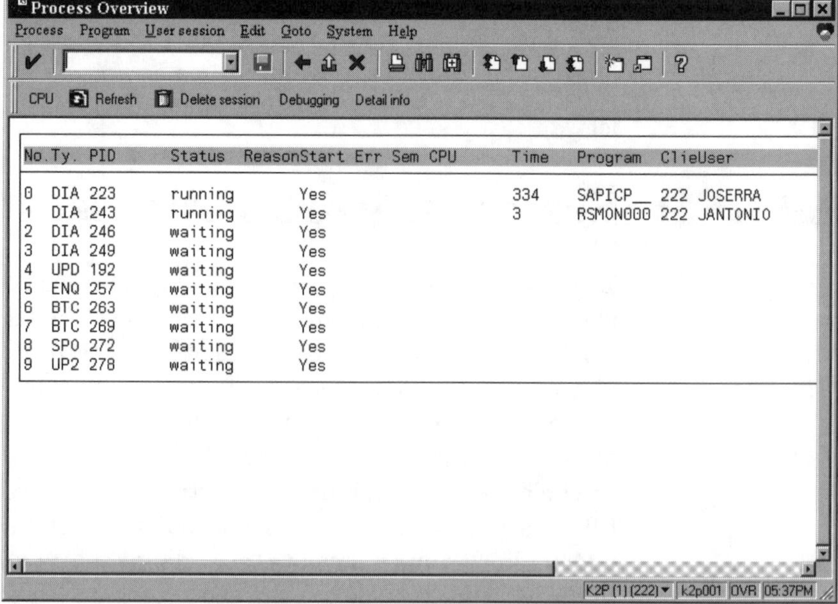

Figure 2-6 Displaying work process within R/3.

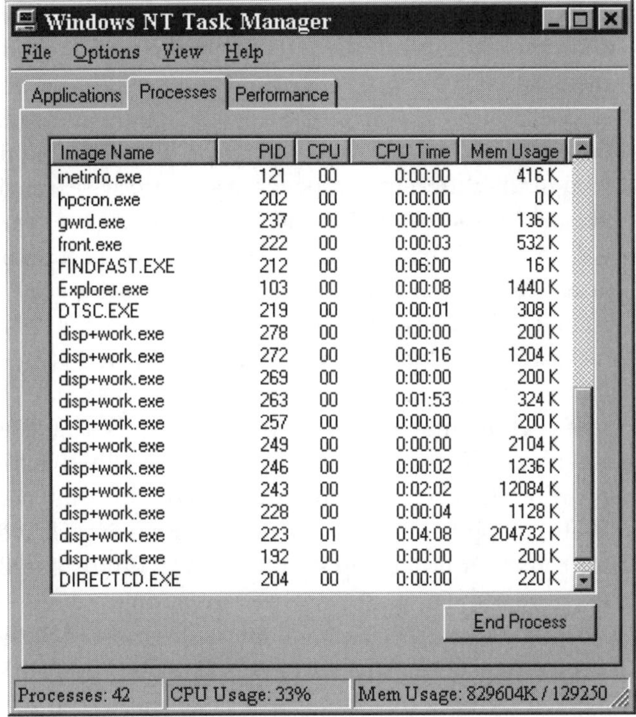

Figure 2-7 Work processes as seen in the Windows NT Task Manager.

deal of resource distribution; otherwise the system would need as many dialog work processes as the number of expected interactive users. It works exactly the same as multiuser operating systems.

The SAP profile parameter that controls the number of interactive dialog work processes per instance is

```
rdisp/wp_no_dia
```

Chapter 4 explains with greater detail the profile parameters.

Depending on the type of business transactions the users are working on, a dialog work process can support from 5 to more than 10 simultaneous users each. This means that 10 dialog work processes could theoretically support approximately 100 users. However, this is just a rule of thumb. *Tuning* this parameter means that if users have to wait long to get a free work process, you should increase the parameter. This, however, has some limitations, such as the total number of processes running on the server and the availability of main memory.

When there is a large number of concurrent interactive users expected in a SAP R/3 system, there will certainly be a number of application servers. Some of these application servers can become special dialog servers, containing a dispatcher process and a number of dialog work processes.

Dialog Step Data Flow. Figure 2-8 shows the flow of a user request through the different components and processes. Initially, the user enters data into the screen fields and presses the *Enter* key. This data is received by the SAPGUI process and is converted to an internal format and immediately sent to the application server dispatcher (1).

The dispatcher checks whether there are available work processes for processing the dialog step. If there are not, the request goes to the request queues (2) until one becomes available. Once a dialog work process is available, the dispatcher sends the user data to the work process (3). Within the dialog work, the task handler is in charge of assigning the corresponding tasks to the internal components (dynpro or ABAP), using the SAP memory buffers, using the roll and page area for user context storage and switching, and finally sending a SQL request to the database (4).

The database system sends the requested data back to the work process (5), which in turn passes it to the presentation server (6). The SAPGUI formats the data and fills up the screen for the user (7).

The time it takes to get from step 1 (user request) to step 7 is known as *response time*. The response time is one of the main indicators of

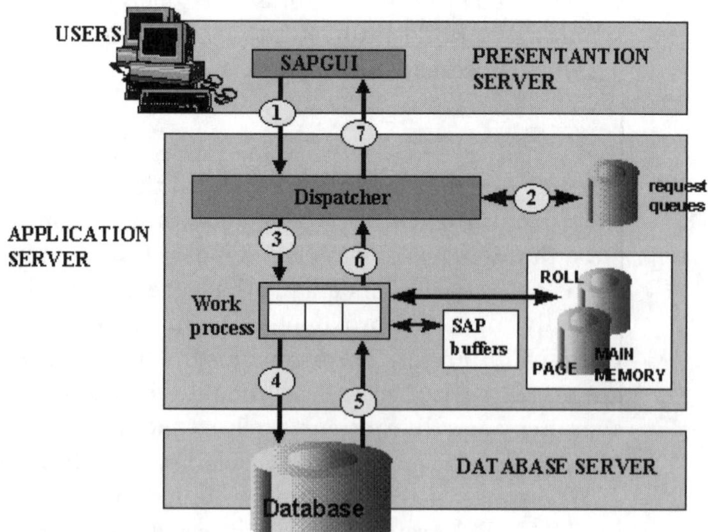

Figure 2-8 Data flow in dialog steps.

how healthy (well-tuned) the system is. A SAP instance profile parameter controls the maximum allowed time for interactive execution of a dialog step:

```
rdisp/max_wprun_time
```

The default value for this parameter is 300, which indicates the length of time in seconds that the dispatcher allows the work process to run. When this value is reached, the dispatcher stops the work process and the user gets a TIME_OUT error.

Background Work Processes

The background work processes are in charge of executing ABAP programs submitted for background execution. Figure 2-9 shows a simple scheme of an application server which includes background work processes.

From an administrative point of view, the background work processes correspond to the batch jobs queues. The ABAP programs submitted for background processing are executed in the planned time by the background work processes. The sequence of program execution is scheduled with *batch jobs.*

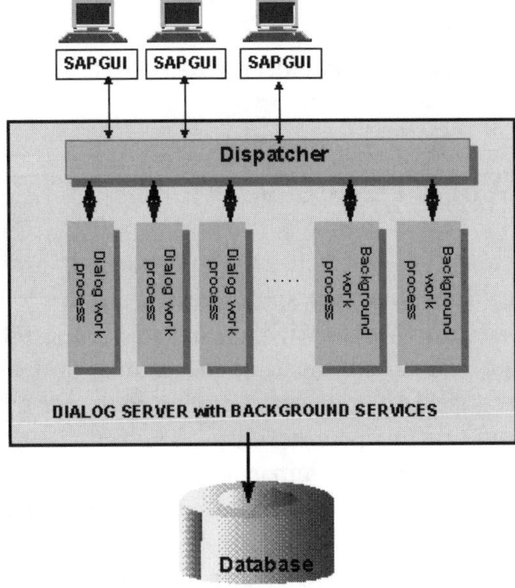

Figure 2-9 Application server with background work process.

Every job can be made of one or several steps that are consecutively processed. A *step* is an ABAP program or an external program.

There are many types of jobs and different ways to submit them for execution. Normally, these background jobs are not immediately processed but are when the system reaches the planned time for execution.

Background processing is very useful for submitting programs requiring long processing times, since interactive execution would exceed the allowed processing time (rdisp/max_wprun_time) and thus abort with a TIME_OUT error, as indicated in the previous section.

There is a batch scheduler which takes care of initiating the jobs at the specified time. The system allows for periodic jobs' execution. This means that programs are submitted with a repetition interval, and when the jobs execute themselves, the first thing they do is plan a new execution time at the required interval. This feature is very useful for control or cleaning jobs within R/3.

The SAP profile parameter that controls the number of background work processes per instance is

```
rdisp/wp_no_btc
```

The background process can be further organized into different types of job queues based on the priorities needed in the particular installation.

Background jobs are very important in the daily management and operation of the system.

In Chap. 11, "SAP Housekeeping: The Computer Center Management System," you will learn how the dialog and background work processes can be automatically switched with the use of operation modes.

Spool Work Process

The spool work process is in charge of formatting the data for printing and passing it to the host spool system. Figure 2-10 includes a simple scheme of a SAP instance with a spool work process.

The spool requests, indicating the printer and the printing format of the spool request, are generated during dialog or background processing and are held on the spool database. The data itself is kept in a special area, known as *TemSe* (temporal sequential objects). There is a profile parameter *rspo/store_location* that controls where the *TemSe* stores the R/3 spool data. It can be either on the database or on a file. Chapter 12 includes more details on the effects of the location of the spool data.

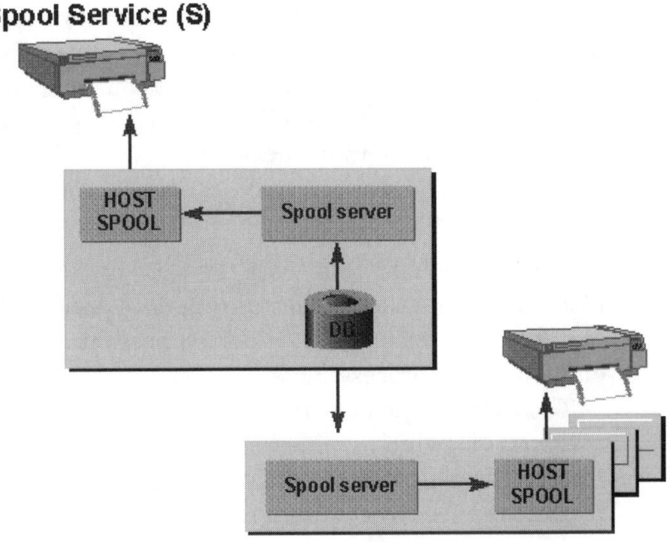

Figure 2-10
Spool work process.
(Copyright by SAP AG.)

When the data is to be printed for the spool job, an output request is generated, which is executed by the spool work process. Once the spool work process has edited the data for printing, it sends a print request to the operating system host spool.

The SAP profile parameter that controls the number of spool work processes per instance is

```
rdisp/wp_no_spo
```

Before release 4.0 this value was limited to one spool work process per SAP instance, although there was the possibility of installing more than one instance per host and getting more than one spool work process. That restriction does not exist anymore with release 4.0 and newer releases.

Enqueue Work Process

The enqueue work process, also known as the lock work process, is in charge of the lock management system. It allows multiple application servers to synchronize their access to the database and maintain the data consistency. In order for the system to run in a consistent manner, it must ensure that when a transaction's dialog steps are handled by different work processes, they retain the assigned locks until the end of the transaction or the intentional release of the lock, even when switching work processes.

Commonly there is only one enqueue work process for a single SAP system; however there are circumstances where, for performance reasons, it might be useful to configure up to four enqueue work processes. R/3 note 127773 contains details. The profile parameter that controls the number of enqueue work processes is:

```
rdisp/wp_no_enq
```

The function of this work process is to protect applications from blocking among themselves during data access. For that reason, a locking/unlocking mechanism must be present. This is the function of the enqueue work process.

The locks (enqueues) are managed by the enqueue work process using a lock table which resides in the main memory. When the processes receive a locking request, the enqueue work process verifies whether the requested lock object interferes with other existing entries in the lock table.

The ABAP applications logic considers that data modifications are usually done when a previous reading has taken place. For that reason, the locking requests are made before the data reading requests.

SAP designed the locking mechanism so that each lock not only needs to be respected by the application server executing the transaction but also by all other servers within the SAP system.

The name of the SAP instance running the enqueue service is included in the common parameter profile, the DEFAULT.PFL file. The parameter is rdisp/enqname = <instance_name>, for example, rdisp/enqname = adminix_C12_00.

Lock objects. The lock objects are special types of objects defined in the ABAP dictionary. The blocking type can be shared (type S), exclusive (type E), or exclusive but not cumulative (type X). The exclusive locks are used to avoid parallel modification of the data, which means that exclusively locked data can be displayed or modified by only one user.

With the shared mode, several users can access the same data at the same time in display mode. As soon as any user processes the data, the remaining users do not have further access to them.

Locks of type exclusive but not cumulative can only be called once. So a lock request will be rejected if an exclusive lock already exists.

When the lock objects are defined in the dictionary, there are two ABAP function modules automatically generated for them: one to lock the object (enqueue) and another function to unlock it (dequeue). These functions are called at the beginning and at the end of a transaction respectively.

If for some reason there are problems between the locking and unlocking of an object, it remains locked until the administrator manually deletes the lock. Refer to Chap. 10 on how to proceed with the locking mechanism management.

The locking object mechanism is intimately related with the SAP logical units of work (SAP LUWs).

Update Work Process

The update work process is in charge of executing database changes when requested by the dialog or background work processes. Figure 2-11 shows a simple scheme of how the update process works.

The dialog work processes can generate database modifications with the corresponding instructions to the database server, independently of whether these work processes run on the same or different machines as the database.

However, when the ABAP language element CALL FUNCTION . . . IN UPDATE TASK is executed, it raises the order for the modification to occur in the update server. Specific update work processes then modify the database accordingly.

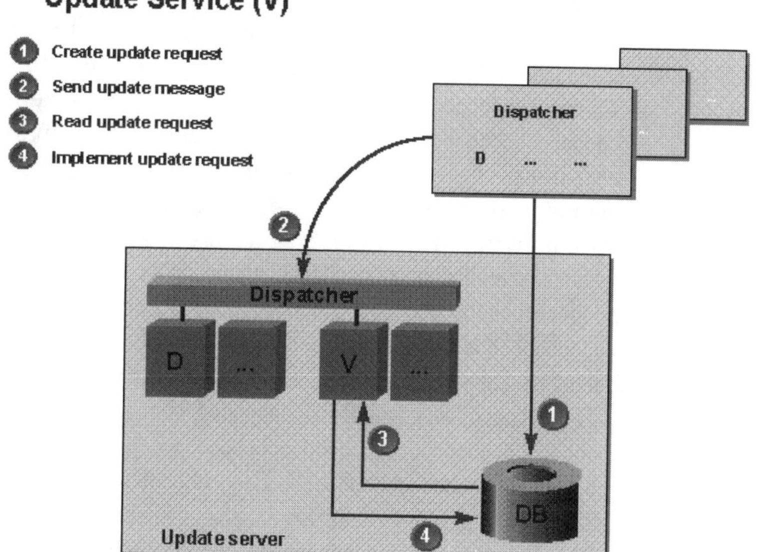

Figure 2-11 Update work process. (Copyright by SAP AG.)

It is recommended to have the update service on the same server as the database for better performance. However, with fast network controllers, it does not make much difference having the update server on a different host than the database.

The update is an asynchronous process, which means that the update requests are processed at the moment and in the order they arrive at the work process. This makes a more homogeneous response time. The drawback is that the transaction might not have finished when another update transaction is waiting.

If for any reason the update transaction cannot be completely accomplished, the user will get a system message and an express mail. Sometimes this is due to database problems, such as tablespaces becoming full and the like.

If the transaction could not finish correctly, the system rolls it back. The rollback of a transaction is possible by having a separate dialog part from the update part. The dialog program first generates log records in the VBLOG table, which are then processed by the update program (run within the update process) once the dialog is finished.

The log records, read by the update work process, contain all the necessary information to make the modifications. During the update phase, the database is modified. The update of a log record can have several parts, known as the *update components.* This division permits the system to structure the objects that make up the update transaction components according to their importance.

An update request can contain a primary update component (V1) and several secondary ones (V2). The time-critical processes are held inside the V1, the less critical within the V2. In order to be able to initiate the V2 components of the log record, the V1 component must have finished. However, the V2 components can be executed in any order and even in parallel if there are enough update processes defined. The execution of primary components (V1) corresponding to different log records can be also done in parallel using several update work processes.

Before release 3.0 of R/3, there was only one type of update work process taking care of both V1 and V2 components. With the release of version 3.0, a new profile parameter was established to indicate the number of update work processes for secondary components, also.

The important profile parameter is rdisp/vbname = <instance name>. This is a common parameter for the full SAP system and therefore is normally in the DEFAULT.PFL file. The other parameters, rdisp/wp_no_vb and rdisp/wp_no_vb2, indicate the number of update work processes of types V1 and V2, respectively. These are defined inside the instance-specific profile parameter file.

If there are error situations during the update, these cannot be solved with user online actions. The active update process component is then stopped. If the errors occurred in the primary component (V1) of a log record, the modifications are rolled back. The log record receives a corresponding status flag and is not taken out of the VBLOG table. Subsequent V2 update actions are not executed.

However, if the interrupted or error component is a type V2, only the modifications done by this particular component are rolled back. The corresponding log record is marked with a status flag and is not deleted from the table. The other components can follow normal update processing.

After an error situation or update interruption, the system automatically notifies the user by express mail about the aborted update and creates an error log entry in the system log. Then it is possible to evaluate and treat the update according to the error message received. Refer to the section entitled "Monitoring Update Records" in Chap. 10 for how to proceed under such circumstances.

Message Server

The message server is a service used by the different application servers to exchange data and internal messages. This server does not have the structure of the typical work processes previously described. However, it acts like a service.

The message server routes the messages between application servers. Since the release of version 3.0, it is also used for license checking and workload balancing together with the SAPlogon utility.

As depicted in Fig. 2-12, there is only one message server per SAP R/3 system. The message server process is the one that makes the application servers exchange messages between them, such as brief internal messages: update start, enqueue, dequeue, batch job start. The communication is established among the dispatchers using the TCP/IP network protocol and the sockets defined in the *services* file.

Every application server has a unique name for the message server. All application servers know which the update server, the enqueue server, and the batch and spool servers are and set those services active, indicating an address to the message server.

The location of the host running the message server is configured in the DEFAULT.PFL common profile. The parameter is rdisp/mshost = <hostname>. Notice the difference from previous parameters such as the update or enqueue services, in which the value of the parameter pointed out to instance name. In this case, the value is a hostname, as included in

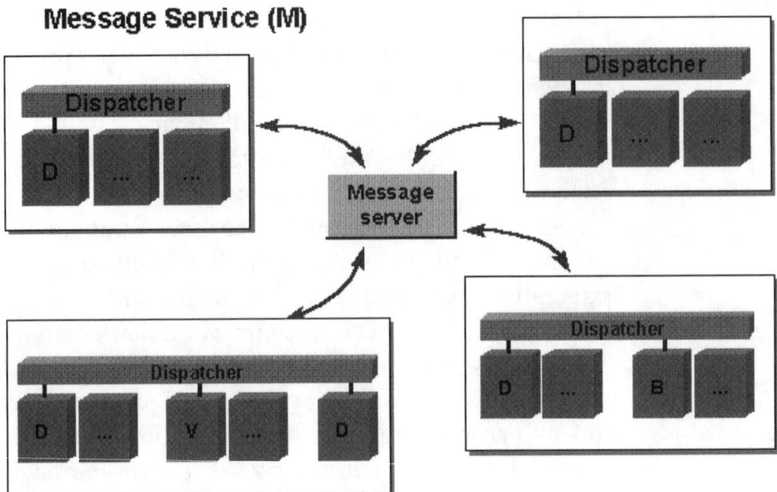

Figure 2-12
Message server.
(Copyright by SAP AG.)

the standard TCP/IP hosts database. The message server host is not restricted to the database server. It can run on any of the hosts that make up the SAP client/server system.

The way this service is started is also different from other work processes. It has its own start execution line in the start profile. Chapter 4 includes more information on the start profiles.

Gateway Server

The gateway service allows the communication between R/3, R/2, and external applications. This service is a CPIC handler which implements the CPIC protocol for communication. This is commonly known as a *SAP gateway.*

The function of the SAP gateway is to exchange larger amounts of data between application servers, in contrast to the message server which only exchanges brief internal and control messages. The SAP gateway exchanges application data, thus the amount of information is larger.

The communication agents can be located on the same system, in another R/3 system, in an R/2 system, and also in an external program. Figure 2-13 shows a simple architecture of the SAP gateway server.

The SAP gateway processes communicate using the TCP/IP protocol in the R/3 side and the LU6.2 when communicating with IBM mainframes running R/2. In the case of Siemens equipment running R/2, the protocol used is UPIC.

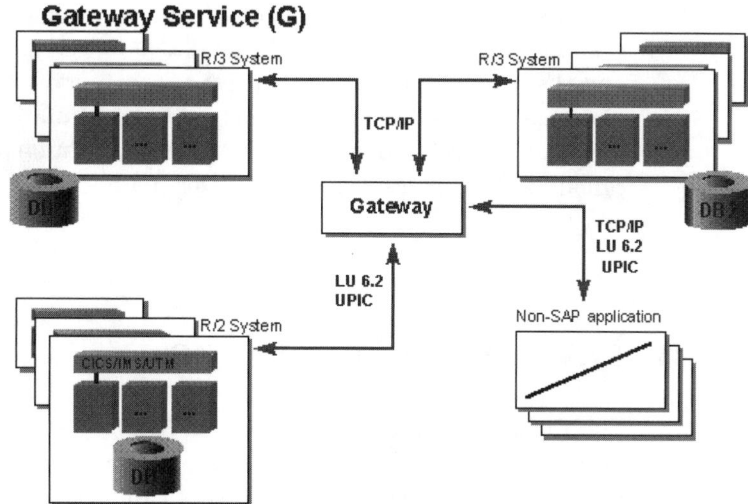

Figure 2-13 Gateway server.

Presentation Interface

The presentation interface is the component in charge of making functionally equivalent the presentation and the handling of R/3, no matter the type of front end used.

For each user session there is a SAP process (SAPGUI) which enables the use of all available presentation possibilities of the corresponding window software. These processes (historically known as *terminal processes*) are in charge, among other things, of managing the graphical elements of the R/3 system.

The connection between the SAPGUIs and the SAP dispatcher is made with an optimized protocol, known as DIAG, in which small data packages are sent through the network.

In the SAP R/3 system, all the menus options, the buttons, and even most of the graphical elements are inside the database. This means that the real screens are not held in the PC software, but are sent on demand. You may notice that the time it takes to go from one screen to another is longer when you are among the first users to log on to the system. As the buffers become filled with cached data, this time noticeably decreases.

The presentation interface allows for upload and download functions from the application server. It also includes possibilities for file transfers and communication with popular Windows applications including MS-Excel, MS-Word, and MS-Access. This is possible, of course, when using a Windows-based front end.

Another feature available in the presentation interface is the SAP graphic utility which establishes a dialog between the ABAP application and the graphic utility in the presentation server for extracting data to make up graphical representations of the information.

You should refer to the SAP online documentation or print document file called SAP Graphics: User's Guide for more information and instructions on the subject.

Database Interface

The underlying database of the SAP R/3 system acts as the main container for all the information managed by the system. The database includes almost everything the users can see on their screens: program source code, screens, texts, menu options, customer information, printer definitions, statistical information, transactional data, and so forth.

The database interface supports different relational databases from different vendors. The main task of the database interface is to convert the SQL requests (ABAP open SQL) from the SAP development environment to the database's own SQL requests. During the interpretation of the ABAP open SQL statements, the database interface makes a syntax check to verify that the statement is correct, and it also automatically tries to make an optimal use (reuse) of the SAP buffers in case a similar SQL statement was requested previously. These buffers are held locally in the main memory of each application server.

Besides using the portable SQL dialect from SAP (ABAP open SQL, previously known as SAP-SQL), it is also possible to directly access the database using ABAP native SQL (previously known as EXEC-SQL) statements. With ABAP native SQL calls, a developer can make specific database SQL calls, which are not supported using the standard ABAP open SQL statements. However, this method is not recommended since the code might not be completely portable or could cause problems during upgrading of the database engine or the R/3 applications.

The database interface also has a cursor caching method. Database cursors are like portions of memory that are allocated by the system to process SQL statements. A *cursor caching method* means that the system tries to reuse, if possible, the access paths which were previously used to process SQL statements. However, this method is not recommended since the code might not be completely portable or could cause problems during upgrading of the database engine or the R/3 applications.

The database is the heart of the SAP R/3 system. It not only is the central source of information for companies' business data, but also the container of user information, software components, documentation, and administrative statistical data to be used when managing or monitoring the system.

One of the most important logical parts of the database is the ABAP object repository, which contains the following:

- *The ABAP dictionary (formerly known as data dictionary).* This is the central source for the definition of objects, such as type and length of fields, indexes, table relationships, and so on. In database terms, these types of definitions are known as metadata. The dictionary is intimately connected to all parts of the business applications and is a core part of the ABAP development workbench. Chapter 8, "ABAP Data Dictionary," deals extensively with the logical management of the R/3 metadata.
- *The ABAP source and executable programs.* Since ABAP is an interpreted language, it can be dynamically regenerated by the application servers (remember the ABAP processor inside the work processes).

The database, of course, includes the data itself. SAP distinguishes three different types of data: master, control, and transaction data. *Master* data contains information that does not change often, such as a user's name, printer's definition, or address of a supplier. This type of data is usually used the same way for similar objects.

Control data is held in control tables and includes system and technical functions of the SAP system.

Transaction data is the most volatile and frequently used information in day-to-day business operations, such as customer orders or accounting transactions including payments, debits, credits, and so on.

The SAP-declared dictionary tables have the corresponding structure in the physical underlying database. The R/3 system handles different types of tables. SAP *transparent tables* are structures that exactly match an underlying database table. With certain database knowledge, users can view or manage these tables directly from the database's own utilities—but this is not advised since it may introduce inconsistencies.

Other table types managed by SAP, which may eventually disappear are *cluster tables,* made of several SAP tables related using foreign keys, and *pooled tables,* corresponding to a set of tables stored in a single table. For more detailed information on these types of SAP tables, refer to the corresponding sections in Chap. 8.

The database interface sends the data read from the ABAP dictionary tables to the ABAP programs by placing it in special work areas (memory buffers known to the work processes). Conversely, the database interface gets the modified data from those areas and sends it to the database.

Software developers can easily declare and work with such areas, since the dictionary is integrated with ABAP. Within an ABAP program, the developer can create additional tables that only exist as long as a program is running. These internal tables can be dynamically enlarged so that it is not necessary for developers to know in advance the amount of memory the internal tables will occupy.

SAP R/3 Communication Protocols and Interfaces

Inside R/3, communication is an overall process which involves most of the components of the systems both internally and to the exterior world (external systems). Communication among systems, modules, and components is based on protocols. The R/3 basis system supports all standard and de facto standard communication and networking protocols.

At the operating system level, the protocol used is TCP/IP. Communication with the database is accomplished using remote SQL calls. Between applications there are many different programming interfaces which use an underlying communication layer, such as CPIC, RFC, ALE, EDI, BAPIs, and others.

The communication interfaces are deployed to integrate all layers of the client/server architecture, from database server to application server to presentation servers. Additionally, they define the channels for the exchange of electronic information, such as the input of data from external systems and the exchange of standardized business information using ALE or EDI.

The communication interfaces are also deployed for sending and receiving mail from the exterior world (Internet, for example) using the standard X.400 mail protocol.

At the programming level, the R/3 system uses the CPIC protocol for program-to-program communication and also includes support for *remote function calls* (RFCs), Microsoft OLE interface, ActiveX, and many other standard interfaces based on objects, such as CORBA, COM/DCOM, and others. Extensive information about communication at the programming level can be found in the R/3 online documentation.

SAP also provides support for connecting and exchanging data and information with traditional mainframes using SNA or other standard protocols.

The system has utilities that enable communication and data exchange with special peripheral devices such as presence card readers and production plant devices.

CPIC. CPIC (Common Programming Interface Communications) is the interface deployed by the ABAP language for program-to-program communication. CPIC was defined and developed by IBM as a standardized communication interface and was later modified and enhanced by the X/Open organization.

The CPIC communication interface is useful when setting up communications and data conversion and exchange between programs. Since CPIC is based on a common interface, an additional advantage is the portability of the programs across different hardware platforms.

SAP divides the possibilities and the scope of the CPIC interface into two function groups: the CPIC starter set and the advanced function calls. This division is simply meant to guide the user and not to restrict the available functions. For instance, the CPIC starter set would just be used for the basic and minimum set of functions shared by two partner programs, such as establishing the connection and exchanging data. The advance calls cover more communication functionality, such as converting data, checking the communication, and applying security functions. For more information on these CPIC function groups, refer to the SAP documentation *BC SAP Communication: CPI-C Programmer's Guide.*

CPIC communication is always performed using the internal SAP gateway which takes care of converting the CPIC calls to external communication protocols such as TCP/IP.

RFC: Remote Function Calls. RFC is a standard programming interface for making remote calls between programs located on different systems. Functions which are developed or exist in a system can be remotely called by another local program. This is particularly useful for data manipulation and processing load balancing between systems. Even when the same functions exist on both systems—called and caller—it is a way of making another system send or receive data, and the remote CPU assigns the needed resources.

RFC is a higher-level logical interface than CPIC, and it makes life easier for programmers since they do not have to worry about implementing communication routines. With the RFC interface, function calls can be accomplished between two SAP systems or between SAP systems and external ones (for instance, with Microsoft Windows applications). The library functions included with RFC support the Visual Basic and C programming languages.

The RFC interfaces come basically with two services:

- A calling interface for the ABAP programs. Any ABAP program can call a remote function using standard programming sentences, providing the remote system has allowed the module to be called remotely.
- An RFC API (application program interface) for programs other than ABAP (non-SAP). SAP even provides an RFC program generator to help implement RFC partner programs in external systems. With these API calls, external programs can call ABAP function modules in SAP R/3 systems (also in R/2). At the same time, with the RFC API, ABAP programs can use functions provided by external programs.

SAP online help and the documentation print files include extensive information about remote programming with RFC and the RFC API.

Memory Management

Starting with release 3.0 of R/3, SAP introduced a new concept in its use of main memory to improve the overall performance of the system, in respect to previous R/3 releases (2.2 and earlier). The main change was to extensively make use of an extended memory management system to optimize the access to the user contexts and thus avoid the overhead caused by heavy roll-in/roll-out tasks of previous releases.

User context is defined as the user data which is kept by the system between dialog steps to continue the processing of the transaction. These data contain such things as authorizations, field information, internal tables, runtime environment management information, and so on. Roll-in is the process of making the data available to the work processes when they need it.

With the extended memory management functions, all user contexts of an application server are held in main memory and are shared by all work processes. In previous releases, the user contexts were in the roll files and had to be copied from one place to another when user sessions were handled by different work processes. With the new memory management, those previous copy functions (copying user contexts to roll areas) are handled by just reassigning pointers in main memory.

With this technique there is a significant improvement in performance, since context switching is a very frequent task when attending to interactive users. In order to observe the real improvements, the system needs more memory and swap space than previous versions.

With SAP releases prior to 3.0, the user context area used by the dialog processes was limited to the size of the roll area. The new memory management allows the size of this area to be extended as the size of user contexts increases. All the data in the user context is directly accessible as shown in Fig. 2-14.

SAP, and not the operating system, takes care of page management for the user contexts which are held in shared memory because SAP's strategy is for openness and thus it is platform-independent.

This shared memory is technically implemented using an *unnamed* mapped file. In UNIX systems, this means that the address space is mapped onto the operating swap space. For more information on memory mapping, refer to the operating system manuals or online help.

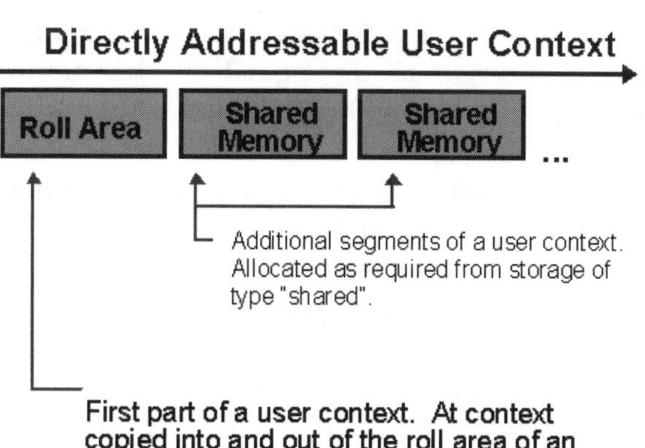
Directly Addressable User Context
Roll Area
Shared Memory
Shared Memory
...
Additional segments of a user context. Allocated as required from storage of type "shared".
First part of a user context. At context copied into and out of the roll area of an work process.

Figure 2.14 Work processes memory allocation. (Copyright by SAP AG.)

To tune and configure memory management, make sure that your system meets all requirements regarding memory and swap space. SAP automatically sets some default parameters depending on your particular configuration. There are some utilities available for monitoring the operation of the memory management to later fine-tune it.

The configuration is accomplished setting parameter values in the system profile. SAP provides a comprehensive manual for administrators full of examples for setting different values for the required parameters that directly affect the mode of operation of the memory management system. Refer to this manual, *BC—Memory Management,* for a detailed description of particular configurations and a deeper description regarding the mode of operation.

Setting the many profile parameters related to memory management can be a very complex job, due to the many relationships of these parameters. R/3 notes 88416 (Zero administration memory management from 4.0A/NT) and 103747 (Performance 4.0/4.5: Parameter recommendations) are a good complement to the memory management online documentation.

The Concept of a SAP Instance

An *instance* is an administrative entity that groups together R/3 components which offer one or several services. These offered services are started or stopped together. All instance components are configured using a common instance profile. For more information on SAP profiles please refer to the section entitled "Profiles" in Chap. 4.

A centralized SAP R/3 system would be made of a unique instance. Another feature which distinguishes the instances is that every SAP instance has its own buffer area, which means that it allocated its own main memory space.

SAP distinguishes between *central instances* and *dialog instances.* Every SAP system has just one central instance, which contains all basic services such as the message server, gateway, update, enqueue, dialog, spool, and background right from installation. Dialog instances, as defined, only contain a set of basic services such as dialog and background work processes from the time of installation.

Administrators can later customize all the services and their server locations by using SAP instance profiles. A central system can be further configured to a distributed system, creating additional instances offering additional services. The usual way of configuring the system right out of the box is to have just one instance per computer; however, providing your systems have enough main memory and processing power, you can install additional instances, which have some advantages.

More information on instances is included in Chap. 4, which deals with the benefits of the SAP system distribution and the components involved in the process.

Building the Client/Server SAP R/3 System

Once all the processes and components which make up the SAP system are known, we can see how all these pieces come together to form a whole client/server R/3 system.

The starting point is a server system (hardware point of view) with the required memory, disks, network controller cards, and operating system.

On this first server, add the relational database management system with its corresponding database processes. At this moment, you have the *database server.* The database is, of course, installed on the disks connected to this computer server.

Now, add basic R/3 services (work processes). We have added a printer to this system to get a connection between the SAP spool work process and the host spool system.

Generically, we link the update and the enqueue work processes to the database. But, as stated in previous sections, there is a database interface component within the dialog and the background work processes that can directly access the database, too.

At this moment, you have the database server and the SAP central instance (because it has all the basic services). From a software client/server point of view, the services provided by the central instance make up an application server.

When the central instance and the database are running together on the same machine, which is usual, this is known as a *database server with central instance,* or simply a *database server.*

In the SAP naming convention, a *service* is a process (such as the message process) or a group of work processes. It is a software concept, and the component that offers those services is called a *server.*

The software components which request those services are known as the *clients.* The clients can be servers at the same time. Since there already is a dispatcher process and dialog work processes, it is possible for presentation servers (clients) to connect to this system (server). It is also possible to configure the directly attached printers or network printers to the SAP system. This would be a centralized system or a two-tier client/server configuration.

Include additional work processes (service types) on a different server, which make up an additional application server. Now it is a SAP R/3 three-tiered client/server configuration. A complete SAP system is the set of clients and server components that make use of or are assigned to the same database.

The connection between the presentation process and the dispatcher is the one that makes the transition between the presentation and application servers. The update process is the one that makes the separation between the application and database servers.

CHAPTER 3

Installation Concepts and Guidelines

The purpose of this chapter is to introduce the reader to the installation of SAP R/3, the software and hardware components and the concepts involved in setting up the system, and the steps required for a fast and successful installation. The goal is to make the installation process easier and more understandable.

This chapter under no circumstances replaces the official SAP installation manuals, since each new R/3 version release might contain differences concerning system set up and installation. Particularly important are the operating system dependencies, where a wrong file or directory permission or incorrect system parameters might lead to R/3 installation errors or unexpected behaviors. The official manuals are often referred to in this chapter.

This chapter's guidelines are based on SAP R/3 release 4.5, and are equally applicable to those releases, such as 4.0, that use the R3Setup installation utility. Previous releases used the R3inst installation utility. Observe, though, that installation is a different process than upgrading.

Due to the open technology of R/3 and thus the number of supported hardware platforms, operating systems, and databases, it is beyond the scope of this chapter to cover all installation variants. For a single SAP system or group of related systems, customers do not usually install different operating systems and databases, except for performing benchmarks and comparisons. Nevertheless, a mix and match of different hardware systems and even operating systems are supported (for example, UNIX systems as database servers and Windows NT as application servers, OS/390 as standalone database servers, and AIX as application servers). Official SAP installation guides contain detailed instructions on how to proceed in these environments. For more information on the latest status of these types of system setups, contact SAP or look it up in SAPnet (sapnet.sap.com).

Customer decisions about hardware platforms are quite variable, but UNIX and Windows NT are the two major operating systems selected. ORACLE is one of the preferred databases, with Informix, Microsoft SQL-Server, and ADABAS D as other choices. There are of course many AS/400 and OS/390 installations, together with the DB2 databases. To explain the making of the decision among different vendors or operating system architectures is beyond the scope of this book, and depends on many factors such as overall system size (number of users, estimated size of database, R/3 business modules to be implemented, batch load, etc.), budget, expected response time threshold, former database know how, and so on.

For the instructive purposes in this book, examples are shown and explained using both UNIX and Windows NT as operating system, and ORACLE and SQL-Server as database, although the general guidelines are completely valid for all other database engines. The only difference would be in the process of designing the file system layout and the actual installation and configuration of the database itself.

CAUTION! If you have a system to use in a nonproductive environment, you can follow these instructions together with those from the SAP manuals, but be aware that the actual installation for productive purposes should only be done by certified SAP R/3 installers; otherwise, SAP does not guarantee its support. It is equally important not to play with installation programs and utilities since that might lead to a complete loss of or extensive damage to files already installed.

Getting Started

Installing the SAP R/3 software successfully, providing all requirements are met, is a process that may last from one to two days, depending on the options and processing power of the hardware chosen. This estimated time does not include postinstallation steps or basis customization.

A good level of expertise with operating systems (UNIX or Windows NT) and management of database systems will ease your way into fast and successful installations. Also, make sure you know the hotline numbers of your nearest SAP subsidiary and your hardware vendor.

These guidelines will not cover such things as failover systems or RAID options, since they are very much dependent on hardware vendor products and configuration utilities. Nevertheless, you can find more information on these and other special topics in Chap. 16.

Elements in a SAP R/3 Installation

When a company decides to implement a SAP R/3 system to fulfill its business information needs, it must be aware that it is probably more difficult to customize the functional aspects of the business; however, all the technical elements involved must be seriously considered to overcome the availability issue. SAP defines *availability* as the fraction of time the system can be used to perform the functions for which it was designed. It does not define it as an isolated hardware or software element, but as a property of the whole information system.

In a SAP R/3 installation, you may encounter the following hardware elements:

- One or several server computers with sufficient main memory and hard disk space
- An appropriate network infrastructure
- Many presentation servers, commonly personal computers, with network interface cards
- LAN servers, which are needed 99 percent of the time
- One or several printers

The following software elements may also be present:

- Server computers operating system and base software kits.
- Graphical operating environment for the personal computers and a supported network operating system.
- SAP R/3 software kits.
- A relational database management system as the SAP information container. This usually comes bundled with the SAP kit.

All previous plus other additional requirements you might need are described in the SAP brochure, "Check list—Installation requirements," which comes bundled in the installation kit.

The third and most important element, which is rare and sometimes scarce, is *people*. Although the system is complex, managing the SAP R/3 system in not so difficult if the right support lines and procedures are in place. Chapter 16 gives some tips about these and other important tasks concerning the operation of SAP R/3.

These items are not a SAP requirements list, but are the set of elements that should be taken into consideration when starting a SAP technical implementation project. Every element is important, and the right configuration of every one—people configuration used to be known as *training*—is what makes the technical implementation a successful base for the project.

Installation Steps

The following installation steps cover the general process of R/3 system installation from the very first phase of sizing to the optional postinstallation choices. The following sections explain the steps, concepts, and all the details extensively. Note that the order of some of these installation steps can be different depending on whether the installation is NT based or UNIX based. Differences are indicated in the corresponding paragraphs. A brief description of each step follows:

1. *Size your SAP system.* *Sizing* is the process of deciding on the size of the system in terms of computing power, physical space needed, network infrastructure, and so forth. Size is a function of the number of users and which R/3 business modules they will work on, how large the database will be, and what the processing power or availability required to meet the system demands is.

NOTE *Sizing is not actually an installation step, but rather a technical implementation issue. However, since calculating and deciding the system's size is a requirement or basic step for any installation, it has been included here.*

2. *Decide on the installation type.* This step answers the question, how will we implement the SAP R/3 client/server approach?
3. *Check the installation requirements.* R/3 will only install if certain minimum requirements are met.
4. *Install and configure the hardware, base software, and network.* Once we get our computer server, we have to get it up and running. You will at least need to install the server operating system, the additional required base software, and configure your network.
5. *Get the R/3 installation notes.* The R/3 installation notes always include last-minute information essential to successful installations. If you don't have access or a user account for entering SAPnet, you can request the necessary notes from your nearest SAP subsidiary by fax.
6. *Installation preparations: adapt systems to SAP requirements.* UNIX systems will require adapting some kernel parameters, swapping space, and sometimes installing additional software. Windows NT requires the installation of products such as the Microsoft Management Console (MMC), and adjustments in NT cache, paging space, NT domain, and other parameters.
7. *Design the layout of file systems and set them up.* Depending upon your system sizing and available resources, you have to design the best way to implement the required file systems.

8. *Install the R3SETUP tool.* R3SETUP is the R/3 installation program that must be first installed with the use of a SAP-provided script file.

The order of the following two points differs between UNIX and Windows NT systems. On UNIX systems, install the R/3 instances first and then the database system; in Windows NT, first install the database software and then the R/3 instances.

9. *Install the SAP R / 3 central instance.* The R/3 central instance is the first piece of SAP software that the installation utility creates and configures. It automatically creates the SAP directory structure and a set of services (work processes) of all available types: dialog, background, update, spool, enqueue, message server, and gateway server.
10. *Install the database system.* This is the process of installing the underlying R/3 database program and creating the runtime and directory structure of the database according to user inputs.
11. *Build and load the database.* Once the database engine is installed from the previous step, the installation utility creates the database structure, and allows you to insert the SAP default database data into the system. At this point, you could decide to import the data from another system (customer system).
12. *Import ABAP program loads.* At this point your SAP system is installed and almost ready for use. This installation step loads ABAP pregenerated programs, so that the system will not have to precompile and generate them when they are first called. This is important for performance reasons.

Installation is almost complete, and you could even start the R/3 system, but the system might not be quite ready. First, you have to apply for your license key or install a temporary license until you get your final one. There are some optional postinstallation instructions which should be taken into consideration. Among them, if your users are not German- or English-speaking people, or if you belong to an international company with subsidiaries in countries with different languages, you will need to import additional language texts into the system.

Now, let's get a closer look at each of these steps.

Step 1: Sizing the System

Sizing may have an impact on the overall installation process. But, if you just want to perform a simple installation test, you can skip this section as long as you have a system with minimum hardware requirements.

Sizing is a complex and inaccurate procedure that involves a few different persons and organizations. A SAP customer usually requires the help of the chosen hardware vendor and of SAP itself. At the same time, these providers pass on to the customers lengthy questionnaires, with data that is fed into a sizing application to calculate the estimated size of the system. The goal of the sizing process is to define three very important figures: how much CPU power is needed (type and number of processors, memory, number of servers), how big the database will be (disk space necessary), and what the minimum recommended network infrastructure to support the SAP R/3 traffic is. The quality of the sizing is just as good as the quality of the data supplied by the customer.

Sizing SAP systems is based on a unit known as the *SAP Application Benchmark Performance Standard* (SAPS). 100 SAPSs are equivalent to 2000 order line items processed in an hour (SD module) or 6000 dialog steps with 2000 postings in an hour (FI module).

Usually the CPU and memory requirements are calculated considering the estimated user population per application module and an approach of transaction volumes at peak times. Every SAP application module can have a different processor power consumption depending on the depth of the transactions, and therefore they are assigned a load factor. Be aware that every SAP release or even the hardware partners could use different factors depending on their technology.

Additional information such as requested average CPU and memory utilization and scalability of the platforms further defines the needed hardware.

Database sizing requires more in-depth business knowledge to be able to fill out the lengthy questionnaires supplied by SAP. Often customers are unable to supply this data accurately. In these cases, the approach usually is to supply a moderate amount of disk space based on similar configurations and later monitor the system growth and add more disk space when needed. This, however, might have some drawbacks including file system redesigns or time-consuming database reorganizations.

SAP has and supplies its partners with a sizing tool to help calculate the amount of disk space needed based on a business questionnaire.

This sizing tool also helps to calculate the estimated tablespace sizes and the biggest tables it will include. This information is particularly useful when customer installations are defined as having a very large database (VLDB). In the R/3 environment a VLDB can be considered a database larger than 30 GB. This is, however, a subjective approach that can be varied as new R/3 or database releases appear.

The section entitled "Considerations for VLDBs" later in this chapter includes some important notes on preparing an installation for a VLDB.

An easy and first approach to sizing can be the *QuickSizer* tool provided by SAP through SAPnet (sapnet.sap-ag.de/quicksizer). With the quick sizing service, SAP customers can make an initial and categorized calculation of CPU, memory, and disk resources, based either on users by application module or on a transaction load profile. The results in terms of SAPSs and average disk volume requirements are immediately available, and customers can decide to pass on this information to the hardware partner directly from the QuickSizer form.

This self-service tool can be used in the initial project phase to gain an approximate idea for planning the systems infrastructure. As the project progresses, and more usage data is available, a double check should be done, either by using the Quicksizer tool again or by directing the information to the selected hardware partner.

A third and sometimes underestimated factor for a correct sizing is the expected network traffic. Usually there are two types of network connections which require appropriate bandwidths: from the application servers to the database server (server network) and from the presentation servers (usually PCs) to the application servers (access network).

The rule of thumb establishes an approximate figure of 1.5 to 2.5 Kbits/sec between presentation servers to application servers. This figure does not take into consideration other network traffic, both R/3 related (printing, downloading, graphics) and non-R/3 related (mail, internet, other client/server applications).

The load between application server and database server (when on different servers) depends on the overall system load, but a minimum of 10 Mbits/sec should be guaranteed.

To calculate the network bandwidth, customers have to know the number of sites and the number of users per site and per module. SAP hardware and technology partners can help in this process. A formula based on benchmark is available for an approximate sizing:

$$C = 16{,}000 * N / [L * (T\text{thinktime} + T\text{response})] \text{ bits/sec}$$

Where

C = required line capacity measured in bits/sec
N = number of users
L = line utilization ($0 < L < 1$). Values of line utilization higher than 50% are not recommended.
Tthinktime = think time between two dialog steps (average = 30 sec)
Tresponse = response time (average = 1 sec)

The R/3 installation kit, as well as the online help, include *Integration of R/3 Servers in TCP/IP Networks,* a valuable manual about the network configuration, which should be carefully read by installers or those responsible for network management.

The sizing of an overall SAP installation has a direct impact on the following elements of the process:

- The installation type (a factor of how many servers and their intended tasks)
- The hardware and network configuration
- The layout and size of the file system
- The installation of the database
- The load of a customer database
- The printing infrastructure and strategy
- The postinstallation steps

The description of this first step is solely intended to make you aware of all the implications of a correct system sizing.

Step 2: Deciding On the Installation Type

Installation type means how to distribute the SAP R/3 services among the available servers. This is the subject of Chap. 4.

In SAP R/3 terms, an instance is a group of processes that provide some specialized services and with a dispatcher process in charge of distributing the user requests to the appropriate work processes.

A SAP installation includes a central instance which by default has the service types dialog, update, enqueue, background, gateway, message, and spool. The names of these services form the acronym DVEBGMS, which you will find often. Notice, though, that *update* corresponds to *V,* since

Verbuchung is the German term for update. The type and number of work processes can be later configured using specific SAP profile parameters.

The server that includes the database management system and the data itself is known as the *database instance* or *database server* in SAP terms, which are slightly different than a SAP instance since the processes are database-specific ones.

A minimal R/3 system consists of a central instance and a database, which are very often located on the same computer, and known commonly as the *database server.* Notice, however, that the database can be installed in a different host than the central instance, in which case it is known as a stand-alone database server.

As stated in the chapter introduction, these general installation guidelines are intended for an installation on a central instance with a database (both on the same computer).

Step 3: Checking Installation Requirements

Besides the hardware on which to install the system, you need the following SAP installation manuals:

- *Getting Started with your R/3 Installation (<Operating System/Database>)*
- *Checklist—Installation requirements: <Operating System>*
- *R/3 Installation on <Operating System> <Database>*
- *R/3 Installation on UNIX: OS Dependencies*
- *Installing SAP Frontend Software for PCs*
- *Installing the Online Documentation*

You also need to have handy the guide for configuring the network (*Integration of R/3 Servers in TCP/IP Networks*) and, if installing additional languages other than German or English, the *Language Import* guide.

The purpose of this chapter, and in general the objective of the book, is to make the reading of these guides easier and more understandable. However, you must pay attention to the specific details and instructions they contain.

Of course, you need the installation software kit, which comes with the set of CD-ROMs commonly referred to as

- *SAP kernel.* This is the first and main CD; it includes the runtime software and the file system templates. Depending on the R/3 release and chosen platform, sometimes it also contains the database runtime software.

- *Presentation.* This includes front-end presentation software for UNIX, Windows, and optional libraries and software subsets.
- *Database software.*
- *DB-Export.* These CDs (two or more) have the database export files to load the standard SAP data into the system.
- *Report Load.* For performance reasons, this CD includes the ABAP loads to speed up execution of programs the first time they are called.

Depending on the release and type of installation (upgrade kits differ from initial installation kits), the software package might come bundled with additional CDs such as the "Language import files," "Online documentation," "Documentation print files," and sometimes kernel patches and other support packages, database upgrades, and documentation.

The minimum hardware required is a certified supported server with a CD-ROM, a network controller, and a minimum of 256 MB of main memory, and about 12 GB of physical disk space. Do not forget a suitable tape drive for making backups.

Although it will not be needed until the installation of the central instance, it is time to decide what the name of your SAP R/3 system will be; in other words, decide on the *SID* (SAP system identification). This name is a three-letter word which must conform to SAP naming rules, such as being uppercase and the first character must be a letter. Some values are not allowed: ADD, ALL, ANY, ASC, AUX, B20, B30, BCO, BIN, COM, CON, DBA, EMS, END, EPS, FAX, FOR, GID, INT, KEY, LOG, LPT, MON, NOT, OFF, P30, PRN, PUT, RAW, ROW, SAP, SET, SGA, SHG, SID, TMP, UID, and VAR. Check the manuals or OSS notes for additional values not permitted. (In SAP installation manuals *SID* is often referred to as *SAPSID*. Both are the same.)

Choose this name carefully, since it must be unique within a group or related SAP systems (usually companywide), and to rename it, the whole system must be reinstalled.

A very popular way to name the systems is: P*nn* (P01, P11, etc.) for productive systems. T*nn* for test systems, and C*nn* or D*nn* for development systems. But this is just a suggestion. It is also very common to find the company initials in the SAP system name.

System types are discussed in detail in Chap. 6, "The Transport System."

Step 4: Installing Hardware, Base Software, and Configuring the Network

Activities included in this step are closely related to meeting the installation requirements for the appropriate platform chosen: R/3 release, operating system, and database. Typical tasks include the physical installation of the equipment and the connection of the storage subsystem (disks, cabinet, RAID controllers) and of the network. The basic purpose here is to get the server up and running, which means that all hardware components must be properly installed. Some of the tasks are, for instance, adding additional disks if there are not enough for SAP, connecting a tape drive, installing new memory modules, and so on.

If you plan to use some type of RAID for the disks, this is also the right time to install and configure the RAID controllers. Some kind of RAID configuration in SAP installations is highly recommended for data security and integrity. Nowadays, hard disks have become a commodity and they are priced reasonably. Chapter 16 further explains the benefits of RAID systems in SAP installations.

Once the hardware is ready, it is time to install your operating system and all the associated software subsets. For your particular server and operating system, SAP might require the installation of additional subsets; check this out in the installation requirements guide.

In your operating system installation, pay attention to the space initially assigned to the file systems created by default, such as the root, user, or temporary file systems. You do not need a very large root file system, (although it depends on the specific UNIX flavor you are using); however, make at least enough space for building three kernel files. Leave enough space for the temporary file system. Sometimes the strangest errors occur when the default temporary directory becomes full.

Beware of swap space. The rule of thumb says that it should be a minimum of three times your memory capacity, with 1.5 GB the minimum size in any case. As an example, for 512 MB of main memory you need a swap area of at least 2 GB. This is a must, particularly since version 3.0 of R/3. Refer to the memory management manual from SAP for more information on how the R/3 runtime system uses the memory.

Configure the TCP/IP network. For doing a simple installation, you have to assign the address and net mask and start the network processes. However, for big installations with several systems, network controllers, and LAN servers, the process can be much more complicated. The section entitled "Guidelines for Distributed Configurations with the R/3 System" in the next chapter contains some notes and advice about this issue. Good examples and additional information can be found in the SAP guide *Integration of R/3 Servers in TCP/IP Networks.*

If you are planning to install additional application servers, install and configure NFS (network file system). For now you do not need to import or export any file systems with NFS; that is a task concerning the installation of additional servers.

Make sure that all the base software you just installed have the appropriate licenses, otherwise some problems could arise when booting your system or trying to use some software.

Finally, some basic UNIX optional setup and configuration tasks may be done, depending on the specific hardware and operating system. For example, when configuring tty ports for remote login, include some cleaning periodic scripts in the *cron* file and add additional hosts to the host database, printer definitions, and so forth.

In the case of Windows NT installations, it is important to install the appropriate operating system release and the Service Packs, as indicated in the installation requirements. Notice that only U.S. English is supported for NT Server software.

Within an NT domain, SAP does not recommend that R/3 servers act either as Primary Domain Controllers (PDCs) or Backup Domain Controllers (BDCs).

Step 5: R/3 Installation Notes

SAP, as well as any other information technology provider, supplies last-minute information and problem corrections through the SAPnet-R/3.

Before proceeding with the installation you must get the current installation notes. The actual note numbers depend on what release version you are installing, and they can be found in your SAP installation manual.

If you don't have a user account to access SAPnet, contact your local SAP office and request the notes. They will send them to you by fax.

For example, for releases 4.0B and 4.5B and platforms UNIX and NT, Table 3-1 indicates the R/3 notes numbers, although you might require more as indicated in the installation manual or referred to within these notes.

SAP notes are updated constantly. If you have the notes from previous installations or from someone else, you should still obtain the latest, unless the note modification date (which is referred to in the field *Set by* at the beginning of the note) is exactly the same.

At this stage before the actual installation has started, you might find it difficult to understand some of the concepts and requirements included in the notes, but try to follow them. They usually contain instructions for all supported operating systems, but you just have to pay attention to your particular one. Occasionally, you will find everything is OK by default and there are no additional corrections to do. (Do not count on it.)

TABLE 3-1
R/3 Installation Notes

Note Number		
4.0B	**4.5B**	**Note Title**
98711	134135	R/3 Installation on Windows NT (general information)
91700	134107	R/3 Installation on Windows NT—Adabas database
98717	134159	R/3 Installation on Windows NT—DB2
98715	134105	R/3 Installation on Windows NT—Informix
91703	134073	R/3 Installation on Windows NT—MS SQL Server
98714	134070	R/3 Installation on Windows NT—Oracle Database
101315	142990	R/3 Installation on UNIX
100125	137480	R/3 Installation on UNIX—OS Dependencies
149066	143047	R/3 Installation on UNIX—Adabas Database
101316	143052	R/3 Installation on UNIX—DB2 Universal Database
101317	143039	R/3 Installation on UNIX—Informix Database
101318	142996	R/3 Installation on UNIX—Oracle Database
80266		Installation of NT Application Servers in a UNIX Environment

Step 6: Adapting Systems to SAP Requirements

For most supported operating systems, SAP R/3 requires that some settings and parameters be modified in order for R/3 to successfully install and run. These parameters are included in the SAP installation guide, *OS Dependencies,* and last-minute adjustments can be found on the latest R/3 notes. The values reflected in the manuals must be carefully checked and strictly complied with.

Very possibly you will have to restart or reboot your system for the parameters to take effect.

For UNIX systems, there is a *memlimits* tool that can be used for checking swap space, heap size, address space per process, and other measurements. This tool can be found on the SAP kernel CD-ROM within the compressed file SAPEXE.CAR. To extract the tool use the following command, substituting <SAPCD> for your mount point where the kernel CD is mounted, and <OS> with the name used for the UNIX option:

```
/<SAPCD>/UNIX/<OS>/CAR -xf /<SAPCD>/UNIX/<OS>/SAPEXE.CAR memlimits
```

Then execute the *memlimits* tool until no errors are found. This might require adjustment of the kernel parameters.

On Windows NT systems some of the installation preparations include the adjustment of the NT cache for maximizing performance for network applications, the installation of some dynamic link libraries (DLLs), and the installation of the Microsoft Management Console (MMC) on release 4.5. On distributed NT environments, this is also a good time for setting up a central transport host.

Step 7: Designing the Layout of File Systems

This step consists of distributing the required file systems into the available physical space (hard disks). For productive installation, this can be the crucial factor for a successful installation and for avoiding performance problems. This procedure will require some thinking, since the configuration and distribution of disks will impact such important aspects of the installation as the data security, performance, application server distribution, and growth estimates.

In SAP R/3 environments, it is highly recommended that the chosen operating system be able to easily reconfigure the available disk space.

The minimum sizes for the required file systems can be found in the corresponding installation manual, as well as in the command files <filename>.R3S, which will be copied to the hard disk when installing the R3SETUP tool. Before actual installation, users have the option of modifying those sizes by editing the R3S command files.

From now on, the SID (SAP system identification) chosen in step 3 will be widely used, since it will be part of the name of most file systems and directories.

The needed file systems can be classified into two types: database-dependent and database-independent file systems.

The database-independent file systems contain the directories needed by the system global SAP data and executables and the SAP instance-specific files and links. These file systems are as follows:

- */usr/sap/trans*—This is the global directory for all SAP servers belonging to the same SAP system group. It is used for transports among the systems. SAP upgrades also use this directory.
- */sapmnt/<SID>*—Systemwide data for one SAP system. Normally this directory will be physically located on the central instance and

its subdirectories exported via NFS to application servers in the case of UNIX systems. On Windows NT, *sapmnt* is the share name for the global directory \usr\sap, which is accessed by the UNC \\SAPGLOBALHOST\sapmnt. SAP directory structure is further explained in the next chapter.

- */usr/sap/<SID>*—Instance-specific data with links to the system-wide data. On Windows NT, *saploc* is the share name for the instance specific directory \usr\sap, which is accessed by the UNC \\SAPLOCALHOST\saploc.

In the case of ORACLE databases, the database-dependent file systems are as follows:

- */oracle/stage/stage_<vno>* (on UNIX systems) or *\ORANT* (on Windows NT systems)—Directory for installation and upgrades of the Oracle database software. *vno* stands for version number.
- */oracle/<SID>*—Location for the Oracle instance SID. Notice that in Oracle terms, an instance is the name of a database. For non-SAP installations, Oracle can have many instances. However, in SAP installations, the Oracle instance and the SAP system name are the same and only one.

NOTE *It is possible to install two SAP instances on one server. However, this is not recommended by SAP in productive operation and requires special instructions.*

- */oracle/<SID>/origlogA*—Original set of first member of Oracle redo log files
- */oracle/<SID>/origlogB*—Original set of second member of Oracle redo log files
- */oracle/<SID>/mirrlogA*—Mirrored set of first member of Oracle redo log files
- */oracle/<SID>/mirrlogB*—Mirrored set of first member of Oracle redo log files
- */oracle/<SID>/saparch*—Directory for archived log files (offline redo log files)
- */oracle/<SID>/sapreorg*—Work directory for database reorganizations and administration
- */oracle/<SID>/saptrace*—Directory where the ORACLE alert and trace files are located.

- */oracle/<SID>/sapbackup*—Used for storing the logs generated by the BRBACKUP tool, as well as the target for backups to hard disk.
- */oracle/<SID>/sapcheck*—Contains the logs of several *sapdba* options such as *-check, -analyze,* or *-next.*
- */oracle/<SID>/sapdata1*—Directory for SAP database files
- */oracle/<SID>/sapdata2*—Directory for SAP database files
- */oracle/<SID>/sapdata3*—Directory for SAP database files
- */oracle/<SID>/sapdata4*—Directory for SAP database files
- */oracle/<SID>/sapdata5* up to */oracle/<SID>/sapdata<n>*—Directory for SAP database files

The minimum number of *sapdata* directories has to be created for the installation to succeed. This number depends on the R/3 version release. It is usually up to the sixth (*/oracle/<SID>/sapdata6*) directory. The number and size of *sapdata* directories is contained within the installation command file DATABASE.R3S or CENTRDB.R3S.

Although it is not the goal of this book to explain the architecture of the Oracle database, a certain knowledge and experience is a requirement to install, support, and manage a SAP R/3 installation. The same applies when the database engine is Informix, Adabas D, or SQL-Server. It is a good idea to have handy the *ORACLE Server Administration Guide* and the *Error Reference Guide,* since a great number of problems encountered during a daily productive operation are directly related to database errors. Chapter 14 contains information explaining the fundamental concepts needed to manage the database from the SAP R/3 point of view.

The Oracle Redo Log Files. The Oracle redo log files, also known as *online redo logs* or *online archives,* are special files used by Oracle to record the changes made to the database during normal operation. These are very important since they will be used in case the changes made to the database due to a recovery situation have to be reapplied.

SAP by default defines four groups of redo log files and places the first and the third in one directory (*/oracle/<SID>/origlogA*) and the second and fourth in another directory (*/oracle/<SID>/origlogB*). The SAP installation also leaves the option of having these sets of redo log files mirrored by Oracle, in which case the first directory is mirrored in */oracle/<SID>/mirrlogA* and the second one in */oracle/<SID>/mirrlogB.* This is the recommended configuration, even if the disks are also mirrored with some kind of hardware or software.

The redo log files work in a round-robin fashion: Oracle writes in the first one, and when this becomes full it starts with the second one until it reaches the fourth one, in which case it will start again with the first one. What happens when switching redo log files is that they are copied to the *archived* directory (only if the Oracle archiver process is started, which is mandatory for SAP installations).

SAP default sizes for online redo logs is 20 MB each. In certain circumstances you can change this value to better fit your needs. The section entitled "Considerations for Oracle VLDBs" later in this chapter explains the effects of the redo log file sizes and explains how to change them.

For performance and security reasons, SAP recommends having each redo log file system on separate disks. The following sections show other alternatives.

Oracle File System Design Guidelines. When distributing the available disk controllers and physical disks into the logical layout of the file systems, there are four main factors to consider:

- *Size.* This is the first and foremost figure to have in mind. For productive installations, remember the notes and guidelines from step 1. In nonproductive or test systems, just use SAP default values.
- *Security (data integrity).* To accomplish a good level of data integrity, some options are RAID systems (mirrored disks), a good backup and restore strategy, and a correct layout of certain SAP file systems, for example, the online redo log files.
- *Performance.* A file system layout in which input/output activity is divided among the largest number of disks will help maintain performance. RAID level 0 (disk concatenation or stripping) also helps.
- *Growth.* Problems of file systems filling up do arrive if they are not sufficiently spaced. Avoid this by having a good strategy (software and hardware) for easily and quickly adding more disks as it becomes necessary.

The basic rules to follow to best approach these factors are as follows:

- Avoid mixing in the same disks file systems with a high I/O activity.
- Do not define SAP database-related file systems together with system or swap disks.
- Do not mix into the same *sapdata* Oracle tablespaces containing the index and the data of the same tables. Installation takes care of this by default, but you have to consider it in case you make some structural changes to the database.

- For security reasons, do not mix the database files with the redo log files or the archive log files.
- If the estimated size of the database is not very large (less than 30 GB) use a mix of small- and medium-capacity disks so that you don't waste so much space when distributing file systems. This has the inconvenience of using up more disk controllers.
- The */oracle/<SID>/saparch* directory must have enough capacity to hold up enough archive files between two successful backups. This size will depend on your expected system activity. It is not recommended to be on the same disk as the *sapreorg* directory because, if a disk failure occurs during a reorganization, having the *archiver* process enabled, you can corrupt your database and will only be able to recover from the last successful backup.

Optimal Configuration. Having considered the previous factors, an optimal distribution of the required SAP file systems would be to have every file system in different volumes or disks (16 disks excluding operating system disks) with the required sizes, and if possible, mirrored by hardware (making a minimum of 32 disks). This, however, has some drawbacks including possible waste of disk space, since some of the file systems are quite small to take up a whole disk (such as, the online redo log files).

Some alternatives are as follows:

- Instead of using RAID level 1 (mirrored disks), try RAID level 5 (use of parity disks). Check this out with your hardware partner. Or, just mirror the database files and the redo log files. Other file systems can be more easily recovered from backups.
- Put together the *origlogA* and *mirrlogB* file systems on a disk and the *origlogB* and *mirrlogA* on another disk. This way, the Oracle process will always be writing on both disks at the same time because it writes synchronously for both the original redo log and the mirrored one. If one disk becomes corrupt, there is always the second one, and Oracle can keep on working with the logical mirrored copy of the corrupted set of logs until you recover from your failure.
- Both the */oracle/<SID>* and the */sapmnt/<SID>* file systems are not especially high in I/O activity. In case of a small number of disks, these file systems could also share the same disk.

Figure 3-1 shows an example of a configuration in which every file system required by SAP is located on a different volume. Figure 3-2 shows an optimal configuration from a logical point of view. It does not show the use

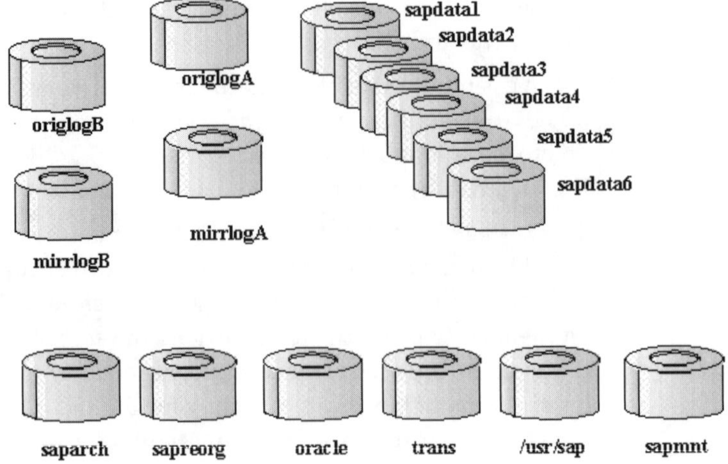

Figure 3-1 Configuration with maximum number of disk volumes.

of any RAID-configured devices. There are, of course, many other possibilities depending on the particular needs of the installation and available resources. Figure 3-3 shows the minimum required configuration, which should be avoided.

The advantage of the configuration example in Fig. 3-1 is that all security measures and even performance measures are set. However, this can be a real waste of disk space and probably disk controllers to evenly distribute the input/output. Another couple of volumes for the operating system and swap or paging space will also be needed.

The example in Fig. 3-2 shows a more balanced configuration in which all security measures are met, and which should also provide a good input/output performance. You could further optimize the configuration

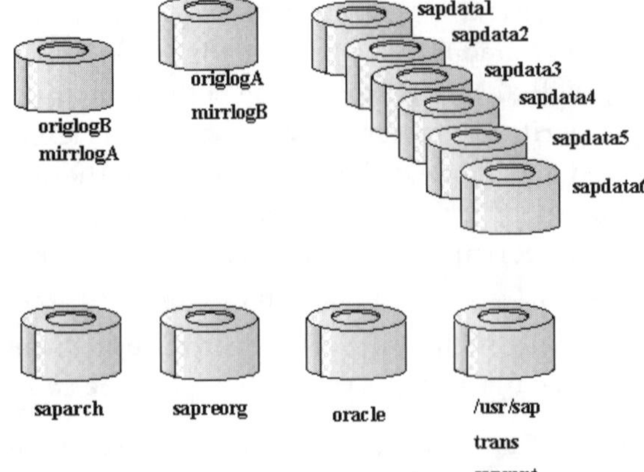

Figure 3-2 Disk layout optimal configuration.

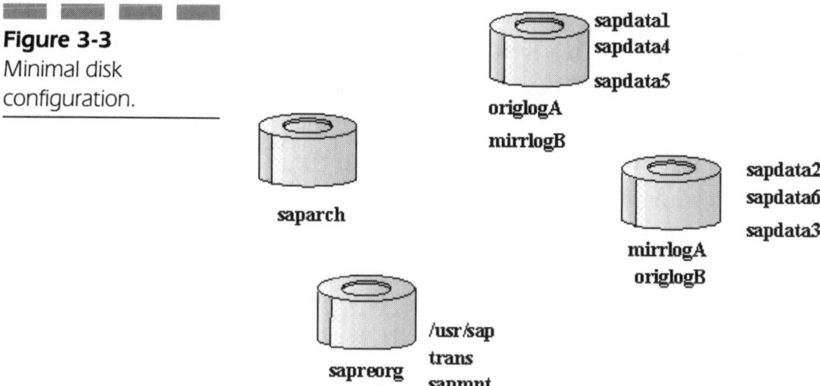

Figure 3-3 Minimal disk configuration.

looking at the specific tablespaces of the *sapdata* file systems, and could place some *sapdatas* in the same volume as long as you do not have both the data and the index tablespace in the same volume. This is mainly for performance reasons. Please consider that performance is a set of factors which depend on the base hardware or software technology used.

The configuration shown in Fig. 3-3 should be carefully avoided and only implemented for test systems or when there is no other alternative, since the security measures are not met. If for budget or technical reasons there are no more volumes available, then a strict backup strategy must be in place in the event any failure occurs.

To continue with installation, decide on and configure your file systems in consideration of the preceding advice and examples to better fit your needs. The way to set up disks and file systems (or raw devices) is very much hardware vendor–dependent. If you do not know how to do this for your particular environment, look at the related section in the SAP installation guide *OS Dependencies* or ask for help from your hardware vendor.

Step 8: Installing the R3SETUP Tool

In the case of an R/3 Windows NT installation, the correct sequence is to install the database software (Step 10) and then follow this step and the next one. UNIX systems can install the database software from the R/3 installation utilities.

From release 4.0 onward, R/3 includes several components for performing and supporting the R/3 installation process. These components are:

- A *shell script* in charge of copying the installation components from the kernel CD-ROM to a local installation directory. On UNIX systems this script is *INSTTOOL.SH;* on Windows NT it is *R3SETUP.BAT.*
- *R3SETUP,* the program that performs the actual installation of R/3 and other components.
- *INSTGUI,* the front end for R3SETUP, is used for watching the installation progress, providing help, restarting installation, and viewing the log files. It can also be started from a remote computer.
- *Command files* (**.R3S*) that contain the instructions for the particular installation process. These files are copied to the local installation directory when running the shell script, and can be edited using the SAPPAD editor before the actual installation. Depending on the platform and release, you can find the following standard command files that serve different purposes:
  - *CENTRAL.R3S,* a command file used for installing a central instance without a database.
  - *DATABASE.R3S,* a command file used for installing a standalone database server.
  - *CENTRDB.R3S,* a command file used for installing a central instance with the database on the same server.
  - *DIALOG.R3S,* a command file used for installing a dialog instance.
  - *GATEWAY.R3S,* a command file used for installing a standalone gateway server.

The procedure on UNIX system must be performed by the privileged user *root.* The following steps are required:

- Create an installation directory with enough free space. Space needs are different according to the platform: allow at least 100 MB. Provide read-write access to the directory.

  The installation directory will be referred as <INSTDIR>. For example:

  ```
  mkdir /temp/install
  chmod 777 /temp/install
  ```

- Mount the SAP kernel CD. The way to do this depends on your UNIX variant. Actual instructions are provided in the *OS Dependencies* guide. You will need a mount point directory, usually */sapcd,* for that. The mount point directory for the CD will be referred to as <CD-MOUNT>.

- Run the shell script:

```
cd <INSTDIR>
<CD-MOUNT>/UNIX/INSTTOOL.SH
```

For example:

```
cd /temp/install
/sapcd/UNIX/INSTTOOL.SH
```

The shell script will automatically copy the installation components from the CD to the installation directory on the local disk.

The procedure for Windows NT systems is slightly different, although the objective is the same. Remember that on NT the database software should be installed first. The script must be run with administrative privileges, either at the NT domain if the system belongs to a domain, or with local administrator privileges if it does not. The procedure should be:

- Create the user group *SAP_<SID>_GlobalAdmin* and the user accounts *SAPService<sid>* and *<sid>adm,* and assign both user accounts the group. Additionally, assign user *<sid>adm* to the group *Domain Admins.*
- Make sure the TEMP variable is defined.
- Create an installation directory. A common one is a new directory *INSTALL* under the home directory of the *<sid>adm* user. For example: *C:\users\<sid>adm\install.*
- Insert the kernel CD in the CD-ROM drive of the server. The drive letter will be referred to as <CD-DRIVE>.
- Either from Windows Explorer or the command prompt, start the program:

```
<CD-DRIVE>:\NT\COMMON\R3SETUP.BAT
```

- The program asks for the <SID> and the directory for copying the files. Follow the instructions by pressing *Next.*

The R3SETUP.BAT script will then copy the required installation components to the installation directory, will provide rights for installation to the user that has run the installation script, and also will add several options within the NT *Programs* menu. Figure 3-4 shows these options. You will finally have to either log off or reboot the system.

At this time it is possible to modify some of the installation command files as well as standard locations and file system sizes. This is done using the SAPPAD editor.

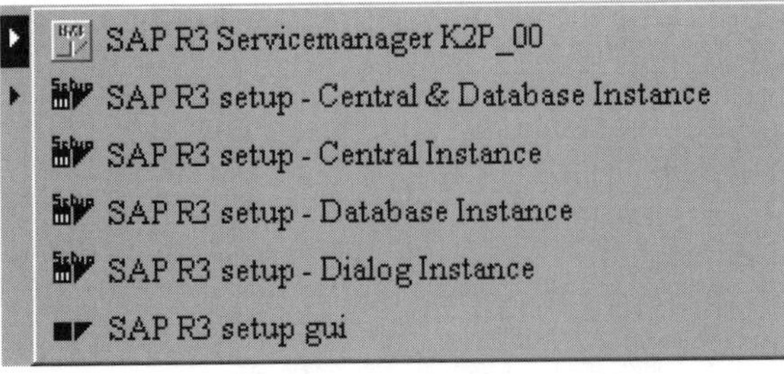

Figure 3-4 R3SETUP installation options.

Step 9: Install Central Instance

As stated at the beginning of the chapter, these guidelines are provided for the example installation of a central instance with database on the same host. Other types of installations are very similar but should be looked up in the installation manuals.

Installation both on UNIX and Windows NT is performed using the R3SETUP tool.

Installation on Windows NT Systems On Windows NT systems, first install the database software (Step 10), then follow step 8 and then this one. Following is the basic procedure:

- Log on using the same user that installed the R3SETUP tool.
- From the NT programs menu, select *SAP R3* (or *SAP R3 Setup for <SID>*) and then, in this case, select *SAP R3 Setup—Central & Database Instance.*
- At this time, the INSTGUI window will open, providing installation information as well as prompting the user for the required parameters such as the SAP system name (<sid>), the system number, RAM, locations of directories, and several others. Enter all appropriate parameters and click *Next* to continue the installation.

In the event of any error, the installation window will switch to the error log view, so that the error can be corrected and the installation restarted.

When the installation of the central instance is finished—which should not take more than 15 to 20 minutes without errors—on NT systems the installation continues with the building and loading of the database. There is no need to log off or exit the installation since the following steps are also performed with R3SETUP.

Installation on UNIX Systems The R3SETUP installation tool on UNIX systems must be executed logged as user *root,* although the tool is provided with *user switch* capability so that it is able to switch to user *<sid>adm* when it needs to.

The option of using the graphical installation frontend INSTGUI is also provided. To use the INSTGUI, make sure that the DISPLAY variable is set correctly, and start INSTGUI before starting R3SETUP.

The installation steps are:

- Change to the installation directory and run the installation program with the corresponding command file:

```
cd <INSTDIR>
./R3SETUP -f CENTRDB.R3S
```

- If using INSTGUI, the window will show the installation progress and information as well as prompt the user for the required parameters, such as the SAP system name (<sid>), the system number, RAM, locations of directories, and several others. Enter all appropriate parameters and click *Next* to continue the installation.

R3SETUP will perform several tasks such as creating the operating system users, groups and services; creating the directories; unpacking the files from the compressed CAR files on the CD and copying them to the appropriate target directories; and setting the right file and directory permissions. It also builds and loads the R/3 database. In the case of UNIX systems with ORACLE, the database software installation tool is called directly from R3SETUP.

In the event of any error, the installation window switches to the error log view, so that the error can be corrected and the installation restarted.

Step 10: Install Database Software

This step discusses the procedure for installing and configuring the database software. For instructive reasons, this step only deals with the Oracle database. The database *server* software is installed only on the host where the database will run. Other instances will only require the installation of *client* database software.

Oracle database software is installed using the *orainst* (*Oracle installer*) program. On UNIX systems, the *orainst* program is called directly from the R3SETUP installation, while on Windows NT it must be independently executed before the actual installation of the central instance.

In the case of UNIX systems, the R3SETUP program calls *orainst* and requests the mounting of the appropriate database CD; optionally you can manually install the Oracle software in a separate terminal and then proceed with the R/3 installation. Enter the requested entries and proceed with the installation. After the database software is installed—which should not take more than 20 minutes if no error occurs—the installation process is now ready for building and loading the database.

For Windows NT systems, the procedure for installing Oracle on the database and central instance server is as follows:

- Insert the Database Software CD (usually called RDBMS CD) in the CD-ROM drive.
- Using Windows Explorer, go to the directory

  ```
  <CD-DRIVE>:\NT\<ARCH>\WIN32\INSTALL
  ```

  (where <ARCH> is either I386 or ALPHA) and double-click on the file ORAINST.EXE to start the *Oracle Installer.*
- The installation program will prompt for a set of entries, where default values are chosen for the particular R/3 installations. Answer the questions, and once on the *Oracle8 Installation Options* window, select *Enterprise Edition* and press *OK* for the software to automatically install.

For some releases it is possible that you may need to install an additional database software patch. Refer to the installation manual for the release you are installing.

On Windows NT R/3 installations the next step would be to install the R3SETUP tool and then the central instance, then automatically proceed to step 11.

Step 11: Build and Load the Database

The building and loading of the database is performed using the R3SETUP installation program. When choosing a database and central instance installation, this step is automatically performed. Otherwise, R3SETUP must be called using the command file DATABASE.R3S.

The building process consists of creating the database structure (the tablespaces in the case of the Oracle database) and locating it in the file systems indicated during the installation or as specified in the command file CENTRDB.R3S. Once the structure has been generated, the installation program will fill up the database with the data included in the export CDs.

For this step the system will require the *export CDs* (usually two, but possibly more). If your server has more than one CD drive or if you are instructed during the installation of the central instance and database to copy the export CDs to a temporary location, the full process can be done without manual intervention.

If they were not specified previously, the R3SETUP program will request some parameters about the configuration of the server system and file locations.

The building, and especially the loading, of the database is the longest process of a SAP R/3 installation, and usually takes several hours.

After a successful loading of the database, R/3 could be started, although there are still some steps that should be followed before starting the application.

Step 12: Import ABAP Report Loads

When the database has been successfully loaded, the R3SETUP tool requests you to insert the CD corresponding to the ABAP report loads.

The ABAP report loads are pregenerated ABAP programs that speed the execution of those programs when they are first called from the R/3 system. The fact that these reports come in a separate CD is due to the fact that they are CPU dependent.

Do as requested by the installation program, inserting or mounting the CD-ROM; confirm the path and proceed with the installation.

Finishing Up

Once the ABAP load is complete and has successfully terminated, the installation program presents an additional step for *Updating MNLS Tables* that is needed in case you need to import languages other than the *Latin-1* type. If this is the case, then you must follow the corresponding manual and SAP notes for importing additional languages. This will require you to start the R/3 system and make some entries in the R/3 language tables.

Check in the SAP installation guides whether you need to perform additional corrections or modifications for your specific operating system.

Since there are some additional steps for completing the installation that have to be performed from within the R/3 system, the following section shows how to install the Windows SAPGUI so you can enter the system and perform those activities.

Installing a Presentation Server On a Windows PC

For logging on to the SAP system, you will at least need to install the presentation interface software, commonly the SAPGUI. The software can be found on the presentation CD that comes bundled in the software kit, or it can be downloaded from SAPnet.

Within the framework and as a result of the *Personalization project,* SAP strategy for the user and presentation interface has evolved toward a concept of a *platform-independent GUI* based on Java technology. However, for the sake and objective of this chapter only the installation of the traditional interface, SAPGUI, is introduced.

SAP R/3 supports several types of platforms for running the presentation software, such as all Windows (3.11, 95, 98, NT), Macintosh, OS/2, and Motif platforms. However, not all SAPGUI releases are supported on the 16-bit platforms (Windows 3.11) and not all additional components can run on non-Windows platforms. Current information can be found in R/3 note 66971.

The process of installing the SAPGUI is in constant change and technical evolution. So, for instance, for releases 3.0, 3.1, and 4.0B the basic installation program was SAPSETUP, which could be used for local and server installations.

However, this has changed in releases 4.5 and 4.6, with new options and procedures for installing and distributing the software, including the new programs SETUP, NETSETUP, and SAPADMIN:

- SETUP can be used for setting up an installation server as well as for performing local installations.
- NETSETUP is used for starting PCs connected to the network that call the installation program located on the installation server. Use NETSETUP for installing the *installation packages* that have been previously defined. These installation packages are collections of components to be installed. This program can be called from a command line, thus allowing installations to be performed automatically by inserting commands in the user's logon script. Later on, users can install or remove packages using the local SAPSETUP program.
- The SAPADMIN program then can be used for defining installation packages, as well as for installing a *NetInstall Service* and a *Service Installation Service* (SIS). The NetInstall Service is a Win-

dows NT service that is called by other programs during the installation, and that is used for executing statements that need administrator rights. A SIS can be installed in one or more computers in a Windows NT domain and is required for using the NetInstall Service.

The following simple guidelines are provided for a local installation of the SAPGUI using the SETUP program for a Windows 98 workstation:

- Insert the presentation CD into the CD drive and locate the program SETUP.EXE, commonly under the directory \GUI\WINDOWS\WIN32. Double-click on SETUP.EXE.
- After the welcome message, the system shows a dialog box for selecting a server or local installation, as shown in Fig. 3-5. Select local installation and proceed by clicking *Next.*
- The program now requests the destination folder for the installation. Specify the target directory and proceed by clicking *Next.*
- The next dialog box is for selecting the components to install. You can choose which components to install by clicking on the component groups, then on *Change option* or *Choose all,* and selecting or deselecting components. Figure 3-6 shows an example of this dialog box. Once the components have been selected, continue the installation by clicking *Next.*

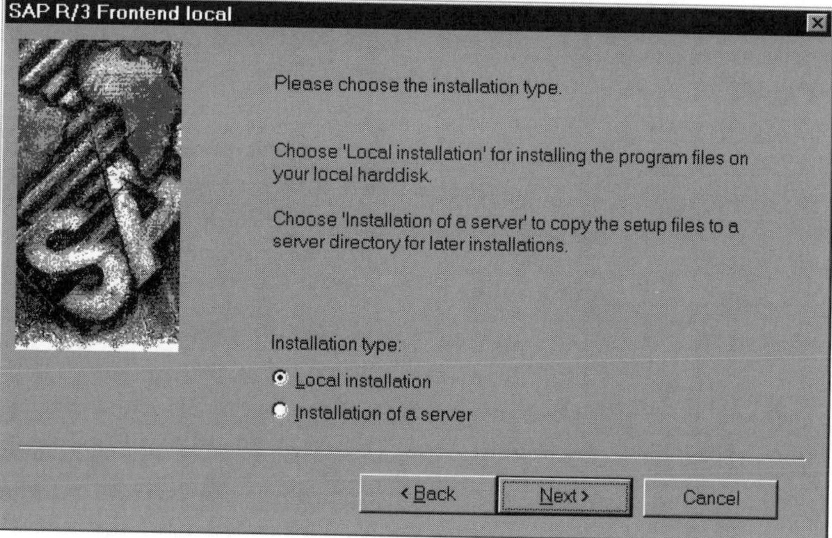

Figure 3-5 SAPGUI local installation.

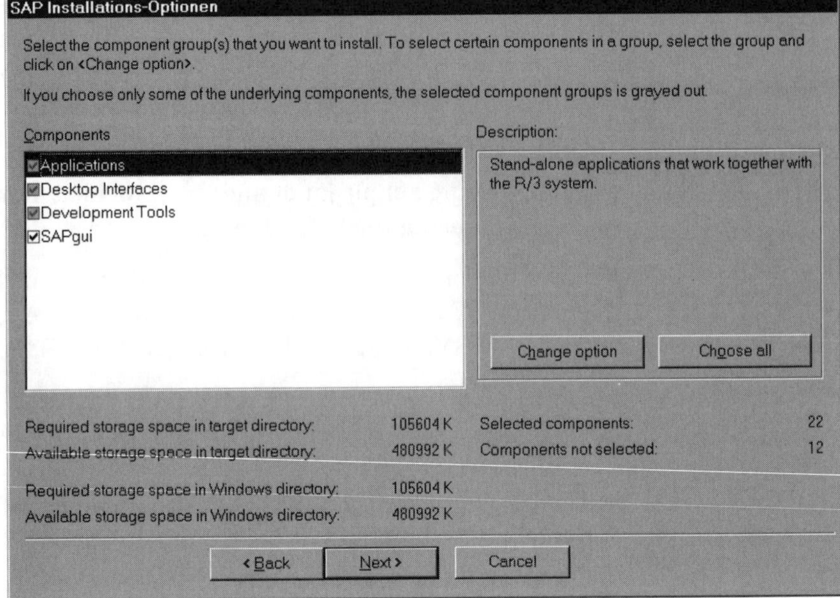

Figure 3-6 Sample dialog box for selecting components.

- The installation now asks for the language of the components to be installed. Most components are available only in English, German, or Japanese.
- The next dialog box asks for the SAPGUI working directory. Choose the path and click *Next* to continue the installation.
- The next entry requests the path to the documentation CD. Enter the drive letter of the CD or the path to the location of the documentation, and keep clicking *Next*.
- The installation requests the name of an application server, the system number, and the SAProuter string for one of your R/3 systems. You can always define additional SAPGUIs using the SAPicon or the SAPLOGON programs. Enter the requested information and proceed by clicking *Next*.
- The installation asks for the icon or program group in which to locate the SAP front end components to install.
- Once all parameters are entered, the installation requests a confirmation. To start the actual installation you must press *Install*.

The installation will finish after several minutes and will ask you to reboot your workstation for changes to take effect.

For other installation options, as well as the package components and ways to configure SAPAdmin for creating and managing packages, please refer to the manual *Installing Frontend Software for PCs.*

Postinstallation Steps

You are anxious to get your hands on the R/3 system, aren't you? Please be patient and read on for some brief explanations about the postinstallation steps, which form part of the complete standard installation.

Some of the most common tasks after a successful installation are as follows:

- The distribution and installation of additional application servers (dialog instances), which are discussed in the next chapter
- Entering the license
- Performing a full backup
- Setting up a printer
- Initializing the correction and transport system
- Installing the online documentation
- Copying clients, and so on

The following sections only discuss some of these tasks, since they are discussed later and in different sections and chapters of this book.

Licensing the Installation

Right after the completion of installation, SAP works using a temporary license that expires in four weeks. So, once installation is finished, you must fill out a license form and send it to SAP, which will send back to you definitive licensing information. Some of the information on that form must be obtained from the just-installed system with the use of the *saplicense* utility.

SAP licenses are handled with the *saplicense* program which resides in the runtime directory /usr/sap/<SID>/SYS/exe/run.

The *saplicense* program has the following options:

- *saplicense -temp,* installs a temporary license until you get your definitive license from SAP

- *saplicense -get,* gets the customer key needed to fill up the license request fax which much be sent to SAP
- *saplicense -check,* gives information about your current installed license
- *saplicense -install,* used when you get your definitive license key to install it permanently in the system
- *saplicense -help,* shows help information about the license

Starting and Stopping the SAP R/3 System

To start the R/3 system, log on at the operating system level using the *<sid>adm* (lowercase) user account which was created during installation. For example, if the SID was defined as DD1, then log in as UNIX user *dd1adm* and enter the password.

To start R/3 on UNIX systems, just execute the *startsap* command. For example:

```
dd1adm> startsap
```

The *startsap* command is really a UNIX *alias* (a symbolic name pointing to something else) that calls the needed start programs.

To stop the system, enter *stopsap* in the command line.

On Windows NT systems, you can start and stop R/3 from within the SAP Service Manager that is located on the NT *Programs* menu, within the *SAP R3* programs group.

The process of starting and stopping the system is explained in detail in the next chapter.

Performing a Full Backup

It should be mandatory to perform a full backup of the system right after finishing the installation, since nobody wants to waste two or three days' worth of effort to install the SAP system again.

If this is the very first backup, it is a good practice to use the operating system backup utilities or other supported backup software to save the whole server files, including the operating system. Before performing a backup, stop the SAP system to leave it in a consistent state.

After you perform this initial backup, you must define a backup strategy including the critical components of the SAP system, such as the database files and the redo logs. This is discussed in detail in Chap. 16.

Remote Connection to SAP

It is also mandatory to make a remote connection to SAP systems as soon as possible. In order to accomplish this, there are some procedures to follow including obtaining the physical connection, the official IP address, and installing and configuring the SAProuter program. Appendix A deals with these topics.

Optional Postinstallation Steps

Depending on the nature of the installation, some optional postinstallation steps may be performed. For example, if the users' language is not German or English, then the users' language may be imported into the system.

The SAP kit comes with a language files CD to import the needed language into the system. To do this, refer to the official SAP manual *R/3 Language Transport.* Do not forget to look up or request OSS notes about possible hints or problems when transporting languages.

Depending on the release, it might be necessary to install the R/3 support packages. The support packages are collections of corrections to R/3 programs and other repository objects. You will have to check the SAP notes to determine which package collections are required for your specific installation.

Further Guidelines for Productive Environments

The purpose of this section is to make the people in charge of technically implementing the system aware that installing the system is not the same thing as having it ready for productive day-to-day business work. There are certain aspects of the R/3 system that, from a technical and management point of view, must be carefully considered. Many of them apply to all installations, and others might not be necessary. All these points are discussed in more detail in different sections of this book.

These points are as follows:

- A backup and recovery strategy for R/3.
- Well-defined technical, functional, and development support lines for the users and developers of the system. This includes hardware and database vendors as well as SAP.

- Cleaning background jobs.
- Definition of daily or periodic tasks for the operation and support teams.
- Database administration.
- Printing strategy.
- System management procedures.
- Definition and setup of the CCMS operation modes and alerts.
- SAP R/3 monitoring (CCMS) and administration, including performance and tuning.
- Network monitoring and administration.
- Users and authorizations management.
- Preventive maintenance and EarlyWatch.
- External systems interfaces and batch input strategy.
- Upgrading the system: SAP, database, operating system.
- Hardware maintenance policy.
- Connection to SAP support servers.
- Implementation quality control.
- Disaster recovery strategy.

Considerations for Oracle VLDBs (Very Large Databases)

Follow the general considerations previously described in the section "Oracle File System Design Guidelines." As a brief reminder, remember that the redo logs have very high input/output activity and should be on different disks than the database data itself. Also, remember to place the data and index files for a tablespace on separate disks, which is standard in the R/3 installation.

However, when considering large databases, where additional tablespaces might be necessary, you may need to do some mixing and matching to place the data and index on different file systems.

The most intensive input/output tablespaces on the SAP system are PSAPSTABD, PSAPCLUD, and PSAPBTABD, as well as corresponding index tablespaces PSAPSTABI, PSAPCLUI, and PSAPBTABI. These tables contain most of the transactional data of users' daily work. At least try to place these three tablespaces on different disks.

The SAPDATA<N> file systems should be used exclusively for the tablespace data and index. Do not mix them with operating system files, swap space, or SAP runtime programs.

The SAPARCH file systems should also be located on a different disk. This file system should be sized properly to avoid the *archiver stuck* problem. This well-known problem occurs if the saparch file system becomes full and the redo log files can't be archived. If this event happens to you, the SAP system becomes inactive, and the update process seems to be in a suspended state.

The size of transaction log files (redo log files) can positively affect the performance. For instance, bigger sizes increase performance but, as a drawback, slow down database startup/shutdown procedures, especially in recover situations. Also, if you lose one redo log, more data is lost. SAP standard size is 20 MB, but you could change that value to 50 MB or even 100 MB. To do that, follow the instructions from the Oracle manuals or request specific instructions from a SAP expert on how to proceed.

!

WARNING! *Before performing any modification on the database, make sure you have a reliable backup and you know what you are doing.*

Increase the capacity of the temporary tablespace, PSAPTEMP. This procedure should be done when first installing the system. When database size exceeds 50 GB, try to increase the size to at least 1 GB. For increasing the size of either the PSAPTEMP or SYSTEM tablespaces, look up the SAPnet notes, since these tablespaces have special instructions for these procedures.

In the creation of additional rollback segments, the SAP rule is that each rollback segment be able to hold the data of about four work processes. If you plan to have more than 40 work processes or if you want to allow the system to share more rollback segments among the work processes, create additional rollback segments. If you do, do not forget to increase the size of the PSAPROLL tablespace.

Another way to increase performance and possibly reduce the time needed for future reorganization is to use the table-stripping procedure. *Table stripping* means to separate large tables from their actual tablespaces and turn them into new tablespaces.

The *sapdba* program includes utilities to perform this without the need to do it manually. Refer to Chap. 14 for more information.

Finally, consider the EarlyWatch service or the Oracle hotline to help you when configuring the necessary Oracle database parameters according to your hardware installation (amount of memory, type and number of processors, version, etc.).

CHAPTER 4

Distributing R/3 Systems

Distribution, in a general sense, means sharing something among several individuals. In SAP R/3 systems, there are many processes, services, printers, users, and so forth. Since SAP R/3 is based upon a client/server software concept, distributing the SAP R/3 system means sharing the provided services among the clients and the servers to optimize the performance and the availability and balancing the load of the system.

This chapter covers the practical aspects of the client/server components of the SAP R/3 system and the benefits of using this architecture. It deals with such issues as identifying which parts of the system can be distributed and how to plan such distribution. It also describes the main factors to consider when setting up the different parts of R/3: sizing, network, load balancing, and availability.

The following sections describe other important and practical details of the R/3 system distribution, for instance, the SAP instance profiles, the operating system directory structure, the process of starting and stopping the system, and which programs you can find under the runtime directory.

When setting up the system, there are details that change depending upon whether a central system or a distributed system is built. Here, you find such things as setting up the central system log (the main repository for R/3 problem and error messages) and awareness of the buffer synchronization (so that users don't say, I can see this data from this system and cannot see it from the other one).

SAP Services Distribution and the Client/Server Architecture

For small installations in terms of number of users (this is relative, but say less than 100), you might not have more than one computer server running your SAP applications. In that case, every service is running in the central system: database, central instance application server, background services, and so forth. The only distributed component is the presentation server (SAPGUI) running on a Windows PC or similar. With such installations, a factor to consider making some kind of distribution is the printing strategy, which could be handed over to the presentation servers (normally Windows PCs) using some type of front end printing.

Centralized SAP Installations

In the case of centralized installations, the system layout looks like the picture shown in Fig. 4-1. If the server is powerful enough, this can be a suitable installation for larger SAP user populations. Moreover, this can be a good fit for starting the R/3 implementation, since the fact that it is a centralized configuration does not mean it cannot scale up to meet the growing demands of the system.

Since the central server in centralized SAP systems configurations is in charge of every R/3 service, you could think of distributing the time among services. Time can be distributed among some work processes such as the dialog and the background by means of operation modes. *Operation modes* are a way of defining how many processes will run during a certain period of time and making the system automatically switch the type of work processes at another period of time. Information on how to set up operation modes is given in the CCMS in Chap. 11, under the section entitled "Working with Operation Modes."

A single centralized instance contains a set of services that are started and stopped together. Commonly, right from a new installation, the instance name is DVEBMGS00 (notice the letters correspond to the different work processes and the last two numbers, 00, are the SAP system number).

When the computer shares these services, the database is usually called the central instance, or database server instance. However, the database could also be installed independently on another computer. Thus, a central instance configuration consists of an application server (dialog, update, background, spool, and enqueue services), a message server, a gateway, and the database system. This is a common configuration for development and quality assurance systems, as well as small productive sites.

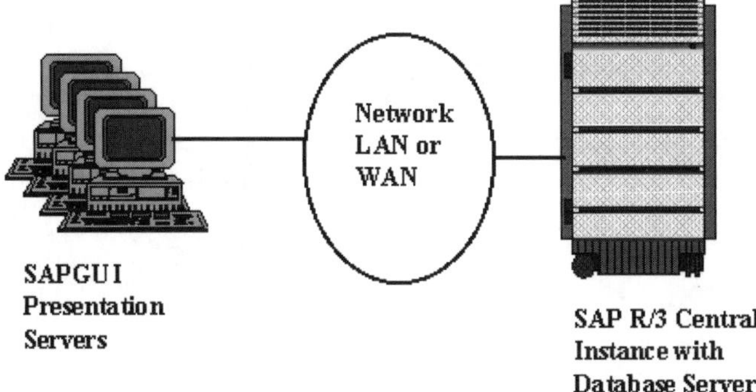

Figure 4-1 Centralized SAP R/3 system.

Notice, however, that the concept of central instance is identified with the R/3 application server typically running the enqueue service and the message server.

The fact that this is a centralized installation does not mean that it is not a client/server from a software point of view and that it would not scale just as well.

The advantages of this type of centralized installation compared to a distributed one are as follows:

- Less management load for installing and administering the system
- Less hardware maintenance
- Less network load

The disadvantages are

- No possibility to distribute SAP services. They all reside on the same central server.
- Performance degradation because the CPU has to share its resources among database services and SAP work processes.
- Less availability—if the server goes down, everything goes down.

This chapter concentrates on bigger installations requiring more than one R/3 server to perform their tasks. From a hardware point of view, additional servers (application servers) are configured to perform the R/3 application logic on behalf of, or cooperating with, the central system. This kind of configuration is known as three-tier client/server systems, as depicted in the example shown in Fig. 4-2.

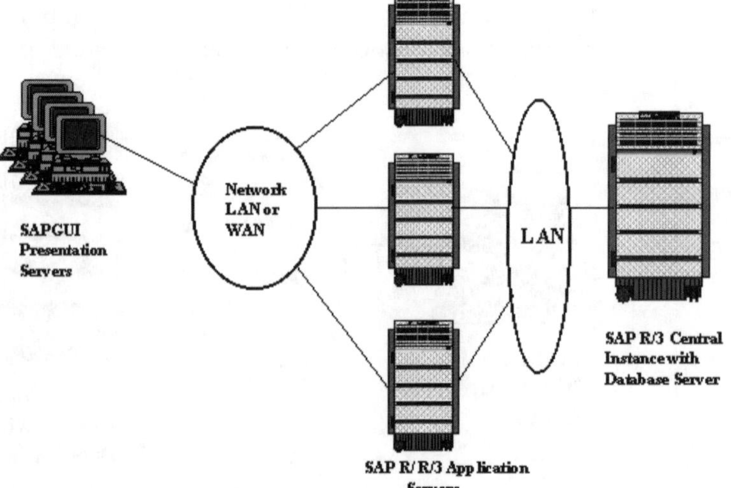

Figure 4-2 Distributed client/server SAP R/3 system.

Factors for Distributing SAP

The factors to consider when planning the distribution of the R/3 system among several servers are as follows:

- *Sizing* (applications modules deployed, number of users) and *expected systems performance.*
- *SAP services.* Some planning is necessary about where to place background, dialog, spooling, message server, update, and so on, and also, how many.
- *SAP profiles.* In distributed configurations, profiles must be shared among the application servers.
- *Load balancing.* Some of the R/3 services can be configured to automatically balance the load on the system.
- *File and program locations.* In distributed configurations, you have two options about where to place the runtime programs: either on the local disks or shared through NFS in UNIX systems. There is also the option to set a mixed environment: some servers with local programs and some other mounting those directories over the network. R/3 instances on Windows NT systems share the same copy of executables located on the *<hostname>\sapmnt* directory, which resides on the central NT host.
- *Backup and recovery strategy.* These can differ slightly from central configurations in the sense that all servers must have a procedure to recover in case of disasters or data loss.
- *Printing strategy.* As you will find in Chap. 14, printing is an issue not to be underconsidered in SAP installations. With several servers there are more available options to define a better printing strategy.
- *System monitoring and maintenance.* Additional work and procedures must exist to manage and monitor the additional servers.
- *Network configuration and monitoring.* Minimizing the communication delays can be a crucial issue for distributed SAP servers. SAP R/3 is a client/server application that requires the TCP/IP transport protocol for the communication between the SAP servers. Remember that the network is one of the critical elements in client/server computing.
- *Maintenance and operation.* Even if the group of the SAP database server and associated application servers can be monitored from a single system, there is more maintenance and system management when the R/3 system is distributed.

The SAP Client/Server Architecture: Advantages and Disadvantages

As stated previously in the overviews of Chaps. 1 and 2, the SAP client/server architecture can consist of several application servers, from a software point of view. These servers can run distributed on separate computers (from a hardware point of view).

Between the SAP application servers of a SAP system, there are client/server relationships in which a server performs tasks for other servers or functions as a client of the same servers. For example, a server can be running the message server for the rest of the system, but at the same time be a client of the update service which is provided by a different server. Presentation servers (normally PCs) are clients of the application servers, and these, in turn, are clients of the database server. This is what forms the client/server architecture.

The advantages of a distributed client/server architecture are as follows:

- Services with intensive input/output demands can run separately on different computers without affecting the performance of the central functions.
- Interactive users load balancing can be achieved.
- There is higher system availability and performance.
- There is high scalability adding additional servers.
- There is greater flexibility. There are many options available depending on the particular needs of an installation.

Disadvantages of these architectures are

- There are higher network loads due to increased data communication exchange among servers.
- Management and maintenance of a distributed system is more complex.
- Service configuration and distribution is not a trivial task.

SAP Servers

The SAP R/3 system is made up of a group of servers and a group of services. Depending on the function they perform, there are three types of servers:

- *Database server.* Basically contains the database engine and associated processes. The database layer contains the database system used by all servers. Since all database systems used by R/3 support remote SQL, it can run separately from the rest of the SAP system. Notice that what distinguishes a SAP system ID (SID or SAPSID) one from another is the unique database for each system.
- *Application servers.* Run the SAP services. The application server layer contains a SAP kernel which can run ABAP programs. It consists of a dispatcher task and a group of work processes. The dispatcher allocates the resources needed to perform the request to its work processes, which carry the request out. Refer to the section entitled "The Dispatcher Process" in Chap. 2 for more information.

  Here, we should point out the difference between an application server and a SAP instance. The concept of a SAP instance was introduced in Chap. 2. The distinction is made on the basis of the hardware or software concept of client/server computing. From a hardware point of view, an application server denotes a computer running application services, while from the software point of view it denotes a group of processes running under the same parameters, with just one dispatcher and a shared common memory pool. This means that a SAP instance is conceptually the same as an application server from the software point of view. But remember that if the server computer has enough memory and CPU power, it could have room for several SAP instances. Nevertheless, if the server computer running the application services has just one SAP instance (which is very common), then server computer = application server = SAP instance.
- *Presentation servers.* Run the SAP front-end interface. The presentation server layer is responsible for displaying the SAP user interface, sending outputs to the user, and receiving the user input to be sent to the application layer of the system.

SAP Services

Service types are the server processes in charge of providing and executing the system tasks. The types of services correspond to the work processes types as described in Chap. 2. Having specialized services makes it possible to support the distribution of the workload by the R/3 system components.

As a brief summary and reminder of what was explained in Chap. 2, the service types are as follows:

- *Dialog.* Perform the dialog steps or interactive processing. With the use of the CCMS operation modes, these services can automatically switch to background processing services or other services types. This is very useful when dividing daily and nightly workloads.
- *Background.* Execute programs submitted for background processing. These services can switch modes with the dialog services.
- *Update.* Execute database changes when requested by dialog or background. There are update types 1 (U1 or time-critical) and 2 (U2 or noncritical).
- *Spool.* Format the data for printing and pass the print job to the host spooler system.
- *Enqueue.* Allows multiple application servers to synchronize their access to the database, maintaining consistency. It's the lock management system service.
- *Message service.* Routes messages between application servers. Since version 3.0 also uses it for licensing, there is only one message server per SAP system.
- *Gateway.* Implements the CPIC protocol.

Depending on the distribution of the SAP servers, the services may be located on the same or different computers.

Guidelines for Distributed Configurations with the R/3 System

As with most big computing applications there is no formula which could result in a perfect setup of the system distribution right from the start. The reasons are that systems workload is not constant and that software upgrades, user population growth, and some type of technical changes always take place. SAP R/3 is no exception, and therefore the correct distribution is a matter of knowing the factors that influence the system and daily monitoring to watch the most relevant figures and take corresponding actions.

A distributed SAP R/3 system is a group consisting of a database server and several application servers. At the same time, a distributed SAP R/3 system is a group of server processes (services).

The following are some guidelines which can help you to plan the best approach for your R/3 system distribution. Additional information can be found in the subsequent sections of this chapter.

1. The database server is a critical point in the whole configuration: without database there is no SAP. The underlying database engine processes are the ones which ultimately access the data for reading, updating, inserting, or deleting it. This means that this server supports the biggest input/output and can become a real bottleneck for the whole system. Depending on the particular sizing and needs of each installation, there are a few things to take into consideration:
   - Keep users from logging in to this system. You can do this by means of network configuration, a load-balancing setup, or by removing the dialog processes. Leave one or two dialog processes for administrative purposes.
   - When installing, plan the file system layout carefully, both for security and performance reasons. If your system requires a very high throughput, think of placing the database files over several different volumes and sharing the load of the disk controllers carefully.
   - The database server can be installed in a completely separate system, so it would not contain any of the SAP-provided services. The CPU then would not have to share its resources between the database and the SAP work processes.
2. The network load between the database server and the application services can become quite high. Size your network accordingly using high-speed connections, for example, FDDI, ATM, and FC, as supported by your particular hardware. Incorrect network configuration, such as connecting an application server to the database server through the access network (the same used for users' connections), causes much higher response times on that application server, mainly due to a higher database access time. This provokes an incorrect and unbalanced load distribution.
3. Common files location. When R/3 services are distributed among several application servers there is at least a couple of shared directories: one for the instances profiles (/sapmnt/<SID>/profile) and another one for the central system log on UNIX systems (/sapmnt/<SID>/global). Additionally, you have to decide whether to share the executables runtime directory /sapmnt/<SID>/exe. Very often this directory is shared by means of NFS (network file

system). The advantages and disadvantages of having this directory local or network-shared is discussed in a later section of this chapter. This does not apply to Windows NT systems.

4. Service distribution.
   - Presentation services should be run only on PCs or dedicated workstations.
   - Dialog services should be moved out of the database server and placed on the specialized dialog servers. Watch the number of available *waiting* dialog processes. If you have too few, users won't be able to log on.
   - Background processes. At the very beginning of an R/3 project you don't actually know how much background job load the system will have. When starting to monitor in the productive phases, you will be able to adjust the number and placement of the needed background work processes. If might even be necessary to leave a whole application server as a specialized background server. In any case, you should be aware and use the CCMS operation modes. With the configuration of the operation modes the system can automatically switch the work process type to background during a defined period of time. For example, it is very common to make some of the dialog work processes switch to background during the night. In periods of light interactive dialog load, you may think of placing some background processes in the database server, since they will be processed faster there.
   - The update server should be as close to the database server as possible. If the database server also includes the central instance, which is very common, leave the update server there.
   - The message server plays an important role both for application server communication and load balancing. Think of placing this service in an application server, since it will also be called by the presentation service interface of the end users.
5. Load balancing. End users should connect to the SAP R/3 system as transparently as possible in terms of which physical application server they log on to. With the help of the message server and the SAPlogon utility, you can define instances to which the users can connect. This facility is very useful both for contingency and for a better utilization of common memory buffers. For example, if one server goes down, users can still connect to the R/3 system.
6. Printing strategy. In a distributed system, an incorrect printing strategy can turn your R/3 average response times into miserable

figures if not planned correctly. In SAP systems, you should distinguish between the spool work process, in charge of formatting and sending the printing jobs to the host spooler, and the host spooler itself. Chapter 14 includes recommendations for planning the printing strategy, but consider having a dedicated server for critical print jobs. The same physical printer can be defined with different logical names, each having a different host spooler, for example. Also, you can define your PC locally attached printer to the SAP spool system. Since release 4.0, the R/3 system also includes support for defining *spool servers* and *logical servers,* making possible the definition and automation of load balancing for printing.

7. Backup strategy. Backup is of course a very essential part of any system implementation strategy. With distributed R/3, there are only slight differences in backup strategies for single or multiple server systems. The most important data to be backed up is the database, which is unique. There is, of course, the SAP and database runtime environment to backup. The strategy must define the procedure for recovering an application server if there is any kind of physical error. Considering that most instance data files are temporary, you should only worry about recovering the operating system and the directory structure for the instance. To be even safer, consider putting some type of disk mirroring on the application servers, which usually do not need much disk space.
8. Number of SAP instances per host. Finally, you could further distribute the services by having additional instances in a single computer server, provided you have enough CPU power and main memory. The benefits of this is that logon balancing is easier, memory can be better used, and there is more choice for service distribution. The drawbacks are that you don't have a unique SAP system number, you have to change some instance parameters, such as the central logging, and you have to maintain additional instance profiles. Additionally, if the server goes down, all the instances will go down as well.

Directory Structure of R/3 Systems

There are several directories containing the files and programs that make up the R/3 systems and that are required for normal execution and operation. The installation process automatically creates these directories, although it is possible to define them manually. Figure 4-3 shows a directory structure under UNIX and Fig. 4-4 shows the same concept under Windows NT on a global host. On dialog instances there is a local path and a global shared path. Both operating systems conceptually have the same directories, although they are implemented differently.

For reasons of simplicity, directories are referred to using the slash (/), which is used in UNIX systems. For Windows NT systems, a backslash (\) is used.

The main directories under R/3 systems are:

- *The physical parent directory of the whole SAP application* (*/usr/sap*). Under this directory you will find the following directories.
- *The transport directory* (*/usr/sap/trans*). The transport directory is used for transporting objects and customizing settings between R/3 systems. This is a global directory within an R/3 network that must be accessible to all systems of the network. Physically, it will be located in a *global transport host* (which can be the production central instance, the development system, or any other). UNIX systems implement the sharing of the transport directory using NFS, while on Windows NT sharing is implemented by the definition of the alias SAPTRANSHOST that is assigned to the transport host. More information on this topic can be found in Chap. 6.
- *The SAP system parent directory, <SID>, for example, /usr/sap/C12.* If more than one SAP system is installed and different SIDs were installed in the same server, then you would have additional directories below /usr/sap, each one with specific instance details.

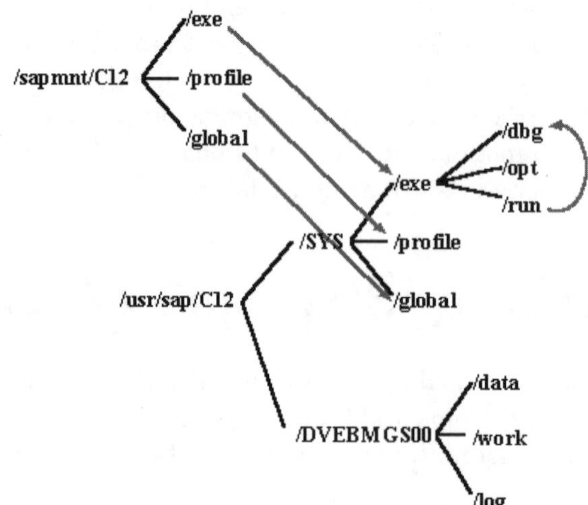

Figure 4-3 SAP directory structure under UNIX.

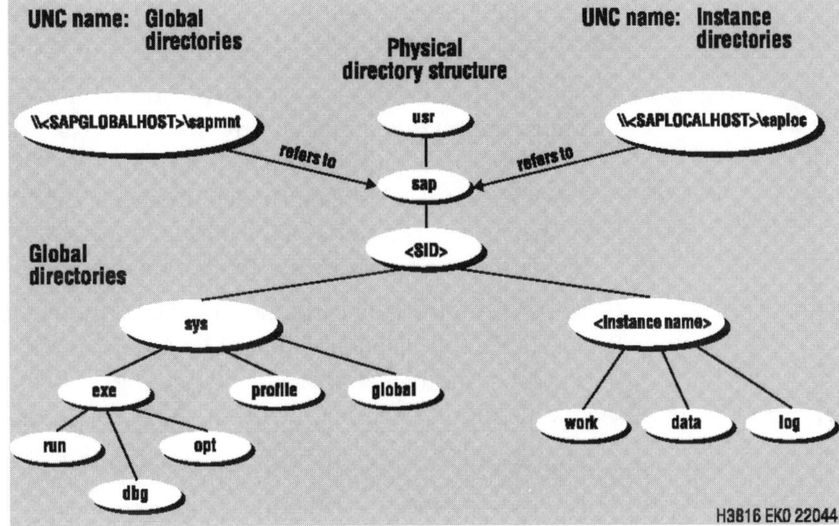

Figure 4-4
R/3 directory structure under Windows NT. (*Copyright SAP AG.*)

Beneath /usr/sap/<SID> you have at least two branches:

1. /SYS directory, containing common and global SAP system files. Below you get the profile, global, and exe directories.
2. <INSTANCE_NAME> directory, (DVEBMGS00 in the preceding example) containing instance-specific directories: data, log, and work. For dialog instances, common names are D00, D01, and so on.

- The SAP mount directory /sapmnt is a directory structure useful for sharing the common files with all systems belonging to the same group. It's a useful method for easily exporting or sharing the directories to other instances. Below the /sapmnt directory, there is also the <SID> which at the same time contains the exe, profile, and global directories which are links (UNIX soft links) to the physical directories under /usr/sap/<SID>/SYS/ as shown in the preceding figure. Windows NT implements this directory structure by sharing the *sapmnt* directory, which is then referred to using the path \\SAPGLOBALHOST\sapmnt.
- There are also directories for the SAP system belonging to the database engine. In the case of Oracle, the whole database system has the /oracle directory as the root for the rest of the needed files. Under the /oracle directory, there are usually two subdirectories: stage, used for database installations and upgrades; and <SID>, for example /oracle/C12, under which the whole database runtime and data files are located.

Let's get a closer look at the SAP final directories. First the system directories:

- The *exe* directory contains all SAP runtime programs and usually additional installed add-on programs (for example, the RFC, CPIC, or SAPcomm libraries). The directory includes three additional subdirectories: opt, where optimized programs might reside; dbg, where programs can run under symbolic debuggers; and run, where the actual runtime programs (the R/3 kernel) are located.
- The *global* directory contains global or common data managed by the SAP application and shared by all instances, for example, the central system log and the batch jobs log.
- The *profile* directory contains the instance profiles: startup profiles, default profiles, and instance-specific profiles.

The specific instance directories contain mostly temporary data files, which are normally deleted (overwritten) when the SAP instance is restarted. There are some exceptions, such as the local system log (which has some storage limit values indicating when to start a new one). The directories are as follows:

- The *data* directory contains mostly virtual storage data for the instance, including the user contexts and roll areas.
- The *log* directory contains all the log entries generated by the instance, such as the local system log. Do not confuse the log and work directories when troubleshooting the system.
- The *work* directory holds all the error and trace information for the instance processes. Error messages and core dumps are usually left at this location. This directory is very useful for debugging or troubleshooting the system, since it contains the instance startup and shutdown log files and all the work processes log files. These log files are preceded by the dev_ prefix. For example, dev_disp is the log file containing the SAP dispatcher messages. You can also see these files from the CCMS monitors.

Kernel Directory: What Do These Programs Do?

As previously stated, in R/3 systems the standard kernel or runtime directory is /usr/sap/<SID>/SYS/exe/run. Technical people have a tendency to want to know exactly what these program files do.

Depending on the specific installation and/or operating system and database, you might find some more program files or even different ones.

Most of the program files in the executables directory are directly used by the SAP processes, by the database administration utilities, or by the installation programs. Some of those programs can be very useful even when the SAP system is down. However, most of them cannot be called directly and will display an error message in your terminal.

WARNING! *Calling directly and using some of these programs can cause severe errors in the system. Do not use them without first checking with the SAP hotline or the SAPnet. The following list is intended for informative purposes only.*

A brief description of what some of the files are for follows:

- *alxxdump.* A test and debugging tool which interfaces with the system alert area. Must be called with the instance profile as parameter and takes you to line-command mode where you can see available options issuing the help command.
- *CAR.* SAP compress and decompress file utility. This may be used manually to extract SAP files from compressed files and is used by the R3INST and the R3SETUP programs.
- *brarchive.* Database utility to perform operations (backup, copy, deletion) of the Oracle offline redo log files (known as archive files). It's an option called from within sapdba, the database administration utility for Oracle. For all sapdba-related files, you can find extensive information in Chap. 14.
- *brbackup.* Database utility to perform online and offline backups with Oracle, called from sapdba.
- *brconnect.* Database utility programs to test the status of the database: up, down, connected, and so on. It's used transparently from sapdba.
- *brrestore.* sapdba utility to restore the database.
- *cleanipc.* Can be used to show or delete SAP IPC (interprocess communication) objects on UNIX systems.
- *coupld* and *codnld*. The transceiver programs for upload (*coupld*) and download (*codnld*) that are needed for receiving data from and sending data to external devices using the PDC interface.
- *coirsrv (only NT).* A program that is used for installing the transceiver modules as NT services.

- *dipngtab.* Used by the installation or upgrade programs for managing generation and activation of tables.
- *disp+work.* Main SAP dispatcher program, called from the sapstart program, which runs as a daemon process and parent of all associated work processes.
- *dpmon.* An interesting utility to display the dispatcher queue process monitor. This can be very useful on those rare occasions when R/3 seems to be in a hanging state.
- *enqt.* A program to display enqueue table entries used by different programs.
- *esmon.* A SAP monitoring program for the extended memory segments used by the SAP processes.
- *estst.* A test program used to display the extended memory segments of the system.
- *evtd.* A utility to test SAP system events.
- *frontend.lst, instance.lst.* Files with the extension lst contain lists of files in a tabular form. These files are used by the sapcpe program to know which of them must be synchronized or updated when the executables directory resides locally in the system, but depends on a central location.
- *gwmon* and all programs starting with gw handle and monitor the SAP gateway server.
- *gwhost.* A program used by the SAP gateway for establishing communication with external systems (SNA and CICS)
- *gwims.* A program used by the SAP gateway for establishing communication with external systems (IMS)
- *gwrd.* The SAP central gateway process
- *initSID.sap.* A template for creating a SAP backup profile. You have to edit it according to your backup needs, change the name of the file to be your own SID, and copy it to the /oracle/<SID>/dbs directory.
- *ipclimits.* This utility displays the maximum number of SAP IPC objects available in the system on UNIX systems.
- *lgtst.* With this utility, administrators can check the connection to the message server. The syntax is *lgtst -H <hostname> -S <message server service name>*, for example:

```
lgst -H copi01 -S sapmsTT1
```

- *memlimits.* A program used to test and tune memory values for the configuration of the extended memory options from version 3.0.
- *mkszip (on Windows NT, since release 4.0).* A program that can be used for backup compression.
- *mlsomadm.* Controls the storage of the logon data for the R/3 system in a coded configuration profile. This is necessary to be able to receive Internet messages in SAPoffice.
- *mlsomail.* Controls the receiving of Internet messages in SAPoffice.
- *mlsopop3.* This program is needed if you want to make an installation of a POP3 (Post Office Protocol version 3) server. Messages from the SAPoffice inbox can then be loaded onto a local storage medium of a POP3 client and be processed there locally. Messages from the POP3 client are sent to SAPoffice via SMTP (Simple Mail Transfer Protocol).
- *mlunxsnd.* Controls the sending of Internet messages from SAPoffice. The messages are passed on to the UNIX mailing program sendmail.
- *msg_server.* The message server. Refer to the "Message Server" section in Chap. 2.
- *msstats (Windows NT/SQL Server).* A program used for collecting statistics and monitoring the Microsoft SQL Server database.
- *niping.* A program to test the connection between SAP hosts with the saprouter program.
- *ntscmgr (Windows NT).* The utility that can be used for handling NT services. Additional programs for setting environment variables and registering keys and commands available for NT are *ntenv2reg, ntreg2cmd,* and *ntreg2env.*
- *R3check.* Useful for checking the consistency of the actions which will be performed by the R3trans utility without actually performing it. The syntax is *R3check <options><control_file>.*
- *R3load.* A program used mainly within installation, upgrade, or system copy utilities for loading R/3 data into the database.
- *R3trans.* R/3 transport program. It was the main program for transport until it was refined in the tp program. It is called by the tp and can perform special actions such as copying clients at the operating system level, performing logical backups, and more. For more information on R3trans, refer to Chap. 6.

- *rfcoscol.* The program used for collecting statistics remotely. It is commonly used in installations with standalone database servers.
- *rfc-ldap (only Windows NT).* The SAP RFC-LDAP (*Lightweight Directory Access Protocol*) gateway.
- *rfcexec.* Can be used for starting RFC server programs and for calling external programs using RFC.
- *rslgcoll.* The system log collector. All programs starting with rslg manage diverse aspects of the log collection.
- *rslgview.* A utility program that allows users to view the system log messages from UNIX. When this command is issued it prompts with a ? sign. At the prompt, type an *h* for *help* on available commands. The syntax is *rslgview pf=profile.*
- *rslgsend.* System log sender.
- *rstrana* and other programs starting with *rstr.* A collection of diverse utilities for tracing, analyzing, and displaying system events.
- *rstsmain.* A program which allows the display and management of TemSe objects (temporary sequential objects) from UNIX.
- *rspomain* and all programs starting with *rspo.* Allow the display and management of spool requests in the SAP system.
- *sapcpe.* The program which copies SAP executables from a central directory to a local-run directory with the purpose of synchronizing versions and having all systems with the same up-to-date versions of programs. It's called by the SAPSTART program.
- *sapdba.* SAP database administration utility for the Oracle and Informix databases.
- *sapevt.* SAP event trigger program. It's used to send events to the background job scheduler for the release and execution of batch jobs.
- *sapftp* is an ftp client that can be called from R/3 using RFCs.
- *sapinstance.* Used to create the necessary files and directory for a SAP instance.
- *saplicense.* SAP licensing program. Administrators must use it to obtain the customer key and later enter the official SAP license when receiving the license key from SAP.
- *sapntchk and sapwntchk.* Programs that can be used for checking configuration problems under Windows NT, including the verification of important profile parameters, hardware configuration, paging, host files, and many others. (Refer to R/3 note 65761.)

- *sapntkill.* Can be used for "killing" Windows NT processes.
- *sapntstartb.* The SAP Service used in Windows NT environment. As of release 4.5B it has been replaced by *sapstartsrv,* which is the SAP Service with DCOM interface.
- *saposcol.* The SAP operating system collector program, which sends all relevant parameters to the R/3 database for monitoring and analyzing.
- *sappad.* The SAP editor for configuration files located on the operating system.
- *saproot.* Program that creates the SAP directory structure.
- *sappfpar.* Used to test and calculate certain profile parameter values to better tune the memory needs of the system.
- *saprouter.* Program that acts as a firewall for managing the access from local R/3 systems to SAP support servers and the SAPnet, and that can also be used for managing the connections in R/3 networks. Refer to the section entitled "SAProuter" in Appendix A.
- *sapsecin (as of release 4.5).* The initialization program for the SAP Security Library.
- *sapsrvkil.* A program that is used for stopping (killing) SAP processes. It is called from the *stopsap* program.
- *sapstart.* SAP startup and shutdown program, which calls the instances start profiles. It's called from the SAP shell scripts files and other parts of the SAP system.
- *sapxpg.* Utility to start external programs from R/3.
- *sdtextD.dba.* sapdba help text in German.
- *sdtextE.dba.* sapdba help text in English.
- *showipc.* A program used for displaying the current SAP IPC objects in UNIX systems.
- *sservmgr (Windows NT).* The SAP Services Manager. It is used for starting and stopping all R/3 services.
- *ssfrfc.* Part of the SAP Security library.
- *startdb.* Shell script to start the Oracle database.
- *startsap.* A program used for starting the SAP system processes.
- *stopdb.* Script to stop the Oracle database. It's called from the *stopsap* script and other programs (such as R3trans, sapdba, or from within R/3) when requested to stop the full system.

- *stopsap.* A program used to stop the SAP system. It is usually called from other programs or shell scripts, or from the Service Manager (Windows NT).
- *tp.* Transport control program. It's used to perform transport functions at the operating system level. Chapter 6 contains more information.

Other programs in the executable directories are used for diverse debugging and testing options from different SAP processes or are used for checking the interface with the operating system, memory, and so forth.

Profiles

A *profile* in the SAP system is an operating system file containing parameters and configuration information of an instance. Since a SAP system might contain from one to several instances, many profiles may also exist. Individual setup parameters can be customized to the requirements of each instance.

The profiles are an essential part of technical and basis settings of the system, and the values they contain play the most important role when tuning the system.

The profiles are used when starting and stopping the system since they are in charge of allocating or deallocating the necessary resources as specified in the profile parameters.

These individual parameters let you customize the following:

- The runtime environment of the instance (resources such as main memory size, shared memory, roll size)
- Which services are available for the instance (which work processes and how many)
- Where other services are located (database host, message server, etc.)

The profile files are located under the directory /usr/sap/<SID>/SYS/profile (logically should point to the directory /sapmnt/<SID>/profile) which is shared by all application servers belonging to the same SAP system (same SID).

These profile files are text files which are structured in the following ways:

The comment lines are proceeded by a # sign. For example:

 # Parameters corresponding to dispatcher functions.

There are lines with parameter value with the syntax

parameter = value.

For example, the number of background work processes running in this instance is *rdisp / wp_no_btc=4.*

Usually, parameters belonging to a group of logically related functions are prefixed by a common root (in the preceding example, the *rdisp /* prefix controls the group of dispatcher parameters within an instance).

All host computers in an R/3 system can access these profiles. It is possible for several R/3 instances to use a single profile simultaneously. Separate profiles are not required for each R/3 instance.

Profiles can be edited and maintained manually using the *sappad* editor, which can be very useful if the system cannot start because of some error in parameters. However, it is strongly recommended that all profile maintenance be performed from within R/3 using the transaction RZ10 (*Edit Profiles*), which is part of the Computer Center Management System (CCMS).

An edited profile is not active (its values are not considered by the system) until the corresponding instance is restarted.

Profile Types

There are several types of profiles available on the SAP R/3 system for correct setup and configuration. These profiles are as follows:

- The *start profile,* which defines the R/3 services to start. There might be as many start profiles as instances.
- The *default profile,* which acts as a common configuration of profile values for instances taking part of the SAP system. There is only one default profile in a SAP system.
- The *instance profile,* which contains specific instance parameter values. There might be as many as the number of instances.

All the SAP profiles are located under a common directory, /usr/sap/<SID>/SYS/profile, shared by all instances belonging to the same SID.

Before continuing with the profile types there are a couple of interesting topics common to profiles: how the variables are handled in the profiles and what the actual value assigned to a SAP parameter is, considering that it can either be in the default profile, the instance profile, or no profile.

Variables Substitution In the Profiles. The SAP profiles include some syntax rules used when substituting parameter values using variables. These rules are very similar to the ones used in normal shell script commands.

The parameter values in the profiles can include the following variables:

- *$(parameter_name)* at runtime is substituted by the value of the parameter specified in parentheses. For example:

  ```
  global_dir_param = '/usr/sap/DD1/SYS/global'
  syslog_param = $(global_dir_param)/SLOGJ
  ```

  Therefore, syslog_param = /usr/sap/DD1/SYS/global/SLOGJ

- *$$* is replaced by the SAP system number. For example:

  `rslg/collect_daemon/talk_port = 13$$` and the SAP system number is 00, then
  `rslg/collect_daemon/talk_port = 1300`

The profiles might also include some *local substitute variables.* These variables only have an effect within the profiles and are not used by the SAP programs. The names of the local variables always begin with an underscore (_) sign and are mainly used for setting other parameter values. For example, if _EXEDIR = /usr/sap/DD1/SYS/exe/run and myparam = _EXEDIR, then myparam = /usr/sap/DD1/SYS/exe/run.

The Values of the Profile Parameters. The parameter values that influence the way the R/3 system allocates resources or services can be set either in the default profile, in the instances profiles, in both at the same time, or in none of them.

The SAP profile parameters are read by the startup program to assign the needed resources to the SAP processes. The parameter values are set by following these rules:

- If a specific parameter appears in the instance profile, this value is the preferred one used by the SAP processes.
- If the parameter is not included in the instance profile, then the system checks whether it is contained in the default profile. If it is there, then the system takes this value for the SAP processes.
- If the parameter is not in any of the profiles, then the default value from the source program code is assumed.

Administrators should ensure that the parameters do not appear in both profiles at the same time on occasions where that's not needed. There are, however, situations where it is convenient to have a particular parameter in the default profile and also in some instance profiles. For example, suppose you want to set the default login language to English in all instances but two, which belong to the Italian subsidiary. In this case, you can set the parameter for the language in the default profile as English and set the system login language parameter to Italian in the two instances to use Italian as the preferred language.

To see a list of all profile parameters in a SAP instance, you can run the standard SAP report, RSPARAM or RSPFPAR. To do so, select *System → Services → Reporting* from any R/3 window, enter *RSPARAM* or *RSPFPAR* in the program input field, and press the *Execute* button. You get a long report list which should be sent to the printer to see it in full, since it usually does not fit on the screen.

Start Profile. The start profile is an operating system file that defines which R/3 services are started. The start profile is a parameter file which is read by the startsap program. Among the services which the start profile can initiate are the message server, the gateway, dialog, enqueue, system log collector and log sender programs, or any other locally defined program.

The start profile is located under the /usr/sap/<SID>/profile directory. These profiles are generated automatically by SAP when the system is first installed. Depending on the release version, the names assigned are either START_<instance_name> or START_<instance_name>_<hostname>; for example, START_DVEBMGS00, START_D01_copi02, where *DVEBMGS00* and *D01* are instance names and *copi02* is the hostname of instance D01.

The start profile includes some general system variables, which are substituted by their real values at runtime, such as the following:

- SAPSYSTEMNAME, which is substituted by the name of the R/3 system. For example, *DD1* as shown in the previous listing.
- INSTANCE_NAME is the variable for the name of the R/3 instance. For example, *DVEBMGS00.*

Besides those general SAP system parameters, the start profile only allows for some specific parameter names and syntax. Those permitted parameters are

- Execute_xx, where *xx* can go from 00 to 99. These lines can be used to start operating system programs or commands to prepare the R/3 system for start. For example, this parameter can be used to set up logical links to the executable programs on the UNIX platforms.

- Start_Program_xx, where *xx* can go from 00 to 99. This parameter is used to start the R/3 instances services in an application server.
- Stop_Program_xx, where *xx* can go from 00 to 99. Know the meaning of this parameter since the word *stop* can be confusing. This parameter is used to start an operating system program, command, or SAP program *after* the R/3 instance is stopped, for example, running the program that stops the saposcol, the saprouter, or the cleaning of shared memory areas which were being used by the R/3 system.

The number *xx* defines the sequence of execution. The programs specified in Execute lines are the first executed. Then the system starts the programs included in the Start_Program parameters. After the specific SAP instance is stopped, then the programs specified in the Stop_Program parameters are started.

To the right of the equal sign in the three preceding parameters, SAP allows for the execution of local programs (located in the same server) or remote programs (located in a remotely connected server).

Programs running on the local server are preceded by the word *local* in the parameter value. In the previous listing you can see that all the lines are preceded by the *local* keyword.

To run programs on a remote host instead of the local host, the parameter values must be preceded by the remote hostname. For example: Execute_00 = copi01 saposcol, where *copi01* is a remote hostname and *saposcol* the name of the program to execute.

Default Profile. The SAP default profile is an operating system file which contains parameter values used by all application servers from the same SAP system.

The name for this profile cannot be changed. It is always called DEFAULT.PFL. The default profile, like all other profiles, is located in the common profile directory of the R/3 system: /usr/sap/<SID>/SYS/profile. There is always one active default profile. Default profiles are also called *system profiles.*

The profile parameters included in the default profile are meant for those values which either are unique in the system, and therefore are the same for all instances, or to enter global parameters to be shared by all instances. Examples of such parameters are the hostname of the database server, the message server, and so forth.

Figure 4-5 includes a listing of the default profile as seen from the operating system. Figure 4-6 shows the same parameter file as seen from CCMS.

The default profile is generated automatically by the system when this is first installed. It includes the usual parameters which follow.

Parameter	*Description*
SAPDBHOST	Hostname of the database server
rdisp/vbname	Name of the update server
rdisp/btcname	Name of the default background server
rdisp/mshost	Name of the message server
rdisp/sna_gateway	Name of the host running the SNA gateway service
rdisp/sna_gw_service	Name of the TCP/IP service to connect to the SNA gateway service
rdisp/enqname	Name of the enqueue server

System administrators can modify or add to the default profile and include any other SAP parameter from the CCMS tool. For new parameters to have effect, the profile has to be activated and all instances belonging to the same SAP system must be restarted.

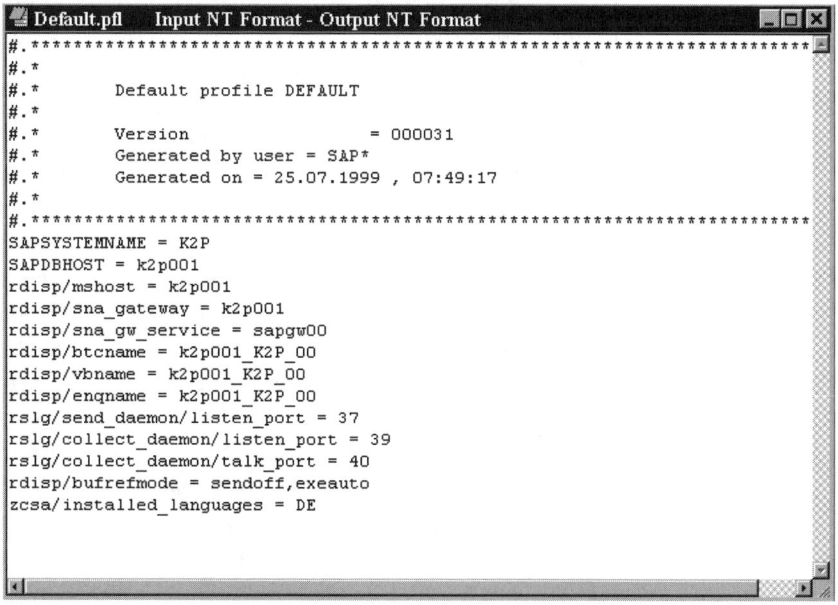

Figure 4-5
Example of default profile.

Default.pfl   Input NT Format - Output NT Format

```
#.***********************************************************************
#.*
#.*       Default profile DEFAULT
#.*
#.*       Version                = 000031
#.*       Generated by user = SAP*
#.*       Generated on = 25.07.1999 , 07:49:17
#.*
#.***********************************************************************
SAPSYSTEMNAME = K2P
SAPDBHOST = k2p001
rdisp/mshost = k2p001
rdisp/sna_gateway = k2p001
rdisp/sna_gw_service = sapgw00
rdisp/btcname = k2p001_K2P_00
rdisp/vbname = k2p001_K2P_00
rdisp/enqname = k2p001_K2P_00
rslg/send_daemon/listen_port = 37
rslg/collect_daemon/listen_port = 39
rslg/collect_daemon/talk_port = 40
rdisp/bufrefmode = sendoff,exeauto
zcsa/installed_languages = DE
```

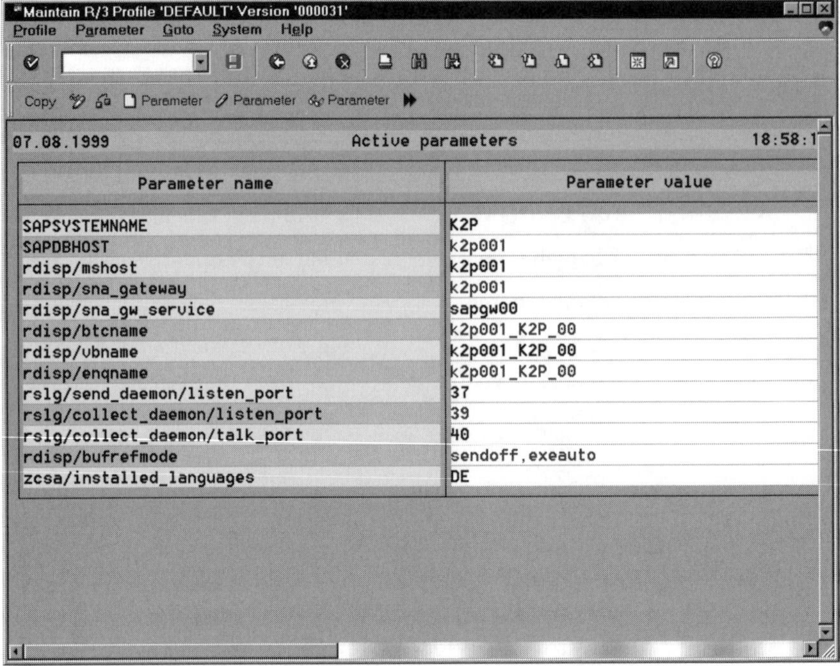

Figure 4-6 Default profile as seen from the CCMS utility.

Instance Profiles. The instance profiles are the third type of profiles and are very important for providing the SAP instances with lots of parameters which directly affect the configuration and resources for the application servers.

The instance parameters typically define how many and what type of work processes are to be started for an instance. They also define the amount of shared memory, the allocation of buffer space and related pools, the instance default login language, and so forth. Parameters set in the instance profiles have precedence over the same ones defined in the default profile.

Instance profiles are automatically generated by the R3setup utility when an instance (dialog or central) is installed. By default, the name assigned to them has the format: <SID>_<instancename> or <SID>_<instancename>_<hostname>, but you can choose any name for them. If you choose a different name than the standard, you should modify accordingly the start profiles to reflect the new names.

It is also possible to use the same instance profile to start SAP instances on different computers. In this case, make sure that the hardware resources available are the same or very similar. You cannot allocate more memory in an instance profile than the actual available memory in the server.

Profiles Maintenance. You should only edit the profiles from the R/3 system using the CCMS profile maintenance tool. Figure 4-7 shows one screen of the maintenance tools in display mode.

Refer to the section entitled "Profile Maintenance Options" in Chap. 11 for extensive information on profile maintenance.

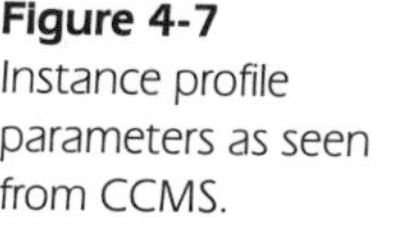

Setting Up the Central System Log

There is a central system log within an R/3 distributed configuration in charge of registering the system events, including warnings, errors, and messages. When installing application servers for a client/server SAP system, the central logging is disabled by default on the application servers. This section explains the process of setting up the central system log on UNIX systems when in a distributed configuration. Additional information about the logging process is given in the section entitled "The R/3 System Logs" in Chap. 10.

Presently, Windows NT does not support central system log. The logging is obtained locally on every NT application server. However, from

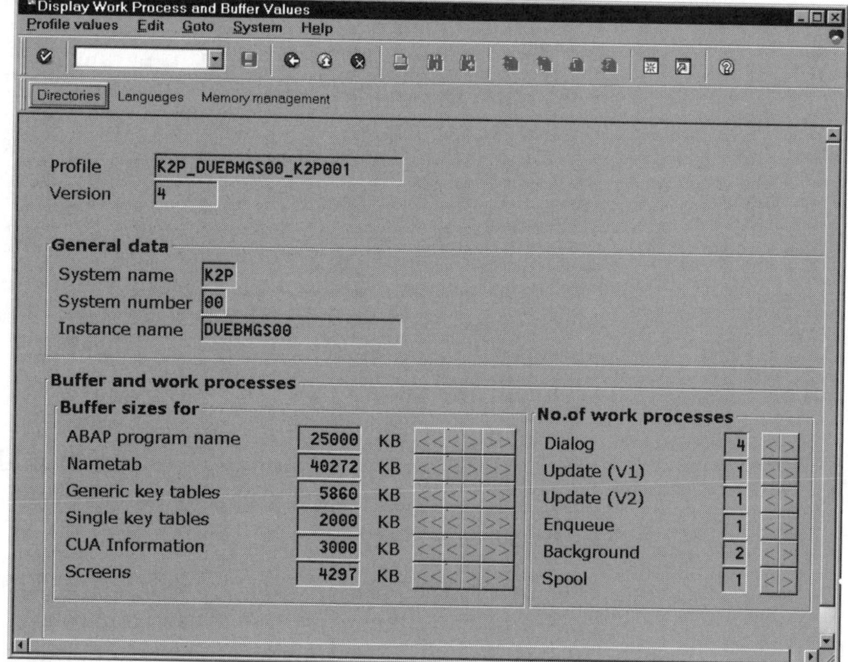

Figure 4-7 Instance profile parameters as seen from CCMS.

any NT server you can automatically log on to other servers to see the system log.

In order to obtain the benefits of the central logging, you have to set up some instance logging parameters.

To display the logging parameters, go to the initial system log screen: *Tools* → *Administration* → *Monitor* → *System Log* (transaction SM21). Then choose *Environment* → *Display SAPPARAM*.

All the system parameters controlling the logging process are prefixed by *rslg*. In order for the central system log to collect the messages sent by all application servers, there are some rslg parameters which must be identical on all instances. The best way to accomplish this is to edit the DEFAULT.PFL file on the central application server. You will probably find most of the parameters correctly set right from installation. However, if there is more than one SAP instance per host, which means that they cannot have the same SAP system number, then you should carefully follow the instructions, otherwise you might receive log messages from some instances and not from other ones.

In order to edit the DEFAULT.PFL, first check the values for the following parameters in all instances:

- *rslg/collect_daemon/host*. This parameter specifies the host where the central log resides.
- *rslg/collect_daemon/listen_port*. Specifies the listening port for the collection process. By default, this parameter is set to 12<SAP-SYSTEM number>, for example, 1200, if your system number is 00. Ensure that the listen port is identical for all instances.
- *rslg/collect_daemon/talk_port*. Specifies the talk port for the collection process. By default, this parameter is set to 13<SAPSYSTEM number>. Ensure that the talk port is identical for all instances.
- *rslg/send_daemon/listen_port*. Specifies the listening port for the send process. By default, this parameter is set to 14<SAPSYSTEM number>. Ensure that the listen port is identical for all instances in your SAP system.
- *rslg/send_daemon/talk_port*. Specifies the talk port for the send process. By default, this parameter is set to 15<SAPSYSTEM number>. Ensure that the talk port is identical for all instances in your SAP system.

Once you have ensured that the system profiles for logging are set appropriately, you have to start the send and collection processes.

The collection process only has to be started on the instance where the central log is to reside. By default on the R/3 system installation, the needed commands are included in the start profile of the central instance. However, you might decide to change the placement of the central logging.

The send process is in charge of forwarding the log messages to the central log, and therefore must be started in each instance of the R/3 system, including the central system. To start the send process, you must edit the start profile for the instance and add the lines as shown in Fig. 4-8. Substitute the values in the figure with your own values. In the example, DD1 is the SAPSID, and DVEBMGS00 is the instance.

If you modified the DEFAULT.PFL in order to set the preceding parameters or included the needed execution lines in the instances START profiles, you have to start and stop the instances in order for the new values to take effect and the new processes to start.

There are additional parameters in the logging process which normally you should not change and which are set correctly by the default installation. Refer to the SAP online documentation for additional information on other parameters.

Buffer Synchronization in Distributed Configurations

When working in the R/3 system, changes made by users to the information they are working with are not immediately updated in the database. This is particularly true in distributed configurations.

In distributed configurations, that is, with several application servers belonging to the same SAP system, every SAP instance has its own buffers.

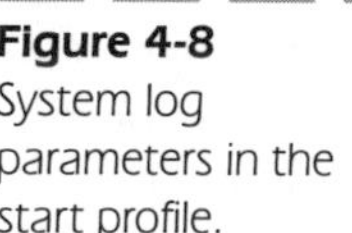

Figure 4-8
System log parameters in the start profile.

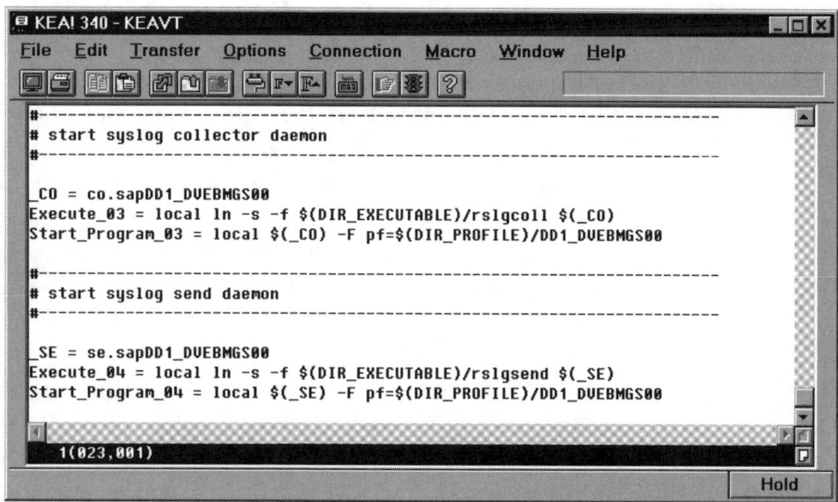
KEA! 340 - KEAVT
File Edit Transfer Options Connection Macro Window Help
#---
start syslog collector daemon
#---
_CO = co.sapDD1_DVEBMGS00
Execute_03 = local ln -s -f $(DIR_EXECUTABLE)/rslgcoll $(_CO)
Start_Program_03 = local $(_CO) -F pf=$(DIR_PROFILE)/DD1_DVEBMGS00
#---
start syslog send daemon
#---
_SE = se.sapDD1_DVEBMGS00
Execute_04 = local ln -s -f $(DIR_EXECUTABLE)/rslgsend $(_SE)
Start_Program_04 = local $(_SE) -F pf=$(DIR_PROFILE)/DD1_DVEBMGS00
1(023,001)
Hold

This could result in data inconsistency when users work on the same data from different servers. A locking mechanism for data access is provided by the enqueue server.

To avoid that, the SAP system provides a way to synchronize the buffers across the application severs. This is known as *buffer synchronization,* or *buffer refresh.*

If the R/3 system is centralized and is made up of only one SAP instance, then buffer refresh is not needed. Data buffered in the SAP system includes many important tables, programs, screens, and so on.

In buffer synchronization, when the system receives any modifying action in the data that is buffered and may have been buffered by another application server, the SAP systems sends *synchronization telegrams,* which are written in the central database table DDLOG. All application servers read from the DDLOG table to check whether their own buffers must be refreshed.

R/3 includes some parameters to control the buffer synchronization. These parameters are rdisp/bufreftime and rdisp/bufrefmode. The *rdisp / bufreftime* parameter sets the value in seconds for the time between two synchronizations. The *rdisp / bufrefmode* parameter affects the mode in which the buffers are refreshed. It admits two values, which are sendon/ sendoff, and exeauto/exeoff.

The first set of values, *sendon / sendoff,* controls whether synchronization is active (sendon) or not (sendoff). The second set controls whether the central instance reads the DDLOG table (exeauto) or not (exeoff).

SAP recommends that when using the transport control program (tp) to perform imports in a centralized SAP system with just one server, to set the buffer mode parameter to rdisp/bufrefmode = sendoff, exeauto. If it is set to exeoff, the instance will not read the DDLOG table, so the changes to repository objects performed by the tp program will not be updated in the repository buffers. Under some circumstances this can cause syntax error messages because the ABAP processor can detect a new version of a program before the buffers are correctly updated.

The buffers are completely erased and reconstructed when restarting the SAP instances. There are also some special commands which can be entered in the command field of the R/3 window to synchronize the buffers in the application server where these commands are issued. For example, entering *$TAB* in the command field refreshes the table buffers, and entering *$SYNC* refreshes all buffers, except for the program buffer.

WARNING! *Handle these options with care and only when instructed by the SAP hotline or an R/3 note. Refreshing the buffers when users are working with buffered tables, programs, or screens might cause some inconsistencies and a decrease in performance.*

Central and Local Storage of Executable Files under UNIX

When implementing a distributed SAP system consisting of several application servers you have to decide whether to install the SAP executable files either locally on the hard disk of every application server or in a central repository of executables from a single server. There is also the option of having some servers share the executable through NFS and others store them locally.

In a standard SAP installation the executables directory is stored on a central host system, usually the central instance. The UNIX directory is /usr/sap/<SID>/SYS/exe/run, where *<SID>* is the SAP system name.

Then, when installing additional application servers (instances), these servers usually share the central directory over the network using standard NFS (network file system). But, after the initial installation, the administrators can decide to store the SAP executables on the local hard disks of the application servers. In these cases, a special program *sapcpe* is used to ensure that the instance updates the executables program files when these are updated in the central server.

SAP recommends storing the executables locally if there is enough local hard disk space available. Depending on the SAP release version and options installed, the needed size is approximately 400 MB. (Look this information up in the SAP installation manuals.)

Each option has its advantages and disadvantages. The choice depends on the hardware, the network, and the operational needs.

Central storage of executables presents the following advantages:

- There is no need for additional storage space on application servers.
- When there are new or updated executable SAP programs, placing them in the central location makes them immediately available for all application servers.
- There is no need to maintain and configure the sapcpe program and associated files to synchronize the updated executable files.

- When the sapcpe program is used, the initial startup of instances is slow because of directories synchronization.

The disadvantages of central storage are

- The network load between the application server and the central server is increased and therefore can result in a decrease in performance, both in the application servers and the central servers.
- The startup of instances is slower because the executables are loaded through the network.
- You have to carefully maintain the NFS configuration and daemons, since, if the central server fails the export process for any reason, the program will be unavailable for all servers.
- If an application server has to make any program swap with active executables because they run out of memory, they actually page over the network, considerably decreasing the system performance.

Based on these criteria, you should decide according to the specific needs of your installation. For example, if all servers are connected with a high-speed network such as FDDI, FC, ATM, or similar, and they all have enough memory, then having the executables centrally located should not be a major problem.

On the other hand, if you have enough local storage space, place the executables on the hard disks of the application servers. If you have servers with less space, you can have a mixed environment. To do this, you must prepare the executables directories and configure the sapcpe program. Defining a master location from which the other servers will update their local files in case there are new or updated programs is required for storing locally.

The actual procedure to set up the directories and the sapcpe program can be found in the SAP online documentation in the system services section within the system administration help books.

Windows NT systems all share the same copy of executables, located on the *<hostname>**sapmnt* directory and normally installed on the central instance.

Starting and Stopping SAP R/3

Starting the SAP R/3 system involves starting the underlying database and all the SAP processes configured to run in all application servers. The type and number of processes are configurable with the start profile and the instance profile parameters. These processes might include the following:

- The operating system and/or network performance collectors
- The central system log collection process
- The CPIC gateway server
- The message server
- The dispatcher processes
- The spool processes
- The dialog and background processes

The SAP R/3 system can be started and stopped by using operating system commands or from within the CCMS utilities. However, for the latter, at least the database server and the central instance must have been started first using the operating system startup commands. In current releases, the database system is not stopped from within R/3 either.

In centralized installations, with just one single server, one start and one stop command are enough for starting or stopping the whole system. However, in distributed configurations, some configuration is needed to start and stop the group of application servers of a SAP system.

Starting the SAP system first requires starting the database and then the instance processes. Stopping is the opposite process: first you have to stop the instance processes and then the database background processes.

For example, you can write a shell script command file that can start the whole system from a single server. In these cases, many people use remote shell commands to execute the start programs in remote computers. Stopping can be done the same way. Remember that using remote commands (for example, rsh, remsh, or similar) can be a security violation in some systems because a list of permitted hosts is necessary. For this, check with your security manager.

To start or stop the SAP system in a UNIX environment, you must log on as user <sid>adm, for example, for SAP system DD1, as user *dd1adm*. The following commands are available.

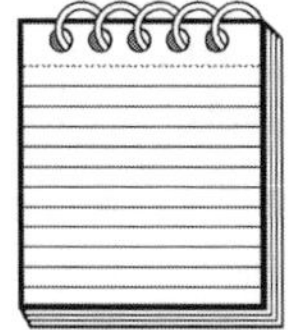

NOTE *The brackets indicate optional parameters where you can choose just one from the list or none at all.*

1. startsap [R3] [DB] [ALL]
   - Using the command, startsap R3, only the SAP instance is started. It is assumed that the database is already running. Otherwise, the instance will not start successfully.
   - With the command, startsap DB, only the database is started.

- Using startsap ALL, the system will first start the database and then the SAP instance. *ALL* is the default setting and can be omitted. If the database is running, it will just start the instance.

2. stopsap [DB] [R3] [ALL]
   - Using stopsap R3, all the instance processes are stopped.
   - With the command, stopsap DB, the system stops just the database. Make sure you first stop the instance processes; otherwise, the SAP processes will "hang" because no update is possible.
   - Issuing the command, stopsap [ALL], the system stops the SAP instance and then the database. *ALL* is the default parameter and can be omitted.

When in distributed SAP installations with several application servers, pay attention to stopping all the instances before stopping the database, which is only located in the database server.

To check if the system has been correctly started or stopped, you can use standard UNIX operating system utilities such as the ps command. From the UNIX system, the SAP processes are prefixed by dw, so, for example, issuing the command

```
dd1adm> ps -eaf | grep dw
```

will show the SAP running processes. If you see no lines from the command output, then no SAP processes are running on this system. *Note: In different UNIX implementations, the options for the ps command might differ.*

Another way to check whether the SAP processes in an application server are running correctly is by selecting *Tools → Administration → Monitor → System monitoring → Process Overview* from the standard SAP monitoring tools. Or, use the CCMS, which permits a check of all the application servers in the system by choosing *Tools → CCMS → Control/monitoring → System monitor.*

In the R/3 startup process, the startsap script calls the sapstart program with the startup profile as the argument. The startup profile is specified in the variable START_FILES which is contained in the script. The script can be found under the home directory of the SAP administration user account, <sid>adm. The actual name of the script is usually startsap_<hostname>_<sap_system_number>, for example: startsap_copi01_00; the script startsap is really a UNIX alias defined in the login environment variables for the <sid>adm user.

When stopping the SAP system, the stopsap script calls the kill.sap script which is located under the instance work directory (/usr/sap/<SID>/SYS/<INSTANCE>/work). The kill.sap script activates the shutdown processing in the sapstart process.

As can be seen, both the start and the stop process of the R/3 system are initiated from the sapstart program, which is located under the executables directory. The syntax of this program is sapstart pf=<start_profile>. For example:

```
tt1adm>/usr/sapC11/SYS/exe/run/sapstart
pf=/usr/sap/C11/SYS/profile/START_DVEBMGS00
```

When the sapstart program is executed, it reads from the start profile to determine the preliminary commands it has to process. These commands are preceded by the Execute_xx keyword, and often they just establish logical links or clean the shared memory.

It then launches the SAP processes as described in the Start_program_xx statements. The *xx* indicates the processing order. However, you should know that sapstart processes the entries asynchronously, which means it will not check the status of one process before proceeding with the next one.

The sapstart process is the mother of all the processes running in a SAP R/3 system. For that reason, when this process is shutdown, all the child processes are shutdown as well.

When in shutdown processing, the sapstart program executes the commands in the start profile and it will wait until all of its child processes terminate or it receives a stop signal from the system. The stopsap script works by sending the stop message to the sapstart program by means of the kill.sap script. This script is very simple, and what it contains is simply the PID of the sapstart process running in the system.

The SAP processes are also shut down asynchronously, and therefore in parallel.

Both the startsap and stopsap procedures are logged into files which are left in the home directory of the SAP administrator user account, <sid>adm. The names of these files are startsap_<hostname>_<sap_system_number>.log and stop_<hostname>_<sap_system_number>.log.

The sapstart program itself logs its processing in a log file located under the instance work directory: sapstart.log. This log file can be seen either from the operating system or inside the R/3 system from the monitoring and tracing utilities.

Starting and Stopping R/3 Under Windows NT

The process for starting or stopping R/3 systems on Windows NT systems is basically the same as under UNIX, except that some of the programs are different, and also Windows NT includes a graphical interface, known as the *SAP Service Manager.* Additionally, Windows NT reads some of the required R/3 variables directly from the *Registry.*

Starting R/3 from the SAP Service Manager requires that the R/3 Service *SAP<SAPSID>_<Instance_number>* (for example, *SAPK2P_00*), be started. This is usually done automatically because the R/3 service is defined for automatic start at system boot by default. In any case, to check whether the R/3 service is running, on the Windows NT server, select *Control Panel → Services* and make sure that the R/3 service has the status *Started.* If this is not the case, you will need to start it manually.

If the R/3 service is started, to start the R/3 system select *Programs → SAP R/3 → SAP Service Manager <SID>_<Instancenumber>.* This program can be located in different places according to the R/3 release. It is recommended that system managers or SAP administrators create shortcuts on their desktops. Press the *Start* button to start the R/3 system. It will start the database first and then the central instance. If the database was already started, then only the central instance is started. The system is completely started when the stoplights turn green. Figure 4.9 shows an example of the *Service Manager.*

Stopping R/3 is also done from the SAP Service Manager, by pressing the *Stop* button. However, this procedure will not stop the database. In the case of Oracle and Informix, R/3 can be stopped using *sapdba,* or the database-specific tools that in Windows NT can be used graphically or from the command line. For Microsoft SQL Server, the database can be stopped from the taskbar.

When the SAP R/3 system includes several instances (application servers), the procedure for starting those instances can be done from the SAP Service Manager of each server, or from the CCMS, once the database and central instance have been started. However, when stopping the full R/3 system, the first things to stop are the application servers, then the central instance, and finally the database.

Figure 4-9
SAP Service Manager.

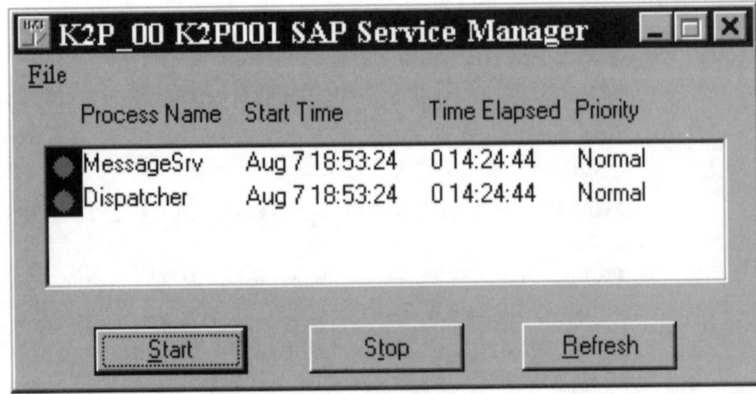

The process of starting and stopping a full R/3 system with several instances has been simplified since release 4.5 of R/3 because installation of R/3 on Windows NT requires the installation of the Microsoft Management Console, which enables starting and stopping all the instances centrally.

Notice, however, that on R/3 installations on Microsoft Server Cluster Services (MSCS), the procedure for starting and stopping the system is quite different on the cluster nodes. Starting and stopping R/3 and the database is done from the Cluster Administration application by selecting the service and choosing the action (Start, Stop, Move, etc.)

User Distribution: Logon Load Balancing and the SAPlogon Utility

SAP provides utilities to configure and efficiently divide the system load among the available servers. The load balancing is provided dynamically. For example, you can define the number of total users allowed to log on in a particular instance and the response time threshold for that instance. With those values the system will decide upon a user logon request which is the best application server for the user to log on.

The process of configuring logon balancing involves two tasks:

1. Configuring the logon groups, which is accomplished from the CCMS utilities within the R/3 system.
2. Installing and configuring the SAPlogon Windows application in every workstation that is going to log on to the R/3 system.

Logon Groups Configuration

System administrators can centrally configure several logon groups containing one or more application instances. When users log on in a defined group, the system automatically selects the instance server, according to the best performance and the number of connected users.

Configuring logon groups is not only meant to balance the load; when enough instances are defined it is also a good way to provide higher system availability for users. For example, suppose you have a SAP installation with one database server and seven application servers running one SAP instance each. Your installation has 400 concurrent users from the SAP application modules: FI, MM, SD, and CO. Every module has 100 users. However, SAP modules support different transactional loads. It's well known that an average SD transaction can be about three times as demanding as an average FI transaction. If you define the following groups:

Group FI/CO, pointing to application servers 1, 2, and 3

Group MM, pointing to application servers 4, 5, and 6

Group SD, pointing to application servers 4, 5, 6, and 7

you get the following advantages:

- Load balancing
- If an application server goes down for any reason (hardware error, maintenance, etc.) users can still connect to the group, which will assign the best application server
- Setting groups of related applications (MM and SD are related, as well as FI and CO) makes a better use of the instance buffers and shared memory, since the probability of having the same called programs or tables in the buffers is high.

In the preceding example, application server 7 is only assigned to SD users because it is the most demanding module among those applications, and also because you can configure this server to allow a smaller number of users with the most time-critical work, for instance, printing invoices, getting orders, and so on. Other very demanding SAP application modules are PP (production planning) or PS (project system).

To log on to the R/3 system, users only need to know the SID of the R/3 system and the name of the logon group. They don't need to specify the hostname or system numbers of the SAP instances.

To create a logon group, from the main menu, select *Tools → CCMS → Configuration → Logon groups.* Or enter transaction code *SMLG* in the command field. This procedure can be done while the R/3 system is running normally; there is no need to stop it.

If there are no logon groups defined yet, the system displays a window with just the name of the current instance. If there are groups already set, then it displays a list with the group names, the SAP instances, and the status of the instances.

To create or edit a logon group, click the *Create entry* button on the application toolbar. The system displays the *Create entry* window, like the one shown in Fig. 4-10. If you only see the first two fields, press the right arrow button to see the remaining fields.

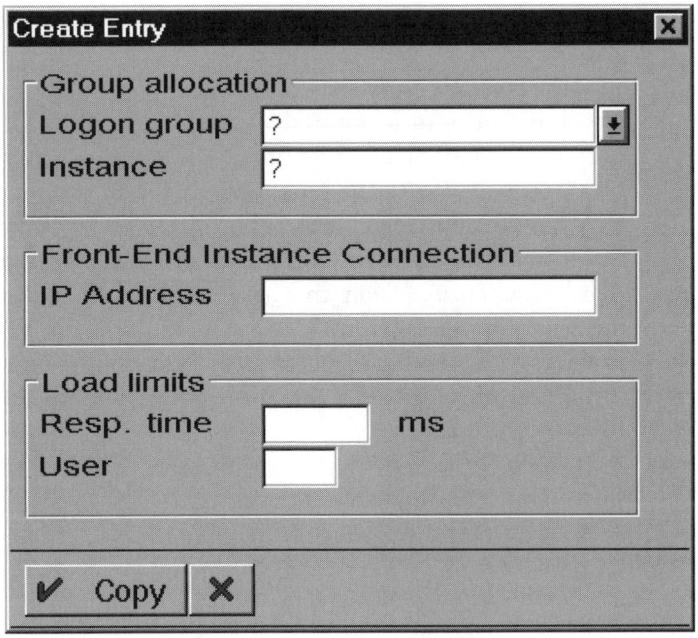

Figure 4-10
Create Entry dialog box for logon groups.

On this screen, you can enter

- *Logon group:* Enter a name for the logon group to be defined. Use a name which can be easily understood. For example, for SD users, set something like "SD group," "SD module," or "Sales." If there were previously created groups, you can click on the possible entries arrow to display or select a group.
- *Instance:* Enter at least one instance for a group. Clicking on the possible entries arrow displays the available SAP instances defined in the system.

To get information about a particular logon group, double click on any line where the group appears. The > button is useful both for editing and displaying the load limit information about a logon group and instance. The screen is extended showing the response time and number of users limit set for that instance in the logon group. These fields are not mandatory; you can leave them blank if you don't want to set any restriction on that group or instance. But, if the response time has been defined for a group in a particular instance, then you have to define a response time limit for every group using the same instance.

When all the information is entered, press the *Copy* button to save your entries.

Define at least another instance for the same logon group. Having a single instance in a group does not make much sense from the point of view of load balancing. It would be the same as logging in with the normal SAPGUI pointing to the hostname and instance number.

From the main logon load balancing screen, administrators can monitor the load of the groups and the users connected. To do this, select *Goto* → *Load distribution* from the menu. The system displays a list with an overview of the current load, showing the performance status of the instances assigned to logon groups. Each application server writes its performance statistics to a memory resident table on the message server every five minutes.

If you want to refresh the performance status of any application server, just double click on the line.

To see the users currently logged on, select *Goto* → *User list* from the menu.

The SAPlogon Application

SAPlogon is a Windows PC program that acts as an interface between the R/3 system and the common SAP user interface, SAPGUI. The SAPlogon program is automatically installed with the SAPGUI.

To start SAPlogon, just double click its icon. Figure 4-11 shows an example.

The SAPlogon menu contains the available servers and logon groups which must be previously defined. You can either add servers or groups manually, or you can request a particular server for the available groups and make it add entries automatically. If it is the first time using it and the menu has not been configured by someone else, it might be empty.

To log on to a SAP system, just click on the entry and press the *Logon* button or simply double click on the entry. When selecting a logon group, the system will select the application server with the best response time. This procedure is accomplished by SAP by means of the message server which logs the availability and response times of all application servers for a SAP system.

SAPlogon Configuration. To make good use of the features of the SAPlogon application, users or the administrator must configure some settings on the logon menu, such as adding servers or groups.

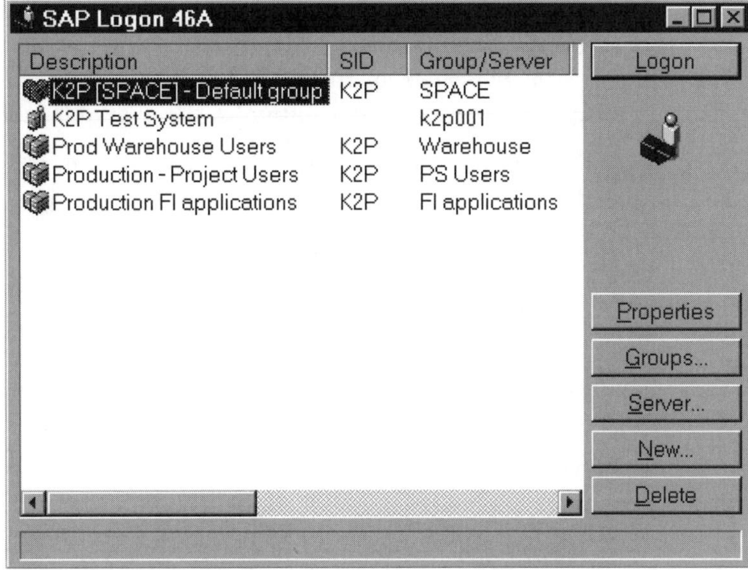

Figure 4-11
SAPlogon main menu.

To automatically add a new server to the menu, select the *Server...* button. A dialog window will show up requesting the data for the new server.

Now you have to specify the SAP system ID, the hostname where the message server is running, and the application server where the SAProuter is running. SAProuter is a special SAP program used for the connection with the message server. There is a section about SAProuter in Appendix A. If SAProuter is not running, you can leave this field blank (select *<NONE>*). You can add servers from different SAP systems to the same SAPlogon menu or even configure a direct access to the SAPnet system.

Upon pressing the *Generate list* button, if there are available application servers, they are displayed in the list box in the window. From this screen, you can decide either to log on to the server (*Logon* button), add it to the list of servers (*Add* button), or do both things at once (*Add and Logon* button). If there are none, then you have to add them manually.

Defining groups is a very similar process. From the main SAPlogon window, select the *Group Selection* button. The system displays a new window which has exactly the same fields as the server selection windows.

Enter the SAP system ID, the message server, and SAProuter information and press the *OK* button. The list box will display the active logon groups in the SAP system. From this screen, you can decide either to log on to the group (*Logon* button), add it to the list of groups (*Add* button), or do both things at once (*Add and Logon* button).

The SAPlogon application also provides the possibility of manually entering new entries or editing existing ones. To add a new entry, click on the *New* button from the SAP Logon menu. In the *New entry* window, enter the necessary information in the available input fields:

- *Description.* You can enter here any short description you want for the server. For example, you can enter the system name or something like *Development System.*
- *Application server.* Specify in this field the name of the host for the application server.
- *SAProuter string.* If you are reaching your server via the SAProuter program, then enter the routing entry here.
- *System number.* Enter the system or instance number of the SAP system to which you want to connect.

If you want to change an existing entry, click on the *Edit* button on the main SAPlogon menu and change the data you want, except for the application server and system number when modifying logon group entries.

The SAPlogon application also includes some configuration options which are not seen directly on the menu. To show those options, click on the top left corner of the SAPlogon window and select *Options.*

Figure 4-12 shows the dialog box displayed on the screen. This dialog box is mainly used for troubleshooting the SAPlogon application or looking for connection problems. The available fields are grouped in two boxes. The first one is the *Saplogon Options,* which includes

- *Language.* This is used for selecting the SAPlogon language. It must have been previously installed, and not all languages are available.
- *Message server timeout.* The value, specified in seconds, is the time the SAPlogon waits for a response from the message server of the R/3 system. The default value is 10 seconds. If you experience timeout problems, then increase this value.
- *Confirmation of listbox entry delete.* When this check box is selected, the system displays a warning before an entry is deleted from the SAP logon menu.
- *Disable editing functionality.* This entry can be used to disable users from modifying logon entries. If the check box is selected, then the buttons in the SAP logon menu (*Edit, New, Delete,* and other options in the entry or group selection menu such as *Add* and *Add and Logon*) are grayed out and can't be used. However, the easiest way to

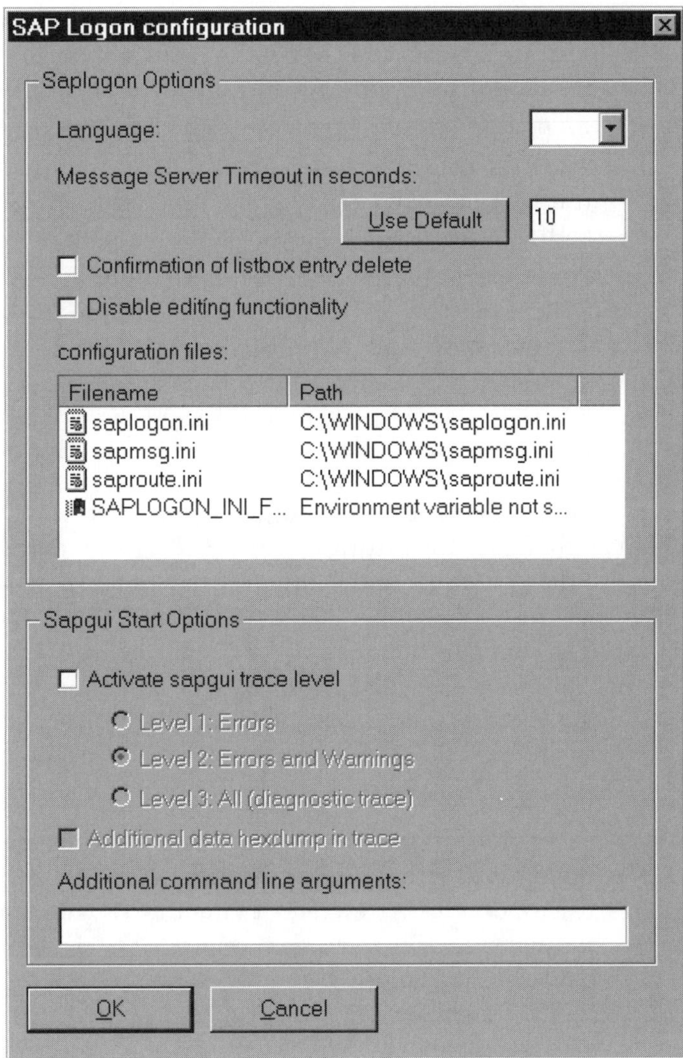

Figure 4-12 *SAPlogon configuration* dialog box.

protect the SAPlogon configuration from editing is to force users to use the SAPLogon-PAD program (SAPLGPAD.EXE), which behaves just like SAPlogon but without editing and configuration options. This is automatically installed with the SAPGUI from R/3 release 4.5.

Newer SAPlogon versions include also a list of configuration files, so that you can edit those files directly.

The second box is the *Sapgui Start Options,* which has the following fields:

- *Activate sapgui trace level.* When this option is set, you first can activate a trace. Then select the radio buttons to the right to choose the level of information which the trace file will record.
- *Additional data hexdump in trace.* This option can only be selected when the trace has been activated. When this option is selected, the trace will include additional memory areas. Please note that having both the trace file and the hexdump activated can result in loss of performance and the generation of very large trace files. When you finish a trace, deactivate those options and delete the trace files.
- *Additional command line arguments.* In this field, you can enter additional arguments to the command line when starting the SAPGUI. Use this field and commands as requested by the SAP hotline in case of problems.

Administering the SAPlogon Application. SAP system managers can configure the settings for the SAPlogon application and then distribute those settings to the end users. In order to do that, they must know what the configuration files are that the SAPlogon application uses.

The configuration files of the SAPlogon are standard Windows system initialization files (INI files) located under the main Windows environment directory (normal locations for this directory are c:\win95, c:\winnt, depending on the Windows version and the users installation directory). These INI files are

- *sapmsg.ini.* This is the initialization file which contains the list of hosts running the message servers. In the following example, the user can connect to SAP systems TT1 and DD1 which are running the message server in the node specified to the right of the equal sign.

  ```
  [Message Server]
  TT1=copi01
  DD1=copi02
  ```

  The first line of the file must contain the [Message Server] keyword. This file is updated automatically when users enter new SAP systems in the SAP logon menu.
- *saproute.ini.* This initialization file contains route strings for the entries included in the SAP logon menu. For example:

  ```
  [Router]
  DD1 Development=/H/copi02/S/sapdp00
  ```

  For every possible connection, there must be a line with the format:

  ```
  <route_name>=<route_string>
  ```

Route strings can concatenate multiple route entries when a connection uses multiple SAProuters. The format for this strings is

/H/<host with saprouter>/S/<service where saprouter is running>/H/....

To see routing examples, refer to the section entitled "SAProuter" in Appendix A.

- *saplogon.ini.* This is the initialization file which stores all the configuration settings, servers, groups, system, routes, and so forth which have been defined for the SAPlogon menu.

Finally, there is a very important file for the SAPlogon to communicate correctly with the SAP system message servers. This communication is established via standard TCP/IP sockets. These are defined in the services file. This file can be located in the same Windows directory or in a different one depending on the TCP/IP software you are using. You must ensure that for each entry in the sapmsg.ini file, you have a corresponding tcp service entry in the services file. These entries have the form of sapms<SID> <socket number>/tcp. For example:

```
sapmsDD1   3600/tcp
sapmsTT1   3605/tcp
```

NOTE *A very typical cause of problems with SAPlogon configurations when editing the services file and including the entry for the message server in the last line is not placing a carriage return after the entry. A way to avoid the problem is not to insert the entry at the end.*

You also must ensure that the service names and numbers are exactly the same as those defined on the SAP servers in the corresponding services file.

If you as administrator want to present for end users the available options with SAPlogon, you have to make a base configuration for them, which is recorded in the saplogon.ini file.

If you don't want users to define their own settings, you have to deactivate the selection options *Groups* and *Server.* In order to preset the settings and protect them against modifications, just copy them to the saplogon.ini file and make sure they have the right entries in the services file. Then make sure they don't have the sapmsg.ini and the saproute.ini files.

With the saplogon.ini file, when users start the SAPlogon application, they have all the selections preset. This is the only one really needed. If you want even better protection against users modifying their entries, you can set the entry *Restricted Mode=1* in the Configuration section of the saplogon.ini file and make this file write-protected.

You can use any of the programs for software distribution available in the market to send those files to all end users connected to the network.

The Network in Distributed SAP R/3 Environments

SAP R/3 is a client/server system, as has often been said. In client/server systems, the network sizing, configuration, and setup play a critical role in distributed environments. A well-planned and -configured network infrastructure significantly reduces the risk of availability problems.

Even if the SAP servers are up and running, when the network lines are down or saturated, from the end-user point of view, the system is unavailable and so is the critical business data.

When planning the network for a SAP R/3 installation, the following factors are important:

- *Sizing the network.* For sizing the network you have to know the types of users and their location and whether they will connect over a local area network (LAN), a wide area network (WAN), or by modem. Soon they may connect using the Internet.
- *Distribution of services.* SAP services can be located on different servers. You have to think whether the services will be statically or dynamically assigned.
- *Monitoring the network.* A good monitoring procedure must be in place to ensure a quick reaction to network problems, such as lines going down, nonresponding servers, router problems, and so forth.
- *Remote connection.* Do not forget to plan the remote connection to the SAP support servers. This process will also need some network expertise and monitoring.

In SAP installations there are two main types of network links: the one established between the application servers and the database server, known as the *server network,* and the one from the end user workstations to the applications servers, known as the *access network.*

The traffic from the end-user workstations to the application server is relatively small, ranging from an average of 1000 to 2000 bits/second. Network traffic between application servers and the database server is much higher, about 10 times more. Additionally, large print jobs can increase considerably the network traffic among the servers. SAP does not recommend installing decentralized application servers that connect to the database servers through WAN networks and routers.

The network traffic has to be calculated considering the number of users, their locations, the expected transaction rates, and so forth. Normally high-speed network controllers are needed to connect the database server to the application servers. For this reason, having at least two network controllers for each application server is recommended. This way, the traffic can be more efficiently routed at the convenience and needs of the SAP installation.

End users working in remote locations over a WAN should have a network connection with enough throughput (number of Kbits per second) to support at least twice the expected average traffic so that the system still can respond efficiently to users' requests even at peak times. A formula based on benchmark is available for an approximate network sizing:

$$C = 16{,}000 * N / [L * (T\text{thinktime} + T\text{response})] \text{ bit/sec}$$

Where

C = required line capacity measured in bit/sec.
N = number of users.
L = line utilization ($0 < L < 1$). Values of line utilization higher than 50% are not recommended.
Tthinktime = think time between two dialog steps (average = 30 sec).
Tresponse = Response time (average = 1 sec).

With the use of the SAPlogon and other utilities, the SAP services can be dynamically distributed over the network. This is accomplished by the tasks performed by the message server.

The network protocol used by the SAP system is the standard TCP/IP. You can find detailed information about the available options when configuring the TCP/IP network with the R/3 system in the SAP manual, *Integration of R/3 Servers in TCP/IP Networks.* In order to fully understand this manual, some network expertise is needed.

CHAPTER 5

Using SAP R/3

The SAP R/3 presentation interface behaves very similarly to any other typical windows application. It does not make much sense for administrators and technical consultants to know and control the kernel of the system without being able to use the basics of the presentation interface. If you are the system administrator, you will very often be requested to give end-user support regarding the SAPGUI features. The purpose of this chapter is to give an overview of the main functions and possibilities of the SAP R/3 windows presentation interface, also known as SAPGUI.

Basic topics such as logging in and out of the system, changing the passwords, the elements of the R/3 window, how to move around, getting help, filling up screen fields, launching and looking at background and printing jobs, and the basics of user sessions and transactions are covered. Advanced topics about user management, passwords, and access rights are covered in Chap. 9.

Logging On and Off the System

Logging on to the system requires the SAPGUI software be installed on your PC or workstation and a valid SAP user identification and password from the system administrator. If you meet these two basic requirements, then you are ready to *log on* to the R/3 system. When you finish your working task, you must *log off.* The R/3 system administrator can automatically log off users when their session is idle for a certain amount of time; this is done with the use of an instance profile parameter.

To access the R/3 system, double click on the SAP R/3 icon. Or, if using the SAPlogon utility, click on the group or server of your choice.

As shown in Fig. 5-1, a new window with the SAP R/3 logon screen appears. This screen has four fields: the *Client,* the *User,* the *Password,* and the *Language.*

In the *Client* field, enter the client number. This numbers defines a whole business entity within the company, or the whole company. Very possibly this field has a default client number in it, which is defined by the system administrator with the instance profile parameter *login/system_client.* In Fig. 5-1, the client is automatically set to *222.* You can accept this value or type over an existing client where you have a user identification.

Once satisfied with the client field, move to the next field by pointing and clicking with the mouse or pressing the *Tab* key.

The next field is the *User* field. Enter the name of the SAP user identi-

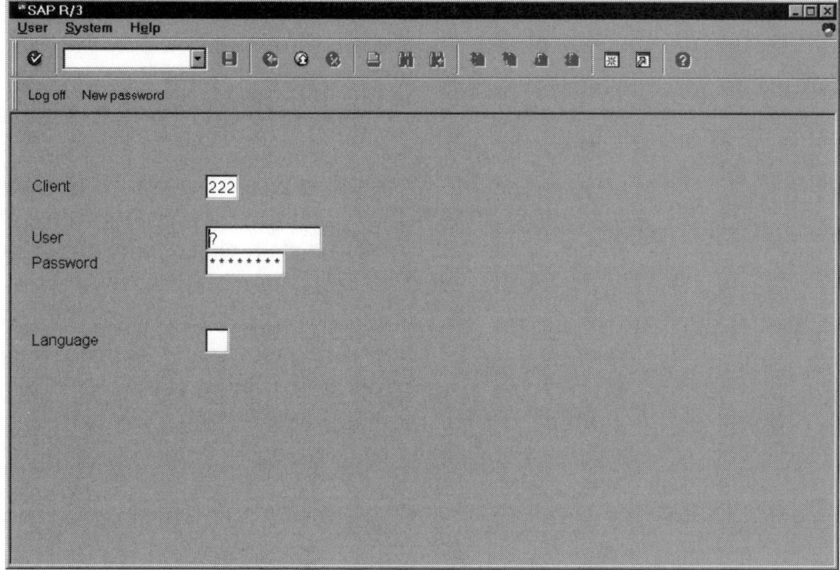

Figure 5-1
Initial SAP R/3 windows for logon.

fication. Users of the SAP system are client-specific, which means that having a user identification (user master record) on one client will only allow access to that particular client.

In the *Password* field, enter the password that has been assigned by the system administrator or the user administrator. If this is the very first time a user accesses the system, pressing the *Enter* key gets a screen requesting the user change the password.

Passwords in the SAP system must follow certain rules. These rules and how the user and the system administrator can change passwords are explained more fully in the next section.

User passwords should be changed at regular intervals to enhance users' security and reduce the risk of intrusions.

The last field on the logon screen is the *Language* field. SAP R/3 supports multinational character sets and languages on the same system at the same time, which is very useful for multinational companies with employees working in several countries and possibly using different languages. SAP R/3 comes bundled with English (language code EN) and German (language code DE). The default language code is defined with the instance profile parameter *zcsa/system_language.* Additional languages have to be imported (installed) by the system administrator. On the same SAP system, different instances can be defaulted to different languages.

When the required fields are correctly completed, pressing the *Enter* key takes you into the R/3 system. If you made a typing mistake in any of the fields, you will see a message in the *status bar* (the bottom part of the R/3 window).

When logging on for the very first time, the first thing you see is the copyright notice. Clicking on the *Continue* button removes the copyright notice.

If the system administrator wrote a system message, this appears in your R/3 window. In this case, pressing the *Enter* key or clicking on the *Continue* button closes the system message dialog box.

In the standard system, the main menu screen is displayed, as shown in Fig. 5-2. Users might get a different menu if the default settings of the user master records were modified to default them to other menus. A more detailed description on setting values for users is given later in this chapter.

When you see this screen, you have successfully logged on to the R/3 system.

Passwords

A *password* is a string of characters (letters and numbers) known to a single user, which prevents other users from accessing the system using that user identification. As stated before, when logging on for the very first

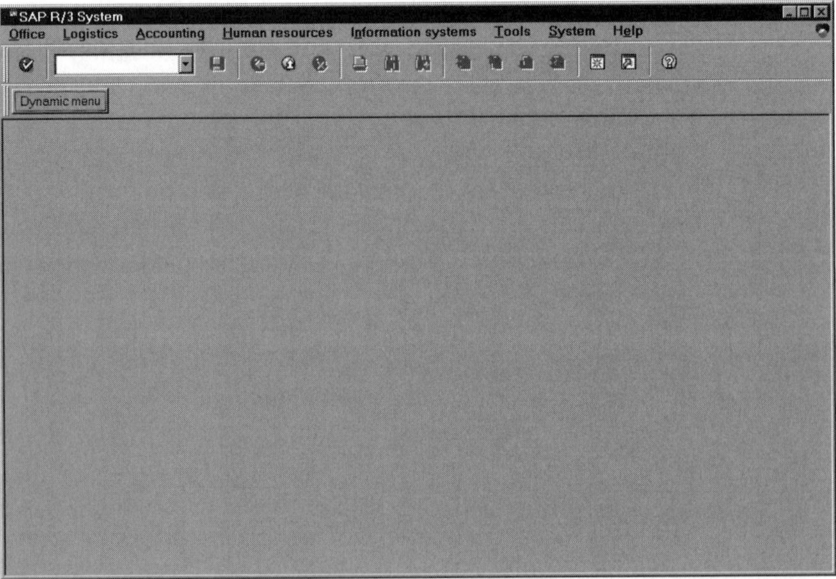

Figure 5-2
SAP R/3 main menu.

time, the new password dialog box is displayed, as shown in Fig. 5-3. There are specific rules for setting passwords.

Password Rules. In the SAP system, users must follow certain rules when entering passwords. Some rules are fixed in the SAP code and others can be set by the system administrator using certain profile parameters or by forbidding entries by specifying values in tables. These administrative topics are dealt with in the section entitled "Password Management" in Chap. 9.

Providing the administrator made no changes, the standard password rules of the system are as follows:

- Password length must be at least three characters long and no more than eight.
- Passwords are not case-sensitive, so, for example, if your password is *laura,* all strings *laura, LAuRa,* and *LAURA* behave just fine.
- Valid alphanumeric characters include all the letters (from *a* to *z*), the numbers, and even the punctuation marks, as long as the password does not begin with a question mark (?), a blank space, or an exclamation point (!).
- You cannot use the string *pass* as your password; nor can the password start with three identical characters (*oooyeah* is an invalid password).
- The password cannot begin with any sequence of three characters which matches the same sequence anywhere in your user ID (*laughu2* is an invalid password if your user ID is *laurab*).
- You cannot use any of the last five passwords.

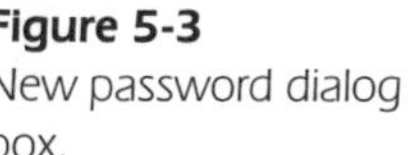

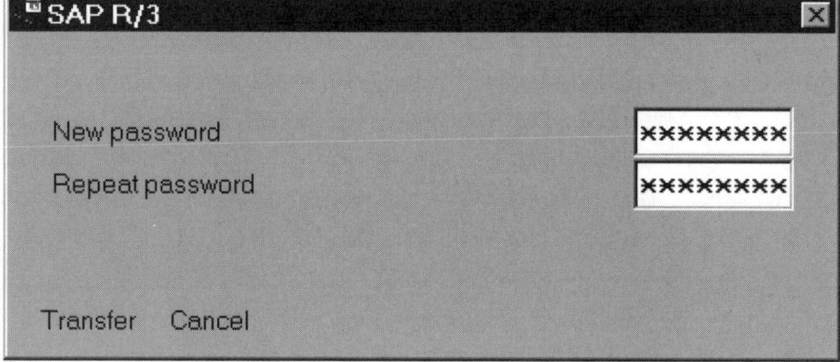

Figure 5-3 New password dialog box.

The following list gives some examples of valid and invalid passwords.

Valid Passwords	*Invalid Passwords*
13071985	pass (it's a system nonpermitted password)
maria099	!jun97 (begins with an invalid character)
hello=98	sapr3 (just because the system manager decided to include it among forbidden passwords)
uandme2	mmmycar (begins with the three identical characters)

System administrators can impose additional password rules, such as forbidding some strings of characters as passwords, setting a minimum password length other than three, setting an expiration time, and so forth. Refer to the section entitled "Password Management" in Chap. 9 for additional information.

Changing the Password. User passwords can be changed by the user owner, by the system administrator, or by any other user with the proper authorization for changing user master records.

Users must change their passwords when logging on for the very first time. The procedure which follows shows how:

When all the logon window fields have been filled up as described in the previous section (client, user ID, password—assigned by your system administrator—and language), pressing the *Enter* key will display the *password change* dialog box, like the one shown in Fig. 5-3.

In the *New password* field, type in your new password, adhering to the previous rules, and click with the mouse or press the *Tab* key to move to the *Repeat password* field; then repeat exactly the same password. This is a security measure to avoid typing mismatches. Next, press the *Transfer* button.

Users must follow exactly the same procedure of changing passwords in case the system administrator changes their passwords.

At any time, users can change their own passwords when logging in. To do so, they have to click on the *New password* button located on the application toolbar. When the fields are complete, the system proceeds with the *new password* dialog box and just follows the previous simple procedure.

It's important to know and make the users aware that they are not allowed to change their passwords more than once a day, unless they are privileged users with certain authorizations.

System administrators might decide to enforce a rule requiring users to change their passwords at regular intervals, say every 45 days. In such cases, the system sends the users a message requesting they do so. When the password expiration interval arrives, the *new password* logon windows automatically appear when the users log on requesting the password change. Users are forced to change the password, otherwise they cannot log in to the R/3 system and will have to contact the system administrator to request a new password.

System Administrator Procedure to Change Passwords for Other Users. Changing passwords for end users is a frequent task for system managers of most computer systems and applications. SAP is no exception. Sometimes users forget their original passwords and need to request new ones. In these cases, the R/3 administrator must follow this procedure.

From the main menu, select *Tools* → *Administration* → *User Maintenance* → *Users,* or, alternatively, go directly to the transaction by entering SU01 in the command field.

In the *User* field, type the user ID corresponding to the user whose password you want to change and then select the options *User names* → *Change password,* or directly press the *Change password* button on the application toolbar. Type in the new password then repeat it in the second field and press the *Copy* button to confirm the change.

Inform the user of the new password. When the system administrator performs this procedure, the system automatically requests that the user change the password when she/he logs on.

Logging Off

Users can log off the R/3 system from any screen. There are several procedures to log off:

1. From the menu bar, choose *System* → *Log off.* You get the *log off* dialog box as shown in Fig. 5-4. The box informs the user that any data or transaction not saved will be lost if continuing with the log off procedure.

   If you are not sure whether the data you were working on was saved, click on the *No* button in the dialog box, and you will be returned to the screen where you were working. Otherwise, press the *Yes* button to log off.

   This procedure will log you off from all your R/3 sessions, meaning it will close off the R/3 windows with the current user sessions.

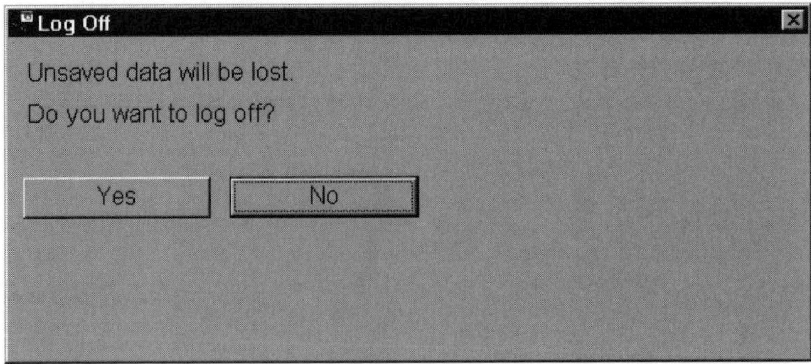

Figure 5-4
SAP R/3 logoff screen.

More information on sessions can be found in later sections of this chapter.

2. Another way to quickly exit all your R/3 sessions is to use the transaction codes */NEND* or */NEX* in the command field. */NEND* asks you to save data; */NEX* does not. With both transaction codes you will be logged off of all your current R/3 sessions.

CAUTION! *Using the /nex transaction will not ask you to save your data. So, if you are unsure whether you saved all your data, do not use this procedure.*

3. Clicking on the *Exit* button ( ) in the standard toolbar located on the R/3 initial screen also displays the *log off* dialog box.

The User Interface: Main Elements of the R/3 Window

This section discusses the main features of the R/3 windows interface and all the elements found in this user environment.

The windows environment of the R/3 SAPGUI includes most of the elements of popular Microsoft Windows applications, following the same style guides and ergonomic design methods. Depending on the nature and functionality of the particular R/3 application screen where the user is doing its tasks, the SAPGUI screens will contain popular check boxes, radio buttons, dialog boxes, icons, push buttons, menu items, and so forth. With the EnjoySAP release (R/3 4.6), SAP has concentrated on improving the user interface, making it easier, more flexible, and more adaptable to job roles. Now included are a better-looking interface, additional drag and drop capabilities, Internet browser features, and integration with the Web and other applications from the SAPGUI. An overview of the EnjoySAP user features is introduced at the end of the chapter.

The R/3 standard windows elements behave exactly the same as any other standard windows applications concerning scroll bars, minimizing a screen, moving windows, setting the active window, and so on. Therefore, reference to standard functions of the windows environment is not included in the following sections.

Figure 5-5 shows an example of an R/3 window from the human resources module which includes most typical elements, including check boxes, push buttons, tabstrips, possible entries input fields, and so on. From top to bottom we have the following items.

The *menu bar* contains the menu items corresponding to the particular R/3 application you are working on. In Fig. 5-5, the application belongs to the human resources modules (*Maintain HR Master Data*). In this application, the menu bar contains eight options: *HR Master Data, Edit, Goto, Environment, Auxiliary functions, System, Help,* and (layout menu). The whole R/3 system includes virtually hundreds of different menu items depending on the task.

Figure 5-5 Typical R/3 window from the HR module.

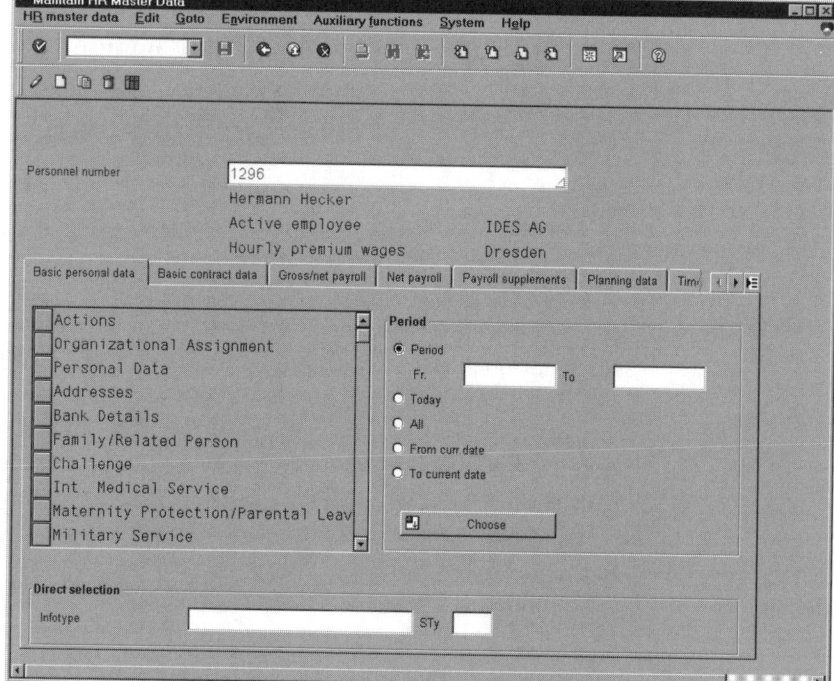

There are three menu options which are always present in every R/3 window: the System, Help, and the menu. The System menu contains groups of functions and utilities which are available to users at all times, including *print, change defaults, jobs,* and so on. The Help menu contains all the available options for the different types and methods of obtaining online help in the system. The menu, or layout menu, has a group of utilities which mainly affects the appearance and behavior of the R/3 windows, such as colors, fonts, grid lines, and automatic tabbing. The following sections describe in detail all the available functions and utilities of these three standard menus.

The next R/3 windows element is the *standard toolbar,* present in every application. It's a collection of icons which perform the most common functions available in the R/3 system. Figure 5-6 shows this toolbar. From left to right you find: *Enter,* the command field, *Save, Back, Exit, Cancel, Print, Find, Find next, First page, Previous page, Next page, Last page, Create new session, Generate shortcut,* and *Help.* Within the standard toolbar, you find the *command field,* which is very important for moving around the system with transactions. The command field also behaves like a *list box* or *history list,* remembering the last commands (transactions) performed.

The icons in the R/3 windows support the *focus* property of many windows applications. This means that if you place the cursor over an icon and wait a couple of moments, the system will show the function or definition of the icon.

The next part of the screen (shown in Fig. 5-7) is the *application toolbar* which normally contains icons or buttons most frequently used in that task or transaction, and from which options may be selected from the specific application menu bar. This design makes it more efficient for end users; however, some screens do not include application toolbars.

The *status bar* is the bottom line of the screen and usually shows informational or error messages to the users (see Fig. 5-8). If the whole message does not fit on the screen, you have the possibility of dragging the message to the left to see the rest of it. The status bar also includes other useful information such as the system data like the ID (K2P), the session number (1), the client (222), the hostname of the application server (k2p001), the writing mode (OVR, overwrite), and the local time. This information is further extended using the down arrow on the system data, so that users can also see the transaction code, user name, program, and response time.

Figure 5-6
Standard toolbar.

Current benefits | Open offer | Event offer | Eligibility | Insurability

Figure 5-7
Example of application toolbar.

Between the application toolbar and the status bar users find the normal working area for particular applications. This working area is the one intended for user input and output and can be made of icons, fields, push buttons, radio buttons, and so forth.

Now let's have a closer look at the most common options.

The Standard Toolbar

The standard toolbar is made of a collection of icons which perform the most common functions in every SAP application. Table 5-1 shows the available icons together with a description of the functions they perform. These functions are also normally available from the menu bar or from the function keys. Some functions, such as those performed by the scrolling icons, can be achieved by using standard windows functions—moving the scroll bars or pressing the *PageUp* and *PageDown* keys on a standard PC keyboard.

The standard toolbar also contains a very important field, the command field, where users can directly enter transaction codes to move directly to other applications or choose a transaction from a history list from the available list entries arrow in the field.

The Screen Layout Menu

The layout menu is used for customizing the display options of the R/3 windows. Figure 5-9 shows the available options under the layout menu. If you are an experienced Windows user, you will find that most tasks are basically the same as those available with the standard functions of the Windows environment.

E: Please enter Purchasing org. | K2P (1) (222) | k2p001 | OVR | 07:39AM

Figure 5-8
Status bar with error message.

TABLE 5-1

Available Icons on the Standard Toolbar

Icon	Description
	*OK* button. Performs the same function as pressing the *Enter* key. It's useful for continuing the transaction and going to the next screen. Also, when users get an error and are presented with a *No application* screen, pressing the *OK* button takes them back to the previous transaction.
	*Save* button. This function is available when there is something to save in the current transaction or application. Otherwise, this button is grayed out. It is sometimes available even if the data was already saved.
	*Back* button. Takes the user to the previous screen in a transaction.
	*Exit* button. This function returns the user to the previous transaction.
	*Cancel* button. The *Cancel* function stops the current transaction and goes back to the previous menu.
	*Print* button. Performs the print function. This is equivalent to choosing *System* → *List* → *Print.* This function is only available when printing report lists or other printable formats such as program codes, traces, and the like.
	*Find* button. Allows users to search for any particular screen in lists, reports, programs code, and so forth.
	*Find next* button. Search for the next occurrence of a previously searched term.
	*Go to first page* function button. The R/3 scrolling functions can be faster than using standard windows functions.
	*Go to previous page* button.
	*Go to next page* button.
	*Go to last page* function button.
	*Create session* button.
	*Create shortcut* button. Can be used for creating an icon in the desktop that can directly call an R/3 transaction, report, or system command.
	*Help* button. Equivalent to pressing F1.

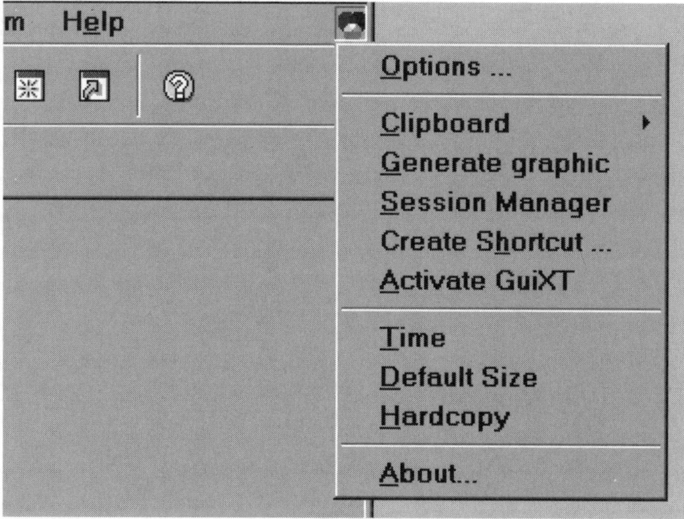

Figure 5-9
Screen layout menu.

Options to configure the layout and behavior of the R/3 windows elements allow you to

- Hide or display the standard toolbar, the application toolbar, and the status bar
- Change the text fonts and the colors of the R/3 windows
- Toggle the display of the system response time or local time in the status bar
- Use the clipboard to transfer information from the R/3 window to other windows applications
- Set the default size of the R/3 window
- Change the behavior of the cursor positioning in fields and set the automatic tabbing function when the input field is complete
- Activate some optional front end components such as the Session Manager or the GuiXT
- Create SAPGUI shortcuts on the desktop

Many of these tasks are performed with additional functions inside the Options menu. For the Options menu, the system displays an additional screen known as the *Options* folder, from which most of the tasks previously introduced are performed. The *Options* folder looks like Fig. 5-10.

Changing the Fonts of the Text Elements. The *Fonts* tab within the *Options* folder can be used for changing the font's appearance and size on the R/3 screens. Figure 5.11 shows the *Fonts* options.

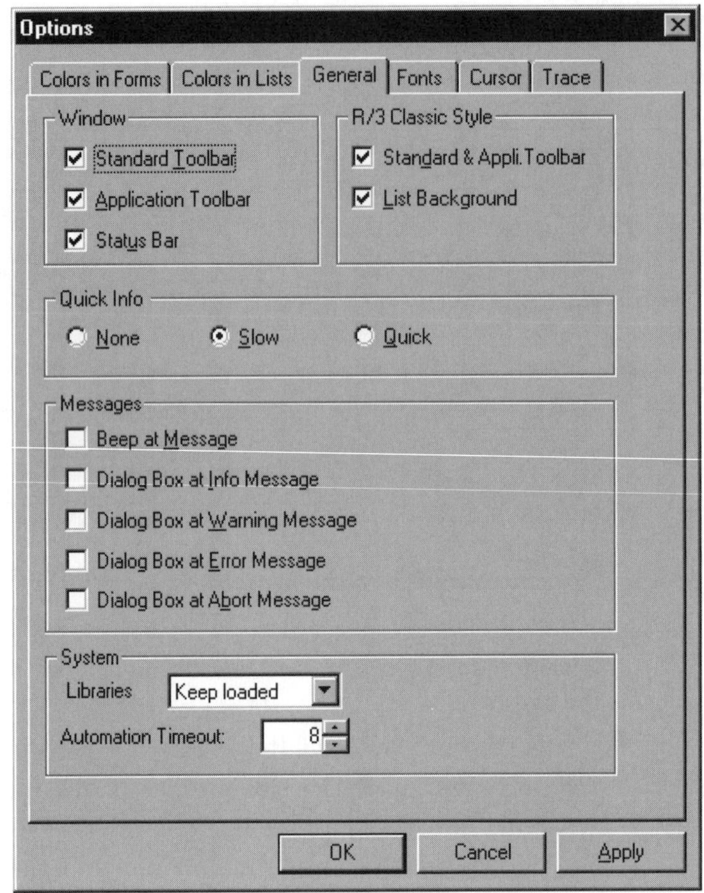

Figure 5-10 The *Options* folder screen.

R/3 allows users to set their own fonts by selecting the *Custom Settings* radio button and choosing the font type and font size. Alternatively, it includes three standard settings (Small, Medium, and Large) that can be adjusted according to user needs.

Depending on your SAPGUI release, you might find instead two options boxes for selecting fixed fonts, which are used in the application input fields and graphic screens, and another for specifying variable fonts that affect the appearance of field names and toolbars.

In any case, in the Preview box, you can see how the fonts will look in the R/3 windows before applying the changes.

Changing the Colors of the R/3 Window. You can change the colors of various elements of your R/3 window, such as input fields, highlighted

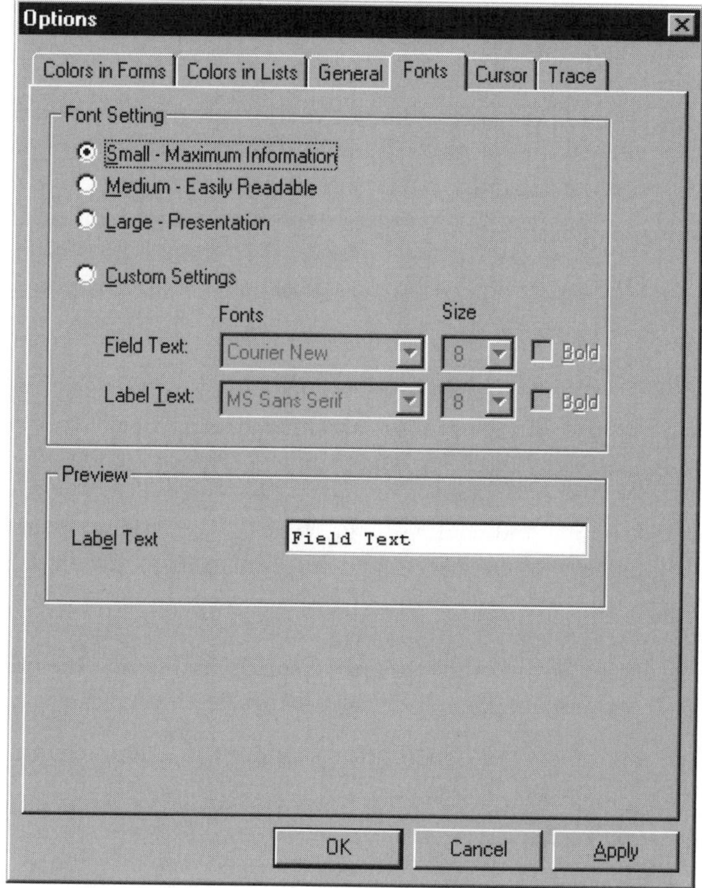

Figure 5-11
Font folder under the *Options* screen.

fields, and lists. Users can choose from available predefined color palettes or can define their own colors. Be careful when you change colors since only the default settings guarantee that all the information on a screen is legible.

The procedure to change colors is slightly different when changing colors in lists. The other changeable elements can be set as follows:

- From the Options screen, select the *Colors in Forms* folder. If you haven't changed the settings previously, the *Color Palettes* field will be defaulted to *Standard*.
- Clicking on the possible entries arrow to the right of *Color Palettes* will display a list of available palettes.
- Select one of the palettes from the list.

For changing the colors displayed in lists, select the *Colors in Lists* folder from the Options screen. You will get the *List colors* dialog box. The *List colors* dialog box contains three columns with seven color choices each. The columns belong to different types of text displayed in lists. The types are normal, intensive, and inverse. Table 5-2 shows the color numbers assigned to specific text types and categories.

You can change either the text color itself or the background color. First, select the color you want to change by clicking over the field or on the radio button to the left. Then, either click on the radio button *Text color* or *Background color.* Clicking on the *Change* button displays the *Color* dialog box.

The *Color* dialog box is very similar to the one used in the configuration of the Windows environment. Select a color from the basic options or create a custom color using the full Windows palette.

Repeat the same procedure for the rest of the colors in lists you want to change and confirm your choices by clicking on the *OK* button or cancel your configuration by clicking on the *Cancel* button.

Hiding and Displaying the Standard Bars. You can decide to display or hide the standard toolbar, application toolbar, and status bar. The system displays them by default. To change the settings:

- Select the *General* folder under the Options menu. Figure 5-10 shows the screen.
- In the figure, you can see three check boxes, each one belonging to a standard bar. The check boxes behave like toggles: on or off.

TABLE 5-2

Color Assignments to Text Types

Color Number	Intensive	Normal
1	Headings	Secondary headings
2	Body of the list (first row only)	Body of the list (either one color or alternating rows)
3	Totals, higher level subtotals	Subtotals
4	Key columns	Highlighted lines/columns
5	Positive threshold value	Inserted lines
6	Negative threshold value	
7	Hierarchy heading	Hierarchy information

- To hide the standard toolbar, deselect the check box next to *Standard toolbar.* To display it, leave the box checked.
- The same method applies to the application toolbar and the status bar. Please notice that if you hide the status bar, all system messages will appear as dialog boxes. This method can be either a pain in the neck or very useful for those users who find it difficult to be aware of the status bar.
- When finished, press the *OK* button to confirm the selections or click on the *Cancel* button to reset your options to the previous settings.

Configuring Automatic Tabbing Between Fields. The R/3 window includes an automatic tabbing feature which can be very useful when users must enter information in many fields and don't want to press the *Tab* key to move from field to field. When the automatic tabbing feature is enabled, the cursor automatically moves to the next field when you reach the end of an actual input field.

AutoTAB only works at the end of an input field. For example, if the a field can hold up to nine characters, and you enter only four, you still have to press the *Tab* key to move to the next input field.

To enable the automatic tabbing, select the *Cursor* folder under the Options menu, and then select the check box next to *Automatic TAB at Field End.* The check box works like a toggle; so, to disable the automatic tabbing, deselect the check box.

Hiding Grid Lines in Lists. You can choose to display or hide grid lines in lists. Lists in the SAP system are represented by screen outputs with lines containing information. There are thousands in the R/3 system. Examples of lists are the output of the user monitoring screen, the jobs overview display, or the output of a report containing the available materials.

When you have lists in your screens, you might decide between two types of grid lines to separate the output lines and fields: regular or three-dimensional (3-D).

To change the display of grid lines in lists, from the Options window, select the *Colors in Lists* folder. To display grid lines in lists, check the box next to *Lines in Lists.* To have the 3-D effect on the grid lines, select the *3D Effects* check box located in the *Colors in Forms* folder as well.

Determining the Cursor Position When Clicking on a Field. R/3 users can decide how they want the cursor to behave when clicking on the blank area of an input field. For instance, the cursor could automatically position itself at the beginning of the field when the user clicks anywhere in a blank field, or it could position itself to the right of any text already entered in the field, considering blank spaces as if they were nulls. Alternatively, users can decide to leave the normal behavior of the cursor positioning, which is to appear exactly where they place it in the field, whether there are blank spaces or not.

Determining the behavior of the cursor positioning depends on the type of tasks users perform most frequently. For example, when the screens they most often use require entering data in many empty fields, it is advisable to make the cursor appear at the end of any text when clicking anywhere behind the text. In such cases, if the input fields are empty, the cursor will position automatically at the beginning of the field, ready for entering data. This is the default setting.

The other setting is to place the cursor exactly in the field position that the user clicks on with the mouse, whether the field is empty or not. This is more suitable for making lots of modifications in fields which already contain data and when users move across fields using the arrow keys instead of the *Tab* key or the mouse.

Cursor behavior is set by selecting the *Cursor* folder in Options menu. In this folder there is a check box with the caption *Cursor to End of Text on Mouse Click.* If this box is checked, the cursor will be positioned at the end of the text of the input field. Otherwise, the cursor will be positioned wherever the user clicks on a field.

Resetting the Default Windows Size. The option *Default size* under the layout menu ( ) adjusts the size of the R/3 window to the default window size. This feature, however, flashes an error message in the status bar if the user does not have the correct windows resolution. And it won't have any effect if the windows still have the default size.

The windows size can be changed by following the normal procedures used in any other screen of other windows applications.

Changing the Time Display in the Status Bar. You can choose whether the system displays the local time or the system response time in the status bar. Response time is the time the R/3 system takes to process a dialog step and present the information back to the users.

This feature is located in the menu and behaves like a toggle between the two time displays, meaning that the time display that appears in the menu changes each time you select the feature. In the standard system, the default time display in the status bar is the local time.

To change the time display from local time to system response time, select *Response time* from the menu. The menu automatically closes and the time display area will remain empty until you perform any function in the system (such as a screen change). Then the response time will appear. The figures shown on the status bars are measured in seconds.

To change the time display from response time back to local time, select *Time* from the menu.

Using the Clipboard. You can transfer the contents of fields onto the clipboard of your windowing environment and then paste them into other fields of the R/3 system or into other windows applications. You can move or copy the contents of fields by using the functions of the *Clipboard* option located in the menu.

The R/3 clipboard functions work very similarly to the clipboard functions of the Windows environment. In many R/3 screens and applications, for example, when working with the ABAP editor, you also have copy and paste functions below the Edit menu. However, options under the Edit menu only work inside the R/3 system and cannot be transferred to other windows applications. The Edit menu usually contains more extensive options than the clipboard.

The R/3 clipboard presents four options: *Mark, Copy, Cut,* and *Paste*. The *Mark* option is useful when selecting several fields to copy and paste. Otherwise, just select a field by clicking and dragging the pointer over the text field and select the most appropriate option. When the *Mark* option is selected, the cursor changes automatically to a crosshair sign. The selection is made by clicking on a corner of the area to copy and holding the mouse and dragging to the opposite corner. The R/3 system will display a rectangle indicating the selected area.

In display-only fields (which cannot be changed) you can copy the contents to other fields, but you cannot *Cut* them.

Shortcuts

Shortcuts are a component of the SAPGUI that works in the 32-bit Windows platforms (Windows 95, Windows 98, and NT), and are very useful for quickly running those functions or transactions that are more frequently used. Shortcuts can be created from the standard toolbar of the

R/3 SAPGUI, or can be manually created (using program *sapsh.exe* or *sapshcut.exe* with parameters). Once they are created, shortcuts appear as regular desktop icons that can even be included in other Windows documents or sent by e-mail.

Shortcuts are automatically installed with the SAPGUI of release 4.5 and EnjoySAP (release 4.6). However, they can be used with release 4.0B, although with limited functionality.

The easiest way to create a shortcut for a particular application is to go to the required screen with regular R/3 menu functions or transaction codes. Once in the transaction for which a shortcut is desired, click on the *Create shortcut* icon on the standard toolbar. Figure 5-12 shows the dialog box for creating shortcuts. Enter the requested logon data and click *OK*.

The system automatically creates a SAP shortcut on the Windows desktop. To run the SAP shortcut, just double-click on the icon. For security reasons the system will display a dialog box requesting the username and password. After a successful logon, the shortcut will take you automatically to the defined transaction or report.

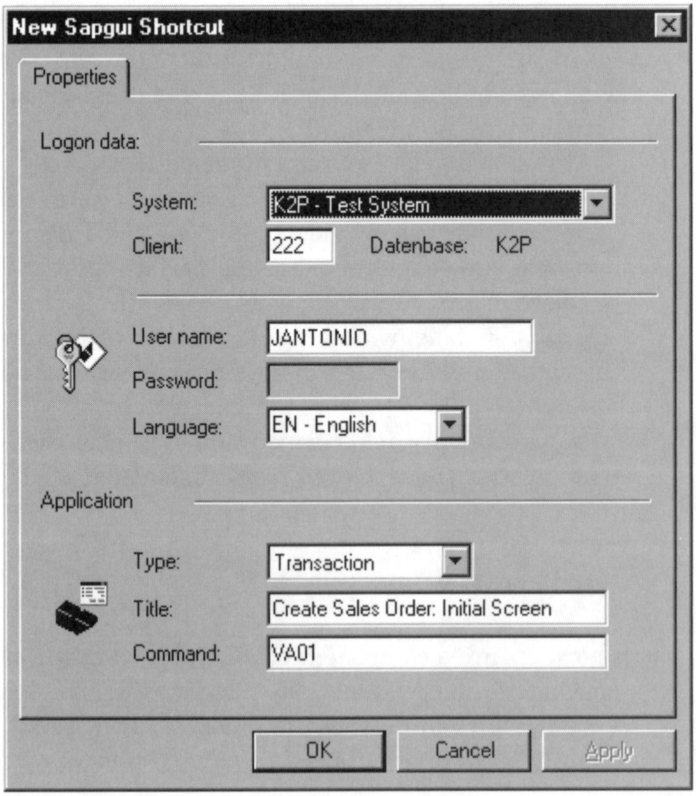

Figure 5-12 Create shortcut window.

Shortcuts can also be used in the current SAPGUI sessions, which eliminates having to enter username and password. There are three options:

- If you drag and drop the shortcut on the existing session, the system will automatically go to the defined shortcut transaction.
- To run the shortcut on a new session, hold the <CTRL> key while dragging the shortcut to the R/3 window.
- To change the shortcut parameters, hold the <SHIFT> key while dragging the shortcut to the R/3 window.

System Status Information

In every R/3 window, users have the option of displaying important information about the system, the user, the transaction, and other data, which can be extremely helpful on many occasions.

The status screen can be accessed by choosing *System* → *Status* from any R/3 window. In the Status window, under the *Usage data* box, you can see what the actual user name, client, language, date, and time are. Most important, though, is the *Repository data* where the system displays the transaction, program, and screen number. This is the way users can locate the transactions they are working on and developers or support personnel can easily locate the specific programs or menus that might have errors.

With SAPGUI release 4.5 and later, part of the status information can also be displayed from the status bar by clicking on the possible entries arrow on the system box.

Working with R/3 User Sessions

Users of the R/3 system can work on more than one task at a time by means of opening new sessions. *Sessions* are like independent R/3 windows where you can perform other tasks. By default, a user can open up to nine sessions and work or move around all open sessions at the same time, without interrupting the work on other sessions. For example, users might decide to have a session open to watch the status of background or printing jobs, while performing their usual tasks in other sessions.

Sessions can be closed at any time, without having to log off the system. However, when a user closes off the last session, this has the same effect as logging off.

The system administrator might decide to limit the allowed number of open sessions to less than nine, since the workload caused by open sessions is virtually the same as having additional users logged on to the system.

Users can create new sessions from anywhere, since the *Create session* function is under the System menu: also, there is an icon in the standard toolbar, available in every R/3 window.

To create a new session, click on the *Create Session* icon, or, from the menu bar, select *System → Create session.* The system will open a new R/3 window with a new session and will place it in front of all other windows, immediately making it the active session. The status bar at the bottom of the screen shows the session number in parentheses beside the SAP system name (SID). The new session will be either the initial R/3 window or the user-assigned initial menu.

There is, however, a faster way to create a new session and a task (transaction) in a single step by using transaction codes in the command field. In order to do that, users have to know the needed transaction code. The R/3 system includes some utilities to help users find the needed transaction codes. When opening a new session with a transaction code, the system displays the initial screen of the transaction in a new session.

To create a new session with a specific transaction at once, you must enter */O<TCODE>* in the command field: front slash (/), the letter *O,* and *<TCODE>,* which stands for *transaction code.* For example, typing */OS001* in the command field and pressing *Enter* will start a new session with the initial screen of the task belonging to transaction S001 (ABAP workbench). Figure 5-13 shows the command field with the example described.

Moving among sessions is like moving among windows in the Windows environment: with your mouse just click on any part of an R/3 window to make that session the active one. In the Microsoft Windows environment, you could also use the popular key combination Alt-*Tab.* Likewise, you can iconize or maximize your windows as you would with any other application.

Ending sessions is easy; however, users should be careful to save data before ending sessions, since the system will not prompt them to save the data unless they are in the last open session—in which case, ending it is the same as logging off the system. When working in different sessions you don't lose any data as long as you don't log off without saving it first.

Figure 5-13 Opening a new session and a new task at once from the command field.

There are several ways to end sessions:

1. Select *System* → *End session* from the menu bar.
2. Press the *Exit* button ( ) on the standard toolbar when located in the higher level task (for instance, the transaction you first called when opening the session or the R/3 main menu).

   Note that ending a session is not the same as logging off. The system behaves in that way only when you are in your last open session.
3. Log off the system completely, in which case all open sessions for the current user are ended.

Moving Around the R/3 System

Users of the R/3 system need to move around to perform their usual work. The SAP system includes several ways to move around. The most usual is by selecting options from the application menus and submenus. This allows users to navigate and choose from the available functions to perform their tasks without the need to memorize keyboard combinations or transactions codes. Navigation in application menus is possible either with the mouse or with the keyboard. Selecting options is just like any other typical windows application: just drag around the menus and click the function you want to start.

Selecting functions just with the keyboard might not be very convenient but it's easy. Pressing the F10 key takes you to the menu bar. From there, you can navigate with the arrow keys: right, left, down, and up. Once you are located over the needed option, just press the *Enter* key. To cancel a selection press the *Esc* key. To cancel the menu bar selection, press F10 again. To move around the R/3 work area, press the *Tab* key to go forward from field to field or *Shift-Tab* to move backward.

Once users working on particular tasks decide to finish their work and go to another application function, they have to move back through the menus and locate their new menus.

Within each specific application screen, usually the most common functions are directly accessible through the push buttons on the standard toolbar and the application toolbar. For example, when working in the initial screen for user administration, you will see the buttons for functions such as *Create, Copy, Change password,* which are the most common ones.

Likewise, clicking and holding the right-hand push button of the mouse (for right-handed people) shows a pop-up box with those usual functions and the equivalent keyboard combinations. This is known as the *function key menu.* The options available under the function key menu differ among tasks. Figure 5-14 shows an example of a function key menu.

Another way to move around, often used by expert users, is by entering transaction codes in the command field. With this method, users can go directly to a task without navigating through the application menus.

Moving Around with Transaction Codes

The R/3 system provides an alternative way of selecting menu options for moving around the tasks and functions of the SAP system by using transaction codes directly in the command field.

Using transaction codes gives users the advantage of moving faster to

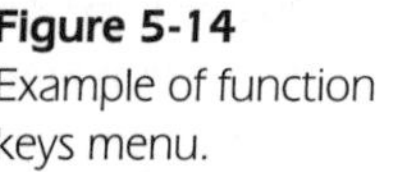

Figure 5-14
Example of function keys menu.

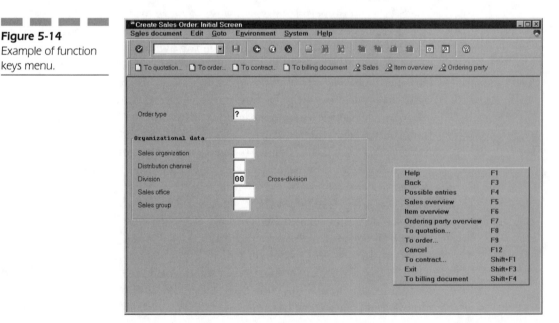

other transactions and also creating a new session with another function at once. When moving with transactions, you can go to any part of the R/3 system, not just the application you are working with. There is, of course, the need for the necessary authorization in order to execute the task.

The disadvantage is that in order to use this method, users have to memorize cryptic transaction codes. A *transaction code* is a four-character code associated with a SAP task. By typing the transaction code in the command field and pressing the *Enter* key, the system takes you directly to the initial screen for that transaction.

Every function within the R/3 system has a transaction code associated with it. There are two main ways to find the transaction code you want to use.

The first way is to first navigate with the menu functions and reach the desired screen. When in the screen, select *System → Status.* You get the status windows, which contains the transaction code in the transaction field.

Another way to find a transaction code is to use the *Dynamic menu* function located on the application toolbar of the system.

An easy way to find a transaction code in the dynamic menu is by clicking on the top line of the application areas and pressing the *Search* and *Search next* buttons.

To move around by entering transaction codes, position the cursor in the command field. Then enter */N* followed by the transaction code, for example, */NS000,* where */N* indicates to end the current task, and *S000* is the transaction code. Transaction S000 is the SAP initial screen. When you are in the initial screen you don't have to enter */N* before the transaction code because there is no task to end. Upon pressing the *Enter* key, the current task is finished and the system takes you automatically to the specified task.

Another way to work with transaction codes but not end the current task is to create a new session and a new task at once, as stated previously and shown in Fig. 5-13. To do that, you must enter */O* and the transaction code. For example, typing */OSE09* in the command field opens a new session in a new R/3 window with the initial screen of the workbench organizer, which is transaction SE09.

The command field includes an entries list indicated by the down arrow on the right side, which is a history list of transaction codes previously entered since you logged on. You could also press the history list and select a transaction from that list. Clicking on a transaction from the list and pressing the *Enter* key displays the initial screen associated with the transaction. A history list display is shown in Fig. 5-15.

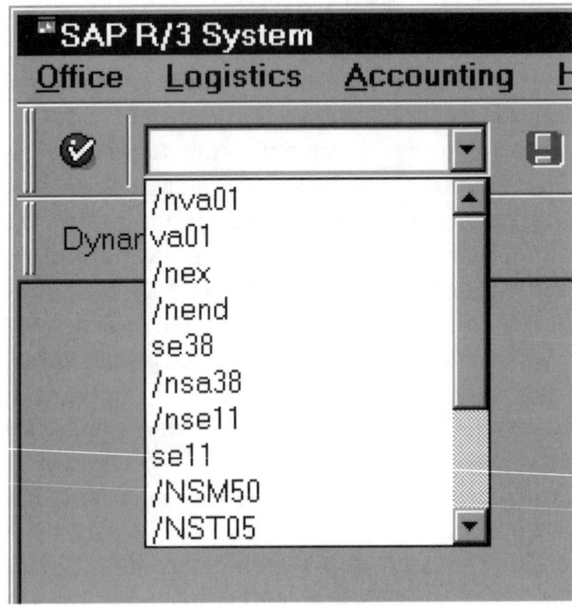

Figure 5-15 Command field history list.

When using the *System* → *Status* function to find the transaction code for the current task, you must be aware that many transactions have several screens associated with them. So, when using transaction codes to move to a task, you can only reach the initial screen for the transaction.

Working with Information

User work on the the R/3 system normally involves entering data into the system or displaying information from it. To perform those functions, users select options from menus, enter data in the input fields, send jobs to the printer, and interact with the system through dialog boxes.

A *field* is a single unit of information, such as a zip code or a last name. Fields have a *field name* (a description) and *field data* (actual data). Figure 5-16 shows an example of some fields in an R/3 window, where *User* is the field name and *SMITH* is the actual data.

There are two fields types in the R/3 windows: *Display* fields and *Input* fields. *Display* fields are fields which show information to the users. *Input* fields are fields where users can enter data.

Fields have different lengths limiting the amount of allowed characters. In the R/3 windows, the field length is determined by the length shown on the screen, or by the length of the database field.

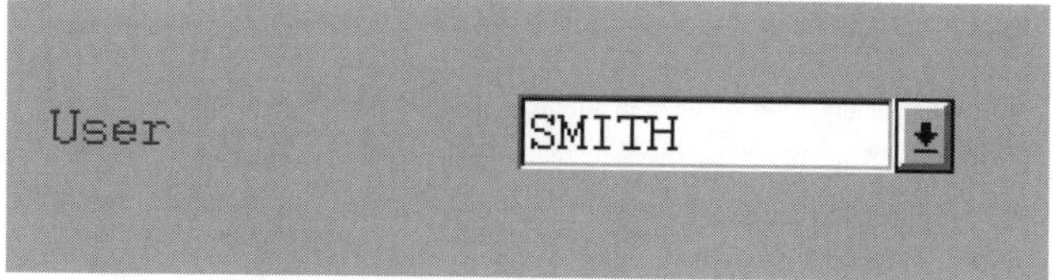

Figure 5-16 Example of field description and field data.

When entering data, users have two common methods available in standard windows applications which require entering information: overwrite (replace) and insert. The default in R/3 is set to replace. The status bar shows the mode (OVR or INS) in which a user is working. To switch methods, just press the *INS* key on the keyboard. It works like a toggle.

To enter data in a field, just position the cursor and type it in. When finished and the field is full, the cursor moves to the next field automatically when autoTAB is enabled. Otherwise, just press the *Tab* key or click on the next field.

Possible Entries for an Input Field

The SAP system provides several types of facilities for helping users fill the data in fields.

Input fields sometimes show a possible entries arrow, where the system can display a list of possible entries. Users select the entry, and the system transfers them automatically to the field.

Another method of finding entries is with *matchcodes* and *search helps.* As their names state, these are methods for helping users find possible entries using different search criteria, that is, using other related fields.

Not all input fields have lists of possible entries. Users do not know if input fields have possible entries, except for search helps which are indicated with a small triangle in the lower right-hand corner.

To display a list of values, position the cursor on the field, click on the possible entries arrow, or press F4. If the field is associated with a matchcode or search help, a dialog box for selecting the search hot key will appear. Select a key to pass to the dialog box for restricting the values for the search, and click on the *Continue* icon. An example of such a list is shown in Fig. 5-17. The list can be long and might not show all entries, in which case it usually includes a function button *Restrict Values,* which can be used for entering additional criteria or reducing the maximum number of hits to further restrict the values that are displayed. It also includes some function buttons for sorting the display or finding a specific entry.

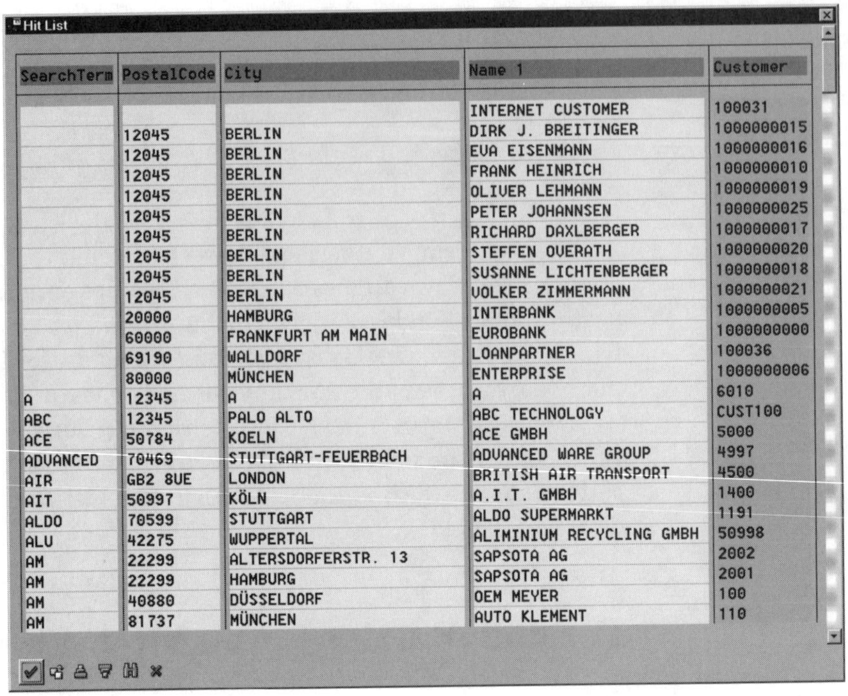

Figure 5.17
Example of a hit list.

Hit List

SearchTerm	PostalCode	City	Name 1	Customer
			INTERNET CUSTOMER	100031
	12045	BERLIN	DIRK J. BREITINGER	1000000015
	12045	BERLIN	EVA EISENMANN	1000000016
	12045	BERLIN	FRANK HEINRICH	1000000010
	12045	BERLIN	OLIVER LEHMANN	1000000019
	12045	BERLIN	PETER JOHANNSEN	1000000025
	12045	BERLIN	RICHARD DAXLBERGER	1000000017
	12045	BERLIN	STEFFEN OVERATH	1000000020
	12045	BERLIN	SUSANNE LICHTENBERGER	1000000018
	12045	BERLIN	VOLKER ZIMMERMANN	1000000021
	20000	HAMBURG	INTERBANK	1000000005
	60000	FRANKFURT AM MAIN	EUROBANK	1000000000
	69190	WALLDORF	LOANPARTNER	100036
	80000	MÜNCHEN	ENTERPRISE	1000000006
A	12345	A	A	6010
ABC	12345	PALO ALTO	ABC TECHNOLOGY	CUST100
ACE	50784	KOELN	ACE GMBH	5000
ADVANCED	70469	STUTTGART-FEUERBACH	ADVANCED WARE GROUP	4997
AIR	GB2 8UE	LONDON	BRITISH AIR TRANSPORT	4500
AIT	50997	KÖLN	A.I.T. GMBH	1400
ALDO	70599	STUTTGART	ALDO SUPERMARKT	1191
ALU	42275	WUPPERTAL	ALIMINIUM RECYCLING GMBH	50998
AM	22299	ALTERSDORFERSTR. 13	SAPSOTA AG	2002
AM	22299	HAMBURG	SAPSOTA AG	2001
AM	40880	DÜSSELDORF	OEM MEYER	100
AM	81737	MÜNCHEN	AUTO KLEMENT	110

To select an entry, double click on it, or click once and press *Enter.* Value is transferred to the field. To change the data in an input field, normally just type over it. If the field is for display only, no change is possible, unless you have a button which can switch between display and change modes. Display-only fields have the same color background as the screen's background.

When working in the R/3 system, some input fields have a question mark in them (?), which means that these fields are *required.* If a particular screen contains a required field, you must enter data into it in order to proceed to the next screen in the task or transaction.

Sometimes users find screens without required fields. In such cases, users can proceed without entering any data. However, in some situations, if data is entered in nonrequired fields, users might have to deal with any required fields associated with them.

Trying to proceed to the next screen when a required field has not been filled out triggers an error message in the status bar, and the cursor is automatically positioned in the required field.

Often you can get help on values to enter in input fields which do not have an associated search help but do have a possible entries list arrow.

This last option is common when the search does not have to mix different views or tables but only has to use the main table associated with a field.

To display a list of entries for a field, just position the cursor on the field. If it has possible entries, the down arrow button appears to the right. Clicking on it displays the possible values. If the arrow does not show, then the field does not have possible entries. To select one of the values shown in the list and transfer it to the field, double click on the desired value.

If the number of entries is very long, it can be limited by using wildcards in the field before clicking on the possible entries arrow. For example, entering *ma** will only display values starting with *ma*.

Facilities for Entering the Same Data Repeatedly

SAP provides functions to ease the input of repetitive data, for example, when filling out invoices, material master records, orders, or even when creating users with similar data. Those facilities can be used with the *Set data* and the *Hold data* functions.

For example, suppose you want to create users with the same profile. You can enter the data once and hold it, using this data for the creation of the rest of the users. The system can transfer automatically the held data to the corresponding input fields. These functions are located under the *System → User Profile* menu. These functions are not available in all the screens. The system will display a message in the status bar when this occurs.

With the *Hold data* function, users can change the data after it is transferred to the input fields. With *Set data,* changes are not possible. This means that *Hold data* is good for occasions when there are small differences in the fields. *Set data* has the advantage that the cursor skips over input fields with held data, so you don't have to move among fields.

Data is held on a screen until a user decides to delete the held data or when the user logs off from the R/3 system. To hold the data on the screen, you first enter the data to be held in the input fields. Then, select *System → User profile* from the menu bar. If you want to hold the data with the ability to change it, choose *Hold data.* If you want to hold the data without changing it and to skip the fields with held data, select *Set data.* If *Hold data* and *Set data* are not available, a message is displayed in the status bar.

To delete the data held on a screen, go to the screen containing the held data to be deleted and choose *System → User profile → Delete data* from the menu bar.

Input Field Default Values with User Parameters

User parameters are other facilities that the R/3 system offers for fast data input. User parameters are associated with certain common fields of the system, but not all. For example, common input fields in many R/3 business applications are *Company code, Plant, Purchasing group,* and so forth. When you define a user parameter for a field, every time and in every screen that the same field appears, it will have the default value specified.

In order to define these parameters, you have to know the technical details of the fields you want to set. To get the parameter name (PID), press the F1 function key for the field for which you want to set the value. This function displays a help screen for the field which includes the button *Technical info* in the bottom part.

Clicking this button, you get the technical information screen for this field: table name, field name, and so on. Figure 5-18 shows an example of

Figure 5-18 Parameter ID field in the technical information screen.

this screen. On the right-hand side, you can see the *Parameter ID* field. In the example, this parameter is *WRK* which corresponds to the plant.

If you always work with the same plant, you can enter this parameter in your defaults. To do so, select *System → User profile → Own data* from the main menu. On this screen, click on the *Parameters* tabstrip, enter the parameter ID code and the default value. Upon pressing the *Enter* key, the system will automatically display the definition for the parameter, as shown in Fig. 5-19. Here, users can enter as many parameters as they like.

Getting Help in the R/3 System

R/3 includes many possibilities to get online help for almost every element of the system. Users can get help with entire applications, for specific functions, for glossary terms, fields, reports, messages, and so on.

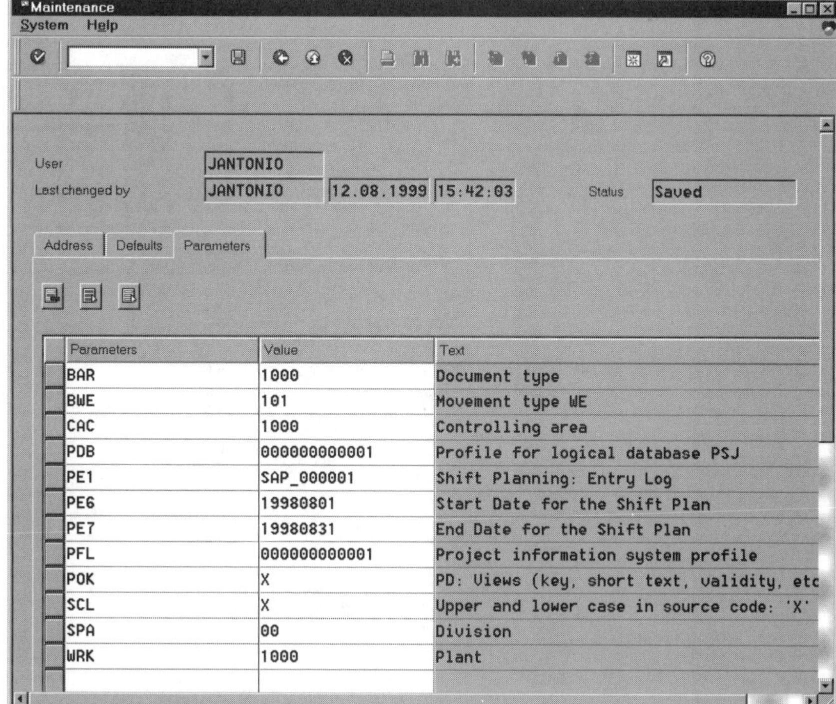

Figure 5-19 Maintaining parameter ID values.

One of the standard menus in every R/3 window is the Help menu, from which users have several options to obtain help. Together with the Help menu, users can press the F1 function key or click on the button to get help on descriptions and explanations on fields, functions, messages, and so forth.

Finally, users can obtain help when entering data in fields. The system often displays many fields either with possible entries lists or with matchcodes associated with them.

Figure 5-20 shows the Help menu. Options included in the menu are as follows:

- *Extended help.* Links with detailed instructions for the tasks, normally calling the online documentation
- *R/3 library.* Links with the initial screen for the online documentation library
- *Glossary.* Contains definitions of common SAP terms related to the current task
- *Release notes.* Includes the release notes for the latest R/3 versions
- *Getting started.* Links to the section "Getting started with R/3" in the online documentation library

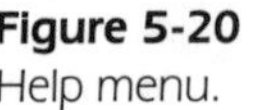

Figure 5-20
Help menu.

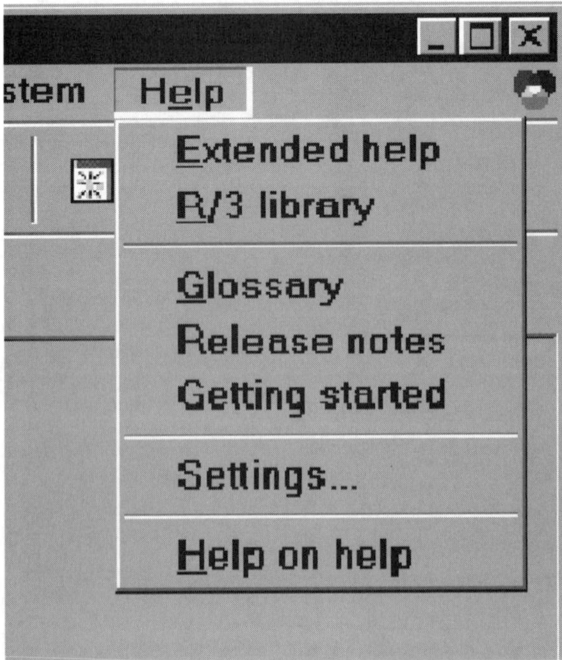

- *Settings.* For deciding whether to display help in a modal R/3 window or use an external help viewer.
- *Help on help.* Describes the features of the help system and how to use it

The online documentation can be always be looked up to see the available help for a specific R/3 application or the basis system. The online documentation is a CD-ROM which comes bundled with the SAP kit and must be installed by the administrator either directly in a CD-ROM drive or can be copied to a LAN server so all users can access it.

The *Extended Help* option is meant to display step-by-step instructions for the task or application you are currently working on. If, when selecting *Help → Extended Help,* there is no extended help available, you get the initial R/3 library screen.

The option *R/3 library* from the Help menu links directly with the online documentation and is presented in HTML or compressed CHM format depending on how the online help was installed and the front end used. From the main menu you can proceed by choosing any application, topic, or area of your interest and then navigate the documentation with the windows hypertext utilities.

With the *Help → Glossary* function, users can look up the meaning of terms related to the current task they are working on. When the meaning of a word or term used by SAP in some application is not clear, choosing the *Glossary* option from the Help menu shows a dialog box with related terms. If it is a long list, use the scroll bars to find the needed term. To display the definition for the term, double click on it.

The SAP system provides help on most fields, input fields, or messages that appear in the R/3 screen. Not all fields have related help available.

To get help on a particular field, position the cursor over it and press the *Help* button or the F1 function key. You get a help screen in which some terms in the help field might appear highlighted. This means those terms are defined in the online glossary. Double clicking on those highlighted terms shows their definitions.

Another way in which the R/3 system provides help is when system or error messages are displayed in the status bar. Double clicking on the status bar shows additional information about the message. Sometimes the additional help on the message includes a hypertext link which can take you directly to a transaction to solve the problem. Another way to get help about the message in the status bar is by positioning the cursor over the message and pressing the F1 key.

When specifying or executing a report, from the execution screen you can get additional information on the report by choosing *Help → Extended Help.*

The help option to display the SAP R/3 release notes can be very useful when upgrading the system or when you want to see what has changed or what is new in the current release compared to previous releases.

The *Help → Release notes* option allows you to search notes by full text or attributes. Or you can see all the notes by clicking on the *Complete list* buttons.

Release notes can be very long, depending on the particular version. To search for release notes, the R/3 system permits users to specify search criteria or attributes.

Attributes are the types of information contained in the release notes. For example, whether it is a correction or a new function, what version it is, if it has an effect on interfaces or batch input, and so forth.

The *Help on help* option explains how to move around the help functions in the R/3 system.

Finally, apart from the options under the Help menu, there is the type of help that the R/3 system offer the users for filling up input fields. This help is provided by means of possible entries lists and search helps.

Working with Search Helps

A *search help* is technically a special dictionary object that came with R/3 release 4.0 for simplifying and replacing previous *matchcodes* (although for compatibility reasons matchcodes still exist). Functionally, search helps are a tool for helping users to find the records they need. Search helps are made up of a collection of search terms. More information on search helps can be found in Chap. 8.

When an input field has a little triangle in the lower right-hand corner you know it has an associated matchcode (see Fig. 5-21). When the input field has a an associated search help, positioning the cursor on it first displays the possible entries arrow. For example, when looking for a specific material, users might not know the material number, but they might remember the provider, the class, the type, the old name, or the description. Materials have a very large number of associated fields. Search helps provide a method of simplifying the search, so users can find the desired value using the search method they know best.

For example, when searching for a material, you could use any of the

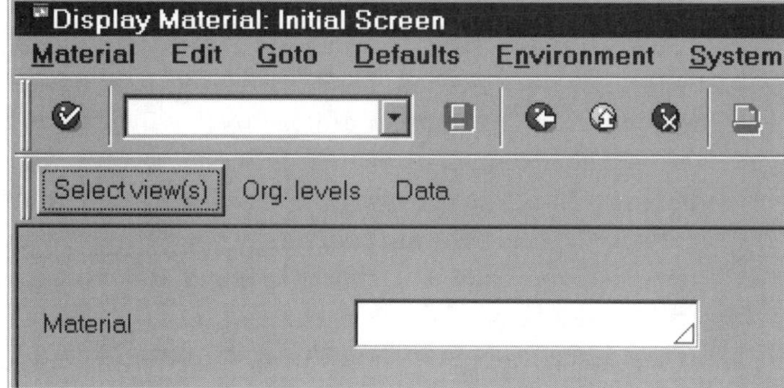

Figure 5-21
Field with search help.

search terms associated with it. Position the cursor inside the input field and press the F4 function key or the entries arrow to get the list of associated search methods (search terms) for the search help. If this is the first time using this search help and there is no default value, a dialog box similar to the one shown in Fig. 5-22 appears on the screen.

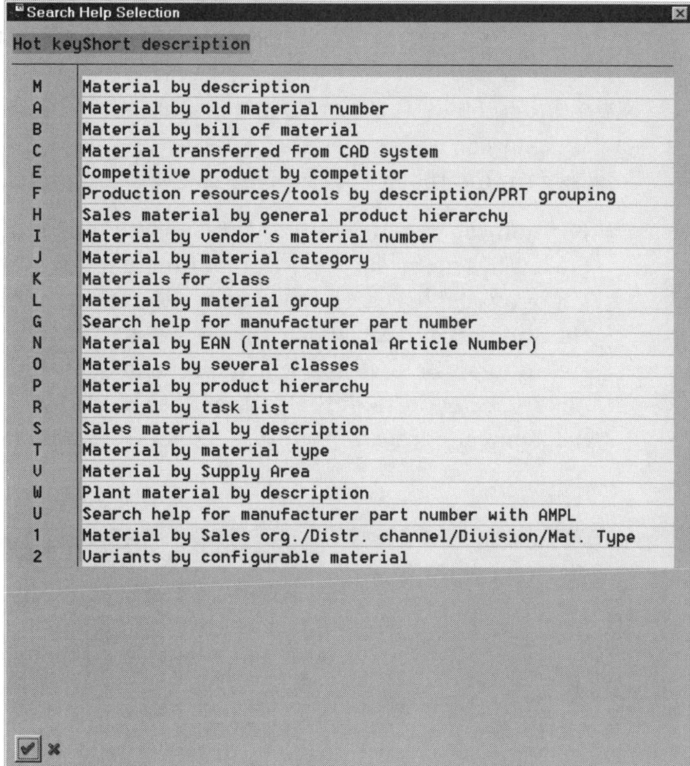

Figure 5-22
Screen with list of search help keys for a particular 203 field.

Each of the lines in the box is a different method for searching the same thing. The first column shows the *search help hot key* which identifies the search method. Double clicking over one of the lines causes the system to display another dialog box in which users must enter the search terms. For example, by selecting the hot key *M* from Fig. 5-22, the system displays a box like the one in Fig. 5-23 with the input fields for the search.

Enter the criteria in the fields or just enter information in those fields for which you know any search criteria; otherwise, leave them blank. The use of wildcards is allowed. For instance, in Fig. 5-23, you could enter *b** in the description field, and the system would display all materials whose descriptions start with a *b.*

The R/3 system includes many predefined search helps, but developers or the data dictionary administrator can create new ones. There are two methods for using search helps in the R/3 system: the *simple method* is the normal way to find values for a field when users do not know which search help to use. The *fast method* is for experienced users who already know the search help to use and also the order of the search terms in the search help.

Using Search Helps with the Simple Method

As stated before, the simple or normal method for using search helps is when users do not know which ones are available in a field. In such cases, users can find the search help by the following method:

- Position the cursor in a field with search help and click on the possible entries arrow or press the F4 function key. A dialog box with a list of available search helps appears in front of the R/3 screen, like the one in Fig. 5-22, which shows the search help list for the material number field. If users have previously used this search help and have selected it, then the system does not show the list of search helps but proposes that key by default without showing the list of

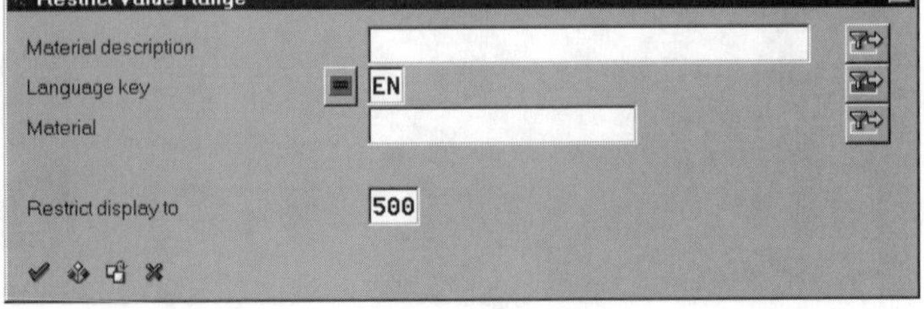

Figure 5-23 Dialog box for a search help.

search helps. Users can select another search help by clicking on the *Other search help* (■) button.

- Then, just double click on a search help to use it. The selected search help will be the default one until users select another. Next time a user lists possible entries for this field, the selected search help will be proposed automatically.

  The search fields for the search help will appear in a dialog box, like the one shown in Fig. 5-23 for looking up a material number.
- Enter the known search terms and use wildcards if needed in the most adequate fields and then press *Enter.* If no search terms are entered, the system displays all the records for that search help. If the list is very large, you can reduce the number of hits by further restricting the value range.
- The system displays all records matching the search terms entered. If no records are found, review the criteria for the matchcode or select a different one by clicking on the *Restrict values* button.
- To transfer the value from the list to the input field, the procedure is the same as that in a possible entries field: just double click on a record or position the cursor over the record and press the F2 function key.

Using Search Helps with the Fast Method

The fast method is intended for experienced users who commonly use search helps to find the needed values in the input fields they use more often. If users know the search help, they just need to enter it directly in the field and press the *Enter* key. To use direct search helps, users first need to know the general syntax.

The general syntax for search helps consists of four parts: an equal sign, a key identifier, periods, and search terms. An example of a search help for the direct method is

=M.material_description.language.material

This example shows the following:

- The equal sign (=) which indicates the beginning of the search help.
- *M,* the search help hot key. In Fig. 5-22, you can see that for this

particular search help, there are many hot keys, each of them having different search fields and different arrangements.

- A period (.) separating every search field. The periods can also substitute for search terms you don't know.
- Search terms between the periods. In the example, substitute material_description, language, and material with search values. Fields must be entered in the order defined for the search help.

Then, to enter a direct search help requires that users know the search help hot key and the order of the search terms. Some examples based on the search help for finding materials follow:

- =M.tubes*.EN finds all material records whose descriptions start with the word *tubes* and have maintenance language *EN* (English).
- =M...12* finds all the material records whose material numbers start with 12.
- =M. finds all the records for matchcode identifier *M*. You do not specify any search term, but the identifier must be followed by a period. In this case, if the records for the material master leave the description empty, the system will not display any record at all.

Working with Reports

Reports in the SAP R/3 system are ABAP programs whose function is to look up information in the database and display it or print it. When end users perform their usual work with the R/3 system, they often need to look up information to analyze, to see business results, to make decisions, or simply to continue the work. This type of extracting, collecting, and formatting of the data held on the database is performed by the SAP reports.

SAP distinguishes two terms in this environment: a *report* is the program itself, and a *list* is the result (the output) of the report.

End users don't have to program the reports themselves since the SAP system includes virtually thousands of preprogrammed reports. These reports can be the result of normal menu function selections, and often users don't even know that they are executing reports, except for the result displayed on the screen or sent to the printer. In these cases, the data already entered in the fields of a screen act as search terms for the reports.

However, sometimes end users, and administrators too, have the need to call a report manually using the functions and facilities provided by the

R/3 system. How to work with reports managing these manual calls is the purpose of this section of the book.

The general reporting facilities of the R/3 system can be found under the *System → Services → Reporting* menu (transaction code *SA38*). With this function, users can start reports when they know the name of the reports. Figure 5-24 shows the aspects of the report selection screen.

To start the report, enter the report name in the field and click on the *Execute* button. Most reports have selection criteria to delimit the scope of the search and the expected results. Some reports, however, do not have selection criteria, so when executing the report, the results are shown immediately.

If the report includes selection criteria, the corresponding screen appears, where users must enter the criteria they want to use for the report results. Criteria are the search terms, and the of use wildcards is allowed.

Once the criteria are entered, press the *Execute* button again or select *Program → Execute in background* from the main menu to submit the report as a background job.

A common way to automatically enter selection criteria is with the use of variants. A *variant* is a collection of predefined criteria to use in

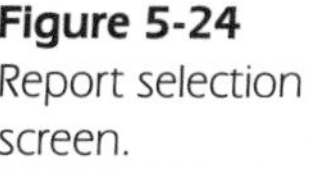

Figure 5-24
Report selection screen.

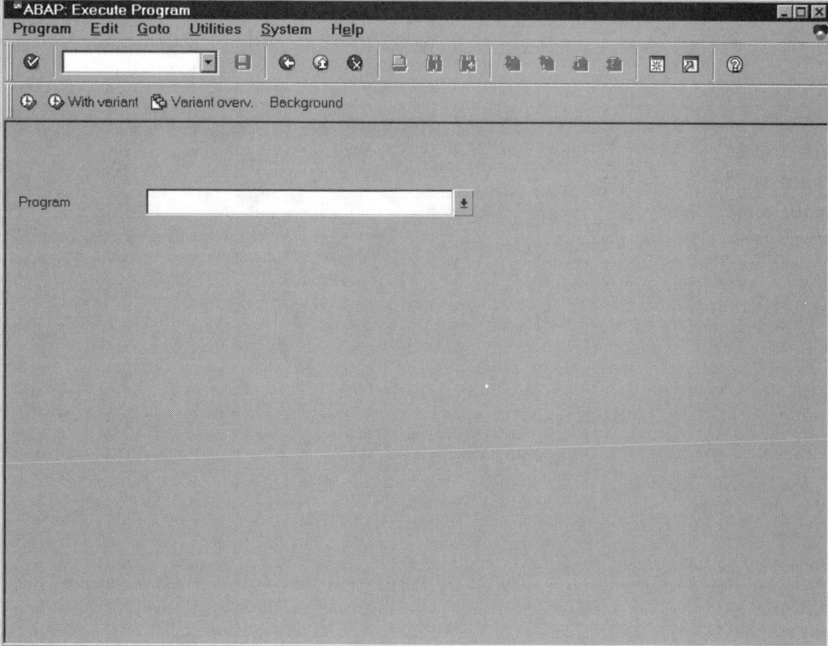

reports. When using variants, users can execute reports with any variant available for that report, in which case, they don't have to enter selection criteria. For example, regional sales managers executing a report to see the sales evolution in their territory can use the same report but with different variants. The only difference in the variants is that in the selection criteria one has region A and another one has region B.

Looking for Reports

To manually start a report with the reporting functions, users must know the report name. In the SAP system, most standard report names start with letter *R*. However, customer-created reports should start with letters *Y* or *Z*.

Reports are grouped in classes, for example, sales reports, stock movements, and projects. Report classes can be very useful for finding report names.

To find report names, from the reporting screen select *Utilities → Find Program* from the menu. The system shows the ABAP program directory search screen, like the one in Fig. 5-25. The report search screen (titled ABAP Program Directory) appears.

In the *program* field enter the part of the report name to search for and use wildcards (* or +). The * wildcard replaces multiple characters, while

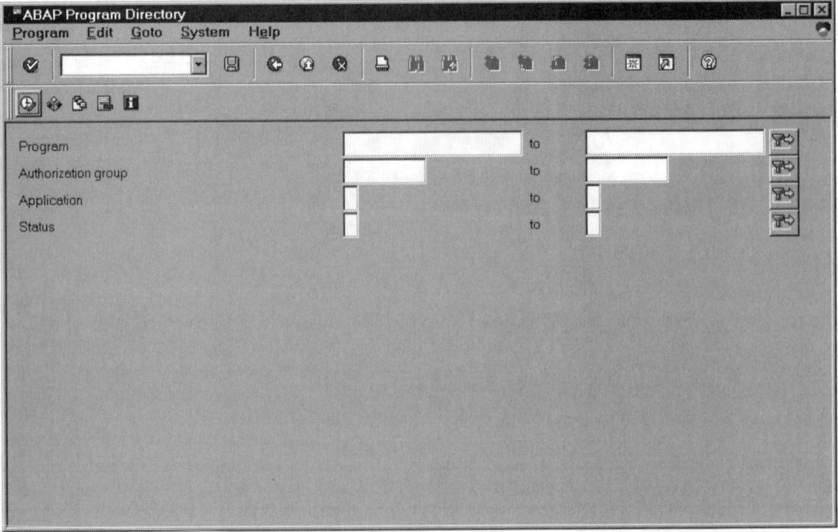

Figure 5-25 Program directory selection screen.

the + wildcard replaces a single character. For example, RSM* will find all reports starting with RSM, and RSPA++00, will find all reports starting with RSPA and ending with 00.

Wildcards can be used anywhere in the field and as often as you want. For example: Z*PS* will find all reports starting with *Z* (customer-developed reports) and having PS anywhere in the middle strings.

Executing Reports

Once the program field is specified, press the *Execute* button. The system will display a list of reports matching your criteria or a list of report classes. If the latter is displayed, you have to double click on any line to display a list of reports belonging to the class. Repeat the process until you find the report needed. Once the report is found, it can be directly called from this screen by positioning the cursor over the line and pressing the *Execute* button or by choosing the *Program* → *Execute* function from the menu bar. The difference with this process in respect to the reporting screen is that if the report requires a variant, it won't allow the execution from this screen.

Users can find the name of the report directly within their usual tasks, so are able to call it even when they are working on different menus or applications. To find the name of the report, first call the report within the normal tasks and select *System* → *Status* from the menu bar. The name of the report appears either in the *Report* field or in the *ABAP program* field.

Using Selection Criteria

The selection criteria are input fields which allow users to delimit the type and amount of information they want the report to process. If no criteria are specified, the result of the report execution can be a long list including data which is not needed for the users. For example, to analyze materials movements in a warehouse, users should enter the warehouse ID as the criteria. The report will process and display only lists matching the selection criteria specified.

But selection criteria are not limited to specific values for the input fields. Some input fields permit the introduction of value ranges and multiple ranges, for example, if you want to display those customers that have been billed between $1000 and $5000 or if you want to search for customers in the states starting with A and C, plus Pennsylvania. As more values are entered in the selection criteria fields, the output can be more specific and the lists will be smaller.

If the system can't return all data because of processing limitations (for example, because it exceeds the maximum time for online processing), it displays a message in the status bar.

Often in a report you find two types of selection criteria:

- *Database selections,* which determine which records are selected from the database
- *Program selections,* which are an additional filter to tell the system which of the fields from the records selected will be displayed on the list

You can get the additional selection options by positioning the cursor in the input field and clicking on the *Selection options* button on the application toolbar. By using the selection options and the multiple selection arrow, users can specify complex search criteria, including multiple value ranges, AND and OR conditions, and so forth.

Working with Reports Variants

A variant is a group of values used as selection criteria or as parameters when calling a report or another type of ABAP program. Variants are attached to a report, what means that a variant cannot be used except for the report for which it was created. The group of values for the selection criteria is saved and assigned a variant name; so every time you want to call a program or a report, instead of specifying the selection criteria, you could call a previously saved variant thus avoiding having to type the criteria over again. In fact, when using variants, the screen for entering the selection criteria does not appear.

Variants are a great help for simplifying data input when launching reports, and they ensure that reports have some selection criteria to limit the results. Users can have as many variants for a report as they wish. Each of them can be used to retrieve different types of information. For example, the same report that retrieves the monthly warehouse inventory could have different variants—one for each warehouse location—so each manager uses the variant according to her or his location.

At the initial reporting screen, when users don't know which variants are available, they can display a list of the variants that are attached to the report, and they can also see the values assigned to the selection criteria. To do that, users just have to enter the report name and click on the *Variants overview* button on the application toolbar. The system displays the available variants. To see the contents, click on one variant to select it, and choose *Variants → Display* from the main menu.

To enter a variant for a report, after calling the reporting function and specifying the report name, click on the *Execute with variant* button. The system displays a dialog box to specify the variant name, as shown in Fig. 5-26. Enter the variant name or click on the possible entries arrow to find which variants are available for the report. Once you select the variant, click on the *Execute* button in the same dialog box.

Creating Variants. To create variants for reports, go to the main reporting screen (*System → Services → Reporting*), enter the name of the report for which you want to create the variants, and select *Goto → Variants* from the menu. The system displays the initial screen for the ABAP variants, or you might get a *Change Screen Assignment* dialog box in cases where the program includes more than one selection screen.

Enter a name for the variant and click on the *Create* button. At this moment, R/3 shows the selection criteria screen for the report specified previously.

In the input fields, enter the criteria and click on the *Continue* button. The system displays the screen for saving the variant with the name you specified already entered in the *Variant* field. Figure 5-27 shows an example of this screen. In the *Description* field, enter a brief description for the variant so that you can distinguish the purpose of the variant when looking at the variants overview.

In this screen there are three check boxes where users can specify environment options for the variant:

- By selecting *Only for background processing,* you tell the system to send the processing of the variant to the background processing system.

Figure 5-26
Variant dialog box.

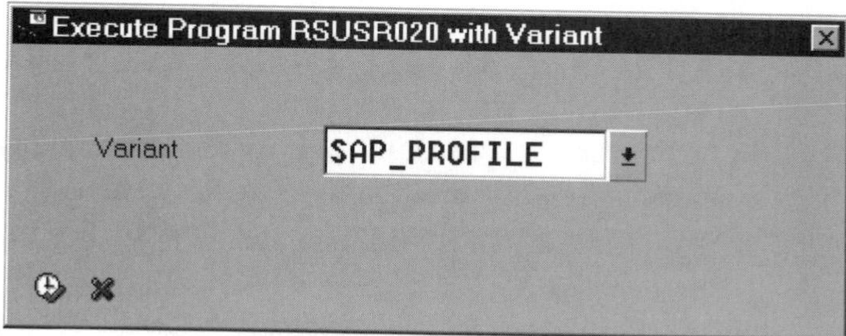

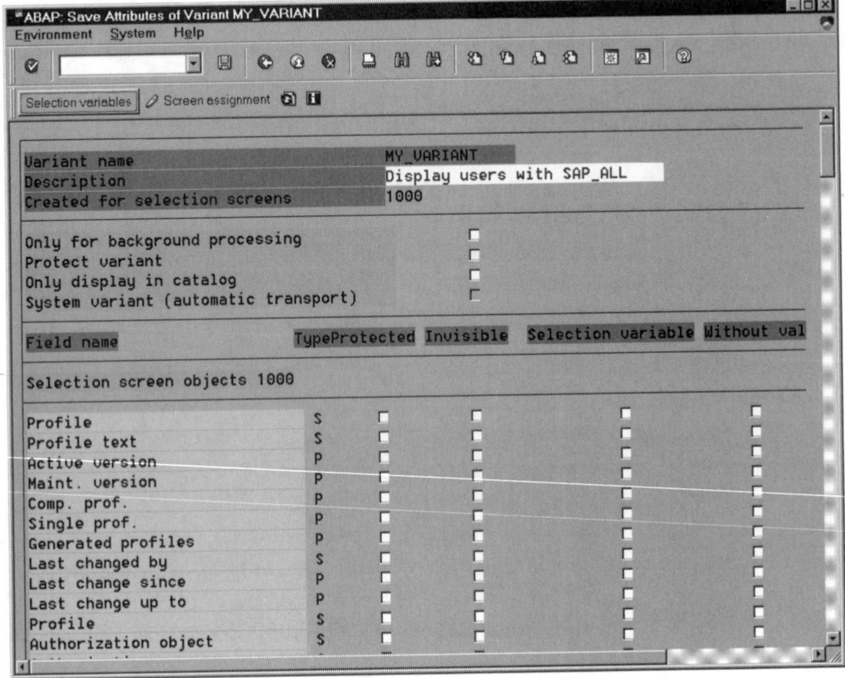

Figure 5-27 Defining attributes for a variant.

- With the *Protect variant* option, only the user who created the variant can modify it or delete it.
- By selecting the check box next to *Only display in catalog,* you tell the system that the variant name will appear in the variant catalog, but not in the input help.

The bottom part of this screen shows additional field attributes corresponding to the specific report for which the variants are being created. Once all needed values are specified, click on the *Save* button in the standard toolbar to save the variant.

Working with Background Jobs

In this section, the use and basic management of background jobs are introduced. More advanced options and information about the background processing system are explained in Chap. 13.

Background jobs are definitions of programs, printing specifications, and start times to be processed by the SAP background processing system. The programs can be either ABAP reports or external programs.

With background processing, the system automatically runs the programs specified in the job at the scheduled time for its execution. There are facilities to monitor the background jobs and for displaying the job's results.

Background jobs have the advantage over traditional online processing that once the job is defined, the background processing system takes care of running it. Otherwise, launching a program interactively locks your session for further input until the program is finished. Remember that in interactive dialog work processes there is a limit on the time a process can be running. If the programs surpass this limit, the system displays an error and the program is canceled. In cases of long-running reports, background jobs are the only way to execute those programs.

Since background jobs can be scheduled to run at any time, another of their advantages is that the execution of long reports can be specified to run at periods with less system load, such as nighttime or weekends.

The background jobs offer a great advantage for defining automatic and periodic execution of the jobs, for example, periodic database cleaning jobs or the system performance collector which runs hourly as a background job. System administrators have to define these jobs only once, and then they are regularly executed at the scheduled times.

A report defined in a background job generates the same output as one run interactively. The output list can be either printed directly or sent to the output controller.

Since job definitions are held on the R/3 database, jobs are available even when the whole R/3 system or the computer itself is restarted. Jobs which were running at the time of a shutdown are canceled by the system, and the owner of the job has to schedule it back.

There are several ways to define and schedule programs for background execution:

- In some of the tasks within the R/3 application, the system automatically schedules long-running reports or programs for background execution.
- From within the ABAP workbench program editor and from several other R/3 screens where programs can be executed, the menu bar or the application toolbar often contain the option to execute the program either online or in the background. Within the ABAP editor, this function is under *Program → Execute → Background.* Upon choosing this option, the system displays the screen for defining and scheduling the job.

At any time and anywhere in the R/3 system, a job can be defined by selecting *System → Services → Jobs → Define Job.* Alternatively, system administrators can also go to the job definition screen by selecting *Tools → CCMS → Jobs → Definition* or directly with transaction SM36, where the job information must be specified. This screen is shown in Fig. 5-28.

Scheduling Background Jobs

The system offers several ways to define background jobs as stated earlier. A job definition basically consists of the following:

- Entering a name for the job.
- Entering the date and time of when to execute the programs.
- Entering the program or programs to be executed in the background. Programs can also contain variants.
- Entering printing information.
- Enter the names of recipients of the spool list.

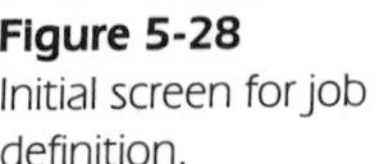

Figure 5-28
Initial screen for job definition.

There are many other options when scheduling a job, such as specifying the host to execute the job, indicating the priority, deciding whether to execute it periodically, specifying a system event instead of time, and so on.

To schedule a job, go to the job definition screen by selecting *System → Services → Jobs → Define Job* from any menu. On this screen, enter a name for the job first. You can choose any meaningful name.

In the *Job Class* input field, you can specify *A, B,* or *C.* Job class *C* is the normal and default value. *A* and *B* are higher priority classes, and users must have authorization for those classes.

Users can enter a target host for background processing or leave it blank for executing it on the default background server. Clicking on the possible entries arrow displays a list of available background servers.

Select the start time for the job by clicking on the *Start date* button. The screen for specifying the start time has many available options. Normal options are either *Immediate,* which schedules the job as soon as you save it, or *Date / time,* which schedules the job for the date and time specified. The other options follow.

NOTE *These options are explained in greater detail in Chap. 13.*

- *After job.* The job will start when another job which must be specified has been completed. In order to use this option, you must know the name of the other job. If you check the box next to *Start status depend,* the job will only start if the previous job finished successfully. Otherwise, the job will not start.
- *After event.* The job will start when the background processing system receives a signal with the event specified. You can see the available events by clicking on the possible entries arrow.
- *At operation mode.* The job will start as soon as the operation mode becomes the active one. Operation modes are a way of configuring how the R/3 system distributes the work processes. This is explained further in Chap. 11.
- *Start on work day (>> button).* The job will start on the day of the month you specify. Upon clicking on the possible entries arrow, the system displays the SAP factory calendar from which you can choose a workday of the month. For example, entering *07* will cause the job to start on the seventh work day of the month. You can specify additional restrictions such as not starting before a specific date and so on.

Check your entries with the *Check* button and, if the system does not complain, save your entries. The system then takes you back to the job definition screen. Now, you must specify the program or programs to execute. Since a job might contain several programs (either ABAP or external programs), the system names them as *steps.*

The system displays the *Create step* screen. Initially, the input fields of the screen are grayed out until you either press the *ABAP program, External command,* or *External program* buttons, depending on the type of program being sent to the background. Clicking on one of the buttons changes the color of the associated input fields. Select over one of the fields and fill in the needed information:

- Enter the user ID under whose authorization the R/3 system will run this background job. By default it uses the current user ID under which the user has logged on.
- Enter the name of the program. If the program has a variant, the system will request that it be entered.
- Enter the language in which you want to receive the output for the report. Remember that R/3 supports many different languages.
- Finally, using the *Print specifications* button, you can specify how to print the results of the programs.

When specifying external programs, such as C programs, shell scripts, or other supported type, the full path name must be specified together with the parameters the program might need, such as options or file names, and the hostname where the program will be executed. Make sure the system can access the specified host and path and that it has the right permissions.

Press the *Save* button to save the job. At this moment, the job is scheduled to be processed by the background system at the specified start date and time.

A job that has been scheduled does not actually run until it is also released. To release a job, the user must have the right authorizations. If the user is not authorized to release jobs, then administrators must release the jobs for them. This is a security measure to better monitor and control the background processing system.

To check the status of your background jobs, select *System* → *Own jobs* from any R/3 screen in the system. If you see a job with status *Cancelled,* it means the job has terminated abnormally. Press the *Log* button to find out the reason for the failure.

System administrators can monitor background jobs graphically from the facilities of the CCMS.

User Printing

All the output lists and almost every other screen in the R/3 system includes a printing function. The most common way to access the printing function is either by clicking on the *Print* button on the standard toolbar or application toolbar or by selecting *System* → *List* → *Print* from any R/3 window.

Printing in the R/3 system is a two-step process which should not confuse users: first they select the print function which displays the print screen. This screen must be filled out, then it will send the list to the output controller and to the printer.

Users have to fill out the print screen to specify some information which is needed by the R/3 spooling system: name of the printer, cover sheet, format, and so on. Once this information is entered, users must click on the *Print* button.

Some applications require users to enter some printing information on a special screen and will not show the print screen.

The Print Screen

Figure 5-29 shows an example of a print screen. On this screen, users normally only have to specify two choices: name of the printer and whether to print immediately or hold the job until requested.

These are the available fields on the print screen:

- *Output Device.* Enter the printer name here or click on the possible entries arrow to display a list of available printers.
- *Number of Copies.* Enter the number of copies for the printed output.
- *Name.* This field identifies the print request in the SAP output controller. This field is automatically set by the system, but users can change it if they wish.
- *Title.* Users can enter here a short description of the print request, so they can easily identify it.
- *Authorization.* This field can contain an authorization code previously defined by the system administrator. It is used to protect users looking at printed data which can be sensitive or confidential.

Additionally, the print screen presents some important spool control

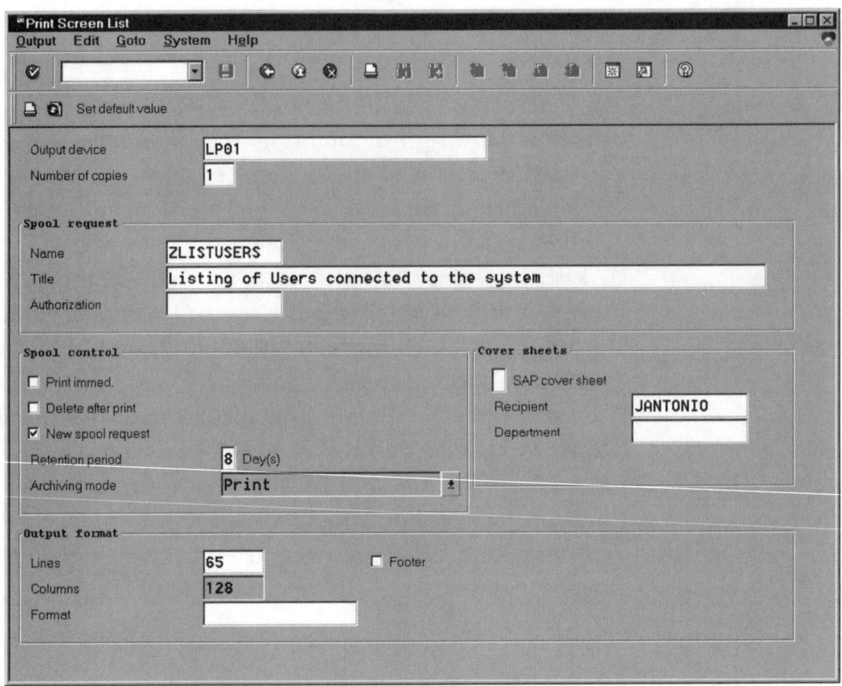

Figure 5-29
Print screen.

fields, which indicate to the SAP R/3 system how to handle the print request.

- *Print immed.* When this option is selected, the system sends the output immediately to the printer. This is a key option since users often forget to check it, and nothing comes out of the printer. If this field is not selected, the print job is sent to the output controller, where you can later print it. Users can have this option selected by default by modifying their own user parameters. To do this, go to *System* → *User profile* → *Own data,* select the *Defaults* tabstrip, and click on the check mark next to *Output immediately.* However, deselecting this option can be useful when wanting to print just a few pages from a long listing, since you can specify pages to print from the output controller but not from the print screen.
- *Delete after print.* Select this option to tell the R/3 system to remove the print request after it has been successfully printed.
- *SAP Cover sheet.* You can use this field to print a cover sheet at the beginning of the print job.
- *Output format fields.* These fields indicate the format used for printing the report or list. The format is automatically set by the system, and users usually should leave these options unchanged.

The print screen includes the *Print* icon on its own application toolbar. Clicking on it creates the output request. If the *Print immediately* option was sent, the job is sent directly to the printer.

Monitoring the Status of Your Print Requests

By selecting *System → Services → Output controller* from any R/3 screen, the system displays the Spool Request screen where users can check the status of their print jobs. On this screen, enter the criteria for the print request you want to search. In normal situations users only have to press the *Enter* key to display the actual print jobs.

Figure 5-30 shows an example of the Spool Request screen. The most important information on this screen is *Output status,* where users can check whether the job has been printed or if any problems have arisen.

Possible values of the output status field are

- *— (Dash).* The print request has been created but has not been sent to the printer yet. This is the normal case when the *Print immediately* check box was not selected. You can send it now to the printer by selecting the request and clicking on the *Print* icon on the application toolbar.
- *Compl.* The print job has completed successfully and should be at the printer.
- *Wait, Problem or another colored message.* There is a problem with completing the print request. To see the problem details, select the

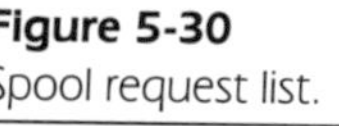

Figure 5-30
Spool request list.

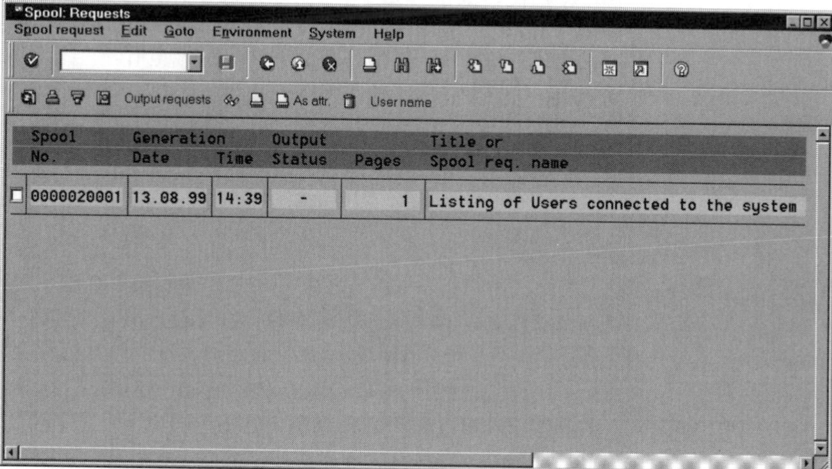

print request by checking the box next to it and press the *Output request* button. On the next screen, select the line again and press the *Display log* button.

Common problems relating to the print functions include *Printer is offline* and *Local PC where the printer is attached is not turned on.*

The output controller also allows users to perform additional functions besides looking at the status of their requests and printing held jobs. For example, they can remove jobs from the system by clicking on the *Delete* button or can display the job output on the screen by selecting the *Display* button.

Additional User Utilities

The R/3 system menu includes some additional utilities which users can find helpful and which they might need from time to time, for example, sending messages to other users or downloading/uploading lists or documents to/from PC files from/to the R/3 system.

The next sections briefly explain how to do this.

Sending Short Messages

To send a short message to another R/3 user, select *System* → *Short message* from any screen. The system displays a screen similar to the one shown in Fig. 5-31. Just write the message in the *Note* area of the screen and specify the recipient name in the input fields below. When you are done, just click on the *Send* button to deliver your message. This is a fast way to call the basic SAPoffice function for sending messages between SAP users.

For more extensive information about the functions of SAPoffice, please refer to the SAP online documentation.

Downloading Files to the Windows PC

Every list generated in the system as well as most screens that generate a print screen can be downloaded to PC files for further treatment or for

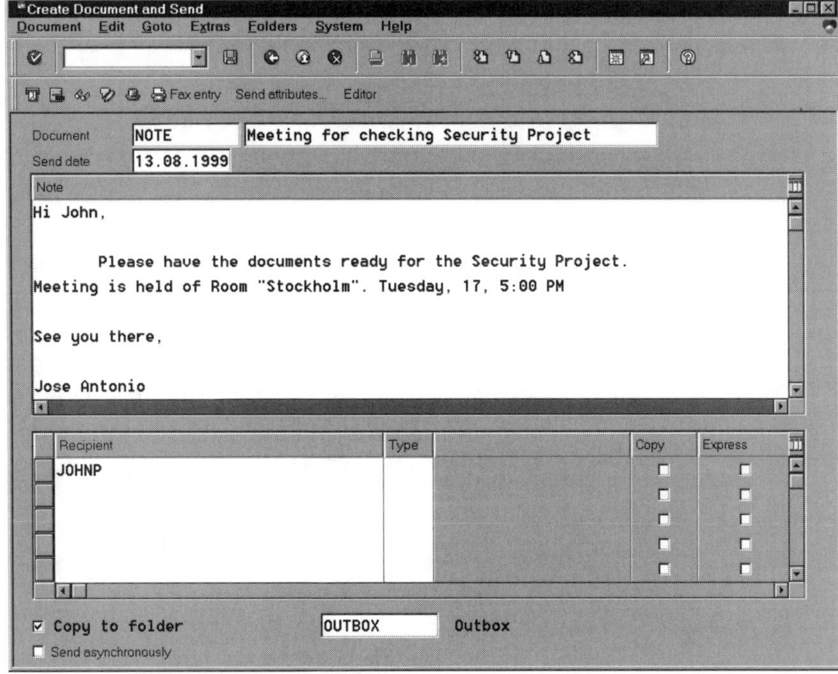

Figure 5-31
Sending a short message.

other analysis or documentation purposes. Similarly, you can upload files from the PC, for example, ABAP source code.

While in the ABAP editor, you can find the upload and download functions under the Utilities menu.

When the screen displays a printable list, you can decide to save it to a local file. To do so, from any R/3 screen, select *System* → *List* → *Save* → *Local file*. The system will display a dialog box with three options from which you can choose your output format. Select the one which best suits your needs and press the *Continue* button.

The system will display another dialog box requesting the path and name of the file in your local PC. It normally shows the work directory path where the SAPGUI is installed. Enter the file name and press the *OK* button. The list will be transferred to your local PC.

TRICK *If you want to override the default path name the download or upload dialog box, go to your user defaults* (System → User profile → Own data), *and set the parameter GR8 to your desired path.*

EnjoySAP User Features

With the EnjoySAP release (SAP R/3 release 4.6), the SAP user interface takes a step forward to a modern, role-based, personal, easy, and flexible end user working environment. It has been, in fact, a release targeting and focusing on users and usability, and on enhancing the system from an *end user* point of view.

Previous R/3 releases included lots of new components, functionalities, add-ons, industry solutions, and technology advances, and also new but not revolutionary user features. The EnjoySAP release has dramatically changed the user interface, going beyond just designing appealing and colorful features, to fundamentally distinguishing between different types of users by delivering a role-based user interface. One of the features included in EnjoySAP most in demand by users is the ability to tailor the interface, so that now users can add their own icons for their most-used functions to the application toolbar. Figure 5-32 shows an example of a screen from the EnjoySAP release.

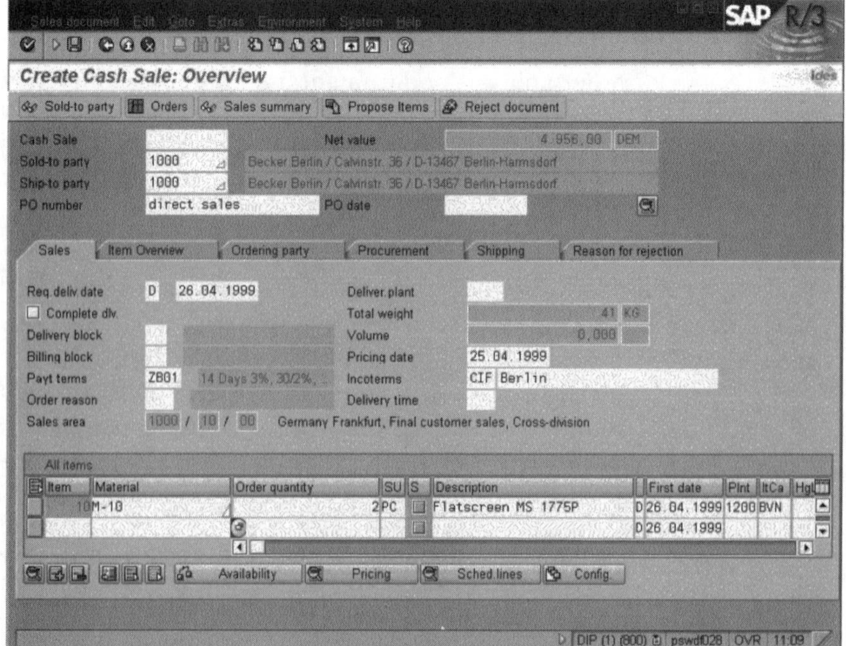

Figure 5-32
Example of interface with EnjoySAP release. (Copyright SAP AG.)

Based on Java and ActiveX technology, integrated with ABAP objects, the user interface acts as a control container, thus providing multiple facilities for interacting with other objects and desktop applications.

Focusing on user needs and new ways to interact with the system, some of the main features and capabilities of the user interface of the EnjoySAP release are:

- Role-based interface with many personalization facilities.
- Redesign of visual and graphical elements for easier recognition of important parts of the applications.
- Easily changeable appearance of screen and screen elements.
- Active environment with integration with other desktop applications.
- Supports for defining favorites in frames, tree structures, tabstrips, and subscreens. Favorites can be R/3 transactions, reports, Web sites, external applications, or other SAP New Dimension solutions.
- Drag and drop capabilities.
- Ability to use the interface as a container of objects such as documents, pictures, sound, and so on.
- Ability for system managers to prepare and customize menus and screens for end users.
- Automatic integration of the authorization system and profile generator with the role-based interface concept.
- Better context-sensitive help.
- Definition of user default values.

CHAPTER 6

The Transport System

The SAP R/3 system includes a collection of tools closely linked to the ABAP workbench and the customizing functions, which are very important for managing and coordinating development and customizing work within a group of SAP systems. These tools form the overall *Change and Transport System* (*CTS*). Figure 6-1 shows a typical diagram of the CTS components, which are explained throughout the following sections of this chapter.

The CTS components are in charge of performing essential functions in the overall development and customization environment, and thus in the implementation process as well as in the operation and support after productive start.

Among the functions of the different CTS tools are:

- Administration and control of new development requests
- Modification and correction to repository objects
- Recording and auditing of all configuration settings and changes
- Configuration of development classes
- Locking of objects to avoid parallel work
- Version management
- Documentation of changes
- Assurance of teamwork development
- Transporting of objects and settings changes among systems
- Logging of transport results
- Setting the system change options
- Recording of where and by whom changes are made
- Configuration of the systems landscape

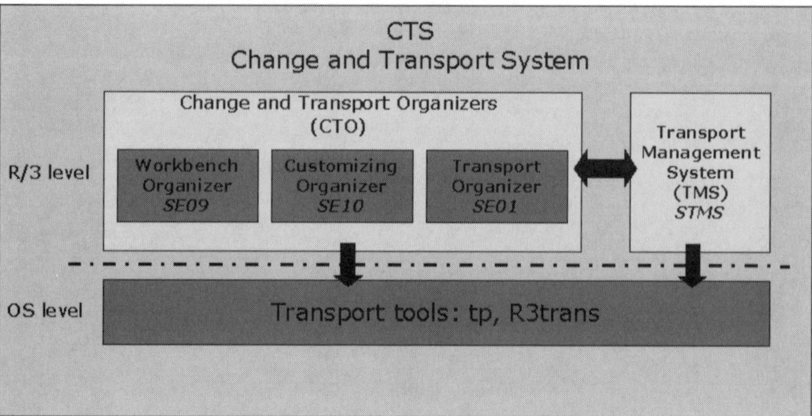

Figure 6-1 The change and transport system.

Additionally, the CTS tools are extensively used and play a fundamental role in the release upgrade process and tools.

The CTS components are made up of the following:

- *Change and Transport Organizers (CTO).* These are composed of transactions SE01 (transport organizer), SE09 (workbench organizer), and SE10 (customizing organizer), which are used for registering the modifications done on repository and customizing objects.
- *Transport Management System (TMS).* In distributed SAP systems environments, the Change and Transport Organizers use the Transport Management System for managing, controlling, copying, or moving, in an orderly manner, the development objects or customization settings among different SAP systems. This process is usually performed between the systems used for development and testing and the productive systems, using predefined transport routes. The transport process consists in exporting objects out of the source R/3 system and importing them into the R/3 target system.
- *Transport tools at the operating system level.* The actual transport process is performed at the operating system level using the transport tools. These tools are part of the R/3 kernel and include the program *R3trans* and the transport control program *tp.* The TMS is linked to those programs so that R/3 allows transports (exports and imports) to be performed within the system using RFC calls. Figure 6-2 shows a simple diagram of the transport process.

Overview of the Complete Process of Transporting Objects from a Source System to a Target System

The workbench organizer and the transport system are some of the most puzzling parts of the technical environment of SAP R/3; this is probably because there is no place for chaotic and unorganized software development or customization. They are actually intended as help functions for having the system development and the modifications under control.

The following summary guideline provides a brief overview of the whole transport chain. This guideline includes the necessary steps for configuring the transport system, although these steps only have to be performed once. The concepts, configuration, and available functions and features of the transport system are explained in the following sections.

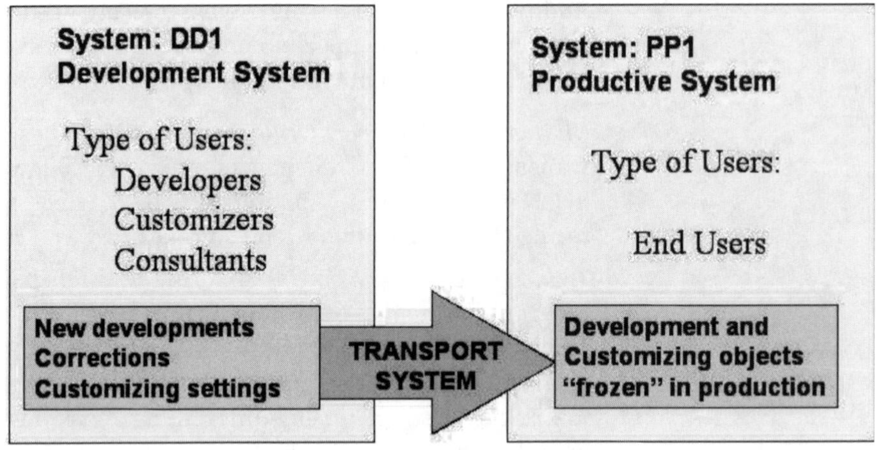

Figure 6-2 Simple illustration of the transport process.

Configuration steps are made up three basic tasks:

1. *Configure the transport directory and TPPARAM.* The transport directory (/usr/sap/trans) is created by the installation program. You have to make sure that this directory can be accessed correctly among systems within a transport group. Within the *bin* subdirectory, there is a global configuration file *TPPARAM* (transport parameter file) that must include entries for each of the R/3 systems taking part in transports. This file must be correctly configured for the transport control program *tp* to function properly.
2. *Initialize the change and transport organizer (CTO).* This is accomplished by transaction SE06 (*Tools → Administration → Transports → Installation follow-up work*) and is one of the first tasks to perform after the installation of the R/3 system. This transaction initializes the basic settings for the CTO, and can also be used for specifying the system change option—that is, which objects and configuration settings can be modified or not within the system. This transaction distinguishes whether this R/3 system comes from a standard installation or from a systems or database copy.
3. *Configure transport systems and routes.* This configuration step is performed using transaction *STMS* (*Tools → Administration → Transports → Transport Management System*) from client 000. The first time this transaction is called, the system creates a *transport*

domain controller, a central system where all configuration is done and then transferred to other systems in the group. The easiest way to configure the systems landscape and transport routes is to select a standard configuration. This can be done by first entering the R/3 systems and then selecting *Overview* → *Transport routes* and *Configuration* → *Standard config.* In this case the TMS will request the roles of the defined systems and set up the transport layer and transport routes for each. For nonstandard configurations or complex system landscapes this process must be manually performed.

In addition to these configuration tasks, it is also important to set the system change options as well as to check the system client settings. These settings define what parts of the system can be changed and recorded by the organizers.

The next steps are:

4. *Create a development class.* The development class acts as a way to group together objects belonging to the same development project. Only objects with an appropriate development class can be transported to other systems. To be able to transport development objects, you must define a class which is not local (such as $TMP) or for test purposes (all starting with *T*). You should define the development class in the range allowed for customers, starting with *Y* or *Z*.
5. *Create or modify an object.* The process of creating a new object (a table or a report, for example) or making a customization setting, automatically asks for the creation of a change request. This request will be transportable as long as the assigned development class, the transport route, and/or the type permits it.

NOTE *The automatic creation of a change request is allowed by the-SAP client settings. You can disable this function and the ability to make changes in the system client independent objects. However, in the rest of this chapter and other chapters, it is assumed that the client allows for changes in the repository and client-independent objects.*

6. *Release and export the transport.* Access the workbench organizer (SE09) or the customizing organizer (SE10) and find the transportable change requests that have not yet been released. Expand the folder to access the change tasks. Change requests are composed by one or more change tasks. First release the tasks and

then release the change request. When the change requests are released, the system performs an export and creates several files at the operating system level.

7. *Import into the target system.* When the group of SAP systems share the same common transport directory, files that have been exported are directly accessed by the target system. Imports can be performed with the *tp* program at the operating system level by logging onto the target system as user <sid>adm, going to the /usr/sap/trans/bin directory, and performing the corresponding call to the program. For example:

```
tp import <transportable change request number> <target SID>
```

   Imports can also be performed within the TMS by accessing the system import queues and performing the imports.

8. *Check log files.* You can check the log files from inside R/3 or at the operating system level. Ultimately, try to display the objects you just imported in the target system.

With these steps, a whole transport process is accomplished. The next sections discuss the concepts, details, options, and possibilities of all the R/3 functions involved.

Transport System Concepts

The change and transport organizers and the transport system deal with topics and concepts, some of which are the same as those used within the ABAP workbench, and some of which are specific to the functions these systems perform. In order to better understand this chapter, the main concepts are introduced in the next sections.

Development Objects

As previously stated, the workbench organizer records and controls changes to development objects as well as new ones. A *development object* is any object created (developed) within the SAP R/3 system.

Examples of development objects are

- ABAP dictionary objects—tables, domains, matchcodes, data elements, and so forth

- ABAP programs, functions modules, menus, and screens
- Documentation
- Application-defined transport objects

The workbench organizer is fully integrated into the ABAP development workbench and the customizing tools. This integration allows users to directly access the workbench organizer functions from the ABAP development workbench. It also allows users to jump directly to the development objects from the workbench editor.

Roles Involved in the Transport Process

The functions of the change and transport organizers allow developers to have the organization and coordination of individual or team development projects. Within the environment of the organizers and transport system, there are two points of view concerning the roles of individuals in charge of controlling and managing the system:

- The R/3 developers and/or the people doing the customizing work are in charge of creating or correcting development objects as well as customizing the system, and thus will create the change requests or use common change requests in a project. Releasing the change requests actually performs the export phase of a transport. When doing this, they should also check the log of the export phase as well as inform the administrator of the status and possibly request that the administrator make the import.
- The R/3 administrator is the person who sets up the transport systems, performs or schedules the imports, checks the result of imports, and finally informs the developers. Administrators have to work both at the R/3 application level and at the operating system level using the transport control program (tp). Since the introduction of the TMS, the most common transport functions, including imports, can be also performed within R/3.

SAP System Group

With the CTO, SAP has established a safer and more controlled environment for the development work among SAP systems. An important concept for the whole process is the SAP *system group,* which is a group of related R/3 systems, each with its own database (its own SID) and its own role in the development and implementation process. Normally, the SAP system group is defined by a common configuration of the TMS (configuration tables) and a common configuration at the operating system level where the group of systems share the transport directory (/usr/sap/trans).

Transports can still be performed when directories are not shared. However, in such cases, administrators must manually copy the export and import files into the corresponding transport directories of the target systems and use special functions of the tp program to be able to perform imports.

Within the Transport Management System, a SAP system group creates a *Transport Group,* which shares a configuration file *DOMAIN.CFG* located in the common transport directory.

Transport Layer

A transport layer is used for grouping all the development objects that will always use the same transport routes within the same development system. Transport layers are assigned to all the objects that come from a specified development system.

This is a central concept for the Transport Management System, and is a requirement to create a transport layer before any development project can start.

Normally there is no need to have more than one transport layer within a SAP systems group, except in those cases where there is more than one development system.

Transport Routes

The transport routes are used for defining the different routes that exist between two systems within the same system group. There are two types of transport routes:

- *Consolidation routes* link a source system, such as the integration (development) system, with a target system, such as the consolidation (quality assurance) system. Every consolidation route is assigned to a transport layer.
- *Delivery routes* are used for linking a source system, such as consolidation (quality assurance) systems, with a target system such as the recipient (productive) systems. The delivery routes are not

assigned to a transport layer, but every object that arrives at a consolidation system via a consolidation route (transport layer) that is also the source of a delivery route is automatically sent to the specified target system using the delivery route.

With release 4.x, any system from the group can be the source of a delivery route, which allows complex transport routes to be established among a group of R/3 systems. If no consolidation route is assigned to a transport layer, or if the transport layer does not exist for the system where objects are modified or repaired, then these modifications are considered local and therefore cannot be transported to other systems.

A well-defined transport and development strategy within a systems group, including the configuration of the transport routes, is extremely important for R/3 implementation and support. The configuration of the transport system is used for managing and automating the process of distributing the development or customization objects among the systems belonging to a group. It is also very important when planning an upgrade project in a systems group, since modifications must be made in several systems and then transported among the various systems to be upgraded.

Change Requests

A *change request* is a list in the system containing the objects to be transported and information on the purpose of the transport, the transport type, the request category, and the target system. A change request is made up of one or more *change tasks*.

When a change request is created, either manually or automatically, the system assigns a number to it automatically, known as the *change request number.* The format of this number is normally *<SID>K<number>,* for example, DD1K900030, where *DD1* is the system identification (SID), *K* is a keyword, and the number is automatically range-generated by the system, which starts at 900001 and does not need to be maintained by the system administrators.

When using the workbench organizer, providing it has been correctly configured, the target system and the type of transport are assigned automatically.

The change requests record all modifications made to development objects or to the customizing settings.

The development objects from the ABAP workbench and customizing are recorded in different request types, known as *request categories,* since each type has its specific management and checks.

The change request category refers to the area to which the objects belong. The system includes two categories:

- *SYST,* which contains ABAP development objects and general customizing (customizing for all clients)
- *CUST,* which contains objects which belong to client-specific customizing

When the changes have been made, and the change tasks have been released, the list of objects is complete and the change request can be released. Transportable change requests are released to the transport system which exports the objects and keeps a record of the transport in logs. When a change request is released, a transport log is automatically created.

To display and check change requests, use the initial screen (request overview screen) from the workbench organizer or the customizing organizer. To access this screen, from the main menu, choose *Tools → ABAP Workbench → Overview → Workbench Organizer* (or call transaction SE09 from the command field). To call the customizing organizer, use transaction code SE10 from the command field. Figure 6-3 shows an example of workbench organizer initial screen. Click on the check boxes to delimit your criteria for displaying change requests and press the *Display* button.

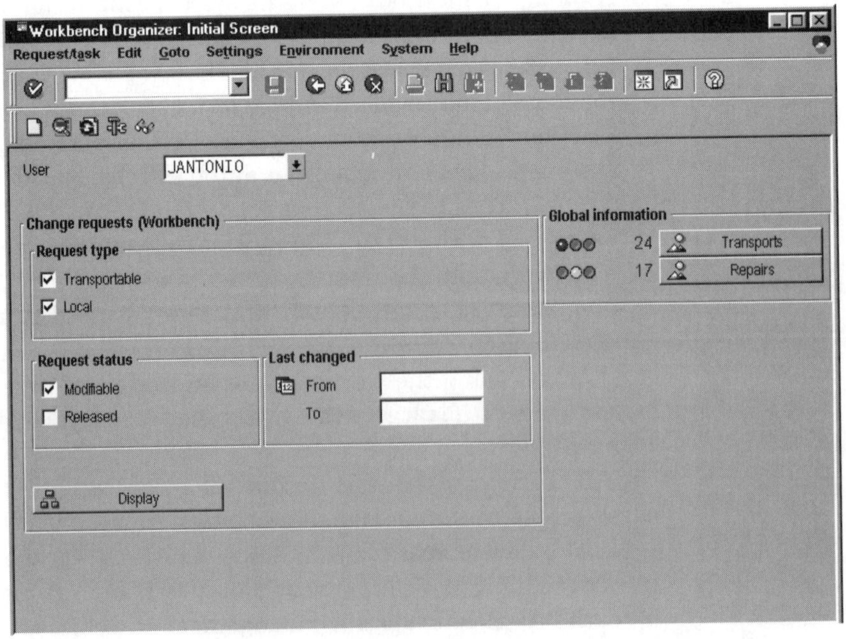

Figure 6-3
Initial screen for the workbench organizer (transaction SE09).

Tasks

A *task* or *change task* in the workbench organizer is a list of objects that are created or modified by a user. In the workbench organizer, tasks can be either development, correction, or repair tasks.

Tasks are held individually by single users. A change request, on the contrary, can contain tasks belonging to different users. Tasks are not transportable by themselves, but only as part of a change request.

Tasks also have a task number, which uses the same number range as change requests and is consecutive. This means that you cannot distinguish tasks from change requests by their numbers.

If you want to search just for tasks within requests, from the initial workbench organizer screen, select *Request/Tasks → Task selection.* Enter the selection criteria, such as task type and status, and return to the main screen. Then click on *Display.* The system will show the list of change requests in hierarchical form, with tasks located one level lower than change requests. You can view tasks by clicking on the + folder sign.

Another option is to select the *Workbench Organizer Tools* icon on the application toolbar (transaction code SE03), then select some of the reports to find tasks and requests within the *Requests/tasks* folder.

When development work starts, usually a system administrator, a development leader, or project manager creates a change request to define tasks for all users involved in the project. Then users start modifying objects or creating new developments which are registered in the tasks belonging to the change request. Once users finish working on their tasks, they must release them. Only when all tasks under the same change request are released can the change request be released and exported.

Development Teams

The method of grouping tasks together in a common change request is what makes the process of having several users working in the same development project possible. The system uses the authorization object S_TRANSPRT to protect the change and transport organizer functions and S_CTS_ADMI for the administration and management of the transport system. To be able to define tasks and requests for other users, a project leader must have the authorization S_CTS_PROJEC. Developers or people in charge of customization need the authorization S_CTS_DEVELO to be able to work at the task level. There are some standard superuser profiles containing these authorizations.

Objects included in tasks or requests become locked against other development work on the same objects until the requests have been released. If this occurs, the lock is removed from the objects. Users on the same team can display and change the objects of other users working on the same project sharing the same change request.

Development Classes

A *development class* is a way of classifying objects belonging to the same development project. Every development object in the system is assigned a development class.

The development classes are objects themselves and, apart from grouping together related objects, also include the consolidation route for the objects belonging to the class. The development classes form the main structure on which the ABAP workbench is based to start development work.

Version Management

Both the ABAP workbench and the organizer provide a version management facility for all the development objects in the system. With version management, users can compare the current version of an object with previous versions, enabling developers to display or restore previously released versions of objects.

To display the version for a particular object, first locate your object by navigating through the change requests and tasks of the workbench organizer. Click on the object to select it, and from the menu select *Object → Versions*. With this facility, administrators have the ability to monitor the development work by seeing what has been modified when and who did it.

Version management is very useful for developers and also very important when performing upgrades, since it allows users to compare previous programs or customer-created programs or tables with those of the new SAP release.

The system stores all versions of objects; they would occupy a lot of space. However, the R/3 system stores them in the form of *delta sets*. This means that it actually has one full version and the differences with the other versions. One version state is rebuilt by applying the deltas over the full version.

Requests Documentation

In order to have complete control over the development process, the workbench organizer system requires that the developers must write some structured documentation for each request. The documentation screen appears automatically when releasing a task.

To display a task or change request–associated documentation, locate your change request or tasks, and from the menu select *Goto → Documentation.*

Repairs and Original Objects

An *object original* is a key concept in the workbench organizer and the transport system, and a correct understanding of it will significantly help you to understand the inner workings of the workbench organizer system.

SAP R/3 repository objects are held in the table TADIR. This table contains the field *SRCSYSTEM,* indicating the source system for the object. The source system is the attribute that is used by the system to determine whether the object is original or not. An original object is a development object (table, report, form, screen, etc.) that has been created in the system in which you are working. When you receive your system and install it, you do not have any original objects in your own system: all objects contained in the repository have been *originally created* at SAP. When the development team creates new reports, tables, or other development objects, then they have originals, as long as they work on them in the same system they were created.

For example, you have a report program called ZRSP0001 which was created in system DD1. This means that the *system owner* (the source system) of the report is DD1. If you make modifications to this program in system DD1, you are making a *correction* to the program. However, suppose you transport this report to system PP1 without changing the system owner of the object. Then, if anyone in system PP1 tries to modify the program, she or he will be making a *repair* to the object, because among the properties or attributes of the program, there is one (*SRCSYSTEM*) which says that the original system for that object is DD1 and not PP1. This is exactly the case when anyone tries to modify original SAP objects in his or her system. Those object modifications are always repairs because the originals are at SAP systems, where they were developed.

The objects' original location is a security measure to ensure that development objects remain consistent for all systems in which they are used, thus preventing parallel work on the same objects and ensuring that an original of each object exists in only one system. Corrections and development work can normally only be carried out on the original object in the original system.

This is a key concept because it makes a fundamental distinction between a correction/development task and a repair task:

- If you modify an object in a system in which it was not created, then you are making a *repair task.*
- If you modify an object in a system in which the object was created, then you are making a *correction task.*

NOTE *There are procedures to make objects appear as originals even if they were not created in the same system where they are being modified.*

The next sections describe in detail the procedures for handling repairs and change requests and how to change the system owner of a particular object.

You can easily find whether a particular object is original in the system you are working. To do so, find the object by navigating either in the workbench organizer or by means of the repository browser (transaction code *SE80*). From the repository browser you can see the original by choosing *Edit → Object directory entry.* Both methods present different screens, but both include the *Original system* field in which you can see the system in which the object was originally created. Notice that table entries do not have this field, since inserting or updating table entries is allowed in any system.

System Types

Depending on the size of your R/3 installation (number of users and business modules to deploy) and the projects planned, you will install several R/3 systems that serve different purposes in your system group.

Normally, the implementation of SAP R/3 in a company requires the installation of several systems (meaning a different SID, which implies a different database server), each of which will serve a particular function. For instance, normally one system is used to carry out development and customizing work; this is later transported to the productive environment which is the real system where end users connect and do their work. Sometimes, though, you also need another system for testing special functions or new modules without affecting either the production or the development environments.

The first distinction to make is that there are two perspectives when talking about system types:

1. The perspective of their function—what they are used for in our installation: development, production, testing, training, quality assurance
2. The perspective of workbench organizer and transport system settings—consolidation, integration, recipient, special development systems

The transport system allows a complex group of SAP systems to be set up. For instance, you can set up several systems for distributing the development projects among them. You can also transfer special development work to another system, or you can finish and freeze the development work and make the transport system automatically distribute it to several other systems.

Of course, if the needs are not so demanding, a couple of systems—one for development and testing, and another for productive operation—will suffice to organize development and testing and productive operation.

System types can be set to special change options to protect them from unwanted development or modifications. To do this, the workbench organizer includes a utility that allows administrators to set the system change options.

System Change Options

With the system change options, administrators decide how to open or close the system to new developments, ensuring the integrity of the system. The available options are suitable for different types of systems and directly affect the functions allowed in the workbench organizer and transport system.

In order to reach and set the system change options, the user must have all the authorizations for the workbench organizer.

To reach the system change options screen, from the workbench organizer initial screen select *Goto* → *Tools* or enter transaction SE03 in the command field. You get a new screen with the tools for the workbench organizer. On this screen, you will see a collection of functions and utilities to perform special workbench tasks. The *system change options* function is located in the *Administration* folder. Open the folder and double-click on the *Set system change option* line. You get a new screen as shown in Fig. 6-4.

The system displays a column table with the name ranges or namespaces for different types of objects.

In order to enable modifications on any type of objects, you must first select the *Global setting* option to indicate whether the objects from the repository or client independent customization can be modified. You can only change system change options in the name ranges when the global setting option is set to *Modifiable.* Click the *Global setting* . . . push button on the application toolbar to display or change this setting.

If you want to enable modifications in any of the name ranges, just select the check box under the *Modifiable* column.

From the *Edit* menu you have the option to select all, deselect all, or *Select all own,* which means that the only modifiable objects are the local and the customer range objects.

System change options can also be set using special command options of the transport control program tp. For example, to set the system to *objects cannot be changed* in system DD1, as a sapdd1 user you can issue the command: tp lock_eu DD1.

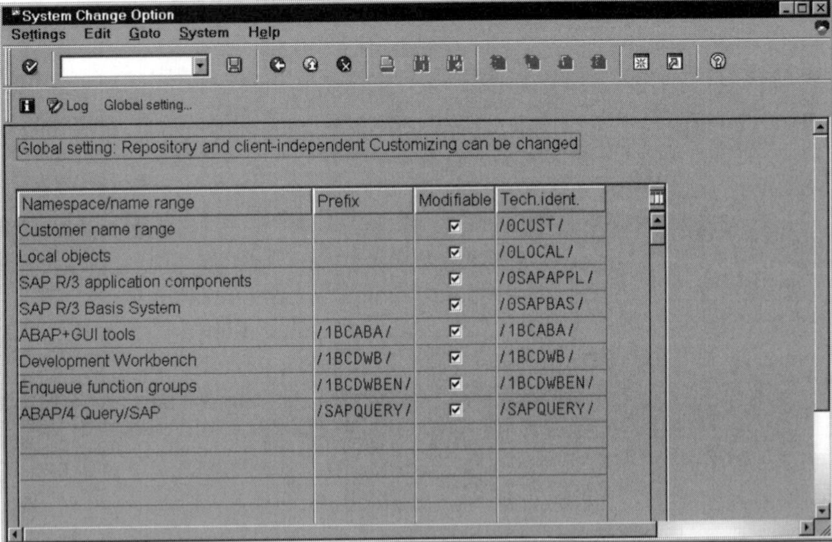

Namespace/name range	Prefix	Modifiable	Tech.ident.
Customer name range		☑	/0CUST/
Local objects		☑	/0LOCAL/
SAP R/3 application components		☑	/0SAPAPPL/
SAP R/3 Basis System		☑	/0SAPBAS/
ABAP+GUI tools	/1BCABA/	☑	/1BCABA/
Development Workbench	/1BCDWB/	☑	/1BCDWB/
Enqueue function groups	/1BCDWBEN/	☑	/1BCDWBEN/
ABAP/4 Query/SAP	/SAPQUERY/	☑	/SAPQUERY/

Figure 6-4
System change option screen.

Functions of the Systems

The type, function, and number of systems are a matter of factors such as budget, size of implementation, critical needs, and so on. However, even in the smallest installations a second system is almost a must, since it is really not a good practice and not recommended by SAP to do the customizing or development work in a productive system.

From the point of view of the workbench organizer and the transport system, the function of the systems as described previously is not really needed. What the workbench organizer needs in the settings is to know which objects can be modified in every system (which system contains the original of the object) and how these changes should be transported to other systems.

Usually development or customization is not carried out directly in productive systems, since the risk of problems is high: a wrong program, a change in a table structure, or an incorrect customization can cause total system unavailability.

However, where there are several systems available, the developers can isolate their work from real production work, minimizing the risk of impacting the productive work of the end users. When the development work is completed and tested, the new or modified objects and programs can then be transported. This object transport can further be tested for integration purposes in another system, or, if that step is not necessary and tests were successful, development objects can be transferred directly to the productive system.

From the point of view of functionality, a training system is often needed as well, although often a different client in the development or test system would normally suffice. If training is going to be intensive, for many users and parallel sessions, then an additional system could be the most convenient option. This training system could be built by performing a copy of the production system.

Development Systems. As the name says, the development systems are where the development work takes place. Normally, the development is carried out for your own objects, this way making these objects originals from these systems. The development system is also used for customizing work which includes functions to create automatically transportable change requests.

From the point of view of the workbench organizer, the development system is the *integration system* for the development classes defined for your own objects.

Original SAP objects can also be modified in these types of systems. You should only do modifications to SAP objects when you need to change the functionality or you receive indications from SAP (SAPnet or hotline) to correct a bug. If this is the case, then you are making a repair.

In development systems, if repairs are permitted, the system change option is normally set to enable modifications on all name ranges including both customer and SAP objects.

Production Systems. The production system is where the end users enter real business data and where the actual business processes run. The production system only contains released versions of your development work. No development takes place in this system, or better, no development should be made in this system. Set the system change option for your production system to *Not modifiable* in the global settings.

The production system is normally the consolidation system for your own development classes and receives transportable change requests with your own development work from the development system.

If for any critical reason you need to perform repairs to the production system, then temporarily change the global settings of the system change option to *Modifiable* to allow modifications in the required name range or namespace.

Test Systems. Test systems, also known as *quality assurance systems,* are used to test the new developments and the customizing settings. Also, they can be used as distribution points of new developments. This does not mean that tests are not performed on the development system; what happens is that test systems often use real data for the integration tests.

Test systems are useful both for preparing the productive environment and for testing new developments with real data after the beginning of production. Often in SAP implementations, not every module or application becomes productive at once; it's a phased project where some applications become productive before others.

When tests are validated, the development objects or customizing work can be transported from the test system to the productive environment.

System Types from the Perspective of the Workbench Organizer and Transport System

The workbench organizer and transport system distinguish between four different types of systems within a group of connected R/3 systems:

- Integration systems
- Consolidation systems
- Recipient systems
- Special development systems

With these system types, the development and transports can be controlled in an orderly manner. This does not mean you need four different systems or that this is a strict scheme to follow. Special development systems are normally not required and are mostly used by SAP itself to develop new or special applications. They won't be dealt with in this chapter.

Figure 6-5 shows a simple scheme with the relationship among these types of systems. These system types are defined when configuring the workbench organizer and the transport system in special tables which hold those settings.

Normally, consolidation systems receive transports which have been released from the integration system. When user installations only have one system for development and one for production, the consolidation system can be the production system. The consolidation systems contain a functioning version of the development.

In larger configurations with three types of systems, the production systems are set as recipient systems and receive the transports previously imported into the consolidation system.

Integration Systems. Integration systems correspond functionally to development systems, where applications or customizing settings is done. When the new developments have been tested, the normal transport route is from the integration system to the consolidation system. In nonproductive consolidation systems, the developments are tested using test data for later transport to the recipient systems.

The restriction on the integration system is that the system does not permit originals to be transported to a consolidation system. Read this sentence carefully: *you can transport from your source system (integration*

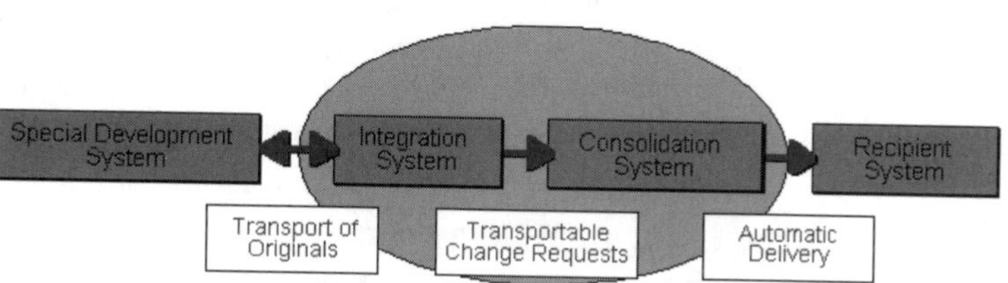

Figure 6-5
Illustration of system types. *(Copyright by SAP AG.)*

system) your originals (new developments) to a target system (consolidation system). However, the system attributes of the objects in the target system indicate that the system original is your source system, which is fine.

What is really restricted by the system is overwriting an original object with the same object with a different attribute as source system. There are, however, special mechanisms for achieving this change. Later in this chapter there is a section about transport types and special transports.

Consolidation Systems. Consolidation systems are set up to receive transports from integration systems. Functionally, they can correspond to either test systems or productive systems. For example, in a group of just two SAP systems, the productive system is configured as the consolidation system. In a group of more than two systems, the consolidation system can be the test system for the new developments and can be used to distribute the new developments to the productive environment, which are then set up as recipient systems.

Once you have established that your developments are free of errors, you can import them into the recipient systems. The users testing the consolidation system have to arrange this with the system administrator responsible for carrying out the transport.

Original objects transported from integration systems to consolidation systems cannot be corrected, but repaired. But, in case an object which has been transported needs to be corrected, the best way is to make the correction in the integration system and transport it back to the consolidation system instead of making a repair. Avoid making repairs as much as possible, or only make them if instructed to do so by the SAP specialists or with advanced corrections from SAPnet notes.

The development class to which an objects belongs is what sets the integration and consolidation system for a development object.

Recipient Systems. Recipient systems are those systems that can receive transports when these have successfully been imported previously into the consolidation system. In order for this process to work, in the workbench organizer settings, all the recipient systems have to subscribe to the consolidation systems.

This is technically accomplished by making an entry in the TASYS table. The section about setting up the workbench organizer later in this chapter includes more information about how to do this.

The recipient systems normally are able to receive only transports of copies when these were previously imported in a consolidation system.

Managing Development Classes

Development classes are used by the R/3 system for grouping together related development objects which belong to the same or similar application areas or similar functions. Development classes are a way in which objects are classified and allow the system to perform certain functions on all objects belonging to the same development classes.

Development classes are held and defined in table TDEVC, which can be maintained from the ABAP repository browser.

To create a new development class, go to the repository browser (transaction SE80), select the *Other objects* radio button, and click on the *Edit* push button.

On the new screen, enter the name of the new class in the *Development class* input field and click the *Create* icon. If the name follows naming conventions, it will automatically include the transport layer and will be linked to the workbench organizer. Enter a short text describing the new development class and save your entries.

Notice how important the definition of the development class for the transport system is. Every development class is assigned a transport layer which defines the route for transports coming from the same development system.

When defining new development classes carefully follow SAP's recommended naming convention:

- Customer objects and test objects should belong to development classes beginning with *Y* or *Z*. This ensures that changes to objects belonging to those classes are recorded in the workbench organizer and therefore can be transported.
- Development classes that begins with a *T* are considered private test classes. R/3 systems always include the TEST development class. When creating a new class of this type, you can specify whether the workbench organizer should control the objects belonging to that class. If you want the workbench organizer to manage that class, select the check box next to *Link to Workbench Organizer* when creating the development class. However, objects belonging to these classes are not intended for transport and are treated as local objects. When creating such a class, the system does not assign a transport layer. If in any case you want to transport objects belonging to those classes, you have two options: special transport as copies or modify the TADIR entry for the object.

NOTE Be extremely careful when modifying the catalog entry for a particular object since it can cause inconsistencies in the system. Follow SAP notes or the instructions of SAP specialists.

- Development classes beginning with *$* are considered local classes. Objects belonging to this class are not managed by the workbench organizer. R/3 systems include the local class $TMP by default. These classes do not have either transport layer, and therefore objects can not be transported.

Every time a new object is created by a developer, it must be assigned to a development class. Actually, the ABAP workbench requests the user enter the development class as soon as the *create object catalog entry* dialog box appears as shown in Fig. 6-6. This information is automatically entered in the TADIR table which is the catalog for the R/3 repository objects.

Development classes can also be the entry point for navigating through the ABAP repository browser.

Figure 6-6 Specifying a development class for an object.

Create object catalog entry

Object R3TR PROG ZTEST02

Attributes

Development class
Author JANTONIO

Repaired
Original system DD1

Master language E
Generated object

Local object | Lock overview

Configuration of the Transport System

The process of configuring from scratch the transport system for a group of SAP systems includes the following activities:

1. Initializing the Change and Transport Organizer
2. Setting up the transport directory and the tp program
3. Configuring the TMS, which includes:
   a. Configuring the transport domain controller
   b. Adding systems
   c. Configuring the transport routes
4. Setting the system change option

When configuring a group of related SAP systems in which the customization, development, and transport systems are organized, there is some information you must know beforehand. This information is basic system landscape design information, and involves the following:

- Which systems are in the group and what their roles are: production, testing, development
- What clients will be created and with what purpose
- Which objects can be modified in the systems
- What will be transported and what the transport routes are
- Whether recipients' systems will be defined to receive transports when these have been imported into consolidation systems

The next sections explain the most important configuration settings for each of these activities.

Step 1. Initializing the Change and Transport Organizer

This initialization is known as *installation follow-up work* or processing after installation because it has to be performed as one of the first activities after the R/3 installation is finished.

This step is accomplished by executing transaction SE06 (*Tools* → *Administration* → *Transports* → *Installation follow-up work*). Figure 6-7 shows an example of this screen.

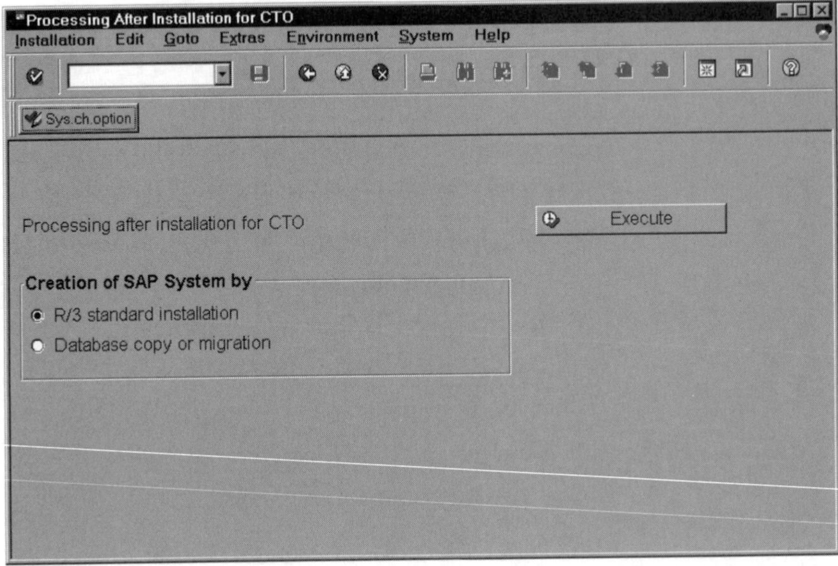

Figure 6-7 Processing after installation for CTO.

This transaction initializes the basic settings for the CTO, and distinguishes whether this R/3 system comes from a standard installation or from a copy of an existing system. It can only be executed once.

On the SE06 screen, specify how the system was installed and click on the *Execute* push button.

When *R/3 standard installation* is selected, the system assumes that it has been installed using the standard R/3 software kits. In this case the program will initialize some basic CTO tables, and there is no need to adjust requests or repairs, since no changes exist. This option should not be used if the system was originated from a copy, since it will create many problems with the change and transport organizer when transports or even upgrades are performed.

When the selection is *Database copy or database migration,* it means that the R/3 system has been created from a copy. In this case it is very important that the system name does not match any other system name within the SAP system group. Systems coming from copies are normally assigned a different role within a group of SAP systems. When this option is executed, the system will request the name of the source system and will ask whether the objects are to be kept as original (new role) or changed to the new system (assuming role from copied system).

Step 2. Setting Up the Transport Directory and the tp Program (TPPARAM)

This second step consists in ensuring that the transport directory (/usr/sap/trans) is shared among a SAP systems group. All systems taking part in the group are included in the global configuration file *TPPARAM* (transport parameter file), located under the *bin* subdirectory of /usr/sap/trans. You must edit this file and make sure all systems have a corresponding entry. If a system is missing, copy another systems entry and change the values (for instance, the parameter <SID>/dbhost = <hostname>).

The transport directory can be shared using NFS on UNIX systems, or using file shares and the alias SAPTRANSHOST or SAPGLOBALHOST on Windows NT systems. The installation program creates the transport directories and subdirectories with the needed files, including an initial configuration or a template TPPARAM file. This file must be correctly configured for the transport control program *tp* to function properly.

Additional information about the *tp* program and TPPARAM are included in following sections of this chapter.

Step 3. Configuring the Transport Management System (TMS)

One of the main functions of the TMS is to create a central system for global transport system configuration and administration. This is achieved using RFC communications between R/3 systems.

The first time a SAP systems group is being installed, one of the systems must be set as *transport domain controller* (as in Windows NT domains). To do this, log onto the R/3 system to be the transport domain controller in client 000, and enter transaction code *STMS* (*Tools → Administration → Transports → Transport Management System*). If there is no domain controller, the system automatically prompts you to create one. It will generate RFC destinations and the TMSADM user, which is used for establishing the communication.

Now you have to include the other R/3 systems. The easiest and most automatic way to do this is to log onto each of the R/3 systems and run transaction STMS from client 000. If the transport directory is shared, the systems will automatically join the transport domain. Once they join, from the domain controller, select the new system and from the menu select *R/3 System → Accept.* Finally, distribute the TMS configuration to all systems in the group by selecting *Extras → Distribute TMS conf.*

Once the systems are configured, the transport routes must be set up to establish consolidation and delivery routes. In regular three-system landscapes, the easiest way is to select a standard configuration. This can be done by first entering the R/3 systems and then selecting *Overview → Transport routes* and then *Configuration → Standard config.* In this case the TMS will request the role of each of the defined systems and set up the transport layer and transport routes for each. For nonstandard configurations or complex system landscapes this process must be performed manually.

Tables that store some of the settings of the TMS are:

- TYST, which contains a list of available SAP systems in a group
- DEVL, containing the transport layers
- TWSYS, which includes the consolidation routes for change requests
- TASYS, which is used for assigning and configuring recipient systems

Other TMS functions are explained in a later section of this chapter.

Step 4. Setting the System Change Option and the Client Settings

Client settings and system change options define the parts of the system that can be modified and automatically recorded by the organizers. Basically, both configurations must allow changes to take place and must be linked with the workbench or customizing organizers. System change options are explained in a previous section. Client maintenance, copy, and settings are explained in Chap. 10.

The Transport Management System (TMS)

The TMS is the transport tool that complements the change and transport organizers for central management of all transport functions. The TMS is used for performing the following functions:

- Defining a central transport domain controller for managing transport configuration in a group of related SAP systems
- Configuring the R/3 systems landscape by assigning roles
- Defining the transport routes among systems within the landscape
- Displaying and managing import queues on each of the systems
- Performing imports of request queues or specific requests
- Performing transports between systems that do not share a common transport directory
- Distributing a configuration
- Testing the configuration
- Displaying the transport logs and parameter files

Within an R/3 transport domain, all systems share a common or reference configuration held in the transport domain controller. Other R/3 systems contain a copy of this reference configuration.

Normally all systems within a transport domain share a common transport directory (usr/sap/trans), although there are situations where this directory is not shared, such as in slow WAN connections, in heterogeneous hardware platforms, or for security reasons. Because of this possibility, there is the concept of the *transport group,* which indicates a group of R/3 systems that share the common transport directory. A transport domain can have more than one transport group.

The next sections explain the main functions and options of the TMS in configuring systems or domains and defining transport routes. The functionality related to managing imports and transport using the TMS is explained in a later section of this chapter.

Configuring Systems and Domains

The transport domain will contain the R/3 system landscape whose transports are being managed jointly. One of the systems will have the role of domain controller, and will hold the main reference configuration. For availability and security reasons, this system is normally the production system.

When transaction *STMS* is started in client 000 on an R/3 system, the following happens:

- If the system is already assigned to a transport domain, the initial screen shows the system's role in the domain.

- If the system has not yet been assigned to a transport domain, it will look for file DOMAIN.CFG in the transport directory to locate an existing transport domain.
  - If a domain exists, the system will prompt to join the domain.
  - If a domain does not exist, a new transport domain is created and the current R/3 system is assigned as the transport domain controller.

When a transport domain is first created, the TMS system performs several configuration actions:

- Creating a transport domain and a transport group
- Creating the user TMSADM
- Generating RFC destinations required for R/3 communications
- Creating the file DOMAIN.CFG in the *bin* directory of the common transport directory

This file contains the TMS configuration and is used by systems joining groups and domains for checking existing configurations. Figure 6-8 shows the TMS initial screen.

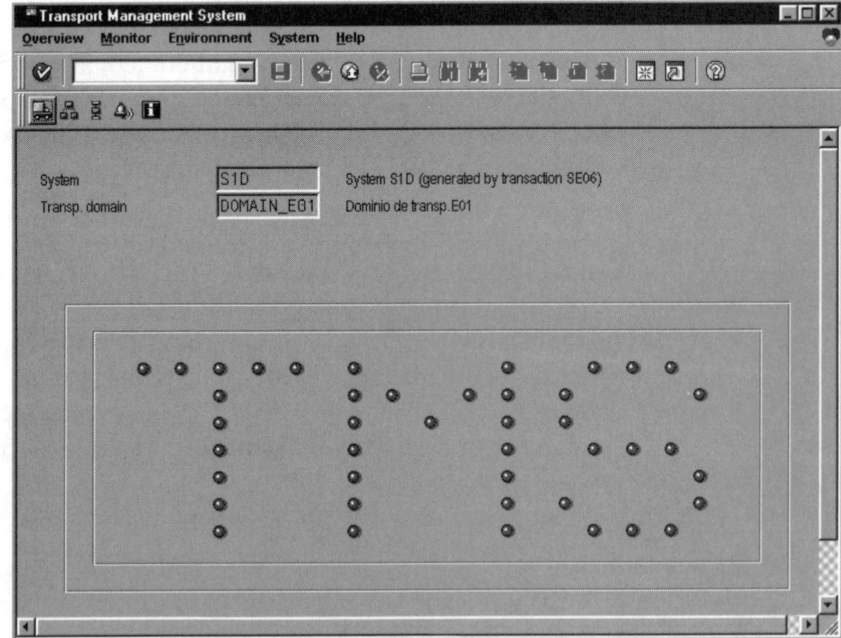

Figure 6-8 Transport management system initial screen.

The TMS allows the definition of a backup domain controller that can take over the functions of the transport domain controller in case of failures. To define a backup domain controller, select the main transport domain controller system, change its definition (*R/3 system → Change*), and enter the system to be used as backup domain controller. Save your entries and distribute your configuration (*Extras → Distribute TMS conf.*).

When configuring the TMS on an R/3 system consisting of several application servers, you can specify the application server to be used for TMS functions. Normally you should select the application server with the highest availability, such as the central instance (the one running the message and/or enqueue server).

Adding R/3 Systems to a Transport Domain. Once the transport domain controller is configured, you have to add other R/3 systems within the landscape. TMS allows the definition of:

- *Regular R/3 systems sharing the common transport directory.* To include these systems, log onto the system to be included in client 000 and start transaction STMS. The TMS will check for the configuration file DOMAIN.CFG and will automatically propose to join the domain. Select the proposal and save your entries. The system status will be waiting to be included in the transport domain. For security reasons, inclusion of systems still needs to be accepted by the transport domain controller. So, log onto the domain controller and go to *Systems.* The screen will display the new system. Select this new system, and choose from the menu *R/3 system → Accept.*
- *R/3 systems without common transport directory.* To include these systems, log onto the system to be included in client 000 and start transaction STMS. In the *Configure Transport Domain* dialog box, select *Other configuration → Include system in domain,* then enter the hostname and system number. Save your entries. The system status will be waiting to be included in the transport domain. As in the previous case, this system must be accepted by the transport domain controller to be active.
- *Virtual systems.* The TMS includes the functionality of adding virtual systems for the purpose of defining R/3 systems that have not yet been installed or are not yet available. These systems are defined in the transport domain controller. In the system overview screen, select *R/3 System → Create → Virtual system.* Enter the system ID and description and save your entries.

- *External systems.* These are like virtual systems but are used for sending transport information or exchanging it with other systems using exchangeable data media. To create external systems, select *R/3 System → Create → External system.* Enter the system ID and description, and the path and description of the transport directory.

Displaying Transport System Status. At any time you can check the systems and the current status of the transport domain configuration in the TMS systems overview. To do this, enter transaction STMS in the command field. In the initial TMS screen, select *Overview → Systems.* Figure 6-9 shows an example of this screen.

The systems overview shows the current status of each of the systems in the *Status* column. You can see whether the configuration is up to date and active or whether there was any error in distributing the configuration. You can display the meaning of the icon symbols by selecting *Extras → Key* or by clicking on the *Key* icon on the application toolbar. Figure 6-10 shows the meaning of each symbol.

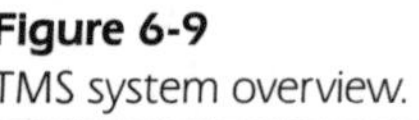

Figure 6-9
TMS system overview.

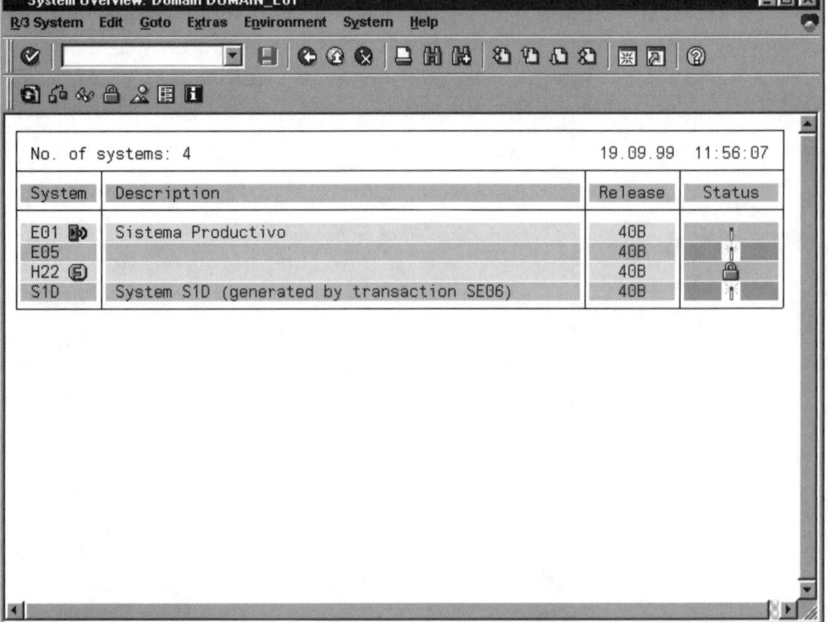

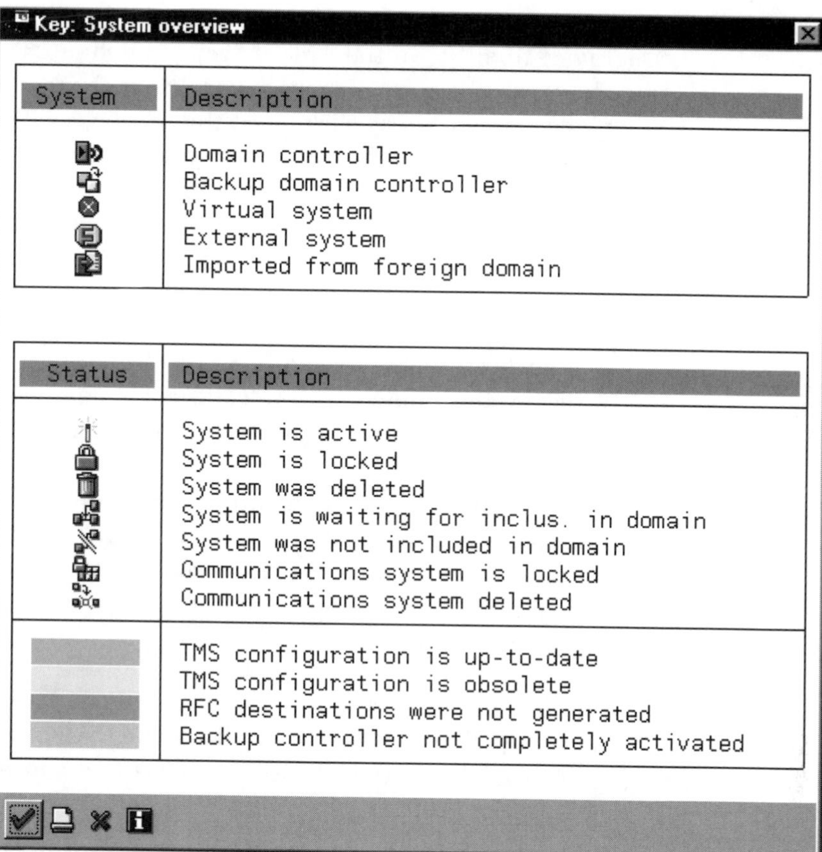

Figure 6-10 Symbols used in TMS system status.

Configuring Transport Routes

Once the domain and systems are configured, you have to specify the transport routes that will be used by the systems. Since many customers' systems landscapes fall into the same categories, the TMS provides some standard system groups that can be used for easily defining routes. When standard system groups are used, the system automatically generates the transport routes. You can select the following standard system groups:

- Single system
- Two-system landscape: development and production
- Three-system landscape: development system, quality assurance system, and production system

Transport routes are configured by selecting *Overview* → *Transport routes* from the initial TMS screen. To define transport routes or use a standard configuration, you have to be in change mode. If you are in display mode, switch by clicking on the *Display* ↔ *Change* icon.

If you select the standard configuration, the current configuration of the R/3 systems will be replaced by these standard settings, although existing objects or development classes will not be deleted. To define a standard configuration, select *Configuration* → *Standard config.* from the menu. The system displays a dialog box with three radio buttons for selecting your required standard configuration. Enter your selection and click *Continue.* Depending on selection, the system will then ask which systems play which role: development, production, or quality assurance. It will then generate the transport routes according to user entries.

If you are not using standard configuration but need to define complex transport systems, you can also use standard settings for initial transport routes and then define additional consolidations or delivery routes.

The TMS includes two types of editors for defining and configuring transport routes:

- A *hierarchical list editor,* where systems and transport routes are displayed in a tree structure. To create transport routes in this editor, from the initial TMS screen select *Configuration* → *Transport route* → *Create.*
- A *graphical editor,* where systems and transport routes are displayed graphically and editing can be performed using the mouse. For accessing the graphical editor, from the initial TMS screen select *Overview* → *Transport routes* → *Go to* → *Graphical editor.* Information on the display areas and on working with the graphical editor can be found in the online documentation.

As introduced in the section on transport system concepts, transport routes can either be of the *consolidation* or *delivery* type. For a standard three-system landscape (development, quality assurance, and production), the transport routes are as follows:

- The *consolidation route* links the development system and the quality assurance system. This transport layer is named Z<SID>, where <SID> is the system ID of the development system.
- A *delivery route* is generated for linking the quality assurance system and the production system.

When developments or changes are made in the development system that include objects whose development class refers to the standard transport layer, these changes are recorded in change requests. These change requests will be transported first to the quality assurance system and then to the production system.

The transport system also creates the consolidation route SAP that is used when changes are made to SAP objects. In these cases, the changes are recorded in *repair tasks* that can be transported the same way.

Notice that you will only be able to create delivery routes for existing consolidation routes.

An example of transport route configuration is shown in Fig. 6-11.

In Fig. 6-11, you will notice in the title bar that the system includes a version number. When an active configuration is modified and saved, the system creates a new version. You can activate a stored version by choosing *Configuration* → *Get configuration* from the transport domain controller on the transport route screen.

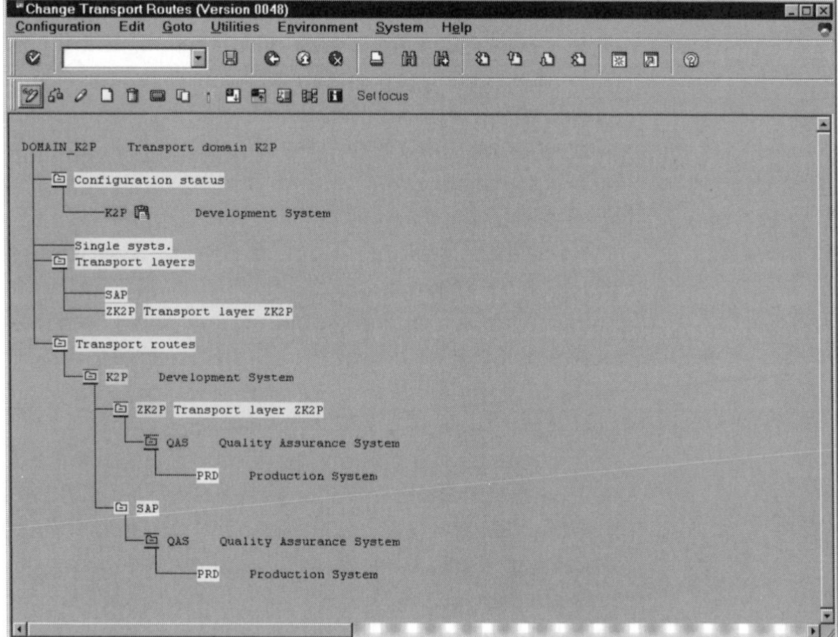

Figure 6-11 Transport route configuration.

Distributing and Verifying TMS Configuration

Before distributing the TMS configuration to other systems in the group, you should first check the configuration. There are several checking options available that should behave without errors before the TMS can function properly. If any errors are found, review your configuration or network settings before proceeding.

Within the transport routes overview screen, select *Configuration → Check* and then either *Local* or *All systems.*

Since all R/3 systems in a transport domain communicate using RFC connections, you should also check these RFC connections in the TMS system overview. Select *Overview → Systems → R/3 System → Check → Connection test* from the TMS initial screen.

To check whether the transport control program *tp* and the TPPARAM file are correctly configured, select *R/3 System → Check → Transport tool* from the *Systems Overview* screen.

Additionally, you should also verify the availability of the transport directories in all systems within the transport domain. Select *R/3 System → Check → Transport directory* from the *Systems Overview* screen.

When the configuration of the transport domain controller is complete, the next step is to distribute the configuration to all other R/3 systems within the transport domain. To do this, select *Configuration → Distribute* from the transport routes overview screen. You can also select *Extras → Distribute TMS conf.* from the systems overview screen.

Once the configuration has been distributed, you must activate the new configuration on each R/3 system within the transport domain. The activation can be performed centrally from the domain controller (by selecting *Configuration → Activate → In all domains*) or locally on each system (by selecting *Configuration → Activate → Local*).

Because changing transport routes can have some impact on R/3 system configuration, the TMS uses the TMSSUP remote function call for the distribution and activation of transport route configurations. For security reasons, this function module requires the administrator to log onto the target system with the target system administrator's user and password.

Working with the Workbench Organizer

The workbench organizer is activated automatically every time a user edits a repository object. The user is able to create or modify the object only if he or she has opened a change request or uses an existing change request in the workbench organizer. Entering objects in requests ensures that all changes made in the ABAP development workbench and customizing are registered. Except in specific instances, all changes to customizing objects such as table entries are registered in the customizing organizer.

The transport system is used to transfer objects from one R/3 system to another. The transport system also takes care of checking and monitoring the results of the transport requests. A transport can be seen as having two phases: an export phase and an import phase.

The export phase is executed automatically from the organizers when users release their transportable change requests. The results of the exports are logged and the files at the operating system level generated. It also performs an import test to simulate the import at the target system so if it finds inconsistencies, you can correct them before actually importing the objects.

The import phase has to be performed by the system administrator at the operating system level or using the TMS, but the results are also recorded in the transport logs and can be checked within the R/3 system.

The transport system allows the following components to be transported:

- New or corrected objects created by customers
- Standard objects from the SAP system
- Table entries

The transportable objects are virtually any SAP objects, including programs, function modules, forms, documentation, table definitions (structure), data elements, domains, screens, menus, print definitions, and number ranges; also, as stated in the preceding list, table entries which are not by themselves development objects, but data, are included, too. Objects or table entries can be transported whether they have been modified or not.

The following sections explain how to proceed to successfully perform transports observing the available options and restrictions of the R/3 system. The transport control program tp is explained later.

Creating Change Requests

Although there are two main types or categories of change requests, SYST (workbench) and CUST (customizing), the flexibility and features of the change and transport organizers are further enhanced, with the possibility of relocating objects, instituting development classes, copying objects, including requests within requests, and so on. Many of the special functions are performed using the *transport organizer* (*SE01*), which is introduced later in this chapter. The following sections and examples deal with the most common and typical tasks to be performed when working with regular workbench and customization tasks and change requests.

There are two basic ways to create a change request:

- *Automatically.* When creating or modifying an object, or when performing customization settings, the system displays the dialog box for creating a change request. It is important to note that any users who need to perform development on the system or modification to SAP object originals must be registered using the SAP Software Change Registration (SSCR).
- *Manually.* Create the request from the workbench or customizing organizer, and then enter required attributes and insert objects.

The manual creation of transports is sometimes very useful when transporting copies of objects to systems outside the system group, when copying specific table entries among systems, or for solving synchronization problems. To create a change request manually in the initial workbench screen, the customizing organizer screen, or the requests overview screen, click on the *Create* icon on the application toolbar. Depending on the *Category* that is selected, the system will ask you to specify a type of request, or will set the request type automatically. Types of change requests are:

- *Transportable change requests.* Regular workbench requests (category SYST) that will contain objects with the correct development classes, and that will have a transport layer and a target system.
- *Customizing requests.* Change requests that will contain customization settings that can either be client dependent (CUST category) or applicable to all clients (SYST category).
- *Local requests.* Requests that will not be transported, mostly because they are meant for use in editing or creating objects for test purposes.

- *Unclassified requests.* Requests whose type is not initially assigned or empty but will be manually entered when appropriate. This option is only visible on the requests overview lists.

To manually create a change request and associated tasks, click on the *Create* icon and specify a type of request. The system will display a dialog box like the one shown in Fig. 6-12. Normally you only have to specify a short descriptive text and enter the usernames to participate in this request. The system will create a task for each of the usernames.

You can also specify special request attributes for qualifying and evaluating change requests. SAP provides several standard attributes, like SAPCORR, SAPNOTE, and so on. You can add your own by editing table *WBOATTR* using transaction SM30.

Releasing Tasks and Requests

When new developments, corrections, or customizing work is complete, developers must release their tasks and requests. To release a task, go to the initial workbench organizer screen. As request types, select the *Transportable* and *Modifiable* check boxes, and deselect other options. Then, click on the *Display* push button, or press <ENTER>. The system will display a list with the change requests that have not yet been released. To list the tasks, open up the change requests by clicking the + sign on the folder signs. The system shows a screen similar to the one shown in Figure 6-13. Position the cursor on the task to be released and click on the *Release* button on the application toolbar. You can figure out which tasks

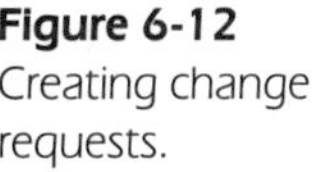

Figure 6-12 Creating change requests.

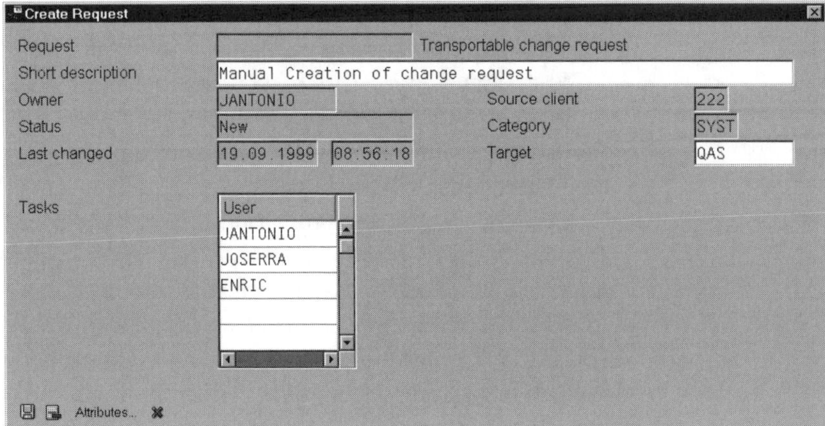

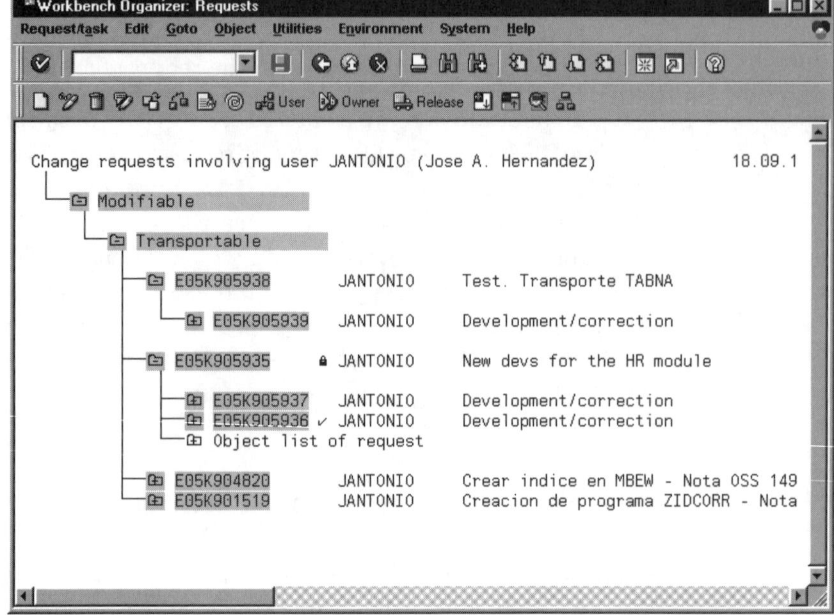

Figure 6-13 Example of displaying requests from the workbench organizer.

have been already released by the color coding (*Utilities* → *Key*). If the task is a repair, the system will display a dialog box asking whether to automatically confirm the repair.

When releasing a task, the system will automatically show the documentation screen for entering whatever descriptive text should be held with the tasks. Enter your documentation in the editor screen, click the *Save* button, and then click the *Back* icon. The system will inform you that the task is being released in response to the change request. If there were any locks on development objects included within the task, those locks are transferred to the change request, along with the documentation for the tasks.

When developers finish working on their tasks and have released them, then requests themselves can be released. This process is almost the same as releasing tasks. Just position the cursor on a transportable change request whose tasks have already been released, and click the *Release* button on the application toolbar. The system will display a message on the screen indicating that the objects are being exported, or you might get an error message if there is any problem with the objects within the change request. If the release is normal, an export run takes place, exporting the object data to operating system files in which the import to the target system takes place. When the request is released the locks on the objects are removed, allowing users to make further changes.

Monitoring Transports and Repairs

The square box *Global information* on the upper right of the initial workbench organizer screen contains two stoplights with a summary of the transports and repairs performed in and out of the system. Click the push buttons to display the associated change requests.

The list of change requests corresponding to the selected categories are displayed in a hierarchical list. You can navigate this list from which you can see the transport logs at the last level of the hierarchy. Double clicking on the line will display the transport log screen, in which you can select the level of detail to be displayed.

An example of the transport log and the codes is shown later in the section entitled "Checking Transport Results," where the return codes of the logs are also explained. If you find the reason for the error and have corrected it, you can select *Transport/Repair → Error corrected* from the menu bar of this screen, which will delete the error from the display. This function is recorded in the transport action log. To see the action log, select *Goto → Action log* from the menu bar.

You can enter criteria for searching and displaying different types of change requests. To display an individual change request or task, or to perform a search, click on the *Display individually* button on the application toolbar. In the dialog box you can enter a request or task number and click *Enter.* If you click the possible entries arrow on this dialog box, the system shows an additional screen for entering criteria and searching requests.

You can also select the request from different user. This is done by entering the user name in the *User* input field.

From the list display, also in hierarchical form, you can navigate and expand the branches until you reach specific objects contained in the tasks.

Transport Rules

When creating transport requests or performing imports, some restrictions must be observed to maintain the consistency of the transported objects.

Transports cannot overwrite or delete original objects or objects under repair in the target system. In special situations, imports that overwrite such objects can be performed with special unconditional modes of the tp program. However, this should only be performed under the instructions of SAP specialists.

You cannot transport copies of objects to a target system (consolidation system) that is not included the consolidation transport route. This is automatically set by the workbench organizer with transportable change requests. The restriction is imposed by the development class of the objects, which indicates the integration system and the consolidation system for the objects.

Transports to any recipient system should only be performed from the consolidation system to which the system has subscribed. These transports are automatically included in the import queue of the recipient systems, as defined in the delivery routes.

Specifying Objects to Transport. When working with tasks and change requests directly with the workbench organizer, the object list is generated automatically when the tasks are released. The task numbers are included within the object list of the transportable change requests.

But you can also enter objects to be transported using the organizer object list maintenance tools, which provide utilities for creating objects lists, copying and pasting, and so on.

To create or modify an object list, select the change request from the request overview screen. You can either include the object directly in the change request or in tasks. Position your cursor on the change request or task, and double-click on it.

The workbench organizer shows the *Display object list* screen. Click on the *Display <—> Change* icon to access the edit mode. The system displays the *Maintain object list* window as shown in Fig. 6-14.

You might not see any empty lines in the *Object list* square box. Select *Edit → Insert line* from the menu bar, or press the *Insert line* button on the application toolbar, or click the *New entries* button to display a full screen with empty lines.

In this screen you can manually enter the objects you wish to transport. There are five columns:

- *PgmId.* The program ID is part of the name of an object type for its use in the workbench organizer and the transport system. Press the F4 key or click on the possible entries arrow to display a list of allowable values. Normally, the R3TR value is used for ensuring the consistency of all related objects in a transport. For example, if you want to transport a new table between systems, the R3TR program ID ensures the transport of all the needed and related objects for the table, including the data elements and domains.

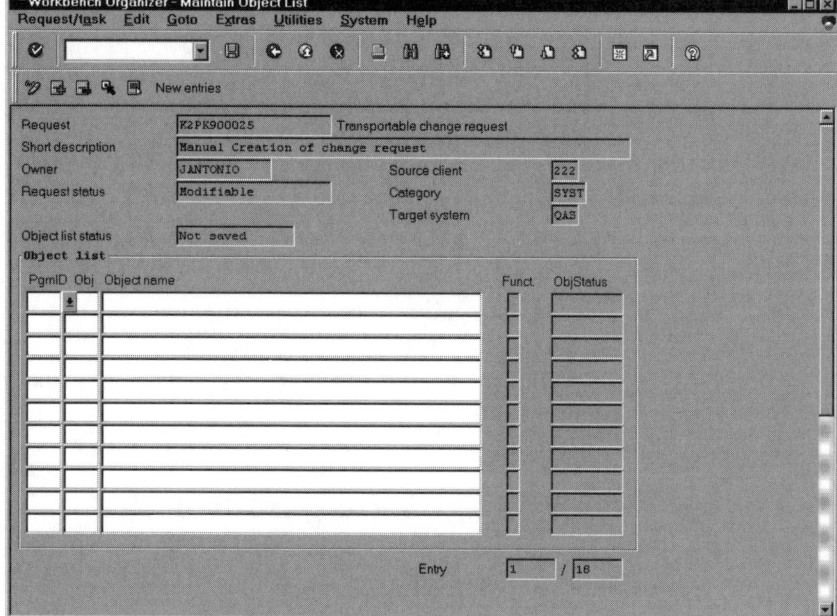

Figure 6-14 Object list maintenance screen.

- *Obj.* This is the object type. The system uses this type to perform the needed operations at the target system. There are hundreds of types, which you can look up by pressing the F4 function key. Most typical are *PROG* which means ABAP source code and CUA definitions, *TABL* for table definitions, or *TABU* for table contents.
- *Obj. Name.* It's the object name, for example, a table name, a program name, a view name, and so forth.
- *Funct.* The function column is normally grayed out. It can be used to specify special functions for an object entry. For example, suppose you want to transport the contents of a long table, but only want to transport those entries that match a particular key value. You can do this with function K. To access this field, select *Extras → Modify object function.* Some object types do not have any object function.
- *Obj. Status.* The object status field is automatically maintained by the system and is mainly a lock indicator.

Protecting a Transport Request. When temporarily finished working on a change request, you can decide to protect it so that no other tasks can be assigned to the request. To protect a change request, locate your change request with the workbench organizer, select it, and choose *Request/task* → *Request* → *Protect.* You can later remove the protection at your convenience.

When a request is *protected,* the objects in the lists get the status locked and this prevents other users from modifying them.

If the system successfully locks all the objects in a change request, the status of the request is set to LOCKEDALL. From the workbench organizer, you see the status as *Protected.*

If the status shows LOCKED instead of LOCKEDALL, it means that some object in the request could not be successfully locked.

If you are going to release and export your requests immediately, you don't need to protect the request. It's a useful function when working for several days on some objects and you want to discourage other users from modifying them.

Checking Transport Results

There are several ways to display the result of a transport. One of them was introduced in the previous section about working with the workbench organizer. Another option for displaying logs is to do so from the requests overview screen by selecting the change requests and then choosing *Goto* → *Transport log.* Figure 6-15 shows an example of the overview of transport logs for a request. Transport logs only exist when the release of the change request has been performed.

There are two main types of logs:

- *Action log,* which logs and displays actions that have taken place: export, test import, import, and so forth
- *Transport log,* which keeps a record of the log files generated by the transport steps

The transport log includes several levels of detail, from a summary information screen to a more detailed output where you can even see exactly which objects have been transported, how long it took, and possible warnings or errors. Figure 6-16 shows an example of a transport log.

Transport logs have several levels of details that you can expand or compress using the icons in the application toolbar. In Fig. 6-16 the transport log for the main import in the production system is completely expanded. Additionally, the upper line on the display shows the location of the log file at the operating system level.

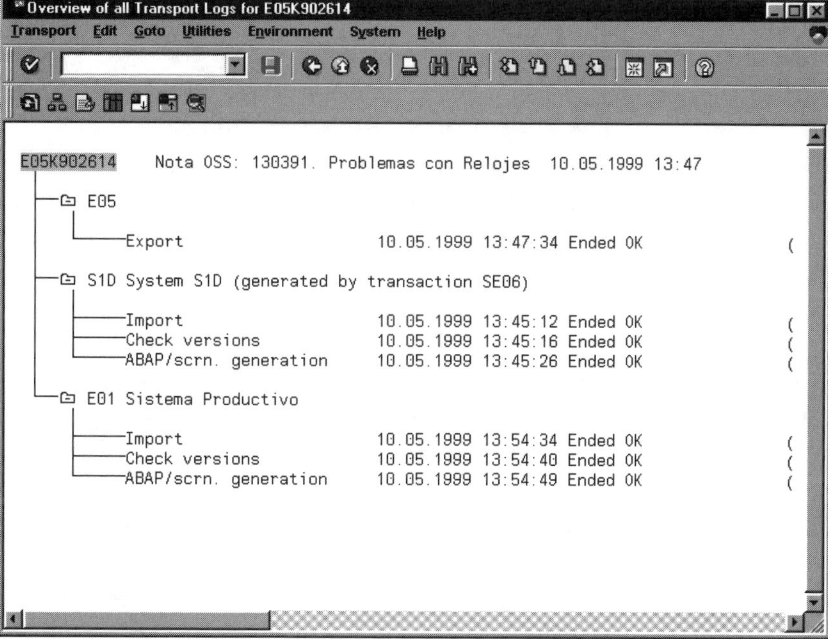

Figure 6-15 Overview of transport logs for a request.

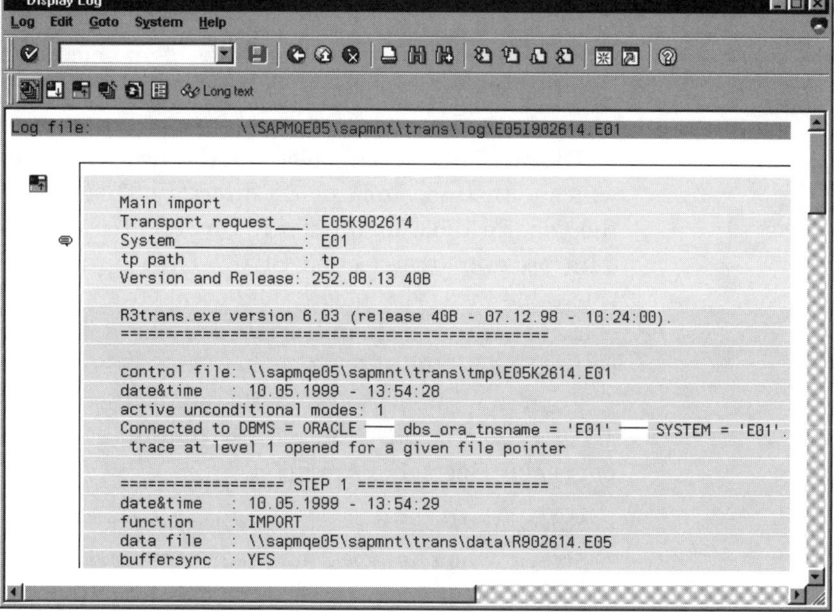

Figure 6-16 Example of a transport log.

The most important information on the transport log is the return code which indicates whether the transport was successfully performed. The codes have the following meanings:

- *0:* The transport was successful.
- *4:* The transport has at least one warning message. The objects in the request have been transported but the system warns that some action might have been improperly set in the transport, for example, when importing an object to a system which was not the original target system.
- *8:* The transport has some severe errors that prevented the objects from being transported. You should look at the error messages and take a corrective action before performing the transport again.
- *12 or higher:* The system has flagged a fatal error. These errors normally are not related to the transport content itself but to some R/3 system error which can be related to the operating system or to the database system. In such cases, perform the basic troubleshooting with the CCMS tools and contact the SAP hotline or look up your error messages in SAPnet.

Object Attributes

As mentioned earlier, the attributes of an object offer important information that directly relates to the way it can be handled by the workbench organizer and the transport system.

The attributes for all objects in the system are held in the TADIR table, which is the repository object directory. This table can be displayed from the general table maintenance function (transaction SM31) or from the data browser (transaction SE16). Only authorized users can maintain this table, however; modifying entries from this table could have unexpected results and should be avoided except if instructed by a SAP note or by SAP support personnel.

From the transport system there are other menu options to display the TADIR table or only the records containing the attributes related to a particular object. For example:

- Selecting *Utilities → Obj. directory entry* from the request overview screen, when an object has been previously selected.
- From the menu of the object list maintenance screen, selecting an object and then choosing *Goto → Object attributes.*

Selecting an object and using one of these options allows you to see the following attributes:

- *Program ID, Object type,* and *Object name.* The identification of an object for the workbench organizer and the transport system. The meaning of these fields is explained in the previous section entitled "Specifying Objects to Transport."
- *Author.* The user ID of the person who created the object or is responsible for it.
- The *development class* of the object, which specifies the integration and consolidation system for the object; therefore, it restricts the allowable transport routes to other systems.
- *Original system (SRCSYSTEM),* for which the object is considered original. It could be the same system in which it was originally created or can be another one if the object was transported changing the authorization.
- An *entry flag (SRCDEP),* which indicates whether the object is under repair or is system-specific. In these cases, the object is protected from being overwritten by other transports.

To find additional information or get reports on tasks, change requests, repairs, and so forth, use the workbench organizer tools (transaction SE03), which are available as an icon in the application toolbar on the organizer screens.

Workbench Organizer Tools

The utilities tools for the workbench organizer and the transport system provide a collection of standard and expert functions, mainly for use by the system administrator, providing facilities for reporting, unlocking, setting the system change options, and other advanced functions over the objects controlled by the workbench organizer.

To use some of the expert functions included within these tools, users need the CTS_ALL authorization. This screen can be accessed from the initial workbench organizer menu by selecting *Goto* → *Tools.* Alternatively, use transaction SE03 in the command field.

To get additional information about the actions or report that each of the functions perform, click on a line and select *Goto* → *Documentation* from the menu bar.

The Transport Organizer

Besides the workbench and customizing organizers, the CTO includes the transport organizer (*Tools → Administration → Transports → Transport organizer,* transaction code SE01), which can be used for performing special transport types such as:

- Transport of copies and relocations
- Object lists
- Client transports
- Preliminary transports from SAP

One of the singular differences between the workbench and customizing requests is that when creating this type of transports there is no assignment of transport routes. Additionally, each of the request types handled by the transport organizer has its own naming convention.

Following is a brief overview of the different selections and request types and what they are used for. When accessing the SE01, you will see the initial screen of the transport organizer with a request type box including four options:

- *Copy transports and relocs.* This option directs you to four different types of requests depending on what you want to do in respect to source system and object originals. The four types of requests are:
  - *Transport of copies.* This type of request can be used for transporting objects from your R/3 system to other R/3 systems, without modifying the original system from the objects.
  - *Relocation of objects without a development class change.* This is comparable to type C transports of earlier R/3 releases. This type of request is used for moving objects to other development systems and changing the original source system while maintaining the development class.
  - *Relocation of objects with development class change.* This type of request is similar to the previous one, but you can specify a new development class for the objects on the target systems. Objects change both original system and development class. These requests can be useful when permanently moving development work to other systems.
  - *Relocation of a complete development class.* This type of request moves a complete development class, and therefore will change the transport layer. You will need to specify both the new development class and the transport layer.

- *Object lists.* This type of request is used for setting up a list of objects that can later be used in other change requests when selecting the function *Include object list.* Object lists do not function as transports and cannot be released. They are transported as objects within other transportable change requests. You can choose any name you want except that first three characters must not be SAP and the fourth must not be K.
- *Client transports.* This special request type cannot be manually created, but can be managed and displayed from this option. The reason for including this type of transport within the transport organizer is to implement some security measures, such as not including client transports in normal import queues.
- *SAP/Partner → Customer.* This option is mainly used by SAP or its partners for delivering developments to customers. If you do not perform developments for delivery to other customers, this option is only used for displaying information.

Performing Transports with the TMS

Up to release 3.1H, the import phase of transports was always performed at the operating system level. Since the introduction of the TMS, there is a full suite of functions for managing transports and performing imports from within the R/3 systems. The TMS uses the *tp* program for performing imports and other functions.

You can still use all the functionality available with the transport control program *tp* and even with *R3trans.* The following sections cover these programs in great detail.

The TMS includes all the security measures to ensure the proper order of imports. It does allow special preliminary transports and the use of unconditional modes, and other special queue functions, similar to the ones found when using *tp.*

All the transportable change requests that have been released are now displayed in the import queues of the target systems. When releasing change requests, the system creates several files in the transport directory (data, control file) and inserts an entry in the import queue of the target system. The import queue is the same as the system import buffer, and as such the file is located under the *buffer* directory.

To access the import queues, access the initial TMS screen *Tools → Administration → Transports → Transport Management System* (transaction code STMS) and then click on the *Imports* icon on the application toolbar, or select *Overview → Imports.* The system will display the import overview screen, with several columns including the system within the transport domain, the description, the number of requests in the queue, and the status.

To display the contents of an import queue, double-click on one of the systems. Figure 6-17 shows an example of an import queue. For performance reasons the TMS only reads import queues the first time it accesses them. If you need the latest queue status, select the *refresh* function.

From the import queue you can display the object list, the logs, the documentation, or the owner. You can do this from the *Request → Display* menu.

To begin the transport process, transport all the requests in the import queue into the quality assurance system. This will automatically insert these requests into the import queue of the delivery systems (normally production systems). Then users should check and test what has been transported into the quality assurance system. If tests are verified, the next step is to transport the full import queue into the production system.

Transport administrators will normally select the *Start import* function, which will request the target client and start importing the queue in

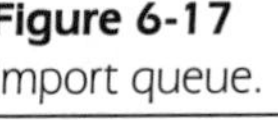

Figure 6-17
Import queue.

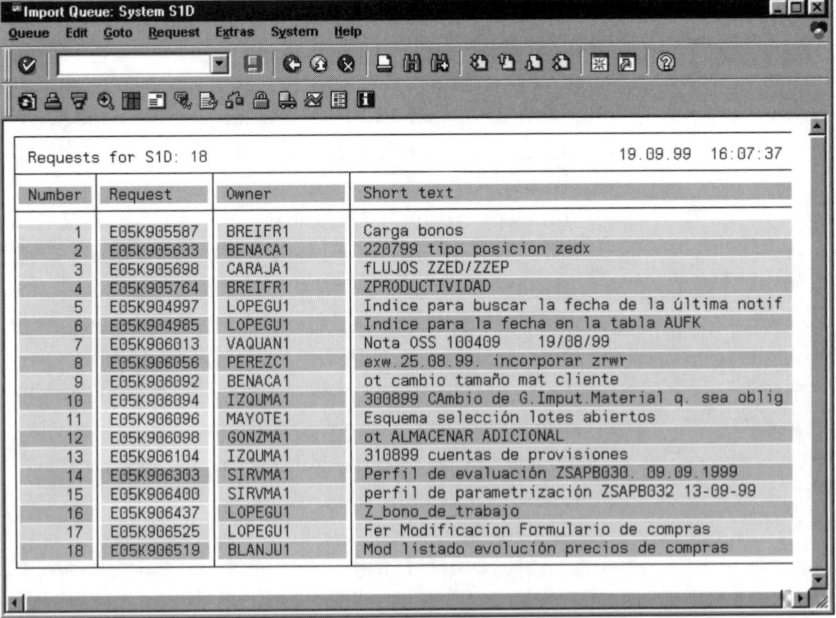

Number	Request	Owner	Short text
1	E05K905587	BREIFR1	Carga bonos
2	E05K905633	BENACA1	220799 tipo posicion zedx
3	E05K905698	CARAJA1	fLUJOS ZZED/ZZEP
4	E05K905764	BREIFR1	ZPRODUCTIVIDAD
5	E05K904997	LOPEGU1	Indice para buscar la fecha de la última notif
6	E05K904985	LOPEGU1	Indice para la fecha en la tabla AUFK
7	E05K906013	VAQUAN1	Nota OSS 100409 19/08/99
8	E05K906056	PEREZC1	exw.25.08.99. incorporar zrwr
9	E05K906092	BENACA1	ot cambio tamaño mat cliente
10	E05K906094	IZQUMA1	300899 CAmbio de G.Imput.Material q. sea oblig
11	E05K906096	MAYOTE1	Esquema selección lotes abiertos
12	E05K906098	GONZMA1	ot ALMACENAR ADICIONAL
13	E05K906104	IZQUMA1	310899 cuentas de provisiones
14	E05K906303	SIRVMA1	Perfil de evaluación ZSAPB030. 09.09.1999
15	E05K906400	SIRVMA1	perfil de parametrización ZSAPB032 13-09-99
16	E05K906437	LOPEGU1	Z_bono_de_trabajo
17	E05K906525	LOPEGU1	Fer Modificacion Formulario de compras
18	E05K906519	BLANJU1	Mod listado evolución precios de compras

the order in which the change requests were previously released. This function is equivalent to the *tp import all* command.

Imports can be started from any R/3 system within the transport domain; however, if you are logged onto any system but the target system, TMS will show a logon window for providing logon information. TMS will establish an RFC connection and start the *tp* program in the target system. When *tp* starts the import, the system closes the RFC connection. When imports have been successful, they are automatically inserted in the import queue for the next system in the transport route.

The status column of an import queue can show different statuses. You can display these statuses by clicking on the *Key* icon on the application toolbar. The queue can have the following statuses:

- *Open* for new requests being added
- *Closed,* meaning that the newly added requests will not be imported during the next full import
- *Running*
- *Errors occurred during import*
- *Import terminated*
- *Import queue could not be read*

Besides importing all requests in the queue with the *Start import* function, the TMS includes many other options. Following is a list of the main functions that can be performed using the TMS import facilities:

- *Closing an import queue.* This is the function of setting a stop mark for preventing imports of change requests that were released and added to the queue after a certain time. To do this, select the queue and choose *Queue* → *Close* from the menu. The TMS then sets a mark so that new requests are positioned after the mark and only requests before the mark will be imported in the next import.
- *Opening the import queue.* Select *Queue* → *Open* to delete the stop mark.
- *Adding requests to the queue.* You can manually add a change request to an import queue by selecting *Extras* → *Other requests* → *Add.* Normally this function should not be used because requests are automatically added. This is equivalent to the *tp addtobuffer* command.
- *Removing requests from the queue.* You can also remove a particular request from the import queue. Select the request, and from the

menu choose *Request → Delete.* SAP's recommendation is not to delete, but to create a new change request with the correction.

- *Performing single imports.* This process is known as performing preliminary imports, as opposed to standard import in which the full queue would be included. To perform the import of an individual change request, click on its line in the import queue and select *Request → Import.* The system displays a dialog box for entering some information. Figure 6-18 shows an example that also displays the expert mode. With the expert mode you can set unconditional modes just as with the *tp* program. Options are:
  - Ignore that the transport request has already been imported (unconditional mode 1)
  - Overwrite originals (unconditional mode 2)
  - Overwrite objects in unconfirmed repairs (unconditional mode 6)
  - Ignore invalid transport type (unconditional mode 9)

  Enter the system client and options and click the *Start import* icon.

  SAP does not recommend this process because there is some risk of creating inconsistencies. However, to minimize the risk, when a single import is performed it remains in the queue and will be reimported the next time the full queue is imported. This guarantees that exports and imports are performed in the correct order.

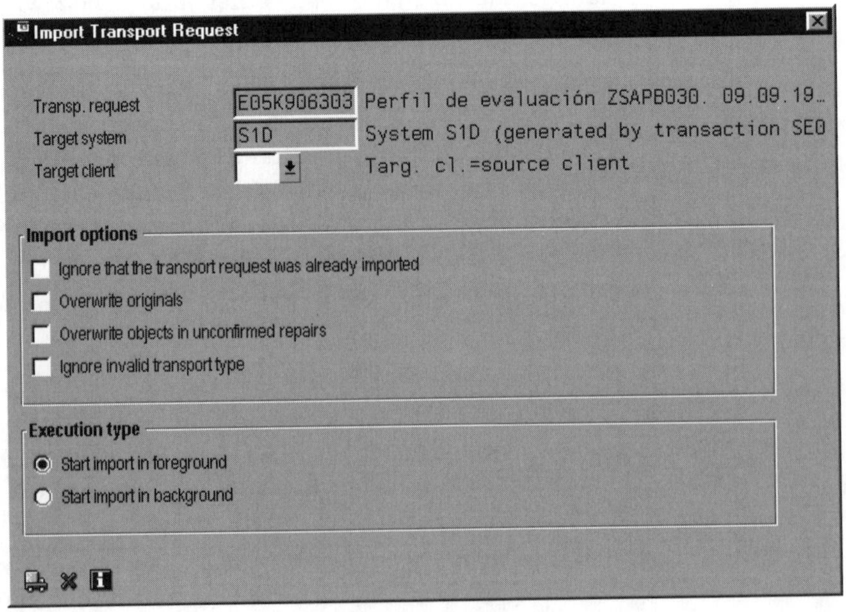

Figure 6-18 Transport request import options.

- *Forwarding a change request.* On certain occasions, you can select the function *Request → Forward* to send a change request to a system outside the predefined transport routes.
- *Transporting between transport groups or foreign domains.* Under the *Extras → Other request* menu, you have several options for reading the import queues on systems whose transport directories are not shared and that therefore are located on other transport groups or domains. You can still perform transports among these systems, but the import queues of target systems must first be adjusted.

Using tp, the Transport Control Program

The transport control program tp is the SAP program that administrators use for performing and planning transports between systems and also in upgrades of the R/3 systems. The tp program is used by the CTO and the TMS.

The tp program uses other special programs and utilities to perform its functions. Mainly, it calls the R3trans utility program. However, tp offers a more extensive control of the transport process, ensuring the correct sequence of the exported/imported objects, since the wrong order can cause severe inconsistencies in the system.

Administrators normally use tp for performing imports; it can also be used for exports, although the normal export process is automatic when releasing change requests. The export phase extracts the objects from the database and places them on files at the operating system level, together with a control file and a transport log. The export phase is done in the source system.

The import phase has to be performed in the target system. In this phase, the exported objects are inserted into the database following the instructions on the control file which came along with the data files of the export.

Importing data causes a refresh (a synchronization) of the SAP buffers which can cause performance problems if this is done often. For that reason, it is a good practice to schedule imports at times of less interactive work, such as at night or on weekends.

Before you can start using the tp program, you should ensure that the tp program is set up correctly and the requirements met. The next section explains how to set up the tp program.

Setting Up the tp Program

The tp program is located in the standard runtime directory of the SAP system. This directory is /usr/sap/SYS/<SID>/exe/run. It is automatically copied in the SAP installation process.

The requirements for using the tp program are as follows:

- The transport directory /usr/sap/trans must exist. This is a requirement for the SAP system installation, so it should be there. Watch out for the correct ownership, which you set to the SAP administrator user account, <sid>adm.
- The transport directory must be accessible by every R/3 system taking part in the transport process. This also includes all the application servers. If an application server cannot access the /usr/sap/trans directory, then you must make sure that the background process for imports doesn't run in this system, otherwise it will fail since it will not find the needed files in the directory.
- The workbench organizer and the transport system must be initialized as indicated in a previous section with transaction SE06, which initializes and updates the needed control tables for transports.
- Transports are only allowed between systems with different names (different SIDs).
- Both the source system and the target system must have at least two background processes each. This is because the transport process automatically schedules and releases the needed jobs.
- You must log on as user <sid>adm to perform transports. Imports with tp always have to be performed in the target system, while exports with tp must be done in the source systems.
- The tp global parameter file, TPPARAM, must be maintained, specifying at least the hostname of the systems taking part in the transport process. This file is explained in a later section of this chapter.
- The import dispatcher process RDDIMPDP and RDDIMPD_CLIENT_<nnn> should be scheduled as background jobs in every system where imports will be performed. These jobs are automatically scheduled by the system when performing a client copy. If for any reason they are deleted, you can schedule these jobs by running report RDDNEWPP. These jobs are defined as periodic event triggered, meaning that *tp* sends a signal (an event) to the R/3 system and the job starts. These events are SAP_TRIGGER_RDDIMPDP and SAP_TRIGGER_RDDIMPDP_CLIENT.

The Transport System at the Operating System Level: Users and Directories. In a group of related SAP R/3 systems which are going to perform transports among themselves, a correct configuration of users at operating system level and of the file directory structure is essential. In a standard R/3 installation, the system correctly sets both the users and the directories. There might be, however, some circumstances where the configuration might change unintentionally or from previous system settings.

The standard transport directory is /usr/sap/trans which is shared by all the systems. Normally, one of the systems holds it physically while others access it via NFS (network file system) or with file shares. This is done so all the systems have access to the exported files and transport logs. Otherwise, a manual copy of the needed files must be performed.

It is equally important to give the right system authorization for accessing this directory. All the subdirectories should have <sid>adm as the owner. To avoid permissions problems, the normal setting is to give read, write, and execute access both to the owner and to the SAP administrator group number, *sapsys.* And, at the same time, this group should be defined the same in all SAP servers. If the group number has been manually created, modified, or previously used by other applications, problems might arise.

Exports are always automatically performed by R/3 using <sid>adm. Imports are performed at the operating system level in the target system and users must be logged on as user <sid>adm to guarantee correct file permissions.

The installation creates the subdirectory structure beneath /usr/sap/trans. The subdirectories are as follows:

- *bin.* Contains the TPPARAM file, which is the global transport parameter file. Normally, the <sid>adm user positions in this directory to perform imports so that the tp program locates the TPPARAM at the default directory. Otherwise, the call to tp must include the location of the parameter file. Optionally, this directory might contain other files such as T_OFF.ALL or T_OFF.<SID>. These files can be used to deactivate permission for all or a particular system to perform exports.
- *data.* This directory contains the transport data files.
- *log.* Under this directory, all the individual and general transport logs, statistics, and trace files are located. Administrators should refer to this directory for troubleshooting functions.
- *buffer.* Contains special buffer files with the SID of every system in the transport group. These files include control information on

the transports that will be imported into other systems and the order of them. A good monitoring and display of the buffers improves the management of all the transport processes.

- *cofiles.* It is the control file directory containing information about the steps of the transportable change requests as well as the return codes.
- *sapnames.* Contains information on SAP users performing exports and keeps track of the status for each change request.
- *tmp.* It is the temporary directory containing some auxiliary temporary files with control flags, semaphores, and so forth.
- *actlog.* This directory includes action log files for all the tasks and change requests. These files are only accessed and modified by the R/3 system.
- *olddata.* Contains archived transport files from other transport directories which are generated when the administrators perform the *tp clearold* command.

Additionally, the system might have two more optional directories:

- *backup.* This directory is used if you are going to perform logical backups with the R3trans program.
- *serial.* This optional directory is needed in the case that the serialization option of tp is used.

TPPARAM: tp Global Parameter File. The tp program uses a parameter file, TPPARAM, located in the bin subdirectory under the transport main directory (/usr/sap/trans) which defines many important parameters that directly affect the way tp works for performing exports or imports.

Every time tp is executed, it has to know the location of the TPPARAM file. For this reason, very often administrators always call tp from the bin directory. Otherwise, the location must be specified with the option pf=. If this option is not specified, then tp must search for the TPPARAM in the current directory. This allows for the creation of different parameter files, when administrators wish to perform special functions or wish to call the tp program from a different location than /usr/sap/trans/bin.

The TPPARAM file can contain lots of parameters which can be either

- *Global,* which are then valid for all the SAP systems in a group.

- *Local,* which are only valid for each SAP system. These parameters are preceded by the system name, for example: DD1/impdp_by_event = yes.
- *Operating system–dependent,* in which case these parameters are preceded by a keyword corresponding to the specific operating system.
- *Database-dependent,* which will contain a prefixed keyword corresponding to the specific database system.

Since there are many allowed parameters in TPPARAM, as with instance profiles, the parameters which are not specified, will take a default value.

Local parameters have precedence over global parameters. This system of precedence allows for having at the same time local and global parameters, which can be used for specifying different parameter values for special systems.

The syntax on the file is very simple: comments are preceded by a # sign. While parameters have the form of <Parameter>=<Value> for global values.

If the parameter is preceded by a SAP system name and a forward slash (/), then the value only applies for that system. For example: DD1/dbhost = copi01.

When the parameters are only valid for a particular operating system, then you enter the keyword or acronym for the operating system and the | sign, for example: as4 | transdir =...Valid keywords for operating systems are aix, hp-ux, osf1, sinix, sunos, wnt (Windows NT), and as4 (AS/400).

Finally, when the parameters are database system–dependent, the parameters are preceded by a database system acronym and the : sign. For example: ora:<parameter>=<value>. Supported acronyms of databases are ora (Oracle), inf (Informix), ada (Adabas D), mss (Microsoft SQL Server), db4 (DB2/400), and db6 (DB2 for AIX).

Additionally, TPPARAM provides predefined variables which can be used when specifying parameters and which are converted at runtime. These variables must be specified with the format *$(var_name),* for example: $(dbname). For a list of predefined variables refer to the online help documentation.

Since there are so many possible parameters in the tp configuration file, just the most important ones are described here:

- *TRANSDIR.* This parameter indicates the transport directory which should be accessible by all the systems in a SAP group and with the same name. All the transport data files and log files are stored in different subdirectories beneath TRANSDIR. In UNIX systems, this parameter is: TRANSDIR=/usr/sap/trans/. In Windows NT systems, this parameter is TRANSDIR=\\<transport host>\sapmnt\trans\.

- *R3TRANSPATH.* Sets the name and location of the R3trans program which is used by the tp control program. The system will find the correct program as long as the imports are performed by the <sid>adm user in the target system, since the SAP administrator user profile includes the right path accesses. In UNIX systems, this parameter is: R3TRANSPATH = R3trans. In Windows NT systems, this parameter is R3TRANSPATH = R3trans.exe.

Following are database-dependent parameters that the tp program needs to establish communication with the SAP system database. Only relevant Oracle parameters are introduced here:

- *DBHOST.* The name of the host with the database server. Both in UNIX and Windows NT systems, this would be DBHOST= <hostname>, for example: DBHOST=copi02.
- *DBNAME.* This parameter sets the name of the database instance, which normally matches that of the SAP system.

Two other global parameters that are always present in TPPARAM are

- *ALLLOG.* This parameter is used to specify the name of the log file which keeps information of the steps for all transports in the system. This file is always located in the /usr/sap/trans/log directory. Default value is *ALOG $(syear) $(yweek),* which indicates that an ALOG file is generated for every calendar week. Example: ALOG9705.
- *SYSLOG.* This parameter specifies the name of the file in which the transport control program keeps information about the imports performed to a certain system. Default value is *SLOG $(syear) $(yweek).$(system).* This generates a SLOG file every calendar week and with the name of the import system as the file extension. These files are also located in the transport log directory. Example: SLOG9708.TT1.

Two useful parameters in TPPARAM for common functions of tp when communicating with the background import job of R/3 are

- *IMPDP_BY_EVENT.* This is a boolean parameter which is either true or false. The default value is true and it means that the tp program will trigger the import background job of the R/3 system (RDDIMPDP) whenever an import takes place. If it's set to false, then the import background job must be scheduled to run periodically to check if there are pending imports. You leave it set to the default true value to avoid hundreds of background job logs. This requires that the additional parameter SAPEVTPATH be set.

- *SAPEVTPATH.* Must contain the complete path to the sapevt program. This program is the SAP event trigger program, which can send signals to the R/3 system. This parameter is only used if IMPDB_BY_EVENT is set to true. Example: DD1/sapevtpath = /usr/sap/$(system)/SYS/exe/run/sapevt.

When tp is called with special option put, there are some parameters in TPPARAM which control the command files for starting and stopping both the R/3 system and/or the R/3 database. These parameters are

- *STARTSAP.* It's the location for the program that starts the R/3 system. The default value is " ", which will not start the system when tp is called with the put function, unless you are performing an R/3 system upgrade, in which case, the upgrade program will modify it when needed. Similarly, the other three parameters, which also default to " " are as follows:
- *STOPSAP.* This is the parameter for stopping R/3.
- *STARTDB.* This is the parameter for starting the R/3 database.
- *STOPDB.* This is the parameter for stopping the R/3 database.

To display the values of the TPPARAM parameters for a particular SAP system, issue this command: tp showparams <sid>; for example: tp showparams DD1.

Additionally with the use of the "–D=<value>" option when calling the tp program, you can temporarily change individual parameter values, only valid for the current tp call. Example: tp import DD1K900052 PP1 "–D stoponerror=1."

For other TPPARAM parameters, please refer to the SAP online documentation under the section *transport control.*

Overview of Options for the tp Program

The tp transport control program allows system or transport administrators to perform all the management functions for the transport system. These functions are specified by entering options when calling tp.

The list of available options can be obtained by issuing a tp help command.

To display help for a particular option of the tp program, call the *tp <command>* where *<command>* is a valid option.

The program tp includes functions for exporting, importing, buffer actions, managing disk space of the transport system, information, and special functions. Only those options which are more useful in normal daily operative tasks are included here. More information about all available options can be obtained from the SAP online documentation library.

Informative options are as follows:

- *tp showbuffer <sid>.* This displays the transportable change requests ready for import to the <SID> system. Example: tp showbuffer TT1.
- *tp count <sid>.* This command option displays the number of requests in the <SID> buffer waiting for import. Example: tp count TT1.
- *tp go <sid>.* This command is just informative, and it shows the environment variables needed for the connection to the database of the <SID> system. This command is executed automatically by tp before logging on to the database. Issuing this command, however, does not log on. Example: tp go TT1.
- *tp connect <sid>.* This is another informative option to check whether the connection to the <SID> database is successful. It logs on to the database and then logs off. It displays a message on the screen displaying the result of the connection.
- *tp checkimpdp <sid>.* The output of this command shows the type of background job which is scheduled in the <SID> system: whether it is event-periodic, just periodic, or not scheduled at all. Example: tp checkimpdp TT1.
- *tp showinfo <transport request>.* This informative option shows the header information of the transport request. You don't need to specify a <SID> system. For example: tp showinfo DD1K900052

Main options for cleaning up the transport subdirectories data, log, and cofiles are

- *tp check all.* This checks the transport directories looking for files which are not needed (not waiting for imports) and have exceeded a minimum age specified by parameters in TPPARAM. These parameters are: DATALIFETIME, OLDDATALIFETIME, COFILELIFE-

TIME, and LOGFILELIFETIME. This parameter displays a list of files which can be deleted and generates a temporary file with the list.

- *tp clearold.* This uses the list file generated by the *tp check all* command and deletes the files included in the list.

Command options for handling the transport buffer are

- *tp addtobuffer <transport request> <sid>.* Adds the transport request to the buffer for the <SID> system and places it as the last request to be imported. If this request was already in the buffer, it modifies its order and places it as the last request. Example: tp addtobuffer DD1K900052 PP1.

WARNING! *Changing the order of transport requests might have unpredictable results.*

- *tp delfrombuffer <transport request> <sid>.* The transport request is deleted from the buffer queue of the specified <SID> system. It does not delete the transport files from the directory. Example: tp delfrombuffer DD1K900052 PP1.

WARNING! *This command can cause changes in the import sequence and therefore might produce unpredictable results.*

- *tp setstopmark <sid>.* This command option sets a special mark in the import buffer for the specified <SID> system. This is useful when issuing the import commands *tp import all* or *tp put,* in which cases the importing only processes those requested before the mark. When the system processes the import of all objects before the mark, it stops itself and deletes the mark.
- *tp delstopmark <sid>.* Deletes a stop mark from the <SID> buffer if it exists.
- *tp locksys <sid>.* This command locks the <SID> system preventing users other than DDIC or SAP* from logging on. This command is normally issued by upgrade utilities. However, users already logged on will not be affected by the call.
- *tp unlocksys <sid>.* Removes the lock on the <SID> system set by a previous tp locksys command.

- *tp lock_eu <sid>.* Sets the system change option of the specified <SID> to *cannot be changed.*
- *tp unlock_eu <sid>.* Sets the system change option of the specified system to the value it had before a previous *tp lock_eu* command.

The main import tp command options are detailed in the following section.

Working with Imports Using *tp*

Although transport administration and performing imports has become much easier using the TMS import functions, it is still necessary to know how the *tp* control program can be used for performing imports.

There are many available command options for performing imports in the R/3 system. Most of them are used for special purposes, such as importing only certain objects, performing activations, and so on.

The main and most commonly used commands for the tp program when performing imports are as follows:

- *tp import <transport request> | all <sid> [options...].* The tp import command has a more complex syntax than the other tp commands, since it allows many options to be specified. The command allows the import of a single transport request or the import of all requests waiting for import in the buffer of the <SID> system (up to a stop mark). Examples are import of a single transport request: tp import DD1K900052 PP1; and import of all pending transport requests for system PP1: tp import all PP1.

  Available options for the tp import command are

  - *U<n>[<m>..].* To specify one or more unconditional modes. The next section describes the unconditional modes available. Example: tp import all DD1 U1.
  - *client<n>* or *client=<n>.* Imports to a specified client. Example: tp import all DD1 client007 or tp import all DD1 client=007.
  - *pf=<TPPARAM>.* Specifies the exact path of the tp parameter file if it does not use the default one located under /usr/sap/trans/bin.
  - *–D"<parameter value".* Changes a TPPARAM value for the current call.
  - *silent.* Writes the output of the command to the dev_tp file located under the SAP instance work directory.

- *tp put <sid>.* Imports all the transport requests registered for import in the SID buffer up to a stop mark. This option will perform a start and stop of the SAP system as specified in the parameters for TPPARAM. If the default values of the STARTSAP and STOPSAP parameters are set to " ", the call to *tp put* won't stop the system. This option is mainly used when upgrading R/3 systems. When the default parameters are set, then *tp put* is the same as issuing a *tp import all.*

In order to perform imports, the administrator in charge of importing the objects into the target systems has to log on at the operating system level as user <sid>adm. Normally, the administrator imports all objects that are in the buffer waiting for an import. Since importing objects might reset the buffers, it is not convenient to launch imports during normal working hours. An alternative is to include a *tp import all <sid>* call in a shell script that can be scheduled using system utilities or specialized software for scheduling the import at more appropriate times.

When performing imports, the tp program performs all the necessary steps depending on the nature of the objects or data which is being transferred. It will perform the following steps:

- ABAP dictionary import. The tp program calls the R3trans utility to import the dictionary objects into the target system. The data is imported inactively so as not to disrupt the normal work in the target R/3 system.
- ABAP dictionary activation. During this phase, the nametabs (runtime dictionary objects) are written inactively, so that the system can keep running. Enqueue modules are not activated during this phase for consistency reasons.
- A distribution program checks whether there are any pending actions to move the new and inactive runtime objects into the active system.
- Next, the tp program performs any required structure conversion for the objects in the transport.
- At this moment, the system can move the new dictionary runtime objects to the active runtime environment. Some inconsistencies could occur if the objects are being accessed by active users.
- The next step is the main import phase where all the data is imported with the R3trans utility. If the data is successfully imported and consistent, an automatic transport to another subscribed recipient system can take place.

- Then the tp program takes care of activating any enqueue modules present in the transport which cannot be handled as other dictionary objects. These modules are directly passed onto the runtime environment.
- The final steps are to import any application-defined objects, set version flags for the imported objects, execute XPRA reports in case of puts, generate any report or screen, and remove the transport request number from the system buffer.

If you get error messages during any phase of the import, tp will stop any further actions. After looking at the log files and finding the cause for the error and solving the problem, you normally can start the import again. The tp program records the point at which the processing should be restarted.

Unconditional Modes in the tp Program. Unconditional modes are options that can be specified for exports or imports with the tp program and are intended for performing special actions on transport requests.

WARNING! *Use only unconditional options when you are sure of what you are doing. Otherwise, this can cause severe inconsistencies in the systems.*

The unconditional modes tell the tp program to overwrite the rules imposed by the objects as defined in the workbench organizer. For example, they allow the import of original objects when that's not permitted by the development class.

Unconditional modes are numbers from 0 to 9, and they can be used in the options part of the tp call. They are always preceded by the letter *U*. Several unconditional modes can be used in the same command. For example: tp import DD1K900052 PP1 U18. This tells the tp to activate unconditional modes 1 and 8.

When using unconditional modes, the transport log usually issues warning messages. These are functions for every unconditional mode:

- *0.* Known as *overtaker.* It can be used for importing from the buffer without deleting it and then it uses unconditional mode 1 to allow another import in the correct location.
- *1.* During an import, the system ignores that this request was already imported, and it can be imported again.

- *2.* During an import, this permits the overwriting of original objects.
- *3.* During import, this allows the transport program to overwrite system-specific objects.
- *6.* This allows for overwriting objects which are unconfirmed repairs.
- *8.* This mode ignores transport restrictions based on the table classes.
- *9.* This mode ignores whether the system is locked for this type of transport.

Managing Special Transports

Usually administrators should perform imports for all the change requests which have been exported for a particular system. This is accomplished by a *tp import all* command. This is the only way that tp can guarantee the right order for importing objects, avoiding some newer versions being overwritten by older ones.

There are occasions, however, when special and individual transports must be used, for example, when performing urgent imports or for transferring client-specific data from different clients. In these cases, you must be extremely careful not to change the order of the individual change requests.

These types of transports require the import for individual transport requests. For example: tp import DD1K900054 PP1.

When performing individual transports, have a look at the buffer (*tp showbuffer <sid>*) and ensure that no other older change requests contain the objects that you are going to import individually. This process can take some time and requires the use of the transport information system.

For performing individual imports, SAP recommends using the unconditional mode 0, which does not delete the change request from the buffer and will be imported again in a normal import, but ensures the correct release order for all change requests of a system. Example: tp import DD1K900078 PP1 U0.

Normally, the data exported from a source client is imported into the client with the same number; however, the tp program permits specifying a different target client on the command line. For example: tp import DD1K900078 PP1 client=007. This type of transport is valid for all the objects in the change requests which are client-specific in the source client.

You should be careful when issuing a *tp import all* command when trying to transport to more than one client. In those cases, the only way is to transport individually every change request to the required target clients.

The Interface Between tp and ABAP

The actions that the tp control program performs are not performed alone. The tp program communicates with the ABAP runtime to execute the needed actions over the transported objects. For example, structure conversion, screen generation, and so forth.

The interface between the tp program and ABAP is handled by the import dispatcher background jobs and the use of two system tables: TRBAT and TRJOB. By looking at the contents of these tables while an import is going on, administrators have another way of monitoring the transports online.

The dispatcher background jobs, as explained earlier, are RDDIMPD and RDDIMPDP_CLIENT_<nnn>, which schedule further jobs when needed. These jobs schedule themselves back to wait for further import steps or new imports.

When a tp command is issued at the operating system level, it sends a signal to the background processing system for the RDDIMPDP to start, makes an entry in the TRBAT table for each transport request to import, and inserts the number of the background jobs in table TRJOB. At that moment, RDDIMPDP starts processing, first checking the TRBAT table to see if there are any pending imports. If it finds an entry, it launches additional ABAP programs as background jobs which will perform the necessary actions on the transport objects. If any step is canceled, RDDIMPDP checks for entries still existing in table TRJOB and tries to restart the action. For this reason, the system needs to have at least two free background work processes.

Table TRBAT contains several fields, including the change request number, function, return code, time stamp, client, special function, and log, which logs online the actions being performed during import. The function and the return code indicate the step being performed and the status. Refer to the SAP online documentation in the transport control section for a description of the function keys and return codes of the TRBAT table.

Overview of the R3trans Program

R3trans is the R/3 system transport program which can be used for transporting data between different SAP systems, even when they don't belong to the same group. For example, it can be used to transport change requests created at SAP which are bug corrections to current programs or new developments. R3trans normally is not used directly but called from the tp control program or by the R/3 upgrade utilities.

R3trans is only directly used in certain circumstances such as for exporting or importing data to or from other SAP systems and also for performing special functions such as SAP logical backups or for managing imports or exports with data from other SAP versions. This, however, can be done only when you are sure that no logical inconsistencies will occur in the transported data.

R3trans supports transporting data between different operating systems or even different database systems.

The syntax for calling the R3trans program is *R3trans [<options>] <control file>*. Options are parameters which indicate what function the program will execute. You can use several options at the same time. At least one option must be specified. The control file further specifies the actions which the R3trans will perform. This is a normal text file with special commands.

R3trans must be called by the SAP system administrator, <sid>adm. Some of the useful options available are

- *R3trans -d,* which checks whether it's possible to connect to the database.
- *R3trans -i <file>,* which imports directly the data from the <file> without the need for a control file.
- *R3trans -t <control_file>,* which performs the functions on test mode. Modifications are not written in the database.
- *R3trans -w <file>,* which writes the transport log to the specified file. If none is specified, the default is trans.log in the current directory.

Information on additional options and how to write control files can be found in SAP online documentation.

CHAPTER 7

Introduction to the ABAP Workbench

This chapter is an introduction to the ABAP developing environment and the ABAP programming language. ABAP stands for *Advanced Business Application Programming;* this is the language in which all the R/3 business modules are written and developed and which customers can use to extend SAP R/3's possibilities.

This chapter is intended to introduce the components involved in the development environment of the SAP R/3 system and to explain what are they used for. It shows how the components of the development environment relate to the R/3 system and what tools are available for developers working with R/3.

This chapter is not intended to teach users to program in ABAP but to provide them with an introduction to the features of the programming language and the concepts used in ABAP development.

Introduction to the Development Environment of the SAP R/3 System

The development environment of the SAP R/3 system is a fully integrated set of development tools, functions, programming languages, and a data dictionary, grouped together under the name *ABAP workbench.*

The ABAP workbench is the kernel for all the SAP R/3 system business applications and the foundation for developing additional functions and applications for the client/server R/3 system.

The ABAP workbench is intended as a development environment that can cover all the phases of a development project, allowing teamwork, organization, and version management even across SAP systems.

The ABAP workbench permits easy transfer of developments among systems, which makes it completely portable among R/3 systems and thus ensures information integrity.

For example, a large part of an R/3 system upgrade is made up of a big collection of programs, function modules, tables, and so forth, which are developed at SAP and are transferred to customer systems using the transport tools. This process is quite automatic and almost transparent to administrators.

The main features of the ABAP workbench architecture are as follows:

- Distribution of applications among servers, where the same application runs across different underlying hardware platforms without modification

- Supports common and standard GUIs
- Transparent communication with other systems, with the interfaces provided by SAP middleware
- Transparent handling of underlying database systems with ABAP open SQL or Native SQL
- Communication with external applications using RFCs and with desktop applications using RFC, OLE2, and ODBC

The development work is based on an object repository, which contains:

- Facilities to create and maintain database definitions, application defaults, and business rules which can be viewed graphically
- The ABAP dictionary, which does central, active management of all application-related descriptive data including table definitions, foreign key relations, and views.

The full integration of the components means that changes in any part have a direct and immediate effect on all applications using those components.

SAP is based on standards: user interface, database development, communications, and programming. It provides the data model for R/3, which contains the relationships between the business applications. The workbench contains a major library of business functions. You can precisely fine-tune R/3 to your special needs.

Overview of the ABAP Workbench Tools

For developing and maintaining the client/server applications of the SAP R/3 system, the ABAP workbench includes a group of tools and utilities to facilitate and perform all the development-related tasks. As a way to introduce them all in a clear picture, Table 7-1 contains a list of these tools classified by the use and purpose of each.

Basic Concepts of the Development Environment

The development environment includes virtually hundreds of functions, many of which are quite common in other types of applications, especially

TABLE 7-1

Overview of Workbench Tools

Function	Tool/Component	Use
Programming	ABAP dictionary	Defining, maintaining, and storing the data dictionary of the SAP R/3 system. Stores all dictionary objects including tables, relationships, documentation, and help information.
	ABAP editor	Creating and maintaining the ABAP programs, editing function modules, logical databases, and screens (DYNPROs) logic programming.
	Function builder	Defining and maintaining the ABAP function modules (general purpose routines which can be called from other ABAP programs). Can be used for designing server or client programs to communicate using RFCs, by creating RFC templates in C or Visual Basic.
	Screen painter	Designing and maintaining the graphical user interface screens in a transactional and client/server environment like R/3.
	Menu painter	Designing and maintaining the menus for the graphical user interface.
	Business objects builder	Two main purposes: (1) Provides all the needed information about the business objects: types, key fields, access methods, BAPIs, and so on. (2) Can create the business object instances at runtime when receiving object-oriented requests.
	Data modeler	Can be used for managing and maintaining the SAP and own data models using the SAP model known as the Structure Entity Relationship Model (SERM). Due to the level of integration with the ABAP workbench, the data modeler can make models using a top-down or bottom-up approach by assigning dictionary tables or views with entity types of the data modeler.
	ABAP query	Can be used to generate report programs without any programming experience, only by navigating the menus that the ABAP query administrator creates for different user groups.
Navigating	Repository browser	Managing and organizing the development objects in a hierarchical form, allowing easy navigation among objects and the development environment. Objects can also be directly managed from the repository browser and assigned to other development classes.

TABLE 7-1

Overview of Workbench Tools *(Continued)*

Function	Tool/Component	Use
	Repository information system	Navigating and searching for the dictionary objects, development objects, and the relationships among objects.
	Application hierarchy	Displaying the development objects from a organizational and application point of view.
	Data browser	Navigating in the data tables of the database. Can be used for locating and displaying the content of several dictionary objects, such as tables and views, and their internal relationships. In some cases, new entries can be made (for tables with maintenance allowed set).
	Business objects browser	Presents the business objects with their within the R/3 application hierarchy and allows navigation among them.
	BAPI browser	Presents the BAPIs with their within the R/3 application hierarchy and allows navigation among them.
Debugging	SQL trace	Tracking the database calls from the system transactions and programs.
	Runtime analysis	Analyzing the performance of the system calls.
	Online debugger	Stopping a program and analyzing the results of the execution of every program statement.
	Computer-Aided Test Tool (CATT)	An integrated tool for facilitating the testing process. Can be used for creating, maintaining, and executing automatic testing and software verification processes. Tests can be conducted for ABAP workbench developments as well as for customizing.
	System log	Keeping track of the errors that occurred during program execution.
Organizing development	Workbench organizer	Controlling and keeping track of development work and team-related development projects and managing versions of development objects.
	Customizing organizer	Same function as workbench organizer, but in this case manages and controls modifications to customization settings.
	Transport organizer	Performing and managing the transports of development objects across different SAP systems.

the features concerning a programming language, such as a sensitive editor, a data dictionary, function library, and debugging facilities.

The SAP R/3 development environment has, however, many of its own functions and features. Within the whole environment there are two basic concepts which have particular importance: development objects and development classes.

Development objects are all the components of an ABAP application: program elements (events, global fields, variants, subroutines, includes), programs code (function modules, reports, module pools), transactions, message classes, dictionary objects (tables, data elements, domains, etc.), and development classes.

Development classes are logical groups of development objects which are related, normally deployed for the same application module, related reports, and so on. This concept is introduced in Chap. 6. Development classes are particularly important for team development, the transport system, and use within the repository browser, application hierarchy, and so forth.

Starting the ABAP Workbench

For starting the ABAP workbench, from the main menu, select *Tools* → *ABAP Workbench* or, alternatively, enter transaction S001 in the command field. Figure 7-1 shows the workbench initial screen. On this screen of the ABAP workbench, there are four available menu options:

- *Overview.* Contains the development system options for getting information, navigation, and development organization. Tools under this menu can be used to find and manage development objects. Figure 7-2 shows this menu.

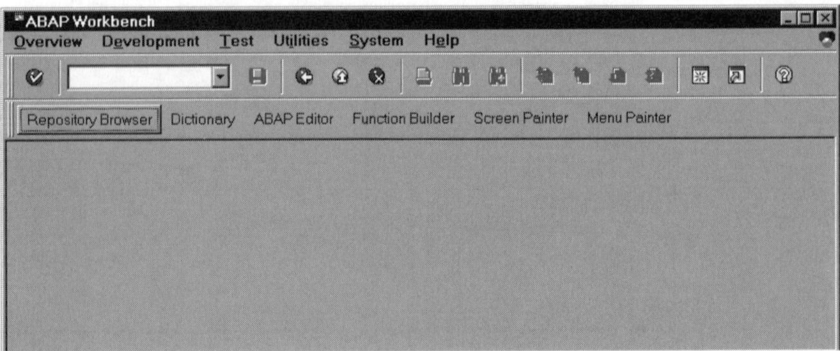

Figure 7-1 ABAP workbench initial screen.

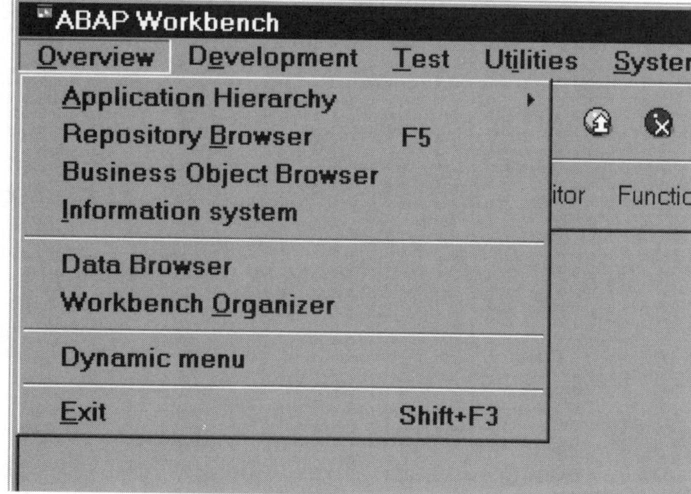

Figure 7-2
Options under the Overview menu.

- *Development.* Includes all the development components to create or modify SAP applications. The most important tools in this menu also appear in the application toolbar. Figure 7-3 shows the available options within this menu.
- *Test.* Includes functions for analyzing and testing complete ABAP programs. Figure 7-4 shows the available menu options.

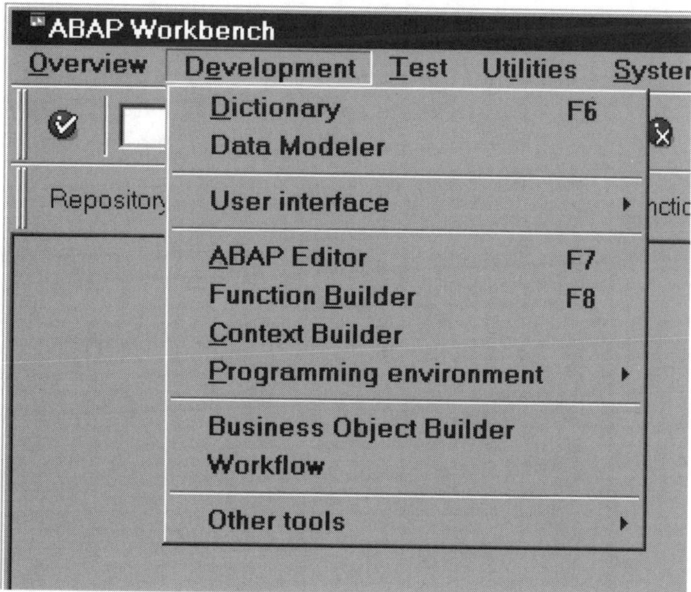

Figure 7-3
Options under the Development menu.

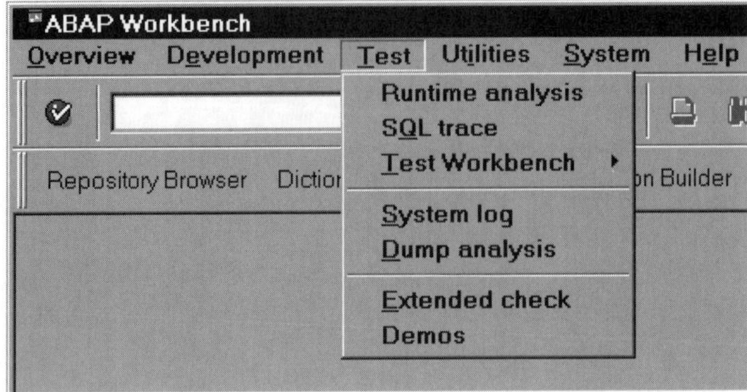

Figure 7-4
Options under the Test menu.

- *Utilities.* Contains additional utilities related to the development environment such as translation facilities, documentation handling, and so on. Figure 7-5 shows the menu options.
  Normally you can access the workbench tools at least two ways:
- Directly from the options menu functions or by clicking the available buttons on the application toolbar
- From the *repository browser* screen or other navigation tools, which automatically launches the tools associated with the development object being treated

In the first case, from the toolbar, you directly access the development tools and enter the object names, while in the second case, you are working with development objects and invoke the tool for each object.

For example, from the ABAP dictionary tool, users are presented with an input field to enter a dictionary object name to work on. However, from the repository browser, you navigate among all your types of development objects; clicking on a report name automatically launches the ABAP editor.

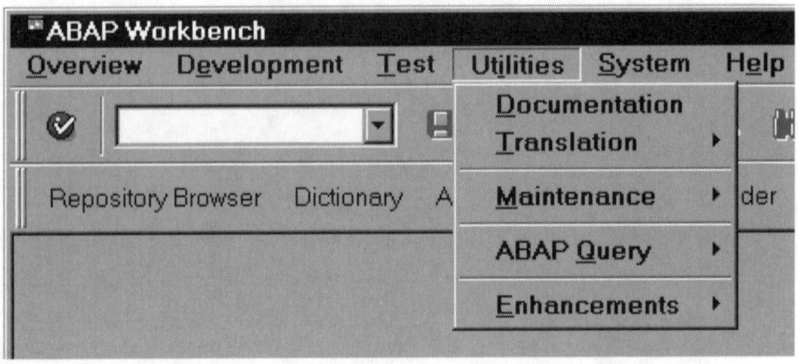

Figure 7-5
Options under the Utilities menu.

Since the SAP development environment is fully integrated both at the object level as well as with the tools used for managing them, the repository browser tool can play one of the fundamental roles in the SAP development environment as the starting point for every development project. For this reason, and because it becomes the most-used navigation tool, it is included in the application toolbar of the workbench initial screen.

The following sections describe and introduce the user to the management of the major workbench tools. Please be aware of the many icons displayed in the application toolbars within the workbench tools. These icons perform the most common functions available from the menu options.

Working with the Repository Browser

As stated earlier, the *repository browser* is the main navigation tool for the development environment which centralizes the organization and management of the development objects grouped by development class. It also can display specific objects or related groups of objects by other criteria.

To display the initial screen of the repository browser, from the initial ABAP workbench screen, click on the *Repository Browser* button or, alternatively, select *Overview* → *Repository Browser* from the menu bar, or enter transaction code SE80 in the command field. Figure 7-6 shows the initial repository browser screen.

On this initial screen, the system presents two options boxes where you can decide whether to work with an object list or with single objects. In the first case, you can navigate through a list of related objects, while in the second case, you must choose the specific object with which you want to work.

Object Lists

When working with object lists, you can decide to enter the development class for which you want to display the object list. Click on the radio button next to *Development Class* and enter the name of the development class or click on the possible entries arrow to list and select one. Next, click on the *Display* function button. Figure 7-7 displays the resulting screen for development class FB0C.

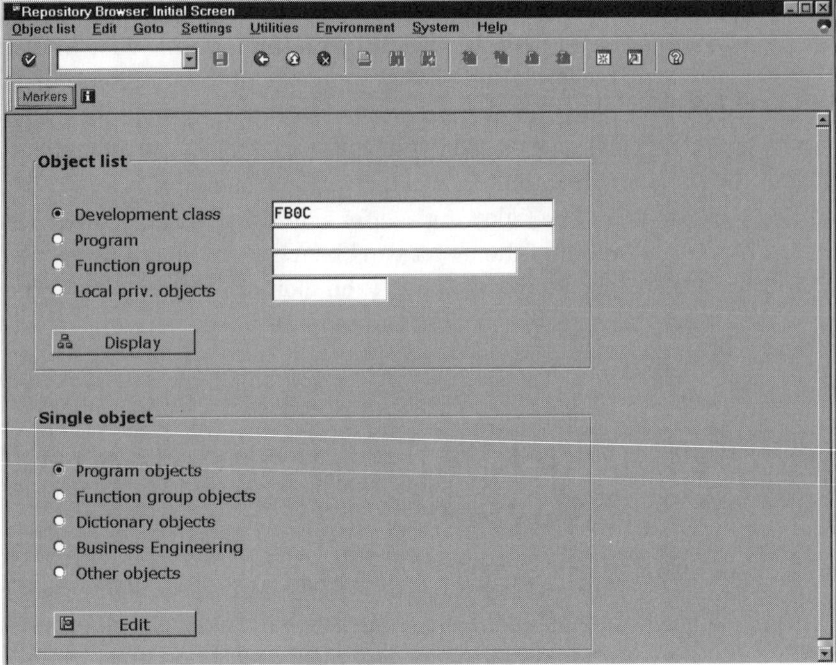

Figure 7-6 Initial screen for the repository browser workbench tool.

As you can see, the system presents the object list in a folder structure with + and – signs to indicate whether the folder contains additional elements or it's the last in the hierarchy. To use those folders for navigation, just position the cursor over the folder sign and click on it, or you can double click on the name of the object, which has the same effect.

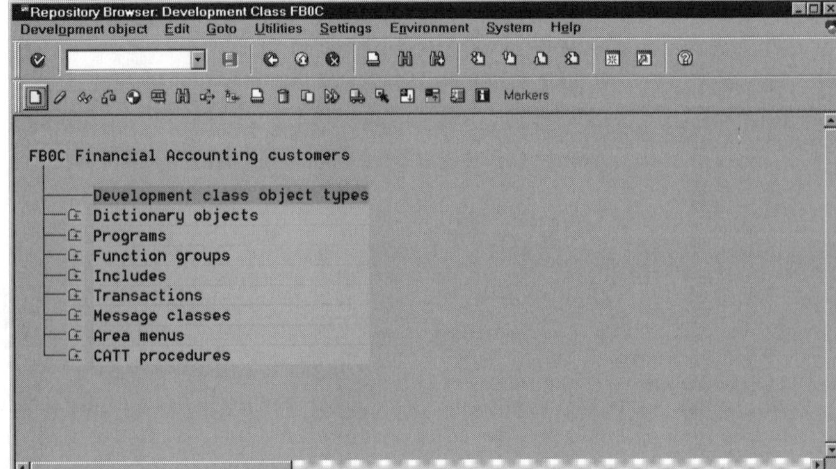

Figure 7-7 Display of development class objects from the repository browser.

There are also other elements in the list, such as the collection nodes, which correspond to the development class object types. Upon double clicking on them, the system displays a screen for creating or maintaining additional development objects under the development class. If you create an object of a type which did not exist previously in the display, the system additionally creates a folder for it.

At the last level of a hierarchy, you can see the objects themselves. By double clicking on an object name, the associated workbench tool is triggered. By double clicking on program names, an additional screen where you can specify other object types is displayed.

Selecting Single Objects

Navigating the system using single objects can be useful when users work for several days in the development object (normally longer-duty tasks such as big programs or function modules). In this case, select the radio button next to the object type and click on the *Edit* button. For example, Fig. 7-8 shows the resulting screen when a dictionary object is selected and the user clicks on *Edit*. On this screen, you can enter a previously created dictionary object to modify, or you can create a new one. In fact, the options available on the screen include most functions you could perform when in the corresponding workbench tool, in this case, the dictionary.

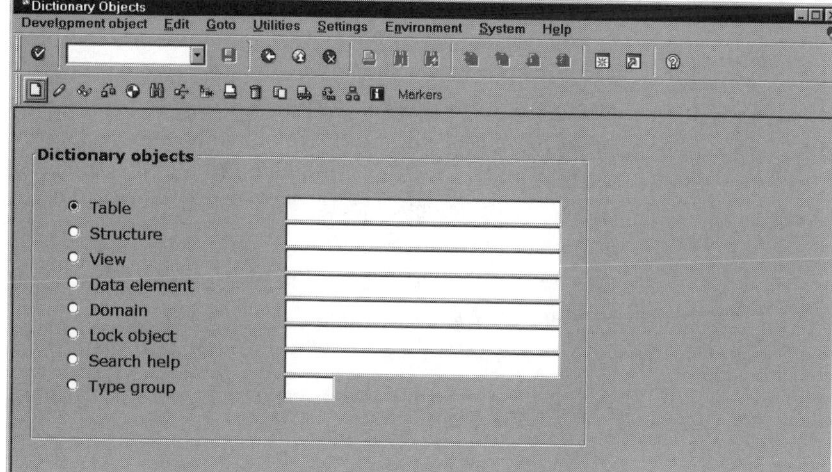

Figure 7-8 Managing dictionary objects from the repository browser.

Maintaining Development Objects from the Repository Browser

As mentioned earlier, you can create and maintain development objects from the corresponding workbench tools: ABAP programs from the ABAP editor, screen layouts from the screen painter, tables from the data dictionary, and so on—but you can also do it from the repository browser.

To create an object of a particular type from the repository browser, you should first have a folder containing that type of object. If there are no folders for that type of development object, then, from the *Object list* display screen, double click on the collection node. The system shows a dialog box requesting the object type to create. Select the type of object and the name and click on the *Create* icon. When creating the object, the system goes to the corresponding workbench tool. When you are finished, the system also will have created a folder for that object type.

To modify an object, you have two options. The first is to select the object from the repository browser list and then click on the *Change* icon on the application toolbar.

The second way is to double click over the object, which will automatically trigger the associated application and the corresponding screen for editing that type of object in display mode. Once on this screen, you will normally see the icon for switching between display and change modes.

From the repository browser, you can also copy objects by selecting them from a folder and clicking on the *Copy* icon. Then you have to give a new name to the new object in the dialog box shown on the screen. If the copied development object has subcomponents, the system displays the additional dialog boxes for selecting which components you want to copy.

Once the components of an object are selected, click on the *Copy* icon again to perform the copy. Note that the system does not allow folders to be copied, but allows several objects to be copied at the same time. To copy several objects, you have to select those objects, and upon clicking on the *Copy* icon, the system guides you to all the needed screens for performing the copy. To select objects from a list, position the cursor over the object and select *Edit → Selection → Sel./desel. Sub-tree* from the menu or click on the icon *Sel./desel. Sub-tree* on the application toolbar or select the function key using the right mouse button.

Navigation Options

The repository browser allows for some customizing to facilitate the navigation among several object lists.

When the list of folders and objects becomes very long, it can be useful to display on the screen only the part which directly relates to a specific object. To do that, from the repository browser list, select the object you want to have displayed and select *Edit → Set focus* from the menu.

The system shows the initial object list but with the focused object with an indication similar to a path name in the upper area of the screen, as shown in Fig. 7-9.

To disable the focus, just position the pointer over the upper objects (pointer shape changes) and click on any of them (for example, the development class).

Another useful option when navigating through objects is the *marker* which allows you to set a mark in those objects or folders used most often, so, instead of navigating to find your objects, you can directly use the saved markers.

The repository browser includes options to define, display, and delete markers. There are three types of markers:

- *Initial Marker.* Used to define the starting point of the object list. When this marker is defined, the system displays this marker when starting the repository browser.
- *Permanent Markers.* Used to define locations within the object lists which will be stored and can be used in different sessions of the repository browser to a maximum of nine.

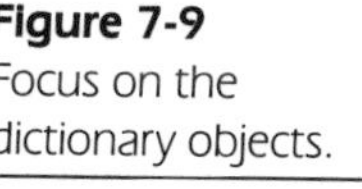

Figure 7-9
Focus on the dictionary objects.

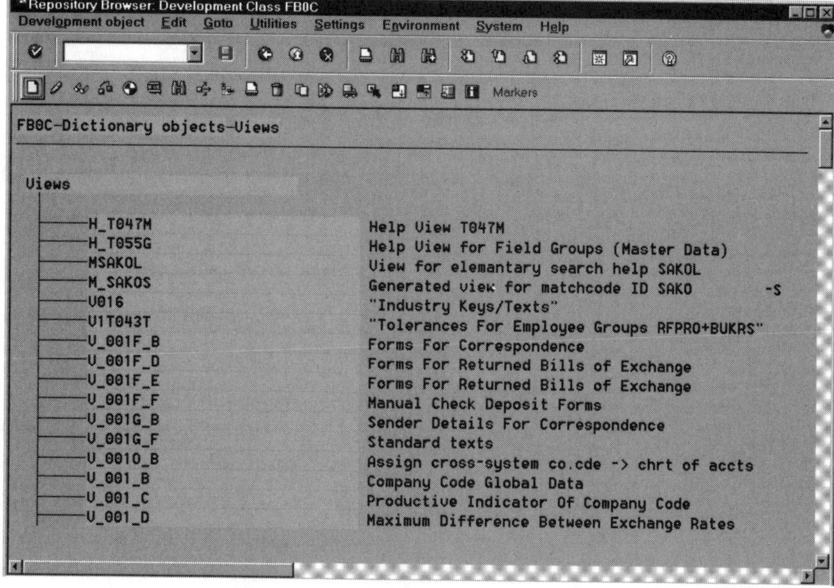

- *Temporary markers.* Used and created automatically by the system to define temporary locations for objects lists but which are not saved between different sessions of the repository browser.

To display the available markers, from the menu, select *Goto → Markers.* In this dialog box you can see the markers already defined and the temporary markers created by the system, and you can save any of the temporary markers to be a permanent one. If you want to delete any of the defined markers, select the marker and then click on the *Delete* icon in the bottom part of the Markers dialog box.

To define a marker, position the cursor on the selected object and choose *Settings → Save marker.* To define the *Initial marker,* first locate the object list screen you want to set as initial, and from the menu choose *Goto → Markers.* Then select the option *Define init. Position.* If you delete the *Initial marker,* the system will display the default screen for the repository browser.

The Repository Information System

The *repository information system* is one of the workbench navigation tools which allows for searching any of the objects belonging to the R/3 system, based on specific criteria.

To start the repository information system from the initial ABAP workbench screen, select *Overview → Information System* or, alternatively, enter SE84 transaction code in the command field.

On this initial screen, the system displays in a hierarchical form the different object types which can be defined in the R/3 system. These object types are represented by folders, each representing different types. These folders can be further exploded down clicking on the + sign to see their contents.

Using the Repository Information System

Since searching among different object types basically presents a report with many input fields for entering the search selection criteria, before starting to search, users have the option of defining some standard settings which can affect the search results and which can be used in further searches.

From the repository initial screen, select *Settings → User parameters.* The system will display a dialog box where you can set

- The maximum number of entries to be displayed in the search
- The type of list selection screen to be displayed in the search. Options are
  - *Standard selection criteria.* This type will select a SAP standard selection screen for each type of object (each type of search).
  - *All selection criteria.* The resulting search list will display all available display fields for the objects.
  - *User-specific variant.* Users can create variants, even with the same name, for the different reports and use them as a collection of search criteria.

Performing Searches

From the initial repository screen, navigate in the object tree until you find the type of object you want to search. Click on an object type to select it, and then select *Objects → Find* or click on the *Find* button on the application toolbar.

The system will display a different selection screen depending on the chosen object type and the user parameter settings. Figure 7-10 shows the screen for searching program objects using standard selection criteria.

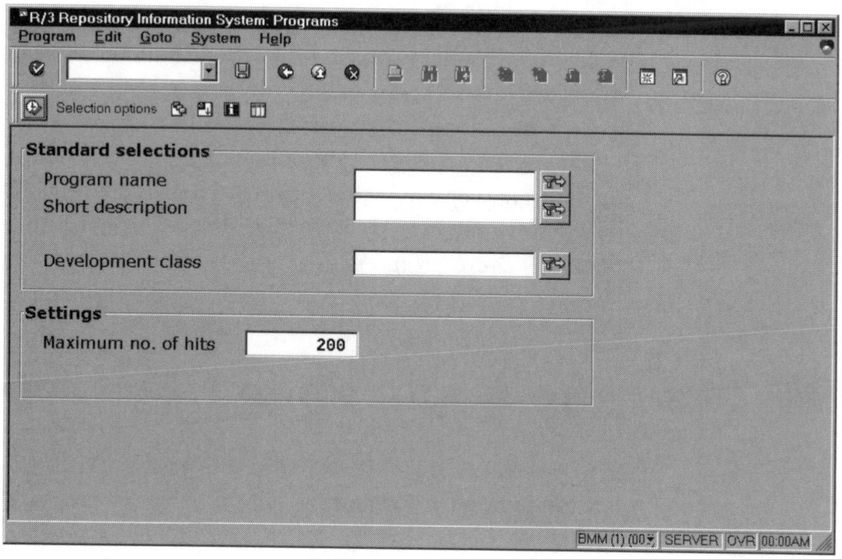

Figure 7-10 Selection screen for finding objects within the repository.

On the selection screen, there are many different input fields for entering search criteria. You can use wildcards, such as the *. After entering the criteria, click on the *Execute* button in the application toolbar.

The resulting screen presents the object list with check buttons and active menu functions depending on the object types. From this screen you can directly manage those objects. By double clicking on any of the objects, the system will automatically trigger the corresponding workbench utility. In the previous example, double clicking on a program object launches the *ABAP editor* utility.

The "Subobject" Utility

From the object list resulting from the repository information system, users can get information about the subobjects corresponding to the object type by clicking on the check button next to the object and then selecting *Utilities → Find sub-objects.*

The system will normally display a dialog box for selecting what types of subobjects are used by the selected objects. For example, users can get the variants (subobjects) contained by a given program.

The *Where-used List* Utility

Once the system displays an object list using the repository info system, you can also find out where in the system a particular object is used. You only have to select the object by clicking on the check button next to the it and then selecting *Utilities → Where-used list* or by clicking on the *Where-used list* icon on the application toolbar.

The system normally displays a dialog box for selecting what type of objects use your selected objects. For example, you can decide to find in which data elements or in which tables a particular domain is used. This utility is common in every workbench tool.

The Application Hierarchy

The *application hierarchy* is another navigation tool within the ABAP workbench, which documents and displays the structure of the developments or the whole application. The application hierarchy includes the whole organization and structure for all the R/3 standard business applications.

When starting the application hierarchy, you can display or manage two types of structures: SAP standard or customer applications.

To start the application hierarchy, from the initial ABAP workbench screen, select *Overview* → *Applic. Hierarchy* and then either select *SAP* or *Customer.* Selecting the *SAP* hierarchy only displays the structure, whereas *Customer* displays full management.

Selecting the *SAP* application hierarchy displays all the modules or functional applications which make up the whole SAP system.

Navigating and expanding the folders, you will find two types of appellation nodes: title nodes and development nodes.

Title nodes are only used for the purpose of documenting clearly the application hierarchy, assigning a title to it. However, *development nodes* have an associated development class which makes a direct link with all the objects assigned to that development class.

Double clicking on any of the development nodes presents a new list with the object types associated with that particular development class.

The lists users can get with the application hierarchy are actually the same as those that can be output using the repository browser for the particular development class.

From the application hierarchy, you can directly search objects belonging to a particular node by selecting the node (function key F9) and then clicking on the *Repository Information System* button, located on the application toolbar.

Using the Data Browser

The *data browser* is the ABAP workbench utility that allows navigation through and the display of the contents of the ABAP dictionary tables. It also allows for creating table entries for tables which allow maintenance in their technical settings. The data browser can be started directly by selecting *Overview* → *Data Browser* from the initial ABAP workbench screen or, alternatively, by entering transaction code SE16 in the command field.

To display a table's contents, enter the name of the table in the available input field and click on the *Display* icon in the application toolbar.

The system will then display the table contents selection screen, where you can enter specific search criteria to restrict the searching.

Enter your search criteria and click on the *Execute* icon to display the table contents. The resulting list is shown in different colors; you can display the legend by selecting *Utilities* → *Color legend* from the menu. The key fields are always displayed. You can also display the incoming foreign key relationship by clicking on the *Check table* button on the application toolbar.

Sometimes when there are too many fields to display, the system shows a previous dialog box for you to select which of the fields you want to display.

The data browser also allows for creating new entries in case the specific table is set with the *Maintenance Allowed* check box within the dictionary.

The data browser facility is also automatically invoked from the dictionary table maintenance screen by selecting *Utilities* → *Table contents*. The difference is that when displaying table contents directly from the dictionary, the system automatically displays the selection screen with the table you are working on.

Introduction to the ABAP Editor

The ABAP editor is the SAP workbench tool for editing the source code of different development objects such as:

- ABAP program source code: reports, include modules, module pools, and so forth. The editor is also used to maintain other components of an ABAP program such as variants, program attributes, documentation, and text elements.
- Code for the flow logic for the screen painter.
- Logical databases.
- Function modules.

The source code of the ABAP development objects is stored internally in the R/3 underlying database together with the generated (runtime) object. Programs are not stored as operating system files. Therefore, if you upload source code from your workstation to an ABAP program, you will have to use the ABAP editor to modify it.

The ABAP editor functions go far beyond normal editing features: it is also a fully integrated tool within the development environment, which means that if you include or declare other objects, you can branch directly to those objects. For example, if in your program you declare a table with the TABLES statement, double clicking on the declared table name within the editor will branch directly to the table definition in the ABAP dictionary.

The ABAP editor also includes syntax verification, test execution, checking the source code, online ABAP help, and code reusability.

To start the editor, just click on *ABAP Editor* from the initial workbench screen or, alternatively, enter transaction code SE38 in the command field. Figure 7-11 shows the initial ABAP editor screen.

From this initial screen you can create, modify, and display any of the available objects as shown on the radio button options on the screen. To work with the editor, click on the radio button of the object type you want to work with, enter a name for the object in the *Program* input field, and then select the corresponding command button to either display or create an object. If you don't know the name of the object, you can click on the possible entries arrow to find or search for one.

From the initial editor screen, the system offers many functions included in the menu options and the application toolbar icons, such as renaming an object, deleting an object, searching, and executing.

Performing functions on the development object triggers the workbench organizer dialog boxes to introduce the change request numbers.

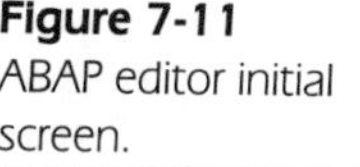

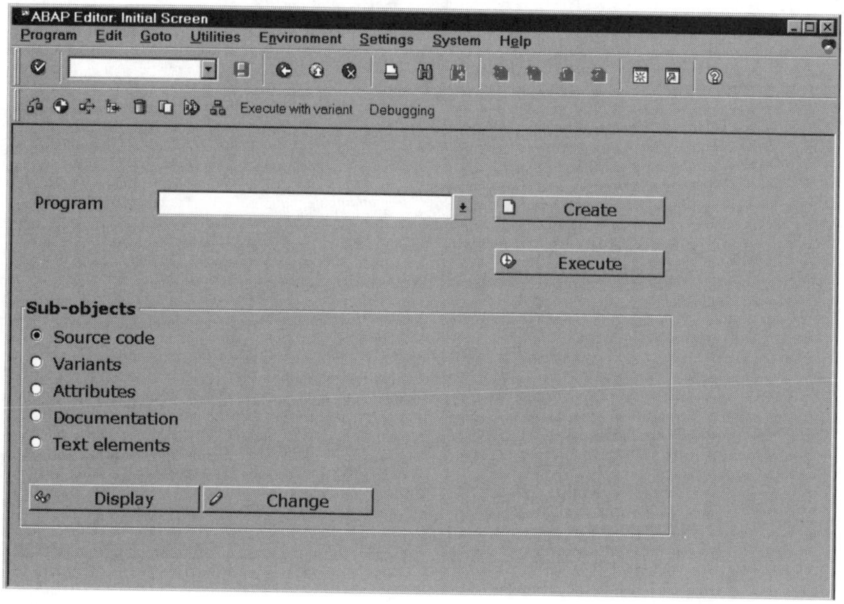

Figure 7-11
ABAP editor initial screen.

Refer to Chap. 6 for information on the workbench organizer and the transport system.

Getting Started with the ABAP Editor

To create a new program, you only have to enter a name in the *Program* input field on the initial screen of the ABAP editor and click on the *Create* push button. Remember to stick to SAP naming standards for customer programs (start them with *Z* or *Y*), otherwise, the system will require a registration key even for programs you create. Figure 7-12 shows the first screen (the attributes screen) when creating a program.

Before getting into the editor operating procedures, it must be clear that the logical sequence when using the editor is as follows:

- Define the program attributes
- Edit the needed source code
- Define the needed test elements for the type of program
- Check and verify the program syntax
- Optionally, create variants

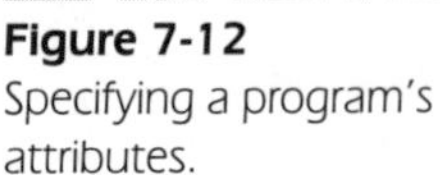

Figure 7-12 Specifying a program's attributes.

- Test/execute the program, either online or with the debugger
- Document the program

The whole process can be accomplished without leaving the ABAP editor. In this way, when creating a new program, the tool presents the *Attributes* display as shown in Fig. 7-12. When displaying or modifying an existing program, by default, the system branches directly to the source code editor display, except if another radio button option is selected from the editor initial screen. However, if you want to display, modify, or execute a nonexisting program, the system will display an error message.

Since the workbench is integrated, you may also access the ABAP editor from many other workbench tools, including the repository browser, function libraries, and screen painter.

Specifying Program Attributes

During the process of creating a new program, the system requests some information to correctly identify and catalog the program. This is the initial *program attributes* screen as shown in Fig. 7-12.

On this screen, you must fill up all the mandatory fields, as you know, which are indicated by a ? sign. The most important fields are as follows:

- *Title.* A brief description of the program identifying its contents or purpose.
- *Type.* Here, you must choose the type of program intended in the code. To see the available types, click on the possible entries list arrow. Figure 7-13 shows available values.

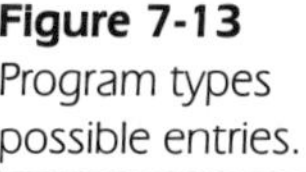

Figure 7-13
Program types possible entries.

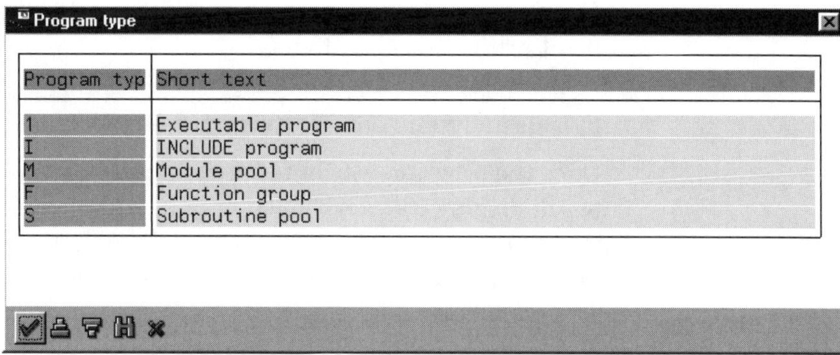

Program type
Program typ
Short text
1
Executable program
I
INCLUDE program
M
Module pool
F
Function group
S
Subroutine pool

- *Status.* Indicates program status. It's not a mandatory attribute. The status can make some of the ABAP editor functions unavailable. Display the available status by clicking on the possible entries list arrow.
- *Application.* This is a required entry which is used for cataloging the program within a particular application. You can also assign the asterisk (*) which indicates that it is not an application-specific program.
- *Authorization group.* You can assign here a group name which can later be used to establish the access control to that program using the SAP authorization system. Specifically, you can use this group in the authorization field, *Authorization group ABAP program,* within the authorization object S_PROGRAM.
- *Development class.* This field indicates the development class to which the program belongs. It is only a display field. The system requests the development class when first creating the program at the time you save the attributes.
- *Logical database.* Indicates the name of the logical database associated with this program (in case of programs of type report). Logical databases are special ABAP programs that reports use to read data from tables.
- *Selection screen.* Used only if the program is a report. If you do not specify a selection screen, the system automatically creates one based on the selection criteria of the logical database and the parameters and select options statements used in the program. In other cases the selection screen must correspond with an additional selection screen of the logical database associated with the report.
- *Editor lock.* It's used to lock the access to this program.
- *Fixed pt. arithmetic.* You can check this field when using fixed-point arithmetic operations.
- *Upper/lower case.* If you select this, the program code (apart from literals and comments) is converted to uppercase.

Once the program attributes are entered, when you save them, the system will display the workbench organizer dialog box, where you have to enter the development class to which the object will belong. You can list the available classes by clicking on the possible entries arrow. Enter your entry and save it.

Next, the system will display the following dialog box to assign a change request to the newly created object.

You can always display or modify program attributes by clicking the *Attributes* radio button on the initial ABAP editor screen and clicking on the *Change* or *Display* push buttons.

The next step is to enter the program source code.

The ABAP Source Code Editor

Although the naming can become confusing, the difference between the ABAP editor as the workbench tool and the ABAP editor as the *source code* editor should be clear.

There are several ways to reach the ABAP source code editor:

- From the ABAP editor initial screen, select the *Source code* radio button and then choose either the *Display* or *Change* push button when the program exists.
- From the *Program Attributes* screen, click on the *Source code* button on the application toolbar once the attributes were saved.
- Double click on a program when displaying objects from the repository browser or related workbench tool.

Figure 7-14 shows the source code editor screen.

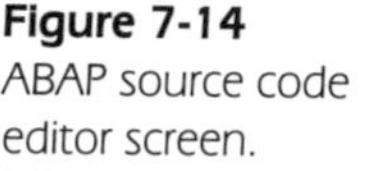

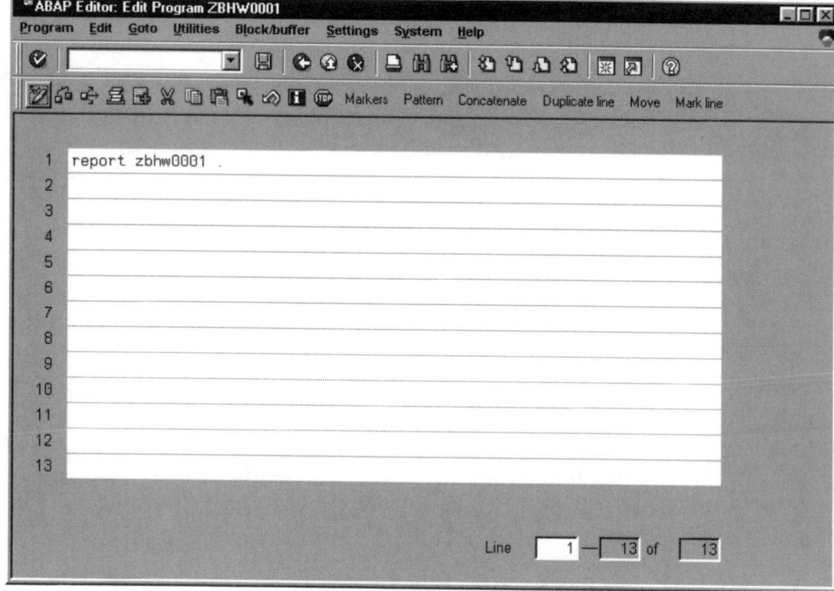

Figure 7-14 ABAP source code editor screen.

The Source Code Editor Interface. The source code editor interface is made up of a normal application and a standard toolbar plus a work area where you actually edit your program code.

The menu bar on this screen contains six standard menu options including all the functionality within the ABAP source code editor. The menu bar options are as follows:

- *Program* (or the specific object being manipulated by the editor). This contains functions affecting the overall object (program), such as generate, check, save, execute, and so forth.
- *Edit.* Under this menu, the system includes internal functions related to editing functions, such as the insert statement, cut, copy, insert to/from buffer, and search/replace.
- *Goto.* Options under the Goto menu are for calling other ABAP editor maintenance functions, such as attributes, text elements, messages, documentation, variants, as well as navigation functions such as markers or navigation stack.
- *Utilities.* This includes access to other workbench utilities such as the data browser, workbench organizer, debugging tools, and so on.
- *Block / buffer.* This menu includes external editing functions related with the windows interface such as the clipboard, comment insertion facilities, and so on.
- *Settings.* This menu allows for defining initial editor settings.

There are several functions to set up the editor working environment:

- *Editor working mode.* You can work in *PC Mode,* similar to a PC word processor, *PC Mode with line numbers,* which additionally includes numbered lines and is the default option, and *Command mode,* which emulates the editor functionalities of the SAP R/2 system.
- *Compression logic.* Allows creation of a program overview organized by logical blocks. When users start the editor, all blocks are expanded; individual blocks can then be expanded or compressed using the corresponding icons. The blocks are defined starting with a comment line beginning *{, and ended with a comment line beginning with *}.
- *Display mode.* You can decide to work with upper- or lowercase. If you choose to work with lowercase, everything will appear in lowercase except the literals and the comments. Users can also decide to work with uppercase only for ABAP keywords.

To define these modes, from the editor screen, select *Settings → Edit Mode,* and make your selections.

Basic Editing Concepts. The SAP R/3 code editor works very similarly to any text processor or program editor. To write code, just place your cursor where you want to enter the text and write the program code. To go to the next line, press the *Return* key.

You can move around the screen using the typical mouse functions or the arrow keys on the keyboard or the scrolling icons from the R/3 windows standard toolbar.

Lines, Blocks, and Buffers. The editor offers several facilities for working with lines, *blocks* (a group of contiguous lines), and *buffers* (intermediate copy of program code which can be transferred).

To work with either lines, blocks, or buffers, you have to select the line or groups of lines to manage. There are two methods to select lines:

- Interactively, by double clicking on the first line to select and then on the last one. The selected line or block switches color to reverse video.
- Using the available Edit menu options or function keys, for example, by positioning the cursor on the first line of the block and choosing *Edit → Select* from the menu. Then repeat the operation for the last line of the block.

When editing code, the system makes available some facilities for copying and pasting code between programs, sessions, and even between systems. These are commonly known as *buffers* or *clipboards.* The ABAP editor has five types of buffers or clipboards: the session buffer, the system buffer, and the clipboards X, Y, and Z.

The *session buffer* is used to perform cut and paste within the same editor session in a single system. Once you leave the editor, the buffer contents are lost.

The *clipboards X, Y,* and *Z* are used for performing cut and paste operations between different sessions in the same SAP system. There is no difference among them; it's just a matter of having more than one buffer.

The *system buffer* is used for doing cut and paste between sessions in different SAP systems, for example, between the development and the productive system. This process should not be confused with transporting objects. It is just a faster process than performing a download and upload operation on the local workstation disk. Table 7-2 presents a summary of these functions.

TABLE 7-2

Clipboard Cut and Paste Options

Buffer	Copy Function	Paste Function
Session buffer	*Edit → Copy to buffer*	*Edit → Insert from buffer*
Clipboard X	*Block / buffer → Copy to X clipboard*	*Block / buffer → Insert from X clipboard*
Clipboard Y	*Block / buffer → Copy to Y clipboard*	*Block / buffer → Insert from Y clipboard*
Clipboard Z	*Block / buffer → Copy to Z clipboard*	*Block / buffer → Insert from Z clipboard*
Clipboard (system buffer)	*Block / buffer → Copy to clipboard*	*Block / buffer → Insert from clipboard*

Line Editing Options. The source code editor includes some utilities for performing some functions in the line where the cursor is positioned (the active line). Some of these functions are directly available from the icons in the application toolbar, but all of them are accessible from the menu bar options as the following list shows.

Menu Option	*Function*
Edit → Edit line → Insert line	Inserts a new line before the active line
Edit → Edit line → Delete line or *Edit → Cut*	Deletes the active line
Edit → Edit line → Split line	Divides the active line into two lines at the position where the cursor is located
Edit → Edit line → Concatenate line	Joins active line with the previous line into a single line
Edit → Edit line → Duplicate line	Duplicates the active line

Searching and Replacing. As with common editing tools, the ABAP source code editor includes functions for searching and replacing text. To perform these functions, from the editor menu, select *Edit → Search / Replace* or, alternatively, as a fast path, click on the *Find* button located on the standard toolbar. The system displays a dialog box where you can enter the text to find and the text you wish to replace it with.

Layout Commands. In order to improve the appearance of the source code on the screen, the editor includes several options; the most common is the *Pretty printer.* The function *Program → Pretty printer* rewrites the program code following the indentation rules as described in the ABAP user guide. This function should only be executed after the program has been checked and contains no syntactical errors.

Saving Program Code

As mentioned previously, programs are stored in the R/3 database when they are saved.

There are several menu options for saving the program source code:

- *Program → Save without check.* The system stores the program in the database without doing syntactical verification.
- *Program → Save as.* The program is saved with another name in the database without doing syntax verification.
- *Program → Save temp. version.* The system stores a temporary program copy in a buffer. This copy is held in the buffer (clipboard) until you perform any other *Save* function. To restore a temporary copy held on the buffer, select *Program → Get temp. version.*

When for any reason (system error, etc.) you leave a program before saving it to the database and a temporary copy was created, when returning to editing the program, the system automatically presents a dialog box where you can decide which copy you want to work with. Available options are as follows:

- *Fetch from buffer (inactive version).* The system takes the temporary copy as it was stored in the buffer. The temporary copy becomes the active program version.
- *Fetch from database and get buffer.* The system fetches the copy stored in the database but it also makes the temporary copy available in the buffer. The database copy becomes the active version.
- *Fetch from database and delete buffer.* The system fetches the copy as stored in the database and deletes the previous temporary buffer.

When in doubt, you can execute the *Compare* function to see the differences between the program database copy and the buffer copy.

Checking Program Source Code

The ABAP editor includes some functions to check and verify the program syntax. Depending on the level of syntax analysis to be performed, there are several commands available.

The most common way to quickly verify the program syntax at any moment is to click on the *Check* icon in the application toolbar, or to select *Program → Check → Current program* from the menu bar. In both cases the system checks the code of the program in the current editor session and the top include if it exists.

You can also perform the syntax check to verify the program with the existing *includes* by selecting *Program → Check → main program.*

In any case, the system will display in the status bar any messages about the syntax errors it found.

If you want to perform a more comprehensive program verification beyond the syntax check, you can select the *Program → Check → Extended program check* from the initial ABAP editor screen. When selecting this function, the system displays a new screen full of check boxes in which you can select the extension of the check to be performed, as displayed in Fig. 7-15. Once the extended check is finished, the system presents a listing with all the errors and warnings grouped by extended verification types.

Editing Help Facilities

The editor includes several options to facilitate and to automate the code writing.

- *Inserting statements templates.* By selecting the *Edit → Insert statement* function, the system allows you to insert instructions templates in which you only have to fill up some input fields; then the system automatically generates a syntactically correct state-

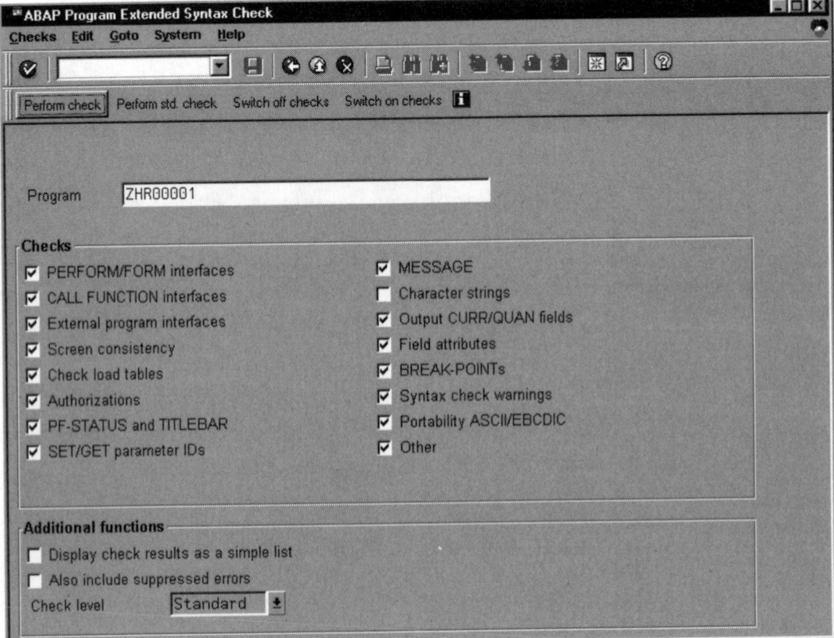

Figure 7-15 Extended syntax check display.

ment and inserts it in your source code. When selecting this function, the system displays a dialog box for selecting the type of statement to include. Figure 7-16 shows this dialog box.

- *Inserting comment lines.* You can automatically insert or remove comments in a block of source code by selecting the functions *Edit → Block/buffer → Insert comment* or *Edit → Block/buffer → Delete comment.*

Comments in the ABAP source code are indicated by entering an asterisk (*) in the first column of a line. If you want to include comments within a code line, you must enter an open double quote sign ("). Everything after this sign is considered comment by the system up to the next line.

- *ABAP programming language help.* At any moment while editing the source code you can look up the online ABAP programming documentation by calling the function *Utilities → help on* from the menu. Figure 7-17 shows the dialog box for selecting help on keywords, tables, and so forth. From this screen, you can also call the full online manual.

Editor Navigation Functions

Often, long programs *include* source code from other programs. For example, when having common data or variable definitions for a group of common programs, developers create a source code program including just those definitions. Then developers do not have to rewrite that code—it's enough to

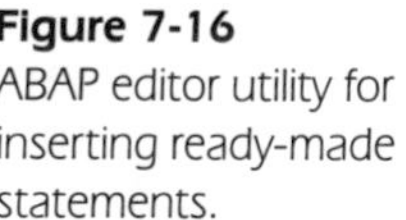

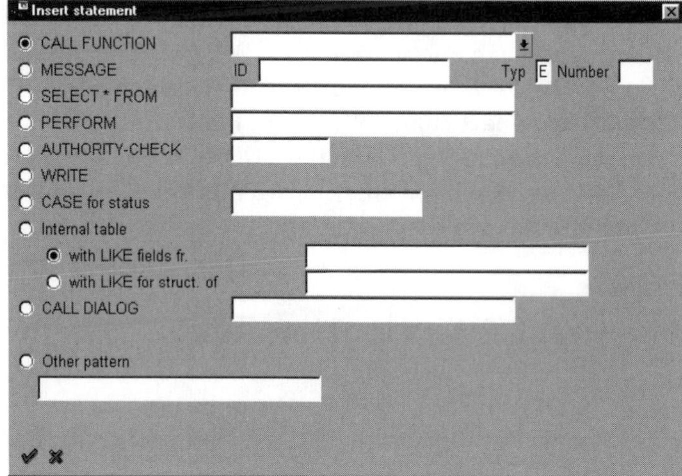

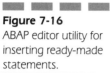

Figure 7-16 ABAP editor utility for inserting ready-made statements.

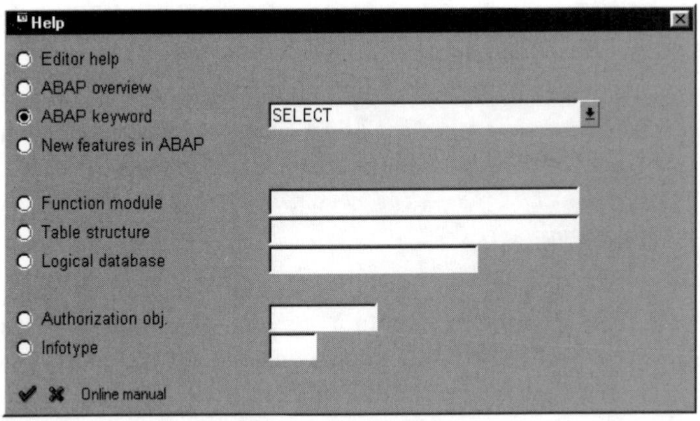

Figure 7-17
Getting help dialog box.

include it from other programs which make use of it. The same procedure applies when creating functions or subroutines. This is common practice in many programming languages, as is use of the .INCLUDE keyword.

Expanding Includes. When using INCLUDE programs within your programs, you can automatically expand the contents of the included program just by double clicking on the INCLUDE line. In this case, you can edit the include program.

You can also display the contents of the include programs by selecting the *Edit → Additional functions → Expand INCLUDE* option from the source code editor menu. Using this option, if you want to make changes to the include program and then save them, you have to select *Edit → Additional functions → Save INCLUDE.*

Main Programs. If you are editing a program which is used in other programs (included), from the editing session you can look up what programs make reference (INCLUDE) to it. To display these programs, select *Utilities → Main programs.* The system displays a list of programs that use that particular INCLUDE. Figure 7-18 shows an example of finding the programs which use the BDCSTAUD program (the source code). This is quite useful for knowing what effects a modification in an INCLUDE might have in other programs.

Special Navigation Tools

The ABAP editor assists users in navigating across program source code in a similar way as the repository browser, and also aids in displaying the

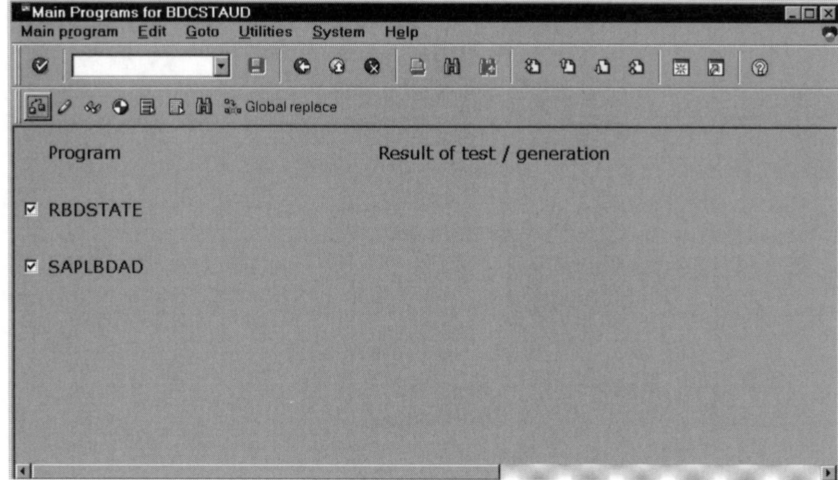

Figure 7-18 Displaying the program list using an include.

hierarchy of the program in order to visualize and move parts of the program. This can be achieved with:

- *Markers.* Allows you to maintain the history of your navigation across code objects. Implicit markers are maintained automatically in the ABAP editor. You can also add your own explicit markers by placing the cursor on a line and choosing *Mark line.* Markers only apply within your current R/3 session. To display the current list of markers, choose *Goto* → *Markers* from the Editor menu.
- *Navigation stack.* Allows you to maintain tracking of the navigation across code objects. To display the navigation stack, choose *Goto* → *Stack.* Users can move to any point on the stack by double-clicking on an item in the stack.
- *Structure hierarchy.* The structure hierarchy displays the structures in programs. To display the structure hierarchy, choose *Utilities* → *Structure hierarchy.* Figure 7-19 shows the ABAP editor display hierarchy of program RSEPSFTP.

Downloading and Uploading Source Code

From the source code editor, you can upload and download program source code from and to your local workstation. These functions are available from the Utilities menu, by selecting either *Upload* or *Download.*

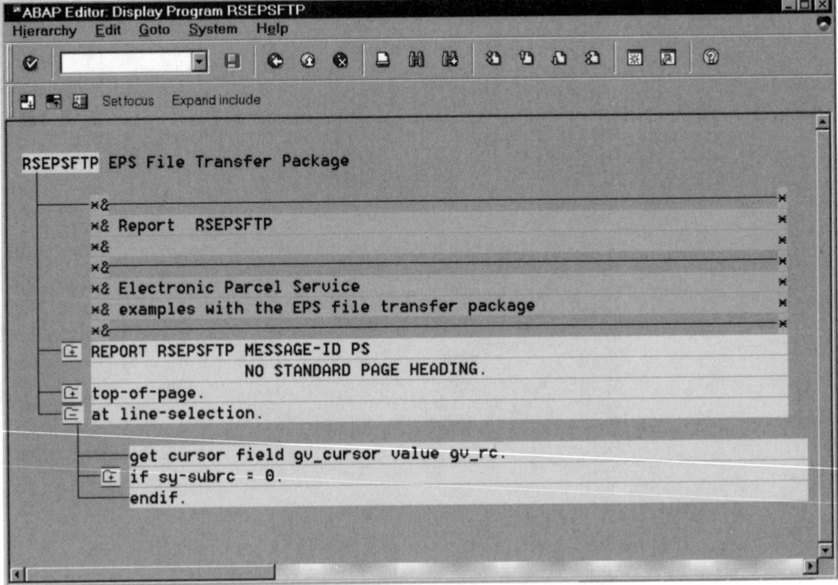

Figure 7-19 Example of structure hierarchy.

The system displays a dialog box for entering the path to your local workstation file.

Normally, you should use the ASCII code for performing these functions.

Special Editor Features

The ABAP code editor includes some special features which work when you double click on different elements of the editing screen. For example, when you double click:

- On a line, the system positions that line as the first line on the screen. This is similar to scrolling through the editor until that line is the first one.
- On an object name, the system displays the object definition, if it exists, or allows you to directly define it.
- On a statement keyword, the editor positions the cursor over the end statement keyword if it exists, and vice versa.

For more information about editing and special features, please look in the SAP online documentation.

Introduction to the Screen Painter

The *screen painter* is one of the ABAP workbench tools that, together with the menu painter, allows you to define and design R/3 screens and to program the behavior of the screens associated with the dialog steps of the R/3 transactions. In other words, these tools allow you to define the *flow logic* for R/3 screens and programs.

A SAP R/3 transaction is executed following the logic associated with each screen and running the ABAP programs which are indicated in the screens' logic. To define how a screen is going to be processed, the screen painter needs four components:

- *Screen Attributes.* The function of the screen attributes is to indicate a screen type and associate the screen object to the SAP system, such as the ABAP programs which are to be executed when at that screen. It also describes the screen order within a transaction.
- *Fields.* Fields are the main screen elements. Fields are defined in the ABAP dictionary or internally in the programs. Field attributes establish relationships between the screen fields as well as define their behavior when end users are executing the transaction.
- *Screen layout.* This function establishes the layout of the graphic elements on the screen, such as input fields, labels, icons, radio buttons, check boxes, and element groups.
- *Flow Logic.* This is the main screen definition for controlling the flow logic of the screen, that is, how it reacts to user inputs and calls associated ABAP modules and programs as defined using the ABAP program editor.

The DYNPRO Concept

DYNPRO, or *dynamic program,* has been quite a common term in SAP naming conventions. A DYNPRO refers to a screen together with its flow logic. Actually, DYNPROs should be considered synonymous with *screens* as created by the screen painter.

The screen painter uses a procedural programming language different than the ABAP language. This language is interpreted by the screen processor rather than by the ABAP processor. For more information, please refer to the SAP official guides.

Starting the Screen Painter

To call the screen painter tool, from the main ABAP workbench, select the option *Development → User interface → Screen Painter* or just click on the *Screen Painter* push button on the application toolbar. Alternatively, enter transaction code SE51 in the command field. Figure 7-20 shows the screen painter initial screen.

On the initial screen painter screen, you can see some radio button options which are used to maintain the elements involved in screen definitions as described previously.

To access any of these options, first enter the program name (type M, Module pool) related with the screen to create or modify and a number for identifying the screen.

You can also start the screen painter from the repository browser by double-clicking on the corresponding screen for a certain program.

In this case, the system goes directly to the initial maintenance screen corresponding to specific *Screen flow logic.* From any of the screen painter screens, you can navigate to other screen painter component maintenance screens.

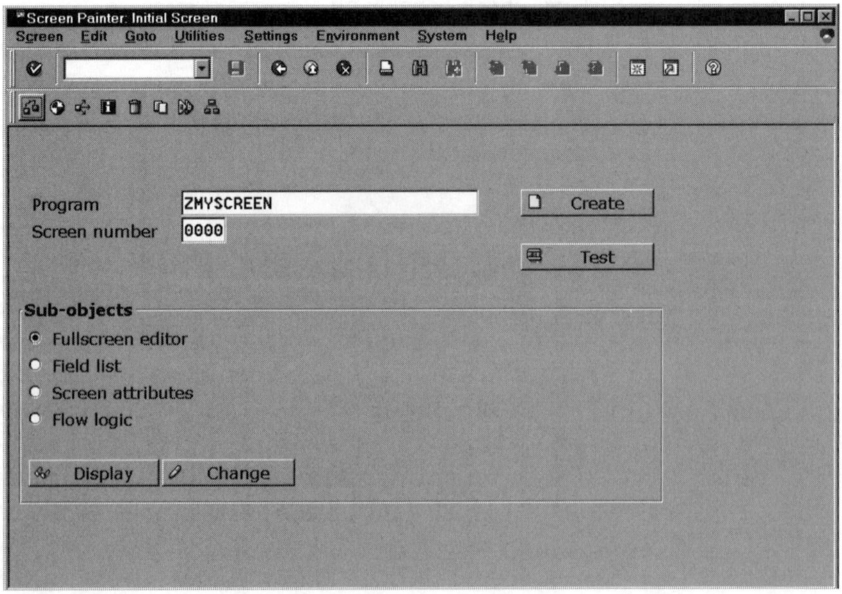

Figure 7-20
Screen painter initial screen.

Using the Screen Painter

Independently of the chosen path to call the screen painter, the process of creating a DYNPRO includes the creation and definition of all the needed screen components. A logical sequence might be the one presented in the following list.

Step	*Screen Painter Menu Option*
Create the screen and attributes	*Screen Attributes*
Select and position the needed fields within the screen	*Fullscreen Editor*
Establish the field attributes to which the screen belongs	*Field list*
Define the screen flow logic with respect to the transaction to which it belongs	*Flow logic*

Creating a New Screen: The Screen Attributes. Enter the name and number for the new screen and click on the *Create* push button located to the right of the *Program* input field. The system will display the *Change Screen Attributes* screen.

Once located on the attributes screen, you have to enter the following information in the required input fields:

- *Short description.* Brief description to identify the purpose of the screen.
- *Screen type.* Normally, you select the *Normal* option for the usual R/3 windows. There are, however, other common screen types such as *Modal dialog box* or *Subscreen*. The *Modal dialog box* screen type is used to establish independent and interactive dialogs (often confirmation dialog boxes) within a screen or transaction. The *Subscreen* type represents "screens within screens" and its logic is controlled from within the original screen.
- *Next Screen.* Number of the screen which must be processed after the current one during the normal transaction logic.

There are other input fields for defining screen attributes. Only the main ones were introduced. Others can also be important for specific applications. Refer to the online help for information on the purposes of other fields in the screen attributes.

Once the screen attributes are defined, you should save them. When all screen elements are defined, you should use the *generate* function for the screen to become active in the runtime system.

On the initial screen painter attributes screen, there are several options in the application toolbar which you can call to navigate directly to define other elements needed for creating screens.

Defining the Screen Layout. Defining a screen layout requires the following steps:

- Setting the fullscreen editor to the needed editor mode
- Starting the fullscreen editor
- Selecting the definition for the fields to insert in the screen using the existing ABAP dictionary field definitions or the existing program field definitions
- Positioning the fields in the screen area using the fullscreen editor
- Defining or converting the fields in graphical elements
- Positioning the graphic elements that are independent of the screen fields
- Defining the attributes of every screen element
- Checking the screen
- Generating the screen

Establishing the Screen Painter Editing Mode. The screen painter includes two editor modes: a graphical one and an alphanumeric one.

The graphical editing mode works similarly to typical Windows applications using popular drag and drop features. This interface works at the presentation level (normally a Windows PC) and must be separately installed when installing the SAPGUI presentation software. The graphical editor is not available on all platforms.

The alphanumeric mode uses a different interface which is a little harder to manage. Results, however, can be exactly the same. While in graphical mode, you can directly position graphical elements in the screen layout; with the alphanumeric mode, you have to select them using menu options.

To select the editing mode you wish to work with, from the initial screen painter screen, select the option *Settings → Graphical fullscreen,* and then you can click the option *Graphical Screen Painter.*

If the graphical editor is not installed on your workstation, the system will display a message in the status bar and will automatically present the alphanumeric mode.

The next sections only introduce the basic functioning of the graphical editing mode since it's a more friendly and practical editor.

Overview of Screen Elements. The main elements in a screen painter editing screen are as follows:

Element	*Description / Use*
Text fields	Free text or field labels for other screen elements. Display-only elements.
Input/output fields	Input and/or display fields.
Radio buttons	Graphical elements associated with an input field. They must be logically associated into a group. Radio buttons allow users to assign entries that are mutually exclusive for a field.
Check boxes	Graphical elements associated with input fields that are normally used in boolean YES/NO operations.
Push buttons	Used for activating a particular function, passing the function code associated with the ABAP processor for the processing of the Process After Input (PAI) modules. This function is only executed when there is ABAP code associated with the push button function.
Group Boxes	Graphical display element that allows several screen elements to be grouped together.
Subscreen areas	Rectangular screen areas reserved for displaying additional screens at execution time.
Table controls	Screen areas that the system creates just like tables, but that are processed as loops. Table controls have a header row, a definition row, and a set of rows and columns (table) that are defined automatically by the system.
Tabstrip controls	A control that functions like a card index file where each card contain fields of one component/screen, allowing users to jump from one to other inside the same

	screen. Tabstrip controls have tab titles, tab pages, and tab environment.
Status icon	Used to display output fields containing an icon.

Basic Concepts in the Fullscreen Editor. To call the fullscreen editor, from the initial screen painter screen, click on the *Fullscreen editor* push button and then click *Change,* or, from the *Screen Attributes,* click on *Fullscreen Editor.* The system will display the graphical screen painter editor as shown in Fig. 7-21.

In the graphical screen painter fullscreen editor includes, you can see the following:

- *The work area.* It's the screen area in which you place the different elements in the screen layout. This is the big, rectangular area.
- *The Element palette area.* This contains the screen element types which can be included within a screen. This area is located to the left of the main area.
- *The Element bar.* This contains specific information about the selected screen element. It's located just below the header line.

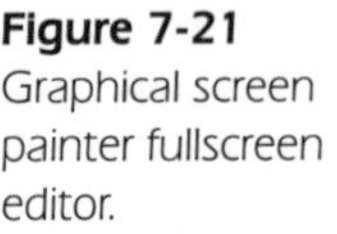

Figure 7-21
Graphical screen painter fullscreen editor.

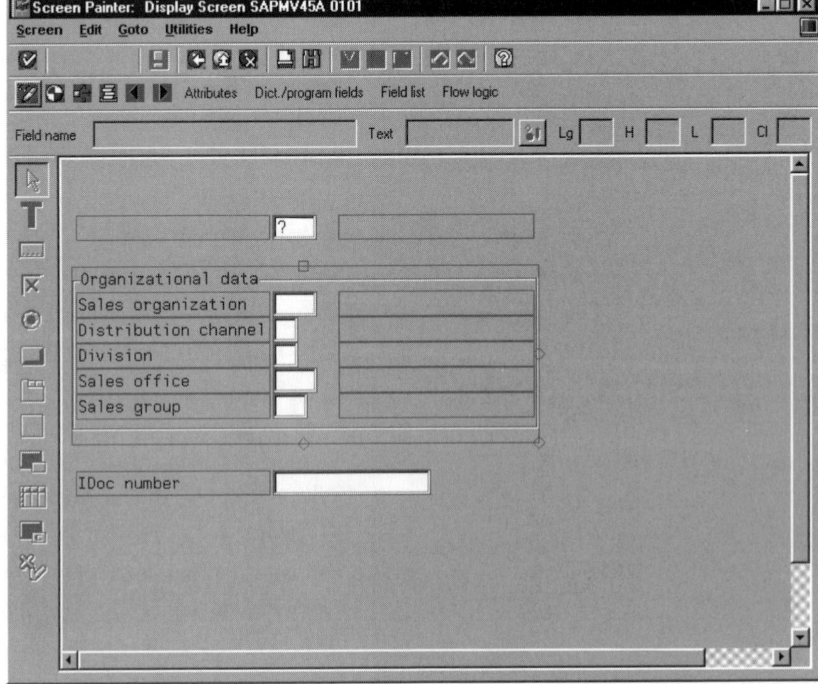

Selecting the Screen Fields Definition. By selecting the push button *Dict/program fields* on the application toolbar from the graphical fullscreen editor or by selecting *Goto → Dict./programs fields,* you can call the screen painter function that allows you to indicate from which information source you want to get the field definitions for the elements to be included in the screen being created. Figure 7-22 shows an example of this screen.

In this dialog box, you have to enter the location where the fields to be used in the screen are logically defined. These definitions can be either in the ABAP dictionary or in the ABAP program in which the screen is based.

To get a field definition, enter the name for the field in the *Table/field name* input field in the dialog box and click on the *Get from program* push button in case the field is defined in the program, or else click on the *Get from Dict* if those fields are defined in the ABAP dictionary. Figure 7-22 shows an example of getting the TADIR table definition from the dictionary. The lower part of the screen displays the field or table field attributes with their logical definitions.

Positioning Fields in the Screen Area. Once you have the field definition in the *Dict./program fields* dialog box, to transfer and position the fields on the screen, you must select one or more fields by clicking on the small push button to the left of each field.

If you want a field to be copied on the screen as an input/output field, then mark the check box under the *I/O field* column. Upon doing this, the field will be entered as *input/output elements.* You can also decide to copy any selected fields as either *Text elements, radio buttons,* or *check boxes* by clicking the corresponding radio button under the *Copy as* column. Only

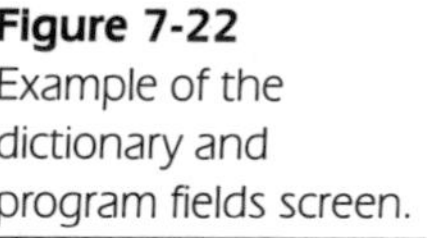

Figure 7-22 Example of the dictionary and program fields screen.

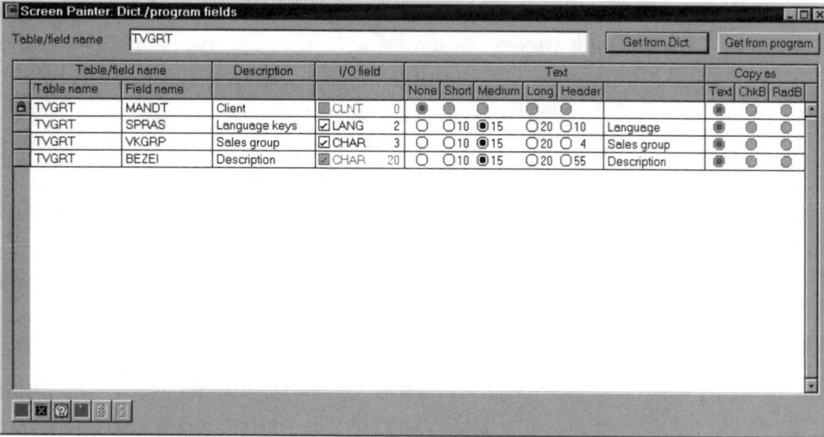

fields which are used as flags (boolean YES/NO values) are allowed as radio buttons or check boxes.

Next, you have to select which of the field labels you want to use. These field labels are the ones defined in the *Data element* corresponding to the particular fields. To do this, just click the needed radio button under the *Test* column.

To transfer your selections to the painter editor area, click on the *Copy* push button. The system will then go back to the fullscreen editor screen.

The system displays a kind of field shadowing with the cursor. Now position the cursor where you want those fields to be located on the screen and just click on the area. The templates for the selected fields will now appear on the screen. Later you can move the fields to make the screen look nicer.

You have to repeat this process for the necessary elements to be included in the screen. You can also position new fields on the screen, whose definitions are not contained in the program or in the data dictionary. In such cases, the system will display a dialog box for entering the field name, associated text, and the field attributes. To do this, from the fullscreen editor screen, just click on the elements available in the *Element Palette* area, define the new fields in the *Element bar,* and position them in the screen area.

With this method, the fields are not associated to dictionary fields, but you can nevertheless create the screen. Since one of the biggest benefits of R/3 is the data integrity, it is advisable to always create screen layouts based on previously defined dictionary or program fields.

Adjusting and Fine Positioning the Screen Elements. After screen elements have been defined and positioned in the main area of the fullscreen editor, usually some fine-tuning is required to make the screen look nicer. Some of the adjusting functions are to resize, move, and delete some of the elements until you get the desired results.

Use the drag and drop features of the windows interface. For example, to move an element, just click on it and, without releasing the mouse button, drag the element to the new position. When performing adjusting, moving, or resizing operations, the cursor changes its shape.

You can also draw boxes over some of the screen elements to make some kind of logical grouping for a nicer display. To do this, you select the *Groupbox* option of the *Palette* tool.

Defining Screen Element Attributes. From the moment they are created, all the screen elements have some attributes which determine their characteristics and behavior. The system groups these attributes in four parts:

- *General attributes.* These include attributes which are directly managed by the screen painter and the fullscreen editor.
- *Dictionary.* The dictionary attributes refer to the behavior of the element as it's defined in the dictionary. These attributes only apply to elements which have been *copied* from the dictionary definition. Some of these attributes are particularly important for the overall functional potential of the screens created with the screen painter: *Matchcode, Parameter ID, SET parameter, GET parameter,* or *Foreign Key.*
- *Program.* These attributes define the method of communication with the program associated with the screen painter from which it's defined.
- *Display.* This sets the behavior of the elements with respect to their display features, such as reverse video, invisible, and so forth.

You can display or maintain these attributes individually or by previously selecting them and then applying a common attribute to the selected elements.

The *Attributes* dialog box. You can display the *Attributes* dialog box by selecting an element and clicking on the *Attributes* push button on the application toolbar. Alternatively, you can also get it by double clicking on an element. Figure 7-23 shows this dialog box. This box only displays the attributes for a single element.

Field List Screen. With the field list screen, you can display a list of all the screen elements together with their screen's attributes.

To call this screen, from the initial menu painter screen, select the *Field list* radio button and then click on the *Display* or *Change* push buttons. Alternatively, from the fullscreen editor screen, you can select the *Field list* function on the application toolbar. Figure 7-24 shows this screen.

On this screen, you can also display at once all the field attributes. In the upper-right-hand side of the screen there are contiguous push buttons with the + and – signs where you can click to expand the display for those attributes and, probably, scroll horizontally to see them all.

The OK Code. The *OK Code* field is automatically created by the system without a name and it's not visible on the screen, but it's necessary to communicate information to the program associated with the screen.

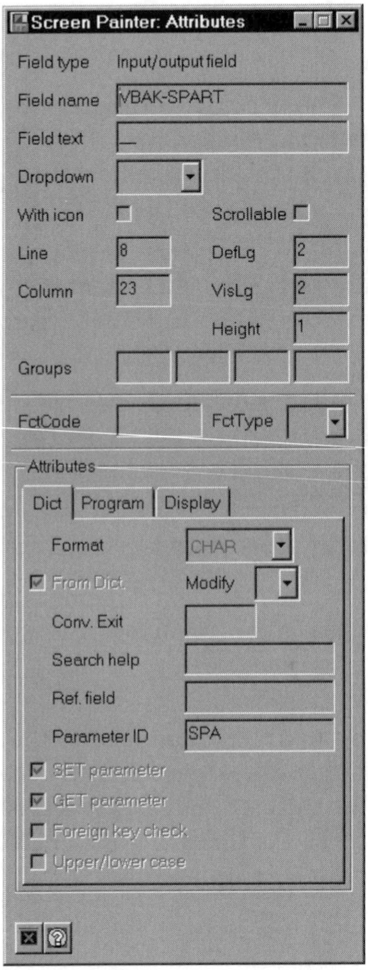

Figure 7-23
Screen painter field attributes screen.

The *OK Code* is an internal field which the system uses in the PAI modules (refer to the next section) to evaluate what action must be taken after user inputs. It is an important element used to evaluate the screen flow logic.

Screen Flow Logic

You can call the flow logic editor of the screen painter by double clicking on a screen object within a repository browser screen object or from the initial screen painter display by entering the screen name and number,

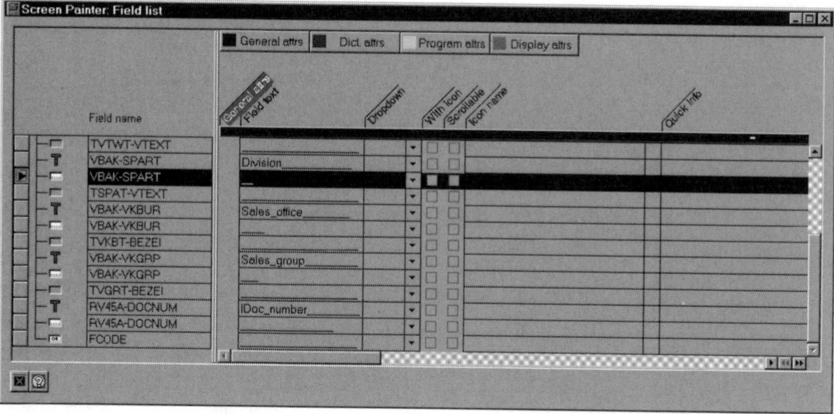

Figure 7-24
Display of the screen painter field list.

selecting the *Flow logic* radio button, and then clicking on the *Display* or *Change* buttons.

When first creating the flow logic for a screen, the system displays two very important modules:

- *The PBO (process before output) modules.* These modules include the code which is executed before the system presents the screen.
- *The PAI (process after input) modules.* These modules are called by the system as a response to user input.

More information about the *OK Code* and the PBO and PAI modules can be found in SAP official documentation about programming ABAP transactions.

Testing and Verifying Screen Painter Objects

Before finishing the editing of a screen, you should use the available screen painter tools to test and simulate how the screen will really appear at execution time.

From all the screen painter component displays, you always have the *Test* function available, either directly by clicking on the *Test* icon in the application toolbar or by selecting the *Screen* → *Test* function from the menu. The system requires you to define the screen size for the testing, and you can even select to test the screen flow logic.

Additionally, you can verify the different screen definition components (syntax, consistency, layout) by calling the available check functions from the menu:

- *Screen → Check → Syntax*
- *Screen → Check → Consistency*
- *Screen → Check → Layout*

Generating a Screen

Once a screen is finished, verified, and tested, you have to *generate* it to be able to use it within an R/3 transaction. To generate a screen, from any screen painter screen, click on the *Generate* icon on the application toolbar or select *Screen → Generate* from the menu.

Introduction to the Menu Painter

The *menu painter* is the ABAP workbench tool for creating and maintaining user interfaces. User interfaces are independent of the screens generated by the screen painter, which means that a program can have several different user interfaces. The opposite is also possible: the same user interface can be used for several screens. However, a user interface is always dependent on a dialog program.

A user interface is made up of a GUI status and a GUI title. From the user point of view, a user interface created by the menu painter contains the following elements:

- *Title bar.* It's the upper-screen line containing the window title.
- *Menu bar.* It's the line right below the title containing the pull-down menu options.
- *Standard toolbar.* It's a toolbar located on the line right below the menu which contains the standard system icons.
- *Application toolbar.* It's the toolbar located under the standard toolbar. This toolbar contains the icons and push buttons defined by the users. These options are also normally available from the menu options.
- *Function keys.* These are special invisible functions that are executed by pressing a key combination or by clicking the right mouse button (for right-handed people) and displaying the available function key box.

Main Menu Painter Objects

As introduced in a previous section, the user interface is independent of the screens generated by the screen painter. However, both interfaces and screens can be associated by means of the object known as the *GUI status.*

The GUI status object is a special element which groups together the following user interface components (when the related screen is of type *Normal*):

- Menu bar
- Standard toolbar
- Application toolbar
- Function keys (not visible)

The other element of the user interface, independent of the GUI status and of the screen, is the *GUI title.*

The three types of objects (including the screen) can be assigned to the same program from within the repository browser. But to really and operatively assign them, the ABAP statements SET PF-STATUS and SET TITLEBAR must be used in the source code of the dialog program (of type M), which contains the transaction logic, the process before output (PBO) module.

Object Hierarchy. Between programs, screens, and interfaces, the following hierarchies are possible:

- A program might have multiple GUI status and GUI titles.
- Multiple screens can be assigned to the same GUI status.
- One screen can be assigned to multiple GUI status and GUI titles, but only one at a time.
- Normally, in a user interface, both the GUI status and GUI title go together.

The Function Concept. When working with user interfaces within the menu painter, functions are very important elements. *Functions* are codes which the system stores in the system field SY-UCOMM for programs or type 1 (reports) or in field OK-CODE for transactions, when the corresponding function key, push button, or menu option menu is executed.

An interface function has the following elements:

Element	Description
Function code	Identifies the function to the system
Function type	Tells the system when or how to carry out a function (see function types)
Function text	Short text to describe the function, for example *Save*
Icon name	Name of the icon to be displayed on a push button associated with a function
Icon text	Text to be output on the push button in addition to the icon associated with a function
Infotext	Text to be displayed in the status bar
Fastpath	Letter combination that allows users to choose functions without using the mouse

Depending on which part of the dialog program you want to execute the code associated to the function, you can define several types of functions as the following shows:

Type	*Dialog Program Part (ABAP Event)*
E	AT EXIT-COMMAND (PAI)
T	Executes the CALL TRANSACTION *tttt* statement, where *tttt* is the function code
S	Executes system functions used internally in SAP standard applications. You should not use type S when creating your own functions.
P	Triggers a function defined locally at the GUI. This function is not passed back to the ABAP program (no SY-UCOMM or OK-CODE). Instead, it is processed at the presentation server. This type of function can only currently be used for *tabstrip controls* (screen painter).

The function code is assigned in the dialog program. The user interface communicates with the dialog program using the SY-UCOMM/OK-CODE field.

Starting the Menu Painter

To start the menu painter, from the main ABAP workbench, click on the *Menu Painter* button on the application toolbar or, from the menu, select

Development → Menu Painter. Alternatively, enter transaction code SE41 in the command field.

From this initial screen you can create, manage, display, and test all menu painter objects. Available options are as follows:

Status	Access and manage all the GUI status elements
Status list	Accesses the list and manages the created objects by double clicking over them
Menu bars	Accesses the list and manages the created menu bars by double clicking over them
Menu list	Presents the list of menu options and allows its management by double clicking over the objects.
F key settings	Lists and manages the function keys
Function list	Lists the available functions codes and maintains them
Title list	Accesses and manages the GUI title lists

Using the Menu Painter

When displaying and managing the GUI status, you access the main menu painter screen. However, when creating a GUI status for the first time, the system first displays a dialog box for entering a short description and the GUI status type.

You can access the main menu painter screen for defining GUI status by entering the name of the status in the input field, clicking on the status radio button, and then clicking on the *Display* or *Change* buttons. You can also access this screen from the repository browser workbench tool, by double clicking on any existing GUI status object, or when creating a new object.

From the repository browser screen you can manage all the available component objects for a status; you can go directly to the maintenance options for the specific status objects from the Goto menu.

If you create all the objects from a specific status screen, then you are using what SAP calls the *stand-alone technique*. The logical sequence when creating a status should then be

1. Create the GUI status
2. Define the menu bars, menu options, and submenus
3. Define the function key assignments
4. Define the application toolbar

5. Create a GUI title
6. Test and generate the status

Creating a GUI Status. To create a GUI status, from the initial menu painter screen, enter the name for the status and click on the *Create* push button. The system displays the dialog box for entering initial data for the status. On this initial screen, you have to enter a short description and select the GUI status type to be associated with the GUI status. Depending on the GUI status type, the user interface will support different menu painter elements.

Upon clicking on the *Continue* button in the previous dialog box, the system displays the main screen for maintaining GUI status, as shown in Fig. 7-25.

GUI Status Type. The GUI status type tells the system which kinds of window and components are usually associated with a given GUI status (for example, a dialog box window never has menu bars or a standard toolbar).

Available GUI status types are:

GUI Status Type	Associated with Windows Having
Screen	Menu bars, standard toolbar, application toolbar, and function keys
Dialog box	Application toolbar and function keys
List	Menu bars, standard toolbar, application toolbar, and function keys
List in dialog box	Application toolbar and function keys

Defining the Menu Bar and Submenus. Once in the screen for maintaining the status, click on the expand icon next to the Menu bar field (shadowed in blue), and the system will display the fields to define the menus that will appear in the menu bar.

To create a menu bar, you have to enter a name in the *Menu bar* input field which will identify that menu bar. Then you have to enter the name for each menu according to the order you want them to appear in the menu bar. You can create up to six menus, although the menu bar can hold up to eight menus and the system automatically includes the System and Help menus.

To create menus, the system allows you to use the standard menu bars as models and then to modify the menus and submenus as proposed by

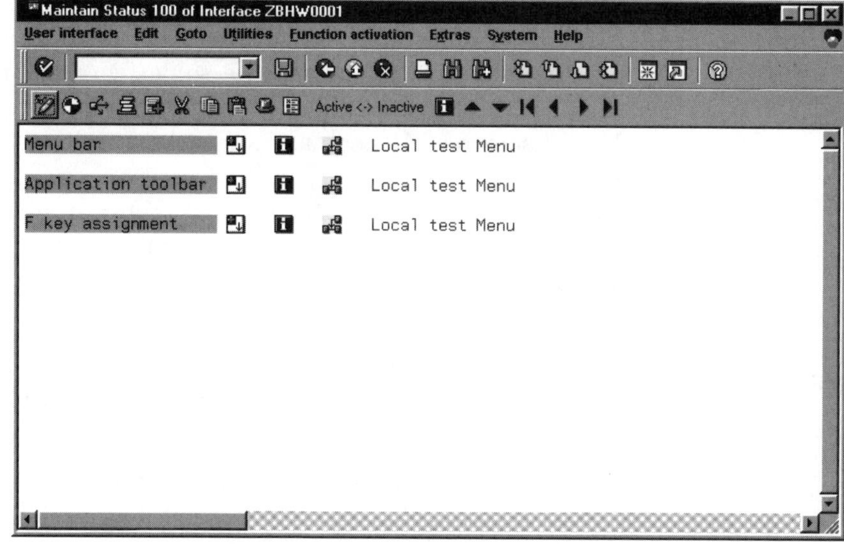

Figure 7-25 Maintaining GUI status.

the system standards. Of course, you can create completely new menus without using any standard as template.

In the first case, click on the folder with the + sign next to *Display standards.* The system will display all the usual menus in the standard menu bar.

In the second case, where you want to create your own menus without using standards, click on the *Hide standards* buttons. The system will clear the fields. At this point, you can write on each field the name for the menus you want to create.

Menu Components. A menu can contain functions, other menus (submenus), and separators. To create components, double click over the menu name. The system will show two columns: *Code* and *Text,* with a maximum of 15 rows. The following list shows the meaning of these components.

Component	*Code*	*Text*
Function	Function code	Name of the option as it will appear in the menu
Separator	<empty>	Position the cursor and from the menu select *Edit → Insert → Separator line*
Submenu	<empty>	Submenu name as it will appear when displaying it

Submenus. To create the submenu components, leave the function column empty, enter a submenu name, and double click on the submenu text. The system will display the same two columns as for defining a menu option as previously described. Follow the same steps. Figure 7-26 shows a screen with menu and submenu definitions.

Defining the Key Assignments. You can define which function should be executed by pressing a key combination or when using the right mouse button function key display. To do this, you must:

- Click on the expand icon next to the *F key assignments* field (shadowed in blue), and the system will display the fields to define the standard toolbar and function key assignments. Figure 7-27 shows an example of this screen.
- Enter the name in the *F key assignment* input field, which will identify that group of F keys to define within the GUI status maintenance screen.
- Fill up the *Recommended function key settings* table with the function code.
- Fill up the *Freely assigned function keys* table with your own codes.

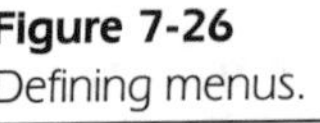

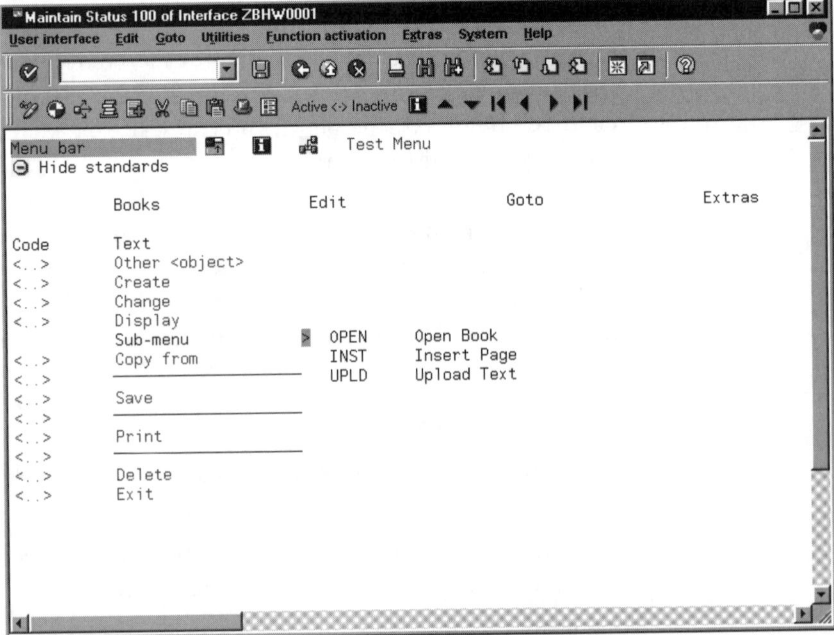

Figure 7-26
Defining menus.

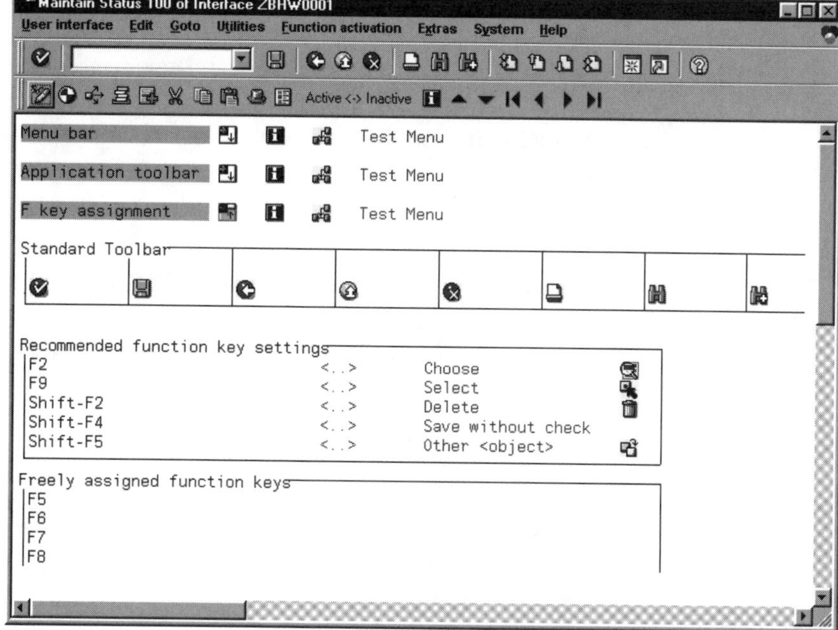

Figure 7-27 Defining the standard and application toolbars.

Defining the Application Toolbar. In the application toolbar, you can include icons corresponding to functions assigned for F keys. For this reason, before defining an application toolbar you must have the F keys previously created. Then, you only have to enter in the function fields for the application toolbar within the status maintenance screen the function code you want to appear in the application toolbar.

Creating a GUI Title

To create a GUI title object, on the initial *Menu Painter* screen, select the *Title* radio button, enter the name for the title, and click on the *Create* push button. On the title screen, enter the title number and the description—the actual text you want to appear in the title of the user interface.

Testing and Generating GUI Status

Similar to most workbench objects, the GUI status must be generated to become active in the runtime system. To generate the status, click on the

Generate icon in the application toolbar or select *User interface → Generate* from the menu.

Previous to this, you can test the user interface by calling the *User interface → Test status* function. The system displays a dialog box to specify the screen number you want to use to test the user interface and the title identifier to display.

Activating and Deactivating Functions

The procedure for activating or deactivating GUI status functions is as follows:

- Display the GUI status.
- From the menu, select *Function activation → In current status.*
- The system shows a dialog window with two push buttons that allows users to display all the functions, both activated and deactivated, from that GUI status.
- Removing the check mark from a specific activated function will deactivate that function. Adding a check mark will activate the function.

If you want to activate or deactivate functions from more than one GUI status, proceed as follows:

- Display the GUI status.
- Select *Function activation → In several statuses.*
- The system displays a dialog window, in which you must enter the code of the function to activate or deactivate.
- The system displays the status of the function on the different GUI statuses where the function is defined.
- Removing the check mark for a GUI status will deactivate the function for that status. Adding the check mark will activate the function.

Introduction to Area Menus

Conceptually, an *area menu* is a transaction which calls other transactions or functions. The difference between it and a normal user interface is that an area menu is a user interface which is not related to any *Dialog program* or any *Screen Painter* screen.

To create an area menu, from the initial ABAP workbench, select *Development → Other tools → Area menus.* The system displays the initial area menu editor as shown in Fig. 7-28.

In the initial area menu editor, enter a code for the area menu in the input field, click on the *Create* button, and enter a description for the area menu. Then, click on *Continue.*

The system will display the *Maintain area menu* screen, which is very similar to the GUI status maintenance screen. In this screen:

- Enter the windows title in the *Title* field.
- Explode the menu bar.
- Enter the menu name in *menu bar* field.
- Double-click on the menu name.
- Enter the transaction function codes in the *Code* column.
- Enter the menu item names in the *Text* column.

After entering this information, save your definition and generate the area menu. You can test this area by selecting *Area Menu → Test.*

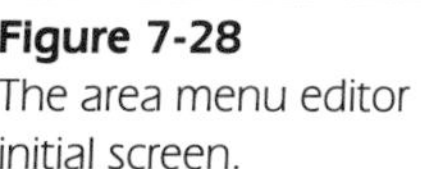

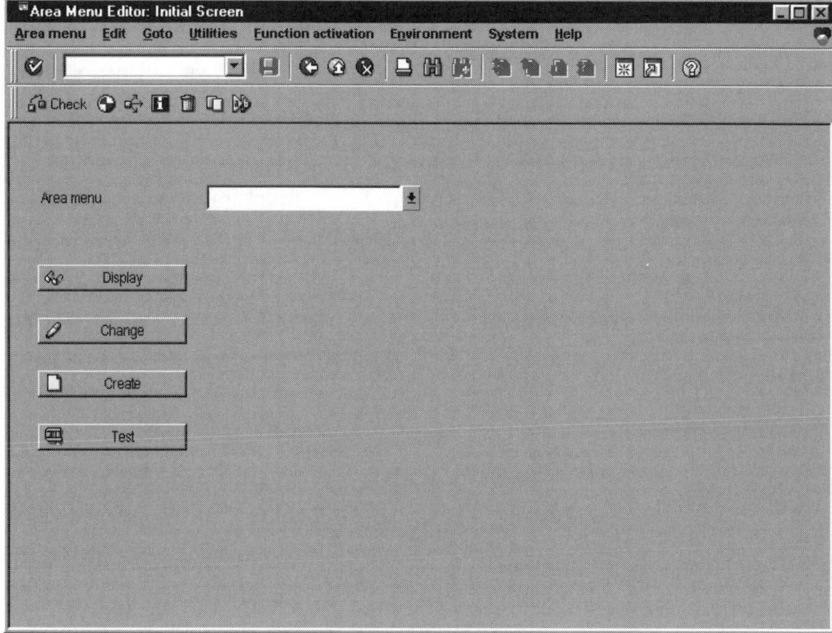

Figure 7-28 The area menu editor initial screen.

The Function Builder

Function modules are general purpose routines created with ABAP code that are available for every developer and from any program. The *function builder* is the ABAP workbench tool which allows you to maintain, control, and perform centralized tests of the function modules.

Function Builder Structure

To understand more easily the functionality described in the next section, an introduction to the different components and concepts which make up the function builder management, both from the point of view of the tool (external view) as well as from the point of view of its internal construction (internal view), follows.

External View. From the point of view of the workbench tool, the function builder is made up of a group of functions. Every function group contains all the routines (function modules) which belong to that function group.

A *function group* is a logical group of function modules having a common relationship among them and sharing a common programming context, such as global variables, at runtime.

For every function module, the system independently manages the following elements:

Administration	Administrative information about the specific function module
Import/export parameter interface	Formal parameter list for the function module input/output together with its characteristics
Table parameter/exceptions interface	Identifies the tables which can be input/output (by reference) to the function module and the definition of the exceptions which are managed by the function module
Documentation	Possible documentation for the function module
Source code	Contains the source code for the function module
Global data	Contains the global data definition for the group of functions (common to all function modules belonging to the group)

Main program	Contains the source code of the main program corresponding to the group of functions

Internal View. For every function group, there is a corresponding *main program*. The system identifies this main program with the name *SAPL<functgrp>*, where *<functgrp>* corresponds to the function group name. For example, for the ZJRS group, the main program would be *SAPLZJRS*.

This program includes references to include objects where the global data is defined for the function group, as well as the source code corresponding to every function module, the code for the subroutines, events, PAI modules, PBO modules, and so on.

The include object where the global definition is stored is named as *L<functgrp>TOP,* for example, *LZJRSTOP.* This include will contain the FUNCTION-POOL statement in the first line and then the common variable declaration section for all the function modules.

The include object where the source code for every function module is defined is identified by the system with the name *L<functgrp>UXX.* For example, *LZJRSUXX.* Within this object there will be an include for every function module that belongs to the function group. This include is known as *L<functgrp>Unn,* where *nn* is a sequential number corresponding to each function module. Within this include, the function source code is located between the instructions FUNCTION <function name> in the first line and ENDFUNCTION in the last line.

You can see some of these internal views in the Administration information.

Working with the Function Builder

To call the function builder main screen, from the ABAP workbench initial screen, click on the *Function Builder* button on the application toolbar. Alternatively, select *Development → Function Builder* from the menu, or enter transaction code SE37 in the command field. Figure 7-29 shows the function builder initial screen.

The next sections present the most common activities when working with the function builder, such as

- Displaying information about a function module
- Searching a specific function module
- Creating a function group

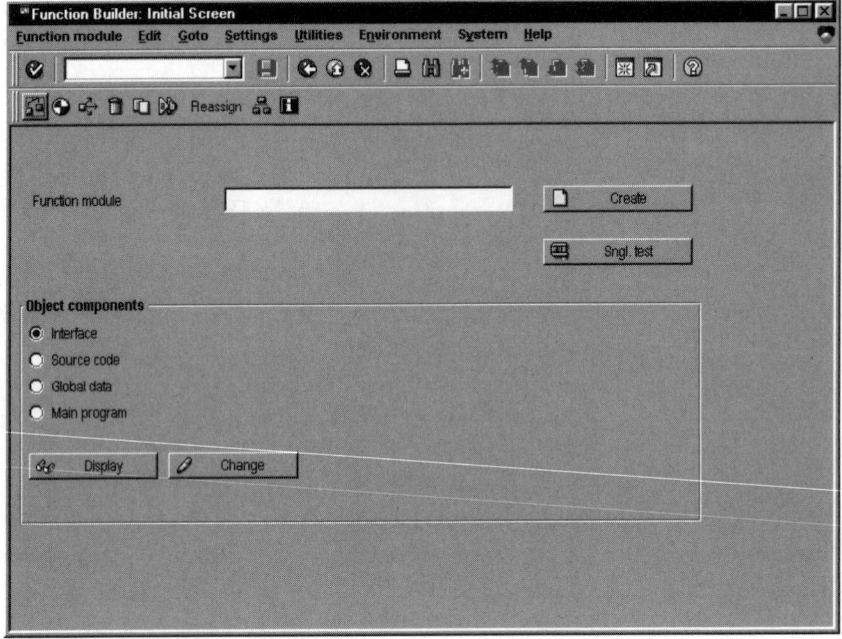

Figure 7-29 Function builder initial screen.

- Creating a function module
- Checking and activating modules
- Testing modules
- Calling functions with RFC

Displaying Information about a Function Module. To know the features and information about a function module, either when they are customer-created or from the extensive collection of standard SAP function modules, you must enter the function name in the input field, click on the radio button belonging to the information type to display, and click on the *Display* button.

The following options (radio buttons) are available for displaying information about function modules:

- *Interface.* Displays the following pages (as tabstrip options)
  - *Administrative* information about the function module such as function group, application area, development class, process type, RFC calls, and so on
  - Information on interface *import* parameters defined for a function module

  - Information on interface *export* parameters defined for a function module
  - Information on interface *change* parameters defined for a function module
  - Information on interface *export* parameters defined for a function module
  - Information on interface *tables*
  - Information on interface *export* parameters defined for a function module
  - Information on interface *exceptions*
  - Function module and parameter *documentation*
- *Source code.* Presents the content of the include object L<functgrp> Unn corresponding to the function module being displayed
- *Global data.* Displays the include object SAPL<functgrp>TOP
- *Main program.* Displays the content of the main program belonging to the function group to which the function module belongs

Searching for a Specific Function Module. To search whether the function builder already has a function which might be useful for your current needs, you can select *Utilities* → *Find* from the function builder initial screen. The system will present the initial screen for the information system corresponding to the function modules. This screen shows a collection of selection fields in which you may enter some information to filter the search.

Alternatively, you can click on the possible entries list arrow next to the *Function module* input field. The system will directly show the input help personal value list. Clicking on the *Information system* push button, you are presented with the same screen as if you had selected the *Utilities* → *Find* function.

Creating a Function Group. If you need to create a new function group to which you want to assign new function modules, from the initial function builder screen, select *Goto* → *Function groups* → *Create group.* The system displays a screen where you can enter the code for the function group and a short description identifying it. By clicking on the *Save* icon the system will automatically generate the main program SAPL<functgrp> and the includes L<functgrp>TOP and L<functgrp>UXX.

Creating a Function Module. To create a function module, you must complete several steps.

First, enter the name of the function module to be created in the function builder initial screen and click on the *Create* button.

The system displays a dialog box where you enter the function group to which you want to assign the function module. In the *Administration* page of the *Create function module* screen, enter the following fields:

- *Application.* Allows you to relate the function module with a specific application area
- *Short text.* Brief description of the function module
- *Copy from.* Name of a function module (from a different function group) from which you want to copy: its ABAP source code, the interface definition, and the documentation
- *Process type.* Indicates how this function module can be executed: with normal calls, with remote function calls (RFC), or in an *in update task* process

By clicking on the *Save* icon, the system will automatically edit the L<functgrp>UXX include and add a new include (L<functgrp>Unn) which corresponds to the function module and where *nn* is a sequential number corresponding to the order of creation of the function module within the function group: the first one will be 00, the second 01, and so on.

Figure 7-30 shows an example of the administration screen for creating function modules, after the entered information has been saved.

Establishing the Interface. To define a function module interface, you must define the formal import, export, and changing parameters as well as communicate the exceptions which might return the function module. To do this, you have five different tabstrips folders in the Create Function module screen (Import/Export/Changing/Tables/Exceptions) for each interface element.

For every interface element, you can define the following fields:

Interface Element	Fields	Description
Import	▪ Import parameters	Name of formal import parameters
	▪ Reference field/structure	Name of data dictionary field defining the former parameter
	▪ Reference type	Internal ABAP type
	▪ Proposal	Parameter default value

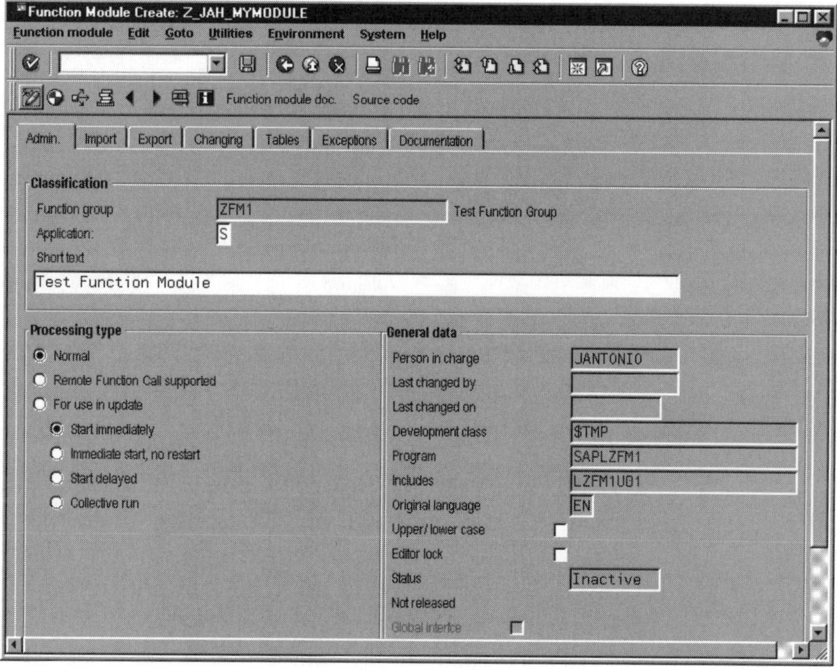

Figure 7-30 Creating a function module.

Interface Element	Fields	Description
	▪ Optional	Indicates whether a parameter is mandatory
	▪ Reference	By reference/by value
Export	▪ Export parameters	Name of formal export parameters
	▪ Reference field/structure	Name of data dictionary field defining the former parameter
	▪ Reference type	Internal ABAP type
	▪ Reference	By reference/by value
Changing	▪ Changing parameters	Name of formal changing parameters
	▪ Reference field/structure	Name of data dictionary field defining the former parameter
	▪ Reference type	Internal ABAP type
	▪ Proposal	Parameter default value
	▪ Optional	Indicates whether a parameter is mandatory

Interface Element	Fields	Description
	▪ Reference	By reference/by value
Tables	▪ Table parameters	Name of formal table parameters
	▪ Reference structure	Name of data dictionary field defining the former parameter
	▪ Reference type	Internal ABAP type
	▪ Optional	Indicates whether a parameter is mandatory
Exceptions	▪ Exception	Name of exception

Editing the ABAP Source Code. When modifying a function module code, you can have two different types of changes: *Global data* or *Main program.* According to the change type, users must check the corresponding radio button on the function builder initial screen and click on the *Change* button.

In each case, the system displays the usual ABAP editor screen with the corresponding program codes and with the name *L<functgrp>Unn* for a main program or *L<functgrp>TOP* for global data.

Checking and Activating

As with all other development environment objects, functions can also be checked and activated. To check and activate function modules, select the following options:

- *Function module → Check*
- *Function module → Activate*

If the system finds any inconsistencies, it will display an error message.

Testing and Performance

The function builder provides extensive functionality for verifying the correctness of functional modules before these are released or before they are called by other programs. To run a test:

- Enter the function name in the input field of initial function builder screen and press the *Test* or *Sgnl. Test* button.
- The system displays the Test Function Module initial screens, including the import and changing fields defined for the function module. Before clicking on the *Execute* button, you must enter appropriate values for performing the test. If you want the test execution to be run in debugging mode, you must press the *Debugging* button. Figure 7-31 shows an example of the Test Function Module initial screen.
- The system shows a new screen with the value of the import, export, and changing parameters, as well as the resulting exceptions and information about the runtime.

The function builder can be used also for storing test executions so that they can be compared later with other runs. To do this, proceed as follows:

- When in a screen with test results, press the *Save* icon, and enter a short text description for the test in the input field of the dialog window.
- From the initial Test Module Function screen, you can access the saved tests by selecting *Test Data Directory.* This option takes you to the *Test Data Directory* screen, where the system displays the stored test execution for that function module.

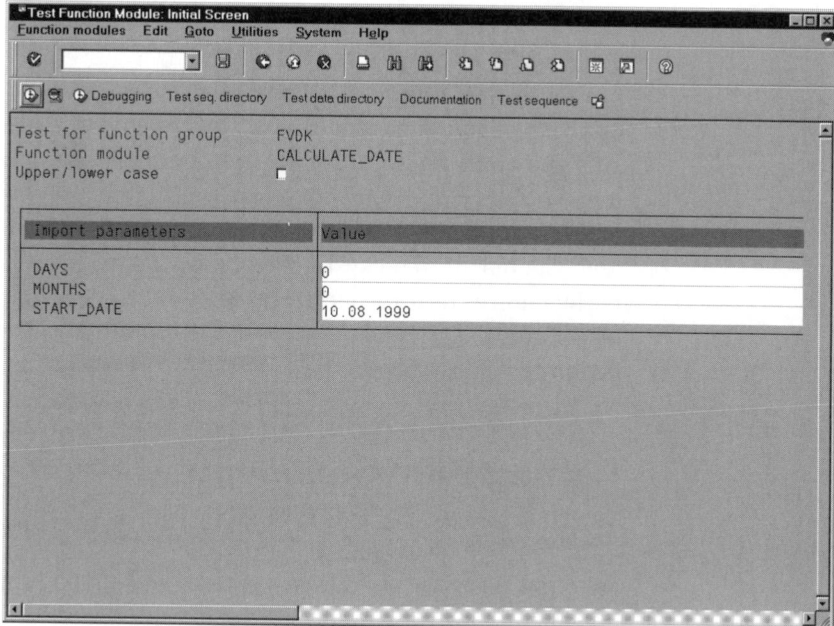

Figure 7-31 Test function module initial screen.

The system provides several alternatives for using the previous test results:

- To get the test data entered on a test, press *Get test data.*
- To display the test results, press *Show test results.*
- To repeat an execution with stored data and compare results, press *Regression test.*
- To execute with data from different tests and compare differences in results, press *Complete test.*

Additionally, if you want to store function module execution sequences (the same test with different sets of test data or different function modules), follow this procedure:

- Once in the initial Test Function Module screen, and before executing the test, press *Test sequence* or select the menu option *Goto → Test sequence.*
- Perform regular test execution (if you want to change function module, select the option *Function modules → Other func. Module* and enter the name of the function module). To finish the test sequence, select the menu option *Edit → New sequence.*

The management and control of the test sequence can be performed from the initial Test Function Module as a unit (by pressing *Test seq. Directory*) or for every execution of the sequence (by pressing *Test data directory*).

Finally, the function builder can also be used for performing runtime analysis of function modules. To do this, users only have to activate the runtime analysis from the function builder initial screen by selecting the menu option *Environment → Test environment → Runtime analysis.* Then users enter the import/changing parameter data and press the *Runtime analysis* button. The system executes the function module and stores the performance data in performance files that are used by the ABAP runtime analysis (transaction code SE30), and takes users to the SE37 transaction for analyzing the information.

Calling Function Modules Remotely with Remote Function Call (RFC)

For SAP R/3 systems to perform the role of RFC function server, two requirements must be met:

1. The offered functions (function modules) must be defined for allowing RFC calls. This is achieved by setting the *Remote Function Call supported* radio button in the Administration tabstrip of the function module.
2. External client programs must call the corresponding function module using the RFC APIs.

For these requirements, the function builder includes some tools to help to create external programs (RFC clients or servers). From the function module import/export screens (in change mode), select *Utilities→ RFCinterfase→ Generate* to obtain C and Visual Basic template programs for programming RFC clients or servers.

The SQL Trace Tool

The SQL trace is a tool that allows you to display and analyze the contents of the database calls that are made by the reports and transactions written in ABAP. Using this facility, you can:

- Display for every ABAP OPEN SQL instruction which SQL embedded (DECLARE, PREPARE, OPEN, FETCH) statements have been executed
- Analyze the consequences for the system performance—for example, which values the system uses for specific database accesses and changes
- Identify unnecessary accesses to the database and where the COMMITs are performed

Creating a SQL Trace

To create a SQL trace, perform the following steps:

- From any R/3 screen, select the menu option *System → Utilities → SQL trace.* Alternatively, enter transaction ST05 in the command field. Figure 7-32 shows this initial screen.
- Set the SQL Trace check box, enter the file path and filename in which to keep the trace log, and click the *Trace on* button.

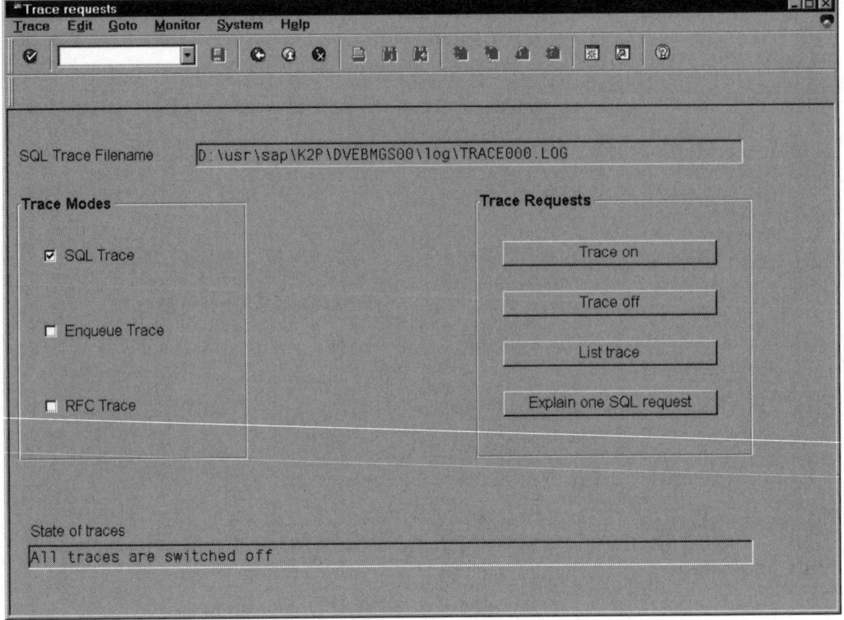

Figure 7-32 Main screen for the SQL trace tool.

- Enter the username for the user under whose privileges the program to be traced is going to be executed. The field status of trace will then be *turned on.*
- Execute the program or transaction you want to trace.
- Return to the SQL trace initial screen (ST05) and press the *Trace off* button.

Analyzing a SQL Trace

To display a previously created SQL trace, perform the following steps:

- From any screen, call the *System → Utilities → SQL trace* menu and click the *List trace* push button. The system will request:
  - *SQL trace filename.* Where the trace was recorded
  - *Trace mode.* Trace to show (SQL, Enqueue, or RFC trace)
  - *Username.* Username under which the trace was created
  - *Period.* Period of time to analyze
  - *Duration.* Operation time to consider during analysis
  - *Operation.* SQL operation to analyze

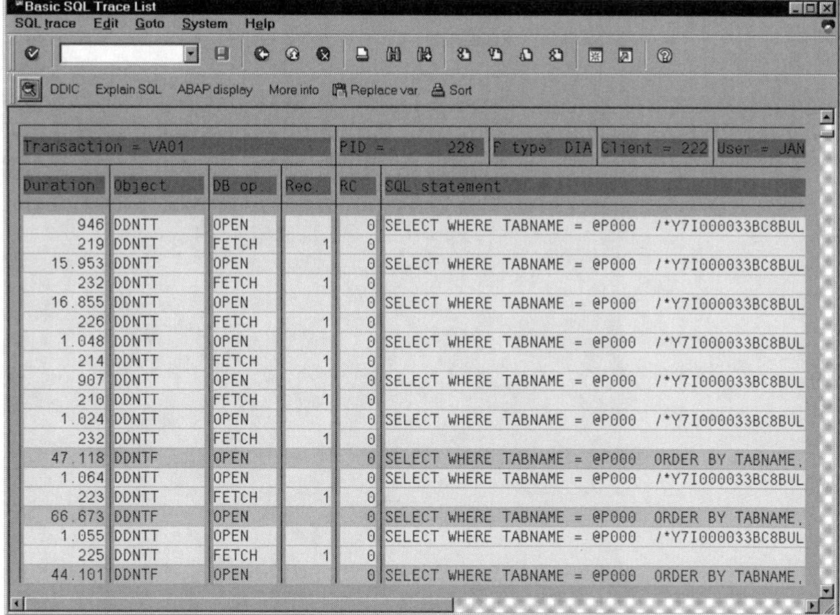

Figure 7-33
Listing the database request for SQL traces.

Then click on the *OK* button. Figure 7-33 shows the resulting screen with the database request lists.

The system will present a listing with all the database calls, indicating when the calls were made, the program, the table accessed, as well as the embedded SQL call operations.

To know which ABAP statement was the source for the SQL operation, position the cursor in the program field and click on the *ABAP Display* button.

To display the dictionary definition information about the accessed table, position the cursor over the *Table* field and click on the *DDIC info* button.

The system also includes a utility for providing detailed information about the SQL operation strategy followed by the underlying database system. To display that information, position the cursor over the line to analyze and click the *Explain SQL* button. Figure 7-34 shows an example.

The system displays the execution plan for SQL statements. Here, you can display the actual SQL statements and discover whether the access is being performed using indexes or is just sequential. This can be quite useful for long-running transactions, especially when database accesses are concerned.

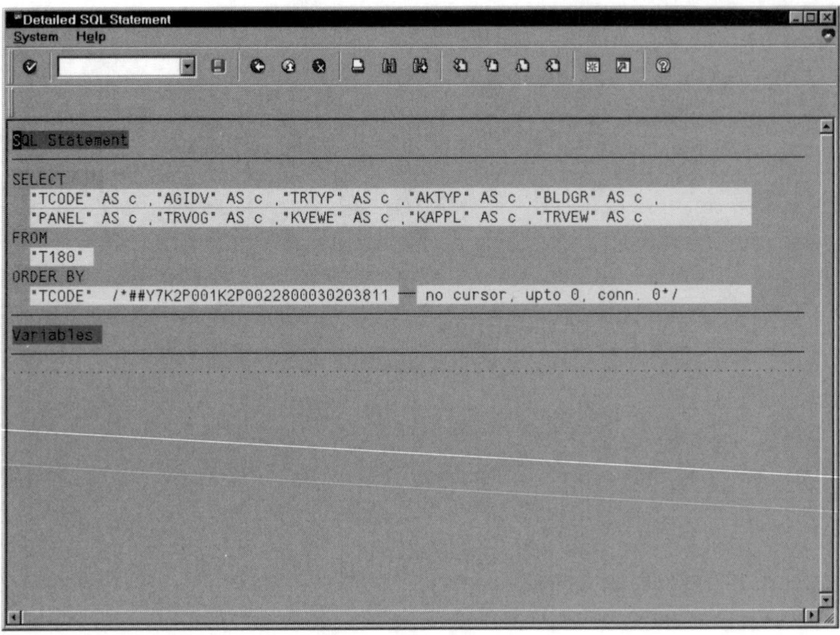

Figure 7-34 Analyzing SQL statements.

Runtime Analysis

The *runtime analysis* is an ABAP workbench tool which is quite useful for analyzing the performance of an ABAP program or transaction. With this tool, the system can display information about the following:

- Execution time
- Executed instructions and the hierarchy ordered by execution time or by instruction category
- Accessed tables and types of access
- Chronological execution flow

This tool can be useful for identifying:

- Which parts of programs have intensive CPU load
- Whether parts of programs are or not correctly structured
- The quantity and type of database access

Creating a Performance Data File (Runtime Analysis)

There are several access points for creating a performance data file used in the runtime analysis tool:

- From the ABAP workbench initial screen, select *Test → Runtime analysis.*
- From the ABAP source code editor, select *Utilities → More utilities → Runtime analysis.*
- From the ABAP editor initial screen, select *Program → Execute → Runtime analysis.*
- From any R/3 screen, select *System → Utilities → Runtime analysis → Execute.*
- Enter transaction code SE30 in the command field.
- From the repository browser, select a program or transaction and then select *Development object → Test/Execute.* When a dialog box appears, select *Runtime analysis* and click *Continue.*

Figure 7-35 shows the initial screen for the runtime analysis. To execute a runtime analysis, perform the following steps in the initial ABAP runtime analysis screen:

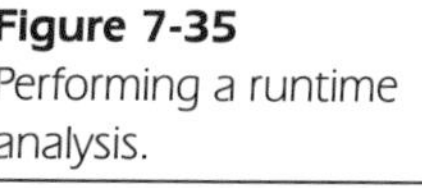

Figure 7-35 Performing a runtime analysis.

- Select the object you want to analyze by clicking on the corresponding radio button *Transaction / Program / Function module.*
- Enter the name of the object to be analyzed in the field next to the radio button.
- Select the options and restrictions for the analysis. (See the following table.)
- Click on the *Measure runtime* icon or *Runtime analysis → Execute.* The system will execute the selected object (program/transaction/function module) and will generate a trace file (performance data file) that can then be analyzed when the execution of the object has finished.

Options	Description
With subroutines	Indicates whether or not the PERFORMs are included in the analysis. By default, they are included. If they are not included, the runtime of each PERFORM is assigned to the program that makes the call.
With internal tables	Includes in the detailed analysis the instructions related to internal tables (COLLECT, APPEND, etc.).
With technical DB info	Logs technical information about the database operations. This option takes a lot of resource consumption, so it is not advisable except for in very specialized situations.
With memory management	Logs the memory management information for the work processes.
Function module	Only logs the calls to a single function module.
Particular units	Only logs the activity of a part of the program. These parts can be defined: ▪ Statically: the instructions SET RUN TIME ANALYZER ON and SET RUN TIME ANALYZER OFF are included to mark the area to be analyzed. ▪ Dynamically: in this case, the beginning and end of the analysis are defined by running, at the required moment, the option *System → Utilities → Runtime analysis → Switch on* or *System → Utilities → Runtime analysis → Switch off.*
All	Keeps a log of all the activity of the program.

The performance data files are created at the operating system level in the instance data directory. These files might occupy a lot of storage space, so be sure to remove files which are no longer needed.

Analyzing a Performance Data File

On the initial ABAP runtime analysis screen, select the *Runtime Analysis → Other perf. File* menu option or just click on the *Perform. Files* push button. The system will display a dialog box for selecting the user or object from which to select the trace corresponding to the performance data file.

According to the previous selection, the system displays a list of the existing trace files. Select a file clicking in the check box next to it, then click on the *Analyze* button.

The system then displays the *Overview Runtime Analysis Evaluation* screen including a bar chart with the total execution times and the statistics for the execution of some of the program actions. Figure 7-36 shows an example.

By clicking on the available buttons, you can analyze several types of information. The following is a summary of these functions.

Button	*Displayed Information*
Hit list	Displays a list with the most "system-expensive" instructions ordered by execution time. The list includes the program,

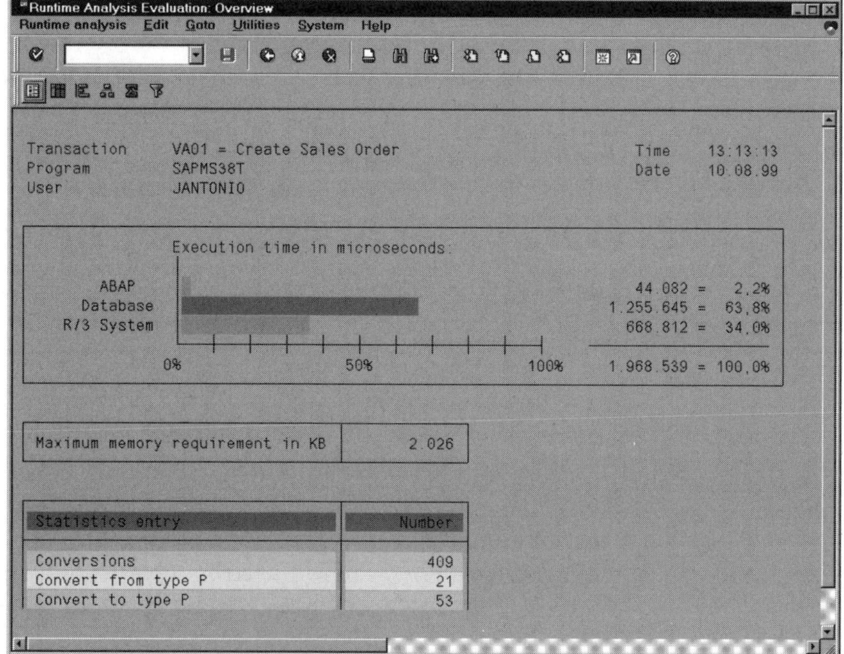

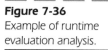

Figure 7-36
Example of runtime evaluation analysis.

number of executions, and type of instructions (ABAP, database, or R/3 system).

Tables Displays the most important tables, the number of accesses, and the time needed for the accesses. It also indicates whether the table is included in any of the buffers.

Group hit list Displays a list with the performed instructions classified by instruction type: PERFORM, MODULE, CALL FUNCTION, and so on.

Call Hierarchy Presents a chronological listing with the flow of calls during the execution of a program or transaction.

For a correct understanding of the output of the runtime analysis, it is important to know the difference between the terms *Gross time* and *Net time:*

- *Gross time:* the total time including the times of all the subcomponents (MODULE, PERFORM, CALL FUNCTION, CALL SCREEN, CALL TRANSACTION, CALL DIALOG, SUBMIT)
- *Net time:* the gross time minus the times of the subcomponents.

It is possible to reduce the number of call types that the runtime analysis presents in the output listings by using a filter. This filter can be activated from the initial runtime analysis screen selecting the menu option *Edit → Display filter* or by clicking on the *Display filter* icon.

Overview of the Workbench Debugging Tools

The *ABAP debugger* is the workbench tool which allows you to stop a program during its execution when a particular condition is met. When the program is stopped, you can use the debugger to display the contents of the tables and variables being used by the program. It also allows you to execute the program step-by-step, reviewing exactly the real flow of the program execution.

When developing, you can use *Breakpoints* and *Watchpoints,* which are elements that establish when to stop a particular program.

Starting the ABAP Debugger

There are many occasions during normal system operation during which the ABAP debugger can be started. When testing or executing programs, the ABAP debugger is automatically started when the system is running a program and finds a breakpoint.

A debugging session can also be started in programs which do not have *Breakpoints* or *Watchpoints* using one of the following methods:

- By positioning the cursor in a report or transaction within the repository browser object list, clicking the *Test/execute* icon, and selecting the *Debugging* mode
- From the ABAP editor, by executing a program choosing *Program* → *Execute* → *Debugging* from the menu
- From any R/3 screen, by selecting the menu option *System* → *Utilities* → *Debug ABAP*

Figure 7-37 shows an example of the debugging screen.

If the program to debug is a system program, to activate debugging you have to select *System* → *Utilities* → *Debug System.* Execute the system

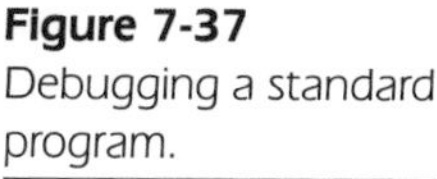

Figure 7-37
Debugging a standard program.

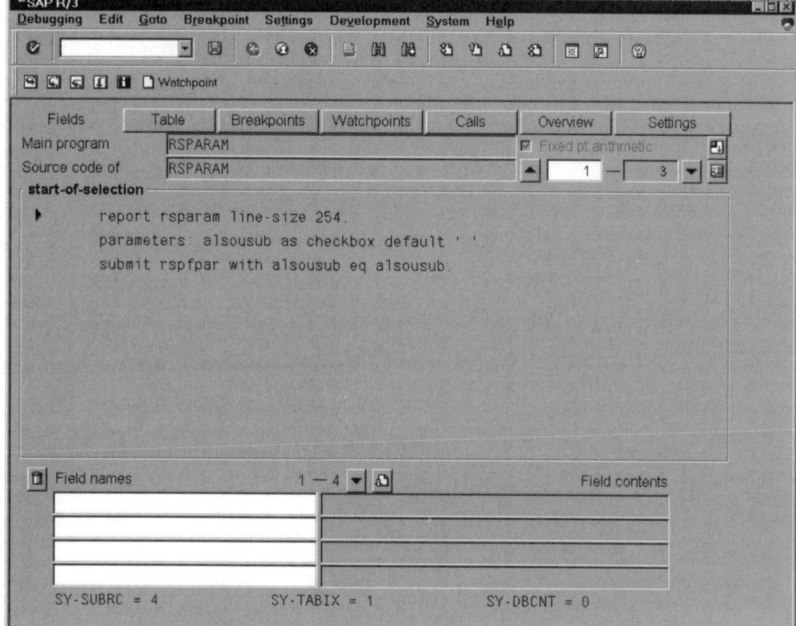

program, and when the debugging session is finished, you have to stop it using *Debugging* → *Debugging off* from the debugging session itself.

Elements of the ABAP Debugger

The ABAP debugger shows the program information using 10 different views that you can directly select from the initial ABAP debugger screen by clicking on the corresponding button or selecting the corresponding menu options from the *Goto* menu. The following table shows a summary of these views. From any view, users can always expand the program area by clicking on the *Expand* icon and can compress the program area with the *Compress* icon (top right side of screen).

View Type	*Information Displayed*
Overview	Presents the program structure—events, subroutines, and modules—indicating which is currently being processed
Call stack	Displays the calling sequence within a particular event, up to the current breakpoint
Fields	The default view that can display the content of up to eight fields
Breakpoints	Displays up to 30 breakpoints
Watchpoints	Displays up to 5 watchpoints and the field contents of the last watchpoints reached
Table	Allows for displaying and modifying the contents of an internal table
Settings	Displays and maintains the current debugger settings
Active programs	Displays all programs needed for program debugging, including system programs
Single field	Displays the contents and technical attributes of a field
Structured field	Displays the contents and technical attributes of a structured field field
Object	Displays the structure of an ABAP object

Breakpoints

A *breakpoint* is a signal within a program that, at runtime, tells the ABAP processor to stop the program execution and to start the ABAP debugger.

The following list shows the breakpoint types.

Type	*Description*
static	Are set up with the BREAKPOINT keyword inside the program, which you can directly display with the ABAP source code editor.
	Are normally used as user-independent breakpoints.
Dynamic	These breakpoints are not visible within the program code.
	Are user-dependent breakpoints.
Watchpoints	Are field-specific breakpoints.
	The program is stopped when the field reaches the values established in the watchpoint.
	Are user-dependent breakpoints.
Keyword/event	These are keyword- or event name–specific breakpoints.
	The program stops just before executing a specific event or keyword statement.
	Are user-dependent breakpoints.

Setting Breakpoints. The following list shows the necessary steps for setting breakpoints.

Breakpoint Type	*Set From*	*Needed Steps*
static	ABAP editor	▪ Enter the keyword BREAKPOINT
dynamic	ABAP editor	▪ Position the cursor over the source code line to have the breakpoint
		▪ Select *Utilities* → *Breakpoint* → *Set* from the menu
		▪ To display the breakpoints: from the menu, select *Utilities* → *Breakpoint* → *Display*
		▪ From the breakpoints list, you can delete them or navigate with them
	ABAP debugger	▪ Execute a program in debugging mode
		▪ Position the cursor over the source code line to have the breakpoint

		• Double click or select the function *Breakpoint → Set / delete*
Watchpoints	ABAP debugger	• Execute a program in debugging mode • Position the cursor over the needed field in the source code • Click the *create watchpoint* button in the application toolbar to get the watchpoint dialog screen • Select the checkbox local watchpoint (if only for the main program) and, for conditional *watchpoints,* enter the value or field to compare in *comp. Field/value* • Click on the *Enter* button • To display the active watchpoints, select *Goto → Watchpoints;* you can then delete *Watchpoints* by clicking the *Delete* icon next to the *Watchpoints*
Key word/ event	ABAP debugger	• From the initial ABAP debugger screen, select *Breakpoint→Breakpoint at→At statement* *Breakpoint→Breakpoint at→function module* *Breakpoint→Breakpoint at→event/subroutine* *Breakpoint→Breakpoint at→System exception* • Enter the keyword name, event/subroutine name, or function module in which you want to set the breakpoint • Click on the *Enter* button • To display the active breakpoints, select *Goto → Breakpoints;* you can then delete *breakpoints* by clicking the *Delete* icon next to the *Breakpoints*

Navigating Through Program Code

During a debugging session, you can navigate through the program and the breakpoints controlling the flow of the program by selecting the available functions included in the ABAP debugger in the form of icons located in the application toolbar. The following list summarizes those functions and buttons:

Single step. Executes a single program instruction, even when the flow is transferred to subroutines

Execute. Similar to *Single step,* but when the program instruction is a call to a subroutine, it executes the whole subroutine and stops in the following line of code

Continue. Executes the program until it's finished or until it finds the next active breakpoint or watchpoint.

Return. Allows for executing the program instructions up to the end of a routine and stops in the line of code where the routine gives the control back to the main program. It is commonly used within routines to exit from them without a step-to-step execution.

Debugger Settings

For different reasons, during the debugging process the flow of the program could leave the debugger's control. The ABAP debugger includes some facilities for defining the behavior of the debugging process in these situations. Following is a list with the available options:

System debugging — Used for allowing the debug process for system programs (type S).

To enable or disable this option, users must select *settings → System debugging.*

Memory monitoring — Monitors whether the session roll area has been modified.

To enable or disable this option, users must select *settings → Memory monitoring.*

Update debugging — Can be used for performing the update function modules within the work process where the debugging is running.

To enable or disable this option, users must select *settings → Update debug. On/off.*

Warnings	Can be used for defining the system behavior when encountering warnings. To enable or disable this option, users must select *settings → warnings on/off* and *settings → cancel on warning.*
In background task: Lock release	Can be used for debugging modules that are executed in the background, but are called from the program being debugged. To enable this option, users must select the check box *In background task: Lock release* within the setting view.

All these options can be displayed and modified in the ABAP debugger setting view.

Displaying and Modifying Field Values

Every time the program is stopped in a program instruction within a debugging session you can display and modify the contents of tables and fields.

Users can display the contents for the following fields:

- System fields
- Program fields
- ABAP dictionary fields (when defined in the program with the TABLES keyword)
- External program fields

In order to do this, in the fields view screen of the debugger, enter the name of the field do be displayed. The system automatically displays the content. Figure 7-38 shows an example of field view within the debugger.

In the case of external programs, you must enter the program name within brackets preceding the field name.

To modify fields values during a debugging session you have to

- Double click on the field to display or change within the code part of the ABAP debugging screen. This will take you to the tables debugging view.

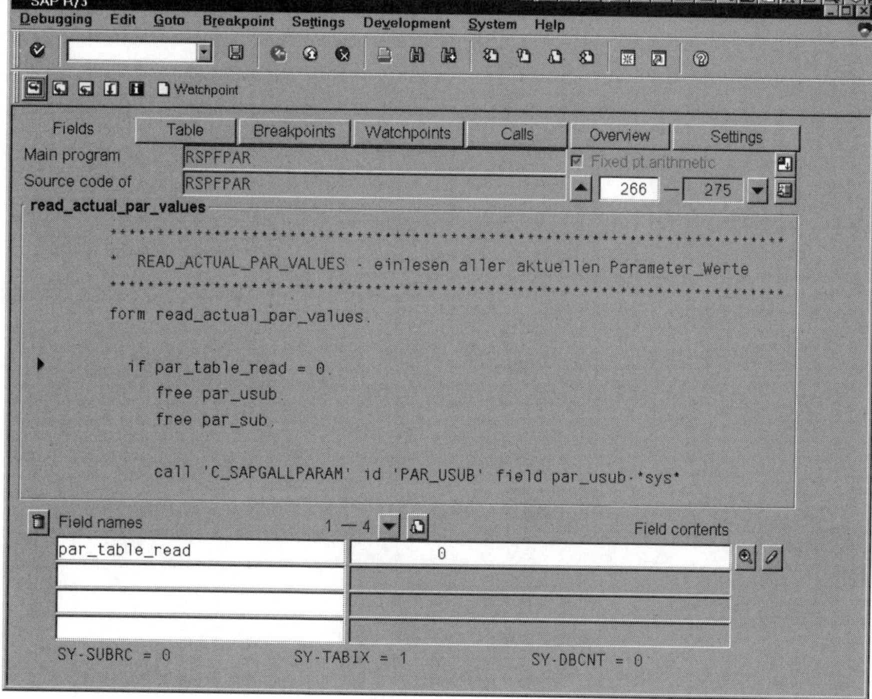

Figure 7-38 Showing a field's contents within the debugger.

- Once in the tables view, enter the new value in the column next to that field and click the *pencil* icon. This action is recorded in the system log.

Displaying and Managing Internal Tables

Upon clicking on the *Table* button from the initial ABAP debugger screen, the system will display the table debugging view. On this screen, you can see the *Internal table* input field, where you have to enter the name of the table to be displayed.

The system will display the input field *Column Header* where it shows the table field names. Under each field, the system displays the corresponding values. If you want to display another table field, or display with a different order, you only have to edit the *Column Header* input field with the required fields and with the order you wish to be displayed.

Within the screen for displaying tables, there are four push buttons available that are meant to provide the following functions:

Push Button	Function	Steps
Delete	*Deleting row*	▪ Position the cursor over the line to be deleted. ▪ Press the *Delete* button.
Change	*Editing row*	▪ Position the cursor over the line and field to be modified. ▪ Press the *Change* button. ▪ Enter the new value in the input field. ▪ Press *Enter.*
Append	*Append row*	▪ Click the *Append* button. ▪ Enter the new value in the input field for the first field of the row. ▪ Press *Enter.* ▪ Enter the fields contents in the newly inserted line, following the same procedure as for editing a row.
Insert	*Inserting row*	▪ Position the cursor over the line where you want to insert a new line. ▪ Click the *Insert* button. ▪ Enter the new value in the input field for the first field of the row. ▪ Press *Enter.* ▪ Enter the fields contents in the newly inserted line, following the same procedure as for editing a row.

Debugging and Database

When performing a debugging process for a program accessing the database, some consideration must be given since some data could be blocked for long periods of time. The ABAP debugger includes a function that can be used for releasing (unlocking) the database by selecting the option *Debugging→ Database→ Commit (unlock).*

If you want to undo all modifications performed to the database since the last COMMIT, then you must use the option *Debugging→ Database→ Rollback.* Although there are occasions where debugging has to be done on productive systems, it is recommended to perform debugging in either the development or test environments.

Introduction to the ABAP Programming Language Features

ABAP stands for *Advanced Business Application Programming.* Before release 4.0 of R/3, the language was known as ABAP/4 (the 4 meant it was a fourth-generation language). With release 4.0B the name was changed to simply ABAP because, although the language maintains most of the best fourth-generation language features and previous syntax and keywords, many object-oriented features have been incorporated in a move to make it a fully capable object-oriented language. It is the programming language that SAP has used to develop all the R/3 business modules and applications, including the system management functions. It is available to customers and developers to extend SAP functionality for their particular needs.

ABAP programs are created and maintained using the workbench tools discussed in previous sections.

Because of its origin and evolution, ABAP retains many of the fourth-generation language features such as:

- It is based on structured programming methodologies, allowing modular programming and reutilization of code.
- It resembles natural English language, making ABAP programs easy to read and understand.
- It's an interpretative language, not compiled. This nature facilitates testing and running earlier versions of programs without the need for constant compilation.
- It can be used both from single report list programming (*report programs*) to complex transaction processing (*dialog programs*).
- It's an event-driven language.
- It's completely integrated with the rest of the workbench tools, such as the screen painter, the menu painter, dictionary, and so on.

- Supports multilanguage text elements. This means that you can create text elements in several languages without modifying the program source code.
- Similar to many programming languages, it includes elements for
  - Variable and data type declarations
  - Flow control elements
  - Operational elements
  - Event elements
  - Functions and subroutines, which can be managed by a central library
- Contains a subset of standard SQL statements enabling transparent database table access independently of the underlying database system being used.
- Provides extensive functions for handling and operating with data types such as dates, strings, floating point numbers, and so on.

The ABAP object-oriented features started together with SAP's strategic and technological move toward working with *business objects* and the introduction of *Business Application Program Interfaces* (BAPIs) within the Business Framework architecture. The *business objects* are included within the ABAP workbench in the *business object repository* (*BOR*).

As an object-oriented language, the new ABAP, from release 4.x onward, incorporates technology principles such as *inheritance, encapsulations,* and *polymorphism* to provide the language with advantages such as lower maintenance costs and greater ease in reusing code.

Basic concepts and features of the ABAP object-oriented programming language are the same as those of other object-oriented languages. The most important are:

- A *business object,* or simply an *object,* represents a type of entity—a customer, a business unit, an account, and so on—containing all its properties. Every object has an *identity* that allows it to be distinguished from other objects.
- *Object classes,* or simply *classes,* specify the structure of the objects belonging to a given class and the definition of the interfaces. Classes are useful for grouping objects with the same structure (attributes, methods, events). Generally, objects are defined using classes. The term *instance* is used for a specific object belonging to a class.
- The object's *attributes* provide the object with its characteristics, describing the current object state.

- *Methods* are the actions that can be performed with the object, indicating the behavior of the object.
- *Events* are used so that the object can inform or be informed of any event or state change on the system to enable the system to react to those events.
- *Interfaces* are another very important feature of objects. They define the method in which objects can be used independently of their internal implementation.

CHAPTER 8

ABAP Data Dictionary

The ABAP dictionary is the central workbench repository utility providing the data definitions and the information relationships that are later used in all the business applications within R/3.

This chapter deals with those aspects of the ABAP dictionary which are most useful and can have more interest for system administrators and developers. In any case, in order to fully exploit the possibilities within the ABAP dictionary, users must understand such topics as

- What is a data dictionary, and what is it used for?
- What is a relational model?
- What is the data dictionary in the SAP R/3 environment?
- What objects does the ABAP dictionary handle, and how are objects defined?
- How does the dictionary treat versions?

The ABAP dictionary can be seen as a logical representation or a superior layer over the physical underlying database. As has been previously mentioned, the supported database engines must comply with the relational data model. This model is strictly followed by the ABAP dictionary, and therefore it is important to know the basic concepts of relational databases: what functionality they provide, how they establish the relations between the different objects and elements, and what operations can be performed on the objects.

Once the concepts of the relational data model are clear, those general terms should be projected over the topic of interest in this chapter: how the relational theory fits with the ABAP dictionary.

Definition of Data Dictionary

A *data dictionary* in computing terms is the source of information in which the system data is defined in a logical way. The data dictionary is the centralized and structured source of information for business applications.

The data dictionary is the core of a well-structured development environment. Around a data dictionary, you can assemble other components of a development environment as a programming language, of context-sensitive editors (CASE type), screen painters and handlers, and so forth.

The elements that make up a dictionary are known as *metadata*. Metadata is the computing term for the data whose function is to describe other data. Actually, the data of the dictionary is not the operational data which tells a customer's address or an article price, but rather is a type of data whose function is to define the semantic or syntactic properties of the operational data, such as the type, length, and relationships.

Currently, the relational databases and the transactional systems in general, all have and all use a data dictionary as the system core.

An advantage of having a data dictionary is avoiding inconsistencies when defining data types that will later be used in different parts of an application; this avoids redundancies and considerably decreases the cost of maintenance.

When a type of data is defined in the dictionary, it is available to any program or function module in the application. A change in the definition of a type of data in the dictionary automatically affects any other data, module, function, or program which has data or variables defined using that modified data type. This can be quite useful when you want to modify all related data types, but at the same time and for the same reason, you must be extremely careful not to negatively affect other system parts (other types or programs) using those data types.

Utility of a Data Dictionary

The data dictionary allows the user to create, modify, or delete data definitions (data types). At the same time, it's a great source of information, not only for the development environment but also for the user—it is a fast and efficient way to answer questions such as which entries exist in a table of the database; what the structure of this table is; this view...; and what the relation between two different dictionary objects is.

The ABAP Dictionary in the R/3 Systems

The ABAP dictionary data is the core of the R/3 development system. It is the source of every definition within R/3, from the very basic domains to the company model. It is totally integrated with the other tools of the development environment.

The integration of the ABAP dictionary with the development workbench is an *active* integration. Activating any modification in the data definitions has an immediate effect in all related ABAP programs, function modules, menus, and screens.

Some of the main available functions in the ABAP dictionary are the following:

- Add, delete, modify, and, in general terms, manage the definitions of the dictionary data (activation, version handling, etc.).
- Preserve the data integrity.
- Be the central source of information. From the dictionary, you can get information about the defined relations between the system tables. It allows direct access to the data in the underlying database system. The dictionary tells whether a table is active, empty, or contains data, and so forth.
- Act as the central layer for software development. The ABAP dictionary is an active component of the SAP R/3 environment. Every created or modified element of the data dictionary (every definition) can simultaneously and automatically be used in every software component which includes that definition.
- The ABAP dictionary is integrated in the development environment and in the R/3 application environment using *call interfaces.* With those call interfaces, the programs can directly access the information stored in the dictionary. At the same time, all the development workbench tools can directly access the data dictionary for creating menu definitions, generating screens, reporting functions, and other activities which always have up-to-date data definition information. For example, when declaring a table inside an ABAP report, there is no need to declare the structure of the table—you only need to declare the name of the table itself. At program generation time, the system directly accesses the data dictionary to look for its structure and properties.
- The ABAP dictionary permits the documentation of the system data.
- Ensures that the data definitions are flexible and can be updated.

Because the R/3 system works in base to an interpretative method, instead of working with original objects, it actually works with internal representations of objects. With this type of operation the system performance is enhanced and has the advantage that the development tools, screen interpreters, database interface, and so forth always access the most current data.

When any of the data dictionary objects are used in other parts of the development workbench, for example, within a source code program or in a screen, the developers only have to enter a table name or position the corresponding field in the screen. The system automatically knows all the object properties and information and automatically creates and initializes all the work areas, symbol tables, and so on.

Entering one or more tables names with the ABAP TABLES keyword allows the system to automatically know, even in the program edition phase, the properties for the tables and fields making up those tables.

For example, if an ABAP report contains the declaration TABLES: TABNA, all information about this table, such as primary key, indexes, field names, and data types, which are all defined in the data dictionary, is retrieved when the program is generated. Any changes to the table do not require the source code for the program to be modified except when explicitly using field names which have been removed from the table structure. When the programs are called after a table structure change, they are automatically regenerated without user intervention, always making the most updated information available by retrieving it from the ABAP dictionary.

The Relational Data Model

A data model is an abstraction of a part of the real world which is represented using formal structures. A relational database basically uses one formal structure known as a table.

A *table* can be defined as a two-dimensional matrix made of rows and columns. It can also be described as a group of records of the same type. Figure 8-1 shows a very simple scheme of tables.

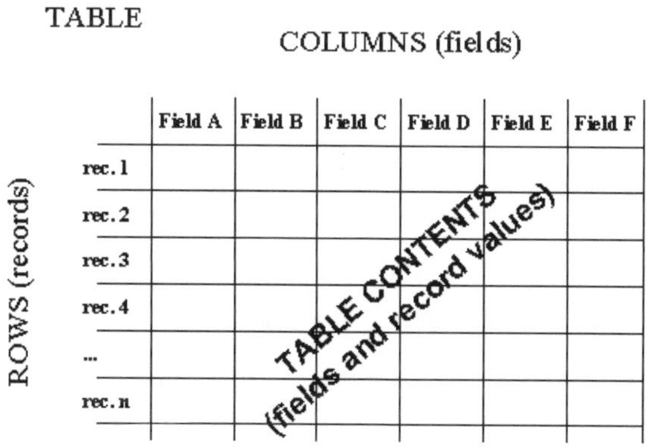

Figure 8-1 Row and column representation of a table.

TABLE

COLUMNS (fields)

ROWS (records)

	Field A	Field B	Field C	Field D	Field E	Field F
rec. 1						
rec. 2						
rec. 3						
rec. 4						
...						
rec. n						

TABLE CONTENTS (fields and record values)

Records are groups of fields based on existing data types. These data types are previously defined in the data dictionary. A table is a similar concept to a conventional indexed file; the difference is that in the relational model the main index is known as the *primary key,* which is made of one or more fields of the record. A record is also known as *tuple* or simply a *row.*

The most significant feature of the primary key is that it identifies univocally one and only one record of the table: a table does not permit records with duplicated primary keys.

However, contrary to the features of the ISAM (Indexed Sequential Access Method) files, the relational model defines relationships among the different tables depending on the system design being implemented.

To establish relationships between two different tables, it's necessary that one of the tables contains some information about the other; normally, that information corresponds to the field or fields that make up the primary key. These relationships between the fields in the source table with primary keys of another table are known as *foreign keys.* These types of relationships mean that somehow there is some redundancy in the relational data model, but the minimum possible. When defining relationships between keys, there are two important concepts to consider, which are further explained later in this chapter: the cardinality and the dependency factors.

To define the data model and the table relationships is not normally a role of the SAP data dictionary administrator, but of the analysts or designers of the functional model. The data dictionary administrator probably is involved in the physical definition of those tables and relationships in the dictionary. Therefore, the administrator of the ABAP dictionary must know how to work and manage the different dictionary objects. Functions such as creating tables, defining data elements and domains, creating indexes, and foreign keys, are common among the functions of a SAP DD administrator.

Concepts of the Relational Data Model

To have a good understanding of the relational data model, you should have a reasonable grasp of the following concepts:

- *Entity.* An *entity* is an object type which can be univocally identified and from which you wish to keep information. For example, in the university data model included for learning purposes in the R/3 system, each of the rows (records) of the UPROF table (university professors) represents an entity.

- *Entity type.* It's the set of entities with common attributes to which you assign a unique name and a unique description. Commonly, this is known as a table. In the SAP example, the UPROF table represents an entity type.
- *Attributes.* An attribute is the description of a characteristic of an entity or entity type. For example, in table UPERS (people at the university), the field *EUNA* (name of university member) represents an attribute for the entity type UPERS.
- *Relationship.* It's the relationship established between two entity types. In a common database language, the following is true:

Entity type:	Table
Entity:	Record (row)
Attribute:	Field
Relationship:	Relation between tables (using foreign keys and having a specific cardinality)

- *Foreign key.* Foreign keys define relationships between tables. One of the most important functions of foreign keys is to ensure data integrity in the relational data model. For example, suppose table T1 is a "persons table" (contains people's IDs and address fields, including the state or region), and table T2 is the "states table" (contains the state or region's ID, i.e., AL, CA, PA, and the state's name). The foreign key provides a relation or link between the two tables T1 and T2. This relation is made by having one or more fields in table T1 (in this case, the field could be *state ID*) pointing to the primary key of table T2.

  Table T1, persons table, which contains the foreign key is called a *foreign key table,* whereas table T2, the states table, is called a *check table.*
- *Cardinality.* Defines the relation type between two groups of data, that is, between two tables. The cardinality of a foreign key indicates how many dependent or referenced records a record in a check table can have. Cardinality is expressed in the form *N:M,* where possible values are:
  - *N* can be either 1 (one and only one dependent record) or *C* (zero or one dependent record).
  - *M* can be either 1 (one and only one), *C* (zero or one), *N* (at least one), *CN* (zero or more).

- *Dependency factor.* The *dependency factor* indicates whether the foreign key field in each record must contain a value and whether this value may be changed.

  If we are building a relationship between two tables, there will be a foreign key linking these two tables. Fields for foreign keys are included in the foreign key table in order to avoid ambiguous references. An example is: table UPROF (professors table) contains, as its primary key, the field *professor number.* Table UKURS (course table) contains courses and also lists professor numbers.

- *Cardinality types.*
  - 1:1 relationship. To one element of table *A* corresponds one and only one element of table *B.*
  - 1:C relationship. To one element of table *A* corresponds at most one element of table *B,* for instance, zero (0) or one element of table *B.*
  - 1:N relationship. To one element of table *A* corresponds at least one element of table *B,* for instance, one or more elements from table *B.*
  - 1:CN relationship. To one element of table *A* corresponds zero or one or more elements of table *B.* Figure 8-2 shows an example of the 1:CN relationship.

  In all the previous cases, table *B* represents the foreign key table, and table *A* represents the check table.

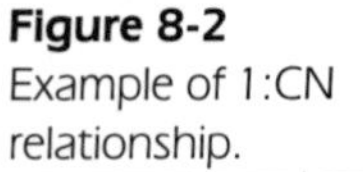

Figure 8-2 Example of 1:CN relationship.

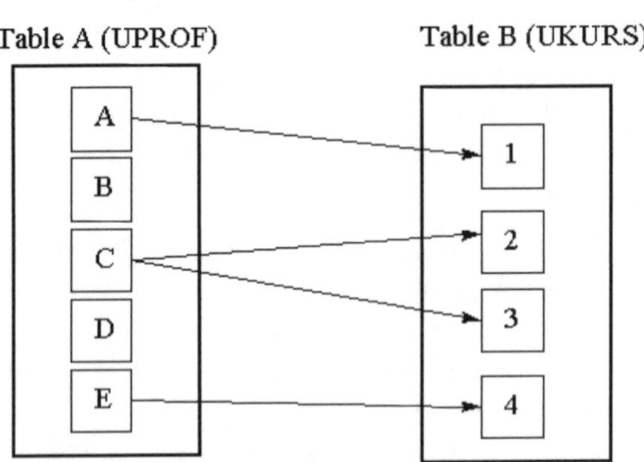

Relationship Types

In a relation mode, several types of relationships between the tables are possible.

- *Hierarchical relationship type.* In a hierarchical relation, an entity type (table) depends on the existence of previous (initial) entity types. The key of the initial entity type is inherited by the dependent entity type. Following the university example, the courses table (UKURS) is a dependent table on the faculties table (UFACH). The primary key from table UFACH is the faculty number (field *FABNR*) while the primary key from table UKURS is the combination of fields *FABNR* and *KRSNR* (course name).
- *Aggregating relationship type.* In an aggregating relationship, an entity type is produced by grouping two or more initial entities. The key of an aggregate table type is the combination of the keys from initial (previous or dependent) tables. In the university example included in R/3, the table of course results and participation, table UKRTB, is an aggregated type of table which is created using tables UFACH (faculty table), UKURS (courses table), and UPERS (people at university). From each of these tables, the new aggregated table, UKRTB, inherits its primary key: FABNR (faculty number), SEMNR (seminar number), and IMMNR (matriculation number).
- *Referential relationship type.* In a referential relationship, an entity type always refers to the initial entity type but is not identified by it. The key of the referenced entity types is not affected by this.
- *Conditional-referential relationship type.* This is similar to a referential relationship. However, the relationship link and therefore the referential aspect is application-dependent (conditionally) for the entity type: the relationship might not always exist. Figure 8-3 shows an example of this type of relationship.

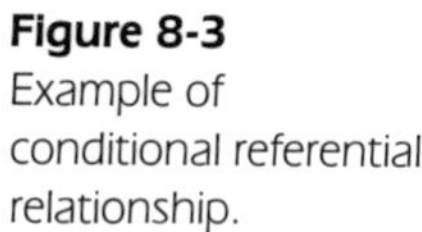

Figure 8-3 Example of conditional referential relationship.

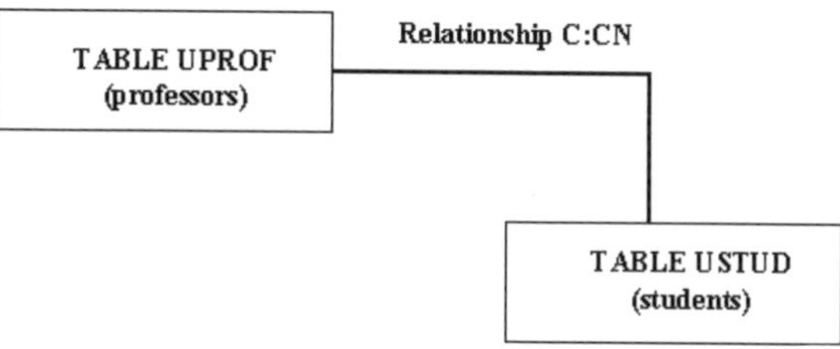

- *Specialization.* Specialization is a property of an entity type. Such an entity type represents a subset of one initial entity type, with the possibility of having additional attributes. The specializing entity type inherits the key of the initial entity type as a key attribute. Figure 8-4 shows an example where tables USTUD and UPROF are specializations of table UPERS.

  The relationship, as represented in the figure, means that there is one and only one element in the UPERS table for each element (record) from the USTUD table. One element from the UPERS table may or may not be referenced in table USTUD; but if it's there, it will be there only once. In other words, if all elements from the UPERS table were students, tables UPERS and USTUD are equivalent in the relationship, and then the cardinality would be 1:1.

Dependency Factors and Foreign Keys

The dependency factor indicates the degree to which a table depends on another check table. It specifies whether a foreign key field should have value and whether this value can be modified without removing the unique identity of the record.

The dependency factor defines the dependency levels from the point of view of the foreign key table.

In SAP R/3, the dependency factor concept is implemented using the *foreign key field type.* Using foreign key field type, you can specify whether the foreign key fields are identifying or partially identifying the foreign key table, that is, whether they contain key fields or key candidates.

The following is copied from SAP online documentation. (Copyright by SAP AG.)

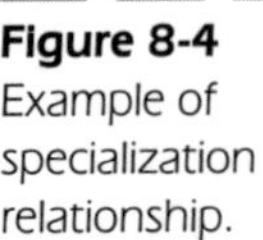

Figure 8-4 Example of specialization relationship.

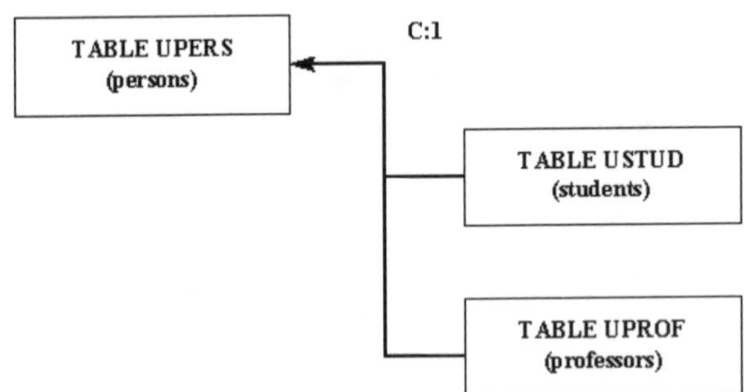

Possible foreign key types are:

- *Non-key-fields / candidates.* The foreign key fields are neither primary key fields of the check table nor do they uniquely identify each record of the check table (key candidates). The foreign key fields are thus not (partially) identifying for the foreign key table.
- *Key fields / candidates.* The foreign key fields are either primary key fields of the check table or else they uniquely identify each record of the check table (key candidates). The foreign key fields are thus (partially) identifying for the foreign key table.
- *Key fields of a text table.* The foreign key table is a text table for the check table. That is, with the exception of the language key field, the key of this table is the same as that of the check table. This is a special instance of the key fields/candidates type.

Entry of the semantic attributes for a foreign key relationship is optional. For this reason, the foreign key field type also provides the option not specified.

Relational Operations

To display, fetch, and manage information and relationships between tables in a relational database system, there are some relational operations available:

- *Join.* The join operator is used to mix several tables into a single one, in which the individual fields for the tables are related to one another by means of conditions. When there is a foreign key relationship among the tables, then the join condition is automatically generated from the foreign key specification.
- *Projection.* The projection operator is used to suppress fields in select or join operations. Or, inversely, only some specific fields are selected (projected).
- *Selection.* The selection operator is meant to suppress records in a select or join operation. That is, a selection operator imposes a filter or condition for the output or result of the operation, for example: SELECT * FROM MYTABLE WHERE MYTABLE-ID > “100” will only select those records from table MYTABLE where the field ID is greater than 100.

These three types of relational operators are meant for dealing with database views and can be combined to make complex operations and conditions.

Starting the ABAP Dictionary

To call the ABAP dictionary, from the main menu, select *Tools* → *ABAP Workbench* and then click on the *Dictionary* button. Alternatively, you can enter transaction code SE11 in the command field. Figure 8-5 shows the initial screen for the ABAP dictionary.

Once at this screen you can see a list of possible dictionary objects which you can select by clicking on the associated radio button. You also have to enter an object name in the input field next to *Object name.*

Below the standard menu, the system has an extensive set of functions which can be performed with the selected object. Not all possible options are discussed here, just the most important ones.

Data Dictionary Objects

As explained in previous theoretical sections, the data in a database are held on structures known as *tables.* The tables can be empty or can contain data, which are then disposed according to a structure type, better

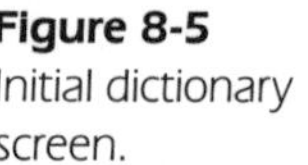

Figure 8-5 Initial dictionary screen.

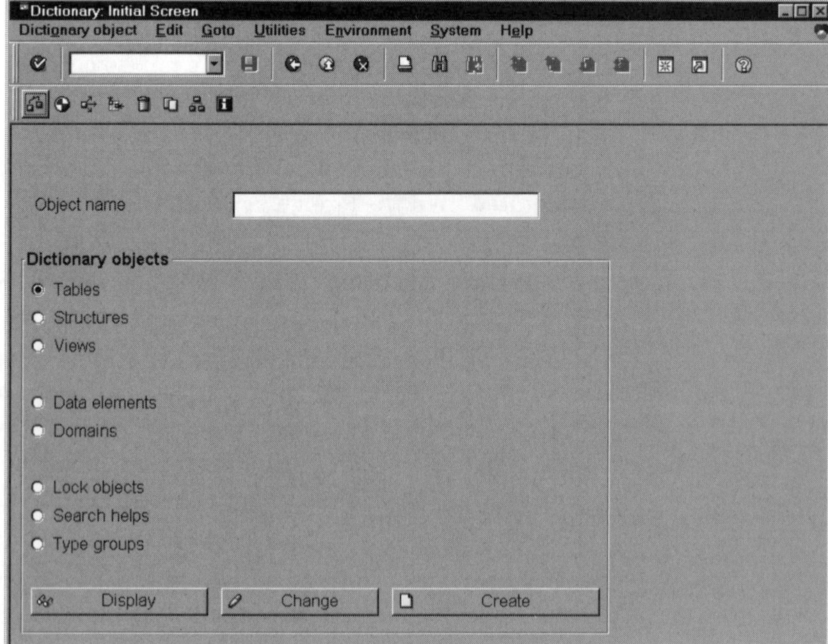

known as a *record*. At the same time, the record is made up of a set of fields, which are defined with corresponding attributes, such as data type, length, and so forth.

In common database naming conventions, a table corresponds to an entity type. A record (row) corresponds to the entity concept, whereas the field is an attribute. From now on, in practical terms, only the terms *table, rows,* and *fields* will be used. The relationship between two tables is known as a *relation*.

The attributes or characteristics of the fields which make up a row in a database table are based on standard type definitions which must exist in the data dictionary. A field only makes sense as a database object within a table. Out of the table context, a field does not exist for the data dictionary. However, the standard types for defining the types for fields are contained in the data as real objects, independently of whether the table exists or not.

Depending on whether this definition is a *semantic definition* or a purely *technical definition,* the ABAP dictionary distinguishes between two dictionary objects: *data elements* and *domains*. These objects are part of the dictionary *metadata*.

The ABAP dictionary can handle eight different object types (see Fig. 8-5):

- *Table.* As previously explained, a table is a two-dimensional data matrix. A table can contain zero or many rows, corresponding to the predefined table structure (entity type). This is, at the same time, a complex structure, which can be made up of one or several fields (attributes). Every row that makes up the database table has the same structure and properties. The fields that make up the structure of the table records, as well as its attributes, permitted value range, and so on, are set when defining the table.
- *Structures.* The object structure refers to the definition of a compound object that does not have any content. It's like a table or a view, but it never has entries: it's only a structure. These types of objects are used in programs for defining data structures or for defining data in the interfaces from the module pools and the screens. The basic difference between structures and tables (or views) is that the structure does not exist at the underlying database system level; however, both tables and views do exist in the database. Structures only exist as definitions in the dictionary. As a result, structures do not need to be activated.
- *Views.* From the relational database point of view, a view is a *virtual* table. It contains data which are really stored in other tables.

The contents for the views are dynamically generated when called from a program or a transaction. In the simplest form, the fields within a view all come from a single table, where you could select all of them or just a few (projections), or select some of the fields of the table according to specific criteria (selection) using the *Select* option. Other, more complex forms of views allow for selecting fields from different tables which are related by foreign keys (join operation). You can also use the three methods combined for creating a view: projection, selection, and join.

- *Data elements.* They are a semantic definition of the properties and type for a table field. It's an intermediate object between the object type *domain* and the table field. A field in R/3 is always associated with a data element, which at the same time is always related to a domain. Some properties of table fields in the SAP environment can only be defined at the data element level, for example, the text elements associated with the fields. As an example, suppose there is a table with the fields *manager_name* and *employee_name.* These fields could have the same technical description—they could be strings with 30 characters—char (30). They would be, however, different at the semantic level: the meaning is different, since they relate to names of people at different levels in company. This difference is only reflected with the text elements associated to the data elements, but it is also useful for the online help which can be associated with the fields.
- *Domains.* They are the formal definition of the data type from a technical and syntactical point of view. They set attributes including data type, length, possible value ranges, and so on.
- *Lock objects.* These types of object are used for locking and synchronizing the access to database records in tables. This mechanism is used to enforce data integrity, that is, two users cannot update the same data at the same time. The lock object definition includes the table or tables which can be concurrently accessed, as well as the key fields for the access. A lock object request is not only used to lock a single record from a table but also to lock a complete logical object. Defining a lock object in the data dictionary automatically generates two ABAP function modules which allows for locking (ENQUEUE) and unlocking (DEQUEUE) the object.
- *Search helps.* These are objects that can be used for assigning input help (using the F4 function key) to fields. These types of objects are new with release 4.0 and are meant to replace the func-

tionality of matchcodes. The main difference between search helps and matchcodes is that *search helps* are physically built based on transparent tables. There are two types of search helps: collective and elementary. Due to the addition of this new type of dictionary object in release 4.0, there is an independent and large section on this subject at the end of the chapter.

- *Type group.* These objects contain ABAP type definitions. From version 3.0 onward, developers can define their own data types based on standard R/3 data types.

For reasons of compatibility with previous R/3 releases, you can still access and use the *matchcode objects,* although the way to access them is through the menu *Utilities → Matchcode objects.* A matchcode object is similar to a table secondary index, which helps to find values for key fields using other field values which are better known. As an example, if you need to find a material number but you only know the description, you can design a matchcode which can look up material numbers using the description. A matchcode definition is a two-stage process:

1. In the first stage, you define the fields from the table or tables to use for the search. If more than one table is used, a foreign key relationship must exist among them.
2. In the second stage, you define the identification of the required matchcodes (IDs) using projection and selection operations based on those fields.

Tables in the ABAP Dictionary

Tables are the basic management objects in the underlying logic of the R/3 business applications. The number of tables of a new and standard R/3 installation exceeds 10,000 in the ABAP dictionary. This fact does not mean you have to deal with all of them. The system manages them in a transparent way for users.

The following three types of tables are available:

- Transparent tables
- Pool tables
- Cluster tables

From an application user point of view, all tables behave and are used for the same purpose. There are no differences either in the properties or in the operation: all of them are relational tables, with their own sets of allowed operations, relations, and so forth; all of them can be managed with standard SQL calls; and all of them can be used for making queries, updates, deletes, inserts, and more.

However, from an administrator point of view, things are slightly different. The ABAP dictionary is a layered software which isolates end users and even developers from the underlying database management system. In other words, the inherent openness of the R/3 architecture makes the use of the dictionary completely transparent, regardless of whether the underlying DBMS is Oracle, Informix, SQL-Server, Adabas, or DB2.

SAP uses these procedures to create more complex data structures than the standard structures provided within the database system. This is done both for performance and for grouping logically related tables. That's why, besides normal transparent tables, the R/3 system also includes tables of type *pool* and *cluster.*

Transparent tables do exist with the same structure both in the dictionary as well as in the underlying database system, exactly with the same records and field descriptions.

However, the other two types cannot be directly queried in the underlying database, since those structures are only logically known at the SAP level. These structures can be found in the database but not in a directly readable form.

Pooled Tables, Table Pools, Cluster Tables, and Table Clusters

These types of tables are not transparent in the sense that they are not legible or manageable directly using the underlying database system tools. They are managed from within the R/3 environment from the ABAP dictionary and also at runtime when they are loaded into application memory.

Pool and cluster tables are logical tables. Physically, these logical tables are arranged as records of transparent tables. The pool and cluster tables are grouped together in other tables, which are of the transparent type. The tables that group together pool tables are known as *table pools,* or just *pools;* similarly, *table clusters,* or just *clusters,* are the tables which group cluster tables.

Not all operations that can be performed over transparent tables can be executed over pool or cluster tables. For instance, you can manage these tables using Open SQL calls from ABAP, but not Native SQL.

These tables are meant to be buffered and loaded in memory, because they are commonly used for storing internal control information and other types of data with no external (business) relevance.

SAP recommends that tables of pool or cluster type be used exclusively for control information such as program parameters, documentation, and so on. Transaction and application data should be stored in transparent tables.

Table Pools. From the point of view of the underlying DBMS as from the point of view of the ABAP dictionary, a table pool is a transparent table containing a group of pooled tables which, when created, were assigned to this table pool.

Defining a table pool requires two key fields, a fixed length field and a variable length field. Table 8-1 shows the structure of a table pool definition.

Fields *TABNAME* and *VARKEY* are the primary keys in a table pool. *TABNAME* contains the name of the pooled table, whereas *VARKEY* contains the primary key for that pooled table. Notice that *VARKEY* only admits character data types, which implies that only character data types are allowed as primary keys for pooled tables.

DATALN is a field which contains the actual length of the record which is written in the next field, *VARDATA*. This field, *VARDATA,* might be a long field, since it contains the other data of the record which do not belong to the primary key.

An example of a table pool is *ATAB*. Another typical example of pools and pooled tables are the matchcodes: while the matchcode data for every matchcode ID can be stored in pooled tables, a table pool is created for every matchcode object, which contains the group of pooled tables belonging to every matchcode ID. More information on matchcodes can be found in the following sections.

TABLE 8-1

Table Pool Definition

Field	Type	Description
TABNAME	CHAR(10)	Table name
VARKEY	CHAR(n)	Maximum key length n =< 110
DATALN	INT2(5)	Length of the VARDATA record returned
VARDATA	RAW(m)	Maximum length of the data varies according to DBMS

Table Clusters. Similarly to pooled tables, cluster tables are logical tables which, when created, are assigned to a table cluster. Therefore, a *table cluster*, or just *cluster*, groups together several tables of type clusters.

Several logical rows from different cluster tables are brought together in a single physical record. The records from the cluster tables assigned to a cluster are thus stored in a single common table in the database.

A cluster contains a transparent cluster key which must be located at the start of the key of all logical cluster tables to be included in the cluster. As well, a cluster contains a long field (*VARDATA*), which contains the data of the cluster tables for this key. If the data does not fit into a field, continuation records are created. The structure of a table cluster is shown in Table 8-2.

Please refer to the SAP online documentation for instructions on how to create, delete, and maintain these types of tables.

Working with Tables

The dictionary includes many functions for working with tables. There are five basic operations you can perform on tables: display, create, delete, modify, copy. Please do not confuse displaying a table with displaying the table entries (table contents).

In order to display a table, it must previously exist; otherwise the system will display an error message in the status bar. For the following example, the table TABNA is used.

TABLE 8-2

Table Cluster Definition

Field	Type	Description
CLKEY1	CHAR(*)	First key fields
CLKEY2	CHAR(*)	Second key field
....	...	...
CLKEYN	CHAR(*)	*n*th key field
PAGENO	INT2(5)	Number of the next page
TIMESTMP	CHAR(14)	Time stamp
PAGELG	INT2(5)	Length of the *VARDATA* record returned
VARDATA	RAW(*)	Maximum length of the data section; varies according to database system

To display this table, from the main dictionary screen, enter the table name in the *Object name* input field with the radio button selected next to *Tables*.

Then, click on the *Display* button at the bottom of the screen, or press the *F7* function key, or, alternatively, select *Dictionary object* → *Display* from the menu. The system will display the table description as shown in Fig. 8-6.

In this screen, you can see table information such as

- Table type, shown next to the name of the object. In the example, it is a transparent table.
- Short text description.
- Name of the user who made the last change, and the date of the change.
- Master language.
- Table status. On the screen, you can see this table is saved and active.
- Development class. For information on development classes, refer to Chap. 6.
- Delivery class, which sets the maintenance group for the table. It controls how tables will behave during client copy procedures, upgrades, and so forth.

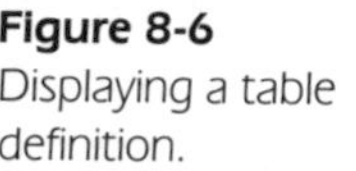

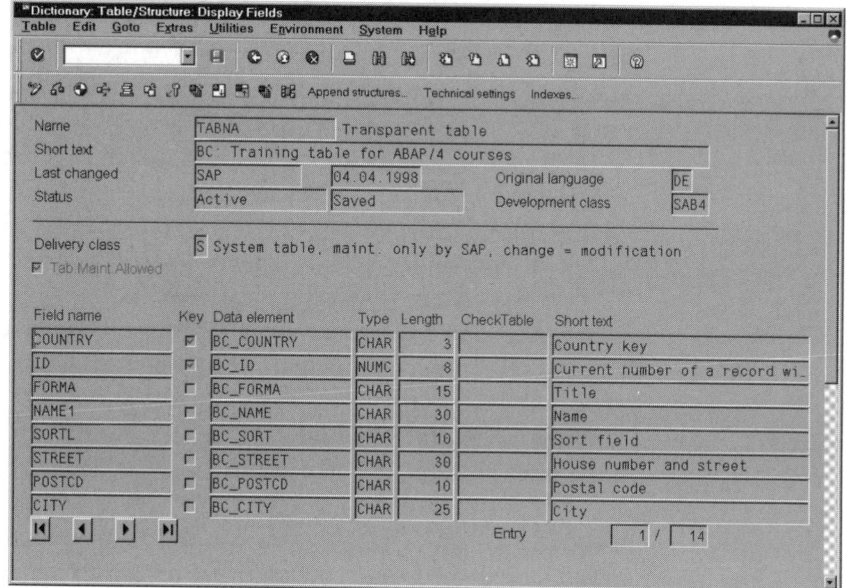

Figure 8-6
Displaying a table definition.

- Tab. Maint. Allowed flag, which indicates whether you can generate a screen for maintaining table entries.

Then, on the lower part of the screen, you can see the table fields with all associated characteristics such as:

- Field name.
- Key indicator. When set, this field is the primary key, or part of it.
- Data element.
- Basic data type.
- Length.
- Check table.
- Short text, describing the field.

Additional information about the table can be displayed by selecting the corresponding functions from the menu or directly from the application toolbar, such as keys, indexes, or technical settings.

Creating a Table. To create a new table, from the main dictionary screen, enter the name of the table in the input field and click on the *Create* button. Remember that customer tables must follow SAP standard naming conventions for customer objects. For instance, start the name with *Z* or *Y,* otherwise they may be overwritten by SAP upgrades.

After clicking on the *Create* button, the system displays a screen similar to the one shown in Fig. 8-6 but with empty input fields. On this screen you must enter a short description, the delivery class, and the table fields, specifying the primary key. When specifying fields, it is also mandatory to enter data elements and domains which must previously exist. Refer to the section entitled "Defining fields," later in this chapter.

Optionally, you can set foreign key relationships with other tables, as well as the maintenance flag and the technical settings. Once you enter all the information, you must save your settings and finally activate it to become effective in the system runtime.

When saving a table, the system requests the development class and a new task (correction) which allow it to be transported and for the version to be managed.

When activating the table you have a defined table structure, but the table still contains no entries.

Copying Tables. If you want to create a new table with a similar definition, it is a good, time-saving practice to copy an existing one and modify it, for example, by adding or deleting table fields, modifying the short descriptions, and so on.

To copy a table, enter the name of an existing table in the input field provided in the initial dictionary screen and click on the *Copy* button in the application toolbar or, alternatively, select *Dictionary object → Copy*. The system will display a dialog box for entering the name for the new table. Then proceed the same way as you would to modify a table.

Deleting Tables. To delete a table, just enter its name and click on the *Delete* icon in the application toolbar. Remember that you can only delete your own tables. You should only delete SAP tables when requested to do so by SAP consultants or instructed by a SAPnet note, which is a rare occurrence.

Modifying Tables. To modify a table, enter the name of the table and click on the *Change* button on the lower part of the screen. The system will display a dialog box requesting the change request number for registering the modification, as explained in Chap. 6.

Defining Fields

Since tables are composed of fields, there are some field attributes that must be defined. These are:

- *Field name.* The name assigned to the field in the table
- *Key flag.* When set, indicates that the field is key or is part of the key
- *Data type.* The data type assigned to the field
- *Field length*
- *Number of decimal positions.* Only applies to numerical field types
- *Short text.* A short description of the field

Assigning data type, length, and short text can be done either by direct type entry or by assigning a data element to the field, in which case the data type, length, and short text are automatically assigned.

When fields are defined without reference to data elements, the system offers limited functionality. So, for instance, there is no F1 help and no foreign keys can be defined for them.

A field can be assigned to the following objects:

- *Search help.* When a search help is assigned to a field or to a data element, any screen containing this field will display an associated search help when the F4 function key is pressed.
- *Reference field* and *Reference table.* For fields that specify currencies (data type CURR) or quantities (data type QUAN), the table field in which these values are to be found must be specified.

Double-click on the field name to make or display these assignments.

Foreign Keys

As stated in a previous section, the relationship between dictionary tables is built based on *foreign keys.*

The relationship is established when defining a field on table A that is a primary key of table B. In this case, table A is known as the *foreign key table,* while table B is known as the *check table.*

There are two working modes for foreign keys that restrict the action of a *select* statement associated with a foreign key relationship between two or more tables. These are:

- *Generic foreign keys*
- *Constant foreign keys*

There are fields that do not make sense when used within a *select* (in the case of generic foreign keys), and other fields (in the case of constant foreign keys), where the values are always constant. For example, in a foreign key relationship defined for four fields of the foreign key table that make up the check table, one of the four fields is defined as generic and another is defined as constant. When performing the *select* associated with the relationship, the generic field is not taken into consideration, while for the constant field, this is compared against the constant defined in the foreign key table.

Fields F3, F4, F5, and F6 from table A (foreign key table) are related to fields V1, V2, V3, and V4 from table B (check table). F5 is defined as generic, and F6 as constant with the value *K.* In this situation, the *select* associated with the foreign key relationship is: select * from B where B–V1 = A–F3 and B–V2 = A–F4 and B–V4 = *K.*

Text Tables

Table A is defined as a text table of another table B when it contains the key for table B and an additional key field that is the language field, with the LANG data type.

Table A can then contain the same entries repeated in different languages.

Keys and Primary Keys

As introduced when dealing with the relational data model, a table record has to be referenced in a univocal way. At the practical level, it means that a part of the information contained in the record will be unique and cannot be repeated in any other table record.

This unique identification information is made up of a table field, or a group of fields, and is known as the *primary key.*

For example, the primary key of table UFACH is made up of a single key, the first one, which identifies univocally every table record. This field is *FABNR.* However, in table UKURS, to identify the primary key the two first fields are needed for avoiding duplicates. These fields are *FABNR* and *KRSNR.*

Technical Settings

Technical settings are special table attributes which help to optimize such table resources as storage requirement, input/output, logged change entries, and so forth. Figure 8-7 shows an example of the screen for maintaining table technical settings.

The most relevant parameters in the technical settings are as follows:

- *Data class.* Establishes the physical area of the database (tablespace) where the table is to be stored.
- *Size category.* Allows you to specify estimated space requirements for the table in the database.

Data class and size categories only are relevant for the Oracle and Informix databases.

These two parameters, data class and size category, are necessary when tables are created in the database.

Further down the screen under the *Buffering* square box, the system allows for specifying:

- Whether the table is going to be buffered. When a table is buffered, it is loaded in the tables buffer from the application server memory, and it will remain there until the application server reboots; then the buffer is reset or the object is swapped out because of insufficient buffer space. Tables are buffered in order to improve an appli-

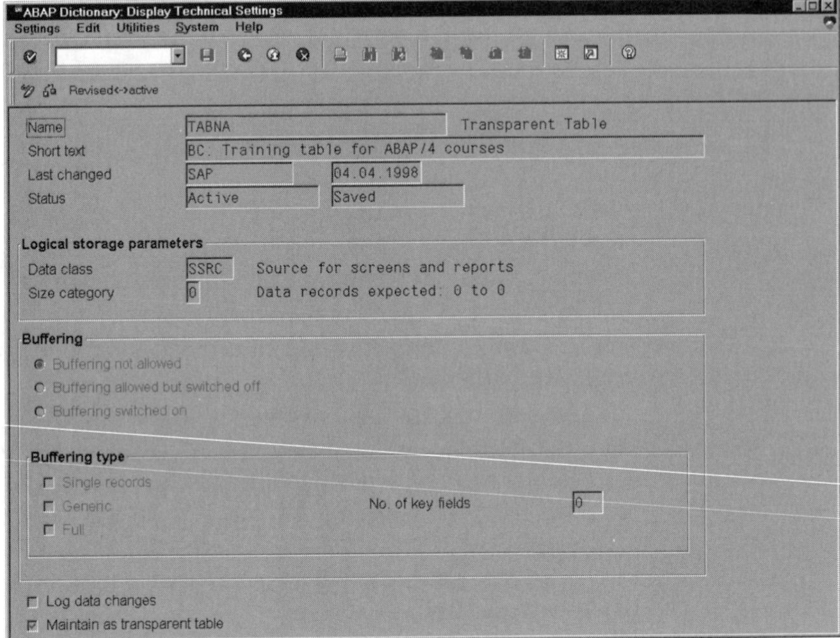

Figure 8-7 Screen for maintaining a table's technical settings.

cation's performance when accessing the table data. However, this is not very appropriate for tables with very high levels of updating activity. Buffering mechanisms within client/server distributed systems require a buffer synchronization procedure for the whole system, that is, for all the application servers. This issue is further explained in Chap. 4.

There are three buffering options:

- *Buffering not permitted.* This option is used for tables that are updated frequently, and in which the latest data must be accessed without waiting for synchronization of buffers between application servers and the database server.
- *Buffering allowed but switched off.* The user or developer responsible can decide whether or not to activate buffering for that particular table.
- *Buffering activated.* This buffers a table, and is used mainly for tables with lots of read access and little or no updating. In this case, the user must also specify the buffering type.

When the table is to be buffered, the *buffering type* must be indicated. Options are:

- *Single records.* The buffer will only store the table record accessed.
- *Generic.* The buffer will store all the table entries that correspond to a specific part of the key that has been selected. For example, if the primary key of the table is made up of the first three fields, and the generic buffering is established using the first two fields, only the records that match the first two fields of the primary key will be stored in the memory buffers.
- *Full.* All table rows are loaded into memory buffers.

Tables buffered using the *Single records* type are included within the TABLP table, while other types are stored within TABL.

For more information on buffering tables, please refer to the chapter "Buffering Database Tables" in the BC ABAP dictionary guide or in the online documentation from SAP.

Since release 4.0 there are two additional options for table technical settings:

- *Log data changes.* Setting this flag enables every change on table records to be kept in a log file. The log file registers the UPDATE and DELETE operations performed directly either by user online transactions or other application programs. For logging to be active, you also need to set the instance profile parameter *rec/client.* This option must be handled with care since it can seriously affect global system performance.
- *Convert to transparent table* or *Maintain as transparent table.* The first flag appears for tables of type pool as well as for all other tables that have been converted to transparent tables.

Generating the Table in the Database

Once a table is defined in the ABAP dictionary, it has to be created physically in the underlying database. The generation is performed automatically when activating the table using the ABAP dictionary functions.

There are, however, certain restrictions: only transparent tables are automatically generated. Pool- and cluster-type tables are not automatically generated since, from the database point of view, these type of SAP tables do not match database tables.

This implies that nontransparent tables cannot have secondary indexes, since secondary indexes, just as tables, must also be generated at the database level.

Indexes

The purpose of defining secondary indexes for tables (only for tables of type transparent) is to enhance the access time when performing select operations on the table. The secondary indexes allow access to the table information on which they are defined, using a different order than the one for the primary key. Physically, they behave like a record table subset, ordered by different criteria.

The secondary indexes do actually occupy physical space in the database; therefore, every table update implies a real updating of the secondary indexes. So, if defining secondary indexes helps the search performance, they, however, slow down the updating process.

The secondary indexes do not need to be unique; duplicates are allowed: a secondary index value can identify more than a record of the table in which it was defined. You may restrict secondary indexes to be unique, however, by setting the property *Unique index.*

To create indexes for a table, from the main table maintenance screen, select *Goto* → *Indexes* from the menu or click on the *Indexes* push button on the application toolbar. If the table already had indexes defined, the list is shown on the screen. From this list, you can create additional indexes by clicking on the *Create* icon. When creating new indexes or when no indexes exist yet for the table, the system displays a dialog box for entering the *Index ID* for the index.

Enter the *Index ID* and click on the *Continue* icon. The system displays the screen for the index maintenance, as shown in Fig. 8-8.

On this new screen, enter a description for the index in the *Short text* input field. Select whether you want the index to be unique by marking the *Unique index* check box, and then enter the fields for the index under the *Table fields* box. You can either manually enter them or display a list by clicking on the *Choose fields* push button.

As you can see in Fig. 8-8, the status line shows that the index is created (*New*) but *Not saved,* and, therefore, it does not exist in the database. The final step is to physically create the index in the database by clicking on the *Generate* button in the application toolbar. The system performs the selected action and shows the activation log if any errors occurred.

Append Structures

An *append* type structure is an information structure (field) which is assigned to a specific table (it belongs to one and only one table). However, a table can have several append structures.

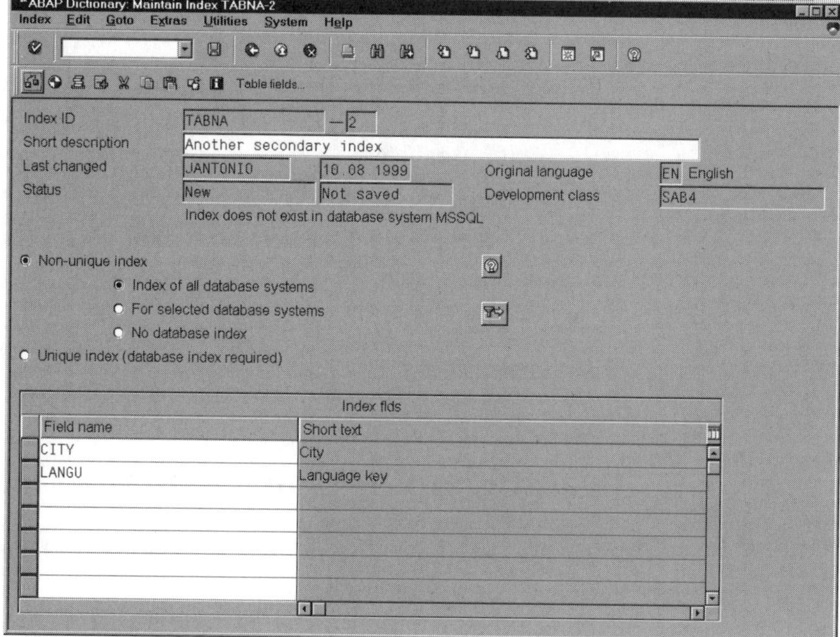

Figure 8-8
Secondary index definition screen.

The append structures are designed as an enhancement concept which allows for adding information fields to standard SAP system tables without modifying their original definition. For example, they could be used for special or add-on customer developments to SAP standard tables if this becomes necessary. Append structures are only allowed for SAP tables and not for your own tables.

For example, when upgrading R/3 from earlier releases, if possible, all the tables and structure fields which were created by the customer are transferred to an APPEND structure during the dictionary adjustment phase.

What the difference is between an append structure and a substructure is that when using an append structure, the table itself is not modified, it only contains a reference to the associated table. However, when adding a substructure, the table itself is changed by adding an *.INCLUDE* line in the table.

This difference is noticeable in the way both types of structures are created. So, for instance, creating an append structure to a SAP standard table can be done in display mode of a table, which means it does not require performing a repair task.

If you want to preserve your append structures against being overwritten by SAP upgrades, remember to name them with the allowed naming convention for customers as indicated by SAP.

The following features and restrictions also apply when dealing with append structures:

- They can only be assigned to one table. If you want to use the fields for several tables, it's better to create a structure and include it in the required tables.
- They cannot contain fields of types VARC, LCHR, or LRAW.
- When new table fields come in with new version releases and you need them as early corrections, it's better to implement a repair than create an append structure. Keep append structures for more customer-oriented developments rather than for implementing SAP-advanced corrections.

Creating an Append Structure

From the initial ABAP dictionary screen, select the name of the table and click on the *Change* or *Display* button.

Note: when creating a new append structure for a table, you are not directly modifying the table definition. So, to create append structures you do not need to modify the table with the *Change* option; it's enough to enter the transaction with *Display* and then click the *Append structures* button. You do not need an SSCR registration number to make a repair, because it is not a repair.

The system displays the *Dictionary: Table / Structure: Change Fields* or the *Display Fields* screen. At this screen, select the *Append structures* option. This displays a dialog box for assigning a name to the append structure. By default, it proposes the name *ZA<table name>*. Leave the proposed name as it is or write over it with your own name and click on the *Continue* button.

On the next screen, the system displays the same screen as if you were creating a normal table or structure; that is, you have to enter a short description and then fill up the needed new fields with the data elements.

Once new fields are defined for the append structure, you have to *save* it. The system requests a new change request number as usual when performing modifications.

Then you have to activate the new structure, which will force a new table adjustment to the database level. Once the append structure is activated (partially active), then you have to activate the table to which it belongs. The system displays a log with the system activation which adjusts the table with the new append structure.

Once the conversion is finished, the append structure appears in a new field in the table as *.APPEND.* Figure 8-9 shows this screen.

To delete an append structure, from the initial ABAP dictionary screen, enter the name of the append structure but (this is important) click on the radio button next to *Structures* or *Tables.* Simply, click on the *delete* icon on the application toolbar or, alternatively, select *Dictionary object* → *Delete* from the menu.

Customizing Includes

Customizing includes are similar to *append* structures, since they allow modification of SAP standard tables when the requirement is to add customer customizing fields to these tables. This type of include can be can be found in several tables or structures. When the include is modified, the modification will automatically affect all the tables and structures containing it, thus preserving data integrity.

SAP delivers standard customizing includes that can be filled by the customer using special customizing transactions. The names of these special includes start with CI_.

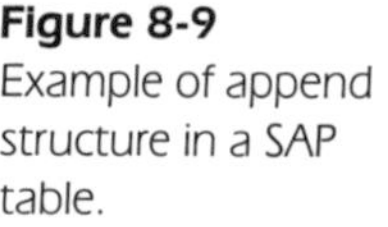

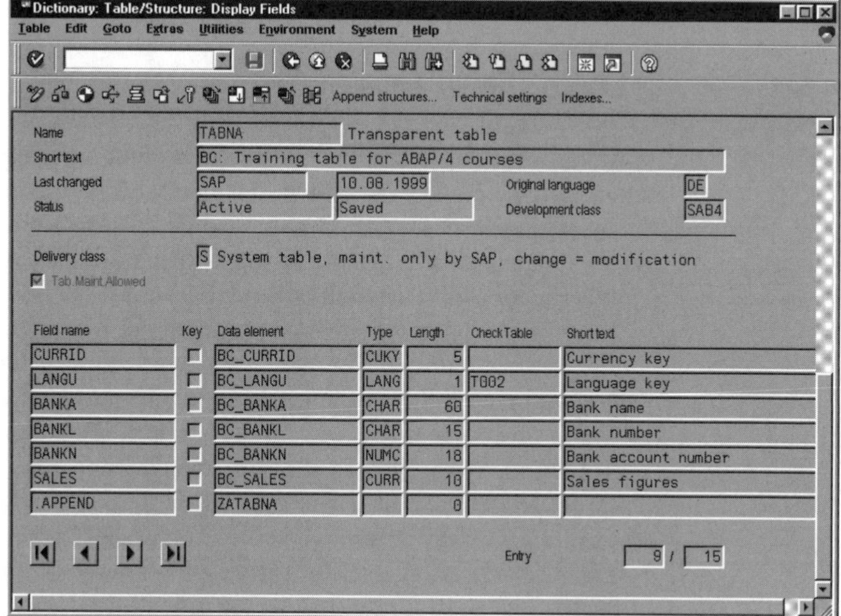

Figure 8-9 Example of append structure in a SAP table.

Substructures

The aim of defining substructures is to save time when working with tables or structure definitions. It is like an include statement in standard programming languages (*INCLUDE* in C or Pascal; *COPY* in COBOL, and so on).

When making a change to a substructure, all the tables, structures, or other substructures which include the modified substructure are also changed automatically. The substructures can be nested (can include other substructures) up to nine nesting levels.

To include substructures, just insert a new field in the table, and then from the main menu select *Extras → Substructures → Insert substructures.* The system displays a dialog box for entering the table name to be included as substructure as well as a prefix input field which allows you to distinguish fields by using this suffix.

The table is included as a substructure. You can then perform several operations with the substructure from the *Extras → Substructures* menu, such as exploding the fields on one substructure or on all.

When you include a table as substructure, you actually include the complete table. If you wish to include only some fields, then you have to select *Extras → Substructures → Insert subst. fields,* but in this case, these new fields become normal table fields which are not adjusted according to the substructure modifications.

Data Elements

A data element describes the role of a domain in a specific business context. An isolated data element does not define the technical attributes for objects, nor the permitted value range. A data element really includes a semantic definition, in other words, it assigns a certain meaning to the table fields which are defined using that data element.

However, the syntactical or technical definition, that is, whether a field can contain integer number, characters, and so on, is defined at the *domain* level. Refer to the next section for more information.

The data element always needs to be defined over a domain. At the same time, a field always needs a data element. This allows all fields with the same technical and semantic settings to use the same data element.

As an example, suppose you have two *PAYMENT* fields in different tables which are referring to the same content, that is, *fixed payments.* These fields can be defined using the same data element, for example,

ZFIXPAYM. However, another table may need a field for *variable payments,* which should not be defined using the previous data element since the *meaning* of both is different, as well as the associated text elements and the documentation.

However, both can use the same domain (*ZPAYDOM*) which only defines the technical settings for the field, in this case a 4-byte integer with a 10-character field length.

Defining a Data Element. There are several ways to define a data element. The most usual is to create the data elements before defining the table fields which later use those data elements for their semantic definitions.

To create a data element, from the main dictionary screen, enter the name for the data element in the *Object name* field and click the radio button next to *Data elements.* Remember to use the customer naming convention. Then, click on the *Create* button. Figure 8-10 shows an example of the screen for defining a new data element.

You have to enter information for the following input fields:

- *Short text.* This is a mandatory field (remember the ? sign). Enter here a description which can later be used as online help, since

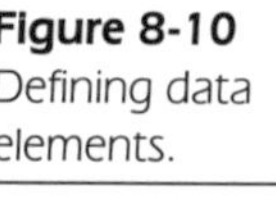

Figure 8-10 Defining data elements.

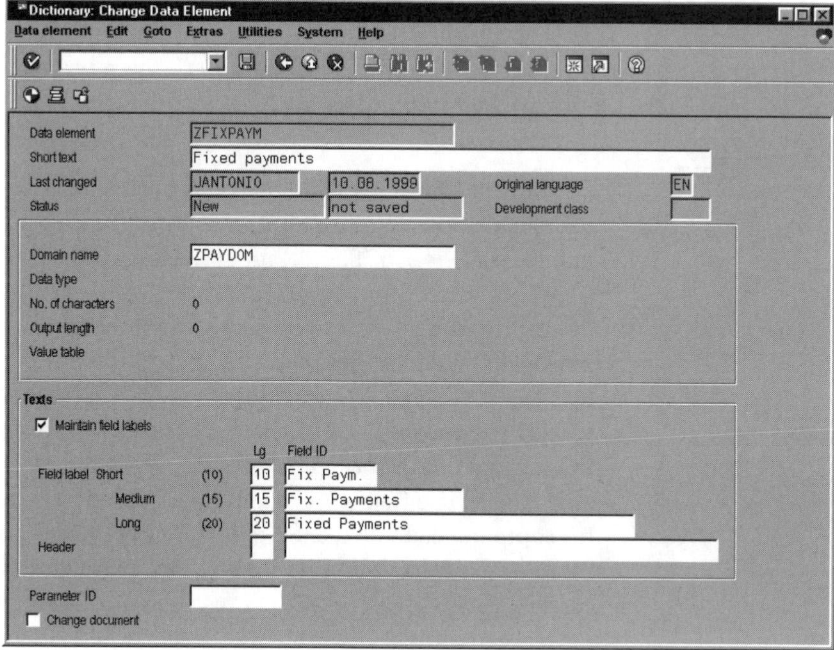

clicking on the F1 function key when a field has this data element assigned will show this description. It can also be used in reports.

- *Domain.* This is a mandatory field, also. If the domain does not exist, SAP can take you directly to the domain definition screen. If you use an existing domain, press the *Return* key to display the settings for the domain. Then it will display the data type, the field length, and the value table, if there is any. If it does not exist, you can create it directly by double clicking on the field. Then the system will display the screen for maintaining domains. This is explained in the next section.
- *Maintain field labels flag.* In current versions, these texts are optional. It only makes sense to deactivate this flag if the data elements are not going to be used in screens. When you use a table field in a system screen, the text displayed for that field can be the text associated with the data element, where you can select either the short, medium, or long settings.
- *Texts elements.* In these fields, you can enter a description for short, medium, and long texts, as well as for the header text. Headers are used when entering data for these fields in tabular forms (columns).

NOTE *Text elements are language-dependent. If you maintain the text elements only in language E (English), these texts will not be available for other logon languages.*

- *Parameter ID.* This is an optional field. With the parameter ID, users can set a default value in their default settings, as was explained in Chap. 5. The parameter ID can also be used in transactions. You can define a parameter ID, which can be used to determine the default values for a field in the user master record. Moreover, when several screens containing a field designated in this way are displayed in succession, the field is automatically filled with the value entered in the first screen of the series. When designing a screen with screen painter, an appropriate attribute must be assigned to the field. For example, if a user only has authorization for company code 001, the fields displaying the company code can be filled automatically by the system with the value 001. For this, the corresponding parameter ID must be entered in the data element for the company code.

- *Change document.* This, too, is an optional field. You may stipulate that a document be generated each time data is changed in a field that refers to this data element. The commercial objects for which a change history is to be recorded are defined using transaction SCDO. Function modules can be generated for these objects, which are then called in the corresponding application programs and the changes logged at runtime. A log entry is generated for each changed field that refers to a data element for which the flag *Change document* is set.

Once the data element definition is complete, click on the *Save* button. Then for the data element to become effective, you must *activate* it. To do that, click on the *Activate* button on the application toolbar.

Note status fields in the data element definition screen when you are defining it, when saving it, and when activating it. These are the statuses:

- Before saving, the status reflects *New* and *Not saved.*
- After saving and before activating, the status shows *New* and *Saved.*
- Once activated, the status switches to *Active* and *Saved.*

Remember that when creating this new object the system displays the dialog box for creating a new change request.

Once the data element is saved and active, it can be used in any table field definition. An interesting property of the data elements is that you can also associate documentation with a data element. To do that, from the data element definition screen, select *Goto → Documentation.* The documentation entered for a data element will be displayed when a user presses the F1 help function key over a screen field.

Available Management Options. When in the data element maintenance screen, you have several utility menu options. These options are quite common for most of the dictionary objects.

From the Utilities menu, you can do the following:

- Display the *Activation log.* This log gives information about how the activation was performed and whether there were any errors in the process.
- Access the *Repository Info system.* The repository info system is briefly discussed later in this chapter.
- Find out where this object is used with the *Where-used list* function, for example, in which table fields it is referred to. It works like a cross-reference pointer.

- Display the tasks and request information associated with the user ID with the *Requests (Organizer)* option which calls the workbench organizer directly.
- Display the version management functions with *Version management,* where you can display, compare, recover a previous version, and perform other functions with the existing versions of an object. This topic is discussed in a later section.

On the Goto menu there are two other useful options. One is *Search help,* which can be used for associating a data element with a search help. When this option is selected, R/3 displays a dialog box for entering the search help and the parameters. Pressing the F4 function help in the parameter field displays the available values. More information on search helps is provided in a later section of this chapter.

From the Goto menu, there is another useful option such as the *Translate.* With the *Translate* function, you can translate the texts associated with the data elements to other languages installed (imported) into your R/3 system.

Working with Domains

Domains, as already mentioned in previous examples, define the technical attributes for a field. Technical attributes set such properties as allowed type and value range which can be entered in the fields. Therefore, fields which have a different use and even a different semantic definition (data element) can make use of the same domains.

If a table field is supported with a data element, which uses a domain with a value table, then the possible entries for the field are restricted to the entries in the value table.

Fields that make reference (are defined) to the same domain are changed (updated) at the time when the domain is activated in order to guarantee the whole consistency of dictionary objects.

Defining a Domain. Before creating a new domain, you have to check whether a domain with the same value range already exists. If this is the case, you should use the existing domain if possible. You can check this by using the available functions within the ABAP repository information system utility.

There are several alternatives for defining a domain. The most usual way should be to create the domain before defining the data elements for table fields. To create a domain, from the initial dictionary screen, enter the name in the *Object name* field, click on the radio button next to *Domains,* and then click on the *Create* button. The system will display a screen like the one shown in Fig. 8-11.

You have to enter information for the following fields:

- *Short text* is a mandatory field. Enter here a description of the domain.
- Display fields below the short text show the name of the user ID as well as the date of the last modification. Under these fields, you can also see the *Status.* These fields change as you perform the *Save* and *Activate* functions, exactly the same as with the data elements.
- Under the *Format* box, you have the input fields *Data type* where you must enter a standard SAP data type. You can select a data type by clicking on the possible entry list button and selecting one of the available types. The *field length* is the number of valid positions for the field without formatting characters such as periods, commas, and the like.
- In the *Value table* input field, you can enter the name of a table. The fields referring to this domain may only assume values contained in

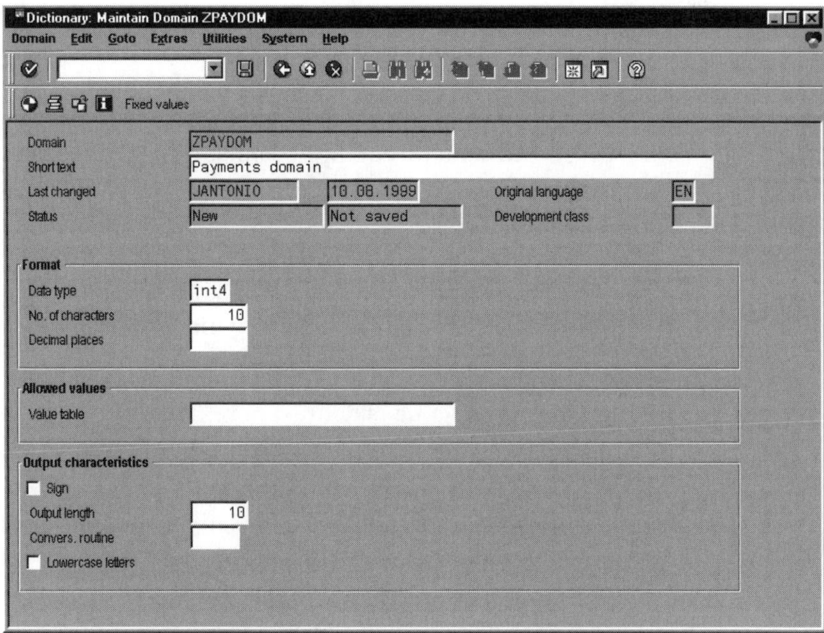

Figure 8-11 Defining domains.

the corresponding field (selected when the foreign key is maintained) of this table. A value table may only be used in a single domain. For the check against the entries in the value table to be made, the corresponding foreign key must have been maintained.

- Under the *Output characteristics,* you might see the *Sign* check box when the selected data type is any of the available numeric data types. In this case, the *Sign* box can be checked to reserve the first position of the output for the number sign.

Once the domain is created, save it and activate it so that it can be used in further objects. You can find information about the activation by selecting *Utilities → Activation log.* When errors occur during the activation process of the domain, the activation log will be displayed automatically. You can also assign documentation for a domain by selecting *Goto → Documentation* from the menu.

You can optionally limit the number of values allowed using a value table as described earlier or by defining fixed values. Fixed values are defined by selecting *Goto → Fixed values.* The system displays a maintenance screen where you can specify fixed value ranges. Values can only be specified for domains of the data types CHAR, NUMC, DEC, INT1, INT2, and INT4. You can specify both values and a value table for a domain. When this happens, all the fields referring to this domain are checked against both the values and the value table, and therefore can only contain values which are contained in both the specified values and in the value table.

In the example shown in Fig. 8-12, you can see that for the domain *UPENUM* there is a value table *UPERS.* No values for fields based on the *UPENUM* domain can be specified if these values do not exist previously in the UPERS value table.

You can set up if a field that refers to a defined domain is an input or an output field, as well as set the editing characteristics. This is useful when creating new screens. You can also control how the fields which refer to this domain are displayed during input/output with the following options:

- *Decimal places.* The number of places permitted after the decimal point for a value is defined here. This field is visible only when a numeric data type (DEC, FLTP, QUAN, and CURR) is chosen.
- *Sign.* If this field is selected, the first output position is reserved for a sign. This field is visible only when a numeric data type (DEC, FLTP, QUAN, and CURR) is chosen.
- *Output length.* Maximum field length including editing characters for input/output of the values. This value is computed automatically, but can be overwritten.

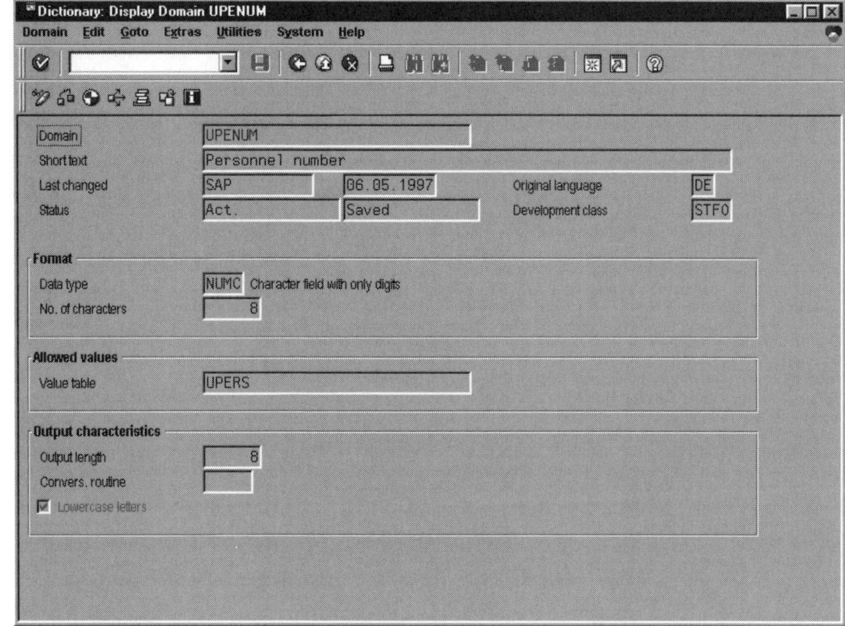

Figure 8-12 Domain with value table.

- *Conversion routine.* This field can be used to change the standard editing format for the values of a domain.

Working with Complex Objects: The Aggregate Objects

Up until here, previous sections explained how to work with the basic objects of the data dictionary. With the basic objects, the dictionary allows for defining more complex structures. For example, using domains and data elements you can define fields for tables and structures. Then, using one or more tables and their relationships, you can define other complex structures such as views, matchcodes, and lock objects, which are known in the SAP environment as *aggregate objects.*

Base Tables in Aggregate Objects

Aggregate objects are based on a table known as the *primary table* of the aggregate object. Other tables can be added to this primary table. These additional tables are known as *secondary tables.* The link between the primary tables and the secondary tables is established by means of foreign key relationships and join conditions. *Transitive* connections (use of intermediate tables) between a primary table and secondary tables are also possible.

The following sections present how the aggregate objects are defined, using examples of creating views, matchcodes, and lock objects. You can obtain further information about these objects from the SAP online documentation in the ABAP dictionary section. However, the aim of this section is to present a useful introduction to understanding the main parts, mainly from the point of view of the R/3 administrator.

Working with Views

A *view* is like a table but with no contents; it is a virtual table. A view is a definition based on the relationship between one or several tables using the permitted relational database operations, for example, select, join, or projections. A view does not physically contain any data. The information is dynamically generated when the view is used at runtime.

The view is a useful method of offering a specific set of application data which can then be associated with certain parts of an application or even with different user profiles. Working with views allows for restricting or limiting the access to information by areas, employees, plants, and so forth. It offers application users the ability to display or manage the information which is really meaningful and useful for their work or the information for which they have access privileges.

This process reduces the need to create new tables with just specific data for each application, which then increases the redundancy and is more costly to maintain. It is also one of the preferred methods for relating the specific modules of business applications which are otherwise logically separated.

View Types. The system offers the following types of views:

- *Database view.* This type is defined just the same way as it is defined in the underlying database. It can use one or several related tables. It supports the three relational operators: join, projection, and selection. Only tables of type transparent are allowed for this type of view.
- *Projection view.* This type allows you to suppress some fields from the display in a transparent table. The projection view is defined

using only the relational operator *projection*. Update, insert, delete, and select operations can be performed.

- *Structures.* These are virtual tables that are made up of several tables. Structures are comparable with tables of type *INTTAB,* internal SAP tables.
- *Help view.* This type is used from transactions when additional help is needed. Help views are used exclusively by the SAP help system. All relational operators are supported. Access is only possible with the SAP help and cannot be seen with either the SAP Open SQL or the Native SQL. For the selection, a function module is generated. For help view definitions only 1:1 and 1:C relationships are possible. This type of view is activated using the F4 function key.
- *Maintenance view.* These views enable the maintenance of a group of related tables using standard SM30 transactions (extended table maintenance) and other special customizing transactions.

Creating Views. From the initial dictionary screen, enter the name of the view in the *Object name* input field and select the *View* radio button. Then, click on the *Create* push button. The system displays a dialog box requesting the type of view to create, as you can see in Fig. 8-13.

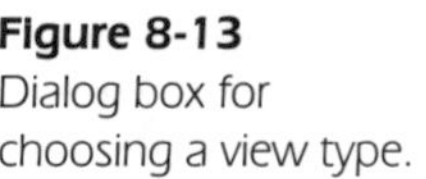

Figure 8-13 Dialog box for choosing a view type.

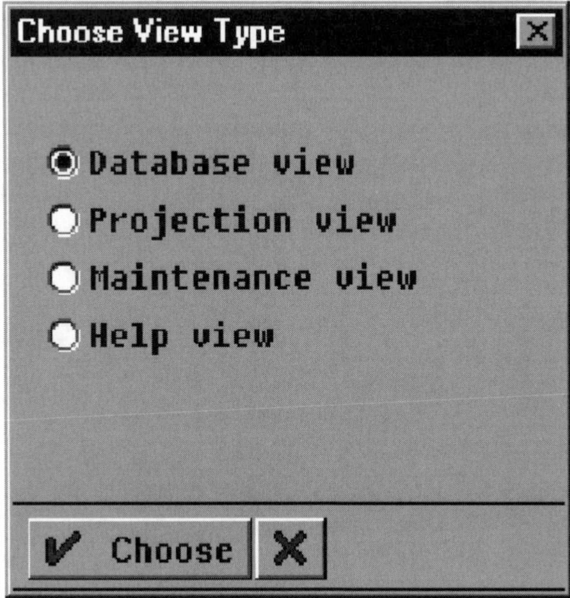

For the example, the database view is chosen. Select the radio button and click on the *Continue* icon. The system then displays the view maintenance screen as shown in Fig. 8-14.

On this screen, there is header information and three table boxes: one for specifying the tables in the view, another one specifying the join conditions, and a third one for selecting the fields for the view. You have to maintain the following input fields:

- Enter a *short text* describing the purpose or contents for the view.
- In the *Tables* box, enter the names of the tables which are to be related for creating the view.
- Next, in the *Join conditions* box, enter the fields names in which the relation between the tables is based.
- Then in the *View fields* box, select the fields you wish to appear in your view. To select the fields, click on the *Table Fields* button on the application toolbar. The system first displays the tables previously entered. To display the available fields, select a table by double clicking on it, then click on the check boxes next to the field names. Finally, press the *Copy* button to transfer the selected fields to the *View fields* box.

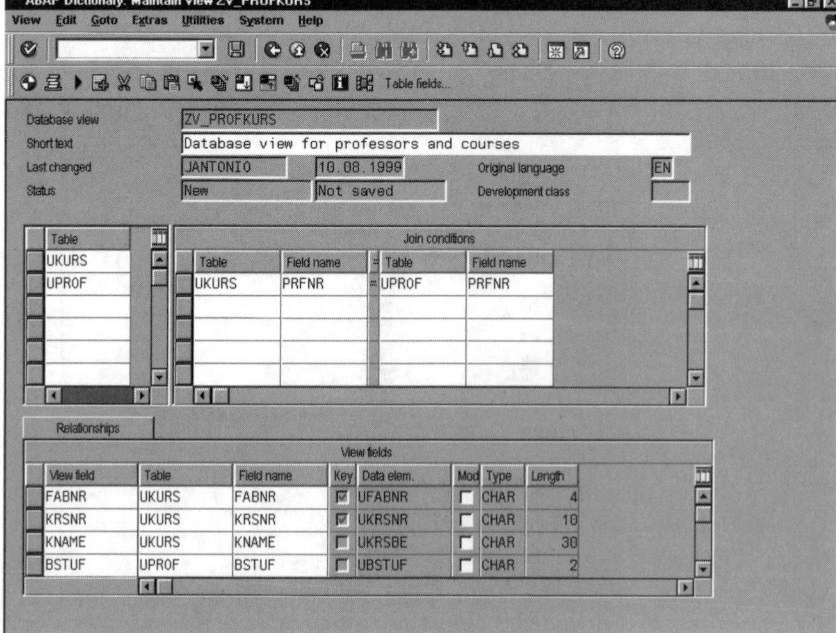

Figure 8-14 Database view maintenance screen.

- Optionally, you can restrict the selection by using the function *Goto → Selection condition.* In the selection condition box, you can enter the following fields:
  - *Table:* Table name
  - *Field name:* Name of the field
  - *Operator:* LK, GT, GE, NE, EQ, LE, LT, LIKE, NOT LIKE
  - *Comparison value:* Constant value for the comparison
  - *AND/OR:* Logical operator to use with two lines of the selection condition
- *Save* your view definition and then *Activate* the view. Upon *Activating* the view in the dictionary, it is automatically created in the underlying database system, as long as the tables also exist in the database. If there are errors, the system displays the error log messages.
- Optionally, you can create some documentation for the view by selecting *Goto → Documentation* from the menu.

To display the table entries matching the view conditions from the view maintenance screen, select *Utilities → Display data.*

When you delete a view you not only delete the view definition in the ABAP dictionary but also you delete the view at the database level. To delete a view, in the initial ABAP dictionary screen, enter the name of the view in the *Object name* field, having the radio button *Views* selected, and then click on the *Delete* icon on the application toolbar.

Working with Matchcode Objects

A matchcode is an aggregate database object which works like a special tool to help search for data records in the system. Matchcodes are particularly useful for searching when the key of a record is not known. A complete section on how users work with matchcodes and search helps was introduced in the section "Working with Matchcodes" in Chap. 5.

Matchcodes require a two-step definition:

- Define the matchcode object, including the relevant tables and fields which make up the matchcode, to be later used by the matchcode IDs.
- Define one or more matchcode IDs for a matchcode object. With the matchcode IDs, you define different search criteria combinations and the screen layout order, based on the information contained in the matchcode object.

Case Study: Creating a Matchcode

The following example illustrates the creation of matchcode objects. The new matchcode object will be named ZENR and will be based on tables UPROF (professors table) and UPERS (persons table), which are included in the standard SAP system for example and training purposes.

To create matchcode objects, from the initial dictionary screen, select *Utilities → Matchcode objects → Create.* For the matchcode object, you have to enter a four-character name complying with the customer name range, that is, starting with *Z* or *Y.* Select the *Matchcode* radio button and then click on the *Create* push button. Figure 8-15 shows an example of this screen.

In order to create the new matchcode object, the following steps are needed:

- First, you have to define the matchcode object's attributes and select the primary table.
- Next, select which secondary tables are used in matchcode objects.
- Then, select which fields make up the matchcode objects.
- Finally, you have to activate matchcode objects.

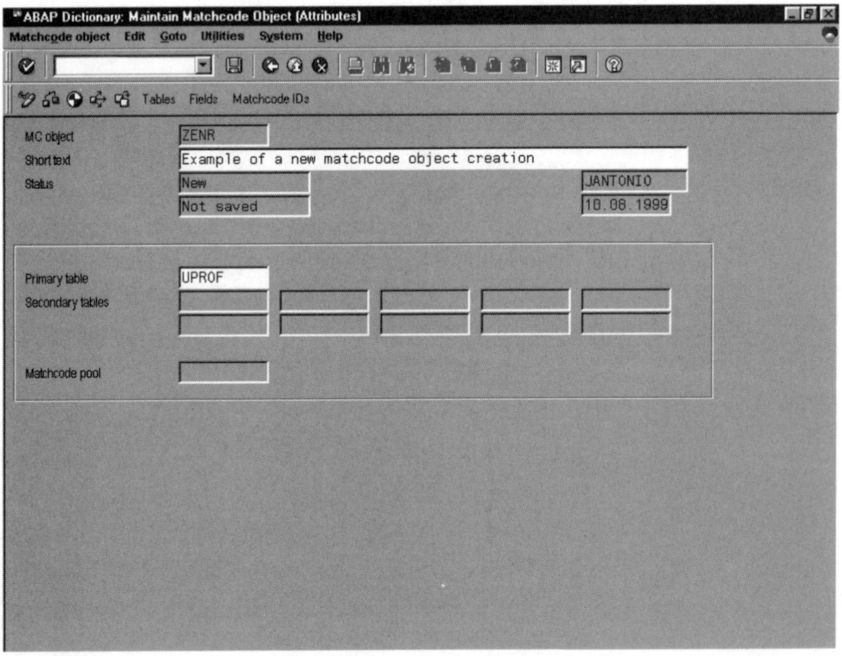

Figure 8-15
Initial screen for matchcode attributes definition.

Defining the Attributes for the Matchcode Object. Once in the initial matchcode definition screen, the definition of the matchcode object requires the following attributes to be entered:

- Enter a brief description for the object in the *Short text* input field.
- Enter the name of the primary table for the matchcode object (in the example, UPROF), and save your entries.

When requested, enter your needed development class and change request number. The following additional information is displayed on the *Maintain Matchcode Object (Attributes)* screen:

- *Secondary tables:* Tables related to the primary table by foreign keys.
- *Matchcode pool:* The name automatically defined for the *Table pools* belonging to the matchcode object is displayed here after the first *Physically stored ID* of the matchcode object is activated.

The table pool is automatically defined in the ABAP dictionary and in the database when the first physically implemented ID of the matchcode object is activated. The name of the table pool contains the prefix *M_* and the name of the matchcode object. The name of the table pool for the matchcode object ZENR will be *M_ZENR*.

Selecting Secondary Tables for the Matchcode Object. For selecting secondary tables, follow these steps:

- Choose the function *Goto → Tables* or just click the *Tables* button on the maintenance screen for the attributes of a matchcode object. The maintenance screen for the table selection of the matchcode object is displayed. For adding secondary tables, just click on the button *Choose sec. tab.* A dialog box appears showing the possible secondary tables for primary table UPROF, that is, a list of all the tables connected by foreign keys to the selected table. Figure 8-16 shows this dialog box.
- Position the cursor on a table you want to include as a secondary table and click on the *Choose* push button. The table is shown on a color background. Repeat this process for all the tables you want to include in the matchcode object. Press the *Copy* push button. In the example, table UPERS is chosen. The system returns to the initial maintenance screen. The selected table is stored as a secondary table and the corresponding foreign key is displayed. Figure 8-17 shows this screen. The mandatory key fields are automatically transferred.

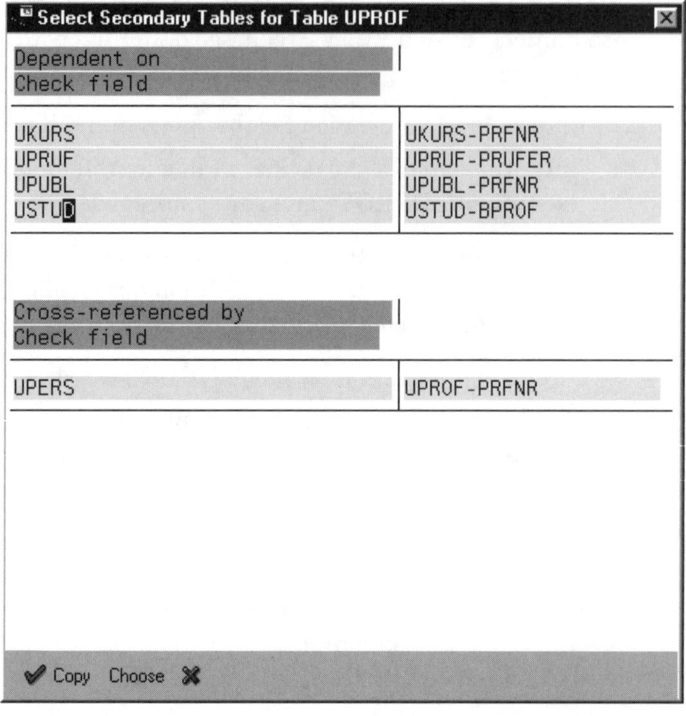

Figure 8-16 Dialog box for selecting secondary tables for matchcodes.

ABAP Dictionary: Maintain Matchcode Object (Fields)

Matchcode object Edit Goto System Help

Choose fields Tables

MC object: ZENR
Short text: Example of a new matchcode object creation
Status: New JANTONIO
Not saved 10.08.1999

Tables
Primary table: UPROF
Secondary tables: UPERS

Fields

Table	Field name	MC field	Key	Data eleme	Type	Length	Tar. fld
UPROF	PRFNR	PRFNR	☑	UPROFNR	NUMC	8	☑
UPERS	EUNA	EUNA	☐	UNAMU	CHAR	20	☐
UPERS	ADRE	ADRE	☐	UADRES	CHAR	40	☐

Fields 1 3

Figure 8-17 Choosing fields for the matchcode.

- Select the fields you want to use by clicking on the *Fields* button. Notice that the field or fields to search must be marked in the check box column *Tar.fld*.
- Save your table selections when all the required tables and fields are included.

Activating Matchcode Objects. Before you can create matchcode IDs, you have to activate the matchcode object. In the maintenance screen for the attributes of a matchcode object choose *Matchcode object → Activate* or, alternatively, click on the *Activate* icon in the application toolbar.

The system records the activation process in the activation log, which can be displayed using *Utilities → Display log → Activate.* If errors occur during activation, the activation log is displayed automatically.

Creating Matchcode IDs. Once the matchcode object has been activated, you can start the definition of the matchcode IDs. Call the matchcode ID maintenance screen from the maintenance screen for the attributes of a matchcode object by selecting *Goto → Matchcode Ids* or by clicking the *Matchcode Ids* button of the *Maintain Matchcode Object (Attributes)* screen.

A list of all existing IDs for the matchcode object is displayed. To define a new ID, click on the *Create* push button. The system displays a dialog box where you can enter any alphanumeric character as the identifier for the matchcode ID. Normally, you should use the digits from 0 to 9 which are reserved for customers. In this example, the number 1 is used. Figure 8-18 shows this dialog box.

When you click on the *Continue* button, the maintenance screen for the attributes of a matchcode ID appears. To define the matchcode ID, the following steps are required:

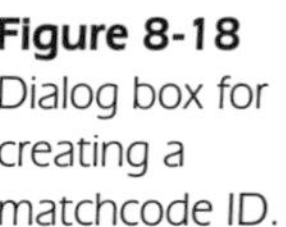

Figure 8-18 Dialog box for creating a matchcode ID.

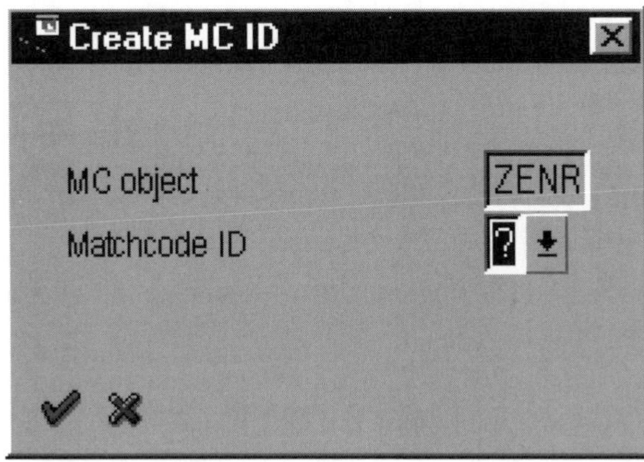

- Enter the general attributes of the matchcode ID.
- Select the secondary tables for the matchcode ID.
- Select the fields for the matchcode ID.
- Optionally, specify selection criteria for the matchcode ID.
- Activate the matchcode ID.

Entering the Attributes for Matchcode IDs. On the initial maintenance screen for the matchcode ID, you have to enter the following information:

- In the field *Short text,* enter a brief descriptive text of what the matchcode ID is about.
- Choose the *Update type* for the matchcode ID. Default value is update type A, which corresponds to transparent IDs. Normally, all IDs should be created as transparent IDs. It's important to notice that this update type is not a physical matchcode ID. The matchcode records, in this case, are set up temporarily at the moment of access to the matchcode (like a view). Types A, S, and P are physical matchcodes. Each one has its own table in the system. You can click on the possible list arrow in this field to display and select a dialog box with the available update types.
- Also, enter some of the optional settings as introduced in the next section. When you are finished, save your entries. Figure 8-19 shows an example of this maintenance screen.

Entering Optional Settings. The following settings are optional:

- *System matchcode.* If this flag is set, it indicates a system matchcode which is used by the SAP software and cannot be changed by customers.
- *Deletion flag.* This flag indicates that the matchcode is not immediately deleted from the database. Instead it retains this deletion flag to identify it for physical deletion in a general deletion operation.
- *Authoriz. Check.* If this flag is set, the system will perform authorization checks for this matchcode ID.

Depending on the update type which has been selected, other fields can be displayed:

- When update types A, S, and P (physical matchcodes) are selected, the system will display the *MC pooled table* field, which shows the

Figure 8-19 Initial screen for maintaining matchcode IDs.

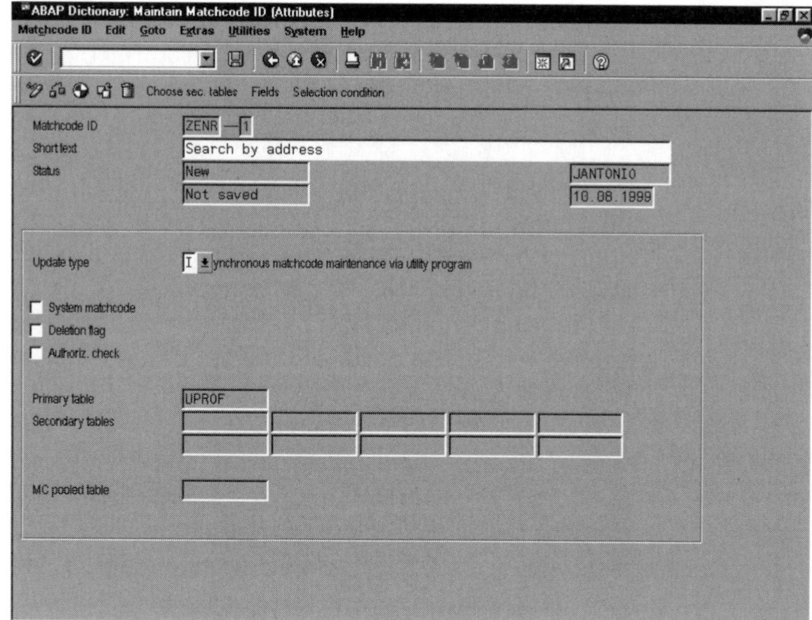

pooled table for the matchcode when the ID has been activated. Notice that the name of the pooled table always contains the prefix *M_* and is made up of the name of the matchcode object and the matchcode ID. Therefore, for ID 1 of matchcode object ZENR, the pooled table name is *M_ZENR1.* Additionally, the system also displays the *Deletion flag* which can be set to prompt the system to assign deletion flags to the matchcode ID records when any of the records in the base table are deleted. That is, the matchcode ID records are not immediately physically deleted, but are deleted at a later time during a mass deletion process. For matchcode IDs of update type P, the deletion flag cannot be set.

Matchcodes of update type *I* or *K* (transparent matchcodes) have been replaced with *search helps.*

Selecting the Secondary Tables for the Matchcode ID. To select secondary tables of a matchcode ID, proceed as follows in the maintenance screen for the attributes of the matchcode ID:

- Position the cursor on the base tables of the ID and select the function *Edit → Choose sec. tables.* A dialog box appears listing the tables linked to the table by foreign keys.

- Select the secondary tables required in the dialog box and press the *Continue* button. The system then returns to the maintenance screen. The selected secondary tables are included in the ID.
- Save the selection of the secondary tables.

Observe that only transparent tables may be selected for transparent matchcodes (update type I). For performance reasons, only *hierarchical relationships* are allowed for dependent tables of synchronous matchcodes (update type S). For performance reasons, when selecting tables for matchcodes of update type S (synchronous updating), only key extensions are allowed for the dependent tables. The selected tables must, therefore, be related hierarchically.

Example: Table T2 is dependent on table T1, while a further table T3 is dependent on T2. The tables are said to have a hierarchical relationship if the key of T2 contains the key of T1 in its first position and the key of T3 contains the key of T2 in its first position. Only with this type of relationship can T2 and T3 be included as secondary tables for primary table T1 for a matchcode to be updated synchronously.

If two tables T2 and T4 are dependent on a table T1, only one of the tables may be included in the matchcode ID in addition to table T1. Exceptions to this rule are text tables. If T2 or T4 is a text table of T1, then both can be included in the matchcode ID.

Selecting Fields of a Matchcode ID. Proceed as follows to select the fields of a matchcode ID:

- In the maintenance screen for the attributes of the matchcode ID, choose the function *Goto → Fields.* The maintenance screen for the matchcode ID appears.
- Position the cursor on a table name and choose *Edit → Choose fields.* The fields of the selected table are displayed in a dialog box. In the example, fields selected are: *PRFNR* from table UPROF, and *ADRE* and *EUNA* from table UPERS.
- You can include a field in the matchcode ID by clicking on the corresponding entry and pressing the *Choose field* push button. The entry is shown on a colored background.

  Once all the fields to be included in the matchcode ID have been selected, click on the *Copy* push button. The selected fields are transferred to the matchcode ID. Figure 8-20 shows an example of selecting fields for the matchcode ID.

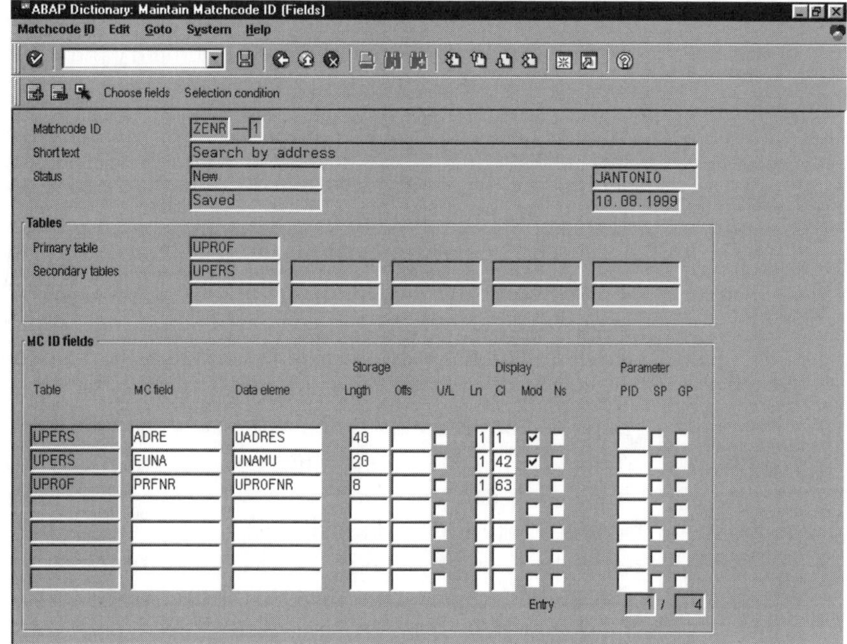

Figure 8-20 Entering fields for the matchcode ID.

Observe that the selection sequence corresponds precisely to the sequence in which the fields are listed in the matchcode ID. The sequence of the fields in the matchcode ID is of paramount importance for later accessing behavior, for example, in connection with the possible entries push button F4. The fields which are most frequently accessed should be placed at the start.

- Save the field selections if you do not wish to choose any of the optional settings described in the following section.

Note that there are some restrictions on selecting the fields.

Additional Settings. There are several optional settings for the fields of matchcode IDs. A brief introduction concerning their significance follows. For more information, please refer to the SAP online documentation.

- *Storage.* The input fields *Length, Offset,* and *Upper/Lower* influence how the matchcode records are saved.
- *Display.* With the *Line, Column, Mode,* and *No show* check boxes you can set the way the matchcode records are displayed.

- *Parameter*: You can define whether the values from the matchcode records can be stored in the SAP memory parameters, such as the PID, the SP, or the GP.

Activating a Matchcode ID. The matchcode ID from the maintenance screen for the attributes of the matchcode ID may be activated with *Matchcode ID → Activate.*

The corresponding database view is created in the database during activation for matchcode IDs of update type I. During activation, a check is made to see whether the corresponding index to support view selection exists in the database. If this is not the case, a warning is given.

Information on the activation process can be obtained from the activation log. You can display the activation log with *Utilities → Display log → Activate.* If errors or warnings occur during activation, the activation log is displayed automatically.

After activating, observe that the screen field *MC view name* is filled with the name *M_ZENR1,* as previously stated.

Before using a matchcode this must be filled with data. To do this, you must use the option *Utilities → Database utility → Build data* from the Matchcode ID screens.

Testing the Matchcode. To test your matchcode ID and display its data, proceed as follows:

- Go to the screen *Maintain Matchcode Object (Attributes).*
- Select a matchcode ID by clicking on the *Matchcode Ids* button on the application toolbar.
- Push on *Utilities → Display MC data.* A pop-up screen appears asking for values for the field of matchcode ID.

Select to continue, then all the data of matchcode ID appears, placed as corresponding to the field sequence of the matchcode ID.

Since, in this example, the matchcode object and matchcode ID have been created using development class ZDES, and not as local objects, it's possible to display the version management for that object.

You can access version management from the *Maintain Matchcode Object (Attributes)* screen by selecting the option *Utilities → Version management.* In this example, this was the only version. However, if you modify any relevant aspects or properties of the object definition, another version would be generated and you can see it using that function.

Later in this chapter, there is a section which discusses version management for dictionary objects.

Working with Lock Objects

In an information system where users can access the same data in a concurrent way it is necessary to have a control system in charge of granting the integrity and consistency of data. In the SAP R/3 system, this synchronization method for user access to data is built on a data-locking mechanism by the definition and use of lock objects over table records.

The locks are established and released by calling function modules which are automatically generated when defining the lock objects in the ABAP dictionary. This synchronization system is independent of the locking mechanism used by the underlying DBMS. This section introduces how lock objects are created, modified, and deleted with some easy examples.

Creating Lock Objects. As previously introduced, a lock object is a dictionary object of the type aggregate. A lock object definition then has a similar structure to other aggregate type objects.

Defining a lock object requires the following steps:

- Defining the attributes for the lock object
- Choosing the secondary tables, if any
- Selecting the arguments and locking type
- Activating the lock object

These steps are presented following an example in which the lock object *EZENR1* is created. Name ranges for customer objects in the case of lock objects normally start with the *EZ* or *EY* character strings.

From the initial ABAP dictionary screen, enter the name for the object in the input field, click on the *Lock objects* radio button, and then click on the *Create* button. The system displays the *Maintain lock objects* screen as displayed in Fig. 8-21.

Enter the *short text* as usual and, most importantly, the name for the *Primary table.* In the example, one primary table will be used (*TABNA*). The flag, *allow RFC,* can be used to enable remote function calls with the function modules generated for the lock object.

Save your settings. Next, select the *Tables* option. The system displays the *Maintain Lock Objects (Tables).* When in this screen, you can

- Select a secondary table
- Select the fields for the lock object

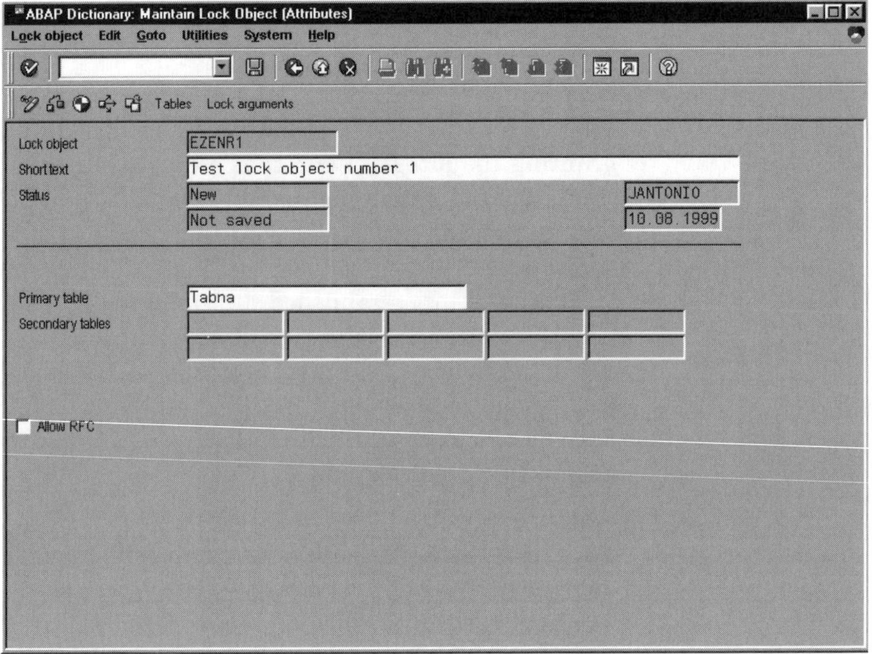

Figure 8-21 Initial screen for maintaining lock objects.

Secondary tables only make sense when there are foreign key relationships with other tables. In the example, table TABNA does not have these relationships.

The second option is to select the lock arguments for the object, that is, which fields are selected by the R/3 enqueue work process to establish the locking mechanism. Assigning values to these fields is how you define the *granularity* of the lock mechanism. The SAP R/3 system can lock objects to the record level.

Lock object arguments are not really selected by developers but rather are imposed by the lock object definition and include all the primary keys for the selected tables in the lock object. Figure 8-22 shows an example of lock arguments without using secondary tables.

You can also select the lock mode. The system has three available lock modes, which you can display by clicking on the possible entries arrow. The system displays a dialog box with the lock mode types.

- *E (exclusive).* The lock data can only be displayed or modified by a single user, who is the owner of the lock over the locked data. Any other request on the lock object is rejected.

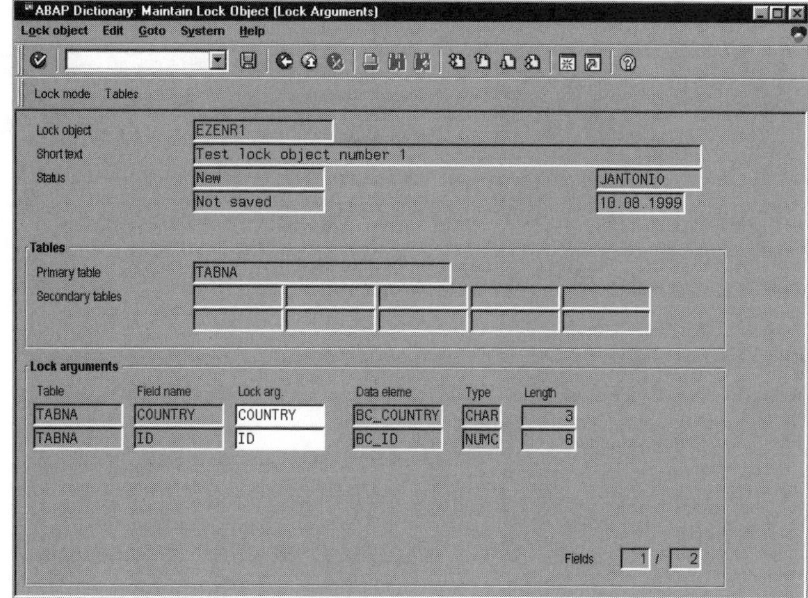

Figure 8-22 Entering the lock arguments.

- *S (shared).* Several users can access the same records simultaneously but only in display mode and except the first one which asked for the lock in update mode.
- *X (exclusive not cumulating).* Locks of type E can be called several times from the same transaction and are removed successively. In contrast, a lock of type X can be called only once. Any other call for such a lock is rejected. A lock of type X is not accepted if another lock of type E is already set. The lock mode can be defined separately for each base table. When a call for a lock occurs, a corresponding entry is inserted into the lock table of the system.

Finally, you have to activate the lock object. Just click on the *Activate* button on the application toolbar or, alternatively, select *Lock object → Activate* from the menu.

To access the activation log, select *Utilities → Activation log.* Figure 8-23 shows the activation log for the EZENR1 lock object. Notice the generation of the enqueue and dequeue function modules.

Function modules ENQUEUE_EZENR1 and DEQUEUE_EZENR1 can then be used from the ABAP programs and transactions.

The ENQUEUE functions are used to set the lock over the selected data depending on the lock object arguments, while the DEQUEUE function module releases the lock over previously locked objects.

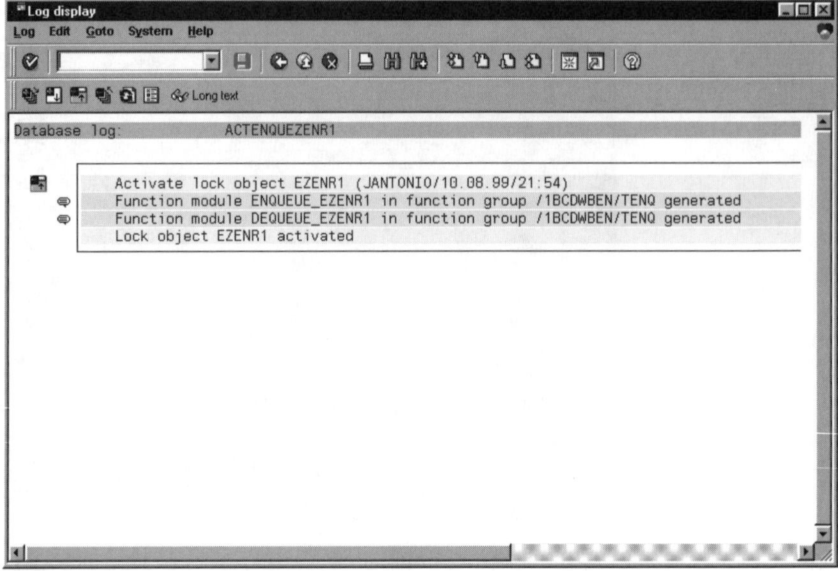

Figure 8-23
Lock object activation log.

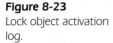

Working with the Database Utility

The interface between the ABAP dictionary and the database is the *database utility*. You can call the database utility from several ABAP data dictionary screens. For example, from the initial screen of the ABAP dictionary, select *Utilities → Database utility.* Figure 8-24 shows this initial screen.

The database utility includes functions for creating, deleting, and converting objects from the ABAP dictionary in the underlying database and even for displaying the table contents.

All relevant objects are supported in the database utility, such as

- Tables
- Table indexes
- Views
- Matchcodes
- Special table types:
  - Table pools
  - Table clusters

Normally, user DDIC, with authorization profiles SAP_ALL and SAP_NEW, has all the authorization required for working with all the utilities of the ABAP dictionary.

Figure 8-24
Initial database utility screen.

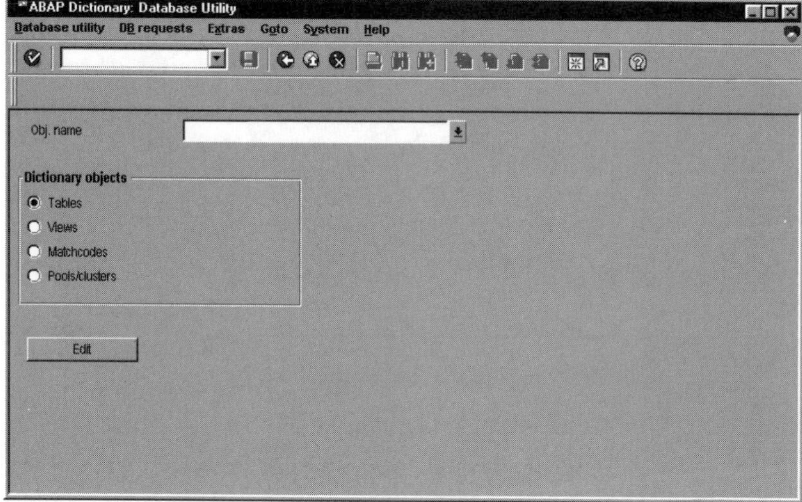

When in the initial database utility screen, as shown in Fig. 8-24, you can select the object class you require, enter the object name in the *Obj. Name* input field, and then press *Enter* to branch to the maintenance screen *Data Dictionary: Utility for Database <object name>* where *<object name>* is the object entered in the input field.

Another way to access the database utilities is from most of the dictionary object maintenance screens. In this case, the initial screen of the database utility is bypassed and you move straight to the maintenance screen for the relevant object class.

The maintenance screens for the individual object classes contain the various database functions available and certain help functions which check whether an object exists, display a restart log for an object (if one exists), or display any programs that may have been generated.

Some additional information on the objects is displayed (for example, the short text). Valid objects are active data dictionary objects.

If you want to edit secondary indexes for a table, you can search for an active index by entering * in the field *Index ID* or by calling the input help function on the field.

If you enter a matchcode without specifying a matchcode ID, the functions always apply to the matchcode object.

If you wish to edit more than one matchcode ID, you can enter * in the field *Matchcode ID.* Matchcode ID selection then takes place online.

The database utility also provides these overview functions:

- *Background logs.* Day logs of the mass table converter can be displayed.

- *Background jobs.* Database jobs to be executed in the background are listed here. There is also a function for deleting background jobs. The restart logs for a background job can be displayed.
- *Restart logs.* The restart logs are displayed here. You can delete a restart log (unlock) or restart processing.

Processing Types

There are three basic functions of the database utility:

- Create database object
- Delete database object
- Adjust database object as redefined in ABAP dictionary

These basic functions may be executed using the following processing types:

- *Direct.* The database changes are carried out immediately. There are some risks derived from this processing type such as a heavy loading of the system and a danger of losing data if data are written to the system during conversion.
- *Background.* A background job is scheduled for the required database changes. You can specify the time at which background processing is to begin.
- *Enter for mass processing.* Choosing this processing type, entries are generated with the relevant function in a system table TBATG. The requests collected together in table TBATG can then be processed in the background later, at fixed times.

To display the jobs that are scheduled for mass processing select *DB requests → Mass processing.* You can also display the logs from background jobs by selecting *Extras → Logs* from the initial database utility screen.

The objects that can be edited from the database utility are as follows:

- Transparent tables
- Indexes
- Views
- Matchcode pooled tables or matchcode views
- Physical table pools or table clusters

With the transparent table you can perform the following functions:

- Create the table, with its corresponding indexes, as it has been defined in the ABAP dictionary.
- Delete the table and all its indexes.
- Activate and adjust the database. If you modify a table definition in the dictionary, this table switches the status to *Revised.* When activating it, if the modifications were structural, then you have to adjust and activate the table at the database level also. There are only two ways to perform this operation:
  - Keeping the data entries (the content) of the table
  - Deleting all the entries from the table, before performing the adjustment

It is also possible to verify if data exists for a table on the database and to check the consistency of table definition, as well as to create and delete database indexes.

Database Utility Functions with Cluster and Pool Tables

The following functions are available when working with cluster and pool tables:

- *Delete data.* The data within a pool or cluster table type are deleted from the physical pool or cluster to which the table was assigned.
- *Activate and adjust the database.* You also have the option to
  - Keep the table entries by storing them in a temporary table
  - Delete the table entries before the adjustment

For the different table types, there are two different options for verifying them:

- *Consistency verification*
- *Data existence verification*

For the other object types such as indexes and views, there are options to create, delete, adjust, and activate them from the database utility also. In the case of views, there is even the possibility of performing a consistency verification.

Database Utility Functions with Matchcodes

As introduced earlier, the database utility can also be used for editing matchcode objects and matchcode IDs.

The operations supported for matchcode objects from the database utility are:

- *Create database table.* Creates the physical matchcode pool
- *Delete database table.* Deletes the physical matchcode pool
- *Compare definition.* Allows comparison of the active version from the ABAP dictionary and the current definition in the database

Two types of functions can be performed on matchcode IDs, depending on whether the matchcode ID is physical or a transparent.

For physical matchcode IDs, available functions are:

- Build data
- Delete data
- Activate and adjust database

Physical matchcode IDs can only be of the A, S, or P type. Their structure is based on pooled tables.

For transparent matchcode IDs, functions supported are:

- Create database view
- Delete database view
- Activate and adjust database

Transparent matchcode IDs are of type I or K, and are very similar to search helps.

Activation in the Dictionary

For a dictionary object to be effective at runtime, that is, for a dictionary object to be available for use within programs, transactions, and so on, it must be in *active* status. For objects to become active, R/3 includes the *Activation* function.

When a table or aggregated object is activated, it is placed at the disposal of the system as a runtime object in a way that makes it available very quickly for the application programs to access the relevant information of new activated objects.

As stated at the beginning of this chapter, the ABAP data dictionary and the ABAP programming language as well as the rest of the workbench tools are completely integrated.

For example, the information for a table object is divided in the ABAP dictionary among domains, data elements, field definitions, and table definitions. The runtime object of the table collects this information for application programs to access in an optimal way.

Application programs and screens receive their information from the ABAP dictionary (metadata). Any change to the metadata affect all the system components related to them: when an object is activated, all objects dependent on it are also reactivated. In other words, the activation of a dictionary object can trigger a chain reaction activation, as many as the number of dependent objects, directly or indirectly.

When a dictionary object is modified, which means that the object previously existed, this operation should be done with extreme care. It is good to know how many objects will be reactivated because of the modification of the first one. For instance, if you modify a domain, when activating it, it will reactivate all data elements, table fields, tables, matchcodes, views, lock objects, or structures which directly or indirectly are based on that domain. At the same time, it will affect all programs in which the previously mentioned object is used.

To know how many and which ones are the effected or dependent objects of the one being modified, you can use the *ABAP repository information system* or the *Where-used list* function.

If there is a structural modification, that is, you change the format or type, most probably the effected tables will need to be readjusted at the database level because of such a change, else, there would be inconsistencies between the ABAP dictionary definition and the corresponding structure at the database level.

From the R/3 release of 3.0 onward, when activating a table or any other object which requires an explicit definition in the database, for example, matchcodes, automatically generate the object in the database. In previous versions—2.2 and earlier—you had to create explicitly the object in the database once activated in the dictionary. So, for instance, an object could exist as active in the ABAP dictionary but be nonexistent at the database level.

There are two ways to activate objects:

- Individually, one by one
- Massively, several at the same time

When the activation is performed massively, it might take quite a long time, then it should be processed in the background system. This type of activation is known as *background activation.*

The mass activation operations are usually used when performing upgrades or new R/3 software installations, as well as when transporting a large or complex number of objects between systems.

The report RDDMASG0 is the program in charge of performing the mass activation. When performing individual activations which include several dictionary objects, special care must be taken in the order in which the objects are activated, since there might be a dependency relation between the objects, for example, between data elements and domains. However, the mass activation system correctly handles the activation order for the list of objects.

To enter the ABAP dictionary objects to be activated, you can use the following methods:

- Change request or task.
- External table. An external table has to be of a pooled table from the ATAB pool and must have the same structure as table TACOB.
- Internal table from within a program. An internal table must have the same structure as table MAGE.

Adjusting Database Structures

At the SAP level, there are always two definitions of a structured database object which can contain data, such as tables, matchcode IDs, and so forth:

- Definition at the ABAP dictionary level
- Definition at the underlying DBMS level

Both definitions of the same objects should always be consistent to be able to work with them without producing errors. This is, of course, normally the case, since when activating one of these objects in R/3, the ABAP dictionary utilities automatically generate the object in the underlying database.

At this point, no inconsistencies exist since there are no modifications from the initial structure defined in the ABAP dictionary.

However, in an object lifetime, it is very possible that the object can be modified. Modifications can affect the structure and the order of the object, for example, the order of the fields of a table. In such cases, it might be necessary to *readjust* the object to the database level, that is, to adapt the new structure of the object in the database according to its definition in the ABAP dictionary.

Determining When an Adjustment Is Needed. There is no need to perform an adjustment in a table where you only change the sequence of fields that are not part of the primary key. However, if you change the sequence of the fields which make up the primary key, or the whole primary key, then you have to readjust the table.

You must adjust the table every time you add or delete a whole field from the table.

Adjustment Modes

There are three modes to readjust a table in the database:

- *Deleting and recreating the table in the database.* Using this method, all data in the table is lost. This consists of deleting the table at the database level and then reactivating it back at the ABAP dictionary level, which then automatically recreates it in the database.
- *Modifying the database catalog (ALTER TABLE command).* In this case, only the definition in the database is modified. If there were any secondary indexes defined for the tables, these indexes must be regenerated.
- *Converting the table.* This is the most complex mode of adjusting a table, but it preserves all data and indexes after the adjustment.

How to Adjust a Table

There are several ways to adjust a table or a matchcode ID. There are also several navigation options for calling the database utility, which contains the needed functions for the adjustment. There also is the possibility of running the adjustment directly from the SE38 or the SA38 transactions by executing the report RDDMASG0 (mass adjustment mode).

In the following example, it is assumed that the table structure in the dictionary has been modified. Since a modification has been performed, there is a need to adjust the structure of the table in the database (old structure) with the new structure as defined in the ABAP dictionary. To do that, you have to call the database utility by following these steps:

- At the initial ABAP dictionary screen, enter the table name in the *Object name* input field, select the radio button *Tables,* and click on the *Change* button.
- If you modify the table structure, for example, by adding a new field, or if the table has been previously modified, then the status is set to *Revised.*

At this point, if you choose to activate the object, the system automatically displays a dialog box requesting the conversion of the table at the database level, that is, adjusting its new definition. In the displayed dialog box, you can click on the *Database utility* push button, to go directly to the database utility functions.

If you did not choose to activate because you were aware of the needed adjustment, you could go to the database utility by selecting *Utilities* → *Database utility* from the initial screen for table maintenance. Figure 8-25 shows an example.

From the database utility screen you can proceed with performing the adjustment to delete the table or to create it, in case it does not exist.

As you can see in Fig. 8-25, under the *Processing type* box, there are three options for performing the adjustments:

- *Direct.* Changes and adjustments are performed online immediately.
- *Background.* The process is launched as a background job at the specified scheduled time.
- *Enter for mass processing.* Selecting this mode, the system enters the object name in the TBATG table, which includes all objects wait-

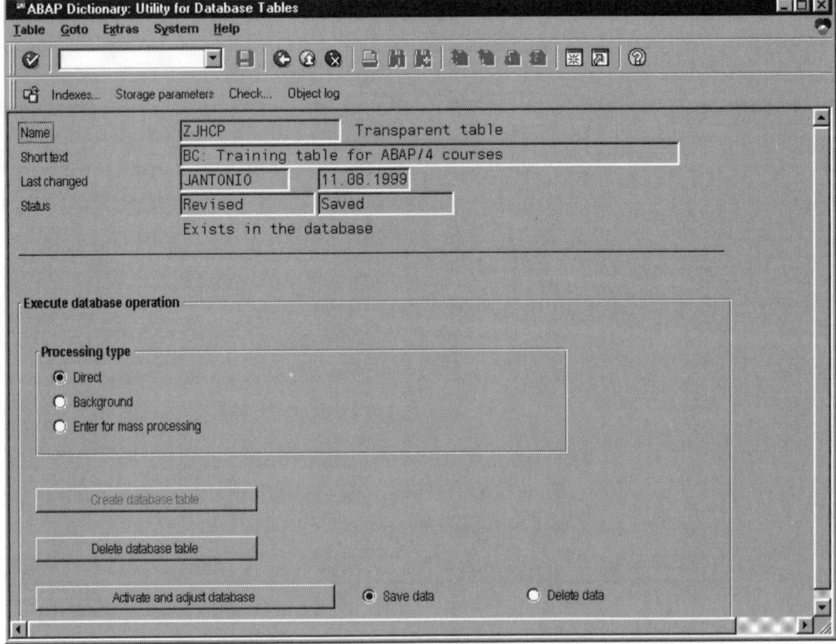

Figure 8-25
Database utilities for tables.

ing for adjustments. With this procedure, you can define a background job to be processed at a later time (for example, at night).

For adjusting tables with the mass processing procedure, you would have to

- Access the database utility. From the table maintenance screen select *Utilities → Database utility* from the menu.
- Then, under the *Processing type* option, click on the *Enter for mass processing* radio button to select this type.
- If you want to retain current table entries, click on the *Save data* radio button, and then click on the *Activate and adjust database* push button. The screen will show a new push button in the application toolbar, *Unschedule,* and a message indicating *Mass processing request: Adjust. The request is not yet assigned to a job,* next to which you get the *Display rest* push button. Figure 8-26 shows how the screen might look.
- Click on the *Display rest* button. The system displays the *List of mass processing request* screen, which contains the list of objects included in the TBATG table, which are the objects waiting for adjustment with the mass processing option. Figure 8-27 shows an example.

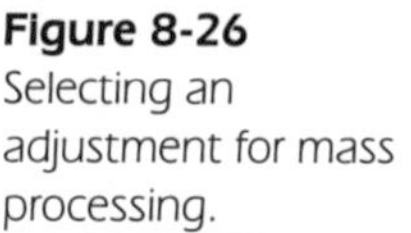

Figure 8-26 Selecting an adjustment for mass processing.

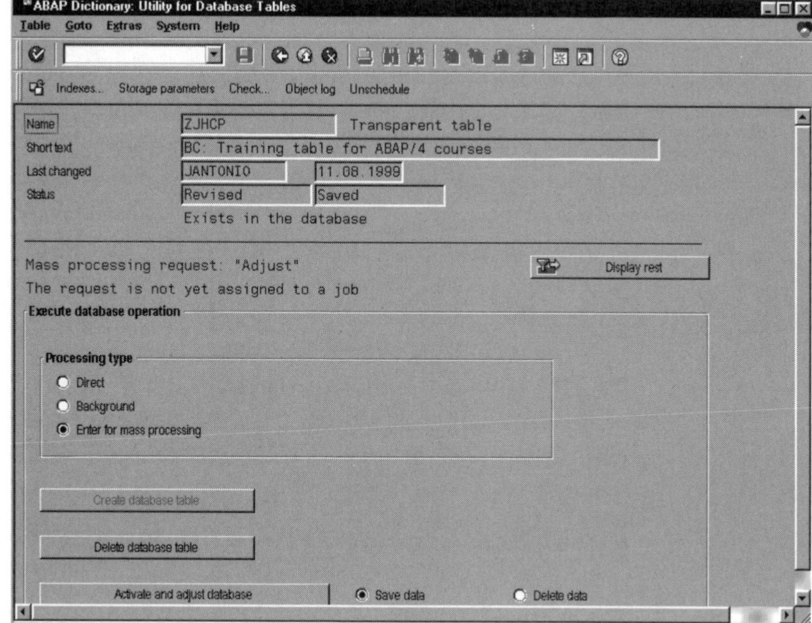

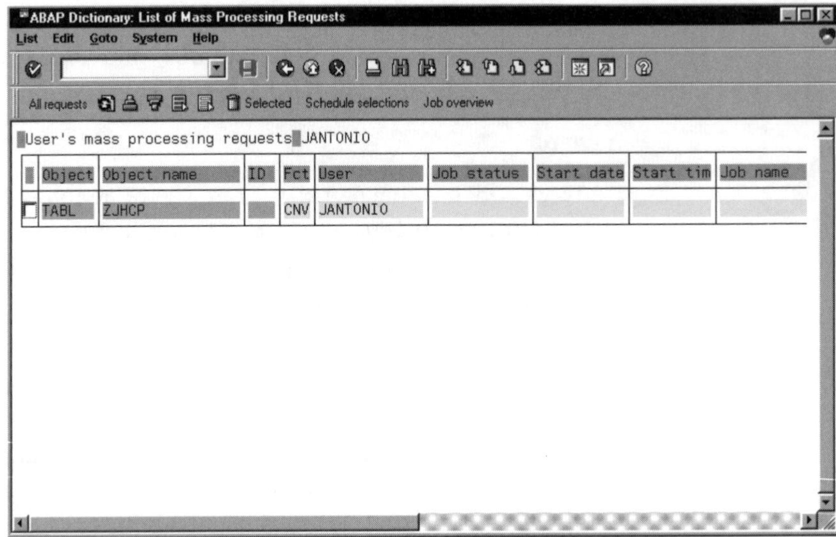

Figure 8-27
The list for mass processing screen.

- Select the objects you want to adjust by clicking on the check box next to each of them, and then click on the *Schedule selections* button on the application toolbar. The system then presents the common background job scheduling options where you have to enter the date and time most convenient for the processing.

The system will display the name and the status of the newly created job, and, on the *List for Mass Processing* screen, the *Job status* field appears with the message *running* if you have scheduled it for an immediate start. In this case, if the adjustment is fast, upon clicking on the *Refresh* button, you will quickly see how the TBATG table is emptied and the adjustment is finished. In this case, the screen displays the message *List is empty.*

You can also display the status of the mass processing using the normal *Job Overview* transaction by clicking the corresponding button on the application toolbar.

When the adjustment is finished you can check the contents of the TBATG table using the *data browser* (transaction code SE16).

For fast and easy adjustments for tables with little or no content, you can submit a job or process the adjustment directly online.

Conversion Process and Restart

The adjustment and conversion process for transparent tables is based on six steps:

- The program is generated, and a lock is set for the table to be converted.
- The table is renamed in the database as a temporary table using the format *QCM<table_name>*.
- The revised version of the table is activated, which means the table is created in the database as a new table.
- The data must be reloaded; this is done from the temporary table *QCM<table_name>*.
- Secondary indexes, if any, are re-created at database level.
- The lock entry set for the table in the beginning is removed in order to allow users and R/3 processes to access the table.

The conversion process is traced in the restart log file because for certain reasons this process can go wrong. In these cases, the lock entry set for the table being converted is not released and the table remains locked so that nobody trying to access it will be permitted to do so.

In order to release the table, the conversion process must be restarted; this can be done after correcting the error that caused the conversion termination. Steps for restarting are:

- From the database utility initial screen, enter the table name and choose *edit*.
- Choose *Restart log*.
- Find out the cause of the error and apply the appropriate corrections.
- Continue the conversion with the option *Restart adjustment*.

Version Management in the ABAP Dictionary

In the SAP R/3 development environment in general, as well as in the dictionary, new objects are defined and created as they are needed. The new objects are created under particular circumstances and development necessities, but, as time goes by, circumstances and needs can vary and changes are needed. When these situations occur, you can decide to delete those objects and recreate them in case the original would be too different or too difficult to adapt, or you can modify the existing ones. Modifying dictionary objects generates new object versions. These modifications should not be confused with adding, deleting, or updating table entries, but are dictionary object definitions, such as the number and type of table fields, secondary tables for aggregate objects, different or new fields for matchcode IDs, and so forth.

When dictionary objects are associated with a development class other than the local, temporary one ($TMP), as objects are modified, the R/3 system keeps all the versions for the object as they are being defined and saved.

These functions are handled by the dictionary version management utilities. With these utilities, developers compare old versions with the current one and can even reactivate an older version.

For example, assume that a table structure has been modified and then the table has been activated. After activation the table becomes active in the runtime, and a program which was using that table suddenly stops working correctly. Using version management utilities, you can quickly recover the previous version which was working correctly, until you find a solution for the situation.

An additional advantage of version management is that it keeps a historical record of the objects and developments.

Version management allows for modifying existing objects without activating them in the runtime: only one object version can be active, and the version management system creates a temporary version when modifying objects, which does not affect the actual system operation.

The SAP R/3 version management system distinguishes three types of versions:

- Versions in the dictionary from the point of view of the object status
- Temporary versions generated during the development process
- Historical versions, which are being kept as objects, are being modified, and the corresponding corrections released

You can access these versions and manage them from the functions available under the Version management menu.

From the point of view of the object status, in the ABAP dictionary, objects can have the following versions (status):

- *New,* for objects which are created from scratch and have not yet been activated
- *Revised,* indicates that an object has been modified after being previously activated
- *Active,* for the objects which have been activated and which are fully operational in the runtime system

- *Partially active,* when objects could not have been fully activated, normally because errors occurred in dependent objects

An additional status is also possible in the case of matchcode IDs: the *deactivated* status. This status means that the deactivated matchcode ID will not be used in the search within the matchcode object. This status is manually set by the users when the ID doesn't seem to be used, but they don't want to delete it.

These object versions are shown in the status field on the objects maintenance or display screens.

The Versions Catalog

The versions catalog is the name assigned by SAP to the functions available under the *Utilities → Version management* menu, which is available from any of the object display or maintenance screens. Figure 8-28 shows an example of the versions screen.

The version catalog displays all the existing versions for a particular object, including temporary and historical versions, if there are any other than the active or revised one.

As you can see by looking at the application toolbar as shown in Fig. 8-28, when in the version catalog, users can display, compare, and

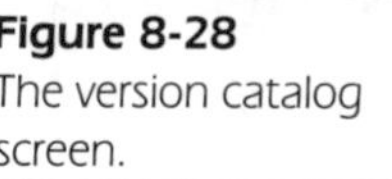

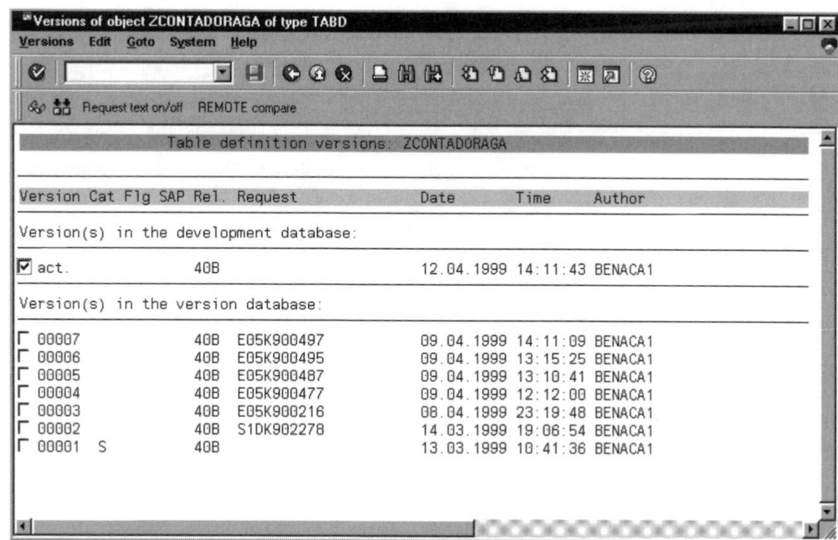

Figure 8-28 The version catalog screen.

retrieve any of the object versions. From this menu, old versions can even be reactivated, although this can generate some activation problems if dependent objects have also been modified or no longer exist.

Figure 8-29 shows a simple example of versions comparison. In this case, no changes appear in the general attributes for the table; however, there was a new field in the new version which could be seen if the screen was scrolled down. The figure shows the *Full display* comparison.

But you can more conveniently display the changes between the objects by selecting *Delta Display* from the application toolbar.

Finally there is also a *Parallel Display* option in which both object versions are displayed next to each other.

The version catalog can even compare versions in other R/3 systems by clicking on the *REMOTE compare* push button on the application toolbar or by selecting *Versions* → *REMOTE compare* from the menu. The system requires you to enter the name of the remote R/3 system which must be connected and accessible from your local system.

To retrieve an old version as an active version, you have to access the particular object in maintenance mode. Then, access the version catalog selecting *Utilities* → *Version management.* Select the version you want to set back as an active version by clicking the check box to the left, and then click on the *Retrieve* push button on the application toolbar.

The system displays a dialog box that displays a message indicating that the version retrieved will be set as a new revised version. If you click

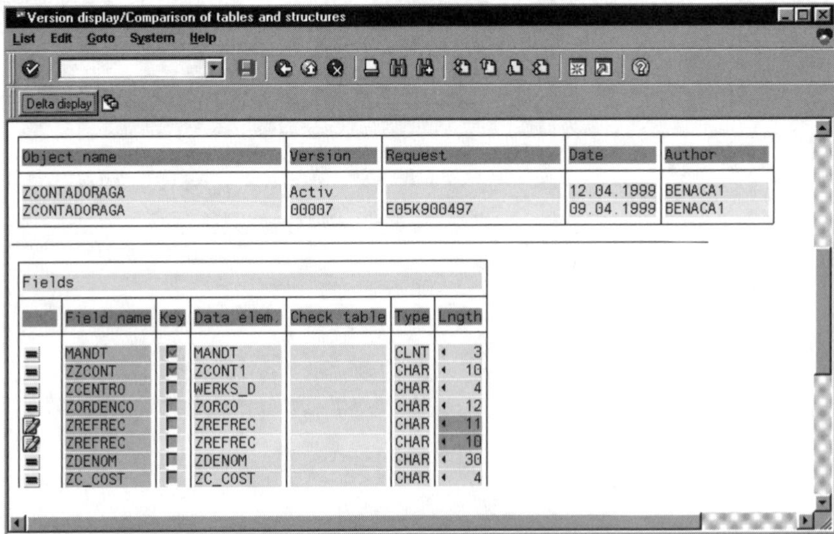

Figure 8-29
Full display versions comparison.

on the *Yes* button to confirm the operation, the object still needs to be activated before becoming the actual *active* version.

If you retrieve an old version, and right away call the version catalog again, you will now see this new version as a *modified* one.

Working with Search Helps

Search helps are used in functions that were usually assigned to matchcode objects. They are accessed by pressing the F4 function key on any screen field that has a matchcode assigned to it.

In order to allow use of a search help in a screen field, developers must explicitly assign a search help to the desired field.

Just as matchcode objects have matchcode IDs, search helps have two options or types, based on *search paths.*

- *Elementary.* When a search help references a single search path.
- *Collective.* When a search help includes several search paths. In this case, when a user presses the F4 function key in a field with a search help assigned to it, the system will offer the option of selecting one of the search paths defined. The value selection and the settings for online behavior are taken from the elementary search helps.

To assign a search help to a table field, you must first create the search help; then, simply position the cursor on the field and select *Goto → Search help for field.*

Creating a Search Help

The following are simple steps for creating both types of search helps.

For creating an *elementary search help,* follow these steps:

1. In the initial ABAP dictionary screen, enter the name for the search help, select the object type *Search help,* and click on the *Create* button.
2. The system shows a dialog box for selecting the search help type. Choose *Elementary search help,* and then *Continue.*
3. Next the system displays the maintenance screen for elementary search helps. Enter a short description in the *Short text* field.

4. The next step is to indicate the selection method for the search help, which can be based on assigning a table, view, or tables with text tables.
5. If it is necessary to change the standard input process using the *F4* function key, you can use the *Search Help Exit,* a function module that can be called from the *F4* help processor under special conditions. Refer to the online documentation for details on this issue.
6. Select the dialog type for the search help. The dialog type defines how a hit list is displayed. There are three options for dialog types:
   - *Immediate value display,* where the hit list will be immediately displayed
   - *Complex dialog with value restriction,* where the users receive a dialog box for selecting the search help
   - *Dialog depending on number of values,* in which case the hit list is displayed immediately when it contains fewer than 100 entries, and if it contains more, the system displays a dialog box for selecting the values
7. Define the search help parameters. The name of a parameter for elementary search help must match the name of corresponding field of the selection method. You also have to indicate whether it is an *import* or *export* parameter by setting the corresponding flag.
8. If users are going to access a search help using a *hot key,* then you have to define a position ID within the field *Shortcut.* All elementary search helps within a collective search help must have different *shortcuts.* Usually, a *hot key* is assigned to an elementary search help when the elementary search help is going to be part of a collective search help. In this case, each of the elementary search helps will have its own *hot key* to identify it.
9. Finally the definition is saved and activated, and the system requests the introduction of a development class to the search help.

Users can see information about the activation of the search help by selecting *Utilities* → *Act. log.*

For creating a *collective search help,* follow these steps:

1. In the initial ABAP dictionary screen, enter the name for the search help, select the object type *Search Help,* and click on the *Create* button.

2. The system shows a dialog box for selecting the search help type. Choose *Collective search help,* and then *Continue.*
3. Next the system displays the maintenance screen for search helps. Enter a short description in the *Short text* field.
4. Enter the parameters for the collective search help. You must indicate whether they are *Import* or *Export* parameters by setting the corresponding flag. Enter the name for the data element that describes the parameter contents in the field *Data elements.* The field *Default value* can be used for assigning a default value that will be used in case no specific value is specified when linking to a field.
5. If it is necessary to change the standard input process using the *F4* function key, you can use the *Search Help Exit,* a function module that can be called under special conditions from the *F4* help processor. Refer to the online documentation for details on this issue.
6. Select *Search helps* to include other search helps within the collective search help. The system displays an *input mask,* where you have to enter the names of the search helps to be included. If you don't want to offer one of the included search helps, set the flag *Hidden* next to it. Save this data.
7. The next step is to position the cursor on an assigned search help and select *Parameter assignment.* In the field *Reference parameter* you have to enter the names of the parameters from the elementary search help to which the corresponding parameters of the collective search help should be assigned.
8. Finally the definition should be saved and activated, and the system will request the introduction of a development class to the search help.

The activation log can be found by selecting *Utilities* → *Act. log* from the menu.

Search Help Structure

There are two types of search help structures, depending on whether the search helps are elementary or collective.

There are basically three aspects that define the behavior and structure of an *elementary search help:* the selection method, the parameters, and the online behavior.

The *selection method* describes the way data is obtained from the hit list. There are three ways, depending on the source of the data:

- When all the data comes from a single table, this table is the only object that has to be defined as the data source for the hit list.
- When the data comes from more than one table, so that data is joined in a view, the hit list data will come from the view that is made up of the related table fields.
- When the hit list data comes from a table that is complemented by a text table, the definition of the data source for the hit list must include both the table and the associated text table.

When a field of the selection method is used for the data collection of the hit list, it is necessary to define a parameter with the same name as the field. This is the case for:

- Fields that are used for performing restrictions in a hit list
- Fields that are displayed in a hit list as an additional column
- Fields with values that must be sent back to the screen

Parameters can be defined either as *import, export* or without specific type, in which case they will not appear within the hit list. All parameters defined can be used for the selection when making the hit list. The parameters that are to be displayed on the screen must be defined as type *export.*

In the example shown on the following pages, for the *USTU* search help, there is a single export parameter that corresponds to the identification number of a university student who is taking courses. Since it is a single field, it has a single export parameter that will *export* its value to the screen from the *module pool* when the user double-clicks over the selected values offered by the hit list.

The online behavior refers to how the hit list should be displayed, as well as the definition of the dialog box that can restrict the value selection.

There are two main aspects to the structure of collective search helps:

- The parameters that make up the interface between the screen mask and the elementary search help parameters assigned to the collective search help
- The search helps assigned to the collective search help, which can be either elementary or collective, providing the possibility of nested search helps

Example: the USTU Collective Search Help

In release 4.0 you can find several standard search helps. This section explains the structure and behavior of the search help *USTU,* from the university examples included in the R/3 system.

To access this search help, from the initial ABAP dictionary screen, enter *USTU* as the object name, select the *Search Help* radio button, and click on the *Display* button.

USTU is a collective search help made up of four elementary search helps (USTUA, USTUB, USTUC, and USTUD), which have been assigned *hot keys* from A to D. This can be seen by clicking on the *Search help* button. Figure 8-30 shows this screen.

USTU has a single parameter, *EUNR,* based on the *UPERSN* data element that represents the number of the university member. This number identifies every individual from the university. This will be the only data type exported to the field *UPRUF-PRUFLING* of the screen *UPRUFEDI-1100.*

You can see the structure of the elementary search helps by double-clicking on them. Figure 8-31 shows the structure of *USTUA.*

In Fig. 8-31 you can see that *USTUA* has a single export parameter, *EUNR,* with the data element *UIMMNR,* which is the matriculation number and which is equivalent to the data element *UPERSN* (because both are based on the same domain, *UPENUM*).

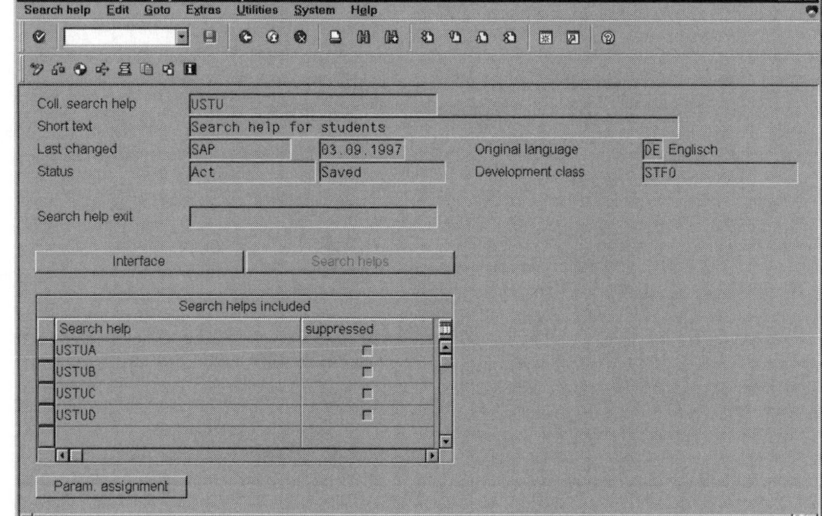

Figure 8-30 Display search help USTU.

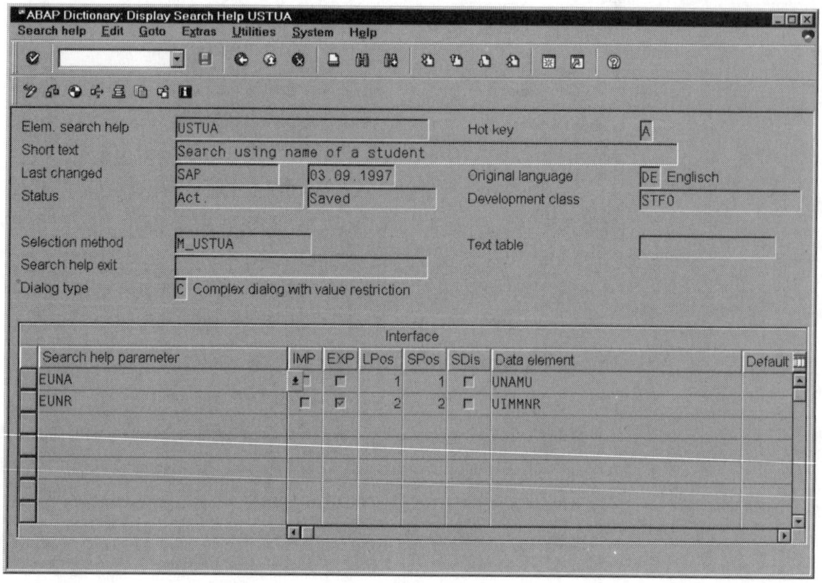

Figure 8-31 Search help *USTUA*.

The other elementary search helps (USTUB, USTUC, and USTUD) from the search help *USTU* have the same export parameter, *EUNR*.

To test how the search help works, from the transaction *SA38* (*Reporting*) or *SE38* run the program *UPRUFEDI*. Figure 8-32 shows this initial screen.

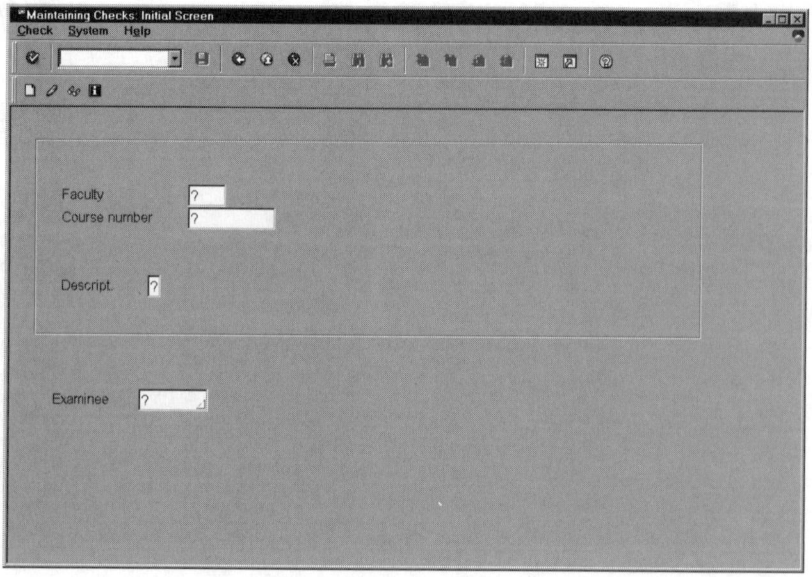

Figure 8-32 Program *UPRUFEDI* for testing search helps.

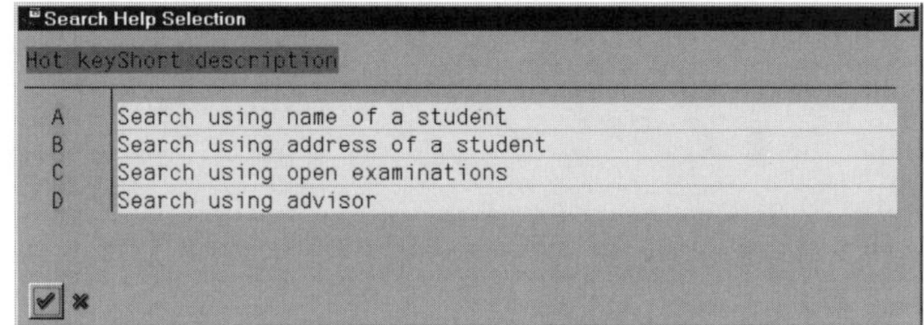

Figure 8-33
Search Help selection.

Enter some values in the first three fields of this screen, and then press F4 on the field *Examinee* or click on the possible entries arrow. If it is the first time this search help has been used, the system displays a Search Help selection dialog box like the one shown in Fig. 8-33. Otherwise it will display the last search help used.

Select one of the elementary search helps offered by double-clicking on it. In the value range dialog box, enter the selected value restriction or the * wildcard, and click on the *Continue* icon.

The system will display the hit list according to your selection. You can transfer your value by double-clicking on any of the entries.

NOTE *The section "Dependency factors and foreign keys" on pages 380 to 381, copyright by SAP AG, reprinted with permission. The sections "Selecting fields of a matchcode ID" and "Activating a matchcode ID" on pages 417 to 420, copyright by SAP AG, reprinted with permission.*

The section on lock modes, on pages 422 to 423, copyright by SAP AG, reprinted with permission.

The section "Processing types" on pages 426 to 427, copyright by SAP AG, reprinted with permission.

The section "Activation in the dictionary" on pages 428 to 430, copyright by SAP AG, reprinted with permission.

CHAPTER 9

Management of Users, Authorizations, and Profiles

The users of the SAP R/3 system are defined internally within the same R/3 system and there is no need for user management at the operating system or database level, except for those special users defined in the standard installations, such as <sid>adm, SAPServices<adm>, ora<sid>, or others, depending on the operating system and database platform.

The users are defined and maintained, and the security of the system is enforced in the user master records with the use of the SAP R/3 authorizations and profiles.

This chapter deals with the general management of user master records and the available fields and options. But the main concern for system administrators and project managers when implementing the R/3 system is how to enforce the right security methods for users' access to the business information. The SAP system provides a comprehensive and flexible way to protect data and transactions against unauthorized use.

In the user master records, users are assigned one or more authorization *profiles.* These authorization profiles are made of a set of *authorizations,* which give access privileges for the different elements of the system. Further down, authorizations refer to *authorization objects* which contain a range of permitted values for different system or business entities within the R/3 system.

Managing authorizations and profiles is a complex and time-consuming task within SAP implementation projects and later maintenance and support. SAP has designed a tool that reduces the time needed for implementing and managing the authorizations, thus decreasing the implementation costs. This tool is known as the *Profile Generator.*

The Profile Generator is a SAP utility available since release 3.0F and productive since the release 3.1G, with the goal of making the configuration and management of authorizations and user profiles easier. It can be used for automatically creating authorizations and profiles and assigning them easily to users. The definition of profiles using the Profile Generator is based on the possibility of grouping functions by *activity groups* in a company menu. This menu will be generated using customizing settings and will only include those functions selected by the customers. *Activity groups* form a set of tasks or activities that can be performed in the system, such as running programs, transactions, and other functions that generally represent job roles.

In this chapter all the concepts are introduced with some practical examples dealing with the process of granting access rights and protecting the system elements. A final section of the chapter covers the topic of organizing the user master record management from the point of view of tasks involved in granting access rights to the users.

Overview of User Administration

As a SAP administrator or support personnel, user handling should not be of major concern if certain rules and guidelines are followed from the beginning of the project. This, however, does not apply to authorization and profile maintenance, which are matters of joint projects and efforts between the SAP functional and technical people. The reason is that usually SAP system managers do not have to deal with such things as granting access to certain users for specific general ledger accounts, cost centers, or production plants. It is the role of the customization specialists, developers, or business consultants to define entities which should be protected by means of authorization objects and to assign or create the corresponding profiles. This task is really important, and it might become a puzzle which can take a lot of time to solve, depending on the degree of security protection desired and the number of users and modules being implemented.

The easy part of user administration deals with such things as creating user master records, changing passwords, helping users define their own default values, and organizing the user maintenance tasks.

Managing User Master Records

Similar to the rest of the R/3 system, where there is a material master, a vendor master, and so on, the user administrative and management functions also has a user master. The *user master records* define the user accounts for enabling access to the system. They contain other screens with additional fields apart from the user ID, some of which are just for information purposes (but are nevertheless important) and others can make life easier for both users and administrators.

The user master records contain all the access information needed by the system to validate a user logon and assign users access rights to the system, such as passwords and authorization profiles.

There is a lot of extra information in a user master record, including which default screen the users will see when they first log on, what printer is assigned by default, and the addresses and phone numbers of users. Some of the fields are just for information purposes, while others have a direct effect on the working environment for the users.

To reach the user maintenance functions via menu options, from the main menu select *Tools → Administration → User maintenance → Users,* or type the transaction code *SU01* in the command field. Figure 9-1 shows the user maintenance initial screen. This screen shows the input field for specifying an individual user for which to perform administrative actions. To find a particular user when you don't know the proper user ID, you can select the possible entries list arrow, and then click on the *List* icon on the dialog box.

To perform functions over a group of users, the system includes some options under the menu *Environment → Mass changes.* This is explained in a later section.

Creating Users

From the user maintenance initial screen, as shown in Fig. 9-1, there are many options available. Normally, the input field for the *User* field is empty, except if you have been working in other user management functions previously in the same session.

User master records are client-dependent, which means that they are separately defined for each client in the SAP system. For example, if user *FREDSMITH* is defined on client 003, but not on client 005, he won't be able to log on in client 005.

To create a user master record you have two options: either define it completely from scratch or copy it from another user or from a reference user you had previously defined. The next sections explain both methods.

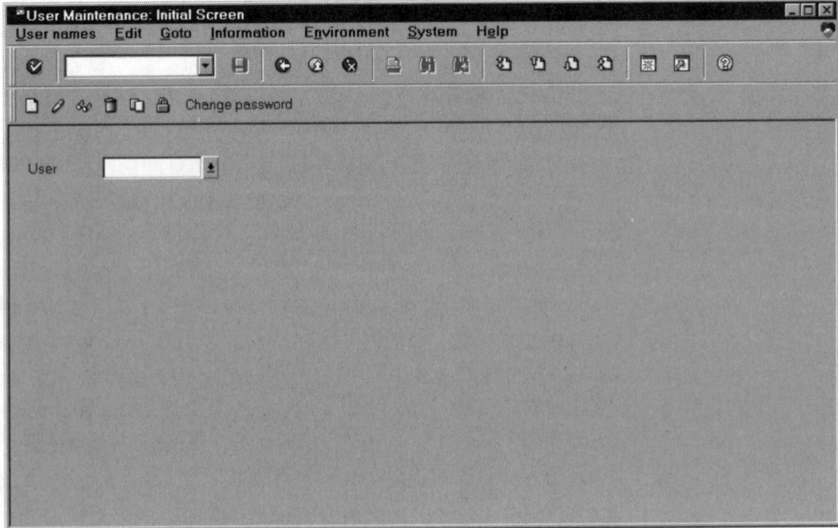

Figure 9-1 Initial screen for maintaining user master records.

Creating New Users from Scratch. From the user maintenance menu, enter the name for the new user and click on the *Create* icon, or with the right mouse button select the F8 function key, or select *User names* → *Create* from the menu bar. Figure 9-2 shows a screen similar to the one you will get. The system displays the different sections of the user master records within the different tabstrips. You might get additional tabstrips if you have security interfaces installed, such as with an SNC-compatible product.

The first data the system displays corresponds to the *Address* information. Here the *Last name* is a mandatory field that must be completed to go to other sections. You can move back and forth between tabstrips by clicking on them. However, any mandatory fields on these subscreens must be completed before you can move to another section.

The most important mandatory field is the password, located under the *Logon data* tabstrip, as shown in Fig. 9-3. Enter a password in the *Initial passwd* field and retype it in the second field (verification field). Also enter the user group, or select it from the list of available groups by clicking on the possible list entries arrow. Users themselves can maintain information corresponding to *Address, Defaults,* and *Parameters* by select-

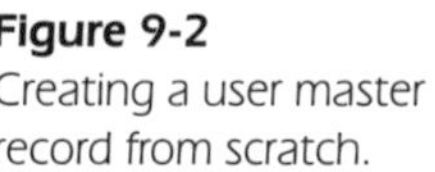

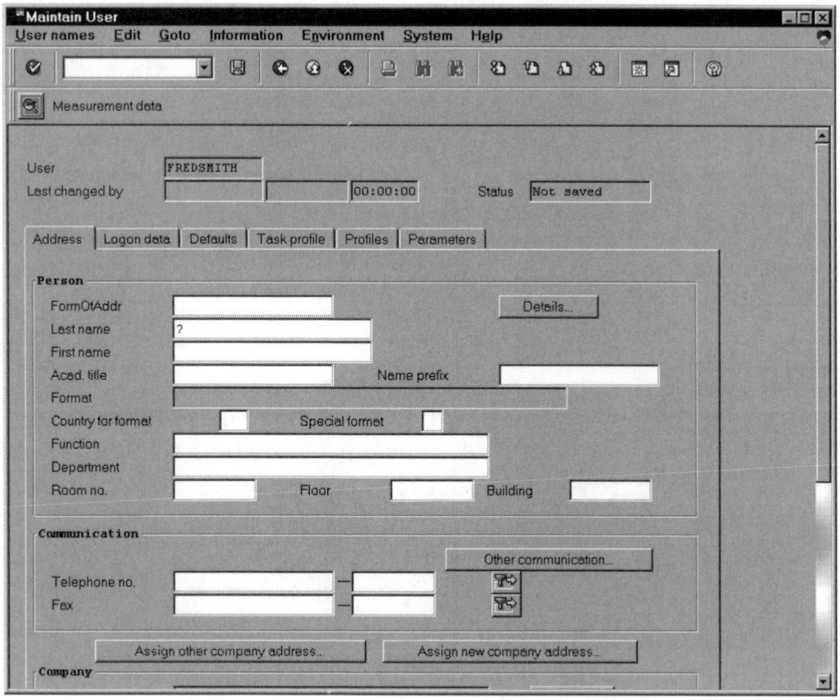

Figure 9-2
Creating a user master record from scratch.

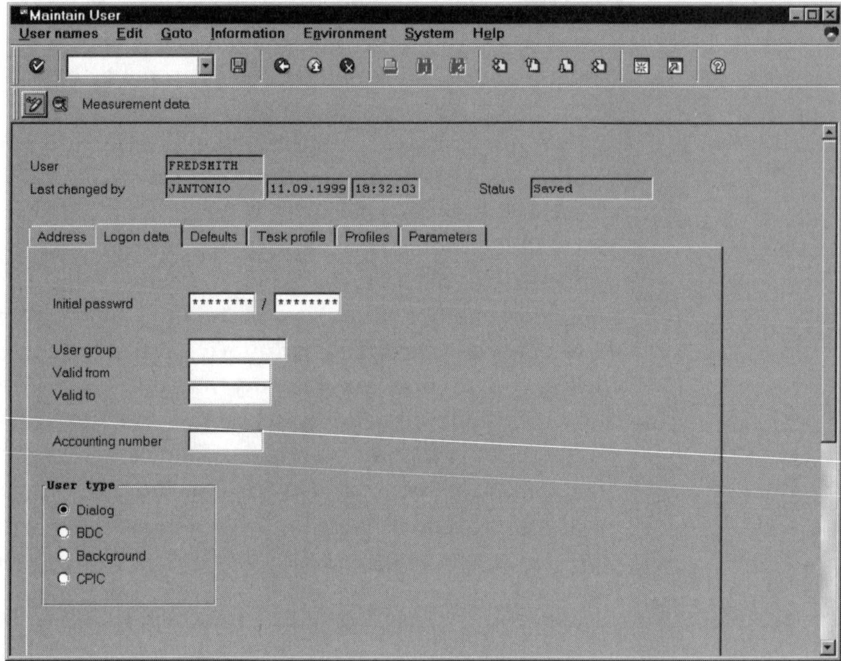

Figure 9-3 User maintenance logon data.

ing *System* → *User profile* → *Own data* if they have the required authorization.

When mandatory fields are completed, you can save the user by clicking on the *Save* icon. It is important, however, to assign at least some authorization profiles or task profiles to the users; otherwise they won't be able to perform any task.

After a user has been created, any modification to the user master fields is performed by entering the user ID in the *User* input field of the initial user maintenance screen, and clicking on the *Change* icon on the application toolbar.

Copying Users from Reference Master Records. Instead of defining all the R/3 users one by one from scratch, it is usually better to define some template user master records and to create new users by copying these templates and changing only some of the fields. Doing it this way reduces the time needed to create users, especially at the beginning of the system life. These models or reference users can be normal R/3 system users. For example, suppose your company is implementing R/3 for managing the sales and distribution, the materials management, and the finances. Possibly there will be users who just take orders in the system, others doing accounting work, and others with different tasks. In these cases, you can create a reference user for the sales module and use that user master record as a reference for creating the rest. The same process can be done for the users of other modules.

To create a new user by copying from a reference user, from the initial users maintenance screen, enter the name of the new user in the input field and press the *Copy* function button from the application toolbar. The system displays a dialog box similar to the one shown in Fig. 9-4.

As you can see from Fig. 9-4, you can decide what parts of the user master record to copy. You might want to copy just the profiles or just the address, in case you want to reuse any of the company address, or even just the defaults. In any case, you will have to specify a new password for the new user. The other values for the following screens can be modified just as if you were creating a new user. To modify any input field value, just write over the field while in *Overwrite* mode.

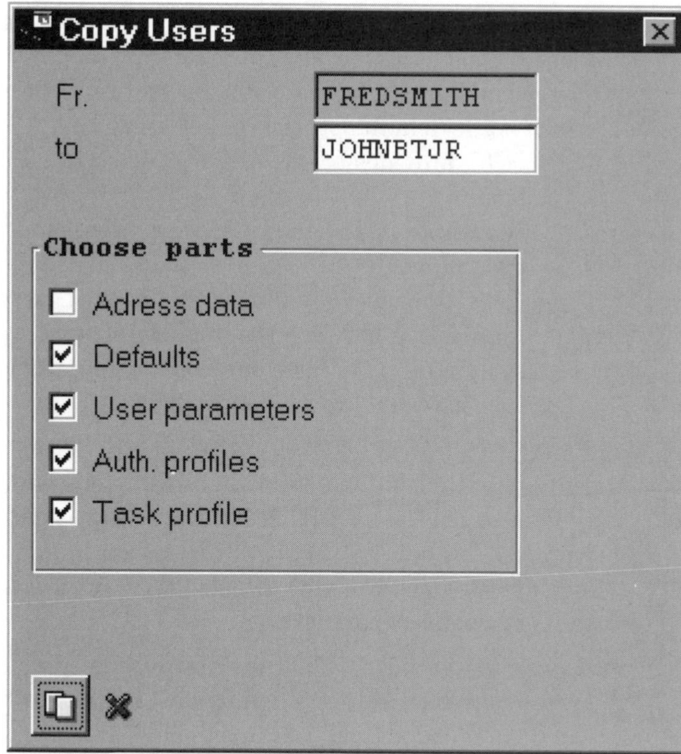

Figure 9-4
Dialog box for copying users.

User Master Records Fields

Whether you are creating or modifying user master records, the R/3 screens for the user maintenance transaction show several input fields. The most important fields are as follows:

- *Initial password.* The password for the first logon with the user ID. The password must be entered twice in a verification field, to make sure there were no typing errors. The next section explains password management from the point of view of the administrator. For an introduction and guide for users, refer to the "Password Rules" section in Chap. 5.
- *User group.* The name of the user master record group to which this user should be assigned. This is a useful field for dividing user maintenance among groups. For example, you can create user administrator master records in charge of a particular group but not of others. Before you can assign a group, it must have been created first.
- *User type.* There are four user types available, each of which provides special access privileges depending on the type of processing. The normal interactive or ordinary user must be of type *Dialog* which is the default. Other types of users are
  - — *BDC,* provides access privileges for processing batch input sessions
  - — *Background,* provides access privileges for processing background jobs
  - — *CPIC,* special system user for the SAP gateway and the communication between the application server processes. The R/3 system needs to have one CPIC user defined to be able to execute external programs from within R/3.

  A user can only be assigned to a user type.
- *Valid.* In this optional field, administrators can enter a period of time in which the user ID is valid. Although this field is often left empty, it can be very useful within a security policy, especially when setting accounts for occasional users such as external consultants or business partners.
- *Accounting number.* You can enter in this optional field any name or number you want to assign to a user as her or his user account. It can be unique for each user or can be shared by a group of users. This field is useful when working with the SAP user accounting sys-

tem, which performs statistics of the usage of the system. If you want to get individual usage statistics, you could enter the same user ID name into this field. For group statistics, a possibility is to enter the cost center, the department name, and so forth. If you leave it blank, the accounting statistics for the user will be assigned to a collective *No account* category.

- *Profile.* A profile gives the user the permission to access specific system functions. *Profiles* are made of a group of authorizations and authorization objects. Profiles can be simple or composite. Composite profiles are groups of profiles (either simple or composite).
- *Task profile.* Administrators can assign a list of individual tasks to users. The task profile defines the user's role within the R/3 system. The system includes three types of objects that can be added to a task profile: position, responsibility, and activity group. The first two objects are directly related to the Human Resources module.

The R/3 system includes a large number of predefined profiles and activity groups matching most common user needs for the different SAP application modules and also for the development and system management functions. To get the list of predefined profiles you can click on the possible entries arrow of the input field for profile. Looking for specific predefined profiles can be done by either looking in the application documentation or by searching the implementation guide (IMG).

There are other ways to search for profiles by tracing authorizations and then using the authorization information system. Both topics are covered later in this chapter.

The system provides facilities for creating your own profiles, using the Profile Generator or manual authorization creation, when the predefined profiles or activity groups are not enough.

Available Defaults and Options for User Master Records

After the first initial screen for user maintenance, the system provides additional screens for entering other user information. You can set, for example, the default printer for a user, the user's address, and values for user field defaults (parameters). The three available screens are *Address, Defaults,* and *Parameters.* These subscreens are accessed by clicking on the corresponding tabstrip within the user maintenance screen.

Users can set their own values and defaults by themselves in the *System → User profile → Own data* menu. The following sections show the available options which can be set by users.

Specifying User Address. The information in user addresses is only used by the R/3 system for documentation purposes. It can be very useful, however, for system administrators when trying to locate a user by her or his name, phone number, and so on. Often companies assign user IDs using letters and numbers which are coded so that it is easier to locate or assign user IDs to system users.

Figure 9-2 shows an example of this screen. As you can see, the *Address* data for a user includes three main information boxes, corresponding to *Person, Communication,* and *Company.* Some of the most important fields in those boxes are:

- *Last name.* In this field you must enter the surname of the user. This is a mandatory field that has an additional use when using SAPoffice.
- *Telephone no. and fax.* These fields can be used for entering the phone number and fax number. When there is an external fax system connected to R/3 using the SAPconnect interface, the fax number must be maintained to avoid error messages in the system log.
- *Company.* You can also enter and maintain the company information for users.

Other information which can be quite useful can be the phone and fax numbers, the cost center, the address, and so forth.

Setting User Default Values. Administrators or users by themselves can set some fixed or default values for some common functions or input fields which they find often while working in the R/3 system. Figure 9-5 shows an example of this screen. Here, you can set the following:

- *The Start menu for the user.* You can set the name of the menu or the transaction which will be started automatically when a user logs on.
- *The logon language.* Setting this field for a user will overwrite the system default when the user logs on. If the language field for the initial logon window of the R/3 system is empty, the language specified in this field is used.

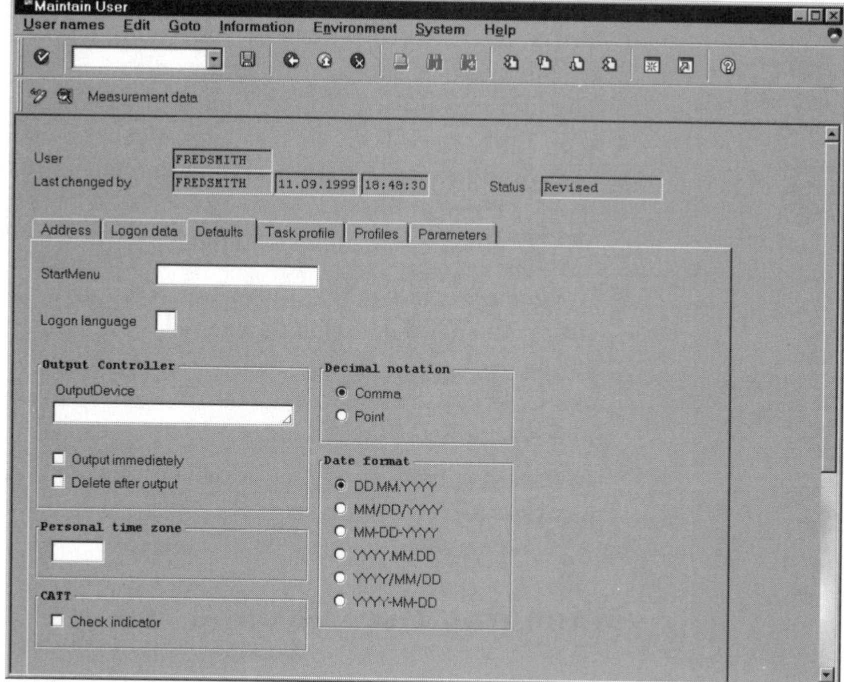

Figure 9-5 Maintaining user default values.

- *The default printer for a user.* This is assigned in the *Output device* field. You can click on the possible entries arrow to display a list of printers.
- *The output controller check boxes.* These are particularly important for handling users print requests. Check the box next to *Print immediately* to have a print job sent directly to the printer; otherwise, it will just send it to the output controller where users can print it later. Setting the box next to *Delete after output* tells the system to delete the job from the spool database after it has been printed. Information and management of the printing system is the topic of Chap. 14.
- *The format for date and decimal points.*

The last check box, *CATT,* is used for special test functions within the computer-aided test tool provided in the SAP system. For information on CATT, look it up in the SAP online documentation.

Setting User Default Values for Parameters. The parameters that can be set on this screen match some fields of the R/3 system. Setting default values using these parameters offers the advantage that every time a user is presented with a screen containing any of those fields, the value is automatically entered in the input field.

The section entitled "Input Field Default Values with User Parameters" in Chap. 5 explains this concept. Remember that at any time users can overwrite those values or change the parameter values by selecting *System → User profile → Own data.*

The parameter screen has two fields:

- *Parameters* refers to the parameter ID, which you can find using the technical information for the field (remember: place your cursor on the field, press F1 and then *Technical info*). You can also list the available parameters by clicking on the possible entries arrow next to the parameter input field.
- In the *value* field, enter the value you want to assign as the default any time an R/3 screen presents that field.

Managing User Groups

User groups within the R/3 user maintenance functions basically serve as a way to divide administration tasks. To reach the user groups screen, from the initial user maintenance, select *Environment → User groups.*

User groups are just assigned a name. So, the only two functions to perform are either *Create* a group or *Delete* a group. To create or delete a group, position the cursor over the group name and click on the corresponding function button.

An additional option, *Adjust,* is used to check whether the defined groups in the system are assigned to any users. In case they are not assigned, the system presents a list with the unassigned groups in case you decide to delete them.

Clients 000 and 001 include a special privilege group, SUPER, which is assigned by default to superusers SAP* and DDIC. To delete the group SUPER, users need special authorization.

Modifying User Master Records

Changes to user master records can be performed by the system administrator with the corresponding authorization or by the users themselves to their own address, defaults, or parameters values. Normal privileged users cannot change, for example, their authorization profiles. They can do that only if they have additional access rights to perform that operation.

The modifications made to a user master record (like a password, a locking, a time period validity, etc.) are only effective the next time a user logs on. Current logged-on users are not affected by those changes.

But administrators can make some changes to the users' access permission by modifying and then activating authorizations and profiles. Changes made to profiles are not effective until the users log on again; however, a modified and reactivated authorization has an immediate effect, even on logged-on users. So, for instance, if an authorization has been changed and then activated, it will immediately affect all users with profiles containing that authorization.

Deleting Users. To delete a single user master record, just enter it in the input box of the initial user maintenance screen and press the *Delete* button on the application toolbar.

Locking and Unlocking Users

Administrators can temporarily set a lock in user master records which prevents a particular user from logging on to the R/3 system. To lock a user, enter the user name in the input field and select the *Lock / unlock* button on the application toolbar, or select *User names* → *Lock / unlock* from the main menu. Locking and unlocking functions work in a toggle fashion. A lock won't have an effect on users who are currently logged on.

The system also enters automatic locks in user master records after 12 consecutive unsuccessful logon attempts. The default value is 12, but administrators can change that by setting an instance profile parameter. Refer to the section entitled "Technical Details: System Profile Parameters for Managing Users and Authorizations" at the end of this chapter.

A user who has been automatically locked out by the system because of unsuccessful logon attempts is also automatically unlocked by the system at midnight. However, a manual lock on a user master record will remain in place until you explicitly delete it.

Making Modifications to a Group of Users

The SAP system does not include many functions to perform over a group of users. The options available are:

- *Deleting all users from the current client.* From the initial user maintenance screen, select *Environment → Mass changes → Delete all users.* The system will present a confirmation screen.

WARNING! This function will delete all users from the specified client.

- *Adding or deleting a profile for all users.* To do this, select *Environment → Mass changes → User profile.* The system will present a screen where you can select which users will be affected by the change.
- *Resetting all user buffers* can be used cautiously by administrators when for some reason there is a need for cleaning the contents of the user buffer table.

Users Information System

The user maintenance functions of the SAP system include a comprehensive information system where you can look up, display, and analyze the users, profiles, or authorizations of the system. The system permits extensive navigation among the information: from users to profiles, from there to authorizations, and so on.

To reach the user and authorization information system, from the main user maintenance menu, select *Information → Information system.* The system displays a report tree corresponding to the authorization information system. These report trees contain several folders, each of which contains different reports. Figure 9-6 shows this report tree. By running different reports from the report tree folders, you can get a list of users, profiles, objects, authorizations, and so forth. The system presents several selection screens to permit searching for different criteria.

Another very useful report collection is the *Change documents* folder reports, which can be used for displaying any modifications made to authorizations, users, or profiles and tells who did the modification.

Password Management

To change a password for a user, click the *Change password* push button on the application toolbar from the initial user maintenance screen. The system will display the new password dialog box where you have to enter

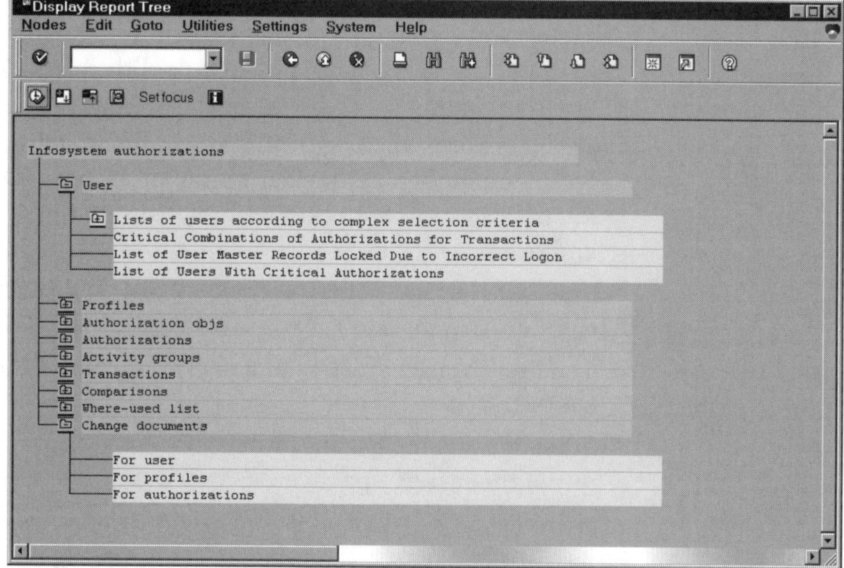

Figure 9-6 Authorization info system report tree.

the password twice to verify that you didn't make any typing mistakes. When system managers change the password for other users, the system requests these users to enter the new password when they log on.

Administrators can change their passwords and other users' passwords as many times as they wish; however, normal privileged users can only change their passwords once a day.

By default and right from installation, there are some standard requirements concerning passwords. Some of the restrictions are set up in the system code and cannot be changed, while others can be changed as required by setting some instance profile parameters or by configuring system tables. For example, system administrators might decide to set up a minimum password length or enter a character string as a nonpermitted password.

On the other hand, passwords are not case-sensitive, so uppercase and lowercase passwords or a mix and match of both cases behave exactly the same.

Password Restrictions and Requirements

The passwords restrictions and requirements are as follows:

- The password cannot be the word *pass*.
- Minimum password length is set by default to three characters. Administrators can change this setting by specifying a greater value in

the instance profile parameter *login/min_password_lng*. If you change this parameter, be sure to do it in the common DEFAULT.PFL so that it has effect on every instance of the SAP system. Maximum password length is always set to eight characters.

- The password can't begin with any sequence of three characters contained in the user ID. For example, if a user ID is *FREDSMITH,* the password cannot begin with the letters: *FRE, RED, EDS, SMI,* and so on.
- The first character of a password cannot be an exclamation point (!) or a question mark (?).
- The first three characters of a password cannot contain a space character.
- When a user changes his or her password, he or she may not use any of the last five passwords.
- Administrators can decide to forbid certain strings to be used as passwords. Users will receive an error message in the status bar when specifying a password which has been forbidden by the administrator. The process of forbidding passwords is explained later.
- A password cannot begin with three identical characters. For example: *aaamy* and *bbbyou* are invalid passwords.
- A user must change his or her password if there is an expiration date in the user master account and the date has arrived.

System managers can decide how frequently the users must enter new passwords. To enforce password changes, set the instance profile parameter *login/password_expiration_time* with a value indicating the number of days after which a password must be changed. For example, if the profile parameter is set to 30, users will be requested to change their password every month. To leave the passwords without limit, the default value *0* is used for this parameter.

With the previous restrictions and other user master records rules, the process of logging on to R/3 requires some more work for the system code to do besides checking the password. For instance, when a user tries to log on with a correct password, the system first checks whether the user is locked. If the user is locked either manually by the system manager or automatically after 12 unsuccessful logon attempts or by a system upgrade, the system displays an error message.

If the user is not locked, then R/3 checks whether the current password has expired. In this case, the system requests the user to enter a new password.

Restricting Password Strings

System administrators can forbid passwords or password strings by entering them in the table USR40. This is useful, for example, to avoid the use of passwords which start with similar words as the name of the company, the river that crosses nearby, and so forth. Table USR40 is maintained with standard table maintenance transactions such as SM30 and SM31 (*System → Services → Table maintenance*).

To specify a nonpermitted password string, you can enter the typical wildcards, * and ?, where the * substitutes a group of characters, and the ?, a single character.

Figure 9-7 shows an example of this table with some of the forbidden password strings. In this example, all passwords starting with the characters *SAP,* containing *R3,* or ending with *2000* are forbidden. This table is client-independent and, therefore, the password restrictions are applied to any system client.

Managing R/3 Superusers

The SAP R/3 system includes in the default installation two special users: DDIC and SAP*. These users have special privileges and must be pro-

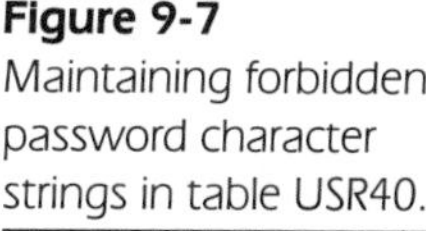

Figure 9-7
Maintaining forbidden password character strings in table USR40.

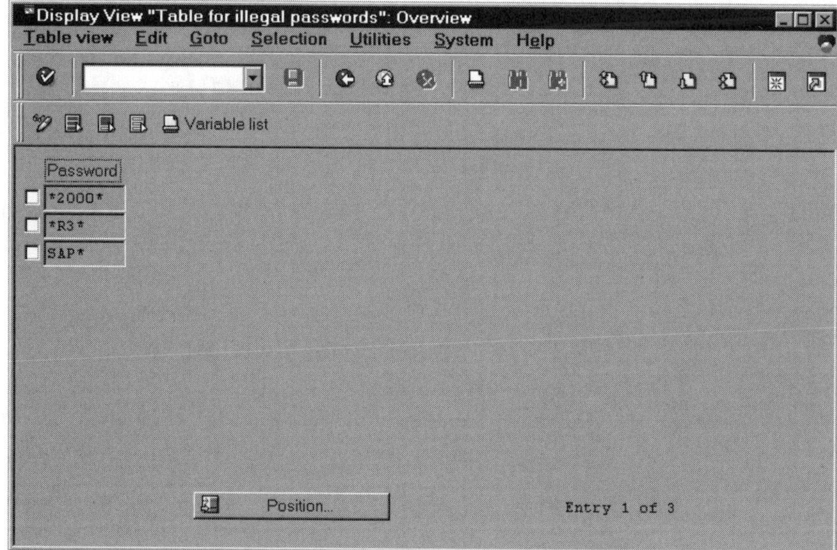

tected to avoid unauthorized access. System administrators should consider a good strategy for managing the superusers of R/3 for security reasons and to ensure system integrity.

The standard installation creates the system clients 000, 001, and 066. The SAP* and DDIC users are created in clients 000 and 001 with standard names and passwords.

User SAP*

SAP* is the standard SAP system superuser, and it's the only system user who does not require a user master record because it's defined in the code itself. When a new client is created for doing a client copy, SAP* is created by default in the new client with a standard password *PASS* and unlimited access rights. In the standard installation, SAP* has the password 06071992 in clients 000 and 001.

The special properties of the SAP* user can be deactivated. To deactivate the properties of the SAP* superuser, you must create a user master record for it, in which case it will have just the authorizations given in the profiles of the user master record.

If a user master record exists for SAP* and then it is deleted, it recovers the special properties assigned by the system code and has the password *PASS* again. When SAP* does not have a user master record, the password is always *PASS;* it cannot be changed, and it's not subject to any authorization check.

Some of the measures to protect SAP* are as follows:

- Change the password in client 000 and 001.
- Create a user master record for SAP* in 000, 001, 066, and the possible new clients you create in the system.
- Turn off the special status of SAP* by setting the instance profile parameter *login/no_automatic_user_sapstar* to a value greater than zero in the common default profile, DEFAULT.PFL. If the parameter is set, then SAP* has no special default properties. If there is no SAP* user master record, then SAP* cannot be used to log on. Be sure to have a user master record for SAP* even when this parameter is set because, if the parameter is reset to the value *0,* the system will again allow the logins by SAP* with the password *PASS.*
- Having a user master record, SAP* behaves like any other user subject to authorization checks. Its password can be changed.

- Create your own superuser account in each system client. This is explained in the next section.
- Delete all profiles from the SAP* profile list so that it has no authorizations.
- Be sure that SAP* is assigned to the user group SUPER which protects the master records from being deleted by anyone not having authorization to delete SUPER master records. The user group SUPER has special status in the user maintenance profiles as delivered by the system. Users within this group can only be maintained or deleted by new superusers, as defined by the SAP standard authorization profiles.

Defining a New Superuser

Defining a new superuser just requires giving him or her a superuser profile with all authorizations in the user master record. The standard profile with full authorization, which is the only one needed to define a new superuser to replace SAP*, is the SAP_ALL profile.

SAP_ALL contains all R/3 authorizations, including the new authorizations as released in the SAP_NEW profile. SAP_NEW is a standard R/3 profile which ensures upward compatibility in access privileges. It's the way to protect users against authorization problems after a new system upgrade. If the upgrade of the system includes new access tests, this profile ensures the inclusion of those new authorization objects needed to validate the new access tests.

User DDIC

User DDIC (from *data dictionary*) is the maintenance user for the ABAP dictionary and for software logistics. It's the user required to perform special functions in system upgrades. Like SAP*, user DDIC is a user with special privileges.

The user master record for user DDIC is automatically created in clients 000 and 001 when you install your R/3 system. It has, by default, the password 19920706. Its difference from SAP* is that it has its own user master record.

To secure DDIC against unauthorized use, you must change the password for the user in clients 000 and 001 in your R/3 system.

User DDIC is required for certain installation and setup tasks in the system, so you should not delete DDIC.

The Authorization System in SAP R/3

The authorization system of the SAP R/3 system is the general term which groups all the technical and management elements for granting access privileges to users to enforce the R/3 system security.

An *access privilege* is permission to perform a particular operation in the SAP system. Access privileges in the R/3 system are granted to users by assigning them authorizations, profiles, or task profiles. By entering such profiles in user master records, you enable users to use the system.

The main features and concepts of the SAP R/3 authorization system can be summarized as follows:

- The authorization system is based on complex system objects with multiconditional testing of system access privileges. The authorization system tests multiple conditions before granting users the permission to perform a task in the system. A multiconditional access test is defined in an authorization object. A multiconditional testing is, for example, to allow users to create, display, or delete information from one purchasing center, but only display information in another purchasing center. The following list shows this concept:

User	*Purchasing Center*	*Permissions*
FREDSMITH	001	Create, Delete, Display
FREDSMITH	002	Display
JGALPJR	002	Create, Delete, Display

- The authorization system uses authorization profiles and activity groups, together with the Profile Generator tool, to make the maintenance of the user master records easier. Authorization profiles are groups of authorizations. Instead of entering every authorization in the user master records, administrators only have to enter profiles.
- Authorization profiles can be either simple or composite. Composite profiles contain other profiles.
- The authorization system uses an activation method. When authorization or profiles are created or modified, they must be activated to become effective.

- The SAP authorization system provides mechanisms for the distribution of the maintenance tasks related with users and access privileges, such as assigning authorizations, activating profiles, managing new authorizations, and so on. These tasks can be done by a single superuser or they can be divided among several administrators.

The R/3 system includes many predefined authorizations, profiles, activity groups, and activity group templates, which cover most of the usual needs for assigning access privileges to users. Before creating a new profile, you should try to use an existing predefined profile or activity group.

The complex objects of the R/3 authorization system are structured in a hierarchical but flexible way, as shown in Fig. 9-8. The next section introduces the main elements of the authorization system. These concepts might seem a bit complex the first time you work with them, so the following section includes a practical step-by-step example where all these topics are used in a real situation.

In order to aid understanding of the authorization system, basic concepts are explained first. Then the manual procedure for creating profiles and authorizations is introduced, and finally the Profile Generator tool and how to work with it are covered.

Authorization Profiles

An authorization profile contains a group of authorizations, that is, a group of access privileges. Profiles are assigned to users in the user master records. A profile could represent a simple job position since it defines the tasks for which a user has access privileges. Every profile might have

Figure 9-8 Hierarchy of authorization system.

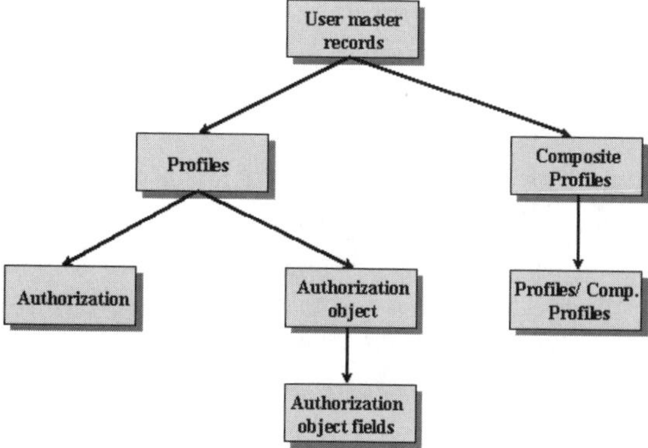

as many access privileges (authorizations) as desired. Profiles can contain authorization objects and authorizations.

Changing the list or contents of the authorizations inside a profile affects all users that are given that profile when this is activated. It becomes effective the next time the user logs on. The change is not effective for users currently logged on.

Composite Profiles

Composite profiles are sets of authorization profiles, both simple and composite. A composite profile can contain an unlimited number of profiles. They can be assigned to users just as profiles in the user master records are.

Composite profiles are suitable for users who have different responsibilities or job tasks in the system. These profiles are sometimes known as *reference* profiles for assigning a larger group of access privileges and having the possibility to better match users with several responsibilities.

Making modifications to any of the profiles in the list included in the composite profile directly affects the access privileges of all users having that composite profile in the user master record.

When displaying profiles on the different SAP screens, there is a flag indicating whether the profile is simple or composite.

Authorizations

The R/3 system uses authorizations to define the permitted values for the fields of an authorization object. An authorization might contain one or more values for each field of the authorization object.

An authorization object is like a template for testing access privileges, consisting of authorization fields which finally define the permitted values for the authorization. Both authorization objects and fields are explained in the next two sections.

An authorization is identified with the name of an authorization object and the name of the authorization created for the object. An authorization can have many values or ranges of values for a single field. It is also possible to authorize for every value (by entering an asterisk, *) or for none (by leaving the field blank). In the example shown in Fig. 9-9, you can see that for the object, *Batch processing: Batch administrator,* there are several authorizations. Each of these authorizations can have different values for the authorization fields within the object.

Authorizations are entered in authorization profiles with the corresponding authorization object. When an authorization is changed and then activated, it immediately affects all users having a profile containing that authorization in their user master records.

The technical names for authorizations and authorization objects have a maximum of 12 positions, but usually they are displayed in the system using short descriptive texts. For customer-created authorizations, the only name restriction is to not place an underscore in the second position of the technical name. Additionally, every customer-created system object should comply with SAP standard style guide and begin either with a *Z* or a *Y* to distinguish it from the SAP original objects, thus avoiding the possibility of being overwritten by a system upgrade.

Authorization Objects

An *authorization object* identifies an element or object within the SAP system which needs to be protected. These objects work like templates for granting access rights by means of authorization fields which allow for performing complex tests of access privileges. An authorization object can contain a maximum of 10 authorization fields. Users are permitted

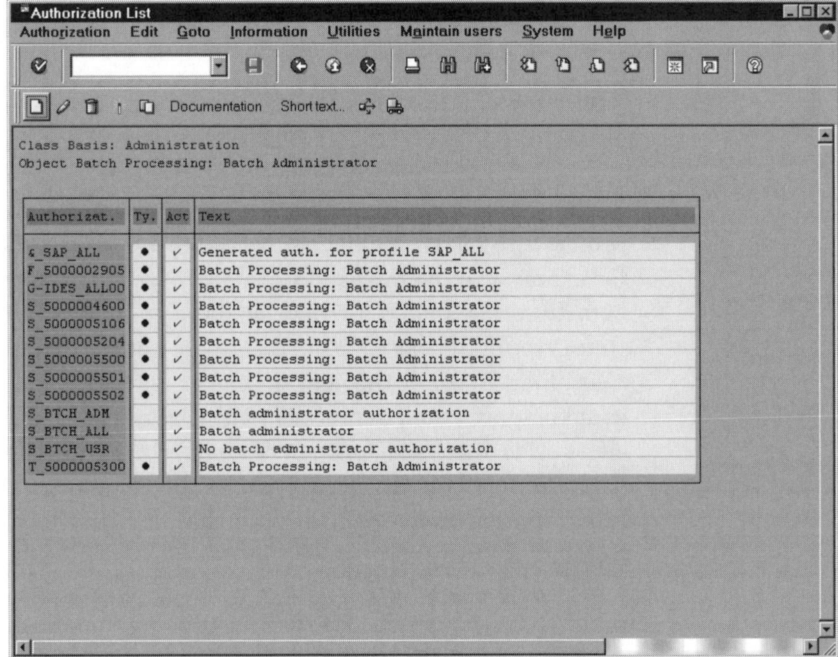

Figure 9-9 Example of authorization list for an authorization object.

to perform a system function only after passing the test for every field in the authorization object. The verification against the field contents is done with the logical AND operator. Users' actions are allowed only if the user authorization complies with the access test for each field contained in an object. With this mechanism, the system can perform multiconditional tests.

As with authorizations, when maintaining authorization objects, the system does not display the names but descriptive text for each object.

Authorization objects are grouped in object classes belonging to different application areas which are used to limit the search for objects, thus making it faster to navigate among the many R/3 system objects.

SAP predefined authorization objects should not be modified or deleted, except if instructed by the SAP support personnel or a SAPnet note. Deleting or changing standard authorization objects can cause severe errors in the programs that check those objects.

Before an authorization object is modified, all authorizations defined for that object must first be deleted.

If you want to use the OR logic to give users access to certain functions, you can define several authorizations for the same object, each time with different values. In the user master records, you assign each of these profiles, which are linked with the OR login. So, when the system tests whether the user has access privileges, it checks each authorization to see if the assigned values comply with the access condition. The system allows access with the first authorization that passes the test.

Authorization Fields

Authorization fields identify the elements of the system which are to be protected by assigning them access tests. An authorization field can be, for example, a user group, a company code, a purchasing group, a development class, or an application area. There is one authorization field that is found in most authorization objects which is the *Activity*. The *Activity* field in an authorization object defines the possible actions which could be performed over a particular application object. For example, activity *03* is always *Display,* so if an authorization contains two fields such as *company code* and *activity* and if the company code field is * (meaning all company codes), the user with that authorization can only display the company codes.

The list of standard activities in the system is held on the SAP standard table TACT, which can be displayed using standard transactions such as

SM30 (*System → Services → Table Maintenance*), SM31 (*System → Services → Ext. Table main.*), and SE16 (*Tools → ABAP Workbench → Overview → Data Browser*). Figure 9-10 shows the contents for table TACT.

The relationship between the authorization objects and the activities is held in table TACTZ. Not all authorization objects have the *Activity* authorization field.

Authorization fields are the components of authorization objects as stated previously. And also, fields are part of the standard ABAP function call AUTHORITY-CHECK.

When maintaining authorizations, the system does not display the real names (technical names) for the fields, instead it shows a description for each field. Table TOBJ contains the fields that are associated with each authorization object; this is how the SAP system knows which fields belong to an authorization object. The fields in an object are associated with data elements in the ABAP data dictionary.

Authorization fields are not maintained from the user maintenance menu, but have to be defined within the development environment.

Normally users do not need to change standard authorization fields, except if adding or modifying system elements and they want those elements to be tested with authorizations.

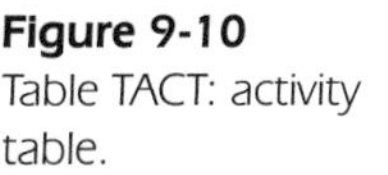

Figure 9-10 Table TACT: activity table.

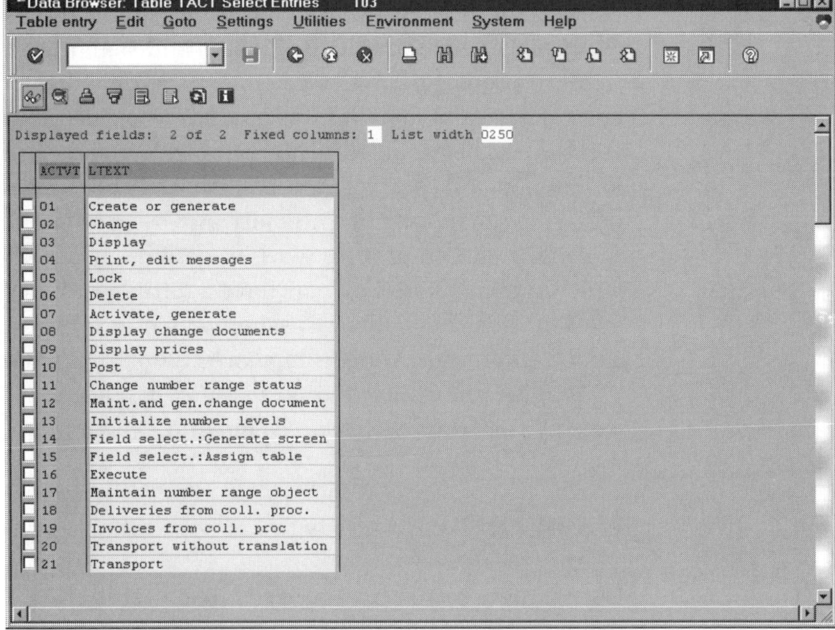

ACTVT	LTEXT
01	Create or generate
02	Change
03	Display
04	Print, edit messages
05	Lock
06	Delete
07	Activate, generate
08	Display change documents
09	Display prices
10	Post
11	Change number range status
12	Maint.and gen.change document
13	Initialize number levels
14	Field select.:Generate screen
15	Field select.:Assign table
16	Execute
17	Maintain number range object
18	Deliveries from coll. proc.
19	Invoices from coll. proc
20	Transport without translation
21	Transport

Activity Groups

The definition of profiles with the Profile Generator Tool is based on the possibility of grouping functions by *activity groups* in a company menu that is generated using customization settings and that will only include those functions selected by the customers.

Activity groups form a set of tasks or activities that can be performed in the system, such as running programs, transactions, and other functions that generally represent job roles. The activity groups and the information they include are what makes the profiles able to be automatically generated.

Activity groups are the basic components needed for working with the Profile Generator tool, which uses them to generate authorization profiles.

An activity group resembles a job role, such as sales representative, accountant, treasurer, system administrator, and so on. Activity groups can include as many single system activities as needed. Single system activities can be transactions, reports, or tasks. These activities can be included in as many different activity groups as needed.

Administrators select transactions or reports from a menu tree, or can select authorizations and save this information as an activity group. This selection is used by the profile generator for determining the necessary authorizations and generating the profiles, which can then be assigned to users. If an activity group contains more than 150 authorizations, the profile generator automatically creates additional profiles.

More properly, activity groups are assigned to organizational objects, such as organizational units, jobs, positions, users, and so on. User master records can be assigned to one or more activity groups. When this type of assignment takes place, the updating of the user master records can be performed manually or automatically by running a background job.

Authorization profiles within activity groups are date dependent, which means that they can have multiple validity periods that cannot overlap. Date dependency assignment of profiles to user master records can be enforced by scheduling background jobs for that purpose.

Activity groups are stored in *Infotypes,* special organizational objects used by the Human Resources module.

User Buffer

User buffers are special areas (tables) containing all the authorizations for the user. These buffers are specific for individual users, and are actually built when the users log on, based on the authorizations contained in the profiles included in the user master record.

When users try to perform activities in the system, the application programs and transaction are checked against the authorization objects and values contained within the user buffer.

The number of entries in the user buffer can be controlled using the profile parameter *auth/number_in_userbuffer.*

The Activation Concept in Profiles and Authorizations

The authorization system allows two versions of authorizations or profiles: an active version and a modified, or maintenance, version. A new or modified authorization or profile cannot be used until it has been activated, since user master records can only contain active versions of profiles.

The activation concept is useful for preventing mistakes when creating new authorizations or modifying existing ones, since the maintenance versions will not affect the system. It is also helpful for dividing the maintenance tasks among several users. For example, some users can define or edit authorizations, while an activation administrator can be in charge of activating the maintenance versions previously created.

The system verification for access privileges is only performed against active versions. Active versions are the only ones which have real effect in the system.

When administrators create or modify an authorization or a profile, then they are working with a maintenance version. In this state, the system displays the status *Revised* in the header of the authorization or profile being modified. When the activation is performed, the maintenance version becomes the active one and replaces automatically the existing version if it exists. The system changes the status to *Active.*

Case Study: From the Authorization Fields to the Profiles, a Practical Example

The next example shows step-by-step how to manually create an authorization based on a standard authorization object. In the example, a new authorization for the development environment is created, allowing users to only perform activities in programs that belong to a particular development class.

From the SAP main menu, select *Tools* → *Administration* → *User maintainence* → *Authorization.* The system will display a screen similar to the one in Fig. 9-11. Notice that this screen shows only the object classes. You can use the scroll bars or the scroll buttons on the standard toolbar to display additional object classes.

Double click over the *Basis: Development Environment* object class to display the list of objects for that class. Notice that the system displays only the descriptive text for the authorization objects. To see the name, click on the *Technical name* button on the application toolbar. Figure 9-12 shows the same objects as the previous figure but with the technical names.

To display the fields associated with the authorization object S_DEVELOP, position the cursor over the line and click on the *Display fields* button on the application toolbar. Figure 9-13 shows the screen display.

The values assigned to any of those fields configure the authorizations for that object. To display the list of existing authorizations for that object, double click over the S_DEVELOP line.

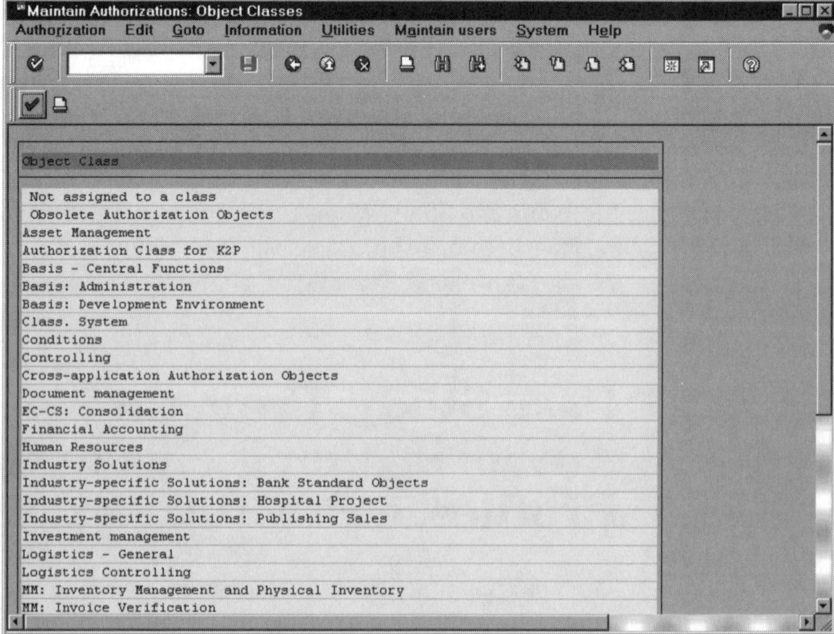

Figure 9-11
Authorization object classes initial screen.

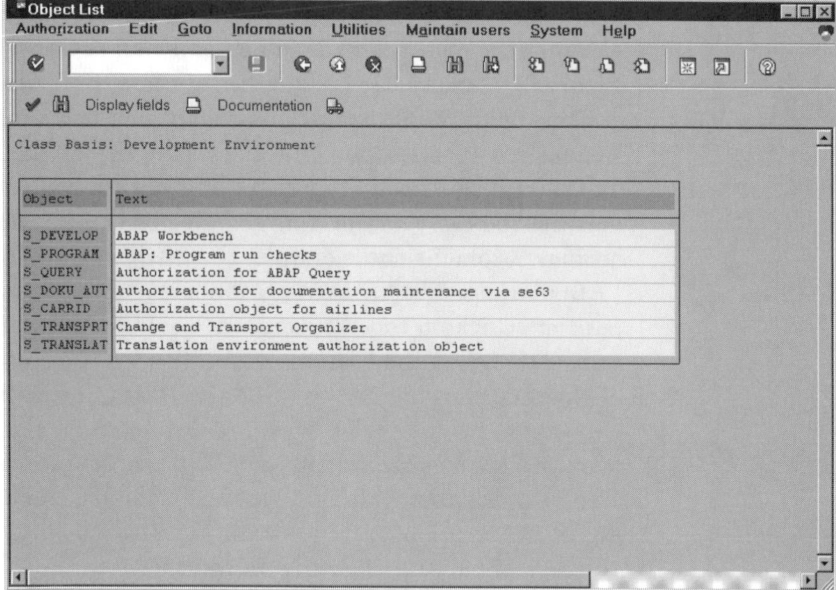

Figure 9-12 Technical names for authorization objects.

The difference between these authorizations is in the values assigned to the fields of the authorization object. To see the field values, double click on any of the lines. In the example, you can create a new authorization from scratch or copy an existing one from the list. Scroll down to look up the field values for the authorization S_DEVELOP (notice that has the

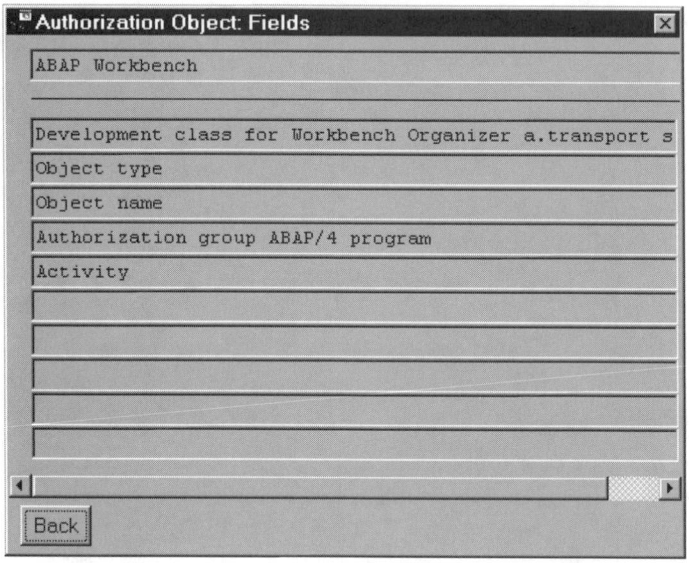

Authorization Object: Fields

ABAP Workbench

Development class for Workbench Organizer a.transport s

Object type

Object name

Authorization group ABAP/4 program

Activity

Back

Figure 9-13 Authorization fields for the object ABAP development workbench.

same name as the object), you can see that it has by default all permissions for the object. This is indicated by an asterisk (*) as the field value. Figure 9-14 shows the field values of the S_DEVELOP authorization.

The standard authorizations should not be changed by the customers. Instead create a new one. Click once over the S_DEVELOP authorization, and then click on the *Copy* button on the application toolbar. The system displays the *Copy authorization* dialog box where you can enter your own authorization. In the example, the new authorization is called *ZZDEVELOP.* Remember that you cannot write an underscore in the second position. Click on the *Copy* button inside the dialog box. The system will go back to the authorization list.

Now you can change the values for the authorization fields and include only access privileges for your own development class, which is one of the fields of the authorization objects. To do so, double click on your newly created authorization, which displays a similar screen to the one shown in Fig. 9-14. Position the cursor on the *Development class for Workbench organizer* field and click the *Maintain values* button on the application toolbar. The system displays a screen like the one shown in Fig. 9-15. This dialog box has several input fields which allow you to limit with single values or using value ranges which will be the permitted development classes for users having that authorization. These input fields include possible entries arrows for selecting available values. In the example, all development classes from ZAAA to ZZZZ are permitted.

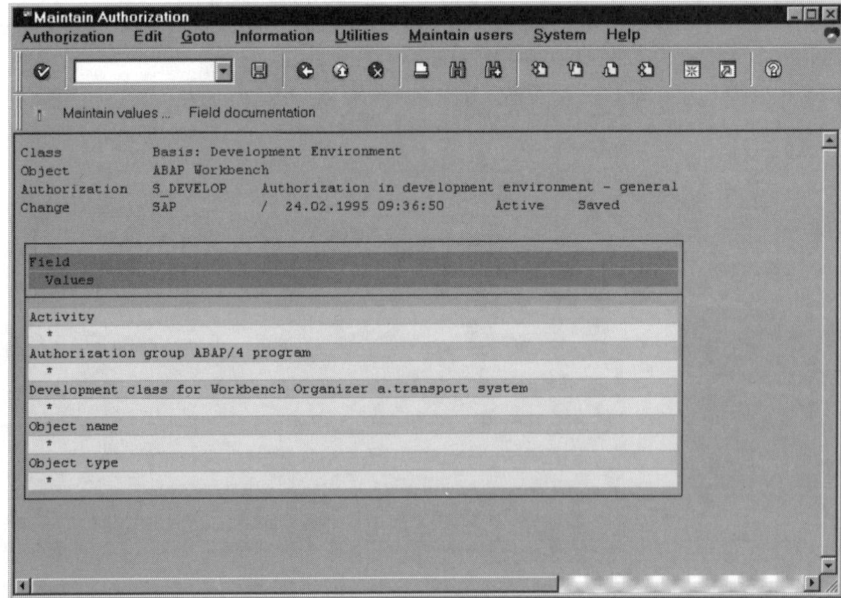

Figure 9-14 Initial screen for displaying and maintaining authorization fields for an authorization.

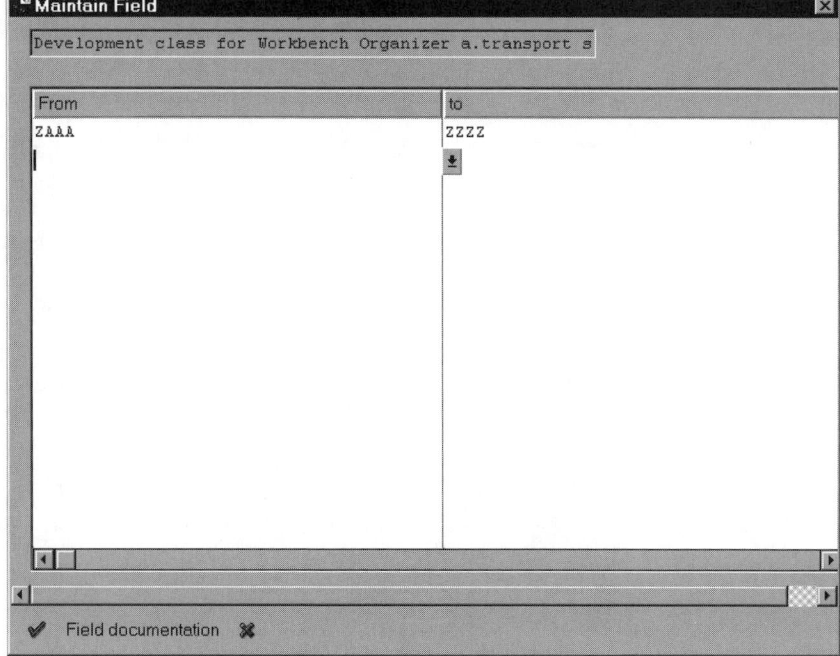

Figure 9-15 Entering values in an authorization field.

Click on the *Enter* button, and finally save your new authorization by clicking on the *Save* button on the standard toolbar. Follow the same procedure for modifying the authorization, so that users can only display system objects belonging to those development classes. In that case, the field value you want to modify is the one corresponding to *Activity.* When modifying the *Activity* field, clicking on the possible entries arrow shows the list of possible activities. Figure 9-16 displays this dialog box. Select the activity *03* which corresponds to *Display.* This tells the system that the user is only allowed to display development objects. Save your new authorization.

Next, for the access privileges to become effective, you have to activate the newly created authorizations. To do that, position the cursor over the authorization, and click on the *Activate* button on the application toolbar. Alternatively, select *Authorization* → *Activate* from the menu. The activation is a two-step process which first shows the defined values for the authorization fields and then activates the authorization. Click again on the *Activate* icon on the application toolbar. You will see a check mark in the *Act.* column.

Finally, those new authorizations have to be assigned to users creating an authorization profile, which is what we enter in the user master records. To create a profile, go back to the initial user maintenance screen and then select *User maintainence* → *Profiles.* Alternatively, you can

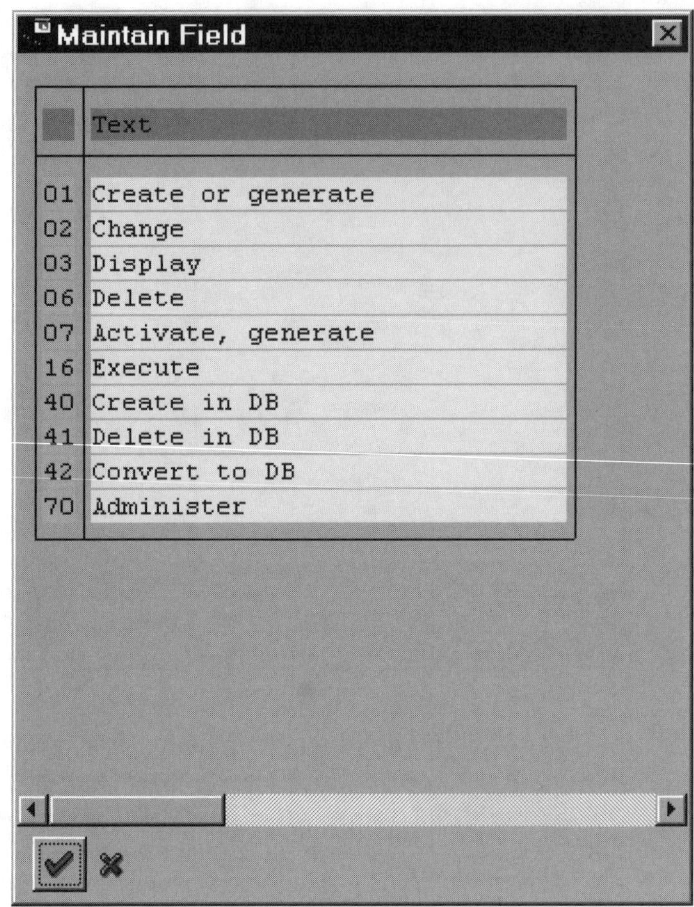

Figure 9-16 List of activities associated with the *Activity* field in the authorization.

enter transaction SU02 in the command field. Figure 9-17 shows the initial screen for profile maintenance.

Since you are going to create a new profile, select the check box next to *Maintained only* under the version box, and click on the *Generate work area* function button. If you select the *Active* option, the system will display the list of all currently active profiles.

Click on the *Create* icon on the application toolbar. The system displays the *Create new profile* dialog box such as the one in Fig. 9-18. In this dialog box, you could decide whether you want to create a simple or composite profile. The system default is simple. Assign a name and a short description to your new profile and press *Enter*.

The system now displays the screen for maintaining the profiles. You now have to insert the authorizations created previously. To do so, click on

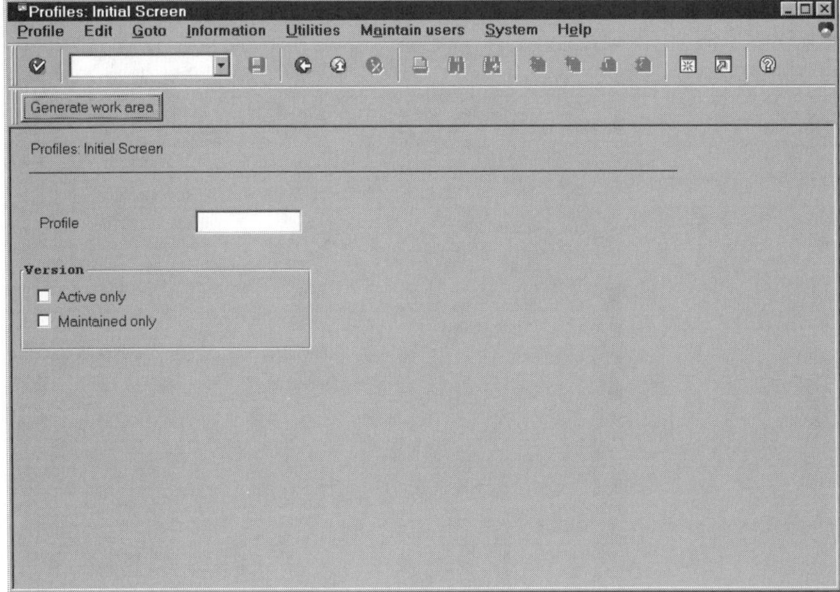

Figure 9-17
Initial screen for maintaining profiles.

the *Insert authorization* button on the application toolbar. You will see the object class list again. Double click on the line corresponding to *Basis: development environment* to get the list of available authorizations for the objects in the class. Locate your authorizations and click on the check boxes next to the object names. Here, you can decide to include as many authorization as you like. Press the *Enter* key and the system will return to the profile maintenance screen and will automatically insert the authorizations selected. Figure 9-19 shows the resulting screen. Notice in the header that the profile is *New* and *Not saved*. For the profile to be assigned to users, first click on the *Save* button to save it. The system will change the status to *Revised* and *Saved*. And, finally, press the *Activate*

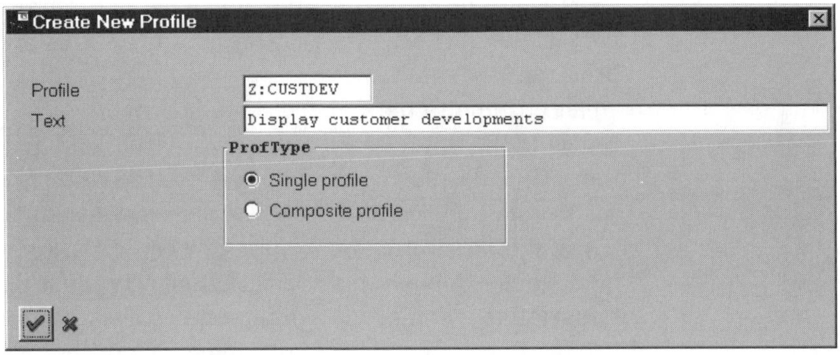

Figure 9-18
Dialog box for creating a new profile.

Create New Profile
Profile Z:CUSTDEV
Text Display customer developments
ProfType
Single profile
Composite profile

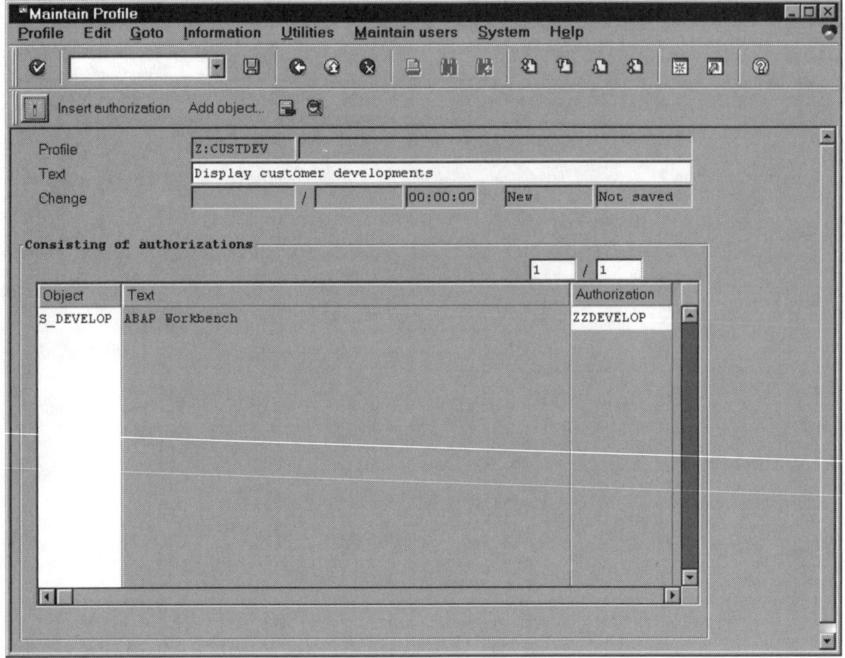

Figure 9-19 Assigning authorizations to the new profile.

button to make an active version for the profile. Once the profile is active, you can insert it in user master records.

Working with the Profile Generator

The Profile Generator is a SAP tool, available since release 3.0F and productive since release 3.1G, that aids in facilitating the management of user authorizations and profiles. Previous to the Profile Generator, there was a great deal of effort involved in the implementation and support of the authorization concept, and this was a costly activity within projects.

The Profile Generator tool was designed by SAP with the objective of reducing the time needed for implementing and managing the authorizations, thus decreasing the implementation costs. SAP recommends using the Profile Generator to set up authorizations.

Using the Profile Generator is very different from manual profile management, where authorization objects must be selected, authorizations defined, and profiles created to be assigned to users later. With the Profile Generator, the management of authorizations is based on the functions and tasks that users will perform with R/3, and the Profile Generator is in charge of selecting and grouping the authorization objects.

The definition of profiles with the Profile Generator is based on grouping functions by *activity groups* in a company menu that is generated using customization settings and that will only include those functions selected by the customers. As introduced in a previous section, *activity groups* form a set of tasks or activities that can be performed in the system, such as running programs, transactions, and other functions that generally represent job roles. The activity groups include information so that profiles can be automatically generated.

In summary, the Profile Generator:

- Can be used to automatically create profiles and assign them easily to users
- Only selects and uses the necessary authorization objects, avoiding excessive validations in the system and thereby improving performance
- Facilitates functional communication between security or the authorization administrator and end users or consultants
- Makes defining and maintaining authorization profiles easier

The Profile Generator can be accessed from the main menu by selecting *Tools* → *Administration* → *Users* → *Activity groups,* or alternatively by entering transaction code *PFCG* in the command field.

The Profile Generator only generates simple profiles. When these profiles have been automatically generated, they cannot be maintained manually.

The following sections introduce how the Profile Generator works, how to configure it, and a basic example of creating activity groups and using automatically generated profiles to assign the activity groups to user master records.

How the Profile Generator Works

Based on a job role, or group of tasks that represents what the users are trying to perform, administrators can identify and select the transactions, reports, or values that are required for users to pass the authorization checks.

Using the Profile Generator tools, the administrator creates activity groups that select the required authorizations from a company menu, and sets authorization values for the authorization objects selected.

Once activity groups are created, the Profile Generator is in charge of retrieving all the authorization objects for the selected transactions. This is accomplished using special check tables.

The Profile Generator then creates the profile or profiles, and then the activity group can be assigned to the user master record.

The user master record is then updated by a direct assignment, which automatically assigns the generated profiles as well. This assignment can be also performed via a batch job.

Once the assignment is done, when the users log on, their user buffer will contain the corresponding authorization that will allow them to pass the authorization checks required for performing their usual jobs.

Configuring the Profile Generator

Before using the Profile Generator for the first time, there are four steps that are required to configure and work with the Profile Generator tool. These steps are:

1. Activate the Profile Generator. The activation of the Profile Generator is based on the instance profile parameter

```
auth/no_check_in_some_cases = Y
```

If this value is not set, users won't be able to see the *Authorization* push button within the activity group maintenance screen.

This is the default value since release 4.0. This profile parameter tells the system to allow certain authorization checks to be ignored in a program. With this setting the profiles will only contain the necessary authorizations. For example, if the installation includes only one company code, administrators don't want to worry about setting authorizations for company code.

2. Set Up the Initial Copy of Profile Generator Configuration Tables. You must run transaction *SU25* to transfer the SAP transactions and authorization objects from SAP tables USOBT and USOBX to the customer tables USOBT_C and USOBX_C. You can then maintain these tables using transaction SU24. Figure 9-20 shows the initial screen for transaction SU25.

Table USOBT includes the relation between the transactions and the authorization objects.

If it is a new installation, just click on the button next to option 1, *Initially fill the customer tables.* If you are upgrading from a previous

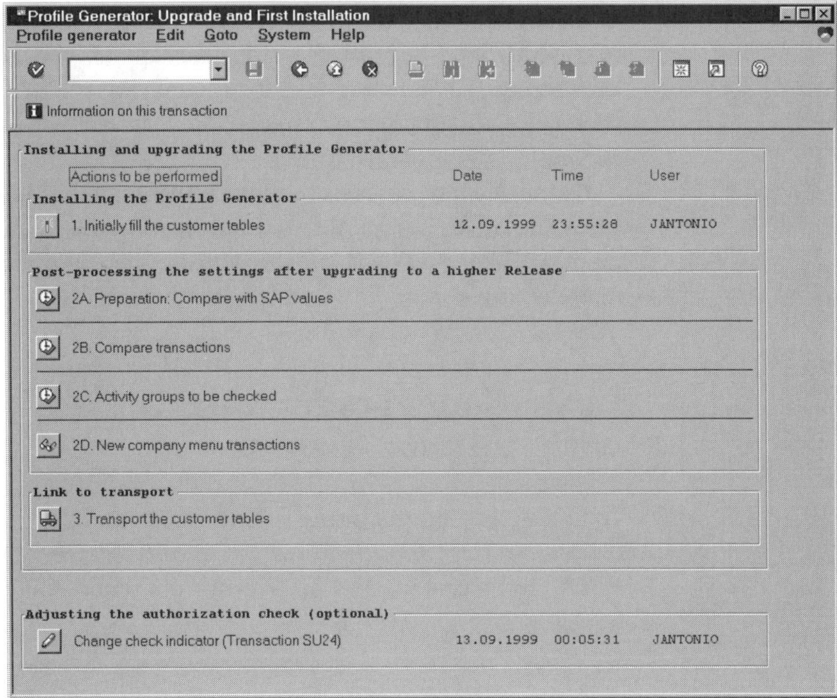

Figure 9-20 Configuring the Profile Generator with transaction SU25.

release, you must use the lower options, but first look up the most recent information concerning your release in the online documentation.

3. Maintain the Scope of Authorization Object Checks in Transactions. This is performed using transaction SU24 (also the last button on the screen for transaction SU25) in order to maintain customer tables USOBX_C (transactions and authorization objects) and USOBT_C (proposed values for authorization objects). This is not a mandatory step, but can be used by customers to maintain their own authorization checks as well as to assign R/3 authorization objects to custom transactions. You can also maintain the assignment for a single transaction, and enforce or suppress the authorization check for any transaction. Additionally, it is possible to maintain the field assignments for the transactions. In any case there is always the possibility of comparing these settings with the SAP standard settings.

The purpose of this transaction is for the administrator to be able to maintain the scope of authorization checks in transactions by:

- Assigning the authorization objects that are relevant to a transaction
- Assigning default values and organizational level defaults for authorization object fields

4. Generate the Company Menu. Finally, after you have run transaction *SSM1* and run all the steps (except transports if not required) on that screen, as shown in Fig. 9-21, generate the SAP standard menu and then the company menu. You can decide which will be the first menu and choose the default reporting tree.

Option 2b can be used to modify the company menu. You have to generate the menu (option 2c) for modifications to take effect. The generated menu will be used by the activity group maintenance functions as a base for selecting application and transactions.

Basic Concepts for Working with Activity Groups

To access the activity group maintenance screen, select *Tools* → *Administration* → *User maintenance* → *Activity groups,* or alternatively enter *PFCG* in the command field. The system will display a screen like the one in Fig. 9-22.

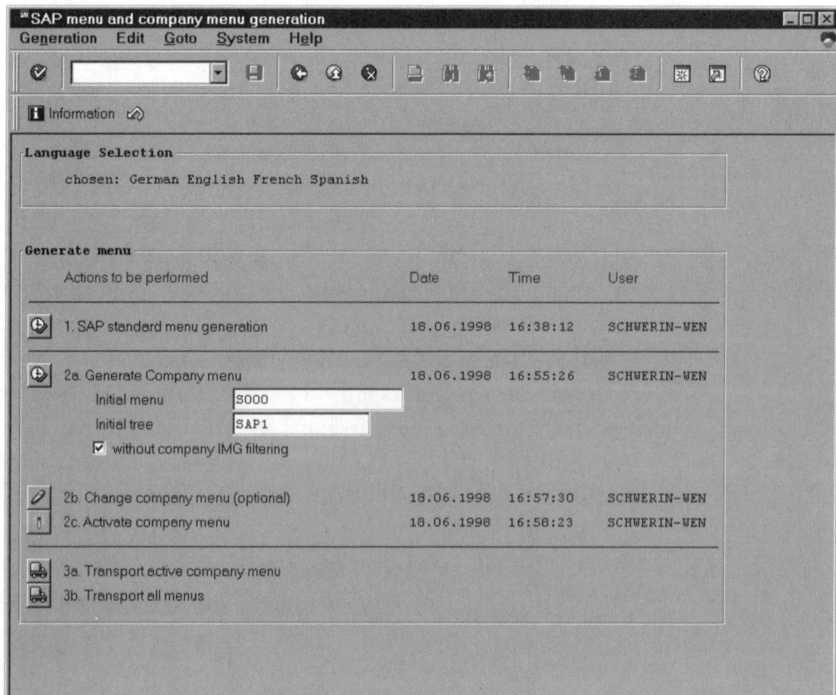

Figure 9-21 Creating the SAP company menu.

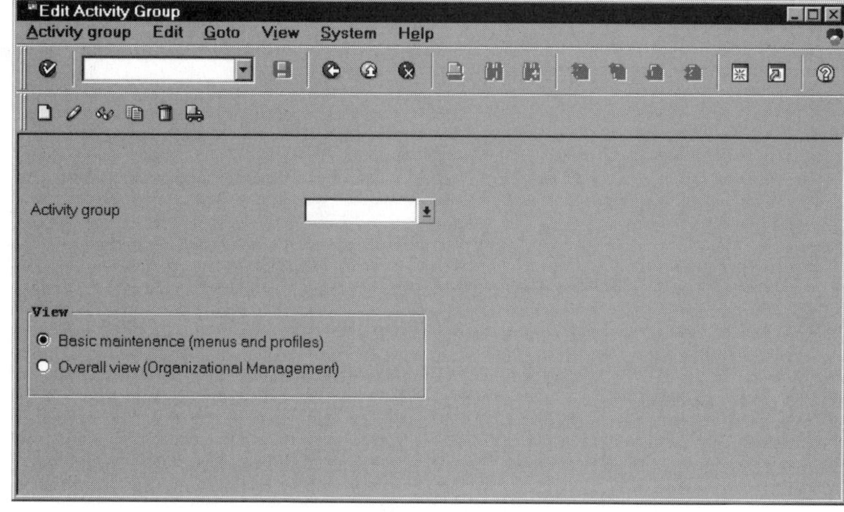

Figure 9-22 Activity group initial screen.

Activity group maintenance includes two different views:

- The *basic maintenance view* allows all functions for activity groups to be accessed and menus and authorizations to be selected. However, this view can only be assigned to user master records, and does not allow for maintaining validity dates.
- The *overall view (organizational management)* is a more comprehensive view that can display all the assignments for an activity group. It allows tasks to be linked with activity group and validity dates to be changed. This view is tightly related to the personnel development HR application, so it is useful for users working in organizational management.

Activity groups are assigned to *agents.* There are several types of agents. The most common is the *user master record;* however, there are other types of organizational agents that can be created within the Human Resource module, such as *organizational units, positions, jobs, persons,* or *work centers.*

Activity groups can be created with or without *responsibilities.* The concept behind *responsibility* within activity groups is based on an organizational object such as position or job role, but this is really a tool that can be used to differentiate the authorization profiles generated with activity groups. This is useful for defining the authorizations for people who perform the same functions but in different company areas: they have the same position but different job roles.

Activity groups with *responsibilities* are used for associating one set of activities with one or more authorization profiles, which can later be assigned to users or agents.

Creating Activity Groups

When creating activity groups, you can decide whether to create them with or without responsibilities. Without responsibilities, the basic steps are:

1. Create the activity group.
2. Select the transactions from the company menu or the work flow tasks (in overall view).
3. Complete the authorizations for chosen activities.
4. Generate the profiles.
5. Assign the profiles to agents (users).

When choosing responsibilities, the basic steps are quite similar:

1. Create the activity group.
2. Select the transactions from the company menu or the work flow tasks (in overall view).
3. Create responsibilities.
4. Complete the authorizations for chosen activities for each responsibility.
5. Generate the profiles for each responsibility.
6. Assign responsibilities to agents (users).

The following example shows how to create a simple activity group for the purchasing department users, providing them with authorizations for creating purchasing orders when the vendor is known (transaction code ME21) and for changing and displaying purchasing orders (transaction codes ME22 and ME23).

These are the steps:

1. Access the main activity group screen by selecting *Tools* → *Administration* → *User maintenance* → *Activity groups,* or enter transaction code *PFCG* in the command field. The system will display the *Edit Activity Group* screen.
2. Enter the name for the activity group, select the basic maintenance view, and click the *Create* icon on the application toolbar. The sys-

tem will display a dialog box for deciding whether to allow responsibilities for the activity group. For this example, select *No.* The system will display a new screen similar to the one shown in Fig. 9-23.

3. Enter a brief description in the *Name* field, and click on the *Menu* push button within the *Activities* box. The system will display the menu tree for the company menu, with all traffic lights red.
4. Click on the plus sign on folders to open their contents. In our example, click on the plus signs on *Logistics, Materials management, Purchasing, Purchase order, Create.* Finally, mark the square box next to *Vendor known.* You will see traffic lights turning to green. On the same level as *Create* and below, mark the square box next to *Change* and *Display.* If you want to display the transaction codes, select *Edit* → *Technical name* → *Technical name on.* Save your selection by clicking on the *Save* icon on the standard toolbar, and click the *Back* icon.
5. You will return to the previous screen. The next step is to maintain the *Authorizations,* by clicking on the *Authorizations* push button. The system first displays a new screen where you have to maintain the organizational levels. In this case, these are the *Purchasing group, Purchasing organization,* and *Plant.* You can

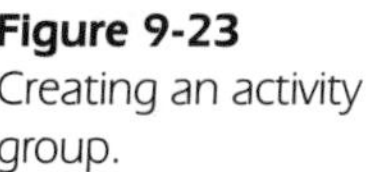

Figure 9-23 Creating an activity group.

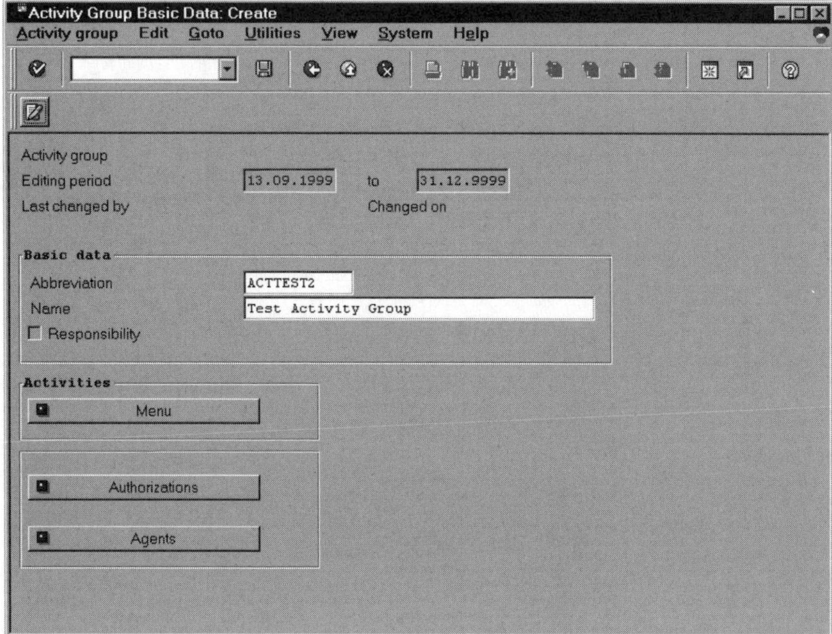

input simple values or ranges, or enter a wildcard such as * to indicate all organizations. Fill in the fields or click on the *Complete authorization* push button if you want to allow authorization on all organizational levels. The system will display the activity group browser view, as shown in Fig. 9-24.

6. Expand the nodes by clicking on the folders or by positioning the cursor on the line and clicking on the *Expand* icon. Notice how the browser view is presented in four levels: authorization object class, authorization object, authorizations, and field values. The system automatically selects the objects and values according to the previous selections. Select *Utilities → Technical names on* to display the familiar authorization objects. Notice also how the profile generator tool has selected the authorization object *S_TCODE* (authorization for transaction start) and provided it with the values of the selected transactions.

7. You have to maintain all pending authorizations before you can generate the complete profile. The maintenance status of the authorizations at every level is shown using traffic lights: green indicates that all values are maintained, yellow that there is some value that is not yet maintained, and red that at least an organizational level is missing. In order to maintain pending or open values, you can click on the individual level so the system

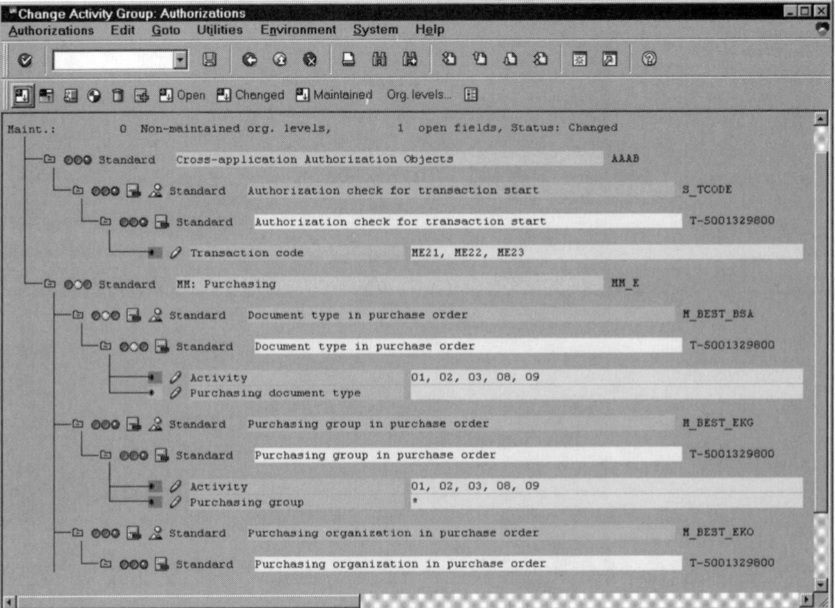

Figure 9-24 Activity group browser view.

will display a new dialog box for entering required field values. Or, you can click on a traffic light and maintain all outstanding fields below, or assign full authorizations. For this example, you can assign complete authorizations for the subtree by clicking the stoplight on the *Standard: Document type in purchase order* line. On the dialog box, click the *Enter* icon.

8. Next, click the *Generate* icon on the application toolbar. The system will display a dialog box for entering the profile name and a short text. You can keep the proposed system name or change it to your own standards. Continue by clicking the *Enter* button. The system will now generate the profile.
9. Go back to the initial activity group maintenance screen. The screen will show green traffic lights for both *Menu* and *Authorizations.* Now assign this profile to one or more user master records by clicking on the *Agents* push button.
10. The system will display the *Maintain Agent Assignment* screen. Click on the *Create Assignment* push button on the application toolbar, or select *Assignment* → *Create* → *Create assignment* from the menu. The system displays a dialog box searching users. Enter an asterisk (*) or other criteria, and click *Continue.* The system will display a list of system users matching your criteria. Select the users by clicking on the check boxes next to them, and click on the *Transfer* push button.
11. If you want the profiles to be transferred to the actual user master records, click the *User master data update* push button. The system will display the data reconciliation program. Click on *Execute.* The system will display the list of users with pending assignment of the activity group. Click on the *Update user master* push button. You can verify that the activity groups and profiles have been effectively transferred by looking up the user master records using transaction SU01. There is the possibility of running a general report for updating all user masters and pending assignments of activity groups by using transaction *PFUD.*

To manage the time-dependent assignments of activity groups, administrators should schedule the report *RHAUTP1* (releases 3.1 and 4.0) or *PFCG_TIME_DEPENDENCY* (release 4.5) to run every night.

The Profile Generator tool includes many additional functions to facilitate the creation and maintenance of authorizations and profiles, such as responsibilities and templates, collections of authorization objects that can be included within activity groups.

Templates are client independent and can be maintained using transaction *SU24*.

For additional information on this and other topics on the profile generator, please refer to the online documentation.

Predefined Profiles and Basis System Authorization Objects

A newly installed SAP R/3 system includes hundreds of authorization objects, authorizations, and profiles which allow a virtually unlimited number of combinations for protecting the system against unauthorized access.

To list the profiles of the system, from the main menu select *Tools* → *Administration* → *User maintenance* → *Profiles.* Select the check box next to *Active only* and click on the *Generate work area* button to display the list of available active profiles.

Some of these profiles are special, such as the SAP_ALL and the SAP_NEW. The SAP_ALL profile includes all the access privileges for the R/3 system and should be assigned only to superusers. The SAP_NEW profile includes all new access privileges which were added to system components of previous releases. SAP recommends adding the SAP_NEW profile to all user master records for compatibility reasons when performing R/3 upgrades. With the SAP_NEW, users can continue to use functions which were unprotected in earlier versions when access tests have been added in new releases.

The following is a short list of system authorization profiles for common basis functions:

- *S_A.SYSTEM.* The superuser's profile for system administrators. It's a simple profile including all the authorizations for the basis system. This profile excludes authorizations for business applications; however, since users with this profile can create and assign authorization and profiles to users, it's virtually a fully privileged user.
- *S_A.ADMIN.* The profile for system operators. It includes less authorizations than the superusers. For example, they are not allowed to modify users belonging to the group SUPER.
- *S_A.DEVELOP.* The standard profile for privileged SAP developers. This profile does not allow users to perform any system administration functions except for those directly related with development.

- *S_A.USER.* The basic profile for normal end users. They have basic authorizations for working in the R/3 system. Many of the authorizations it contains allow users only to perform the display activity over functions.
- *S_A.CUSTOMIZ.* This profile can be assigned to end users and consultants who need to work with the customizing functions.
- *S_A.TMSADM.* This profile provides access to the transport management system functions and is used by the RFC user TMSADM.
- *S_A.SHOW.* This is a simple profile that provides display access to most basis functions. It is suitable for occasional users, visitors, or auditors.

Tracing Authorizations

The R/3 system includes some options to find the authorization for any transaction or function a user performs in the system. This is quite useful when looking for an authorization denial problem or when defining profiles when you want to specify exactly what authorization objects a particular transaction checks. The two methods available in R/3 for finding authorizations are the authorization check transaction (SU53) and using the system trace.

The *system trace* is a more general purpose tool used mainly by developers or system administrators which can provide a great detail of information and can be used to trace other user sessions.

Transaction SU53 is more specific for authorization error analysis but can only be used for the current user sessions. However, SU53 is a faster and more direct method for finding an authorization denial problem. Transaction SU53 can be accessed from the menu *System → Utilities → Displ. auth. check.*

Using the System Trace for Tracing Authorizations

The SAP system includes extensive tracing and debugging utilities. You can find more information about tracing in Chap. 10. This section covers just the simple process of activating and displaying a trace concerning authorization checks.

To start the system trace, from the main menu select *Tools → Administration → Monitor → Traces → System trace.* The system displays the initial tracing screen.

From this screen, select *Trace switch → Switch, edit.* The system displays the available trace options and switches, one of which is the *authorization check.* Make sure you mark the check box next to *authorization check*.

In the *Write options* field, select the value *write trace to disk.*

The system trace can be used for recording which are the authorization checks performed by the system using your own user ID or using other users' sessions.

To limit the trace to your own user ID or another user ID, enter the name of the user ID you want to trace in the field *General filter* by clicking on the possible entries arrow and then selecting it from the list.

To activate and start the tracing process, select *Trace switch → Editor save → In active system* from the menu. The trace will start recording every system function you or the entered user performs. So, if you are looking for an authorization problem or just want to find a particular authorization check, open a new session and go to the screen, function, or transaction you want to analyze.

Once you are finished you should stop the system trace. Go back to the session where you activated the trace, and if you are on the tracing screen, stop the trace by selecting *Trace switch → Immediate switch → Stop.*

Now you should look at the trace file generated. To display the trace, select *Trace file → Choose file,* or simply *Trace files → Standard,* from the menu. The system displays a list of traces. Position the cursor over the file to be displayed and click on *Display file* or *Choose file.*

The trace file contains the authorization objects, authorization fields, and values that have been tested while you have been performing system functions. Authorization tests are displayed in the following format: *<Authorization object>:<Field>=<Value tested>*. But you can display a more legible view of the authorization check by clicking over the entry. Figure 9-25 shows an example of the trace file showing an authorization check for object M_MATE_ST.

Using the SU53 Transaction

The transaction SU53 can be used to analyze a function when getting the error *You are not authorized to* in the status bar. When you get this message, enter *SU53* or */NSU53* in the command field. Alternatively, you can

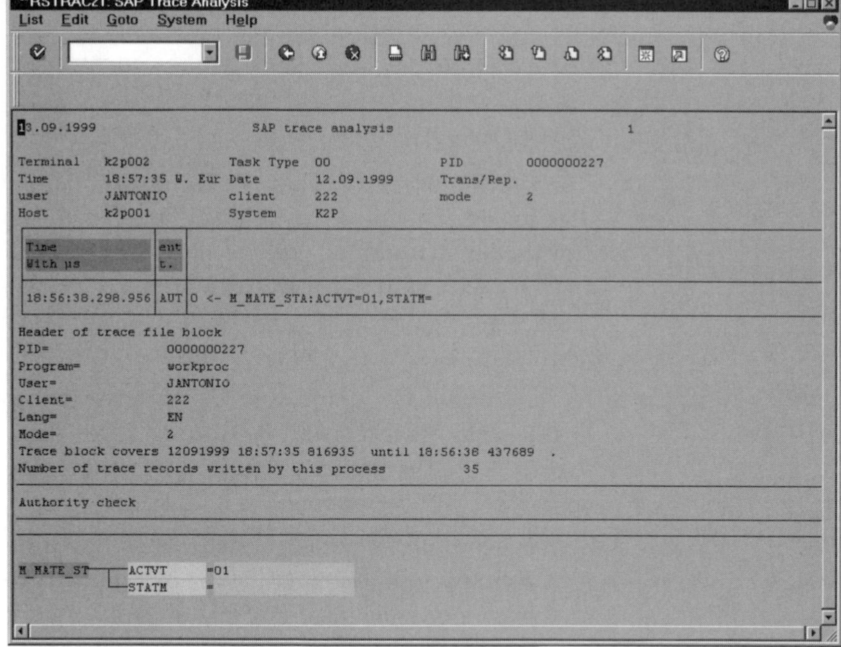

Figure 9-25 Result of a trace analysis for an authorization object.

select *System* → *Utilities* → *Displ. auth. check* from any R/3 screen. The system will display the authorization object and value for which you were not authorized.

Transaction SU53 can also be used from any of your open sessions and not only from the one in which you got the authorization error message. However, you cannot use SU53 to analyze other users' authorization errors. In those cases, administrators should instruct users to reproduce the error and then to enter the transaction SU53 in the command field to receive information about the authorization error messages they got.

Organizing the Maintenance of the Authorization System

The SAP authorization system offers many options for organizing the administration of users, authorizations, and profiles, making it quite flexible when defining roles.

Depending on the type, size, and security restrictions, an installation can have a single superuser for all users and authorization system maintenance to several decentralized administrators with different maintenance functions and limited authorizations.

SAP recommends that for enforcing maximum system security customers divide the maintenance of the user and authorization system among three types of users:

- *User administrators.* They are in charge of creating and modifying user master records. User administrators can set user parameters, edit the list of assigned profiles, and so forth. User administrators cannot create or activate authorizations or profiles. User administrators can be further divided by assigning them authorization maintenance to certain user groups.
- *Authorization administrators.* These users are able to define or modify authorizations and profiles; however, they are not permitted to activate authorizations or profiles. Authorization administrators only work with *active* versions of authorizations and profiles.
- *Activation administrators.* They are in charge of activating profiles and authorizations. This type of administrator is no longer able to change the authorizations or profiles but can only activate existing revised versions of profiles and authorizations.

Dividing the maintenance responsibilities among different administrators can increase the security of the system against unwanted actions over user master records, authorizations, and profiles. Another advantage is the decentralization of the user administration. In big installations with hundreds of users, it can be a good practice to divide up user maintenance functions by department, building, regional office, and so forth.

To implement these administrative roles, the superuser uses authorizations to limit which user groups are maintained by user administrators and which authorizations and profiles can be maintained or activated by which administrators. Since the superuser can limit and restrict the access rights, the decentralized administrators do not need to be high-level technical staff. They can be normal company users.

As a superuser, you can define new profiles for these administrators using the standard S_A.ADMIN profile as a template and changing the allowed field values corresponding to authorization objects such as *user group, authorizations, authorization profiles,* and mainly setting the *Activity* field values.

Refer to the SAP online documentation in the "Users and authorization" help file for details on setting values for dividing up administrative roles.

Creating New Authorization Checks

Although the R/3 system includes virtually all authorization objects and checks to test whether users can access the system functions, customers might add new development objects and functions to extend the system capabilities. In such cases, customers might also need to include a new authorization check.

R/3 provides several ways to include new authorization checks for custom-developed objects or transactions, the most important being:

- By assigning an authorization object to a transaction code in the transaction table TSTC and using authorization object S_TCODE
- By programming the authorization check using the ABAP standard statement AUTHORITY-CHECK
- By assigning authorization groups to tables, maintaining table TDDAT, and using authorization object S_TABU_DIS
- By using authorization object S_PROGRAM and using program authorization groups by maintaining table TPGP

Using Authorization Checks with Table TSTC

Transaction codes are associated with system functions, started normally by choosing menu options. Table TSTC is the transaction code table where the transactions are associated with the system functions or menu options. As you have seen often, transactions can be called directly from the command field by entering their codes.

The system uses authorization object S_TCODE each time a transaction is executed to check if the users have authorization for starting that transaction. This object is automatically included in the profiles with the corresponding values when using the Profile Generator. This object is not checked when transactions are not directly called, such as the case of CALL TRANSACTION statements within ABAP programs.

Table TSTC also allows for the assignment of an authorization object to a transaction. When a user starts this transaction, the system checks the user authorization for the transaction. This type of authorization check is direct and there is no need for programming.

You can display or maintain table TSTC using the standard table maintenance function *System → Services → Table maintenance* or, alternatively, SM31.

In table TSTC, you can associate any authorization object with a transaction and can also specify the values that the user must have to pass the authorization check.

Remember that you can always know which is the current transaction for the function where you are currently located by selecting *System → Status* from the menu.

This type of authorization check is enforced both when the transaction is called from a system menu option or when entering the transaction code in the command field. However, if the transaction is called indirectly from another function which includes the CALL TRANSACTION statement, the system does not check the authorization. Therefore, if your transaction is critical, it's more secure to program the check with the ABAP AUTHORITY-CHECK instructions.

Using the ABAP AUTHORITY-CHECK

To use the AUTHORITY-CHECK statement for checking authorizations in your programs, you must follow some steps, which may or may not be required depending on the check you want to program:

1. Define and create authorization fields for the new authorization test. The contents of the authorization fields are the values that the program will really test.
2. Define the authorization object containing the newly defined authorization fields.
3. Assign the authorization object to an object class. You can use any existing class; however, it is recommended to assign customer authorization objects to customer authorization object classes, starting with the letters *Y* or *Z* to distinguish them from SAP predefined classes.
4. Finally, program the checking of the authorization using the ABAP AUTHORITY-CHECK standard statement.

Defining New Authorization Fields. Authorization fields are defined from the ABAP development workbench. To reach this function, from the main menu select *Tools → ABAP Workbench → Development →*

Other tools → Authorization objects → Fields. The system displays a screen with three function buttons under the authorization fields box. For defining your own authorization fields, you should select *Customer,* otherwise your own authorization fields could be overwritten by an R/3 release upgrade.

Before creating new fields, remember that you can use SAP-defined authorization fields in your authorization objects. For example, you can use the common *Activity* authorization field (ACTVT) in your own authorization objects.

As a requirement before defining a new customer authorization field, the structure ZAUTHCUST must have been created previously. However, when it's the first time creating an authorization field, the R/3 system checks for this structure and, if it does not exist, it takes you automatically to the ABAP dictionary function to create it.

To create this structure, from the ABAP workbench initial screen (transaction S001), click on the *Dictionary* button, enter the ZAUTHCUST in the input field, click the radio button next to *Structure,* and then click on the *Create* function button in the bottom part of the working R/3 window area.

You are presented with the initial screen for creating a table. Enter a short description. You don't need to define any fields for this structure, since the field maintenance function will automatically insert your authorization fields in it. Save your table and be sure you assign the change request to one of your own customer development classes.

For information about defining tables, data elements, domains, and foreign keys, refer to Chap. 8. For detailed explanations on the change request, development classes, and workbench organizer functions, refer to Chap. 6.

Once you have the ZAUTHCUST structure, on the authorization field maintenance screen, you can enter the names for your own authorization fields and assign them to a dictionary data element. Remember to name your fields according to the SAP style guides, starting with *Y* or *Z.*

You can define ranges of values using associated domains or assign foreign keys to the authorization fields.

Defining New Authorization Objects. To create or define a new authorization object for a function or transaction which needs to be protected, select *Tools → ABAP Workbench → Development → Other tools → Authorization objects → Objects.* Figure 9-26 shows an example of this screen.

You have to assign your objects to an object class. From the object class screen you can create your own by clicking on the *Create* button and entering a name and a description for the class.

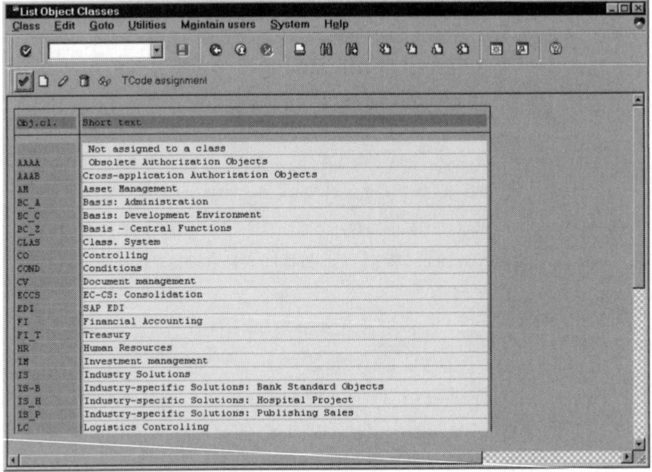

Figure 9-26 Object class list selection.

Once you have your object class created, from the object class list screen you can double click on your class name to reach the authorization object screen, and then click on the *Create* button to define a new authorization object.

Enter the name for the new object, a short description, and the authorization fields you want to associate with this object. An authorization object can have a maximum of 10 authorization fields which will be used to perform multiconditional testing for accessing the protected system function. You can also enter documentation in the new object specifying the purpose of the object creation.

You should not delete or modify standard objects defined by SAP since that might cause errors in the SAP programs calling those objects.

For creating your programs and using the AUTHORITY-CHECK standard ABAP statement, refer to the SAP online documentation on the ABAP workbench.

Technical Details of Tables and Instance Profile Parameters for Users, Authorizations, and Profiles

The next few sections summarize some of the most important dictionary tables the SAP system uses internally to manage user master records, authorization, and profile-related information, as well as some of the important profile parameters which can directly affect the functions of the user and authorization maintenance.

Technical Details: User- and Authorization System–Related Tables

When administrators modify, create, or update user master records or define authorizations or profiles, the system updates the tables where it internally keeps the information. To know which are the tables used by the user and authorization maintenance functions can be of importance, for example, in transports, system upgrades, and for general database maintenance.

User-related tables cannot be directly seen as with the table maintenance function (*System* → *Services* → *Table maintenance*), except for the table with forbidden password strings, USR40. Some of the other tables are as follows:

- USR01 contains the runtime data of the user master records
- USR02 is the table containing logon information such as the password
- USR03 includes the users' address information
- USR04 contains the users' authorizations
- USR05 is the users' parameter ID table
- USR06 contains additional data for users
- USR07 includes values for last failed authorization check
- USR08 is the table for user menu entries
- USR09 contains user menus
- USR10 is the table for user authorization profiles
- USR11 contains the descriptive texts for profiles
- USR12 is the user master authorizations values table
- USR13 contains the descriptive short texts for authorizations
- USR14 contains the logon language versions per user
- USR30 includes additional information for user menus

Users and profile and authorization change history data are held in tables USH02, USH04, USH10, and USH12. The system includes other tables related to user master records which are the transparent versions of some of the previous tables. These are UST04, UST10C, UST10S, and UST12.

Tables related with authorization objects and authorization fields are as follows:

- TOBJ is the authorization objects table containing the authorization fields for each.
- TACT contains the list of the standard activities authorization fields in the system. Refer to Fig. 9-12 for an example.
- TACTZ is the table which defines the relationship between the authorization objects and the activities in those objects containing the *Activity* authorization field.
- TDDAT is the table needed for assigning authorization groups to tables used by authorization object S_TABU_DIS.
- TSTC is the transaction code table where authorization objects and values can be defined.
- TPGP is used for relating application areas with program authorization groups.
- USOBT is the standard SAP table that relates transactions with authorization objects.
- USOBX is the SAP check table for USOBT containing the transactions and authorization objects.
- USOBT_C is a customer table, copied initially from the SAP standard, that relates transactions with authorization objects.
- USOBX_C is the customer check table for USOBT_C containing transactions and authorization objects.

Technical Details: System Profile Parameters for Managing Users and Authorizations

Parameters directly affecting the user management functions are as follows:

- *login/fails_to_session_end.* Indicates the number of times that a user can enter an incorrect password before the system closes the logon window. The default value is 3, but you can set it to any value between 1 and 99.

- *login/fails_to_user_lock.* This parameter sets the number of times a user can enter an incorrect password before the system automatically locks the user out. If this happens, the user is automatically unlocked at midnight. The default value is 12. Possible values are from 1 to 99.
- *login/system_client.* Sets the default system client. This client is automatically filled in the client field of the logon screen, although users can overwrite it.
- *login/min_password_lng.* Specifies the minimum password length. Default value is 3, but you can specify any value between 2 and 8.
- *login/password_expiration_time.* Indicates in number of days the period of validity for passwords. When the expiration time arrives, the user is asked to enter a new password.
- *login/no_automatic_user_sapstar.* Disables special properties for user SAP* when this parameter is set to a value greater than 0.
- *rdisp/gui_auto_logout.* Specifies the number of seconds a user session can be idle before being automatically logged off by the system. This parameter is deactivated by setting the value to 0. A user session is considered in an idle state during the period of time in which its terminal process (SAPGUI) does not transfer or communicate with the application server. By default, this option is not activated. For example, developers working in the ABAP editor for a long period of time can be considered *idle* to the system if they do not perform any function other than editing.

WARNING! *Be extremely careful using this option with the type of users working in your installation. With the auto-logoff function activated, the system does not perform any checks nor does it save the data from the user sessions. The system does not show the logoff confirmation dialog box.*

If setting the auto-logoff option, be sure to set a large value for those instances in which users might have long idle times.

- *auth/no_check_in_some_cases.* This parameter is set to switch off special authorization checks by customers, and is the main parameter for activating the Profile Generator tool. Values can be either Y (yes) or N (no).

- *auth/no_check_on_tcode.* If this parameter is set to value Y (yes), then the system does not perform an authorization check on object S_TCODE.

To make the parameters globally effective in a SAP system, set them in the default profile, DEFAULT.PFL. To make them instance-specific, you must set them in the profiles of each application server in your SAP system.

CHAPTER 10

General Administration Utilities

This chapter covers all those administrative areas and management tasks which are difficult to classify under any other section or chapter. These administrative tasks deal with the basic monitoring and management of the components which make up the SAP R/3 system.

The R/3 system offers a very extensive collection of programs, menus, and utilities for performing administrative tasks. Most of them are located under the functions provided from the *Tools → Administration* menu (transaction code S002).

This chapter concentrates on the basic monitoring facilities. Both the performance monitoring and the extended utilities of the CCMS are dealt with in the next chapter. The transport system utilities are explained in Chap. 6.

The basic utilities include the following:

- Checking the consistency of the system installation
- Displaying and monitoring all the application servers
- Displaying and monitoring the system work processes
- Displaying and monitoring the user sessions
- Posting system messages to all logged-on users of a SAP system to inform them of any particular events such as closing the system for upgrades, backups, and so on
- Managing the SAP update records in charge of performing the changes in the database
- Displaying and managing the SAP lock entries on the database objects
- Locking and unlocking transaction codes
- Using the client copy functions
- Analyzing the dump files generated by abnormal termination of ABAP programs
- Using the tracing and logging facilities to analyze system problems

Basic SAP R/3 System Administration

The functions available for the basic administration of the SAP system form the group of transactions which should be performed on a regular basis in the daily operation and management of the system. These functions are the responsibility of the R/3 system administrator and/or the system operator. Whenever a problem is detected while doing basic administration it has to be reported and solved as soon as possible.

Administrators can help prevent problems from occurring by following certain monitoring practices.

In the event problems are detected, the monitoring and administration facilities can help to isolate the problem and solve it more quickly. Having an operator or administrator manual and maintaining an internal incidence log will greatly reduce the time it takes to solve a particular problem in cases where it has happened previously.

In case a problem cannot be solved quickly enough, SAP system administrators should contact the SAP hotline or enter the problem in the SAPnet support services (formerly OSS).

Checking the Installation

Every time a SAP instance is started, the system automatically checks whether there are any inconsistencies. You can manually check the system status for inconsistencies by selecting *Tools* → *Administration* → *Administration* → *Installation check.*

When you call the installation check, the system looks into the table which collects system events and performs the following checks:

- That the critical database structure definitions are identical in the data dictionary and in the SAP kernel, including tables such as SYST, T100, TFDIR, TSTC, and so on.
- That the SAP kernel release number matches the number stored in the database

Displaying and Monitoring the SAP Instances and Application Servers

Using transaction code SM51 in the command field or by selecting *Tools* → *Administration* → *Monitor* → *System monitoring* → *Servers* from the menu options, you can display the instances or application servers of the SAP system, as shown in Fig. 10-1. The display will show only those servers which are active. This should be one of the first monitoring tasks

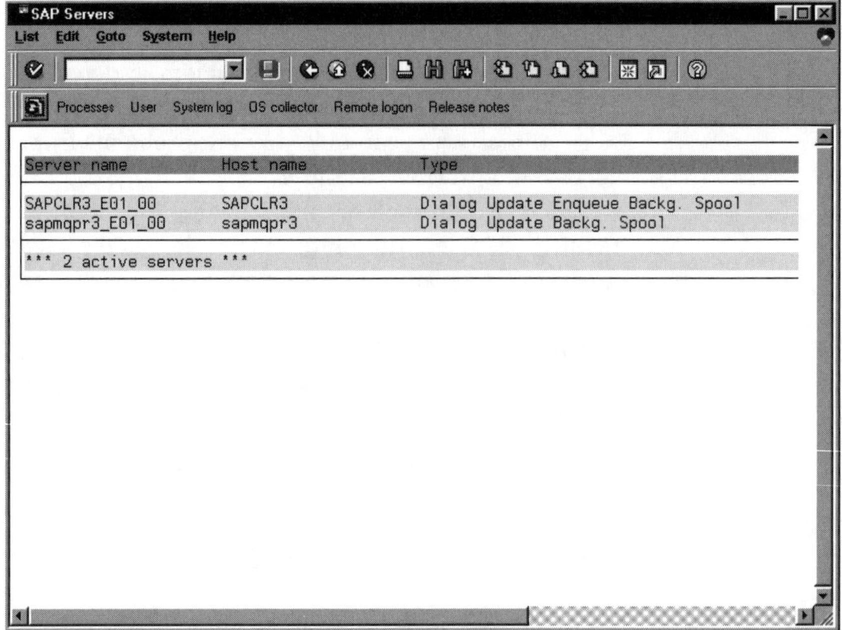

Figure 10-1 Server monitoring display.

run by the administration to determine whether all application servers are up and running.

The application servers shown on the screen are the ones which have registered themselves—the ones which have connected to—the message server. If for any reason the message server process dies, you won't be able to see the servers.

On the application server display, you can see several fields which give specific information about the SAP instances. These fields are

- *Name.* It's the name of the SAP instance. The name is made up of the hostname of the server, the SAP system name (SID), and the SAP system number.
- *Host.* It's the hostname in which the SAP instance is running.
- *Type.* The type of work processes for which the application server is configured.

From this monitoring screen you can further display which users are connected to any of the instances shown on the screen or see what processes are running by selecting the *User* or *Processes* button on the application toolbar. By using these functions, the system takes you to exactly the same transaction as if you were going directly to the user or work process monitoring transactions.

On this screen, there are additional options which you can access from the Goto menu or directly by clicking on the push buttons on the application toolbar. Main options are

- *System log.* Displays an instance system log
- *OS collector.* Calls the operating system performance monitor for summary statistics on the status of the host platform on which a SAP instance is running.
- *Remote logon.* Performs a SAP remote logon to any of the servers in the system.
- *Traces.* For displaying the so-called developer trace files and some other files of the global profile directory.

From the *SM51* transaction, an interesting and very useful option for system administrators when monitoring, tuning, and troubleshooting the system is to look up the status of the dispatcher queue. This information can be obtained by selecting the application server and then choosing *Goto → Queue information.* Figure 10-2 shows an example of this screen.

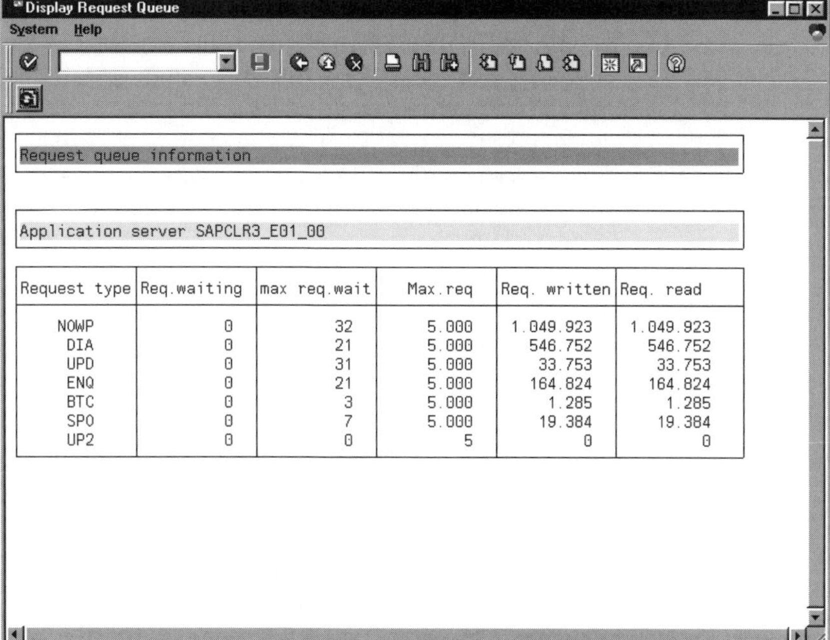

Request type	Req.waiting	max req.wait	Max.req	Req. written	Req. read
NOWP	0	32	5.000	1.049.923	1.049.923
DIA	0	21	5.000	546.752	546.752
UPD	0	31	5.000	33.753	33.753
ENQ	0	21	5.000	164.824	164.824
BTC	0	3	5.000	1.285	1.285
SPO	0	7	5.000	19.384	19.384
UP2	0	0	5	0	0

Figure 10-2 Request Queue information display.

There are several columns in the request queue display, including the work process type, the number of requests waiting in the dispatcher queue to be processed, and the maximum number of requests that had to wait. If there are frequently many requests waiting, it might indicate locking problems or too few work processes. These numbers are reset every time the application server is restarted.

Monitoring the System Work Processes

To display the status of the work processes of the application server where you are logged on to, select *Tools* → *Administration* → *Monitor* → *System monitoring* → *Process overview* (transaction code *SM50*). Administrators should regularly monitor the system processes to determine if the number and configuration is appropriate. The process overview offers only a snapshot of the processes, so you have to press the *Refresh* button to get a better view of what's going on.

Notice that you can only display the processes of your local system. To display other server processes, call the server monitoring transaction explained in the previous section and, from a selected server on the list, select the *Processes* function.

The SAP work processes correspond to operating system processes. You could also monitor these processes from the operating system. In fact, the field *PID* matches exactly to the *Process Id* of the underlying operating system. With a UNIX command such as *ps -eaf|grep dw,* you can see the SAP processes. On Windows NT systems you can see the processes from the *Task Manager* as *disp+work.*

The SAP runtime directory (/usr/sap/<SID>/SYS/exe/run) contains some monitor programs which allow you to see some of the work processes and the dispatcher from the operating system. Refer to the section entitled "SAP R/3 Directory Structure" in Chap. 4 for more information.

The work process overview presents detailed information in different columns. Notice that in order to see all the available columns you might have to scroll horizontally using the scrolling buttons on the bottom part of the screen. The columns in the work process overview screen show the following information:

- *No.* Refers to the internal ID number of a process. It is useful for identifying messages in the system log belonging to a work process.

- *Ty.* It's the type of work process. Chapter 2 explains in detail each of the SAP work process types. On this screen, you can find the following types:
  - *DIA.* Dialog work processes, in charge of executing interactive dialog steps
  - *UPD.* Update work process for executing U1 update components (refer to the section entitled "Updating Process Concepts" later in this chapter). In charge of critical updates on the database
  - *UP2.* Update work process for executing U2 update components. In charge of performing secondary updates on the database
  - *ENQ.* Enqueue work process in charge of setting and releasing lock objects
  - *BTC.* Background work processes, in charge of executing background jobs
  - *SPO.* Spool work process in charge of the SAP spooling system (formatting and printing)
- *PID.* Process identification number of the work process which matches the PID of the operating system process.
- *Status.* Shows the current state of the work process. Observe that the process overview screen always offers a snapshot of the processes. So, upon pressing the *Refresh* icon, it can change. Possible process status are
  - — *Running.* The process is executing a system request.
  - — *Waiting.* The process is idle and waiting for any system request.
  - — *Hold.* The process is held by a single user. Although a *Hold* state can be normal, having too many processes in hold state affects the system performance.
  - — *Killed* or *Complet.* The process has been aborted with the *Restart* option set to *No.*
  - — *Stopped.* Due to system or application error, the process has stopped and could not restart automatically.

  When the process overview displays many processes with status *waiting,* it means that the system load is low. When this happens, the SAP dispatcher will try to allocate the same work process for a user, and thus avoid rolling in and out the user contexts.
- *Reason.* This column displays a mnemonic code displaying the reason for a work process with a *hold* status. Some of the reasons can be activities performed by the lock mechanism, the update process,

debugging, CPIC tasks, or RFC requests. If the reason columns display *Priv,* it means that a work process has been reserved for a private use in a particular ABAP transaction requiring a large paging storage. This mechanism prevents the rolling in and out of the user contexts and the ABAP paging.

- *Start.* This column has either the values *Yes* or *No* and indicates whether the work process will be automatically restarted in the event of an abnormal termination. Normally, this field is set to *Yes* but you can switch the restart status by selecting the function *Restart after error* from the Process menu.
- *Err.* Contains the number of times a work process has terminated abnormally.
- *Sem.* This column can contain the number of the semaphore on which a work process is waiting. Normally, this field is empty. However if you notice that a semaphore number appears often, it might indicate some performance problems in the system and might need some parameter adjustments.
- *CPU.* Contains in number of seconds the CPU time consumed by a work process.
- *Time.* Indicates the elapsed execution time used by the work process for the dialog step that it is currently processing. This column usually contains a small figure. When it displays a large figure, it might indicate that the process is being held in a debugging session.
- *Program.* This column contains the ABAP program that is currently executing.
- *Client.* Indicates the SAP system client where the session is being executed.
- *User.* Contains the user ID whose request is being processed.
- *Action.* Under this field the system shows the actions being performed by the running program. These actions are the same as those recorded by the system performance monitor which is activated by default with the profile parameter *stat/level.* This column might display actions such as *sequential read, insert,* or *direct read.*
- *Table.* This column displays the name of the tables being accessed, if any.

There is more detailed information available from the process overview screen which you can display by selecting the work processes and then clicking on the *Detail info* button on the application toolbar. With this option, in addition to all the information from the overview screen, the system displays statistical information about the work process such as the memory, development environment, and database usage.

From the process overview display, you can perform additional options by selecting them from the menu item *Process.*

You can terminate a work process with or without generating a core dump file in the operating systems, which can be used for debugging. Before canceling a work process, you should select the menu function *Restart after error,* either with options *Yes* or *No,* to indicate whether the process which is to be canceled should restart or not, after being manually terminated.

By selecting a work process and then selecting the *Process → Trace → Active components* option from the menu, you can activate a trace and choose what is to be traced in the work process, which is stored in the so-called low-level *developer traces* files (dev files). Figure 10-3 shows the available tracing options for the work processes, where you can decide the level of tracing information to get.

To display a trace, choose the work process and, from the menu, select *Process → Trace → Display file.* More information about the system tracing facilities are provided in a later section in this chapter.

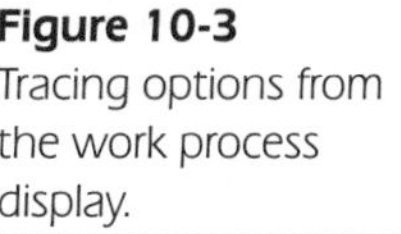

Figure 10-3 Tracing options from the work process display.

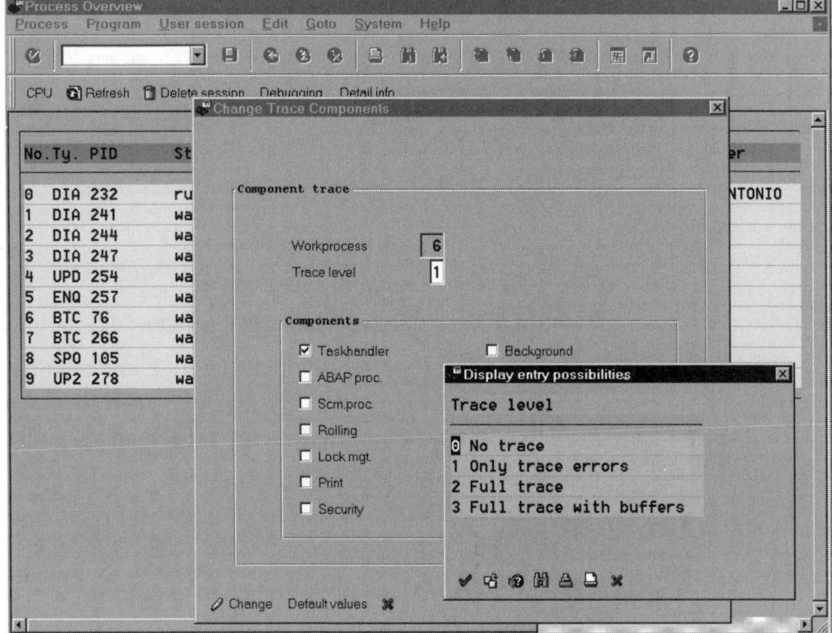

By selecting the work process and clicking on the *Delete session* button on the application toolbar you can also delete a user session and release the work process. However, you should avoid performing this function from this overview, since the work processes can be attending several users, and you could unintentionally affect other users' work. Rather, you should delete a user session from the *User overview* screen, as explained in the next section.

Finally, by selecting any work process that is currently executing a program, you can decide to put that program into debugging mode. To do this, select the line of the work process and click on the *Debugging* button on the application toolbar. The system displays the ABAP debugging facility and locks the work process for exclusive use. Refer to the online SAP documentation for more information on this facility. An overview is presented in Chap. 7.

Monitoring and Managing User Sessions

To display the users which are active in your current system, you can directly use the transaction code SM04 in the command field or, from the menu options, select *Tools → Administration → Monitor → System monitoring → User overview.* Notice that with this transaction you can only see which users are active in the same server where you are logged on. There are several ways to see which users logged on to other application servers:

- Select the *User* function from the SAP servers overview display
- From the main menu, select *Tools → Administration → Monitor → Performance → Exceptions / Users → Users; global.* Alternatively, use transaction code AL08.

The user overview screen includes the following fields:

- *Cl.* displays the SAP system client the user is logged on to.
- *User* contains the name of the user ID. Sometimes this field might appear blank when users are in the process of connecting, and also when the system itself is performing special functions with users SAPSYS or SAPCPIC.
- *Terminal* displays the name or address of the presentation terminal from which the user is connected to the application server.
- *Tcode* displays the current transaction code in which the user is working.

- *Sessions* shows the number of external sessions opened by the user. An external session is manually created by the user with the *System → Create session* option. The maximum number of external sessions per user is six.
- *Int. Sess* indicates the number of internal sessions that are automatically created by the system when navigating through transactions. Internal sessions are like hierarchy or navigation levels when performing system functions. The maximum number of internal sessions is set to nine.
- *Trace* can be ON or OFF, indicating whether the user has an active trace.

Besides monitoring the users' activity, from the user overview screen you can perform the following functions:

- Delete external user sessions. To do this, select the user from the overview screen and click on the *Sessions* button. The system displays a dialog box with the user sessions. In this dialog box, select the session to delete and click on the *End session* button.
- Delete all user sessions at once. From the user overview screen menu, select *Edit → Delete user.*
- You can take over a user's session if for some reason the user has lost access to the SAPGUI or stopped due to other problems. To do this, you can select *Edit → Copy session.* If this process is applied to a normal user, the user will lose the SAPGUI on his or her workstation.
- Display the memory being used by the logged-on users by selecting *Goto → memory.*
- Display brief information about the user by selecting it from the overview list and clicking on the *User info* button. The system will show the information as entered in the address screen of the user master record.

Posting System Messages

The system manager often has the need to post messages to all users connected to the system for administrative functions, such as for informing them of the time the system will be shut down for maintenance, backups, and so on. For that purpose, the R/3 system includes a utility for administrators to post brief messages to users by selecting *Administration → System messages* from the main administration menu. Alternatively, they can enter transaction code SM02 in the command field. If there are no messages created, the system will display the screen indicating that the system message list is empty.

To create a system message, click on the *Create* icon on the application toolbar. The system displays a dialog box like the one shown in Fig. 10-4. Enter the message in the input text lines provided for that purpose. Users can create as many messages as they wish, with a maximum length of three lines.

You can decide to display the messages to all logged-on users in the whole SAP system or only to the users logged on to a particular application server.

By using the expiration fields provided you can decide when a message will automatically be deleted from the system.

The system displays the message as a pop-up box in the user sessions. It will display it only once to each user, either when they log on or, for users who are already logged on, as soon as they interact with the application server.

Before continuing to work, users must clear the messages by pressing the *Enter* key or clicking on the *Continue* icon.

When there are messages already created, users can change the message either to modify the text, change the expiration date, or the server.

Individual messages or all posted messages can be deleted from the system by selecting them and clicking on the *Delete* icon.

This transaction, by default, is not protected with any authorization objects, so any user in the system is allowed to post a message.

This function is not intended for sending messages or notices to particular users. To do that, use the *Short message* function available from the

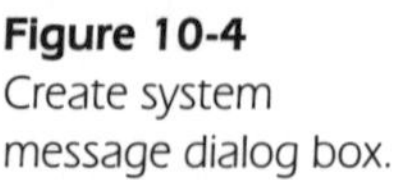
Create System Messages
System message text
System will shutdown tonight from 23:00 to 23:30 for
maintenance. Please do not release jobs for that time.
Your friendly admin !!
Server
Expiration
14.08.1999
23:00:00

Figure 10-4 Create system message dialog box.

System menu. This is actually a fast path to SAPoffice functions and it's available to all authorized users.

Displaying and Managing Update Records

The update work processes are in charge of making and recording the changes in the SAP underlying database as users work normally in the system.

The update work processes perform their functions when the ABAP applications are programmed with the statement *IN UPDATE TASK.* This type of updating is performed asynchronously in the system, meaning that the programs leave update records in a queue to be processed and then continue the execution. The following section discusses the main concepts related to the update processes.

Normally, the updating processes run without management intervention; nevertheless, R/3 includes utilities to monitor, check, and perform management operations on the updating process, which can be very useful in case problems arise. When updating errors occur, normally the user requesting the update receives an express SAP message and an alert is triggered in the CCMS monitor.

The update functions are located under the administration menu, and then *Monitor* → *Update.* Alternatively, enter transaction code SM13 in the command field. The system displays the initial update screen as shown in Fig. 10-5. From this initial update screen, you can perform the following functions:

- Display the system update records with error status or which have not yet been processed
- Activate and deactivate the updating in the whole SAP system
- Display update statistics
- Display the data on the erroneous update records and reprocess them, either in real or in test mode
- Send waiting update records for processing after a deactivation/activation of the updating
- Delete update records

Be sure to understand clearly how the updating process can affect the system before performing any management options on update records.

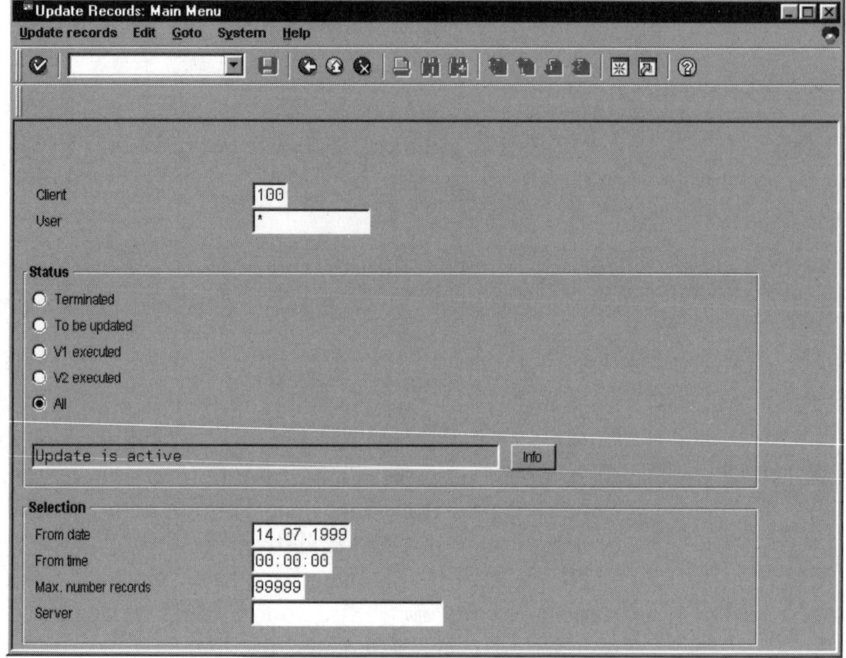

Figure 10-5 Update process monitoring initial display.

Update Process Concepts

Several of the work process types of the R/3 system update the database. The dialog and background work processes include a database interface which can directly update the database. But these processes might also make use of the update work processes for updating the physical database in an asynchronous way. This section deals with the updating as performed by the update work processes.

If the transactions programmed in the ABAP business applications have been designed for asynchronous updating, then in the database commit phases, the transactions pass the update records to the update work processes, which finally perform the changes in the database.

The update records contain both the data and the instructions on how to modify the database. These update records also have an update record header which is created by the transaction requesting the update. The headers of the update records are used for monitoring and managing the update processes.

An update record might have several update components in charge of making different changes to the database. Update component types modify different database objects. The R/3 system distinguishes between primary (U1 or V1) and secondary (U2 or V2) update components.

Primary update components, known as *U1 components,* are in charge of the critical updates of the database and have priority over the secondary update components, U2.

Critical updates of the database are the most usual, including posting financial documents, receiving sales orders, launching a production order, and so on. Secondary updates are lower priority changes such as calculating totals or preparing statistical information.

The SAP dispatcher always assigns a higher priority to U1 components to perform the update as soon as possible; they are always processed before the U2 components.

These types of update components are completely transparent to users and system managers, since they are programmed in the application transactions. However, developers must consider the update components when defining new customer transactions.

A group of update components of both types in an update record is processed sequentially by a single work process of an application server. U2 update components are always processed by the U2 update work processes. Should no U2 update work process be available in the application server, then the U2 components are processed by the U1 update work process.

Distribution of Update Work Processes

The profile parameters rdisp/wp_no_vb and rdisp/wp_no_vb2 define the number of update work processes running in an instance. A U2 work process can only process U2 update components.

The update work processes can be running on more than one server, in which case the system will perform server load balancing to distribute the update requests among the available work processes. For performance reasons, many installations define most of their update work processes as "close" to the database as possible, that is, on the same server as the database server.

Every 10 minutes the system checks the availability of the update servers and refreshes the information for the application servers. When a server is down, the update requests are reallocated to active update servers.

As a security measure to ensure that the update process does not get saturated with update records, the update servers process synchronously every 100th update. When this happens, the program that requested the update will wait until all pending updates have been processed. Then the program will resume execution.

This is particularly useful for large data load programs or background jobs which perform many updates and which could potentially fill up the processing capacity of the update server.

Monitoring Update Records

From the main menu for monitoring the update records, as shown in Fig. 10-5, there are several input fields and radio buttons for selecting update records. When entering selection criteria, you can use wildcards for selecting all update records. You can select using the following criteria:

- *Client.* Enter here the SAP system client or an * to indicate all clients.
- *User.* You can specify the user ID whose transaction generated the update record.
- *Status.* With this radio button, you can indicate the type of update record:
  - *Terminated.* Indicates that the update records terminated with errors. This status corresponds to internal status ERR.
  - *To be updated.* Will show records which have not yet been processed.
  - *V1 executed.* With this status, you select those update records for which the U1 part has been successfully processed.
  - *V2 executed.* It's the status for selecting those update records which have successfully processed the U2 component.
  - *All.* To display all the update records regardless of their status.
- *From date* and *From time.* These are used to specify the date and time range in which to display update records. Successfully processed update records are automatically deleted by the system and will not appear.
- *Max. Number records.* This is used to limit the number of update records to be displayed.
- *Server.* This is used to indicate which update server is in use in case there is more than one update server configured in the SAP system.

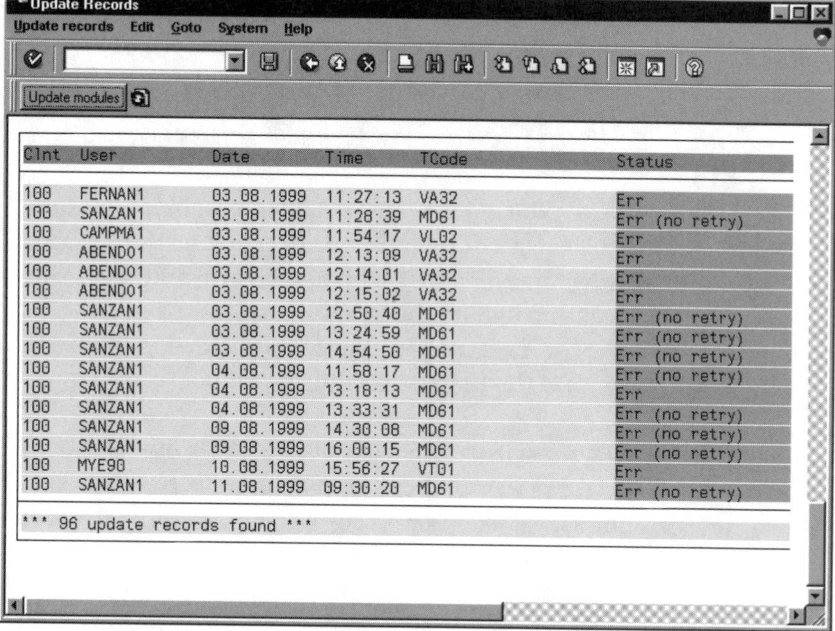

Update Records

Update records Edit Goto System Help

Update modules

Clnt	User	Date	Time	TCode	Status
100	FERNAN1	03.08.1999	11:27:13	VA32	Err
100	SANZAN1	03.08.1999	11:28:39	MD61	Err (no retry)
100	CAMPMA1	03.08.1999	11:54:17	VL02	Err
100	ABENDO1	03.08.1999	12:13:09	VA32	Err
100	ABENDO1	03.08.1999	12:14:01	VA32	Err
100	ABENDO1	03.08.1999	12:15:02	VA32	Err
100	SANZAN1	03.08.1999	12:50:40	MD61	Err (no retry)
100	SANZAN1	03.08.1999	13:24:59	MD61	Err (no retry)
100	SANZAN1	03.08.1999	14:54:50	MD61	Err (no retry)
100	SANZAN1	04.08.1999	11:58:17	MD61	Err (no retry)
100	SANZAN1	04.08.1999	13:18:13	MD61	Err
100	SANZAN1	04.08.1999	13:33:31	MD61	Err (no retry)
100	SANZAN1	09.08.1999	14:30:08	MD61	Err (no retry)
100	SANZAN1	09.08.1999	16:00:15	MD61	Err (no retry)
100	MYE90	10.08.1999	15:56:27	VT01	Err
100	SANZAN1	11.08.1999	09:30:20	MD61	Err (no retry)

*** 96 update records found ***

Figure 10-6 Example of update record with error status.

Figure 10-6 shows an example of the resulting screen when looking for terminated update records. From this screen, by selecting the record and then choosing *Goto → Update header* from the menu, you can display the header of the update record, needed by the update process to manage the records. Figure 10-7 shows an example of the update header. The update header includes management data which shows specific information

Update Header

Update 19990810155627111186SAPCLR3.0002
Client 100
User MYE90
Lang. ES
Account
Report SAPMV56A
TCode VT01
Enqueue SAPCLR3.000219990810155627111186
Context :S:
Info 16
VB-Rc 9
Status Update was terminated
UpdateSrv SAPCLR3_E01_00
Error text
00 671: ABAP/4 processor: BCD_ZERODIVIDE

Figure 10-7 Update header example.

about the update record and which can be useful for finding the problem in the system log.

Available Update Functions

From the monitoring update menu, there are functions to help you locate the causes of updating problems, functions for looking at the data which was contained in the update record, and also utilities for processing or repeating update records.

The next section contains an overview of the management options within the update monitoring menu.

Processing and Repeating Update Records. From the Updated records menu, there are two options to manually start, restart, continue, or repeat the processing of update records. These menu functions are *Update* and *Repeat update.*

With the *Update* option, you can decide to update records which have not yet been committed and which are waiting to be processed. These records have either the status INIT or AUTO.

INIT status indicates that an update record has all the needed components: header, update function modules, and the data, but has not yet been processed.

Records with *AUTO* status are flagged in update records which have been marked for processing as the update process restarts. This situation might happen when the updating process has been deactivated.

Within the Post menu option, select whether you want to process *All records* or a *single* update record.

With the *Repeat update* function, you can request the system to reprocess update records carrying status ERR, which means they have terminated abnormally. You should, however, analyze the cause of the error before proceeding.

When an update record terminates abnormally, it automatically releases the lock held on the objects for updating. This means that the user who got the error might have tried to manually enter the same data again and therefore update the database. If you, as administrator, are not aware of that fact and repeat an update, you can cause severe inconsistencies in the database. Therefore, as a step before repeating an update record, contact the user or users with the update errors to see if they can reenter the data in the system. If the users do not know or do not remember the data, you can help them by looking at the actual data fields and tables with the update records *Display data* and *Display RF documents* functions.

When repeating the processing of an update record, you can select either the U1 or U2 update components. However, the U2 components will not be processed unless the U1 have been successfully processed. Normally, the U2 update takes place immediately after the U1 update, but it's not asynchronously performed from the U1.

From the *Repeate update* menu you can decide whether to select *All records* or *Single* to repeat abnormally terminated update records.

Deleting Update Records. Once you are sure the update record has been processed, either by manually reentering the data or by repeating the update process, you can delete the update records. To do that, from the update menu, first enter the criteria for selecting the records to delete. The system will display a list with the update records that met the criteria. On this new screen from the Updated Records menu, select *Delete* and then either *all records* or *single* to delete just the one you have selected.

When deleting update records the system releases any locks held on the objects.

Displaying and Resetting Update Statistics. You can display a report for the update activity in the SAP instance where you are currently logged on. This report can be seen by selecting *Goto → Statistics* from the first update monitoring screen.

In this report, you can see information such as number and status of update requests, database activity involved in the update processing, and runtime statistics.

You can reset the statistics to zero. From the initial monitoring menu, select *Update Records → Reset → Statistics* and then you can either choose *local,* for resetting the statistics just on the current application server, or *global,* for resetting the statistics in all update servers.

Activating and Deactivating Updating. If a severe system error takes place but the system did not crash, such as, for example, a tablespace overflow, it sometimes might be useful to deactivate the updating as a security measure to prevent all coming update records to be aborted by the system, in which case users must enter the data back and process again the erroneous transactions. You could deactivate the updating, correct the system problem, and then activate it again and reprocess all the pending update records.

To deactivate updating systemwide, from the initial monitoring update menu, select *Update* → *Deactivate*. When performing this function, users will get a message in the status bar indicating that updating has been paused.

When the system updating is deactivated, all the transactions in the system, including background processing, are paused and users are disabled from generating update requests; however, when updating is reactivated, they can continue to work without losing any data. Background jobs continue from the point they were paused.

To reactivate the updating process, select *Administration* → *Update* → *Activate* from the initial update screen.

Basic Troubleshooting with Updating

Usually the list of update records will appear empty. If, when many users are connected, you often click on the *Refresh* icon, then you will see some update records with the *Init* or *Auto* status. The *Err* status indicates an aborted update record.

Update problems are normally flagged in the system alert monitor under the ABAP posting parameter within the ABAP errors section.

Although the update monitoring and management functions include many functionalities for handling the update records, when an update error occurs, as basic troubleshooting the system administrator should do the following:

- Analyze the cause of the problem in the updating
- Try to solve the underlying problem which caused the error
- Repeat the update processing or, depending on the type of error, request the user repeat the data entry which performs the update. Contacting the user to reenter information is always the safest way.

Analyzing Update Errors. Start by entering the search criteria for abnormally terminated update records in the first update monitoring menu. For example, mark the radio button next to *Terminated* or *All*, enter the time period selection, and press *Enter*. The system will display a list of update records, as shown in Fig. 10-6.

Mark the record with the *Err* status by clicking on it, and select *Update modules* from the application toolbar. Or, directly double click on it. The system displays a list of the update function modules which were to be processed for the update record. Figure 10-8 shows an example of the update modules.

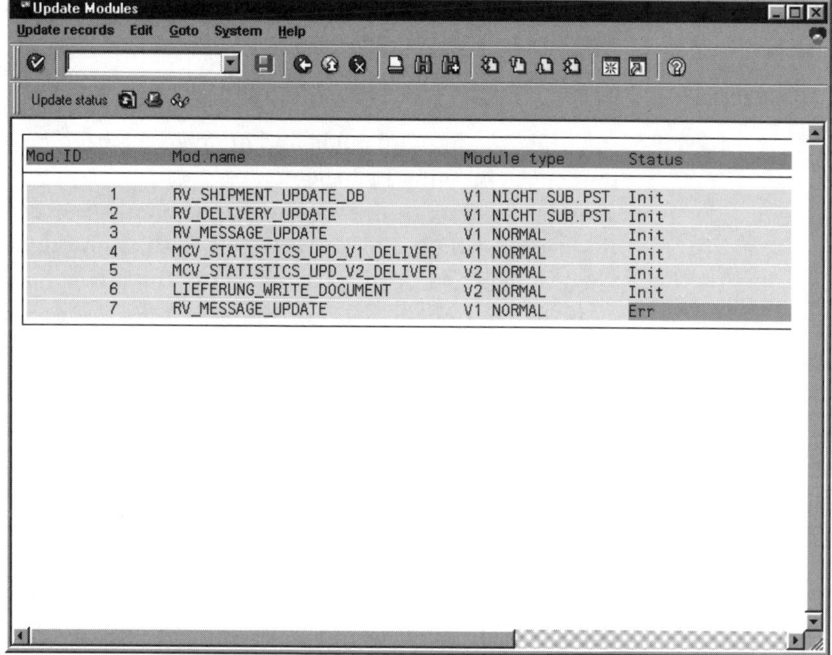

Figure 10-8 Update modules display.

The list near the top of the screen shows each of the modules for the update record, together with their processing status. To display the error information, click on the module with the error status (*Err*) and select *Update status* from the application toolbar.

The status dialog box shows the error message associated with the abnormal termination. The error text includes an error code, which you can use for searching SAPnet for R/3 notes in case you cannot solve the problem yourself. The bottom part of the window includes the *ABAP short dump* function, which you can use to display more detailed information about the error.

Additionally, you should look in the system log and look for messages relating to the update's abnormal termination. The most common reasons for aborted updates are database-related problems, such as tablespaces becoming full.

The function *Update records* → *Test* can be used to repeat an aborted update record without making database modifications. This *test* function actually makes changes to the database but then rolls them back after the update record is either complete or ends in errors again. If the test completes successfully, it means that it was a temporary problem which has been resolved. Otherwise, you will get a new error message. This function should not be used in productive systems since it may cause inconsistencies if the data cannot be rolled back.

An experienced administrator with a strong ABAP background can also select *Updated records → Debugging* to put the update function module under debugging mode and analyze the problem with the ABAP development debugging utilities.

After analyzing and correcting the cause of the problem, either the update record should be repeated with the update utilities or the user should be asked to reenter the data. The latter method is the safest one.

If the user needs help remembering the data to enter, from the update modules display, like the one shown in Fig. 10-8, you can select *Goto → Display data* to find which data was entered for that update module.

The system displays the format of the update data, with the names of the single fields and tables for the screen. You can double click on any of the columns to see what value was entered in the fields.

If the update data was generated for a financial application, instead of choosing *Display data,* select *Goto → RF documents.*

If you need to reprocess the update record again or finish up the unprocessed components, proceed as indicated in the previous section, "Processing and Repeating Update Records."

Displaying and Managing Lock Entries

Lock entries are system objects in charge of protecting the integrity of the data by synchronizing the access, so users cannot modify the same data at the same time. The lock objects are defined in the ABAP dictionary as a way of locking a data object. This is explained in Chap. 7.

To display and perform some basic operations on lock entries, from the main administration menu, select *Administration → Monitor → Lock entries* (transaction code *SM12*). Figure 10-9 shows this display.

This screen works like a selection criteria display. You can select lock entries for displaying by client, user, specific tables which have locked rows, and by lock entry arguments. By entering the wildcard * in the client and user, the system displays all current lock entries.

Clicking on the continue button will display the list of current lock entries, as shown in Fig. 10-10. The display includes the following columns:

- *Cli* refers to the SAP system client.
- *User* shows the SAP user ID holding the lock.
- *Time* indicates the time when the lock was generated.

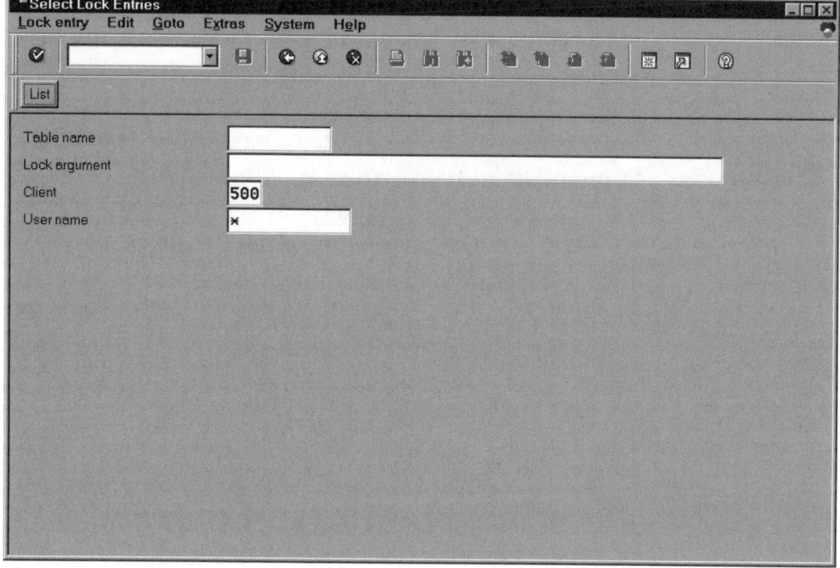

Figure 10-9 Lock entries initial selection screen.

- *Shared* is an indicator which tells whether the lock object is shared or not. With shared lock objects, more than one user might lock the same data.
- *Table* includes the name of the table with locked rows.
- *Lock argument* shows the fields used by the lock entry.

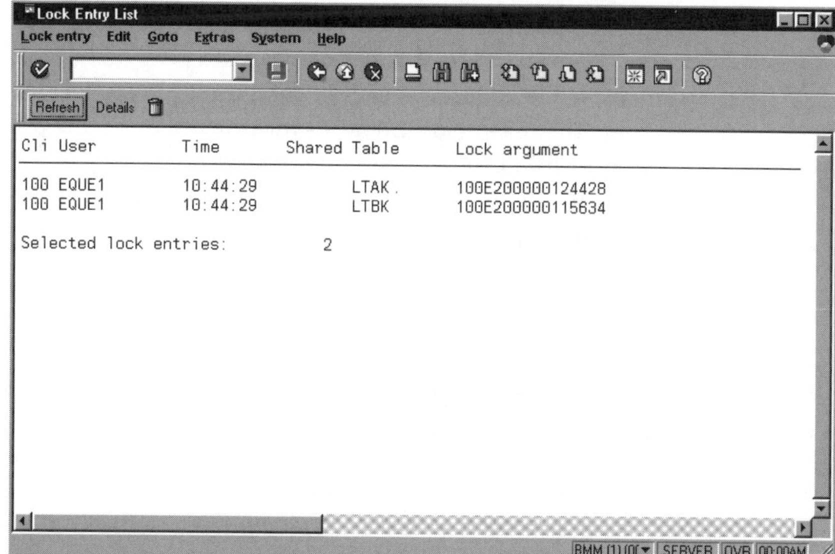

Figure 10-10 Example of lock entries list.

Lock entries are deleted automatically by the system when the programs release the data objects. However, it might sometimes be useful to display and possibly manually delete the lock entries when a system error has occurred and the dispatcher cannot release the lock. For example, this might happen in cases where users shut down their systems without logging off from R/3 in an orderly manner. If this happens, users will not be able to access the locked data.

To display additional information about a lock entry, click on any of the entries from the list and select the *Details* button on the application toolbar. This window shows interesting information such as the transaction code being performed by the user, the application server hostname, and the lock object name.

Troubleshooting of Lock Entries

Frequent monitoring of lock entries should be a common practice by either R/3 administrators or operators, since unreleased locks can block other users from working in the same transactions for updating information.

Normally, the locks are automatically released when transactions are committed or when users are finished working on the data.

Special attention must be given to locks which are held unreleased for several hours. Although this is not always a cause for alert, since in special circumstances such as long-running background jobs which update the database, it can be a completely normal process.

The lock monitoring functions offer the utility to manually delete unreleased locks. However, you should not delete locks directly before analyzing the reason for the lock. Once you discover the problem and solve it, the lock will automatically be released.

As much as possible try to avoid manually deleting lock entries, and do it only when you are sure that it will not affect an update process, a background job, or an active user. Otherwise, it might lead to data inconsistencies.

Some of the most frequent reasons for unreleased locks are as follows:

Abnormal termination of the SAPGUI. If users shut down their PCs without logging off R/3, or if the SAPGUI terminates for other reasons, such as network or communication problems, the user session may remain active in the SAP system. If this happens while the user had lock entries, sometimes these locks remain unreleased since the user is no longer active in the system, and therefore they cannot be automatically released.

In these cases you can manually release the lock either by deleting it from the lock entry list, or you can log off the user from users monitoring screen in the application server where the user was logged on. This information can be found in the lock entry details window. The user will not be able to reclaim the old lock before the abnormal termination and must redo the work again.

To manually delete a lock entry from the lock entry list, click on the line holding the lock you want to release and click on the *Delete* icon from the application toolbar, or select *Lock entry* → *Delete* from the menu bar.

Inactive SAPGUI. Another common reason for holding a lock for a long period of time is when users currently working on the system leave their presentation services with unfinished transactions. Before manually deleting a lock entry which is preventing other users from working in the same tasks, try to locate and directly check with the user. Otherwise, you should either manually log off the user or delete the lock if this is seriously preventing other users' work. However, make sure the lock is not coming from an important background job. You can check this in the *WP no.* in the lock entry details window.

Problems in update processing. When there are update modules which are unprocessed by the system, these modules do not release the locks. The update process only releases the locks when either the update records have been completely processed or they have abnormally terminated with an error status. Only update modules with status *INIT* or *AUTO* (unprocessed updates) can hold locks.

Normally, the lock entry list will highlight those entries which are held by update processes, especially by U1 update components. If you press the Refresh button often on the lock entry list, you can sometimes see highlighted entries, which are released very quickly.

From the entry lock details window you can also distinguish lock entries held by the update processes because they have the *Backup flag* set.

To correct this situation, before manually deleting a lock entry, you should investigate the cause of the update problem. Refer to the previous section on update monitoring and troubleshooting on how to proceed. For example, check that updating is activated and that the update work processes are running. Once the update problem is solved, the lock will automatically be released.

Testing for Other Locking Problems. Previous basic troubleshooting only covered the problems related to unreleased lock entries, assuming that the lock mechanism was working correctly. There are, however, situations when the problems might affect the whole enqueue process.

The *Extras* menu options from the initial lock entry screen provides some useful diagnosis functions which will automatically pinpoint problems in the enqueue server. The available options are

- *Statistics.* The system displays a small report with the enqueue statistics.
- *Diagnosis.* With this function, you can test whether the enqueue process is working correctly. The R/3 system will test the locking environment and will report the found problems, if any.
- *Diagnosis in update.* With this option, the system performs a test with locking objects contained in update tasks.
- *Function info.* This option presents a brief but interesting summary of how the enqueue process works and which are the requirements. The fact that the system profile parameters must be correctly set for the enqueue server, message server, and enqueue work process deserves special mention.

TRICK *The Lock Entries screen contains a hidden menu that should be handled with care. You can get this extra menu by entering TEST in the command field. The system will display an additional menu entitled* Error handling, *which is used in special cases for advanced troubleshooting of the enqueue processes. For instance, you can activate a log of the enqueue process and display the file, so you can establish exactly where the locks are being set or rejected.*

Working with the Client Copy Options

The information contained in the SAP R/3 system, and thus in the database, can be classified in two groups:

- Data which is client-independent, and therefore valid for all of them
- Data which is client-dependent, and only available in the specific client

The client-dependent data is treated by the R/3 system in its own special form. When a user is logged on in an R/3 session in a particular client, the user is only able to see data which belongs to that client or data which is client-independent.

The way R/3 internally implements this is by having the client field as a key field in the records which belong to tables which are client-dependent. An easy way to test this is by accessing directly with the database tools and doing an SQL select statement in one of those tables. There are a few thousand tables which are client-dependent. These tables always include the client field (known as *MANDT*) as part of the primary key. This field always has table T000 (the clients table) as a check table.

Internally, the underlying SAP database system, like in the preceding example, does not know about the limits imposed by the client within the R/3 system. However, the ABAP Open SQL statements normally only know about the client in which the users are logged on.

The client concept allows for having several work environments within the same SID. These work environments are treated as different business entities, although they are often used for testing, demo, training, different customizing modules, and so on, which makes it very normal to find several clients under the same SAP system.

The SAP system, as was introduced in previous chapters, includes three standard clients from the standard installation: clients 000, 001, and 066.

Client 000 is the reference client with a complete society model and with sample data. SAP recommends not to work in this client for productive purposes, except for those administrative tasks which are performed in client 000.

Client 001 is a copy of client 000, which customers can use to start the customizing work or use also as a reference client.

Client 066 is a special client used by the SAP service personnel to perform the preventive maintenance service, EarlyWatch.

Apart from the standard SAP clients, customers can create their own, as many as they consider necessary. Pay attention, however, to the storage needed for having too many clients.

The R/3 system includes functions for creating, copying, and deleting clients, as well as the necessary options to access the client data without altering the consistency or integrity of the database. It's important to use the SAP-provided functions for managing clients and not to perform them with database utilities since there is a high risk of creating inconsistencies in the system.

Right after installation, to start working with the R/3 system, one of the first post-installation steps is to create a new client. When the client is initially created it contains no data. From this newly empty client, administrators have to decide whether to fully copy another client into it or copy just parts. Initially, your reference clients for copying are the SAP standards. Then when your installation has more clients, the source client for the copy can be any of the existing ones in the system.

The next section explains the functions that SAP makes available for doing client copy management functions.

Client Copy Tools

The system includes five tools to perform client copy functions. All these tools are available from the *Tools → Administration → Administration → Client admin.* menu. Options under this menu are

- *Client maintenance,* transaction SCC4. It's the function for maintaining system clients: creating new ones, modifying attributes, and so on.
- *Client copy.* It's the main client copy function and includes two options:
  - *Local client copy,* transaction SCCL. It's the function for copying clients within the same SAP system.
  - *Remote client copy,* transaction SCC9. It's the function for copying clients among different but connected SAP systems.
- *Special functions.* Includes special functions for client maintenance such as deleting clients, comparing tables between clients, or copying a client in base to transport request. Menu options are:
  - *Special functions,* transaction SCC1.
  - *Delete client,* transaction SCC5.
  - *Table analyses,* transaction SCU0.
- *Client transport.* It's the function for performing client copy transport functions and includes two options:
  - *Client export,* transaction SCC8.
  - *Postprocess import,* transaction SCC7
- *Copy logs,* transaction SCC3. This option presents the list of the client copy logs and allows copy progress to be monitored.

All these options are explained in the following sections.

Creating a New Client

To create a new client for being the target of a client copy, you first have to define that client. The client definition is performed by selecting *Administration → Client admin. → Client maintenance* from the initial administration menu or, alternatively, by entering SCC4 transaction code in the command field.

You can also access this function from the customizing functions by selecting *Tools → Business Engineer → Customizing → Basic functions → Set up clients* from the main menu. From this screen, select the *Define client* option by clicking on the *Execute* button. The system displays a message warning that you are going to update a table which is client-independent.

The system displays the client table, T000. In this table you can define additional clients or modify the information of the already-defined clients. If the table is in display-only mode, click on the *Display/Change* icon to set the table to maintenance mode. Figure 10-11 shows this screen.

To create a new client, click on the *New entries* button. You get a screen like the one shown in Fig. 10-12.

On that screen, you must enter the client number in the corresponding required input field. Enter a descriptive text and other optional informa-

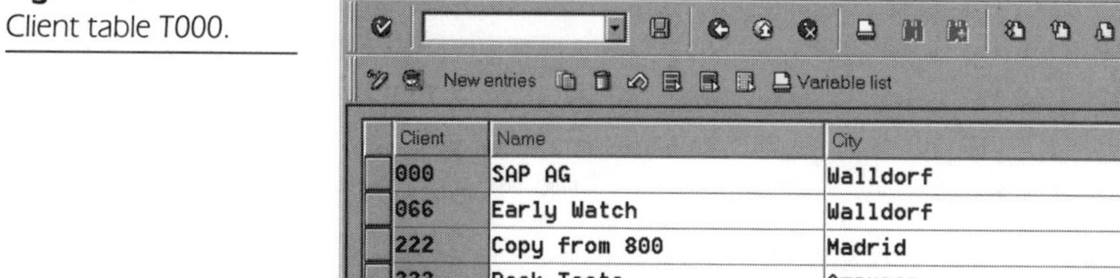

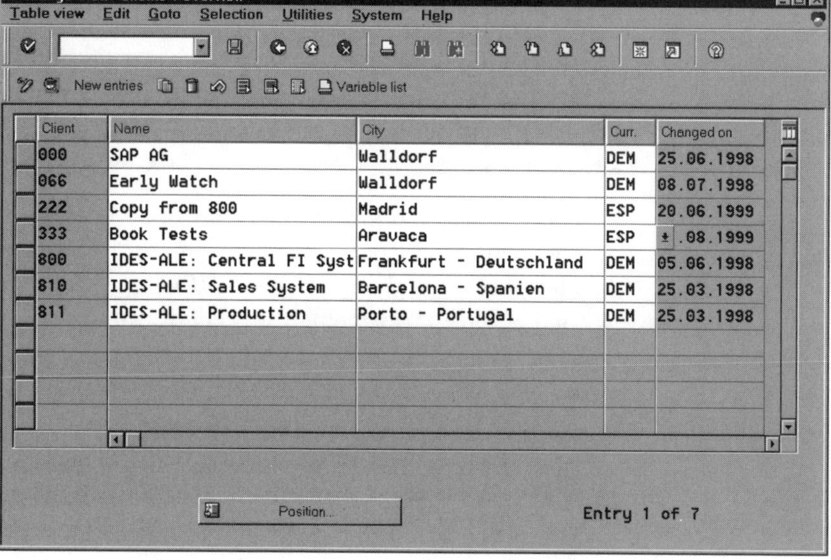

Change View "Clients": Overview
Table view Edit Goto Selection Utilities System Help
New entries
Variable list
Client Name City Curr. Changed on
000 SAP AG Walldorf DEM 25.06.1998
066 Early Watch Walldorf DEM 08.07.1998
222 Copy from 800 Madrid ESP 20.06.1999
333 Book Tests Aravaca ESP .08.1999
800 IDES-ALE: Central FI Syst Frankfurt - Deutschland DEM 05.06.1998
810 IDES-ALE: Sales System Barcelona - Spanien DEM 25.03.1998
811 IDES-ALE: Production Porto - Portugal DEM 25.03.1998
Position...
Entry 1 of 7

Figure 10-11 Client table T000.

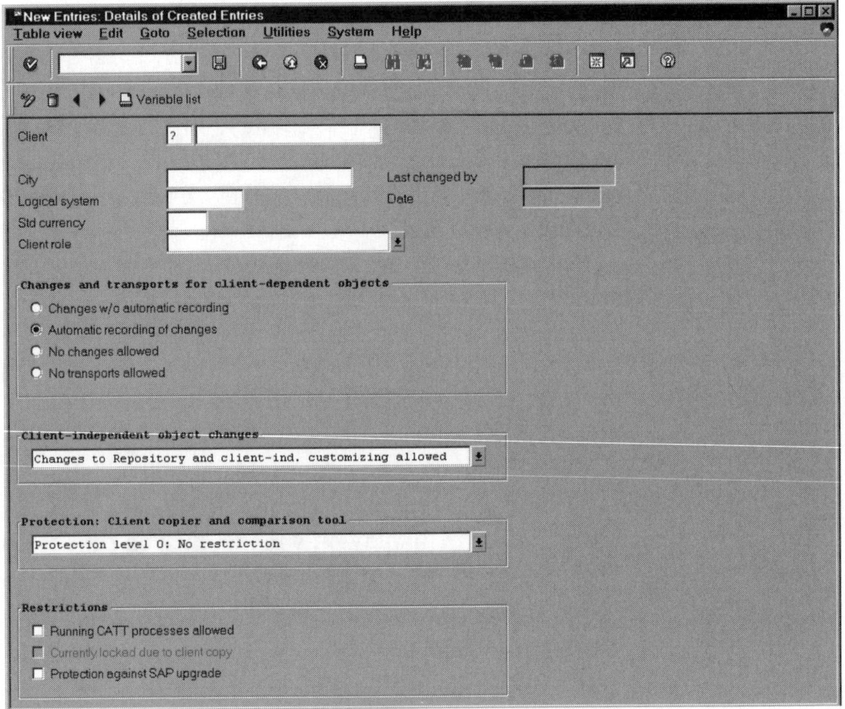

Figure 10-12 Defining a new system client.

tion in the available fields. When your input is complete, click on the *Save* button to save the new entry.

Changes and Transports for Client-Dependent Objects. When creating new clients, there are four options to consider for client-dependent objects according to the possibility of changing client customization and possible transport to another clients or systems. These options are:

- *Changes without automatic recording.* When setting this option the client can be customized, although the system will not automatically generate *change requests.* If users later wish to transport customizations performed on this client, the transport requests must be manually created. This flag is not usually set except for test or demo clients and is not suitable for development and customization.
- *Automatic recording of changes.* With this option, customizing is allowed on the client, and all changes are included on *change requests* that can later be transported to other clients or systems. This is the usual configuration for developing and customizing clients on development systems.

- *No changes allowed.* This option does not allow any modifications to be performed on the client. In this case the client is protected (locked). This is a usual configuration for productive clients where customization should not be performed. It is possible, however, to export the customization settings of this type of client using manual generation of a transport request.
- *No transports allowed.* Changes are allowed with this option; however, customization settings cannot be transported either automatically or manually.

Client-Independent Object Changes. This setting establishes which clients are authorized to perform maintenance of client-independent data. The fact that client-independent data exists and is common to all existing clients means that a change in any of this data affects all system clients. Client-independent data includes all repository objects (programs, table definitions, screens, and so on) as well as some common types of client customizing.

Four possible options for this setting are:

- *Changes to repository and client-independent customizing allowed.* With this option there are no restrictions on this client for changes and development.
- *No changes to client-independent customizing objects.* This option allows for development on repository objects but not on client-independent customizing.
- *No changes to repository objects.* This option lets users perform client-independent customizing but no development or modifications to repository objets.
- *No changes to repository and client-independent customizing objects.* This setting prohibits any client-independent modifications and is common on productive systems.

Client Copier and Comparison Tool. This option is a security measure used for avoiding undesired client copies or client overwriting and for prohibiting access for the purpose of comparing customization settings with those of other external clients. The three options are:

- *No restriction.* There are no restrictions, so a copy could be duplicated or compared.
- *No overwriting.* Client cannot be overwritten by a client copy. This should be the standard setting for productive clients.

- *No overwriting and no external availability.* Client is protected against read access by other clients—for example, comparing the customization settings using client comparison tools.

Restrictions. Client definition can additionally include several special restrictions:

- *Start of CATT process allowed.* This flag allows this client to be used as a test client within the R/3 Computer Aided Test Tool (CATT).
- *Currently locked due to client copy.* The system sets this flag automatically when a client copy is in process, thus disabling work on this client temporarily until the client copy is complete. When the copy is finished, the program releases the lock and unsets this flag.
- *Protection against SAP upgrade.* This flag can be used for preventing a SAP upgrade from overwriting customization settings on this client. This is a very special option that should be carefully used in accordance with SAP upgrade instructions and particular installations.

Requirements for Creating Clients and for the Copy Process

When creating new clients there are some requirements which must be considered. One of the main factors is the storage requirement. Creating a new client is like creating a new structure inside the database. So, before actually creating and copying the client, you should ensure there is enough space for it. This can be done by executing a client copy in *test mode,* which outputs the database space requirements for the new client in the copy log. SAP recommends approximately 200 MB of free space for a client with no application data. In the case of an Oracle database, this space is distributed mainly in the following tablespaces:

Table Space Name	*Minimum Value*	*SAP Recommendation*
PSAPPOOLD	24 MB	>50 MB
PSAPPROTD	20 MB	>25 MB
PSAPSTABD	15 MB	>25 MB
PSAPPOOLI	40 MB	>50 MB
PSAPPROTI	3 MB	>5 MB
PSAPSTABI	1 MB	>5 MB

Other restrictions that apply during a client copy process are as follows:

- No users should be working on either the source or target clients, since this might cause inconsistencies. Administrators should lock users on the source client for entering the system. Only SAP* and DDIC are allowed to log on to the system.
- The client copy should run in background and if possible at night. In this case, ensure that no background process is scheduled to run in the source client which could modify the database at the time the client copy process is running because it can cause inconsistencies in the database just as normal logged-on users would.
- In order to launch a client copy, the following authorizations are needed:
  - S_TABU_CLI allows the table maintenance in all system clients
  - S_TABU_DIS permits the content of the CCCFLOW table to be modified
  - S_CLIENT_IMP permits data import when doing a client copy
  - S_DATASET_ALL allows log files to be written in the file system
  - USER_PRO permits copying user profiles
  - S_USER_GRP permits the user master records to be copied
- When users need to create and export object lists for a client export, the following authorization might be also required:
  - S_TRNSPRT allows functions to be performed within the transport system
  - S_CTS_ADMI is the authorization for performing administrative functions on the transport system

For some of the activities and operations that are needed for defining a client, authorization S_CTS_ALL is required.

As the system superuser, SAP* has all the needed privileges to launch a client copy. SAP recommends performing the operation with SAP* or with a self-defined superuser having all the system access privileges. For more information on defining superusers, refer to section entitled "Defining a New Superuser" in Chap. 9.

Be careful when copying a source client over an existing client, since the process will first delete all the tables' contents in the target client before importing the new data from the source client.

If the source client includes very large tables, it can result in long runtimes and also there is the risk of rollback segments overflow. When possible, enlarge rollback segments before performing a client copy.

When copying clients between different SAP systems, copy only the client-dependent tables. Copying client-independent tables can only be performed when the target system has not been customized yet; otherwise, the copy process will overwrite the existing tables and this might leave the target client in an inconsistent state.

Depending on how—what is copied—the client copy is performed, you must watch out for the system number ranges. SAP distinguishes three different situations:

- When customizing and application data are copied, the number ranges are copied together with data because application data refers to number ranges.
- When only customizing data is copied and application data is deleted, the number ranges are reset.
- When only customizing data is copied but the application data is not deleted, the number ranges and application data are retained.

According to the table and table class selection, these are selected based on *delivery class.* This setting determines whether the entire table or only part of it (the client-dependent part) is copied. All customizing tables will be copied except those with the following delivery classes:

- *L:* these tables should be empty on the target system.
- *A:* application tables.
- *W:* system tables, which are internally filled.

Copying a Client in the Same System

Copying a client requires the following steps:

- Defining the new client
- Logging into the new client with user SAP* and password PASS
- Selecting a copy profile and a source client and launching the client copy
- Checking the copy log

When you have defined a new client as indicated in the previous section, you can automatically log on to the new client with user ID SAP* and password PASS.

Once logged on in the target client, from the main menu, select *Tools* → *Administration* → *Administration* → *Client admin.* → *Client copy* →

Local copy or, alternatively, enter transaction code SCCL in the command field.

In the *Selected profile* input field, you have to enter a profile which tells the function what to copy. The SAP system includes a group of predefined profiles. Click on the possible entries list arrow to display a list of the available copy profiles. Figure 10-13 shows the resulting dialog box.

If you want to copy the whole client, including users, customizing, master, and transaction data, select the SAP_UAPP profile.

If the profile selected includes user master data, enter the source client for the user master in the *Source client user masters field.* In the *Source client* input field, enter the source client for the copy.

It is advisable to perform a *test run* before the real execution of the copy. The test run informs you about storage requirements and possible problems when copying clients.

Finally, you have to execute the copy. Depending on the chosen copy profile, these functions can take a considerable amount of time. Therefore, it is recommended to execute the client copy functions in the background. You should only execute them online when copying users master data only.

Deleting Clients

There are several possibilities in R/3 for deleting a whole client. The first one is by using the standard *client delete* transaction, SCC5.

Log on in the client to be deleted and make sure no users are logged on to this client. Then, from the main menu, select *Tools → Administration → Administration → Client admin. → Special functions → Delete client* or enter transaction code SCC5 in the command field. This function also gives you the possibility of specifying whether you also want to delete the entry from the client table T000.

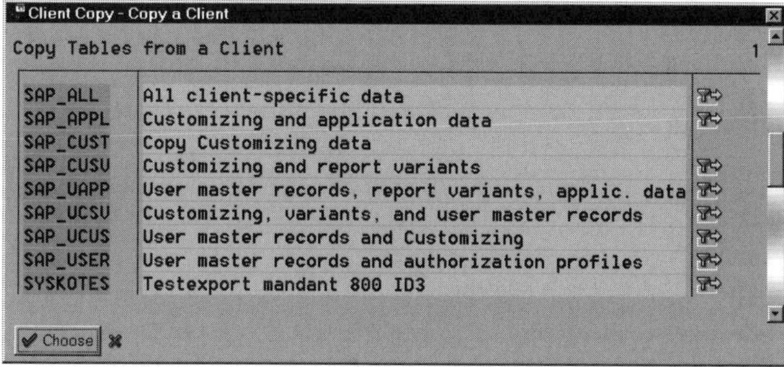

Figure 10-13
Entries list for copy profiles.

You can execute this function online or launch it in the background. You can check the client deletion process by looking at the log with transaction SCC3.

Deleting a Client with R3trans. Clients can also be deleted using the R3trans programs, which can be the fastest way. For example, suppose that the SAP system name is TT1 and the client to delete is 010. To delete this client, log on at the operating system level as user tt1adm and access the /usr/sap/trans/bin directory (i.e., cd /usr/sap/trans/bin).

Using a standard editor create a control file, for example, delcli.ctl, with the following text:

```
clientremove
client=010
select *
```

where *010* is the client number to be deleted. Save the file and execute the command:

```
R3trans -w delcli.log -u 1 delcli.ctl
```

Status After Deletion. After deleting a client, the space is not automatically freed from the database, although these free areas can be filled up with new data.

When a client has been deleted and a new client is created and then copied, the space which was freed can be reused by the new client.

To immediately restore the free space after a client delete, you should perform a database reorganization. This is only recommended in cases where the deleted client had a lot of data and you don't expect to reuse that space. And also in case, for performance reasons, you want to fill up the gaps left for the deleted data.

Client Copy Logs

Any of the client copy functions generate a log file which can be displayed by using transaction SCC3. From the administration initial menu, select *Administration* → *Client admin.* → *Copy logs.* The system displays a list with the target clients for the copies, number of runs, and date of last run, and a short status text.

From the initial screen you can select the copy log you want to display and navigate to see the full details of a copy process. To do this, double click on the needed client line. The system displays the list of logs. Select one to display the client copy log analysis. Then to display the full copy log, select *Log* from the application toolbar.

Restarting a Client Copy Process

If for any reason (such as database storage problems) the copying process has been canceled, when trying to reexecute the same copy process, the system allows you to restart the copy at the point where it was previously terminated, using the same parameters as before.

The client copy programs use the client copy control flow table, CCCFLOW, which includes checkpoints. When you are presented with the option of restarting the copy process but you don't want to use the restart option, select the *NEWSTART* option.

Transporting Clients Between Two SAP Systems

Example: suppose you want to copy client 005 from a source system TT1 to target system DD1. The target client can be 005 or any other client.

If the client does not exist in the target system, DD1, first log on to the target system in any existing client and create the new client by using the standard function, for example, *Tools → Administration → Administration → Client admin. → Client maintenance.*

If the client already exists in the target system, you should first delete it. Refer to the previous section on deleting clients.

Log on in the source system in the client you want to copy (to export). In this example, system TT1 and client 005. Enter transaction SCC8 in the command field or, alternatively, select *Administration → Client admin. → Client transport* from the initial administration menu. Enter the same data as you would in a normal copy procedure between clients in the same system, and select the *export* option. You must select what you wish to transport by using one of the existing copy profiles, as shown in Fig. 10-13. Copy profile management is explained in the next section. Execute the copy in the background.

When the export is finished, you get the following files in the transport directory:

- Data files:
  - /usr/sap/trans/data/ROnnnnnn.TT1
  - /usr/sap/trans/data/RTnnnnnn.TT1

- Control files:
  - /usr/sap/trans/cofiles/KOnnnnnn.TT1 (client-independent objects)
  - /usr/sap/trans/cofiles/KXnnnnnn.TT1 (client-dependent long texts)
  - /usr/sap/trans/cofiles/KTnnnnnn.TT1 (client-dependent tables)

  where <*nnnnnn*> is a system-generated transport number.

Now you have to import those transport files manually using the *tp* transport control program. The transport order is:

- TT1KOnnnnnn
- TT1KTnnnnnn

Now, log on at the operating system level as user *dd1adm,* and go to the *bin* transport directory. Remember that TT1 is source system, DD1 is target system, and *005* is the example client number. Commands are:

```
tp addtobuffer TT1KOnnnnn DD1
tp import TT1KOnnnnn DD1 client005
tp addtobuffer TT1KTnnnnn DD1
tp import TT1KTnnnnn DD1 client005
```

After importing the KO and KT, you have to run transaction SCC7 in the target system for the import postprocessing, in which text files are automatically imported. Check the transport log for errors.

For releases before 4.0, the process is a bit different: log onto the target system (DD1) and client (005) and run the report *RSCLIIMP.* You can run this report using the standard transactions *SA38* or *SE38.* Enter the report name and click on *Execute.* When this report is executed, the screen will request you to enter the command filename. In this example, the command file is *TT1KTnnnnn.* This report is useful for ensuring that the import was performed consistently. It is very important that this report be run on the target client; otherwise you will not know for sure if the *tp* commands ended successfully.

Sometimes RSCLIIMP can report errors during verification of the existence of previous imports. The checks and actions performed by the RSCLIIMP report are also achieved by the RSCCXSUB report without verifying the existence of a previous report.

If the texts have also been exported, they must be imported by running the RSTXR3TR report, assigning the */usr/sap/trans/data* directory as the input parameter, where the text data file has been previously exported with the SCC2 transaction.

On the RSTXR3TR selection screen, you must enter the needed information in the following input fields:

—Transport request: TT1KXnnnnn

—Dataset name: /usr/sap/trans/data/SXnnnnn.TT1

—Mode (Export/import): Import

This report has to be executed in the target client.

Copying Individual Tables Entries Between Clients

In addition to the previous functions and transactions used when performing client copy functions and the associated reports, SAP provides additional reports which can be very useful when managing information among system clients. These reports are as follows:

- *RSCLXCOP.* Copy/delete specific tables from a client.
- *RSCLCCOP.* Copy specific tables from a client. This reports client copy using a command file.
- *RSDBVCOP.* Copy variants between clients.
- *RSTXFCOP.* Call copy styles.
- *RSTXSCOP.* Call copy styles.

These reports do not make any entries in the CCCFLOW table and therefore do not allow the restart option.

Other possibilities for copying individual table entries between clients is, for example, by programming in ABAP the transfer of the data to a file and then loading that file on to the target client. And finally, you could transport the table contents by creating a transportable change request and entering the table contents in the transport editor. For table contents, use the R3TR TABU <table name> option. However, you should avoid using these last two options which can cause inconsistencies in the system data.

Copying Tables Entries Between Two Different Systems

There are several ways to copy table entries between two different SAP systems. One of the most efficient is by using the R3trans utility. The tp program could also be used; however, the transport control program tp performs many additional checks and imposes some restrictions on the table types to be transported.

For example, assume that, after a client copy between two SAP systems, a table content could not be completely copied to the target system (import phase) because the table reached the maximum number of extents in the underlying database. You can avoid having to perform a whole import again by transporting a single table with R3trans. The general procedure to do this is as follows:

1. Create the control file for the export
2. Run the control file in the source system
3. Check the export log
4. Create the import control file in the target system
5. Run the import control file in the target system
6. Check the import log and the data in the target system

Example of Copying Table Entries Between Clients and Systems. The following example shows the copying process of the contents of a table from the client 002 in system C12 to client 010 in system T12.

After verifying the client copy log, due to some storage problems in table MOFF, this table could not be completely copied. To avoid having to perform the whole client copy process, just the entries on table MOFF from the source client will be copied to the table MOFF on the target client 010 in the target system T12.

1. In the source system (C12), create a control file, for example, expmoff.ctrl with the following content:

   ```
   export
   client=002
   select * from moff where mandt = '002'
   ```

2. Run the R3trans utility with the previous control file: R3trans -w expmoff.log -u 18 expmoff.ctrl

   The R3trans syntax and options are discussed in Chap. 6. While the *-w* flag indicates the log file, the *-u* flag sets unconditional modes for the transport. In the export phase, unconditional mode 1 indicates the system to ignore the wrong status of transport requests. Mode 8 allows direct selection of tables when the default modes are not allowed.

   By default, the previous command generates the data file *trans.dat* in the directory where the export has been executed. If both source and target systems share the transport directory, it won't be necessary to copy the *trans.dat* file. Otherwise, you must use available tools for file transfer, for example, ftp.

3. Check the export log file, expmoff.log, and verify it did not contain any errors.
4. Once in the target system, create the import control file, for example, impmoff.ctrl, with the following content:

```
import
client=010
```

5. Then execute it with the R3trans tool: R3trans -w impmoff.log -u 248 impmoff.ctrl

   By default it uses the data file *trans.dat* generated by the previous command file.

   The unconditional modes used in the import phase are: 2 for enabling the overwriting of the original, 4 which ignores that the transport request was intended for a different target system, and 8 which allows for importing tables which are restricted by their table types.

   If you use the default options for the import, you do not need a control file. The import can be performed directly with R3trans -i <file>.
6. Check the import log file, impmoff.log, to check that the import runs fine without errors. You can also log on to the target client, 010, in the target system and look up the table contents with standard dictionary utilities, such as the data browser (transaction code SE16).

The R/3 System Logs

R/3 includes extensive log facilities to display and possibly correct the problems and errors occurred during system operation. All servers in a SAP system record the events in system logs. Central system logging is not currently available for Windows NT and AS/400 systems.

There are two types of system logging: local and central. The *local* logs the ones registered by each individual application server. In a distributed system, you can configure a central system log which collects the log records of all servers. In order to have a central system log, you must configure it. This is explained in the section entitled "Setting up the Central System Log" in Chap. 4.

Physically, the individual application server log files (local system logs) are stored under the specific instance directory /usr/sap/<SID>/<INSTANCE_NAME>/log, with the name SLOG<INSTANCE_NUMBER>. For example, for SAP system K22 and instance D03, the log file would be: /usr/sap/K22/D03/log/SLOG03.

Each individual application server or instance writes the log messages in a single circular file. When the file reaches the maximum allowable size, a log switch takes place and the system starts overwriting the file from the beginning. The maximum allowed size of a log file is specified in the system profile parameter *rslg/max_diskspace/local*.

However, when the central system log is configured, it uses two files: an active file and an old file. The active file contains the current log. When the active file reaches the maximum length specified in the system profile parameter rslg/max_diskspace/central, the system performs a log switch. The system deletes the old log file, copies the active file as the old log file, and creates a new active log file. This process is performed transparently for the administrator and does not offer any notification when it replaces the old log.

The central system log is located under the SAP-shared global directory /usr/sap/<SID>/SYS/global. The name of the central old log file is usually *SLOGO,* while the active central log file is by default *SLOGJ.* Both names can be modified using system profile parameters.

Local log files are continuously updated, while there is always a short delay in the update of the central log. This is due to the fact that the send process of the application servers are executed periodically and have some time of inactivity.

There are several ways to access the system logging functions:

- From the main menu, select *Tools → Administration → Monitor → System log*
- From the performance menu, select *Exceptions / Users → Exceptions → System log*
- Directly by entering transaction code SM21 in the command field

The system displays the initial screen for the system logging functions, like the one shown in Fig. 10-14. This screen presents several input fields where you can enter some selection criteria to filter the display of the system log messages.

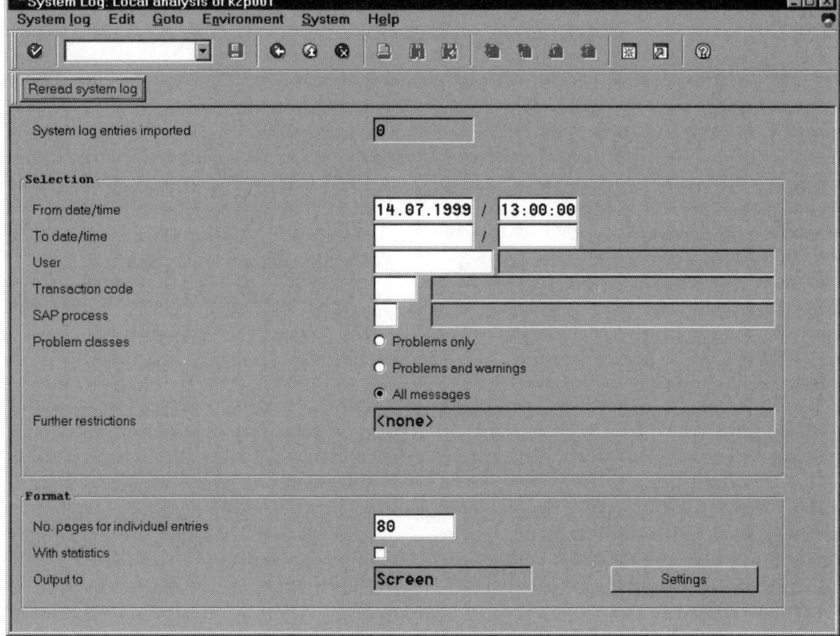

Figure 10-14 Initial screen for the system log.

The System Log Selection Criteria Screen

The first time this transaction is called, the application toolbar shows only the *Reread system log* push button. But after log entries have been read, the system will display additional push buttons:

Re-display only is useful for showing the same system log which was last read, but allows you to enter further selection criteria.

Read in system log is useful for retaining the log data read previously and specifying new criteria. This way the system will mix information from two different selection criteria.

The following selection criteria are available:

- *From date / time* and *To date / time.* Specify the time interval for the log display.
- *User.* Enter here the user ID you want to search for log messages. There are two special users which can be used in this display. By entering *CPIC* in this field, you can display log events which are initiated by SAP instances at the request of other instances. Enter

user SAPSYS to display messages generated by the background processing system.

- *Transaction code.* To display messages concerning an individual transaction.
- *SAP process.* You can use this selection field to display log messages related with a particular SAP work process or service. The following values are available:
  - DP to indicate the dispatcher processes
  - D<*n*> to indicate a work process number as displayed by the process overview screen. For example D1, D2, and so forth.
  - VB to select updating processes messages
  - V<*n*> to select update work processes by number
  - S<*n*> to select messages generated by the spool work processes
  - MS to select messages from the message server
- *Problem classes.* With this radio button option, you can select to display only problem messages, problems and warnings, or select all kinds of messages, which is the default selection. Notice that selecting *All messages* includes such things as the start of work process, the change of operation modes, and so on.
- *Instance name.* This field appears only when you select to display the central system log. You can enter here the name of one of the SAP instances.

The next options within the *Format* box can be used for setting how you want the log display:

- *No. pages for individual entries.* Enter here the maximum number of pages you want to see in the log report. By default, it is 80, excluding the preface and summary pages.
- *With statistical analysis.* When this check button is selected, the report shows a summary of the log analysis.
- *Output to.* It's the device to output the report. The default is the *screen* output. To change this value you must click on the *Settings* button. Clicking the *Settings* button displays a new dialog window with additional formatting options for the report log.

The layout dialog box permits for selecting additional columns in the report log, as well as directing the output to the printer.

System Log Types

The R/3 system utilities allow you to display other instance logs from a single place. These options are located under the *System log → Choose* menu.

The following options are available:

- *Local system log.* It's the default selection when calling the system log transaction. The system will display only the log messages belonging to the current application server to which you are logged on.
- *Remote system log.* With this option, you can read system logs from an application server other than the one you are currently logged on to. When you select this option, the system includes the *Instance name* input field in the selection screen, where you have to enter the name of the remote instance.
- *All remote system logs.* By selecting this option, the system will display the logs for all of the SAP instances which make up the SAP system. This is useful for Windows NT systems where there is no central system log.
- *Central system log.* The central system log can be displayed in distributed systems as long as it has been previously configured. Its difference from the previous option is that a central place collects the log messages by all application servers (or instances) which have been configured to send their messages. Chapter 4 includes a topic on how to configure the central system log.

Displaying the Log Report

Once you have selected the criteria and the type of log, click on the *Reread system log* button on the application tool bar. The system will display in columns the log messages. Figure 10-15 shows an example.

You can get additional information about any of the log entries by double clicking on them or by selecting them and clicking on the *Details* icon.

You can use the R/3 scrolling icons to display the summary information of the report on the first page. On the last page of the report, the system displays a table of contents for the report.

Often you will see that the *User* field in the report is empty. This normally indicates system messages, such as startup or shutdown, operation mode switches, buffer resets, rollbacks, and so forth.

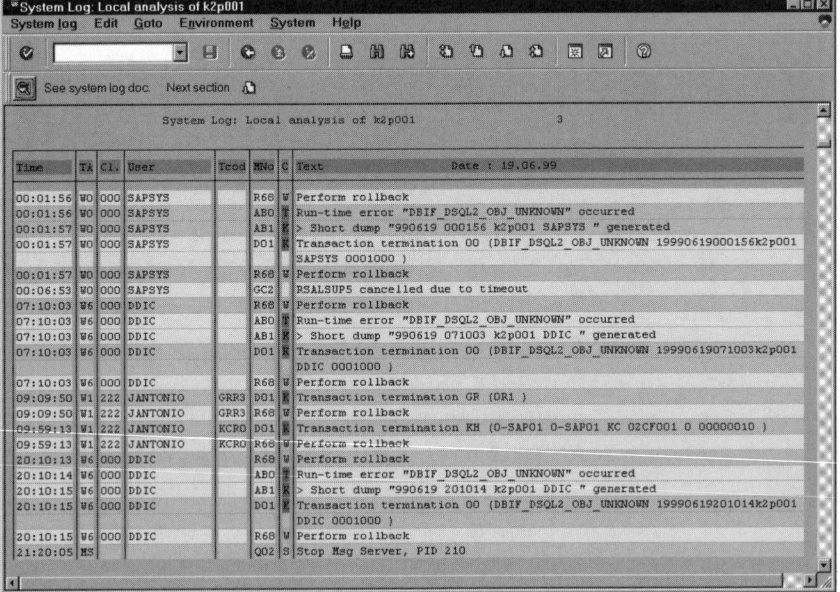

Figure 10-15 System log report.

Log Message Codes

The column titled *MNo* in the log report shows the log message codes, which are associated with a type of log event. Most of these codes have associated documentation explaining the cause of the log and, in case of errors, the possible cause of the error.

To see this information, first double click on a log entry to display the detail screen.

In this screen, you can see the documentation for message codes. You can also display the short text documentation for the message code, by selecting the *See system log doc.* from the application toolbar. There is not always log documentation available.

You can also instruct the system to ignore certain codes by selecting *Edit → Ignore messages* from the menu. When you perform this function, the next time you request the log report, the system will not display messages with the ignored code.

When you select the *Ignore message* function, the system will include that code on the inclusion/exclusion screen. This screen can only be managed from the expert mode. The system log expert mode is discussed later in this chapter.

System Log Environment Utilities

Within the system log display, the Environment menu provides some useful information about the system logging functions. The options are

- *Display SAPPARAM.* Use this function to get the system profile parameters directly related to the logging process. Notice that all logging parameters are prefixed by *rslg.*
- *Show authorizations.* Select this option to display the needed authorizations for managing the system log, as you can see in Fig. 10-16.
- *Clocks.* Shows the system clocks used for setting time stamps in the message logs. This is a useful function in distributed environments to test whether the different application servers have their clocks synchronized.
- *Process status.* Use this function to display the current state of the system log's send processes.

Figure 10-16 System log related authorizations.

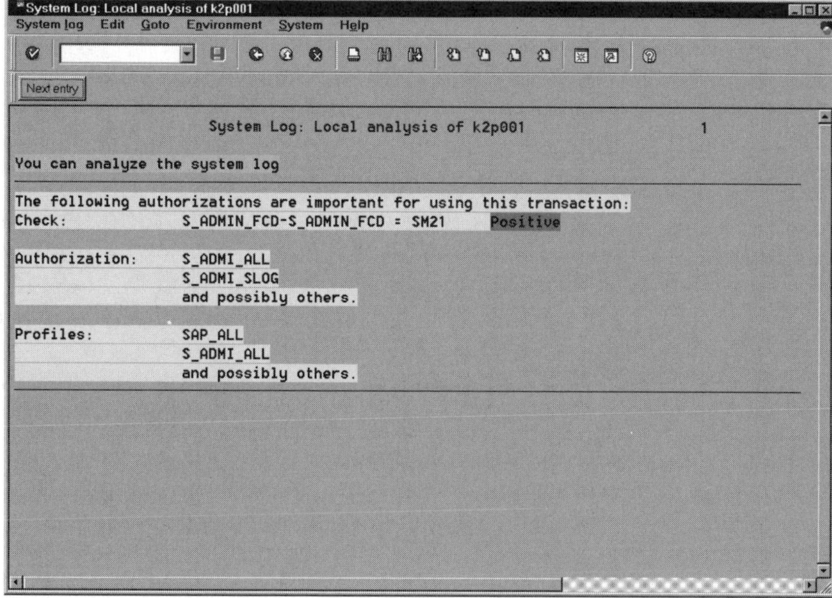

Using the System Log Expert Mode

The system log includes two modes for log analysis: normal and expert. The normal mode is the default and standard one. To switch to expert mode you must explicitly select it by choosing *Edit → Expert mode* from the menu.

When selecting expert mode, there are additional selection options. First of all, the system log selection screen presents two additional push buttons: *Attributes* and *Message IDs.* By selecting *Attributes,* the system displays a new dialog box, where you can enter additional selection criteria (expert selections).

These additional fields are mainly intended for use by SAP specialists when doing more extensive troubleshooting. In this dialog box, you can further restrict log events by programs, program classes (K, S, T, W, X), positions on file segments, development classes, and so on. For additional information on these selection fields, please refer to the SAP online documentation.

The other expert option, *Message IDs,* can be used to exclude certain message codes from displaying in the log report. These are the same system log message codes which can be used in the CCMS monitors to trigger log alerts. To display or even download a list of available system log messages, run the ABAP report RSLG0011.

Displaying ABAP Short Dumps

The R/3 system includes some special utilities for analyzing the cause of program errors. When serious program errors occur the ABAP processor terminates the current program and the development workbench generates a so-called short dump.

An ABAP *short dump* is a list which includes extensive information about the possible causes of the error and the guidelines to solve it.

Short dumps are kept in the system database in a special table called *SNAP.* This table must be frequently checked since it might soon become full in number of extents.

When users have a serious program error, the short dump is immediately presented in the R/3 display and is also kept in the database for later analysis. The analysis is a task reserved either to experienced system administrators, development personnel, or SAP specialist.

An ABAP short dump includes information such as:

- What happened and why the program was aborted
- What program and where in the code the error is located

- What can you do to solve the problem
- What the error message keywords are to use for searching the problem
- What the values of the most relevant system variables are at the time of the error
- What tables were being used at the moment
- Management data such as user, transaction, application server, and so on, that produced the error
- Whether any other programs were affected

When a short dump appears on the screen, the user can use the ABAP debugging facility to track the program code where the error exactly occurred.

Choosing the *back* function right after the generation of a short dump, takes the user back to the last active menu in the system before getting the error.

To analyze the error at a later time, the administrator must select the function *Monitor → Dump analysis* from the main administration menu. Alternatively, enter transaction code ST22 in the command field. You can also look for short dumps from the system log report. Figure 10-17 shows the initial menu for short dump analysis.

On this screen, you can see how many short dumps have been generated in the current day and the previous day (yesterday).

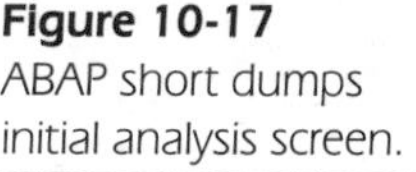

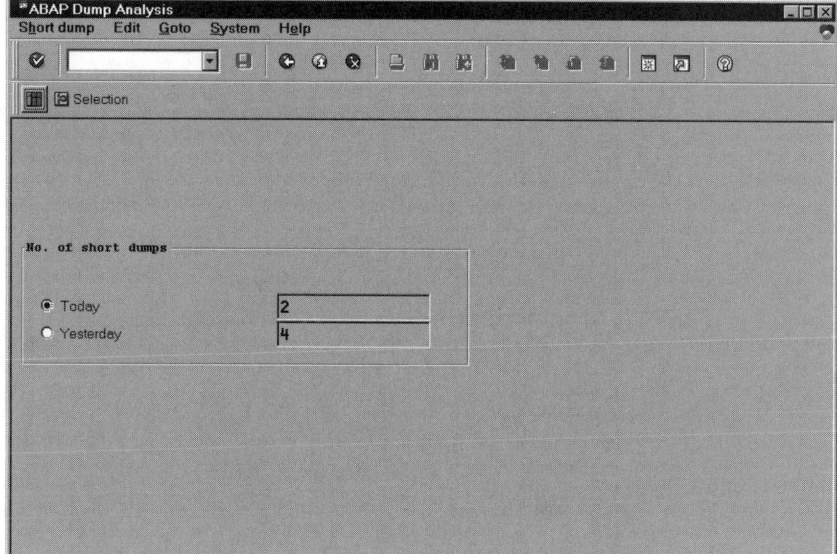

Figure 10-17 ABAP short dumps initial analysis screen.

If you want to see the list of these recorded short dumps, select the day and click on the *Display list* icon. If you want to search for specific short dumps or short dumps from previous days, then click on the *Select short dump* button on the application toolbar.

Whatever you choose, the system will display a list of short dumps. Double clicking on any of them will display the dump analysis screen, just as it was displayed at the time it happened. Figure 10-18 shows an example of a short dump.

Short dumps are not precisely "short" and they can have more than 25 pages of text. For that reason, the analysis screen presents the *Overview* function, so you can step directly to the most interesting information for the analysis.

The overview list can be divided up into 20 categories. To make reading easier, you can double click on any of the lines to directly access the required information. The initial sections contain administrative and informational data about the problem that caused the error. The last parts include more technical information, including the program source code, internal and system variables at the time of the dump, and table values.

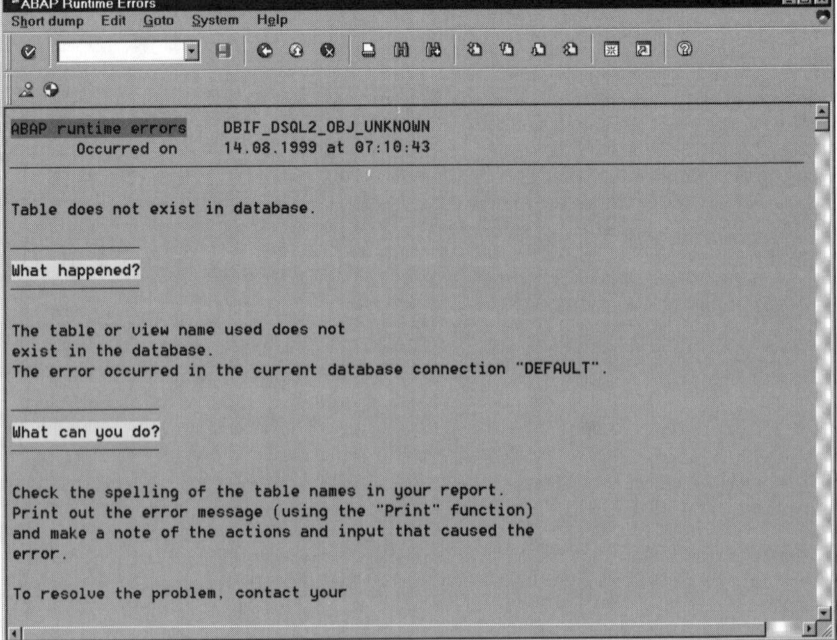

Figure 10-18 Example of an ABAP short dump.

While in the analysis list display, you can select whether there are any particular short dumps you want to keep for further analysis. To do that, select the short dump and click on the *Keep/Release* icon or, from the menu, select *Short dump → Keep/release.*

Sometimes there are recurrent problems which can cause many and periodical short dumps. For this reason, you should often delete old short dumps and reorganize the table SNAP. This can be done from the dump analysis menu by selecting *Goto → Reorganize.* The system displays how many days you want to keep. Another organization measure is to submit a periodic background job which automatically deletes old short dumps.

Another useful option for displaying the general status of a SNAP table and the number of runtime errors in the system can be found by selecting *Goto → Statistics* from the ABAP dump analysis initial screen.

The System Tracing Utilities

Besides the system log and the ABAP short dumps, the R/3 system includes many facilities to debug, follow, and keep track—in other words, *trace*—its internal operations. The information provided by the different tracing functions is highly technical and it's primarily used for solving problems in the system or trying to optimize the performance and/or the coding of the ABAP programs.

The basic tracing utilities available are

- System traces
- Developer traces generated by the SAP processes
- SQL traces for analyzing the database accesses
- ABAP program traces

This section covers the basic handling and configuration of the system traces and developer traces. Both the SQL traces and ABAP program traces are mainly used by developers. These types of traces offer more extensive functionality and are accessed from the development workbench, together with the debugging tools. Information about these traces can be found in the SAP online documentation regarding the workbench tools.

The three main system tracing options are available from the *Tools → Administration → Monitor → Traces* menu: SQL trace, system trace, and developer traces.

The Next sections will explain how to use the system and the developer traces.

Using the System Trace

The system trace functions can be set up to include a very extensive group of technical information which can later be used by expert administrators, developers, or SAP specialists to solve or tune specific system problems. This section does not cover how to analyze those files, but how to configure and set up system traces, which is not an obvious matter by navigating through the menus.

Each process in a SAP instance has its own trace buffer, where it writes the tracing information before being transferred to disk, if this option is selected.

Call the *System trace* function by selecting *Monitor → Traces → System trace* from the main system administration menu. Alternatively, enter transaction code ST01 in the command field. Figure 10-19 shows the initial screen for the system trace. This screen shows the following fields:

- Under the *SAP Trace for* box, the system displays the SAP system name, SAP system number, and hostname where to activate the trace.

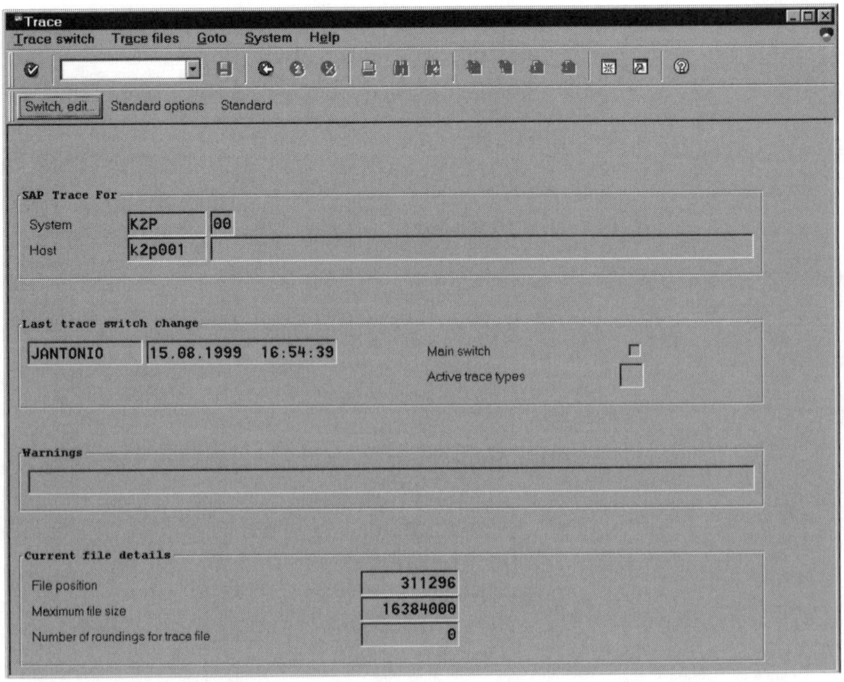

Figure 10-19 System trace initial screen.

- The *Last trace switch change* box includes information about who was the last user to switch (activated or deactivate) a trace and when. The *Main switch* check box will be selected when the tracing is enabled. The *Active trace types* displays a coded number indicating a group of traces which are running at the moment. When this field is grayed out, it means that no active traces in the current session are running at the moment.

The fields on this screen are not directly modifiable from this display, but they will be automatically updated by the system according to the chosen trace switches.

The application toolbar shows three push buttons:

- *Switch, edit.* This option is available from the menu by selecting *Trace switch* → *Switch, edit.* Selecting this function will display the main screen for defining what, when, how, and where to trace.
- *Standard options.* From the menu you may also select *Trace files* → *Standard options.* The system will display a dialog box where you can set global standard options for the trace sessions, such as what to trace and if you want to restrict the trace to a particular user, program, or transaction.
- *Standard.* You can select from the menu *Trace files* → *Standard.* This function displays the list of available trace files for displaying the contents and further analysis.

For configuring the system trace, from the initial tracing screen, select *Trace switch* → *Switch, edit* or click icon on the application toolbar. The system displays a new screen with the available traces, options, and switches. Figure 10-20 shows this screen.

The trace switch display has five parts, included in different boxes. The left part of the display corresponds to *Editor contents* options, while the right-hand side of the screen contains options for trace filter management.

The following is an overview of each of these parts:

- *Trace types.* Under this box you must check what is to be included in the trace files. For example, to trace the ABAP program calls, you must click on the *Detail view* icon to *Call from ABAP prog.* The system will display an additional dialog box for selecting the type of ABAP calls to be traced. If you want to trace authorizations, you must select the check box next to *Authorization check.* For the trace types which do not have a check box, but do have a push button, you can also set the trace options from the *Goto* → *Edit details* menu. If

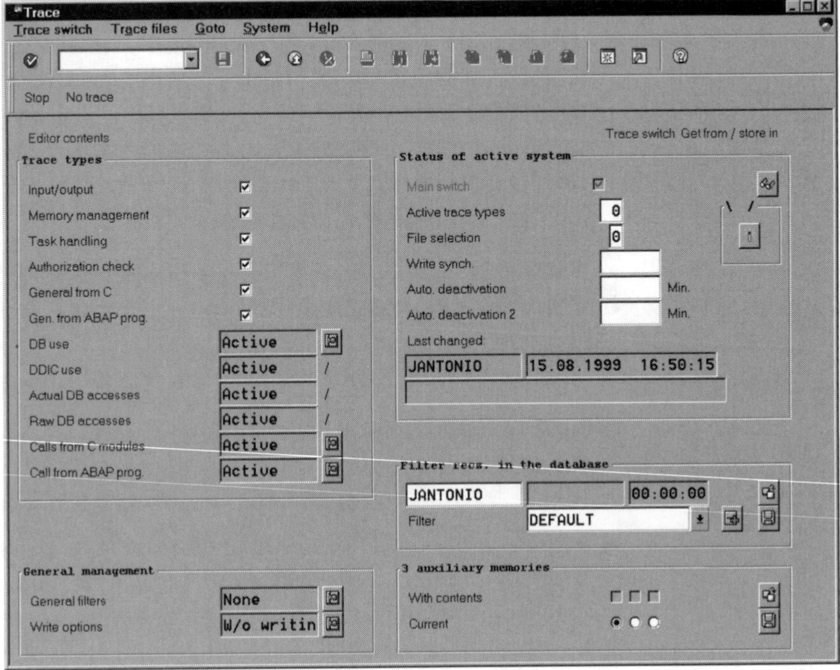

Figure 10-20 The trace switch editor.

you do not select any available type, the trace file will not contain any information.

- *General management.* Under this option there are two important fields:
  - *General filters* can include general tracing restrictions as set in the *Standard options* setting. These settings can be overwritten, however, and include additional restrictions regardless of the trace type. You can access this function from the menu by selecting *Goto → Edit details → General filters.*
  - *Write options* displays a dialog box for entering how the system will write the trace. You must set here the option *Trace: Write to disk* if you want the trace to be written to a trace file. Figure 10-21 shows this dialog box.

  If you select the check box next to *Write unbuffered,* the trace entries will be written directly to disk without going to the trace buffer. This, however, will reduce the system performance.
- *Status of active system.* This shows the actual status of the system tracing process. If you can't see any options configured, load configuration by selecting *Trace switch → Editor load from → From*

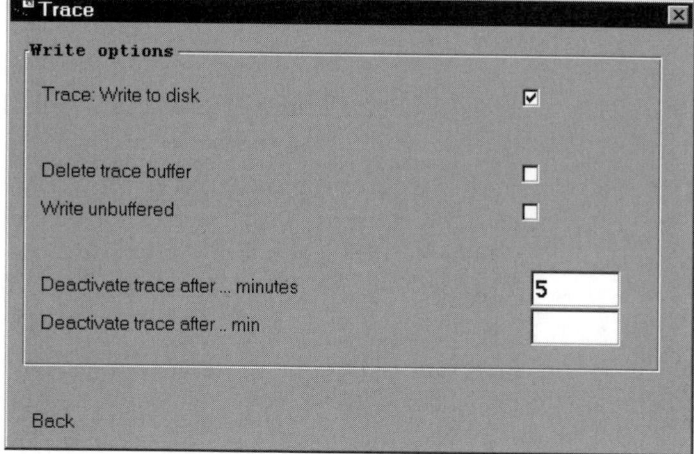

Figure 10-21 Dialog box for trace write options.

active system. The *Active trace type* will automatically be filled according to the selected traces. In the *File selection* field, you can enter any value from 0 to 9 and from A to Z. This value will be substituted in the variable as defined in the rstr/file profile parameter. The default value of this profile parameter is /usr/sap/<SID>/<instance name>/log/TRACE+00, and the chosen letter substitutes the + sign. So, for example, for system TT1, instance DVEBMGS00, an *A* as file selection will point to the trace file /usr/sap/TT1/DVEBMGS00/log/TRACEA00.

- *Filter recs. in the database.* The first field by default includes the user ID of the current user. You can limit the trace to a certain user ID or enter an * to trace all users. You can click on the possible entries list arrow to select any of the system users. This is not recommended, though, because the size of the trace file can be very big and heavily affect the system performance and also because it would be soon overwritten by new entries since trace files are circular. In the *Filter* field, you can enter a name for your trace editor selections to store them in the database. It works like a report variant. To save a filter, from the menu, select *Trace switch* → *Editor save in* → *Database (new)* or just click the *Save changed filter records* icon next to it. You can load a filter from the database by first selecting the filter and then choosing *Trace switch* → *Editor load from* → *From database*.
- *3 auxiliary memories.* This is used to load or store the trace editor contents in temporary buffers.

Practical Example: Setting and Displaying a Trace. The basic steps to start the tracing process and display a trace file are as follows:

1. Call the system trace utility by selecting from the main menu *Tools → Administration → Monitor → Traces → System trace.*
2. From the main trace screen, click on the *Switch, edit* button to define the trace types in the trace editor. You must select at least one type of event to trace. It is also particularly important to select the *Write to file* option. Notice the *File selection* input field.
3. To start the tracing process, select *Trace switch → Editor save → In active system* from the menu or click the *Activate trace* icon. The trace will start recording every system function for the user entered in the filter record. It's normally your own user name or another user ID you selected.
4. Once you or the user is finished in the programs or transactions which you wanted to trace, you should stop the system trace. Go back to the session where you activated the trace, stop the trace by selecting *Trace switch → Immediate switch → Stop trace.* or click the *Stop* button on the application toolbar. You should wait a couple minutes to allow the system trace to write the buffer contents to disk before displaying it.
5. Now you should look at the trace file generated. To display the trace, go to the initial trace screen and click on the *Standard* button. The system displays a list of trace files.
6. Double click on any of the files to display their contents. A trace file might be quite long, so you have to scroll down as necessary. The file includes a header showing the editor options for the trace as well as administration information.
7. Scroll down the file as necessary. You can display additional information on trace entries by double clicking on them. For information on how to interpret the highly technical contents of the trace files, please refer to the SAP online documentation and to the specific SAP notes on tracing.

System Tracing: Technical Details. The system traces are written in circular files, as specified in the *File selection* option. If you do not change the file selection, the trace is always written to the same file. These files are located by default in the instance log directory, that is, /usr/sap/<SID>/<instance name>/log.

When a trace file becomes full, the system starts writing again from the beginning of the file. The trace file might include several tracing sessions. In this case, it will include some messages indicating where one trace ends and a new one begins.

Before writing the trace entries to disk, the traces use internal buffers which are being transferred to disks as they become full.

You can specify both the maximum size of trace files and the path name for the trace files using instance profile parameters. All the tracing parameter names begin with the *rstr* prefix. The parameters you can maintain are

- *rstr/file.* Enter here the absolute path name for the trace files. By default, the system sets the log directory of the SAP instance. The trace file name is *TRACE+<system number>*, where the + sign is the variable substituted with the *File selection* value from the editor, and *<system number>* is the SAP system number or the instance number. For example: TRACEA00.
- *rstr/max_diskspace.* You can enter here the maximum amount of disk space in bytes which can be allocated to the trace files. By default, this value is approximately 16 MB.

Using Developer Traces

The system *developer traces* are log files which contain technical information about the SAP work processes and other programs. They are normally used by specialized personnel, especially by SAP support, when looking for problems in the SAP kernel or the runtime programs.

These traces can be useful also for administrators, since some of the files sometimes contain the explicit reason and explanation for system errors.

To display the list of developer traces, from the monitoring menu, select *Traces → Developer traces.* The system will display a list with the title *Error log files* as shown in Fig. 10-22. These files are actually operating system files located under the work and profile directories. To display the contents of any file, just double click on them, or select *Log file → Display* from the menu.

When you display any of the files, lines beginning with the **** ERROR* => message, contain error information. The error lines can be useful for displaying what functions and what operations caused the error message.

If any of the entries are also writing system log entries, then the line begins with ****LOG <message ID>*.

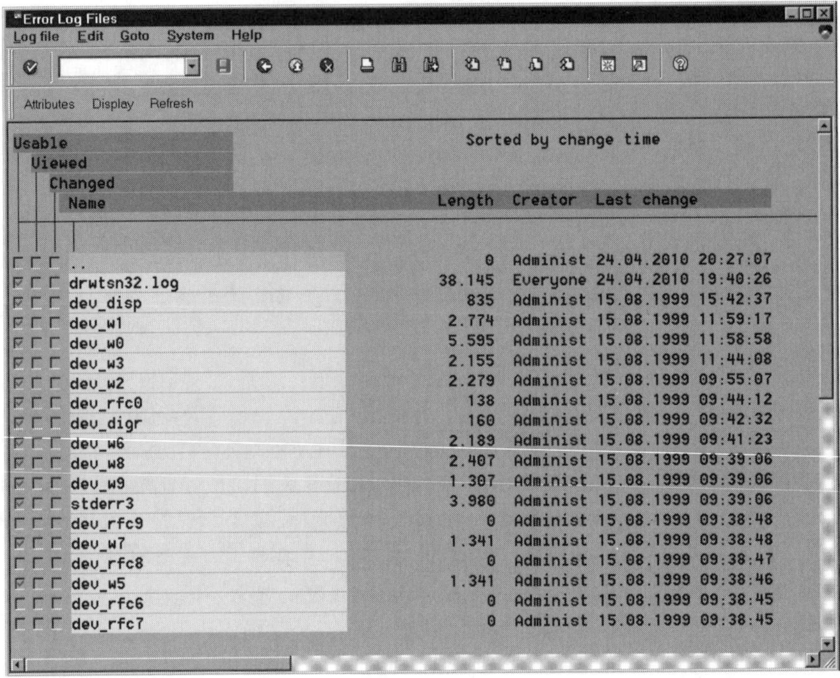

Figure 10-22 Display of the list of developer traces files.

The names of all the developer trace files start with the character string *dev*. The following list shows the developer trace file names.

Component	*File name*
Dispatcher	dev_disp
Work processes	dev_w<n>, where <n> is the number of the work process
Dynpro (screen processor)	dev_dy<n>
Roll	dev_ro<n>
Paging	dev_pg<n>
Database interface	dev_db<n>
ABAP processor	dev_ab<n>
Enqueue process	dev_eq<n>
System logging	dev_lg<n>
Message server	dev_ms
SAPGUI	dev_st<logon name>
APPC-server	dev_appc
Transport program calls	dev_tp
Remote function calls	dev_rfc<n>

The list of files displayed by the SAP system as shown in Fig. 10.22 may also include any other files which are found on the work instance directory.

You can set the level of tracing to be included in the developer trace files by adding the options to the start command lines of any SAP program. The start commands are normally located in the startup profile of the SAP instances. Available options are

- *TRACE=0.* No trace is written to files.
- *TRACE=1.* Write error messages in the trace file.
- *TRACE=2.* Write the full trace.
- *TRACE=3.* Write the full trace including data blocks.

You can set any of the above trace options for the whole instance, by entering the rdisp/TRACE=<n> parameter in the instance profile file.

CHAPTER 11

SAP Housekeeping: The Computer Center Management System (CCMS)

The *computer center management system* (CCMS) is a collection of tools and utilities which allows you to monitor, manage, and configure the R/3 system. The CCMS toolset supports most of the system management functions needed for an R/3 system from within the same R/3 system.

The CCMS provides a series of graphical monitors and management utilities, including functions for the following:

- Starting and stopping SAP instances
- Monitoring and analyzing the workload of the underlying operating systems, the network, the database engine, and the SAP system itself
- Automatic problem detection with the use and configuration of alert thresholds
- Definition of operation modes with 24 hours unattended work process automatic reconfiguration
- Instance profile checking and maintenance
- Logon load balancing
- Centralized management of usual activities of the printing system, database, and background system
- Data archiving functions

The CCMS manages a very large amount of highly technical information, which can only be understood with a deep knowledge of the operating system, underlying database architecture, network, and the R/3 internals. For that reason, this chapter is not intended to be a substitute for the official SAP documentation on CCMS, but it is to help you understand the concepts of the system and present the available features. Included are several examples of those utilities which can be more useful in the daily operation and maintenance of the system.

Some of the features which are accessed from the CCMS are dealt with more specifically in other chapters. For example, for background job monitoring, analyzing, and configuration, refer to Chap. 13. SAP servers group load balancing is introduced and explained in Chap. 4, and common administration utilities are introduced in Chap. 10. Instances and instance profiles are covered in Chaps. 2 and 4.

Due to the introduction of the new monitoring architecture with release 4.0 and the maintenance of the familiar alert monitors of releases 3.x, Chap. 12 deals exclusively with the alert monitors.

Introduction to Common R/3 and CCMS Concepts

CCMS is a great management tool for R/3 administration that includes virtually hundreds of functions. This fact, at the same time, implies there is an overwhelming amount of information which is not always easy to understand. Realistically, it may be more practical to get acquainted with the most common concepts and the most useful operations of the CCMS. Then, to get deeper details and further help in any part of the CCMS, you should make use of all the included help options in the R/3 system, especially by pressing the F1 key on any available fields, and then using the *Extended help* function for the specific topic. For deeper technical information, you should refer to the SAP online documentation.

The following are the main concepts with which to get familiar when operating the CCMS:

- *R/3 instances.* An instance defines the resources needed by a SAP application server, such as memory configuration, number and type of services provided (work processes), and so on. Every R/3 instance has its own memory buffers and is controlled by a single dispatcher process. R/3 instances are identified with an instance name, normally with the syntax *<hostname>_<SID>_<system number>,* for example: *copi01_TT1_00.* For every R/3 instance, the system creates separate directories under the /usr/sap/<SID>, automatically generates the instance profiles, and inserts some entries in several operating system files such as the /etc/services. R/3 instances are created when the R/3 system is installed and also when installing additional dialog servers.
- *Instances profiles.* The SAP system profile files include the group of parameters which sets the values for the resources needed by the R/3 instances, as well as for the number and location of the R/3 services in a SAP installation. These files are initially generated when installing the SAP system and additional dialog instances. Types and parameter syntax of these files are explained in the section entitled "Profiles" in Chap. 4. From version 3.0 onward, these files must be maintained only with the available utilities within the CCMS. This is explained in the section entitled "Maintaining Profiles" later in this chapter.
- *Operation modes.* With operation modes, system managers define how they want the SAP services to be allocated and started in the

configured R/3 instances. Their main use is to automatically switch work process types to better distribute the available resources. For example, you can define operation modes to have many dialog work processes during normal working hours which can automatically switch to background work processes during night operation for processing background jobs scheduled at night.

- *Control panel.* The control panel is a central monitor which presents an overview of the whole SAP system status and is where most management functions can be performed, such as changing operation modes, starting and stopping instances, and so on. The control panel includes many different views for displaying status, alert, performance, or error information.
- *Monitors.* R/3 includes several monitors, both list-oriented and graphical, which allow for online monitoring of the system. Monitors display the alerts defined in the system. Monitors can be configured to work to dynamically refresh the information at periodic intervals. This feature and the color coding makes a valuable tool for fast problem detection and corrections. Since release 4.0, SAP R/3 offers a monitoring architecture with new monitors and alert management, to which external monitoring tools can be easily added. The new monitoring architecture follows SAP's strategy of overall object orientation.
- *Alerts.* Alerts are important predefined system events which are constantly monitored. SAP includes alerts for the database, the operating system, the network, and R/3 components. System managers can define alert thresholds, that is, the values which will make the system show an alert message when a specific event or system condition occurs. Alerts can be simple warnings or critical errors. For example, system managers can configure the alert thresholds to trigger an alert when a file system exceeds 80 percent of the available space. For reasons of compatibility with releases prior to 4.0, besides the new monitoring architecture, SAP includes the possibility of defining and managing alarms with tools from previous 3.x releases.
- *Performance and workload statistics collectors.* The R/3 system incorporates several collector programs and background jobs which keeps a record of both current workload statistics and history workload for the operating system, the database, the network, and the R/3 system. The different workload monitors permit a fine analysis of performance problems, as well as a big help for the preventive maintenance of the whole system.

Administrator Duties with the CCMS

The available facilities provided within the CCMS should be regularly used and maintained by the system administrators both for keeping a smooth operation and making the most out of the available resources. The information recorded with the CCMS monitors and collectors is also needed by the SAP personnel when troubleshooting the customer systems and performing the EarlyWatch sessions.

In general, system administrators should do the following:

- Configure the CCMS:
  - Configure the instances and operation modes
  - Configure the alert thresholds
  - Configure and submit the performance collectors
  - Configure the logon groups
- Use the CCMS for:
  - Online alert monitoring
  - Performance problems analysis
  - Importing and maintaining the SAP system profiles

Even though the CCMS is shipped with some default values to provide the basic functionality of the system, before using the full capacity of the CCMS immediately following SAP installation, there is some configuration work to do. The following sections in this chapter will show you how to perform those tasks.

Starting the CCMS

To start the CCMS, from the main R/3 menu, select *Tools → CCMS.* Alternatively, enter transaction code SRZL in the command field. Figure 11-1 shows this initial screen where you can see the main CCMS functions.

To work with the CCMS, you must have the authorization S_RZL _ADM. This authorization object only has the *Activity* field. Assigning activity value 01 (create or generate) to the authorization gives administrator authorization, while an authorization with the value 03 (display) will only allow users to show the information in the CCMS.

Figure 11-1
CCMS initial menu.

Maintaining Profiles

From version 3.0 onward, the CCMS has included convenient tools for maintaining all the SAP system profiles: the DEFAULT.PFL, the start profiles, and the instance profiles. Although these files are kept at the operating system level under the /usr/sap/<SID>/SYS/profile directory, you should edit the SAP profiles using this tool, since the R/3 system keeps records of them also in the internal database.

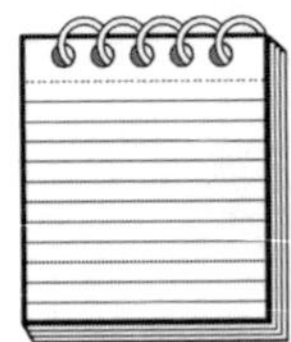

NOTE *Only in those cases where the system cannot be started because of profile value problems should these files be edited at the operating system level.*

With the new tool, the system keeps versions of profiles and permits editing very conveniently using a friendly windows interface. An additional advantage of using only the CCMS profile maintenance tool is that the system checks the consistency of all the parameter values and displays any problems or errors it detects.

The profile maintenance tools keep a copy of the profiles in the database, although the real files still remain at the operating system level. The CCMS, however, has the ability to create or modify the operating system files. This process is known as *activating* a profile.

Initially, however, the profile maintenance tools do not have any profiles to work on, and you must import them. So, *importing* a profile is the process of copying the profile files into the R/3 database as a reference copy.

Maintaining the profiles this way is very important since they define the basis for the instance definitions and operation mode tasks.

To start the profile maintenance tool, from the CCMS initial menu, select *Configuration → Profile maintenance.* Alternatively, use transaction RZ10 in the command field. The system displays the initial edit profiles screen for maintaining system profiles as shown in Fig. 11-2.

Importing the Profiles: First-time Maintenance

Before being able to maintain the profiles within CCMS, the files on disk must be imported to the R/3 system for the first time.

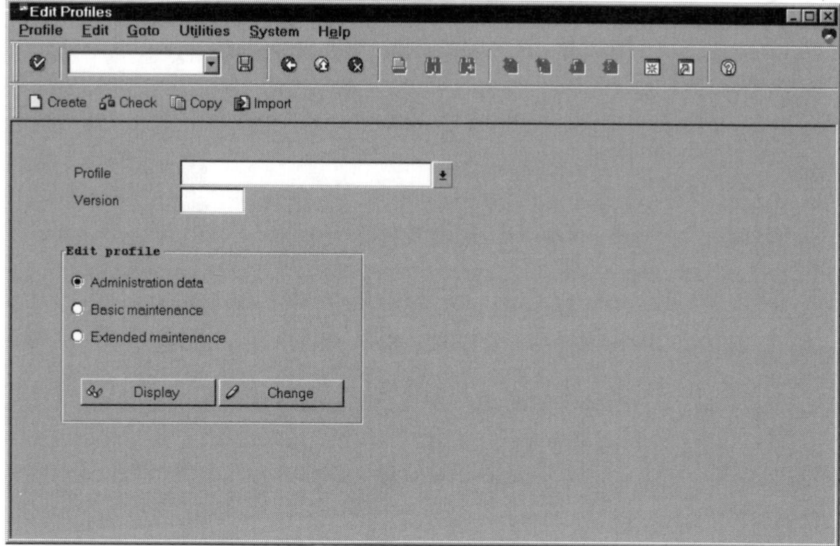

Figure 11-2 Initial screen for profile maintenance.

To import all the profiles of the active R/3 instances, from the edit profile initial screen, select *Utilities → Import profiles → of active servers.* R/3 accesses the profile directory and imports all the SAP system profiles in use, such as the DEFAULT.PFL (common to all instances), the start profiles, and the instance profiles, and copies them all in the database with their actual names. R/3 will check the imported profiles and display a log on the screen. If, for some reason, you had to edit the profiles at the operating system level, you can import them again as needed.

You must import the profiles to be able to define the operation modes.

The reverse action is to modify the profile parameters with the maintenance tool and then copy them to the operating system files. To do this, select the modified profile in the profile input field and click on the *Activate* icon on the application toolbar or select *Profile → Activate* from the menu. However, the modifications in a profile will not have any effect until the instance is restarted.

Profile Reference Server

For each profile, an application server is assigned by the CCMS profile maintenance tool. This server is used to test the profile. This is useful in instances with heterogeneous environments with different operating systems and servers with different physical resources.

You can have the same reference server for several profiles, especially when the equipment has the same operating system, the same physical resources in terms of memory, and it's assigned the same number and type of work processes, and so on.

Profile Versions

Every time you modify a profile, the system creates a new version but keeps the old one in the database. The file at the operating system is overwritten when saving the changes and activating it. At the operating system level, the old file is assigned the .BAK extension.

The system only allows activating the most recent version of a profile. If you want to activate an older version, you must first copy the old version into a newer one.

Reports RSPARAM and RSPFPAR

You can always look at the current active parameter of an instance by running the RSPARAM or RSPFPAR reports. These reports must be submitted in the specific instance, it does not show global parameters. You can search for any particular parameter string by clicking on the *Search* icon.

The difference between these reports is that RSPFPAR can be used for displaying a range of parameters (whether substituted or not) and also that users can request a short parameter description on the report output.

The resulting list presents two parts. The first part shows the parameters in the form before the substitute variables are replaced. The second part of the report displays the real values of the instance parameters.

Profile Maintenance Options

Modifications to the profiles are sometimes, although not often, needed for tuning the system, for changing the placement or number of the SAP services, or when changing the physical system resources, such as adding additional memory. Sometimes these changes will be suggested by the SAP technical personnel in EarlyWatch sessions.

If you use the same instance or start profiles for several instances, you could delete the files which were generated by the R3SETUP tool but which are not used by the system. You should be careful, however, when doing this since the script files for starting the SAP system, startsap_<hostname>_<number> and stopsap_<hostname>_<number>, make a call to these profile files; so you should change those scripts accordingly.

Editing Profiles. Enter the profile name or select it from the possible entries list. The version is automatic. The options box *Edit profile* includes two command buttons, *Display* and *Change,* with three associated radio button options:

- *Administration data.* For any of the profile types, the administration data includes information such as the name and location of the operating system file, the date and time of modification and generation, user name who changed it, and the reference server for parameter checking.
- *Basic maintenance.* This is very useful since it does not present parameters with technical names, so there is no need to memorize them. The available options depend on the type of profile but normally include the basic and most important profile parameters. The basic maintenance option presents the profile parameters in a very convenient modifiable form, with push buttons and so on.
- *Extended maintenance.* This presents the operating system profile file in R/3 list form without the comments. Allows for maintaining profiles at the individual parameter level. From the extended maintenance screen, it is possible to create additional parameters which are not set in the profile and therefore assigned from the internal SAP code.

To edit a profile, you must know what type of parameter you are looking for.

When modifying a profile, the system will automatically include a comment in the file indicating the date, time, user ID of who did the modification, and what the old value of the parameter was.

When finished editing a profile, you must first *Copy* the new values and then select *Profile* → *Save* or click the *Save* icon to store the profile in the database. When saving profiles, the system automatically performs a consistency check.

If you want the profile parameters of an edited profile to be effective the next time an instance is restarted, you have to transfer the modified profile to the operating system level. You do this by selecting from the menu *Profile → Activate*, although commonly the system will automatically request you to activate the profile after it has been saved.

A full example of editing profile parameters is included in the section "Example: Maintenance of an Instance Profile."

Checking Profiles. At any time, but especially after importing or modifying any of the system profiles, you should check the consistency of the profiles. This check includes from spell checking to verifying all the imposed conditions on parameters. The system, though, will automatically check when saving or activating, and presents a check log.

When the SAP system checks a profile it also checks that all profiles are consistent among themselves; for example, it would not allow two different message servers in different profiles.

To check the consistency of any profile, from the main screen, select the profile and version and click on the *Check* icon, or, from the menu, select *Profile → Check.*

When an application server is started, the system checks that the profile information stored in the database matches that of the operating system files. If there are differences, the alert monitor will display an alert message.

You can always check and compare the profiles against the file on the operating system by entering the profile name in the input field and selecting from the menu *Utilities → Check all profiles → of active server.* Or you can compare against the profiles in the operation modes by selecting the menu option *Utilities → Check all profiles → In operation modes.* Also, you can compare the selected profile in the profile name input field with the active profile.

Importing Individual Profiles. When a profile has been modified at the operating system level or a new dialog instance has been installed, you should import the new profiles. First, you have to create a new profile and then you have to import it.

On the initial maintenance screen (Fig. 11-2), enter the name of the profile and click on the *Create* icon, or select *Profile → Create* from the menu.

The system presents the initial screen for entering the administration data, such as the description, the profile type, the file name (include the whole path), and the reference server. Enter the requested information and save your inputs. The system transfers the data to the database. Then proceed by selecting *Profile → Import* on the basic profile maintenance transaction screen.

The system displays a dialog box where you have to specify the profile file at the operating system level. To display the available files, click on the possible entries list arrow. The values for the profile will be transferred and checked for errors. You can now edit the profile and save it into the database. You can also use the copy function to make a copy for another profile with similar values.

Deleting Profiles. You have two options to delete profiles from the database:

- To delete a single profile, on the initial edit profile screen, enter the name and version in the corresponding input fields and then select *Profile → Delete → Individual profile.*
- To delete all versions of a profile, select *Profile → Delete → All versions → of a profile.*

The system will remove the entries from the database and will display a dialog box requesting whether you also want to delete the files at the operating system level.

Automatic Adjustments of Buffer Pools in the Instance Profiles. For every instance, R/3 includes several groups of memory buffers which are used for the communication among the instance work processes. A group of memory buffers is known as a *pool.*

These pools are distributed in the shared memory segment of the server operating system and greatly depend on the memory size of the server. You cannot allocate more physical memory than available. Be sure to consider that memory is also used by the operating system processes and the database background processes.

It is quite difficult to balance all the buffer size parameters in their corresponding tools. In previous versions it was a task mainly performed by the SAP specialist and was the cause of problems when starting the SAP instances when someone tried to manually adjust those pools.

With the new profile maintenance tool, the procedure of adjusting buffer sizes in their respective memory pools has been automated, and the R/3 system presents the needed values compared with those offered by the system. If there are inconsistencies, an error message is displayed in the parameter list.

Example: Maintenance of an Instance Profile

This section shows an example of the options available when maintaining an instance profile. The same procedure applies when, instead of instance profiles, the start or default profiles are selected.

From the initial edit profile screen, enter the name of the instance profile. You can display the list of profiles by pressing the F4 function key or by clicking on the possible entries list arrow. Select the requested profile. The system will automatically display the latest version.

Select the radio button next to *Administration data* and then click on the *Change* button. The system will display the *Edit profile management data* screen as shown in Fig. 11-3.

The administration data includes the name and version of the profile, which cannot be modified, and a short description. It describes basically the type of profile, the name of the file at the operating system level, and the reference server. To save any changes, click on the *Copy* button.

Go back to the previous screen, and now select the *Basic maintenance* function. Figure 11-4 shows this screen.

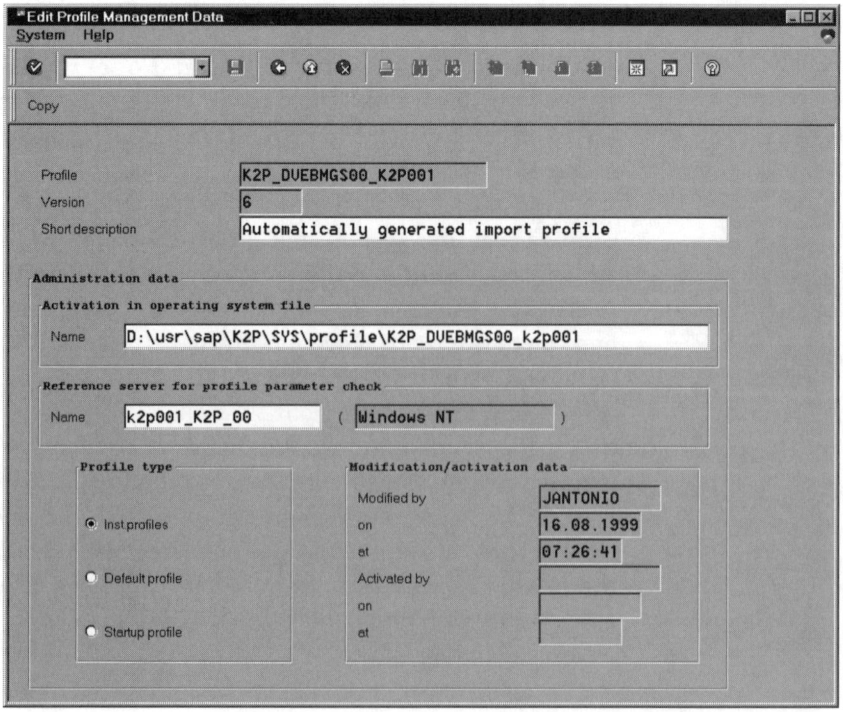

Figure 11-3 Editing profile management data screen.

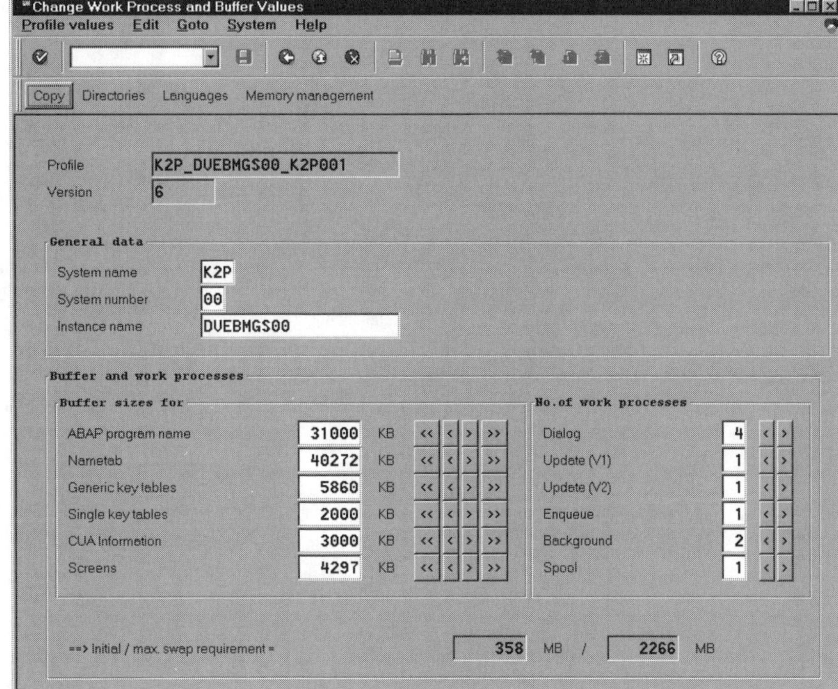

Figure 11-4 Instance profile basic maintenance screen.

Initially, the system displays the work processes and the buffer values, which you can adapt to suit your needs. To increase or decrease any of these values, click on the push buttons next to the parameters. The > sign increases the number in one, while the >> sign adds one thousand to the values. The signs < and << decrease the values. Notice that if you decrease any of the values, the system will check the buffer values and display an error message if it detects inconsistencies.

From this screen, you can also access additional basic parameter information for the instance such as the supported languages, the operating system directories, or the memory management. Figure 11-5 shows the display for the *Advanced Memory Management* edit screen. Notice that the system automatically calculates the swap space requirements when changing any of the parameters.

Finally, go back to the initial profile maintenance screen and select *Extended maintenance.* Clicking on the *Change* button will display a screen similar to Fig. 11-6.

The extended profile maintenance allows each parameter to be treated individually. The list includes all the parameters which are defined in the

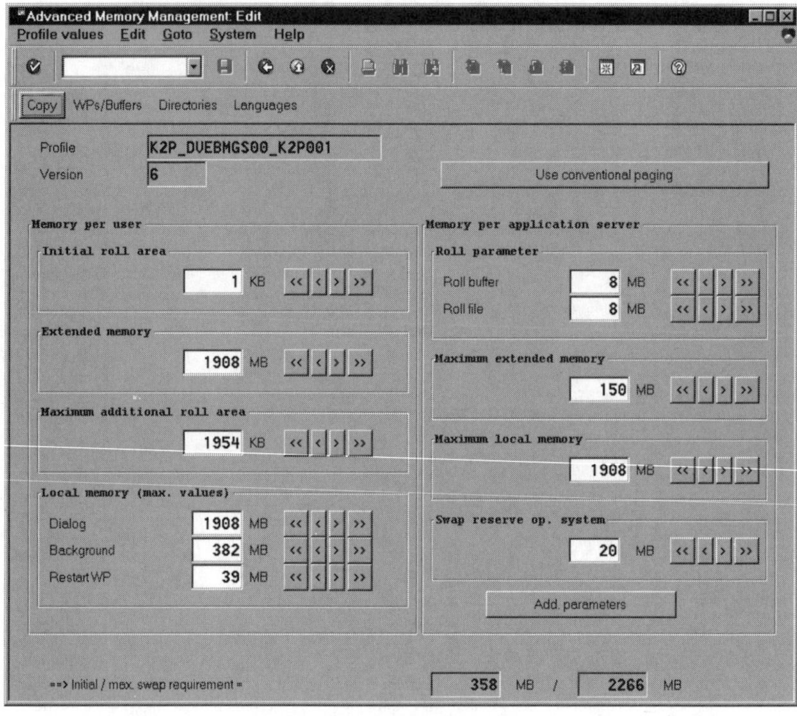

Figure 11-5 Advanced memory options when editing instance profiles.

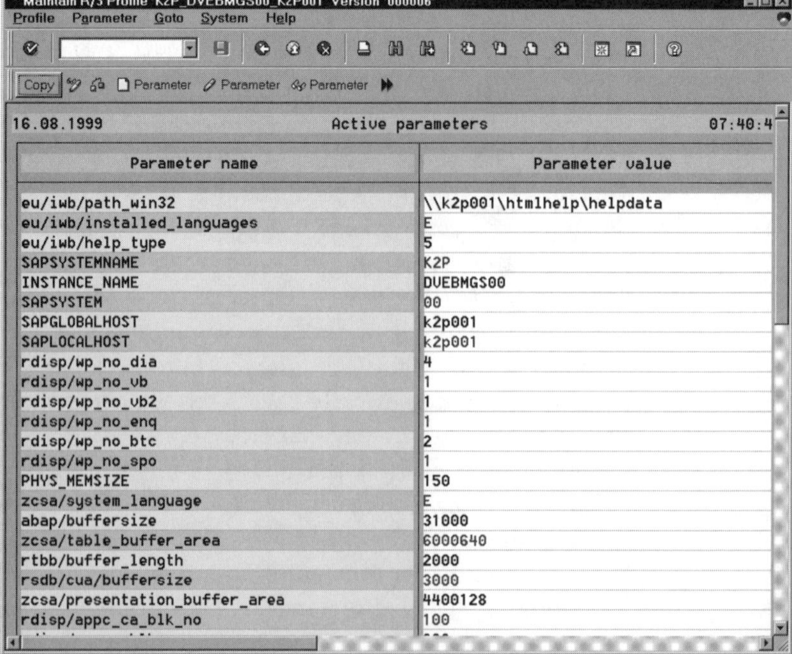

Figure 11-6 Instance profile extended maintenance display.

instance profile, but does not include active default parameters which are assigned by the system code.

From this screen, you can modify or delete existing parameters or create new parameters as long as they exist in the SAP system.

To create a new parameter, click on the *Create* icon in the application toolbar. The system will show a screen like the one in Fig. 11-7.

NOTE *Creating parameters requires those parameters to exist on the R/3 system; they are just not explicitly included in the instance profiles and therefore are taken by default when they are not present in the profiles.*

On this screen, you can enter the parameter name, or you can display the list of all available R/3 instance parameters by clicking on the possible entries list arrow.

You can navigate through all the parameters defined in the profile by clicking on the *PARAM+* and *PARAM-* buttons from the application toolbar.

Figure 11-7 Example of adding a new parameter to the instance profile.

Working with Operation Modes

Operation modes are the way the R/3 system allows for flexible configuration of the available services (work processes), thus optimizing the availability of the system resources. With operation modes, you can define how many work process types will be available and can automatically switch to other types at certain hours. When an operation mode switch takes place, there is no need to restart the instances.

Operation modes are defined at the instance level. An instance is assigned to one or several operation modes. The operation mode definition includes

- The number and type of work processes for an instance. The total number of work processes cannot be modified.
- The time and schedule when the services will be available.

The most common example of how operation modes work is to have two operation modes for every instance: *Normal working hours* (defined to run from 07:00 AM to 18:00 PM) and *Night time* (defined to run from 18:00 PM to 07:00 AM). During the *normal working hours* operation mode, the instance must have many dialog processes to be able to attend the user online requests. But when users leave work, the system might continue working, especially with scheduled background jobs. Then the *night time* operation mode automatically switches most of the dialog work processes to background work processes.

Example: assume that your central R/3 system has a total of 10 work processes available. For this system, you can define the *Normal working hours* operation mode with the following work process distribution: 5 dialog, 1 background, 1 update1, 1 update2, 1 enqueue, 1 spool. In order to be able to process data more efficiently in the background, you can define the *night time* operation mode with the following work process distribution: 2 dialog, 4 background, 1 update1, 1 update2, 1 enqueue, 1 spool; of the 4 background work processes, 1 work process is reserved for job class A. Remember that you must leave at least one dialog work process with the background services.

Configuring Operation Modes

To set up an operation mode, from the main initial CCMS screen, select *Configuration → OP Modes / Servers,* or enter transaction code RZ04 in the command field.

The screen *CCMS: Maintain Operation Modes and Instances* is displayed. From this screen, you can create and change operation modes and instances. Existing operation modes are listed as they were previously defined. If you have not defined any operation mode yet, the system displays the <DUMMY> operation mode, which is a nonproductive operation mode.

To configure an operation mode, the instance profiles must be correctly set up, since the operation modes will use the instance and start profile information for performing their tasks.

There are four required steps for the configuration:

1. Define an operation mode.
2. Define the instance.
3. Assign the instances and the work process distribution to the operation mode.
4. Maintain the operation mode timetable.

Defining Operation Modes. To define a new operation mode, from the initial screen for maintaining operation modes and instances, click on the *Create* icon in the application toolbar. Figure 11-8 shows the resulting screen.

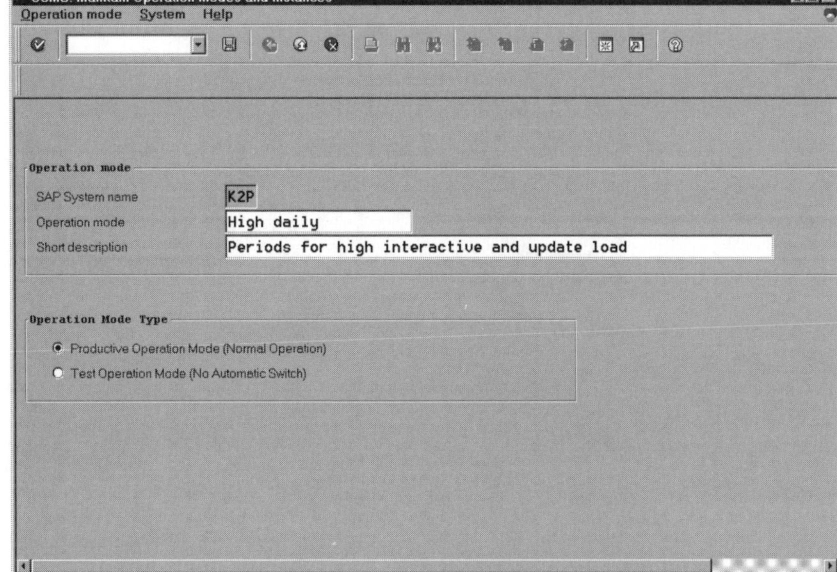

Figure 11-8 Creating an operation mode.

Enter the name and a short description for the operation mode in the provided input fields. Then in the radio button options box *Operation mode type,* you have to decide whether to define a productive operation mode or a test one.

A *productive* operation mode will make effective and automatic mode switches and are used in normal R/3 operation. *Test* operation modes can only be switched manually. Normally, select productive operation modes.

After entering the data, click on the *Save* button. Now you are ready to assign the new operation mode to an instance.

Define/Configure CCMS Instances

If you click the *Instances/profiles* button while in the initial screen *CCMS: Maintain Operation Modes and Instances,* the system shows the instances to which different operation modes are assigned (in the *OP mode view*). For creating or defining a new instance, you must select *Profile → Create new instance.* Figure 11-9 shows the *Maintain Instance Data* screen in which input fields must be entered for correctly configuring the instance:

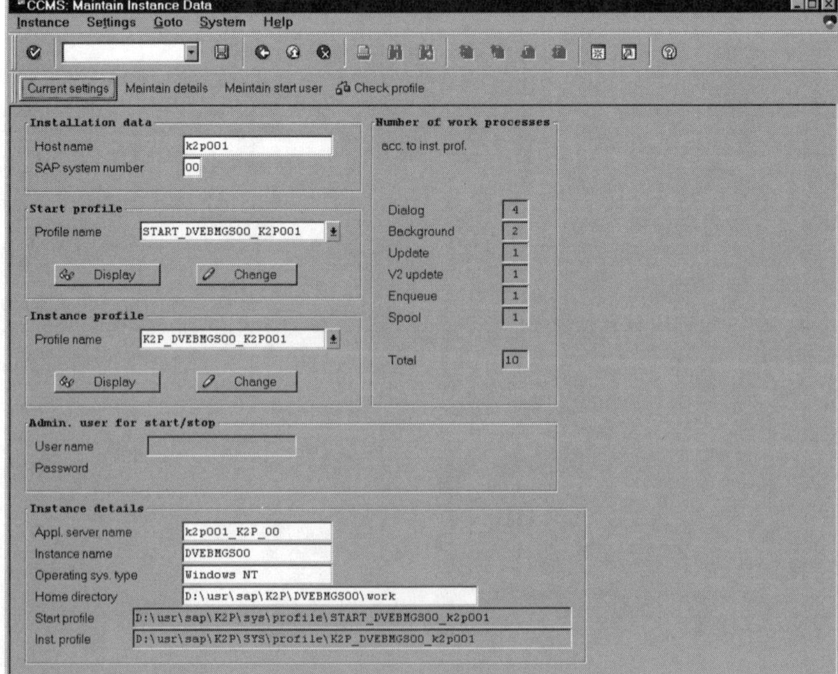

Figure 11-9 Maintain Instance Data screen.

- *Hostname.* Should contain the hostname of the instance.
- *SAP instance number.* Refers to the SAP system number, which must be unique.
- *Start profile name.* Refers to the instance start profile as defined in the CCMS. For a list of values, you can press the F4 function key or the possible entries list arrow.
- *Instance profile name.* Refers to the instance profile as defined in the CCMS. You can also display available values.

Pressing the *Return* key at this moment will fill up the rest of the screen fields. The fast way of creating an instance is to simply enter the *Hostname* and click on the *Current settings* button on the application toolbar; the system will then fetch all the profile data automatically from the active instance.

By selecting *Maintain start user,* you can additionally configure the user data for starting or stopping the instance.

Next, click on the *Save* icon on the standard toolbar, or select *Instance → Save.* The system will save the instance data and check the configuration. Once the information is confirmed, and only when creating the instance for the first time, the system displays a dialog box *CCMS: Maintain Work Process Distribution,* where you select an operation mode for assigning the instance. You are asked whether you want to assign the instance to additional operation modes.

Assigning Operation Modes to Instances

Assigning operation modes to instances does not have any effect on the instance profile or directories which were created during the R/3 installations or with the profile maintenance tool. It has a direct connection, though, for checking the consistency of the defined number of work processes in the profiles against those which can be defined in the operation modes.

To assign an instance to an operation mode, from the main CCMS screen, select *Configuration → OP Modes / Servers.* The system displays the list of operation modes already defined.

Click on the *Instances / OP modes* button on the application toolbar to display all the instances with productive operation modes. Figure 11-10 shows an example of this screen. The system displays the list of operation modes for every active instance with information about the number and

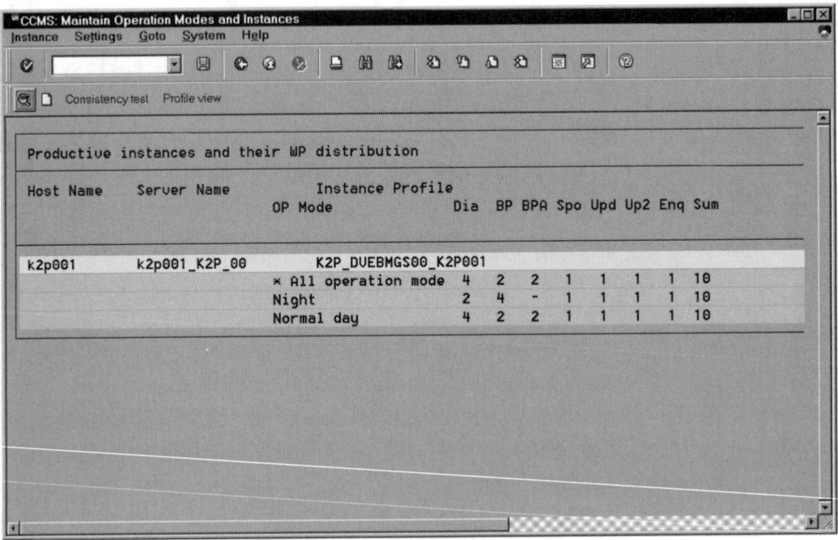

Figure 11-10 Screen for maintaining instances and operation modes.

type of work processes assigned to them. Note that the total number, under the *Sum* column, should be the same for a single instance, regardless of the operation mode.

To assign a newly created operation mode, click on one of the lines in the list of operation modes, and from the menu select *Instance → Maintain instance → WP distribution.* The system will display a new window for defining the work process distribution for the instance, like the one shown in Fig. 11-11.

In this dialog box, click on the *Other operation mode* button. The input field *for Operation Mode* becomes available for modification. Click on the possible list arrow to display the list of defined operation modes.

Notice that the system includes the * to indicate *operation mode–independent.* This mode is useful for defining the work process distribution using only the profile parameters defined for the instance.

Enter or select your new operation mode, and click the *Enter* icon to go back to the work process distribution dialog.

Following the rules and restrictions for changing the work process distribution (refer to the next section), increase or decrease the number of work processes as needed by your new operation mode, and click on the *Save* icon. The system will return to the instance list and your operation mode is then saved and assigned to the instance.

The next step is to configure the timetable for operation mode switch.

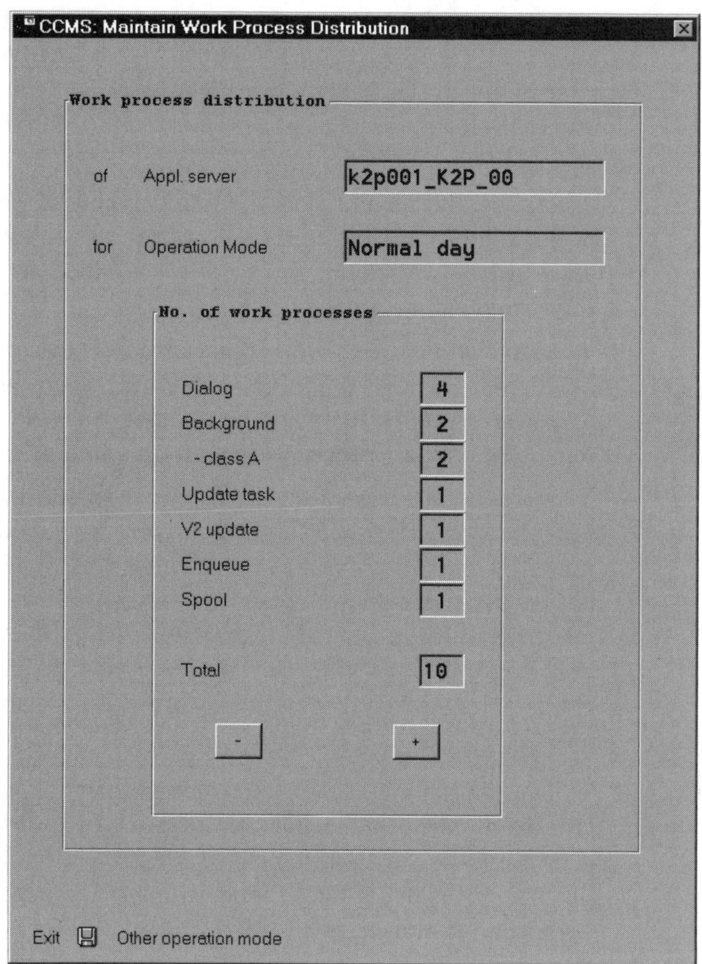

Figure 11-11 Dialog box for work process distribution with operation modes.

Restrictions on Work Process Distribution

When switching operation modes, the new instance settings should be based on the existing profile definitions in the operating system. That is, the number of work processes and important directory path names should be consistent.

When distributing the number and type of work processes among the instances and operation modes, there are some rules which must be observed:

- The total number of work processes is generated when the instance is started at the operating system level and cannot be changed. To change the total number of work processes, you have to modify the instance profile parameter values accordingly and restart the instance.
- The number of dialog work processes is not changed directly, but is automatically calculated as the total number of work processes minus the number of the other work processes. You must always leave at least two dialog work processes, since they are needed for correct system operation.
- You can change the number of background work processes, and even set it to 0 as long as there is at least one background process in the SAP system. If you increase the number, you will see how the system automatically decreases the number of dialog work processes.
- Background processes for class A jobs are a subset of the number of background work processes. You can reserve as many background processes for class A jobs as the number of defined background work processes. If all background work processes are reserved for class A, users without the needed authorization (S_BTC_ALL) will not be able to release jobs while the operation mode is effective. Regular users usually can only define jobs of type C (normal priority jobs).
- The number of spool processes cannot be changed.
- The number of update work processes (both V1 and V2) can be increased or decreased as needed but cannot be set to 0. If an instance does not have any update process, then it cannot have any update process using an operation mode change. It would first have to be defined on the instance profile.
- Enqueue work processes should be left normally unchanged. Only one of the instances offers the enqueue service. If the instance has an enqueue process, it can be changed under certain limitations (1 to *n* or *n* to 1) but can never be set to 0. Modify this value following the instructions from the SAPnet notes or SAP specialists.

Configuring the Timetable for Operation Mode Switches

Scheduling automatic operation mode switching offers two ways:

- *Normal operation.* Defines 24-hour cycles for the operation modes switches.

- *Exception operation.* Allows for the definition of an exceptional time period for the activation of an operation mode. This mode will only be executed once in the specified date and time interval.

From the control panel, you can manually perform operation mode switches or simulate a switch before entering in productive operation to test if any errors occur.

To simulate a switch, from the CCMS main screen, select *Control/ Monitoring → Control panel → control → Switch OP mode → Simulation.*

To maintain the operation mode timetable for normal operation, from the CCMS main menu select *Configuration → OP mode timetable.*

Select the radio button next to *Normal operation (24 hr)* and click on the *Change* button. The system displays the timetable for the 24-hour cycle. By default, the system displays 1-hour intervals, but you can change it to smaller periods from the *Edit → Time period* menu when in maintenance mode.

You have to select a time range by double clicking on the start time and on the end time. The system changes the colors of the intervals to indicate they are selected.

To assign an operation mode, click on the *Assign* button on the application toolbar. The system will show a dialog box, where you can click on the possible entries list arrow for displaying the available operation modes. Figure 11-12 shows this process.

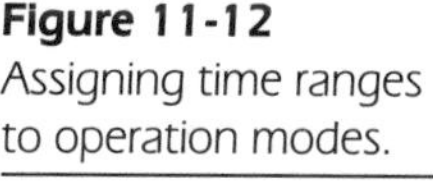

Figure 11-12 Assigning time ranges to operation modes.

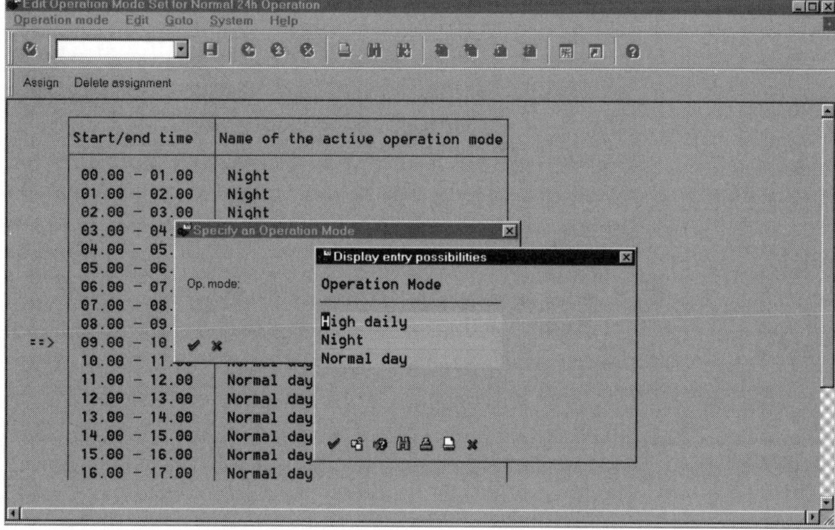

Select the operation mode and click on the *Enter* key to assign it to the time period chosen. Save your changes.

You must define the whole 24-hour range for operation modes to work. You cannot leave any time period unassigned, otherwise the switch will not be possible and can cause problems in the background processing system.

To define an exception operation, select the radio button next to *Exception operation* and click on the *Change* button. Proceed with the normal operation for assigning operation modes to the timetable. The only difference is that you have to specify a date for the exceptional operation to work. The system provides the functions *Day+1, Day–1,* or *Specify a day.*

Checking the Consistency of Operation Mode Configurations

After modifying any of the CCMS configurations, you should check whether the operation modes, profiles, and instance definitions are consistent and correctly defined. This check will inform you of any potential problems which should be corrected before restarting an instance or the whole SAP system.

To do a consistency check, from the productive instance list, like the one shown in Fig. 11-10, select *Instance → Consistency test.*

Operation Mode Switching

Operation modes switch automatically at the times defined in the timetable (using the system program SAPMSSY2) or when the system starts or when there are no active operation modes (using the system program SAPMSSY6). When operation modes are switched, the R/3 system work processes are redistributed automatically without stopping and restarting the instances.

Only the work process types are changed. For example, a work process used as a dialog process can be switched for use as a background process.

A new process type will not be activated until the process is completely free, normally in a waiting status. For example, if a background job is running a long report and must be switched to dialog work process, the switch will wait until the job has finished and the background work process is free. This means that sometimes processes may not be switched immediately but at the next possible time. Processing is not interrupted.

Normal system operation continues uninterrupted during the operation mode switch.

Operation mode switches are recorded in the system log. The old process type and the new process type are recorded for each switched work process.

Manual Operation Mode Switch. You can manually switch operation modes at any time from the control panel. To do that, two steps are necessary: first define which will be the new active operation mode, then perform the operation mode change for one or all active instances/servers. To perform this from the CCMS main menu, select *Control / Monitoring → Control panel.* By default, the system displays the instance status and the operation mode. Click on an instance, and then select *Choose OP mode.*

The system displays a list of the available operation modes. Choose the one you want to switch to. The system will switch the operation mode and return to the initial screen. You may see the status *non-standard operation mode* because they are still running in the currently active operation mode.

For the second step, you have two options:

1. Change the operation mode for a single instance.
2. Change the operation mode for all instances.

To switch the operation mode on one instance/server, select the instance by double-clicking on the server line (change color) and then selecting *Control → Switch OP mode → Selected server.*

To switch the operation mode on all servers, select *Control → Switch OP mode → All servers.*

The servers remain in the manually activated operation mode until the next switch time. The system displays an error message if the operation mode switch cannot be performed on all the chosen servers.

Technical Details: Operation Modes

The system component in charge of performing the operation mode switch is the ABAP program SAPMSSY2, which is the job scheduler. For this reason, automatic operation switches can only be performed if there is at least one job scheduler and one background work process in the system.

When a SAP instance is started, it runs without an operation mode. It will start the work process number and types as defined in the instance profile.

The ABAP program SAPMSSY6 is in charge of switching the operation mode of a system for the first time. This program runs cyclically in intervals defined by the parameter rdisp/autoabaptime. By default, this parameter is set to 300 (seconds).

In every cycle, the SAPMSSY6 program collects alert values, checks the profiles, and creates dummy operation modes.

The operation mode status is checked during these intervals, and the mode assigned in the timetable is automatically activated. If, in the current time interval, there is no operation mode assigned, an operation mode will not be activated. This will cause a status error.

The SAPMSSY6 program only switches operation modes in cases where the R/3 instance is not running any operation mode. Within the first five minutes after system startup, the system is switched to the operation mode defined in the timetable.

If you perform a manual active operation mode switch, the SAPMSSY6 program will switch back to the operation mode as defined in the timetable.

The SAPMSSY6 program can be run manually from the control panel by selecting *Utilities → Diagnosis → Run SAPMSSY6.*

Overview of the CCMS Monitors

CCMS includes very extensive monitoring utilities and functions. This section gives you an overview of the available monitor and gives you enough information for you to understand and interpret the different CCMS monitors.

The CCMS monitors provide functions for the following:

- Checking system status and operation modes
- Locating and eliminating potential problems as quickly as possible
- Early diagnosis of potential problems, for example, resource problems in the host or database system that could adversely affect the R/3 system
- Analyzing and tuning the R/3 system and its environment (host and database systems) in order to optimize the throughput of the R/3 system

Under the monitoring utilities, a distinction must be made between the following:

- *System monitors.* In charge of displaying an overview of the SAP instances status and alerts
- *Alert monitors.* Online monitors capable of automatic problem detection and display. Due to the new monitoring architecture since release 4.0 and the extensive information it contains, *Alert Monitors,* for both 3.x and 4.x releases will be explained in detail in the next chapter.
- *Performance monitors.* Specialized monitors which analyze and help to tune the different components of the SAP system such as the database, the operating system, the buffers, or the network

Although some of the monitors run independently keeping a record of the components activity, they also offer a high degree of integration. For example, from the system monitor you can reach the alerts monitors. The alert thresholds defined will impact the performance monitors, and so on.

The CCMS monitors are the most important tools available for evaluating the performance of the R/3 system and analyzing the possible source of problems.

System administrators should make daily checks of the critical performance components and react quickly to system alerts.

The CCMS provides graphical monitors for continuous runtime monitoring of the complete R/3 environment. When using the graphical monitors, you should normally set the automatic refreshing option to constantly display the current system status.

The CCMS also provides list-oriented monitors for higher-detailed analysis. You can generate comprehensive statistics for system tuning and for error analysis.

The CCMS also independently monitors other important components surrounding the R/3 system, for example, the operating system and network services and the database system. The CCMS can also report potential problems automatically using alerts.

The R/3 Control Panel

The control panel gives you an overview of system activity. You can get information on alerts, performance, buffers, and system logs. You can check whether instances were started correctly and whether instances are running in the correct operation mode, that is, whether automatic operation mode switching is possible.

If you are using profiles, you can use the control panel to check whether the profiles were changed, including changes made to comments, without activating them. When a profile is changed, you get an alert.

To start the control panel, from the main CCMS menu, select *Control/ Monitoring → Control Panel*. Alternatively, enter transaction code RZ03 in the command field. A list of host systems and instances of your R/3 system is displayed, together with the status, alert text, and the active operation mode.

From the control panel you can do the following:

- Start or stop instances
- Maintain operation modes and instances
- Log on to a host system or instance
- Display the R/3 system log and process traces
- Stop the R/3 system
- Display and maintain the alert thresholds of the system

To perform operations on one server, simply position the cursor on the line with the server before performing the operation. It is not necessary to double click on the server to select it. However, to select more than one server, double click on each server.

If the control panel displays a message in the *Alert text* column, you can find out the reason by selecting the server and then choosing *Monitoring → Status details*. The system will display a dialog box with the reason and details for the alert. Many of the alerts are derived from deviations in the configuration data and the real data.

Control Panel Views. The information in the control panel can be displayed in several different ways, each one containing different data. Figure 11-13 shows the available views menu options. When in a view, you can click on the *Next view* or *Previous view* buttons on the application toolbar to navigate through all of them.

These views are as follows:

- *Standard view.* This is the default view when accessing the control panel. It shows initial alerts, operation mode, and server status information.
- *Alert view.* This is a list monitor which display the alerts of the main system components.

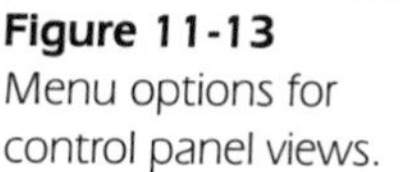

Figure 11-13
Menu options for control panel views.

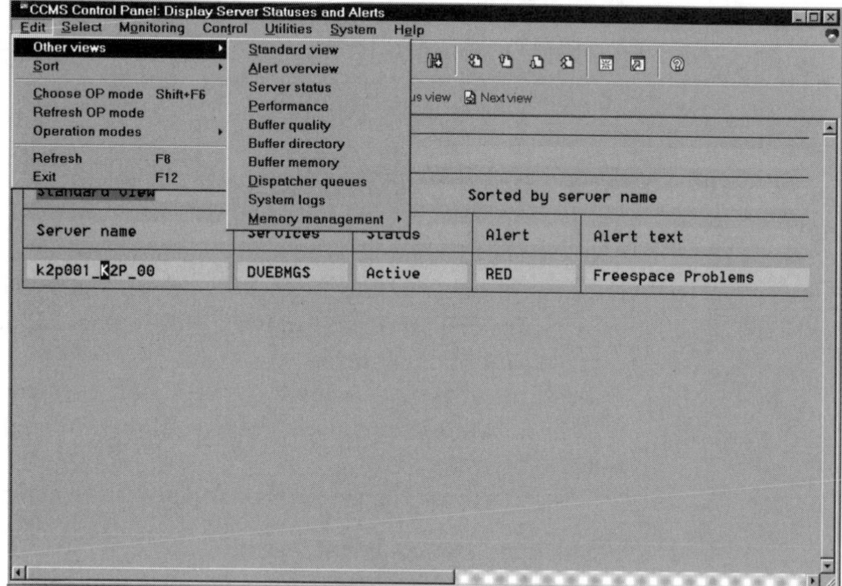

From the alert details screen you can further display more specific alert messages and information by double clicking on any of the summary lines.

- *Server status view* shows only server status information.
- *Performance view* shows the number of logged-on users, wait time, and response time for the dialog and update processes.
- *Buffer quality view* shows the buffer quality in percent collected for the last 90 minutes.
- *Buffer directory view* shows the number of directory entries that exist for each buffer type.
- *Buffer memory view* shows the statistics of the memory utilization for each buffer type.
- *Dispatcher queues view* shows the work process queues utilization statistics for the instance. Normally, this view should display 0 percent for all queues. A larger value might indicate that the system is having problems supporting the current workload.
- *System log view* shows the number and frequency of system log entries and the alert messages in the system log

- *Memory management views* allow you to either display absolute memory values including as swap or extended memory, or use percentage values by selecting *relative values.*

The System Monitor

The SAP system monitor is a graphical global monitor which shows all the configured instances in an R/3 system. The database and the SAP instances are displayed in a networked graphical form with colored boxes representing the instances.

Inside each of those colored boxes is information about the name of the instance, the host server, and the type and number of work processes running in the instance.

From the system monitor you can do the following:

- Start and stop SAP instances
- Display instance details
- Display the alerts details for a selected instance
- Log on to an active SAP instance directly from the monitor
- Display system trace files
- Change the operation mode for an instance

To access the system monitor, from the initial CCMS menu, select *Control/Monitoring → System Monitor.* Figure 11-14 shows an example of this monitor. The colors of the boxes indicate the instance status. You can display a legend listing of possible statuses by selecting *Settings → Legend* and then selecting a position.

The system monitors includes two views:

- *Startup View.* Monitors the status of the instances with regard to the current operation modes. From this view you can control startup and shutdown of instances. An instance box with red color indicates that the instance is not active, while green means active and correctly configured. The white color means an unknown state. The green color with white diagonal lines indicates that the instance is not configured, while the green color with red diagonal lines means that the instance is incorrectly configured with respect to the operation mode.
- *Alert View.* Shows instance alert status information. When selecting an instance in this display and selecting from the menu *Con-*

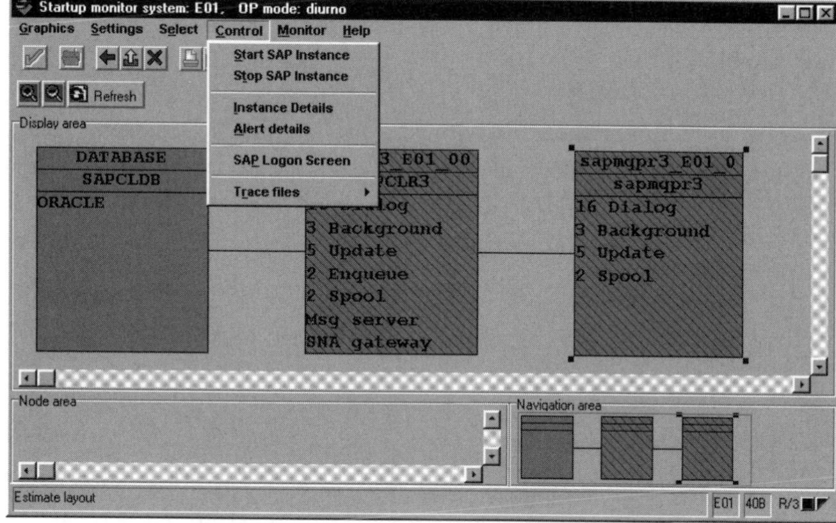

Figure 11-14 Startup system monitor.

trol → *Alert details,* the system displays a new graphical window displaying the same information as the alert view from the control panel. The color codes indicate the type of alert for the instance: red, yellow, or green. The gray color means that the instance is not active, while the white represents an unexpected status.

To switch between system monitor display modes, from the menu, select *Monitor* → *Startup View* or *Monitor* → *Alert View.*

You can display the alert status message for each instance in the status bar automatically when moving the cursor over an instance by selecting *Settings* → *Info* → *On.*

Performance Monitors

The R/3 performance monitors are specialized in providing detailed analyses of individual components of the system, such as the database, the network, the operating system, and the R/3 processes.

The performance monitors periodically collect statistical information on the system components activity and present it in a more convenient form. With these statistics, system administrators can check the system status and performance.

The statistical information is collected using the RSCOLL00 program which is scheduled to run hourly. The information is archived during days, weeks, and months in the database table MONI.

To access the performance monitors menu, from the main CCMS screen, select *Control/Monitoring → Performance menu.* Or, enter transaction code STUN in the command field. The system displays the initial performance menu screen. From this screen, you can access all the system components performance monitors, all the alert monitors, and all the statistical workload analyses.

Configuring the CCMS Monitors. In order for the performance monitors to collect information, there is some configuration work to do, such as activating the statistical profile parameters and submitting the SAP collector background job.

You can display the statistical profile parameters from the performance menu by selecting *Workload → Analysis → Goto → Parameters → Local profile.*

The performance monitors collect every user action which performs a communication with the dispatcher process. This statistical information is buffered in the SAP instances and then written to an operating system file. It is consolidated by the collector background job which writes the information into the R/3 performance database tables. The main performance table of the R/3 system is a special table called MONI, whose contents cannot be displayed using normal methods.

It is highly recommended that your system have the statistical performance collectors activated, since their information is very valuable for solving and analyzing performance problems.

Statistical information is activated by setting the instance profile parameter stat/level to a value greater than 0.

The Performance Data Collector Program and Background Job. The ABAP report RSCOLL00 is the data collector program in charge of collecting the performance statistical data and storing it in the MONI table, and also in the PAHI table.

The data collected includes information about the R/3 instances and parameters, the operating system, and the database. This data is first collected and then analyzed and reorganized by the data collector program.

In every installation, administrators must submit a background job which executes the RSCOLL00 program hourly. This job is usually called *SAP_COLLECTOR* or *SAP_COLLECTOR_FOR_PERFMONITOR* and must be submitted by user DDIC in client 000 to run periodically every hour.

The RSCOLL00 program uses the special table TCOLL (data collector configuration table), which includes the list of specific collector programs and the running dates and times for each of those programs. This table comes predefined by SAP. Although modifications are possible, make them only in accordance with SAP guidance. To access and maintain this table, from the performance menu initial screen, select *Workload* → *Analysis* → *Environment* → *Collector frequency.* Figure 11-15 shows this table's contents.

The data collector programs only need to run centrally on a single server which will communicate via CPIC with the rest of the SAP instances as required.

You can decide how much data and how many dates should be kept on the MONI table. Call the MONI table reorganization screen by selecting *Workload* → *Analysis* → *Goto* → *Parameters* → *Performance database* from the initial performance menu. You can modify the retention values by clicking on the *Modify parameters.* These parameters might have some impact on the overall system performance, so you should proceed with caution when changing them. Figure 11-16 shows this screen.

In table MONI, program *RSSTAT60* maintains two kinds of records: detailed statistics (daily and cumulative weekly and monthly statistics) and compressed long-term data (statistics for comparison with other servers or periods). During a reorganization run, *RSSTAT60* uses daily data for updating longterm data and deletes all data for which the resi-

TCOLL list

Report	Days of Week							Hours of Day																								Repe-titions	System
	Mo		We		Fr		Su	0		2		4		6		8		10		12		14		16		18		20		22			
RSAMON40	X	X	X	X	X	X	X	X	X	X	X	X	X	X	X	X	X	X	X	X	X	X	X	X	X	X	X	X	X	X	X	1	C
RSDBPREV	X	X	X	X	X	X	X	X		X		X		X		X		X		X		X		X		X		X		X		1	C
RSEFA350					X																			X								1	C
RSHOSTDB	X	X	X	X	X	X	X	X	X	X	X	X	X	X	X	X	X	X	X	X	X	X	X	X	X	X	X	X	X	X	X	1	*
RSHOSTDC	X	X	X	X	X	X	X	X		X		X		X		X		X		X		X		X		X		X		X		1	C
RSHOSTPH	X	X	X	X	X	X	X										X			X							X					1	*
RSORA811	X	X	X	X	X	X	X													X							X					1	C
RSORAPAR	X	X	X	X	X	X	X									X					X						X					1	C
RSORATDB	X	X	X	X	X	X	X								X													X				1	C
RSORAWDB							X													X												1	C
RSSTAT60	X	X	X	X	X	X	X				X																			X		1	C
RSSTAT81	X	X	X	X	X	X	X													X					X						X	1	C
RSSTAT83	X	X	X	X	X	X	X	X	X	X		X	X	X	X	X	X	X	X	X	X	X	X	X	X	X	X	X	X		X	1	C
RSSTAT90	X	X	X	X	X	X	X														X						X					1	*
RSSTAT98	X	X	X	X	X	X	X					X			X			X			X			X			X					1	*
RSSTATPH	X	X	X	X	X	X	X										X			X						X						1	*
RSTUNE80	X	X	X	X	X	X	X										X					X								X		1	*

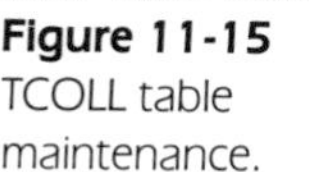

Figure 11-15 TCOLL table maintenance.

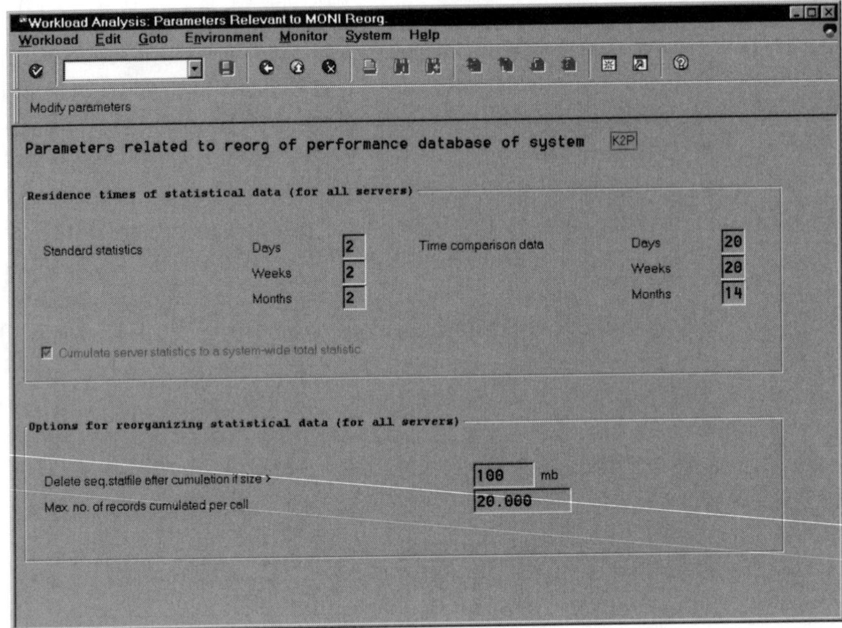

Figure 11-16 Parameters for performance database reorganization.

dence period (defined in MONI performance database parameters, see Fig. 11-16) has expired. *RSSTAT80* runs periodically, and when MONI reorganization has not been performed in the last two days, it starts program RSSTAT60 to do the reorganization using the MONI reorganization parameters (*Workload → Analysis → Goto → Parameters → Reorg. Parameters.*)

Workload Monitor

The workload monitor is the CCMS component in charge of storing all the R/3 system statistical information. With the information provided by the workload monitor you can analyze the behavior for any or all servers of your SAP installation.

The workload monitor includes several types of views, which are very useful for analyzing how the system is being used, what the peak times are, which are the most frequently used transactions, the transaction types, the memory profile, and so on.

The workload monitor uses the information that has been collected by the data collector, and therefore allows for the analysis of both current time periods, daily analysis, and for previous weeks and months. This statistical information is the key for analyzing whether the current system configuration is still enough to support the number of users, SAP applications, and workload as it was a few months ago. For example, if you see that average response time is increasing every week or month, it can either be the result of increasing system demands or it might indicate a potential system configuration problem. You can also analyze differences in response times between different application servers.

Some of the available functions within the workload monitor include convenient graphics functions which display the same information for friendly graphical analysis.

You can call the workload monitor from the initial CCMS menu by selecting *Control/Monitoring* → *Performance Menu* → *Workload* → *Analysis.* Alternatively, use transaction code ST03 in the command field.

The system displays a list of active and inactive application servers. From this screen, you can choose any of the servers by clicking on them before selecting a function, or you can compare server workloads by selecting any of the functions under the *Goto* → *Performance database* → *Analyze all servers* menu options.

To display the workload overview for a specific server, click on the *Choose for analysis* button on the application toolbar. The system will display the pop-up window *Choose server name* for selecting either a particular server or the whole SAP system by choosing *Total.*

Make your selection and click on the *Enter* icon. Next, the system displays an additional dialog box for choosing the time period for the analysis. Choose the needed time period. Remember that the periods held on the performance database are those defined for the reorganization of the data collector.

The system will display the workload overview screen for the selected server and period, like the one shown in Fig. 11-17.

On the bottom part of the overview screen under the *Task types* box, you can select whether to display the total for all system task types or only for dialog, update, background, spool, or RFC tasks.

In the application toolbar, you can select to display the same statistical information but organized by the following methods:

Time profile, which is very useful for displaying the system's most busy time periods and also for further tuning the CCMS operation modes. When selecting this function, the system presents the time profile in a list form. Clicking on the *Graphics* button on the application toolbar will display an additional graphical window, like the one shown in Fig. 11-18. From this example, you can see that the peak number of dialog steps are concentrated between 9:00 A.M. and 16:00 P.M.

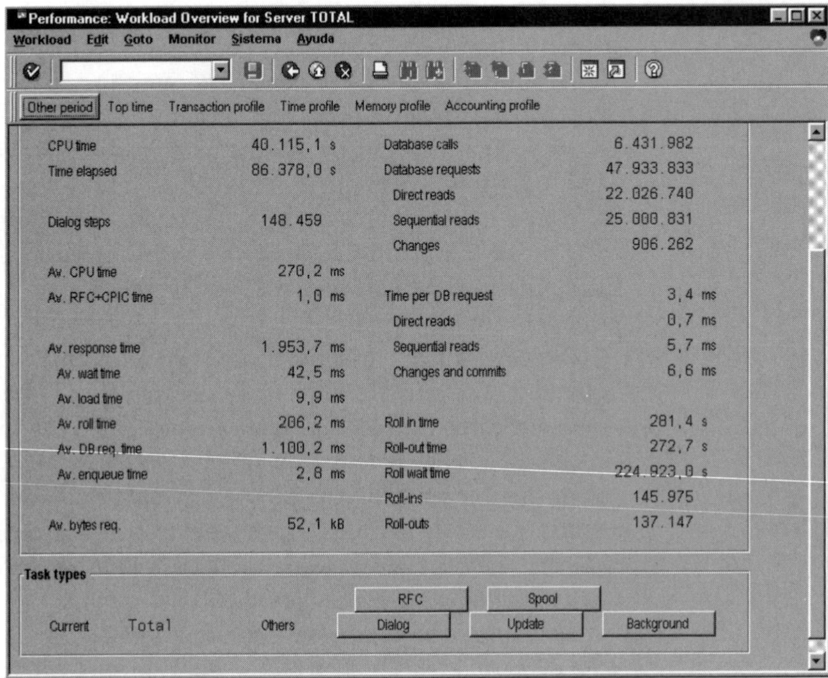

Figure 11-17 Workload overview display.

Figure 11-18 also includes an extensive collection of push buttons to show the aggregate information using different concepts. This is a common feature of most workload graphics.

Other functions available from the workload overview screen are the *Transaction profile,* the *Top time,* the *Memory profile,* or the *Accounting profile,* if you have set up the corresponding user groups.

The workload overview screen, as shown in Fig. 11-17, displays the following information:

CPU time. Indicates in seconds the total CPU time needed for completing the SAP process requests. The ratio between the CPU time and the elapsed time should not fall below 5 percent, since a low percentage might indicate input/output bottlenecks.

Average response time. The response time is measured as the time period from which a work process is instructed by the dispatcher to execute a function to the time it takes to return the information to the SAPGUI. It does not include the time it takes to get from the SAPGUI request to the SAP dispatcher. The average response time is measured in milliseconds and should normally lie below 1500,

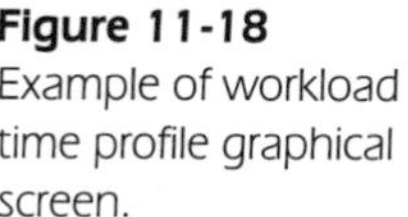

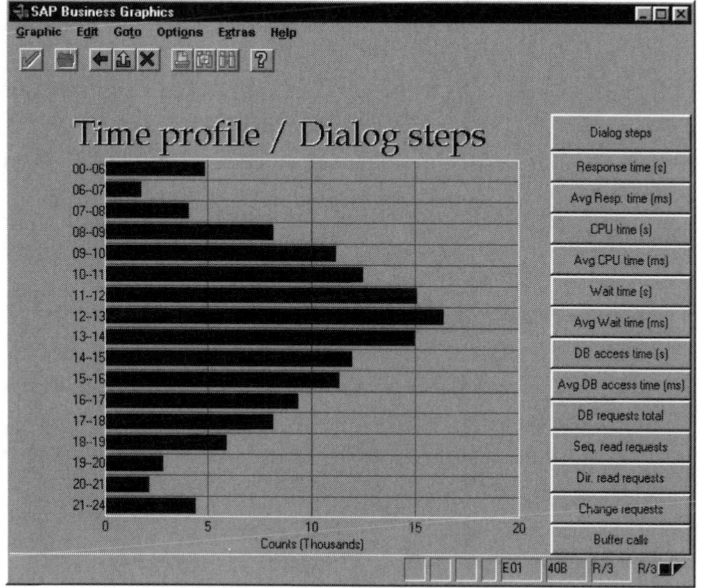

Figure 11-18 Example of workload time profile graphical screen.

that is, 1.5 seconds. Administrators should pay particular attention to this time, since this is the time users are really waiting for the system to return control to their online tasks.

Average wait time. It's the time that a dialog step waits in the dispatcher queue for a free work process. The average value should be below 100 milliseconds, otherwise, it might indicate that the number of configured work processes is not enough to cope with the system load.

Average CPU time. Measures the average CPU time used by the work process.

Average load time. It's the average time needed to load and generate ABAP programs and screen information from the database.

Database calls. Measures the total number of parsed requests sent to the database.

Database requests. Includes the total number of ABAP requests for data in the database. The system performs these requests with the database interface of the work processes which are then parsed into individual database calls. When the information requested is stored in the SAP buffers, there is no need for database calls to the database server. For this reason, the ratio between the database calls and database requests is interesting since it indicates the efficiency of table buffering.

Time per DB request. Measures the performance of the database. Good values for *direct reads* should not exceed 10 milliseconds, while for *sequential reads* should be below 40 milliseconds.

These are the fields with the most interesting information. For help on the meaning of other fields in the workload overview display, please refer to the SAP online documentation.

To access or select specific details of the workload performance history from the initial workload monitor screen, click on the *Detail analysis menu* from the application toolbar. In the workload detailed analysis menu, you can display from the current server performance history to the overall SAP system or compare performance statistical analyses among all servers.

Work Process Load Monitor

Another monitor included within the CCMS is the work process load monitor, which can be used to analyze the systemwide load on the work processes running on all active instances. To call this monitor, from the CCMS main screen, select *Control / Monitoring → All work processes.* The system displays the *Systemwide work process overview* screen with a list of the current work processes.

To get work process load information, on the overview screen double click on the instance name. The system displays a new window with information about the chosen work process.

On this screen, you can see detailed information about the work process including the action it is actually performing, the program, screen, client, and the user which is currently assigned to the work process. From this screen, you can put the program into debugging mode or you can cancel it.

To display additional information about the system status, select the *Next view* icon.

You can set some display and information settings by using the *Process list → Settings → Change* option, for example, to specify whether you want to see the connections in the status line, or if you want to display RFC information. Additionally, you can select to display your own work processes information.

This monitor can be mainly used for analyzing a potential problem in the system performance which may be caused by a particular work process.

If you want to filter and select work processes by using some selection criteria, click on the *Select process* button on the application toolbar. The systemdisplays a screen where you can enter the selection criteria and click on the *Continue* button to display the information.

Operating System Collector and Monitor

The R/3 system lies over an operating system, from which it uses such important resources as CPU, physical memory, physical disks, file systems, paging space, and network. These resources are absolutely critical for the performance of R/3. For this reason, the CCMS performance monitors also include extensive information about these resources and allow for setting alerts on operating system elements.

When administrators detect performance problems, the operating system monitor is one of the first places to look for analyzing the possible reasons for the problems. Sometimes a suspicious figure in this monitor does not mean a problem in the operating system itself. For example, a locking problem or an erroneous or extremely large SQL statement can raise the CPU load to its maximum.

The operating system monitor collects the information using the *saposcol* program at the operating system level. The saposcol program is provided by SAP as part of the standard installation and is automatically started when the SAP instance is started.

To access this monitor, from the initial performance menu (transaction code *STUN*), select *Operating system* → *Local* → *Activity*. The system displays a snapshot of the operating system activity on the system where you are currently logged on. Figure 11-19 shows an example.

The system displays snapshots in 10-second intervals, including information about the CPU, memory, swap, disk, and LAN network. You can click on the *Refresh* icon to get new snapshots of actual operating system activity.

To display information about any of the particular areas for the last 24 hours, double click on any of the fields of the display. The system shows information which can also be seen in graphical form by clicking on the *Graphics* button.

To see additional information related with any of the monitored components or about other operating system data such as configuration parameters or the performance database, click on the *Detail analysis menu* button on the application toolbar. Click on any of the available push buttons on the display to obtain the needed information.

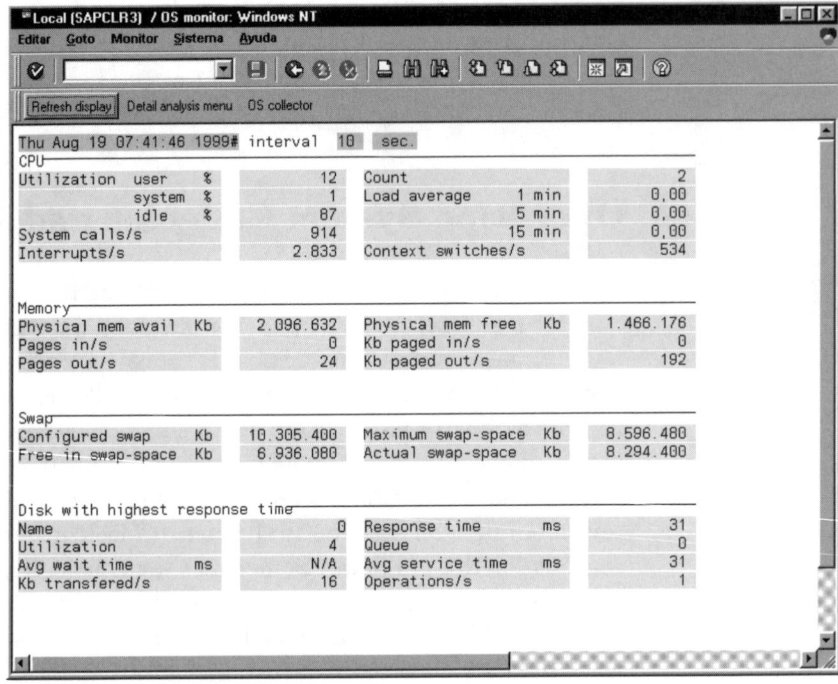

Figure 11-19 Initial screen for the operating system performance monitor.

From the detail analysis menu, you can look up operating system information from any of the previous 24 hours. If there is no data for a particular hour, it will not be displayed.

From the detail analysis menu you can also compare recent days and recent servers, since the data collector program stores the information from saposcol in the performance database.

To display the relevant operating system kernel parameters, select *Operating system → Local → System configuration* from the initial performance menu. The list shows the parameters as defined in the kernel configuration file together with their active values.

To display the changes made to the system kernel parameters, select the *Parameter Changes* button.

The *LAN Check by Ping* option performs a ping operation over a group of R/3 servers, including presentation servers, offering information about the time it takes communication packets to travel from servers, number of lost packets, and so forth. This information can be a useful indicator of the network performance.

The ping utility is a standard program used in the TCP/IP protocol which determines whether a remote host is reachable and the time it takes for network packets to travel between a source and a target system.

From the operating system monitor (transaction code *OS06*) you can also check the status of the disks and file systems by selecting *Goto → Current data → File system monitor.*

NOTE *To have snapshot information on Windows NT systems about throughput activity on disks (input/output), you have to run the program* diskperf -y *on the server. This information will not be available until the system is rebooted.*

The Operating System Collector Program Saposcol. The saposcol program runs as a background process in the operating system, and it is executed independently of the R/3 instances. It is constantly collecting information about the server resources, specifically about the CPU, memory, swap space, physical disks, LAN network, and file systems. The saposcol program makes all the collected data available to the SAP instances using shared memory areas, which are periodically read by a dialog work process.

The saposcol program can run constantly even if the SAP system is stopped. If this is the case, the program writes the information in an operating system file.

The saposcol program collects system information for every 10 seconds as well as for every hour of the last 24 hours. The data collector background job, normally called *COLLECTOR_FOR_PERFORMANCEMONITOR,* takes the data out of the shared memory and stores it in the performance database.

Another collector program supplied by SAP, *rcfcoscol,* is started with remote function calls and can collect operating system information out of servers without R/3 instances, such as stand-alone database servers.

The saposcol program is located under the SAP runtime directory and is automatically started the first time the R/3 instance is started on a server. However, stopping the SAP instance will not stop the saposcol program.

You can also manually start the saposcol program at the operating system level or even from within the R/3 system. If there is another saposcol program running which is collecting data, you cannot start a new saposcol.

When the saposcol program is started, it performs an initialization and reserves an area of shared memory based on the system resources to monitor.

The saposcol program writes the error and status information in the *dev_coll* file, which is located by default in directory */usr/sap/tmp* or the home directory of the owner of the program. On Windows NT systems, this file is usually located in C:\. Under this directory, it also creates and reads data from the file *coll.put* which is used as a temporary data storage area by the program when R/3 instances are not running.

The saposcol program does not have to be stopped when R/3 is down, since it keeps collecting data which it can later transfer to the performance database. And, particularly, it should not be stopped with *kill* commands, otherwise the data in shared memory will not be correctly flushed and you will not be able to start a new saposcol program.

You should stop saposcol only if you are going to restart the server. To stop this program in an orderly manner, you should issue the command *saposcol -k.* Before the saposcol program stops, it writes the data from the shared memory to the file *coll.put.*

The data in the *coll.put* file will later be imported when a new saposcol program is started and will make it available to the R/3 performance data collector.

To monitor the saposcol program from R/3, call the operating system monitor, like in Fig. 11-19, and click on the *OS collector* button on the application toolbar. The system will display the OS collector screen. By clicking on the *Status* button you can see all the information about the saposcol program. From this screen you can start and stop the saposcol program, you can display the log file (dev_coll), check the current status of the program, and you can also switch the details mode on or off.

Since the saposcol program is constantly running in the background and collecting operating system information, it may use a lot of operating system resources. There are two options to reduce the saposcol CPU load. The first one is to set the *Details* mode to *off* from the OS collector screen. This mode tells the saposcol program that it does not need to collect all the details during every run cycle.

The second method is to run saposcol in *idle* mode. In this mode, saposcol only collects data every minute instead of every 10 seconds. If a work process does not read the collected data from shared memory, then it does not need to be collected every 10 seconds. When the data has not been read during five minutes, then saposcol switches to idle mode. However, when in idle mode, if a process reads the data from the shared memory, the saposcol switches back to normal mode collecting data every 10 seconds. Even in idle mode, saposcol collects enough information to have good performance statistics every hour.

You can run saposcol in dialog mode and display the collected information at the operating system level. To do that, as user <sid>adm, enter *saposcol -d.* The system will display the collector command prompt (*collector>*) where you can enter interactive commands to display information. For help on the available options refer to the CCMS online documentation. You can display available options by entering *help* at the command prompt. To exit this utility, enter *quit*.

Buffer Performance Monitors

A *buffer* in computing terms is a temporary memory area which helps to transfer data between programs. Because buffers reside in memory, the transfer of information is much faster than accessing it from physical disk storage. For this reason, buffers play a very important role in the overall system performance.

The SAP R/3 buffers reduce the physical database accesses by holding the data most frequently used and making it available to the processes of an instance. Once the data is available in the buffers, the workload is sensibly reduced because the work processes do not have to repeatedly access the database to get the same information.

There is, of course, both a locking and a synchronization mechanism to prevent both the modification to buffered data from different application systems, as well as for making available the buffered information to other application servers.

The R/3 system has several types of buffers for holding dictionary data, programs, screens, and even company-specific data, such as the *factory calendar* which usually remains unchanged during normal system operation.

The SAP buffer monitors let you analyze the performance of the buffer sizes to get an overview of whether the configured values are good enough or need some further tuning and adjustments.

Each SAP instance has its own buffers. So, in case an application server has more than one instance, each has its own buffer areas. Sometimes, the buffers are known as *client caches* because they are located in the application servers (that is the client from the point of view of the database server).

The SAP buffers can be either located in memory areas which are local to individual work processes or can be located in shared memory areas accessible by all the work processes of an instance.

To meet some operating system restrictions on the number of allowed shared memory allocation per process, SAP has grouped together some of the buffers in shared memory segments known as *pools*.

While displaying SAP instance profile parameters you can see the size values assigned to several R/3 buffer pools. These parameters have the syntax *ipc/shm_psize_<nn>* where *nn* is the pool number, for example, *ipc/shm_psize_40*.

Buffer Types. The R/3 system includes seven groups of buffers in the system shared memory. These groups are as follows:

- *Repository buffers.* These buffers contain the active table and field definitions (metadata) of the ABAP dictionary. These buffers are also known as *dictionary buffers* or *nametab buffers* (*NTAB buffers*). When a table or field definition is activated in the R/3 system, an entry is made in these buffers. The repository buffers include four buffers in shared memory:
  - *TTAB buffer,* containing the table definitions, which are held on table DDNTT
  - *FTAB buffer,* containing the field descriptions corresponding to table DDNTF
  - *IREC buffer,* containing the initial record layout which is initialized depending on the field type
  - *SNTAB buffer,* containing a brief summary of the TTAB and FTAB buffers
- *Table buffers.* Table buffers contain table entries. Whether tables are buffered or not and the way tables are buffered can be set using the ABAP dictionary technical settings utility. There are two table buffers:
  - *TABLP buffer* is the partial table buffer, also known as *single key buffer,* which stores single record table entries.
  - *TABL buffer* is the generic table buffer, or *generic key buffer,* which stores a range of table entries, that is, a group of records with their field values. Sometimes the generic table buffer can contain all the record entries for a table. This is called *full buffering.*
- *Program buffer.* Contain the generated and executable versions of the ABAP programs. This buffer is also known as the *PXA buffer* (program execution area) or *ABAP buffer.* This buffer uses the tables D010L (ABAP loads), D010T (texts), and D010Y (symbol table) for storing its contents.

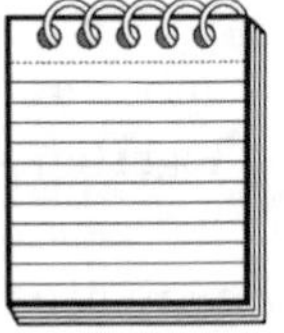

NOTE *Tables D010L, D010T, D010Y, DDNTT, and DDNTF, as well as some other repository related tables, are only found on the physical database and do not have corresponding ABAP dictionary definitions.*

- *GUI buffers.* These types of buffers contain the R/3 graphical elements such as screens, menus, pushbuttons, icons, and so forth. There are two GUI buffers:

  - *Presentation buffer* contains the generated R/3 screens (dynpro loads). This buffer is also known as the *screen buffer.*
  - *Menu buffer,* or *CUA buffer,* stores graphical objects for the presentation interface, such as menus, icons, and push buttons.

- *SAP roll and paging buffers.* These buffers contain part of the roll and paging areas for the SAP instances. There are additional roll and paging areas located on the roll and page files on disk. The roll area is used for storing user contexts when the user process is *roll out* of a work process. The paging area is used for storing larger data such as internal tables.
- *Calendar Buffer.* The R/3 calendar buffer contains all the defined factory and holiday calendars. These calendars are kept in the tables TFACS and THOCS.
- *SAP Cursor Cache.* This is a special type of buffer which holds reusable SQL statements. A good cursor cache ratio significantly improves performance since it reduces the process of parsing SQL statements. This buffer is database-dependent and should not be changed without SAP guidance since it can affect other system areas.

All the buffers can be adjusted with their respective parameters in the instance profiles. However, you should be very careful when doing so, since it affects the overall sizing of the pools, the needed operating system swap space, and the available physical memory.

Working with the Buffer Monitor. The buffer monitor utilities include an extensive list of functions for analyzing and tuning the size and quality of the SAP buffers. To call the buffer monitor, from the initial performance menu, select *Setup / Buffers* → *Buffers* or, alternatively, enter transaction code ST02 in the command field. Figure 11-20 shows the initial buffer monitor screen, also known as the *tune summary* overview. The information displayed on the tune summary screen includes only the buffer and memory usage information for the instance where you are currently logged on.

The buffer overview screen has four parts displaying specific information. These parts are buffers, SAP memory, and call statistics. To see them all, you probably have to use the R/3 window scrolling functions. For each of the parts, there are different assigned columns with the related performance and statistical information.

To see the *cursor cache,* select the option *Goto* → *Current local data* → *SAP cursor cache* → *ID cache.*

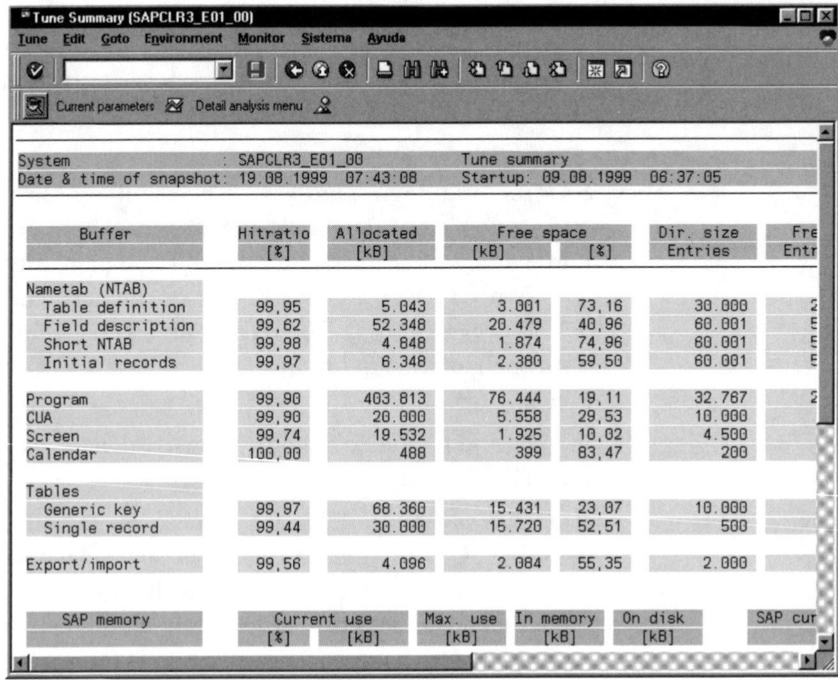

Buffer	Hitratio [%]	Allocated [kB]	Free space [kB]	Free space [%]	Dir. size Entries	Fre Entr
Nametab (NTAB)						
Table definition	99,95	5.043	3.001	73,16	30.000	2
Field description	99,62	52.348	20.479	40,96	60.001	5
Short NTAB	99,98	4.848	1.874	74,96	60.001	5
Initial records	99,97	6.348	2.380	59,50	60.001	5
Program	99,90	403.813	76.444	19,11	32.767	2
CUA	99,90	20.000	5.558	29,53	10.000	
Screen	99,74	19.532	1.925	10,02	4.500	
Calendar	100,00	488	399	83,47	200	
Tables						
Generic key	99,97	68.360	15.431	23,07	10.000	
Single record	99,44	30.000	15.720	52,51	500	
Export/import	99,56	4.096	2.084	55,35	2.000	

SAP memory	Current use [%]	Current use [kB]	Max. use [kB]	In memory [kB]	On disk [kB]	SAP cur

Figure 11-20 Tune summary screen for buffer monitoring.

- *Buffers.* In the first column of the display you can see the names for each of the buffer types. For each of them, the following columns are available:
  - *Hit Ratios.* A hit occurs when a SAP object is accessed from a buffer. A hit fails when the objects have to be accessed directly from the database. The hit ratios indicate the percentage of hits. This is a quality indicator. As it approaches 100 percent the better the buffer since the performance is increased with buffer accesses.
  - *Allocated Size.* This column contains in KB the size allocated to buffers. It differs a little bit from the available buffer size, since a small part of the buffer size is used for management purposes.
  - *Freespace.* Contains in KB the available free space in the buffer. The percentage is a good indicator for right sizing this buffer.
  - *Dir size entries.* Contains the number of directory entries for the buffer. Sometimes, even when the buffer has free space, objects cannot be loaded because there are no more free directories. The directory contains the pointers to the location of the buffered objects.

- *Free directories.* Shows the number and percentage of free space of directory entries for the buffer.
- *Swaps.* This column indicates the number of swaps, i.e., the number of times an object has to be taken out of a buffer for making room for another object. Swapping occurs when a buffer doesn't have enough free space or free directory entries.
- *Database Accesses.* This column shows the number of database accesses indicating the number of times when objects could not be read from the buffers and had to be accessed by directly accessing the database.

When critical situations occur in any of the buffer columns, the system displays the figures in red.

- *SAP Memory.* This part of the display includes information about the SAP memory areas used by the system such as the rolling and paging areas and the extended and heap memory. Columns to the right contain information about the current and maximum use and the sizes allocated in physical memory and in disk files. You can get additional details about any of the entries by double clicking on the line.
- *Call Statistics.* Under this section, the system displays access statistics for the data, which can reside either in buffers or in the physical database. The screen displays the different types of table accesses (select single, select, insert, update, delete), together with the hit ratios, ABAP processor calls, and database statistic calls for each type of access. You can notice that no hit ratios exist for the *Update, Insert,* and *Delete* calls, since they always have to be passed to the database system.
- *SAP Cursor Cache.* The R/3 system cursor cache stores parsed SQL statements such as the SELECT statements which can be reused avoiding the SQL parsing preparation processing. The SAP cursor cache has a fixed size and cannot be tuned.

From the tune summary screen, you can access additional buffer performance information. By clicking on the *History* button you can display the buffer history and analyze whether the sizes have been correct by comparing several days activity.

You can further analyze individual buffers, memory, and table call statistics from the Detail analysis menu. On the buffer overview, click on the *Detail analysis button* on the application toolbar.

Regarding memory configuration, SAP recommends allocating more memory to the buffers rather than distributing it to the database. However, when allocating more memory than required, you could waste memory space which can cause excessive system paging on the operating system.

From the tune summary screen you can even see the specific buffered objects, such as tables or programs. To see them, double click on the particular buffer. The system displays a detailed screen for the buffer. On this detailed screen, you can select the *Buffered Objects* button, which will display an alphabetical list of the objects currently contained in the buffers. Figure 11-21 shows an example of the buffered programs.

Tuning buffers is critical to improve the system performance. The first advice is to buffer as much data as possible because it will reduce physical database accesses which are more costly than memory accesses. At the same time, buffering reduces the network traffic between application servers and the database server.

Optimal buffer sizes depend on many factors such as the system sizing, average workload, database system, operating system resources, and so on. Tuning buffers is a matter of constant monitoring and periodical adjustments as required by the system performance evolution.

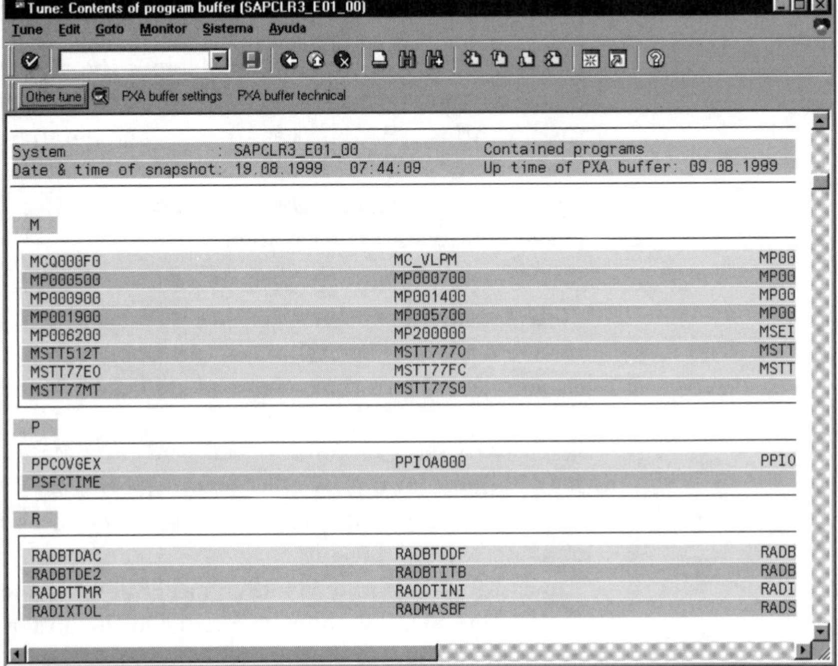

Figure 11-21 Example of buffered program objects.

While small buffers can cause many object swaps and physical database accesses, large sizes can cause costly operating system paging. In any case, as more physical memory is available, the better the buffers can be tuned.

All the buffer sizes can be tuned by setting the corresponding instance profile parameters. The CCMS profile maintenance tool can help to check the consistency of the buffers and memory pools.

Buffers should not be adjusted too often due to special workload circumstances such as large initial data loads or long end-of-period running reports.

You can see the current buffer parameters by clicking on the *Current parameters* button on the application toolbar of the buffer overview screen.

Database Performance Monitor for the Oracle Database

The database performance monitor performs extensive checks on the database system allowing for comprehensive analyzing and monitoring. The performance collectors constantly feed the database statistics tables with historical and statistical information about the database. This information can be accessed from any application server on the system.

Administrators should use this performance monitor for the following tasks:

- Checking the current database component sizes and the space-critical objects
- Looking for lost indexes either in the ABAP dictionary or the database
- Displaying a forecast of database storage needs
- Analyzing performance problems in the database
- Getting data for tuning programs with database access

To quickly detect and react to database problems, you should define database alert thresholds which can be monitored online and graphically from the alert monitors.

These database monitors have been fully programmed by SAP in ABAP to feature a common set of monitoring and performance utility tools for analyzing the database system. In the case of the Oracle database, SAP uses the information provided by the database engine in its many system views and tables, known as *dynamic performance tables* or *V$ tables.*

The performance menu includes four menu options for the database:

- *Activity.* It's the main entry point, and from the many functions and menu options available you can access all the database performance functions.
- *Exclusive lock waits.* It's the function for analyzing whether a process is exclusively holding a lock and other processes are locked waiting for the resource held by the other process.
- *Tables/indexes.* This option shows the summary information about the database structure, number of files, missing indexes, tablespace growth, statistics, and so on. Figure 11-22 shows this screen.
- *Parameter changes.* This is the function which keeps records on any database parameter modifications in the configuration file init<SID>.ora.

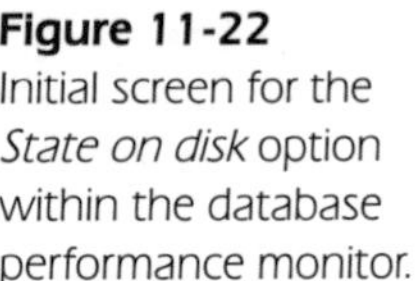

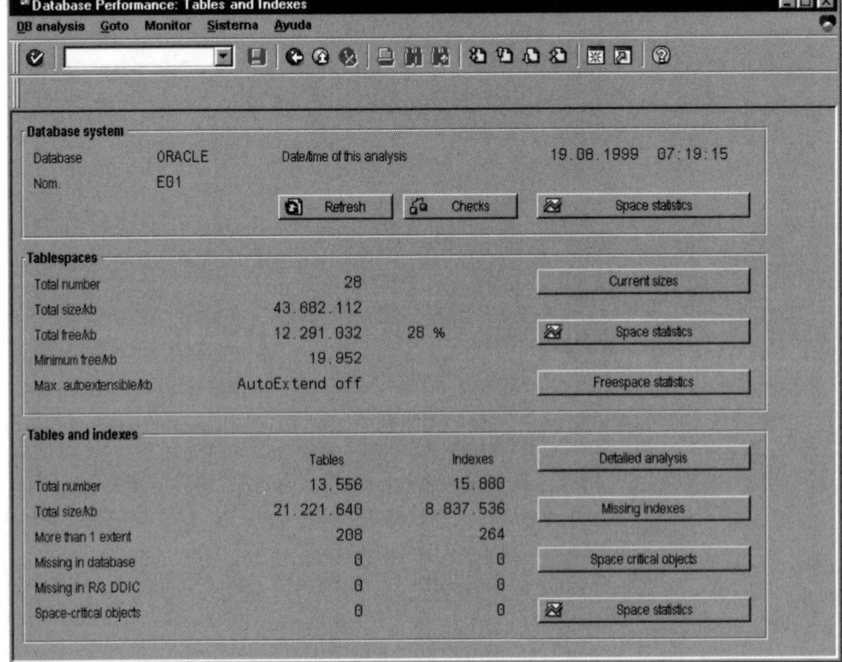

Figure 11-22 Initial screen for the *State on disk* option within the database performance monitor.

To access the database performance information, from the initial performance menu, select *Database → Activity*. Alternatively, enter transaction code ST04 in the command field. The system displays a summary overview of the database activity, as shown in Fig. 11-23.

The summary information provided by the database performance monitor includes the most important indicators for the Oracle database. You need some previous knowledge of the Oracle database to understand each of these indicators. An overview of the Oracle database architecture is presented in Chap. 15. As a brief introduction, these indicators are as follows:

- *Data buffer.* It's the buffer which holds the Oracle blocks in shared memory. The main indicator to watch is the *Quality* which should approach 100 percent for optimal performance. When an Oracle process requests a data block and is already found in memory, the quality improves.
- *Shared pool.* It's an area within the Oracle SGA (system global area) which holds several memory structures as the data dictionary cache and the shared SQL statements. It's an important area since the possibility to reuse SQL statements because they are already in memory can improve performance. The quality of these indicators is better closer to 100 percent.
- *Log buffer.* Contains information about the changes being made to the database before the Oracle log writer process (LGWR) writes the buffer information into the online redo log files. For better performance, allocation fault rates should be as close to 0 percent as possible.
- *Calls.* Displays the number and type of calls that the SAP processes request to the Oracle database.
- *Table Scans.* This is an indicator of how data is being accessed. A table scan is a sequential access that occurs when the database must read all the data blocks from a table on disk. A large number might degrade performance. Since this type of access does not use an index, which is acceptable when tables are small (short tables), but not when the amount of data is large. In this case, an index should be preferable, and you should analyze the SQL statements and the possibility of creating indexes for these tables. Table scans are alerts indicators. The default threshold value is 10 table scans every 10 seconds. The number of table scans should be reduced as much as possible. Can be caused by missing indexes in the database or incorrect SQL statements.

- *Table Fetch (Oracle).* Table fetches are indexed accesses to the database, where Oracle performs the search by the rowID of the data block containing the data.
- *Sorts (Oracle).* Indicates the total number of rows and whether the sorts were performed in memory or disk. Sorting is a common operation of the SQL statements when they need to order the results of a query or join operation or an index creation. Sorting degrades performance but it is a necessary feature. It is better doing the sorting in memory than on disks.

From the overview display, you can also access the performance history database by clicking on the *Previous days* button on the application toolbar.

To display the full-featured performance and information functions, click on the *Detail analysis menu* button on the application toolbar. From this detailed screen, you can access a vast information store about the database. This section briefly discusses only some of the available options which are used more often. For the other functions, please refer to the SAP online documentation and the database reference manuals.

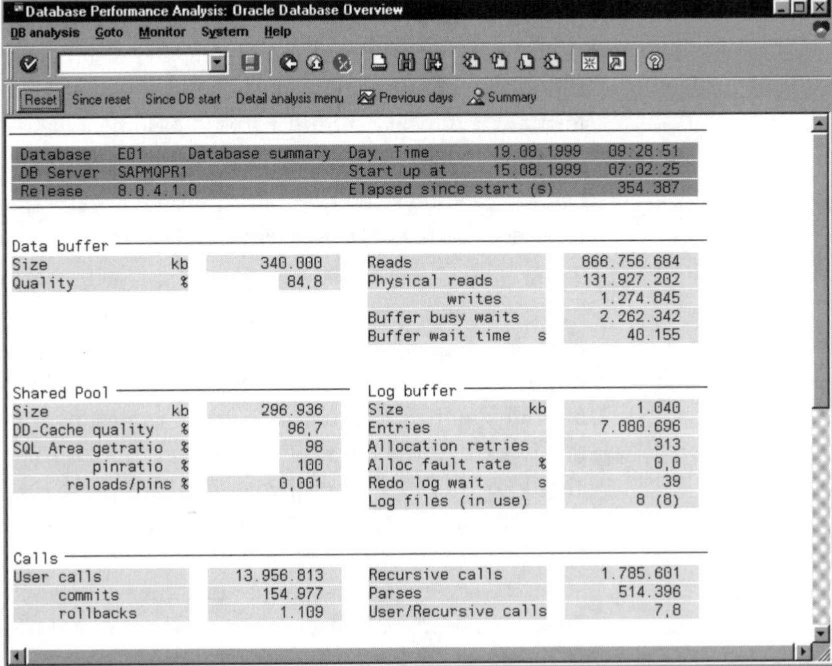

Figure 11-23 Summary overview of database performance analysis.

To give you an idea of how much information the system holds, you can display any of the Oracle dynamic performance tables (V$ tables) by clicking on the *Display V$ values* button.

One of the most useful options for getting detailed information about the database structure is selecting *Database* → *Tables/indexes* from the initial performance monitoring menu (Fig. 11-23). From here you can check things such as lists of missing indexes, detailed table and tablespaces analyses, and space statistics, including forecasts based on the utilization statistics stored in the performance database.

CHAPTER 12

Alert Monitors

As introduced in Chap. 11, R/3 includes a large variety of monitoring functions for helping system managers to maintain and control the SAP systems. *Alert monitoring* is one of the most extensive capacities, having been largely modified and enhanced since release 4.0 with the introduction of a new monitoring architecture. However, to make the transition easier for those system managers whose equipment does not meet the extensive requirements of the new alert monitors, SAP has also retained the alert monitoring functions from previous 3.x releases.

The R/3 system keeps records of many system activities, error situations, and alerts, and it does this from many different places. Alerts are most commonly displayed using the alert monitors, or from the CCMS control panel, as introduced in Chap. 11.

This chapter has two parts. The first deals with the management of system alerts in releases 3.x, which is present on earlier versions; the second introduces the new monitoring architecture and includes an overview of main concepts and handling of the alert monitors in releases 4.x.

Managing SAP System Alerts (3.x)

The CCMS alert monitors are graphical tools for online problem detection. These graphical monitors are specially coded with colors indicating the level of severity of the detected alarms. Alerts, as introduced in the control panel in Chap. 11, can also be seen in list form.

The alert system is specially designed for online monitoring and is a helpful preventive tool for anticipating performance problems in the various SAP components, thus improving the system availability.

The main SAP system alert monitor (releases 3.x) can be started from the initial CCMS screen by selecting *Control/Monitoring* → *Alert Monitor (3.x)* or also from the Alert menu within the main performance menu. There are two groups of monitors:

- The global alert monitor, which includes global components of the system common to all instances, such as:
  - The SAP system monitor
  - The database monitor
  - The network monitor
- The local alert monitors, are server specific monitors which will display different information depending on the server you are logged on to. These monitors include:

— Operating system monitor
— File system monitor
— Call statistics
— Current workload

The remote monitors allow for displaying performance data in remote SAP servers. For example, to display the SAP system monitor for a particular instance, select *Alerts → Global → SAP system*. The monitor screen shows the list of instances. Upon clicking the left push button on the display, the system performs a remote logging into the selected instance.

The right column in the display shows the overall status alert, and the middle column shows the alert text, if any. Red color means a critical alert, yellow means warning, and green indicates no alert.

By clicking on the middle push button, you actually display an overview of the instance-specific alerts. Figure 12-1 shows an example of this alert monitor. On this new display, you can get additional performance and alert information by clicking on the push buttons in the left column. Where there are any yellow or red alerts, the rightmost part of the display includes additional push buttons for acknowledging or resetting the alerts.

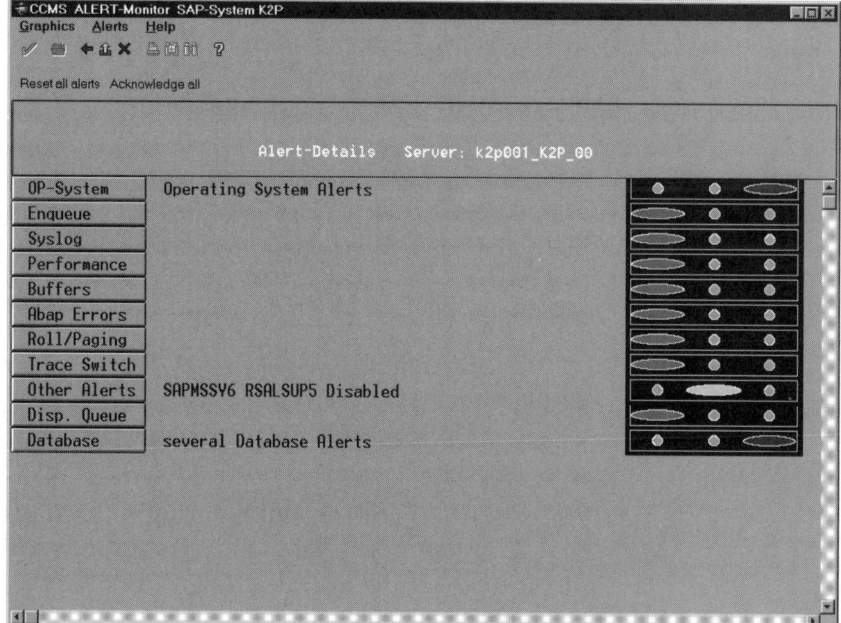

Figure 12-1 Graphical alerts monitor.

Acknowledging and Resetting Alerts. When there are red or yellow alerts while displaying the alert details in any of the system monitors, these alerts will remain with the current status until the system administrator either resets or acknowledges the alerts.

There is a difference between resetting or acknowledging alerts. *Acknowledging* an alert means that you are aware of the current alert situation, and you want to temporarily clear the alert situation. This is useful, for example, when a problem cannot be immediately solved and you don't want to constantly see the alert. When you acknowledge an alert, temporarily, the current statistics values are set at the new alert threshold. If these new thresholds are newly exceeded, a new alert will appear. To acknowledge an alert, just click on the *Acknowledge* push button to the right of the alert.

However, *resetting* alerts will clear the existing statistics for the alert and set the statistic values to 0. (Note that neither resetting nor acknowledging makes any permanent change to the database.) Resetting alerts is useful for clearing alerts which are temporary. For example, when you know there is a peak situation which will soon automatically be solved. The threshold values remains the same, so if the value is exceeded again, the alert will be triggered again. To reset an alert, click on the *Reset* push button to the right of the alert.

In other situations, you might decide you want to prevent an alert from being triggered at all. You can deactivate that alert from the alert overview display as seen from the control panel (transaction code *RZ03*) by selecting the alert and then choosing *Settings → Disable* from the menu. To activate the alert again, select *Settings → Enable.*

Color Coding in the Global Alert Monitor

The colors in the global alert monitor have the following meanings:

- *Green.* System is OK, without alerts. The current value is under the defined threshold.
- *Yellow.* Indicates a warning situation. The current value is slightly above the threshold, although it is not a critical problem.
- *Red.* A critical problem has occurred which can severely affect system performance. The value is above the acceptable threshold. Administrators should always analyze and solve the problem as soon as possible.

Color Coding in the Performance Indicators

Some of the performance monitors include special colored bars indicating the activity level of a system component in relation to the defined threshold value.

Figure 12-2 shows an example of the database alert monitor with the performance indicators. (In this figure, you cannot distinguish the colors, only the levels of gray. Look it up in your own system by selecting *Alerts → Global → Database system* from the initial performance menu.) The left side of the bar represents no activity, or value 0, while the rightmost side of the bar represents the threshold value.

You should turn on the automatic monitoring with the *Monitor on* push button to refresh the performance data every 10 seconds. You may change the refresh period in multiples of 10 seconds. This is useful because the activity level is highly variable in a running system, and alert thresholds come and go frequently.

In general, the colors have the following meanings:

- *Yellow.* When the whole bar is yellow, it means no activity at all; therefore, it's indicating a warning. As activity increases, the bar shows the green color on the left-hand side.

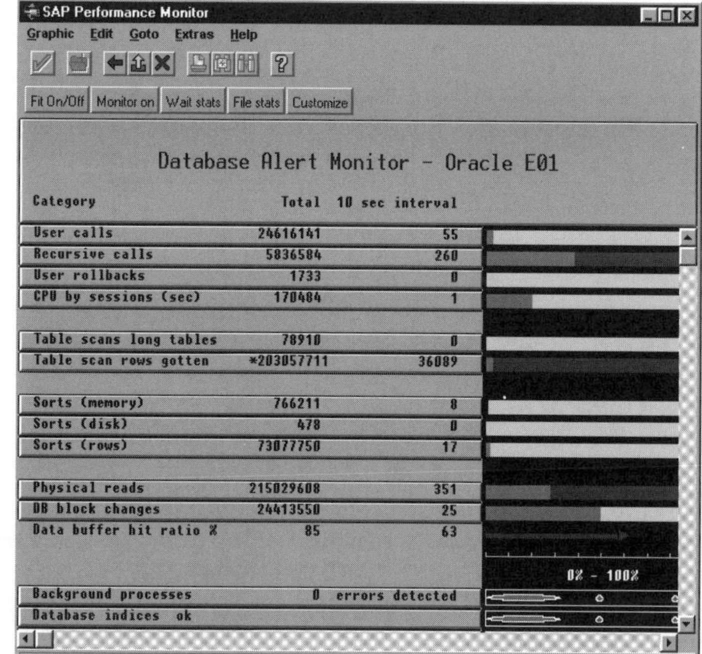

Figure 12-2 Example of performance indicators in the database alert monitor.

- *Green-yellow.* The activity of the component is below the threshold value.
- *Green-red.* The activity is above the defined threshold value.
- *Green.* This represents the current level of activity. If the whole bar turns green, it means that the level of activity is the same as the threshold value.
- *Red.* This represent the percentage by which the threshold value has been exceeded.

Setting Alert Monitor Thresholds

A newly installed SAP system includes a predefined set of threshold values for the alert monitors. When any of the R/3 system components exceeds the threshold value, the system triggers an alert.

These predefined values might not be suitable for all installations, since there are many differences in terms of overall system and database sizing, hardware platform, operative indicators, expected availability, and so on.

To suit every customer monitoring need, the CCMS includes utilities for defining the threshold values. Sometimes these values cannot be set right from system installation, but after a reasonable amount of system uptime. A periodic monitoring of the system and the maintenance of good workload statistics should help to fine-tune both the system and to redefine the allowable thresholds. Responsible persons for monitoring and setting alerts should not use information from special peak situations of heavy workload, but use instead the average figures as reflected by the statistical workload information.

For alert monitors 3.x, all alert thresholds are maintained either from the CCMS control panel or from the CCMS configuration menu. Both options arrive at the same transaction RZ06. For example, from the CCMS initial screen, select *Configuration → Alert monitor → Thresholds (3.x)* or select *Control/Monitoring → Control panel → Monitoring → All threshold values.* The system displays a list with the application servers and the database.

From this centralized utility you can either display or set the needed alert thresholds for every server (database or application). It is not necessary to log onto the specific SAP to define or display its alert thresholds.

To display the current alert threshold for an instance, select one of the available instances and click on the *Display* button. Figure 12-3 shows an example of the result.

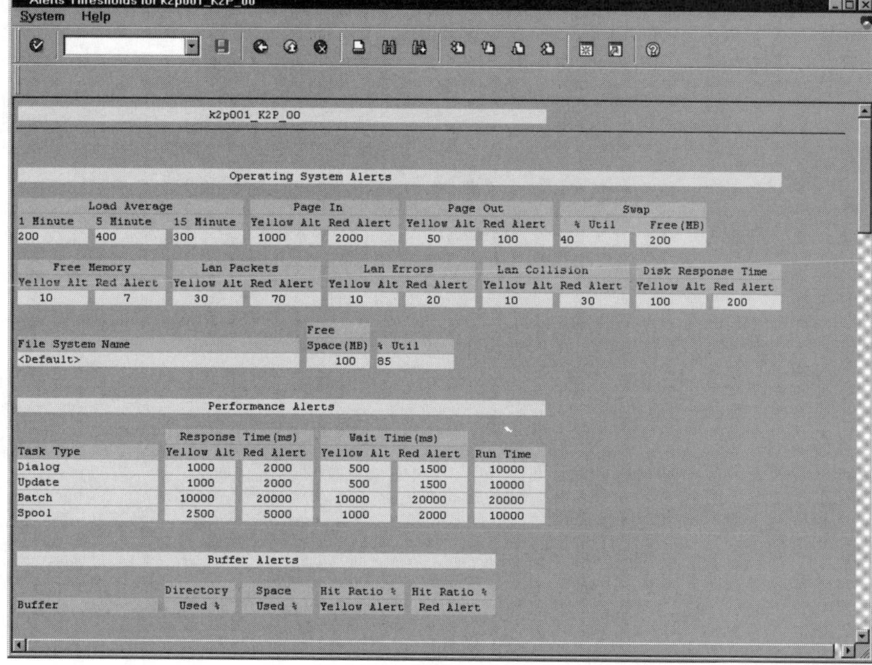

Figure 12-3
Alerts thresholds display.

In order to set the values for the different alert thresholds within the SAP components you need a deep knowledge of the system. There is, however, the option of using the SAP default threshold values to start and fine-tune it after some time of productive work. To do this, you have to define global threshold values for the database and the network, as well as specific server thresholds for the operating system, buffer, system log, performance, and other general R/3 system alerts.

In the case of database thresholds, click on the database server line and press *Change*. Then, in next screen, press *Set to SAP defaults* or set your own thresholds. To define the server thresholds from the Maintain Alert Thresholds screen, click on the server line and then press *Change*. Figure 12-4 shows the resulting screen. In the application toolbar there are four options:

- *Copy from server.* With this option the system displays a list of servers plus the <SAP default> settings, which you can use to copy any of the existing alert threshold values to the current server. If any of the alert thresholds are not defined, the copy will not be performed. The <SAP default> values cannot be changed.

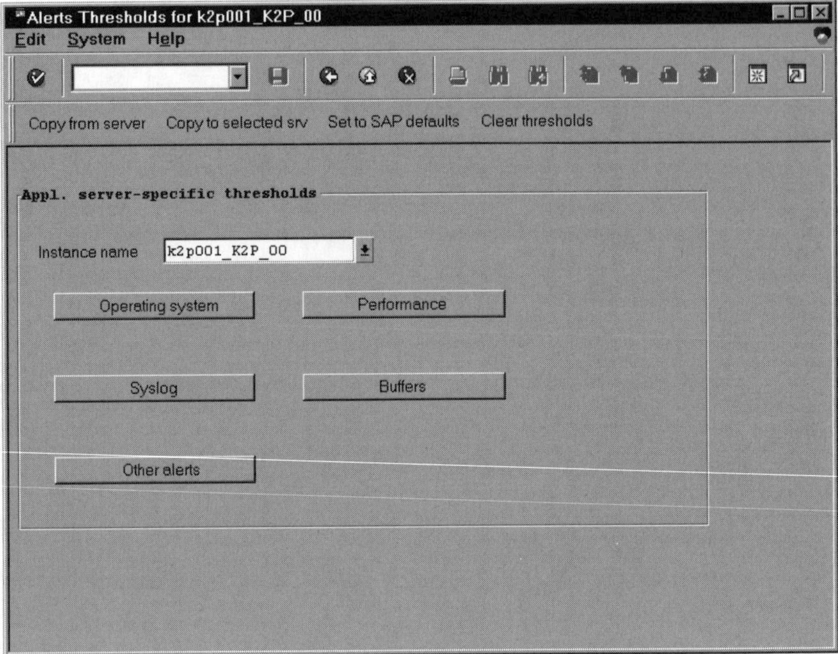

Figure 12-4 Alerts thresholds initial maintenance screen.

- *Clear thresholds.* This option will delete all the alert threshold values defined in this server except for the <SAP default>.
- *Copy to selected srv.* With this option you can copy the alert threshold values from the current server to any other system server which you can select from a following dialog box.
- *Set to SAP defaults.* Using this option will set all the alert thresholds to the <SAP default> predefined values.

There are two groups of thresholds: global and per server. The *global* thresholds are a set of values which are unique for the whole SAP system, such as the database and the network. The *per server* thresholds can be individually set for every server instance. When in any of the alert types for the per server thresholds, you always have the option to copy other server values or SAP defaults values as previously defined.

The next sections include a brief summary of some of the most important threshold alerts for each alert type.

On this screen you can also see five push buttons that can take you to the corresponding alert threshold maintenance screen. On these screens you will always see the four previously explained options on the application toolbar, as shown in Fig. 12-4.

Database Alert Thresholds. Database alert thresholds are specific to the underlying database system used by the SAP system. In this section, only the Oracle databases are covered.

There are several input fields for specifying database alerts, and all of them are important. The following, however, is just a list of the most common. For more information on the other fields, please refer to the SAP online documentation. Figure 12-5 also shows the database alert threshold options, which are as follows:

Refresh Alert Monitor in 10 sec Interval. This parameter appears in some of the other monitors and is used for specifying the time interval in which the database alert monitor will refresh the display when the monitor is turned on. If the value is 3, the database monitor will refresh the display every 30 seconds. This parameter is quite important since other alerts will make statistical performance calculations based on the time frame specified here.

Quality %. This parameter indicates the percentage of the database buffer reads against total reads. SAP recommends setting an alert if the value is less than 75 percent. By default it is set to 90 percent.

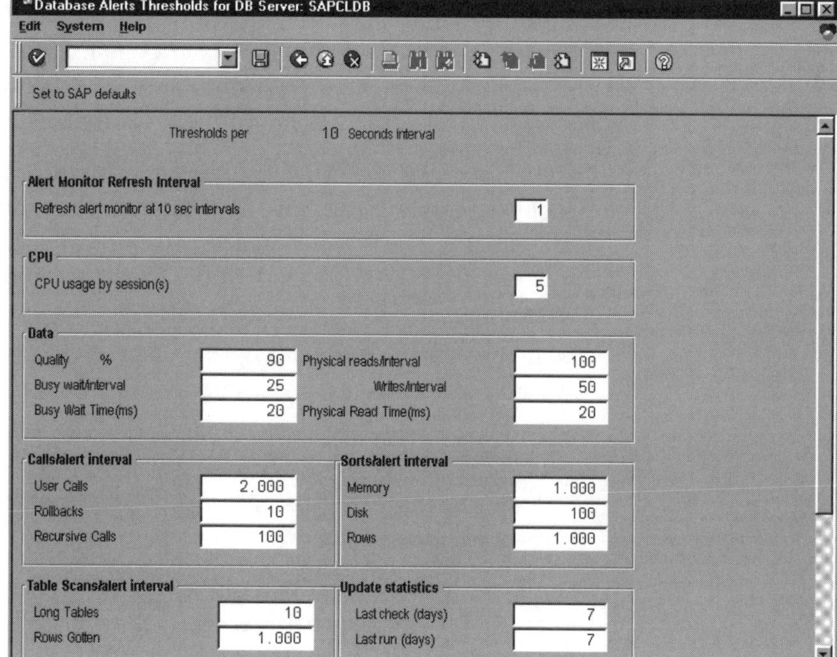

Figure 12-5 Database alerts thresholds maintenance options.

Disk under the *Sorts* box. This indicates the number of sorts for every refresh interval. The number should normally be less than 10 percent of the sorts performed in memory since disk sorts negatively affect the system performance.

Remaining Space In Archive (KB). Indicate here the value under which the system should trigger an alert if there is less space in the file system containing the Oracle archived redo log files. The directory is normally /oracle/<SID>/saparch. If this file system becomes full, you will get an *archiver stuck* error.

Using BrBackup (1->Yes, 0->No). Set this flag to 0 in case you are deploying a backup strategy which is not based on the SAP standard BRBACKUP utility for Oracle databases. Otherwise, you will be getting a continuous red alert. If you do use BRBACKUP, leave this value at 1.

Most Recent Backup Age Allowed (in days). Enter here the number of days for which an alert will be triggered in case the date for the most recent successful backup exceeds this value. This only applies when using BRBACKUP.

Network Alert Thresholds. To maintain the network alert thresholds, select *Edit → Additional threshold → Network threshold* from the Maintain Alert Thresholds screen. With the network alert thresholds you can have your system network segments monitored. When selecting this option, additional to the refresh time interval, the system presents three initial options for creating, deleting, or modifying network segments:

Change Segment. The system presents a dialog box with the available segments. Select one network segment and the system will display the alert values which you can further maintain. You can always copy the threshold values from the predefined <Default> segment.

Create Segment. With this option you can define a set of alert threshold values for a new network segment by entering the name and TCP/IP address of the segment. After entering the information the system displays the alert maintenance screen.

Delete Segment. Use this option to delete the alert threshold values for an existing segment.

The network alert threshold maintenance screen includes many technical parameters for triggering either yellow or red alerts relating to the use and quality of the network packages in the SAP R/3 communications.

You should contact your network administrator for fine-tuning and defining these alerts, or use SAP default values.

Operating System Alert Thresholds. The operating system alert maintenance screen displays the alert thresholds for several monitors within the CCMS. Figure 12-6 shows this screen.

The following operating system alert options are some of the most common:

CPU Load Ave/Min. Enter here in units of 100 the number of processes per minute allowed in the CPU queue. In the Fig. 12-6, the red alert is triggered if there is an average of four processes per minute in the CPU queue.

Free Memory (MB). Enter here in number of megabytes the amount of memory which can be left free before the system triggers the alert. In Fig. 12-6, if there is less than 7 megabytes of memory free, the system will generate an alert.

Utilization %. The monitor will generate an alert if the swap space used is higher than this figure.

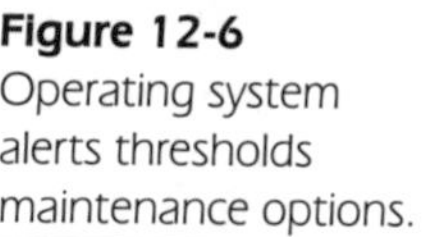

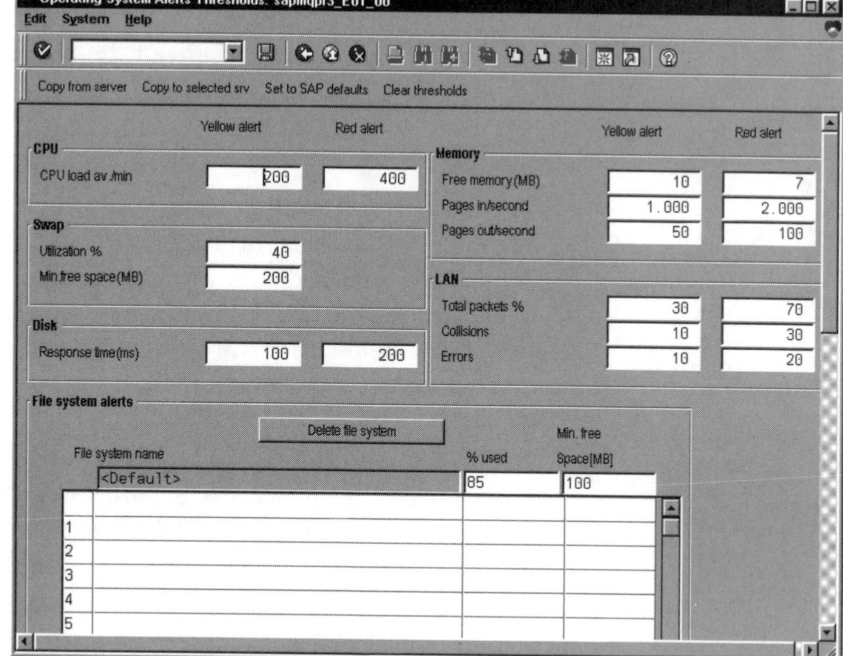

Figure 12-6 Operating system alerts thresholds maintenance options.

Min. Free Space (MB). This is under the *Swap* box. The system will trigger an alert if the swap space is less than the percentage entered in this field. Notice that with the extended memory management functions from version 3.0 onward, swap space can now be further used by the work processes.

File System Name. The *File system alerts* box includes a table where you can enter the file systems you want to display in the monitors. This file system will be monitored in relation with utilization and free space parameters.

% Used. This is the utilization parameter for the file system specified previously. Enter here the percentage amount over which an alert will be triggered if the used spaced exceeds this figure. When this value is reached, first the monitor generates a yellow alert. If the used space surpasses this figure by 10 percent, a red alert is triggered.

Min. Free Space (MB). The system will trigger an alert when a file system has less free space than the value specified in this field. This value in megabytes indicates the minimum free space in a file system before triggering the alert.

Performance Alert Thresholds. The performance alert thresholds include some basic and important value indicators for the R/3 work process types on every instance. If any of the application servers do not have these alert threshold values defined, the system uses the SAP default values.

There are the alert indicators:

Response Time. In this column enter the acceptable response time in number of milliseconds for the different work process types. For both the dialog and update work processes, a good response time should be less than 1000 milliseconds (1 second). An average response time of less than 1.5 seconds for dialog work processes should also be acceptable for installations with many network WAN connections.

Wait Time. The *wait time* is the time a user request spends in the SAP dispatcher queue before being processed by a work process. SAP recommends that a good value for the wait time should be less than 1 percent of the response time, for example 10 milliseconds.

Run Time. Enter in this column the number of milliseconds for an acceptable runtime of a work process before it generates an alert.

System Log Thresholds

The CCMS alert threshold maintenance tool also allows for filtering the system log message codes that are sent to the alert monitors. The system log threshold maintenance screen includes two parts. On the left, there is a column where you can enter ranges of system log ID messages. And the right column is for specifying single system log IDs.

When a message from the syslog range occurs, an alert will be triggered, as long as the specific message ID is not *disabled* in the single syslog ID column.

In the syslog range columns, you can enter up to 20 ranges of message IDs. The ranges can go from A00 to ZZZ, and if you overlap ranges the system will automatically join them together as appropriate.

You can find out the meaning of the syslog ID message by clicking on the *Syslog Overview* button or by clicking on the possible list arrow in the single ID columns.

Clicking on the *Set to SAP defaults* button will include the SAP default list of system log alert thresholds.

On the left part of the window, the *Syslog* ranges present the following options:

From ID. Lower range value for the syslog ID. The first available system log ID is A00. You can display a list of possible values by clicking on the possible list arrow or pressing the F4 function key.

To ID. Upper range value for syslog ID. The last available system log ID is ZZZ.

Delete Range. Use this function to delete a system log range from the alert maintenance screen. You have to position the cursor on the line of the system log range to be deleted.

On the right-hand side of the window, you can enter filtering information in base to single system log IDs. You can use these options to indicate a single system log which should *not* trigger alerts. Or, alternatively, you can enter single system log ID not included in the ranges that you want to trigger alerts.

The single system log ID column admits a maximum of 100 entries. Additionally, the system will automatically delete redundant entries if they overlap with ranges. For example, if you enable alerts for the range B00 to MZZ and also indicate that alerts should be triggered for the single syslog ID, ME1, with the *Alert on* box checked on, this last ID will automatically be excluded from the system list.

On this part of the screen, you have the following options:

On. It's the most important indicator to enable or disable alerts for a single syslog. If this box is selected an alert will be triggered when the syslog ID occurs. Otherwise, what it does is to exclude or suppress the alert for this syslog message.

ID. Enter here valid system log IDs or select them by clicking on the possible list arrow.

Text. This display field will be automatically filled when first entering an ID and pressing the *Enter* key. It includes a short description of the system log IDs.

On this screen, you have also the following options:

Maximum Number of Syslogs. You can enter here the threshold for the number of system logs generated since the system startup. If the number of system logs exceeds this limit, an alert will be triggered.

Maximum Number of Syslogs per Hour. You can enter here a threshold value indicating the maximum number of system logs generated per hour.

Buffer Alert Thresholds. Buffer settings and buffer alerts can be set per individual SAP instance. The system will use the SAP default values for buffer alerts if they are not maintained. Figure 12-7 shows this screen.

The buffer alert threshold maintenance screen is structured with the buffer types on the left part of the screen and four columns where you can enter the requested threshold values for each type of buffer with regard to the quality, directory used, and space used. More information on buffer types can be found later in this chapter.

On the buffer threshold maintenance screen you find the following buffer types:

Name Tab Buffers. These buffers, known commonly as *nametab* buffers and also as *R/3 dictionary* or *repository* buffers, contain the data definitions of the SAP fields and tables. There are four types of nametab buffers:

Table Definition. This buffer indicates the number of entries which can be stored in the four types of nametab buffers.

Field Description. This buffer contains the field catalog for the dictionary buffers.

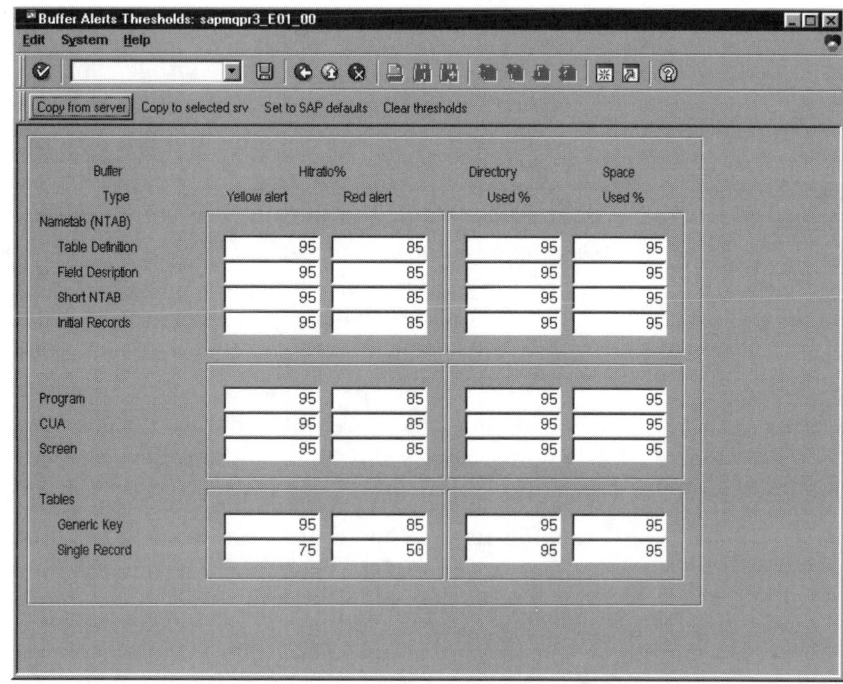

Figure 12-7 Buffer alerts thresholds maintenance options.

Short NTAB. Includes the buffer for the short nametab buffers.

Initial Records. This buffer includes the initial records for the nametab buffer.

Other buffers are as follows:

Program. This buffer holds the generated ABAP programs.

CUA. This is the *common user access* buffer which stores the graphical objects for the interface, such as menu bars, push buttons, and so on.

Screen. The screen buffer holds the R/3 screens (dynpros) which are used by the ABAP programs.

Tables. The table buffers include the database table entries buffers. There are two types of table buffers:

Generic Key. The generic key table buffer holds a group of table entries or a range of records with its values. It can hold all the table entries for a table.

Single Record. This buffer holds single table entries. This is the buffer which might take more time to approach a high degree of quality.

All the previous alert buffers are measured with the following options:

Hit Ratio %. This ratio is a percentage which is calculated as Hit Ratio % = Buffer Reads/Total Reads * 100. For most buffers, the optimum performance should be approaching 100 percent. Normally, for all buffers except the single table key, a red alert should be triggered if this value is under 80 percent.

Directory Used %. For each of the buffers there is an associated directory entry table, which work like fast pointers. If the directory table is full but there is still space left in the buffer, this space cannot be used, since the system cannot include the entry in the directory. So, having space in the directory for the buffer is as important as having free space in the buffer. The alert value should be approximately the same as the yellow alert for the hit ratio.

Space Used %. This alert value measures the percentage of the buffer used. When there is no space left in a buffer for additional objects, some of the objects will be swapped out to make room for the new objects.

Other Alert Thresholds. Finally, there is a group of miscellaneous alert thresholds including such SAP system components as the enqueue, roll, paging, and dispatcher use. These alert thresholds can be set for each individual SAP instance.

The screen for *Other alerts* as shown in Fig. 12-8 presents the following options:

Roll File Used %. This alert value represents the ratio of the used roll space divided by the total space of the roll file. Enter here the percentage above which an alert will be triggered. Default SAP value for triggering alerts is 90 percent.

Paging File Used %. This field represents the same type of ratio as the previous alert: paging used space divided by the total paging space on the SAP instance.

Enqueue Directory Used %. Enter here the threshold for the enqueue directory fill level.

Enqueue Entry Used %. This value represents the percentage of the enqueue entry usage. If the system exceeds this value, you might have processes waiting too long for setting locks on system objects.

Dispatcher Queue Used %. The alert threshold value entered in this field is applicable to any of the six dispatcher queues, one for each work process type: dialog, update, batch, spool, enqueue, and V2

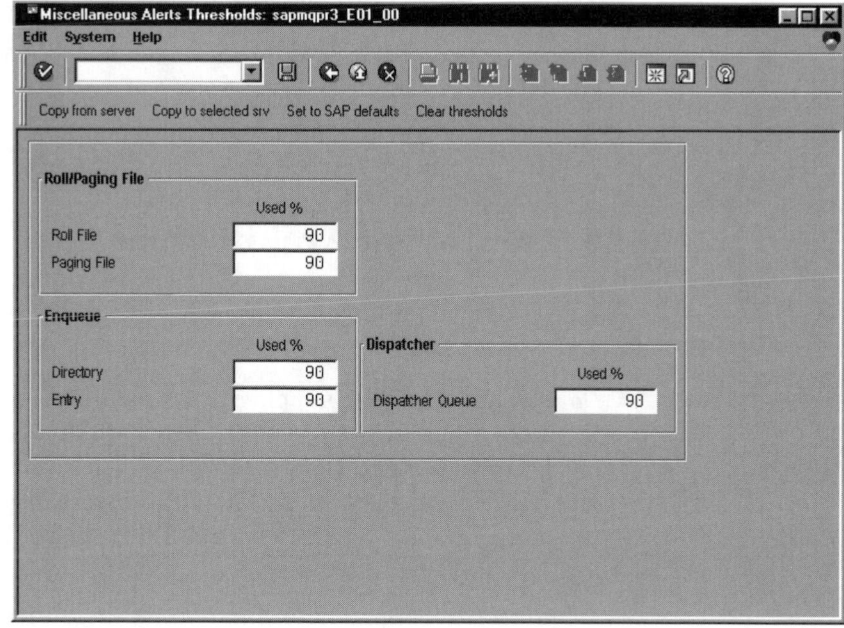

Figure 12-8 Miscellaneous alerts thresholds maintenance options.

update. You can get the status of these queues from the control panel by selecting the server and then selecting the dispatcher queues from the Alert Details screen.

Alert Monitors with Releases R/3 4.x

With release 4.0 or R/3, SAP introduced a new monitoring architecture within the CCMS based on advanced object-oriented technology. The alert monitor 4.x is based on and developed using this new monitoring architecture.

The 4.x alert monitor includes the following added features over previous 3.x releases:

- Dynamic generation of alerts on each system being monitored
- Assignment of analysis tools for different types of alerts or alarms
- Easy display, logging, and management of occurring alerts with a convenient alert browser

- Ability to adapt monitoring tools to system managers' requirements
- Ease of integration with external tools and applications using APIs and BAPIs
- Ability to manage alerts from several R/3 systems environments

4.0 Monitoring Architecture

The new monitoring architecture, shown in Fig. 12-9, is made up of the following main components:

- *Data suppliers.* Data suppliers are programs that collect information from different parts or components of the R/3 systems and the related environment. Data suppliers keep information related to different *Monitoring objects.* Initially, the system includes active data suppliers for host systems where SAP is running, both application instances and database.
- *Monitoring objects.* These objects represent different elements or system components that can be monitored within R/3 or a related environment. Monitoring objects are created by *data suppliers,* which are also in charge of collecting information about the monitoring objects. Each type of information that can be collected for a

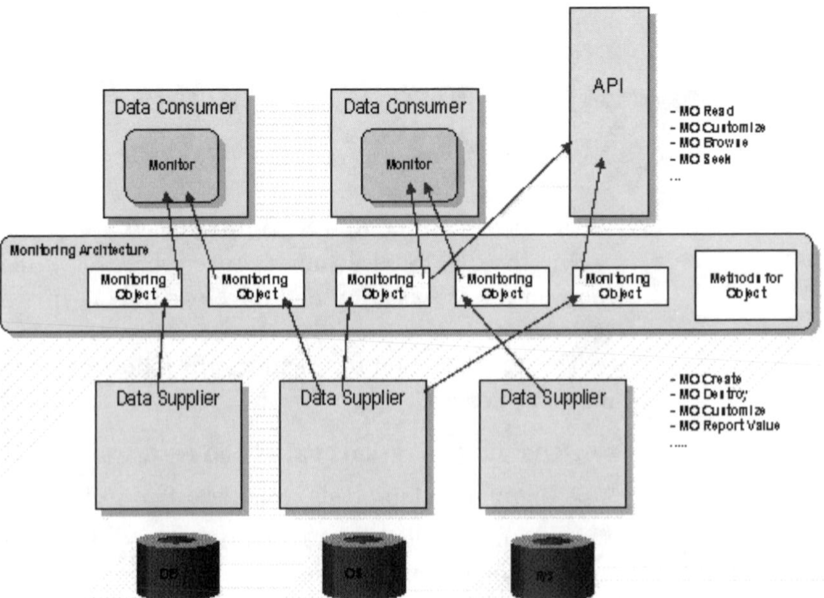

Figure 12-9 Monitoring architecture. (Copyright by SAP AG.)

monitoring object is known as an *attribute.* For example, a monitoring object can be *swap space* and its attribute *space used,* with a value of 10 percent, which is the data collected by the data supplier.

- *Data consumers.* These are programs that, depending on the monitoring object status, process the object information collected from data suppliers. This information is used for management, monitoring, and analysis. Like the data suppliers, the data consumer programs are linked to monitoring objects using BAPIs, so they can be either R/3 or external programs.

An additional concept and type of monitoring functionality is provided by *message containers,* which can hold logs and traces from different parts of the system, making this information available for the alert monitors.

The initial application of the new monitoring architecture is the *Alert Monitor 4.x,* which is made up of the standard data consumer provided by SAP in standard installations.

Based on the information provided by the data supplier, the alert monitor (*data consumer*) includes the following functionalities:

- Triggering alerts in case of errors or warning, and displaying them in different colors.
- Managing and displaying detailed information about the monitoring object, as well as permitting changes in its configuration, such as the definition of alert thresholds
- Assigning on-alert tools to the monitoring objects, so that automatic reaction to alerts can be configured
- Assigning analysis tools to the monitoring object for the analysis and determination of the causes for alerts

The following sections introduce the main concepts and components needed for working with the alert monitor 4.x.

Monitoring Tree

The alert monitor displays information about monitoring objects using hierarchical trees—known as *monitoring trees* (MTs)—of the different system components to be monitored. Each node of the tree corresponds to a *monitoring tree element* (MTE). There are three types of MTEs:

- *Monitoring attributes.* These MTEs are directly related to the monitoring object, its attributes, and its values. They can be classified as *performance, single message, heartbeat, message container* (can trigger alerts), and *text* (only used for descriptions).

- *Monitoring objects.* These are used for grouping together several monitoring attributes that are linked to the same object.
- *Monitoring summary nodes.* These nodes are used for grouping MTEs of both monitoring objects and monitoring attributes. These nodes can be either real (containing data that can be saved) or virtual (pointing to real MTEs but unable to be saved).

Figure 12-10 shows an example of MTEs obtained by expanding the tree of one of the monitors, for example and for a start of the basic monitor.

Monitors and Monitor Sets

The alert monitor included in release 4.0 or R/3 includes a preconfigured *basic monitor,* offering an MT with nodes that can all be currently monitored. System managers can create their own *personal monitors* (that is, new MTs) for simplifying the activity of monitoring by suppressing nodes from the standard MT, or for differentiating types of monitoring. Addi-

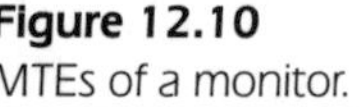

Figure 12.10 MTEs of a monitor.

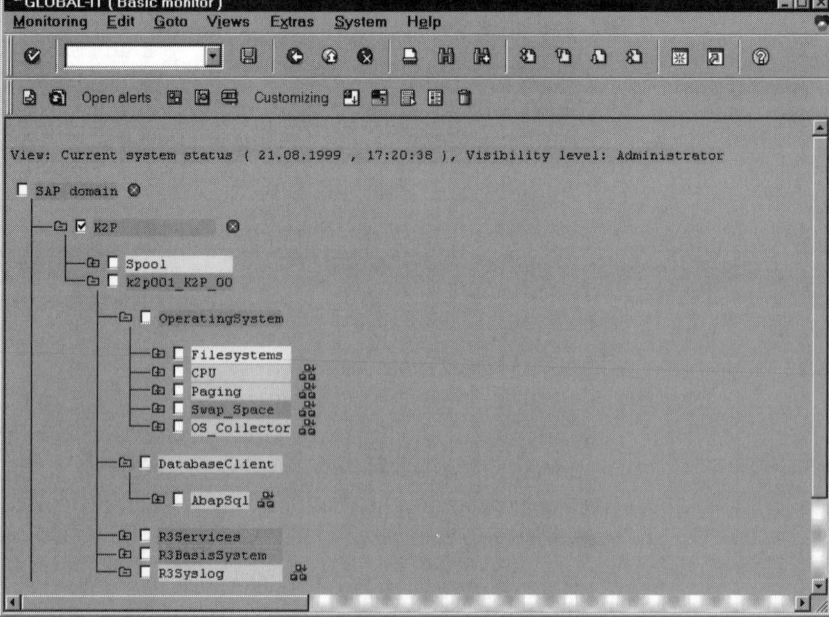

tionally, system managers can organize monitors in groups, known as *monitor sets.*

The monitor set tree is the higher level within the monitoring hierarchy of the alert monitor, and within it you can find the various monitoring trees or MTs.

The process of creating a monitor set is based on copying a set that was already created. Initially it is necessary to copy one of the SAP standard sets in order to later maintain them with the required monitors and MTs.

Creating a Monitor. Creating a new monitor is quite convenient when starting from the basic monitor, which contains all the available monitoring elements. The process of creating a new monitor based on the basic monitor follows:

- From the initial R/3 screen, select *Tools* → *CCMS* → *Control/Monitoring* → *Alert Monitor* (*4.0*), or alternatively, enter transaction code RZ20 in the command field.
- Expand the monitor sets in the Monitor Set screen, and select the basic monitor. Select the options *Edit* → *Load Monitor* or click on the *load monitor* icon. Normally, the system displays the Open Alerts view from the basic monitor; if it does not, select the view by selecting *Views* → *Open alerts.*
- Before selecting the option *Monitoring* → *Create,* expand the MT depending on the monitor to be created and select the modes you wish to include in it. Figure 12-11 shows an example.
- The system displays the MT without a name. With the selected options, you can modify the settings and save them by choosing *Monitor* → *Save monitor* or by clicking the *Save* icon on the standard toolbar.
- Enter the name of the new monitor in the input field. The system will display the Open Alert view of the new created monitor.

Modifying a Monitor. To modify a monitor, from any of the monitor views, select *Monitor* → *Change name* if you want to change the monitor name, or select *Monitor* → *Change* if you want to change the structure of the corresponding MT. In the latter case, the system will display the expanded structure of the basic monitor with the selected MTEs of the monitor that you want to change. If you want to expand the structure with new MTEs, just select them. If you want to delete some MTEs, just deselect them. Finally, save the changes by selecting *Monitor* → *Save monitor* or by clicking on the *save* icon.

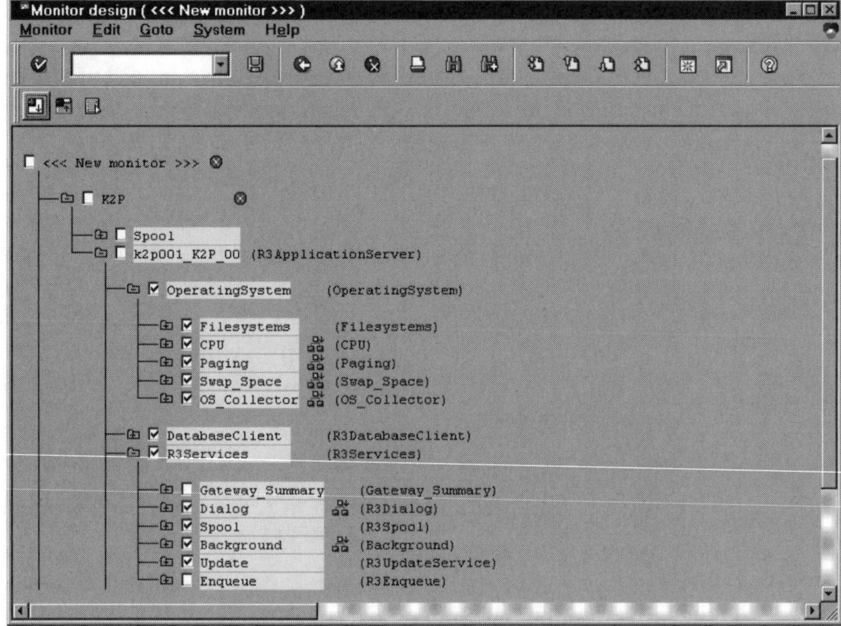

Figure 12-11
Creating a monitor.

Navigating Across Monitors (Monitoring Tree)

Navigating monitors basically means navigating through the MTs. Each monitor or MT has two possible views:

- *Current status.* Shows an overview of current alert values.
- *Open alerts.* Displays the nonprocessed alerts in the system.

There are color codes for the MTE nodes that have the following meanings:

- *Green.* The component works correctly.
- *Yellow.* A warning alert has occurred.
- *Red.* A problem has occurred in the system.
- *White.* There is no information about this node that has been provided by any data supplier.

When an MTE has an alarm, the corresponding color code is automatically transmitted to superior hierarchical nodes.

The usual management of the 4.x alert monitor should start with displaying the *current status* of the corresponding monitor to determine the status of the monitored objects. Then display the *Open Alerts* view to check on possible problems or warnings that could have appeared in the system since the last control. Once the cause of the problem has been analyzed and removed, the last step is to confirm the corresponding alert.

Next is a brief overview of how to use the different views.

Current Status View. To reach one of the monitor views, double-click on the corresponding monitor within the CCMS *Monitor Sets* screen. The system displays the last monitor view that was previously used. If you want to change the view, select it from the *Views* menu options, or click on the corresponding icon on the application toolbar. Figure 12-12 shows an example of the current status view of the basic monitor with administrator level display.

Expanding the MT nodes, you can reach the monitoring attributes nodes in which the system displays the most relevant information about the corresponding monitoring objects. You can get more information by clicking on the *Display detail* button on the application toolbar or selecting *Edit* → *Nodes(MTE)* → *Display details.* The system displays the rele-

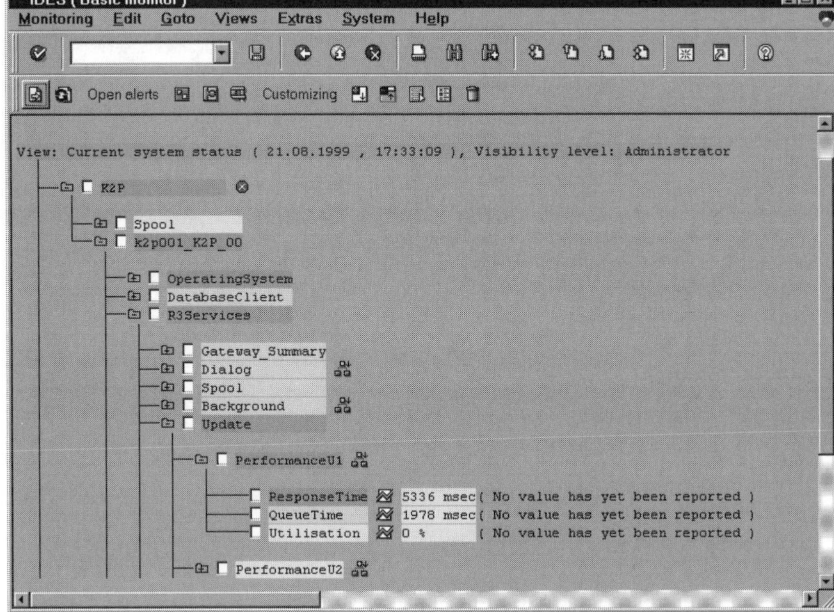

Figure 12-12 Basic monitor current status view with display at administrator level.

vant information about the monitoring object during the last 30 minutes and the last 24 hours. An example is shown in Fig. 12-13.

You can also display the information related to the MTE definition by selecting *Edit → Nodes(MTE) → Display MTE description.*

In cases where there is an analysis tool assigned for the MTE, from this view you can run the analysis by positioning on the selected MTE and running the option *Edit → Nodes(MTE) → Analyze* or by clicking the *start analysis tool* on the application toolbar. In the latter case, if the selected attribute does not have an associated analysis tool, there will be a message in the status bar.

Open Alert View. This view can be reached from the CCMS Monitor Sets (RZ20) by double-clicking on the corresponding monitor. If the system displays the *current status* view, click on the *Open alerts* icon on the application toolbar.

As in the current status view, you can expand the nodes with alarms, which can be distinguished based on their color, until you reach the corresponding attribute. Once the attribute is reached, you can display it and read the corresponding alert.

If you don't want to navigate until you reach the attributes that are triggering the alerts, you can position on any red or yellow node and click

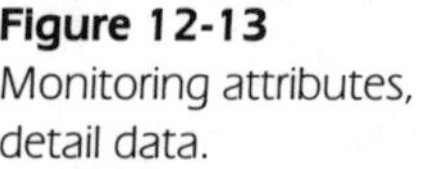

Figure 12-13 Monitoring attributes, detail data.

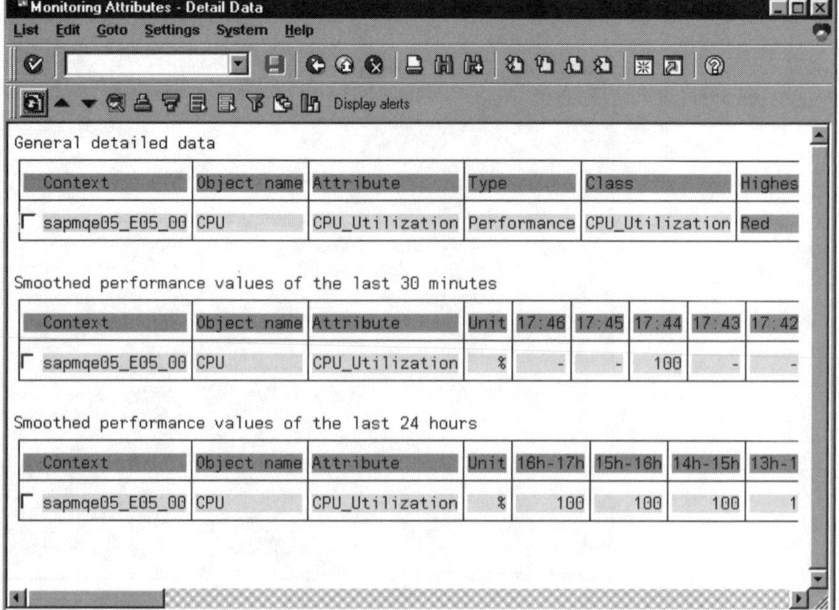

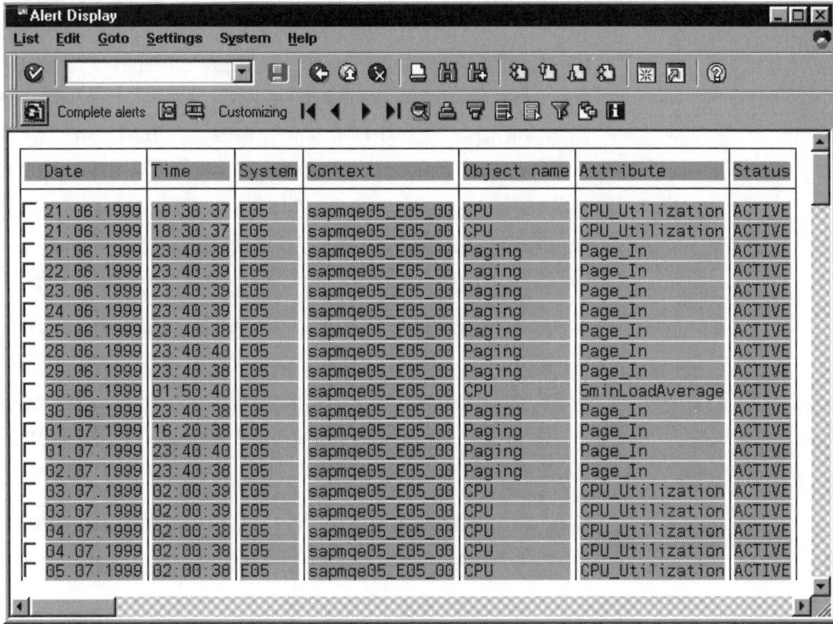

Date	Time	System	Context	Object name	Attribute	Status
21.06.1999	18:30:37	E05	sapmqe05_E05_00	CPU	CPU_Utilization	ACTIVE
21.06.1999	18:30:37	E05	sapmqe05_E05_00	CPU	CPU_Utilization	ACTIVE
21.06.1999	23:40:38	E05	sapmqe05_E05_00	Paging	Page_In	ACTIVE
22.06.1999	23:40:39	E05	sapmqe05_E05_00	Paging	Page_In	ACTIVE
23.06.1999	23:40:39	E05	sapmqe05_E05_00	Paging	Page_In	ACTIVE
24.06.1999	23:40:39	E05	sapmqe05_E05_00	Paging	Page_In	ACTIVE
25.06.1999	23:40:38	E05	sapmqe05_E05_00	Paging	Page_In	ACTIVE
28.06.1999	23:40:40	E05	sapmqe05_E05_00	Paging	Page_In	ACTIVE
29.06.1999	23:40:38	E05	sapmqe05_E05_00	Paging	Page_In	ACTIVE
30.06.1999	01:50:40	E05	sapmqe05_E05_00	CPU	5minLoadAverage	ACTIVE
30.06.1999	23:40:38	E05	sapmqe05_E05_00	Paging	Page_In	ACTIVE
01.07.1999	16:20:38	E05	sapmqe05_E05_00	Paging	Page_In	ACTIVE
01.07.1999	23:40:40	E05	sapmqe05_E05_00	Paging	Page_In	ACTIVE
02.07.1999	23:40:38	E05	sapmqe05_E05_00	Paging	Page_In	ACTIVE
03.07.1999	02:00:39	E05	sapmqe05_E05_00	CPU	CPU_Utilization	ACTIVE
03.07.1999	02:00:39	E05	sapmqe05_E05_00	CPU	CPU_Utilization	ACTIVE
04.07.1999	02:00:38	E05	sapmqe05_E05_00	CPU	CPU_Utilization	ACTIVE
04.07.1999	02:00:38	E05	sapmqe05_E05_00	CPU	CPU_Utilization	ACTIVE
05.07.1999	02:00:38	E05	sapmqe05_E05_00	CPU	CPU_Utilization	ACTIVE

Figure 12-14 Alert display.

on the *Display Alerts* button to activate the alert browser, which will display all the alerts pertaining to the selected node branch.

The number of alerts displayed depends on the level of the selected node. Figure 12-14 shows an example of the alert browser screen.

The alert browser shows all the alerts sorted by alarm type and attribute, and includes all the utilities needed for selection and treatment, such as filters, ascending and descending orders, and so on.

In both the alert browser and the screen corresponding to *Open view,* you have the option to confirm the corresponding alert by clicking on the *Complete alerts* button on the application toolbar, or by selecting *Edit → Alerts → Complete alerts* when the corresponding MTE attribute is selected.

From either view type, you can establish the level of detail to display, and under which type of activity should it be displayed. These options can be found on any monitor view by selecting *Extras → Display options.*

Customizing Alerts

Customizing is the process of setting values and parameters in order to adapt and define the behavior required for the alert monitor when alerts occur as well as the way alerts are handled and displayed by the corresponding monitors or MTEs.

Within this customizing process, there are several types of settings:

- *General settings.* These settings mainly affect the management of the alert—for instance, to which users should it be visible, how many alerts should be kept, and so on. Table 12-1 shows the general settings options.
- *Performance settings.* These setting are used for defining the behavior for alert thresholds. Table 12-2 shows the performance settings options.
- *Single message settings.* These settings are related to the behavior when error messages appear. See Table 12-3 for these settings.
- *Tool assignment.* This type of setting can be used for assigning different tools to MTE attributes (monitor attribute). Table 12-4 shows tools types and settings.

Since the number of MTEs within a monitor can be quite large, setting all these values for each of them can be quite time consuming. For this

TABLE 12-1

General Alert Settings

Setting	Scope	Description
Message class	All MTEs	Message group from which to fetch message texts
Message number	All MTEs	Message number within message class
Visible for user level	All MTEs	Indicates for which activity type the MTE is displayed. The following options are available: ▪ *Monitoring:* Operator user ▪ *Detail analysis:* Administrator level ▪ *Developer analysis:* Developer level
Weighting of alerts to be triggered	Attribute MTE	
Maximum number of alerts kept	Attribute MTE	Maximum number of alerts to be stored by an MTE
Which alerts should be kept	Attribute MTE	Indicates which alerts will be kept. The following options are available: ▪ *All* ▪ *The newest* ▪ *The oldest* ▪ *As current status*
Do not trigger alerts within the first . . . seconds	Attribute MTE	Specifies number of seconds to wait and not to show the alert

TABLE 12-2

Performance Settings

Setting	Scope	Description
Comparative value	Attribute MTE	Indicates with which value to compare. The following options are available: ▪ *Last reported by* ▪ *Average in the last hour* ▪ *Average in the last quarter of an hour* ▪ *Smoothing over last 1,5,15 minutes*
Threshold values	Attribute MTE	Definition for alert thresholds for different alert levels and corresponding color code Options are: ▪ *Change from GREEN to YELLOW* ▪ *Change from YELLOW to RED* ▪ *Reset from RED to YELLOW* ▪ *Reset from YELLOW to GREEN*
Display unit	Attribute MTE	Indicates the threshold unit
Conversion factor	Attribute MTE	Can be used for defining a threshold conversion factor
Message class	Attribute MTE	Message group from which to fetch texts for performance message text
Message number	Attribute MTE	Message number within performance message class

reason SAP introduced several *customizing components,* which can be used for facilitating definition and management tasks:

- *MT classes.* These provide classification for defining a virtual group of nodes of an MT with a predefined general setting.
- *Customizing groups.* This allows for defining a virtual group of attribute notes, with common general, performance, or single message settings,
- *MT-specific elements.* In this case the setting is defined for a specific node.

These components can be created for use in different situations or intervals such as night and day, and therefore the system also includes *customizing variants.* When a variant is activated, the corresponding settings (for example, alert thresholds) take effect. For example, you can assign the attributes for the general customizing settings to a group *ServiceDefaultCust.* The same settings then apply for all monitoring attributes in the group, and to maintain the settings you only have to maintain the customizing group.

TABLE 12-3

Single Message Settings

Setting	Scope	Description
When should a message lead to an alert	Attribute MTE	Indicates under which circumstances an error message should trigger an alert. Options are: ▪ *Always (at every message)* ▪ *Message value (color) has changed* ▪ *The message sent has changed* ▪ *Never*
Change of value upon alert generation	Attribute MTE	This setting can be used whether you want to edit or change the value when an alert is generated. Options are: ▪ *Copy value unchanged* ▪ *Red transferred as yellow* ▪ *Yellow transferred as red* ▪ *Red is transferred as yellow and yellow as green*

Customizing Tasks

Monitoring customization includes performing the following tasks:

1. Maintain required *customizing components* by assigning values to the settings.
2. Define and release necessary tools.
3. Assign tools to MT classes or MT specific elements.
4. Activate the required customizing variant.

For maintaining or creating customizing components, from any of the monitor views select the menu option *Goto* → *Universal customizing,* or alternatively enter transaction code RZ21 into the command field. The system displays the *Monitoring: Setting and Tool Maintenance* screen, shown in Fig. 12-15.

From this screen you can display existing customizing components by selecting the component and clicking on the *Display overview* push button. You can display available tools for an MT class or for a specific MT element, or you can display the tool definition or type. To do this, just select the option radio button and click on the *Display overview* push button.

To create a new customizing component, click on the *Create Group/MTE Class* icon on the application toolbar. The system shows a dialog screen for selecting the type of customizing component and the type of setting you want to create.

TABLE 12-4

Tool Types and Settings

Setting	Scope	Description
Start the tool every . . . seconds	Attribute MTE	Indicates the interval for execution of the collecting tool.
In absence of values, deactivate after . . . seconds	Attribute MTE	When a collecting tool does not send any data for the specified period, it is deactivated.
Collecting tool	Attribute MTE	Determines the data and then transfers it to the corresponding attribute.
On-alert tool	Attribute MTE	When an alert is generated, the corresponding on-alert tool is triggered, normally informing the system manager or exporting the data to to an external tool.
Analysis tool	Attribute MTE	These tools provide additional information about the problem that is causing the alert and can be automatically executed from the alert browser.

Depending on the selected type, the system will display the corresponding setting screen, in which you have to specify the name for the customizing component and the name for the associated customizing variant. Then you have to maintain the setting options, as detailed previously in Tables 12-1 through 12-4. Once the settings are maintained, save your definition.

For maintaining different customizing components, you have to follow a similar process for displaying them and, when in the display screen, switch to change mode by clicking on the *Change* icon on the application toolbar.

To create customizing variants, select the menu option *Customizing → Customizing variants → Create.* The system displays a dialog screen for entering the name of the variant and a short description before confirming the definition. For displaying existing variants and status, select *Customizing → Customizing variants → Overview.*

Tool Definition and Release

For defining a tool and releasing it for a particular activity type, from the *Monitoring: Setting and Tool Maintenance* screen (transaction *RZ21*) se-

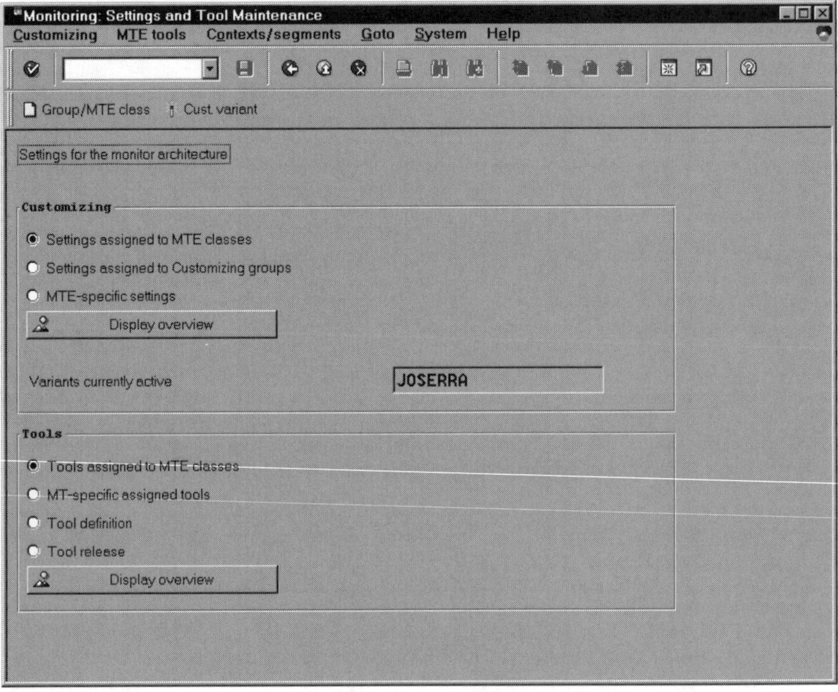

Figure 12-15 *Monitoring: Settings and Tool Maintenance* screen.

lect the menu option *MTE tools → Tool definition → Create.* The system displays a screen similar to the one shown in Fig. 12-16.

The following list describes the main input fields you have to fill in when defining a new tool:

- *Tool name.* Name of the tool for the alert monitor.
- *To be executed.* Name of the program or object to be executed. Available options are *Report, Function module, Transaction,* and *Logical command.*
- *Execute tool on.* Where the tool will be executed. Options are *Any server, The local server of the MTE to be processed, DB server,* or *Specified server.* In the last case you must indicate the hostname of the required server.
- *Execute tool for.* Whether you want that the tool to be executed for only a single MTE or for several. Options are *Individual MTE* or *Table of several MTEs.*
- *Control of tool execution.* How the tool can be executed. Options are *In dialog process, In background,* or *Manually executable only.* There is also the option of specifying that the tool be executed auto-

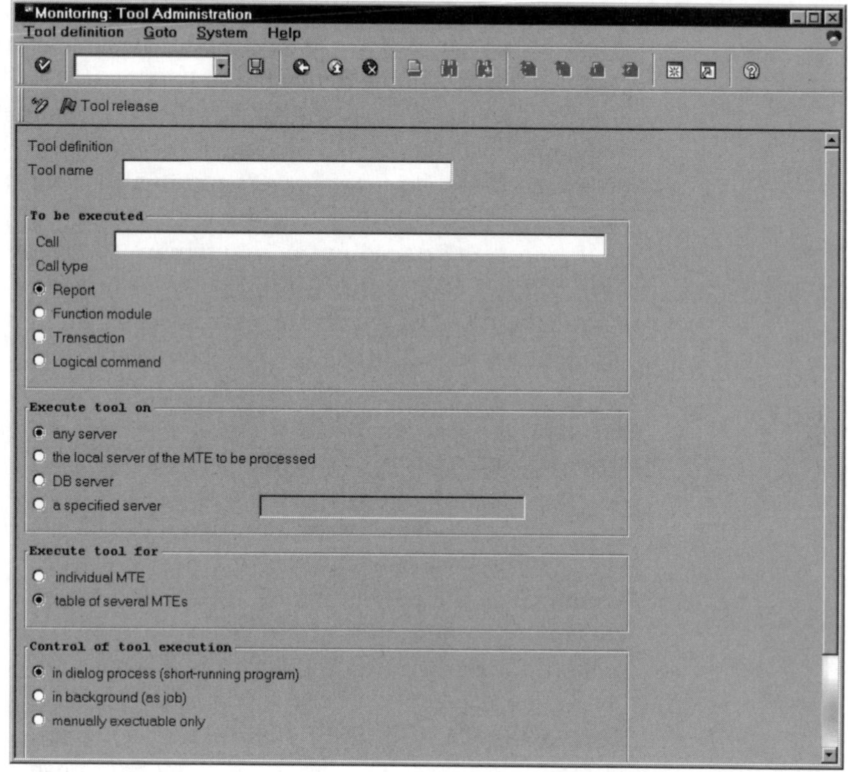

Figure 12-16 *Monitoring: Tool Administration screen.*

matically after each system start-up (by selecting the check box *Execute tool directly after system start-up*).

Once the settings are entered, save the tool definition by clicking on the *Save* icon on the standard toolbar.

Once a new tool is defined, you must assign a tool type. To do this, click on the *Release* button on the application toolbar. The system shows a dialog screen for specifying the type. Available options are: *Collecting, On Alert,* or *Analysis.* Finally, save your definition.

For maintaining tools, select the option *MTE tools → Tool definition → Overview* from the menu. The screen displays all defined tools. Just double-click on one to select and maintain it.

Assigning Tools to MT Classes. The system includes the option of assigning the required tools to a specific MT class. To do this, from any monitor view select the option *Extras → Tool assignment → To MTE class.* The system displays an overview with all MT classes with tool assignment, sorted by MT class. If this is an assignment for an MT class that still has not been assigned to any tool, click on the *Create* button on the application toolbar, and in the dialog box enter the name of the MT class and the names of the tools to be assigned in the corresponding fields by selecting radio buttons. If no type is assigned, you can mark the option *No tool.* By selecting the option *Inheritance,* you can also decide that the tool type will be inherited from the MT hierarchy.

If you want to modify the assignment to an MT class, on the list of assigned MT classes select the check box and click on the *Change* icon. Then proceed to maintain the assignment just as in the case of the creation of a new one.

Assigning Tools to MT-Specific Elements. To assign tools to a specific element, from any monitor view select an MTE and choose the option *Extras → Tool assignment → To node (MTE).* The system shows in display mode the assignment of the corresponding MTE using tabstrips, one for each type of tool. For maintaining the assignment, click on the *Change* icon, and then proceed by indicating for each tool type the tool to be assigned. If you don't want to assign tools, indicate either that there is no tool or that this is inherited from the MT hierarchy.

Activating Customizing Variants. To activate customizing variants, from the RZ21 screen click on the *Activate* push button or select *Customizing → Customizing variants → Activate* from the menu. In the dialog box, select the name of the variant to be activated.

To display defined customizing variants and check their status, select the option *Customizing → Customizing variants → Overview* from the menu.

More information on extensive options and concepts about the alert monitors can be found in the online documentation and on SAPnet.

Features with Later R/3 Releases

Release 4.0 was the starting release for the new object-based monitoring architecture and the first applications based on it, such as the alert monitor 4.x. Although extensive functionality was included, there were still some weak points. These are being enhanced constantly by SAP.

With release 4.5, the alert monitor includes dynamic selection and updating of the monitoring functionality, which means that now system managers who define their own monitors can make their selections based on rules instead of on static MTEs. For instance, they can choose to display all swap space used in all monitored systems, and R/3 will select the corresponding elements matching the selection.

With the EnjoySAP release (4.6), when the alert monitor is started the system displays the user's own monitors automatically. Also included are monitor templates, a higher collection of monitoring objects, and an easier process for defining analysis tools.

CHAPTER 13

Background Jobs

The SAP R/3 system includes functions that allow users to work noninteractively, or offline. These functions are handled by the background processing system.

Users normally work interactively with the R/3 system. *Interactively* means they are working online, they input data into the application screens, and the system responds. The interactive service is provided to the users through the dialog work processes.

There is, however, the option of working noninteractively, or offline. *Noninteractively* means that instead of executing programs and waiting for an answer, users can submit those programs for execution at a more convenient, planned time. This type of work is performed by the background work processes.

Introduction to Background Processing

The execution of programs in the background are submitted in the form of *background jobs,* or simply *jobs.*

There are several reasons to submit programs for background execution:

- The interactive user sessions are always *fighting* to get a free dialog work process for their requests.
- The maximum allowed time for online execution is defined in a SAP parameter profile (rdisp/max_wprun_time) which normally should not exceed 300 seconds. This means that for ABAP programs whose processing time would exceed that parameter, users would get a TIMEOUT error and an aborted transaction. To avoid these types of errors, you could submit jobs for background processing.
- You can continue to work in the system while your program is executing—this is the most important reason to run background processing jobs. When working online with a long processing report, you cannot interact with the system and have to wait until it finishes or the dispatcher throws you out if you exceed the time limit.

This does not mean that interactive or online work is not useful. Both types of processing have their purposes. Online work is the most common one: entering business data, displaying information, printing small reports, managing the system, and so on. Working interactively or online requires the person to be present to interact with the system. However, with background jobs, the system does not need user input or users have already provided the input in the job definition.

Background jobs are used mainly for the following tasks:

- To process large amounts of data, for example, to get a quarterly report of sales, a monthly warehouse movement report, data load from external systems, and so on.
- To execute periodic jobs without human intervention. A couple of easy examples are jobs needing everyday reports of the total incoming payments or periodic cleaning jobs submitted by the R/3 system manager which take care of deleting obsolete data, such as old log files, ABAP dumps, and so on.
- To run programs at a more convenient, planned time other than during normal working hours, for example at night and on weekends, when there are usually less interactive users.

For example, if interactively running a report that takes two or three minutes to finish, the R/3 session in which the report is executing will be busy until the report execution ends. During that time, the user cannot interact with the session. Instead, the user could have scheduled it for background processing, creating a background job and specifying the name of the report. When releasing the job, the system will execute it in the background but will give the user the control of the R/3 session so he or she can keep on working and interacting with the system.

Jobs executing in the background are working online with the R/3 system, so any actions performed by the program steps, such as locking a table or updating the database, will have an immediate effect just as if an interactive user was running the same program.

Background jobs execution is handled with the background work processes. The way to implement the background work processes depends on the particular needs of the SAP installation.

In any case, when installing an R/3 system for the first time, the system configures by default the background processing system in the central SAP instance with a number of background work processes depending on the hardware configuration.

The number and location of background work processes is configurable both with SAP system profile parameters and with the use of the CCMS operation modes. With operation modes, system managers can define some work processes to work as dialog during certain hours and then switch automatically to background processes without the need to restart the application server instances. For more information about the operation modes, refer to Chap. 11.

Background Jobs

A SAP background job defines the program or group of programs which are going to be executed by the background work processes. In order to do this, the job must be defined. SAP includes several utilities to define, manage, monitor, and troubleshoot the background jobs.

Figure 13-1 shows the initial screen for job definition. You can get to this screen from many different places: by entering transaction code SM36 in the command field, by selecting from the initial SAP screen *Tools* → *CCMS* → *Jobs* → *Definition,* or selecting *System* → *Services* → *Jobs* → *Define jobs* from any R/3 screen.

Components of the Background Jobs

A background job has the following components:

- *Job name.* Defines the name assigned to the job.
- *Job class.* Indicates the type of background processing priority assigned to the job.

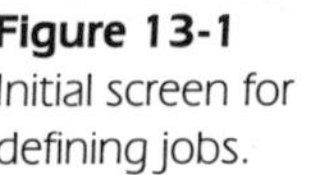

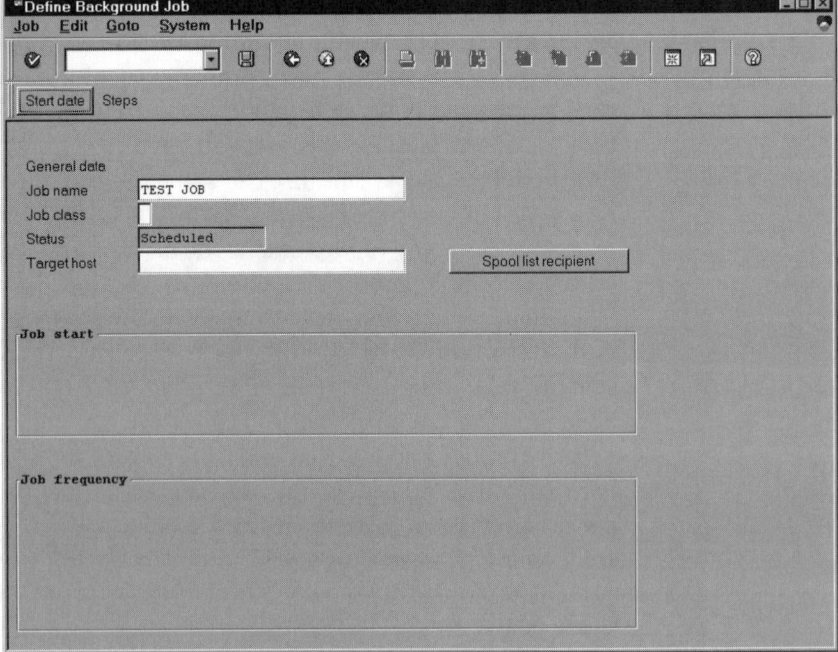

Figure 13-1 Initial screen for defining jobs.

- *Target host.* It's the SAP instance where the job will be executed.
- *Job steps.* A job step defines the program (either ABAP or external) which will be executed.
- *Start time and repeat interval.* Define when the job will be started and whether it should be periodically executed.
- *Job print lists.* These lists specify the printing parameters for the job output.
- *Job log.* The logs for the jobs include log information about the job execution such as starting time or any other information coded in the programs.
- *Job spool recipient list.* A recipient list can be used for specifying one or more recipients who will receive automatically the spool list generated by the job.

All these components of background jobs are explained in greater detail in the following sections of this chapter.

Starting Background Processing

Starting background processing means to reach any type of job definition screen in order to specify the needed data for the background execution of programs. There are several ways to start the background processing system:

- From the initial job definition screen as shown in Fig. 13-1.
- From the ABAP reporting service screen. From any menu, you can select *System* → *Services* → *Reporting,* then enter the report name. The reporting screen includes the option for background execution by selecting *Program* → *Background* from the menu.
- From the ABAP workbench editor. On the editor initial screen, enter the name of the program in the input field and select *Program* → *Execute* → *Background* from the menu.
- Sometimes working with business applications, especially navigating through the many information system and reporting functions, the system allows for background execution.

The last three methods mentioned are virtually the same thing, though the system can display different selection screens. With these three methods of starting background processing, after indicating *background execu-*

tion, the R/3 system displays the *Execute report in background* screen. The job will have automatically included the report as the first job step, whereas the user has to enter additional job definition fields, such as the job class, target host, start time, and so on.

Defining Background Jobs

Starting background jobs is a two-step process: you first define the job and then you have to release it.

When users define a job and save it, they are actually *scheduling* the report, that is, specifying the job components, the steps, the start time, and the print parameters. So, to schedule a job is the same thing as to define it. More precisely a *scheduled* job is a job definition which has been saved.

When users schedule programs for background processing, they are instructing the system to execute an ABAP report or an external program in the background.

Scheduled background jobs, however, are not actually executed until they are released. When jobs are released, they are sent for execution to the background processing system at the specified start time.

Jobs are released automatically if the user is authorized to release jobs, and they automatically start the execution in the background system if the user has chosen the *start immediately* option.

Both the scheduling and the releasing of jobs require authorizations. Standard SAP users have authorization which allow them to schedule jobs; however, releasing jobs is a task normally assigned to the system administration and requires another authorization. Protecting the releasing of jobs with authorization enables system administrators to better monitor and maintain the background system and allows the available resources to be better distributed. The drawback is that scheduling jobs is such a common task that it can surpass the administrator's ability to maintain the whole system. Therefore, reserve some time for studying which users should be allowed to release their own jobs.

When users do not have release authorization, the start time or frequency they specify does not have any affect at all, except for informing the administrator in charge of releasing them of their preference for executing the job. Administrators or users with authorization for releasing jobs can change the start time specifications and the interval.

The authorization objects which control the background jobs are described later in this chapter under the section entitled "Authorizations for Background Jobs."

When scheduling jobs, users can specify several steps, each having a different report or program. Each step has its own attributes, such as authorized users or print parameters. The same job can contain steps with ABAP reports and steps with external programs or commands (this is explained more fully in a later section).

When defining jobs, users also have the option of scheduling a program as a separate job or modifying an existing job which has not yet been processed and adding it to the list of job steps.

Users, and especially administrators, should avoid having too many released jobs during normal, operative working hours, since the system processes the background jobs during online operation where there are available background work processes. Remember that a background job will perform the same tasks as if the functions were performed online. So, if a background job does lock a table or updates the database, it will have an immediate result and can affect the work of online users.

This chapter deals basically with job definition and with the management options available; however, background jobs can also be defined from the development workbench by programming them. More information on how to define background jobs using the ABAP programming interfaces can be found in the SAP online documentation in the section, "Programming with the Background Processing System," within the section "Basis Programming Interfaces."

Job Definition Fields

As introduced earlier, to schedule or define a background job, there are some input fields which must be filled. From the initial job definition screen as shown in Fig. 13-1, you can see in greater detail which are the job definition fields and what their intended functions are.

Job Name. The job name identifies the job. You can specify up to 32 characters for the name, including letters, numbers, and space characters. Try to give a name which will easily identify the function of the job; also, you could use the same starting letters of words for related types of jobs, since the name will often be used to display lists of jobs.

Job Class. The job class determines the priority of a job. The background system admits three types of job classes: A, B, and C, which correspond to job priority. Class A is the highest priority class; class B is the next priority class; and normal jobs have the C class, which is the lowest and default priority for most jobs. To schedule jobs with higher priority, users must have special authorizations or request the administrator to change the priority of the job. Job classes are very useful when you need to reserve some of the background work processes for scheduling important or more critical jobs.

You can reserve background work processes for class A jobs. This can ensure that class A jobs will always have free processes so that they can be executed (in case there are no more class A jobs waiting for work processes reserved for class A). Class A jobs can be processed as well by normal background processes, and they have priority over regular class C or class B jobs.

With this method, administrators can decide how they want to use background processes of type A:

- Work processes for critical tasks, such as type A, and two-level priority for job classes B and C
- No background work processes reserved for class A jobs, so that regular three-level priority is used

The advantage of having work processes reserved for class A jobs is that even when there are many released jobs of class C waiting to be processed because all work processes are busy with other jobs, these normal-priority jobs will not use the reserved work processes intended for jobs with the class A. Therefore, even in high-load background situations, administrators can release important jobs by assigning a higher priority job class.

To reserve background work processes for class A jobs, you have to configure the instance operation modes with the CCMS utilities. Refer to Chap. 11 for more information.

Target Host. This field is used to specify the hostname of the server where the background job is to run. You can select the hostname by clicking on the possible entries list arrow and choosing one of the hosts from the list. However, this field is normally left blank, which instructs the system to execute the job in the system with the lightest work.

Because of the possibilities for distributing the SAP R/3 services, not all servers might offer background services (run background work processes), and it's also possible to configure one or several servers just for background processing.

The target field host is used mainly when, for any reason, a job must be processed on a particular server. Some of the reasons to do that might be: a job will read operating system files only accessible from a particular server, the printer defined for the job output is only defined in that server, and so forth. For example, you should be particularly careful when performing change request imports in a system with several servers. In order for the background job RDDIMPDP not to fail the first time, all SAP servers where background jobs might run should have access to the common /usr/sap/trans directory; otherwise, you should specify a target host for the importing jobs.

Commonly, jobs do not require a target host for being executed, since the CCMS system with the help of the message server is responsible for distributing the load among the available background servers.

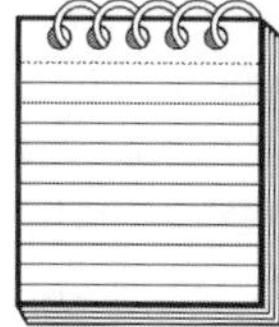

NOTE *Do not confuse this target host, which specifies a host running background work processes, with the target host as specified when defining external programs as job steps. It can be the same, but not necessarily.*

Job Steps

Once the general job definition fields are entered, you have to click on the *Steps* function button to define which are the programs that will be executed as part of the job. Figure 13-2 shows an example of the initial *create step* screen.

Figure 13-2
Screen for creating a job step.

Create Step 1

User JANTONIO

Program values

ABAP program | External command | External program

ABAP program
Name
Variant
Language

External command (command pre-defined by system administrator)
Name
Parameters
Operat. system
Target host

External program (direct command input by system administrator)
Name
Parameter
Target host

Check | Control flags

There are three types of steps which can be defined depending on the nature of the program to be executed. You can notice these types by looking at the buttons on the program values box shown in Fig. 13-2. These types are

- *ABAP programs.* With this option, you can specify the execution of ABAP reports as steps of a background job. Module pools or functions groups are not allowed for definition as steps.
- *External commands.* These are predefined commands that should have been previously defined by the system administrator. Normal users with the required authorization can schedule these job steps. Since this is a way of executing programs or commands outside R/3, for security reasons users have to specify the operating system type and cannot change the predefined arguments.
- *External programs.* These programs are unrestricted operating system programs or shell scripts that require batch administrator privileges. There is no need to define these commands using transaction SM69. The requirement is that the computer must be reached from within the SAP server and have either remote shell support, a running SAP gateway, or a SAP instance that is on the reach of a SAP gateway.

Clicking on the command functions buttons for the type of step actually changes the available command buttons on the lower part of the screen.

The following sections explain how to schedule steps and the requirements and parameters which can be used.

Scheduling ABAP Programs as Job Steps. When scheduling ABAP reports as job steps, there are several type parameters which can be specified. The most important one is usually the selection criteria for the execution of the report as it would be normally specified when launching the report online. A group of selection criteria is saved in variants. Refer to Chap. 5 for a description of report variants.

When an ABAP program is specified as part of a background job, if it needs selection criteria, the variant must have been previously created, otherwise you will not be able to save the ABAP step.

To define an ABAP program as a job step, from the initial job definition screen, press the *Step* button, and then click on the *ABAP Program* button on the *Create step* screen. Then proceed as follows:

- The *User* input field will be filled automatically with your own user name. But you can select another user name which will be used by the system to check the authorizations for the running job. You can only enter another user name if your own user is authorized to do so.

- Enter the name of the ABAP program in the *Name* input field.
- If the ABAP program has selection fields, you must enter a variant in the *Variant* input field. If you don't know the name of the variant, click on the *Variant list* button and select one. If you don't have any variant defined, you have to first define at least one variant, otherwise the system will not let you schedule the job. You can leave this field blank only in the case that the program does not require variants.
- Finally, in the *Language* input field, you can select a different language than the default, which is the one used when logging in to the system. Since SAP R/3 is a multilanguage system, there might be some language-dependent texts in the program which will be affected by the value of the *language* field.

In the definition of steps with ABAP programs, you can also specify print parameters to instruct the system on where and how to print the job output.

When finished entering the needed information in the input fields, you can check your definition by clicking on the *Check* button. The system will display a message in the status bar if it finds any errors in the job definition. If there are no errors, click the *Save* icon to save your step.

Scheduling External Commands. Both external commands and external programs are executed by means of the *sapxpg* program. This program is called either by a remote shell (*rsh, remsh,* and others) or by the SAP gateway (the usual way under Windows NT systems).

External commands to be scheduled must have been previously defined by the system administrator (transaction code *SM69* or *Tools → CCMS → Configuration → External commands*).

To define these commands as job steps, first click on the *External command* push button on the *Create step* dialog box.

On the *Name* input field, click on the possible entries arrow to select one of the available external commands. Only the commands available for the target operating system can be successfully executed.

The *Parameters* input field is used for specifying additional flags or parameters for the command.

Select *Operating system* from the available options, and the *target host* where the command will be executed.

Finally, verify the definition by clicking on the *Check* icon. If no errors are found, proceed by saving the step definition.

Scheduling External Programs. You can schedule external programs as job steps. These external programs can be of any type as long as they can be reached from the R/3 server and the host where the program resides can execute the program itself. It can be any compiled or executable program, shell script, and so forth.

The step definition for external programs allows you to include any parameters the program needs in a complete transparent way. The error messages generated by external programs are included in the log file for the background job.

To enter an external program as part of a job, when on the *Create step* screen, click on the external program. The system will change the colors for the relevant input fields while graying out the field for the ABAP programs. Notice how the command buttons in the lower part of the screen change as well, depending on the type of program.

Enter the following information for the external program:

- *Name.* Enter the name and path of the external program. You should enter the path to ensure that the program can be found in the target system except if the program is in the search path of the SAP user with which the R/3 gateway was started (normally the <sid>adm user). For example: enter /home/dd1adm/copy.sh, instead of entering just copy.sh.
- *Parameter.* Enter here any parameters, flags, or options that the external program might need. For example, if the program /usr/bin/ps needs the option *-eaf,* enter this value in the parameter field.
- *Target host.* You have to enter here the hostname of the server where the external program is to be executed. This host must be reachable from the R/3 server.

R/3 includes some special options for submitting external commands or external programs, which can be reached by clicking on the *Control flags* button which appears on the screen for creating a step with external programs. Figure 13-3 includes the new dialog box shown by the system when selecting this function.

With the control flag options, you can activate a trace for the external programs, and also direct the output and error information to the job log. But the most interesting option within the control flags is the *Job to wait for external program to end.* By selecting the *Yes* radio button option, the SAP system will start the external programs as service programs in the host where they are started, which means that they will remain active in the system.

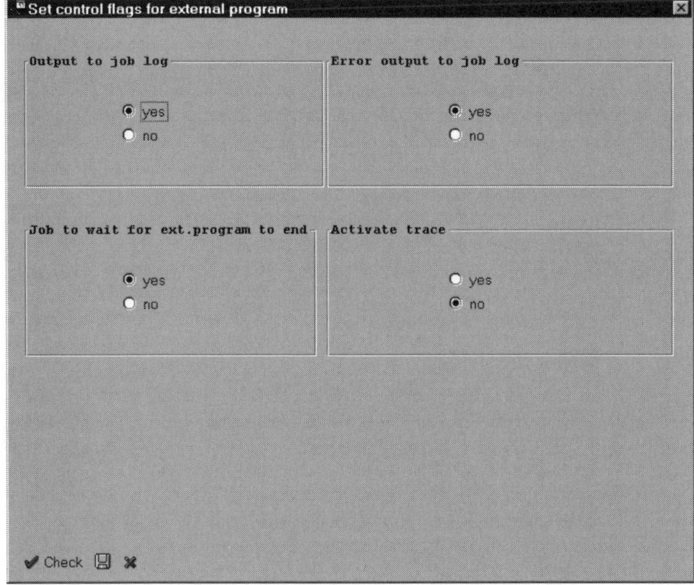

Figure 13-3 The control flag display for external programs.

When starting these types of service program which do not terminate, these programs return control to the SAP background system which terminates the job as soon as it has been started.

Defining the Start Date and Time for the Job

For background jobs to execute, you have to specify their start time. R/3 provides many options which virtually cover most needs both for defining start-time criteria and for defining a repeat interval. In any case, jobs are not executed until they are released, independently of the start time defined.

Start time can be defined before or after the definition of the job steps. However, if no start time is specified, the job will be saved but will never be executed unless the system or job administrator modifies a job and defines a start time and then releases it.

To define a start time, click on the *Start date* button on the initial job definition screen. Figure 13-4 shows the resulting display.

The system provides the following start options:

- Immediate start
- At a specified date and time

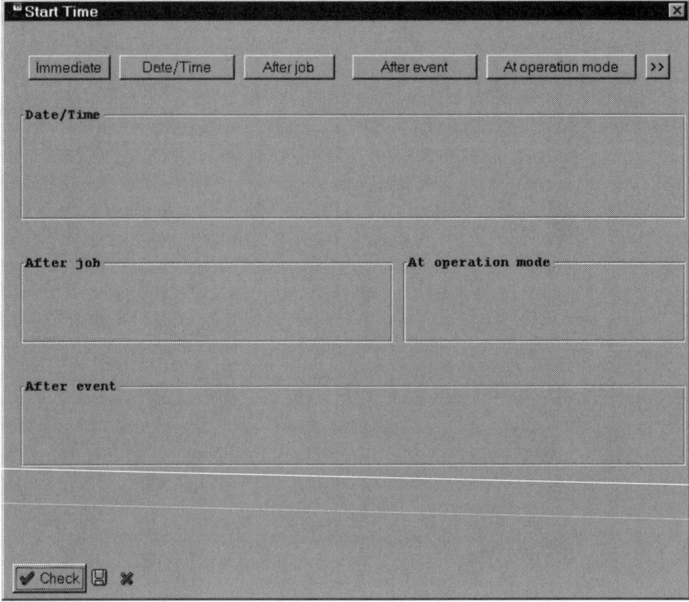

Figure 13-4
Job start options.

- After receiving a system event
- At change of operating mode
- After termination of a preceding job
- On a specific work day

For those jobs which need to be periodically executed, R/3 also provides the facility to specify a repeat interval, which can be assigned to every start option.

The following sections cover available start options one by one.

Immediate Start. For immediate start jobs, the background processing system sends the jobs for execution as soon as they are released. The immediate start jobs are released by clicking on the *Save* icon.

When users define *immediate* as the start option, the background scheduler processes the job immediately if there are available background work processes. If there are no background work processes available, the job will wait in *Released* status until one of the background work processes becomes free. This also applies if the job class is B or C (normal priority) and the free work processes are reserved for class A.

If, when defining the job, the user specifies a target host, immediate start jobs will also wait for execution if there is no free background work process in the specified host, even if there are free background work processes in other hosts.

When no target host is specified, immediate start jobs are evenly distributed among the available background processing servers.

When selecting the *Immediate* option, the system includes this information within the *Date/time* box and presents additional options on the same screen, such as the check box to specify whether it's going to be a periodic job and whether you want to specify additional restrictions for the start time of the job.

Users not having authorization for releasing jobs cannot use the *Immediate* start option.

Date and Time. The *Date/time* option allows you to specify the date and the time when the job will be processed. When you click on the *Date/time* button, the system opens input fields under the *Date/time* box to allow for entering the start data, and also how it automatically shows the *Periodic job* check box and additional function buttons on the bottom part of the screen.

In the input fields, enter the requested start date and time. You can either type the requested information or click on the possible entries arrow to choose a value. In this case, when selecting dates and time, similar to the rest of the R/3 system, clicking on the arrow for a date will display a dialog box with a calendar.

Sometimes, it might not be convenient for the job to be released for execution if there are no free work processes available at the specified date and time. In these cases, the system allows for restricting the job not to start after a specified date and time by entering that information in the input field *No start after*.

Specifying periodic intervals for execution and additional start restrictions are explained in the following sections.

After Job. The *After job* start option lets you specify starting a background job after the execution of a previous job. Figure 13-5 shows the list

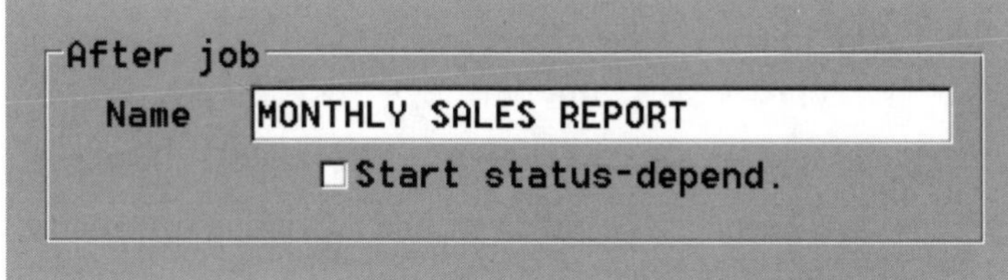

Figure 13-5 Specifying a job after a predecessor.

box displayed by the system in which you enter the name of the previous job.

The *After job* option includes the check box *Start status-depend* which is used to specify whether to start the job independently of the status of the previous job or only execute the job if the previous job was finished successfully. Selecting the check box indicates the background system to start the job only if the previous job was successful.

The *After job* option is quite useful for defining "cascaded" jobs which need to be executed one after another.

After Event. With the *After event* start option, users can define jobs which will be executed when the system triggers a specific event. *Events* are signals which indicate that a certain condition, phase, or stage has been reached, for example, that the SAP system has just been started, a certain database operation has been performed, and so forth. Events can be triggered by ABAP programs, by the SAP system itself, or by using the *sapevt* program from the operating system.

Starting background jobs by sending events is quite useful especially in situations where there is an interface or relation between operating system processes and SAP. Two typical examples are as follows:

- When imports are performed with the tp program, it sends the SAP_TRIGGER_RDDIMPDP event. When the SAP system receives the event, the background job RDDIMPDP is automatically started, since it is scheduled to run after receiving this event.
- When receiving sequential files for processing by a batch input session in the background, you can have a shell script or program which periodically looks for the requested file. When it finds the needed sequential file, it can trigger an event to the SAP system to start the background job which processes the batch input program.

It is also possible to specify the jobs started after events to be periodic. This means that when the job is triggered, the first thing it does is to automatically reschedule itself for the next time it receives the event.

You can display a list of available events by clicking on the possible entries arrow. Or you can create your own events. To do that, from the main menu, select *Tools → CCMS → Jobs → Define events.*

A practical example is:

1. Create a new event, for example, MY_TEST_EVENT.
2. Define a job with a simple ABAP report and select the *After event* start option.

3. Click on the event possible list arrow and select your newly defined event. Save the job. It will be released.
4. Login at the operating system level as user <sid>adm and trigger the event by using the command *sapevt "MY_TEST_EVENT" pf=/usr/sap/<SID>/SYS/profile/<instance_profile>,* for example, if the <SID> is *DD1* and the instance profile *DD1_DVEBMGS00,* the full command is *sapevt "MY_TEST_EVENT" pf=/usr/sap/DD1/SYS/profile/DD1_DVEBMGS00.*
5. In the R/3 system, check that the job has been started.

At Operation Mode Change. Another option for starting background jobs is when the system changes the operation mode. This option can be quite useful for system or job administrators when having to reschedule many jobs for other users at a more convenient time in order to optimize system resources and performance. For example, if when changing the operation mode, the system is configured to switch many dialog processes to background work processes (for example, in operation modes defined for nightly or weekend operation), it may be a better time to schedule the jobs which could not be processed during a normal operation mode.

To define a job *at operation mode change,* click on its function button and enter the operation mode name in the input field. More information on operation modes can be found in Chap. 11.

Additional Start Restrictions. The system includes an option to restrict the job start time to a specific workday linked with a factory calendar. This option can be useful when jobs are not needed on holidays or weekends, but only on certain workdays, for example, background jobs that generate production orders or project worksheets which are only required for operative users who do not work on holidays or weekends.

Restrictions on workdays and the factory calendar can only be applied to jobs with the *Date/time* start option. To specify start restrictions, when in the *Date/time* option, click on the *Restrictions* button. Figure 13-6 shows the dialog box that the system displays.

In the restrictions for start date dialog box, you can define jobs to execute only on workdays and decide how the background system will behave in case the scheduled job's planned start is on a nonworking day. The system allows you to either cancel the job, always execute it, move it to the next workday, or move it backward to the previous workday.

Relative Start Option. The last available start option is to specify the number of workdays relative to the beginning or end of a month

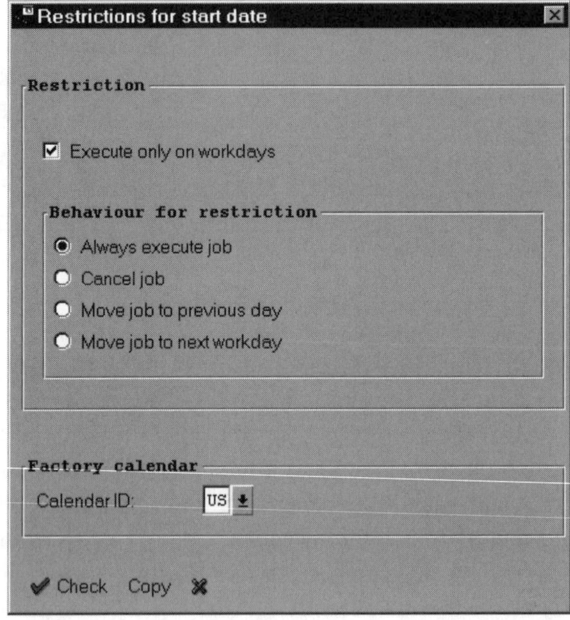

Figure 13-6 Specifying start restrictions.

when a job should be started. As with every option in the system that uses workdays, it must be linked with a factory calendar. To display the dialog box for specifying relative start times, press on the >> icon on the initial *Start date/time* screen. The *Period* input box is specified in number of months. For instance, *02* means that the job will be repeated every two months.

Defining a Repeat Interval Period

The background processing system allows for defining a repeat interval for jobs that you want to execute periodically. For example, administrators can run cleaning background jobs everyday, sales managers can have a sales report run in the background every month, and so on.

To define a repeat interval period, you first define a start option. The dialog box automatically shows the *Periodic job* check box. Select this box and then click on the *Period values.* The system displays a new pop-up box like the one shown in Fig. 13-7.

This figure has five standard options: hourly, daily, weekly, monthly, and *Other period.* To select any of the periodic values, just click the push button.

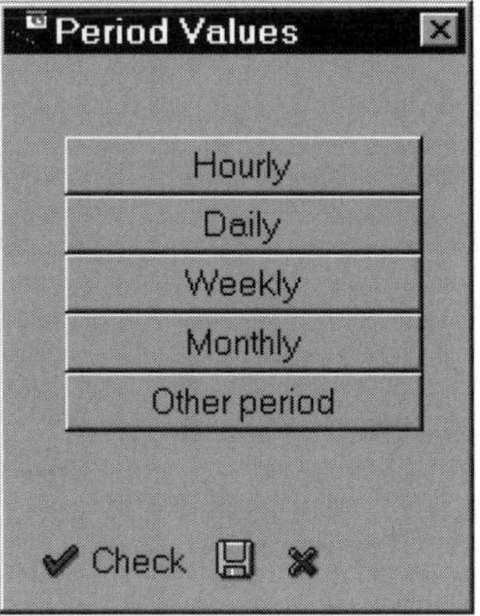

Figure 13-7 The periodic value pop-up box.

With the fifth option, *Other period,* you can specify virtually any repeat period option. Enter the desired values in the corresponding input fields.

When specifying a repeat interval for jobs started with the *After event* option, you cannot specify a repeat time value; instead, when the job is defined as *periodic,* the system will reschedule it every time it is processed.

Specifying Job Print Parameters

Often, the result of an ABAP program or external program makes database modifications which are not output in lists. Often, too, the result of a background job is a report list, which can be passed directly to the printing system, either as an output request or directly sent to the printer. You can also send the spool output to a list of recipients.

When defining ABAP reports which generate report lists, you can decide to define the print parameters for the background jobs. To do that, click on the *Print specifications* button which appears in the dialog box for ABAP step creation. The *background print parameter* screen is virtually the same as any other print request generated in the SAP system. Enter the requested print specifications and save the settings.

Specifying the Spool List Recipient

As stated in the previous section, a new feature of release 4.0 is the possibility of automatically sending to a group of recipients the result of a job that includes a spool request. The system allows this output to be sent both to in-

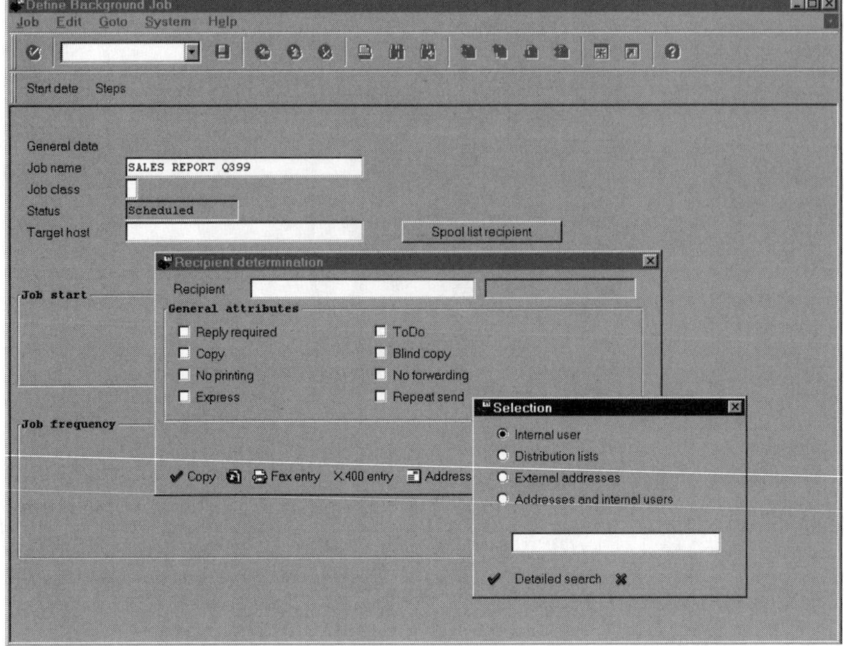

Figure 13.8 Spool list recipient options.

ternal users or by other external means (internet mail, fax, and so on) if these communication types have been previously configured in the system.

To send the output of a job to a recipient or group, click on the *Spool list recipient* push button on the initial job definition screen. The system will display a dialog box for determination of recipients, as well as additional flags that will be attached to the message. Clicking on the possible entries arrow in the *Recipient* input field opens an additional dialog box for selecting the type of user or messaging system. Figure 13.8 shows these screens.

Make your required entries and press the *Copy* icon to transfer the information to the job definition.

Basic Management Operations on Background Jobs

Previous sections explained the process of defining and scheduling jobs. This section covers additional management options to handle modifying, monitoring, and controlling background jobs. Users can display a list of their own jobs by selecting *System* → *Own jobs* from any R/3 menu.

The most important background job managing operations are as follows:

- *Checking the status of jobs.*
- *Modifying jobs.*
- *Deleting jobs.* Some time after a job has been processed, you should delete it to release system resources. You have two options for deleting a job: manually, job-by-job or automatically, using a reorganization program that deletes jobs that are beyond a date line.
- *Viewing the job log.* If a job has been aborted, you should view the job log for the cause of the failure.

Most basic management operations are performed from the job overview screen. To reach the job overview screen, first, from the main menu select *System* → *Services* → *Jobs* → *Job overview* or, alternatively, enter transaction code SM37 in the command field. Figure 13-9 shows the initial screen for selecting jobs.

On the initial screen, enter the selection criteria for the jobs you want to look for. On the job selection screen, you can specify job name, user name, a date and time interval, job status, and so forth. Wildcards, such as the asterisk sign (*) are allowed. Do not forget to enter the event name

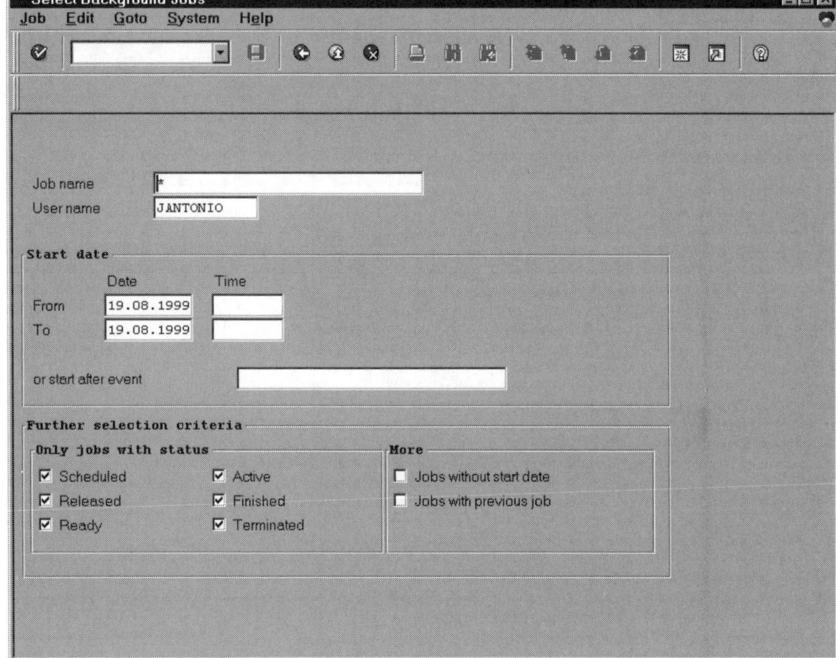

Figure 13-9 Background jobs main selection screen.

or an * to select jobs which are started after event, even when they are already finished in the date and time range.

Once the criteria is specified, click *Enter* to display the job overview for the requested selection. Figure 13-10 shows an example of a *Job overview* screen. This screen includes several menu options that allow you to perform common monitoring and management tasks over a job or a group of selected jobs.

The next sections explain some of these common tasks.

The Job Status

A job can have one of the following statuses: scheduled, released, ready, active, finished, canceled. They indicate the following conditions:

- *Scheduled.* The job has been created but still has not been released to run. A scheduled job will never execute unless it is released.
- *Released.* The job is released to run at the time or condition specified in the start options.

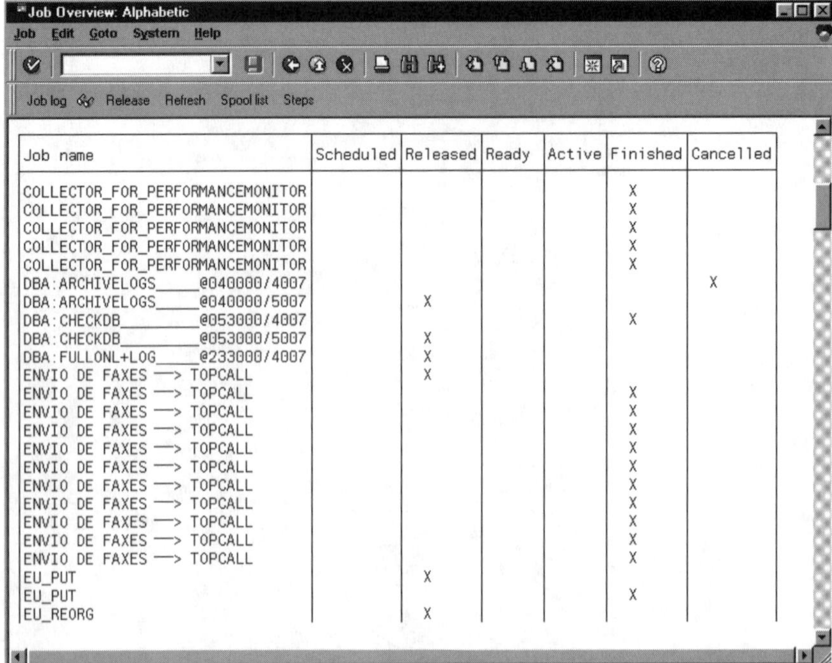

Job name	Scheduled	Released	Ready	Active	Finished	Cancelled
COLLECTOR_FOR_PERFORMANCEMONITOR					X	
COLLECTOR_FOR_PERFORMANCEMONITOR					X	
COLLECTOR_FOR_PERFORMANCEMONITOR					X	
COLLECTOR_FOR_PERFORMANCEMONITOR					X	
COLLECTOR_FOR_PERFORMANCEMONITOR					X	
DBA:ARCHIVELOGS_____@040000/4007						X
DBA:ARCHIVELOGS_____@040000/5007		X				
DBA:CHECKDB_________@053000/4007					X	
DBA:CHECKDB_________@053000/5007		X				
DBA:FULLONL+LOG_____@233000/4007		X				
ENVIO DE FAXES —> TOPCALL		X				
ENVIO DE FAXES —> TOPCALL					X	
ENVIO DE FAXES —> TOPCALL					X	
ENVIO DE FAXES —> TOPCALL					X	
ENVIO DE FAXES —> TOPCALL					X	
ENVIO DE FAXES —> TOPCALL					X	
ENVIO DE FAXES —> TOPCALL					X	
ENVIO DE FAXES —> TOPCALL					X	
ENVIO DE FAXES —> TOPCALL					X	
ENVIO DE FAXES —> TOPCALL					X	
ENVIO DE FAXES —> TOPCALL					X	
EU_PUT		X				
EU_PUT					X	
EU_REORG		X				

Figure 13-10
Job overview list.

- *Ready.* The start date and time has arrived and the job is waiting to be executed. This status is not seen very often. It is a short period of time before the job changes to an active status.
- *Active.* The job is running, being executed.
- *Finished.* The job has ended successfully.
- *Canceled.* The job has ended with errors.

Modifying Scheduled Jobs

A job which has been released can be canceled, which reverts its status to *Scheduled.* To do this, from the job overview list, select the job, and then, from the menu, choose *Job → Schedule job → Cancel.*

To release a scheduled job, from the menu, click on the *Release* button on the application toolbar or select *Job → Schedule job → Release.*

From the job overview screen, administrators can also change the definition of a job which has not yet been processed. By selecting the job and then choosing *Job → Change* from the menu, authorized users can modify the start time, the steps, print lists, restrictions, and so on.

Other available options under the Job menu are as follows:

- *Copy* is used to copy a job with another name.
- *Move* is the option available for changing the target host of a job.
- *Capture* is a function to intervene in an active job in order to interrupt it or put it under debugging mode.
- *Check status* is useful in situations where, due to system failures, shutdowns, and the like, it's not clear that the status of the job is the real one.

For jobs which are already finished or have been canceled, you can display the job log by selecting the job and clicking on the *Job log* function button on the application toolbar.

To display the details of individual jobs, select the job and click on the *Display* button on the application toolbar. From the job display screen, you can look further at the rest of the job information like the steps, start time, repeat interval, print specifications, and so forth.

Deleting Jobs

Background jobs become very numerous in productive R/3 installation and so do the number of job logs and job-related information. It is a good practice to periodically delete all the jobs which have already been processed and are no longer needed. Deleting jobs removes the associated job log and the internal table entries.

There are two ways to delete jobs: manually, by selecting jobs from the job list display and then choosing the *delete* function from the menu, or automatically, by defining one or several jobs which periodically clean up old jobs. The standard ABAP report RSBTCDEL is used for this purpose. You can create several variants which delete only those jobs specified in the selection criteria. You can find more information about other useful cleaning jobs in the SAP notes.

Be careful when deleting jobs which are predecessors of other jobs, since those jobs will no longer be started, although you have the option of rescheduling them by assigning a different start option.

Displaying Job Logs. Every background job generates a job log after execution; job logs are only available for finished or canceled jobs. They record the messages which are issued by the programs specified in the job steps. The messages of the job log are language-dependent.

These logs can be very useful for finding the cause of errors, problems, and failures or for tracing important parts of a job. If no problem occurs in the job execution, the job log simply contains the start time and finish time of the job and an indication of the start of every job step. Sometimes, depending on the nature of the executed program, it might also contain internal program information, such as statistical information. These messages are output to the log file using the MESSAGE keyword of ABAP.

To display the log for a job, select the job from the job overview list and double click over it, or click on the *Job log* button on the application toolbar.

For each job log a job file is created at the operating system level. These are usually located under the SAP system global directory (/usr/sap/<SID>/SYS/global) and are managed within the TemSe (temporary sequential objects) database. These log files should not be deleted manually in the operating system, since they are managed by the SAP system and their deletion can cause inconsistencies in the TemSe database. The log files are automatically deleted by the system when the jobs are deleted.

Analyzing Canceled Jobs

A canceled job indicates that the program terminated with some kind of error. The nature and cause of the error can be diverse: program error, wrong variant, system shutdown, restart of instance, locking problems, authorization problems, and so forth.

To find the cause of error, you should first display the job log. If the job log includes any error messages, look into the system log to find additional information. You can select the background work process as the criterion. To do that, you first have to find the process number of the background work process in the process overview display.

If a program defined in a job step caused an abnormal termination of an ABAP program, look into the short dump list. The procedures, concepts, and information about the system log and the ABAP short dumps can be found in several sections in Chap. 10.

General procedures for analyzing problems with the background system and an overview of basic troubleshooting is contained in the following sections.

Authorizations for Background Jobs

Regarding background jobs, there are also certain operations and data that require protection. The SAP system includes three standard authorization objects for handling and administering background jobs and the background system:

- *S_BTCH_ADM.* It's the authorization for the administrator of the background processing administrator.
- *S_BTCH_NAM.* It's a general authorization for specifying user names when defining and releasing background jobs.
- *S_BTCH_JOB.* It's the authorization for allowing or restricting operations on background jobs.

Administrators with all the authorizations can display jobs in all SAP clients and perform all types of job operations: canceling, copying, deleting, and so on. They may also submit jobs of higher priority, such as class A or B jobs.

Users without any of these authorizations are only allowed to define and schedule jobs of normal importance. Class C jobs are assigned by default.

Using the Graphical Job Monitoring Tool

Within the CCMS monitoring functions, the SAP system includes a utility for graphical job monitoring. To display the job scheduling graphical monitor, from the main menu, select *Tools → CCMS → Control/Monitoring → Job schedul. Monitor.* Figure 13-11 shows an example of the SAP graphics display for monitoring jobs.

The graphical job monitor is quite useful for looking at the available resources for background, the status of jobs, estimated runtime, operation mode switch, and so forth.

The background processing system manages a statistics database used for making estimates of job processing times. This is particularly useful with periodic jobs. For jobs without runtime statistics, the monitor shows an estimate with the minimum length.

In the left column of the display under *Job server,* the monitor shows how many background work processes are available identified with the name of the host system.

The ruled horizontal line on top of the display shows the time unit used for monitoring. The broken vertical line shows the current time. The monitoring tool shows the jobs as rectangles where you can click to dis-

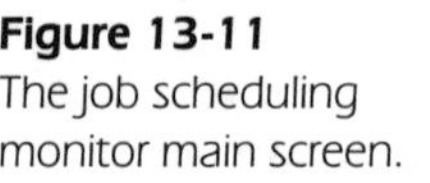

Figure 13-11
The job scheduling monitor main screen.

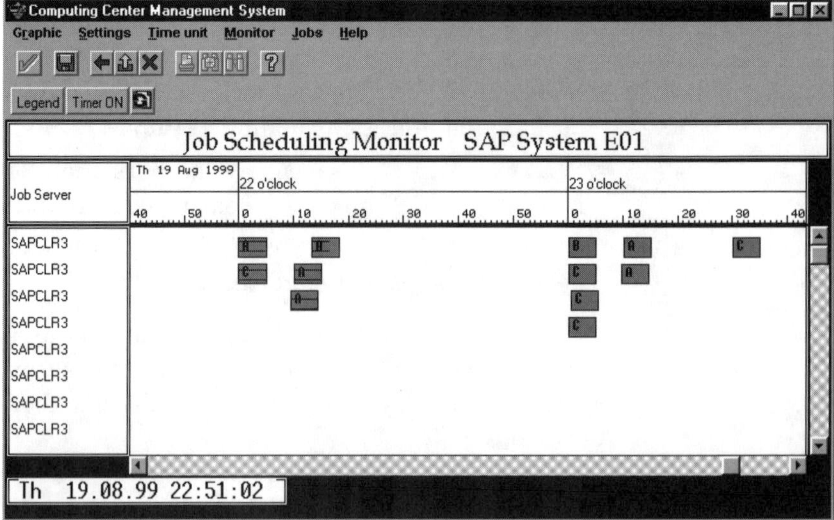

play an overview with information about the particular job. The length of a job rectangle shows the approximate amount of time that the job requires for processing. For a finished job, it actually shows the time it took to complete.

The status of a job is indicated by its colors. To display a legend of the meaning of each color, click on the *Key* button on the display toolbar.

Watch out for long yellow bars with shading which might indicate a problem in the background scheduler or blocked work processes. Many red bars with >>> shading (estimated runtime exceeded) might indicate that the program is not running correctly.

The graphical job monitoring tool can quickly give an idea of the load distribution among the available background work processes. From a general display, you can see if the system is executing jobs evenly among the available background servers.

The job monitor uses an additional alert monitor, which automatically reports any errors related to the background processing such as canceled jobs.

With release 4.5, the background processing system was integrated into the new alert architecture and CCMS monitors.

To the right of the current time, the rectangles are for jobs which are waiting to be processed.

On the menu bar of the graphical display, there are several functions available to configure the monitoring utility, as well as for displaying and managing jobs.

The time unit menu allows you to change the time measurements on the display. By default it is set to minutes, but you can compress or expand the display by selecting another time unit such as hours or days.

With the Jobs menu, administrators can display job logs and job overview information and can change the job information. To perform any function under this menu, first select the function and then click on the job. For example, you can select *Check job status* from the Jobs menu and then click on any job in the display. The system shows a dialog box indicating whether the job status is OK or not.

By clicking on the *Timer on* button, the system automatically updates the job display every three minutes.

Using the *Monitor → Customize* function, you can decide to set some standard values for displaying jobs under the monitoring tool. For example, you can decide how many hours you want to have for displaying canceled jobs, what the standard expected runtime assigned to jobs without statistics is, and so forth.

Troubleshooting the Background Processing System

There are several options in the SAP system for monitoring and troubleshooting the background processing system. These options include utilities which can be used from the general administration monitoring utilities to extensive CCMS analysis tools. Where to look and what functions to use depends very much on the type of errors, which can range from configuration problems to authorizations or runtime problems.

In general, the order to look for background job problems can be:

- Displaying the job log and analyzing the job status
- Using the general monitoring utilities to analyze the background work processes and the system log
- Using the graphical job scheduling monitor
- Using the CCMS general analysis tools

Displaying the Job Log and Analyzing the Job Status

To display a job log and analyze its status, you must access the job overview list from a previous job selection screen. This screen may be accessed from many different places in the R/3 system. For example, directly by entering the SM37 transaction code in the command field or by selecting *Tools → CCMS → Jobs → Maintenance* from the main menu.

Enter the criteria for restricting the jobs to analyze and then display the job or list of jobs.

The first operation on a selected job will be to see its status and check it for possible errors by using the *Job → Check status* function. If the real job status is OK, the system displays a message in the status bar.

If you suspect an active job is running for a longer time than normal, maybe because it started to loop, you can put it in debugging mode by selecting it and then choosing *Job → Capture.* The system will display a debugging window where you can analyze the program code. The running program stops and you can debug it. From the debugging window, you can continue to execute the job at the point it was stopped. This option is only available for ABAP steps and not for external programs.

Analyzing the Work Processes and System Log of an Application Server

Another step in the analysis of problems with the background processing system is to display the general process overview monitor. From the main menu, select *Tools → Administration → Monitor → System monitoring → Process overview.*

The two types of work processes to look for are the background work processes and the dialog work processes. The *Type* column (*Ty.*) shows the type of work processes: *BTC* for background (batch) and *DIA* for dialog. And the *Status* column displays whether these processes are running, waiting, and so on.

The first column of the process overview (*No.*) shows the number of the work process. This number can be very useful if you later want to analyze the system log and want to restrict the search to problems with that particular work process.

The process monitor shows other interesting information such as the program it is executing at the moment, the user under which the job is running, and so forth.

Selecting one of those processes, you can get further detailed information by clicking on the *Detail info* button; or, you can also display the trace file by selecting *Process → Trace → Display file.*

With the system log, you can also analyze system errors, messages, or warnings regarding the background processing system. You can restrict your search just to the background work processes by entering the number in the *SAP process* input field.

The CCMS Job Analysis Tools

Within the computing center management system (CCMS) there is a set of utilities which can be used to analyze and monitor the background processing system. To reach these tools, from the main menu, select *Tools → CCMS → Jobs* and then the available options.

The three tools which are used for analyzing the background system are *Check environment, Background objects,* and *Performance analysis.*

Checking the Background System Environment. The CCMS utility *Check environment* is used for analyzing the configuration and the status of the background environment. To reach this function, from the CCMS initial screen, select *Jobs → Check environment.* Figure 13-12 shows an example of the initial screen for performing simple tests on the background system.

These utilities check all the necessary conditions which must be met for the background processing system to work correctly. This analysis utility is helpful in determining if all the elements of the background system are configured and if there is any missing parameter.

The analysis tools include two types of tests:

- *Simple tests.* These tests are used by the system to check if the profile parameters are correctly set and if the SAPCPIC user exists, since it is needed for starting external programs. These tests can be performed on a single background server or on all of them. To launch this test, from the initial screen click on the *Execute* button.
- *Additional tests.* These tests perform more extensive tests on the background processing system such as authorizations, consistency of the database tables and the TemSe database, status of background servers, and whether the dispatcher of a SAP instance has any entries in the queue for background processing. To reach these expert mode functions, from the initial screen select *Goto → Additional tests.* Figure 13-13 shows this screen.

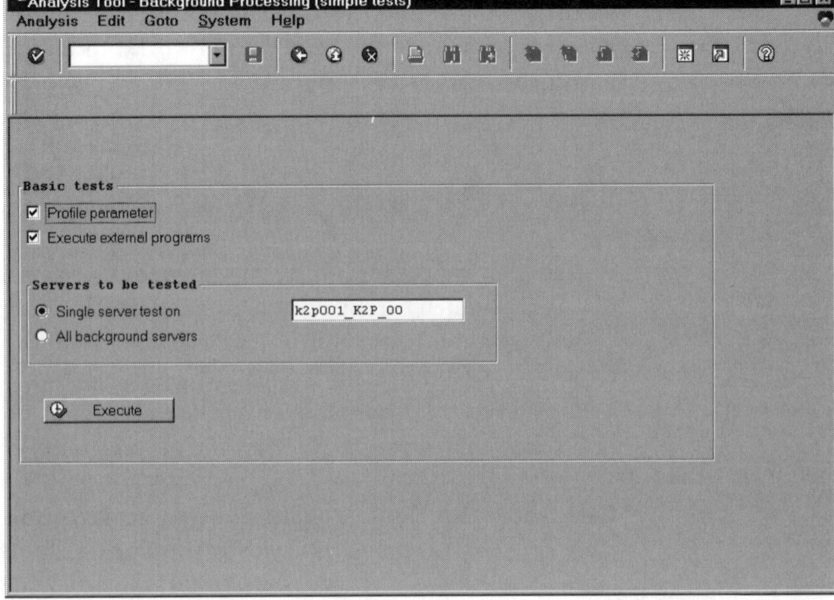

Figure 13-12 Initial screen for the simple test of the background processing system.

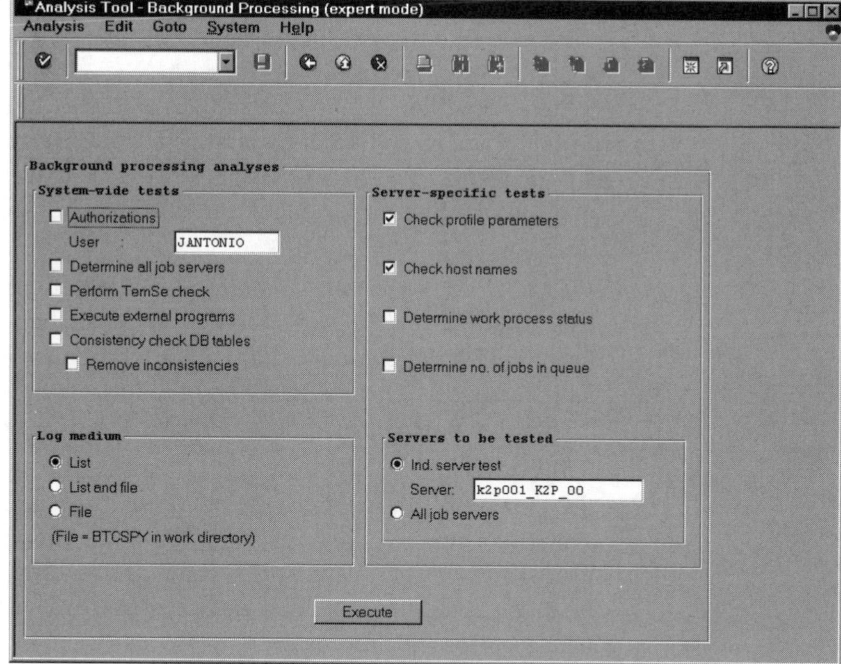

Figure 13-13 Initial selection screen for the export mode in background system analysis.

Job information is stored internally using several R/3 tables. With these additional tests, the system can find if there are any consistency problems in those tables, such as a missing index, duplicate entries, existence of all job data, and so forth.

The results of the tests can either be displayed as a list or written to the file BTCSPY in the working directory of the application server to which you are logged on.

Analyzing the Background Objects. The system background objects are the elements or control objects which make up the runtime environment for processing jobs. To reach this function, from the CCMS initial screen, select *Jobs → Background objects.* From this initial screen you can either display or maintain these objects. Select a function to display available background objects.

These objects are as follows:

- *Time-driven scheduler.* It's the component of the background system responsible for starting jobs which have a start date and time specified. This scheduler is also responsible for starting jobs defined with a scheduled start option, such as *After event, After job,* or

At operation mode, which could not be started at their scheduled time for some reason, for example, because there were no free background work processes.

The scheduler is started by the SAP dispatcher in the period indicated by the rdisp/bdctime instance profile parameter. It is started in a dialog work process. For this reason, it is important that every instance configured for background processing must have at least one dialog work process.

- *Event-driven scheduler.* When the R/3 system receives any events, this scheduler is in charge of checking in the background system for any jobs which must be started after that event. If there are jobs waiting for the event, this scheduler starts them.

  The event driven scheduler also runs in a free dialog work process of any server.
- *Job starter.* The job started is another component of the background system in charge of starting the jobs and performing some preparatory functions for the job such as reading the needed data from the tables and starting the job steps. This object runs in a background work process.
- *Switch operation modes.* This object is used to initiate the switch of operation modes in a dialog work process. This component is triggered by the time-driven scheduler which uses an internal timetable to check if an operation mode has to take place.
- *Zombie cleanup.* This background object is in charge of checking whether there are jobs with the wrong status after a system restart. For example, after a power down and restart of an application server, no jobs should have a ready or active status with an initial start time previous to the restart. The *zombie cleanup* sets the status of those jobs to either finished or canceled.
- *Starter for external programs.* This background object is the component that allows external programs to be started as part of a job step. An external program is started from the background work process in which the job is running.

Every background control object can be maintained separately. The maintenance consists of either defining and activating any of the objects or activating the trace information for them. On the initial screen for background objects, select *Maintain.*

In the first column, the list shows an entry for each host, and in the right column an entry for the object. From this screen, you can create an object by clicking on the *Create* icon, or you can modify the control information of the object.

With the *Action log* button, you can display when the job was last run and when the trace was last activated.

To modify an object, select the object and click on the *Change* icon. The system will display a dialog box will display a dialog box where you can activate or deactivate the object itself or the tracing. To display the list of available traces, you must use the transaction code SM51. You can reach this function from the main menu by selecting *Tools* → *Administration* → *Monitor* → *System monitoring* → *Servers* and then choosing a server and selecting *Goto* → *Traces* from the menu.

The background objects are also stored internally in system tables.

Analyzing Job Performance. Under the Jobs menu in the CCMS is the *Performance analysis* function. With this function, administrators can analyze the runtime of jobs which are either active, finished, or canceled.

When using this function, the system presents a selection screen for delimiting the jobs to be analyzed. Clicking on the *Execute* button will display a list of jobs together with the runtime statistics. If you want to look for additional information about a particular job, just double click over it.

Common Background Job Problems

The following list summarizes some of the typical problems that can be found in the background processing system and the check actions to perform to solve the problem. When no solution is found, log on to the SAPnet system and report your problem.

First, perform the initial checks as the following describes. As a common practice for all of the typical problems, display the job log, the system log, and finally use the CCMS job analysis tool.

- *Job was not started.* First, check the job start time definition and ensure it has a start date and that the user who defined the job has authorization to release it. If the start date has been reached, check that there are free work processes in the background servers, especially if a target host was specified.

  If the job was to be started after an event, define a dummy job to test the event. If there are problems with the sapevt program, check the background objects and enable a trace for the event-driven scheduler.

- *Cannot display the job log.* This can indicate that the job log could not be created in the application server because of wrong permissions, the global directory is not correctly mounted on the application server where you tried to look at the job log, or there are inconsistencies in the TemSe database.
- *Job has been canceled.* Jobs can be canceled for many different reasons. The first step in analyzing canceled jobs is to display the job log to see if there are any error messages. If the message text is not enough, from the menu, select *Goto → Long text.* Common problems relate to runtime errors of the ABAP processors, authorization permissions, inaccessible operating system files when the programs read or write to external systems, and so forth.
- *An external program cannot be started or canceled.* The following R/3 system components play a part in the processing of external programs in a job: the background work process which starts the external program, the background control object, and the SAP gateway which starts the sapxpg program. The sapxpg program is in charge of starting the external program and sending back job information.

  For external programs, you should first check the job log and the system log. Then make sure all the requirements for starting external programs are met. You can use the *Job → Check environment* function to analyze this.

  It is equally important that the sapxpg program lies in the search path of the user which starts the SAP gateway, normally the <sid>adm user, and that the file permissions are correct.

  For external programs running on a different host than the background jobs, the host must communicate with the SAP gateway through the TCP/IP socket and also must allow the remote system to perform *remote shell commands.* This means that an entry is required in the services file in the remote host plus an entry in the .rhosts file in the home directory of the owner of the gateway ID on the remote host.

  Remote commands are started using the command *remsh,* or *rsh,* which is set in the instance profile parameter gw/remsh. You should test at the operating system level whether the target system is prepared to allow the execution of programs from another system.
- *Job remains in status active.* Sometimes you can find jobs with active status even after a system restart. It can also happen that there is an inconsistency between the real status of the job and the entry in the corresponding job table.

In any case, you should verify the real status of the job by looking at the job overview and then selecting the *Check status* function.

If it is an ABAP program, you can try to *capture* it to put it in debugging mode in case it is in an infinite loop status.

In the case of an external program, you should log on at the operating system level and check whether the process is still running there, otherwise you might have a problem starting external programs.

Look at the background object to see if the zombie cleanup is activated. If it is not, create or change the object so that it automatically deletes the zombie job.

CHAPTER 14

The SAP Printing System

SAP provides its own spooling and printing system within the R/3 application to enable a uniform interface for all printing functions, independently of the system platforms supporting both the printing devices and the application services. This is one of the features of the open client/server architecture of the R/3 system.

Printing is an issue within R/3 which should be seriously considered and carefully planned in the early technical implementation phases of the R/3 project. After the R/3 system starts in productive operation, system managers should monitor and manage all the operations related to printing.

Printing functions are intimately associated with and supported by the R/3 spool work processes as well as by the operating system spool system. When an R/3 application server is configured for running at least one spool work process, then it's considered a *spool server.* This does not mean that the application server is not running other types of SAP services. However, there might be installations where there is a heavy printing demand, and one or more dedicated spool servers might be required. These servers can be small, dedicated workstations with a high-speed network connection to the other servers, which are used for connecting and configuring the host printers used by the SAP system.

The next sections of this chapter introduce the SAP spool system architecture, the management and definition of the printing devices and spool servers, and the spool system troubleshooting and planning considerations for a printing strategy.

Among the basic features of the SAP spool system are the following:

- Manages the output requests for printing, for the SAP communication server, and for the archiving devices
- Provides a uniform interface for different host spool systems
- Supports local, remote, and PC printing
- Supports multiple print and output devices, formats, paper types, and character sets

Important features have been added that greatly improve the SAP R/3 spool system functionality over that in version 4.x. Some of these new features can be summarized as follows:

- Better look of spool administration transactions
- Multiple spool work processes per instance
- Open interface to external output management system (OMS)
- Spool accounting exit

- Workload balancing
- Other management facilities

Printing from the user's point of view is covered in the section entitled "User Printing" in Chap. 5.

Elements of the Printing System: Concepts of the SAP Spool System Architecture

Printing in the SAP system is accomplished by the SAP spool system. The SAP spool system is in charge of handling all the system print requests, as well as managing the output for other R/3 components such as the communication server, which can be used for EDI and FAX devices or for the optical archiving systems. The SAP R/3 spool system can also be integrated with external output management systems (OMSs). In release 4.0 and onward, the new access method E implements the spool system's XOM interface to external OMSs. For more details about OMSs, refer to the *R/3 BC Printing Guide.* In this chapter, the spool system is explained from the perspective of the printing needs, which also involves faxing when using fax devices connected to Windows systems, and which actually behave as printer ports.

Handling print requests basically involves the following:

- Formatting the data according to the specified print parameters and for a specific device type
- Sending the formatted data for output to the host system where the printing or faxing device is connected

Figure 14-1 shows a diagram of the spool system operation. This diagram represents how several SAP system components can generate different types of information output ready for printing, such as reports, mail messages, lists, and graphics. When users request printing for the output generated, they are actually sending the request to the SAP spool system. This process is known as generating a *spool request.* These spool requests can either be sent to the host spool, or they can be held in the SAP spool system for later printing.

Two other servers or processes generate special types of spool requests. These servers or processes are SAPcomm (for FAX and EDI) and SAP

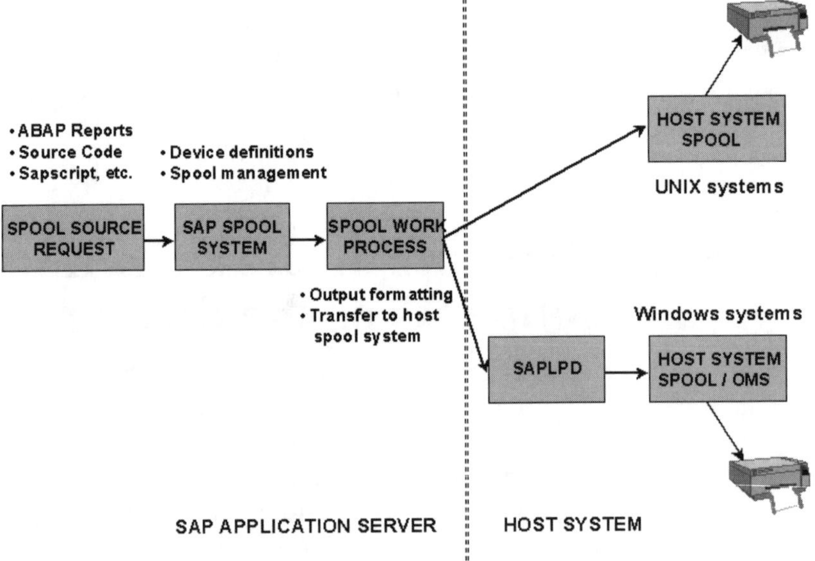

Figure 14-1
The SAP spool system operation.

ArchiveLink (for document archiving). These components use the spool system as a repository.

When a spool request is actually sent to a printer or fax device, it is first passed to the SAP spool work process, which is in charge of formatting the output and then sending this print job to the host spool system. Printers or faxes which are remotely connected in Microsoft Windows systems are first transferred to the SAPLPD transfer program which communicates with the Windows print manager.

If the SAP application server where the spool work process is running and the host system are actually the same server, then this is considered *local printing;* when these systems are different, then it's considered *remote printing.* A special type of remote printing is when the host system is a Windows PC running the SAPLPD transfer program; this type of printing is known as *PC printing.* These types of connections are important for defining the output devices within the spool system and are defined using the SAP access methods.

Printers or other output devices defined in the SAP R/3 spool system have a primary spool server designated—that is, a server with one or more spool work processes running on it. This server is in charge of processing spool requests for those printers and devices. If the primary spool server becomes unavailable, it is possible to specify an alternate spool server in order to process the spool requests from those printers and devices.

The host spool system is the ultimate component in charge of sending the print job to the physical printer. This is basically how the printing system works in SAP R/3. However, even if it might seem very simple, it is actually a little bit more complicated, especially when defining new device types, print controls, formats, and so on, as will be explained in subsequent sections. For now, the following is a closer look at the basic spool and printing system concepts:

- *Spool request* is the SAP naming convention for *output job* or *print job,* but in SAP terms, a *spool request* is made up of the spool request record (administrative information to manage the print jobs), the data which is sent to the printing device, and the actual output requests. A spool request is not necessarily meant just for printing, it can also be generated for other communication or archiving devices.
- *Output requests* are the component of the spool request which actually formats the output data and sends it to the host spool system to be printed. You can submit multiple output requests for a single spool request. You can, for example, have a spool request printed on different printers or reprint a request if it could not be printed successfully the first time.
- *Access methods* are how the SAP spool work process communicates with the host spool system.
- *SAPscript* is SAP's own text editor, which is used for creating and formatting documentation in R/3, such as online help, forms, implementation guide texts, mail messages, and so on.
- *List output* is a generic name for the output which is generated by ABAP reports, and which is not formatted using SAPscript. The spool system handles both types of output: that generated by SAPscript text editor and the results of an ABAP report.
- *Forms* define the page layout for texts, report lists, and the like, which are specially prepared for display or for printing.
- *Layout sets* are maps of the output pages, which specify where the text is placed (filled) on a page and what its attributes are.
- *TemSe* stands for the *temporary sequential* object database, which is a special place where the R/3 system stores the spool request data and other R/3 objects such as the background job logs.

The SAP spool system is not only responsible for handling the spool and output requests, but it's also the R/3 component containing the functions for managing output devices, device types, device drivers and initialization, device formats, character sets, and so forth. It's actually a complete interface which converts all types of SAP output into the required output device format.

The Spool Work Process

Every printer or other type of output device defined in the spool system requires an associated spool work process, which will take care of handling all spool requests for the specific devices. It's also possible to have the same printer defined (with different names) for being managed by different spool work processes. This is sometimes done for contingency situations when an application server might be stopped.

As introduced both in Chap. 2 and in the previous section, the spool work process is one of several types of SAP work processes running on an application server that formats the data in a spool request and then sends it to the host spool system.

Actually, the spool request contains a reference to the data, the specific output device (printer), and the printing format. The data itself is kept in the TemSe database.

When the spool system sends the request for actual printing, it then generates an *output request* (or print request), which is handled by the spool work process. To generate the output request, the spool work process converts the spool request into a device-specific (printer-specific) output stream. Performing this conversion requires:

- Translating (resolving) SAP device print controls into actual printer commands, adding initialization strings corresponding to specific device types
- If needed, converting the character set used within the SAP system to the character set understood by the output device
- Formatting the data for generating the output request using the printer driver assigned to the device type for SAPscript output

The spool work process will finally send the data to the host spool system, and, in the case of PC printing, to the SAPLPD program, which communicates directly with the Windows print manager.

The SAP profile parameter that controls the number of spool work processes per instance is *rdisp/wp_no_spo,* which can be maintained from the CCMS instance profile maintenance utility.

Since release 4.0, you can define more than one spool work process per server even if there is only one instance installed in the application server.

One big advantage of enabling the definition of more than one spool work process is the possibility of sending parallel output requests from the same R/3 instance. Before release 4.0, only one spool work process was allowed per instance; and considering that work processes were not multithreaded, the output requests were sequentially processed, so a request was not handled until the previous one was finished.

Having several spool work processes per instance avoids bottlenecks caused by such things as communication problems between spool work processes and printing devices (PCs, network printers, LAN connections, and others) that could be temporarily turned off or unavailable. With multiple spool work processes, these other requests can be handled by additional free spool work processes.

Before R/3 release 4.0, the spool server assignment and spool server work process were static, so that each device was assigned to a specific server that only had one spool work process. Since release 4.0, it is possible to implement spool load balancing by using spool server groups. This is known as *dynamic spool assignment.*

Spool Servers, Hierarchies, and Load Balancing

As discussed in the previous section, dynamic spool server assignment was introduced with release 4.0, allowing for printing load balancing.

Spool servers provide greater flexibility in defining and configuring printing systems in R/3 installations. Spool servers can be configured on the basis of different attributes, and there is also the possibility of defining different types of spool servers. There are two types of spool servers:

- Real or physical
- Logical

A logical server is mapped directly or indirectly to a real spool server. Logical servers are given a name pointing to another logical server or to a real server. Relationships between spool servers, whether logical or real, define different hierarchies.

A hierarchy is a dependency relationship of different levels that define priorities when spool requests are being managed by the spool servers within the hierarchy.

A hierarchy is established when a spool server, whether logical or real, is assigned an alternative spool server. Hierarchies can be as complex as required.

There is a relationship between a spool server and its alternate spool server. If the server is logical, then there is an additional relationship between the logical server and the server it is pointing to, which can also be either physical or logical. Output requests assigned to logical servers are processed by the real server.

For example, a SAP R/3 system made of two application servers, *ntsap_NT1_00* and *ntsap_NT2_00,* has two logical spool servers *Logical_NT1* and *Logical_NT2.* These logical servers are defined as *Nonexclusive spool servers,* have *Production print* (type P) as their server class, and are mapped to real spool servers *ntsap_NT1_00* and *ntsap_NT2_00,* respectively. Additionally, logical server *Logical_NT1* has *Logical_NT2* as an alternate server. Figure 14-2 shows the hierarchy relationship.

The horizontal relationship represents the mapping between a logical server and another server (either logical or real). The vertical relationship links the logical server with an alternate server (either logical or real).

The definition and configuration of logical spool servers can be performed and tested on development system, then transported to production systems at a later time with minimal and quick adjustments.

When logical servers are defined as *Nonexclusive spool servers,* they are enabled for the process of load balancing, which means that the system will take into consideration both the logical server and the alternate server when calculating and finding the most appropriate server for processing output requests.

Server Selection. When the R/3 printing system is going to process an output request, one of the steps to be performed is selecting the spool server. By default, R/3 commonly has the static selection option for choosing the spool server, meaning that this is a constant definition and does not allow for load balancing.

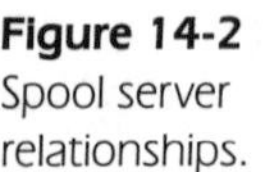

Figure 14-2 Spool server relationships.

Using dynamic spool server selection, the system can automatically balance the load of the spool processes by means of assigning alternate servers.

Dynamic selection of servers has certain limitations when using local R/3 printing, such as access methods C and L. Refer to the latest SAPnet notes and the online printing guide for current status.

Defining Spool Server

To create a new spool server, go to the main spool administration menu by selecting *Tools* → *CCMS* → *Spool* → *Spool administration* from the initial menu (transaction code *SPAD*). Then select *Configuration* → *Spool server* or click on the *Spool server* push button. Switch to change mode by clicking on the *Change* icon. Then click on the *Create* icon on the application toolbar or select *Spool server* → *Create* from the menu.

Fields on this new screen have the following function:

- *System name.* This is the name of the server. You can assign any name, although R/3 normally defaults to hostname_SID_instance_number—for example, *k2p001_K2P_00.*
- *Short text.* This is located right below the system name for entering a brief description of the server being defined.
- *Server class.* Indicates the class of server. Available values are:
  - *V*: High printing volume
  - *P*: Production printing
  - *T*: Test server or test printing
  - *D*: Desktop printing
- *Logical server.* Selecting this flag defines the spool server as a logical spool server. This selection will force users to define the field *Mapping* that will appear when the *Enter* key is pressed or the definition is saved.
- *Mapping.* Only appears when defining logical servers, in which case users must select the server to which a logical server must be mapped.
- *Nonexclusive server.* Activating this option removes the static spool server selection. By default all output devices are handled exclusively by a single spool server. This flag is useful when the primary spool server is unavailable, because the system can redirect the spool requests to an alternative server. This flag is also selected for

enabling printing load balancing. The system will look for the best or least loaded spool server based on the defined spool server hierarchy.

- *Alt. Server.* This is the name of the alternate spool server. It can be used by the system if the primary spool server assigned is not available, so it will be able to process pending spool requests. This alternate spool server can be either real or logical.

Managing Spool Requests

There are several ways of calling the spool request management functions:

- From the main menu, select *Tools → CCMS → Spool → Output management*
- From any menu, select *System → Services → Output controller*
- Directly enter transaction code SP01 in the command field

Figure 14-3 shows an example of this screen.

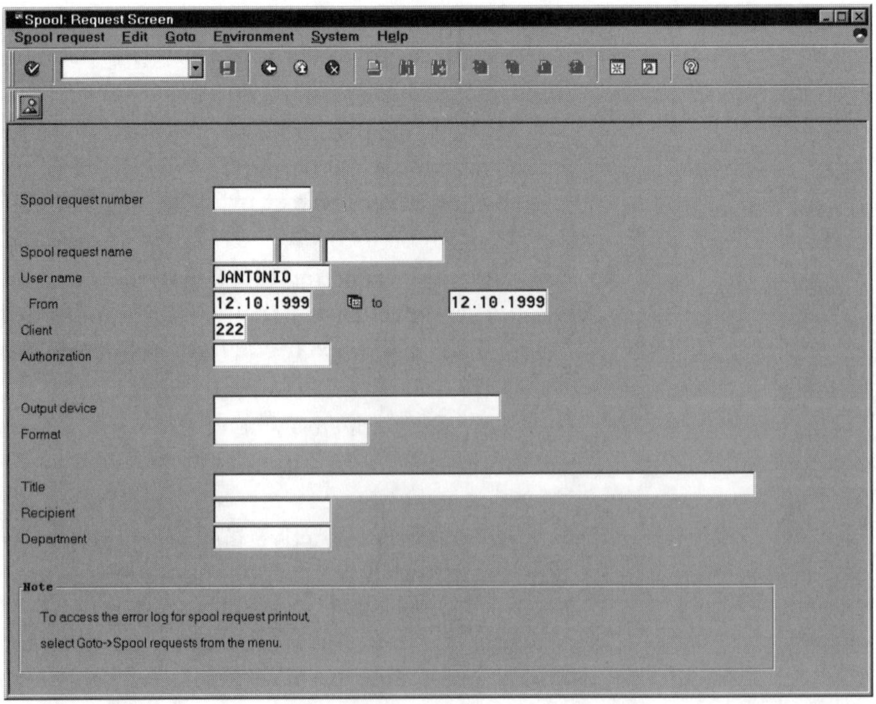

Figure 14-3 Initial output controller display (SP01 transaction).

This initial output controller display behaves like a selection screen, where you can search spool requests by spool request number, spool request name, user name, date, client, and so forth. By default, the screen always presents the logon user name, the logon client, and the system current date—but these parameters can all be overwritten.

Once the selection criteria is entered, just press the *Enter* key or click on the *Overview* (*Continue*) icon on the standard toolbar to display a list of spool requests matching the criteria. The spool requests which have been successfully printed and for which the user had selected the flag *Delete after print* are automatically deleted from the system, and therefore will not appear on this list. On this screen, the system displays information about the spool requests arranged by columns. These columns are

- *Spool no.* It's the spool request number as it has been automatically assigned by the system.
- *Generation date.* Date in which the spool request was generated. This column can be toggled with the client and user name information by clicking on the *User name* push button on the application toolbar.
- *Time.* Time when the spool request was generated.
- *Output status.* Indicates what the status is of the spool request. The system can display the following output statuses:

  ----: For this spool request no output request (order to print) has been generated.

  Wait: The output request is waiting to be processed by the spool system. It has not yet been sent to the host spool system.

  Process: The spool work process is formatting the spool request to be sent to the printer.

  Print: The host system spool is processing (printing) the SAP output request.

  Compl: The output request has been completed and successfully printed.

  <F5>: This status indicates that there is more than one output request for the same spool request. You can double click on this status field to show all the associated output requests or, alternatively, select the check box to the left and click on the *Output request* push button on the application toolbar.

  Problem: A problem has occurred during the output request processing. The printing might have been generated; however, it might not be correct or correspond actually to the expected printed format.

Error: There is a severe printing error. No output request is generated at the physical printer.
Archive: For spool requests that were sent to an archiving device. The spool request has been processed by the spool system and is waiting for archiving.

- *Pages.* Indicates the number of pages of the output request.
- *Title.* Displays the title of the spool request if the user entered one when submitting a spool request, otherwise the system by default shows as the title the type of request, the device name, the program, and the first three characters of the user name.

From this spool request screen, you can perform several useful functions as introduced in the following sections.

Printing and Displaying Spool Requests

To create an output request (to actually send to the printer device), select the spool request from the list by marking the check box to the left of the entry, and then just click on the *Print* icon in the application toolbar or, from the menu, select *Spool request* → *Print.*

There is also the option of sending the output to the printer after actually displaying the spool request on the screen. To do this, from the spool request list, select the entry by marking the check box, and click on the *Display* icon. The system will show the *Spool request <number>* screen. From this new screen, you also have a print icon in the application toolbar.

On the *Spool: Display* screen, you can specify displaying the spool request in hexadecimal format by clicking on the *Display hex.* push button.

By default, the maximum number of lines displayed in this mode is 1000 or, alternatively, 10 pages of a SAPscript document. You can, however, specify a different number by selecting *Number of lines* in the application toolbar.

Displaying and Modifying the Spool Request Attributes

When in the spool request list screen, you can display the attributes for any request by double clicking on the entry. The spool system distinguishes between attributes I and II. Attributes I show the spool request attributes, while attributes II show print request information. You can toggle between the attributes by clicking on the corresponding push button on the application toolbar. Figure 14-4 shows a screen with spool request attributes (I).

From the attributes screen, you can modify the spool request attributes if you want to send the spool request to the printer again (generating a new output request). And, as an interesting point, notice that the attributes display includes an authorization field which can be used to limit which users can access the output request for displaying or printing it again.

The attributes II screen includes information such as the number of copies, priority, SAP title page, or the *Delete after print if no errors* flag.

Displaying Output Request Log Files

If any errors occur during the processing of the spool requests, you can display the log information from the spool request list screen. To do that, double click on the entry to select it, and then select the option *Display log.* You can display more information about the error by clicking on the *More info.* push button on the application toolbar.

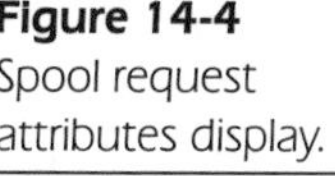

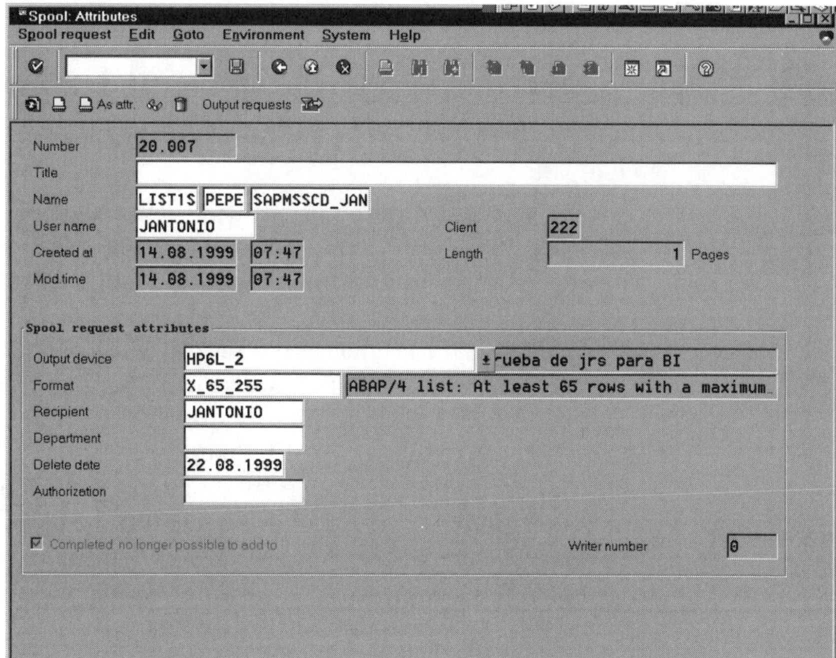

Figure 14-4 Spool request attributes display.

Deleting Spool Requests

There are several ways to delete spool requests:

- Automatically, by setting the flag *Delete after print* when creating output requests.
- Interactively, from the spool request list, by selecting the required entries and clicking on the *Delete* icon.
- Calling the *Spool → Spool Administration* menu from the CCMS initial screen, then selecting the option *Delete obsolete spool request.* The system displays a new screen with several deletion options.
- With the periodic background job RSPO0041. Job RSPO0041 manages the TemSe database, with options for removing any spool data file that is corrupt or orphan.

  When deleting a spool request, the system removes:

- The spool request itself and associated table entries
- The print file
- All output requests that were generated for that spool request

Connecting Printers to the Operating Systems Spool

Before you can define a new printing device in the R/3 system, the printer must be physically installed and configured in the host operating system that is running the host spool system, and thus managing the spool request sent to that device.

Printers can be connected to several types of operating systems: UNIX systems, Windows or Windows NT, AS/400, and others, and can be connected either locally (physically attached to those servers) or remotely (through the network). SAP R/3 supports all those types of connections, although the concept is slightly different. From the point of view of the access methods, *local printing* means that the spool work process is running on the same server as the host operating system spool, and *remote printing* is when the servers are different and connected through the network. A third way, known by SAP as *PC printing,* is when printers are configured on Windows PC systems through the print manager. There is also the option of *local PC printing* even when the printers are not defined at the SAP level.

At the same time, there are many vendors, models, flavors, print protocols, and so on for the printers. Not all understand the same printing language, or support the same printing features and possibilities.

Before you can define a new printer device within the R/3 system, it's absolutely critical that you define, configure, and test the printer on the host system where the printer is connected. Only then can you be sure that the printer can be defined and will function properly within R/3.

For setting up printers on the operating system spool, every hardware vendor and operating system has its procedure. The SAP official documentation (the *BC Printing Guide*) includes instructions on how to set up printers in most of the supported operating systems. You can look in this documentation or the official administration manual of your server operating system for more information.

When printers are not directly connected to the host systems but are connected remotely to the network, commonly they use the TCP/IP protocol. In these cases, you must ensure that the printer is accessed by the network and test that it prints correctly. For instance, their IP address must be included in the *hosts* server file or in the domain name servers.

As requirements for proceeding with the definition of printers within R/3, the following information is needed:

- Printer or spool queue name at the host system
- Model and type of printing device
- Printing protocol supported: PCL, POSTSCRIPT, and so forth

Defining R/3 Printer Devices

For the R/3 system, a printer is defined as an output device, just like a fax or optical archive equipment.

The R/3 system includes an extensive spool administration transaction for defining and managing all aspects of printing configuration and output devices. To call this transaction, from the initial R/3 menu, select *Tools → CCMS,* and then *Spool → Spool administration* or, alternatively, enter transaction code SPAD in the command field. Figure 14-5 shows the initial spool administration screen. It has two parts:

Since release 4.0 it is possible to define the initial screen for spool administration: system managers accustomed to previous releases can

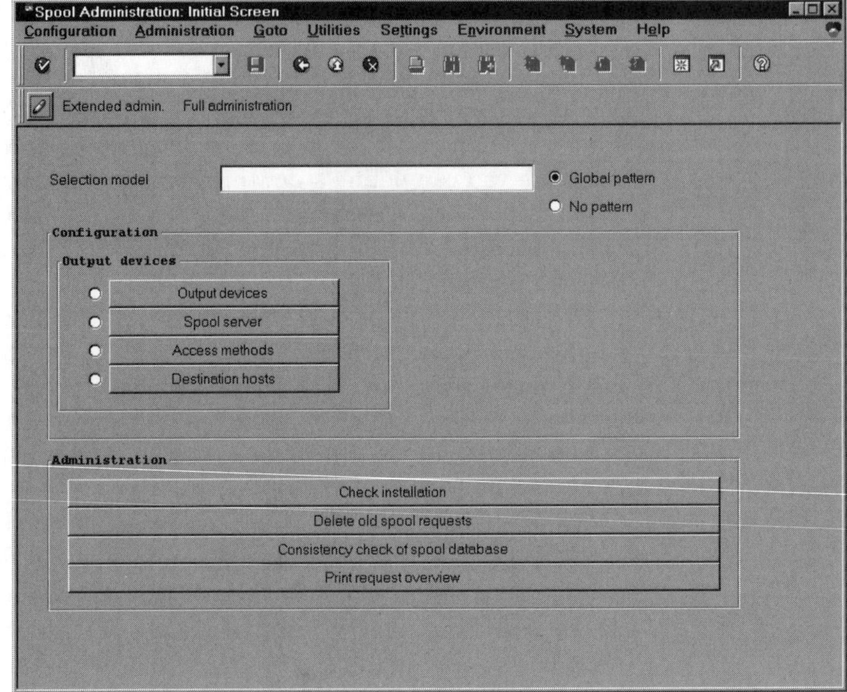

Figure 14-5 The Spool Administration initial screen (SPAD transaction).

use the old initial administration screen or can decide to switch to the new one. To select the initial spool administration screen that will be displayed when calling transaction SPAD, from the menu *Settings* → *Configuration* select the option required.

The initial administration screen has several parts that will show more or fewer components depending on whether simple, extended, or full administration is selected. Fields and options for the simple screen are:

- *Selection model* field. This field is designed as an improvement in the method of selecting spool objects. For example, if there is a collection of device types whose names begin with ZZ, then by entering in the selection model field and selecting the *Global pattern* radio button, it is possible to search for all device types whose names begin with ZZ. If, on the contrary, the *No pattern* radio button is selected, all device types are listed.
- *Configuration.* This includes four items in the simple administration screen that are the only options for output devices:
  - — *Output devices:* this option is used for displaying, managing, and defining devices.

- — *Spool server:* this option shows all spool servers defined in your system, and is also used for creating new spool servers or deleting existing ones.
- — *Access methods:* this option shows all possible access methods, and can display devices or output requests for each existing method.
- — *Destination hosts:* this option displays a list of destination hosts, associated devices, and possible errors.

When full administration is selected, the screen includes additional options for configuration of device types, output management systems, character sets, and text pools for title pages. These options are explained in several sections throughout the chapter.

- *Administration.* The lower part of the screen includes four push button functions that are used for administrative purposes, including deleting old spool requests, performing checks and consistency checks of the spool system, and displaying a list of print requests.

In this section, only the process of creating a new printer—a new output device—is explained. In following sections, all the other options are described with the help of a case study.

To change or create a new printer, from the *Spool Administration* initial screen, click on the *Output devices* push button, or select *Configuration* → *Output devices* from the menu bar. On this screen, select the change mode by clicking on the *Change* icon on the application toolbar. The system will display the list of current output devices. On this screen, click on the *Create* icon for defining a new output device. Figure 14-6 shows the new display.

To define a new output device you must at least fill up the required entry fields (those which include the ? sign). Notice that the system already has filled up some default values.

Fields on this screen are as follows:

- *Output device.* It's the name of the device as it will be known to R/3 users.
- *Short name.* You can enter a four-character short name, just as in releases prior to 4.0.
- *Device type.* Corresponds to the device model for the printer, fax, archive, or other output device. You can click on the possible entries arrow to show a list of available device types as included in the standard system. If the printer you want to connect does not exist and there is no compatible model, you might have to define your own device type.

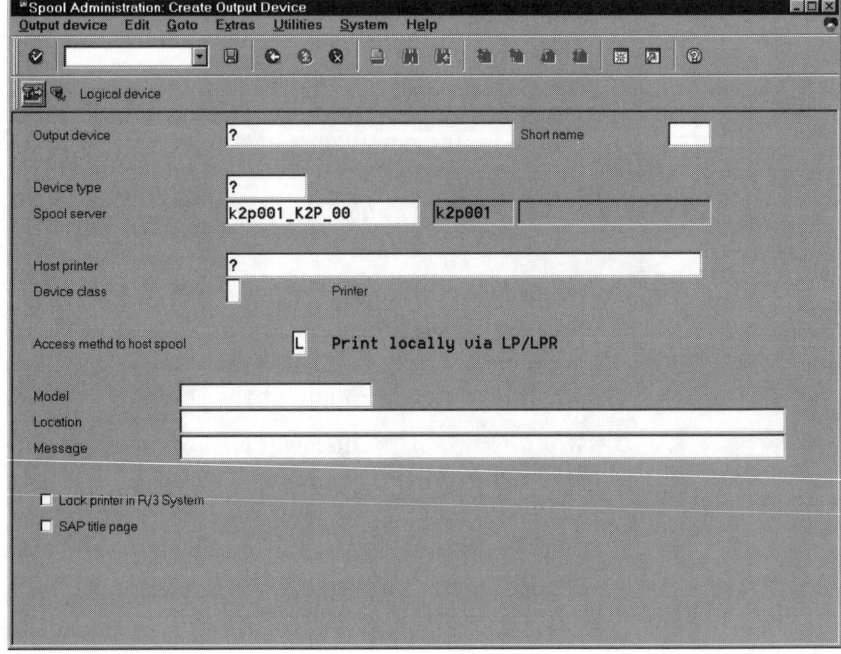

Figure 14-6 Screen for creating new output devices.

- *Spool server.* It's the name of the SAP instance running a spool work process. If there is more than one SAP spool server, you can select it from the available list by clicking on the possible entries arrow.
- *Host.* This is a display field which shows on which host server the spool work process is running.
- *Host printer.* It's the name of the printer exactly as it's defined at the operating system level. In Windows systems, it might be something like LPT1:, LPT2:, or even a UNC name such as \\my-server\myprinter.
- *Device class.* Shows the device type. Figure 14-7 shows the dialog box with the available device classes. For printers, which is the most common class, leave this field blank.
- *Access method.* The access method specifies the communication path between the SAP spool system and the host spool system: it's the method used by the SAP spool to transfer the data to be printed to the host spool system. Access methods specify how and when the print formatting is processed for the subsequent transfer and processing by the host spool system. You can display a list of the available access methods by clicking on the possible entries list arrow.

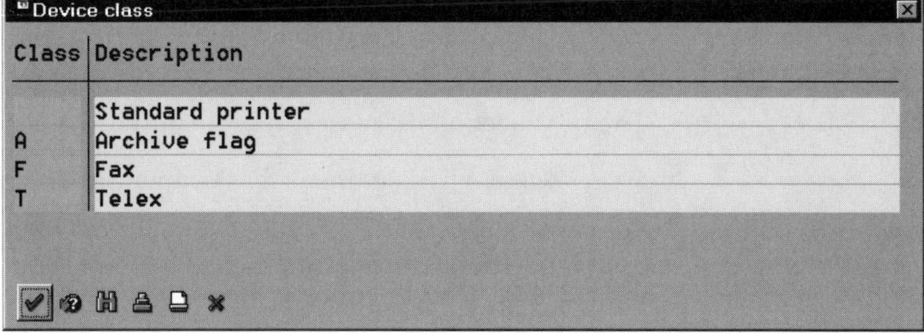

Figure 14-7 Dialog box with available device classes.

For definitions of printers as output devices, you should select between the following:

An access method for *local printing,* that is, when the SAP spool work process and the host spool are running on the same host. In this case you must choose between:

- Access method *L.* Suitable for UNIX systems, where the SAP spool system stores the print job as an operating system file which is sent to the host spooler using the typical lpr or lp commands. The exact command is specified using an instance profile parameter. With method *L,* the SAP system can query the host spooler about the status of the output request.
- Access method *C.* This is used for Windows NT systems and, in this case, no operating system file is generated. The SAP spool system directly passes the data to the Windows print manager.
- Access method *E* is intended for printers that must be connected over an external output management system.
- Access method *F,* known as front end printing, can be used for output requests that should be printed locally on a user's PC.
- Access method *I* is intended for use with archiving devices.

An access method for *remote printing,* as specified when the SAP spool work process runs on a different server than the host spooler. In this case you can choose between:

- Access method *U.* This is remote printing with the Berkeley protocol. If you enter access method *U,* press the *Enter* key. The system will display an additional input field, *Destination host,* where you must enter the hostname where the printer is configured and which is handling the operating system spool requests.
- Access method *S.* This is remote printing using SAP protocol.

  - Access method *X*. This is the method intended for SAPcomm device types.
  - Access method *Z*. This can be used for IBM AFP devices.

  The next section discusses in more detail the access methods.

- *Model name.* This name is for documentation purposes only.
- *Location.* This field is intended for informative purposes only. You can enter a brief description here about the printer and where it's located. This is an optional field.
- *Message.* Together with the previous *Location* field, this is another field for informative purposes which can be used for administrators to display a special message when users select this printer as the output device. It's an optional field. When it is left blank, the system will show the informative text as entered in the *Location* field.
- *SAP title page.* When this check box is selected, the output device by default prints out a SAP title page (a cover sheet).
- *Lock printer in R/3 system.* As an administrator, you can use this field to temporarily lock a printer from being used within R/3.

On the *Spool Administration: Change Output Device* screen, there is an additional screen that can be called by clicking on the Next Screen icon (right arrow near of the upper left corner). Figure 14-8 shows this second screen, where you can specify the following items:

- *Lang. cover sheet.* To specify the language for the text included in the title page (cover sheet).
- *Host title.* If there is a space character, the SAP cover sheet will not be printed. Options D or X force printing of printer defaults or the SAP cover sheet, respectively.
- *Monitoring using monitoring infrastructure.* When this flag is set, the system monitors the spool requests. Some caution must be exercised when using this flag, since massive monitoring of output devices can affect the system's performance.
- *No longer ask for print requests in host spool.* When this option is set, the SAP spool system does not request the output status to the host spool system. Setting this option might be good for performance reasons; however, once the print request is successfully sent to the host spool system, the output controller will not check the actual status of the printing, so that if there is any error at the host system spool, the SAP system will not know.

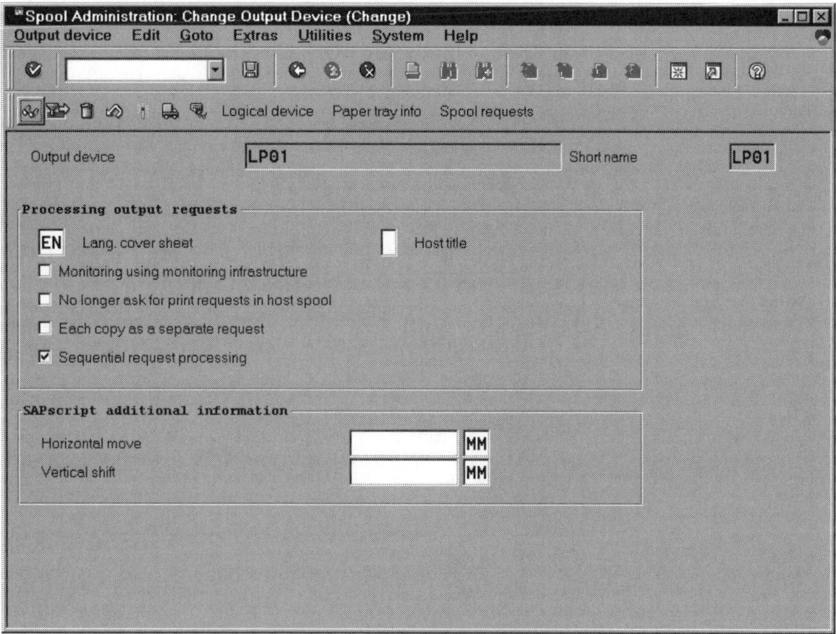

Figure 14-8 Additional options for defining output devices.

- *Each copy as a separate request.* The system can generate as many output requests as the number of copies specified for printing.
- *Sequential request processing.* In R/3 version 4.0 you can have more than just one spool work process for a server. If you want to assure that spool requests generated for a given device are processed sequentially, set this flag. Otherwise spool requests could be reordered during processing.
- *SAPscript additional information.* Options included here are intended for SAPscript, in case you need to change or shift the SAP-script output.

Logical R/3 Output Devices and Device Pools

Since release R/3 4.0 it is also possible to define logical printer devices. Logical printer devices are virtual devices that must be mapped against existing defined printer devices in the system.

When creating a logical printer device, what the system actually defines is a device of access type P or *Pool Device,* mapped against only one physical device. In this sense, a *Logical Device* can be considered as a *Pool Device* with one and only one physical device assigned.

About Pools. Device pools have the purpose of grouping devices of the same type (for example, PostScript printers) using a unique device name, thus permitting the spool requests directed to that pool to be printed by any of the devices assigned to the pool.

This type of device definition is completely equivalent to well-known logical printer queues of many operating systems, where a print job directed to the logical queue is output by any of the physical queues defined for the logical queue.

In SAP R/3, what is assigned to the pool is not the physical printer itself but the output device, which can be either logical or physical. When the device is a logical device, it must be directly or indirectly mapped to a physical device.

A device pool covers two basic functions of the printing devices:

- Sending spool requests to all printing devices associated with a device pool
- Balancing the load of print requests among the devices that make up the device pool, avoiding possible spool bottlenecks

Defining a Logical Printer Device. To define a logical printer device, from the initial *Spool Administration* screen select the option *Output devices.*

Then click on the *Create* icon from the application toolbar. The system displays the *Spool Administration: Create Output Device* screen as shown in Fig. 14-6.

Proceed as usual, by filling in all required fields; then, instead of clicking on the *Save* icon, click on the *Logical device* option in the application toolbar. This will lead you to a new screen, as shown in Fig. 14-9.

In the field *Mapping to,* enter an existing device on your R/3 system and save the new definition.

Defining a Device Pool. To define a device pool, select *Output devices* from the *Spool Administration* initial screen. Then click on the *Create* icon from the menu bar. The system displays the *Spool Administration: Create Output Device* screen.

Fill in the required fields and select P as access method. Save the definition by clicking on the *Save* icon.

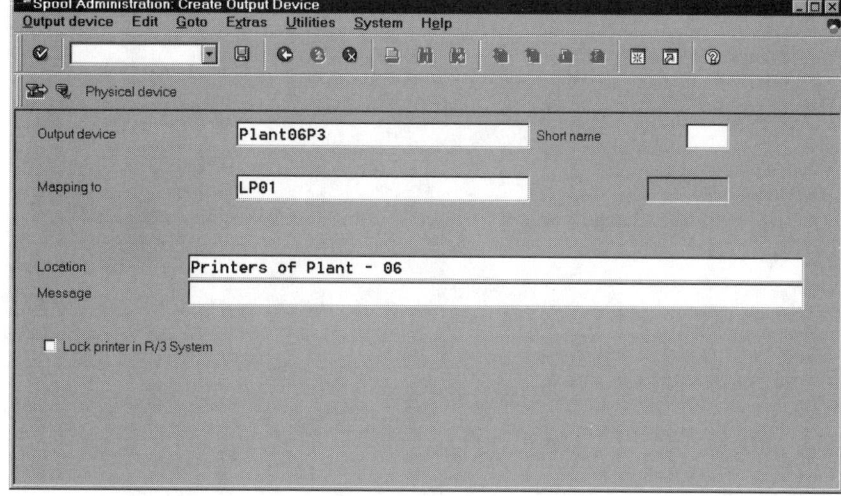

Figure 14-9 Defining a logical device.

The system displays a dialog box with an information message stating that "the device pool must contain at least one device." Click on the *Continue* icon to proceed to next screen.

On the new screen, just as if a logical device was being defined, enter the following information:

- *Mapping to.* You can enter the first printer device of your pool in this field, or leave it empty.
- *Location.* Description information.
- *Message.* Messages to users who use this output device. If this field is empty, then the location message is displayed.

Next, click on the *Physical device* option. The system will display a new screen as shown in Fig. 14-10.

Select *Device pool* from the application toolbar. A new screen will be shown where you will be able to update the device list for the pool just created.

In this new screen, you must also select the pool function:

- *Send to a device pool.* This is the option for balancing printing among devices.
- *Send to all devices in pool.* This option can be used when you need to send the same print job to all devices at the same time.

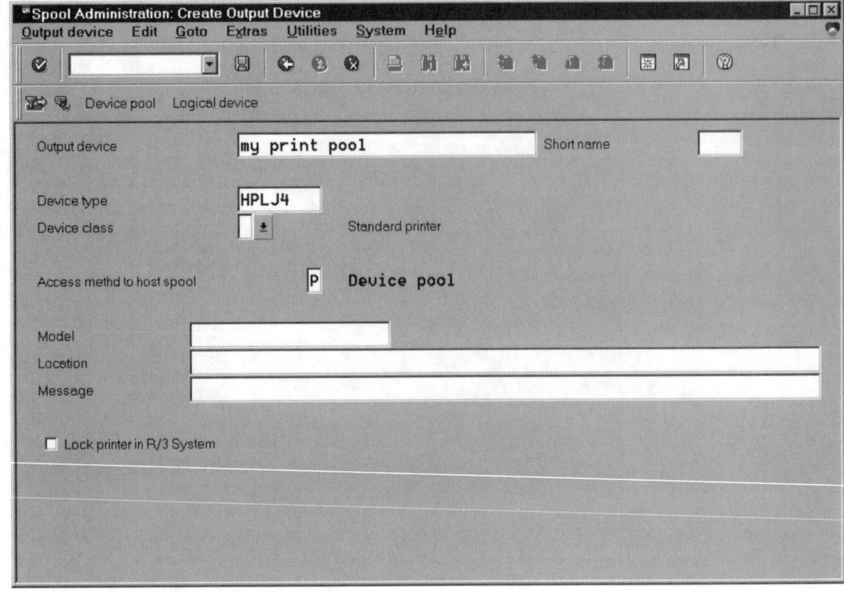

Figure 14-10 Defining the physical device.

Enter the devices on the device list column and click on *Continue.* You will be returned to previous screen. Just click on *Save* to finish the definition of the device pool.

Introduction to the SAP Access Methods

Access methods are very necessary not only for defining the type of printing (local, remote, PC printing), but for defining the printing performance parameter, since the way the data is transferred from the SAP spool to the host spool affects the final throughput. Not all access methods are supported by all the operating systems and types of connections.

A brief description of the available access methods follows:

- *C—Direct operating system call.* This access method is commonly used for local printing when defining output devices which are managed by Windows NT systems. The spool work process and the print manager which drives the printer are running on the same server. This is applicable even to printers which are *shared* in the LAN. Behaves similarly to access method *L* in UNIX systems. Access method *C* does not allow for requesting status information from the SAP spool system to the Windows NT print manager.

- *I—Archive service.* This access method is for defining an output device to be used as an archiving system. You can define a printer as an archive service. When doing this, and users send documents to the spool system, these documents can be transferred directly both to the archive system as well as to the actual printer.
- *L—Print locally via LP/LPR with signal.* The SAP spool work process will use a command to transfer the spool requests to the host spooler. The actual commands, such as lp or lpr, are operating system–dependent, and are set in the SAP instance profile parameter rspo/host_spool/print. Both the spool work process and the host spool are running on the same server. This method is not supported under Windows NT systems, instead you must use access method *C.*
- *P—Device pool.* This special access method is used for defining device pools. This method is available from release 3.0D onward. With device pools, output requests can be sent to more than one printer at a time, and also they can be used for defining several printers to perform automatic print load balancing. Devices that compose a *device pool* must be *local,* which means that they must be accessible from the host spooler or print manager where the spool server resides.
- *U—Print on LPDHOST via Berkeley protocol.* This access method is used for implementing remote printing or even PC printing when the SAP spool work process is running on a different host than the server where the printer is connected. With access method *U,* the spool work process will transfer the formatted data to the target host spooler through the network link. Since there is the possibility of printing large volume jobs, this method is not recommended for slow WAN connections, since it might slow down the processing of other print requests. This method can be used for UNIX, OS/2, and Windows printers; however, it is not supported in some of the operating systems.
- *S—Print on LPDHOST via SAP protocol.* This access method is used both for remote printing and PC printing. It uses a special SAP communication protocol which includes data compression, transmission of the SAP title, and so forth. Access method *S* might be slower than method *U* and is mainly used for printers which are defined using the SAPWIN device type.
- *X—SAP comm.* This method is used for devices which are managed by the SAP spool system and handled by the SAP communication server, such as FAX, Telex, and EDI.

- *F—Print on front end (locally) via SAPLPD.* This is a variant for local or front end printing. This access method is designed for those end users who require printing on their local (or default) assigned or attached printer, which has not been defined on the R/3 system as an output device. In these cases the R/3 dialog work process handling the user process sends the formatted request to the SAPLPD or *lpd* process, according to the type of workstation. If the SAPLPD process was not previously started, the system will start it automatically. More information about local PC printing can be found in a later section.
- *Z—Command interface spool exit.* This method exists for compatibility reasons but is being replaced by access method E from release 4.0 onward.
- *E—Command interface/RFC interface to OMS.* This access method is designed for output requests that will be sent to an output management system (OMS) that is compatible with R/3 printing commands.

Definition and Logical Components of Output Devices

For the R/3 system, the normal operation of an output device (printer) requires that all the logical components are correctly defined and configured. The SAP system includes most of the predefined settings for most output device types, so, actually, administrators only have to define new ones when using devices or special formats or character sets which are not included in the standard SAP system. Figure 14-11 shows a simple diagram of these output devices' logical components. There are some elements which are only needed for SAPscript output.

The next sections deal with these components in more detail. The following list contains an overview of the purpose of each component of an output device:

- *Output device (printer).* It's the actual physical printer as configured at the operating system level.
- *Device type.* The *device type* is actually the interface between the output device and the other components. It contains the full printer characteristics and attributes. A device-type definition can be used for all printers of the same type.

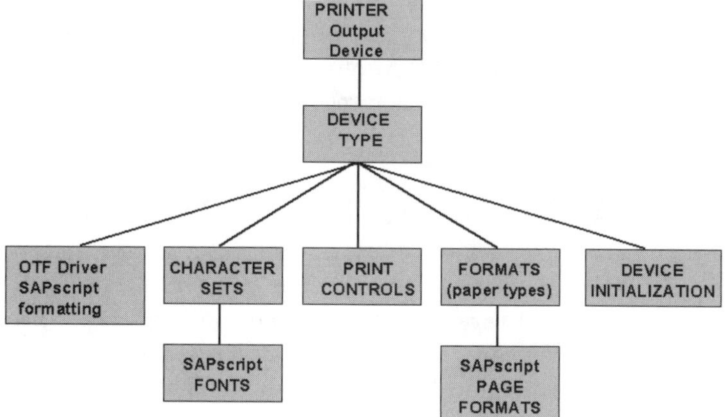

Figure 14-11 Components of an output device definition.

- *OTF driver.* It's the driver used by SAPscript to format output for devices of this type. The name *OTF driver* is derived from the function accomplished, since it is the component in charge of converting the internal SAPscript format—known as Output Text Format (OTF)—to the native format of the device.
- *Character sets.* This component specifies which character sets are available for printing or display in devices of this type. These sets contain the coding which make a device generate a particular character or symbol.
- *SAPscript fonts.* For SAPscript output, the R/3 system maintains its own fonts, font metrics, and character sets, which are used for printing and formatting text with nonproportional fonts. These fonts determine the appearance of the characters: Courier, Times Roman, Arial, and others. If the output device does not support any of these fonts, SAPscript converts them to a similar one supported by the device.
- *Print controls.* This component contains the printer command sets, making them available to the SAP spool system. The command sets contain the escape sequence needed for controlling typical printer operations, such as setting boldface, starting new page, and so on.
- *Formats (paper types).* This component specifies how the output will appear on the paper. It mainly contains the settings for establishing paper sizes, such as *Letter, DINA4,* and so forth.
- *SAPscript page formats.* It's only used by SAPscript output and specifies the printable area and whether the orientation of the format is portrait or landscape.

- *Device initialization.* This is the group of printer commands which are used for configuring a particular output device for printing within the SAP system. A device initialization is made up of the device-type definition together with the defined formats.

Defining New Device Types

Creating a new device type is needed in those cases when the SAP standard software does not include your particular printer or device type. A new device type can be defined either from scratch or by copying an existing one and then modifying it. The same device type can be used for printers which are of the same model.

To define a new device type, from the initial *Spool Administration* screen, select the *Full administration* screen by clicking on the corresponding button on the application toolbar. With *Full administration* you can display the device type options. Next, select the *Device types* push button. The system displays the available device types. On this screen click on the *Change* icon.

To define a new device type from scratch, click on the *Create* icon on the application toolbar. If you want to define it based on another similar device, click on the *Copy from* push button. After selecting one of the two options, you will get a new screen where you can enter the new device type, name, and other data such as driver for SAPscript and printer character set. Depending on the option selected, the new screen will be either the Create device type screen, where none of the screen fields have default values, or the Copy device type from XXXXXX screen, where default values inherited from the source (copied) device are used. Figure 14-12 shows what this screen looks like when a device type is being created from scratch.

Enter a name following SAP standard naming conventions for customer objects (starting with character *Z*) and right below, there are the following fields:

- *Name.* Enter here a brief definition or description for the device type.
- *Driver.* Name of the print driver for SAPscript. The driver makes the conversion from the output format of SAPscript OTF to the print format of the device type. Clicking on the possible entries list arrow displays the available standard entries.

  The most common drivers for defining new device types for common printers are

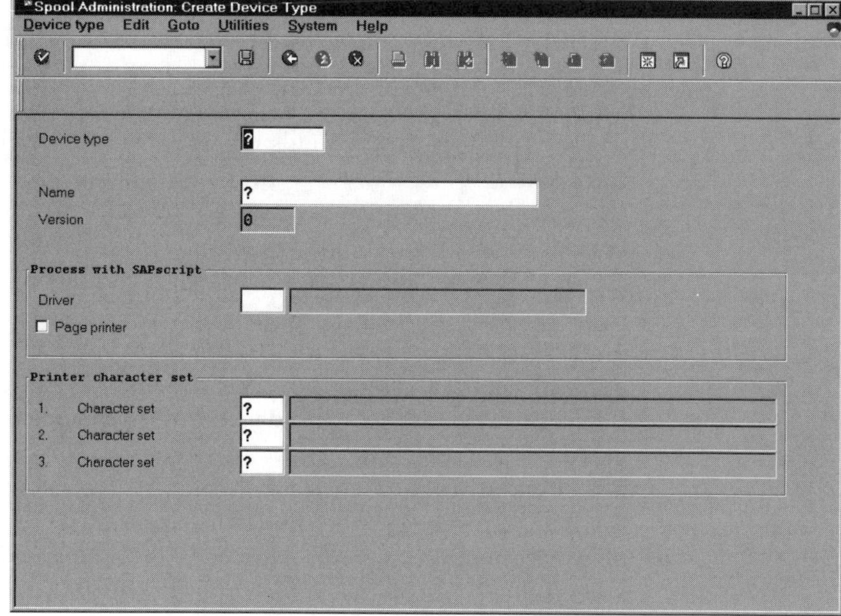

Figure 14-12 Screen for defining a new device type.

- *HPL2.* For standard HP Laserjet printers working in HP PCL4 or PCL5 printing formats or for compatible printers.
- *POST.* For standard POSTSCRIPT printers.
- *PRES.* Drivers for Kyocera printers working in PRESCRIBE mode.
- *STN2.* Standard driver for line printers (new driver).
- *STND.* Standard driver for line printers (old driver).

- *Page printer.* You can select this check box when the printer device is capable of preformatting a whole page or document before it's actually printed, for example, with the POSTSCRIPT drivers.
- *Printer character set.* Since printers might use different character sets than those of the application servers or host systems, the spool system needs to indicate the character set for the device types. In this field, you must enter the code for the character set which is supported by the device type. You can look up the list of supported character sets in the printer manual.

The character set represents the possible characters used by the system with its equivalence in the ASCII or EBCDIC coding. The ASCII character set might vary among different vendors. There are several widely used codes according to some standard normalization organizations, such as ISO, but also some vendors have come out with their own character sets and coding, such as IBM, DEC, HP, SNI, or SAP itself. You can click on the possible entries arrow to display the list of available character sets.

There are three input fields for character sets. Only the first is used by the system, so normally the three input fields have the same value. The character set chosen for the device type must be supported by the printers using such device types. For example, if for a Digital printer you select the character set code 2101, check that it corresponds to the character set supported by the printer, either in native mode or by emulation. For instance, for device type DECLA75P, there is the character set 2101. This character set represents the correspondence between the characters and their ASCII representations, depending on the printer type and operative mode. For example, the character *1* (one) is represented in ASCII as the hexadecimal value *31* or decimal value *49*. Generally the ASCII codes for the first 128 values (from 0 to 127) are quite standard. The most noticeable differences start in the extended ASCII mode, when representing the special characters, tildes, umlauts, national characters, and so on.

You can display and compare the character sets with the device type being defined from the *Spool Administration* (full administration) screen by selecting the radio button *Character sets,* and then clicking on the *Display* button. The system displays a list with all available character sets. For example, select character set *2103* and then the option *Edit character set.* The system displays the character set definition for the code 2103 as shown in Fig. 14-13.

Once fields have been filled in, just click on the *Save* icon. The system will then display the common dialog boxes for entering the development class and the change request number.

Managing Printer Character Sets

The standard SAP R/3 system includes many character sets. It is only necessary to include new character sets when new devices to be connected only support different character sets.

Defining a new character set will be available for use in the spool system. There are two ways to associate a character set to a printer or to an output device.

- Enter the character set code in the device-type definition, just as mentioned before.

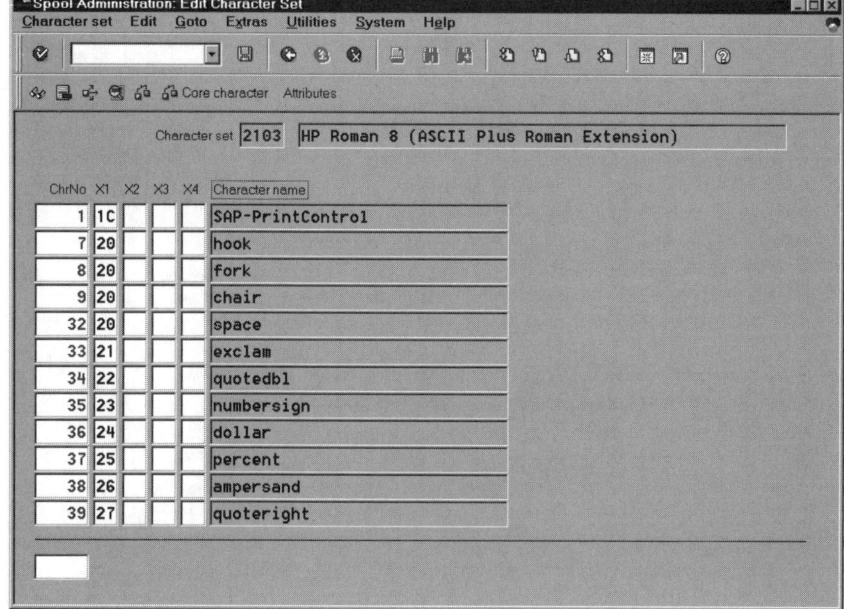

Figure 14-13 Displaying character codes for a character set.

- Select a character set code using the SAPscript print controls S0000 or SF<nnn>.

When creating a character set, you have to enter the manufacturer name from the list of manufacturers. You can display this list by selecting the option *Char. set manufacturers* from the initial *Spool Administration* screen.

If the manufacturer's name is not on the list, you can create it. From the *List of manufacturers* screen, click on the *Create* button. Enter the data for *Manufacturer* and a *Short name* and save your entries.

The next step is to define the new character set itself. From the initial Spool Administration menu, select the *Character sets* push button. The system will display the *List of character sets* screen, as shown in Fig. 14-14.

The new character set can be created from scratch using the *Create* option, or you can define it based on an existing one using the *Create from* option, which might be easier.

Selecting the *Create from* option, the system will display a new screen like the one shown in Fig. 14-15. As can be seen, most fields already have the default value as assumed from the original. On this screen, a new code for the new character set should be assigned using the customer number range, from 9000 to 9999. Values in the other entry fields can be over-

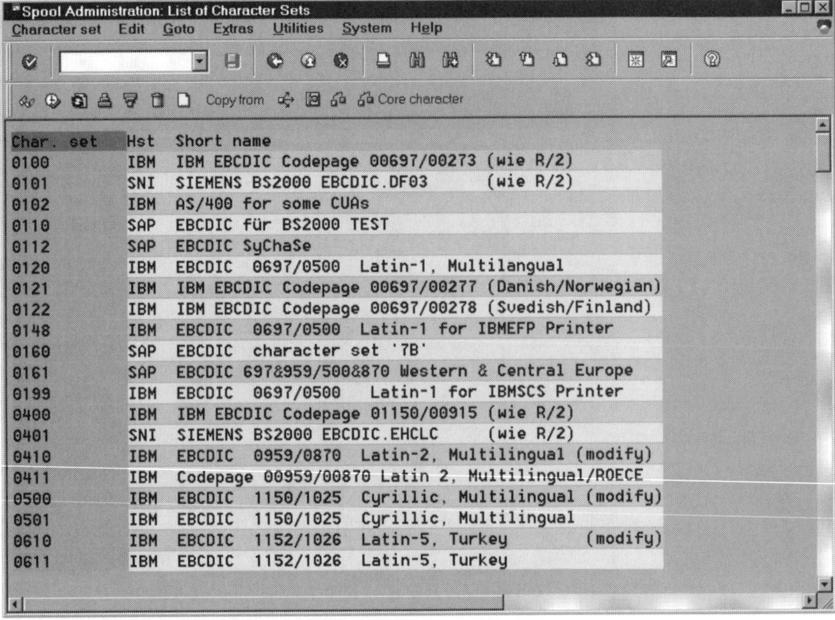

Figure 14-14
Standard list of character sets.

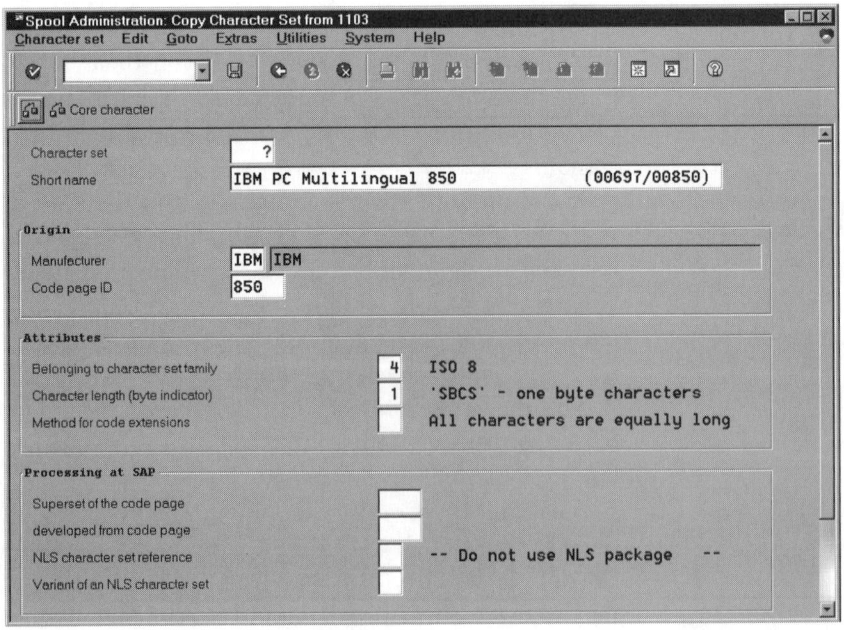

Figure 14-15
Creating a character set from a copy.

written with your own new values. In the *Short name* field, enter a brief description for the new character set.

For a detailed description of the purpose of the other fields on this screen, please refer to the SAP official online documentation in the *BC Printing Guide.*

Once the new character set is defined, the system returns to the *List of Character Sets* screen, where you can edit the new character set by selecting the *Edit character set* function on the application toolbar. If it's a newly created character set, then you have to fill up the equivalence table or, if the character set was created using the *Create from* option, adjust those values. As an example, Fig. 14-16 shows the first part of the Digital character set 2101. On this screen, you can see several columns:

- *ChrNo* is the character number in decimal format for the ASCII equivalent to the symbol (character) defined.
- *X1* has the same coding, but in hexadecimal form.
- *Character name* includes the short description for the characters.

Character sets must be activated to take effect. Please refer to the SAP R/3 *BC Printing Guide* for more information.

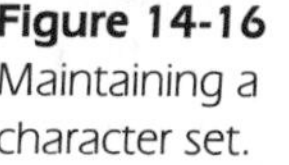

Figure 14-16 Maintaining a character set.

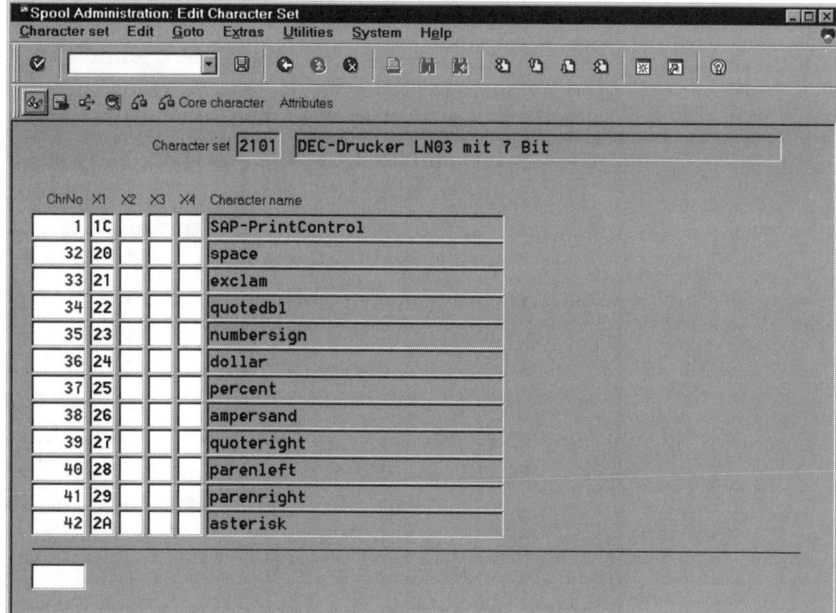

Character Set Naming Convention. Character sets created by customers must begin with 9. However, standard character sets follow a naming convention made up of four digits.

- First number is the basic code range:
  0 - EBCDIC
  1 - ASCII
  2 - Single-byte and double-byte character sets
  4—Double-byte character set
  9—Reserved for code pages defined by user
- Second number specifies a country range:
  1–3: Countries with Latin alphabets (North and South America, Western Europe, Africa, and Australia)
  4–6: Counties with non-Latin alphabets (Eastern Europe, Asia, Arab countries)
  7–9: Reserved for special languages
- Third and fourth digits make up a sequential number.

Working with Print Controls

The SAP R/3 provides a standard set of *printing controls* which behave like sequences of printing instructions, which are converted or translated into escape commands sequences controlling how text is printed by the specified output device. These escape command sequences must be compatible with the printer-specific language—the printer must understand these escape commands.

The print controls can manage such things as font size, bolding, italics, underline, and so on. For example, assume that you want to use a print control that tells the printer to print with a 12cpi font, italics, and normal intensity; this print control could be defined as *SF012*. According to the target output device, the content for this print control might be different; for instance, if the target printer is a Digital LA210, the print control must include an escape command sequence such as *1B5B32771B5B317A;* if the target printer is an HP LaserJet or an IBM Proprinter, then the escape sequence is different. This fact indicates that with the same print control, you can work with different types of printers and get the same result, making the definition of the escape sequence completely independent of the result of a report or form within the R/3 system. In fact, the print controls are the technical translations (mapping) between the SAP world and the output devices.

Print controls are used both for printing SAPscript text as well as for other types of print output, such as reports. The SAPscript output uses print controls which are distinguished by standard SAP naming conventions: all print controls for SAPscript start with the character *S.*

Once a new output device has been created, it's necessary to assign it the print controls. There are two ways to assign print controls:

- Create them, one by one, from the *Edit Print Control* screen
- Create them by using a copy from a similar device and then modify the needed controls

Defining New Print Controls. To define new print controls, from the initial *Spool Administration* screen, click the push button next to *Device types.* The system displays a list of devices. Select the device for which you want to create the print controls and click the *Print controls* button on the application toolbar. The system displays a new screen, *Edit print controls,* as shown in Fig. 14-17. On this screen, you find the following columns:

- *PrtCtrl.* It's the name for the print control sequence.
- *V (variant).* This field indicates how the escape sequences are to be handled:

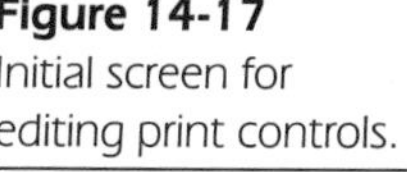

Figure 14-17 Initial screen for editing print controls.

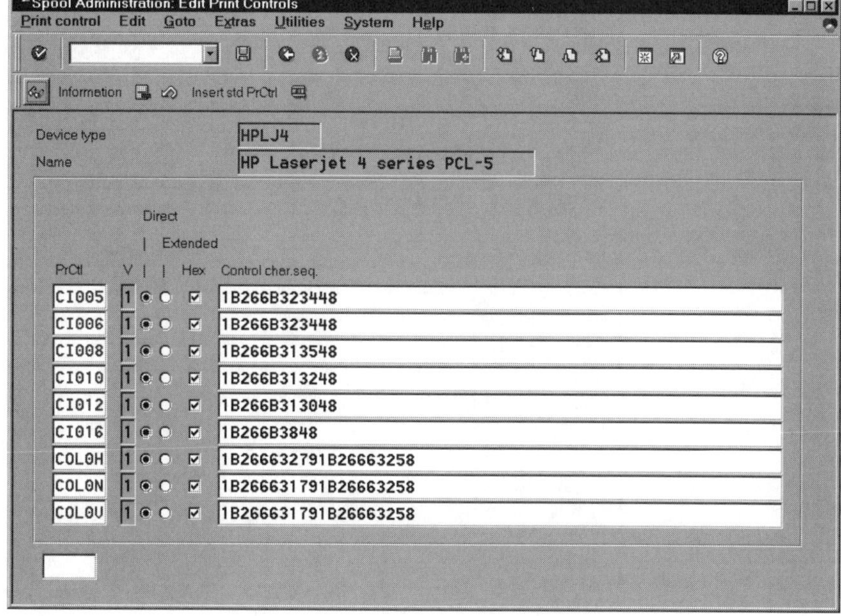

1: Enter the print control as defined in the text. All the SAPscript print controls are defined using this variant.
5: The control code is entered only once in the text, based on a prefix (ESCAP) and a SUFFIX.

The value of the variant field is set by activating the radio button to the right of the field. The first radio button (*Direct* column) sets a value of 1, and the second radio button (*Extended* column) sets a value of 5.

- *Hex.* This option is the escape sequence containing hexadecimal data.
- *Control char. Seq.* This field is used for entering the appropriate escape sequence according to the specifications for the print control. For example, for the device ZDECMT60 in Fig. 14-18, the print control *SF002* has the escape sequence *1B5B34771B5B317A*. This is an escape control sequence for a Digital DEC LA210 printer working in native mode. This sequence defines the *Horizontal Pitch* and the *Vertical Pitch*. Thus, the sequence *1B5B* represents the character *CSI,* which is the same as the combination *ESC[*. Next, the hexadecimal values *34* and *77* indicate that characters must be written with 8.25 characters per inch. The next control sequence, after the

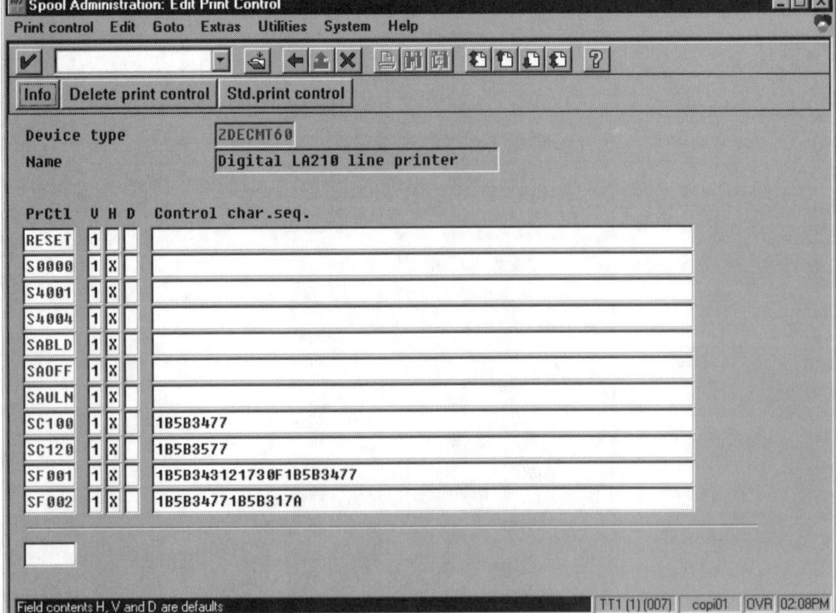

Figure 14-18 Editing print controls after a standard print control was transferred.

second *1B5B,* is the set for the vertical pitch, *31* and *7A,* which indicates to write 6 lines per inch.

When a new print control which was not included in the standard SAP R/3 system is defined, first it must be created with the option *Insert standard print control.* Upon choosing this option, the system displays a list of missing standard print controls for the device.

To define a new print control, select one from the list of standard print controls by double clicking on it. The system automatically includes it in the print control list, where you can edit it and set the needed values. For example, if you select the standard print control *RESET,* the system goes back to the previous screen and inserts it in alphabetical order.

Predefined Print Controls. This section is taken from SAP documentation. (Copyright by SAP AG.)

The list below shows the print control keywords that have been predefined by SAP for use in the SAP system editor and in ABAP PRINT-CONTROL statements. You should not alter the use of any of these keywords. Otherwise, printing may produce unpredictable results.

Note that SAP*script* uses its own private set of print controls when it formats text for output. These print controls are listed separately in the next section.

- **<xx>BEG:** Per formatting group, marks the start of a region that is to be formatted. Reserved for future use.
- **<xx>END:** Per formatting group, marks the end of a region that is to be formatted. Reserved for future use.
- **BAROF:** Ends bar code printing.
- **BARON:** Starts bar code printing.
- **BC<nnn>:** Prints a barcode.
- **CI<characters>:** Specifies the character pitch (characters printed per inch). The character pitches in existing CI print controls are three digit numbers which are read without a decimal place. For example, character pitch 10 is represented by the control code CI010. The system reads the value as "10".
- **CO<nnn>:** Obsolete. Has been replaced by predefined print controls COL<xx> of the FORMAT instruction.
- **COL<xx>:** Sets list colors for color and halftone printing. These print controls are associated with the ABAP statement FORMAT.
- **ESCAP:** Defines the prefix for an escape sequence.

- **FO<nnn>:** Specifies the font.
- **LI<lines>:** Specifies the leading (lines printed per inch). The leadings in existing LI print controls are three digit numbers which are read without a decimal place. For example, a leading of six lines to the inch is represented by the control code LI006. The system reads the value as "6".
- **LM<nnn>:** Sets the left margin.
- **RESET:** Reset sequence for returning a printer to its standard settings.
- **SABLD:** Starts boldface printing.
- **SAULN:** Starts underlining.
- **SAOFF:** Stops boldface printing and underlining.
- **SEPAR:** Defines the separation character to place between consecutive printer control codes.
- **SI<nnn>:** Font size. The font sizes in existing SI print controls are three digit numbers which are read without a decimal place. There is no convention for entering font sizes at this time. Select SI001 for a normal font size, SI002 for a larger font.
- **SUFFX:** Defines the suffix for a printer control code.

SAPscript Print Control List. SAPscript reserves the use of the print controls for the drivers that are used with the different device types. For information on other reserved print controls, please refer to the SAP online documentation *BC Printing Guide.*

There is a special print control which deserves a special mention. With the *SF<nnn>* print control, it's possible to define specific user fonts with SAPscript for a particular output or print device, assigning a user-defined control sequence. To make the SF<nnn> print control available for SAPscript, it must be entered within the *SAPscript font maintenance function.*

This is demonstrated in the case study described later in this chapter.

Managing Page Formats

Page formats are used for specifying page attributes, such as the orientation and the size. With this information, SAPscript can distribute and fill the page so that the text can fit correctly. For example, a page format can be used or defined for printing four labels on a page. If you use a standard page format for this operation, the standard listing for the labels is truncated. However, with a page format that widens the logical print window for SAPscript, the operation can be successfully completed.

To define a new page format, from the initial *Spool Administration* screen, click the *Page formats* button. The system displays the *List of Page Formats* screen.

On this screen, you can either click on the *Create* push button or the *Copy from* push button. The system shows a new screen for creating a new page format. In Fig. 14-19, the format from the standard *INCH4* was chosen to copy. The following fields must be filled up:

- *Page Format.* Name for the new page format, according to the permitted value range for customers, for example, *ZINCH4*.
- *Orientation.* Page orientation, which can be either portrait or landscape.
- *Paper size.* Width and length of the paper, entering both the value and the measurement units, must be specified. You can select between inches, characters, millimeters, centimeters, or points.

To use page formats with SAPscript, the name must match the name defined for the corresponding format (paper type) as explained in next section.

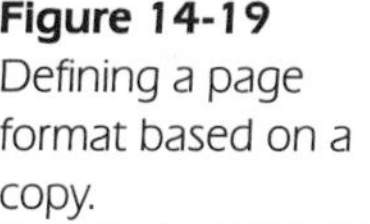

Figure 14-19 Defining a page format based on a copy.

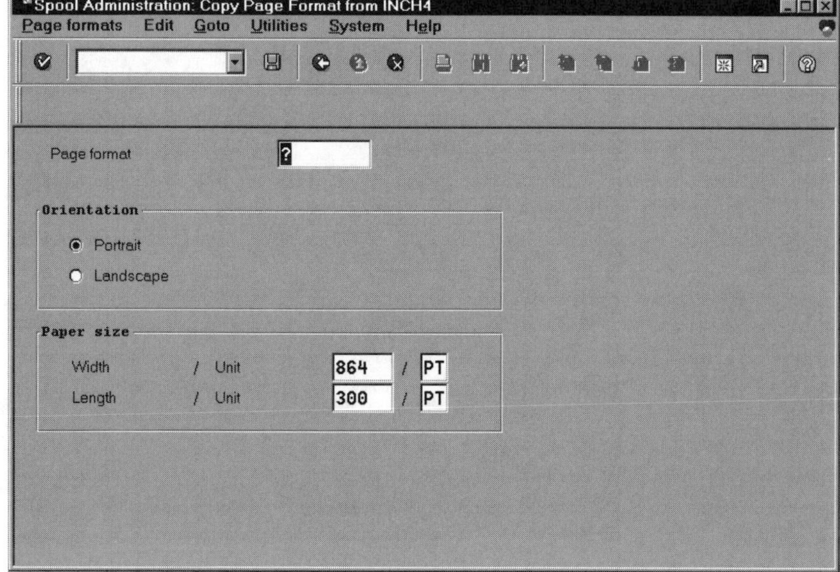

Managing Formats

To be able to perform the *Device initialization* function, it is necessary to have some formats (paper types) defined. In other words, for initializing any device type defined in the system, thus making it available for printing, it must have an associated output format that was previously defined.

When defining a format, you need to identify which page format is going to be used, so that it can be assigned the right orientation. For example, the paper type *DINA4* can be used with two page formats *DINA4,* one with landscape orientation and the other one with portrait orientation.

To display or manage available paper types, from the initial *Spool Administration* screen, select the *Formats* button. Figure 14-20 shows the list of the standard defined paper types.

The SAP spool system reserves the paper type formats starting with an *X* for printing ABAP lists and reports. For example the *X_65_80* format means to print every page with 65 lines and 80 characters wide. The *X* formats use nonproportional fonts, assuming that printers use a 12-inch paper length.

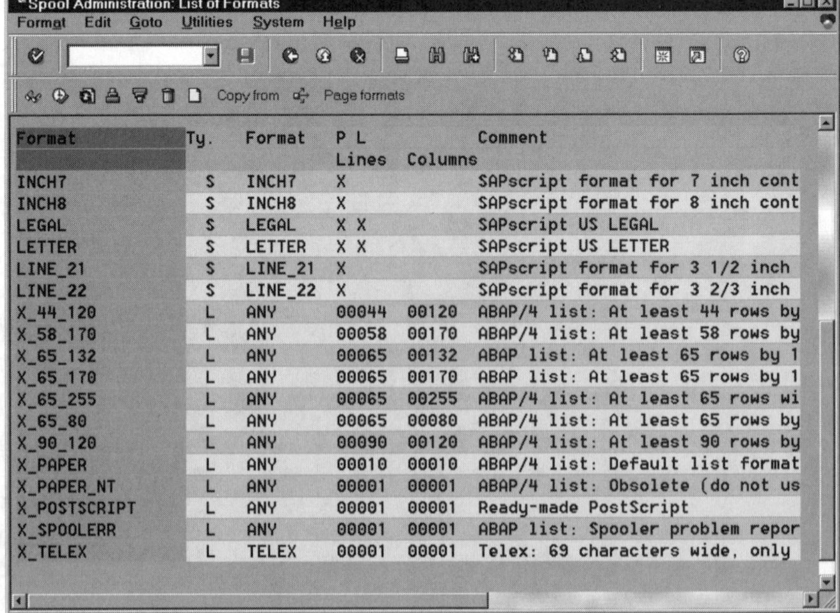

Format	Ty.	Format	P L Lines	Columns	Comment
INCH7	S	INCH7	X		SAPscript format for 7 inch cont
INCH8	S	INCH8	X		SAPscript format for 8 inch cont
LEGAL	S	LEGAL	X X		SAPscript US LEGAL
LETTER	S	LETTER	X X		SAPscript US LETTER
LINE_21	S	LINE_21	X		SAPscript format for 3 1/2 inch
LINE_22	S	LINE_22	X		SAPscript format for 3 2/3 inch
X_44_120	L	ANY	00044	00120	ABAP/4 list: At least 44 rows by
X_58_170	L	ANY	00058	00170	ABAP/4 list: At least 58 rows by
X_65_132	L	ANY	00065	00132	ABAP list: At least 65 rows by 1
X_65_170	L	ANY	00065	00170	ABAP list: At least 65 rows by 1
X_65_255	L	ANY	00065	00255	ABAP/4 list: At least 65 rows wi
X_65_80	L	ANY	00065	00080	ABAP/4 list: At least 65 rows by
X_90_120	L	ANY	00090	00120	ABAP/4 list: At least 90 rows by
X_PAPER	L	ANY	00010	00010	ABAP/4 list: Default list format
X_PAPER_NT	L	ANY	00001	00001	ABAP/4 list: Obsolete (do not us
X_POSTSCRIPT	L	ANY	00001	00001	Ready-made PostScript
X_SPOOLERR	L	ANY	00001	00001	ABAP list: Spooler problem repor
X_TELEX	L	TELEX	00001	00001	Telex: 69 characters wide, only

Figure 14-20 List of available formats.

Formats for SAPscript. For SAPscript, the names of *Page formats* and *Formats (Paper types),* must match; for example, the customer page format *ZINCH12* must have a corresponding customer format also known as *ZINCH12.*

The list of the standard formats used by SAPscript can be found in the *BC Printing Guide* within the online documentation.

Device Initialization

A device initialization in the SAP spool system consists of associating a device type with a format, to which a set of initialization commands is assigned which are specific for the output device.

From the full administration setting of the *Spool Administration* screen, click on the *Device types* button. The system will display the list of device types. Select the device to be associated with a format by positioning the cursor over its name, and click on the *Formats* push button on the application toolbar. A new screen appears, showing the list of *formats* for device types defined for selected device type. You can select any format from the list by double-clicking on the *format* required. The system will display a new screen for maintaining the format associated with the device type. Figure 14-21 shows an example.

On this screen, there are certain lines which have a check box already selected. Each one of these lines represents a set of commands or escape sequences for the device type, which are meant to perform the assigned functions described to the right of every line, for example, the function *Printer initialization.*

You can display or edit the available functions. To edit, click on the line and select the *Edit* option or just double click on it. The system displays the edit screen for the control file (escape sequences) for the selected function for the device. In Fig. 14-22, you can see the edit screen for the function *Printer initialization.*

Special Characters for Device Initialization and Printing Controls. Table 14-1 shows the list of special characters and their descriptions for device initialization. A practical example of generating an initialization for a device can be seen in the following case study.

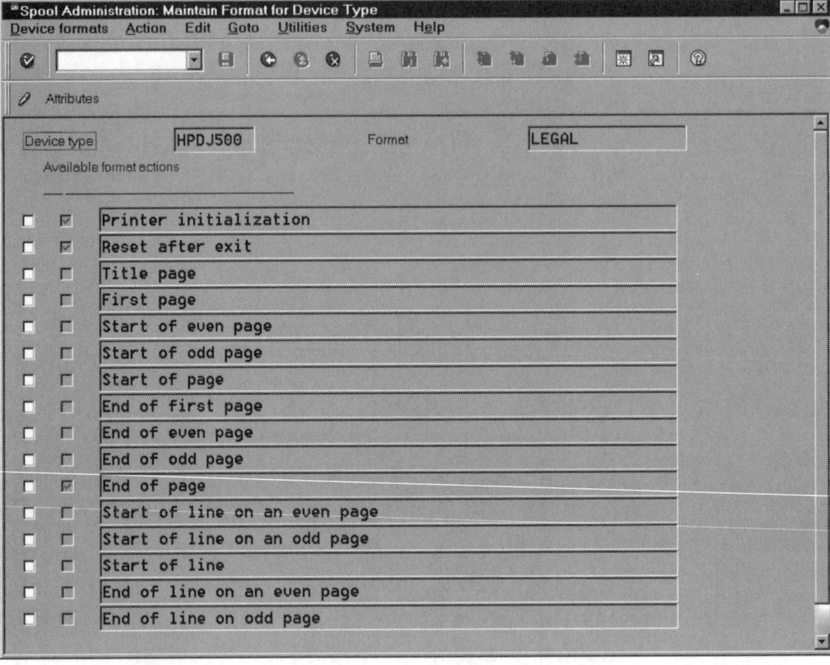

Figure 14-21 Maintaining formats for device types.

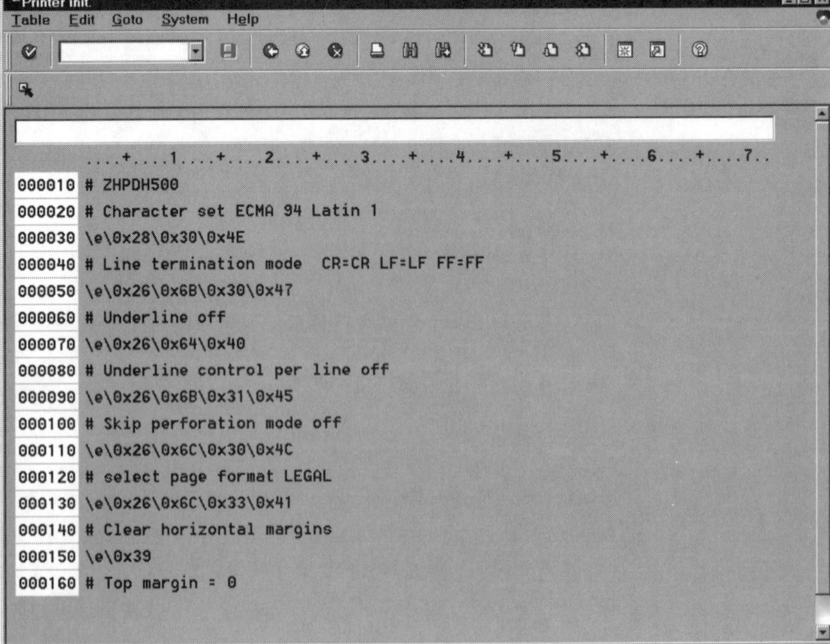

Figure 14-22 Escape sequence for printer initialization.

TABLE 14-1

Special Characters for Device Initialization

Character	Description
\e	Escape symbol. The hexadecimal value is 1B.
\0x	Indicates that the next two characters represent a hexadecimal number (a byte). If *Convert flag* is set in the output device definition, the character set of the hex characters is automatically converted at output.
\0y	Indicates that the next two characters represent a hexadecimal number (a byte). The character set of the characters is never converted. The characters are transferred to the output device in the representation of the character set in which they were stored.
#	Comment (first character in a line). This line is not sent to the output device.
\n	New line (line feed). Hexadecimal value *0A*.
\r	Carriage return. Hexadecimal value *0D*.
\f	Form feed. Hexadecimal value *0C*.
\s	Space character. Hexadecimal value *20*.

Case Study: Defining a Printer and Creating a New Device Type for It

In this example, a new device type for supporting the DEC LA210 printer is defined. The settings which have been configured for this printer are just one set out of many other possible settings, which were configured this way for the particular needs of an installation.

When trying to define a new printer for the R/3 system, first you have to check if the model already exists as a device type. To check this, use transaction SPAD and display all available device types. In this case, since it does not exist, a new device type must be created.

The easiest and fastest way to define a new device type is by copying it from a similar printer type and then modifying it. This process requires the following steps:

1. Definition of the device type
2. Definition of the print controls for the new device type
3. Device initialization for the formats
4. Fonts used for SAPscript.

Definition is started from the initial *Spool Administration* screen using the well-known transaction SPAD. Click on the *Full administration* button to switch to full administration if you don't get the additional options.

To define the new device type for the DEC LA210 printer, the Mannesmann Tally MT600 printer, which has similar features, was used. To copy the definition of this device type, from the initial *Spool Administration* screen, select *Utilities* → *For dev. types* → *Copy device type* from the menu bar. The system shows a new screen, like the one in Fig. 14-23.

In the *Copy device type* input field, enter *MT600,* and in the target field *to device type,* enter *ZDECMT60.* Then, click on the *Execute* icon and proceed generating the device type. When executing this function, the system will display a list with the number of entries copied.

You can go back to the initial screen by clicking twice on the *Back* icon in the standard toolbar or pressing the F3 function key twice.

Once you have the new definition based on a copy, you must proceed with modifying the definition to adapt it to the specific characteristics of the new printer. To do this, select *Device types* button. The system will display the list of available device types. Scroll down until you find the new device, ZDECMT60. Double click on this device to modify it.

The system will display the new device with exactly the same settings as for the original device from which it was copied. Change the description in the *Name* field and leave the driver as *STN2,* which corresponds to a line printer.

Also change the character sets to a compatible code, for example, *2101* which corresponds to an LN03 printer with 7 bits, which is compatible with the LA210 printer. This information can be found in the printer manual.

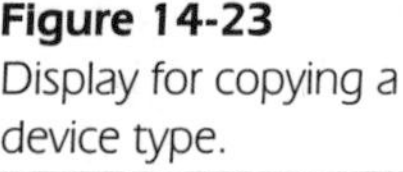

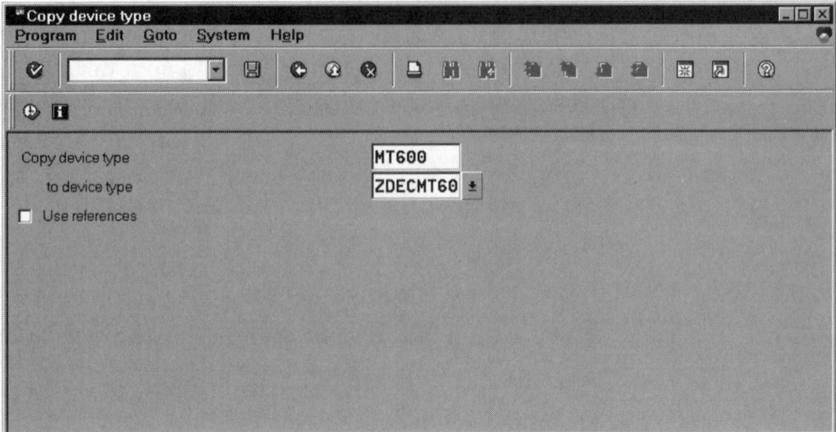

Figure 14-23 Display for copying a device type.

Click on the *Save* icon and proceed to modify the following:

- The print controls, normally those referring to the fonts used by SAPscript, such as those starting with *SF.*
- Device initialization, which must adapt every associated page format for the device.

For this printer, there was the need to define and modify some of the fonts used by SAPscript. To do this, from the initial R/3 menu, select *Tools* → *CCMS,* and then *Spool* → *Font maintenance.* The system displays a screen like the one in Fig. 14-24. Select the radio button *Printer fonts/AFM metrics,* and then click on the *Change* option. The system will display a new screen with the list of device types.

The SAPscript fonts defined for a device type must also exist as print controls. You can display the font maintenance screen for a device by double clicking on the corresponding device type line. Figure 14-25 shows the fonts for the newly created device type ZDECMT60. In the figure, new fonts have been defined already.

You must ensure that the fonts are consistent with the definition of the print controls displayed in the font maintenance screen. Those fonts must be defined to enable printing with those fonts from a SAPscript form. Otherwise, the spool request might produce problems or errors, being unable to generate the output request.

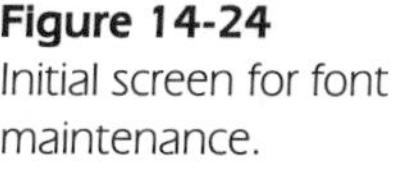

Figure 14-24
Initial screen for font maintenance.

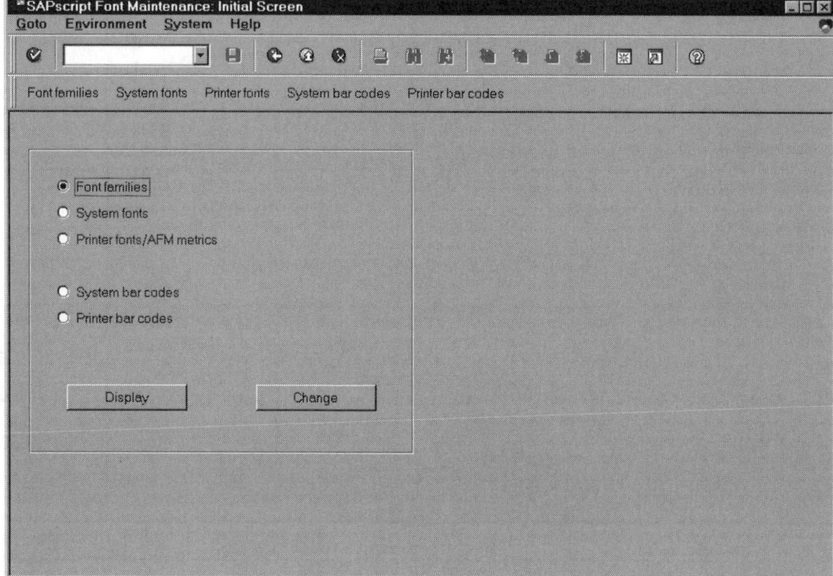

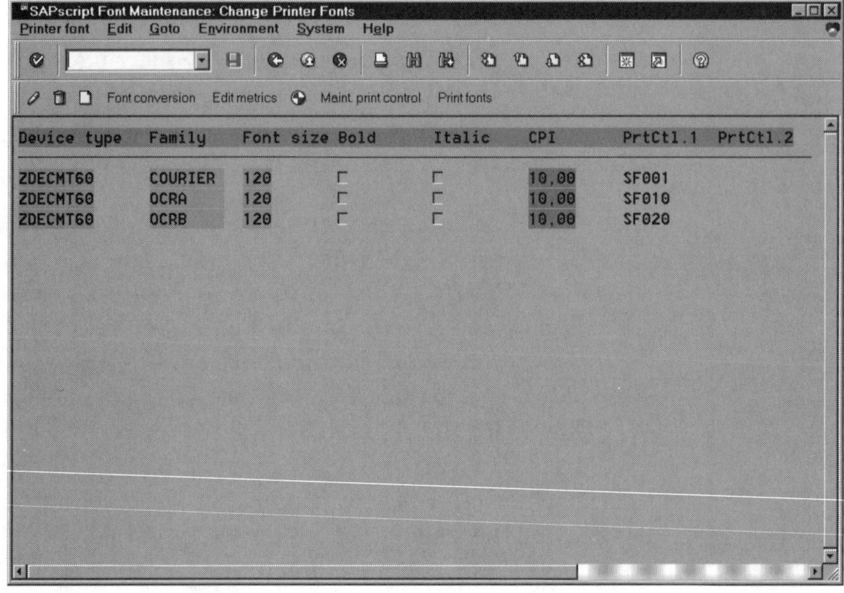

Figure 14-25 Changing and defining printer fonts.

User-defined print controls must start with the *SF* string followed by three digits, for example: *SF001.*

You can define new print controls either from the initial *Spool Administration* screen, as introduced in an earlier section, or from the *Change printer fonts* maintenance screen by clicking the *Maint. print control* push button on the application toolbar. For example, upon selecting the *SF001* print control and clicking the mentioned button, the system displays a dialog box where you can enter the associated escape sequence. Figure 14-26 shows this dialog box.

The SF print controls to be defined must include the escape character sequence meeting the requirements needed for SAPscript.

SAPscript Font Maintenance: Maintain Print Control

Device type ZDECMT60

Print control SF001

Variant 1

Hexadecimal switch X

Standard setting

Control char.seq. 1B5B343121730F1B5B3477

Figure 14-26 Defining a print control from the *Font Maintenance* screen.

Sometimes the definitions for several print controls are the same. The reason is that when working in native mode some font types such as bolding or italics for any of the font sizes were programmed for this printer mode.

However, they are defined this way to avoid conversion errors from SAPscript. The escape control sequence for the printer is described in the specific technical printer manual, in this case in the *LA210 Letterprinter Programmer Reference Manual.*

You can verify and test the existing print controls from the *Spool Administration: Print Control* screen, selecting the device type to check, and then selecting the option *Test print control.*

Every time you define a new SAPscript font with an associated print control, you must generate (activate) the new font or else it will not be available. For example, you define a new font for device type ZDECMT60 from font family Courier, size 120 and attribute bolding, 10 cpi, with an associated print control SF022. Then you include the appropriate escape sequence, as explained earlier, and save. You have now defined a new font with its print control for device type ZDECMT60, but the font is not yet available. To make it available, you must generate it.

Initializing the Device Format

From the initial *Spool Administration* screen, select *Device types,* and on the next screen, select the new device type *ZDECMT60* and click the *Formats* push button on the application toolbar.

The system displays a new screen with the list of *formats* defined for device type ZDECMT60, previously selected. All the formats associated with that device type must be examined in order to adapt its escape sequences to the new device. If the escape sequences of the source device, from which the copy has been done, are very similar to those of the new device ZDECMT60, for every *device type-Format* couple there will be little or nothing to modify. The purpose of this example is to adapt the *device type* ZDECMT60 and the *Paper type* DINA4 to the correct escape sequence values for the printer type being defined.

Next, select the *format* DINA4 by double-clicking on it. The system will display the new screen shown in Fig. 14-27. On this new screen, you have several options:

- Edit an existing action
- Copy the full format

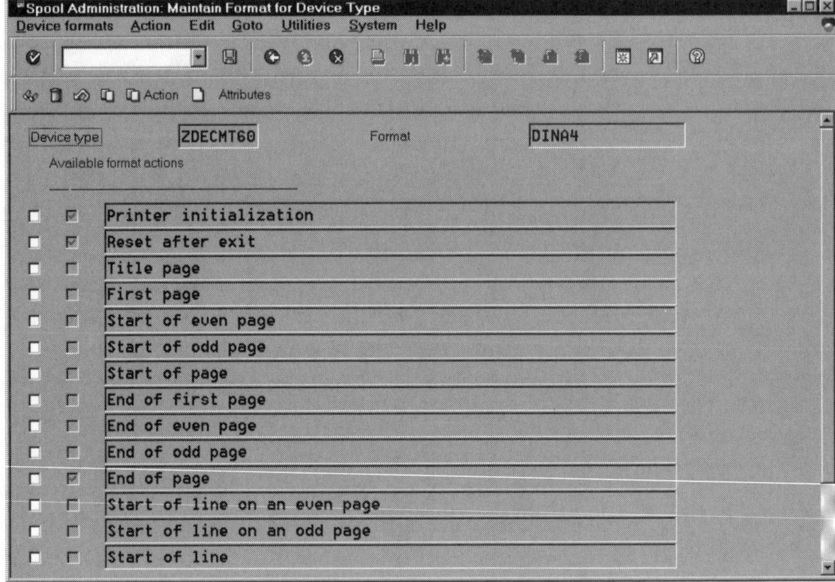

Figure 14-27 Example of formats for device types.

- Copy an action
- Create a new action

In this context, by *action* you must understand the actions as defined on the right-hand side of the display, such as *Printer initialization, Title page,* and so on. These actions might have some content, that is, might be programmed. If the actions are not programmed, the *flags* column does not contain an *X* mark (this column is located to the left of the action).

In case of a new definition, when the device type was created using a copy from a different device, the actions are already filled with the same content as in the original. They will be empty if the type was newly created. In that case the *Copy format* option should be used, and the dialog box that the system should display is shown in Fig. 14-28. Here you should enter the source device type and format, and click on the *Copy reference* icon.

In this *Case Study* all formats for the new device are already copied from device type MT600, including its actions. So here it is only a question of adapting all actions for every format to the new device ZDECMT60. All the actions available for every format are marked with a flag in a column to the left of the action name, as shown in Fig. 14-27.

The next step is to edit, one by one, the programmed escape sequences to adapt them to the new printer, since it's usual that escape sequences for the control and management of the printers be different.

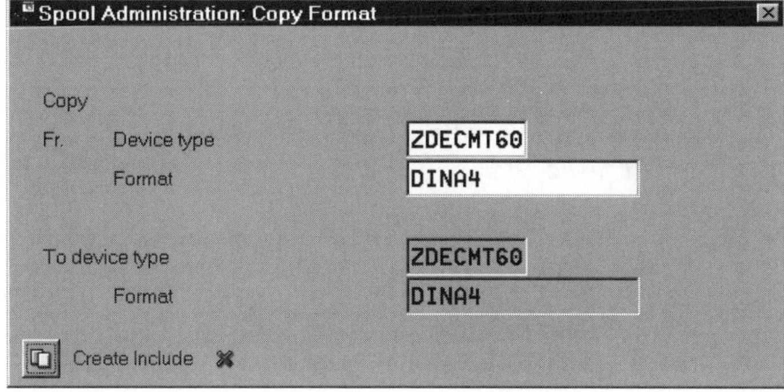

Figure 14-28 Dialog box for copying formats from another device type.

The example in Fig. 14-29 lists the full text for the action *Printer initialization.*

To indicate the start of an escape sequence, the combination used is *\e*. To indicate that the next character sequence is in hexadecimal format, use the string *\0x*. Within the *Print control* descriptions, the whole control sequence is directly written in hexadecimal values.

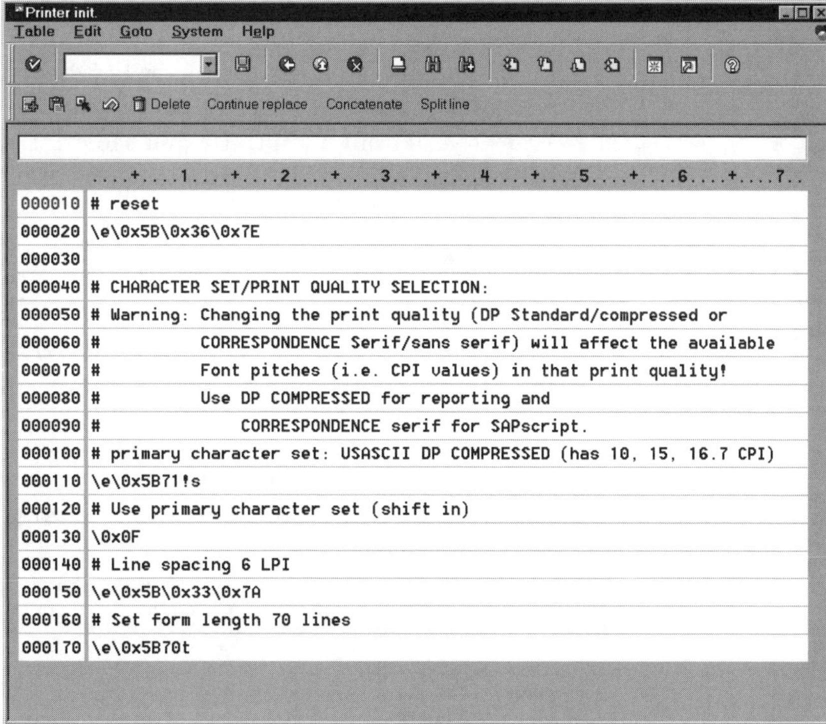

Figure 14-29 Printer initialization.

When working in the R/3 system, forms might need additional page formats, for example, the INCH12 type, but with the largest length and width for the printable area. Once a new page format is created, it can be combined with a device type to have a new *Device type - Page format* association, that is, a new initialization for the *formats for device type.*

It must be observed that if the *format (paper type)* is not defined, the page format will not be able to perform the initialization. So, it's a requirement to have previously defined the *format (paper type),* and to assign it to the corresponding *Page format.* In the example, the *Page format* and the *Paper type* are created with the same name: *ZINCH12.* The link or association between the device type with the *Page format* is made using the *format (paper type).*

Once these components are created, you only have to run the initialization for the *formats for device type* and create or copy the actions you wish to perform with such device.

Front End Printing

The SAP R/3 spool system provides a facility for printing using a local PC printer, even if this device is not defined within the spool system.

In order to use front end printing, in the print screen list, users must indicate one of the following device names as output devices, depending on the type of workstation:

- Windows PCs: LOCL
- Apple Macintosh: LOPS
- UNIX workstation PostScript printers: LOPS
- UNIX workstation HP PCL-5 printers: LOHP

Once the correct output device is selected, the system can submit the print job. The print file is transmitted to the destination workstation.

For Windows PCs, SAP R/3 automatically starts the SAPLPD program if it has not previously been started.

For UNIX or Macintosh workstations, the document is printed on the lpd printer with the name _DEFAULT. The printer must be defined at the UNIX or Macintosh level.

In order for front end printing to work properly, there are minimum requirements. In the first place, you must define an output device with the name LOCL, LOPS, or LOHP, indicating access method F, and _DEFAULT as host printer name.

Then, the front end workstation requires the following.

- For PC Windows workstations:
  - — SAPGUI software (version 3.1G or greater).
  - — SAPLPD (which is automatically installed with SAPGUI).
- For UNIX workstations:
  - — SAPGUI software (version 3.1G or greater).
  - — UNIX must define a printer with the name **_DEFAULT**.
  - — Process lp or lpd (depending on UNIX family) must be running.
- For Macintosh workstations:
  - — SAPGUI software (version 3.1G or greater).
  - — lpd shareware (install a special lpd printer daemon for Macintosh, in order to work as a UNIX system).
  - — Printer with the name **_DEFAULT** must be defined for the LPD process on the Macintosh.

NOTE *The status of the output request will be set to* Completed *as soon as the request has been sent to the front end workstation in charge of processing it. The only messages the R/3 system will keep record of are those dealing with the communication between the R/3 application server and the workstation.*

The SAPLPD Driver Program

The SAP R/3 system includes a tool that facilitates the definition of printers which are connected to the presentation servers (PCs) and not to the application servers. These printers can be locally connected to the PC or can be network-shared printers.

The communication between the SAP spool work process and the host spool system at the Windows PC is done using the SAPLPD transfer program, which is run on the Windows PC which has the printer or printers configured within the print manager.

The SAPLPD transfer program is needed when

- You wish to have printers or fax machines which are connected to the PC with Windows operating systems (Windows 95, 98, NT, etc.).

- You have printers or fax machines connected to NT servers which are not configured as R/3 application servers.
- You have configured a printer on a Windows NT application server with device type *SAPWIN*.

The SAPLPD program is automatically installed together with the SAPGUI. To run it at the PC, the following requirements must be met:

- The presentation server must run a supported operating system and environment, such as Windows 95, 98 or NT.
- The TCP/IP network protocol must be compatible with Winsockets, such as Microsoft TCP/IP, Novell LAN Workplace, and so forth.
- The file SAPFAX.DLL must be used to connect faxes to Windows systems as output devices.

Depending on the SAPGUI release, SAPFAX.DLL is often not automatically installed, but it can be found on the Presentation CD-ROM that comes bundled in the R/3 software kit.

Starting SAPLPD

As with any other Windows program, you can start the SAPLPD either by double clicking on the *SAPLPD* icon or by copying the icon program to the Startup window or Startup menu so that when the Windows system is started, the program is automatically started as well.

There is also the possibility of installing a network-shared version of the SAPLPD program, instead of a local one. In this case, you must ensure that the program working directory points to a local directory with write permission.

A user only needs to be running one instance of the SAPLPD program on the Windows PC. This instance can accept output requests from any of the configured SAP systems or application servers, as long as the output device is conveniently configured in the SAP systems; for example, as the host system, the output device must include the PC TCP/IP hostname which must be reachable from the application server.

The SAPLPD process temporarily stores all the printing requests in local files. This is not needed, however, when the output devices are defined as SAPWIN. In this case, the output requests are transferred directly to the Windows GDI interface without the need of intermediate temporary files.

The Temporary Sequential (TemSe) Objects Database

The spool system uses the TemSe (temporary sequential) objects database to store print data. The TemSe database is also used for storing background processing job logs and other sequential text objects that are temporary in nature.

The SAP R/3 system includes two menu options for handling the TemSe database, one for administration and another one for displaying the contents. This menu can be selected with *Tools → Administration → Spool → TemSe administration* or *TemSe contents.*

Since the TemSe database can hold a lot of job logs or print data files, it is convenient to schedule the report RSPO0041 periodically as a background job for removing and reorganizing the log files.

The functions for displaying or managing the TemSe contents should only be used in exceptional cases when wishing to analyze some specific problems. If you manually delete TemSe files, the background processing system or the spool system might issue some error messages when trying to display or delete log files.

Particularly for the spool system, the TemSe database stores the data from the spool requests, which can be displayed using the *Display contents* function. To do that, you first have to enter the selection criteria on the *TemSe: Request screen.* The system will display a list where you can recognize spool jobs because they have the syntax *SPOOL <number>*. Select one and click on the *Contents* push button on the application toolbar.

If needed, you can reorganize the TemSe database, which will remove old objects from the database, by selecting the menu options *TemSe database → Reorganization* from the main TemSe administration menu.

TemSe has two main storage options. Spool request data can be stored either in the R/3 database or in the file system of the OS of the host. This can be customized with the profile parameter *rspo/store_location.*

When file storage is used, by default data is stored in the R/3 global directory—for UNIX systems, in /usr/sap/<SID>/SYS/global. You specify the default TemSe storage method in the system profile of each application server, so you are able to specify a mixed storage method—that is, you can specify different storage methods for different spool servers.

The Spool System and FAX Solutions for R/3

There are two main alternatives to send faxes from the SAP R/3 system:

- Use the SAP communication server options, which are also used for managing other types of communication protocols such as EDI or mail. In this case, the spool system acts merely as the holder of the communication requests. This option requires compatible devices with the R/3 system communication server software. Refer to the SAP Web pages or to your local subsidiary for finding the certified vendors of this type of fax solution. With this type of solution, devices are defined with access method *X*. This method is being replaced by SAPconnect on newer R/3 releases.
- Use the SAPLPD transfer program and the SAPWIN device type to use a Windows-driven fax device (for example, a local PC fax-modem or a Windows shared fax) and use it as a normal printer port. In this case, observe that not all Windows FAX solutions are completely integrated. This means that only certain Windows FAX software will make the SAP system request that you enter a FAX number. Otherwise, you enter the fax number indirectly at the Windows application.

Troubleshooting Printing Problems

The following is a list of possible steps to perform when you notice printing problems in the system. These problems can be very different: no printing at all, slow printing, printing garbage, and so forth.

In any case, you should

- Check and monitor the spool work process from the *Process overview* transaction as well as from the operating system spool (print daemon or print manager). Also, check that the message server is working properly.
- Particularly, check that you can print normally from your operating system.
- Find which printer is causing the problems. Use transaction SP01 *System → Services → Output controller*. Check the output request attributes, the log files, and the size of the print job.

- For remote printers, check the network connection.
- If a print job has been printed out but contains unreadable characters, check whether the device type is the most appropriate, whether the printer is working in emulation mode, and what the access method is for the device.
- When nothing is output at the printer and the output controller is in wait status, check the system developer traces and the system log and look for time-out messages. Check that all application servers running spool work processes are reachable.
- If the job has status *Complete* or *problem* and nothing is output at the physical printer, it might be related to a wrong output device definition, a problem in the host spooler, the physical printer, or the SAPLPD transfer program. Carefully check the access method.
- If printing is very slow, possible causes might be lost indexes in the spool tables, too many spool table entries, slow WAN connections, or incorrectly defined access methods. Often you will need to review the printing strategy about distribution of output devices in several application servers according to their expected volume and size of print jobs. Refer to the SAP online documentation and the SAPnet about some interesting planning strategies for the spool system.

As an additional analysis method, carefully check the spool profile parameters.

SAP Printing System Administration Tasks

The SAP printing system and associated tasks are a subset of those general administration tasks for the daily operation of the SAP system.

R/3 system managers should be in charge of the following tasks:

- Periodically checking and monitoring the spool system, both at SAP and at the operating system level. Use the CCMS and workload monitor to check the spool work process performance.
- Deleting old spool requests or scheduling the background job which automatically deletes them.
- Defining new printers, device types, and other device elements.

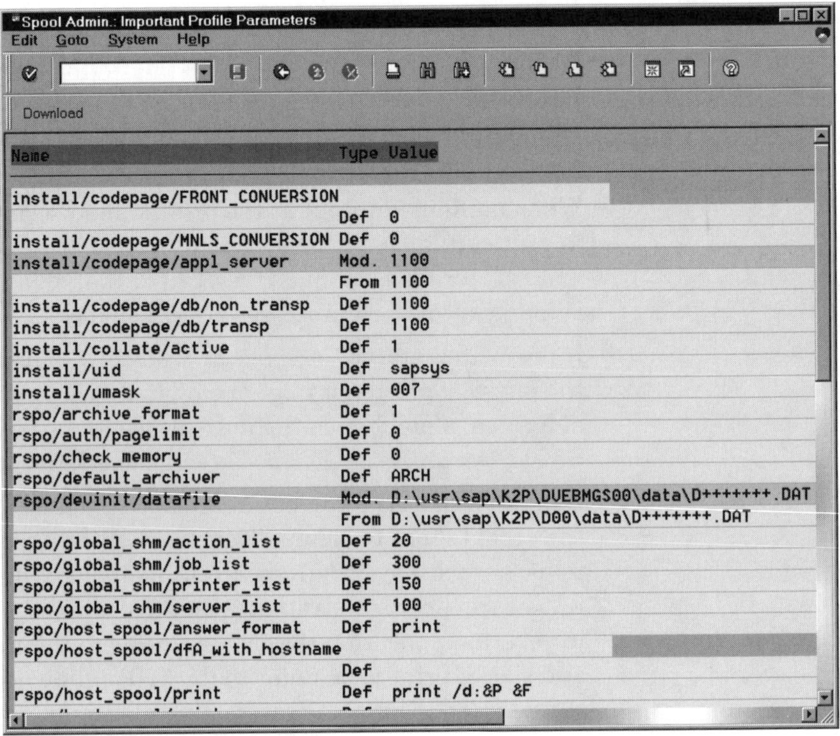

Figure 14-30 Display of the instance parameters for the spool system.

- Using the statistical information of the system for fine-tuning the planning strategy.
- Troubleshooting the spool system.

From the initial *Spool Administration* screen, there is a push button in the lower part of the screen, within the *Administration* box, which can be used to check the consistency of the spool system. Call this function by clicking on the *Consistency check of spool database* push button.

Spool System Instance Profile Parameters

To display the instance profile parameters directly related to the spool system, from the initial *Spool Administration* screen, select *Utilities* → *Display SAPPARAM*. Figure 14-30 shows an example. If you need to change any of these parameters, use the profile maintenance functions available within the CCMS. These utilities are described in Chap. 11.

CHAPTER 15

SAP Administration for Oracle Databases

While Chap. 8, "ABAP Data Dictionary," presented the R/3 data from the "internal" or logical point of view for the business application and the development environment, this chapter discusses all aspects of the administration of the underlying database system that is used by SAP R/3 as the container of the business and system information. This chapter only covers the R/3 administration-related issues concerning the Oracle database.

SAP has included many monitoring functions for managing the database within R/3, and for those tasks that cannot be directly performed right now within R/3, it has provided a comprehensive tool for making the administration of the database easier.

This tool is a character cell menu-driven program called *sapdba* that greatly facilitates the database administration for R/3. However, in order to use the facilities provided by *sapdba,* a good knowledge of the database architecture is greatly required.

R/3 contains many database management functions within the CCMS, including scheduling backups and running the optimizer statistics.

As part of the Oracle database system, R/3 also includes the Oracle server manager tool (*svrmgrl, svrmgr 23,* or *svrmgr 30,* depending on the platform and the Oracle release), which is a database administration tool that can be used to issue manually SQL statements for managing, monitoring, and performing database operations. SAP highly discourages using the Oracle server manager to change the system data, since it might cause severe inconsistencies in the system. Use it only at request of the SAP personnel or as instructed by official notes or documentation.

In this chapter, *SID* refers to the SAP system name identification, and *DBSID* to the SAP database name—database instance—identification. Normally, when a single Oracle instance is installed in a SAP database server, both are the same, so it will be referred to by the generic SID. For the examples contained in this chapter, the SID variable will be *TT1*.

A well-defined database administration is also a critical factor for the successful support and maintenance of the whole SAP R/3 system. In this chapter, the usual term *DBA* refers to the *database administrator,* which is the role reserved for the person in charge of managing the database.

This chapter is written to be operating system independent, although it is mostly based on UNIX and Windows NT. As most readers know, there are some variations between these systems in the way directories are dealt with and some different terms.

UNIX deals with variables using the notation $VARIABLE_NAME, while in NT the notation is %VARIABLE_NAME%.

The directory separator sign used in UNIX is the forward slash (/), while for Windows NT the backslash (\) is used.

Introduction to the Oracle Database Architecture Under R/3 Systems

One of the SAP R/3 openness strategy components relies on database systems complying with standard SQL calls which must follow the relational data models. Oracle is one of the RDBMS (relational database management systems) adopted by many SAP R/3 customers.

The Oracle database system is installed as part of the standard R/3 installation, as you learned in Chap. 3. When Oracle is installed, it creates a directory structure under the directory pointed out by the ORACLE_HOME environment variable. In SAP installations, this directory is normally /oracle/<SID>. For example, in the R/3 system TT1, it is /oracle/TT1.

An additional directory needed in the installation is the *stage* directory, which is used for upgrading Oracle versions. The directory structure of the Oracle database under SAP is covered in the next section.

This section intends to give you an idea of the basic components of the Oracle architecture and how it is integrated into the R/3 environment. It does not cover the architecture of the Oracle parallel server option (OPS).

Very basically, the Oracle database is made up of:

- *A collection of database files.* The most important files from a general R/3 point of view are the data files, the control files, the redo log files, the archived log files, the parameter initialization file, and the alert file.
- *Oracle and SAP runtime programs and the background Oracle database processes.* The main Oracle background processes are Oracle listener, DBWR, LGWR, ARCH, CKPT, PMON, and SMON. These will be described later in this chapter. For every SAP R/3 work process, there is a shadow database process that is like a dedicated server process in charge of supporting permanent database requests.
- *Areas in main memory.* The Oracle database uses a memory region known as SGA (system global area) where the data is buffered (cached). This region is shared by all background processes. The SGA is subdivided into several structures, each with a particular function. Another memory area is the program global area (PGA), which is used by a single ORACLE process, and it's not shared.

Figure 15-1 shows an example of these components.

Figure 15-1 Oracle database architecture: simple diagram of components.

Database memory areas

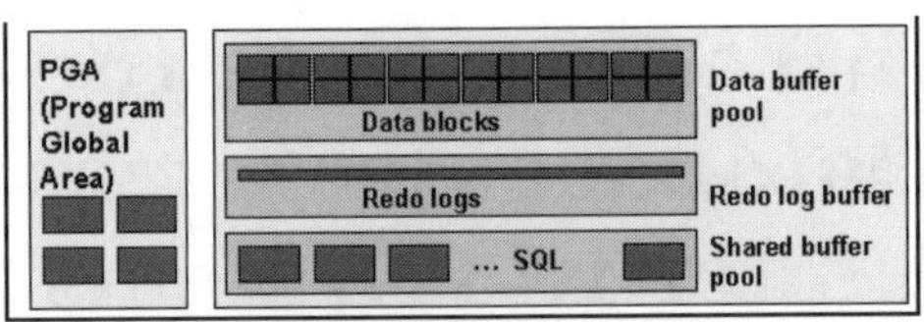

SGA (System Global Area)

Database Background processes

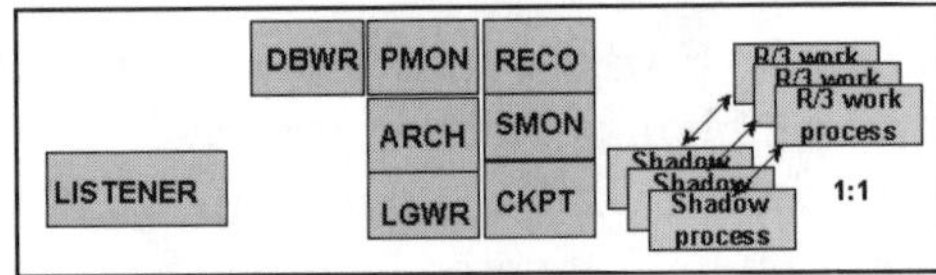

Database files

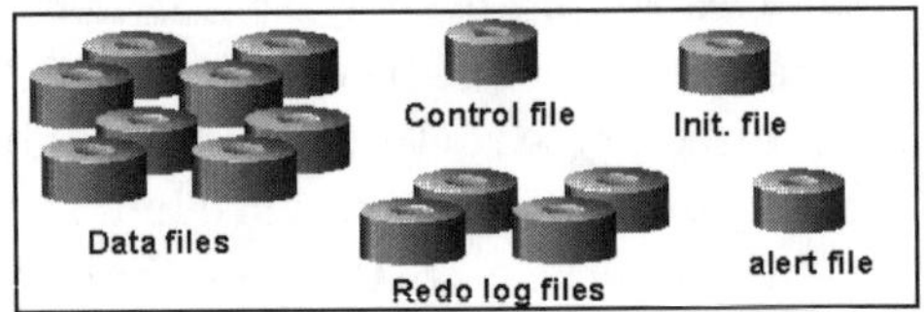

Oracle Directory Structure for R/3

In a SAP R/3 Oracle installation, you find the following directories:

- */oracle/<SID>/sapdata<n>.* Here, <n> is a number from 1 to the number of needed directories. The sapdata directories contain the Oracle data files that make up the Oracle tablespaces. These are the files that contain the actual R/3 data. By default, depending on the SAP release, the system needs five or six sapdata directories. You can create more at your installation convenience.
- */oracle/<SID>/origlogA.* Contains the original set of the first member of Oracle redo log files.
- */oracle/<SID>/origlogB.* Contains the original set of the second member of Oracle redo log files.
- */oracle/<SID>/mirrlogA.* Mirrored set of first member of Oracle redo log files.
- */oracle/<SID>/mirrlogB.* Mirrored set of second member of Oracle redo log files.
- */oracle/<SID>/saparch.* It's the directory containing the archived log files (offline redo log files).
- */oracle/<SID>/sapreorg.* It's the work directory for performing database reorganizations and administration.
- */oracle/<SID>/sapcheck.* Includes log and analysis files as generated by the sapdba command mode commands.

- */oracle/<SID>/sapbackup.* Contains the log files of the database backup and archive backups. It can also contain directories for making disk backups.
- */oracle/<SID>/saptrace.* Contains the background and user process trace files, including the main Oracle alert file.
- */oracle/<SID>/dbs.* Contains the initialization file for Oracle as well as a mirrored copy of the control file, help texts for the sapdba program, and the parameter files for the sapdba and brbackup utilities. On Windows NT systems, these files are located under the *database* directory.
- *Other directories such as bin and rdbms.* These contain components of the Oracle database system, such as the runtime programs, utilities, audit logs, network utilities, messages files, and export/import utilities.

Oracle Environment Variables

During the installation phase and during Oracle database upgrades, it is very useful to know the existing database environment variables used by SAP with Oracle. Following is a list of the main ones.

Environment Variable	Description	Standard Value
ORACLE_HOME	Default home directory for the database software, and also for the home path of the database administrator.	/oracle/<SID> (UNIX) <drive>:\orant (Windows NT)
ORACLE_SID	Refers to the system identification of the database instance. In SAP installations where only a database instance is installed, it is the same as the SAP system identification (<SID>).	<SID>
SAPDATA_HOME	Directory of the database files.	$ORACLE_HOME/
DBS_ORA_TNSNAME	Points to the database identifier <SID> from the tnsnames.ora file.	<SID>
ORA_NLS		$ORACLE_HOME/ocommon/nls_722/admin/data
ORA_NLS32		$ORACLE_HOME/ocommon/nls_733/admin/data
ORA_NLS33		$ORACLE_HOME/ocommon/nls/admin/data

The Parameter File init<sid>.ora

The init.ora file is the initialization and configuration file for the Oracle database. In R/3, this file is called *init<sid>.ora* (for example, *inittt1.ora* for SAP system TT1). This file is located under the *dbs* directory on UNIX systems and under the *database* directory on Windows NT systems.

This file contains the system parameters that configure the database. When the database is started up, this file is read by Oracle to determine such configuration parameters as the name of the database instance, the system global area (SGA) and other database buffer sizes, the name and location of the control files, the name of the rollback segments, the number of maximum database files, and many others.

There is a very long list of allowed parameters for the configuration file init.ora. Some of these parameters only work in certain operating systems. Although many of the following topics will include references to some parameters in this file, for a complete description and available options in the init.ora file, please refer to the official Oracle documentation.

This is a very important file for the correct functioning of the database and should be frequently backed up. It's a critical file for tuning the database performance.

Data Storage: Tablespaces and Data Files

The database data is stored in logical entities known as *tablespaces.* Tablespaces are Oracle logical storage objects, working like folders that contain the database table data or the indexes. Every tablespace corresponds to one or more physical data files located on one or several disks. The reason for this logical storage object is to increase the flexibility when managing the database-allocated space. For example, a DBA can reorganize single tablespaces, back up or recover a tablespace, increase or reduce the size, put a tablespace offline, and so on. When creating a database object such as a table or an index, you always have to specify which tablespace will contain it.

Every tablespace has a name and some storage parameters. Under R/3 installations, the SAP names of the tablespaces follow a certain naming convention.

There is always a special tablespace called SYSTEM that contains the dictionary information of the database; that is, the data the database needs to manage itself. This tablespace cannot be taken offline during normal operation.

One of the most common R/3 problems—when it is not sufficiently monitored—is tablespaces becoming full.

The sapdba program includes all the needed utilities to manage tablespaces.

Although tablespaces are the most common storage objects to deal with, there are additional storage objects in the database system. The relation among these objects is shown in Fig. 15-2. These are the other storage entities:

- *Oracle block.* It's the smallest physical storage unit in the database. The size is always a multiple of the operating system block size, so it can be different depending on the operating system. The size is defined in the parameter db_block_size in the init.ora file. In SAP installations, for performance reasons, the size is usually 8096 bytes (8K).
- *Extent.* It's a logical storage unit made up of a contiguous collection of Oracle blocks. A collection of extents is a *segment.*
- *Segments.* There are several types of segments in the database. Two of the most common are *data segments,* which contain table data; and *index segments,* which contain index data. There are also rollback segments, temporary segments, and bootstrap segments. When any database object is created, an initial extent is assigned to the object's segment. When the object requires additional space, more extents are allocated to the segment. The first block of the first extent contains the *segment header,* which itself contains the *extent map* and the free list information.

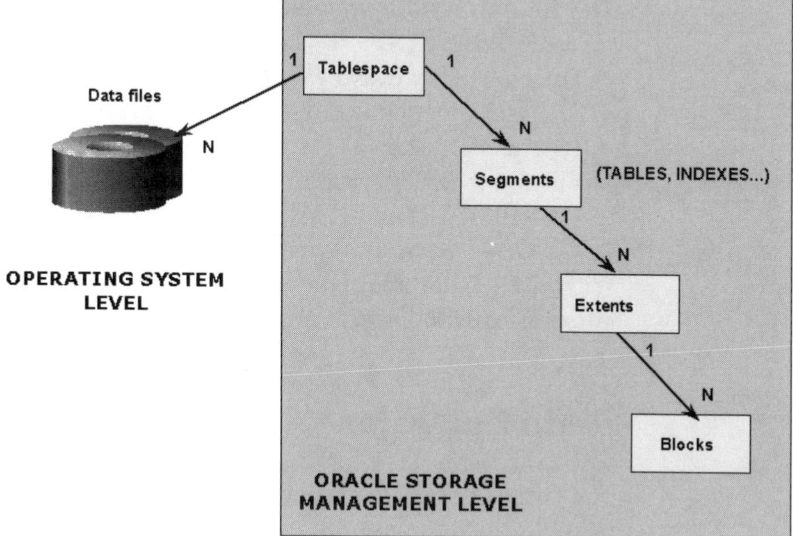

Figure 15-2 Relation between storage objects.

The *tables* are the objects containing the database data. The size of the tables increases proportionally with the number of records they contain (number of rows).

Indexes are objects associated with tables that are used to speed up the search and execution of SQL statements. Creating or deleting indexes does not affect the associated table. When the data in the tables is frequently modified, for example, in tables with transactional data, the index can even grow faster than the associated table. It is normally better for performance and space management reasons to maintain the index segments in separate tablespaces than the associated tables. Standard SAP installation follows this principle.

Rollback segments are segments that store the "before image" of the information when a database transaction has modified that information. In case of problems, or just in the case someone changes her or his mind, this information can be used for *rolling back* transactions to the state they were in before the modification, and it is also used for transaction recovery. To *roll back* a transaction means to restore the value of a particular data block before it was modified.

Temporary segments, as the name indicates, are segments that the database system uses temporarily for doing join or sort operations or for creating indexes. For large database sizes in the R/3 environment, administrators should allow extra temporary space, which can increase performance when dealing with large tables or indexes. In the SAP system, the temporary segments are stored in the tablespace PSAPTEMP. It is a common rule to assign this space a size twice as big as the size of the biggest index.

The SAP R/3 Tablespaces. The SAP naming convention for the tablespaces is PSAP<TSP><D | I>.

The prefix is always *PSAP,* except for the SYSTEM tablespace. The *<TSP>* is a mnemonic name indicating the tablespace contents, and the suffix can be either *D* for data tablespaces or *I* for index tablespaces, except for the rollback and temporary segments tablespaces. Examples are PSAPBTABD and PSAPDOCUI.

Table 15-1 below contains an overview of the standard R/3 tablespaces. With the sapdba tool you can create additional tablespaces, which will automatically follow the SAP naming convention.

Redo Log Files

The Oracle database system uses the redo log files to record the changes made to the database during normal operation. These files are open and

TABLE 15-1

Tablespaces Under an Oracle R/3 Installation

Tablespace Name	Description
Oracle system tablespaces. **These tablespaces do not contain R/3 data but are required for the operation of the database.**	
SYSTEM	Includes the internal Oracle dictionary.
PSAPROLL	Contains the rollback segments.
PSAPTEMP	Temporary tablespace for internal processing.
BASIS tablespaces. **These tablespaces contain the R/3 Basis environment data.**	
PSAPEL<rel>D/I <rel> = R/3 release	Contains loads for the development environment. Are release-dependent (for example, PSAPEL45BD for release 4.5B).
PSAPES<rel>D/I	Contains the sources for the development environment in this release.
PSAPLOADD/I	Contains the ABAP report loads and screens.
PSAPSOURCED/I	Contains the ABAP report sources and screens.
PSAPDDICD/I	Includes the ABAP dictionary.
PSAPPROTD/I	Includes control and log tables.
APPLICATION tablespaces.	
PSAPCLUD/I	Contains the system cluster tables.
PSAPPOOLD/I	Contains the system pool tables (i.e., ATAB).
PSAPSTABD/I	Contains master data, transparent tables.
PSAPBTABD/I	Contains transaction data, transparent tables.
PSAPDOCUD/I	Contains documentation tables.
CUSTOMERS tablespaces.	
PSAPUSER1D/I	Includes the customer tables.

online while the system is running; therefore, they are also known as *online redo logs.*

The redo log files work in a circular way. When the database is first started up, any changes are written to the first (or current) redo log file. When this redo file is full, then it writes to the second one, and, at the same time, makes a copy of the finished online redo log file to the *archived* redo log directory, in case the archive mode is enabled. When it finishes writing in the fourth redo log (in the case of a default R/3 installation), the system starts again in the first one. Figure 15-3 shows this process.

The redo log files are very important for the Oracle database since they are used in case of database recovery and reapplying changes to the database in case of an abnormal shutdown. If an online redo file is lost, the database can only be recovered up until the time the gap occurred.

The SAP R/3 standard database installation creates four redo log files of 20 MB each, separated under two different directories, origlogA and origlogB. It also gives the option to have these files logically mirrored under the mirrlogA and mirrlogB directories. An online redo log group is made of one original redo log file and its mirror copy. In case of corruption by any of the files, the system can still use the mirrored copy until the problem is resolved. SAP strongly recommends having these files mirrored, either logically as supported by Oracle, or physically by disk mirroring technologies.

Archived Redo Log Files

The archived redo log files (archived copies of the old online redo log files) are created when the database is operating in ARCHIVELOG

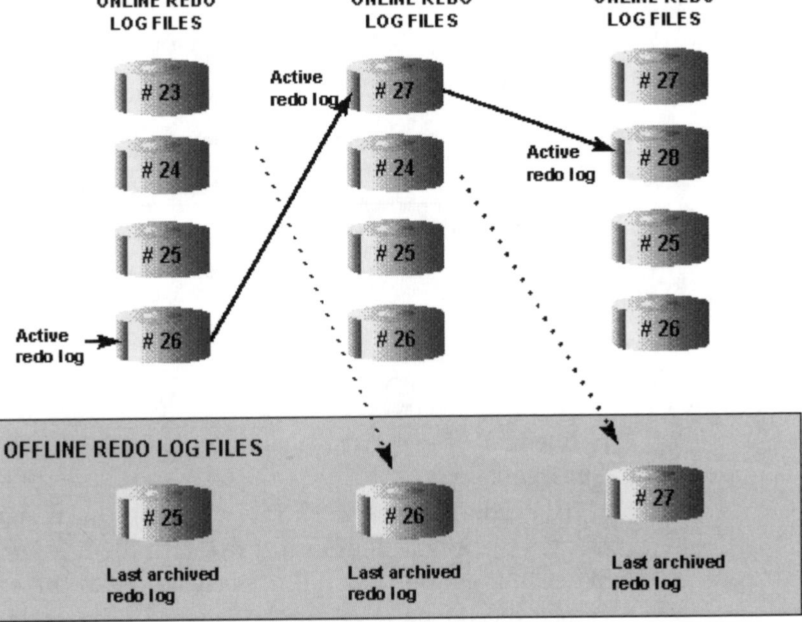

Figure 15-3 Redo log files and archived redo log files: mode of operation.

mode. You have the choice to operate the database in this mode or in NOARCHIVELOG mode.

The copy process of the online redo log files to the archiving directory is performed by the Oracle archiving process (ARCH), which is started by default in the R/3 environment that includes the needed parameter values in the initialization file init<sid>.ora. These parameters are as follows:

- *log_archive_start = true.* Indicates to automatically start the Oracle archive process when the database is started. These parameters enable the automatic archival mode.
- *log_archive_dest.* Indicates what is the archiving directory for the offline redo log files. By default, SAP sets this value as *ORACLE_HOME / saparch / <SID>arch,* where *ORACLE_HOME* is an environment variable that normally points to /oracle/<SID>. Also, *<SID>arch* is a prefix for the archived files that is completed with a log sequence number and the *.dbf* extension (for example: /oracle/TT1/saparch/TT1arch865.dbf).

Make sure to have enough free space in the archiving directory, since if it becomes full, the archive process will not be able to archive any more redo logs and the database will be stopped. This is known as the *archiver stuck* error.

ARCHIVELOG mode is absolutely necessary to be able to perform online backups. It is also necessary for performing logical database recoveries when a media failure has not occurred but a logical failure, such as a privileged user deleting an unwanted table. SAP and Oracle strongly recommend that you operate the database in this mode.

The archive redo log files should be periodically backed up to tape or other media to have a consistent backup strategy. SAP has included the brarchive utility within sapdba to back up these files.

Control File

The control file is another very important piece of the database. This file contains the schema of the database: names, location, status, and states of all the data files and online redo log files. The control file is essential for normal operation of the database. As part of the database startup procedure, Oracle reads the control file to locate the data files and the online log files. If the control file is lost due to a media failure, a new control file can be created. However, if you only have one copy and lose it, it will be almost impossible to recover the database up to the final consistent state.

This would cause some downtime for the database, so it is suggested to maintain at least three copies of the control file, each on a separate disk or volume. SAP includes the needed parameter in the init<sid>.ora file to mirror this file in three different places (three different disks or volumes if you have set the file systems that way). The parameter that sets the control file location is *control_files*. An example is:

```
control_files = (?/dbs/cntrl<SID>.dbf,
?/sapdata1/cntrl/ctrl<SID>.dbf, ?/sapdata2/cntrl/ctrl<SID>.dbf)
```

Notice that the question mark is an Oracle placeholder that is normally substituted in the parameter file by the ORACLE_HOME environment parameter value.

As part of the backup procedures, in addition to the data files and log files, the control file should be copied as well.

The Alert File

As part of the Oracle trace files, which are used in problem analysis and diagnosis, SAP includes the saptrace directory under the home directory of the ora<sid> user.

The saptrace directory includes two directories for different types of tracing: background and usertrace. The *usertrace* directory includes trace files generated by user processes, while the *background* includes tracing from the Oracle background processes and the alert file, alert_<SID>.log.

This file is not critical for database operation, since Oracle can create another one automatically, but it is, however, extremely important in discovering database system problems and errors, especially in recovery procedures.

The directory locations are defined in the init<SID>.ora initialization parameter file.

The alert file continuously collects all the database system activities (not transactions), such as database start and stop, backups, tablespace storage modifications, redo log switch, and error messages. When database problems occur, you can look into this file to find out what happened and obtain the Oracle error message number.

This file is constantly appended with new message information. It is not a file that is created every time the database system is restarted. It is therefore quite important, and, for that reason, sapdba does not include any option to clean it up.

You can see this file from the R/3 application by calling *Tools* → *Administration* → *Monitor* → *Performance* → *Database* → *Activity.* Then click on the *Detail analysis menu* button. On the new push button menu, click on the *Database message log.*

Oracle Memory Areas

Oracle database processes use several memory areas during normal operation. These memory areas are particularly important for understanding how the Oracle processes work and how to optimize performance. Remember that memory operations are always faster than those on physical disks.

The most important memory area allocated by Oracle is the *system global area,* commonly referred to as the SGA. This area is shared by all the concurrent users connected to the database instance. Sometimes this area is also known as *shared global area.* In R/3, the most typical database user is the SAPR3 user.

The SGA parameters are defined in the init.ora initialization file, and its size is displayed by Oracle when starting the database.

The SGA contains two parts:

- A fixed size part holds information about the instance and the database that is needed for the normal background processes operation. This size cannot be changed and depends on the platform, the release version, and other important factors.
- The variable part might be affected by many of the init.ora parameters. This part is tunable.

Among the parameters that most affect the SGA are the following:

- The parameter db_block_size specifies the size of an Oracle block in bytes. In SAP systems, this is usually 8096.
- The parameter db_block_buffers is the total number of data buffers in the SGA. The product db_block_buffers × db_block_size defines the size of the *database buffer,* or *buffer cache,* which is the total amount of space that the database allocates in the SGA to buffer data blocks.
- The parameter *shared_pool_size* specifies in bytes the amount of space that the SGA reserves to cached and shared SQL statements.
- The parameter *log_buffers* indicates the size in bytes for the space allocated to the redo log buffers. These buffers contain the changes made to the data before they are actually written to disks.

Introduction to Oracle Background Processes

The Oracle processes are responsible for executing different tasks in the database system. These processes are permanently and concurrently running in the system when the database is started.

The Oracle system distinguishes between user processes created for executing user applications and Oracle processes. The Oracle processes can be of two types: server processes and background processes. *Server* processes in two-task environments are the counterpart of user processes. The *background* processes are the main database system processes in charge of performing the main functions of the database engine. A set of background processes together with the SGA is called an *Oracle instance.*

The Oracle background processes perform different tasks in the database operation. The type and number of background processes running for an instance depends on the actual database configuration. The following list only reflects those common processes running in the Oracle SAP R/3 environment:

- *Oracle listener.* This process is responsible for connecting the R/3 work processes and their dedicated oracle shadow processes when they are in different nodes. This is a network connection that uses TCP/IP as communication protocol. To accept connections on the database server, the listener must be running. The Oracle utility *lsnrctl* (NT: *lsnrctl80*) is used to start and stop the listener and to check the status of SQL*Net connections. In UNIX systems, the process *tnslsnr* is started. On Windows NT, the service OracleTNSListener is started.

The following three operating system files are used in a NET8 configuration. These files can be found in the ORACLE_HOME subdirectory network/admin (NT: net80\admin) on each application server and on the database server:

- *tnsnames.ora.* Contains a list of service names for all databases that can be accessed in the network.
- *sqlnet.ora.* Contains client-side default domain information and optional diagnostic parameters used for client tracing and logging.
- *listener.ora.* Used only on database server machines. Contains Oracle system IDs for which the listener can receive connections and various control parameters used by the program *lsnrctl.* The default R/3 system profile should contain the entry

```
dbs/ora/tnsname = <SID>
```

- *Database writer (DBWR).* It's the background process in charge of writing data blocks from the database buffer to the data files on disks. Usually the DBWR process is optimized automatically to reduce input/output to disks and only write to physical disks when requested by other transactions needing the SGA memory areas.
- *Checkpoint (CKPT).* The CKPT process sends a signal to the database writer process (DBWR) at checkpoint. It then updates the headers of the control files and data files. This process is not enabled by default.
- *Log writer (LGWR).* It's the process responsible for writing redo log entries from the redo log buffers to the online redo log files on disk. When the checkpoint process is not running, the LGWR process is also responsible for updating the headers of the control files and data files with the latest checkpoint.
- *System monitor (SMON).* This process is started automatically by Oracle when the database is started. The SMON of an instance is responsible for recovering the database after an abnormal termination, recovering, or rolling back transactions that were not processed because of the crash. It is also responsible for cleaning up temporary segments that are not being used.
- *Process monitor (PMON).* The PMON process is also started automatically by the database system and is responsible for performing process recovery; for example, when a user process or a server process fails. It also cleans and releases any resources that were being used by the failed processes.
- *Archiver (ARCH).* The ARCH is only present when the database operates with automatic archiving. This process is responsible for copying the redo log files to the archive area (disk or tape) before they are overwritten by a new redo log file. This only happens, though, if the ARCHIVELOG mode is set, which is the default and recommended state in R/3 installations, and the only way to perform point-in-time (partial) database recoveries.

Other Oracle processes which are not normally found on current releases and without the OPS option in R/3 installations are the *Lock (LCKn)*, *Dispatcher (Dnnn)*, *Recoverer (RECO)*, and the *Server (Snnn)* processes. For more information about these processes and others, refer to the actual Oracle documentation.

Oracle databases under Windows NT use the *thread* implementation. This is a similar concept to the processes on UNIX systems. The most visible difference between the platforms is that on Windows NT systems all Oracle processes except the listener form a single Oracle process. In Windows NT, the Oracle listener is normally started as a service called OracleTNSListener, which enables all network communications.

Startup and Shutdown of the Oracle Database

When the database is normally started using the *svrmgrl* command *startup* or *startup open,* the database system goes through several stages. These stages are, in this order: nomount, mount, and open. You can use these options to start the Oracle database system only up to one of those stages.

- The first stage is *nomount.* In this phase, the Oracle system reads the initialization file init.ora to initialize the SGA, locate the control file, and start the background processes. This stage is useful for some recovery functions and is also the stage for creating a new database for the first time. To start the database up to this stage, use the command:

```
svrmgrl> startup nomount
```

- The next stage is *mount.* During this stage, Oracle reads the control files holding the database schema to find the location of the data files and online redo log files. The database instance is mounted and gets an instance lock. This stage is useful and needed for performing some important recovery functions as well as some of the database storage management, mainly those commands starting with the keywords *ALTER DATABASE* (although these statements can also be issued in the open stage), such as relocating data files, taking a data file online or offline, creating redo log groups, and so on. To start the database up to this stage, use the command:

```
svrmgrl> startup mount
```

- Finally, during the *open* stage, the database instance opens the database: data files and online redo log files. If during this stage the system detects a previous abnormal termination, a recovery is automatically performed using the online redo log files. To start the database up to this stage, use the command:

```
svrmgrl> startup open
```

  or just

```
svrmgrl> startup
```

When you have more than one Oracle instance (normally not the case in R/3), these commands are followed by the DBNAME.

These are the three stages when starting the database; there are, however, other command options for the *startup* command. For more information, please refer to the official Oracle documentation.

Stopping the database with the *shutdown* commands presents three options: normal, immediate, and abort.

- With a *normal* shutdown, the system ensures a consistent database state and does not require recovery during the next startup. The normal shutdown process will wait until all database users complete their tasks and disconnect from the system. It will also complete the ongoing transactions, clean the database buffers, and update the headers of the data files and the control files. Then it dismounts the database and stops the database instance. In summary, it's the recommended way for stopping the database gracefully. In R/3, it is the usual way of stopping the database, since stopping the R/3 instance will disconnect the database users. It is also the way to stop the database from performing an offline backup. To stop the database normally, use the command:

  ```
  svrmgrl> shutdown normal
  ```

  or just

  ```
  svrmgrl> shutdown
  ```

- The *immediate* shutdown option is sometimes needed when, for some reason, the database needs to be stopped immediately, such as when an important object has just been deleted or when the DBA needs to modify initialization parameters because sessions are exhausted. When the immediate option is used, Oracle does not wait for users to disconnect. The SQL statements being processed by Oracle are terminated, any uncommitted transactions are rolled back, and the database instance is stopped. Nevertheless, the database stops in a consistent state, and no automatic recovery is required in the next database startup. To stop the database immediately, use the command:

  ```
  svrmgrl> shutdown immediate
  ```

- The *abort* option is used in emergency situations where the other shutdown options fail, such as when one of the Oracle background processes aborts, when there is a media failure, or when the control file gets corrupted. Using the *shutdown abort* will cause the database to terminate immediately all current SQL requests without rolling back the uncommitted transactions. After stopping the database with the abort option, the database is not stopped in a consistent state; for that reason, the next time the database is started, it will perform a crash recovery. You should only use this shutdown option when absolutely necessary. To stop the database with the abort option, use the command:

```
svrmgrl> shutdown abort
```

Introduction to Cost-Based Optimizer

As of R/3 release 4.0, the cost-based optimizer determines the most effective strategy for retrieving database data. The access strategy used depends on the information in the:

- Queried table (or tables, for a view or join)
- Fields specified in the WHERE clause of the SQL statement
- Indexes defined for the tables queried

The cost-based optimizer computes the cost of several strategies for accessing the tables, and chooses the one that requires the smallest number of data accesses. To calculate the cost of a strategy, the optimizer requires statistical information about the tables and indexes of the database, such as:

- Number of table or index rows and number of blocks allocated for the object
- Number of distinct values in each column of the table

The statistical information for a table or index is stored in the Data Dictionary of the database. To collect the statistical information, the Oracle SQL command *analyze table* is used.

This cost-based optimizing functionality can be managed from inside R/3 (CCMS) or with the tool *sapdba.*

SAP R/3 Database Administrator Common Tasks

R/3 database administration is a very important role within the overall R/3 implementation and support projects. This is a very common role in many database-oriented applications, which are most of the current business applications. This role is commonly referred to as *DBA* (*database administrator*).

The following list reflects some (but probably not all) of the tasks that are usually assigned to DBAs:

- Design and maintenance of the physical database layout, covering things such as ensuring that data segments and index segments are located on different volumes, managing the location of main files, sizing and forecasting the database growth, and so on. The DBA should help and actively collaborate with the rest of the R/3 technical staff in the system sizing and design.
- Database backups, including the backup strategy definition: what to back up, when, where, and with what. The DBA also should be responsible for defining the tape and volume management, the tape drive maintenance, checking the backup logs, and so on. Within the backup strategy, the recovery procedures should not be left aside; they are at least as important as the backup itself. In the SAP R/3 environment, it should be a good practice to thoroughly test the backup/recovery strategy before going into productive operation.
- Database security maintenance, such as user and password administration, checking and monitoring database network connections, and possibly database accesses using external tools (such as ODBC and RFC).
- Checking and monitoring the database performance. These tasks should include a daily or periodical checklist of the database status, including fragmentation level, number of extents, overflow problems, file systems problems, and so on. Within the R/3 environment, this task also includes the maintenance of the main profile parameter files such as init<SID>.ora, init<SID>.sap, and so on.
- Perform the cost-based optimizer activities and procedure to ensure a correct performance, avoiding old, nonexistent, or imprecise statistical information and analyzing the different possibilities as to why the CBO could result in performance problems.
- Database storage management, including tasks such as adding data files to tablespaces, modifying internal storage parameters, taking care of the log archive area, backing up these archived logs, planning database reorganizations, designing and performing export/imports, and so on. It is also recommended to draw a map of the sapdatas file systems, including the tablespaces and data files.

- Database problem analysis and escalation procedures. The DBA should actively report, solve, and document common database problems. The use of a tool for reporting incidence should be taken into consideration.
- The DBA should become familiar with the ABAP dictionary and also collaborate in developments of new objects and lend a hand when new SAP applications are getting ready for the productive phase.

Introduction to sapdba

For administering the Oracle database, SAP provides the sapdba utility, which greatly simplifies the tasks involved when managing the database. With sapdba, you can perform practically all functions required in an R/3 installation concerning the underlying database. It is even possible for administrators without a deep knowledge of the *svrmgrl* tool to be able to perform almost all the needed tasks. Another advantage of using sapdba for database administration is that all actions performed with the tool are logged, so that the system keeps a record that can be checked for reviewing the operations that have been performed.

The sapdba utility is needed for performing functions that actually cannot be run within R/3; therefore, they are run at the operating system level, normally with user ora<sid>, which is created by SAP as part of a standard R/3 installation under Oracle. The SAP administrator account at the operating system level, <sid>adm, can also be used for performing certain database actions (not the privileged ones), but in order to do that you have to change the permissions for the *sapdba* program and, if it does not exist (although this is typically done in the installation), create the user OPS$<SID>adm as *identified externally* at the database level. The correct permissions for the *sapdba* program are:

```
rwsr_xr_x oratt1 dba
```

To set these permissions, log onto the database server at the operating system level, with root privileges, and perform the following operations:

(Example for system TT1:)

```
# cd /usr/sap/TT1/SYS/exe/run
# chmod 4755 sapdba
# chown oratt1 sapdba
# chgrp dba sapdba
```

To create OPS$<SID>adm as *identified externally* at the database level, the parameter OS_AUTHENT_PREFIX=OPS$ must first be defined in profile init<SID>.ora. Then you have to connect to the database as *internal* and perform the following operations:

(Example for system TT1:)

```
svrmgrl> create user ops$tt1adm identified externally default
tablespace psapuser1d temporary tablespace psamptemp;
svrmgrl> grant dba, connect, resource to ops$tt1adm;
```

You can only run the sapdba utility from the host where the database system was installed.

For the correct management of the database, there are a couple important environment variables that must be set. These variables are defined in the login script files of the database administration user (ora<sid>): ORACLE_HOME and ORACLE_SID.

Internal Database Users and Passwords

In order to control and manage the data access, the Oracle database includes a record of internal database users. Database users can be created with the standard Oracle tools, as well as granting or revoking accesses, privileges, and so on, to enhance the system security. Normally, the R/3 installation does not need to create internal database users. In fact, when R/3 is first installed, the database system includes the standard privileged users sys and system. Additionally, R/3 creates the SAPR3 Oracle database user, which is the owner of all SAP R/3 objects.

To connect to the database, you must always enter a user name and password, except when the password is the system standard.

When the sapdba utility connects to the database, by default, it uses the Oracle user *system*, which has full privileges for starting and stopping the database, creating and deleting database objects, recovering the database, and so on.

For directions on how to create Oracle users, please refer to the official database administration guides.

So, if you haven't changed the system password (*manager*) during the R/3 database password change phase, you can start the sapdba program with full privileges by entering the sapdba command at the operating system prompt:

```
oratt1> sapdba
```

Figure 15-4 shows the sapdba initial menu screen.

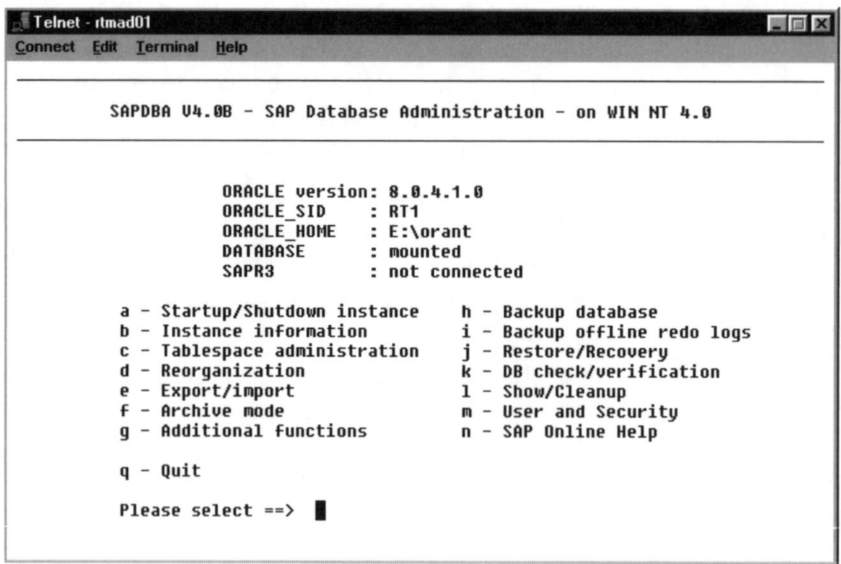

Figure 15-4 The initial menu of sapdba.

If you don't use the standard system password, you have to enter a password when calling sapdba. The following options are available for starting sapdba and specifying DBA users other than the standard:

- *oratt1> sapdba -u <user>/<password>* With this command, you specify a privileged database user different from the standard user system. However, you should avoid using the *-u* option, since the user and password are visible and displayable in the process list. You can also use the *-u* option with the format sapdba -u
- *oratt1> sapdba -l <user>/<password>* It is also used for entering sapdba with a different DBA user than the standard. This is the option to use when launching sapdba with the UNIX cron utility, for example. The difference from the *-u* option is that the password is not visible in the process list, although it is visible when entered interactively.
- *oratt1> sapdba -U internal/<password>* With the -U option, you start the database as the superuser *internal.*

Command Mode sapdba

Besides the *-u, -l,* and *-U* options, sapdba also allows for being called with several other command options. This can be very useful when creating command scripts for performing automatic database management and monitoring operations.

This is a brief introduction to those commands. The full reference and documentation for these commands can be found in the SAP online library.

- *oratt1> sapdba -p <path/profile>* The *-p* option can be used to specify a sapdba initialization profile different than the standard init<sid>.sap profile (for example: *sapdba -p /oracle/TT1/dbs/myprofile*). If the alternative profile file does not contain all the values, sapdba uses standard default values.
- *oratt1> sapdba -e <number of extent>* The *-e* option sets the default value for the number of extents when performing extent checks with sapdba.

Options *-u, -l, -U, -p,* and *-e* will display the sapdba initial menu. However, when you call sapdba with one of the following command options, the sapdba initial menu will not be displayed:

- *oratt1> sapdba -h* This is the help option. It displays a summary overview of the sapdba command options.
- *oratt1> sapdba -check* Generates a log file giving extensive overview information about the database structure. The log is left in the sapcheck directory under the Oracle home directory. This check might last several minutes. You can submit it in the background. In fact, it is recommended that you regularly—daily or every other day—submit this check function so as to get into a single report the current statistics of the database system.
- *oratt1> sapdba -analyze <tablespaces|tables>* This option is used when reorganizations are pending for checking the space situation of the tablespace specified and when creating current statistics for the cost-based optimizer using *sapdba -analyze DBSTATCO.* The *<tablespaces>* parameter admits the Oracle percent-sign placeholder for indicating several tablespaces, as well as entering individual tablespaces separated by commas. This option can be a lengthy procedure, perhaps even lasting several hours depending on the tablespace analyzed. So use it with care and refer to the current SAPnet notes and the SAP documentation before performing analysis. The *-analyze* option admits several other optional parameters.
- *oratt1> sapdba -checkopt <tablespace(s) | table | key_word>* This command option checks whether a table(s) has missing or obsolete statistics to be used by the database optimizer and update table

DBSTATC (Control Table for Optimizer Statistics). Initially, requirements table DBSTATC contains the most critical 430 tables with information about its requirement flag, method (E: Estimate; C: Compute), and accuracy. This table should not be too large.

The results of this check can be:

- Insertion in table DBSTATC if:
  - — Statistics already exist and change is greater than threshold
  - — The method has changed
- Marking with a requirement flag when:
  - — The current number of records is less than 200,000 and percentage change is greater than threshold, or
  - — The current number of records exceeds 200,000 and is less than table_record_old, and absolute change is greater than threshold, or
  - — The current number of records exceeds 200,000 and table_record_old, and change is over 100%
- Removal from table DBSTATC if the TOBDO date is older than 30 days, it is an optimizer table, no customer flag is set, and Active = A
- *oratt1> sapdba -next <tablespaces>* Can be used to modify the NEXT storage parameter.
- *oratt1> sapdba -startup* Performs a normal database startup.
- *oratt1> sapdba -startup_dba* Starts the database in restricted mode (DBA mode).
- *oratt1> sapdba -shutdown* Performs a normal shutdown of the database.
- *oratt1> sapdba -shutdown_abort* Stops the database using the shutdown abort option. Refer to the previous section on starting and stopping the database.
- *oratt1> sapdba -check_db_open* Checks if the database is already started.
- *oratt1> sapdba -cleanup* Deletes the log files according to the expiration values defined in the sapdba profile.
- *oratt1> sapdba -r <path/timestamp>* Starts a database reorganization using the restart scripts previously generated. It should only be used when submitting the reorganization in the background.
- *oratt1> sapdba -export <tablespaces/table>* You can use this option to export the objects specified (a tablespace, a set of tablespaces, or a

single table). By default, the export is performed to /dev/null, which means that it does not generate an export dump. This procedure is useful for testing the tablespace for corrupt data blocks.

When using sapdba with commands, the program returns status codes that you can check in your scripts with the usual $status variable. Possible codes are as follows:

- 0 Operation successfully finished
- 1 General error
- 2 Operation could not be started
- 3 The log file could not be opened
- 4 Wrong environment
- 5 sapdba could not determine which Oracle version is installed

When you start the sapdba program with any of the command options that do not display the initial menu, instead of specifying the password directly, you can specify it by means of a data file that is passed onto the command. This way, the password will not appear in the operating system process list (command ps). For example, *oratt1> sapdba -check -l system < /oracle/home/mypass* where the file */oracle/home/mypass* contains the password.

Configuring sapdba: The Initialization Profile init<sid>.dba

The sapdba utility uses a set of parameters that can be defined in an initialization profile file. These parameters describe initial values for many of the functions that can be performed by sapdba and related utilities. Some examples are: type of backup, default file compression, size of export and import buffer, and so on.

This file is located by default under the /oracle/<SID>/dbs directory in UNIX systems, and *\orant\database* in Windows NT systems. And the default name is init<SID>.dba. If this file does not exist, sapdba uses standard default set parameters. When calling sapdba in command mode, you can overwrite the parameters set in the initialization profile by using a different profile. You do this using option *-p.*

In menu mode, you can always overwrite default values with new ones just by selecting the needed option and changing it. Some of the available parameters are volume_backup, tape_size, cpio_flags, compress, and backup_mode. For a complete and current list of parameters and the actual permitted values, please refer to the SAP online documentation.

Any changes made to the profile parameters will be active when starting the sapdba program.

***sapdba:* Display Settings.** To get a correct screen display of the sapdba program, you must correctly set both the LINES and COLUMNS environment variables (operating system specific), as well as the TERM variable on UNIX systems. sapdba displays correctly using 24 lines by 80 columns.

The TERM variable must be set according to your terminal type. Typical terminal variable *vt100* will work correctly for most terminal emulation programs and operating systems.

You can configure the number of lines for the screen display of the sapdba menus. By default, it is set to use 24 lines. However, if your display has fewer than 24 lines, you can get a correct display of sapdba by setting the LINES variable before calling the program.

You should also make sure that the UNIX *at* command functions properly. The sapdba program uses the at command for launching reorganizations to be processed on the background. You normally have to add the ora<sid> user to the at.allow file. Refer to the UNIX help or documentation for the command at.

sapdba Log Files. The log files generated when performing sapdba functions are kept either in the sapreorg directory or in the sapcheck directory.

Although sapdba logs all the functions performed when using the tool, it does not log by default the result of an operation. If you want to keep the results of a specific check, you have to set the log option to *yes.*

For example, if you perform the freespace and fragmentation check within the Tablespace administration menu, you can decide to keep the results of the check in a log file by setting the log checks option (option b) to *yes.* In this case, a log with the form <timestamp>.ext is generated under the sapreorg directory.

You set the log check option by simply selecting the option. It works like a switch: if it is set to *no* (default), it is changed to *yes* and vice versa. Setting the option to *yes* is only valid for the current menu. If you go back to another menu, the option is set back to *no.*

Using the sapdba Expert Mode

To enhance the internal security when using sapdba, you can set the expert mode and assign it a password for protecting the most important (or critical) functions of the tool. You can then restrict the access to some of the functions that can only be performed when someone identified as the expert enters the password. These protected functions are the ones that could most negatively affect the system if used incorrectly.

When these functions are protected by the expert mode, anytime a user using sapdba tries to perform any of those, the system will display a message indicating that it is protected. To proceed, the user must identify him- or herself using the expert mode function. In this way, knowing the expert mode password is equivalent to having privileges for performing those critical functions.

NOTE *The expert mode is not supported on Windows NT platforms.*

To call the expert mode, from the initial sapdba screen select option *m—User and Security* and then option *a—Expert mode*. Figure 15-5 shows this screen.

First of all, if you want to manage the expert mode functions, you have to identify yourself as the expert. Select function *a—Switch expert mode,* and enter the expert password in the lower part of the menu as requested by the system.

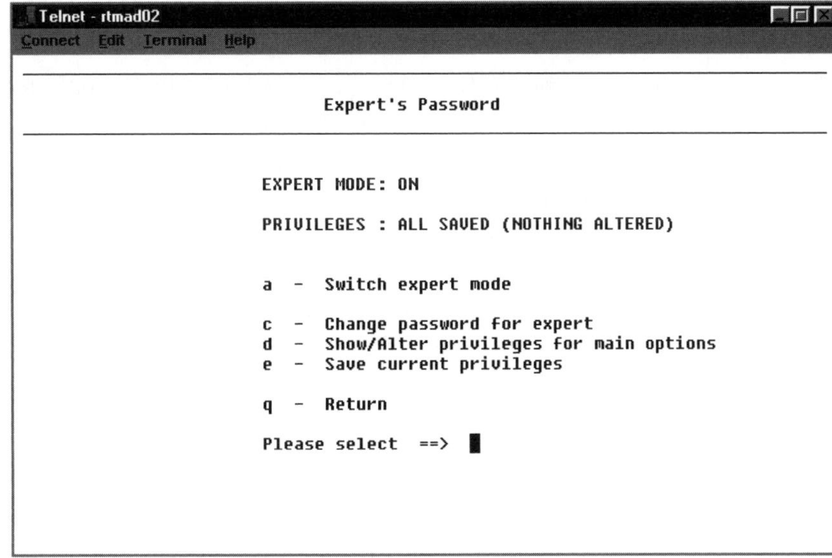

Figure 15-5 The sapdba expert mode screen.

If the password is correct, the system activates the expert mode, and the entry *EXPERT MODE: ON* appears at the top of the menu.

If the user doesn't know the password, she or he can only use the option *Show / Alter privileges for main options* to check what functions have been protected with expert mode.

Using the expert mode, you have the ability to lock the following sapdba menu options:

- *START / STOP.* When protected, it locks the option *Startup / Shutdown instance.*
- *TSP_ADMIN.* When protected, it locks the options *Tablespace administration → Alter tablespace, Add Datafile,* and *Create tablespace.*
- *REORG.* When protected, it locks the following reorganization options: *Reorganize single table or index, Reorganize list of tables and indexes, Reorganize tablespace, Reorganize tablespace and data files,* and *Move / rename data files of a tablespace.*
- *EXP / IMP.* When protected, it locks the export/import option.
- *ARCHIVE_MODE.* When protected, it locks the options *Archive mode → Toggle database log mode* and *Toggle automatic archival.*
- *EXEC_SQL_SCRIPT.* When protected, it locks the option *Additional functions → Execute SQL scripts.*
- *BACKUP.* When protected, it locks the options *Backup database* and *Backup archive logs.*
- *RESTORE.* When protected, it locks the options *Check (and repair) database* and *Restore / Recovery.*
- *CLEANUP.* When protected, it locks the option *Show / Cleanup → Cleanup log files / directories.*
- *ALTER.* When protected, it locks the option *Reorganization → Alter / show table or index storage parameters.*

To display which functions are protected, or if you want to protect additional ones, first identify yourself as the expert if you haven't done so yet, and then select option *d—Show / Alter privileges for main options.*

To apply or remove the protection for any of the available functions, just enter the function's number. When you are finished, press *q* (quit) to go back to the previous menu. If you have made any changes, you will notice that there is a reminder in the privileges display. You still must save your privileges using menu option *e—Save current privileges.* (The privileges are stored in the database table SAPDBAPRIV, so if the database is not up and running, sapdba cannot save any changes to the privileges.)

Expert Mode Password. To set the expert mode password for the first time, select option *b—Set initial password for expert* from the expert menu. The system will request you enter a new password and confirm it a second time.

The password is stored in encrypted form in the file passwd.dba under the /oracle/<SID>/passwd directory. Make sure to protect this directory by assigning it the root owner. However, when the password is protected, you might need to change the owner back to ora<sid> before changing the password.

Normally, the password is changed from the expert's menu using the same option. However, if you forget the password, you must first delete the passwd directory and set the password again just as if it were the first time you entered it.

Displaying Status Information About the Database Instance

Status information about the database instance is automatically shown in the upper part of the sapdba initial screen. You can also display status information about the database instance by selecting option *b—Instance information* from the initial sapdba menu. Figure 15-6 shows this screen.

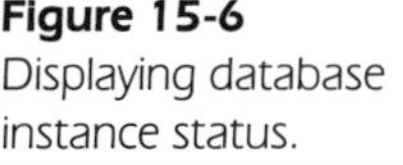

Figure 15-6 Displaying database instance status.

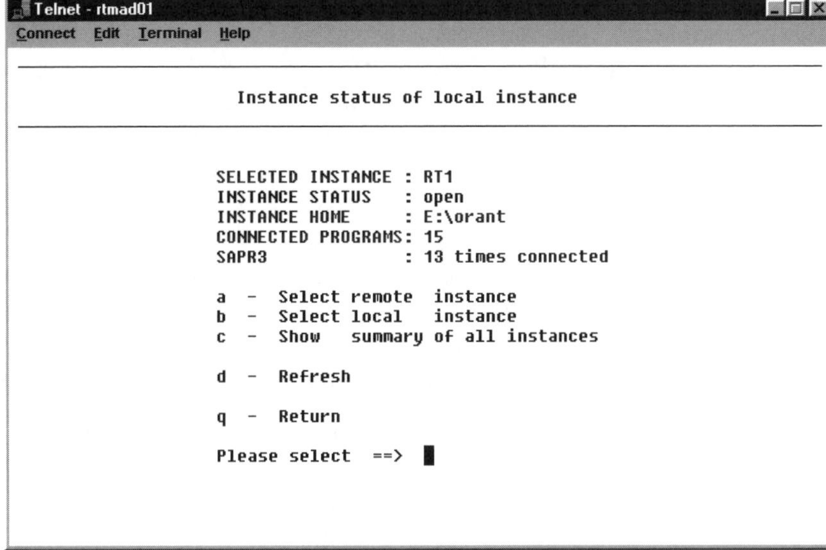

Telnet - rtmad01
Connect Edit Terminal Help
Instance status of local instance
SELECTED INSTANCE : RT1
INSTANCE STATUS : open
INSTANCE HOME : E:\orant
CONNECTED PROGRAMS: 15
SAPR3 : 13 times connected
a - Select remote instance
b - Select local instance
c - Show summary of all instances
d - Refresh
q - Return
Please select ==>

However, for non-OPS installations, this option does not provide any additional information than the one shown on the upper part of the initial sapdba screen.

As you can see in the figure, the system displays:

- *SELECTED INSTANCE.* Shows the name of the database instance.
- *INSTANCE STATUS.* Indicates whether the database instance is up and running (*open*) or shut down (*Instance shutdown*).
- *INSTANCE HOME.* Shows the value for the ORACLE_HOME environment variable.
- *CONNECTED PROGRAMS.* Shows the number of database user programs (mainly the SAP R/3 processes plus the sapdba program itself) connected to the database.
- *SAPR3.* When connected, it means that the R/3 instance is up and running.

Starting and Shutting Down the Database from sapdba

From both the sapdba command mode and menu mode, you can start and stop the Oracle database using some of the available options described in the previous section about starting and stopping the Oracle database.

Remember that you can also start and stop the database by using *startsap DB* and *stopsap DB,* although these commands are only used for the *normal* startup and shutdown options.

From the sapdba menu, select the option *a—Startup/Shutdown instance.* The system displays a new menu as shown in Fig. 15-7. From this menu, you can access the available modes for startup and shutdown by selecting either options *a* or *b.*

You can use the refresh option (*c*) to update and display the current status of the database in the upper part of the screen.

When selecting the startup menu option (*a*), the system allows for starting the database only with the following modes:

- *Startup normal.* This will start the database for normal productive operation.
- *Startup restricted.* This mode will start the database in restricted-session mode, which will be exclusive for database administrators

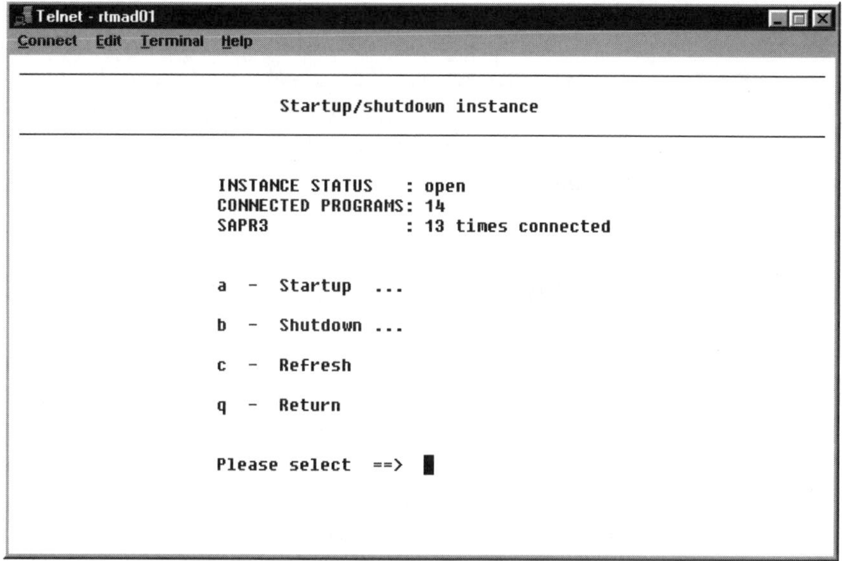

Figure 15-7 Initial menu for starting and stopping the database from sapdba.

and useful for performing management tasks such as reorganizations. You can only start the database this way if it is not open. Otherwise you must shut it down before starting the restricted mode.

If you want to start up the database using other modes such as *mount* or *nomount,* you have to do it from the *svrmgrl* tool.

Selecting option *b—shutdown* will display a new menu.

You can stop the database using several shutdown modes. Details about these modes are described in a previous section. Available options are as follows:

- *Shutdown normal.* This option will stop the database normally and leave it in a consistent state, and it's the recommended way to do it. You can only stop the database this way when SAPR3 is not connected; that is, the R/3 instance was previously stopped.
- *Shutdown immediate.* The database is shut down as soon as connected users finish their current tasks (transactions are finished). However, since in SAP R/3 installations, user processes are held by SAPR3 itself, the database won't stop until R/3 is stopped. Using this mode leaves the database in a consistent state, also.
- *Shutdown abort.* This option should only be used in emergency situations such as when other shutdown options could not stop and close the database. Emergency situations might be related to hard-

ware failures affecting the database volumes. Using this option will stop the database immediately, regardless of connected users or active transactions. This means that the database will be left in an inconsistent status, which will require a database recover at the next database startup. Avoid using this shutdown option except when absolutely necessary.

Displaying Log Files and Log Cleaning Tasks

The initial menu option *l—Show/Cleanup* is used for displaying and cleaning up the log files generated by sapdba (including the backup log, reorganization logs, etc.) as well as removing the oldest ones.

You can also display the initialization profiles for the Oracle database (init<sid>.ora), for the sapdba profile (init<sid>.dba), and for the brbackup/brarchive profile (init<sid>.sap).

To display the profiles and the log files, from the initial sapdba menu, select the option *l—Show/Cleanup* and then select *a—Show log files/profiles.* The system displays a new menu, as shown in Fig. 15-8, where you can display the log files and the profile parameter files just by selecting the option letter.

```
Telnet - rtmad01
Connect  Edit  Terminal  Help

                         Show log files / profiles

          a  -  SAPDBA log files
          b  -  SAPDBA daily check log files
          c  -  SAPDBA main log
          d  -  SAPDBA struct log
          e  -  BRBACKUP log files
          f  -  BRARCHIVE log files
          g  -  initRT1.ora (ORACLE profile)
          h  -  initRT1.sap (BRBACKUP, BRARCHIVE)
          i  -  initRT1.dba (SAPDBA profile)

          q  -  Return

          Please select  ==>
```

Figure 15-8 Available options for displaying log files and profiles.

You should try to purge old log files periodically as well as Oracle audit and trace files. You can do this from the Show/Cleanup menu by selecting option *b—Cleanup log files / directories.*

From this menu, select the type of files you want to delete. In any case, you should retain the previous day's log files. Also, it is recommended that you delete files that are 30 days old. The system will request you to specify how old the log files must be in order to be deleted.

Please observe the following considerations when deleting old log files:

- Deleting logs for brbackup and brarchive processes will make it so that these logs will no be longer available for display within the CCMS functions.
- If a logged action performed with sapdba contained an error mark in the main log, the log will not be deleted from sapdba.
- If you need to restore a backup for which the log file was deleted, you will have to first restore the backup log.

Setting and Switching the Archive Log Mode

Archiving log mode must be normally started for SAP R/3 installations under the Oracle database. In order to start it automatically, enter the needed parameters in the init<sid>.ora file as stated in the previous section "Archived Redo Log Files."

There are situations in which you might consider it convenient for performance reasons to temporarily disable the archive log mode and enable it back again. For example, you can disable it for performing certain lengthy reorganizations or full database imports.

In any case, make sure you always have a consistent backup of the situation before you disable the archive log mode.

There are several ways to switch the archive log mode:

- Manually, using the *svrmgrl* tool by issuing the ALTER DATABASE ARCHIVELOG or ALTER DATABASE NOARCHIVELOG commands.
- Within sapdba, from the initial menu, select option *f—Archive mode.* The system will display the archive mode menu, as shown in Fig. 15-9.

In any case, to change the archive mode, the SAP R/3 instance must be stopped and the database must not be *opened.* When trying to change the

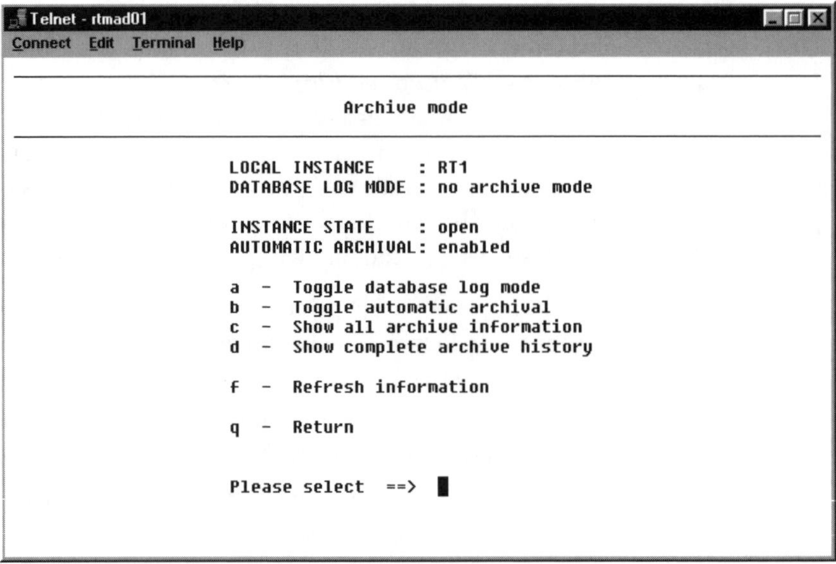

Figure 15-9 Switching ARCHIVE log mode from sapdba.

archive log mode while the database is open, the system will request to shut it down to be able to achieve the operation. If SAP is up and running, you won't be able to change the archive mode either.

Tablespace Administration with sapdba

The sapdba function *c—Tablespace administration* is used for performing usual database administration tasks such as checking the free space or space problems in the tablespaces, extending the available tablespace storage, and creating new tablespaces. The next sections explain in detail all the available options. Figure 15-10 shows the Tablespace administration menu.

Please note that SAP recommends that if any structure change is performed in the database while managing tablespaces, as in when adding new data files, you should always perform a backup to avoid problems recovering a database with structural changes. In fact, after such changes, the system will automatically display the backup menu to allow you to start the backup right away. If you are going to perform several modifications in an administration session, you can wait to finish with all your changes and then perform either a backup of all the modified table-

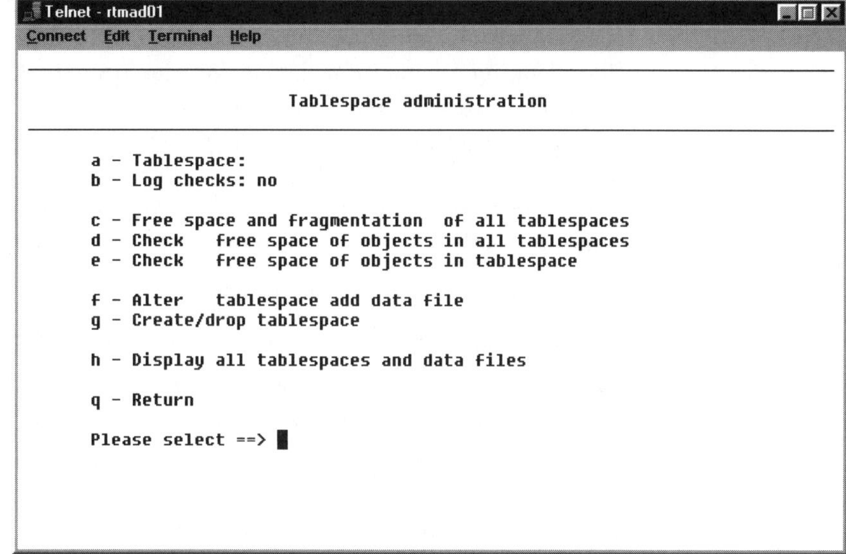

Figure 15-10 Initial menu for tablespace administration.

spaces or a full backup of the whole database. Whether you choose to perform the backup immediately or not, sapdba will make a copy of the old and new control files and leave them in the reorganization directory /oracle/<SID>/sapreorg/<timestamp>. These files are saved with the names *cntrl<SAPSID>.old* and *cntrl<SAPSID>.new.*

You can manage tablespaces using the Oracle server manager (svrmgrl) tool. However, sapdba presents the advantage that it automatically follows SAP naming conventions and will automatically check possible constraints (available storage, for example) as well as supply recommended values for file-system destinations, sizes, and other parameters. The sapdba will notify you of errors before performing an operation with tablespaces.

The tablespace administration menu offers options for managing individual tablespaces as well as performing global checks to all the database tablespaces. When working with individual tablespaces, you must first enter the tablespace name using option *a.* Otherwise, leave this option blank.

The menu option *b—Log checks* can be set to *yes* to store the checks performed in a log file (<timestamp>.ext) under the work directory (sapreorg).

The next sections describe all other tablespace administration options.

Checking the Free Space and Fragmentation of Tablespaces

Under the Tablespace administration menu, you will find several options for checking the available free space. These options should be regularly checked (at least once a day) to prevent one of the most typical problems in R/3 system operation: failure due to insufficient contiguous space. When looking at this information, you can quickly decide to extend one or more tablespaces to avoid those problems.

Using option *c—Freespace and fragmentation of all tablespaces* will display an overview of all current allocated space and the free space remaining together with other useful information. An example is presented in Fig. 15-11. The screen presents the following information:

- *Tablespace.* Indicates the tablespace name.
- *Total.* Total tablespace storage space indicated in kilobytes.
- *Allocated.* Indicates in kilobytes the space that is already allocated (occupied) by database segments (data, indexes).
- *%-Alloc.* The percentage of allocated space in relation with the total space. This is probably the main data to look at. If you find that this figure is over 85 or 90 percent, you might consider reorganizing or, better, extending the tablespace by adding new data files. Reorganization is explained later in this book.
- *Files.* Number of data files conforming the tablespace.
- *Free areas.* Number of areas that can be further allocated by the tablespace when the segments need to be extended. A high number probably means that the tablespace is highly fragmented.

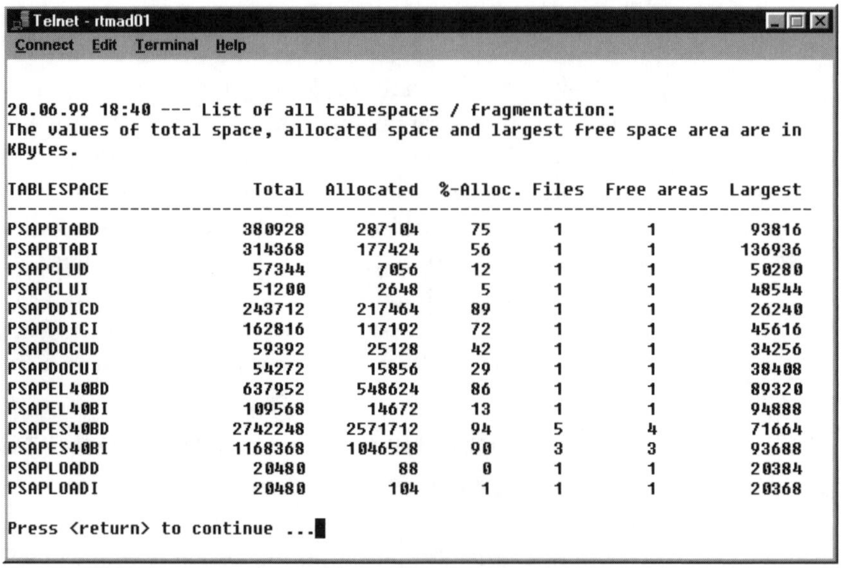

Figure 15-11 Example of a list for free space and fragmentation of tablespaces.

Telnet - rtmad01

Connect Edit Terminal Help

```
20.06.99 18:40 --- List of all tablespaces / fragmentation:
The values of total space, allocated space and largest free space area are in
KBytes.

TABLESPACE                 Total  Allocated  %-Alloc. Files  Free areas  Largest
---------------------------------------------------------------------------------
PSAPBTABD                 380928     287104      75       1          1      93816
PSAPBTABI                 314368     177424      56       1          1     136936
PSAPCLUD                   57344       7056      12       1          1      50280
PSAPCLUI                   51200       2648       5       1          1      48544
PSAPDDICD                 243712     217464      89       1          1      26240
PSAPDDICI                 162816     117192      72       1          1      45616
PSAPDOCUD                  59392      25128      42       1          1      34256
PSAPDOCUI                  54272      15856      29       1          1      38408
PSAPEL40BD                637952     548624      86       1          1      89320
PSAPEL40BI                109568      14672      13       1          1      94888
PSAPES40BD               2742248    2571712      94       5          4      71664
PSAPES40BI               1168368    1046528      90       3          3      93688
PSAPLOADD                  20480         88       0       1          1      20384
PSAPLOADI                  20480        104       1       1          1      20368

Press <return> to continue ...
```

- *Largest.* Size in kilobytes of the largest free area within the tablespace. This information is important when, for instance, the tablespace contains tables or indexes with a new extent size larger than the largest area available in the tablespace. In that case, even if there is free space, the creation of the new extent would fail. Cases like this indicate fragmentation problems.

This information will enable database administrators to decide whether a reorganization might be needed, although, as you will see in following sections, it's better, easier, and faster to extend a tablespace before reorganizing it.

Using the tablespace administration options *d—Check free space for objects in all tablespaces* and *e—Check free space for objects in tablespace,* administrators can check whether any tablespaces can overflow if additional extents are allocated to them. With option *d,* you check all tablespaces, while with option *e,* you must specify the tablespace to check.

When selecting these options, the system will display a prompt requesting the number of extents to be checked. As a result, the system will display a list of tables or indexes that would overflow if the database would allocate the number of extents specified. By default, it usually checks for the creation of one additional extent.

If the system finds no overflow problems in case of extent allocation, it will also be reported. Figure 15-12 shows an example of checking the

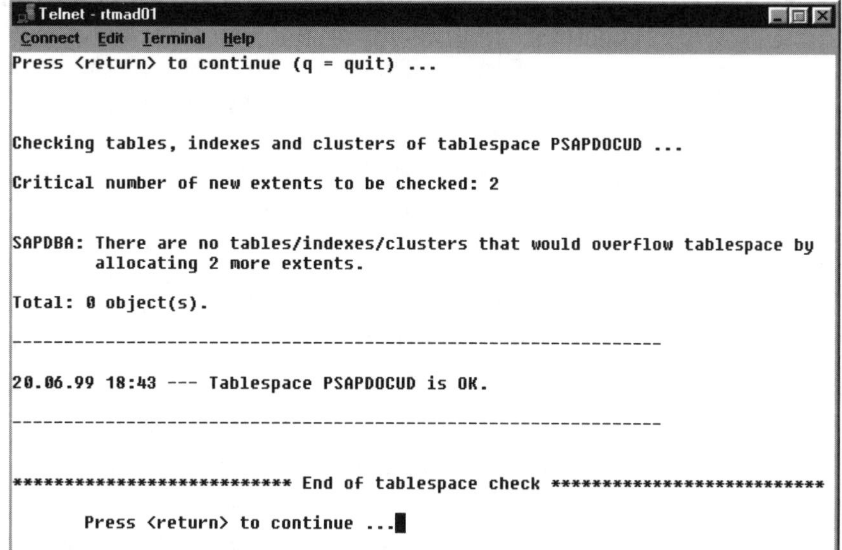

Telnet - rtmad01
Connect Edit Terminal Help
Press <return> to continue (q = quit) ...
Checking tables, indexes and clusters of tablespace PSAPDOCUD ...
Critical number of new extents to be checked: 2
SAPDBA: There are no tables/indexes/clusters that would overflow tablespace by allocating 2 more extents.
Total: 0 object(s).
20.06.99 18:43 --- Tablespace PSAPDOCUD is OK.
*************************** End of tablespace check ***************************
Press <return> to continue ...

Figure 15-12 Checking extents overflow.

PSAPDOCUD tablespace for the allocation of two additional extents. In this example, the system displays no problems.

If the system displays an overflow problem allocating a single extent, you should extend the tablespace as soon as possible.

Remember that you can also check for space-critical problems within the database workload monitors within the performance menu.

There are two other options within the tablespace administration that are used for looking at the files or raw devices that are being used by the tablespaces.

Using option *h—Display all tablespaces and datafiles* the system displays the tablespaces together with the datafiles at the operating system level with the size of the files.

Extending Tablespace Storage Space

If a previous check shows that there is little free space in a tablespace, or if fragmentation problems might produce a tablespace overflow, then one of the possible solutions is to add more space to a tablespace. Another solution, in case of fragmentation problems, can be to reorganize the tablespace.

Adding extra space is achieved by adding new data files. You can do this while the R/3 system is running or when it's stopped; however, the database always needs to be started.

To add a new datafile: from the tablespace administration initial menu, first enter the tablespace name using option *a* and then select option *f—Alter tablespace Add Datafile.* In UNIX environments, the system will first ask if you want to use file systems or raw devices for the new data file. If you decide to use raw devices, please refer to the Oracle and SAP recommendations that you can find in the official documentation guides. In Windows NT environments, the system displays a new screen like the one shown in Fig. 15-13.

On this new screen, the system shows the tablespace name in the header and it also displays by default some suggested values for the new data file. You can, however, change those default values for the size and path of the new data file to adjust them for your needs. Options available in this menu are as follows:

- *File system or raw device (UNIX only).* Indicates whether the new data file is going to be created in file systems or raw device.
- *File size.* The sapdba program provides a suggested size for the new data file calculated in base to either some profile parameters in

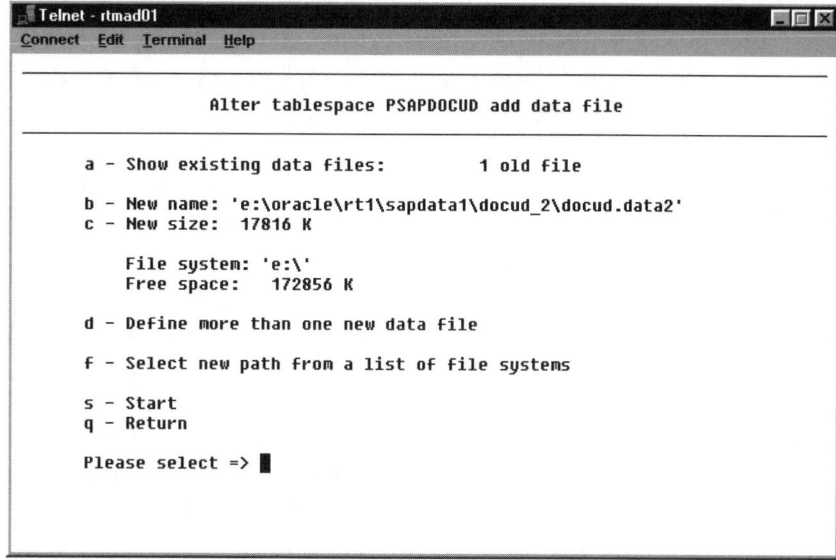

Telnet - rtmad01
Connect Edit Terminal Help
Alter tablespace PSAPDOCUD add data file
a - Show existing data files: 1 old file
b - New name: 'e:\oracle\rt1\sapdata1\docud_2\docud.data2'
c - New size: 17816 K
File system: 'e:\'
Free space: 172856 K
d - Define more than one new data file
f - Select new path from a list of file systems
s - Start
q - Return
Please select =>

Figure 15-13 Menu for extending tablespaces.

the init<SID>.dba file or as a percentage of the total tablespace size. You can enter option *b* and modify this value according to your own growth estimates. On Windows NT systems, as shown in Fig. 15-13, this is option *c—New size,* where you can additionally decide the drive letter for storing the file system.

- *Select path.* By default, sapdba has set a path that complies with SAP standards for placing data and index tablespaces in different file systems. Selecting this option will display a list of all the sapdata directories, highlighting which directories are already used either by the tablespace and the associated data or index tablespace. Please, when choosing a path for a new data file, remember that if data and index tablespaces are located in the same disk volume, a performance loss may result. On Windows NT systems, this is equivalent to option *b—New name,* although the system provides a predefined name that is compliant with SAP naming standards.
- *Alter suggested path.* The sapdba programs display the default directory path for the new data file according to the SAP naming conventions or the one you selected with the previous option. If you choose a different one, it will check if the file system has enough free space for holding the new data file. This option is *f—Select new path from a list of file systems* on Windows NT.

- *Display current files.* The system displays the number of data files already allocated to the tablespace and the total number for the database. On Windows NT this function is available under option *a—Show existing data files.*
- *Define more than one data file.* This is available on Windows NT systems when, due to storage limitations or for big tablespaces, you need to specify more than one data file to be created at once.
- *Start (Add datafile).* Select this option to start the creation of the new data files. When this happens, the system will first check the consistency of the block sizes between the Oracle and the operating system blocks. If it finds a mismatch, the process will prompt you to continue the process. If there are any errors while this process is running, an error message will be displayed. Please stop the process and look at the log files (alert file and the log file generated in the sapreorg directory) to analyze and solve the problem before proceeding.

After the new datafile has been successfully created, the sapdba program will automatically show the menu for backing up the database.

When adding new datafiles, make sure you do select sizes large enough to have free space for a long period of time, especially for tablespaces that grow very quickly, even if this means to waste some extra storage space for some time. It is better and safer to have a lot of extra space than to continuously add new data files and perform new backups every time.

At the database level, a new data file is added by issuing an *ALTER DATABASE ADD DATAFILE* statement. The sapdba program will always perform a backup of the old and new database control files in the work directory (sapreorg).

Data Files Naming Convention. The sapdba utility will always add new data files using the SAP standard naming convention for directories and data-file names. The naming convention is as follows:

- For the directory: /oracle/<SID>/sapdata<n>/<tablespace name>_<file name>
- For the file name: <tablespace name>.data<file number>

where *<n>* is the sequential number for the sapdata directory; *<tablespace name>,* often referred to as *<TSP>,* is the mnemonic name for the tablespace; and *<file number>* is another sequentially assigned number for the data file in the tablespace. Notice that this number appears both in the subdirectory created for the new data file as well as in the data file itself.

The sapdba tools always tries to create the new data file in the same sapdata directory where the last data file (the one with the largest sequential number) was created. For example, suppose you were adding the fourth data file for the PSAPBTABD tablespace in the TT1 database. The third one was created as:

```
/oracle/TT1/sapdata2/btabd_3/btabd.data3
```

Then, if you accept the SAP suggested path for the new data file and there is enough free space in the volume, the fourth data file would be created as:

```
/oracle/TT1/sapdata2/btabd_4/btabd.data4
```

If you specify a different path because there is not enough storage to hold the new file, the sapdata directory will be different, but the subdirectory and the file name will be the same.

SAP allows you to specify nonstandard paths (directories) for the new data files; however, the sapdba tool will first create the data file in the specified nonstandard path, but it will also create a symbolic link between the standard path and your directory.

This way of functioning with symbolic links is what is used when working with raw devices.

Extending Special Tablespaces: SYSTEM and PSAPTEMP. The sapdba tool can also be used to extend the size of special tablespaces such as SYSTEM and PSAPTEMP. However, you must be extremely careful, since once SYSTEM has been extended, it cannot be reduced except by performing complicated reorganizations. You can find notes in SAPnet about this issue.

The PSAPTEMP tablespace can be extended as long as the SAP system has been stopped and there are no processes using temporary segments.

Creating New Tablespaces

The sapdba tool supports creating completely new tablespaces as long as they follow standard SAP naming conventions (PSAP<TSP><D|I>). PSAPROLL and PSAPTEMP can also be created with SAPDBA, but not the SYSTEM tablespace. To call this option, first enter the tablespace name using option *a* in the tablespace administration initial menu and then select option *g—Create / drop database.* The system will ask whether you want to create the new tablespace in a *file system* or *raw device.* Make your selection. Next, the system will display a screen like the one shown in Fig. 15-14 when using file systems.

When creating a new tablespace that is going to hold either a SAP index or data, you must ensure that both tablespaces will be created and also ensure that both will be created in different file systems (sapdatas). The sapdba tool will verify whether both tablespaces (data and index) exist and will display a message. It does not create the counterpart automatically. Obviously, when creating the first one, the other one does not yet exist, but you can continue the process.

Before creating new tablespaces, you should know beforehand what data is going to store, as well as calculate the growth estimates, since you must specify the size and storage parameters for the new tablespaces.

Depending on whether you have chosen file system or raw device, the system displays different options:

- *File system or raw device (UNIX only).* The menu displays whether you will be creating the tablespace in a file system or on raw devices and gives you the option to choose again. Please refer to the Oracle and SAP recommendations found in official documentation for working on raw devices.
- *File size (UNIX) or New size (NT).* Enter the approximate size for the initial datafile of the tablespace. Make it big enough for holding

Figure 15-14 Menu for creating new tablespaces.

```
Telnet - rtmad01
Connect  Edit  Terminal  Help

                    Create tablespace PSAPJAHD

   b - New name: 'E:\oracle\RT1\sapdata1\jahd_1\jahd.data1'
   c - New size:  1600 K

       File system: 'e:\'
       Free space:    172856 K

   d - Define more than one data file
   e - Default storage parameters

   f - Select new path from a list of file systems

   s - Start
   q - Return

   Please select =>
```

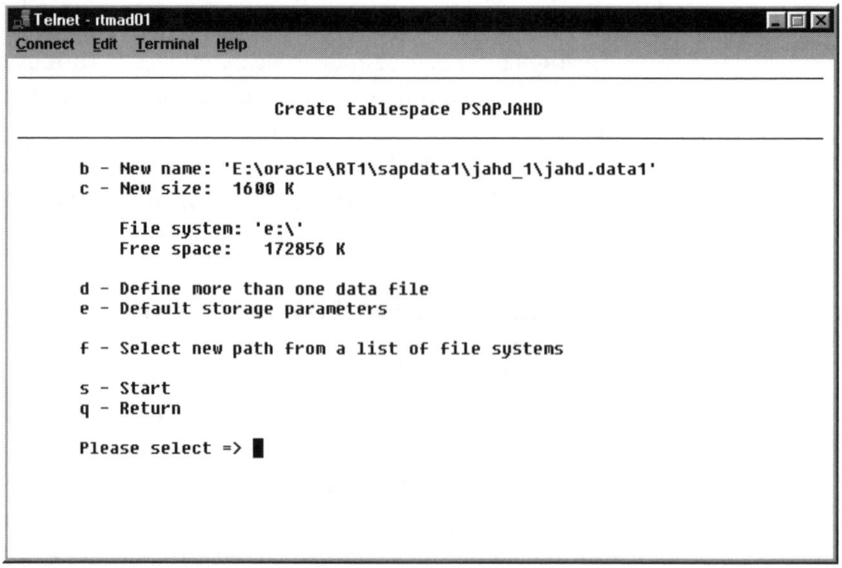

the requested data as well as for additional free space to avoid storage or fragmentation problems. Do not leave the default value, which is usually twice the Oracle block size.

- *Select sapdata path.* When selecting this option, the system displays the list of all the sapdata directories with a mark of data files already in use by its corresponding data or index tablespace (if it exists). For a tablespace that still does not have a counterpart data or index tablespace, select the sapdata that you think might be the most convenient, then remember to create the other in a different sapdata.

Using the *Select sapdata path* option for defining the new data file name offers the advantage that the system will display which directories and what free space are available.

- *Alter suggested path.* The sapdba tool shows the default path following SAP standard naming conventions for tablespaces and data files, or it will display the one you entered using the previous Select path option. If you select a different one, the system will check if there is enough free space for adding the data file. This option is *f—Select new path from a list of file systems* on Windows NT.
- *Default storage parameters.* Although the system displays some standard storage values, you can change them all. Refer to storage parameters at a later section. When table or index segments are later created in this tablespace, these will be the default values used for them.
- *Start (create tablespace).* Select this option to start creating the tablespace. As usual, the log is created in the work directory sapreorg, which can be found by the time stamp.

Introduction to Database Reorganizations Using sapdba

A *database reorganization* is the process of *solving* certain storage problems that develop during the normal operation of the database. These problems are related to the very dynamic database operation and its influence on the database storage environment, such as the creation of extents, the need to add many additional data files, the internal fragmentation, and so on. Ideally, reorganizations should be done as infrequently as possible, because they cause system downtime and can be quite time-consuming.

DBAs should plan ahead for reorganizations. The periodicity will depend on many factors, but it can be a good practice to plan one reorganization every two or three months and then perform all the needed reorganizations in a row so that, for instance, the same previous backup can be used for all of them.

There will be situations, however, when reorganizations will be absolutely necessary, especially when

- The database has reached the hardware limits with respect to the number of extents or number of data files. This possibility will hardly be the typical case, but it can happen.
- The database has performance problems due to the high number of extents, block chaining, and internal fragmentation.

When first installed, the database has an initial status where all database objects are stored in the initial extent and where the tablespaces occupy just one or two data files.

As normal work is being done in the database, such as adding and deleting data, tables, and indexes, the following changes occur:

- *Creation of additional extents* for tables and indexes to make room for new data.
- *Creation of additional data files* for tablespaces when there is not enough free space to create new extents.
- *External fragmentation* problems in tablespaces can occur as the database system automatically generates new extents as more storage is needed when creating new data records. Then, when tables or data records are deleted because they are no longer needed, the tablespaces can become full of *freespace gaps.* These gaps occur when the free storage space available have units that are smaller than the requested extent size, then the space is lost. This problem is no longer so critical, as current releases of Oracle handle these spaces more efficiently.
- *Internal fragmentation* is a problem that happens when the fill level of the data blocks changes. As new data is being added and/or deleted, some blocks are filled completely, while others are not completely occupied. In this last case, the space is used inefficiently. The opposite situation is known as *block chaining,* and it happens when data records occupy more than one block; in these cases, additional blocks are allocated by the database, which must then follow a chain from the first data block to the following data blocks, compris-

ing the data record. The block-chaining problem might have some performance impact, since there will be higher input/output for accessing disks and reading the data, especially in connection with sequential accesses (table full scans) to the table data.

Even when these types of events and changes happen in the database, the time it takes for the SAP system to access the data is not severely affected, since most accesses are performed using indexes. Fragmentation problems impact database performance when accesses are performed without indexes and when input/output bottlenecks develop in the physical disk volumes.

What Can Be Solved with Reorganizations?

Performing reorganizations, you can solve some or all of the problems that develop when operating the database, as described before. You actually reorganize the storage allocated to the database and make a better use of the available space. A reorganization can also have a significant positive impact on system performance.

When reorganizing, you may do the following:

- Merge all the data from an object and compress all the extents into one single extent (the initial extent)
- Merge all data files from one tablespace into a single data file
- Defragment the database: merge the freespace segments into larger ones
- Resolve data chaining by arranging data blocks from the same records contiguously
- Reduce the level of internal fragmentation by balancing the fill level of the data blocks

In summary, reorganizing allows you to start again from a new "storage optimal" situation of the reorganized database elements.

When Is a Reorganization Needed?

Reorganization might be especially needed in two situations:

- When, after a database analysis, the system shows database storage problems, such as internal fragmentation, that are causing performance problems

- When it is absolutely necessary to avoid problems related to the limitations of the database system and the operating system; two limitations can apply, depending on the Oracle release:
  - *Maximum number of extents per table/index.* The maximum number of extents is defined in the segment storage parameter MAXEXTENTS. For an Oracle block of 8 K (the usual size for most operating systems), the usual default software limit was 505 extents in Oracle releases previous to 7.3. From release 7.3 onward, this restriction does not apply, and MAXEXTENTS can be set to UNLIMITED. For performance reasons, SAP's recommendation and usual value is 100. If the parameter MAXEXTENTS is set to 100 and that value is reached, the database cannot create additional extents for the object. You have to either change the parameter to a higher value or reorganize the object.
  - *Maximum number of files per database.* The number of files in the database includes the data files, the redo log files, and the control files. The default software limit is 254 files. The hardware limit is set to 1022 files in most operating systems. This number is hardly reached in SAP installations. This number is set in the parameter db_files in the init<sid>.ora file. If you are approaching this number, you could reorganize on a tablespace basis to reduce the number of data files.

It is important to notice that database storage problems can often be solved by adjusting certain storage parameters instead of performing reorganizations. So, before carrying out reorganization, you must analyze whether a reorganization is really needed or if it can be avoided.

Analyzing Whether a Reorganization Is Needed

The sapdba tool provides several functions for performing reorganizations, for changing storage parameters to avoid reorganizations, and for analyzing if reorganizations are really needed. To access those functions, from the initial sapdba menu, select option *d.* Figure 15-15 shows the initial reorganization menu.

One of the most useful functions, because of the extensive information it can provide, is option *a—Check extents and fragmentation* within the sapdba reorganization menu. Figure 15-16 shows this menu.

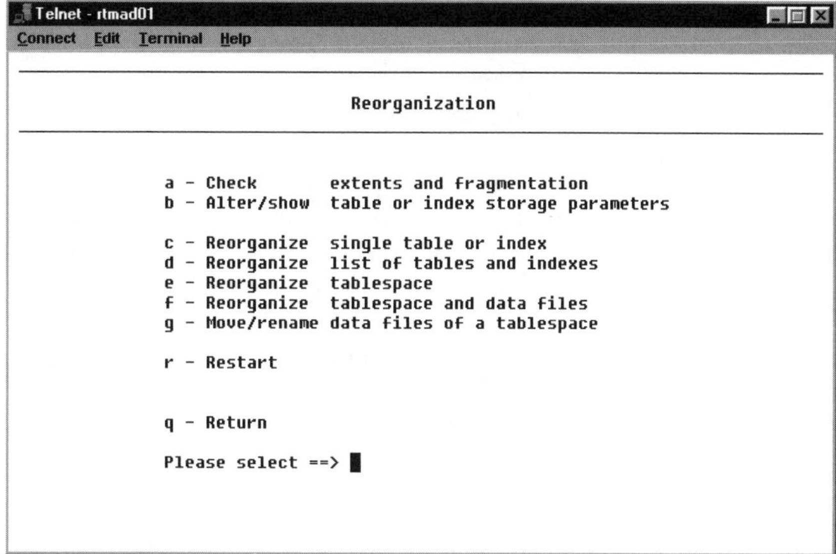

Figure 15-15 Initial menu for the sapdba reorganization options.

The following sections describe how to use available options under this menu to analyze the state of the database storage to determine whether reorganization is needed. Many of these checks can also be performed using the database performance functions within the R/3 CCMS. However, sapdba always includes current information, whether the perfor-

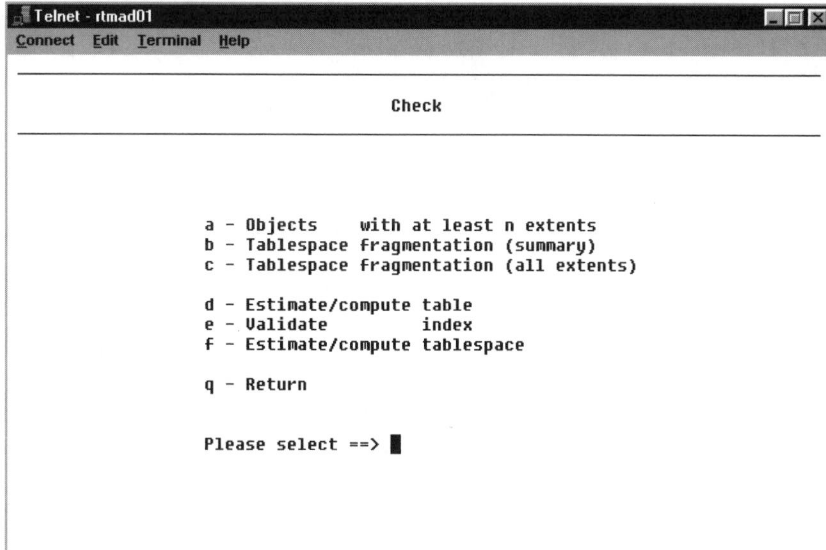

Figure 15-16 Menu for checking objects and fragmentation.

mance database might not show up-to-date information, since the collector program runs certain checks only at specified hourly intervals.

Analyzing Extents. To analyze the actual database extents, from the reorganization initial menu, select option *a—Objects with at least n extents.* Figure 15-17 shows the new menu displayed by the system.

Most SAP R/3 objects have a maximum number of extents (storage parameter) set to 100, and some have a value of 300.

From this new menu, select option *d—Number of extents* to set the criteria for the check. In Fig. 15-17, the check is restricted to objects with at least 50 extents. This option is useful for listing the objects that might need to be reorganized due to a large number of extents.

By default, this function checks all objects in the database, but you can restrict the search by tablespaces (selecting option *a*) and also by single objects (selecting option *c*).

In most sapdba functions, you can specify the Oracle wildcard (placeholder) % for specifying several objects. This placeholder corresponds to the standard Oracle function *LIKE*.

When you have specified the check criteria, enter *s—Start* for performing the check. If, as a result of the check, you find many objects approaching the software limit for maximum number of extents, you might start thinking about a reorganization.

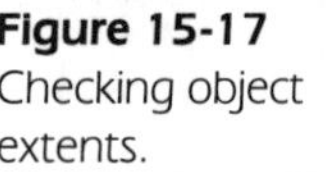

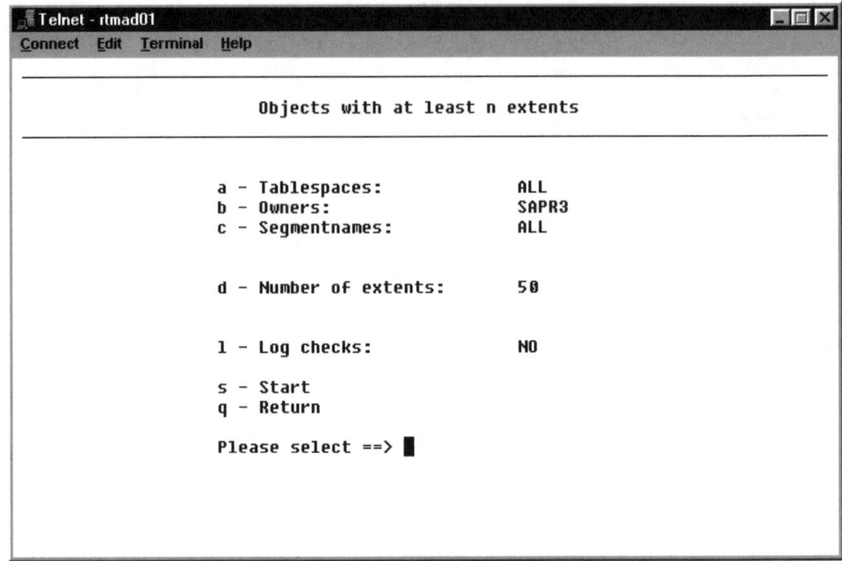

Figure 15-17 Checking object extents.

If the check shows extent problems, there are two ways to temporarily avoid a reorganization. Both have to do with changing storage parameters:

- Increasing the number for maximum extents
- Increasing the size for the NEXT storage parameters

These methods are explained in later sections.

Analyzing the Fragmentation. After analyzing which are the critical extents by using the previous option from the reorganization menu, you can further display and check the level of fragmentation in the tablespaces. While a very similar option is available on the tablespace administration menu, the reorganization menu provides more detailed and extensive checks and information. Analyzing the fragmentation includes the following options:

- *b—Tablespace fragmentation (summary).* Displays summary information about the fragmentation level of the specified tablespace, including number of objects, allocated extents, free space areas, free fragments, number of data files, largest free space area, and available storage space.
- *c—Tablespace fragmentation (all extents).* Displays very detailed information about all segments and their extents for the selected tablespace. For example, you can display specific fragmentation details of certain database segments by restricting the check to those objects that showed a larger number of extents.
- *d—Estimate / compute table, e—Validate index, f—Estimate compute tablespace.* Can be used for analyzing the actual allocated storage space and the actual occupied space. For example, a table can have 10 MB allocated because of its initial extent size; however, it might really contain just 2 MB of data. These options must be handled with care, since they are long-running processes and they lock access for users to those objects. Therefore, you should only start these options when no users are connected or after setting the restricted mode. With these options, you can analyze individual tables (option *d—Estimate / Compute table*), individual indexes (option *e—Validate index*), or all objects of a tablespace (option *f—Estimate / Compute tablespace*).

These options use the Oracle functions *ANALYZE TABLE <table name> ESTIMATE / COMPUTE STATISTICS* and the *ANALYZE INDEX <index name> VALIDATE STRUCTURE.*

The result of these analyses can be used when specifying a new storage size for the objects to be reorganized. For example, you might use those values for reducing the size of some objects (using option *Reduce object: yes*). However, you must always take into consideration the recommended safety margin for letting at least a 20 percent free space for the objects.

You can also perform the intensive fragmentation and free space analysis by using the sapdba *-analyze* command option, which calls the same Oracle ANALYZE and COMPUTE statements. Please refer to the SAP online documentation for available options, syntax, and restrictions.

Reorganization Types

With sapdba, you can perform several types of reorganization. You should always try to choose the reorganization type that is most convenient for solving the current storage problems as well as anticipating provisions for minimizing future ones. Besides reorganizing the full database, there are three available reorganization types:

- *Reorganization of single tables or indexes.* This type of reorganization consists in merging all the object (table or index) extents into a larger initial extent, when the default *compress extents* option is set to *yes.* This type of reorganization by compressing extents can be performed as long as there are sufficient contiguous areas in the overall tablespace. The sapdba tool will perform the needed checks before reorganizing to make sure it can be achieved. The Oracle database additionally merges the free space fragments it finds in the tablespace. This type is the fastest and an easier method of reorganization, although in especially large R/3 tables, such as ATAB, it might take many hours. Figure 15-18 shows a picture of this type of reorganization. This type of reorganization is performed using the option *c—Reorganize single table or index* from the reorganization menu. Similarly, option *d—Reorganize list of tables and indexes* will also produce the desired effect with the difference that you can specify a group of objects in a previously created ASCII file containing the list of objects.
- *Reorganization of a tablespace.* This type of reorganization will merge all the objects it contains (tables or indexes) using one extent per object. It will also merge all the free space in the tablespace into one larger segment per every data file. Figure 15-19 shows a simple diagram of this type of reorganization. This type of reorganization is

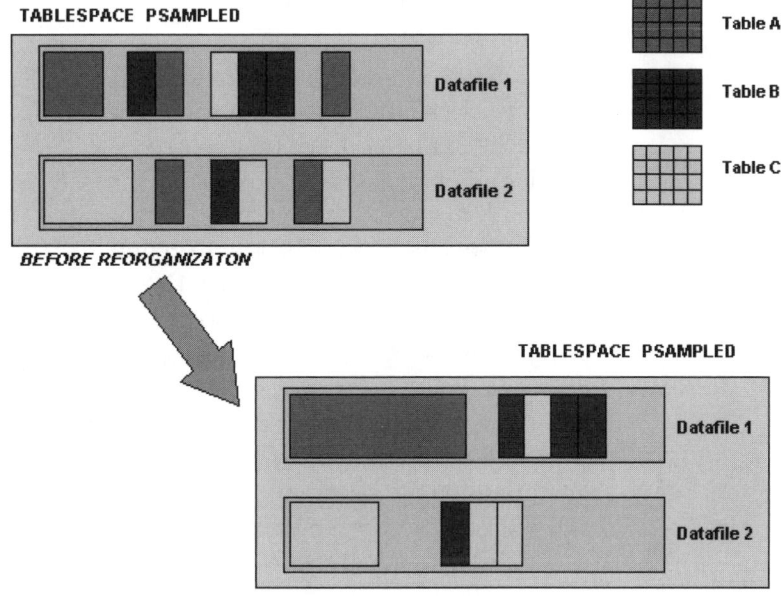

Figure 15-18 Simple diagram for reorganization of single objects.

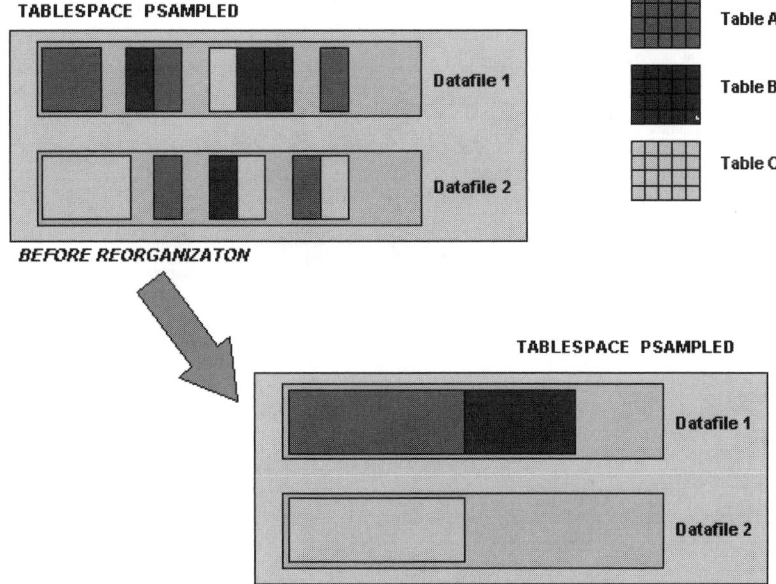

Figure 15-19 Simple diagram for reorganization of tablespace.

performed selecting option *e—Reorganize tablespace* from the reorganization menu.

- *Reorganization of tablespaces with data files.* This type of reorganization works similarly to the previous one, but additionally it will merge the data files of the tablespace into a single data file (or into a smaller number of data files) as long as the file size is smaller than the limit imposed by the operating system. Most 32-bit operating systems set this limit to 2 GB; others (mainly 64-bit operating systems) do not have this limitation. Figure 15-20 shows a simple diagram of this type of reorganization. This type of reorganization is performed using option *f—Reorganize tablespace and data files* from the reorganization menu. This might be the most complicated reorganization type since you must be especially careful deciding the number and placement of the new data files. When because of operating system limitations on file sizes you need more than one data file, the sapdba tool will suggest to write the contents of the old data files into a number of files with equal size, and it will try to write them into the same directory following standard SAP naming conventions. So, you must also ensure that there is sufficient storage space available. In any case, sapdba will check for all restrictions and report on any problem.

Related with this last type, the reorganization menu option *g—Move / rename data files of a tablespace* allows you to change the path for the data files of a tablespace without reorganizing it.

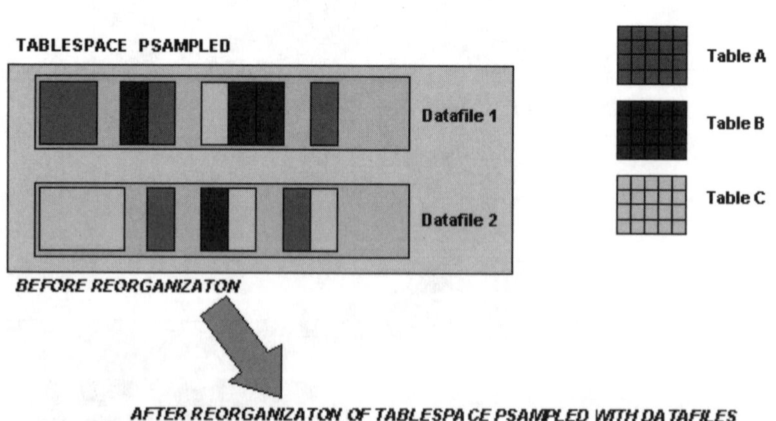

Figure 15-20 Simple diagram for reorganization of tablespace with data files.

The following sections deal in detail with how to proceed for carrying out these reorganization types; but before going on, it's important to have a good idea of the storage parameters managed by the database system, since they are the key to understanding the real reorganization process. Some of these parameters have been mentioned already in several previous sections.

Storage Parameters

A correct understanding of the storage parameters can certainly help when making reorganizations and also for avoiding them. Setting all of the parameters at optimal values for all database objects can be a difficult task.

Before and during some phases of a reorganization, you can manually change important storage parameters. However, some of the parameters in the following list should not be changed manually by DBAs unless they are real Oracle database experts or when they are instructed by SAPnet notes or SAP consultants to do so.

A brief description of the most important storage parameters follows:

- *INITIAL.* It's the size of the first object extent. When using the option "Compress extents = yes" during a reorganization, the total size occupied by the object extents plus the initial extent is merged into a new and larger initial extent. HINT: When reorganizing, you can assign a larger value for the INITIAL parameter when you know it is a table or an index that grows very quickly. You can also reduce the size.
- *NEXT.* Indicates the size of the new extents that the database creates as it needs to add new data to the objects. This value can be entered manually or can be calculated automatically by SAP using tables DD09L, TGORA, and IGORA. These tables store the size category and suggested next extent sizes for the database objects. HINT: To avoid reorganizations because the number of extents is reaching the limit, you can change the NEXT parameter value to a larger size, in which case fewer extents will be created.
- *MAXEXTENTS.* Indicates the maximum number of allowed extents for the database segment (table, index, rollback). It's normally set to 100 for Oracle block sizes of 8K. This parameter can be increased or set to UNLIMITED in emergency situations.
- *MINEXTENTS.* It's the starting number of extents when the object is created. It's normally always set to 1, except in rare situations where the INITIAL extent is split in several data files because of space problems or limitations.

- *PCTINCREASE.* This parameter sets in percentage the growth factor for creating new extents. For example, if it was set to 10, every new extent would be 10 percent larger than the previous one. In SAP, this parameter is always set to zero, otherwise tables could grow exponentially and overflow some tablespaces in short order. When set to zero, all new extents always have the size set in the NEXT parameter.
- *PCTFREE.* This parameter specifies the percentage of the data blocks that is not filled with data but rather is reserved for later updates or changes that might occur to those data blocks. The default value in SAP installations is 10 percent.
- *PCTUSED.* Indicates the percentage of space in the data blocks that Oracle will try to fill before allocating a new block. Normally, if a data block is full, no more rows can be added to it until the percentage of the used storage falls below the value indicated by this parameter. This parameter cannot be specified for indexes. The SAP default value for PCTUSED is 40 percent.

Those are the most important parameters that you will normally deal with when performing reorganizations. There are other Oracle storage parameters that you can find in the official documentation.

Avoiding Reorganizations: Changing Storage Parameters

You can temporarily avoid carrying out reorganizations by modifying some storage parameters, especially MAXEXTENTS and NEXT.

These parameters can be changed using the option *b—Alter/show table or index storage parameters* from the reorganization menu. Figure 15-21 shows this menu.

As introduced earlier, the usual limit for tables and indexes in the SAP system is set normally to 100 extents for an Oracle block size of 8K. If the object reaches this limit and the database tries to allocate an additional extent, an extent overflow error will occur, and it won't be possible to create it.

To solve this problem, you can temporarily and as an emergency solution raise the value or set it to UNLIMITED. You then must solve this situation as soon as possible in the next planned reorganization. When a reorganization takes place, the object's MAXEXTENTS parameters are automatically set to the standard value.

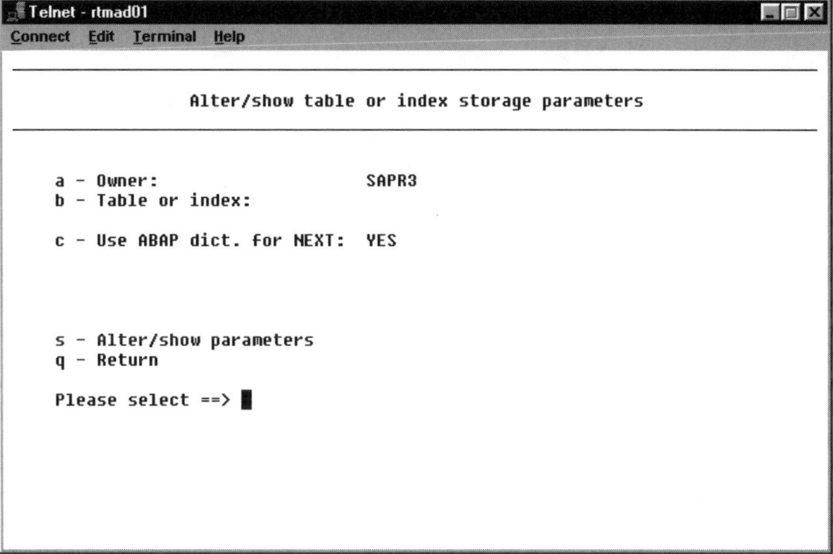
Alter/show table or index storage parameters

a - Owner: SAPR3
b - Table or index:

c - Use ABAP dict. for NEXT: YES

s - Alter/show parameters
q - Return

Please select ==>

Figure 15-21 Initial menu for showing or modifying an object's storage parameters.

Similarly, if you notice that the number of extents for some tables or indexes grows relatively quickly and approaches the MAXEXTENTS limit, you can also increase the value for the NEXT parameter, thus making the new extents larger. When you increase this value, it means that more data blocks can be allocated per new extent, so less extents will be needed for holding the same data volume, thereby decreasing the growth pace for the number of extents.

To change any of these parameters in the menu shown previously in Fig. 15-21, select option *b—Table or index name* to enter the object's name. For option *c—User ABAP dict. for NEXT,* when set to *yes,* the sapdba tool will use the values found in SAP tables DD09L and TGORA/IGORA to calculate and suggest the new value; otherwise, it will suggest a new value based on current sizes. Make your choice and select option *s—Alter/show parameters* to proceed. The system will display a new menu with the object's storage parameter information, as in the example shown in Fig. 15-22.

On this new menu, you can either accept SAP's suggested values as shown in the middle column, or set your own by selecting the options *b, d, e,* and *f.* After selecting an option and, if needed, entering your own values, to perform the actual change, select the commit option *s.*

An easier way of adjusting the NEXT storage parameter for all the objects in a tablespace is by regularly using the sapdba command line option *-next.* This option will automatically adjust the values of the NEXT

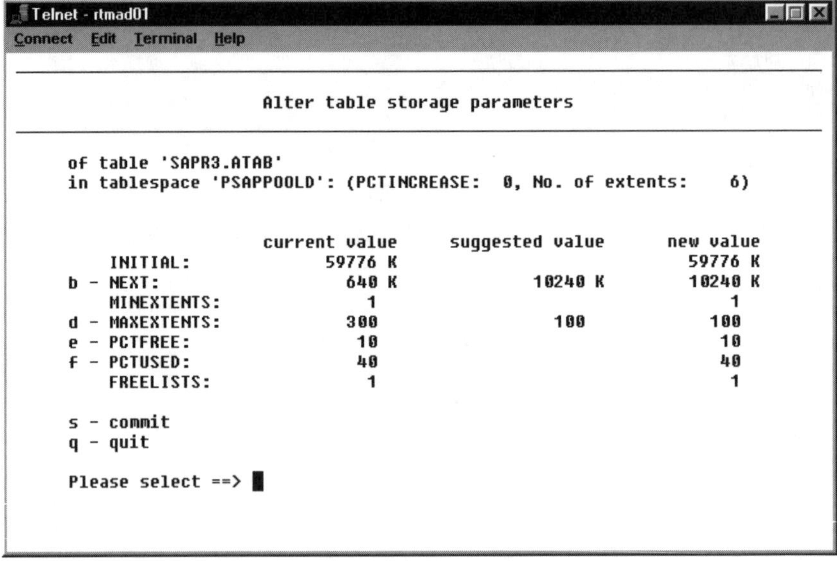
```
Telnet - rtmad01
Connect  Edit  Terminal  Help

                         Alter table storage parameters

    of table 'SAPR3.ATAB'
    in tablespace 'PSAPPOOLD': (PCTINCREASE:  0, No. of extents:    6)

                          current value     suggested value       new value
        INITIAL:               59776 K                              59776 K
    b - NEXT:                    640 K             10240 K          10240 K
        MINEXTENTS:                1                                    1
    d - MAXEXTENTS:              300               100                100
    e - PCTFREE:                  10                                   10
    f - PCTUSED:                  40                                   40
        FREELISTS:                 1                                    1

    s - commit
    q - quit

    Please select ==>
```

Figure 15-22 Example of options for modifying an object's storage parameters.

parameters according to the growth of the objects within the tablespace. It's somehow similar to setting manually the PCTINCREASE parameter.

The syntax of the *-next* option is *sapdba -next <tablespace/s>*. This option works by adjusting the NEXT parameter according to the values contained in the SAP tables DD09L, TGORA (for tables), and IGORA (for indexes) and comparing them with the current values. If no entry for an object exists in these tables, the NEXT parameter is calculated in base to the current NEXT value or 10 percent of the total allocated space.

Additional storage parameters that can be modified to optimize the occupancy of data blocks in the database, therefore avoiding reorganizations, are PCTFREE and PCTUSED. But these processes should only be performed by experienced database administrators.

Considerations Before Performing Reorganizations

Although reorganization is not a really difficult process, you must take all the precautions necessary for its successful completion; and, in case it doesn't complete successfully, you should be able to restore the status of the database to what it was before the reorganization. For this reason, you should consider the following before performing reorganizations:

- Be sure to analyze whether the reorganization is really needed and that you cannot avoid it using some of the methods described earlier about changing storage parameters.
- Decide on the type of reorganization to perform: single objects, list of objects, tablespace, or tablespace with data files. An alternative type is to perform a reorganization of the full database by doing full export and import. This is described in following sections about export/import procedures.
- Check your system limits and resources: be sure to know your operating system and database parameters, such as the Oracle block size and storage limits, and also be sure to have sufficient space in the work directory (sapreorg) for holding the files generated during reorganizations.
- When reorganizing tablespaces without data files, you should also be sure that the tablespaces to hold reorganized objects have enough free space, for example, when you are going to use reorganizations to move database objects to different tablespaces.
- Reorganization will require you to stop the SAP system, thus causing downtime. Usually, these processes must be performed out of normal working hours or on weekends, so try to bundle your reorganizations to avoid further system downtime.
- Since certain reorganizations might take a long time, be sure to allow a sufficient time window, considering the time it might take to get the database back to its state before the reorganization in case of severe errors. To get a time estimate, you can check if a similar reorganization has been performed before by looking at the main log reorg<SID>.log. To shorten the time, try to carefully follow some recommendations on speeding up reorganizations. Refer to the following section.
- Perform a backup or follow the SAP-recommended backup concept for reorganizations, which you can find in the online documentation. This concept basically recommends that you perform a full backup before tablespace reorganizations, and, in the case of single-object reorganizations such as tables or indexes, you could, instead of a backup, perform a previous import for the objects, which is also a secure way of protecting the data. The backup concept also applies *after* the reorganization; for instance, you should also perform a backup after a database structural change, such as the reorganization of tablespaces with data files.

- For special tablespace reorganizations, besides following the general recommendations, try to find related notes on SAPnet. Special tablespaces are, for example, PSAPTEMP and PSAPPOOLD. You can find a few notes relating to problems encountered by users when reorganizing these special tablespaces.
- Finally, you must stop the SAP system to run reorganizations. The database must be up and running. It should be started in privileged mode (restricted) to avoid other users logging in. It is recommended you start a reorganization right after starting the database, since no locks will yet exist on the database objects.

Speeding Up Reorganizations

Certain types of reorganizations might need long running times to complete. In those cases, you can try to use several methods to speed them up. Please be careful when using some of these methods, and, especially when changing parameter values in some initialization files, do not forget to set them back to their original values.

There are many possible procedures to speed up reorganizations.

Changing Certain init<sid>.ora Parameters. Besides changing the setup of rollback segments, which is described elsewhere, there are two parameters that might beneficially influence the time it takes for carrying out a reorganization. These parameters are sort_area_size and db_file_multi_block_read_count.

The sort_area_size parameter will be used to speed up sorting processes while reorganizing. As recommended by SAP in the official documentation, you increase the value for sort_area_size to 8,388,608 (1024 buffers of 8K blocks each).

The db_file_multi_block_read_count parameter indicates the number of blocks that can be read or written per database operation. SAP recommends increasing this value to 64.

To change these values, stop the database system, edit the init<sid>.ora file and make a copy of those lines with the original values, then comment out one of them using the number sign (#) at the beginning of the line and modify the value in the copied line. Then start up the database again for the values to become active.

When the reorganization has finished, and before starting productive operation of the SAP system, set back the original values by deleting the new added lines and removing the comments from the original ones.

Temporarily Disabling the Archive Log Mode. Because the reorganization uses export and import procedures, there might be a lot of transactions (in the import phase) going on in the database, which can generate many archive redo logs. So, before long reorganizations (full database, big tablespaces, ATAB, or other long tables), you should probably disable the archive log mode if the SAP backup concept is to be strictly followed. Otherwise, you might get redo log file gaps and affect the recovery procedures.

Disabling archive log modes offers the advantages of minimizing the input/output generated by the archiver process, avoiding possible archiver-stuck problems, and you will not need to back up extra archive logs.

After a reorganization is finished, a full backup is mandatory, and the archive log mode must be enabled again before starting productive operation of the SAP system.

The *commit=no* Option and the Big Rollback Segment. These two recommendations are the ones that have shown a reduction of time for a long reorganization of about one-third and even one-fourth.

In certain Oracle versions, and especially when importing long records, the import tool performs a commitment of changes for every record, instead of getting the full array of records with the exp_imp_buffer value. So when performing a reorganization that involves long records (i.e., ATAB), manually change the import script's *commit=yes* parameter to *commit=no.*

For this trick to be much more effective, you should also create a new and big rollback segment of at least the size of the longest table in a tablespace. You can determine this size by issuing the following svrmgrl command:

```
svrmgrl> select max(bytes) from dba_segments where tablespace_name
         = '<tablespace name>' and segment_type = 'table';
```

Then you will have to create the tablespace to hold the big rollback segment, the rollback segment itself, and put it online. If possible, place the new tablespace in a different disk volume as other sapdatas. You can do this also from the svrmgrl tool:

```
svrmgrl> create tablespace PSAPBIGROLL datafile
         '/oracle/<SID>/sapdata7/bigroll_1/bigroll.data1' size>;
svrmgrl> create rollback segment BIGROLL tablespace PSAPBIGROLL
         storage (INITIAL <size/10> NEXT <size/10> OPTIMAL
         <size/5>;
svrmgrl> alter rollback segment BIGROLL online;
```

Next, with the SAP system stopped but not the database, set offline all other rollback segments except for SYSTEM and BIGROLL:

```
svrmgrl> alter rollback segment PRS_1 offline;
...
svrmgrl> alter rollback segment PRS_n offline;
```

Edit the init<sid>.ora file to comment out the rollback_segments line (usually one of the last in the file) and, in its place, write down your created rollback segment:

```
rollback_segments = (BIGROLL).
```

Stop and start the database for the new parameter to be effective.

After the reorganization, set back all the usual rollback segments online (PRS_1, PRS_2 . . .) *before* putting offline BIGROLL. Change back the init<sid>.ora parameters and stop and start the database again. If you think you might need this procedure several times, you can leave the big rollback segment off-line and commented out for other occasions. Otherwise, you might drop the tablespace and then delete the associated datafile.

Performing Processes in Parallel. The most time-consuming processes of a reorganization occur mainly in the export/import phase but also when generating the indexes for very long tables. The sapdba system supports performing several processes in parallel in any of those phases. To do that, you have to set up the degree of parallelism for these processes in the init<sid>.dba profile file. The degree of parallelism sets the number of parallel processes that will be running for performing a specific action. It should not be higher than 2 or 3 times the number of CPUs of the database server.

To set a default degree of parallelism for the export/import process, set the profile parameter exp_imp_degree to a value higher than 1. To set a default degree of parallelism for the index creation process, set the profile parameter index_degree to a value higher than 1. By default, both parameters are set to 1. In any case, you can interactively enter the degree of parallelism for index creation in the available reorganization-type menu options. It does not make sense to set a degree of parallelism for reorganizing single objects.

WARNING! *Do not confuse performing several processes in parallel which are meant for the same reorganization with performing parallel reorganizations, that means launching different reorganizations. You should never perform more than one reorganization in parallel.*

Miscellaneous Tricks. There are other possibilities to decrease the time it takes for reorganizations to complete, although the improvement by these miscellaneous tricks are hard to measure. These possibilities are as follows:

- *Extending the temporary segment tablespace PSAPTEMP.* This tablespace should be large enough to hold the largest database index. This is a good practice, not only for reorganizations, but also in normal operation.
- *Temporarily disabling disk mirroring.* Depending on the disk mirroring technology, whether this is performed by software or hardware, it takes some CPU time. Temporarily disabling disk mirroring could provide a small increase in performance; however, you should balance the consequences.
- *Increasing processes priority.* Using operating system utilities, you can find which processes run the reorganizations (for example, the imp program and the shadow Oracle process) and you might manually increase the priority of the associated processes. Please handle process priority changes with care. In some UNIX operating systems, this is achieved with the *nice* and *renice* commands. In Windows NT systems you can do this from the Task Manager.

Running Reorganizations

To start a reorganization, please observe the points indicated previously in "Considerations before Performing Reorganizations" and "Speeding Up Reorganizations." To be able to recover an error situation while reorganizing, it's particularly important to follow the SAP backup concept.

Before starting to reorganize, remember to stop the SAP system and start the database in restricted mode for exclusive use by the administrator.

Basically, when any type of reorganization is run with the sapdba tool, the following things happen:

- The system checks the requirements and creates the scripts that will actually perform the reorganization.
- Database objects (its data contents and definition) are exported to dump files.
- Database objects are dropped (deleted) from the database.
- Database objects are newly created (defined) in the database, often using different storage parameters.
- Database objects (contents) are imported back into the database using the previously exported dump files.
- Other related objects are regenerated (indexes).

When a reorganization is performed using the sapdba functions, the preceding procedures take place in two phases: a preparation phase and a main phase.

The Preparation Phase. The preparation phase, in which the system creates all the needed script for performing the reorganization: export script for creating the export dump files, import script, restart script, SQL scripts for dropping and creating database objects, and so on. The type and number of scripts depend on the reorganization type. For each type of script and object, the system generates a log file under the working directory (sapreorg) below one or more <timestamp> subdirectories.

In this preparation phase, sapdba determines if the SAP instance is running by checking whether the database user SAPR3 is connected. If this is the case, it will issue a warning message. It will also check that free space in data files as well as storage requirements in file systems is enough to hold the reorganization.

At the end of the preparation phase, when all the scripts have been created and the checks performed, sapdba will offer the option of starting the scripts immediately, in batch, or at a later time. Figure 15-23 shows an example of the system output on the preparation phase.

The Main Phase. The main phase is in charge of processing the scripts created in the preparation phase, thus performing the real reorganization. Before starting the reorganization, the system will make sure that

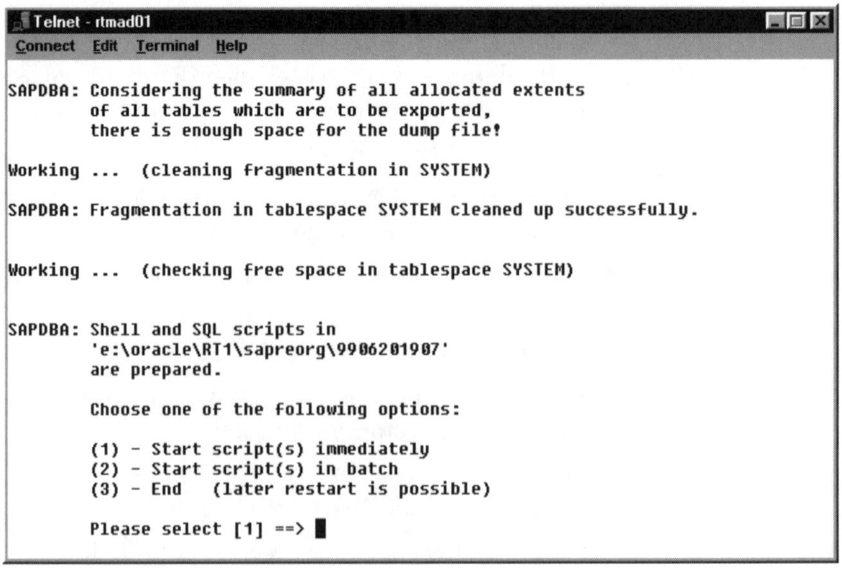

Figure 15-23 Running reorganization up to the end of the preparation phase.

```
Telnet - rtmad01
Connect  Edit  Terminal  Help

SAPDBA: Considering the summary of all allocated extents
        of all tables which are to be exported,
        there is enough space for the dump file!

Working ...  (cleaning fragmentation in SYSTEM)

SAPDBA: Fragmentation in tablespace SYSTEM cleaned up successfully.


Working ...  (checking free space in tablespace SYSTEM)


SAPDBA: Shell and SQL scripts in
        'e:\oracle\RT1\sapreorg\9906201907'
        are prepared.

        Choose one of the following options:

        (1) - Start script(s) immediately
        (2) - Start script(s) in batch
        (3) - End   (later restart is possible)

        Please select [1] ==>
```

the user SAPR3 is not connected. Otherwise, the reorganization will be terminated.

The sapdba tool will process the reorganization by running the previously created scripts:

- It will first process the export phase, in which the object's contents and definition are exported into an export dump file in the work directory.
- Next, objects (and contents) are deleted from the database. Notice that, because actual deletion occurs, it is important to have a backup, since if a severe error occurs in the next steps, the database can be severely damaged, and only a recovery from backups might be possible.
- There is a script in charge of creating the object's definition, probably with modified storage parameters as before the reorganization. For example, by setting the INITIAL extent to the size of the whole table or index.
- Next, the data is imported back into the newly defined objects.
- Depending on the reorganization type, other scripts will be performed, such as index creation.

Performing Reorganizations Using the sapdba Reorganization Menu

From the initial sapdba reorganization menu as shown in Fig. 15-15, there are several menu options for performing reorganizations. From the initial menu, you select the reorganization type (for example, option *e—Reorganize tablespace,* which will display a new menu with several options as shown in Fig. 15-24). These menus will contain slightly different options depending on the chosen reorganization types.

There are, however, common options for all reorganization types that are introduced in the following sections. Those other options that are type-specific will be explained in the corresponding section. All the following options can be changed interactively before starting the reorganization.

Working Directory. It's the directory in which the reorganization scripts and the log files are created. The default directory is /oracle/<SID>/sapreorg. You can change this directory when necessary.

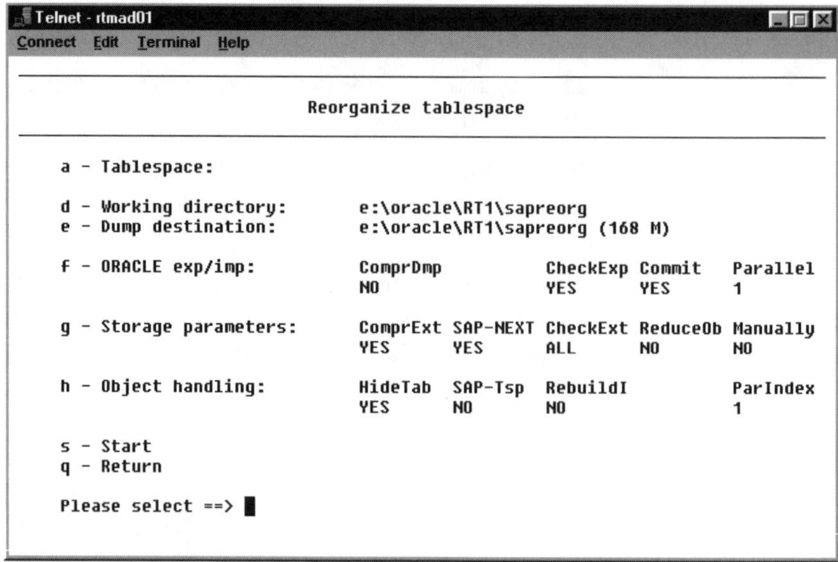

Figure 15-24 Example of reorganization menu: tablespace.

Dump Destination. It's the directory or directories that will hold the export dump files generated during a reorganization. In some options, such as reorganization of tablespaces with data files, you can enter several directories. The default value is normally /oracle/<SID>/sapreorg, but you can also modify this default by setting a different directory value in the parameter exireo_dumpdir within the init<SID>.dba. Although, normally, export dumps are written to disks (which is faster), you can also specify one or more tape devices as dump destinations.

As you can see in Fig. 15-24, the tool automatically shows the available space in the specified destination. Make sure there is sufficient space to hold the exports for the objects to be reorganized, although sapdba will report a warning message in this case. The storage needed might be reduced by selecting compression within the data transfer method for tables (within option *ORACLE exp / imp*), although the system checks will not take compression into consideration when calculating space needed for reorganization.

If you are using tape drives instead of disks, please check the SAPnet notes and read carefully the SAP instructions in the online documentation.

Transfer Method for Table Data (ORACLE exp/imp). The transfer or dump method specifies which tool will be used for performing the data export and import. By default, sapdba uses the Oracle export and import tools (exp and imp). There are two other available tools, SAP unload/SAP load and SAP unload/ORACLE SQL*Loader. Some of these tools are supposed to be faster; however, they are used less than the usual exp/imp method. In this edition, only the Oracle export/import tool is explained. For information on and release availability of the other tools, please refer to the SAP online documentation.

Selecting the option *f—ORACLE exp/imp* will display an additional menu like the one shown in Fig. 15-25. In this new menu you can select the transfer method and other options, such as:

- *Create table . . . as select.* This is an additional and complementary method for data transfer in reorganizations that basically consists of creating auxiliary new tables before reorganizing the actual table. This method presents two advantages: it saves time and it is useful for table stripping (moving tables to other tablespaces). However, this method cannot be used for reorganization of tablespaces with data files or with tables containing LONG columns.
- *Compress dump file(s).* Select this option if you want to compress the export dump files to save space in the dump directory, or select the default value *no.* When selecting *yes,* the output of the export file is sent to the compress UNIX command before the file is actually written. Compression is not available for exporting to tapes.
- *Check dump file.* This option is mainly used when exporting dump files to tape. It performs a read check of the dump file.

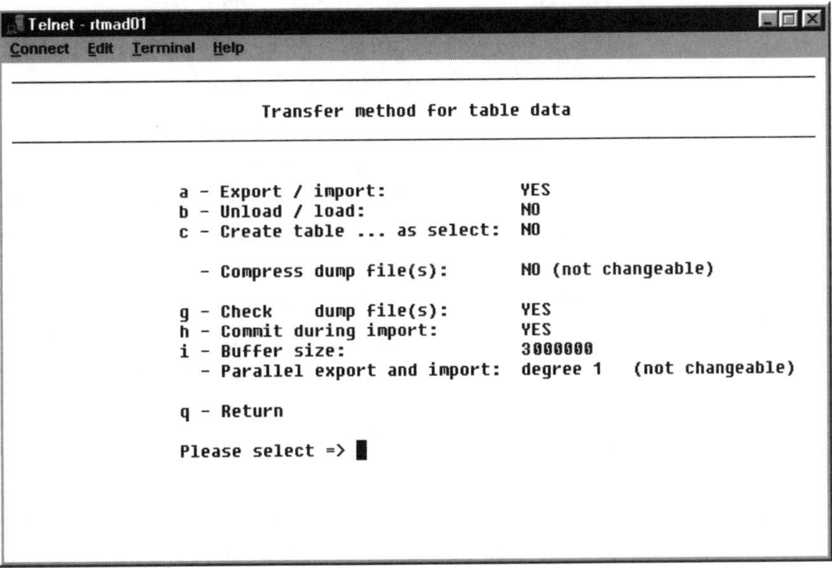

Figure 15-25 Menu for selecting the export/import method of a reorganization.

- *Commit during import.* When using the default value *yes,* an Oracle COMMIT statement is sent to the database after importing the data in the buffer. For tables with long records, setting this value to *no* can improve performance.
- *Buffer size.* Default value of 3,000,000 will provide approximately 3 MB of buffer space for performing exports and imports.
- *Parallel export and import.* This option can only be set in certain situations. It instructs the system to perform the export/import procedure in parallel.

The next sapdba reorganization option corresponds to the group of parameters that have direct influence on the object storage options.

Compress Extents. The default value is yes, which means that the reorganization will compress all the object's extents into one larger INITIAL extent. Refer to the previous topic on storage parameters. In cases where the INITIAL extent would be bigger than the biggest available datafile in the tablespace, sapdba will divide it into several parts.

Use ABAP Dictionary for NEXT. Default value is yes which means that the system will calculate the value for the objects NEXT storage parameter from the SAP tables DD09L and IGORA/TGORA.

Check Space (CheckExt). This option is set to ALL, indicating that all the extents should be checked. If a value of NO is entered, the objects will be restored without any change.

Reduce Object Size. Setting this option to "yes" will affect how the tool will calculate new storage parameters for the objects being reorganized. It will try to reduce the allocated storage space for the objects using the Oracle functions ANALYZE TABLE<table name> ESTIMATE STATISTICS or ANALYZE INDEX <index name> VALIDATE STRUCTURE (for indexes). For example, this option can calculate and reduce an object's INITIAL extent, which has a lot of free space. The default option is *no.*

Change Storage Manually. If you wish, you can manually change the storage parameters for the database objects (indexes, tables, tablespaces), which are being reorganized. The default value is *no,* which means that the storage parameters are set automatically by the tool. Please refer to the previous topic on storage parameters.

Manually changing storage parameters must be done in coordination with the values chosen for other previous options such as *Use ABAP Dict. for NEXT, Compress extents,* and *Reduce object size* following certain criteria.

For example, you can manually change the value for the INITIAL extent to make it larger when you expect a table or index to grow very quickly, and you would like to have enough room to hold the data without the need to create new extents. On the other hand, you could make it smaller when data in the object has been deleted, and you don't expect new data for it.

Similarly, you can manually change the size for the NEXT parameter when you expect fast-growing tables or indexes and want to avoid a rapidly increasing number of extents, or if you want to plan a stable "extent situation" for a longer term.

The next group of options are grouped under *Object handling,* which includes several utilities that can be used in some of the reorganization types. These will be shown on the menu when available. Options are:

- *Hide tables during reorganization (HideTab).* If this option is set to yes, the system will temporarily rename the table or tables being reorganized.
- *Use ABAP Dict. for tablespace (SAP-Tsp).* This option can be used in some types of reorganizations when deciding to move tables to the tablespaces defined in the ABAP Dictionary.
- *Rebuild Index (RebuildI).* When this option is set, sapdba issues the Oracle statement ALTER INDEX REBUILD. This is useful both when reorganizing indexes without tables and when reorganizing tablespaces and data files without using the index tablespaces.
- *Reduce data file size (ReduceFi).* This option can be used when it is necessary to reduce the size of the data files. The system will make the calculations and will add a 10 percent security margin.

Parallel Index Creation (ParIndex). You can enter here when you want to run more than one process in parallel for the creation of indexes. This option is useful when the database servers have more than one CPU. The default value is *degree 1* (no parallel processes).

For all types of reorganizations and associated sapdba menus, you have to specify the objects to reorganize. Normally, you do this with option *b* (in the case of single table or index) or *a* (for other reorganization types). When specifying object names, you generate a list of objects using the Oracle wildcard character (%), which acts as the LIKE function. For example, to generate a list of tables starting with *TBT* you could enter *TBT%.* The sapdba program will present the list where you can choose the table to be reorganized.

The next sections explain how the specific reorganization types are carried out as well as the specific menu options for each of them, while Table 15-2 displays a summary of the main scripts and log files with the naming conventions used in different reorganization types.

TABLE 15-2

Script and Log Files in Reorganizations

Log/script	Description
reorg<SID>.log	Main log for reorganization
<timestamp>.rli	Log for list of objects reorganization
<timestamp>.rtc	Log for tablespace reorganization
<timestamp>.rtd	Log for tablespace with data files reorganization
<timestamp>.rmv	Log for move or rename data files of a tablespace
restart.rsi	Restart file for reorganizing single object
restart.rli	Restart file for reorganizing list of objects
restart.rtc	Restart file for reorganizing tablespace
restart.rtd	Restart file for reorganizing tablespace with data files
restart.rmv	Restart file when changing table file allocation
exp<TSP>.sh	Export script
dro<TSP>.sh	SQL script for deleting objects
tab<TSP>.sql	SQL script for creating table definitions
imp<TSP>.sh	Import script
ind<TSP>.sql	SQL script for index creation
con<TSP>.sql	SQL script for constraints creation
imc<TSP>.sh	Import script for constraints
alt<TSP>.sql	SQL script for deleting of index statistics
drc<TSP>.sql	SQL script for deleting constraints
exc<TSP>.sh	Script for generating several export files
swi<TSP>.sql	SQL scripts for launching security mechanisms in reorganizations
dro<TSP>.sql	SQL scripts for deleting (dropping) objects
del<TSP>.sh	Scripts for deleting files and directories
ren<TSP>.sql	SQL scripts for renaming data files
tsp<TSP>.sql	SQL scripts for creating tablespaces
grants.sql	SQL script for defining grants

Reorganizing Single Objects: Tables or Indexes. To reorganize an index or a table, from the initial reorganization menu, select option *c—Reorganize single table or index.* Figure 15-26 shows this menu.

As a security measure, following the SAP backup concepts recommendations, you could export the table (with the R/3 system stopped) before starting the reorganization.

Select option *b* to enter the name for the table or index. Choose any other option at your convenience according to the concepts described in previous sections.

During the reorganization of a table or index, you might decide to move this database object to a different tablespace (a way of performing *table stripping*). To do that, select option *h—Object handling,* then select the *SAP-Tsp* option and enter the name for the target tablespace. SYSTEM, PSAPROLL, PSAPTEMP, and any other tablespaces that do not conform to SAP standard naming conventions are not allowed. When you move a table from its original tablespace to a different one, the system will automatically move the index to the associated index tablespace.

Then, select *s* for starting the reorganization process.

In the preparation phase, the sapdba utility will check for space problems (import check) and ensure that reorganization is possible. An example of such a check is shown in Fig. 15-23 on a previous section. It generates the shell scripts and SQL scripts for performing the reorganization in the main phase and also creates the restart file.

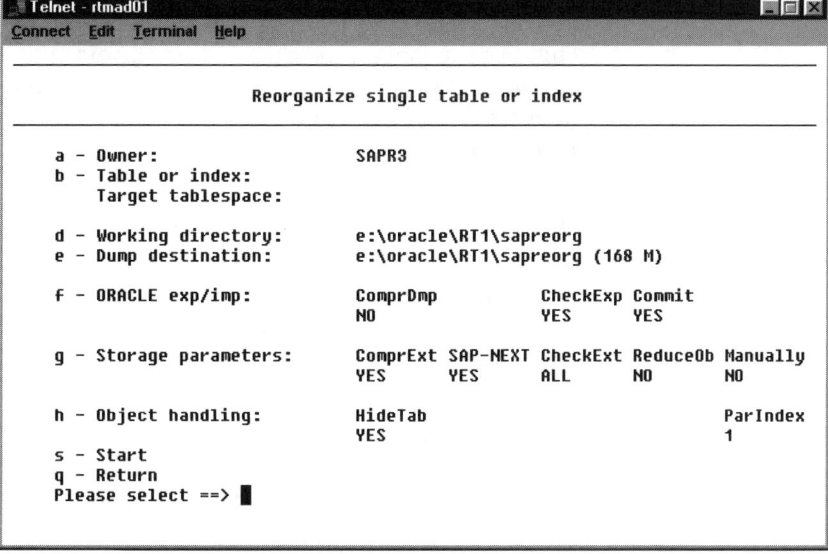

Figure 15-26 Menu for reorganizing single database objects.

The restart file is a very interesting file, since it shows exactly what is the execution order for the generated scripts. This is discussed in a following section.

Refer to Table 15-2 for the list and naming convention of the scripts.

Next, the system requests you to select whether you want to perform the actual reorganization (main phase) either immediately (*1*), start the scripts in batch (*2*), or end (*3*). Choose the most appropriate considering that, for starting reorganizations in batch, the *at* UNIX command must be configured to allow the ora<sid> or <sid>adm user for scheduling background jobs.

Sometimes it's useful to choose option *3—End (later restart is possible)* when you want to look at the scripts before they are actually executed or manually modify any of the scripts or even the restart file. Any manual change should be handled with care. Only experienced administrators or Oracle experts should modify them.

When executing the scripts, the system will:

- Export the data to a dump file
- Delete the object
- Create (define) the table with new calculated or manually entered storage parameters
- Import again the table contents and/or recreate the index

Reorganizing a List of Tables and Indexes. You can reorganize a list of database objects selecting option *d—Reorganize list of tables and indexes* from the sapdba reorganization menu. But before you choose this option, you first have to create the list file including the objects to reorganize.

This list file is a simple ASCII file containing a line for each object to reorganize. The format for the object name is *owner.object;* for example, *SAPR3.T082T,* where *SAPR3* is the owner and *T082T,* the table. Since SAPR3 is the default owner for most objects, you can omit it and just enter an object name (table or index) per line.

The option *SAP-Tsp* within the object handling utilities is usually set to NO, indicating that the system should place the objects to be reorganized in the standard tablespaces as defined in the SAP data dictionary using tables TGORA (for tables) and IGORA (for indexes).

After entering your needed selections in the menu, enter option *s* for starting the reorganization.

In the preparation phase, the actions that take place to reorganize a list of objects are the same as those to reorganize single objects. If the list includes just one object per tablespace, it will do an import check for the single object, while if there is more than one object per tablespace, the system will perform an import check for the tablespace.

The only other differences will be in the log and script files generated. In object-list reorganizations, the logs carry the *rli* extension. Refer to Table 15-2 for the list and naming convention for the scripts generated during different reorganizations.

The system will present the same options for starting the reorganization: immediate (*1*), batch (*2*), or later with restart (*3*).

Reorganization of Tablespaces Without Datafiles. As it was introduced and shown in Figs. 15-19 and 15-20 previously, you can reorganize tablespaces with or without data files. Reorganizing with data files is useful when you wish to reduce the total number of database files or when a tablespace has been extended too often using small data files instead of larger ones. Otherwise, the reorganization of tablespaces without data files is most often used.

For both types of tablespace reorganization (with or without data files), it is particularly important to perform a previous full backup. After a reorganization is successfully finished, you should also perform another backup of at least the reorganized tablespaces.

To reorganize a tablespace without data files, select option *e—Reorganize tablespace* from the reorganization menu. Figure 15-24 shows this menu.

Select option *a* to enter the tablespace name. If you want to change any of the storage parameters, reorganization directories, or wish to perform the index creation in parallel, select the corresponding menu option as introduced in the previous section. Then select *s* for starting the reorganization process.

In the preparation phase, sapdba will generate the SQL and shell script files as well as the restart file. For this type of reorganization, the log files have the extension *rtc.* Refer to Table 15-2 for the list and naming convention of log files.

The system will also perform a tablespace *import check:* it will calculate whether the object extents belonging to the tablespace can be stored in the data files.

After a successful check, the system presents again the three options for running the scripts (the main phase): immediately (*1*), in batch (*2*), or later with the restart script (*3*). Make your selection.

When the scripts are run, they will perform the following tasks:

If the *HideTab* option is set, the script will temporarily rename the tables to be reorganized.

Then, all the index statistics and the constraints are deleted. Then, all the tables and indexes of the tablespace will be exported to one or more export dump files.

Next all the tables and indexes will be deleted.

Using specific Oracle functions, all the free-space fragments on the tablespace data files are merged.

The table definitions are then created, and the table contents are imported. For index tablespaces, the indexes are recreated.

If necessary, any additional tablespace-related objects such as grants and constraints are imported.

Reorganization of a Tablespace with Data Files. For reorganizing a tablespace with data files, select option *f* from the initial reorganization menu. Figure 15-27 shows the resulting menu.

This menu presents the same options as reorganizing a tablespace without data files with the small difference that within the *Object handling* option you have the opportunity to select the *ReduceFi* (Reduce data file) option if you want to reduce the size of the new data file (or data files). Notice that, in most operating systems, you will not be able to reduce all data files to a single one; namely, if the total size is bigger than 2 GB. So, if you expect bigger sizes, the system will normally try to distribute the available storage into files of the same size.

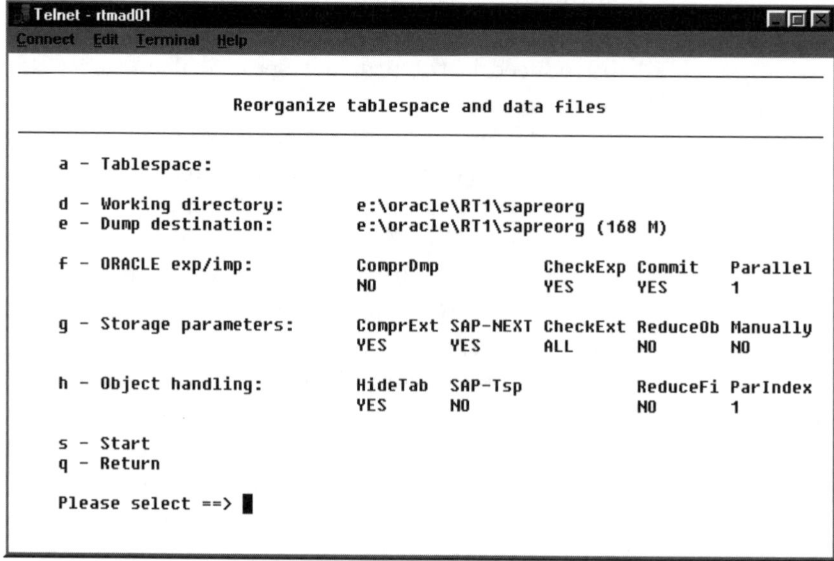

Figure 15-27 Menu for reorganizing a tablespace with data files.

Enter the name of the tablespace using option *a—Tablespace* and make any other changes to the sapdba proposed values as you need. Then start the process by selecting option *s*.

Logs for this reorganization type carry the *rtd* extension. Refer to Table 15-2 for the list and naming conventions of all reorganization scripts.

In the preparation phase, sapdba will calculate the number, the directories, and the sizes for the new data files of the tablespace. If the new tablespace data does not fit into a single data file, it will suggest several files. It checks that there is sufficient storage space in the file system to hold the new data files.

As usual, it generates the SQL, shell scripts, and the restart file.

If the checks are successful, the system presents the three options for running the scripts (the main phase): immediately (*1*), in batch (*2*), or later with the restart script (*3*). Make your selection.

When the scripts are run, they will perform the following tasks:

- Delete the index statistics and constraints
- Export the table contents, indexes, and, if needed, other related tablespace objects
- Perform some safety mechanisms
- Delete the tablespace and all the data files; when the directories contain a single file and do not contain any other file not related with the tablespace, the directories are also deleted
- Create the new directories and datafiles following SAP standard naming conventions
- Using specific Oracle functions, it will merge all the free space fragments on the entire database
- Create (define) the new tablespace and import the tables and indexes, and, if needed, other related objects such as grants and constraints

Moving or Renaming a Tablespace Data File. This is an additional option within the reorganization menu which, although it does not really perform a reorganization in the database sense, changes the database structure. This is option *g—Move / rename data files of a tablespace,* which can be used to change the location of data files in the file system. This is a very useful function when you need to perform changes in the physical or logical layout of the disk volumes, such as when adding additional disks, changing disk types, and so on. Figure 15-28 shows this new menu.

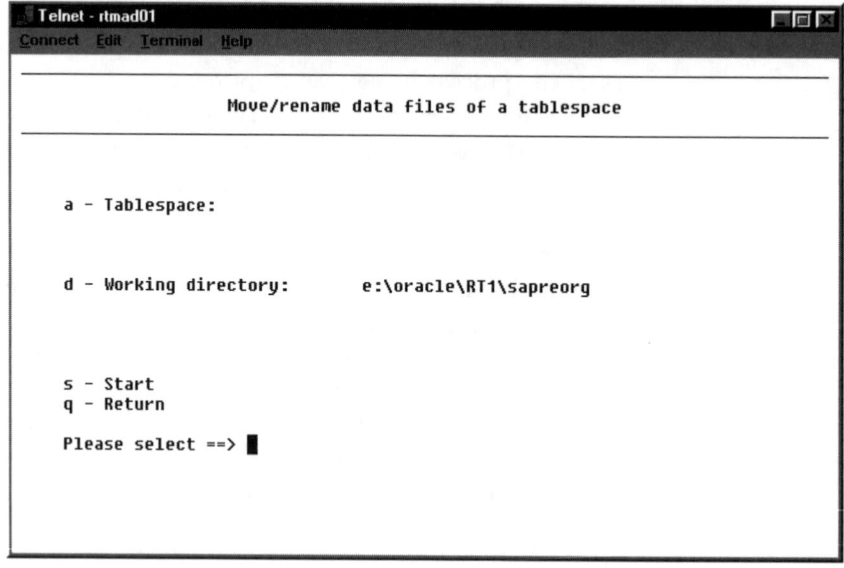

Figure 15-28 Menu for moving or renaming the data files of a tablespace.

Because the file allocation is stored in the database file scheme (the control files), moving or renaming data files is considered a structural change; therefore, a backup of at least the related tablespace is necessary after performing this operation.

In this menu, select the tablespace from which you want to move the data files using option *a—Tablespace.*

Enter *s* for starting the operation; this will guide you through the whole reorganization process. It will show warnings if it detects any problems. The logs for this operation carry the *rmv* extension. The system will perform the following functions:

- In the preparatory phase, the new data files are defined using the user-supplied parameters for the new data-file paths. It generates the SQL and shell scripts plus the restart file.
- It will also make a check to see whether there is sufficient storage space for the data files in the chosen paths.
- To perform this operation, the database must not be open. Therefore, the first thing the program performs in the main phase is to try to put the database into a mount stage. To do that, it will issue a shutdown immediate command to stop the database and then a startup mount.
- Then, it will create the new data files and directories as well as delete the old files as well as directories if they do not contain any other files. If necessary, it will perform the renaming of files.

- Finally, it will save the old and new control files and open the database.

Restarting a Reorganization

You might need to restart a reorganization, either because a simple error occurred or you decided to perform the reorganization at a later time. Sometime it might be useful to perform reorganizations up to the preparation phase, where all the scripts have been generated and then perform all reorganizations in a row at a more convenient time.

However, in serious error situations, it is better to repeat the whole process instead of restarting it. If an error has occurred, you have to solve the problem before restarting the reorganization.

Depending on what the error situation is and at what point of the reorganization the error happened, if the error is serious, you would do better to reset the database to its initial status before the reorganization.

If the error happened in the preparation phase when generating the scripts, nothing has really been altered in the database, so you can solve the problem and start over. Here, restart is not possible because some scripts might be missing.

However, if the error took place after the export phase and the process already has dropped (deleted) database objects (tables, indexes, tablespaces, etc.), you cannot repeat the process from the beginning. Instead, you have to solve the problem and perform the restart process. Remember that if the problem seems serious (refer to your Oracle error reference guide and SAPnet notes), you would do well to reset the database to its initial status by recovering from a backup or from a consistent export file. Then report your problem to SAP.

Before restarting a reorganization, look up the log file generated for the reorganization operation. The log files have the name <timestamp>.<ext>, where *<timestamp>* is the date and time the operation was performed and *<ext>* is the extension for the type of reorganization. Look up possible extensions in Table 15-2. You can find log files either from the *Show / Cleanup* function within sapdba or by manually searching for the file in the sapreorg/<timestamp> directory.

Check these files for warnings or error messages. If there are any, you should analyze them and solve the problems before proceeding.

After the log has been checked, you can restart a reorganization by selecting option *r* from the main reorganization menu within sapdba. Figure 15-29 shows the restart menu.

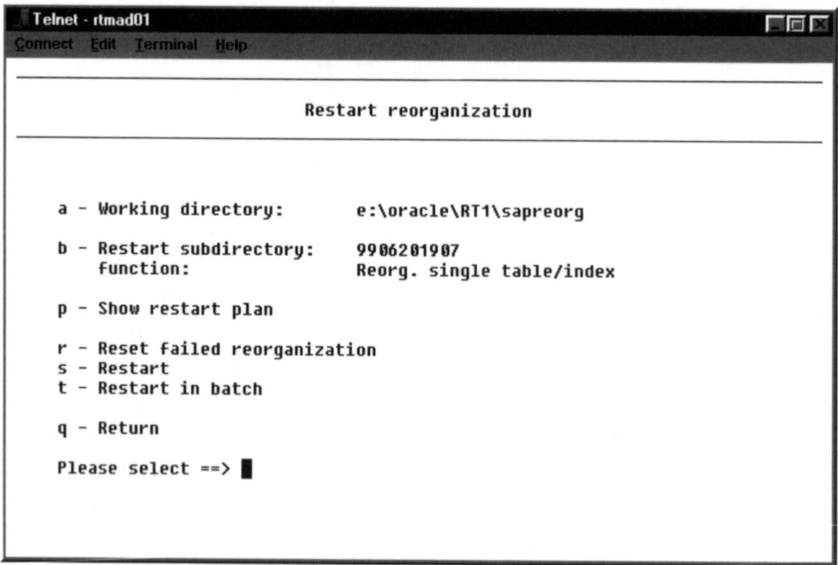

Figure 15-29 The restart reorganization menu.

As a default, option *b—Restart subdirectory* includes the <timestamp> directory corresponding to the last reorganization operation performed, if it finds one. When this occurs, it also shows a short description in an additional function line.

If this is not the function you want, select option *b* and enter your reorganization subdirectory.

You can then show the functions to be performed with the restart file by selecting option *p—Show restart plan*. The system will display the scripts to be executed.

If you agree with the plan, you can proceed by selecting *s—Restart* or *t—Restart in batch*. The system will then proceed as in the main phase of the particular reorganization type.

Restart files have the format restart.<ext>, where the file extension *<ext>* indicates the function and reorganization type of the scripts. For the list of possible functions during the reorganization, refer to Table 15-2. The restart files contain the right ordered scripts that are required for performing the reorganization, as well as some script indicators that indicate if the scripts have already been successfully processed or not. Note that you should not change the order of the scripts, since it will alter the whole reorganization flow.

The possible script indicators are as follows:

- *Y.* The script has been processed successfully.

- *N.* The script has not yet been processed or has failed. This is the normal indicator when reorganization has not been started.
- *S.* This indicator might appear only for import scripts, which have been started but could not be successfully processed by sapdba due to an unexpected error. This is an intermediate stage when processing import scripts.

When a reorganization takes places, at its main phase, all the scripts that have the *N* indicator are processed. When they are successfully finished, its status is changed to *Y.* For import phases, the system sets the intermediate *S* indicator until the import is completely and successfully finished.

If the import did not run successfully and sapdba finds the *S* indicator, then it will delete the contents of all the tables that were already imported and resets the indicator to *N* so it can be processed again after solving the problem that caused the error.

Restart options are also available for the export/import procedures in another sapdba menu.

Exporting and Importing Database Objects

The sapdba tool includes a menu option with several functions for exporting and importing database objects. With these functions, you export and import all types of database objects: tables, indexes, views, grants, and so on. You can decide to export and import both the database object definitions and contents.

Notice than performing an export will make a static copy of the exported objects. This means that this export should only be used as the source of a following import when the database contents have not changed. Exports and imports cannot be used for recovery procedures.

You cannot use exports to import into a different system (database) since the relationship among the elements is too complex (foreign key relationships, check tables, and so on).

Functions offered in the export/import menu cannot be used for exporting and importing the full database. To do this, there are other options, mainly with the R3SETUP installation tool or by manually using the Oracle import and export utility programs (imp and exp or impst and expst). The following section contains a practical guideline for performing a full database export and import between different systems, or even to the same system, under certain circumstances.

Export and import functions within the sapdba menu can be used for

- Performing operations in the same database.
- Backing up single objects (table or index data) before a reorganization. Since it's assumed that no productive activity can be performed during reorganizations, exported objects could be reimported into the system in case of problems.
- Running import scripts for previously generated exports.
- Saving definitions for database objects. When exporting structures, the system creates the scripts needed for redefining the objects.

There are, however, other utilities within the SAP R/3 systems that can be used to perform the same or similar export/import operations: using the transport system or using the R3trans utility program.

Export and import procedures are sequenced in the following phases:

- In the first phase, the system creates the necessary scripts for the export and import of the selected objects, either for only the structure, the contents, or both.
- For export functions, in the second phase, the previously created export scripts are processed.
- For import functions, the system processes the script for importing the object definitions and their contents.

These are practically the same operations as those performed during a reorganization. In fact, as mentioned earlier, reorganization procedures are based on export and import operations.

To access the export and import functions, from the initial sapdba menu, select option *e—Export/import.* Figure 15-30 shows this menu.

From this menu, the system offers several export and import options. When calling any of those available menu options, sapdba will show an additional menu where you can choose which parameters to use. These new menus are very similar to the ones shown on reorganization menus, and the options such as *Working directory, data transfer method, Use of ABAP Dict for NEXT, Storage Parameters, parallel index creation,* and so on, have exactly the same meaning and perform the same functions as explained in the section on reorganization in this chapter.

Similarly, you must meet the storage requirements for allowing sufficient space for the export dumps and must conveniently size the tablespaces to hold imported objects. The system will check all the space requirements, but, contrary to the reorganization processes, sapdba will not check if the import will run successfully.

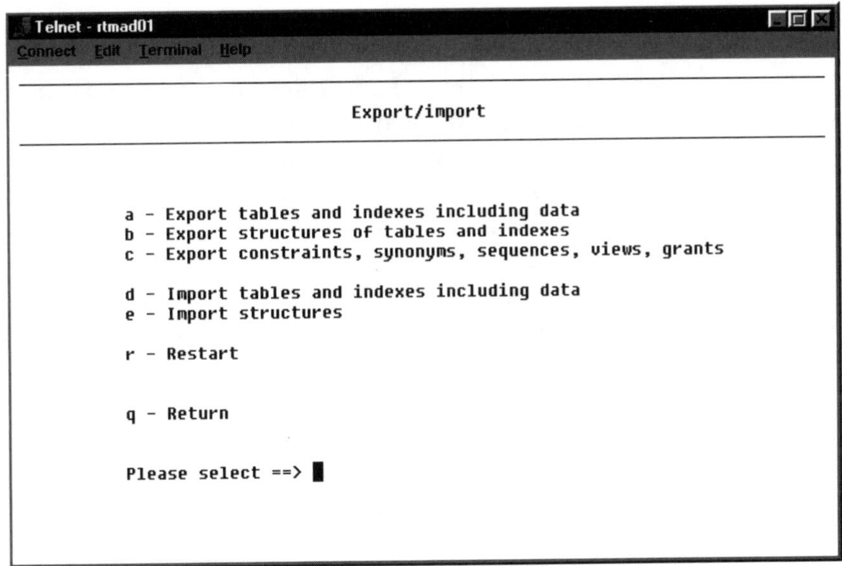

Figure 15-30 Initial menu for export and import functions.

Notice that exports or imports that include data should be performed with the database started in restricted mode. However, you can export database object definitions with the database up and running.

To carry with any export or import function, after checking the requirements and stopping the SAP system, select the most appropriate type (menu option), which is self-explanatory.

Then, change the required parameters, and proceed by selecting *s—Start.*

Export and import functions generate similar log, script, and restart files as reorganizations. These files are stored under the working directory, normally sapreorg/<timestamp>. The file extension meanings can be found in Table 15-2.

Case Study: Guidelines for an Export/Import Procedure of a Customer Database

WARNING! *The following example can only be followed under the circumstances and with the requirements described. For productive installations, please contact a SAP or Oracle specialist who can guide you through this type or other types of copying a full customer database. Since there are other possibilities and situations, you can, however, apply some of the following concepts to complement other solutions.*

In the following example, a full database copy from the development system to a test system is performed. No backup copy and restore is used in this case, since the SAP system names (SID) are to be preserved differently. This is the starting situation:

The source system is the development system, with the name SS1. The target system is a test system, with the name TT1, and SAP R/3 is installed in both systems with the same SAP and Oracle versions.

The procedure for performing the full export and import differs slightly depending on the total size of the export file. In this example, it is assumed that the operating system environment will support the file size generated by the export. Some 32-bit operating systems have some restrictions on this issue of files not larger than 2 GB. If the estimated size for the export dump file is larger than the size supported by your operating system, then a different procedure must be followed. Possibilities are to perform the export to named pipes, to tapes, to several dump files, and so on.

Guidelines are as follows:

1. For safety reasons, perform a full offline backup of both system databases.
2. SAP instances must be stopped in both systems. The database must be started in administrator mode.
3. Check the actual total space for the tablespaces of the source system (SS1). To do this, you can use the sapdba functions:

```
c - Tablespace administration
        c - Freespace and fragmentation of all tablespaces
```

4. Using the same functions in the target system (TT1), make sure that this system has at least the same total space as the development system. For those tablespaces that are not large enough, and also for those in which the source system had a large *%-Alloc,* you should extend the tablespace size by adding new data files. You can do this from the sapdba menu:

```
c - Tablespace administration
        f - Alter tablespace Add Datafile
```

5. In the source system, verify you have a working directory large enough to hold the export dump file. If needed, add new disks to get a sufficiently large volume.
6. Perform the export in the source system in the working directory. In the example, use the Oracle exp utility. On Windows NT systems, this utility is *exp80* (for Oracle 8 databases). You can either make a shell script or use it interactively:

```
orass1> cd /oracle/SS1/sapreorg
orass1>exp
```

The system will request a user name and password. Enter the privileged user name and password (usually SYSTEM and MANAGER).

Then it will request the array fetch buffer size. You can either leave the default value (4096) or enter a bigger one, such as 20,490.

Next, the exp tool requests the name for the export file. For the example, it will be called *export.dmp.* Notice that this file is created in the current directory. In this example, the directory is /oracle/SS1/sapreorg.

Next, the system requests what is to be exported: *(1)E(ntire database), (2)U(sers), or (3)T(ables): (2)U>.* Enter *1* for entire database.

To the following questions, select the default answer *yes:*

```
Export grants (yes/no): yes >
Export table data (yes/no): yes >
Compress extents (yes/no): yes >
```

The *exp* utility has many options and can be also called using a parameter file. Depending on the Oracle release, other options might appear. Choose standard or default settings except those indicated in the example.

After the last prompt, the system starts exporting the full database into the export.dmp file.

The following command performs the same operation:

```
exp userid=system/manager buffer=20490 full=y file=export.dmp
compress=y rows=y grants=y
```

While the export is being performed in the source system, certain activities can be performed in the target system.

HINT *Especially for very large databases, there is an exp option that can dramatically reduce the time needed for the export. This is based on using the DIRECT flag to Y. The DIRECT option specifies that a direct path must be used instead of the conventional export PATH. What this means is that the system will bypass the evaluation buffer in the SQL command processing layer. Some restrictions apply, however, in the sense that this method cannot be used for columns of type REF, LOG, or BFILE or object type columns including VARRAYs and nested tables.*

7. To speed up the import process in the target machine, you can follow the recommendations in the reorganization section, mainly creating and putting online a big rollback segment. In the example, as user oratt1, do the following:

```
oratt1> sqldba lmode=y
sqldba> connect internal
sqldba> create tablespace PSAPBIGROLL datafile
          '/oracle/TT1/sapdata7/bigroll_1/bigroll.data1'
          size 1000M;
SQLDBA> create rollback segment BIGROLL tablespace PSAPBIGROLL
        storage (INITIAL 10M NEXT 10M MAXEXTENTS 121
        OPTIMAL 20M);
SQLDBA> alter rollback segment BIGROLL online;
```

Next, set offline all other rollback segments except for SYSTEM and BIGROLL:

```
SQLDBA> alter rollback segment PRS_1 offline;
...
SQLDBA> alter rollback segment PRS_n offline;
```

Edit the init<sid>.ora file to comment out the rollback_segments line (usually one of the last in the file) and, in its place, write down your created rollback segment:

```
rollback_segments = (BIGROLL).
```

Stop and start the database for the new parameter to be effective. You can check that the only rollback segment (besides SYSTEM) is working by issuing the command:

```
sqldba> monitor rollback segments;
```

8. In the target system, you must delete the full database contents, not the database structure. In 3.1 releases, this option was included within the R3INST tool. Another option is writing a simple Oracle script to output the list of all the tables to a text file:

```
SVRMGRL> SPOOL <filename.txt>
SVRMGRL> SELECT TABLE_NAME FROM DBA_TABLES WHERE
OWNER='SAPR3';
SVRMGRL> SPOOL OFF;
```

Then edit this text file and add the statement DROP TABLE SAPR3. to each table, and also add a semicolon at the end of each statement. This is better done with an editor supporting macros or search/replace capabilities. When you have this file ready, you can rename it to something like DELETE_SAPTABLES.SQL.

The next step is to run this procedure:

```
SVRMGRL> @DELETE_SAPTABLES.SQL
```

WARNING! *This will delete the tables and the full contents of the database. Please be sure to follow this procedure only under the circumstances mentioned in this section.*

9. To speed up the import process, also disable the ARCHIVELOG mode. You can do this from sapdba or from the SQLDBA tool

when the database is only in mount stage by issuing the command:

```
sqldba> alter database noarchivelog;
```

10. Once the export running in the source system is finished, you have to copy it to the target system TT1. You can use the ftp utility, and place the export.dmp file in the working directory /oracle/TT1/sapreorg.

11. Now you can perform the import in the target system. Do it in the working directory sapreorg. You can also launch it interactively, but it's better using a simple script such as:

```
echo IMPORT START IN T11 - 'date' > import.log
nohup imp userid=system/manager full=y buffer=3000000
file=export.dmp
show=n ignore=y grants=y rows=y commit=no indexes=y 2>&1 >>
import.log
echo END IMPORT TT1 - 'date' >> import.log
```

Notice in this simple script the *commit=no* statement, which is very important to reduce the time it takes to perform the import, especially when importing tables with long rows such as ATAB.

You can edit a script like that one and launch it in the background. Then the import can be monitored by looking at the import.log file with the UNIX command:

```
tail -f import.log.
```

Figure 15-31 shows an import in process.

Figure 15-31 Example of a running import.

```
. . importing table                  "CUXREF"          0 rows imported
. . importing table                   "CVEP1"          0 rows imported
. . importing table                   "CVEP2"          0 rows imported
. . importing table                   "CVER1"          0 rows imported
. . importing table                   "CVER2"          0 rows imported
. . importing table                   "CVER3"          0 rows imported
. . importing table                   "CVER4"          0 rows imported
. . importing table                    "D000"          0 rows imported
. . importing table                 "D010INC"     211579 rows imported
. . importing table                   "D010L"       7001 rows imported
. . importing table                "D010LINF"       5054 rows imported
. . importing table                   "D010Q"       5281 rows imported
. . importing table                   "D010S"     216803 rows imported
. . importing table                "D010SINF"     216075 rows imported
. . importing table                   "D010T"     132676 rows imported
. . importing table                 "D010TAB"     252867 rows imported
. . importing table                "D010TINF"     136929 rows imported
. . importing table                   "D010Y"       5152 rows imported
. . importing table                   "D020L"       3058 rows imported
. . importing table                "D020LINF"       3048 rows imported
. . importing table                   "D020S"      43168 rows imported
. . importing table                "D020SINF"      43176 rows imported
```

12. After the import has finished, which might last a few hours, check the log files for the import to make sure that no errors occurred.
13. You can perform a new full backup now of the TT1 system.
14. Before starting the SAP system TT1 with the new fully imported database, you have to enable the ARCHIVELOG mode and change the initttl.ora parameters for setting back the original rollback segments.
15. Then you could start SAP R/3, which will require a few changes to be fully operative:
    - You probably have to enter again the license, since it is stored in a couple internal tables. After a full import, this system has the license data for the source system SS1, which is not valid, since it's hardware-dependent.
    - You have to configure back the workbench organizer and the transport system. When using transaction SE06, specify option *Database copy.*
    - Check your printer connections (transaction code SPAD), your RFC connections (transaction code SM59), your profile parameters, and the background system.

This can also be a fast procedure for reorganizing the whole database. There are many other tools, versions, and requirements for performing similar operations.

Backing Up the Database

External factors, physical errors, and logical errors can cause system downtime and may lead to data loss if you do not have a suitable backup strategy. Your backup strategy must be designed according to the needs of your company and must be carefully tested before your R/3 system goes live and after any changes to the backup strategy.

Oracle RDBMS administration must include *database backups* to save the data stored in the data files of the tablespaces, the log information recorded in the currently active online redo log file, and the administration data stored in the parameter and control files. It must also include saving *offline redo log file backup,* offline copies of the previously completed online redo log file.

Both types of backups are necessary in case there is a need to recover the database to a point in time as close as possible to when data loss occurred.

To perform these tasks, SAP provides the following backup tools:

- BRBACKUP: This program backs up the data files, the control file, and the database redo log files when necessary. It can also back up the offline redo log files of the database in case of a *Consistent Online Backup.*
- BRARCHIVE: This program backs up the offline redo log files of the database.
- BRRESTORE: This program can restore all files belonging to the database system from the backups performed by BRBACKUP and BRARCHIVE using the log files recorded by these programs.

Since release 4.0, it is possible to execute the database backup using BRBACKUP (online and offline modes) and the backup of the offline redo log files using BRARCHIVE in one run.

It is important not to forget that your backup strategy must include backing up all components that make up the system. Besides the database, the backup strategy of R/3 environments should also include the operating system and other R/3 related files such as archiving objects, R/3 interfaces, SAP executables, and others.

The sapdba program uses the brbackup utility to back up the database files, including the control files and the online redo log files. With certain settings, it can even back up nondatabase files like the SAP environment directories. The brbackup utility can be called directly from the command line or can be most conveniently used with option *h—Backup database* from the initial sapdba menu.

Backups using the brbackup tool can also be run within R/3 using CCMS functions. From CCMS, you can schedule backups as well as display the sapdba log files, including the backup logs.

The brbackup utility is only one of the possible ways to implement a backup strategy, but it's the only one, for the moment, that SAP supports directly. Refer to the next chapter for other backup strategies and possibilities.

Before using the brbackup utility, there are certain preparations that should be performed:

- Decide backup types and cycles, determining whether to perform online (system running normally) or offline (system stopped); whether to perform daily backups, backups three times a week, and so on.
- There is a brbackup parameter initialization file that must be set and configured. The file name is *init<SID>.sap* and is located under the Oracle dbs directory. Usually, /oracle/<SID>/dbs. In Windows NT systems, this file is located in the *\orant\database* directory.

- You have to select the tape drive configuration. For performance reasons, tape drives or tape loaders with hardware compression offer better backup speeds. Although tapes are the most common devices for backups, there are other options and device types.
- Before backup, you should initialize the tapes. Brbackup always requires a tape label.
- Consider the time it takes for completing a backup. The backup performance will be a function of the database size and the tape drive speed.

If you want to use software compression with the backups, you have to use one of the sapdba functions to calculate the compression rate before you can perform a backup with the compress option set to *yes.*

Following topics introduce the brbackup tool and the most important options and parameters. More extensive information as well as the full list of available parameters can be obtained in the SAP online documentation. For information on supported third-party backup solutions interfacing with brbackup, please refer to SAP itself or its hardware partners.

SAP Backup Concept and Security Recommendations

SAP makes the following recommendations to eliminate risks as far as possible when backing up and restoring your database:

- Make sure that you have activated the archiving of the online redo logs (mode ARCHIVELOG) in all databases.
- Make sure that the mirrored control files are stored on separate disks.
- Mirror the online redo logs on separate disks (at operating system level and/or using Oracle resources). The mirroring of online redo log files, supported by Oracle, can be set up when installing the database system.
- Install online redo log files, offline redo logs files (archived redo log files), and data files to separate disks.
- Make sure that the block sizes (8K) of the database system and the operating system are the same. This might differ on some operating systems. Verify the most important database parameters.
- Familiarize yourself with the tablespace structure of the SAP system and monitor the critical tablespaces.

These recommendations are applicable independently of the chosen backup strategy, and regardless to whether brbackup is the tool for performing the backups.

The brbackup Menu Options

From the initial sapdba menu, select option *h—Backup database* to call the menu-driven brbackup utility. Figure 15-32 shows the initial menu for backing up the database.

The key factor for performing backups with brbackup is to decide the type of backup. You can run backups in either of the following ways:

- *Offline.* It's a consistent backup of the database after it has been shut down. The SAP system is not available while the backup runs, but recovery procedures are easier.
- *Online.* Runs while SAP system is active, so there is no availability interruption. It might have some negative effects on performance, so it's better to schedule online backups at times where there is not much online activity. To perform online backups, it is mandatory that the database runs with the ARCHIVELOG mode enabled.

Since release 4.0, it is possible to perform a *Consistent Online Backup.* This procedure includes a database backup in online mode, containing

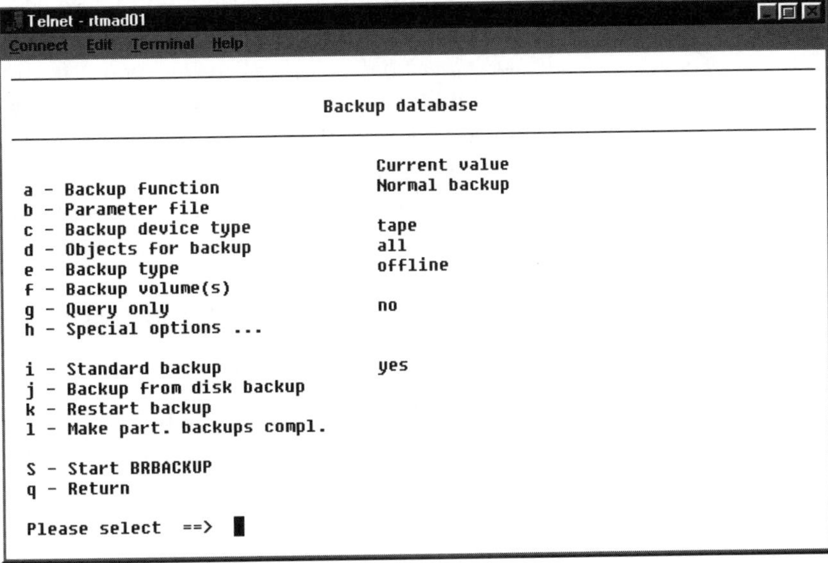

Figure 15-32 The brbackup main menu.

logically consistent data as well as the offline redo logs files that are generated during the backup. These offline files are all saved to the same volume as database files.

The init<SID>.sap initialization profile contains the default value for database backup with brbackup. Right after a new SAP installation, the default value is normally complete offline backup to local tape without compression.

To change the default value, you have to edit the initialization profile. However, you can interactively select other values while using the brbackup utility.

Before running the first backup, you must initialize some tapes and possibly edit the initialization profile to check or edit the tape device and tape length.

There are many options within the backup. Some are not available on all operating systems, and they also differ among *sapdba* versions. Here some of the most common options are introduced:

- *Backup function.* Default value is to perform a normal backup, but selecting this option will display an additional menu for selecting the required backup operation.

  You have to choose from one of the following options:

  Normal backup. This is the normal and default value when the tapes need not be initialized.

  Initialize BRBACKUP tape. Select this function for initializing one or more tapes. When performing this operation, the system will display a reduced menu for selecting additional options:

  — *Check before initialization = no.* If you opt not to check the label, you can initialize any tapes and even overwrite existing SAP volumes.

  — *Check label before initialization = yes.* If you select this, the system will check the label and only allow for initializing SAP tapes when the locking period has expired.

  — *Number of tapes.* This is to specify the number of tapes to be initialized.

  Show information in tape header. The system will display the information contained in the tape header, if any. Since the backup always writes a tape header in all volumes used, this function is useful for checking the type, date, label, and backup type on the tapes.

Determine compression rates. If you want to perform backups with compression, you must run this utility so that the system can estimate the compression rate for the backups. This rate will be calculated by simulating a backup of the files specified with option *g—Objects for backup.* Running this function can take as long as performing an actual backup. If you want, you can specify two or three big tablespaces. Notice, though, that the compression rate can change as the system is in productive operation, since the fill level of the data files can rapidly change. So plan to run this function once a month or once every other month.

- *Parameter file.* The default value is init<SID>.sap, but you can use different initialization profile files. For example, you might wish to create a specific file for calculating compression rates, for initializing tapes, for performing different backup types, and so on. With this method, you avoid having to change parameters online all the time. To enter another parameter file, select this option and specify the name of the file.
- *Confirm backup parameters.* The default value is *no,* which suppresses some of the brbackup confirmation messages. When set to *yes,* the system will stop and display all the confirmation messages. Then the user must confirm the function to continue.
- *Language.* You can select the language for the brbackup messages. Only English (default) and German are available.
- *Backup device type.* The system will display a list of available device types supported by brbackup. The default value is to perform backups to local tape devices, but you can also choose:

  disk. Select this option to perform backup to disk volumes.

  pipe. Select this option to backup to tape devices in a remote system using commands that must be specified in the parameter initialization file.

  tape_auto. Select this option for performing backups to tape devices that support automatic tape loading and switching. Selecting this option will suppress the messages for changing tapes.

  pipe_auto. It's a combination of the last two options. It's used to back up to an automatic tape loading and switching device located in a remote system.

  util_file and *util_file_online.* These are the options that allow for third-party backup solutions integrated with brbackup.

You must enter here the name of a third-party program that must comply with the SAP backup interface program backint. Please refer to SAP for a list of certified backup partners and solutions complying with the backint interface. When using an external backup program, if necessary, you can use the *Backup utility parameter file* option to specify a file containing parameters needed for the external backup solution.

disk_copy. This can be used for copying the database to a disk using the same directory structure.

tape_box and pipe_box. These are used for jukeboxes and autoloaders. In the first case (*tape_box*) the devices must be locally accessible; in the second case (*pipe_box*) they can be remotely accessible.

- *Objects for backup.* The following options can be specified:

  all. It's the default value for backing up the whole database.

  all_data. This option can be used for backing up all the data tablespaces, excluding indexes.

  sap_dir / ora_dir. Choose this option to backup the SAP directories and the Oracle directories without the database data files.

  tablespace name. This option is used for backing up a single tablespace.

  File_ID or *File-ID1 - File-ID2.* Select this option to back up one or more files by specifying the Oracle file ID or a file ID area.

  Generic Path. Use this option for backing up a particular file, specifying the whole path. You can also specify a generic directory path, in which case the whole directory contents will be backed up.

  Object list. You can specify to back up several objects by separating the names with commas.

- *Enter password interactively.* This option can be used to enter interactively the database administrator password. The default option is *no.*
- *Query only.* When selecting this option, the system displays three possibilities:

  no. It's the default value for starting the selected backup function. The backup will be normally started.

  with tape check. No backup will be performed. The system will check and display which backup tape or tapes will need to be mounted for the backup. It checks that the required tapes are mounted in the drive.

without tape check. No backup will be performed. The system will only display which tape or tapes are needed for performing the backup.

- *Backup volume(s).* You can enter here the backup volumes (tape labels) to be used for the backup. When none are specified, the system will use the next sequential volume as specified in the initialization profile, and as recorded in the backup logs. If you need to specify more than one tape, you must separate every label with commas.
- *Compress.* When selecting this option, the system will display the three possible entries:

  no. It's the default value for performing backups without compression.

  yes. Software compression is performed, using previously calculated compression rates, with backup function *Determine compression rate.* When this option is used, the tool will compress the backup files into the working directory before transferring to the backup device.

  hardware. Select this option for backup devices with built-in hardware compression.
- *Verification after backup.* Choose whether you want the utility to perform a verification of the backed-up files. Verification will markedly increase the total backup time. The default option is no verification.
- *Backup type.* Use this option to specify the most important parameter for running the backup. Options available are:

  offline. This is the default option. You can launch an offline backup if the SAP system has been shut down. The brbackup utility will stop the database itself.

  offline_force. The system will shut down immediately without checking if the SAP system is up and running.

  online. This option will perform a backup of the database while the SAP system is running. Operating the database in ARCHIVELOG mode is mandatory.

  online_cons. This is the option used for performing *consistent online backups,* where the archived redo logs generated during the online backup are copied to the same backup volume.

  offline_standby. This mode is one of the options for supporting backup on a standby database. With this mode the standby database is stopped. This configuration is only used in disaster recovery.

offline_stop. This is an option used for standby database configuration. The database is not started after backup, but set to mount standby status.

online_split and offline_split. These two modes, introduced in release 4.x, support the split mirror disks backup, which is especially suitable for large installations for avoiding downtime. The *online_split* mode sets the tablespaces temporarily to backup mode while the disks are being split. The *offline_split* mode stops the database while the disks are being split.

- *Level of parallel execution.* Indicates the number of possible copy processes that can be running in parallel. The default value 0 indicates that the number of processes will be the same as the number of available backup devices.

After entering the needed options in the menu and mounting the required tapes or other selected backup devices, start the backup by selecting option *s.* While the backup is being run, the screen displays the backup size, the progress, and the estimated end time for completion. It will also display a system message when an error occurs or when the backup is finished.

Running a brbackup writes backup logs in a summary log file back<SID>.log under the sapbackup directory. The progress of a backup is left in a detail log file b<timestamp>.<ext>.

The brbackup utility can be also used at the command line, which allows for writing shell scripts for automating and scheduling backups. For detailed information about the brbackup command options as well as all available parameters in the initialization profile init<sid>.sap, please refer to the SAP online documentation.

Backing Up the Archived Redo Logs: brarchive

The brarchive is the utility provided by SAP to back up the Oracle-archived redo log files. Backing up the archived log files is required for having a consistent backup and recovery strategy. You can only perform point-in-time recoveries or partial database recoveries by having the archived redo log files conveniently saved. For recovery procedures, all the archived redo log files from the last consistent backup must be available in the correct sequence. If any redo log file is missing, a recovery will only be possible up to the gap point.

Actually, the archived files are essential for recovering logical error situations, such as the erroneous deletion of system objects. If you want to restore the situation up to the point before the deletion, you can only do it with the archived log files.

The brarchive utility is called from the sapdba menu or invoked in the command line.

By default, the archived redo log files are automatically written by the Oracle archiver process in the saparch directory. The location can be changed by altering the parameter in the init<sid>.ora file. This directory must have been conveniently sized. But it's as important to define a convenient strategy for backing up and then deleting the archived redo log files from this directory, since these archived files are being constantly populated as the users work with the system. If this directory becomes full and no more archives can be written, the system issues the *archiver stuck* problem message, which will stop the database operation.

Archiving Backup Strategies and Requirements

Using brarchive should be part of an overall backup strategy. The only way to avoid the use of brarchive is by performing another type of operating system backup that includes these files. However, using brarchive and sapdba offers some management advantages such as tape labeling control, automatic archive log finding, and recovery.

For installations with lots of productive and concurrent users or with a lot of background processing, there must be a constant monitoring operation over the available space in the archive directory. You can make a simple script that checks this out, say, every half hour, and sends a warning message when available storage falls below 20 percent. There is a CCMS alert checking this. As an alternative for avoiding disk space problems, you can also use the *fill tape permanently* option.

The SAP installations default size for the redo log files as well as the archived files is 20 MB, but this value can be changed for allowing more transactions per redo file. You must consider how many archived files can be backed up, as well as when to launch them, to calculate the devices needed.

For example, suppose in the installation a full offline backup is performed every day at midnight. Normal user activity starts at 07:00 A.M. and lasts until about 20:30 P.M. A possible strategy for backing up the archives could be starting it at 12:30 P.M., then making a second copy, and finally deleting the saved logs. All these backup operations can be performed using brarchive.

As an even safer strategy, you could have an automatic procedure that copies every generated archived log file to another computer as long as you control and keep the sequence exactly.

As with brbackup, the brarchive utility settings are stored in the init<sid>.sap initialization profile, which must be set before you start to use it. Similarly, the tape devices to be used for the backups have to be initialized.

Normally, for backing up archives, you could use different tape devices and tape capacities than those for backing up the database, since it will normally be a much smaller volume.

The SAP system and the database status is independent to perform a backup of the archive redo log files. It does not matter if they are started or stopped.

The brarchive Menu Options

From the sapdba initial menu, call the brarchive utility by selecting option *i—Backup archive logs*. The system displays the Backup archive logs menu, similar to the one shown in Fig. 15-33.

The menu will show the default options as configured in the init<sid>.sap initialization profile: saving the archive log files to a local tape device without compression. Change the parameters as you deem necessary.

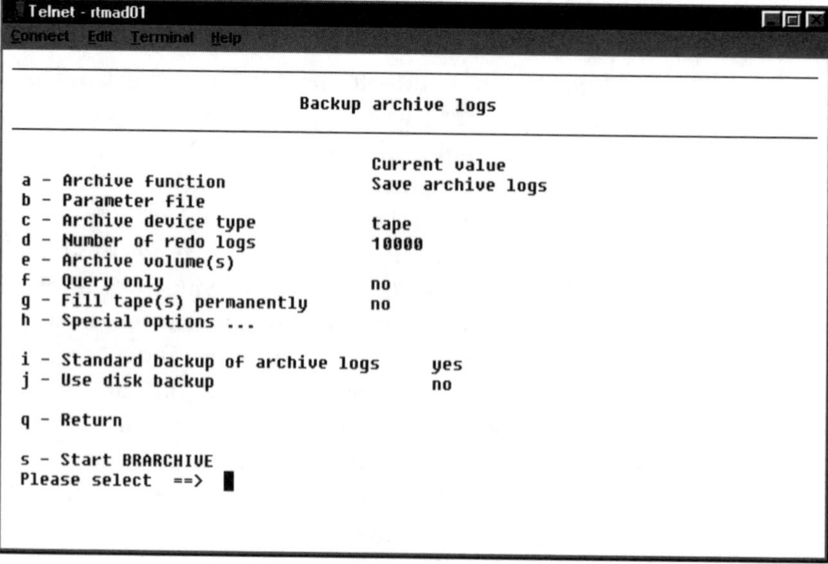

Figure 15-33 The brarchive main menu.

The brarchive utility writes its operations into the summary log file arch<SID>.log and, for every backup, it writes a log file with the syntax *a<encoded timestamp>.<ext>*. You can display these files using the Show/cleanup menu (item *l*).

The archiving menu includes the following options:

- *Archive function.* The brarchive utility includes many different functions. A comprehensive archiving strategy will involve performing several of these functions. When selecting this function, the system will display an additional menu. On this new menu, the following archive functions are available:
  - *Save archive logs.* It's the default value for normal backup of the archives that have not yet been saved.
  - *Make second copy of archive logs.* Performs a second backup of the archive logs previously saved.
  - *Double save archive logs (parallel).* Backs up the archive logs on two tape devices in parallel.
  - *Save and delete archive logs.* Performs the normal save operation and deletes the archive files as they are saved. In this and other functions that delete archive files, the brarchive utility uses the log files to identify which files were already saved or deleted. If any offline redo log file was not successfully archived, it won't be deleted.
  - *Make second copy and delete archive logs.* Performs a second copy of the archive files and then deletes them.
  - *Double save and delete archive logs.* Performs the same operation as the previous option using two tape devices in parallel.
  - *Delete saved archive logs.* Deletes the archive files already saved.
  - *Delete copied archive logs.* Deletes only archive files that were saved twice.
  - *Make second copy and save archive logs.* Makes a second copy of already-saved archive files and then saves all new archive files that have been generated in the meantime.
  - *Make second copy, delete, and save archive logs.* Performs the same operation as the previous option but additionally will delete the already saved archive files.
  - *Initialize BRARCHIVE tape.* Initializes one or more tapes or backup devices. The system will display a new reduced menu for selecting additional options:
    - *Check before initialization = no.* If you choose not to check the label, you can initialize any tapes and even overwrite existing SAP volumes.

- — *Check label before initialization = yes.* The system will check the label and only allow for initializing SAP tapes when the locking period has expired.
  - — *Number of tapes.* Here you can specify the number of tapes to be initialized.

  Show information in tape header. Shows the information contained in the tape header (volume label).

  Stop BRARCHIVE run with fill option. Stops a backup of archive files that was previously started using the option *Continue until end of tape.*

- *Parameter file.* The default file is init<DBSID>.sap, but you can create and enter here any other parameter file that can be useful for having default values when performing different backup functions.
- *Confirm archive parameters.* The default value is *no,* which suppresses some of the brarchive confirmation messages. When selecting *yes,* the system will stop and display all the confirmation messages. Then the user must confirm the function to continue.
- *Language.* You can select the language for the brarchive messages. Only English (default) and German are available.
- *Archive device type.* The system will display a list of available device types supported by brarchive. The default value is to back up the archive files to local *tape* devices, but you can also choose:

  tape_auto. Select this option for performing backups to tape devices which support automatic tape loading and switching. Selecting this option will suppress the messages for changing tapes.

  pipe. This option performs backups to tape devices in a remote system using commands which must be specified in the parameter initialization file.

  pipe_auto. It's a combination of the two preceding options. It's used to back up to an automatic tape loading and switching device located in a remote system.

  disk. Backing up archive files to disk is only done in exceptional cases, such as in parallel server (OPS) configurations, or in connection with a two-step archiving (first to disk, then to tape).

  util_file and *util_file_online.* These are the options that allow for third-party backup solutions integrated with brarchive. You must enter here the name of a third-party program that must comply with the SAP backup interface program backint.

Please refer to SAP for a list of certified backup partners and solutions complying with the backint interface. When using an external backup program, if necessary, you can use the *Backup utility parameter file* option to specify a file containing parameters needed for the external backup solution.

tape_box and *pipe_box* are used for jukeboxes and autoloaders. In the first case (*tape_box*) the devices must be locally accessible; in the second case (*pipe_box*) they must be remotely accessible.

- *Number of redo logs.* The default value is set to 10,000 to make certain that all the archive logs are backed up. It's very unlikely an installation gets more than 10,000 archives. You can change this value to specify the number of archive files to be backed up. For example, by specifying 5, the brarchive utility will save the five oldest archive logs.
- *Enter password interactively.* This option can be used to enter interactively or not the database administrator password. The default option is *no.*
- *Query only.* When selecting this option, the system displays three possibilities:

  no. It's the default value for starting the selected backup function. The backup will be normally started.

  with tape check. No backup of the archive files will be performed. The system will check and display which tape or tapes are required for the backup. The system also checks that the required tapes are mounted in the drives.

  without tape check. No backup of the archive files will be performed. The system will only display which tape or tapes are needed for performing the backup.
- *Archive volume(s).* You can enter here the backup volume (tape label) to be used for the backup of the archive. When none is specified, the system will use the next sequential volume as specified in the initialization profile and as recorded in the backup logs. If you need to specify more than one tape, you must separate every label with commas. However, if the archive files to be saved do not fit into a single tape, you have to start brarchive again to back up the remaining files.
- *Compress.* When selecting this option, the system will display the three possible entries:
  - *no.* It's the default value for performing backups without compression.

- *yes.* Software compression is performed. When this option is used, the tool will compress the backup files into the working directory before transferring them to the backup device.
- *hardware.* Select this option for backup devices with built-in hardware compression.

- *Verification after backup.* Choose whether you want the utility to perform a verification of the backed-up files. The default is *no.* Verification will increase the total backup time.
- *Fill tape(s) permanently.* When selecting the default option *no,* the system will back up the specified archived files according to the archive function chosen. However, selecting *yes,* the brarchive utility will immediately back up new archive files as they are being generated. The process will stop when the backup device is full, when the specified number of archive files is reached, or when it is manually stopped with the archive function *Stop BRARCHIVE run with fill option.*
- *Use disk backup.* This option can be used for performing the backup of the archive log files that were previously copied to disk in a two-step strategy.

To carry out the backup of the archive logs, select the needed parameters in the menu and mount the tape or other specified device. Then, to start the backup, select the option *s.* While the backup of archive files is being run, the screen displays the backup size, the progress, and the estimated end time for completion. It will also display a system message when an error occurs or when the backup is finally finished.

As with brbackup, the brarchive utility can also be called from the command line, which allows for writing shell scripts for automating and scheduling backups of archive files. For detailed information about the parameters and command options available with brarchive, please refer to the SAP online documentation.

Following is an introduction to advanced backup facilities that were introduced in *sapdba* with release 4.0 and that can be used in complex scenarios and with special requirements for backup strategies. Many of these options combine both the *brbackup* and *brarchive* utilities.

Specific information on available commands and use can be found on the online documentation.

BRBACKUP and BRARCHIVE in One Run

Especially for small and midsize installations, the advantage of the one-run strategy is the possibility of having both database and offline redo log backups together in a single set of tapes (*volume_backup*), reducing the number and type of the tapes used and the administrative workload. This strategy also allows unattended online/offline backups to be performed. This backup strategy also supports multiple tape devices and parallel backup to several different devices (e.g., tape and disk).

There are two options for making the backup in one run:

- Tape administration runs under control of BRBACKUP (*BRBACKUP <database backup options> -a <offline redo log backup options>*)
- Tape administration runs under control of BRARCHIVE (*BRBACKUP <offline redo log backup options> -a <database backup options>*)

The first option (brbackup -a) is recommended by SAP for the one-run strategy. In this strategy, BRBACKUP uses the tapes defined in *volume_backup* and performs the following steps:

— Checks the volume label.

— Backs up the tape header files (.tape.hdr0) and profiles (init_ora, init_sap).

— Backs up the database files.

— Calls BRARCHIVE using the options given after *-a* and then writes the offline redo log files to tape after the backed-up database files (without checking the label and without header file).

— BRARCHIVE backs up all logs (BRBACKUP and BRARCHIVE logs).

With the one-run strategy, the maximum number of offline redo log files that can be backed up is the number that can still fit on the tape after the database backup. Therefore, you must check regularly whether the tape capacity is sufficient. If necessary, you should use larger tapes, an additional tape station, or another backup strategy.

Consistent Online Backup

A consistent online backup is a database backup that, while performed in online mode, contains logically consistent data. The offline redo log files generated during the backup are saved to the same volume (as the database files) with BRBACKUP. After the offline redo log files are imported, the online backup can be completely recovered. This type of backup can be done while the database is active.

Is important to know that the backup of the *offline redo logfiles* using BRBACKUP in a consistent online backup runs completely independently from the BRARCHIVE backups.

To make a consistent online backup, start *BRBACKUP -t|-type online_cons* or set the parameter *<backup_type> = online_cons* in the *init<SID>.sap* profile.

To reload the offline redo log files saved within BRBACKUP, use the command *BRRESTORE -m|-mode archive_logs.* To reload a complete consistent online backup, use *BRRESTORE -m full.*

Completion of BRBACKUP and BRRESTORE Backups

The capability to complete partial backups of sapdba utilities can be used in different circumstances:

- For making BRBACKUP runs complete
- For making BRARCHIVE runs complete
- For performing partial backups

These processes are available in the standard backup menus, and use the *-fillup* option of the BRBACKUP and BRRESTORE tools. Backups can be completed either because it was decided to perform a partial backup, or to continue a cancelled backup.

Two-Level Backups

The two-level or two-phase backup consists of using *disks* as intermediate devices for backups. The objective is that the copy process of files is generally faster on disks than on other devices.

In the first phase of the backup, BRBACKUP backs up to disks. In the second phase files can be backed up from the disk to the tapes.

BRRESTORE is capable of restoring two-level backups to their original locations.

Standby Database Backup Scenario

Another important addition to the R/3 backup tools is the possibility of having a standby database server that has the function of covering a special backup strategy as well as creating a disaster recovery scenario. The principle basically consists in having a copy of the primary (productive) system in another system (standby) and applying the redo logs as they are being generated. The standby database is in a mounted standby status, and cannot be opened until the switch takes place.

This type of scenario has some advantages and some drawbacks. Some of the advantages are:

- The risk level in the installation is low, since all the system components are duplicated and can be in different locations.
- In the event of a restore and recovery, the risk of downtime is minimized by enabling the almost immediate availability of the standby system.
- The backup process does not use the productive systems resources, and therefore does not affect the system's performance.

Some of the disadvantages of these scenarios are:

- High cost
- Complex installation and maintenance
- Need for a high-availability solution (switchover) that can be used for quickly switching systems

Some of the backup options for setting up this type of configuration have been discussed in previous sections. Besides the hardware and software configurations, it will mainly require the use of the device types and backup types as *offline_standby, offline_stop,* and *standby.*

For actual configuration options, please refer to the SAP online documentation.

Split Mirror Disks Backup

The principle of this type of backup is to have mirrored copies of database files on disks that can be temporarily detached, attached to a second host for backup, and then resynchronized. The advantage of this type of configuration is that downtime for backup is minimized. BRBACKUP supports this type of configuration both for online and offline backups, and includes all the required options for performing the backups in the second host and then resynchronizing the disks.

In the case of offline backups with split mirror disks, the R/3 system must be shut down for a few minutes for the process of detaching the mirror; right after that the system can be started again. In online backups there is no need to shut down R/3.

In order to set up this type of backup strategy, some software configuration must be performed on the hosts. The *init<sid>.sap* parameters must be configured as well—for example, setting the split commands and the backup types.

Asynchronous Verification of Backups

Asynchronous or deferred verification of backups has the advantage of decoupling the process of backup from the verification, thus reducing the time required for backup completion.

Verification options include using BRBACKUP -verify (option -w), BRARCHIVE -verify, or BRRESTORE -verify, this last option being an independent verification of backups.

These verifications, which mostly include volume comparison or tape readibility, can be complemented by a check of the internal Oracle block structure using the DB_VERIFY tool. This tool is invoked using the option *use_dbv* together with the BRBACKUP or BRRESTORE programs.

Introduction to Database Restore and Recovery Concepts and Procedures

During operation of the database, different types of software problems and hardware failures might arise and cause data inconsistencies, and the only solution to reset the database to a consistent situation would be to perform a restore and recovery of the database using previous backup copies.

The number of problem situations as well as the changing circumstances when errors do occur make it quite difficult to cover comprehensively in a few pages all possibilities for the restore and recovery procedures in SAP R/3 installations. The next sections introduce the concepts and the available tools, whereas more detailed information can be found in official SAP and Oracle documentation.

Restore and recovery should only be performed by experienced database administrators, since a wrong analysis of the situation or a mistaken function might lead, in the worst case, to loss of important business data.

For this reason, it is important that a comprehensive backup and restore strategy is well-defined and tested before actual productive operation of the R/3 systems. Tests should include the largest number of possible circumstances for both physical and logical database errors. Chapter 16 includes a section on backup strategies.

The key to a successful strategy is to understand clearly the elements underlying the database architecture, the critical database files and processes, and the backup and recovery concepts.

The next topics deal only with the Oracle database backup and restore concepts and procedures as supported by the sapdba tool and related utilities. For backing up and restoring other nondatabase files, you can use sapdba or any other standard operating system or third-party backup tools. These other files, such as the SAP executables, Oracle runtime, or operating system files, are normally more *static* and can be restored from normal backups without affecting the consistency of the database data.

A recovery is the full responsibility of the database administrator. Since this can be a complex procedure, options on available menus should be protected by expert mode.

When in a situation where a restore and recovery seems to be needed, the first step should be to analyze the error situation, then check the SAPnet notes, and, when in doubt, contact the SAP hotline for support in the recovery procedure. This is a good place to stress the importance of testing and documenting a backup and recover procedure while building and configuring the technical infrastructure in the implementation phase of SAP projects.

Recovery Concepts

Understanding the recovery concepts basically requires you to understand how the Oracle database system works, what and where the database files are, and how and when those files are modified.

The database files needed in a consistent form for the correct operation of the database are the control file (including the mirror copies), the data files, the online redo log files, and the offline redo log files (archived log files).

A *consistent database* is the usual operative status of the database when all the files have the same internal *timestamp,* when the control file contains the actual scheme of the database files, and when there are no damaged or missing database files.

As introduced in previous sections, using the standard tools in the SAP system, the first three types of files (control files, data files, and online redo log files) are backed up to a backup device using the brbackup utility. Similarly, the archived redo log files are backed up to a backup device using the brarchive utility. When the database needs to be restored and recovered, all types of database files are restored to the server physical disks using the brrestore utility. A difference should be made between the concepts of restoring and recovering.

Restoring is the process of transferring (copying) any or all of the database files needed for a recovery from the backup media (usually tapes) to the server disks, where those files will be needed by the utility programs. Restoring is a physical process. Regardless of the fact that backups are performed at the tablespace level (Oracle storage concept), the restore process is always performed at the data-file level (operating system files). Restoring is not sufficient for having the database operative.

Recovering is the process of setting the database to a consistent state using files that were previously restored. There are several types of recovery: full database recovery, partial recovery (only some files are missing), or *point-in-time* recovery, which is the process of setting the database to the consistent state of a past date and time.

When restoring or recovering, you must watch out for database *structural changes.* A structural change occurs, for example, when you add new data files to tablespaces, reorganize tablespaces with data files, or move or rename data files. This is important because the redo log files do not contain the database statements for performing those operations. This type of situation can cause many problems, and must be handled with Oracle utilities if certain precautions are not taken into account in the backup strategy, like performing a backup when such structural change occurs. This is the reason why sapdba options that change the database structure always ask for a backup to be performed.

Before recovering, an error analysis should be performed. The error analysis mainly involves checking the Oracle alert file as well as the possible trace files generated by either the standard background processes or the user process. In SAP installations, these files are normally located (if standard settings have not been changed) under the /oracle/<SID>/saptrace directory and then in the subdirectories *background* and *usertrace.*

Database crash or error situations can be of the following types:

- *Logical or software errors such as a background process error, internal SQL statement error, or whole-instance error derived from an operating system crash.* These types of errors are normally recovered automatically when the database is started again.
- *Logical user errors, such as unintentional deletion of important data.* In such cases, a logical recovery (point-in-time recovery) will

be needed unless the objects affected were previously exported either by using standard sapdba or Oracle tools or even with R3trans, in which case an import could be performed. These errors can be hard to solve, since the internal logical structure and relationship among the R/3 tables and objects is very complex.

- *Hardware or media errors such as disk failures and file corruption.* These errors can be recovered by having a proper backup and restore strategy that includes the backing up of the archive files. The sapdba program includes the needed utilities for performing most types of restore and recovery procedures when these errors happen.

What Is Supported with sapdba?

The sapdba tool can be used for restoring the full database and individual files and for performing recoveries of the full database. Some database error circumstances, such as the loss of all the control files, defective online redo log files, or structural database changes, cannot be automatically solved with sapdba tools, and recovery must be performed manually using the Oracle tool SVRMGRL.

The sapdba tool can be used for restoring and recovering the database after the loss of any data files belonging to any of the SAP tablespaces as well as the SYSTEM, PSAPTEMP, and PSAPROLL tablespaces.

The sapdba tool includes several restore and recovery options within the *Restore / Recovery* menu. The next sections explain in detail what can be done from sapdba.

Requirements for Database Recovery with sapdba Utilities

For sapdba to be able to assist and perform recoveries, some requirements must be met. *Only* if these requirements are met can sapdba perform the automatic recovery functions. They have to do with the availability in undamaged form of all the files that will be required for the recovery procedure:

- In order to find the location of the database files and the archived redo log files, sapdba needs the brbackup and brarchive logs to be available. For this reason, it's important not to delete these logs too soon. If the logs are not available, the first thing to do is to find them and restore them.

- Copy of the lost database data files
- Copy of all the redo log files (archived log files) that were generated from the time the copy of the database files used for the recovery was created to the time of the error.
- Copy of the control file and the mirrored copies (normally three in SAP installations).
- Copy of at least one of the members of the online redo log groups.

Especially if either of the last two requirements are not met, you will have to rebuild those files using specific procedures and the SVRMGRL tool.

Partial Restore and Complete Recovery

All the options for restore and recovery are included within the *Restore / Recovery* menu. Figure 15-34 shows this menu.

The first option, *a—Partial restore and complete recovery,* can be used for performing the recovery of the database up to the current time. Access this menu by selecting option *a.* On previous R/3 releases this was called the *Check and Repair database* menu. Figure 15-35 shows this menu.

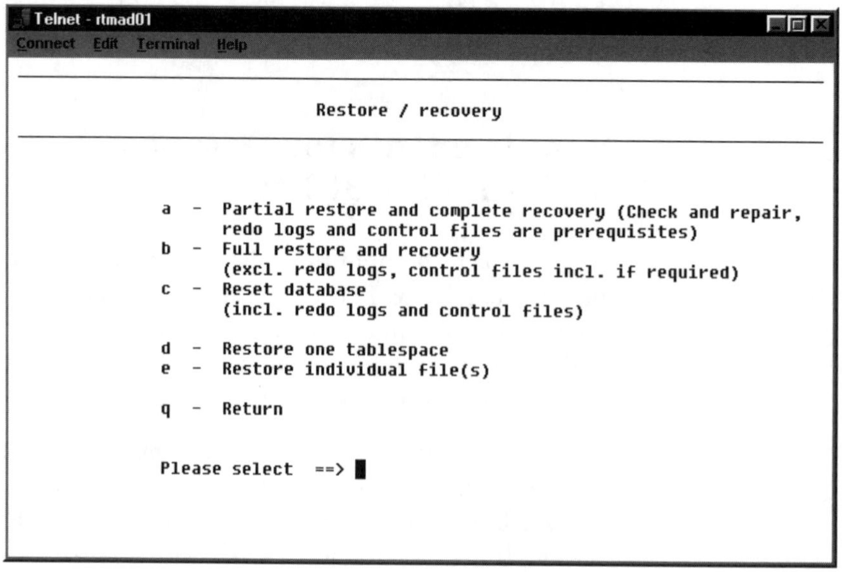

Figure 15-34 The sapdba restore and recovery menu.

```
Telnet - rtmad01
Connect  Edit  Terminal  Help
______________________________________________________________

                    Restore / recovery
______________________________________________________________

    a  -  Partial restore and complete recovery (Check and repair,
          redo logs and control files are prerequisites)
    b  -  Full restore and recovery
          (excl. redo logs, control files incl. if required)
    c  -  Reset database
          (incl. redo logs and control files)

    d  -  Restore one tablespace
    e  -  Restore individual file(s)

    q  -  Return

    Please select  ==>
```

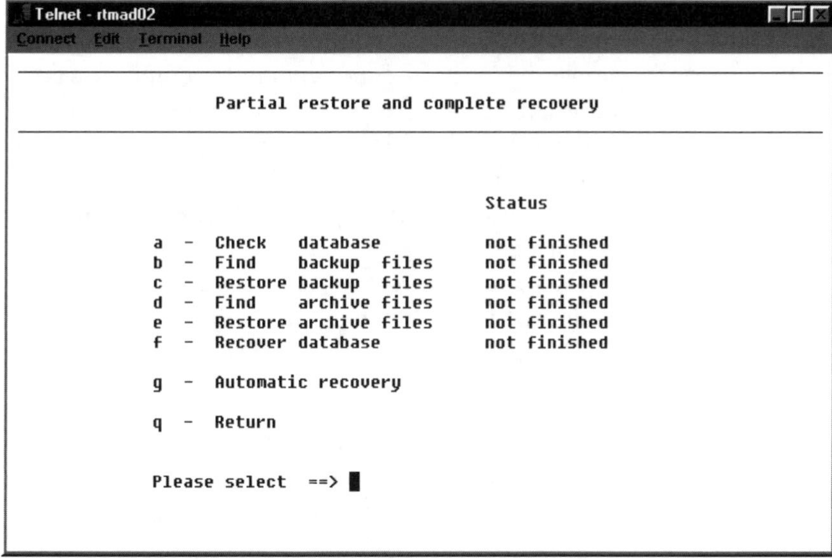
```
Telnet - rtmad02
Connect  Edit  Terminal  Help

                  Partial restore and complete recovery

                                                   Status

          a  -  Check   database                   not finished
          b  -  Find    backup  files              not finished
          c  -  Restore backup  files              not finished
          d  -  Find    archive files              not finished
          e  -  Restore archive files              not finished
          f  -  Recover database                   not finished

          g  -  Automatic recovery

          q  -  Return

          Please select  ==>
```

Figure 15-35 Partial restore and complete recovery menu.

In this and subsequent menus, the system displays several recover options together with the status for the operation. Possible status messages are as follows:

- *not finished.* The process is not yet completed. This is the normal status when the operation has not been performed.
- *not needed.* The process is not required.
- *finished.* The process has completed successfully.
- *not allowed.* This process cannot be executed.

From this menu you can either perform an automatic recovery (option *g*) or perform a step-by-step recovery using the menu options from *a* to *f*.

When choosing the automatic recovery option, the system will process all the actions needed and guide the administrator in all the necessary steps as required, such as stopping the SAP system, mounting specific tapes, and so on. The system will prompt in every step for continuing or canceling the recovery. With automatic recovery, the system will always try to use the latest available backup as recorded in the log files, together with all the archived log files for recovering up to the current time.

If any error happens during the recovery, the system will go back to the initial menu and display the status of every function performed. After solving the error situation, the recovery process can be resumed manually from the first menu option with status *not finished.*

The manual recovery procedure requires you to perform all the functions displayed in the menu in the same order that they appear on the screen. This is absolutely mandatory, since the recovery process needs the information gathered in previous steps to proceed. In any case, the system will check and forbid you to enter a function when the status of previous functions is not set to *finished* or *not needed.*

The status of the options changes dynamically as steps are being performed.

This database recovery process generates the log file <timestamp>.rcv under the work directory sapreorg.

The next topics introduce briefly what is achieved in every manual recovery function.

Checking the Database. With this first option, sapdba checks the internal Oracle V$ tables for database errors that could prevent any further operation. The checking function can perform two types of tests:

- The first one is an online *quick check* of the database files, which is performed while the database is open. This quick check will not alter the option status (*not finished*) and therefore no restore or recover option is possible. After it finishes the check, it will prompt the user to continue with a more comprehensive and safe test. To continue, you should first stop the SAP instance processes if they were running.
- The next is the *safe check.* With this check, the database will be stopped and then started up to the mount state since it's the only way to guarantee that the information in the Oracle V$ tables is current. The safe check will test the status of all the data files, tablespaces, control files, and redo log files.

  As a result of a safe check, three situations might result:

- The check discovers errors that cannot be solved with sapdba, such as control files missing. Status will be set to *not finished,* and you can't continue the recovery with this tool. You must use SVRMGRL manually.
- The check shows that some data files are damaged and need recovery. In this case, sapdba generates the list of required data files for the recovery that are needed for further processing. The status is set to *finished.*
- If the check didn't find any errors, the status is set to *finished* and all other function status indicators are set to *not needed*. No further recovery is necessary.

Finding the Backup Files. Option *b—Find backup files* is used for locating and selecting the backups that are needed for recovering the damaged files. This information is needed for the next restore process. For finding the files, this option uses the available brbackup logs.

The new menu shows the following available options:

- *Start finding backup files.* This option must be used in order for sapdba to find where the backup copies for the lost files are located. SAP will display a list of the most recent brbackup files for each lost file.
- *Show the list of damaged files.* The system presents a list of the lost files and the backup files where they are located. The system will display a message if it does not find one or if the lost file is not required because there is already an older one that can be used.
- *Show the list of backup files.* With this option, you can specify for which lost files you want to display the available backup files.
- *Select a backup file for restore.* You can use this option to specify a different backup file than the sapdba-proposed one to perform the restore. The backup file selected here will be the one used for the restore. The selected backup file is flagged with *SELECTED FOR RESTORE.*
- *Select a BRBACKUP run for restore.* You can use this option to specify which backup copy (brbackup) should be run for every lost file. This is a useful option if you don't want to restore files from different backup runs and want to overwrite sapdba-suggested backups.

After finding the backup files and specifying any additional selection, press *q* to return to the main menu. The status will be changed to *finished,* and the recovery process can be continued.

Restoring the Backup Files. Selecting the menu option *c* will invoke the brrestore utility for restoring physically the selected files from the backup media (usually tapes) to their original directory. This option is only supported in connection with the recovery in process. It cannot be used independently for restoring old database files.

WARNING! *The files restored will overwrite the existing database files with the same name and location.*

When selecting this function, sapdba displays a new menu from which you can start the restore. You can also modify the restore parameters, but this is not normally recommended or needed since they are automatically set using the backup logs.

Restoring with this sapdba function is not supported when a structure change has occurred in the database from the time of the backup file and the time for the recovery.

The restore process will start and, during the process, will check if there is sufficient storage space and that all backup files are available. During the restore, sapdba displays warning or error messages when any file is to be overwritten. When problems are detected, the restore process will pause and allow the administrator to solve it and proceed. When a file is to be overwritten, you have the option to stop the restore process.

During the restore process, the system displays all the information and status of the files being restored. After a successful restore, the status for this option is changed to *finished.*

Finding the Archive Files. Similar to the process of finding the database data file in the copies of the brbackup, this function must be used to locate the archive log files needed for the recovery. The sapdba utility uses also the main brarchive log, arch<SID>.log, for finding the valid backups of the archives logs that can be used for recovering the lost or damaged database files.

Selecting this option will display a new menu with three options:

- *Specify first archive file to be found / restored (Current setting: <number>).* The number indicates the first archive file that needs to be found. This number is determined and suggested by the sapdba tool. If needed, you can change this number. Remember, though, that if there is an archive log file missing from this starting file and the situation to be recovered, the recovery process is not possible.
- *Show the list of archive files.* With this function, you can display which archive files will be required for the recovery process.
- *Start finding archive files.* You have to select this function for finding the archive files needed for the recovery of lost or damaged files. By looking at the brarchive log files, the system will search for archive files that are already in backup devices, but it will also search the archiving directory for files not yet backed up.

Exit to the main restore menu for continuing the process. If the function is successful, the status is changed to *finished.*

Restoring Archived Files. As with the restoration of backup files, selecting the menu option *e* will invoke the brrestore utility, which will physically restore the needed archive files from the backup media (usually tapes) to the saparch directory. You will not need to use this operation if all the needed archive redo log files are already (or still) located in the archiving directory. If the directory is full, it will automatically remove the archive logs that have been already used, and, additionally, the utility also supports restoring while the recovery is in process.

When selecting this function, sapdba displays a new menu where you can start the restore of the archive files on tape. You also have the option for modifying the restore parameters, but this is not normally needed.

During the restore process, the system displays all the information and status of the files being restored, such as the files found and the log sequence number. After a successful restore of archive files, the status for this option is changed to *finished.*

Recovering the Database. After all previous options have been successfully finished, the option *f—Recover database* can be processed to start the recovery of the database.

When the process starts, the system displays information about the recovery steps: the starting point for the recovery, whether it can be performed in a single step, the scripts that were created for performing the recovery, and then the main recovery process itself. The database will be sent into a recovery state, and the needed archived redo logs will be applied. If the system needs additional archive files that could not be restored previously, it will prompt you to mount the device to restore the archives, as other archives have been applied and then deleted. The process can then continue.

When the recovery procedure is finished successfully, the status in the initial check and repair database will be set to *finished,* and sapdba will again open the database.

Restoring and Recovering the Database: Further Options

While the *Partial restore and complete recovery* option allowed for recovering the database up to the current time, sapdba includes other types of restore and recovery options such as restoring a full database backup; performing a point-in-time recovery; recovering individual missing or damaged control files, data files, or tablespaces; and others. Performing any of the available restore and recover functions will overwrite existing system files, so it's convenient to protect them with expert mode—when available—and it ensures that they are only performed by experienced database administrators.

The next topics introduce the options in the previous menu and the functions that can be performed.

Full Restore: Resetting the Database. The option on the Restore/recovery menu, *c—Reset database (incl. redo logs and control files),* can be used to completely reset the database to the state it was at the time of the corresponding full offline backup used for the restore. With this function, the system uses the brrestore utility for restoring all the database files, including the control file and the online redo log files and all the mirror copies.

When selecting this function, the system presents a new menu, shown in Fig. 15-36, with three options. Depending on the option chosen, the database will be set to the status of the backup restored, or it can be further recovered.

The system options are as follows:

- *Restore database and startup open (no recovery possible).* The system will restore the full database and open it. The database will have this status from the time the backup was performed. All data-

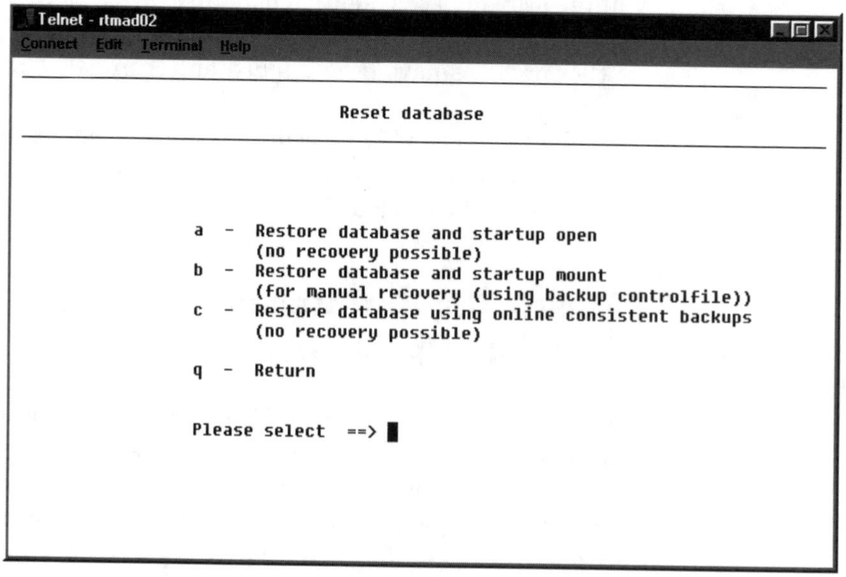

```
Telnet - rtmad02
Connect  Edit  Terminal  Help

                         Reset database

        a  -  Restore database and startup open
              (no recovery possible)
        b  -  Restore database and startup mount
              (for manual recovery (using backup controlfile))
        c  -  Restore database using online consistent backups
              (no recovery possible)

        q  -  Return

        Please select  ==>
```

Figure 15-36 Reset database options.

base data from the time of the backup up to the time the database was last stopped is lost. No further recovery is possible. Additionally, some problems might arise regarding the archive log files sequence numbers as well as the brbackup and brarchive logs and volume initialization. After analyzing the particular situation, please refer to SAP online documentation and SAP notes for how to proceed.

- *Restore database and startup mount (for manual recovery (using backup control file)).* Using this option will restore the complete database, but it will only be mounted (not opened). Further actions will require the manual administrator intervention for recovering the database using the Oracle svrmgrl tool. A manual recovery of the full database is performed with the statement *RECOVER DATABASE*. The option *USING BACKUP CONTROLFILE* has to be used in all situations where the control file is not the current one, but a previous copy.

Notice that this function with manual recovery can be performed normally with an automatic database recovery using the functions available in the sapdba menu Partial restore and complete recovery.

- *Restore database using online consistent backups (no recovery possible).* This is a similar option to the first one, and can be used for restoring a complete backup including the redo log files that were saved in the same backup volume. After the restore, the database will have the status it had when it finished the online backup—that is, it will include all the redo log files that were generated while the backup was running.

Full Database Restore and Recovery: Extended Options. Another option under the Restore/recovery menu is primarily intended for performing point-in-time recovery; that is, to recover the database up to the selected time. This can be the only solution to a logical problem such as the unintentional deletion of important database data. When you know exactly at what time the deletion occurred, you can restore the database up to just before it happened. However, consider that all database data from the point of the recovery up to the current time will be lost.

To access this function, select option *b—Full restore and recovery (excl. redo logs, control files incl. if required)*. The system will display a new menu as shown in Fig. 15-37.

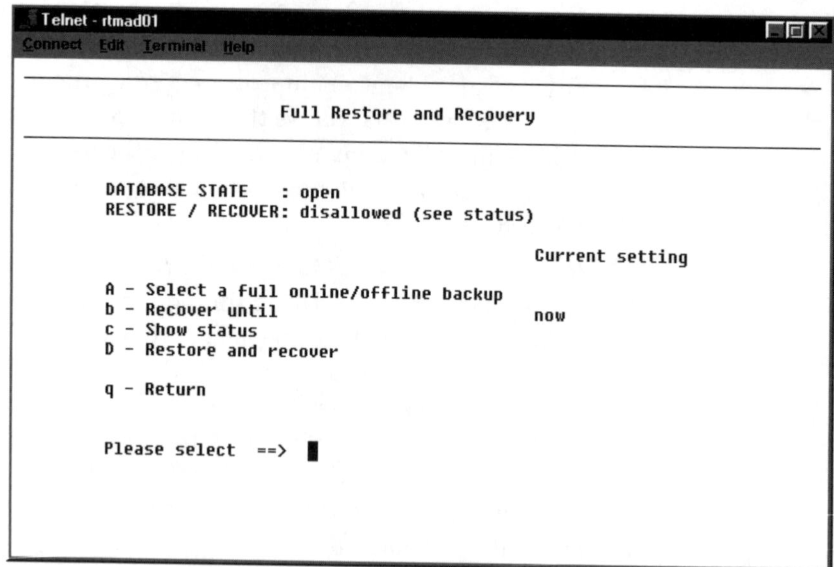

Figure 15-37 Full restore and recovery menu options.

The first thing to do is to choose option *a* for selecting a full database backup (brbackup) from which to perform the restore. The system will display a list of all backup runs as stored in the main backup log. Only successful backup runs can be chosen.

Then select option *b—Recover until* to specify the point in time for the recovery. The default option is *now,* which performs a full recovery up to the current time. Otherwise, you can specify a date and time with the format *YYYY-MM-DD HH.MM.SS.*

Observe the restrictions after a partial or point-in-time recovery concerning the archive log sequence as well as the main sapdba logs for brarchive. Check out also whether there has been any structural changes between the time of the full online or offline backup and the point in time specified for the recovery.

You can check the information about the recovery process before proceeding by selecting option *c—Show status.* The system will display which options have been chosen and which backups and archive logs will be necessary. This option will also display any warnings or messages about whether the recovery will be possible with the specified parameters.

To start the restore and recovery process, select option *D—Restore and recover.* Again, observe that any restore process will overwrite any existing database files.

The restore and recover process generates under the sapreorg directory the log files <timestamp>.rsn for recovering until now, or <timestamp>.rsp for point-in-time recoveries.

Restoring Individual Tablespace

There might be special occasions (such as disk failures or corrupted data files) where it is necessary to restore single tablespaces. You can do this by selecting option *d—Restore one tablespace,* from the initial restore and recovery menu. The system will request the tablespace name as well as the list of backup runs that can be used for the particular restore. It will present a new menu for specifying restore parameters.

If the parameters are correct, to start the restore process (with brrestore), select option *q—Return to restore process and continue.*

The database will be stopped for the restore, and after the data files belonging to the tablespace have been restored, the database will remain closed. Since probably this tablespace (data files) belong to a previous date and time, a recovery using the archive logs must be performed to bring the database to a consistent state. If you have not restored old control files or old online redo log files but only old data files, you can update these data files up to a current and consistent situation (perform a recovery process) using the available functions in *Partial restore and complete recovery.*

Restoring Individual Files

As an additional option, in connection with the brrestore program, sapdba allows for restoring individual files, including nondatabase files that might have been backed up using brbackup. Notice, though, that in case of restoring files with these options, the system merely copies the files from the backup device to the original location without performing further checks. So, in case database files are old, a recovery will probably be needed.

To call these options, from the initial restore and recovery menu, select option *e—Restore individual file(s).* Figure 15-38 shows an example of this menu after a file type has already been selected.

In this menu, the first thing to do is to decide which type of file is to be restored. Select option *A—File type.* The system will display an additional menu with all the file types you can select to restore. Please notice that some of these types can only be restored if they were previously backed up using brbackup. Figure 15-39 shows this new menu.

As you can see from the menu, no less than *all* possible file types in a SAP installation can be restored with these functions. Select the required file type and enter option *q* to go back to the previous menu. Depending on the type selected, the initial Restore individual file(s) menu will be updated with a status message. For example, upon selecting *Offline redo*

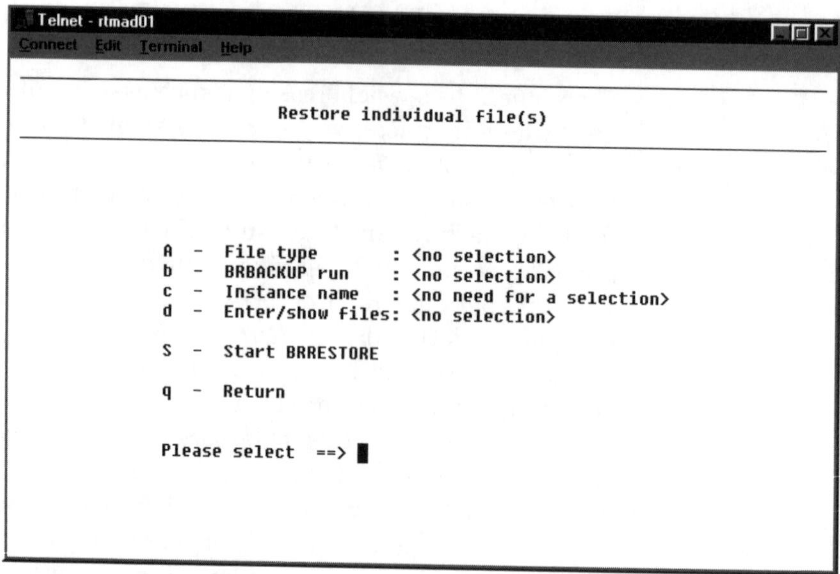

Figure 15-38 Options for restoring individual files.

logs (archive files), the system will inform you that no brbackup run will be needed for restoring, since these files are backed up using brarchive.

If you select profiles or summary log files, the system can restore them from any available tape, since they are always copied in the backup procedures.

Figure 15-39 Available file types for restore.

```
Telnet - rtmad01
Connect  Edit  Terminal  Help

                    Select file type for restore

     NOTE: Profiles and log files can only be restored from a tape!

       Current selection: <no selection>

       a -  Non-database files
       b -  Data files
       c -  Control file
       d -  Online redo logs
       e -  Offline redo logs
       f -  ORACLE and SAPDBA profiles
       g -  BRBACKUP/BRARCHIVE profile (init.sap)
       h -  SAPDBA main and struct log file
       i -  Summary BRBACKUP/BRARCHIVE log file
       j -  Detail BRBACKUP/BRARCHIVE log file

       q -  Return

       Please select  ==>
```

Other file types, such as nondatabase files, tablespace data files, control files, or online redo logs, will require you to enter the brbackup run from which to perform the restore. Selecting option *b—BRBACKUP run* will display a list of available backups as stored in the main backup logs and allow you to choose the needed backup.

Depending on the chosen type, you might have to select option *d—Enter / show files*. In any case, the system will display whether is it *<not needed>* or *<no selection>* has been made. The following entries must be made:

- For online redo log files, you must enter the group numbers.
- For archive files, you have to enter the log sequence number.
- For other file types, the system displays a list with all the relevant files and directories, with a flag indicating whether the file has been selected for the restore (*Res yes*) or not (*Res no*). You can change this flag by selecting the item number. Only those files with the *Res yes* flag will be restored.

To start the restore process, select option *s*. The system will display the menu for specifying the restore parameters. If necessary, change those values, and select the option *q—Return to Restore individual file(s) and continue*. At this moment, the actual restore process is restarted.

Remember that, as stated in the introduction to this topic, sapdba uses the brrestore utility to produce a merely physical restore: transfer (copy) the requested files from the backup device to the server disks. Nevertheless, if brrestore finds that the selected files for the restore still exist in the original location, it will display a warning message and pause for the administrator to confirm that the old files should be overwritten.

The system will display the operations performed during the restore process as well as prompt the users for entering and mounting requested tapes and such.

The restore log is stored in the file <timestamp>.dba under the sapreorg directory. Check out this file for any warning or error messages in case a further recovery is needed.

Introduction to Recovery Functions Using SVRMGRL

SVRMGRL is an Oracle tool for DBAs to manage the database system. As introduced in previous sections, most restore and recovery functions can be performed automatically within the sapdba program, which is in charge of calling the appropriate Oracle database management statements. There are, however, occasions when it might be necessary to perform manually these statements to recover the database after certain problem situations. The SVRMGRL tool is useful, and it's probably the only way to solve these problems.

This tool and the procedures should be used only by expert Oracle database administrators. Extensive information about this tool can be found in official Oracle documentation. This section only introduces the use of the tool with respect to possible database problems. You can also find additional information in the SAPnet and in the SAP online documentation.

WARNING! *An incomplete or erroneous recovery might lead to complete loss of data. Before performing any recovery functions, be sure to have a backup copy. If possible, use the SAP or Oracle hotline for specific recovery directions. Do not use this tool if you are unsure of what you are doing.*

It is always recommended first to try to restore or recover the database using normal sapdba functions. But, if your backup strategy is not based on SAP-recommended brbackup and brarchive utilities, then you have to design your own restore procedures.

Restore procedures with external backup tools can involve the use of SVRMGRL for recovery database, both complete or partial.

When using SVRMGRL, there are two main management statements that can be used for managing the database structure and the recover process: ALTER DATABASE and RECOVER. Additionally, for certain situations you might need to create a new control file or a new data file, tablespace, online redo log, and the like, all of which are handled with the available options for the CREATE command.

SVRMGRL uses mainly the RECOVER command to recover databases. This command admits recovering full databases, tablespaces, or data files. The options are

```
SVRMGRL> RECOVER DATABASE [options,…]
SVRMGRL> RECOVER TABLESPACE [options,…]
SVRMGRL> RECOVER DATAFILE [options,…]
```

For the full syntax of these SVRMGRL commands and when to use them in specific recovery situations, please refer to the official Oracle documentation as well as SAP online documents and SAPnet notes.

CHAPTER 16

SAP R/3 Technical Implementation and Operation

This chapter is intended to cover an overview of the tasks involved in the technical implementation of the SAP R/3 system as well as those aspects of the daily operation and support of an R/3 system or group of related SAP R/3 systems. The guidelines provided in the next sections show some examples of how different companies approach the maintenance and support of the R/3 systems, both before and after the R/3 systems start in productive operation. Depending on the size, number of users, and configuration of the particular installations and specific company requirements, some of the procedures described here might be only suitable to a certain extent. Some companies might not need so many policies and procedures, while some others might find them short.

This chapter is based on several technical implementation projects for big customers. Each one had special requirements, staff issues, physical resource restrictions, and a unique definition of how critical the R/3 business applications were. Think of these guidelines as a generic approach to SAP technical implementation and operation, taking or adapting what you consider useful and disregarding those aspects that do not apply to your specific case.

What Does *Implementing R/3* Mean?

Implementing R/3 basically means using the SAP R/3 application software to solve the information needs of the business.

There might be too many steps to accomplish the goal; it all depends on many factors, probably the most important of which is to what extent the standard R/3 application software matches the business process requirements.

Other critical factors are users and management commitment, both for change and the overall success of the system implementation.

SAP R/3 includes several tools and extensive documentation to facilitate the system implementation. These tools and the implementation manuals can be accessed from the SAP online documentation or directly within the R/3 system from the *Tools → Business Engineering* menu.

SAP provides the following:

- *The Customizing Manual.* To *customize* is to adapt the SAP R/3 software to the business. This manual provides a comprehensive guide of the overall process and includes references to the other guides. Within R/3, all customizing functions are accessed from the menu *Tools → Business Engineering → Customizing.*

- *The procedure model* and *ASAP* (*AcceleratedSAP*). These are the two SAP solution sets that include not only a methodology for implementation but other types of documents and services for providing a global solution for implementation projects. ASAP will soon completely replace the procedure model. The procedure model was introduced in 1995 and was a big step toward making the implementation process easier and providing a framework for it. Included in release 3.0 of R/3, ASAP was introduced in the United States in 1996 as a solution for quick implementations, but it has evolved into a full-featured solution.

The *procedure model* is the SAP core tool describing the activities needed to implement SAP. It provides a detailed project plan of all the steps and tasks involved when customizing R/3. You can access the procedure model from the R/3 system using the menu options *Tools* → *Business Engineering* → *Customizing* → *Basic functions* → *Procedure model.* (On release 4.5 this path has been removed.) The procedure model includes active links to the documentation, R/3 transactions, notes, customizing, and so on, and allows for project management monitoring and analysis.

ASAP goes beyond just methodology by providing a large number of tools and utilities that simplify the implementation process and cover extensive SAP and SAP partner implementation services, such as training, support, consulting, and so on. Differences between these solution sets are explained in Table 16-1.

TABLE 16-1

The Procedure Model and ASAP

Procedure Model	ASAP
German model	American model
Integrated into R/3	Independent tool
General view at a high level	More detailed view of activities and tasks
4 phases	5 phases
Includes project management	External project management
Online help and hypertext	Accelerators: documents, templates, tools, presentations, models, databases
R/3 reference model	R/3 business engineer (includes reference model)
Implementation solution	Complete implementation solution
Considers reengineering/BPR	Little reengineering
Long project?	Quick projects? (6 months/9 months)
—	Question and answer database
Will be replaced by ASAP	Will replace the procedure model

- *The IMG* or *Implementation Guide.* This tool includes a step-by-step guide to customizing, with direct links to all necessary transactions to adapt the selected R/3 modules or applications. Using the IMG it is possible to train end users (especially key users) in the customization techniques and options so they can configure the system themselves according to their business and organizational needs. The IMG includes utilities to manage the so-called *customizing projects.* Using these project management utilities, consultants decide which parts of the system are to be customized, and institute projects for which the system automatically generates a hierarchical list of the necessary customization steps for the selected application modules. The IMG is accessed by opening the customizing main menu and then selecting the necessary functions or utilities under the *Implementation Projects* menu. The IMG is used for configuration, and includes around 10,000 configuration objects in the latest versions. Actually, there is no need to customize all those settings, but only the ones relating to the business process modeling or reengineering. Subsets of the IMG are set up using IMG projects, which can be generated by selecting and including those applications or components that are part of the project. The tool will also automatically select any previously required customizing object, even if the object was not selected.

- *The R/3 Reference Model.* The model that describes the business processes included in the standard R/3 system as well as the relationship among the different application modules. You can access the reference model from the *Tools* → *Business Engineering* → *Business Navigator* menus.

In the process of implementing and customizing the R/3 applications, there are two types of tasks from the business, application, and computing points of view: functional tasks and technical tasks.

Functional tasks encompass those activities concerned with adapting the R/3 software to the business requirements.

Technical tasks comprise the full support to those functional tasks, and most importantly ensure the correct functioning of the application software components and the computing systems in which R/3 is being implemented.

This chapter deals only with the technical part of the R/3 implementation.

Technical Implementation with ASAP

As was introduced in previous section, AcceleratedSAP (ASAP for short) is SAP's implementation solution for R/3 projects. ASAP goes beyond just methodology by providing a large number of tools and utilities that simplify the implementation process and cover extensive SAP and SAP partner implementation services such as training, support, consulting, and so on.

The path proposed by SAP to reach the goal of successful implementation projects is based on the idea of facilitating a quick implementation of SAP R/3 and guaranteeing the quality. To achieve a fast, a high-quality implementation, ASAP is based on the following issues:

- Defining clearly the mission and the scope of the project. A clearly defined project scope is key in adjusting time planning and in making sure that projected costs closely match real costs.
- Increasing the feasibility of realizing a detailed plan at the beginning of the project.
- Standardizing and establishing a single project or implementation methodology, as defined by ASAP itself.
- Creating a homogeneous project environment.

To realize these objectives, ASAP provides the project team with a methodology and with tools, training, and services, as well as a process-oriented project plan known as the ASAP Roadmap.

Some of the tools provided by ASAP are:

- Implementation assistant
- Question and answer database
- Business engineer
- SAP project team training
- SAP support and services
- Knowledge corner

The ASAP solution set is delivered in a CD-ROM that is installed independently of R/3, although there is a connection between some of the tools and the IMG. ASAP is release dependent and is constantly updated. SAP provides periodic updates on SAPnet.

SAP also launched the TeamSAP initiative to provide coaching and training to partners, and a certification program so that customers can be confident of the quality of consultants helping them. TeamSAP is normally positioned as a three-component solution, or as a coordinated network of:

- Processes, represented by the ASAP solution set
- People, including prepared and certified consultants
- Products, represented by the R/3 Business Framework architecture

TeamSAP is SAP's commitment to its customers' implementation success, full application life cycle support, and ongoing changes. In this line, SAP plays an important role in coaching and auditing the quality of projects.

The *ASAP Roadmap* is the project plan of the methodology. It is a well-defined and clear process-oriented project plan that provides a step-by-step guide during the life of the implementation project.

The Roadmap is made up of four major phases, each one describing the main work packages, activities, and tasks needed to achieve the expected results. Together with activities and tasks, ASAP provides descriptions of all the processes, tools, training, services, and documentation that will be useful for carrying out these activities.

The ASAP solution set deals also with the technical aspects of the implementation, and includes many papers, utilities, and templates for helping project managers to address the many technical issues involved.

Technical issues appear in every phase of the ASAP implementation roadmap. As of release 4.0, these are the main work packages:

- Phase 1, the *project preparation phase,* includes a work package consisting of the *Technical Requirements Planning*, mainly used to perform an initial sizing and procure the initial hardware.
- Phase 2, the *business blueprint phase,* includes the work package *Develop System Environment*, which comprises the activities for installing and configuring the development system, including the definition of first system administration procedures.
- Phase 3, the *realization phase,* is the longest phase and includes many technical activities. Most importantly for technology- and infrastructure-related tasks, it contains the work package *System Management*, which is made up of a collection of activities such as:
  - Develop System Test Plans
  - Define Service Level Commitment

- Establish System Administration Functions
- Set up Quality Assurance Environment
- Define Production System Design
- Define Production System Management
- Set up Production Environment

- Phase 4, the *final preparation phase,* contains work packages for system management that target specific activities for the productive environment, especially for conducting system tests. It is also important to perform a quality check on technical issues in this phase.
- Phase 5, the *go live and support phase,* is an important overall phase for the full project team, providing extensive support and guarantees that the systems work as expected. This includes all infrastructure components and support of the basis system.

Getting Ready for Implementing and Supporting R/3: An Approach to Roles

Figure 16-1 shows a possible organization for the group of people which plays a role in the use, implementation, and support of the SAP R/3 system. Theoretically, this approach should not differ much from the IT organizations set in place for supporting other types of demanding and critical business information systems. There are, however, factors that make the technical aspects of R/3 differ from other business applications.

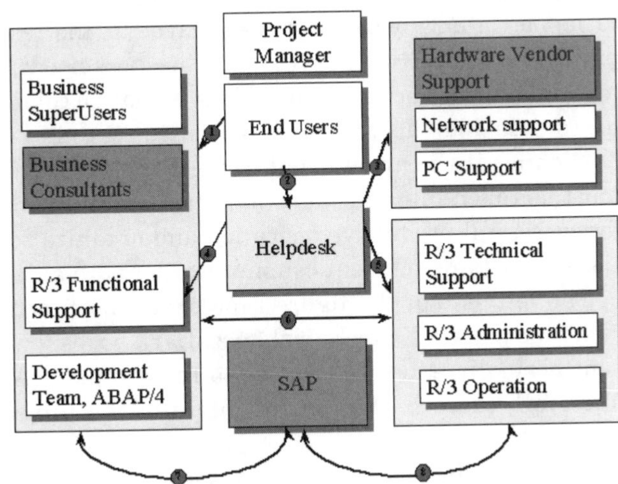

Figure 16-1 An approach to roles and organization for implementing and supporting R/3 systems.

The number of people and the actual management organization to which they belong will heavily depend on the size and budget of the company and the size and importance of SAP R/3. Of course, several of the roles that are presented in the following discussion can fall upon a single person.

Many companies decide to have their helpdesk or even their entire IT department outsourced to external and competent organizations.

Figure 16-1 shows the roles as they have developed in different SAP R/3 projects. This is just one approach, and many other organizations and structures are possible. Depending on the complexity and size of the project, some of the roles could further be divided into more atomic ones, although most typically several roles are assumed by single persons or organizations.

An additional note to consider is that part of the existing IT staff in a company, with some additional R/3 training, could well share some of their current IT tasks with new staff members. For instance, there is no need to have a network administrator just for SAP. Network managers only have to add additional systems to monitor and watch for a correct network layout and configuration.

The number of roles, and of types of activities to be performed on SAP projects, is extremely large, as described in ASAP, ranging from project manager to power user, from layout developer to helpdesk provider. These are all described in the ASAP paper on organization and roles, which not only defines the functions of the roles but also the time commitment expected, depending on the project complexity.

The first and most important entity that every person or role in the organization must consider is the *business* itself and the mission. SAP R/3 might be implemented because corporate management made a strategic decision to support a new business model, maybe as the result of a reengineering process for supporting the changing business needs to compete in a global market. What is for sure and obvious is that no company should invest in a new system like this without expecting to get some benefit from it.

Looking at the arrows that connect the different roles in the figure, it must be taken into consideration that one of the most important aspects for successful productive operation and organization among all the entities is a fast and efficient communication path among them.

The left side of the figure represents the functional roles, while the right one shows the technical ones. Dark boxes with white letters represent normally external entities to the company. And in the center and above all, there is the central figure of the project manager (or managers).

The following is an overview of the roles as pictured.

End Users. Users of the business applications that do the work of feeding the system information and obtaining results to help in the decision-making process. End users usually have a partial but very important vision of the business, and sometimes they are the ones who know the very specific details of some business processes. For this reason, the end users also feed information to the business superusers (arrow 1).

End users will probably be the largest group in terms of people, and they will be the main requesters of functional and technical support. Normally, in a good organization, end users should not directly call the application experts but instead call a form of helpdesk that can be a first line of support which redirects the call to the appropriate person or organization (arrow 2).

Business Superusers. The group of expert users with a comprehensive knowledge of the business. This group is usually the driver of the whole SAP R/3 project and should be made up of people who can make fast decisions. Normally, they belong to the *steering committee* for the project and assign a project manager or project leader for each of the business areas on which the implementation is based. For example, one leader may be appointed to the FI treasury module, another one to the materials management, another to sales, and so on.

Business Consultants. In medium-size to large companies, management often requests an impartial view of the business and help in the implementation techniques, the know-how of the R/3 application software, and the ability for knowledge transfer. Because of the business nature of these projects, it is quite common to find *external business consultants* in most SAP projects. These consultants may also have the responsibilities of project managers or project management assistants. As stated in Chap. 1, SAP has a large number of consulting partners, including the biggest consulting firms plus hundreds of smaller local consulting companies.

SAP Functional Support. Some of the participants in the group of business superusers make up the next group in the figure, *SAP functional support*. The function of this group is to help in the customizing of the system as well as solving user problems that directly relate to business processes and applications (arrow 4). It is also the function of this group to lead the corrections, enhancements, or new developments in the system according to user requests. Usually, this group is in charge of training the end users in their specific modules as well as receiving support calls that might relate more to functional system aspects than technical problems. This team is called in when a user gets an error after posting a financial document, or when a user needs a higher customized report of the inventory, and so on.

The R/3 functional support might rely on an internal or external development team as well as the overall support of the technical group (arrow 6).

The Development Team. This team is only necessary when new developments are needed. When only the development of simple reports is needed, the technical support group could assume some of the development functions. However, in preproductive stages of the R/3 implementation, some help might be needed for tasks such as massive data loads from legacy applications and development of batch input programs, business-customized menus, screens, and so on. Developers need to stay in very close contact with the functional group, since this group is supposed to know the business and user requirements. At the same time, a developer will often need the help of the technical group for things such as system requirements, database resources, and transport requests (arrow 6).

The SAP Technical Support Group. This team is in charge of all the technical aspects of the R/3 installations. This group gives continuous support to the development and functional teams participating actively in the technical parts of R/3 projects. It is usually also the second-level line for solving users' technical problems (arrow 5). This group can be subdivided into R/3 technical specialists, R/3 system administrators, and operation personnel. In small R/3 installations, all functions can be assumed by a single person as long as the procedures to maintain the system are well documented and mostly automated.

The technical group must have a wide range of skills, including client/server computing, operating systems, database and R/3 expertise, and good knowledge about PC technology and even networking. These technologies can be totally or partially supported by existing technical groups as shown in the upper right of the figure, such as the network support or PC support groups, besides having maintenance contracts and support with the corresponding hardware vendors.

Some of the functions of this group could be handed over to existing IT resources. For example, if there are operating system managers, they could well assume the management of new servers once the architecture of R/3 is introduced to them.

Just as a brief summary, here is a list of functions that are normally assumed by the R/3 technical and administration group:

- *Administration of the operating system, database, and sometimes even the network.* This includes such things as doing all typical functions of DBAs, such as reorganizing the database, monitoring storage, backups, and the like.
- *Administration and monitoring of R/3.* Includes management of background jobs, users, the authorization system, the printing system, interfaces, the correction and transport system, remote communications, profile and instance maintenance, tuning, and so forth.
- *Defining and implementing the system backup and recovery strategy.*
- *Solving and reporting technical problems as they are being logged in the system.*
- *Support for new modules going into production by allowing sufficient space, checking technical settings of tables, doing previous exports/imports, and so on.*
- *Support for all kind of maintenance upgrades, including the installation and configuration of corrections to the system such as support packages, kernel patches, and so on.*
- *Support and implementation of new technical or crossfunctional projects in the R/3 environments such as the implementation of the workflow, EDI server, archive link, Internet server, and mail.*
- *Implementing the Early Watch suggested recommendations and corrections into the system.*
- *Always observing the highest system availability.*

The R/3 Operation Staff. These people can be responsible for checking system critical log files such as backup logs and the system log and reporting the observed problems. This staff can also be responsible for the system and database backups as well as doing daily backups of the archived redo log files. Even when this process is automated without manual intervention, someone has to check the log and change the tapes sometimes. This staff can also periodically check some of the system monitors and the states of spool and background systems.

In any case, the administration and operation group should design a comprehensive guide such as an administration and operation manual that can be easily followed by anyone who could eventually substitute for or help this group.

The Helpdesk. This is the central support group in charge of receiving user calls and doing first-line support (arrow 2). This group must be actively in touch with the rest of the support groups (arrows 3, 4, and 5), so, for example, if network lines are not available for whatever reason, or the SAP system has been shut down for maintenance reasons, the helpdesk can quickly assess the situation and react to and answer user queries. This group might use one of the many available helpdesk software applications, including features such as automatic call transfer, problem logs, and incidence recorders.

The Role of SAP Itself in the Big Picture. The demand for getting SAP services such as the installation and implementation of the R/3 systems should be understood as the project goes along. SAP offers an extensive range of services, especially with SAPnet and Early Watch, and should actively assist in overall support, both functional (arrow 7) and technical (arrow 8). You might consider SAP for the following activities (and maybe some others):

- On-site and remote consulting (both functional and technical)
- Main source for project team training
- Help in stress testing definitions
- Collaboration in a quality check before going productive

Finally there is the central figure of the *project manager,* who has overall responsibility for the success of the implementation project after going live, supporting the project, optimization, and continuous change management. The project management itself constitutes a very important implementation issue.

The next sections introduce some of the main activities and issues concerning the technical implementation of the R/3 system.

Introduction to R/3 Technical Implementation

As it was introduced earlier, the R/3 technical implementation comprises the activities needed for supporting the overall customizing as well as ensuring that all the software and hardware components of the R/3 systems work properly, from the very beginning of the project to, most importantly, the productive stages.

Actually, most of this book is devoted to the activities involved in the SAP R/3 technical areas, often known as the basis system. Most of the tasks involved in the technical implementation can be found in both ASAP and the procedure model. This book's approach to these technical activities is not supposed to replace but to complement and explain the concepts, with the purpose of making those activities easier to implement and easier to understand.

Figure 16-2 presents a diagram with some numbered circles showing the main activity areas involved in the technical implementation. The diagram is a generic approach or template to a more detailed technical project plan, which should be adjusted depending on the project scope.

In this diagram, only three milestones have been established:

- *Start.* This is the starting point for the R/3 technical implementation. Usually, this technical starting point comes soon after implementation start, during initial project preparation. Other previous activities in the overall R/3 project can include prepared documentation such as the project plan, the definition of organization, roles and responsibilities, and possibly some basic training. A word of caution is that the project plan often does not take into consideration all aspects of technical activities, and usually underestimates the resources needed to perform them.

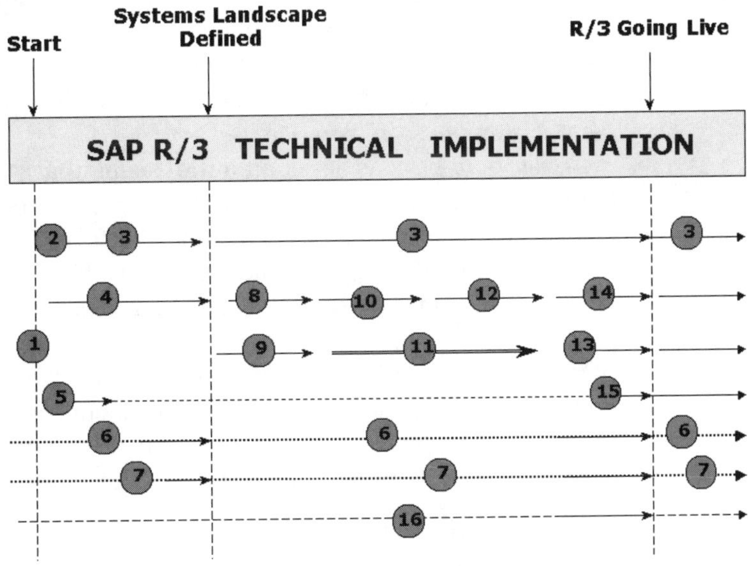

Figure 16-2 Technical implementation diagram.

- *Systems landscape (productive environment) defined.* At this point, the systems infrastructure might have been correctly sized according to the business needs. A suitable systems landscape (development, integration, production) should be defined. The systems architecture design should contemplate additional technological requirements such as the network, security, contingency, and information integrity strategy. This milestone marks the beginning of most critical projects, so that technical issues may be resolved before productive operation is started.
- *R/3 going live.* At this point, final users start real work, which means entering real data, searching for real and meaningful information, and so on. Going live (productive start) marks the distance in terms of transactional data between the development or test systems and the productive one. Availability becomes a critical factor that can severely affect the business.

The technical activity areas pictured in the aforementioned figure are briefly introduced. Timing each phase is a matter of specific project needs, although some ongoing tasks, such as systems administration, last as long as the application itself. Detailed explanations can be found in different chapters and sections of this book.

Activity areas are as follows.

1 **Infrastructure and Requirements Planning.** This is the first project task involving technical issues. It is the planning phase where the initial infrastructure requirements—servers, workstations, networks, and so on—are specified. This is achieved by performing an initial system and network sizing. At this stage it is advisable to procure the development system as soon as possible.

This should be considered an initial sizing that will probably change as the first phases of the implementation start and more information is gathered about infrastructure requirements. Although it is advisable to perform this sizing of production systems, it is quite difficult to actually size the systems properly at this stage. The sizing issue is covered in a following section.

2 **Development System Installation and Configuration.** Despite previous training and initial project documentation, this will probably be the first activity in the technical implementation. Some of the tasks in the development system installation and configuration are

- Installing the hardware, software, and network components
- SAP R/3 software installation

- SAP front-end installation (SAPGUI) for the functional and technical group
- Setting up the SAP online documentation
- Protecting SAP superusers
- Defining development users and initial authorizations
- Defining and setting up some printers
- Defining and implementing the backup strategy for the development system
- Setting up the delivery system and client copy procedures
- Scheduling cleaning background jobs

The outcome of these tasks must be a development system ready for starting hands-on R/3 customizing.

3 **SAP R/3 System Administration and Operation.** From the moment the development system is installed and configured, there is a need to maintain and administer the system. These tasks will be needed as long as the R/3 software keeps running the business applications. Among the tasks of the R/3 system administration, full support to functional consultants should not be forgotten.

The mission, roles, and responsibilities of system managers and operators as well as the description of their tasks can be documented in the *Procedures Guide.* More explicit information such as the physical and logical description of the systems, as well as the detailed instructions for operating the system, can be written down in a SAP R/3 administration and operation manual.

The following sections in this chapter introduce some useful hints for developing these guides.

4 **Productive System Landscape Definition.** Another activity area that is very important because it will set a milestone, is to define the productive system landscape and architecture. Support from the project management and functional team will be required. Tasks in this area involve the following:

- Defining the number and type of R/3 systems: production, development, integration, training, and so on. It is important to remember that the systems landscape also includes the definition of a structured client concept and client copy strategy.
- Calculating the initial database size and the storage growth expectations

- Defining system backup strategies
- Defining high availability requirements, such as switch-over or cluster systems, and contingency plans
- Sizing the networking needs: calculating expected throughput and bandwidth for LAN, WAN, remote connections, and so on
- Defining the helpdesk strategy for technical issues

The result of these activities might take the form of an RFP (request for proposals) to be sent to hardware vendors, as well as provide the basis of the technical project plan to be implemented before going into productive operation.

5 **Configuring and Managing the Remote Connection with SAP.** Right after the development system has been installed, it is very convenient to establish the remote connection to SAP support servers, especially for getting access to the SAPnet services, which are an invaluable tool for the whole project implementation, both functional and technical. Tasks involved in this activity are

- Getting and configuring a remote connection
- Registering the connection with SAP
- Establishing security policies
- Configuring SAProuter
- Registering the SAPnet ID user accounts

6 **Project Technical Documentation.** This is also an ongoing activity for the life of the project. As you can see in the preceding diagram, there is probably some documentation before the actual technical implementation start point. Throughout the project, at least the following technical documents must be worked out:

- *The procedures guide,* describing the overall project organization, mission, people, roles, and responsibilities. Might also include specifications shared by both functional and technical people, such as development methodology for the project or the rules for the transport system. Particularly important is to cover aspects such as contingency planning (i.e., what to do when systems are unavailable), although this might be a separate manual or document. With this one as well as with other manuals it's also important to define the change management: how to handle changes in the systems, in the documents, in the organization, and so on.

- *The administration and operation manual,* containing detailed descriptions about the systems architecture and detailed instructions about full system operations including operating system management, database administration, R/3 management and monitoring, fail-over operation, backup procedures, and so on. The cornerstone to this manual is to include step-by-step instructions on how to perform all tasks needed in the operation of SAP R/3 systems.
- *The technical validation test specifications* is a document that can be prepared for testing the technical requirements and specifications before the system becomes productive. Tests can include simulating disk or power failures, network lines breakdown, deletion of important files, database and recovery, archiving, security issues, and so on.
- *The user guide.* The development of this guide is not actually the role of the technical team, since it should be more functionally oriented, depicting users working in the system business applications. The technical support group might collaborate in those initial sections in the guide describing how to move around the system, how to manage passwords, and the like. Introductory topics are described in Chap. 5.

There might be additional documentation for project plans, preparations for going live, migration, and so forth. These will be very specifically designed for particular installations.

7 **Technical Training.** Training should be an integral part of the SAP R/3 projects. SAP training has been normally imparted by SAP itself, although there might be other companies, such as SAP partners, in the SAP learning services business.

Alongside the project life, your company might contract some technical consultants for doing jobs or tasks for which your own personnel is not yet prepared. Be sure not only to receive training courses but to actively "train yourself on the job" by participating in or understanding what other consultants do.

SAP R/3 training areas to be received by technical support personnel should include

- R/3 architecture and administration
- CCMS
- Authorization system

- Development of workbench tools and, if needed, ABAP and interfaces
- Software logistics (transport system)
- Specific database system administration
- Management of the R/3 data dictionary
- Optionally, when the projects require it, add-on cross-application modules such as workflow, EDI, and ArchiveLink

It is possible that technical staff should not only receive courses but also prepare specific training materials for others: think for example of an introduction to R/3 for helpdesk personnel, a technical overview, and the company-specific rules for the workbench organizer and transport system for the development team, use of the business workflow, and so on.

The timing for receiving or teaching those courses should be included in the project plans, and, in any case, extensive training must be received by the R/3 technical group before the system can become operative.

8 **Productive Systems Installation and Configuration.** This stage marks the beginning of a new phase after the productive systems architecture has been defined and is available. Tasks under this activity area include the following:

- Installation and configuration of hardware, base software, and network components, including RAID systems and backup devices.
- Optionally, for high-availability systems, installation of switch-over hardware and software. The configuration must be done during or after installation of R/3.
- Installation of database and R/3 central instance.
- If the database data is coming from an export file such as the development system, performing a *customer import* into the new system.
- Defining and mounting NFS shared file systems, if any.
- Installation of additional R/3 instances in application servers.
- Initial distribution and configuration of the SAP services, including the definition of operation modes (CCMS). Further tuning and optimizing of the system load is an ongoing task that should be assumed by system administration and operation, after the system starts in productive operation.
- Configuration of the SAProuter for accessing the SAP remote support servers.

- Scheduling periodic cleaning and administration background jobs.
- Together with the functional group and based on the procedures guide, defining the rules for user master records creation, along with the authorization and profiles concept.

Some of the most technical configuration tasks for the productive systems continue in installation, development, configuration, and test of technical infrastructure.

9 **Test System Installation and Configuration.** This is an optional activity area, only needed for those customers who have defined a system landscape including a test system, known also as integration or quality assurance system.

Tasks basically consist of the following:

- Installation and configuration of hardware, base software, and network components
- Installation of SAP R/3
- Defining and implementing a backup strategy for this system

Further tasks will depend on the actual use you want to assign to this system. Just as a reminder, an integration system can be used for

- Testing new developments before going productive
- Testing data load and interface procedures
- Testing the operating system, software, and R/3 migrations
- Functioning as a standby server in emergency situations (as long as the right procedures are defined)

10 **Transport System Configuration and Management.** Once all the systems are installed and initially configured, it is time to configure the transport system. The configuration of the transport system should be the same for a group of related SAP systems belonging to a common system landscape—for example, development, test, and production systems. Since the introduction of the Transport Management System (TMS), the configuration is synchronized automatically among the systems.

Some of the necessary tasks are:

- Sharing the common *transport* directory /usr/sap/trans, either with NFS in UNIX systems or by setting a global transport host using shares on Windows NT

- Running transaction SE06 in every system (as part of the post-installation steps)
- Setting the system change option according to system roles
- Configuring transport routes and transport layers
- If necessary, configuring the TPPARAM file

Management of the transport system will include such things as defining when and how the imports are performed, as well as log checking. For more information on these topics, refer to Chap. 6.

11 **Installation, Development, Configuration, and Test of Technical Infrastructure.** Based on technical requirements, there might be a lot of work in this activity area to get the system's infrastructure working properly. Although some might be optional, the tasks being implemented at this stage should cover the setup, configuration, and test of the following technical elements:

- Backup and recovery strategy, including hardware and software, integration with the R/3 CCMS, parameter settings, and tape labeling and storage.
- Configuration and tests of high-availability software. If possible, test contingency situations: what to do if . . . , how to redistribute SAP services, and so on.
- Optionally, develop and implement an *operator's menu:* a central place where operators can easily perform the tasks that have been assigned to them. An operators menu can be developed using shell scripts and might include such functions as starting and stopping the SAP systems, scheduling backups, displaying and cleaning log files, disk and file system monitoring, and spooling control.
- Set up and test the communication with external systems, including the remote communication with SAP support servers.
- Together with the developers and functional group, prepare the systems for testing massive data loads and run periodic interface tests with the batch input procedures or other tools.
- Test system monitoring with the CCMS, as well as general R/3 administration and operation, including user administration and authorizations, background jobs management, and extensive database administration procedures.
- Set in place the technical support strategy with the helpdesk.

Some of these tests might be performed using the test system, while others such as the switch-over software might require the full infrastructure of the productive environment. In any case, at this stage many backups and recoveries will be needed, so be sure that your procedures work properly in every condition.

12 **Printing Strategy and Front-end Services Installation and Configuration.** Even in paper-free computing environments, for SAP R/3 installations, printing should not be taken as an obvious task. Careful planning and considerations are needed for avoiding long printing wait times as well as collapsing network lines. An incorrectly defined printing strategy might lead to degradation of overall system performance.

Printing strategy as introduced in Chap. 14 is defined based on many different factors that should be as clear and specific as possible, at least for the start of production. They can later be adjusted as needed.

The same thing happens with the installation and distribution of the SAP front-end software and services.

So, before R/3 productive operation, these tasks should also be addressed:

- Carefully plan the printing strategy, considering number of printers, expected volume, locations, critical printing, remote printing, and so on.
- Physically install the printers. Define and test them at the level of the operating system.
- Configure and test the printers within the spool administration facilities of the SAP system.
- Test and avoid situations where printers attached to application servers can lead to inability for user printing.
- If needed, configure and test SAP logon groups.
- Decide on the front-end installation and distribution strategy. Install the SAPGUI software and the SAPlogon in all user workstations. Consider migration strategies when you need to update the front-end software.
- Install the online documentation CD for user accesses and define the strategy for possible updates.

13 **Data Load.** This activity area is part of the "preparing for going live" plan. It should be performed with great coordination between the functional and technical teams. Some of the tasks that need to be addressed are as follows:

- Transfer objects and data from the development system
- Load master data from legacy or external applications
- Implement and test the periodic interfaces with external applications
- Enter manually needed data and information
- Check consistency of entered data

14 **Final Tests Before Going Live.** Just as the previous activity area, this requires full teamwork for checking and testing the overall system functionality. These tests should be supported by the validation test specifications documents, both technical and functional.

Up to now many tests have been performed, for example in activity areas 11, 13, and so on. Now it's time to put it all together. At this stage stress testing should be defined and performed, simulating user loads, peak times, printing, interfaces, and general user handling of the application.

It is also the time to check the quality of the project, including the processes and functions, the user and administration documentation, and so on.

As part of the preproductive test, make sure users understand and follow the contingency procedures: what to do in case of system unavailability, whom to call, and so on.

15 **Preproductive Maintenance Service.** As was introduced in the first chapter, EarlyWatch is the SAP preventive maintenance service. Before going into productive operation and as a way to validate the productive system parameters and configuration, make sure to contact SAP to perform this first Early Watch service. This service requires that the remote connection be set up and established.

Normally, this initial service is free of charge; you should, however, contact SAP for current details.

After the SAP specialist performs the system analysis and sends you the EarlyWatch report, be sure to implement and test the suggested changes and solve any problems you find before starting productive operations.

Once the system becomes productive, you may or may not decide to keep on with this service.

There is another SAP special service for this stage, known as the *going live check*. This is a SAP consulting service that verifies that the main requirements and preparations have been carried out, verifies systems resources and main productive and support strategy, and gives advice on open points or weak points found during the check.

16 **Optional Technical Projects.** Optionally, there are several technical areas that might or might not be implemented in initial R/3 projects. Some of this project might go along with the initial productive preparations or might be part of additional projects. Most of these additional projects fall normally into the cross application module areas, where both the design and implementation should be shared by the functional and technical teams.

The following list reflects some of these optional projects:

- Implementation of an archiving strategy with or without optical archiving solutions (ArchiveLink). Besides SAP standard software, this type of project requires third-party software and hardware.
- Implementation of business workflow processes.
- CAD integration.
- EDI integration.
- Application Link Enabled configurations.
- Electronic commerce and Internet transaction server (ITS) setup and installation.
- Configuration of supported external devices, such as timing equipment, plant control devices, and so on.

Many of the tasks and activities included in this R/3 technical implementation diagram are explained in different sections and topics throughout this book. The more organizational aspects and documentation tasks are the subjects of the following sections in this chapter.

Introduction to a SAP R/3 Procedures Guide

The goal of a procedures guide, also known as *operating procedures,* is to define the rules of the game when working and operating the SAP system. It should include clear norms, answering questions such as what, when, why, and who. This manual should identify roles and responsibilities in the implementation and operation of the systems. It should not be confused with an administration and operation manual, which goes into more specific details about the system architecture operation and administration, providing clear "how to" steps to daily operation.

The rules in the procedures guide might range from a clear definition of the R/3 implementation goal to who is allowed to enter the computer room (data processing center).

The following list provides an approach to the contents that can be included in a procedures guide:

- Introduction to the procedures guide
  - Goal of the implementation and operation of the system
  - Project scope
  - Team roles and organization
  - Systems and application architecture description
    - System landscape definition
    - Business applications definition
- User management procedures
  - Authorization and profile security measures
  - Management of users leaving the company
- Functional implementation procedures
  - Enhancements and change requests management
  - Developing methodology
  - Guide for implementing new modules
  - Functional test procedures
- Technical implementation procedures
  - System administration and operation rules
  - Backup strategy
  - Front-end installation and distribution strategy
  - Printing strategy
  - Networking procedures
  - Systems fail-over procedures
  - Daily operation tasks
  - Rules for implementation of new technical projects
  - Technical test procedures
- Cross-functional application procedures
  - Workbench and transport system rules
  - Use of SAPoffice and business workflow
- Migration strategy
  - Hardware upgrade procedures
  - Software upgrade procedures
  - SAP R/3 application upgrade
- User support management and organization
  - Support guidelines
  - Helpdesk organization

Keeping records of problems and incidences
Escalation of problems

- Personnel issues
  Training procedures
  People backup and holidays permissions
- Contingency procedures
  System crash procedures
  Emergency situations guidelines
  Disaster recovery procedures
- Security issues
  Remote connection procedures
  Access to SAPnet
  Access to the computer room
- Procedure for making changes to this guide

You can extend or compress the contents of this list as the scope of your installation requires. You can, for example, add some of the guidelines included in the SAP procedure model (although this is intended mostly for the implementation before starting productive operation), or you can also include the meetings and approval procedures.

Now, to answer the question, who is in charge of preparing such a document? it should be a collective work of the project team with the consent and approval of the company managers. Also, many of the consulting and partner companies may offer the service of preparing this kind of document.

The following sections cover some of the topics in the guide as well as other important documents, especially in the technical arena, that should be prepared in SAP R/3 installations.

The Administration and Operation Manual

The goal of this manual is to provide systems information easily and quickly to technical support personnel and step-by-step instructions on how to perform the most usual administration and operation tasks. This way, not only can this guide help to have the system functioning properly, but it can also be very useful for a backup person in case someone from the technical team must be absent from work for any reason.

This manual must comply with the rules and procedures established in the procedures guide. To what extent there should be only one manual or a set of two (administration and operation) is a matter of the specific company organization.

The administration and operation manual will include two types of information: detailed descriptions of the systems and step-by-step instructions. You can either decide to put them all together or enter an instruction code within the descriptions, leaving the instructions ordered by code at the end of the manual.

If you intend to describe *all* the administration and operation tasks, the manual can become very large, so a little effort must be made to include only those descriptions and instructions that are most important for the system, while others can be referenced, either in other manuals or in the official documentation. Diagrams and pictures can be very useful for this type of guide.

Just as in the procedures guide, the following is an approach to the possible contents that should be included in this manual:

- Systems information
  - Hardware and software inventory
  - Physical layout of disks and file systems configuration for every system
  - Support hotline numbers
  - Hardware maintenance
  - Software maintenance
  - Instructions for computer and operating system startup and shutdown
  - Instructions for handling disks: adding, removing, and so forth
- Error situations
  - Logging and escalating problems
  - Instructions for notifying users with system messages
- SAP R/3 startup and shutdown
  - Normal procedures
  - Error situations
- Backup procedures
  - Tape management: labeling, schedules, types
  - Starting backups
  - Checking backups
  - Recovery procedures
  - Archiving backup procedures
  - Backup error conditions
  - Backup problems and incidence log
- System monitoring
  - Alerts definition
  - Systems

Network
Processes
System logs
Backups
Batch input
System performance quality (buffers, workload, etc.)
Storage and free space

- SAP R/3 general maintenance and administration tasks
  Cleaning procedures
  Background processing management
  Handling priority jobs
  Changing system parameters; profile maintenance
  Printers and spool management
  Archiving management
  Definition of operation modes
  Authorization management
  General accounting control
- SAP R/3 database maintenance
  Checking database state
  Adding space to tablespaces
  Reorganization procedures
  Export/import instructions
- Administration of the transport system
  Performing imports
  Checking imports
- SAPGUI and SAPlogon
  Installation instructions
  Upgrade and distribution policies and instructions
- Users management
  Users at operating system level
  User master records: add, change, delete
  Changing passwords
  Locking user access to the system
  Unlocking users
- Security management
  Security at the presentation: virus protection and access restrictions
  Security at the server level
  User password control
- Accessing SAPnet
  SAProuter configurations

Registering new users
Enabling remote access to the systems

- Guide changes management
  Guide availability
  Quality controls
- Appendix A: Instruction index
- Appendix B: Instructions

Systems Management

The issue of managing the system while providing technical support is important before and after going live. It is import beforehand because systems management must be performed from the moment the development or integration system is installed and while customization is being performed.

Systems management is the continuous process of monitoring, administering, supporting, optimizing, and securing the systems, with the objective of having a stable platform for the smooth execution of business processes.

The best systems management is proactive (anticipating tasks and problems) rather than reactive (dealing with tasks and problems only when they occur). A proactive approach to system management can be achieved by having operating procedures and a daily and periodic checklist in which the main systems indicators are checked and issues resolved.

Topics related to systems management include:

- *What are the roles involved in R/3 systems management?*

  Ideally, system managers of SAP systems should play several roles as defined in the operations manual. But this will be highly dependent on the size, complexity, and scope of SAP systems. Very complex installations require a clear definition of administration roles, such as R/3 system manager, database administrator, network administrator, R/3 operator, transport system administrator, security manager, authorizations administrator, desktop infrastructure administrator, R/3 technical consultant, supervisor, and so on.

  As a starting point for defining the administration procedures, roles, and responsibilities, you can use the guidelines provided in the previous section or the operations manual template included within ASAP.

- *How and when is training done, and what skill sets are necessary?*
  Technical training is a very time-consuming activity in SAP implementations due to the fact that there are large numbers of different and complex tasks to be performed—most of them continuously. The complexity of the training is closely related to the many components and layers of the technical infrastructure: operating system, database, R/3 basis components, data dictionary, network, client-server computing, security, authorizations, and perhaps development.
  SAP has an extensive education offering on technical training in the form of several knowledge products and self-training material. The availability of resources such as a test system helps a great deal in the technical learning process. Often SAP partners have R/3 technical consulting services that can help in the initial phases of systems management while transferring their knowledge and experience to customers.
- *How many people are required for administering SAP systems?*
  In implementation projects there is always the question of how many resources are required. For instance, if an implementation project lasts for one year, how many basis consultants are needed, and are they needed all the time or just during some phases? The answer is never accurate. The following estimation is based on experience and customer answers.
  Small and simple R/3 installations for up to 50 users and 2-system landscapes might be adequately administered with two system managers doing most of the tasks and external resources for occasional help.
  More complex installations, and those customers in a continuous process of adding new technical components, will require a much larger staff. Experience has shown that installations that implement at least 4 application modules with more than 200 users or more than 100 printers, that connect R/3 with EDI, faxes, and external devices, and that are distributed over several geographical locations require a minimum of 4 people with the appropriate skill sets for systems management and support.
- *Who will support systems managers?*
  Systems managers can get support and take their problems or questions to SAP using SAPnet or SAP customer support. Often, the support of the hardware or software partner will be required when there are problems with the servers or operating system components. Additionally, the best support for system managers is updated and accurate documentation of their tasks, roles, and responsibilities. An

approach from SAP not only for advancing training but also for managing and searching documentation is the Knowledge Warehouse (infoDB).

Skills Sets for Systems Managers

Project managers and other responsible persons in the organization, such the IT manager, often ask what skill sets are necessary for the job positions of systems management within the project team.

Following is an overview of the technical areas that need to be supported by systems managers or technical consultants:

- *R/3 Administration:*
  - — Installations
  - — User administration
  - — Security and profile administration
  - — Configuration and management with CCMS: monitoring, operation modes
  - — Client copies
  - — Transport system administration
  - — Management of batch
  - — Front end installation and distribution strategy
  - — Administration of spool system and printing
  - — Configuration of R/3 for remote connection with SAP
  - — Definition of R/3-related alerts within the CCMS monitors
  - — Correction of bugs by applying SAPnet notes
  - — Application of patches (support packages, legal change packages, kernel patches)
  - — Workload analysis and performance tuning
  - — Support of the functional team with data loads and interfaces
  - — Assistance in the technical areas of cross-applications such as ALE, archiving, or work flow
  - — Assistance in the connection of external software or devices, such as fax, EDI, mail, GIS, CAD, and so on
  - — Assistance in upgrading projects
- *Database Administration:*
  - — Design and maintenance of the database backup and recovery strategy
  - — Assistance in tuning the database
  - — Reorganization of the database

  - Management of database space allocation
  - Rebuilding of missing indexes or creation of new ones
  - Definition of database alerts
  - Definition of database administration and operation procedures
  - Planning for and design of database preventive maintenance
  - Securing of access to the database
  - Assistance for developers in tuning customer programs or reports
  - Performance of recovery tests
  - Design and documentation of database administration procedures

- *Systems Administration:*
  - Installation and maintenance of the operating system
  - Setup and configuration of disk volumes and file systems
  - Assistance in operating-system-related tuning
  - Installation of operating system patches or corrections
  - Monitoring of usage and tuning of performance
  - Backup and recovery
  - Installation and configuration of additional software
  - Automation of periodic system tasks
  - Support for hardware maintenance or upgrades
  - Configuration of network protocols
  - Maintenance of shared file systems
  - Control of system security

- *Network Administration:*
  - Design and configuration of the R/3 server network and the R/3 access network
  - Configuration and maintenance of the remote connection to SAP
  - Management of network security
  - Maintenance of the saprouter
  - Assistance in the configuration of remote connections with R/3
  - Provision of access for remote users
  - Support for the setup and connection of external services like Web browsers or the Internet Transaction Server (ITS)
  - Configuration and maintenance of routers and other network devices

R/3 includes many tools and utilities for managing and monitoring the R/3 systems. Most chapters in this book are intended for helping system administrators.

Having an administration and operations manual, and a process for incidence logging, can decrease the time needed for solving problems if similar situations have occurred previously and the resolution procedure is known.

The easiest escalation procedure for system managers is to search SAP-net or request SAP's support.

Planning Systems Management

The process of managing the R/3 system can be eased by careful planning during the implementation phase. Some of the activities to be performed during previous phases are:

- Training the technical team
- Planning the technical infrastructure and scalability
- Designing, writing, and maintaining technical documentation
- Testing systems infrastructure and systems management procedures
- Carrying out advanced training for the technical team
- Getting acquainted with the SAP support lines and services
- Designing a clear helpdesk and support strategy and communicating efficiently
- Focusing on proactive systems management

Operation Checklist

One of the best ways of performing proactive systems management is to do a daily and periodic monitoring of the status of the main systems components. This is the operation daily checklist, usually carried out by R/3 operations. The following tables include some of the R/3 indicators that must be periodically checked.

While most checks are performed using R/3 standard transactions, some must be performed at the operating system level using operating system applications and tools.

Checks at the host operating system level and network level include:

R/3 Transaction	Description	Purpose of Check
—	Status of servers	Check that all R/3 servers are up and running.
RZ02	System monitor	From within R/3, check that all systems are running on their scheduled operating mode. Display the alert view and analyze problems.
—	Disk space	Check that no file system is full.
—	Backup status	Check result of backup when launched with OS applications or other external software.
SM51	SAP servers	Display all available application servers.
SM50	Process overview	Display the status of processes (continuous daily monitoring task).
OS06	OS monitor	Display the status of main OS indicators and determine whether figures indicate problems.
AL16	OS alert monitor	Display OS alerts for correcting and documenting problems.
OS03	Parameter changes in OS	Check whether some changes have been done at the system kernel.
—	LAN/WAN	Check the LAN/WAN connections.
SMGW	Gateway monitor	Check gateway connection status.
ST08/ST09	Network alert monitor	Display, analyze, and document any detected network problems.

Checking the R/3 environment:

R/3 Transaction	Description	Purpose of Check
SM21	System log	Display and analyze warning and error messages generated in the last few hours. Errors that generate short dumps should be quickly corrected and documented.
ST22	ABAP dump analysis	All ABAP dumps should be displayed and analyzed.
SM04/AL08	User overview	Display users and their activities. Check unauthorized access and logon balancing. Determine whether there are any phantom users (users who have lost their connections).
SM37	Background jobs	Check that all expected background jobs run successfully and that periodic jobs are scheduled and released for next run. Check jobs log. Communicate cancelled jobs to users.
AL01	SAP alert monitor	Check SAP systems alert. Communicate red alerts to system managers.

R/3 Transaction	Description	Purpose of Check
RZ01	Graphical job monitor	Check the runtime statistics for background jobs. This is a procedure for optimizing the performance of a batch and for fine-tuning the scheduling of jobs and distribution of background work processes.
SM13	Update records	Check whether update process is running and active. Aborted update transactions should be analyzed and corrected.
SM12	Lock entries	Check lock entries. Those entries that remain in the lock table for a long time should be analyzed and corrected.
SP01	Spool request overview	Check problems with spool and output requests. Check logs and possible causes of printing problems. Check printer connections and host spoolers. Check possible problems on PC or front end printing.
SP12	TemSe administration	Check consistency of temporary sequential database and launch a reorganization if not scheduled in a background job.
SE01/SE09/SE10	Transport system logs	Check all transports logs from previous period, analyze warnings and error messages, and communicate them to the person who requested the transport.
STMS	TP transport log/transport system at the OS level	Check warning and error messages from the SLOG file corresponding to the TP transport control program.
ST03	Workload analysis	Display and check the main performance and statistical values of the system. The average response time by process type gives a good idea of possible performance or system problems.
ST02	Buffer tune analysis	Display and check the quality of R/3 buffers and analyze red spots (free space problems, swaps, and so on).
SM35	Batch input logs	Display and check the periodic batch input logs and communicate errors to the application responsible for correction.
AL11	Display SAP directories	Display the work directory and search for log and error files from the SAP instance. Report any warning or error.

Checking the database is one of the most critical activities for ensuring the consistency and stable operation of the R/3 systems. It can be done using SAP tools (*sapdba*) for the ORACLE and INFORMIX database, using standard R/3 transactions or specific database management system utilities.

R/3 Transaction	Description	Purpose of Check
—	Check free space	Check and verify the free space on database data devices (tablespaces, dbspaces, etc.) and check space left on log directory.
—	Check DB logs	Check the database alert log.
DB12	SAPDBA logs	Verify the log of the last backup and free space in the log directory. Verify the log of the last backup of archive files when neccesary.
DB02	Storage management	Display the status and growth of the database. Monitor the percentage of free space. Monitor the database fragmentation and the optimizer statistics when necessary.
—	Missing indexes	Monitor whether there are missing indexes in the data dictionary of the database.
—	Critical space objects	Check for the existence of any critical object that could cause database problems when growing.
ST04	Database logs	Display the database error log.
—	DB consistency check	Perform a database consistency check.
AL02	Database alert monitor	Display, acknowledge, and analyze all the database alerts.

These checks and others that your installation might need can be recorded in some form of daily check log that can then be analyzed or kept for statistical reasons.

These logs and checks are not only useful for reacting quickly to system problems, but they also can help in identifying system performance degradation. In any case, a SAP-comprehensive set of statistics within the performance menu also provides more extensive statistical information.

Organizing the Workbench Organizer and Managing Transport Requests

Either as an independent section within the procedures guide or as an appendix for the developing methodology used in R/3 environments, it is important to define the rules that must apply for the transport system.

Chapter 6 is devoted to explaining the workbench organizer and transport system concepts and management. Refer to that chapter and SAP official documentation for additional operative information.

The R/3 workbench organizer and transport system takes care of controlling quite automatically new developments and corrections; however, a misuse of available options can lead to unwanted results. To avoid such results, some type of procedures are needed.

The following is a list with the topics that should be extended to define the customer-specific rules:

1. *Transport system setup rules*
   - The configuration is only done in the transport domain controller. When any changes are made to the configuration, this will be distributed using the available TMS options.
   - There will be a *virtual system,* known as DUM, used for special transports.
   - Transport routes will be defined as standard configuration for groups of three systems, such as development, QAS, and production.
2. *Development classes*
   - Are defined in the development procedures
   - Do not use local ($TMP) development classes except for training purposes
   - Make sure a new development class is transported to or defined for all systems in the group
   - Changes to object development classes are not allowed and must be requested of the system administrator
3. *Naming conventions*
   - Follow SAP standard naming conventions
4. *System change options*
   - System change options for production systems, such as global settings, will be set to *Not Modifiable* so that no repository objects or customization can be performed in these systems.
   - System change options for development and test systems are set to *Modifiable.*
   - If consultants or SAP notes indicate that emergency repairs are required in the production system, the system manager will temporarily set the system change option to *Modifiable.* As soon as the repairs are released and confirmed, the system change option must be set back to its original value.
5. *Tasks and change requests*
   - Tasks are assigned by the development responsible for the users. These tasks will be released by their developers.

- Change requests will be created by the development responsible, which is also responsible for releasing them.
- For small developments and corrections, the developer can create her or his own tasks and change requests.
- It is forbidden to use another group's change requests.

6. *Repairs*
   - Are strictly forbidden except when coming from a SAP note
   - Apply only if strictly necessary for applications
   - Are performed in development systems, tested, and, if accepted, transported to other systems
   - Are not to be left unconfirmed
7. *Performing imports*
   - Imports can be used to test a system at any time, except when receiving other indications.
   - Imports are always performed by the system or transport administrator after receiving the import request form.
   - Imports to productive environments must be preceded by imports to test environments, when possible.
   - For performance reasons, importing to a production environment is restricted to once a day at 2:00 A.M., right after backup. For security reasons, only imports that are in the buffer before 8:00 P.M. will be performed.
   - In urgent or exceptional situations, partial or special imports to a productive system can be performed after receiving management authorization.
   - Developers are responsible for checking both export and import logs.
8. *Special management options*
   - Transporting between different clients in the same system is restricted to the system administrator.

Bear in mind that a wrong transport or an out-of-sequence import can cause a lot of damage to your system, so be sure to establish some organization and rules to avoid such situations. In the preceding example procedures, it is significant that the import to production system is performed right after backing up the system, so that at least you could recover the state of the system as it was before the transport in case some critical errors occurred.

You can surely come out with additional rules for managing and controlling your transport system.

Information Integrity Issues

Information integrity refers to those issues concerning both the quality and consistency of the data managed by the system (*logical integrity*) as well as those issues having to do with the hardware elements and system availability (*physical integrity*).

When there are errors in the system that affect the logical integrity such as wrong user inputs and unintentional deletes, these issues are either resolved using the system's own application facilities or by having a comprehensive backup and restore strategy. It must be pointed out that logical integrity can be a more difficult issue than physical integrity.

However, the physical integrity and therefore the system availability (for unplanned downtime) can only be achieved by means of redundant hardware components, thereby avoiding *single points of failure.*

In SAP R/3 installations and any other business-critical applications, some advisable hardware and software elements can be used to avoid system downtime by reducing the single points of failure. These include:

- Use RAID technology for mirroring disks, which can avoid system downtime caused by a single disk failure.
- Set up high availability systems, which can take over the other's functions in case of a system crash.
- To protect against power failures, attach your system to a UPS (uninterrupted power supply). Also consider having double power supplies for all hardware elements: disks, servers, network hubs, and so on.
- Set up double network links to protect against network failures.
- Store your backup tapes in fire-resistant cabinets.

Further security can be achieved by defining a disaster recovery scenario. This is a service that can be provided by many hardware vendors as well as big service and consulting firms.

Both logical and physical information integrity issues have been faced by SAP in a project they have dubbed a "zero downtime" project. A following section discusses some of the concepts covered by this project.

An Approach to Backup Strategies in SAP Installations

The backup and restore strategy is a critical issue in the technical implementation and operation of a SAP R/3 system installation.

Backup and restore strategies are meant for the following tasks:

- Avoiding the loss of critical system data in case of failures (either hardware or software)
- Recovering from a logical integrity error (this is the *only* way to do so)
- Protecting the business
- Allowing full-system copies
- Safeguarding critical management operations

When studying what backup strategy would best fit your needs and requirements, you must first consider the backup factors that can affect the choice of the backup solution or strategy.

The following is a list of factors that directly influence backup strategy decisions:

- *System availability.* The first issue to consider is the amount of downtime for backup your systems can accept. It can range from no downtime, or a 24×7 systems operation (24 hours a day, 7 days a week), to other possibilities, such as 24×6, 15×5, and so on. For instance, if you decide on any of the 24-hour operations, then your only choice at the moment is to perform the available types of *online backups.*
- *What to back up.* You must consider whether you are going to back up the full system, including the operating system files, SAP runtime files, and the database. Critical to SAP backup strategy is to back up the full database, since it's the piece of the application that changes most frequently. Other system files can be backed up only at periodic times (such as once a week) or on those occasions where changes took place. You can define a consistent backup strategy by having different backup periods for different types of file systems. In SAP installations, you also have to consider the backup of the archive log files.
- *Size of files to back up.* Together with the previous factor, the size of the files to back up will affect the time it takes the backup to complete. Consider also the estimate growth of the system and database files.
- *Backup performance.* Consider the maximum allowed time for a backup to complete.
- *Type of backup.* You can decide whether to perform either full or incremental backups, although for the database, an incremental is not recommended since the tablespace organization makes most of

the database files change just by starting the database. Based on the system-availability factor, you can also decide whether to perform online or offline backups. Additionally, you can decide to verify the backup procedure. A mix and match of available types is also possible.

- *From where to back up.* You must also decide if you are going to perform backups with the same system where the data is located or if you are going to use a different server for doing backups and restores. Currently, there are many client/server backup solutions. In any case, you have to consider also the CPU, input/output, and network capacity, both from the server to back up and the server from which to back up.
- *When to back up.* You have to decide the dates, times, and frequency for performing backups. This decision will be affected by other factors such as the system availability, the expected backup performance, and the size of the files to be backed up. You must consider what is the right period between two full backups, especially for large backup volumes.
- *Backup devices.* The hardware market can offer simple tape drives to the most sophisticated automated tape robots, which can perform backups using several tapes in parallel. You could also consider backup to other devices such as disk volumes, optical devices, CD-ROMs, and so on. For volume, performance, and growth-estimate reasons, you must consider what are the most convenient backup devices.
- *Backup management tools.* You must also consider what software or tools you are going to use for managing backup. You should try to find the software that offers the most extensive features but which should be at the same time easy to use and, above all, reliable. Another consideration is to decide whether you want to use the SAP-offered tools, such as *brbackup* for the Oracle databases, or other tools that can be integrated with it using the *backint* interface.
- *Backup tapes management.* In the backup strategy, you must also decide how the tapes or other backup media are going to be managed: how to label them, what their retention and recycling periods will be, where to store them, and so on.
- *Restore procedures.* Often you find a quite clear backup strategy, but then when there is a need to restore what was previously backed up, lots of problems are found. Defining a restore procedure is not easy because there are so many possible recovery situations:

from simple copy procedure (backup and restore) to a single file missing. The point is to define the possible situations where a restore might be needed and to test it.

When checking your requirements against the previous factors, you might come up with a solution that best fits your company needs. The main message must be to test and monitor your backup and restore strategy before going into productive operation.

The next sections show some possibilities of backup strategies mainly concerning how the backup is performed.

Performing Backups with brbackup

As it was introduced previously in Chap. 15, brbackup is the utility provided by SAP to perform backups in the R/3 systems for Oracle databases.

The brbackup tools have been improving in later versions. Currently, they support online and offline backups as well as backing up other system files besides the database. Since release 4.0, they also support two-level backup (first to disk and then to tape), performing brbackup and brarchive in one run, backup of data tablespaces only, partial backups also useful for completing backups with errors, standby database server, and other features.

Using the backint interface, you can use brbackup together with other third-party software and hardware, allowing for greater performance and different management interfaces.

The brbackup advantages are as follows:

- Full support from SAP.
- Comprehensive tape management.
- Integration with sapdba and the restore and recovery procedures.
- You can schedule backups from within SAP R/3.

The main disadvantage of brbackup is that it might be slow, and it must be run from the same database server, which can affect the system performance.

Operating System Backup Utilities

Every hardware vendor and some third-party software companies offer many backup hardware and software solutions. Using this type of utility usually offers the advantage of being faster and more flexible than br-backup, and many of them can run in a client/server mode, therefore avoiding the need to run the backup in the same database server.

Some of the operating system backup utilities can make a backup of several servers using the same devices. For example, backups can be made of several SAP systems or even the application servers.

The disadvantages of these solutions are that they are not supported directly by SAP, and you cannot perform online backups, since the system must be stopped to shut down the database in a consistent state. Several database and software vendors are developing methods to allow for online backup in a client/server fashion also.

The Triple-mirror Approach

This solution is based on both software and hardware elements and can be best applied in systems with a high-availability configuration. Figure 16-3 shows the initial layout.

This approach consists of having every disk with two additional mirrored disks: actually there is a lot of redundancy since the same information is copied in three different volumes.

The backup will be performed in the standby switch-over system that has the tape devices connected.

At a certain point, the system is stopped to have the database in a consistent state. At that moment, the third mirror is detached from its volume so that the two mirrored disks continue their normal operation. This third mirrored disk is then passed to the switch-over system that mounts the file systems contained on the disks, then it starts the backup. Figure 16-4 shows this situation.

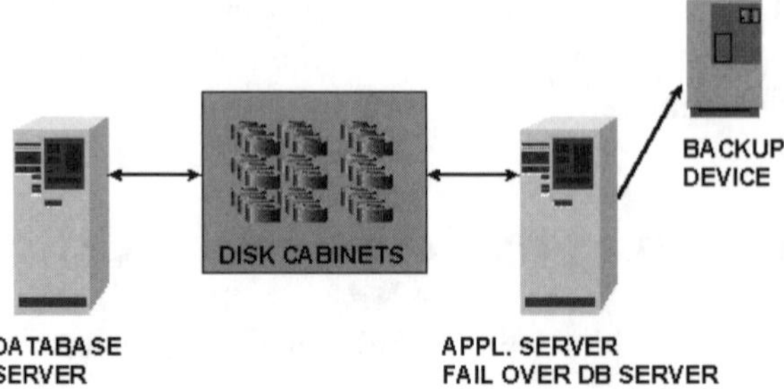

Figure 16-3 Backup using triple-mirror approach, initial situation.

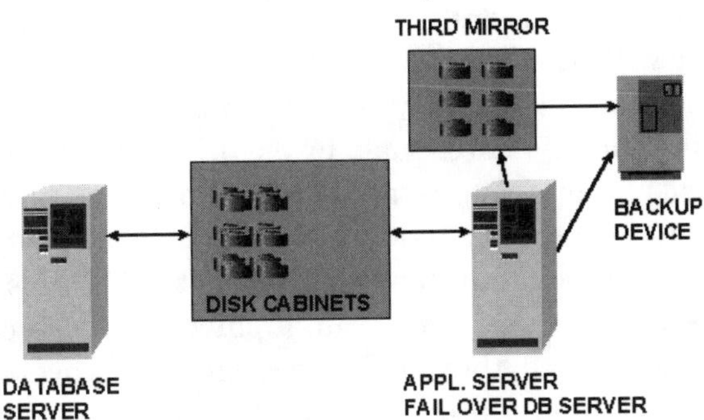

Figure 16-4 Backup using triple-mirror approach, third volume detached.

At this moment, SAP can be started again in the original system. With convenient hardware and software tools for stopping SAP, detaching the third disk, and starting again, the application might take less than ten minutes.

When using only one server, the third disk must be mounted in a different location, the backup devices must be connected to the database server, and the backup must be performed by the same server, which can degrade system performance.

When the backup is finished in the standby server, the third mirror is put back online to synchronize for the next backup. You don't need to stop the application again. This synchronization process might slightly affect system performance, especially input/output. The trick is to measure carefully the input/output bandwidth of the disk controllers.

The advantages of this approach are minimal downtime for offline backups and extra safety with the three mirrored copies. In case of failure, before starting to synchronize the disks back, make sure a full backup copy resides on the disks of the third mirror.

The disadvantages of this solution are that it is costly and it requires many disks and disk controllers. It only allows for offline backup, so the system is stopped, however minimally. Synchronizing back the disks online can be costly to I/O and CPU.

Standby Database Server and the Roll-forward Approach

This solution consists of having an additional server based on a complete offline copy from the database server. The standby database server can be located in a different building, even many miles apart, but be connected with reliable network lines.

Once both servers are in the same initial state, the original database server will be constantly sending the archive redo log files or transaction logs to the standby server, which can then by applied (rolled forward) either synchronously or asynchronously so that both servers are almost in the same database situation. The only difference will be in the time it takes for the archive redo logs to be sent and then applied.

With this solution, you can perform the backups in the standby server. While the backup is going on, archive redo logs cannot be applied; but once it's finished, they are all sequentially recovered.

This solution presents the drawback that recovery procedures can be more difficult. Another disadvantage is that it can be costly to maintain an additional server that cannot be used for anything else. However, with this approach, you don't need to stop the original database system for backups. Additionally, this backup solution can serve the purpose of covering part of a disaster recovery situation.

An Introduction to High Availability and Cluster Systems

Availability in a general computing sense is the period of time in which the system can be used to perform the functions for which it was designed and implemented. The opposite of availability is *downtime.*

Downtime can be of two natures:

- *Planned downtime.* Performing offline backups, database reorganizations, and hardware upgrades
- *Unplanned downtime.* System crash, disk failure, electrical power failure, software system error, network failure; and so on.

Availability is not defined as an isolated hardware or software element but as a property of the group of the system elements. For instance, even when neither the software or the server hardware presents errors but when in fact the network lines are broken, prohibiting users from performing their usual work, you have what is defined as a downtime situation.

SAP project managers should clearly understand that the key measure of system availability is not the time the servers are up and running (the system manager's point of view) but rather the perception by the end users.

The SAP high-availability project was known as the *zero downtime project,* and its goal was to reduce to a minimum both planned and unplanned downtime. To reach that goal, SAP is investing and developing, together with its main partners, software and hardware solutions.

When thinking of availability in the R/3 environment, the following factors should be considered:

- What are the availability needs of the business? Is it 24 hours, 7 days a week (24 × 7)?
- Reasons for a planned downtime: software upgrades (R/3, operating system, database).
- Reasons for unplanned downtime: hardware and software unexpected failures.

One of the first components that has been developed by SAP hardware partners to maximize availability and minimize the unplanned downtime is the switch-over systems (fail-over systems) or cluster systems. These types of systems consist of a group of hardware and software elements that basically consists of:

- At least two servers (normally database server and application server) sharing a common group of disks.
- Reacting to servers, disks, or network failures: when a system crashes, the SAP services are automatically passed onto the standby server, and vice versa.

The switch-over system mostly works by dynamic assignment of SAP services to TCP/IP addresses using TCP/IP alias addressing facilities.

A nice advantage of the switch-over system is that when there is the need for hardware upgrade or service maintenance, services can be manually switched over to the other system without interrupting normal system work.

You must remember that having switch-over systems will require an additional SAP license, since this is attached to the network controller card of the server. SAP usually has provided this additional license free of charge when registering the switch-over software and systems.

Normally, each hardware vendor provides its own switch-over or cluster solution, except in the case of Windows NT systems, where SAP is supporting the Microsoft Service Cluster System (MSCS).

Extensive information about high availability can be found on the R/3 online documentation or on SAPnet.

Performance and Tuning Basics

Performance is the measure of system response time to user requests, either interactively or in batch configuration. Performance problems in R/3 systems can greatly impede the overall acceptance of the systems as well as cause serious financial damage to companies. Therefore this issue must be seriously considered and planned for. Performance and tuning are closely linked to system monitoring and administration.

Performance is affected by the following factors:

- System sizing and hardware resources
- Disk input/output throughput
- Network infrastructure
- Number of concurrent users and workload transaction profile
- Background processing
- Online reporting
- Printing strategy
- Local developed programs and transactions
- Size and fragmentation of database
- Service distribution
- Configuration of technical infrastructure
- Buffer resets by transports
- Other connected services and applications

Tuning is the process of optimizing performance, and consists of setting and configuring the hardware and software components with the goal of having better system response times. In other words, it is the technique by which systems can perform the same processes in less time. In order to achieve optimization of available resources, system managers and technical consultants have to closely monitor system workload profiles and statistics and take corrective actions. These actions can be performed on:

- Scalability, by configuring additional hardware resources if CPU or memory bottlenecks are detected
- Operating system parameters and configuration: memory management, disk input/output, swapping, and so on
- Database parameters and design
- SAP parameters: buffers, processes, instance profile parameters

- R/3 service distribution: batch, printing, operation modes
- Optimization of programs and reporting
- Optimization of database accesses
- Archiving

Activities for a continuous improvement of performance take place in the going live productive support phases. This is usually done via the process of workload analysis and tuning.

Often the most time-consuming transactions are those that have been locally developed. End users may dislike going through large numbers of R/3 screens in order to perform a single transaction, and so request the consulting company to make a new transaction chaining required fields into a single screens. This is a dangerous process, since what used to be several dialog steps, processed at the clerical level (usually measured as a 30-second think time between two dialog steps), are now processed in a row by the system. This can affect performance, especially on those operations where the business process includes dozens of line items.

Frequent transports into productive systems have a negative effect on performance, since, for example, when programs are changed and transported, they must be reloaded into the instance buffers, causing buffer fragmentation that might provoke buffer swaps and that decreases the buffer quality.

Workload Analysis

Workload analysis is part of the performance monitors. The goal of the information provided is to optimize the system's performance by finding what causes problems and bottlenecks, and which programs or transactions have a longer average response time or consume more system resources.

The analysis of the performance data of the R/3 system and the performance monitor are the base tools for finding problems and bottlenecks in the system, and can be used for taking optimization actions.

Workload analysis is based on several monitors:

- Performance database of the main workload monitor (transaction ST03), which displays very important information about the performance status of the systems.
- Work process overview, which can be used for displaying information about the status of current processes and finding stopped processes or long-running transactions.

- Operating system monitor, which can be used to display important information about operating system activity such as CPU utilization, memory, swap or disk utilization, or top CPU processes. The monitor collects both snapshot and statistical information.
- Database monitor, which shows the status of the database and main indicators of the quality of SQL access, data cache, dictionary cache, and so on. It also displays information about the status and fragmentation of the data files.
- Buffer monitor, which provides very useful information for displaying the quality of the instance parameters for the different SAP buffers and the utilization of the main memory. Bottlenecks in buffer usage are usually indicated by an excessive number of swaps.

When analyzing performance problems, it must be first described whether the full system and every user is affected by a given problem, if it always occurs and if it is reproducible, or whether it only happens sometimes.

There are many solutions and approaches for improving performance and tuning the system:

- Contracting preventive maintenance services like EarlyWatch.
- Proactively performing monitoring and systems management, and performing a daily and periodic checklist that should be documented.
- Analyzing the statistics and load profiles using the workload monitor.
- Checking the quality of development by debugging and optimizing local programs and transactions. SAP tools such as debugger, SQL Trace, and Runtime Analysis can be of help in this process.
- Performing extensive system and stress tests.
- Distributing the load among available instances and servers.
- Using offline reporting tools.
- Archiving and deleting obsolete data from the database.
- Applying patches and corrections to standard programs.

Workload analysis options are introduced and discussed in Chap. 11.

Introduction to Helpdesk

The support of R/3 systems consists of solving all types of problems and questions that arise during the operation of the SAP systems. Supporting

SAP users and SAP systems is one of the main activities during and after going live.

If support is not provided in an efficient and timely manner, users will not be able to perform their jobs as expected, systems will not be stable, many questions will remain unanswered, and many application and technical issues will remain unresolved. This can severely affect business operations.

There are many reasons why problems exist or can arise:

- System bugs
- Human error
- Lack of knowledge
- Problems with continuous data migration, conversion, and interfaces
- Technical infrastructure problems: PCs, printing, batch, network connections
- Others

Problems are better solved when postimplementation support is planned in the first phases of implementation. There are, however, several typical mistakes and problems encountered when establishing the support staff or helpdesk procedures after implementation. Some of these are:

- Lack of proactive support and communication
- Lack of training
- Poorly documented support requests
- Unclear helpdesk processes

A good support strategy is based on proactive systems management and application management, as well as on a well-established, trained, and organized helpdesk.

Figure 16-5 shows one of many possible models for designing a helpdesk process within a SAP support strategy.

Besides documentation and other sources of information, end users typically have two lines of support:

- Key users or department superusers who are normally close to the business operations and who have helped during the implementation phase. These persons can sometimes help end users with basic operations questions, doubts, or problems related to the applications.
- The helpdesk, as the central source of support.

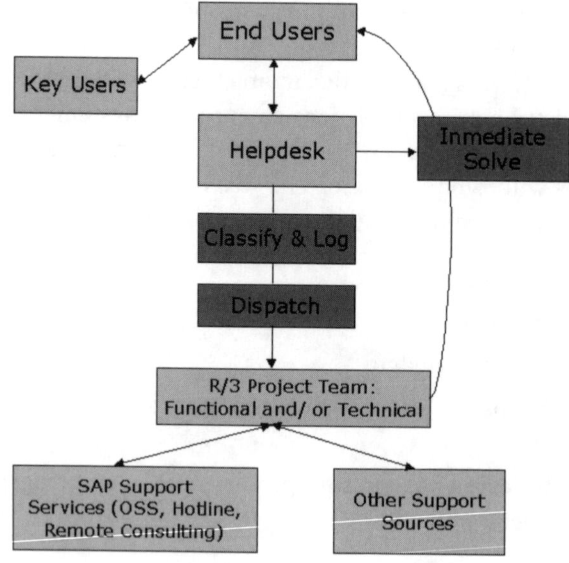

Figure 16-5
Approach to helpdesk strategy.

On many occasions, the helpdesk should be able to provide an immediate solution or answer to end users—for instance, the existence of a network problem on one of the lines, instructions for changing a password, SAPGUI connection parameters, and so on.

On the other hand, the helpdesk will most typically log and prioritize the users' calls and dispatch calls to appropriate expert support.

Expert support is normally provided by the R/3 project team, including functional and technical personnel and even developers. These people are knowledgeable about business processes and systems functioning. Often they are responsible for calling users back with answers and documenting problems for later occasions.

Finally, when the project team is not able to solve those problems, it can use SAP support services such as SAPnet or SAP customer support services. There are other sources of support, such as hardware partners, database vendors, or other software or service companies.

Besides having a defined helpdesk process, there are several other requirements for establishing the helpdesk. Most important are:

- Defining what will be supported
- Establishing levels of priorities
- Implementing hours of operation and methods for contacting support and logging calls

- Establishing standards and procedures for support
- Establishing service levels and response times for callback
- Assigning helpdesk roles and responsibilities
- Establishing communication channels
- Developing helpdesk logistics: equipment, phones, faxes, facilities
- Implementing the helpdesk application
- Providing needed skills and resources
- Developing an escalation process
- Providing initial and continuing training

The number and skills of the support staff personnel will largely depend on the size of the user base, as well as the scope (modules) and status (continuous change and open projects) of the R/3 implementation. For instance, only a small number of support staff personnel will be necessary for small and closed implementations, whereas large and open implementations may require many support staff people, both technical and functional, including developers.

For medium to large and complex implementations, a larger support and helpdesk staff will be required. This is closely related to the issue of the resources needed after implementation (after going live).

Common recommendations for resources after going live are:

- At least two consultants or business superusers for each of the R/3 application modules being deployed.
- A strong technical team, with at least two basis experts plus a systems manager and a good database administrator. At least two of these people must have thorough knowledge of how to monitor performance and tune the systems.
- One or two ABAP programmers when there is the need for additional reporting or development, and also for upgrade projects.

Large companies and value contract SAP customers with several R/3 installations and intensive support needs are advised to create a Customer Competence Center (CCC).

The task of beginning the planning process for defining the postimplementation support is included in the project preparation phase within the ASAP Roadmap.

Supporting SAP: Troubleshooting

As introduced in previous sections, problems, errors, or incidences may be detected either by end users through the helpdesk or by proactive monitoring and systems management.

Intimately linked with the support process, as the cornerstone of efficient support, is having a defined and proven method for problem resolution and troubleshooting in the technical, development, and functional areas.

Troubleshooting documentation and methods provide support personnel the means to analyze and find the causes of problems so that corrective action may be taken at a later time.

The most difficult task in correcting problems (as in healing sickness) is to make the most accurate diagnosis.

Functional problems must be analyzed and solved by the R/3 project team or reminder functional consultants. In order to diagnose functional problems, it is imperative to be able to reproduce them, and, when needed, to debug them.

Resolution will often mean changing some customization settings, applying patches to standard R/3 programs, or modifying locally developed programs. The process will require making changes in the development system and then testing them before transporting the new settings or objects into the productive system.

A Basic Technical Troubleshooting Handbook

A technical troubleshooting handbook, documenting the basic procedures for problem resolution and problem escalation, might be a very valuable tool for any system manager or technical support person.

Here we present a brief overview or scheme of such a handbook to be completed for specific hardware, operating system, database, and R/3 system landscapes:

I. First steps: identification and problem type analysis
   1. Perform initial analysis.
      A. Identify if something has changed (software or hardware installation, scripts, profile parameters, database structure).
      B. System (hardware) is down:
         - Check console messages.
         - Reboot and keep important system log files.
         - Check hardware components.

- — Analyze with diagnosis tools.
- — Escalation procedure: call hardware support.

2. Check main log files.
    - Analyze with diagnostic tools.
    - Start up/shut down log files.
    - Check operating system log files.
3. Identify other problems (startup/shutdown, disks and operating systems, database, operational R/3, performance).

II. Startup and shutdown problems (R/3 and application servers)

1. Check processes or services at operating system level.
2. Check whether database is up.
3. Check connection with database (i.e., tnsping, R3trans -d).
4. Check whether file systems are full.
5. Check for network problems in the server network.
6. Check backup log for problems after backup.
7. Check for problems after system crash.
8. Check for problems with PDC file server.
9. Check file permissions and authorizations.
10. Manually start up or shut down database and then the application server.
11. Check hosts and services files.

III. Operating system problems

1. Check operating system log and event viewers.
2. Check disks and file systems.
3. Check directories and permissions.
4. Check path names.
5. Check security.

IV. Database problems

1. Starting and stopping database
    - A. Refer to startup problems.
    - B. Check database specific error log file.
2. Database storage status
3. Check database error numbers.
4. Check database alerts.

V. R/3 application operational problems

1. Check whether all users are affected.
2. Check whether there is no work at all, or whether work is just limited.
3. Check whether application servers are available (SM51).
4. Check with standard monitoring transactions: SM50, SM04, SM12, SM13, ST22, SM37, SP01.

5. Check trace files on work directory (/usr/sap/<SID>/<instance>/work).
6. Check SAP systems alerts.
7. Analyze database problems.

VI. Specific operational problems
1. Problems with printing
   A. Check network.
   B. Check SP01/SPAD spool request logs.
   C. Check system log.
2. Problems with batch input
   A. Check directories and files.
   B. Check SM35 logs.
   C. Check system log.
3. Problems with lock entries
   A. Check lock entries.
   B. Check update process.
   C. Call user.
4. Problems with update process
   A. Check update process.
   B. Check database.
   C. Check network connections.
5. Problems with enqueue
   A. Check database.
   B. Check instance parameters.
   C. Check operating system processes.
6. Problems with message server
   A. Check processes.
   B. Check network.
   C. Check log files at work directory.
7. Problems with background processing
   A. Check job log.
   B. Check background system consistency.
   C. Check file systems.
   D. Check system log.

VII. Performance problems
1. Perform workload analysis.
2. Perform debugging.
3. Perform runtime analysis.
4. Perform SQL trace.
5. Check for operating system problems.
6. Check disks for input/output bottlenecks.

VIII. Resolution process
1. Search or SAPnet notes for hints, solutions, or workarounds.
2. Escalation: enter message on SAP hotline or SAPnet.
3. Enter problem on hardware partner hotline.
4. Follow problem actions and SAP indications.
5. Apply patches and corrections; test and verify results.

IX. Problem and resolution documentation

SAP Operation and Maintenance Basic Laws

Experience in several SAP implementations has led to the discovery of some operational *laws* for keeping a SAP system in a productive state. This list is not complete; you can probably make it longer, or you can make it shorter by automating most of these laws in fewer, more complete checks.

These are some *laws* for the technical administration and operating of the SAP systems, and in general for the planning and design of the technical infrastructure:

- Daily tasks are *daily!*
- Do not undersize your SAP systems. Be especially generous allocating the amount of memory for your application servers.
- Backup strategy is the cornerstone of safety. Do not leave room for unconsidered events to happen.
- Have enough preconfigured disks ready for adding extra space to your SAP file systems.
- Check database critical objects. Do not let database file systems and data files grow beyond 85 percent.
- Get (ask for) a test server. It can be useful for operating-system, database, or SAP upgrades; also for SAP transports and for a sound and safe backup and recover strategy. So, before taking anything to a productive state, test it.
- Log your incidences from the very beginning, no matter how silly the solution may have been. The question is not to find out a wrong permission in a file but to avoid the situation the next time it happens (and it will!).

- Monitor your network. SAP client/server R/3 relies on the network. So, even if the SAP system is up and running, a network (not nervous) breakdown will negatively impact the availability of productive deployment of the system.
- Do not forget your printers. (Have you ever seen the face of a trucker waiting for his transport route for more than half an hour?)
- Think of what procedures are in place in case SAP becomes unavailable for a long period of time (*long* is, of course, a subjective qualifier, which can go from 10 minutes to several days). Do not think of how much money the company loses because of this (can cause depression and insomnia).
- Contract the EarlyWatch service. Prevention is better than cure!
- Design and communicate a clear procedure for end user technical support. Don't just put a nice framework on a Web page!
- Optimize the infamous Z programs (customer programs). For an unknown reason, these are always the programs with longest runtimes.
- Put a high availability system in your (SAP) life.

APPENDIX A

SAProuter and Remote Connection to SAP

SAP has built a worldwide service network as part of its strategy to support and communicate with its customers in the most effective way. Service has been a key factor for the success of the SAP R/3 product, both for its mother company as well as for its customers, who rely on the R/3 applications for handling mission-critical business processes. SAP service comprises all phases in the life of a SAP R/3 project: from implementation and preproductive states to the daily productive operation of the system. SAP offers a wide range of service packages in an effort to cover the whole spectrum of customer service needs. SAP is currently providing most of its online information and support services through SAPnet (sapnet.sap.com). The former Online Service System (OSS) is now called SAPnet-R/3 front end. Chapter 1 of this book includes an overview of SAP services, but you can find extensive and current information about these and other services by visiting the SAP Web page at www.sap.com.

Remote Connections to SAP Support Servers

As previously indicated, to use the described online services, SAP customers must set up a remote connection to one of the SAP support servers.

The official SAP manual, *Remote Connection to the R/3 Online Services,* contains detailed information about this process. In that guide, you can also find addresses and phone numbers of official institutions, support centers, and service providers that can help you configure your connection. The required forms are also included. Additionally, SAP offers a service package, *rcPack,* for establishing remote connections.

The *Remote Connection to the R/3 Online Services* guide normally comes bundled with the software kit, and you can also find it in the Online Help or Print Files CD-ROMs.

The type of remote connection and the service providers available will vary according to your geographical situation. SAP guides you through the process of choosing what is the best option for you. SAP provides several support centers to assist customers with technical questions regarding the remote connections and configurations of the components involved. A simple diagram of the remote connection is presented in Fig. A-1.

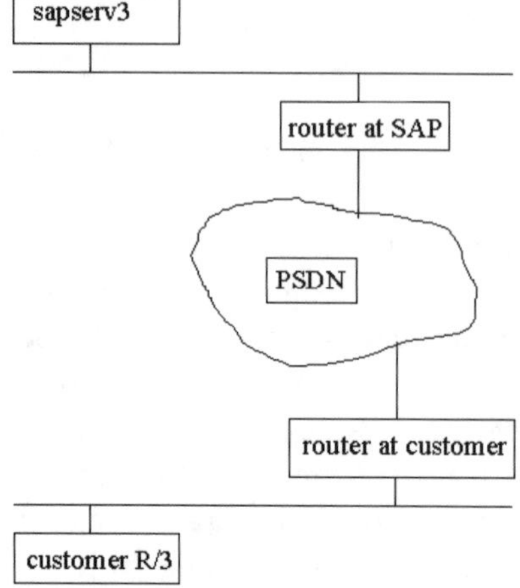

Figure A-1 Simple diagram of connection between customer R/3 system and SAP.

The next section provides a summary with the guidelines for setting up and establishing the remote connection. This guideline is based on the SAP guides and general user experience.

Guidelines for Establishing a Remote Connection to SAP Service Network

The following steps show the general procedure for getting the remote connection to SAP support servers:

1. According to your company needs, existing communications infrastructure, geographical location, and budget, you have to select one type of remote connection (X.25, ISDN, frame relay, etc.) and one of the available service providers, applying for the appropriate communication lines and connections. In the previously referenced guide, SAP has included useful information to help you in the process and has also established some regional support centers specialized in remote connection consulting.
2. The remote connection must use an official assigned IP network address. If you do not have one, you have to apply for such an address or you can let your service provider assign one to you. Normally, you will need at least two official addresses: one for the R/3 server itself and another one for the router that connects it to the Internet.

3. SAP will assign you the support server nearest to you depending upon your geographical location. Available support servers and their locations are:

Server Name	*Location*
sapserv3	Walldorf (Germany)
sapserv4	Foster City, San Francisco (USA)
sapserv5	Tokyo (Japan)
sapserv6	Sydney (Australia)
sapserv7	Singapore (Singapore)

   SAP's phenomenal growth indicates that it may install additional support servers. Search the SAP Websites or call your nearest subsidiary if you need additional information about current support servers.

4. Once you have a support server assigned, you have to fill out and send SAP a form with the names of the contact people at your end. This information will be used by SAP to contact its customers for administrative reasons or in case problems with the connection arise.
5. Using the remote connection data sheet form that you can find in the appendix of the previously referenced guide, provide SAP with the information necessary for establishing the physical remote connection. On this form, you have to specify such things as connection type (X.25, ISDN, frame relay), technical details such as network addresses, and the IP address of the node that will be acting as SAProuter. The *SAProuter* is a special SAP program that acts like a firewall system and enables the connection for the group of systems that conforms to the SAP installation. With the SAProuter, all servers are able to access the SAP support servers without the need of each having a physical remote connection. The SAProuter program, the available options, and configuration are further explained later in this appendix. At this stage, for this information, just specify the TCP/IP host address of the node at your end that you want to use for connecting to SAP.
6. SAP will process your data and send you back the information from their end: the TCP/IP address of the SAP support server assigned and router address, and technical details about X.25, ISDN, and so on (for example, the X.25 number). Then, you and your network administrator have to finish configuring the remote network connection. An overview of common network configuration is presented in the next section.

7. Once the connection is established and tested, you have to configure the SAProuter program and the technical parameters for accessing the SAPnet-R/3 front end. At this point, you should already have the corresponding user names and passwords as requested by SAP in step 4. You can then log on to the SAPnet-R/3 front end and test your connections.

Configuring the Network Connection

Once the physical network connection has been installed, some configuration work is needed to establish the actual connection and log in to the SAP support servers. Some TCP/IP network expertise is required in this process. You might need the help of your company network manager, or you can request support from SAP or the consulting partners.

Normally, the server used for connecting to SAP should have two network interface cards, so that you can independently route the network traffic at your convenience.

You will need to configure the TCP/IP routing and enter the hostname addresses in the hosts database.

Communication between your R/3 servers and the SAP support servers is established using the TCP/IP protocol. It means that the corresponding software and host database must be defined and configured. For instance, you must define in your hosts database (usually the file /etc/hosts in the UNIX system or the file \winnt\system32\drivers\etc\hosts on Windows NT systems) the name of the SAP support server (sapserv<n>) assigned to your location. The name and TCP/IP address is given to you by SAP as a reply to the remote connection data sheet.

Once SAP receives and processes the customer data, adding your host and TCP/IP addresses to their database, access is allowed through its firewall system (*saprouter*). It will send back to you the following or similar information:

IP address router at SAP

Technical details, such as the X.25 calling number if the connection is through X.25 lines

IP address of the sapserv<n>

IP address for the X.25 interface at customers' side

Figure A-1 shows a very simple diagram of the connection between a customer R/3 installation and the SAP support systems.

The router at your site must be configured and the connection tested, especially between your router and the router at the SAP site. Do not confuse the router physical equipment used in wide area networks (WANs) with the SAProuter program.

Then, the hosts database file must be updated to include the following addresses and hostnames:

```
# IP router address at your site
  XXX.XXX.XXX.XXX          <hostname>
# IP SAP assigned support server address
  XXX.XXX.XXX.XXX          <hostname>
```

The *XXX.XXX.XXX.XXX* is substituted with the TCP/IP address. For example, *1.1.1.1. <hostname>* is the name of the host as defined in your network setup.

If your network is using a domain-name-resolving protocol such as DNS, you might not need to add the hostnames, since they will be automatically obtained from the name server.

The TCP/IP address is a 32-bit address made of 4 digits (8 bits each) separated by a period. Theoretically, each address part can range from 0 to 255.

According to your specific operating system network utilities, you have to configure correctly your routes; that is, you have to tell your system how to reach other parts: A typical UNIX command for adding routes is the route command. For example,

```
# route add -net <address> <hostname>
```

To test that the route has been correctly updated, you can issue a netstat command; for example:

```
# netstat -r
```

As a result of this command, you should see your newly added route.

Once the systems and routers are correctly configured and SAP has recognized and added our systems, you can test if you have a physical connection to the SAP support servers by issuing a simple ping command.

You should make several tests:

- Test the connection from your router to the SAP support server. If this test fails, it might indicate that the router is not correctly configured or your system is not yet allowed into the SAP network.

- Test the connection from your SAP R/3 server to your router. If this test fails, it might indicate that the routes are not correctly configured.
- Test the connection from your SAP R/3 server to the SAP support server. If this test fails after previous tests were completed, there may be a communication problem, or the server may not be updated in the SAP database.

When issuing a command such as # *ping sapserv<n>* and you get the *sapserv<n> is alive* or similar message, then the communication between systems is working fine. If you do not get it, or the system does not respond, or you get an error message, review your procedure and contact the SAP support centers.

Security issues are discussed in a following section.

The next step is to configure the SAProuter program to enable the communication between your servers and the SAPnet-R/3 front end system.

SAProuter

The SAProuter is a SAP program located in the runtime directory, /usr/sap/<SID>/SYS/exe/run/saprouter, which is part of the R/3 system installation. The SAProuter works like an intermediate agent in the network for connecting R/3 systems. It can be set up to act like a firewall system, which grants or denies access to your network or R/3 servers.

You have to configure SAProuter for connecting to the SAPnet-R/3 front end as well as for enabling SAP to perform online services.

With the SAProuter program running on one of your local R/3 servers, all the presentation servers (PCs with the SAPGUI) and all the application servers can connect to the SAP network using just one connection point. Then, it is sufficient to define the link between the SAP server and the host running the SAProuter, and between the clients and the SAProuter. This procedure efficiently divides the communication between the application servers and the clients.

For SAP, the whole customer installation (the group of R/3 servers, both database and application) can be accessed via a single TCP/IP address, which is the one in which SAProuter is running. This means, then, establishing a remote connection between the customer and SAP is therefore reduced to reaching the customer's SAProuter host.

With the proper configuration, the SAProuter can be made into an effective instrument for controlling and managing SAP communication within and outside of the customer network.

Network connections between R/3 systems that are established through SAProuter present as an additional advantage that the SAP administrator does not have to route every system that is part of the R/3 network. You can even use SAProuter for establishing connections between servers when there are nonunique TCP/IP addresses.

The SAP support server will only need access to the server that is running the SAProuter at your end. So, for example, it can allow the Early-Watch staff to perform its service to a different SAP system in your network than the one running SAProuter.

The SAProuter program can make indirect connections between two different IP networks (different subnets), but the access is restricted to the application layer. This means that it allows connection between a client software (for example, SAPGUI) and the application server software (R/3 services).

SAProuter is completely hardware-independent, since SAP has used a network interface layer (NI layer), which provides a common interface for all the hardware platforms and operating systems. You don't need to maintain different SAProuters when in heterogeneous environments.

Setting Up SAProuter

SAProuter is a program that, in the most simple form, just needs to be started in the server that is going to act as the R/3 SAProuter server. It can also be started in other servers as an intermediate point of access.

There are basically four steps to follow for setting up SAProuter:

1. Test it with the *niping* program.
2. Create or edit the route permission table.
3. Start the program.
4. Define the route strings for network access with SAProuter.

This process is quite straightforward, but before going into the details, you have to understand how to define *route strings* which are the TCP service connection ports used by SAProuter.

Route Strings and Service Ports. To use SAProuter for establishing connections, the programs that call it must define the route in the form of a route string. A route string contains an entry for each host server it needs to reach. If there is more than one host entry, the preceding ones must be running SAProuter.

You can configure SAProuter to access multiple hosts and multiple services. This is accomplished by defining route strings. The route string might contain as many entries, or substrings, as needed. A single route strings syntax is

```
/H/<hostname>/S/<service>/W/<password>
```

where */H/* precedes the hostname and is a mandatory field. For every hostname, you can specify a TCP service name for the connection after the */S/* indicator and a password following */W/*. If you do not specify these fields, the route string assumes the default values. The default service value (*/S/*) is 3299, and the default password (*/W/*) is blank (no password).

Here are a couple of examples.

1. In the most simple case, as shown in Fig. A-2, a Windows PC SAPGUI client can connect to an R/3 server (server2) through an intermediate server (server1) running SAProuter. The client will use the following route string: /H/server1/H/server2/S/sapdp01.

In this example, server1 is running SAProuter using default TCP service 3299 and without a password—that's why it does not have /S/ and /W/ entries; server2 is an R/3 server that is accessed at the application level using service port sapdp01. This will be the case of a SAP system number 01 in server2 with standard port sapdp01 (number 3201).

2. In the second example, as shown in Fig. A-3, server2, which does not have a remote connection to SAP support servers, will use server1 running SAProuter as the entry point to the SAPnet-R/3 front end system.

You can analyze the route string:

The first part, */H/server1/S/sapdp99/W/my_pass,* indicates the SAProuter server at your site, which is running at the default service port (could be omitted) and is password-protected.

The second substring, */H/sapservn/S/sapdp99,* is the SAProuter running at SAP, which will finally connect you to the ossserver at service port

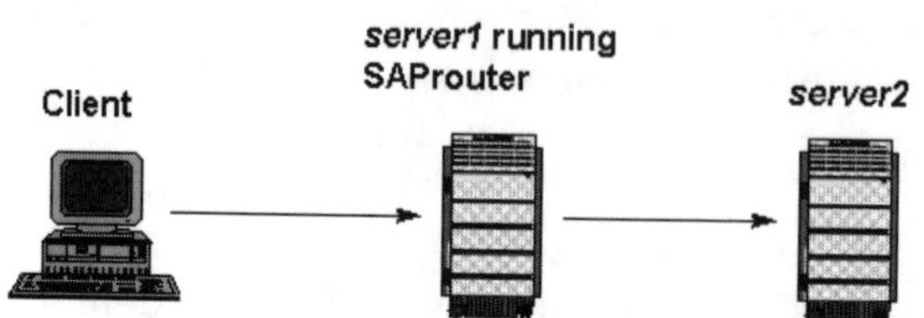

Figure A-2 Route string from a client to a server host using SAProuter.

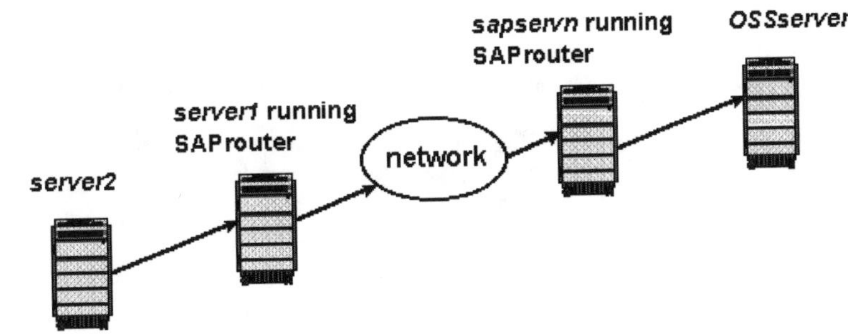

Figure A-3 Route string for connecting customers' R/3 servers to SAPnet (OSS) servers with SAProuter.

/H/server1/S/sapdp99/W/my_pass/H/sapservn/S/sapdp99/H/ossserver/S/sapdp01

sapdp01 using route string */H/ossserver/S/sapdp01.* (Of course, this is just an example. Actual server names and service ports must be obtained by SAP official documentation and will vary depending on your geographical location.)

By default, the SAProuter program uses TCP port 3299 (normally named *sapdp99* in the /etc/services file) to establish an application-oriented connection.

SAProuter can be defined to run in the range 3200 to 3299, although SAP recommends the upper range, since the lower range normally is used by the application servers.

To use a different TCP port for SAProuter, you have to start the program with the *-S* option. In these cases, you have to make sure that the service port is defined in all route access strings.

Testing SAProuter with niping. You can simulate SAProuter connections using the SAP-provided program called niping (network interface layer ping program). This program is located in the SAP standard runtime directory. Figure A-4 shows the system layout for the test.

For this test, it is very convenient having several windows open for connecting to the three servers, for example, in a workstation, or having several telnet sessions in your Windows environment. You can simulate the whole process using a single server by running the programs in the background.

In the preceding example, server1 is running the SAProuter program; server2 is simulating a SAP application server; and server3 is establishing a connection to server2 using server1 as the router.

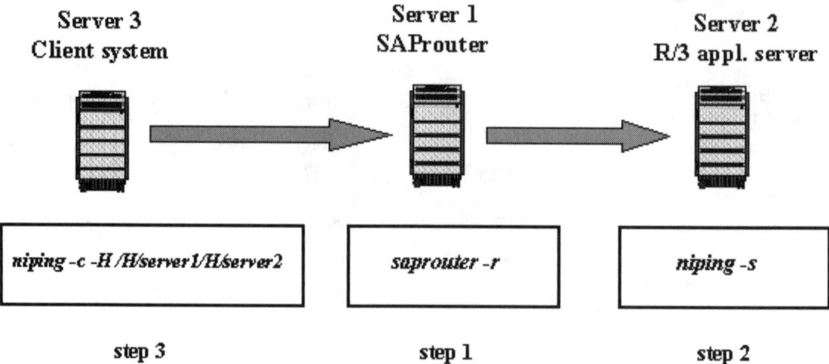

Figure A-4 Testing SAProuter with niping.

First of all, start the SAProuter program in server1. To do that, log in as user <sid>adm (you can also start it as root, but then you have to write the whole path to the program) and start the program by issuing the following command:

```
# saprouter -r
```

Log in on server2 and start the listening server by issuing the command:

```
# niping -s
```

Finally, test the connection from server3 by logging in and issuing the command:

```
# niping -c -H /H/server1/H/server2
```

If everything is correctly configured, as a result of the previous command, the system should display the message:

```
connect to server o.k.
```

Defining the Route Permission Table. To enhance security, each SAProuter can have its own route permission file (table), which specifies the routes, TCP services, and passwords allowed or denied access. If no route permission table exists, it means that all connections are allowed.

By default, when the SAProuter program is started, it looks for the route permission file saprouttab in the user's current directory (normally <sid>adm). In Windows NT systems, this file is usually located in the *system32* directory of NT. You can specify a different file with the *-R* option when starting saprouter.

Figure A-5 shows an example of a permission route table exactly as you can see it, as the output of starting saprouter without options. Notice in the first column in the file, a *D* means *deny access,* while *P* means *permit access.*

SAP recommends that you should always use passwords for enhancing the security. Then, before SAP consultants want to establish a connection to your system, you have to give them the password.

Starting SAProuter. As you probably know by now from the previous examples, the SAProuter program is started by issuing the command *saprouter -r.* You should normally start it automatically at system start, for example, by entering the start command in one of the UNIX *rc* files. In Windows NT systems, saprouter can be installed as a *service* using the *ntscmgr* program, which will start saprouter every time the system is restarted.

Remember to start it with user <sid>adm; else, you have to specify the whole path to the program.

To stop the program issue the command *saprouter -s.*

You can see the list of available options by simply issuing the command *saprouter.* Figure A-6 shows part of the screen you get.

Figure A-5
Basic example of the route table file.

```
# this is a sample routtab : ----------------------------------------
D     host1                    host2      serviceX
D     host3
P     *                        *          serviceX
P     155.56.*.*               155.56
P     155.57.1011xxxx.*
P     host4                    host5      *           xxx
P     host6                    localhost 3299
P     host7                    host8      telnet
S     host9
P0,*  host10

# deny routes from host1 to host2 serviceX
# deny all routes from host3
# permit routes from anywhere to any host using serviceX
# permit all routes from/to addresses matching 155.56
# permit ... with 3rd byte matching 1011xxxx
# permit routes from host4 to host5 if password xxx supplied
# permit information requests from host6
# permit native-protocol-routes to non-SAP-server telnet
# permit ... excluding native-protocol-routes (SAP-servers only)
# permit ... if number of preceding/succeeding hops (saprouters) <= 0/*

# first match [host host service] is used
# permission is denied if no entry matches
# access control is disabled if no routtab found
# service wildcard (*) does not apply to native-protocol-routes
# --------------------------------------------------------------------
```

```
C:\users>saprouter

SAP Network Interface Router, Version 31, January 12 1998

start router : saprouter -r
stop router  : saprouter -s
soft shutdown: saprouter -p
router info  : saprouter -l (-L)
new routtab  : saprouter -n
toggle trace : saprouter -t
cancel route : saprouter -c id
dump buffers : saprouter -d
flush   "    : saprouter -f
start router with third-party library: saprouter -a library

additional options
-R routtab   : name of route-permission-file  (default ./saprouttab)
-G logfile   : name of log file               (default no logging)
-T tracefile : name of trace file             (default dev_rout)
-V tracelev  : trace level to run with        (default 1)
-H hostname  : of running saprouter           (default localhost)
-S service   : service-name / number          (default 3299)
-P infopass  : password for info requests
-C clients   : maximum no of clients          (default 800)
-K [myname]  : activate SNC; if given, use 'myname' as own sec-id
-A initstring: initialization options for third-party library

expert options
-B bufsize   : max. queuelen per client       (default 500000 bytes)
-Q queuesize : max. total size for all queues (default 20000000 bytes)
-W waittime  : timeout for blocking net-calls (default 5000 millisec)
-M min.max   : portrange for outgoing connects, like -M 1.1023
```

Figure A-6 Command options for the saprouter program.

Example of Route Definitions: Setting Up the Connection to the SAPnet-R/3 Front End. The example in this topic is based on a typical customer installation with the following components:

- *Server1.* In the example, the hostname is *mazda* (this name results from the fact that the SAP system manager got a new car). This is the only server at a customer site connected to SAP; it is running SAProuter. Server mazda is the development R/3 application server. The SAP system name is C12.
- *Server2.* In the example, the hostname is *rimut.* This is the productive system, which is not directly connected to SAP support servers. The SAP system name is P12.
- *SAPserv.* In the example, sapserv3 is the SAP support server assigned to this customer. This server is on the SAP end; it is running SAProuter at service port 99.
- *OSSserv.* In the example, the oss002 system. This is the final server; it offers the SAPnet-R/3 front end application services in port 01.

Figure A-7 shows a connection diagram for this environment.

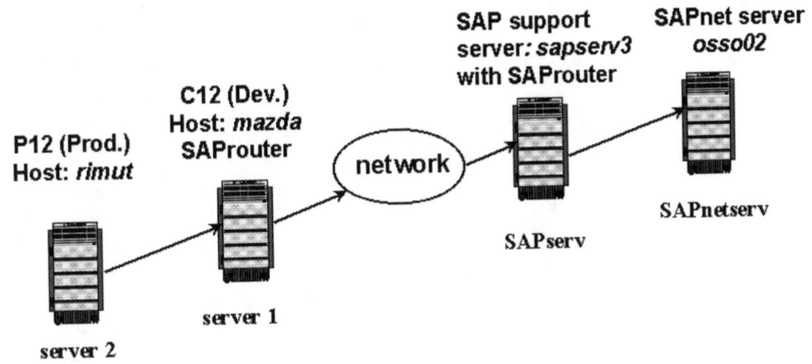

Figure A-7 Example of connecting two servers to SAPnet-R/3 front end.

Actually, the route string definitions will be directly handled by the system when entering the appropriate information in the technical settings for the SAPnet-R/3 front end access from customer systems.

It is assumed that the /etc/hosts file is updated in both servers (mazda and rimut), including the IP address of sapserv and the needed network routers.

Even without the SAProuter server, mazda already should have access to sapserv3.

The first step is to start saprouter in the server. Log in as user <sid>adm and issue the command *saprouter -r.*

Next, log onto the R/3 system with a user ID that has authorization for setting up the connection to the SAPnet-R/3 front end. From the main menu, select *System → Services → SAP Service.* Alternatively, enter transaction code OSS1 in the command field. The system will display a screen like the one shown in Fig. A-8. If all the settings were already configured, clicking on *Logon to the SAP Online Service System* will access the SAPnet-R/3 front end and present the logon screen.

NOTE *Please observe that many R/3 releases still refer to the Online Service System (OSS), even though the name has been changed to SAPnet-R/3 front end, since it is SAP's strategy to provide all services using the Web.*

From the menu, select *Parameters → Technical Settings.* The system will display a screen for setting the parameters. Clicking on the *Change* button allows you to enter the needed parameters in the input fields. Figure A-9 shows an example of a configuration. Notice that when you call

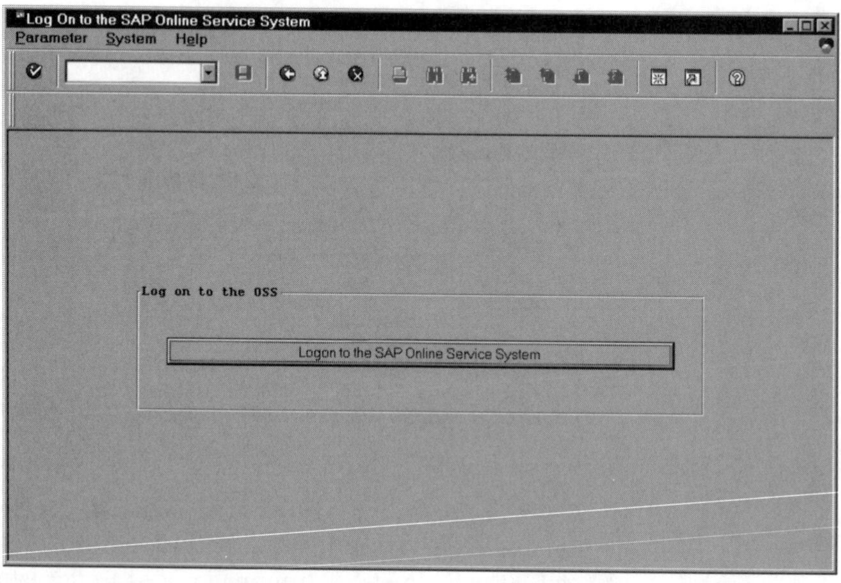

Figure A-8
Initial screen for transaction OSS1.

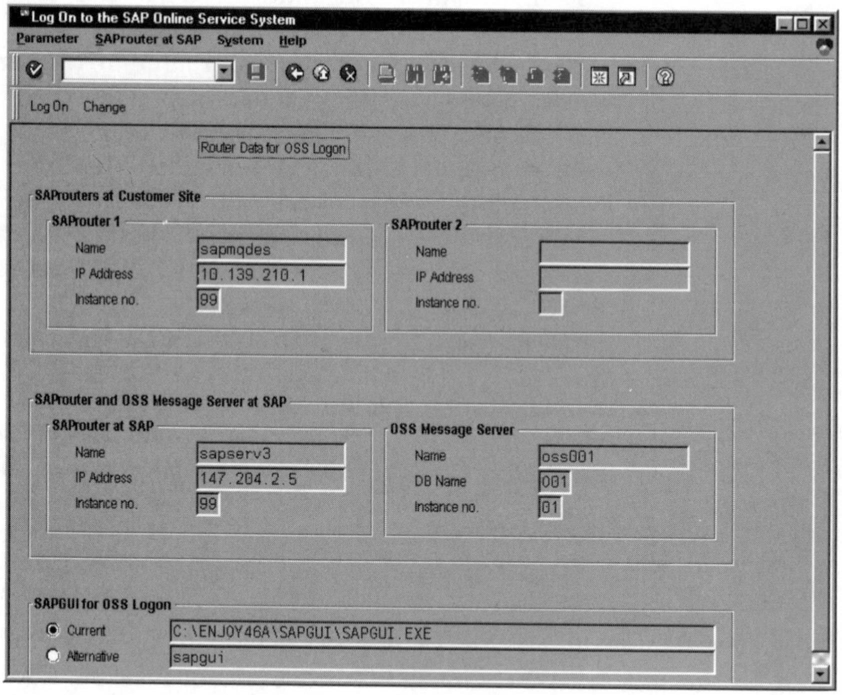

Figure A-9
Example of technical settings configuration for OSS1.

Log On to the SAP Online Service System
Parameter SAProuter at SAP System Help
Log On Change
Router Data for OSS Logon
SAProuters at Customer Site
SAProuter 1
Name sapmqdes
IP Address 10.139.210.1
Instance no. 99
SAProuter 2
Name
IP Address
Instance no.
SAProuter and OSS Message Server at SAP
SAProuter at SAP
Name sapserv3
IP Address 147.204.2.5
Instance no. 99
OSS Message Server
Name oss001
DB Name 001
Instance no. 01
SAPGUI for OSS Logon
Current C:\ENJOY46A\SAPGUI\SAPGUI.EXE
Alternative sapgui

this screen, the parameters for the SAProuter at SAP and the OSS message server already include some default values.

These parameters automatically define a route between a client system (such as a Windows PC) and the SAPnet-R/3 front end system. Users, however, do not need to enter such a route; they can enter the SAPnet-R/3 front end as long as it can access the mazda system and have authorization for using SAPnet-R/3 front end. The permission route string would look like the following:

```
/H/sapmqdes/S/sapdp99/H/sapserv3/S/sapdp99/H/oss002/S/sapdp01
```

You can configure extended connectivity and network security options using and running two saprouters instead of one. The configuration is performed in the screen shown in Fig. A-9.

Remote Connection Security Issues

Normally, the remote connections from customer systems to SAP support servers using official Internet addresses create some form of security concerns, which is perfectly understandable. Customers at first do not like the idea very much, although they do like the benefits of the remote online services. After discussing the security issues, a large majority of, if not all, customers will finally set up the remote connection.

These are the security issues to take into consideration:

- Enforce your firewall system restrictions by the available software and also by defining access lists in the physical routers.
- Normally, connections are established from customers' systems to SAP support servers using *outgoing-only* circuits. This means that it's the customer who opens the connection; then, SAP can access your system using the open channel.
- Create an access permission routing table and assign permission only to specific SAProuters. Assign passwords to the allowed routes.
- Only the SAP support servers are directly connected to customer systems and vice versa. SAP has implemented the following security measures at its end:

  All types of operating system access are disabled, except for anonymous ftp.

  Access is restricted both with SAP firewall and SAProuter.

Only specific persons are allowed to maintain the SAP support servers.

SAP telnet sessions to the customer system are supported using the SAProuter software, as long as the customer opens the telnet service connection and provides SAP personnel with a user and a password.

No direct Internet access is available at SAP servers.

- You can monitor the remote connections by checking the SAProuter log file and using the *Monitor → System monitoring → User overview* function from the administration menu.
- You can use the echo mode in your session to monitor the consultants' activities.
- You can create R/3 user master records for SAP specialists on demand and delete them right after the session; or you can manually lock the user until the next session.
- You can always activate and deactivate the remote connections using the service connection functions within the SAPnet-R/3 front end. Within this function, you can even set a time limit on the connection.

APPENDIX B

Managing Batch Input Sessions

When a company decides to implement the SAP R/3 system to manage business-critical data, it usually does not start from a no-data situation. Normally, a SAP R/3 project comes in to replace or complement existing applications which do not cover actual business needs or applications that become functionally and/or technologically obsolete as the business demands evolve and grow.

In the process of replacing current applications and transferring application data, two situations might occur:

- The first is when application data to be replaced is transferred at once, and only once.
- The second situation is to transfer data periodically from external systems to SAP and vice versa. There is a period of time when information has to be transferred from existing applications to SAP R/3, and often this process will be repetitive.

During the implementation of a SAP R/3 system, some of the important issues to plan and design for are

- Treating the existing historical and master data in the systems which are to be replaced
- Establishing a data communication and transfer policy between the SAP R/3 system and other external and operative information systems

SAP R/3 includes sufficient mechanisms to handle both issues and for allowing the data interchange between the SAP systems and other information systems. From the available and increasing number of methods, the batch input has been and still is the most popular and widely used.

The use of batch input procedures to enter data in the SAP database has the following features:

- Can process large data volumes in batch
- Can be planned and submitted in the background
- Can be processed automatically, without human intervention
- Uses standard SAP transactions, just as if the data was manually entered

The data load using batch input procedures is accomplished in two stages. In the first stage, the functional analysis and the programming permits filtering and generating the data which will later be loaded into the SAP database (generation of batch input session); the second stage has to do with the administration of the data load processes, that is, the management of the batch input sessions.

Among the tasks of the R/3 system administrator, daily checking of batch input can be of major importance. The system includes many utilities which will help in the management, monitoring, and control of the batch input sessions. To call the initial screen for the available utilities for batch input management, select *System* → *Services* → *Batch input* → *Edit,* or, alternatively, enter transaction code SM35 in the command field. Figure B-1 shows this initial screen.

This initial screen is used to select the batch input sessions to work with. After entering the selection criteria, click on the *Overview* icon, or press the *Enter* key. The system will display the list of sessions in your system. Following figure B-2 shows an example.

With the available utilities of the batch input system, administrators can perform the following tasks:

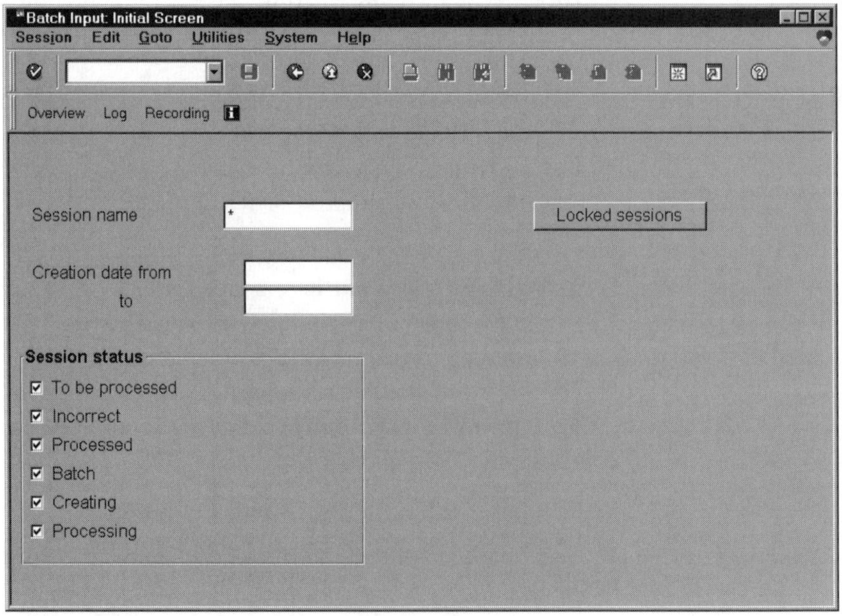

Figure B-1 Initial screen for batch input session management.

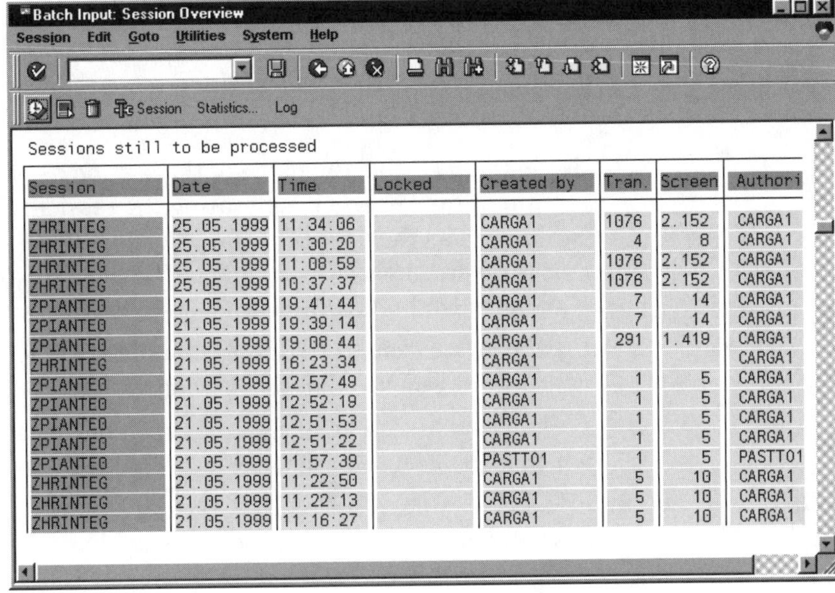

Session	Date	Time	Locked	Created by	Tran.	Screen	Authori
ZHRINTEG	25.05.1999	11:34:06		CARGA1	1076	2.152	CARGA1
ZHRINTEG	25.05.1999	11:30:20		CARGA1	4	8	CARGA1
ZHRINTEG	25.05.1999	11:08:59		CARGA1	1076	2.152	CARGA1
ZHRINTEG	25.05.1999	10:37:37		CARGA1	1076	2.152	CARGA1
ZPIANTEO	21.05.1999	19:41:44		CARGA1	7	14	CARGA1
ZPIANTEO	21.05.1999	19:39:14		CARGA1	7	14	CARGA1
ZPIANTEO	21.05.1999	19:08:44		CARGA1	291	1.419	CARGA1
ZHRINTEG	21.05.1999	16:23:34		CARGA1			CARGA1
ZPIANTEO	21.05.1999	12:57:49		CARGA1	1	5	CARGA1
ZPIANTEO	21.05.1999	12:52:19		CARGA1	1	5	CARGA1
ZPIANTEO	21.05.1999	12:51:53		CARGA1	1	5	CARGA1
ZPIANTEO	21.05.1999	12:51:22		CARGA1	1	5	CARGA1
ZPIANTEO	21.05.1999	11:57:39		PASTT01	1	5	PASTT01
ZHRINTEG	21.05.1999	11:22:50		CARGA1	5	10	CARGA1
ZHRINTEG	21.05.1999	11:22:13		CARGA1	5	10	CARGA1
ZHRINTEG	21.05.1999	11:16:27		CARGA1	5	10	CARGA1

Figure B-2
The *session overview* screen.

- Process the batch input sessions to incorporate data into the SAP system. This is the main function of the utilities. Sessions submitted in the background from these utilities are processed immediately. To process them at a later time you have to use the RSBDCSUB report.
- Debug your batch input sessions by running them interactively in two modes: executing step by step or displaying only errors.
- Display and analyze the session logs and the session contents, including the data and screens. You can display the session before or after it has been processed.
- Lock batch input sessions, preventing users from processing them.
- Delete batch input sessions and associated log files.
- Release sessions to be executed again after system failures.
- Record the new batch input session, with selected transactions and screens for generating a new batch input session. Recorded batch input sessions can be edited and modified.

Batch input sessions can be processed using the background program RSBDCSUB, which creates jobs for automatically submitting sessions in the background at the requested time.

The next section shows how to work with each of these functions.

The Sessions Overview: Selecting Sessions

From the initial batch input selection screen (Fig. B-1) you can enter several criteria to select batch input sessions:

- *Session name.* It's the name of the session as entered in the batch input program, or when generating the session. You can use wildcards, such as the asterisk *, for selecting all sessions or use specific session names. For example, *FISES** will select all sessions starting with the *FISES* character string.
- *Creation date from / to.* Enter a date interval for selecting sessions which were generated in that period of time.
- *Locked sessions.* Clicking on this push button selects sessions which have been intentionally locked which prevents users from processing those sessions.
- *Session status.* Batch input sessions can have the following statuses:

  To be processed. Session has been generated and entered into the sessions queue but has not yet been processed.

  Incorrect. Session has been processed but contains errors. The successful transactions might have been processed, though. An incorrect session can be processed again, but before doing that you have to analyze what happened.

  Processed. Session has been successfully processed. You only see sessions with this status if they were generated using the KEEP option. Otherwise, they are automatically deleted. In any case, the system prevents a successful session from being run again.

  Batch. Session has been scheduled for background processing.

  Creating. Session is being generated.

  Processing. Session is being processed.

Once you have entered the selection criteria, you can either display the list of sessions logs, by clicking on the *Log* icon in the application toolbar, or you can display the sessions list by pressing the *Enter* key or clicking the *Overview* icon.

Logs only exist for sessions which have already been processed.

The Sessions List Screen. Figure B-2 shows the session list overview screen, which is automatically grouped by session status. This screen contains several columns with the following information:

- *Session.* Contains the session name.
- *Date/time.* These two fields contain the date and time when the batch input session was generated.
- *Locked.* This column is either empty, when the session is not locked, or contains a date, which indicates that the session has been locked until the specified date.
- *Created by.* Contains the user ID who generated the session.
- *Tran.* Contains the number of transactions which are to be processed by the session.
- *Screen.* Contains the number of screens which are to be processed by the session.
- *Authorization.* Indicates the user name under whose authorization the session is to be run in case of batch processing.

From this screen you can also display the sessions log, but most importantly you can process and debug the sessions, display statistics, analyze sessions, delete them, and so forth.

Processing Batch Input Sessions

Processing batch input sessions is the actual execution of the transactions and data entry into the SAP system. As has been indicated in previous sections, the system simulates the manual data entry and performs the same consistency checking.

The system can only process batch input sessions which have not yet been processed or have finished with the *Incorrect* status, and which are not locked. There are two ways of processing batch input sessions:

- Automatically, using the report RSBDCSUB to submit the sessions for processing in the background.
- Interactively or online, using the batch input management utilities.

Usually, when the interfaces with external systems have been established using batch input programs and sessions, the actual processing is performed automatically, using the RSBDCSUB report with variants.

However, there are occasions when it is convenient to perform interactive or online processing, such as for correcting a session or for initial testing purposes.

Running Sessions Automatically with RSBDCSUB. Using the RSBDCSUB report for processing batch input sessions is the normal way when systems are in productive operation. It is assumed that the batch input program and sessions generation have been tested and normally work correctly.

To process sessions automatically you should:

- Create the needed variants for the RSBDCSUB report
- Schedule a periodic background job for the RSBDCSUB

To call the RSBDCSUB, select *System* → *Services* → *Reporting* from any menu. Enter *RSBDCSUB* in the *Program* input field and click on the *Execute* icon. The system shows the criteria selection screen for this report. On this screen you should select which sessions will be automatically run. The system, by default, will process all sessions with status *to be processed* and *incorrect*.

Enter your criteria and save the settings as a variant by selecting *Goto* → *Variants* → *Save as variants*. Repeat this process as many times as needed.

Next, call the background job definition screen (transaction code SM36) by calling *System* → *Services* → *Jobs* → *Define job* and create as many jobs with the RSBDCSUB as needed. For example, you might have a specific batch session input which only executes once a month; another might be daily, and so on.

When sessions are run in the background system, R/3 will use the authorization of the user submitting the background job to check the authorization for the session. So, be sure to submit these jobs with all needed authorizations.

If the RSBDCSUB job is manually executed from the usual reporting transaction service SA38, it processes all sessions immediately. In background execution, when the scheduled execution time of the RSBDCSUB job arrives, it automatically checks for those sessions waiting for processing and runs them all immediately.

Running Sessions Interactively. As indicated earlier, this method of running sessions is normally used when testing, debugging, or correcting sessions.

Batch input sessions processed online will use the authorizations of the user running them, which might or might not be the user who generated the session.

To process a session online, from the session list screen, select a session and click on the *Process* icon, or just double click over the session name.

The system will display a dialog box for specifying the run mode and some additional functions such as an extended log, setting dynpro standard size, or expert debugging mode. Figure B-3 shows this dialog box.

Table B-1 shows the three ways to run a session online:

Display all mode is normally used in the first tests of the batch input sessions, while *Display errors only* is used while correcting transactions for sessions already processed. In any case, users can switch display modes interactively.

When running sessions online, either in *Display all* mode or *Display errors only* mode, the system offers several command utilities for interacting with the batch input sessions. These commands can be entered in the command field while the sessions are being processed. The following list shows these command codes:

Command Field Code	*Description*
/n	Terminate current batch input transaction and set as incorrect
/bdel	Delete current batch input transaction from the session

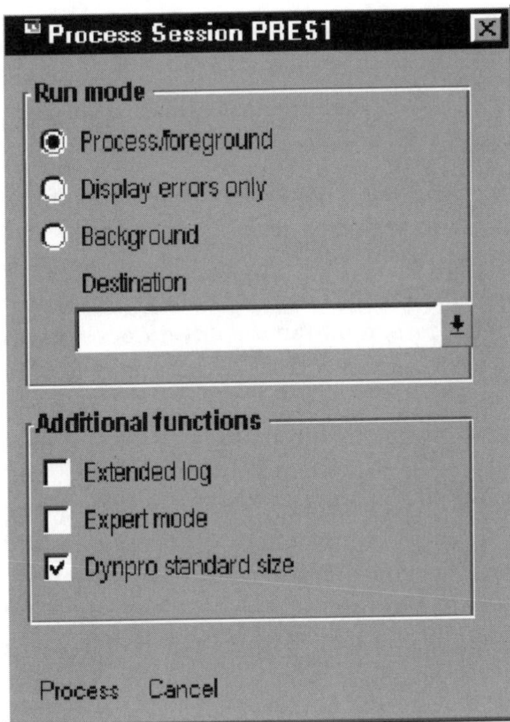

Figure B-3 Dialog box for processing batch input sessions.

TABLE B-1

Run Modes for Online Processing of Batch Input Sessions

Mode	Description
Process/foreground	The system will display all dialog steps and allows you to interactively step through the transactions and correct the possible errors. This is also known as *display-all* mode.
Display errors only	In this mode, the system will only stop and show the screen for those transactions which have not yet been executed and contain errors. If no errors occur, the system will process the session normally, although online.
Background	This mode behaves as it would when you submit a batch for immediate processing, without the need of releasing it. The system does not display the dialog steps. The system will give you back control of the SAPGUI as soon as the session has been submitted. *Display all mode* is normally used in the first tests of the batch input sessions, while *Display errors only* is used while correcting transactions for sessions already processed. In any case, users can switch display modes interactively.

/bend	Terminate processing of the whole batch input session and set status as incorrect
/bda	Switch display mode to process session on-screen (display all) instead of display only errors
/bde	Switch display mode to display only errors instead of process session on screen.

Based on your needs, you must choose one of the three run modes and click on the *Process* push button.

Processing a Session in the Foreground. Processing batch input sessions in the foreground in *display all* or *display errors* mode offers the advantage that you can correct and change the data as it is being entered by the sessions.

If the session was in status *incorrect* because it was previously run but contained some errors, when it is processed again, the system will automatically skip transactions which have been successfully processed previously. This is very important, otherwise, it could generate database inconsistencies, such as trying to duplicate records.

Additionally, the interactive processing allows the user to call other screens in the same transaction. When doing this, you must return to the initial screen defined in the sequence to continue processing the session.

For online step-by-step processing of the session, you just need to press the *Enter* key for every screen. The system will perform the new dialog step entering the data recorded in the batch input session.

If you want to modify any of the values in the screen, just write over them before pressing the *Enter* key.

To switch from *display all* mode to *display only error* mode, enter code */bde* in the command field and press *Enter.* Inversely, to switch from *display only error* to *display all,* enter code */bda* in the command field.

Deleting Transactions and Interrupting Online Sessions Processing. While processing a session online, you can decide to delete a transaction from the session. To do that, enter code */bdel* in the command field. Consider, however, that this action removes the transaction from the session and cannot be executed again if the session is restarted. A delete transaction will only be available in the session log file and within the analysis options in case the session was generated with the KEEP option.

A very useful function, especially for testing large batch input sessions, is the */bend* code. Entering */bend* in the command field cancels the transaction being processed and interrupts the execution of the full session. The system marks then this session as *Incorrect,* but it's kept in the sessions queue and can be processed again if required.

This option can be used for example to run the first few transaction of a large session. When those transactions are tested to determine whether they work correctly as expected, you can cancel the session and submit it to the background processing system. The correct transactions will not be processed again.

In case you discover errors in the first few transactions, you can stop the session and solve the problems before resuming execution.

Results of Sessions Processing

There are several possibilities as the result of the batch input session processing. If you ran the session interactively and do not cancel it with the */bend* code, you have to proceed until the system displays the message saying that the batch input processing is terminated.

When the session was generated using the KEEP option within the BDC_OPEN_GROUP function module, the system always keeps the session in the queue, whether it has been processed successfully or not. However, if the session status is *Processed,* it cannot be run again. In these cases, you have to manually delete it to remove it from the queue.

When session processing is successfully completed and the KEEP option was not set, it will be automatically removed from the session queue. You can only display the log file for the session.

If the batch input session is terminated with errors, and therefore appears in the session list with status *Incorrect,* it can be processed again. Remember that this status is set as soon as any of the transactions in the session have been aborted. In those cases, the system keeps processing the correct transactions. The log file contains those transactions which were incorrectly processed. The system only flags transaction errors with messages of type E (error) and A (abnormal termination).

To correct an abnormally terminated session, you can use some of the available functions to analyze what happened, and then you can use any of the interactive processing modes to correct those errors.

The analysis functions allow to determine which screens and values produced the error. If you find only small typing errors for very few transactions, you can correct them interactively. Otherwise, you might need to modify the batch input program which generated the session or even the data file. After making those changes, you have to generate the session again, making sure that it does not include those transactions which were previously completed.

Analyzing Batch Input Sessions

You can analyze sessions to display the transactions, data, and screens which were processed or are going to be processed. That means that you can analyze the sessions before or after the session has been run.

To analyze a session, select one from the session overview list, and then choose *Goto* → *Analysis* → *Analyze session* from the menu or click on the *Session* push button on the application toolbar. The system displays a dialog box, as shown in Fig. B-4, where you select whether to display the content of data (*old analysis*) and whether you want to analyze all transactions or only the incorrect ones.

If you choose to analyze all transactions, the system will show the *Analyze Batch Input Sessions* screen with the session being analyzed. When you double-click on the session, the system displays all the session information and possible errors. From this screen you can access the session log or the session data.

If you selected the *Contents* (*old analysis*) radio button, then the system displays three columns with the transactions, the status of the processing, and the screen numbers. Figure B-5 shows an example. When the status column is empty, it means that the transaction has not yet

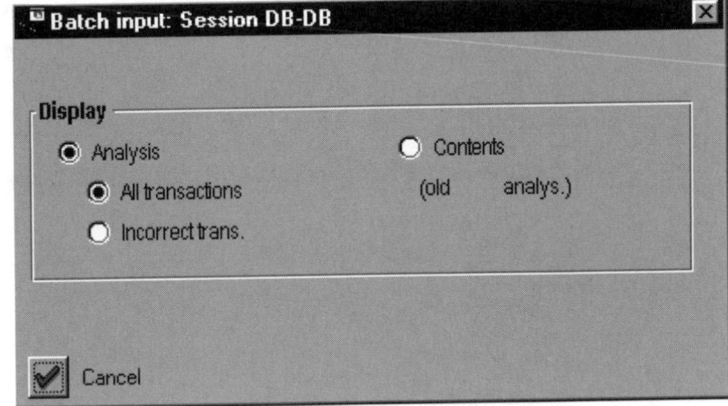

Figure B-4
Options for analyzing batch input sessions.

been processed. It might also contain the *Processed, Incorrect,* or *Deleted* values.

For small sessions, the system only shows the list of transactions and, in the application toolbar, the push buttons *Log* and *Data.* However, for large sessions, the system displays additional buttons which allow you to read the sessions in blocks to prevent time-outs. You can move forward and backward in sessions blocks.

In the session analysis screen, you can display the contents for a particular transaction by selecting a line in the display and then clicking on the *Data* push button. Figure B-6 shows an example.

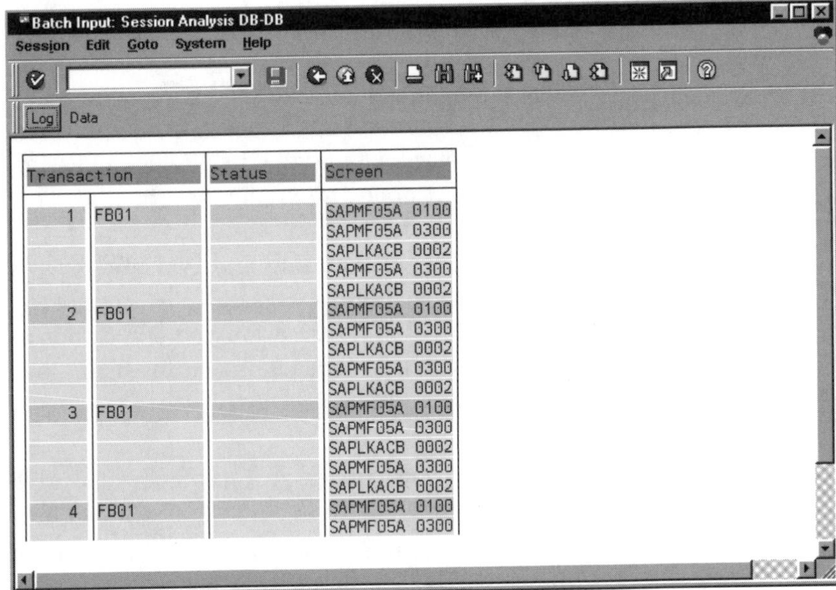

Figure B-5
Session analysis screen example.

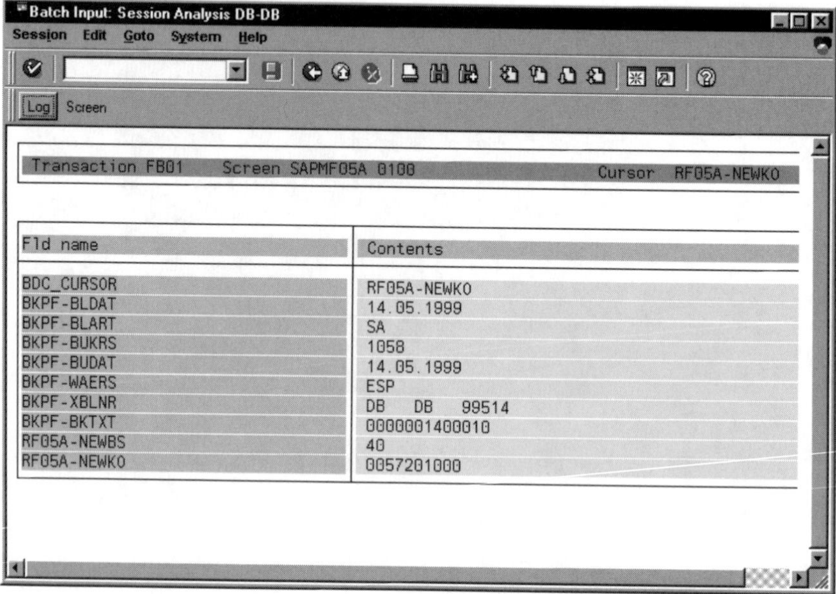

Figure B-6
Displaying data from a session analysis.

You can see exactly the contents for each of the fields of the batch input structure. By clicking on the *Screen* push button from this display, you can branch exactly to the actual screen for the transaction being processed in the session.

Displaying the Sessions Summary Statistics

Another function that can be used to analyze and display the actual status of a batch input session is the *summary statistics.*

From the sessions overview list, select a session and click on the *Statistics* push button on the application toolbar. The system will display a new screen with the sessions summary.

This statistical information is very useful for a quick look at how many transactions have been successfully or incorrectly processed out of the total ones. With this information you can decide whether it's worth processing the incorrect transactions online or if a modification of the batch input program might be necessary.

Displaying Session Logs

The system generates a log for all the batch input sessions which have been processed. If the session has not been run, it does not yet have a log.

For successfully processed sessions which did not have the KEEP option set, you can display the log from the initial batch input screen (Fig. B-1) by entering the selection criteria and clicking the *Log* push button on the application toolbar. The system will display a list of sessions, where you can display the log by either double clicking over them or by selecting them and then clicking on the *Choose* push button.

For incorrectly processed sessions, you can display the log from the overview list or the analysis screen by clicking on the *Log* push button.

The sessions log file contains information about the transactions being processed by the session, as well as reports any problems it encounters during the processing. The last part of the log contains summary information about the session.

Deleting Sessions

Normally, batch input sessions are deleted automatically from the sessions queue after they have been successfully processed. Sessions with the KEEP option set are held in the queue until the user or administrator explicitly deletes them.

To delete a session, select one from the session overview list and click on the *Delete* push button on the application toolbar or choose *Session* → *Delete* from the menu bar.

Deleting a session which was processed already will allow you to also delete the session log.

Restarting Abnormally Terminated or Interrupted Sessions

During the processing or the generation of batch input sessions, the system might present some problems, such as the shutdown of the R/3 instances, power failure, and so on, which can lead to the abnormal termination of the batch input sessions.

In these special system problems situations, sessions can retain the status *Creating* or *Processing*. To find out the actual situation, you can look up the system log, the background job log, or the session log.

Normally, you discover that a session terminated abnormally because its status remains the same after a long period of time. If processing a session usually takes one hour at night, and the next morning it is still in the *Processing* list, it's probably because it has been interrupted due to some system problem.

Before restarting a session, make sure that it has truly been abnormally terminated. Also, check with the process monitors whether there is any activity going on in the dialog or background work processes.

To restart a session that was interrupted, select the session from the overview list and choose *Session → Release* from the menu bar. The system sets the session status to *Processing.*

Restarting a session is completely safe because the system automatically skips all the transactions which were successfully completed in a previous run.

If the system problem interrupted the session generation, the safest way is to delete the session from the queue and run the batch input program again to regenerate the session.

Locking and Unlocking Sessions

Locking a batch input session prevents the session from being run until a specified date. Locking sessions might be useful for avoiding unwanted sessions (such as incorrect sessions) from being run or for setting specific run dates and also for preventing unintentional runs.

To lock sessions, select them from the overview list and then choose *Session → Lock* from the menu bar. The system will display a dialog box asking you to enter the date up to which it must hold the lock.

To unlock a locked session, mark the session and select *Session → Unlock* from the menu. The system removes the lock date.

Displaying Session Queue Information

Batch input sessions are internally managed in the sessions queue (table APQI). You can display management information about a particular session by selecting it from the overview list and then choosing *Goto → Queue* from the menu. Figure B-7 shows an example.

Table APQI is used to manage other system queues as well. For this reason, not all fields are relevant for the batch input sessions. The most important session queue management fields are as follows:

- *GROUPID.* Contains the session name.
- *QID.* The internal identification of a session.
- *MANDANT.* Indicates the client in which a session is to be processed.

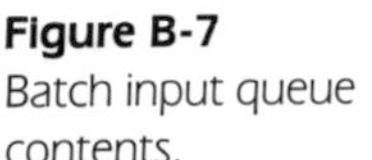

Figure B-7
Batch input queue contents.

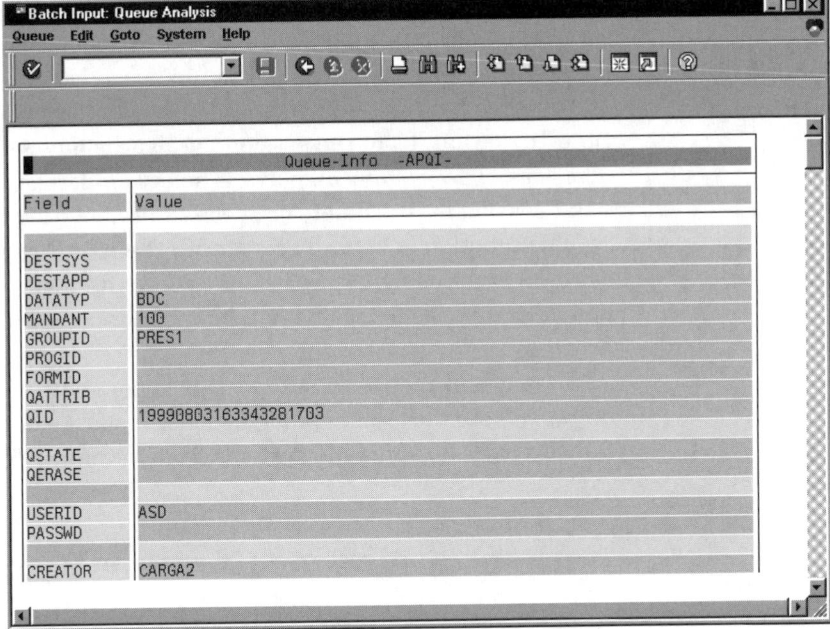

- *QSTATE.* It's either blank or contains a character indicating the status of the batch input session. For example, *E* indicates *error.*
- *QERASE.* It's a control flag which indicates whether the session will be automatically deleted. If it is not marked, it indicates that the KEEP option is set. If it contains the *X* mark, it indicates that it will be deleted after successful processing.

Batch Input Session Management Tasks

With regard to batch input sessions, system administrator tasks mainly consist of the following:

- Submitting the background jobs for automatic batch input session processing
- Checking the sessions log every day and informing developers of errors
- Cleaning up the session queue and the log files

The batch input log file is normally located in the SAP system global directory (/usr/sap/<SID>/SYS/global) with the name *BI<SID><Instance_*

name>. When a session log is manually deleted, the system sets a deletion flag, but it does not remove the occupied space. To physically restore the log space, a reorganization of this file is needed.

You can clean up old session log files by performing a log reorganization. To do that, from the session log list display, select *Folder → Reorganize logs.* The system displays a selection screen where you can enter what session logs to delete or specify to remove logs older than *n* days.

This function is actually executing the ABAP report RSBDCREO (you can look it up using the *System → Status* function). The system will only delete those session logs for batch input sessions which have already been processed.

It's a good practice to submit this report periodically (perhaps once a day) to delete those session log files because it reduces the batch input log file size, which avoids file systems from becoming full unintentionally.

Authorizations for Running Batch Input

There are three aspects of authorizations to keep in mind when working with batch input programs and sessions:

- *Running batch input programs.* These are the programs which generate the sessions. For these programs, there is no need for special authorization other than the normal object for running ABAP programs, such as S_PROGRAM. So, any user with the S_PROGRAM authorization can generate batch input sessions.
- *Processing batch input sessions online.* Since the sessions execute actual transactions, the system performs the same authorization checks as if the user was performing the transactions online.
- *Processing sessions automatically with RSBDCSUB.* The user only needs to have authorization for submitting background jobs. Once the session runs, the system will check the authorizations for the user who created the session.

Common Batch Input Errors

During the generation of a session, or during the actual execution, some of the most typical errors which might happen, besides a system failure, can be as follows:

- The batch input BDCDATA structure tries to assign values to fields which do not exist in the current transaction screen.
- The screens in the BDCDATA structure do not match the right sequence, or an intermediate screen is missing.
- On exceptional occasions, the logic flow of batch input sessions does not exactly match that of manual online processing. This can be discovered by testing the sessions online.
- The BDCDATA structure contains fields which are longer than the actual definition.
- Authorizations problems.

INDEX

A

B

C

D

E

F

G

H

I

J

K

L

M

N

O

P

Q

R

S

T

U

V

W

X